LETTERS

AND

MEMORIALS

OF

STATE

VOL. I.

AMS PRESS
NEW YORK

From a curious Limning   drawn by Isaac Oliver
in the Collection   of Dr Richard Mead.

The Right Honourable
Sr PHILIP SIDNEY,
Knt

To William Perry of Penshurst Esqr this Plate is humbly inscrib'd by G. Vertue. 1745.

LETTERS

AND

MEMORIALS

OF

STATE,

In the REIGNS of

Queen MARY, Queen ELIZABETH, King JAMES, King CHARLES THE FIRST, Part of the Reign of King CHARLES THE SECOND, and OLIVER's Ufurpation.

Written and collected

By Sir HENRY SYDNEY, Knight of the Garter, Ambaffador in *France*, four Times Lord-Juftice of *Ireland*, and thrice Lord-Deputy of that Realm, in the Reigns of Queen MARY, and Queen ELIZABETH, and Lord-Prefident of *Wales*, &c.

The famous Sir PHILIP SYDNEY, and his Brother Sir ROBERT SYDNEY, Lord-Governor of *Flufhing*, and Lord-Chamberlain in the Reign of King JAMES.

ROBERT, the fecond Earl of *Leicefter*, Ambaffador to the Kings of *Denmark*, and *France*, and Lord-Lieutenant of *Ireland*, in the Reign of King CHARLES THE FIRST.

PHILIP Lord Vifcount *Lifle*, Lord-Lieutenant of *Ireland*, by Authority of Parliament, and one of the Council of State of the Commonwealth; and of his Brother Colonel ALGERNON SYDNEY, one of the faid Council of State, and Ambaffador to the Courts of *Denmark* and *Sweden*. Together with Letters of the other Minifters of State, with whom they held a Correfpondence.

The whole containing

The Antient State of *Ireland*; with CHARACTERS and private MEMOIRS.

ALSO,

The Antient Government of the PRINCIPALITY of *WALES*.

The Wars between the *Spaniards*, and the STATES-GENERAL in the *Netherlands*.

Negotiations between the COURTS of ENGLAND, FRANCE, &c.

The INTRIEGUES of the feveral COURTS of Queen ELIZABETH, King JAMES, and King CHARLES THE FIRST.

With other remarkable Tranfactions, both at Home and Abroad, during thofe Times, not hitherto known.

Faithfully tranfcribed from the Originals at *Penfhurft Place* in *Kent*, the Seat of the Earls of *LEICESTER*, and from his Majefty's Office of Papers and Records for Bufinefs of State.

Whereunto is added,

Genealogical and Hiftorical OBSERVATIONS: Alfo MEMOIRS of the LIVES and ACTIONS of the *SYDNEYS*, and their Noble Anceftors, the DUDLEYS, GREY, TALBOT, BEAUCHAMP, BERKLEY, and LISLE; and a Defence of ROBERT DUDLEY Earl of LEICESTER, wrote by Sir PHILIP SYDNEY. Collected from Records, their Laft Wills and Teftaments, Original Papers, Authentick Manufcripts, and our moft approved Hiftorians.

By *ARTHUR COLLINS*, Efq;
AUTHOR of the PEERAGE of *ENGLAND*.

VOL. I.

LONDON:

Printed for T. OSBORNE, in *Gray's-Inn*. MDCCXLVI.

Library of Congress Cataloging in Publication Data

Collins, Arthur, 1682?-1760, ed.
   Letters and memorials of state in the reigns of Queen
Mary, Queen Elizabeth, King James, King Charles the
First, part of the reign of King Charles the Second, and
Oliver's usurpation...

   1. Great Britain--History--Elizabeth, 1558-1603--
Sources. 2. Great Britain--History--Early Stuarts,
1603-1649--Sources. 3. Great Britain--History--
Commonwealth and Protectorate, 1649-1660--Sources.
4. Sidney family. I. Title.
DA350.C7 1973   942.06   72-997
ISBN 0-404-01632-4 (v. 1)

Original size of this book was 9 X 14. This edition has
been reduced to 7 X 10.

Reprinted from the edition of 1746, London
First AMS edition published in 1973
Manufactured in the United States of America

International Standard Book Number:
Complete Set: 0-404-01631-6
Volume I: 0-404-01632-4

AMS PRESS INC.
NEW YORK, N. Y.   10003

To the Honourable the

Lady *MARY SHERARD*,

And to the Honourable

ELIZABETH PERRY,

Grand-Daughters, and Heirs,

Of the Right Honourable

ROBERT SYDNEY,

Earl of Leicester, Viscount and Baron Lisle, Baron of Penshurst, and Lord Sidney.

SHOULD these Memoirs and Letters appear in the World under any other Patronage, whilst a *SYDNEY* is still subsisting, I might be justly upbraided, of the Want of paying a due Homage to the Memory of your great and noble Ancestors, who have so highly deserved of their Country.

Thefe are MONUMENTS of their most famous ACTIONS, which never will fade, or decay, but appear shining Examples of Prudence, Knowledge, Experience, Worth, and Honor, to the latest Posterity,

terity. It is indeed remarkable, that there are exact Parallels of your Progenitors, amongst the Chief of the *Romans*: For what *Tacitus* observes of *Agricola*'s excellent Conduct in *Britain*, is matched by Sir *Henry Sidney*'s in *Ireland*: In his Military Capacity, also considered as a *Roman*, he obtained the *Opima Spolia*, in killing, with his own Hand, *James Mac-Connel*, the principal Leader of the *Scots*: An Honour snatch'd but by Three in that State, greedy of Glory, *viz. Romulus*, *Cassius*, and *Marcellus*: And lastly, as a thorough paced *Roman*, he consumed his Patrimony in the Nation's Service, and was on his Death buried, like *Valerius*, at the publick Expence.

In Sir *Philip Sidney*, we behold *Marcellus* and *Mecænas* united, who, with the strongest Eloquence, could at once teach the best Rules of Poetry, and most gallantly and bountifully rewarded Men of Letters and Science : Who as a Soldier, like *P. Decius Mus.* Successfully executed the antient Silence in March, and afterwards freely rewarded the Partners of his Victory out of his own Purse : And also, like *Decius*, devoted himself in Battle to his Country.

In *Algernon Sidney*, we have, in one View, *Brutus* and *Regulus*. As the First, a Destroyer of Tyrants and Tyranny; as the Latter, a Despiser of Banishment, and even Death itself, when they came in Competition with uttering his Sentiments for his Country's Benefit.

Your

DEDICATION.

Your noble Grandfather, when Lord *Lisle*, and your Uncle, the Earl of *Romney*, were foremost in the List of those, who, at the Revolution, drove hence our *British Tarquin* : The latter being primarily consulted in that solemn Event, and chief Minister to that King, who secured to us a R A C E to reign over us, rather exercising the Valour, Moderation, and Virtue of *Roman* Consuls, than imperious Kings. But why dwell I on these, since, as an Author has observed, your illustrious Forefathers, and all your eminent Relations, have been ever Patrons of Wit and Arms, and leading in the Race of Glory.

Your Female Predecessors have been also Illustrious in their several Ages.

The Duchess of *Northumberland* was the greatest Example in Fortitude of Mind in Adversity, and of modest Virtue ; and whose Wisdom, Care, and Prudence, restored her overthrown House, even in a Reign of Cruelty and Tyranny.

The Countess of *Suffex*, from her private Fortune, made a very ample Provision for the Support of Learning and true Religion, and devoted even her Plate, and Ornaments, to those pious Ends.

The Lady *Pembroke* had that Judgment and Learning, as to be little less famous, than her

renowned

renowned Brother, the Author of the *Arcadia*, and which he dedicated to her Name and Virtues.

Lady *Sunderland* is celebrated for her matchlefs Beauty, Virtue, and excellent Endowments, who fupported the Royal Clergy in her Neighbourhood, in the Times of Anarchy and Confufion. So likewife, it is verified in your Defcent, by your unblemifhed Merits, That Greatnefs of Soul and Genius are inherent in your 'Blood and Lineage.

As I apprehend, that an Attempt to celebrate your Polite Demeanour, and Virtuous Accomplifhments, in this Publick Manner, may be difagreeable to you, I fhall therefore only beg your Permiffion, to fubfcribe myfelf,

Your moft Obedient,

and moft Devoted

Humble Servant,

ARTHUR COLLINS.

THE

THE
PREFACE.

FORMER *Editors of State Papers, having said so much of the Uses, to which they may be applied by the Readers of History, and all agreeing, That they are the most proper Means of conveying down to Posterity just and authentick Accounts of the Transactions to which they relate. I shall make no Apology for my Undertaking, but proceed to give some Account of the Collection before me.*

THE *Title Page will inform the Publick, that these valuable Political Remains belonging to the* SYDNEY *Family, were selected out of the Manuscript Repository at* Penshurst, *and his Majesty's Paper Office at* Whitehall : *But it may be necessary to premise a few Words, concerning the Persons to whom we are obliged for them, and the Nature of their Correspondences ; from whence the Reader will judge, what Information, or Amusement, he may expect to find in the Work itself.*

SIR Henry Sydney *enjoyed the most distinguished Employments in* Ireland, *in the Reigns of Queen* Mary, *and Queen* Elizabeth : *And our Historians agree, that he first civilized the* Irish, *by bringing them under Obedience to the Laws of* England. *The Progress he made through the whole Kingdom, at four several Times, is very judiciously and exactly related in his Letters to Queen* Elizabeth, *and the Lords of the Council ; which shew the lamentable and disorderly State, that the Natives then laboured under from their Tenures, barbarous Customs, want of Commerce,* &c. *as well as the Difficulties he surmounted in making any Sort of Reformation amongst them. They are the only Accounts of the Affairs of* Ireland *during that Time, which can be depended upon ; and the Prudence and Vigour in Government, the Justness of Observation, and the clear and manly Sense, which appear through the whole Course of Sir* Henry Sydney's *Dispatches, are sufficient Reasons for not suffering them to lie concealed any longer in the dusty Corner of a Library.*

SIR Philip Sydney, *his Son, is allowed to be as accomplished a Character, as this Nation, or, perhaps, any foreign one, ever produced. It is to be wished more of his Letters were preserved ; but the few which Time hath spared us, will, for that Reason, be considered, as the greater Rarities. His*
Defence

Defence of his Uncle the Earl of Leicester, *in Anſwer to* Parſons's Commonwealth, *is now firſt printed from the Original* MS.

SIR Robert Sydney, *the younger Brother, copied after ſo ſhining a Pattern ; and by his Virtues and Services, obtained the Title and Honours of Earl of* Leicester. *As he was curious in laying out for Intelligence of the remarkable Events of his Time, he kept a Correſpondence with* Rowland White, *the Poſt-Maſter, a notable buſy Man, who conſtantly writ over to him at* Fluſhing *(when he was Reſident there as Governor) the News and Intrigues of the Court ; and being employed by him in Commiſſions to his noble Relations, and the Miniſters, was entruſted by them, with ſeveral ſecret Paſſages, for the Information of his Patron. To give one Inſtance out of many, I ſhall only add, that in Mr.* White's *Letters, are contained ſeveral Particulars, hitherto paſſed over in Silence, by the Hiſtorians, of the Earl of* Eſſex's *Favour, Troubles, and Fall.*

WHEN *Sir* Robert Sydney *was in* England, *Sir* William Browne, *Deputy-Governor of* Fluſhing, *in the Reign of Queen* Elizabeth, *and Sir* John Throgmorton, *in the Reign of King* James, *conſtantly tranſmitted to him the principal Tranſactions in the* Netherlands, *particularly thoſe of the Army ; as did alſo Prince* Maurice, *and ſome other of the Generals. Under this Correſpondence, the Reader will find an exact Journal of the famous Siege of* Oſtend, *which held out four Years againſt the Flower of the* Spaniſh *Forces in* Flanders. *There is alſo an Account of the Circumſtances relating to the Delivery of the Cautionary Towns to the States General, which is looked upon, as not the ſmalleſt Error, of the weak Adminiſtration of* James the Firſt.

ROBERT, *the ſecond Earl of* Leicester, *was poſſeſſed of fine natural Talents, and a larger Share of Learning, then uſually falls to Perſons of his Rank. His Character may be found in* Clarendon, 8vo, *Vol.* 3. *Page* 201. *He was much employed in Buſineſs during the earlier Part of his Life, and carefully preſerved Copies of his own Letters, relative to the Publick, and of ſuch as were ſent him of a publick Nature. He held a cloſe Correſpondence with the moſt conſiderable Perſons of the Court of King* Charles the Firſt, *particularly, with his Lady's Brothers,* Algernon *Earl of* Northumberland, *Lord High Admiral of* England, *and* Henry *Lord* Percy *of* Alnwick, *Maſter of the Horſe to King* Charles the Second, *when Prince of* Wales, *and afterwards his Chamberlain, and Favourite to the Queen Mother.*

THERE *ſubſiſted the ſtricteſt Friendſhip between theſe three Noblemen, to their Deaths : And the two laſt imparted to the Earl of* Leicester, *the private Intrigues of the Court, from* 1636, *to the Breaking out of the Civil Wars.*

THERE.

The PREFACE.

*THERE are two Volumes of his Lordship's Letters, with the Instructi-
ons and Answers from the King, and Secretaries of State, in his Majesty's
Paper Office, which have been examined, and such of them transcribed, as
were wanting of what he had laid up at* Penshurst, *to which I have in proper Places referred.*

AS the Reader may probably have expected to find in the Earl of Leicester's *Dispatches, more particular Accounts of the Occurrences of the*
French *Court, and of the great Events of the War, then carrying on against the
House of* Austria, *by the enterprising Genius of Cardinal* Richlieu, *it may
be right to apprise him, that my Lord left those Subjects to* Augier, *his Secretary ; and that the Editor has seen in the Paper Office, several Volumes of
that Agent's Letters, who never failed transmitting to the Secretaries of
State, the News, and publick Relations of* Paris. *But the Reader may con-
sult the general Histories of* Lewis the Thirteenth's *Reign upon them, as*
Le Vassor, Le Clerc's *Life of* Richlieu, Pere Bougeant, Grotii Episto-
læ, &c.*

*MY Lords principal Business, was the Management of a Treaty for Re-
covery of the* Palatinate, *which, I shall say the less of, as it is handled at
large in his Dispatches ; but cannot help observing, that though it be a Transf-
action of Consequence, none of our Historians mention it ; neither is the Treaty itself to be found in* Rymer. *Another Point, and that of no small Delicacy, was, to watch over the Motions of the* French *Court, with Regard to*
Scotland, *wherein his Lordship acquitted himself with great Vigilance and
Address.*

HIS Son, the Lord Viscount Lisle, *being of the Council of State, and
of the House of Commons, his Letters disclose some material Passages in both
those Assemblies ; but of these few are printed, our Collection swelling to a
greater Bulk, than could be comprised in two Volumes.*

THE Letters of Algernon Sydney, *contain Accounts of his Negotiation, as a Mediator between* Sweden and Denmark, *wherein the Policy
and Views of the Northern Crowns are laid open in a masterly Manner.
Whilst he was on that Ambassy, the Restoration of* Charles the Second *was
carrying on ; and when it afterwards took Place, his Friends prevailed on
him to forsake his Native Country, till his Principles and Attachments to the
Commonwealth might not be remembered with such Resentment, as he had too
much Reason to expect. He left his Affairs in* England *in a very entangled
Condition, whereby he was a great Sufferer in his private Fortune, whereof
he complains in his Letters to the Earl of* Leicester *his Father ; yet with a
Spirit that shews a manly Contempt of worldly Advantages. His Travels
through* Germany and France to Rome, *are interspersed with many Histo-
rical Passages, Characters, and Descriptions, expressed with so much Life
and Candour, as to merit both Attention and Belief.*

VOL. I.   c   *THE*

The PREFACE.

THE Exactness of the Errata, will, I hope, in some Degree, reconcile my Readers to the Incorrectness of the Printer; many of the Sheets being work'd off at the Press, when I was busied in compleating this Collection.

I am willing to flatter myself, that the Notes which are occasionally subjoined to the Bottom of the Page, may be thought of Use, either in bringing the Reader a little better acquainted with the Family, or Character, of some Person, who makes a Figure in the Correspondences, or in adding a Supplemental Fact, to illustrate, or point out more fully, some Passage in the Collection.

I will not deny, that some Things have crept into it, which might, on a second Review, been omitted; but unavoidable Accidents have already so long delayed the Publication of the Work, that I was afraid of trespassing further on the Patience of my Subscribers. And, therefore (to borrow a Phrase from the Ghost in Hamlet) *Am now come Abroad, to render up my Account, with all my Imperfections on my Head.*

May 8, 1746.   A. C.

A LIST

A
LIST
OF THE
SUBSCRIBERS.

THE Right Hon. Charles Earl of Ailef-bury. *Large Paper.*
The Right Hon. Charles Earl of Arran.
The Right Hon. William, late Lord Aberga-venny.
Dr. Adams, Mafter of Sydney College in Cambridge for the Library.

His Grace Henry Duke of Beaufort. *Large Paper.*
Her Grace the Duchefs of Bolton.
The Right Hon. Richard Earl of Burlington. *Large Paper.*
The Right Hon. William Earl of Bath. *Large Paper.*
The Right Rev. Jofeph Lord Bifhop of Briftol.
The Right Hon. Francis Lord Brook. *Large Paper.*
The Right Hon. Allen Lord Bathurft. *Large Paper.*
The Right Hon. Lord Vifcount Bateman.
The Right Hon. Charles Lord Baltimore.
The Hon. Thomas Lennard Barrett, Efq;
Philip Bennet, of Whitcombe, in Com. Somerfet, Efq; Member of Parliament for Bath.
Edmund Bull, of Poland-Street, Efq; *Large Paper.*
John Bonnell, Efq; *Large Paper.*
John Brown, Efq;
The Rev. Mr. John Butler, of Wateringbury, in Kent.
The Rev. Mr. Birch.

His Royal Highnefs William Duke of Cumberland. *Large Paper.*
The Right Hon. Philip Earl of Chefterfield, Lord Lieutenant of Ireland. *Large Paper.*
The Right Hon. Charles Lord Cadogan.
Sir Kendrick Clayton, of Flower, near Godftone, in Com. Surry, Bart.
Thomas Carew, of Crocomb, in Com. Somerfet, Efq;
James Cocks, Efq; Member of Parliament for Ryegate.

His Grace William Duke of Devonfhire.
His Grace Lionel Duke of Dorfet.
The Right Hon. William Earl of Dartmouth.

The Right Hon. Thomas late Lord Vifcount Deerhurft.
Benjamin Dry, of Sevenoak, in Kent, Efq;
Captain William Daffy. *Large Paper.*

The Right Hon. John Earl of Egmont.
The Rev. Mr. Exton.

The Right Hon. Benjamin Earl Fitz-Walter.
The Right Hon. William Earl Fitz-William. *Large Paper.*
The Right Hon. Thomas Lord Vifcount Fauconberg.
The Right Hon. Thomas Lord Foley.
Thomas Fairfax, of Newton-Kyme, in Com. Ebor, Efq;

The Right Hon. Francis Earl of Godolphin.
The Right Hon. John Earl of Granville. *Large Paper.*
The Right Hon. John Lord Gower. *Large Paper.*
The Lady Elizabeth Germain. *Large Paper.*

The Right Hon. Algernon Earl of Hertford, only Son and Heir-apparent of his Grace Charles Duke of Somerfet. *Large Paper.*
The Right Hon. Charles Earl of Hallifax. *Large Paper.*
The Right Hon. William Earl of Harrington. *Large Paper.*
The Right Hon. the Lord Archibald Hamilton.
Robert Hucks, Efq; deceafed. *Large Paper.*
James Hannot, of Rey-Houfe, in Effex, Efq;
Mr. George Holmes, Deputy Keeper of the Records in the Tower.
Edward Horn, Efq;

The Hon. Mrs. Knight.
Nigell Kingfcote, Efq;

The Right Hon. Henry Earl of Lincoln. *Large Paper.*
The Right Hon. Thomas Earl of Leicefter. *Large Paper.*
The Right Hon. Henry Vifcount Lonfdale *Large Paper.*

James

James Lane, Efq; Richmond Herald.

His Grace Charles Duke of Marlborough. *One Large Paper, and two Small Paper.*
His Grace John Duke of Montagu. *Large Paper.*
His Grace William Duke of Manchester. *Large Paper.*
The Right Hon. George Earl of Macclesfield.
The Right Hon. Thomas Earl of Malton.
The Right Hon. James Earl of Morton.
The Right Hon. Charles Earl of Middlesex, Son and Heir-apparent of his Grace the Duke of Dorfet. *Large Paper.*
George Montagu, Efq;
Edward Medley, junior, of Frifton, in Com. Suffex, Efq; *Large Paper.*
Nicholas Mann, Efq; Master of the Charter-House.

His Grace Thomas Holles Pelham Duke of Newcastle. *Large Paper.*
The Right Hon. James Earl of Northampton. *Large Paper.*
The Right Hon. Francis Lord North and Guilford.
Mr. John Nickolls, junior, Fellow of the Royal Society.

The Right Hon. Henrietta Cavendifh Holles Countefs Dowager of Oxford. *Large Paper.*
The Right Hon. Robert late Earl of Orford. *Large Paper.*
The Right Hon. the Countefs of Orford. *Large Paper.*
The Right Hon. John Earl of Orrery. *Large Paper.*
The Right Hon. Charles Lord Offulftone, Son and Heir apparent of the Earl of Tankerville.
The Right Hon. Arthur Onflow, Efq; Speaker of the Houfe of Commons. *Large Paper.*
Mr. William Oldys.

His Grace William Duke of Portland.
The Right Hon. John Earl of Portfmouth. *Large Paper.*
The Right Hon. John Lord Vifcount Percival.
The Right Hon. Henry Pelham, Efq; Chancellor of the Exchequer.
Sir Walter Parker of Ratton in Com. Suffex, Bart.
William Perry, of Penfhurft Place in Kent, Efq; *One Large Paper, two Small Paper.*
William Pitt, Efq; Paymafter General of his Majeftys Forces.
John Plumptree, Efq;
Jacob Prefton Efq;
Mr. Thomas Prefton.

His Grace Charles Duke of Richmond. *Large Paper.*
His Grace John Duke of Rutland, *Large Paper.*
The Right Hon. William Henry, Earl of Rochford. *Large Paper.*

The Right Hon. Sir John Rufhout, Bart.
John Roberts, Efq;

The Right Hon. John Earl of Sandwich.
The Right Hon. Anthony Earl of Shaftfbury. *Large Paper.*
The Right Hon. Samuel Lord Sandys. *Large Paper.*
The Right Hon. Edward Southwell, Efq; Principal Secretary of State for Ireland.
Sir Hugh Smithfon, Bart. one of the Knights of the Shire for Middlefex. *Large Paper.*
The Hon. Charles Stanhope, Efq;
Sir Brownlow Sherrard, Bart. *Large Paper.*
John Scrope, Efq; joint Secretary of the Treafury.
Andrew Stone, Efq;
Sidney Stafford Smythe, Efq;
Thomas Sidney, Efq;
The Rev. Mr. Scottow, Prefident of Bennet's College in Cambridge.
The Rev. Mr. Stevens.

The Right Hon. Pattee Vifcount Torrington. *Large Paper.*
The Hon. Thomas Townfhend, Efq;
Sir Peter Thompfon, Knt.
John Temple, of Moor Park, in Com. Surry, Efq;
Dr. Thorp, of Rochefter, M. D.
The Reverend Mr. Edward Tart, Mafter of the Leicefter Hofpital in Warwick.

The Right Rev. Ifaac Lord Bifhop of Worcefter.
The Right Hon. Horatio Walpole, Efq;
The Hon. Edward Wortley Montagu, Efq; Uncle to the Earl of Sandwich.
Sir Thomas Wilfon, of Uckfield in Com. Suffex, Bart.
Sir Charles Wyndham, of Orchard, in Com. Somers, Bart. *Large Paper.*
Sir Thomas Webfter, of Battle-Abby in Suffex, Bart. *Large Paper.*
Browne Willis, of Waddon Hall, in Com. Bucks, Efq;
James Weft, Efq; joint Secretary of the Treafury.
Matthew Wife, of the Priory in Warwick, Efq;
Lee Warner of Walfingham Abby, in Norfolk, Efq;
James Wittewronge, of Rothamftead, in Com. Hertford, Efq;
John Walfh, Efq;
John Warburton, Efq; Somerfet-Herald.
The Reverend Mr. Williams, Rector of Penfhurft in Kent.
Henry Wefton, Gent.

The Hon. Philip Yorke, Efq; Son and Heir apparent of Philip Lord Hardwick, Lord High Chancellor of Great-Britain. *Large Paper.*
John Yate, Efq;

THE

THE

CONTENTS

OF THE

FIRST VOLUME.

Letters and Memorials of State.

The CONTENTS.

Mr.

ADDENDA & CORRIGENDA.

PAGE 19, Section 3, Line 1, for 25, read 35. P. 29. f. 5. l. 2. In the Account of Sir *Andrew Dudley*, after *fo unfortunate an End*, add, He diftinguifhed himfelf in the Wars of *France*, in *Henry the Eighth*'s Reign, and againft the *Scots*, in *Edward the Sixth*'s Time. In 1548, 2 *Edw.* VI. being Governor of *Broughtierag*, he was befieged by Monfieur *de Biron*, with a Body of 8000 *French* and *Scotch*, and a Train of Artillery; but as *Hollinfhed* relates, p. 993, *by the valiant Prowefs of Sir* Andrew Dudley, *and the* Englifh *under him, they were repelled, and left their Siege with Difhonour.* After which the Earl of *Argyle*, with his Highlanders, befieged it,
                                                            with

with as little Effect, and was forced alfo to retire from before it. P. 31, f. 5. l. 14. after married, add, *June* 3, 1599. *King* Edward's *Journal*, p. 14, 15. P. 32. f. 1. l. 4. after proclaimed, *dele* and crowned. P. 33. f. 3. l. 4. for Sir *John*, read Sir *Edward*. P. 35. f. 2. l. 30. *I will at my Yeres Minde have fuche devyne Service, as myne Executors fhall thynke mete.* It may be proper to explain this. The Word Yeres fhould be Hearfe; and the Duchefs (for the Sake of her Children) prudently waved profeffing herfelf a Proteftant, and if any Romifh Superftition was to be exercifed at her Funeral, fhe left it to her Executors, and not as her own Act or Defire. P. 48. f. 5. l. 2. for not long after, read, two Years after, and add. Our Hiftorians fay, particularly *Camden*, from whence it is taken, to blacken the Earl of *Leicefter*, that this was a hafty Marriage. But the Truth is from the Depofitions in the Evidence Room at *Penfhurft*, and other Authorities, that the Earl of *Effex* died in *Sept.* 1576 (See the Letters, p. 140) and the Earl of *Leicefter* married his Widow, 21 *Sept.* 1578. See p. 69 in the Lives, which is taken from the Depofitions on Oath, in the Baftard *Dudley's* Cafe, in the faid Evidence Room at *Penfhurft*. P. 64. f. 1. l. laft, after *Difproof*, fhould be the following Paragraph which (by Miftake in copying) is incerted l. 67. As to the *Dudleys*, he deals much harder withal, but no whit trewer, &c. P. 69. l. 29. for *Tirlanghe*, read *Tirlaughe*. P. 70. l. 5. for I can, read I came. P. 78. f. 4. l. 5. after Church, add, in the *Tower* of *London*. P. 89. f. 2. l. 3. for 14, read 24. P. 96. f. 7. l. 1. *Hollinfhed* (in *Caftra. Chron.* p. 1553) gives this Account of the Lady *Mary Sydney*. ' The 9th Day of *Auguft* next following [the Deceafe of Sir
' *Henry Sydney*] died the moft noble, worthy, beneficent, and bounteous Lady, the Lady *Mary*
' *Sydney*, his only Spoufe, and moft dear Wife, eldeft Daughter to that renowned Duke, *John* late
' of *Northumberland*, &c. &c. moft zealoufly godly, and penitently, as by the Teftimony of fome
' honourable, and other grave Perfonages, is well avouched. During the whole Courfe of her
' Sicknefs, and efpecially a little before it pleafed Almighty God to call her to his Mercy, fhe
' ufed fuch godly Speeches, earneft and effectual Perfuafions to all thofe about her, to exhort them
' to Repentance, and Amendment of Life, &c. as pleafed the Hearts of many that heard her. And
' though they before knew her to exceed moft of her Sex, in fingular Virtue and Quality; as good
' Speech, apt and ready Conception, Excellency of Wit, and notable eloquent Delivery: Yet her
' Difcourfe then amazed and aftonifhed the Hearers; and left the World loved and honoured by all
' who knew her, and the renowned Houfe whereof fhe was defcended.' P. 98. f. 2. l. 3. The famous *Waller* gives this Encomium on the Tree:

Go Boy, and carve this Paffion on the Bark
Of yonder Tree, which ftands the facred Mark
Of noble *Sidney's* Birth, &c.

P. *ib.* f. 3. l. 11. for *the Junfeen*, read *tho' I unfeen*. And S. 4. l. 4. after Chamber, incert, juft at this Time * *Charles the Ninth* was heaping treacherous Favours on the Proteftants, in Order to trepan the Admiral of *France*, and his Party, to *Paris*, at the King of *Navarre's* Wedding, when the Proteftants thinking themfelves fecure by that Marriage, were barbaroufly maffacred on 24 *Aug.* 1572. Whereby it is probable, this Favour was by that bafe Prince, conferred on Sir *Philip Sydney*, the better to cover his barbarous Defign. P. 102. f. 5. l. 2. after Inftances, this fhould have been added in. *See the Life of* Spencer *prefixed to his Works*, p. 4. *wherein the following Account is given*: ' It
' is faid *Spencer* was a Stranger to Sir *Philip Sydney*, when he had begun to write his *Fairy Queen*;
' and that he took Occafion to go to *Leicefter* Houfe, and to introduce himfelf, by fending in to Sir
' *Philip*, a Copy of the 9th *Canto*, of the firft Book of that Poem. Sir *Philip* was much furprifed
' with the Defcription of Defpair in that *Canto*, and is faid to have fhewn an unufual Tranfport, on
' the Difcovery of fo new and uncommon a Genius. After he had read fome Stanza's, he bid his
' Steward give the Perfon, that brought thofe Verfes, Fifty Pounds; but upon reading the next
' Stanza, he ordered the Sum to be doubled. The Steward was no lefs furprifed then his Mafter,
' and thought it his Duty to make fome Delay, in executing fo fudden and lavifh a Bounty: But upon
' reading one Stanza more, Sir *Philip* raifed his Gratuity to Two-hundred Pounds, and commanded
' the Steward to give it immediately, left, as he read further, he might be tempted to give away his
' whole Eftate.' P. 120. f. 6. l. 1. for 1602, read 1604. P. 132. f. 4. l. 6. for as, read at. P. 142. f. 5. for has, read as. P. 144. f. 5. l. 4. after are, *dele* already. P. 147. f. 2. l. 1. after *Waller*, add, amongft many other, has thefe:

That cloven Rock produced thee, by whofe Side,
Nature to recompence the fatal Pride
Of fuch ftern Beauty, plac'd thofe healing Springs,
Which not more Help, than that Deftruction brings.   *Waller's* Poems, p. 95.
And Page 97, thus:
Ye lofty Beeches, tell this matchlefs Dame,
That if together ye fed all one Flame,
It could not equalize the Hundredth-part
Of what her Eyes have kindled in my Heart.

P. 149. f. 6. l. 4. after Month, add, The *Wednefday* after he died (which was on *Sunday*) he was cut open, and in his Bladder was found a Stone, as large as a big Lemon, and of that Shape, and weighed fix Ounces. P. *ib.* f. 7. l. 3. after aged, *dele* more then 80, and incert 77. P. 152. f. 1. l. 13. for ment, read Merit. And the fame Page, f. 2. l. 5. after Government, add, which was by King, Lords, and Commons, as he repeatedly declares, particularly Page 115, in thefe Words: *And if I fhould undertake to fay, There never was a good Government in the World, that did not confift of the three fimple Species, of Monarchy, Ariftocracy, and Democracy, I think I might make it good.* Alfo to the fame Effect, p. 132. When he might begin thefe *Difcourfes on Government*, cannot be fo well determined, but it appears plainly, that the greateft Part were wrote about the latter End of King *Charles the Second's* Reign, having Reference to many People then living, whom he Perfonally names. P. 169. l. laft but one, for his, read the King's. P. 178. f. 6. l. laft, for 1727, read 1737. P. 180. f. 2. l. 2. for 6, read 7. P. 238. fect. 2. l. laft, for 1578, read 1577. P. 256. f. 2. l. 1. for *Edward*, read *Edmund*. P. 328. in the Notes, l. laft, for his, read the; and after COUNCIL, add, to his prefent Majefty.

* *Harleian Mifcellany*, Vol. VII. p. 318, &c.

MEMOIRS

OF THE

LIVES and ACTIONS

OF THE

SIDNEYS,

And their Noble ANCESTORS,

THE

DUDLEYS, De GREY, TALBOT, BEAUCHAMP, BERKLEY, and LISLE.

THE *Sidney* Family being firſt ennobled in the Name of *Liſle*, I ſhall begin my Account in tracing their Barony to the preſent Time. Of the Name of *Liſle*, there were anciently ſeveral Families, denominated from the *Iſle of Wight*, the *Iſle of Ely*, &c. But the firſt, I meet of this, is *Bryan de L'Iſle*, a Perſon of great Note in his Time, ranked amongſt the Barons in the Reign of King *John* [a]; and, in the third Year of that King, paid an hundred and twenty Marks, and a Palfry, for the Wardſhip and Marriage of the Heir of *William Briton*. In 6 *John*, he took to Wife [b] *Maud*, Daughter and Heir of *Thomas*, the Son of *William de Seleby*. In 9 *John*, he was made [c] Governor of the Caſtle of *Boleſover*, in Com. *Derb.* and, in 12 *John*, gave [d] an hundred Pounds to the King for his Welcome out of *Poiċtou*. In 13 *John*, he was imployed [e] in fortifying and victualling the Caſtle of *Cnareſburgh* (ſo written in that Age) in *Yorkſhire*; but was [f] then reputed, by ſome, one of the King's evil Councellors.

On 25 *May*, 1213, 15 *John*, the King, from *Temple Ewell*, writes to *Farrand* Earl of *Flanders*, that he had received his Letter, and that he [g] ſends *William* Earl of *Saliſbury*, *Reginald* Earl of *Bologne*, this *Brian de L'Iſle*, and two more with Credentials to him. Alſo, the ſame Year, when the King, by Deed, dated 3 *Oct.* 1213, ſealed with a golden Seal [h], reſigns to God, and his holy Apoſtles St. *Peter* and St. *Paul*, to his holy Mother the Church of *Rome*,

---

[a] Rot. Pip. 3 Joh. Dorſ. and Somers. [b] Clauſ. 6 Joh. m. 10. [c] Pat. 9 Joh. m 2 [d] Rot. Pip. 12 Joh. Linc. [e] Rot. Pip. 13 Joh. Comp. Br. de Inſula. [f] Mat. Paris Hiſt. 231, 23. [g] Rymer's Fœdera, Tom. 1. p. 172. [h] Ibid. p. 176.

to his Lord Pope *Innocent the Third*, and his Catholick Succeſſors, the King-doms of *England* and *Ireland*, with whatſoever belongs to them, for Pardon of all his Sins, and thoſe of his Kindred, as well living as dead. To hold the ſame as in Fee of the Church of *Rome*, promiſing to pay for ſuch Tenure yearly one-thouſand Marks, *viz.* ſeven-hundred Marks for *England*, and three-hun-dred for *Ireland*; having already, by the Legate, paid to the Church of *Rome* one-thouſand Marks Sterling. And thereto were Witneſſes *Simon*, Archbiſhop of *Canterbury*, *W.* Biſhop of *London* ; *P.* Biſhop of *Wincheſter* ; *E.* of *Ely* ; *H.* of *Lincoln* ; *W. de Gray*, Chancellor ; *William de Longſpe* Earl of *Saliſbury*, the King's Brother ; *R.* Earl of *Cheſter* ; *W. Mareſcall*, Earl of *Pembroc* ; *Ro-bert de Roſſe* ; *William* Earl *Ferrers* ; *S.* Earl of *Wincheſter* ; *W. Briwere*, *Pe-ter Fitz-Herbert*, *Matthew Fitz-Herbert*, and this *Brian de L'Iſle*, Sewer.

In 17 *John*, he [i] accounted for the Fermes of the Honour of *Peverel* and *Boleſover*. And, when the Barons grew imperious and turbulent, he [k] was one of the Perſons principally intruſted with the King's Forces in *Yorkſhire* ; whereupon he had [l] the Lands of *Robert de Percy* and *Peter de Plumpton* (who were then in Arms in thoſe Parts) given to him for his better Support in that Service.

In 18 *John*, he [m] had Command to fortify the Caſtle at *Boleſover*, and to hold it againſt the rebellious Barons ; but, if he could not make it tenable, then to demoliſh it, whereby they might not have Advantage by it.

In 1 *Hen.* III, when thoſe Barons had poſſeſſed themſelves of the Caſtle at *Montſorel* in Com. *Leiceſt.* he was [n] one of the chief Commanders of thoſe Forces ſent to beſiege it ; as alſo of thoſe [o] at the Battle of *Lincoln*, where the rebelli-ous Barons, had an intire Overthrow. In which Year, being again [p] conſti-tuted Governor of *Cnareſburgh* Caſtle, and having found [q] much Benefit by the War, he was not inclined to leave that Imployment when a Peace was ſettled, as the Hiſtorian relates. But it appears on Record, that he was one among the Barons of the King's Party, who ſigned the Treaty of Peace, between King *Henry the Third*, and *Lewis*, eldeſt Son of *Philip* King of *France*, at *Lambeth*, 11 *Sept.* 1217, 1 *Hen.* III.

In 2 *Henry* III, he was one of the Barons [s] the King commiſſioned to give to *Lewelin*, Prince of *Wales*, Poſſeſſion of the Lands of *Wenhunwen* in *Wales*, and in *Mungumer*, whereof he was diſſeized in the Time of the War between King *John* and his Barons, to hold till the Heir of the ſaid *Wenhunwen* came of Age. And, ſtanding much in Favour with the King, he was, in 5 *Henry* III, made [t] Warden of all the Foreſts throughout *England*: Alſo, in 6 *Henry* III, had his [u] Commiſſion for the Government of *Cnareſburgh* Caſtle renewed. In 7 *Henry* III, he was [w] conſtituted Governor of the Caſtles of *Peke* and *Boleſover* ; and the ſame Year obtained [x] a Grant in Fee Farm of the Lordſhips of *Cnareſburgh*, and *Burrowghbrigge*, to hold at the ancient Ferm, *i. e.* fifty Pounds *per Ann.* during the King's Pleaſure.

In 8 *Henry* III, on thoſe Diſputes between the King, and divers of his Barons (which occaſioned the Earls of *Cheſter* and *Leiceſter* to put themſelves in Arms) he [y] ſtood firm to the King. And with *Hubert de Burgh*, Juſtice of *England*, and other Barons [z], wrote to Pope *Honorius*, deſiring thoſe Traitors in his Dominions may not be allowed to return into *England*.

In 9 *Henry* III, he was joined in Commiſſion with *Hugh de Nevile*, to in-quire [a] by the Oaths of Jurors, the Bounds of the Foreſts throughout *England*, and to certify what ought to be disforeſted, purſuant to the great Charter. In 13 *Henry* III, he was [b] again made Governor of the Caſtle in the *Peke* ; and, in

---

[i] Rot. Pip. 17 Joh. Comp. Br. de Inſula.　　[k] Mat. Paris 176. n. 30.　　[l] Clauſ. 17 Joh. m. 11.　　[m] Pat. 18 Joh. m. 8.　　[n] Mat. Paris 293. n. 30.　　[o] Ibid. 295. l. 8. [p] Pat. 1 H. III. m. 7.　　[q] Mat. Paris 300. n. 20.　　[r] Rymer, Tom. 1. p. 221.　　[s] Ibid. p. 226.　　[t] Pat. 5 H. III. m. 4.　　[u] Pat. 6 H. III. m. 6.　　[w] Pat. 7 H. III. m. 5. [x] Clauſ. 7 H. III. m. 10.　　[y] Mat. Paris 320. n. 8.　　[z] Rymer, Tom. 1. p. 264.　　[a] Mat. Paris 324. n. 30.　　[b] Pat. 13 H. III. m. 3.

16 *Henry* III, obtained [c] a new Grant of the Guardianſhip of the Caſtle and Honour of *Cnareſburgh*, and Caſtle [d] of *Peke*.

In 17 *Henry* III, he was conſtituted Sheriff of *Yorkſhire* [e], as alſo Governor of the Caſtles of *Scardburgh* and *Pickering* ; and, in 18 *Henry* III [f], was once more made Governor of *Boleſover* Caſtle, in which Year he died ; and his Accounts for thoſe Truſts are [g] but for one Half of the ſaid Year. Alſo, the ſame Year, *Thomas Briton* and *Alice* his Wife, *William de Glamorgan*, and *Ralph de Scopham* [h], were found to be his Heirs, and had Livery of his Lands, paying an hundred Marks Fine.

There was alſo in the ſame Age *Hugh de L'Iſle*, who, in 13 *John* [i], gave two-hundred Marks, and an Horſe of Price, for the Marriage of *Catharine* his Daughter and Heir. And, in 15 *John*, *William de Cantilupe* [k] paid two-hundred Marks for her, to be a Wife for his Son.

Contemporary with the ſaid *Brian*, and *Hugh*, and probably their Brother, was *Robert de L'Iſle* [l], Son of *Ralph de L'Iſle*, Grandſon and Heir of another *Ralph de L'Iſle*. Which *Robert*, having been in Arms with the rebellious Barons againſt King *John* [m], had his Lands ſeized ; but, in 1 *Henry* III [n], returning to Obedience, had [o] Reſtitution of them, lying in the Counties of *Lincoln*, *Kent*, *York*, *Norfolk* and *Suffolk*. Alſo, the ſame Year, having married [p] *Roheſe*, Widow [q] of *Robert de Tatſhall*, and one of the Daughters and Coheirs of *John de Wahul*, paying (with *Robert de Baſingham*, who had wedded *Agnes* the other Coheir) two-hundred Pounds to the King for their Relief [r], had Livery of that Inheritance.

This *Robert* is ſaid to have married another Wife [s], *Iſabel*, Daughter and Heir of *Warine-Fitz-Warren*, Lord of *Heyford-Warine*, in Com. *Oxon* ; but by Record it appears [t] that he married *Alice*, Daughter and Heir of *Henry*, ſecond Son of *Warine*, Son of *Gerold*, with whom he had the Lordſhip of *Heyford-Warine*. It is further ſaid [u], that he gave one Part of the *Vill* of *Newmarket*, with *Caſſandra* his Daughter, to *Richard de Argenten* ; and that *Robert de L'Iſle* was his Son and Heir, which alſo appears from the Record before cited relating to the Manor of *Heyford-Warine*.

This laſt *Robert de L'Iſle* was [w] Lord of *Rugemont* in Com. *Devon*, or *Rubemont* (as ſometimes wrote) by Deſcent from his Anceſtors, and, in 48 *Henry* III, was [x] conſtituted Governor of the Caſtles of *Marlborough* and *Lutgareſhull*, in Com. *Wilts*. But, in 49 *Henry* III, taking Part with the rebellious Barons, was by them (the King being then their Priſoner) [y] made Governor of *Newcaſtle upon Tine*.

In 10 *Edw*. I, he [z] had Command from the King to be at *Worceſter* on *Whitſunday*, with Horſe and Arms, to march with him againſt the *Welſh*, who had taken *Roger de Clifford*, Senior, Priſoner, and had invaded the Lands of his Subjects with Fire and Sword. And *Gerard de L'Iſle* was alſo ſummoned at the ſame Time. When this *Robert* died, I do not find, but he left Iſſue [a] *Robert de L'Iſle de Rugemont*, ſummoned among the Barons in the Reign of King *Edward the Second*, of whom I ſhall hereafter treat, and *Warine de L'Iſle*.

Which *Warine* [b], in 26 *Edw*. I, was in the Wars of *Scotland*, as [c] alſo in 28 *Edw*. I. In 1 *Edw*. II, he was made [d] Governor of *Oxford*, and, the Year after, of *Windſor* Caſtle [e], and Warden of the Foreſt there.

---

[c] Pat. 16 H. III. m. 1.　　[d] Ibid. m. 9.　　[e] Pat. 17 H. III. m. 5.　　[f] Pat. 18 H. III. m. 15.　　[g] Rot. Pip. 18 H. III. Ebor.　　[h] Rot. Fin. 18 H. III. m. 2. & Rot. Pip. 19 H. III. Somers.　　[i] Rot. Pip. 13 Joh. Northampt. & Rot. Pip. 2 H. III. Buck. & Bedf.　　[k] Rot. Fin. 15 Joh. m. 2.　　[l] Jekyl's Barones Extincti. MS. p. 111. b.　　[m] [n] [o] Clauſ. 1 H. III. m. 4.　　[p] [q] Rot. Fin. 1 H. III. m. 1. & 5 H. III. m. 2.　　[r] Rot. Fin. 1 H. III. m. 1.　　[s] Barones Extincti.　　[t] Plac. coram Rege ap. Weſtm. T. Trin. 3 E. II. pro Manerio de Heyford-Warine.　　[u] Baron. Extinct. præd.　　[w] Ibid.　　[x] Pat. 48 H. III. m. 3.　　[y] Pat. 49 H. III. m. 27.　　[z] Rymer's Fœdera, Vol. 2. p. 190.　　[a] Baron. Extinct.　　[b] Rot. Scoc. 26 E. I. m. 7.　　[c] Rot. Scoc. 28 E. I. m. 14.　　[d] Rymer, Tom. 3. p. 78.　　[e] Rot. Fin. 2 E. II. m. 16.

In 4 *Edw.* II, he was [f] again in the *Scottish* Wars ; and, in 5 *Edw.* II, the King sent his Mandate to *Warine de L'Isle*, Constable of *Windsor* Castle. That, whereas he had ordered *Elisabeth*, the Wife of *Robert de Bruce*, to remain in that Castle [g], he therefore commands him to provide such Apartments as are sufficient for her and her Family.

In 7 *Edw.* II, he was [h] once more in the *Scottish* Wars ; but, in 14 *Edw.* II, having been [i] much oppressed by the *Spencers*, he put himself in Arms with other of the Barons. And, following *Thomas* Earl of *Lancaster* [k], shared with him, and the rest of his Adherents, in their ill Success.

The King being present at *Pontefract*, the *Monday* after the Annunciation of the Virgin *Mary*, 1322, 15 *Edw.* II. *Thomas* Earl of *Lancaster*, this *Warine de L'Isle*, and others, were brought before him [l], in the Presence of *Edmund* Earl of *Kent*, *John* Earl of *Richmond*, *Audomar de Valence* Earl of *Pembroke*, *John de Warine* Earl of *Surry*, *Edmund* Earl of *Arundel*, *David* Earl of *Athol*, and other great Men of the Kingdom : When it was deposed, That *Thomas* Earl of *Lancaster*, and his Adherents, opposed the King's Passage over *Burton-Bridge*, for three Days, and slew some of his Men. And that, the King seeking another Passage, the Earl, &c. perceiving it, set Fire to the Town and left it, taking the Field, and displaying their Colours in an hostile Manner : But, when they saw the King coming, quitted their Post, flying in Disorder, committing in their Way great Plunder, till they came to *Borough-Bridge*, where being opposed, by some of the King's Party, they engaged them, and slew several, but at length, he the said Earl was taken, and his whole Body routed. For which Treason, Murders, Plundering, Burning, and Robbing, the said Earl was sentenced to be hanged ; but, in Respect to his noble Birth, the King remitted two Parts of his Sentence, and only ordered his Head to be severed from his Body. That *Warine de L'Isle*, *William Touchet*, *Henry de Bradeborn*, *William Fitz-William*, and *William Cheney*, also taken for the same Crimes and brought by the Marshal before the King and his Peers, should be drawn and hanged.

Stow relates [m], That the before-mentioned, all Barons, were hanged and quartered at *Pontefract*. By the Inquisition taken in 1 *Edw.* III, the Jury found that this *Warine de L'Isle* died seized [n] of the Manors of *Kingston*, *Bouden*, and *Flanflore*, in Com. *Berks*, *Mundeford* in Com. *Norfolk*, and *Kislingbury* in Com. *Northampton* ; and that *Gerard* his Son and Heir, was at that Time twenty-three Years of Age : *Alice* his Wife also surviving, who [o] was Sister and Heir of *Henry le Tyes*, one of the Barons of the Realm, who also taking Part with *Thomas* Earl of *Lancaster* [p], suffered Death for it at *London*.

But in 1 *Edw.* III, it [q] was determined in Parliament, that all Persons, who, in the Time of King *Edward* his Father, were in the Quarrel of *Thomas* Earl of *Lancaster*, to prosecute *Hugh le Despencer*, Senior, and *Hugh le Despencer*, Junior, should repossess their Lands, &c. And the King issued Mandates to the respective Sheriffs to restore them to the Possession thereof ; and those of *York*, *Essex*, and *Norfolk*, were commanded to deliver Possession to *Alice*, late Wife of *Warine de L'Isle*.

The said *Alice* in 4 *Edw.* III [r], procured the King's Pardon for herself ; and in 6 *Edw.* III, obtained [s] a Charter for a Market every Week, on the *Wednesday*, at her Manor of *Pensans* in Com. *Cornub.* also, for a Fair there to begin on the Eve of St. *Peter ad Vincula* (commonly called *Lammas*) and to continue five Days after that Feast. Likewise [t], for a Fair at *Mushole*, in the same County, to begin on the Eve of St. *Bartholomew* the Apostle, and to continue five Days after.

[f] Rot. Scoc. 4 E. II. m. 13.   [g] Rymer, Tom. 3. p. 202.   [h] Rot. Scoc. 7 E. II. m. 5.
[i] Knighton 2547. n. 50.   [k] Ib. 2539. n. 10.   [l] Rymer Tom. 3. p. 936 & seq.
[m] Annals p. 220.   [n] Escaetr. 1 Edw. III. m. 15.   [o] Clauf. 1 Edw. III. p. 1 m. 15.
[p] Walfingham, p. 95.   [q] Rymer Tom. 4. p. 258. & seq.   [r] Pat. 4 Edw. III. m. 17.
[s] Cart. 6 Edw. III. n. 29.   [t] Ibid.

In 10 *Edw.* III, ſhe had alſo [u] a Charter for free Warren, at *Chilton-Teys, Draycot,* and *Lidyerd,* in *Wiltſhire* ; *Hordwell, Kingſton L' Iſle, Bethel-king, Fauclere,* and *Budone,* in Com. *Berks* ; and *Shirebourne* in Com. *Oxon,* which was the capital Seat of her Brother's Barony. She had alſo Liberty to incloſe two-hundred Acres of Wood, two-hundred Acres of Waſte, in *Chil-ton-Teys* ; three-hundred Acres of Wood, a hundred Acres of Waſte in *Budene* ; and an hundred Acres of Wood, with forty Acres of Waſte, in *Shirebourne,* to make a Park.

Gerard her Son, in 7 *Edw.* III. [w], was in the *Scottiſh* Wars, in which Year happened [x] one of the greateſt Victories, that ever the *Engliſh* Nation ob-tained againſt the *Scots,* who attempted to raiſe the Siege of *Berwick* ; and that Town, after the Battle, being immediately ſurrendered to King *Edward,* has been in Poſſeſſion of the *Engliſh* ever ſince.

In 9 *Edw.* III, he was again in the Wars of *Scotland,* being then [y] of the Retinue of *Richard Fitz-Allan* Earl of *Arundel,* one of the [z] ſtouteſt and chief Commanders of the *Engliſh* Forces, under King *Baliol,* who entered *Scot-land* from *Berwick,* on the Twelfth of *July :* Whilſt King *Edward,* the ſame Day, paſſed over the *Solway* Frith, on the other Side, as had been appointed. And both Armies met with little Reſiſtance, by the almoſt exhauſted Powers of the *Brucians,* ſo that they ravaged the Country at their Pleaſure ; but, for their Succeſs, I refer to our Hiſtorians.

In 12 *Edw.* III, he [a] was in that Expedition then made by the King into *Flanders,* who with a Royal Navy of five-hundred Sail, ſet out from the Port of *Orewel,* near *Harwich* in *Suffolk,* on the Sixteenth of *July,* and arrived at *Antwerp,* on the Twenty-ſecond following. The King with his Army, ſtaid in *Brabant* that Summer [b], and on an Interview with the Em-peror, at *Cologne* ; it was ſo glorious and magnificent, that according to the Eſtimation of the Heralds there, who accompanied them, four great Dukes, three Archbiſhops, and ſix Biſhops, thirty-ſeven Earls, and of Barons, Banne-rets, Knights, and Eſquires, ſeventeen-thouſand were preſent.

It is not to be doubted, but this *Gerard d' L' Iſle* continued with the King and his Forces, whilſt he was Abroad [c], who to his great Coſt, waited in *Brabant,* for the Coming of the Emperor's Forces, till the Firſt of *September,* 13 *Edw.* III. And ſoon after, entering *France,* the *French* faced the *Engliſh,* at *Vironfoſſe,* reſolving to give them Battle ; but, though their Army conſiſted of one-hundred and five thouſand Men, headed by the King of *France* himſelf, *John* King of *Bohemia, Charles* King of *Navarre, David* King of *Scotland,* and the whole Power of *France,* yet after promiſing Battle, they ſhamefully retreated from King *Edward* [d], whoſe Army was very unequal in Number.

The King thereupon, waſting Part of the Realm of *France,* returned to *Ant-werp* [e], where he kept his *Chriſtmas,* with great Splendor, the Queen, and her Ladies, and his Army remaining ſtill with him ; and, for the greater Solem-nity, he ſent for his eldeſt Son Prince *Edward,* Duke of *Cornwall,* &c. who paid his Duty to him.

The Year after, the King took on him the Title and Arms of *France,* and publiſhed his Letters Monitory to his Subjects of that Kingdom, to own his Authority as of their rightful King, and to come to his Protection. And im-mediately thereupon [f], all the People of *Flanders* yielded to him, as true and rightful King of *France,* and ſubmitted themſelves and their Country to his Go-vernment. And being determined to purſue the War in *France,* with Vigour, the next Summer, the King left his Forces in *Flanders,* under the Earls of *Sa-liſbury,* and *Suffolk,* with his Queen and Children, and came to *England* to ac-quaint the Parliament with his Proceedings.

[u] Cart. 10 Edw. III. n. 43.   [w] Rot. Scoc. 7 Edw. III. m. 24.   [x] Barnes's Hiſt. of Edw. III. p. 79, 80.   [y] Rot. Scoc. 9 Edw. III. m. 28   [z] Barnes p. 95.   [a] Rot. Aleman. 12 Edw. III. m. 6.   [b] Barnes p. 120, 121, 122.   [c] Ibid p. 134, & ſeq.   [d] Ibid. p. 146.   [e] Ibid p 147.   [f] Ibid p. 158, 160.

How long this *Gerard d' L' Isle* staid with the Army, does not appear; but it is evident [g], from Records, as well as our Historians, that he was in the Wars of *France*, in 20 & 21 *Edw*. III. *Barnes*, in his History of *Edward the Third*, p. 340, relates that the King went on Board, at *Southampton*, in the Close of *June*, with the Prince of *Wales*, and most of his Nobles, and among them he particularly mentions the Lord *Gerard d' L' Isle*, and his Kinsman the Lord *John de L' Isle*. By contrary Winds they were put by Landing at *Bordeaux*, and being drove back to the Coasts of *Cornwall*, the King commanded his Pilots to direct their Course for *Normandy*, and on the Eleventh of *July* happily arrived with his Fleet at *la Hogue*. To relate the particular Successes of the King is not any Part of my Design; I shall only observe, that he took several strong Towns, and came before *Paris*; and laid the Country in Ashes, near the Walls of that City, which the *French* King abandoned. King *Edward*'s Letter, in Answer to King *Philip*, is so memorable, that I shall recite it, as an Honour to this Lord *Gerard d' Lisle*, and those noble Commanders with him [h].

Edward, *by the Grace of God*, King *of* France, *and* England, *and Lord of* Ireland, *unto the illustrious Lord*, Philip *Earl of* Valois.

Sir Philip of Valois,

'WE have read your Letters, wherein you signify unto us, that you
'will combate with our whole Power, between St. *Germain de Prez*,
'and *Valgirart de la Paris*, or between *Franconville* and *Pont-Oyse*, this *Thurs-*
'day, or on *Saturday*, *Sunday*, or *Monday* next following; provided that nei-
'ther we, nor our People, do any Damage, Spoil, or Waste. Whereupon we
'give you to know, that, through Assurance in God, and the clear Right
'which we have to the Crown of *France*, which you usurp injuriously, to
'the Disherison of us, our Country, God and Right, we are come not in any
'Pride, or Presumption, into our said Realm of *France*, holding our Way
'towards you, to make an End of the War between us: But that, when it was
'in your Power to have Battle, you caused the Bridges to be broken down
'between you and us; so that we could not approach unto you, nor pass the
'Water of *Seyne*, till we were come to *Poissy*, and there we took Order to re-
'pair the Bridge, which you had caused to be broken; and we tarried there
'three Days, waiting for you and your Power, which you have assembled;
'unto which Place you might have come, either on the one Side, or the other,
'at your Pleasure. And, because we cannot have Battle with you, we have
'taken a Resolution to pass further into our said Realm to comfort those that
'are our Friends and faithful, and to chastise those who are rebellious unto
'us, whom you unjustly call your Subjects. And surely we will stay in our
'said Realm, without Departing, till we have atchieved our War, as far
'as we may, to our Advantage, and the Grievance of our Adversaries.
'Wherefore, if you are desirous, as your Letters report, to fight with us, and
'to save those whom you claim as your Subjects (if you will let us know,
'at what Time you will come) you shall find us ready in the Field to en-
'counter you, by the Help of God: Which Thing we ardently desire for the
'Benefit of *Christendom*; seeing that you will not vouchsafe either to offer, or
'admit of any reasonable Way of Peace with us. But we are not all advised
'to be directed by you, nor to accept of Place and Day of Battle from you
'on the Conditions above-written. Dated at *Anneville*, this *Thursday*, the Se-
'venteenth of *August*, in the Year of our Reign of *France*, the Seventh, and of
'*England*, the Twentieth.

Soon after, was fought the famous Battle of *Cressy*, where King *Edward* gained an intire Victory, though the *French* were four to one. And it is me-

[g] Rot. Franc. 21 Edw. III. p. 1. m. 9. & Rot. Franc. 21 Edw. III. p. 1. m. 18.　　　[h] Barnes
P. 349.

morable

morable that he came before *Calais*, on *Thursday* the last of *August*, the same Year, according to *Du Chesne*; but others [i] say, the Seventh of *September*; and laying Siege to that strong Town, notwithstanding it was carried on with great Application (all Means being used to divert the Siege) it did not surrender till the Fourth of *August* 1347, 21 *Edw.* III. It has been already proved, that this Lord *Gerard d'L'Isle* was with the King, during the whole Time, so that this short Summary of the two Year's Campaign will not I hope be thought a Digression, since it was so much to the Honour of the Nation.

The next Mention, that I find of him, is in 24 *Edw.* III. when the King at *Rotherhith*, the Eighth of *September* 1350, sent his Mandate to *Bartholomew de Burghersh*, Constable of *Dover* Castle, and Warden of the Cinque Ports, to permit [k] this *Gerard d'Lisle*, with his Servants and seven Horses, to pass the Seas in his Journey to *Rome*. On what Account, he went thither, is not said, but Mandates [l] were sent, at the same Time, for several Barons, and Persons of Distinction.

In 28 *Edw.* III. [m], *Elisabeth*, Widow of *Edmund de St. John*, is said to be his Wife. She [n] was Daughter of *John* Lord *Strange* of *Blackmere*, but whether he had a former Wife I do not find: In the same Year he was in *England*, and among those Barons in Parliament at *Westminster* [o], who constituted *Richard de Wymondeswold*, and others, their Proctors, to consent on their Parts, to what shall be agreed on, between the King's Ambassadors, and those of *France*, before the Pope, not judicially, but as a private Person. And he is therein wrote *Gerard d'Lisle*, Lord of *Stowe*.

In 31 *Edw.* III, he had [p] also Summons to Parliament, amongst the Barons of the Realm. And, in 33 *Edw.* III. [q], was again in the Wars of *France* with the King [r], who on the Feast of St. *Simon* and *Jude*, the Twenty-eighth of *October*, 1329, embarqued on Board the *Philip* of *Dartmouth*, at *Sandwich* in *Kent*, and having a fair Wind made the Port of *Calais*, that Evening. *Barnes* relates [s], that the King's Summons, at this Time had been particularly severe, for none [t] were permitted to stay at Home, between the Age of twenty and sixty, without some special Exemption; and after many Thousands had been turned back, there remained [u], at least, a hundred-thousand of the most chosen Men. And, to receive them and their Provision, there lay at *Sandwich* one-thousand one-hundred and twenty-three Sail of Ships, some of which had returned from *Cálais*, after Conveying the Duke of *Lancaster*, with a prodigious Quantity of Provisions to be laid up in Magazines, against the King's Coming. How the Army proceeded, I refer to our Historians and shall only observe [w], that this Lord *Gerard d'L'Isle* was with the King, when he came before *Paris*, and continued with him till the famous Peace made at *Bretigny*, near *Chartres*, in 34 *Edw.* III. where the two eldest Sons of *England* and *France* solemnly swore to uphold the Articles of the said Peace; King *John* of *France* being then Prisoner in *England*. But this sacred and solemn Oath, which the Duke of *Normandy* (eldest Son of King *John*) took for the Performance of the said Treaty, was most treacherously broke by him in the Reign of the same King *Edward*, when he thought he had an Advantage of the King of *England*. And it may justly be said, that all the Kings of *France*, since, have kept no Treaties with any of the Powers of *Europe*, further than for their own Interest.

The King landed [x] at *Rye* in *Kent*, the Eighteenth of *May* 1360, 34 *Edw.* III; and this Lord *Gerard d'L'Isle* departed this Life the same Year [y], leaving *Warine*, his Son and Heir, of full Age.

[i] Knighton, p. 2588. [k] Rymer Tom. 5. p. 681. [l] Ibid. [m] Rot. Fin. 28 Edw. III. m. 12. [n] Jekyl's Baron. Extinct. *MS*. [o] Rymer ib. p. 797 & seq. [p] Clauf. de iisd. Ann. in Dorso. [q] Rot. Franc. 33 Edw. III. m. 9. [r] Rymer Tom. 6. p. 141. [s] Hist. of Edw. III. p. 566. [t] Knighton, p. 2623. n. 10. [u] Mezeray & Mat. Villani l. 9. c. 53. p. 539. [w] Rot. Franc. 34 Edw. III. [x] Ashmole's Life of King Edw. in Hist. Ord. Gart. p. 662. [y] Clauf. 34 Edw. III. m. 12.

Which *Warine de L'Isle*, in his Father's Life-time, *viz.* 30 *Edw.* III, was with *Edward* Prince of *Wales*, in *Gascony*; and it is very probable was also with him, in 33 & 34 *Edw.* III, in that Royal Expedition into *France* made by the King, wherein his Father, the Lord *Gerard de L'Isle*, served.

In 43 *Edw.* III, he [a] was made Governor of the Town of *Portsmouth*; and on the Twenty-ninth of *September*, 1369, 43 *Edw.* III, was commissioned with *Thomas del More*, Lieutenant of *Richard* Earl of *Arundel*, Constable of the Castle of *Porchestre* [b], to enquire into the Damages each Person had suffered by the *French*, in Burning of the Town of *Portsmouth*. That this *Warine de L'Isle* was in the Wars of *France*, the same Year [c], appears on Record; and in 46 *Edw.* III, being then a Knight Banneret [d], was retained by Indenture, to serve the King in the Wars of *France*, for one whole Year, with twenty Men at Arms, and thirty Archers. Of which Men at Arms himself, being a Banneret, four Knights, and five Esquires, were Part.

In 47 *Edw.* III, he covenanted [e], that *Gerard de L'Isle* his Son, should marry *Anne*, the Daughter of Sir *Michael de la Pool*, Knight, who was to give her nine-hundred thirty-three Pounds, six Shillings, and Eight-pence, for her Portion.

In 51 *Edw.* III, he [f] obtained License, to make a Castle of his House at *Shirbourne* in Com. *Oxon*.

In 1 *R.* II, he [g] was again in the Wars of *France*; and, in [h] 3 *R.* II, went into *Ireland*. And having been summoned to Parliament [i], amongst the Barons from 43 *Edw.* III, till 5 *R.* II, inclusive, departed this Life [k], the Twenty-eighth of *June*, 6 *R.* II, being then seized of the Manor of *Wengrave* in *Buckinghamshire*, *Stow* in *Northamptonshire*, *Chilton-Foliot* in *Wiltshire*; *Kingston-Lisle*, *Colcote*, and *Ordeston* in *Berkshire*; *Sherbourne*, *Noke*, and *Fretewell* in *Oxfordshire*; *Alwarton* and *Trevarnayk*, in the County of *Cornwall*; and *Charlton*, *Tattercote*, *North-Bovy*, and *Langdon*, in *Devonshire*.

His Wife was *Margaret* [l], Daughter and Heiress of *William Pipard*, Knight, [m] Son and Heir of *Thomas Pipard*, Knight, summoned to Parliament among the Barons in 17 *Edw.* III, and a Descendant from *Ralph Fitz-Nicholas* [n], Steward of the Houshold to King *Henry the Third*; and by that Title, I find him, in 11 *H.* III, when [o] he was a Witness to the King's Promise of giving an Equivalent to *Isabel* Countess of *Angolesm*, in Consideration of her Dowry, in *Normandy*, *Aquitain*, and *Poictou*. Also the same Year, having the [p] Title of Sewer to the King, he was sent with *William* Earl of *Pembroke*, Marshal of *England*, and others, to the Princes of the Empire at *Aunvers*, to treat with them, about a League to be made between the Emperor and the King. The Year after, 12 *H.* III, he was [q] sent with *Philip de Albini*, to *Lewis* King of *France*, to compleat the Truce between the two Kings, as enjoined by Pope *Gregory the Ninth*. On the Twenty-fifth of *August*, 14 *H.* III, the King declared, That the Truce concluded with the King of *France* [r], by this *Ralph Fitz-Nicholas* his Steward, to hold till *Sunday* after *Midsummer-Day*, is prorogued till *Lady-Day*. He was in most Transactions of that King's Reign; and in 38 *H.* III, bearing the Title of Steward to the King, he [s] was a Witness to that Grant made by *Edward*, the King's eldest Son, with the Assent of his Father, to *Elianor*, Sister of *Alfonsus* King of *Castile*, of the Castle and Town of *Tickhull*, *Stamford*, and *Grantham*, and the Castle and Town of *Peck*, with their Appurtenances, for a Thousand Pounds Land. And when she comes to be Queen, he promises to add five-hundred Marks more of Land. This was in Order to his Marriage.

[z] Rymer Vol. 5. p. 844.   [a] Ib. Tom. 6. p. 633.   [b] Ib. p. 638.   [c] Rot. Franc. 43 Edw. III. m. 8.   [d] Ex Autogr. penes Tho. Com. Elgin. An. 1659.   [e] Clauf. 47 Edw. III. in dorso m. 28.   [f] Pat. 51 Edw. III. m. 32.   [g] Rot. Franc. 1 R. II. p. 2. m. 14. [h] Pat. 3 R. II. p. 2. m. 4.   [i] Clauf. de iisd. Ann. in dorso.   [k] Esc. 6. R. II. n. 47. & Clauf. 6 R. II. p. 1. m. 20.   [l] Clauf. 50 Edw. III. p. 2. m. 25.   [m] Baron. Extinct. præd.   [n] Mat. Par. in An. 1257.   [o] Rymer's Fœdera, Tom. 1. p. 288.   [p] Ib. p. 295. [q] Ib. p. 302.   [r] Ib. p. 315.   [s] Ib. p. 519.

This

This *Ralph Fitz-Nicholas* being so eminent a Person, I thought it not improper to mention him, as *Margaret Pipard* the Wife of the said *Warine de L'Isle* was his Heir, by whom he had Issue one Son *Gerard de L'Isle*, who died before him, so that, at the Time of his Decease, *Margaret* was his Daughter and Heir. But, before I treat of her, I shall give some Account of her Brother *Gerard de L'Isle.*

It is before recited, that, in 47 *Edw.* III, his Father covenanted for him to marry *Anne* Daughter of Sir *Michael de la Pool*, Knight ; and, at the Coronation of King *Richard the Second* [t], the King knighted *Edward*, Son of *Edmund* Earl of *Kent* ; *John* Son of *Thomas* Lord *Roos*, of *Hamelack* ; *Robert de Grey* of *Rotherfield* ; *Richard* Son of *Gilbert* Lord *Talbot* ; *Gerard* Son of *Warine de L'Isle*, *Michael* Son of *Michael de la Pool*, *Richard de Ponynges*, *Robert de Haryngton*, and *Thomas de la Mare*, giving to each of them large Presents. This Sir *Gerard de L'Isle* [u] was afterwards in the Wars of *France*, and being taken Prisoner, with *Michael de la Pool*, and *John de Beurle*, the King, the Twentieth of *January* 1379, 3 *R.* II, sent *John Gavison*, and others, to ransom them, and those, appointed to the Custody of the Ports of *Dover* and *Sandwich*, had the King's Mandate for to let them pass without Molestation. It may be presumed, he died under his Imprisonment, for he was dead before his Father, and, in 6 *R.* II, *Margaret* his Sister [w], was sole Heir to the said *Warine* Lord *L'Isle*, and, at that Time, the Wife of *Thomas* Lord *Berkley*, and of the Age of twenty-two Years.

In the Evidences at *Berkley* Castle, it appears that she was married to *Thomas* Lord *Berkley* in 41 *Edw.* III, at *Wengrave* in *Buckinghamshire*, the Lord *L'Isle's* House ; and that when his Father, *Maurice* Lord *Berkley*, died (*viz.* in 42 *Edw.* III. [x]) he was but in the sixteenth Year of his Age. Also, when *Gerard de L'Isle*, her Brother, died, her Father, *Warine* Lord *L'Isle*, went to *Berkley* Castle, and made it his Residence in his latter Days. And his Son-in-Law, having the Prospect of so great an Estate, covenanted [y] with him, *That he and the Issue which he should beget on his Daughter, would, after his Death, always use, and bear the Arms of the said Lord* L'Isle ; which were, *Gules, a Lion passant Argent.* The Lordships and Lands, which he had by her [z], were the Mannors of *Charleton, Tetcote, Clonton, Norbery, Langdon, Donn-Cary,* and *Larkbear,* in *Devonshire* ; *Wengrave* in *Buckinghamshire* ; *Stow* and *Church-Brampton* in *Northamptonshire* ; *Chilton-Foliot, Nethercote, Draycote, Horewell, Chikeld, Frishedon,* in *Wiltshire* ; *Kingston-L'Isle, Hordwell, Colect, Ordeston, Buden, Caldicote,* and *Cakewood,* in Com. *Berks* ; *Shirebourne, Noke, Fretwell,* in *Oxfordshire* ; and *Aylwerton, Trevernake, Pensans, Moshole,* in the County of *Cornwall* ; besides divers Advowsons of Churches, and many Lands and Tenements in other Places.

Which Lady *Margaret* died [a] at *Wotton-under-Edge*, 20 *Martii* 15 *R.* II, and lieth buried in the Parish Church there, under a fair Tomb : *Thomas* her Husband surviving her a long Time, who [b] made his Will on *Sunday*, the *Purification of the blessed Virgin, An.* 1415 (3 *H.* V.) and bequeathed to the Fabrick of that Church, wherein his Body shall happen to be buried, a Cross gilt, with all the Relicks included therein : To his Daughter the Countess of *Warwick*, his best Pair of Mattins, as also one gilt Cup, with twenty Pounds contained therein : To *James* his Nephew, his next Heir Male (being Son of *James* his Brother, deceased) his best Bed, and great Cup of Jet, as also twenty Coats of Mail, twenty Breast-plates, and the like Number of Lances : *And, departing this Life at his Mannor of* Wotton-under-Edge, *on* Tuesday 13 July, 5 *H.* V, [c] left *Elisabeth*, then the Wife of *Richard Beauchamp*, Earl of *Warwick*, his only Child by her the said *Margaret*, Heir to the Lordships and Lands of her Mother, as before-mentioned ; and was, at the Death of her

---

[t] Rymer, Tom. 6, p. 157, & seq.   [u] Ibid. p. 230.   [w] Rot. Fin. 6 R. II. m. 25.
[x] Esc. 42 Ed. III. n. 12.   [y] Ex Autog. apud Berkley.   [z] Ibid.   [a] Abbot Newland's Pedigree in Castro de Berkley.   [b] Ex Regiſtr. Chichley Vol. 1. 306, b. in Offic. Principal Cantuar.
[c] Esc. 5 H. V. n. 50.

Father, thirty Years of Age. She also brought to the Earl of *Warwick* all those Lands, whereof her Father died seized in Fee-Simple, or Fee-Tail General, which were about thirty Lordships, in the Counties of *Gloucester*, *Bucks*, *Wilts*, *Northampton*, *Devon*, *Cornwall*, *Oxon*, *Berks*; the City of *London*, *Bristol*, and other Places, besides Advowsons of Churches, &c.

The said *Richard Beauchamp*, Earl of *Warwick*, was one of the greatest Peers of the Realm, and signalized himself by many brave Actions in the Reigns of *Henry the Fourth*, *Fifth*, and *Sixth*, and [d] used these Titles in his Charters, *Ric. de Beauchamp Comes de Warrewyk & de Aumarle, Seignior L'Isle, & Capitayne de Roven.*

By his Testament, bearing Date [e] at *Caversham* in *Oxfordshire*, 8 *August*, 1435, 15 *Henry* VI, he appointed his Executors to cause a goodly Tomb of Marble to be erected in the Abbey of *Kingswood* in *Gloucestershire*, over the Grave of *Elisabeth* his first Wife. And departing this Life the last of *April*, 1439, 17 *Henry* VI, as his monumental Inscription sheweth, on his magnificent Tomb, in our *Lady* Chapel in *Warwick*, left Issue, by the said *Elisabeth* his first Wife, three Daughters, his Heirs, viz. [f] *Margaret*, born at *Goodrest* in *Wedgnok-Park* near *Warwick*, the next Year after the Battle of *Shrewsbury*, who was second Wife to the famous *John Talbot* Earl of *Shrewsbury*; *Eleanore*, born at *Walkinston* in *Essex*, 9 *Henry* IV, first married to the Lord *Roos*, and after to *Edmund Beaufort*, Marquis of *Dorset*, and Duke of *Somerset*; and *Elisabeth*, born in *Warwick* Castle, Wife to *George Nevile* Lord *Latimer*: Which *Margaret*, Wife to the Earl of *Shrewsbury* [g], died at *London*, 14 *June* [h], Ann. 1467, 7 *Edw.* IV, and was buried under the Choir of the Cathedral of St. *Paul*, commonly called St. *Faith*'s Church, in *Jesus* Chapel [i], where a Monument of one-hundred Pounds Value should have been erected, but, instead of it, this Inscription only remained on a Pillar there [k]:

" Here, before the Image of *Ihesu*, lyeth the worshipful and right noble La-
" dy, *Margaret* Countess of *Shrewsbury*, late Wife of the true and victorious
" Knight, and redoubted Warriour, *John Talbot* Earl of *Shrewsbury*, which
" worshipfully dyed in *Guien* for the Right of this Land, the first Daughter,
" and one of the *Heirs of the right famous renowned Knight*, Richard Beau-
" champ, *late Earl of* Warwick, which died in *Roan*, and of Dame *Elisabeth*
" his Wife; the which *Elisabeth* was Daughter and Heir to *Thomas* late Lord
" *Berkley*, and on his Side; and of her Mother's Side, Lady *L'Isle* and *Tyes*.
" Which Countess passed from this World, the XIIII Day of *June*, the Year
" of our Lord 1468. On whose Soul the Lord have Mercy."

The said *John Talbot* Earl of *Shrewsbury*, having distinguished himself by many brave Actions, was, in 31 *Henry* VI [l], constituted Lieutenant of the Dutchy of *Aquitain*, and under him [m] had these Captains of his Men at Arms and Archers, viz. *John* Viscount *L'Isle* (his eldest Son by *Margaret* his second Wife) Sir *Robert Hungerford*, the Lord *Molins*, Sir *Roger Camoys*, Sir *John L'Isle*, and *John*, the Bastard of *Somerset*: And, in Consideration of his great Charge, in that high Employment, had a [n] Grant of the Thirds, and Third of the Thirds, which were reserved to the King there.

The same Year he marched into the Enemies Country [o], took *Bourdeaux*, and put a Garrison into it; whereupon divers remote Cities sent to him [p], promising to submit to his Authority. Thence hearing the *French* had besieged *Chastilion* [q], he advanced and gave them Battle, which, for a long Time, stood doubtful; but this renowned General, having been [r] smitten from his Horse by a Cannon Bullet, died on the Spot, and his whole Army, thereupon giving Way, was pre-

---

[d] Dugdale's Warwicksh. p. 329.   [e] Ex Regist. vocat. Rous. Fol. 141. in Offic. Cur. Prerog. Cantuar.   [f] Dugd. Warw. p. 329. b.   [g] Ibid.   [h] Esc. 7 E. IV. n. 44.   [i] Stow's Survey of London, p. 369. a.   [k] Ibid. and Camden's Remains, p. 378.   [l] Rot. Vascon 31 H. VI. m. 6.   [m] Ibid. m. 4.   [n] Ibid.   [o] Polydore Virgil. p. 501. n. & 20.   [p] Ib. n. 30.   [q] Ibid. p. 502.   [r] Ibid. n. 10.

sently routed. This fatal Accident happened [s] 20 *Julii*, 31 *Henry* VI, as the Inquisition taken after his Death shews ; but, his Body being conveyed into *England*, and interred at *Whitchurch* in Com. *Salop*, a noble Monument is erected there for him, in the South Wall of the Chancel, with this Inscription, whereby it appears he was slain on 7 *July*:

Orate pro Anima prænobilis Domini, Domini Johannis Talbot *quondam Comitis* Salopiæ, *Domini* Furnival, *Domini* Verdon, *Domini* Strange *de* Blackmere, *& Marefchalli* Franciæ, *qui obiit in Bello apud* Burdews, VII° Julii, Mccccliii.

He had Issue [t], by *Margaret* his second Wife before-mentioned, *John Talbot* Viscount *L'Isle*, Sir *Humphy Talbot*, and Sir *Lewis Talbot*, on whom he [u] entailed, in 21 *Henry* VI, the Mannors of *Penyard*, *Credenhil*, and *Strangeford*, in Com. *Heref.* Sir *Humphry Talbot* married *Jane*, Daughter of *John Champernon* [w], and *Elisabeth* his Wife, but died without Issue by her, before the Year 1504 : For then the said Lady *Jane Talbot* made her Will, dated the 10th of *January*, wherein she orders her Body to be buried in the Choir of the Church in the *Minories*, without *Aldgate, London*, nigh the Body of Mrs. *Anne Montgomery*, late the Wife of *John Montgomery*, Esq; and that her Executors cause a convenient Stone to be laid over her Grave, with the Picture of a dead Corpse, and Escutcheons of Arms of her late Husband Sir *Humphry Talbot*, and her, with a Title and Writing underneath, desiring all good People to pray for the Soul of her late Husband, who resteth buried at St. *Catharine*'s Mount, and her Soul. *Probat* 4 *Oct.* 1505.

The said *John Talbot* Viscount *L'Isle* [x], in respect of his Descent from *Warine* Lord *L'Isle*, viz. Son of *Margaret*, eldest Daughter and Heir of *Richard Beauchamp* Earl of *Warwick*, by *Elisabeth* his Wife, Daughter and sole Heir of *Thomas* Lord *Berkley*, by *Margaret* his Wife, Daughter and sole Heir of the said *Warine* Lord *L'Isle*. And, in Consideration that the said *Warine*, and all his Ancestors, were seized *inter alia* of the Lordship and Mannor of *Kingston L'Isle*, in Com. *Berks*, and had the Name, Dignity, Barony, and Lordship of *L'Isle*, Time out of Mind, and had Place in Sessions, and other Privileges in Parliament, and Councils, as other Barons of *England* had for the same Time. And by Reason of the Affinity in Blood of the said *John Talbot*, Son of *John* and *Margaret*, as also being possessed of the said Lordship and Mannor of *Kingston L'Isle*, and for other special Considerations, the King grants to him, his Heirs, and Assigns, the Name and Title of Baron *L'Isle*, in as ample Manner, as the aforesaid *Warine*, or any of his Ancestors, enjoyed the same, Witnesses *John* Archbishop of *Canterbury* Chancellor, *William* Bishop of *Lincoln*, *William* Bishop of *Sarum*, *Humphry* Duke of *Gloucester* the King's Uncle, *John* Duke of *Exeter* his Kinsman, *Humphry* Earl of *Strafford*, *William* Earl of *Suffolk* Steward of the Houshold, Sir *Ralph de Crombwell*, and Sir *Ralph Boteler* Treasurer, *Adam Molynz* Keeper of the Privy-Seal, and others, dated at *Westminster*, 26 *July*, 22 *Henry* VI, by Writ of Privy-Seal, and by Authority of Parliament.

And, 30 *Oct.* 30 *Henry* VI, in [y] Consideration of the great Actions of his Ancestors, his own Loyalty, and Services, the King created him Viscount *L'Isle*, to him, and the Heirs Male of his Body, and gives him Place and Precedency, next to *Henry* Viscount *Bourchier* ; and grants to him an Annuity (for Support of the said Honour) of twenty Marks, payable out of the Issues of the County of *Salop*.

The Year after, 31 *Henry* VI, his Father being constituted Lieutenant of the Dutchy of *Aquitain*, and he one of the Captains under him (as hath been observed) he was by Indenture retained to serve the King there [z], for one Quarter of a Year, with two Bannerets, four Knights, seventy-three Men at Arms

---

[s] Esc. 32 H. VI. n. 29.   [t] Registr. de Wyrksop.   [u] Clauf. 21 H. VI. m. 5. in dorso.
[w] Ex Registr. Holgrave, qu. 38.   [x] Cart. An. 22 H. VI. n. 23.   [y] Cart. ab An. 27 usque 39
H. VI. n. 22.   [z] Ex Autog. penes Cleric. Pell.

on Horseback, and eight-hundred Archers on Foot ; receiving, for himself, six Shillings *per Diem* ; for his two Bannerets, four Shillings each ; for his seven Knights, two Shillings each ; for the Men at Arms twelve Pence, and, for the Archers, six Pence a Piece. But, in the Battle of *Chastilion*, before recited [a], he had the hard Fate to be slain with his Father ; being then seized [b] of the Mannors of *Wrockwardine*, *Chefwordine*, *Sutton-Madoc*, *Brogton*, *Tafley*, *Abberbury*, and *Batterley*, in Com. *Salop*.

He married [c] *Joan*, Daughter and Coheir of *Thomas Chedder*, of the County of *Somerset*, Esq; Widow of *Richard Stafford*, Esq; by whom he left Issue [d], *Thomas Talbot* Viscount *L'Isle*, his Son and Heir and two Daughters [e] ; *Elifabeth*, married to *Edward Grey*, after created Baron and Viscount *L'Isle*, and [f] *Margaret*, to Sir *George Vere*, Knight, who had no Issue by her : Which *Joan*, his Wife, surviving him, died in 7 *Edw.* IV [g], at which Time, *Thomas* Viscount *L'Isle*, her Son and Heir, was nineteen Years of Age, and then married to [h] *Margaret*, Daughter to *William Herbert* Earl of *Pembroke*.

This *Thomas Talbot* Viscount *L'Isle*, being but [i] ten Years of Years of Age, at the Death of his Father, was committed [k] to the Tuition of *Margaret* Countefs of *Shrewsbury*, his Grand-mother, who had only twenty Marks *per Annum* allowed for his Maintenance, during his Minority. And, after his Marriage, having much Contest with *William* Lord *Berkley* (after Marquis of *Berkley*) concerning certain Lands and Lordships, his Right, from *Margaret* his Grandmother aforesaid, had the hard Fate to be slain in a Skirmish, between the same Lord *Berkley* and himself (with their Followers) at *Wotton-under-Edge* in Com. *Glouc.* 20 *Martii*, 10 *Edw.* IV, leaving his two Sisters his Heirs, as beforementioned.

G R E Y, Baron *L'Isle* and Viscount *L'Isle*.

THE Barony of *L'Isle* being granted, as before-mentioned, to *John Talbot*, and the Heirs of his Body, it reverted, on the Death of *Thomas* Viscount *L'Isle* his Son, to his Sisters and Coheirs, of which [l] *Margaret* dying without Issue, *Elifabeth*, the eldest, became sole Heir ; and was married to Sir *Edward Grey*, Knight [m], second Son of Sir *Edward Grey*, Knight, Lord *Ferrers* of *Groby*, in Right of his Wife *Elifabeth*, Daughter to *Henry*, and sole Heir to *William* Lord *Ferrers* of *Groby*, her Grandfather.

This Sir *Edward Grey*, therefore [n], in 15 *Edw.* IV, had the Dignity and Honour of Baron *L'Isle* conferred on him, and the Heirs of his Body, by the same *Elifabeth*.

The Preamble to the Patent sets forth [o], That *Warine* Lord *L'Isle*, deceased, being seized *inter alia* of the Lordship and Mannor of *Kingston L'Isle*, with the Appurtenances in *Berkshire*, had Issue a Daughter *Margaret*, Wife to *Thomas* Lord *Berkley*, and, after his Death, the said Lordship and Mannor descended to the same *Margaret*, and had Issue between them their only Daughter and Heir, *Elifabeth*, married to *Richard Beauchamp* Earl of *Warwick*, who left Issue by her *Margaret*, *Eleanor*, and *Elifabeth* : Which *Margaret*, the Daughter of *Elifabeth*, *John Talbot*, Earl of *Shrewsbury*, took to Wife, and had Issue by her *John Talbot*, Knight, unto whom the said Earl of *Shrewsbury*, in Part of the Property of the said *Margaret* (she being seized of the said Mannor and Lordship, and of all such Lands, &c. which were of the aforesaid *Elifabeth*, the Wife of the said *Richard*, at her Death, according to a Partition thereof made, between the same *Margaret* and her aforesaid Sisters) granted the Lordship and Mannor aforesaid, to him and his Heirs. And that he, the said *John*, had Issue Sir *Thomas Talbot*, Knight, late Viscount *L'Isle*, and *Elifabeth*, now the Wife of Sir *Edward Grey*, Knight, Lord *L'Isle*, and also *Margaret*, late the

[a] Esc. 7 E. IV. post Mort. ejusd. Johan. Viscecom. L'Isle.   [b] Esc. 38 H. VI.   [c] Lel. Coll. Vol. 3. p. 210.   [d] Esc. 32 H. VI. n. 38.   [e] Esc. 9 & 10 E. IV. n. 58.   [f] Orig. 10 E. IV. Rot. 11. n. 15.   [g] Esc. 7 E. IV. n. 4.   [h] Ex Vet. Script. in Castro de Berkley.   [i] Esc. 32 H. VI. n. 38.   [k] Clauf. 37 H. VI. n. 40.   [l] Cart. 15 E. IV. n. 18.   [m] Ex Stemmate de Gray, 4. D. 14. in Coll. Arm.   [n] Cart. 15 E. IV. n. 18.   [o] Ibid.

Wife

Wife of Sir *George Vere*, Knight, and died. After whofe Death, the Lordſhip
and Mannor aforeſaid deſcended to the ſaid *Thomas*, as Son and Heir of the
ſaid *John*. After whofe Death, it deſcended to the aforeſaid *Eliſabeth* and *Margaret*, as Siſters and Heirs of the ſame *Thomas*: Which ſaid *Eliſabeth*, Sir *Edward Grey*, Knight, took to Wife; and afterwards, the aforeſaid *Margaret*
died without an Heir of her Body begotten, whereby the ſaid Sir *Edward
Grey*, Knight, and *Eliſabeth* his Wife, are ſeized of the ſaid Lordſhip and
Mannor, in Demeſne as of Fee in Right of the ſaid *Eliſabeth*, and had Iſſue
between them, lawfully begotten, *John*, and others. The King, therefore, in
Conſideration, that *Warine de L'Iſle*, and all his Anceſtors, had and obtained
(by Reaſon of the Mannor and Lordſhip aforeſaid) the Name and Dignity of
a Baron, and Lord of *L'Iſle*, from the Time whereof the Memory of Man is not
to the contrary; and that he, and all his Anceſtors, by ſuch Name, obtained
Place and Sitting, and other Preheminence in the Parliaments and Councils of
the Kingdom, as other the Barons of *England* had: Alſo, contemplating
his princely Eſtate, rendered more ſublime by the Number of Subjects, and the
Royal Throne ſo much the more exalted, and the Government of the Kingdom eſtabliſhed, when there are in it Men of noble Condition, and of eminent
Quality, *&c.* Therefore grants to the ſaid *Edward*, that he and his Heirs, on
the Body of the ſame *Eliſabeth*, ſhall hereafter be eſteemed, taken, and reputed
to be Lords and Barons *de L'Iſle*, and as Barons, Nobles, and Peers of the Kingdom, *&c.* according to the Eſtate of the ſaid Barony of *L'Iſle*, of ancient Time
belonging or appertaining, as well in Seſſions, as in all and every other the
Preheminences, *&c.* as the aforeſaid *Warine*, or any of the Barons, occupying
or holding the aforeſaid Lordſhip, *&c.* Witneſſes *Thomas* Cardinal Archbiſhop of *Canterbury*; *Thomas* Biſhop of *Lincoln*, Chancellor of *England*; *George*
Duke of *Clarence*, and *Richard* Duke of *Glouceſter*, the King's Brethren;
Henry Earl of *Eſſex*, Treaſurer of *England*; *Anthony* Earl *Rivers*, Chief Butler
of *England*; *Thomas Ruſſel*, Clerk, Keeper of the Privy-Seal; Sir *Thomas Stanley*,
of *Stanley*, Steward of the Houſhold; Sir *William Haſtyngs*, of *Haſtyngs*, Chamberlain of the Houſhold, and others. Dated at *Weſtminſter*, 14 *March*, 15 *Edw.*
IV.

This *Edward Grey* Lord *L'Iſle*, in 14 *Edw.* IV, was, by [p] Indenture, retained
to ſerve the King in his Dutchy of *Normandy*, and Realm of *France*, with
ſeven Spears, and fifty Archers, for a whole Year; and, on that [q] Account,
received for the firſt Quarter's Wages, 172 *l.* 18 *s.* He was alſo with the King,
13 *Auguſt*, 1475, 15 *Edw.* IV, in the Field on the Side of a Village, called
Seyntrie, within *Vermandoſe*, near *Peron* [r], when, with the Aſſent of him and
other Lords, the Offers, made by the *French* King for a Ceſſation of Arms,
were accepted. In 1 *R.* III, he [s] was created Viſcount *L'Iſle*, in Conſideration (as
the Preamble of the Patent recites) of his noble Deſcent, and the Services that
he and his Anceſtors had performed. And, in 4 *Henry* VII, he was conſtituted [t]
one of the chief Commiſſioners for chooſing Archers in the County of *Warwick*,
for the Relief of *Britanny*.

By his laſt Will and Teſtament [u], which bears Date, 17 *July*, 1492, and
the Probate thereof the 25th of *Auguſt*, in 7 *H.* VII, he ordered his Body to
be buried in his Tomb in the new Chapel of our Lady, begun by himſelf to
be built in the College of *Aſtley*, where the Body of *Eliſabeth*, his late Wife,
lay buried.

He bequeaths to *Jane* his Wife, during her Life, all his Lands and Tenements purchaſed in *Warwickſhire*; as alſo, all his Lands in *Chilvercoton*, and
Mannor of *Bedworth*, &c. in the ſame County, appointing her to cauſe ſome of
the ſaid Lands to be amortiſed, to endow and find a Prieſt perpetually to ſing
in the Chapel of *Aſtley* before-mentioned, for his Soul, and the Soul of his

[p] Ex Autog. penes Cleric. Pelles.　[q] Rymer, Vol. 12, p. 846.　[r] Rymer, Vol. 12. p. 14
& ſeq.　[s] Rot. Cart. 1 R. III. m. 3.　[t] Pat. 4 H. VII. in dorſo. m. 20.　[u] Ex
Regiſtr. vocat. Dogget. qu. 13. in Cur. Prærog. Cantuar.

late Wife *Elisabeth*, as also, for the Soul of the said *Jane*, and all Christian Souls.

He bequeaths to *Margaret*, his Daughter, his Standing-cup covered, all gilt, and his Salt of Gold. To *Anne* his Daughter, which is married, a Standing-cup covered, all gilt. To *Elisabeth* his Daughter, a Standing-cup covered, all gilt, and a Salt covered, all gilt. And whereas he had intended to marry his Son and Heir, and with the Money given to him, by Reason of the said Marriage, to have preferred and married his said two Daughters, which resteth yet undone, to his great Discomfort: He wills that *Jane* his Wife, to whom, before all other Persons, he assigns the Rule and Governing, as well of his said Son, as of his Daughters, if she may obtain the Ward and Marriage of his said Son, and his Lands: That then she shall marry his said Son and Daughters, for their Honour and Weal, after her Discretion. And whereas he, and *Elisabeth* late his Wife, by their Letters Patents under their Seal of Arms, ordained his well beloved Brother *Thomas Grey*, their Steward of the Mannor of *Drayton* in Com. *Stafford*, with an annual Fee of 20 *l*. He requires and strictly charges, as well his Son and Heir, as all other Persons who shall have the Ward and Marriage of his said Son, as they will answer before God, that he or they suffer him to enjoy the said Office, during his Life, with the said Fee. And bequeaths to him a standing Cup of Silver covered, a Salt of Silver gilt, two of his Gowns, one of black Sattin furred, and the other with Cloth lined with Silk. Also two of his young Horses, and two Mares, in his Park of *Drayton*. The Residue of his Goods, Chattels, &c. after his Debts, and his Burial, and Funeral Expences paid, he bequeaths to *Jane* his Wife, whom he makes his sole Executrix, concluding:

And I beseech my especial and singular good Lord, the Archbishop of *Canterbury*, Chancellor of *England*, and the right worshipful and my full trusty Friend, Sir *Reynold Bray* Knight, to be the Supervisors of the said Testament. And to be good and special Mediators, unto my most beholden Sovereign Lord the King, for my said Wife and Children; lowly beseeching his Grace, to have them in his most noble Favour, Tuition, and Defence. And to suffer my said Wife to have the Ward, Marriage, Rule, and Guiding of my said Son and Daughters, before all other Persons. And I beseech my said Sovereign Lord, as for a poor Remembrance, to receive of my said Executrix my Tablet of Gold, enamelled of the Salutation of our Lady. And my said good Lord Chancellor, my high Standing-cup covered, of Silver, gilt and enamelled with Imagery. And also, my singular Friend *Bray*, a Cross of fine Gold set with a Ruby, and five Pearls, and my Gown of Crimson Velvet furred.

He left no Issue, by *Jane* his second Wife; but by *Elisabeth* his first Wife, beforementioned, Daughter of *Thomas Talbot* Viscount *L'Isle*, he had a Son *John*, who succeeded him, and three Daughters, viz. *Margaret*, Wife of *Henry Stafford*, Earl of *Wiltshire* [x], who died without Issue by her, 24 *March*, 14 *H*. VII. *Anne* second Daughter, Wife of Sir *John Willoughby* [y], Son and Heir of Sir *Henry Willoughby*, of *Wollaton* in Com. *Nottingham*, who [z] died without Issue by her in 3 *Edw*. VI; as appears by Inquisition taken at *Nottingham*, 23 *March*, 4 *Edw*. VI; wherein the Jury found, that Sir *Edward Willoughby*, Knight, was his Brother, whose Son and Heir, *Henry Willoughby*, Esq; was Cousin and Heir to the said Sir *John Willoughby*, and was killed in encountering the Rebels, at *Norwich*, 27 *August*, 3 *Edw*. VI, leaving *Thomas* his Son and Heir eight Years, nine Weeks, and one Day old. *Elisabeth*, the youngest, was first [a] married to *Edmund Dudley*, Esq; of the Privy-Chamber to King *Henry the Seventh*, by whom he was Father of *John* Duke of *Northumberland*; and was, in second Marriage, the Wife of Sir *Arthur Plantagenet*, who thereupon, in 15 *Henry* VIII, was [b]

---

[x] Ex Registr. Hornor. 31. in Cur. Prærog. Cant.   [y] Esc. 4 Edw. VI. n. 85 in Cur.
[z] Dugdale's Warw. p. 757 & Esc. 4 Edw. VI. n. 85 in Court of Wards.   [a] Esc. 20 H. VII.
[b] Pat. 15 H. VIII. p. 1.

advanced

advanced to the Dignity of Vifcount *L'Ifle*, with Limitation thereof to the Heirs Male of his Body by the fame *Elifabeth*.

John Vifcount *L'Ifle*, Son and Heir of *Edward*, was made [c] one of the Knights of the *Bath*, in 19 *Henry* VII, at the Creation of *Henry* Prince of *Wales*, and [d] died on the 6th of *September*, in 20 *Henry* VIII, leaving *Muriel*, his Wife (one of the Daughters of *Thomas Howard* Duke of *Norfolk*) big with Child, who was delivered 7 Days after his Deceafe, of a Daughter, named *Elifabeth*.

By his Laft Will and Teftament, bearing Date the 6th of *September*, 1504 (20 *Henry* VII.) wherein he writes [e] himfelf *John* Vifcounte *Lyfle*, of hole and parfitte Mynde, and fomewhat difeafed and feke in Body. *Firft*, I bequeth my Soule to Almighty God, to our Lady Saynt *Mary*, and to all the Saynts in Heven, and my Body to be buried where it fhall pleafe my Lord Trefaurier, and my Lady, my Wife, to ordre and difpofe for me.

He bequeaths to the Mother-Church of *Salifbury* 10 *s*. to the Church of *Drayton-Baffet*, a Gown of black Velvet, to make a Veftment ; to the Chapel of *Kingfton-Lyfle*, a Pair of Veftments, at the Difcretion of the Lady his Wife, and to the Church of *Sparfal* a Pair of Veftments.

He bequeaths to *Thomas Blount* his Gown of *French* Tawney, lined with black Sarcenet, two other Gowns, his Coat of black Damafk, and his grey Hobby. To his Coufin *Thomas Hungerford*, his Gown of black Camblet furred with Fox, his Doublet of crimfon Sattin, his Doublet of black Sattin, and his Riding-Coat of black Velvet. He bequeaths to *Richard Bennet*, his Chaplain, 4 Marks, and the like Sum to Sir *Oliver Poole*, his Chaplain ; and Legacies to his Servants, which were numerous. And wills, that his Executors find a devout Prieft to fing for his Soul two Years after his Deceafe.

He bequeaths to his Uncle *Thomas Gray*, and Dame *Ifabel* his Wife, a Fee of 20 *l. per Annum*, out of his Mannor of *Drayton-Baffet*. And to *Thomas Blount*, for Term of his Life, a Fee of 10 Marks, for the Exercifing and Keeping of the Office of the Bailyfhip and Parkerfhip of *Chaddefley-Corbet*, in the County of *Worcefter*, befides all other Grants made to him, according to the Letters Patent under his Seal. And having enfeoffed *Thomas* Lord *Howard*, *Edward Howard*, Knight, *Oliver Poole*, Clerk, and *Thomas Baffet*, Gent. in his Mannor of *Paynefwick*, in the County of *Gloucefter*, the Mannor of *Ribbesford*, with the Advowfon of the Church, and *Chaddefley-Corbet*, in the County of *Worcefter* ; the Mannor of *Bedworth*, with the Advowfon of the Church, in the County of *Warwick*, and his Mannor of *Kybworth*, in the County of *Leicefter*, by feveral Deeds bearing Date 5 *September*, 20 *Henry* VIII. His Will is, that *Thomas Blount* fhall have, for his Life, 20 Marks Annuity, out of his Mannor of *Chaddefley-Corbet*, clear of all Charges : Alfo, that the faid Feoffees make a good and fufficient Eftate in Law to his Lady Dame *Muriell*, his Wife, of the Remainder of the faid Mannor of *Chaddefley-Corbet*, and in all other the Mannors, with the Advowfon of all the Churches aforefaid, with their Appurtenances, to hold for Term of her Life, the Remainder to his right Heirs for ever in Fee ; and further bequeaths to her the Refidue of all his moveable Goods, after his Debts paid, and his Will performed ; and conftitutes her and *Thomas Blount*, Executors. Which Will was proved 8 *October*, the fame Year 1504.

It is further apparent, that *Elifabeth*, his only Child, before-mentioned, was not born till after his Deceafe, as he makes no Mention of her in his Will. But, in 4 *Henry* VIII, Sir *Charles Brandon*, Knight [f], obtained a Grant of her Wardfhip and Marriage ; and, in order thereto, was advanced to the Degree and Honour of Vifcount *L'Ifle*, and to the Heirs Male of his Body, by *Elifabeth Grey*, then Vifcountefs *L'Ifle* [g], as fhe is ftiled in the Patent, 5 *Henry* VIII ; but, fhe dying before Solemnifing and Confummation of the faid Mar-

---

[c] Anftis on Knights of the Bath, 4to, p. 47.   [d] Efc. 20 H. VIII. & Dugd. Warwickfh. Vol. 1. p. 466.   [e] Holgrave, qu. 17.   [f] Pat. 4 H. VIII. p. 2.   [g] Pat. 5 H. VIII. pars 1.

riage [h]

riage [h], he, in 15 *Henry* VIII, resigned the said Patent of Viscount *L'Isle*, to be cancelled in Chancery, in order to the King's granting the said Honour to *Arther Plantagenet*, and his Heirs Male, by *Elisabeth*, Sister and Heir of *John Grey* Viscount *L'Isle*.

I am not unapprised, that *Dugdale* [i] (who quotes *Brook* for his Authority) reports, that the before-mentioned *Elisabeth*, contracted to Sir *Charles Brandon*, was the first Wife of *Henry Courtney* Earl of *Devon*, and that she died without Issue by him ; but it is evident from the said Patent, of 15 *Henry* VIII, that she died affianced to Sir *Charles Brandon*, before Consummation.

Having thus proved, that *Elisabeth*, sole Daughter and Heir of *John* Viscount *L'Isle*, died without Issue, the next, in Succession, was *Elisabeth* [k], Sister and Heir to the said *John* Viscount *L'Isle*, who was first married to *Edmund Dudley*, Esq; by whom she had Issue [l], *John* Duke of *Northumberland*, her Son and Heir ; but, by *Arthur Plantagenet* before-mentioned, she had no Male Issue. I shall therefore now recite the principal Actions of the said *Edmund Dudley*, and his Descendants.

The said *Edmund Dudley* was the Son and Heir of *John Dudley*, Esq; [m] second Son to *John* Lord *Dudley*, Knight of the Garter, and *Elisabeth* his Wife, Daughter of Sir *John Berkley*, of *Beverston* in *Gloucestershire*.

Which *John Dudley*, Esq; had to [n] Wife *Elisabeth*, one of the two Daughters and Coheirs of *John Bramshot*, Esq; Lord [o] of the Mannors of *Gatton*, *Calbourne*, and *Whitwell*, in the *Isle of Wight*, as also of the Mannor of *Bramshot*, in Com. *Southamp.* from whence his Ancestors were denominated [p], who were Heirs of the Families of *Tregois*, *Boham*, and *Lisley* ; and their Son and Heir, *Edmund Dudley* [q], was 36 Years of Age on his Mother's Death, the 12th of *October*, 14 *Henry* VII.

Having been trained up in the Study of the Laws at *Grey's-Inn*, where his Arms were [r] then set up in a Window of the Chapel (which is a further Evidence of his Descent) he was such a Proficient, and his eminent Abilities were so conspicuous, that, in 1 *Henry* VII, that prudent Monarch made Choice of him to be one of his Privy Council, though he was then but in the 23d Year of his Age, *propter prudentiam singularem, fidem, & gravitatem* [s], saith *Polydore Virgil*.

In 1492, 8 *Henry* VII, he was one of those great Men in the King's Army near *Bologne* [t], who offered Propositions to King *Henry the Seventh*, for a Peace to be concluded between *England* and *France*, and requested him to comply therein : And accordingly the King commanded *Robert* Bishop of *Bath*, *Giles de Aubeny* Lord of *Aubeny*, Knight of the Garter, and Lieutenant-General of the Town and Marches of *Calais*, to treat with those deputed by the *French* King [u] ; and in the Articles signed at *Pontile* near *Turon*, the 6th of *November*, 1492, the Duke of *Bedford*, Uncle to the King, and Admiral of *England*, Deputy of the *Cinque-Ports*, Keeper of the Privy-Seal, and the King's Lieutenant in *Calais*, was appointed Conservator of the said Peace. And, in 10 *Henry* VII, he obtained the Wardship and Marriage of *Elisabeth*, Daughter and Coheir of *Edward Grey*, Viscount *L'Isle*, as I have before recited.

In 14 *Henry* VII, 1499, the King calling together the three Estates of the Kingdom to meet at *Westminster* [w], he was, with the Lord *Dacre* of the *South*, and *Richard Sackfield*, Esq; those of that Part of the Temporal Lords and Commons of the Diocess of *Chichester*, who assented to, and signed the Peace made with *France*, at the Staples on the Sea near *Bologne*, the 3d of *November*, 1492.

---

[h] Pat 15 H. VIII. pars 1. in Capella Rot.   [i] Baronage of Engl. Vol. 1. p. 642.   [k] Pat. 15 H. VIII. p. 1. ut supra.   [l] Ex tumulo Amb. Comes Warw. fil. and hær. Joh. Duc. Northumb. in Capella St. Mar. in Warw.   [m] Ex Stemmate apud Penshurst penes Gul. Perry, Arm.   [n] Esc. 14 H. VII. &   [o] 2 H. VIII. & ex Tumulo Ambros. Comes Warw. apud Warw.   [p] Ex Stemmate ut supra   [q] Esc. 14 H. VII.   [r] Dugdale's Orig. Jurid.   [s] Polyd. Virg. p. 567. n. 10 & 569. n. 30.   [t] Rymer's Fœdera, Vol. 12. p. 490.   [u] Ibid. p. 499.   [w] Ibid. p. 710 & seq.

In

In 19 *Henry* VII, being then [x] Speaker of the Houfe of Commons in Parliament, he was to have been called to the Degree of Serjeant at Law, on the
13th of *November*, but petitioned that he might be difcharged from taking
that Degree [y]. Whereupon the King directed his Precept to *William* Bifhop
of *London*, then Lord-Keeper of the Great-Seal, commanding his Forbearance
to make out any Writ for that Purpofe. The next Mention, I find of him, is in
22 *Henry* VII [z], when he obtained a Grant of the Stewardfhip of the *Rape* of
Haftings, in Com. *Suff.*

But whether he, with Sir *Richard Empfon*, another Lawyer, difcerning King
Henry to be of a frugal Difpofition, did firft project the Taking Advantage
againft fuch as had tranfgreffed the Penal Laws, by exacting from them the
Forfeitures according to thofe Statutes [a] : Or, whether the King perceiving fo
fair a Gap open, to take vaft Sums of Money from his Subjects, and finding
thofe Perfons fit Inftruments for his Purpofe, put them on fuch Courfes for fill-
ing his Coffers, is not clearly made out. But thefe were they whom he conftituted [b] his *Judices Fifcales*, of whom the Lord *Verulam* faith, Dudley *was an eminent Man, and one that could put hateful Bufinefs into good Language.* Their
Courfe was (as the fame Author [c] obferved) to proceed fecretly to the Outlaw-
ry againft Men, and then feize their Eftates.

But King *Henry the Eighth*, in the firft Year of his Reign, having, by
his Proclamation [d], divulged, that whofoever had received Injury by the Injuftice of any, fhould, on Complaint to him, have Redrefs. This Liberty fo encouraged thofe who had fuffered (and were fufficiently imbittered againft them)
that nothing would then fatisfy but their Lives ; on which the King gave Way,
as *Stow* relates, that they might be legally proceeded againft.

Thereupon this *Edmund Dudley* was committed to the *Tower*, and being arraigned at *Guildhall* in *London* [e], on *Monday, July* 16, 1509, 1 *Henry* VIII, before *Edward* Duke of *Buckingham*, *Henry* Earl of *Northumberland*, *Thomas* Earl
of *Surry*, *George* Earl of *Shrewfbury*, *Thomas* Earl of *Derby*, *Thomas* Prior of St.
John's of *Hierufalem* in *England*, Sir *Charles Somerfet*, Knight, Lord *Herbert*, Ste-
phen Jennings, then Mayor of the City of *London*, Sir *John Fineaux*, Knight,
Sir *Robert Rede*, Knight, *John Boteler*, *William Grevile*, Sir *Thomas Lovel*,
Knight, Sir *Edward Poynings*, Knight, Sir *Henry Marney*, Knight, Sir *Thomas
Englefield*, Knight, and Sir *Thomas Drury*, Knight, Juftices to inquire, *&c.* on
an Indictment of divers High Treafons : And, being thereupon convicted, was
beheaded on *Tower-hill* (with *Empfon*, who had been tried at *Northampton*)
on the 28th of *Auguft*, 2 *Henry* VIII, by the King's fpecial Precept [f], and was
buried in the *Black-Fryers* Church.

He was a long Time imprifoned in the *Tower* before he fuffered ; and it was
reported, the Queen had procured him a Pardon, as *Stow* relates [g], but the importunate Clamours of the People brought him to that unfortunate End. During his Confinement, he wrote a Book, intituled [h] *Arbor Reipublicæ*, dedicated
to King *Henry the Eighth*, but never came to his Hand, as *Stow* writes.

In the Catalogue of the Manufcripts [i] of *England* and *Ireland*, printed at *Oxford*, 1697, it is faid to be among the Manufcripts of *William Bromley* of *Bag-
ington* in *Warwickfhire*, Efq; and this Account is given of it :

" The Tree of Commonwealth, by *Edmund Dudley*, Efq; late Counfellor to
" King *Henry the Seventh*, the fame *Edmund* being, at the Compiling thereof,
" Prifoner in the *Tower*, in 1 *Henry* VIII."

The Effect of this Treatife confifteth in three efpecial Points :

---

[x] Herbert's Hift. of H. VIII. p. 6.   [y] Billæ Sign. 19 H. VII.   [z] Pat. 22 H. VII. p. 2
[a] Bacon's Hift. of H. VII. p. 209.   [b] Polyd. Virg. p. 613. n. 10.   [c] Hift. of H. VII. ut
antea.   [d] Ibid.   [e] Petit. in Parl. for Reftit. of his Son, 3 H. VIII.   [f] Stow's Annals,
p. 409.   [g] Ibid. p. 488.   [h] Balei Cent. XI. de Script. Brit. p. 72.   [i] Cat. Lib. MS. Ang.
& Hib. Oxon. Tom. 2. p. 102.

First, Remembrance of God, and the Faithful of his holy Church; in the which, every Chriſtian Prince had Need to begin.

Second, Of ſome Conditions and Demeanors, neceſſary in every Prince, both for his Honour, and Aſſurety of his Continuance.

Third, Of the Tree of Commonwealth, which toucheth People of every Degree, of the Conditions and Demeanors they ſhould be of.

The Lord *Herbert*, in his Life of King *Henry the Eighth*, gives [k] this Account of him:

" *Dudley*, a Gentleman of Birth, and of ſuch Parts, as he was choſen
" Speaker of the Parliament in 19 *Henry* VII, having, with *Empſon*, exceeded
" their Bounds, were deteſted of all, but eſpecially the poorer Sort, who found
" it eaſier to hate than to pay. And new and ſtrange Crimes were found and
" objected againſt them, as appears on their Indictment on Record, wherein
" they are accuſed of Conſpiracy againſt the King and State. And *firſt*, that
" during the Sickneſs of the late King, in *March* laſt, they ſummoned cer-
" tain of their Friends to be in Arms at an Hour's Warning; and, upon the
" Death of the ſaid King, to haſten to *London*. Out of which, and other Cir-
" cumſtances, it was collected by the Jury, that their Intention was to ſeize
" on the Perſon of the new King, and ſo to aſſume the ſole Government: Or,
" when they could not attain this, to deſtroy him. Of which Crimes, how
" improbable ſoever, *Dudley*, in his Trial at *Guildhall, London, July,* 16,
" 1509, and *Empſon* at *Northampton*, were found guilty by the Juries. And,
" the importunate Clamours of the People prevailing with the King, he,
" for Satisfaction to the Commonalty, commanded their Heads to be ſtruck
" off, doing therein (as thought by many) more like a good King, than a
" good Maſter."

This *Edmund Dudley* [l], had to his firſt Wife *Anne*, Daughter to Sir *Andrew Windſor*, Knight; and, to his ſecond, *Eliſabeth*, Daughter of *Edward* Viſcount *L'Iſle*, before-mentioned, who ſurvived him, and was ſecondly married to Sir *Arthur Plantagenet* Viſcount *L'Iſle* [m], ſo created in 15 *Henry* VIII, by rea-ſon of his ſaid Marriage with her, and to hold and enjoy the ſaid Title to him and his Heirs Male, begotten on the ſaid *Eliſabeth*, Siſter, and (then) ſole Heir of *John Grey*, late Viſcount *L'Iſle*. By her firſt Huſband *Edmund Dudley*, ſhe had Iſſue three Sons [n], *John, Andrew,* and *Jerome*; alſo a Daughter *Eliſa-beth*, married to *William* Lord *Stourton*.

John Dudley, the eldeſt Son, was ſcarce [o] eight Years of Age at his Father's Death, and had to his [p] Guardian *Edmund Guilford*, Eſq; of the Body to the King, who, by his Petition [q] exhibited in Parliament, 3 *Henry* VIII, obtained [r] a ſpecial Act for the Repeal of the ſaid *Edmund*'s Attainder, and Reſtitution of the ſaid *John* his Son, in Name, Blood, and Degree, ſo that he might en-joy all his Father's Lands, &c.

Being, therefore, ſo very young, many Years paſſed before he appeared in any publick Employment; but, in 15 *Henry* VIII, being in the 22d Year of his Age, he was in that Expedition under *Charles Brandon* Duke of *Suffolk*, General of thoſe Forces ſent into *France* againſt the Duke of *Bourbon*, and, for his valiant Behaviour [s], was then knighted by the ſaid Duke of *Suffolk*.

In 19 *Henry* VIII, he [t] accompanied Cardinal *Wolſey* into *France*, who was then ſent Ambaſſador there; and, in 26 *Henry* VIII, being ſtiled [u] the King's Servant, he had a Grant of the Office of Maſter of the Armory in the *Tower* of *London*, for Life, with the accuſtomed Wages of twelve Pence *per Diem* for himſelf, and three Pence *per Diem* for his Groom.

---

[k] Hiſt. Eng. Vol. 2. p. 3 and 4.   [l] Ex Stemmate Famil. de Dudley apud Penſhurſt.   [m] Pat. 15 H. VIII. p. 1.   [n] Ex Stemmate.   [o] [p] [q] Petit. in Parl. 3 H. VIII.   [s] Stow's Annals in 15 H. VIII.   [t] Ibid. An. 19 H. VIII.   [u] Pat. 26 H. VIII. p. 1.

In 31 *Henry* VIII, he was [w] Mafter of the Horfe to the Lady *Anne* of *Cleve*; then landed in *England*, in order to her Marriage with King *Henry*: And, in 32 *Henry* VIII, in thofe triumphant Jufts, holden at *Weftminfter*, on 1 *May*, and feveral Days after, he was the firft and principal of the Challengers againft all Comers, being in fumptuous Apparel, and his Horfe trapped with white Velvet. And, growing further into the King's Favour, he was on [x] the 12th of *March*, in 34 *Henry* VIII, advanced to the Title of Vifcount *L'Ifle*, in Confideration (as the Preamble fets forth) not only of the acceptable and laudable Services of his beloved and faithful Subjeft, Sir *John Dudley*, Knight, varioufly done; but alfo his Vigilance, Forefight, Faithfulnefs, Valour, and illuftrious Defcent. To hold the faid Title to him and the Heirs Male of his Body, and to enjoy Seat and Place in Parliament among the Vifcounts of the Realm of *England*, and in all other the King's Dominions, with a Grant of an Annuity of 20 Marks; payable half-yearly, out of the Revenues of the Counties of *Warwick*, and *Leicefter*, by the Sheriffs of the faid Counties.

In the fame 34 *Henry* VIII, he was [y] conftituted Lord High Admiral of *England* for Life; at which Time, Sir *John Hayward* [z] gives this Charafter of him: That he was a Perfon very comely, and of a Spirit highly afpiring, neither wanting Skill, Induftry, or Refolution to attempt great Matters.

In 25 *Henry* VIII [a], he commanded a Fleet of 200 Sail, and landed the King's Army at *Leith* in *Scotland*, to which Place they fet Fire, and having wafted *Edinburgh*, and fcoured thofe Seas, he landed 28 *July* in the Haven at *Bologne* in *France*, with 900 Men: And having valiantly behaved at that Siege, on the Surrender thereof, he was left by the King his Lieutenant there, in *Sept.* 1544, with fufficient Forces, and Direftions what to do on all Occafions.

Soon after, the Dauphin coming before the Place with an Army of 52000 Men, and laying clofe Siege thereto [b], he made a gallant Defence, though the Walls were much fhattered: And, when the Dauphine had entered the bafe Town, divers of the *Englifh* being flain in the Defence of it, he, by a brave Salley, beat out the *French* again, with the Lofs of above 800 of their Men, then efteemed the beft Soldiers in that Realm.

On 8 *Jan.* 1546, 37 *Henry* VIII, the King ftiling him [c] his beloved and faithful Counfellor, Sir *John Dudley*, Knight of the Garter, Vifcount *L'Ifle*, Baron *Malpas*, Lord High Admiral of *England*, *Ireland*, and *Aquitain*, orders him, on the Intreaty of the King of *Portugal*, to permit all Perfons carrying Wheat to that Country to pafs unmolefted.

On 27 *March*, 1546, the King (as the Patent [d] imports) fully confiding in the Loyalty, Wifdom, Valour, Induftry, Diligence, Experience, and Integrity of his moft beloved Coufin and Counfellor, *John* Vifcount *L'Ifle*, Lord High Admiral of *England*, *&c.* conftitutes him his Lieutenant-General, and Commander in Chief of all his Forces at Sea, defigned to go againft the *French*, with Orders to invade their Dominions, and impowering him to mufter all Officers and Soldiers, *&c.* and to hear and determine all Caufes thereto belonging, as well relating to Life, *&c.* With a Mandate to all Perfons to be obedient to him.

Whereupon he landed 5000 Men upon their Coafts, fired *Treport*, and other Villages, with the Lofs but of one Man; and, the *French* making Head againft him, he offered them Battle [e], which they refufed, returning with the Lofs of all their Coft, as my Author obferves.

The fame Year being [f] ftiled *John* Vifcount *L'Ifle*, Baron of *Malpas*, and *Somerie*, Knight of the Garter, Lord of *Baffet* and of *Teys*, and Lord High Admiral of *England*, *&c.* he was impowered with *Cuthbert* Bifhop of *Durham*, and *Nicholas Wotton*, LL D. Dean of *Canterbury* and *York*, to take the Oath of *Francis* the *French* King, for obferving the Articles of Peace, figned

---

[w] Hollinfhed, p. 919. b. n. 10. [x] Pat. 34 H. VIII. p. 3. [y] Ib. p. 7. [z] Life of E. VI. p. 16. [a] Stow's Ann. Herbert's Hift. of H. VIII. in Hift. of Eng. Vol. 2. p. 248. [b] Life of E. VI. ut fupra, p. 17. [c] Rymer's Fœdera, Tom. 15 p. 84. [d] Pat. 37 H. VIII. p. 13. in Rymer, ut fupra. [e] Life of E. VI. ut antea. [f] Rymer, Vol. 15. p. 98.

in

in the Tents of the Field near the Town of *Campens*, in the Confines of *Ardres* and *Guifnes*, 7 *June*, 1546 : At which were alfo prefent *Henry* the Dauphin, the Duke of *Brittany*, the Cardinals of *Lorrain*, *Ferratia*, *Bellay*, *Caftilione*, and *Mendon* ; *John* of *Bourbon*, Count *de Anguyen* ; *Charles de Bourbon*, Duke of *Monpenfier* ; the Lord *Hennebault*, Admiral of *France* ; with many other Bifhops, Earls, and Barons of *France* : And, of the *Englifh*, *Henry Manners*, Earl of *Rutland* ; *Edward* Lord *Clinton*, and others : And our King took the Oath, 7 *Auguft*, 1546.

On 16 *Oct*. following, he [g] was impowered, with the Archbifhop of *Canterbury*, the Lord Great-Mafter of the Houfhold, the Treafurer of the Houfhold, and others, by their Warrants made out to the Treafurers, Receivers, and all others having the King's Money in their Hands, to pay all Perfons every fuch Sum or Sums of Money, as they fhall appoint by their faid Warrant, for paft Reward, Conduct, Entertainment of Garrifons, Ordinary or Extraordinary, Fortifications, Provifion of Victuals, Ordnance, and all Kind of Munition, and for all and every other Thing or Things, concerning the Expedition of any of the King's Affairs : And, that fuch Warrants fo iffued out by them, from 28 *Sept*. laft paft, fhall be a fufficient Difcharge to the faid Treafurers, Receivers, &c. againft him and his Heirs and Succeffors, and to remain in full Force till *Eafter* next.

King *Henry the Eighth* now drawing near his End, I find no further Mention of him in that Reign, other than by the Laft Will and Teftament of that Monarch, bearing Date the 30th of *December*, 1546, 38 *Henry* VIII, he was [h] appointed by him one of his Executors, *Willing, commanding, and praying them, to take on them the Occupation and Performance of the fame. And that they be Counfellors of the Privy-Council with our faid Son Prince* Edward, *in all Matters concerning both his private Affairs, and publick Affairs of the Realm, and that none of them prefume to meddle with any of our Treafure, or do any Thing appointed by our faid Will, alone, unlefs the moft Part of the whole Number confent, and by Writing agree to the fame ; but that the moft Part of them may lawfully do, what they fhall think moft convenient for the Execution of our Will, without being troubled by our faid Son, or any other, for the fame.*

And, by his faid Will, *for the Kindnefs and good Service, his faid Executors had fhewn unto him*, he bequeaths to each of them the following Legacies : *Firft*, To the Archbifhop of *Canterbury*, 500 Marks ; to the Lord *Wriothefley*, 500 *l*. to the Lord *St. John*, 500 *l*. to the Lord *Ruffel*, 500 *l*. to the Earl of *Hertford*, 500 *l*. to the Vifcount *L'Ifle*, 500 *l*. But, to the reft of them, he left only 300 *l*. each, *viz*. to the Bifhop of *Durham*, Sir *Anthony Brown*, Sir *William Paget*, Sir *Anthony Denny*, Sir *William Herbert*, Juftice *Montague*, Sir *Edward North*, Sir *Edward Wotton*, and Dr. *Wotton*.

In lefs than three Weeks after the King's Death, he was, by the Protector, removed from being Lord High Admiral, though, by Patent from the late King, he held it for Life [i]. And, on 17 *Feb*. 1547, 1 *Edw*. VI, Sir *Thomas Seymour*, Brother to the Protector, had a Grant of that Office in as full and ample Manner, as Sir *John Dudley*, Lord Vifcount *L'Ifle*, Baron of *Malpas*, Lord *Baffet* of *Drayton* and *Tyaffe*, High Admiral of *England*, &c. held or occupied the fame. However, as fome Compenfation, he [k] was the fame Day, 17 *Feb*. 1 *Edw*. VI, created Earl of *Warwick*, *by reafon of his Defcent through his Mother, from* Margaret *the eldeft Daughter and Coheir of* Richard Beauchamp, *Earl of* Warwick ; and was alfo made Great Chamberlain of *England*. Likewife, foon [l] after, he obtained a Grant of *Warwick* Caftle, the Seat of his Anceftors, with the Mannor, and divers other great Lordfhips and Lands in that County.

In the firft Year of King *Edward the Sixth*, being [m] made Lieutenant-General of the Army, then fent into *Scotland*, by his Conduct and Courage principally,

---

[g] Rymer, Vol. 15. p. 102. 　　[h] Ex Regiftr. vocat Allen, qu. 32. in Cur. Prærog. Cantuar.
[i] Rymer, Vol. 15. p. 127. 　　[k] Pat. 1 E. VI. p. 6. 　　[l] Pat. 1 E. VI. p. 9. 　　[m] Life of E. VI. p. 15.

I

that fignal Victory was obtained over the *Scots* at *Mufcleborough* ; and, obferving the Valour and Deportment of fuch who were under his Command, he
[n] conferred the Honour of Knighthood on feveral of them, being impowered
to reward thofe he found meritorious.

On 4 *March* 1 *Edw.* VI, bearing [o] the Title of *John* Earl of *Warwick*, Vifcount *L' Ifle*, Baron of *Malpas* and *Somery*, Knight of the Garter, Lord *Baffet* of
Drayton, and *Tyaffe*, and Great Chamberlain of *England*, he was commiffioned
with *John* Lord *Ruffel*, Keeper of the Privy-Seal, *Thomas* Lord *Seymour* of *Sudley*, Knight of the Garter, and Lord High Admiral, and Sir *William Paget*,
Secretary of State, to fettle all Matters with the *French* Ambaffadors in *England*, relating to the Peace made between King *Henry the Eighth*, deceafed, and
Francis the *French* King ; as alfo the Boundaries of the Marches of *Bologne*, &c.

In 3 *Edw.* VI, he commanded [p] all thofe Forces fent againft the Rebels in
Norfolk, headed by *Ket*, a Tanner, of which having flain about 5000, he took
Ket himfelf, and fettled all in Quiet there. Alfo 28 *Oct.* 1549, 3 *Edw.* VI,
the King recites [q], that, in Confideration of the good and faithful Services of
John Earl of *Warwick*, Vifcount *L' Ifle*, Knight of the Garter, Great Chamber-
lain of *England*, and Prefident of the Council of the Principality of *Wales*, he
grants to him the Office of Lord High Admiral of *England*, *Ireland*, *Wales*,
Calais, and *Bologne*, and Marches of the fame ; of *Normandy*, *Gafcony*, and
Aquitain, and High Admiral of his Fleet and Seas, with the fame Powers as
Sir *Thomas Seymour* Lord *Sudley* had, which were very extenfive.

After which, furrendering [r] his Letters Patents into the *Chancery* to be cancelled, of the Office of Lord High Chamberlain of *England*, *William*, Marquis
of *Northampton*, and Earl of *Effex*, was appointed thereto, 4 *Feb.* 1550, 4 *Edw.*
VI. And, on the 20th of the fame Month and Year, the King recites, That
whereas *Henry the Eighth*, late King of *England*, granted to his moft beloved Coufin and Counfellor, *Charles*, late Duke of *Suffolk*, deceafed, the Office of Lord
Steward of the Houfhold, by the Name of Great Mafter of the Houfhold, or
the Great Mafter of the King's Houfhold : And, whereas by Act of Parlia-
ment in *May*, 22 *Henry* VIII, it was enacted, That during the Time the late
Duke of *Suffolk*, and his Succeffors in the faid Office, fhould enjoy the faid
Poft of Lord Steward, they fhould be called Lord Steward of the King's
Houfhold, as by the faid Act appears. That attributing much to the Loy-
alty, Wifdom, and Virtue of his beloved Coufin and Counfellor, *John* Earl of
Warwick, &c. [s] and having always experienced his Conftancy in the Chriftian
Religion, his Valour in War, Sedition, and Riots, his friendly and faithful In-
clination towards him, and defiring his Abode and Refidence in his Palace, and
Attendance on his royal Perfon : By Advice of his Privy-Council, he grants to
the faid Earl of *Warwick*, the Office of Lord Steward, or Great Mafter of his
Houfhold for Life, with all Fees, Wages, &c. as the faid Duke of *Suffolk*,
Earl of *Wiltfhire*, or any Steward of the King's Houfhold, held or enjoyed.
And commands, that the faid Earl of *Warwick* have his Letters Patent with-
out Fine or Fee, great or fmall, to his Ufe to be paid.

In 5 *Edw.* VI, he was employed [t], with *William* Marquis of *Northampton*,
in an Ambaffy to the *French* King ; and, on 20 *April*, the fame Year [u], was
conftituted Earl Marfhal of *England*. And, after being [w] made Warden of all
the Marches towards *Scotland*, he was, 11 *Oct.* the fame Year [x], advanced to
the Dignity of Duke of *Northumberland*, at which Time there was no other
Duke, except his Brother, the Duke of *Suffolk*, Father of Lady *Jane*.

Being therefore, fuperior to all others in Titles of Honour, and in Authority
and Power ; and obferving the King very declining in his Health, he afpired to fettle the Crown in his Family, and, to that End, brought about the Marriage of the
Lord *Guilford Dudley*, his fourth Son (his three eldeft having Wives living) with
the Lady *Jane Grey*, eldeft Daughter to *Henry* Duke of *Suffolk*, by *Frances*, Daugh-

[n] MS. in Offic. Arm. [M. 9.] f. 50. b.   [o] Rymer's Fœdera, Tom. 15. p. 135, & feq.
[p] Stow's Ann. in 3 E. VI.   [q] Rymer, p. 194.   [r] Ibid. p. 203.   [s] Ibid. p. 208.
[t] Life of E. VI. p. 123.   [u] Pat. 5 E. VI. p. 4.   [w] Ibid. p. 7.   [x] Pat. 5 E. VI. p. 4.

ter to *Mary*, second Sister to King *Henry the Eighth*. After which, by his Interest, and Power, a Patent was sealed by the King for the said Lady *Jane*'s Succession to the Crown on his Demise, excluding his two Sisters, *Mary* and *Elizabeth* [y]. Which Letters Patent were subscribed by all the Privy-Council, as also the greatest Part, both for Number and Power of the Nobility, the King's learned Council, and all the Judges, except Sir *James Hales*, one of the Justices of the *Common-Pleas*. ' Some (as Sir *John Hayward* recites) being guid-
' ed by particular Interest, for that they were possessed of much Monastery
' and Chantry Land; which, if Religion should alter through Queen *Mary*'s
' Coming to the Crown, they might be in Danger to lose; and others by Fear
' of, or Obligation to this Duke, then so potent, and almost absolute in the
' Government of the State, whereby it was supposed he could make any Title
' good, either by his Authority or his Sword.'

But I leave it to the Reader's Judgment, whether it may not be more justly said, they feared an Alteration in Religion, on Queen *Mary*'s Accession to the Throne, through which View they were induced to alter the Succession. Sir *John Hayward* further relates [z], ' That he contrived to get the Princess *Mary*
' into his Hands, causing the King to write his Letters for her Coming to him
' in his Sickness. But she, being made sensible of the Design, when she was
' within half a Day's Journey of *London*, diverted her Course another Way.'

Being greatly in Favour with the King, he procured to himself many beneficial Grants. On 19 *May*, 5 *Edw*. VI, the King [a], in Consideration of the true, faithful, and acceptable Services, of his dear Cousin and Counsellor, *John* Earl of *Warwick*, Earl-Marshal of *England*, and Great Master and Steward of his Houshold, grants to him, his Heirs, and Assigns, for ever, the capital Mansion of *Otford*, together with the Mannor of *Otford*, in *Kent*, and the two Parks thereto belonging, with all Rights, Members, and Appurtenances thereto belonging, in the said County of *Kent*.

On the Demise of King *Edward the Sixth*, the Lady *Jane Dudley* was proclaimed Queen, 10 *July*, having been conveyed from the Court at *Greenwich*, to the *Tower*; where she [b] was received as Queen, according to the Letters Patents, signed by King *Edward*, 21 *June* last past. The 12 *July*, the Queen and the Council with her in the *Tower* had Advice, That the Lady *Mary* was at *Keninghall* Castle in *Norfolk*, with the Earl of *Bath*, Sir *Thomas Wharton*, Son to the Lord *Wharton*, Sir *John Mordant*, Son to the Lord *Mordant*, and many of the Gentlemen of that County; and that the Earl of *Suffex* and his Son, *Henry Ratcliff*, were also coming to her.

On which the Council immediately concluded, to send the Duke of *Suffolk*, with other Noblemen and Forces, to fetch the Lady *Mary* to the *Tower*; but the Queen his Daughter with many Tears requested the whole Council, that her Father might remain with her; and thereupon the Council [c], as my Author observes, persuaded the Duke of *Northumberland*, to take it upon him, *Saying that no Man was so fit therefore, because, he that had atchieved the Victory at* Norfolk *once already, was so feared, that none durst once lift up their Weapon against him; besides, that he was the best Man of War in the Realm, as well for the Ordering of his Camps and Soldiers, both in Battle, and in their Tents, as also by Experience, Knowledge, and Wisdom, he could animate his Army with witty Persuasions, and also pacify and allay his Enemies Pride, with his stout Courage, or else dissuade them, if Need were, from their Enterprise. Finally, said they, the Queen will in no wise grant, that her Father should take it on him, wherefore, we think it good, if it may please your Grace, it lieth in you to remedy the Matter.*

It appears from the same Author, and others, that the Duke was not forward to take on him the Enterprise, being jealous of the Fidelity of the Council to him, and that during his Absence, they would more easily be wrought

[y] Heyward's Life of E. VI. p. 173, 176.   [z] Ib. p. 178.   [a] Pat. 5 E. VI.
[b] Stow's Annals, p. 610.   [c] Ibid.

I   on on to deliver up the Queen his Daughter-in-Law. However, the very same Night, he sent for both Lords, Knights, *&c.* that were to go with him ; and, the next Morning early, called for his Armour, at *Durham* Place, where he appointed all his Retinue to meet ; and by his Order, Carts laden with Ammunition, *&c.* and Field-pieces were sent forward [d]. Also, that no Time might be lost, he the same Morning, went to the *Tower*, and moved the Council to send their Powers after him to *New-Market*, as had been before determined, which they promised to do. At which Time, he is said to make the following Address to the Council [e] :

' My Lords, I and these other noble Personages, with the whole Army,
' that now go forth, as well for the Behalf of you and yours, as for the Esta-
' blishing of the Queen's Highness, shall not only adventure our Lives amongst
' our Adversaries in the open Fields, but also we do leave the Conservations
' of ourselves, Children, and Families at Home here with you, as altogether
' committed to your Truth and Fidelities, whom if we thought ye would,
' through Malice, Conspiracy, or Dissension, leave us your Friends in the Bri-
' ars and betray us, we could as well sundry Ways foresee and provide for
' our own Safeguards, as any of you, by betraying us, can do for yours.
' But now, upon the only Trust and Faithfulness of your Honours, whereof
' we think ourselves most assured, we do hazard our Lives, which Trust and
' Promise, if ye shall violate, hoping thereby of Life and Promotion, yet shall
' not God count you innocent of our Bloods, neither acquit you of the sacred
' and holy Oath of Allegiance, made freely by you, to this virtuous Lady
' the Queen's Highness, who by your, and our Enticement, is rather by
' Force placed thereon, than by her own Seeking and Request. Consider also
' that God's Cause, which is the Preferment of his Word, and Fear of Papists
' Entrance, hath been (as ye have here before always said) the original Ground,
' whereupon ye even at the first Motion granted your good Wills and Con-
' sents thereunto, as by your Hands Writing appeareth ; and think not the
' contrary, but, if you mean Deceit, though not forthwith, yet hereafter God
' will revenge the same.
' I can say no more but in this troublesome Time, wish you to use con-
' stant Hearts, abandoning all Malice, Envy, and private Affections. I have
' not spoken to you in this Sort upon any Distrust I have of your Truths,
' of which always I have hitherto conceived a trusty Confidence ; but I have
' put you in Remembrance thereof, what Chance of Variance soever might
' grow amongst you in my Absence ; and this I pray you, wish me not worse
' good Speed in this Journey, than you would have to yourselves.' On
which one said :

' My Lord, if you distrust any of us in this Matter, your Grace is far de-
' ceived, for which of us can wash his Hands clear thereof? And if we should
' shrink from you, as from one that was culpable, which of us can excuse
' himself to be guiltless thereof? Herein your Doubt is too far cast. I pray
' God it be (said the Duke) let us go to Dinner ; and so they sat down. Af-
' ter Dinner, the Duke went unto the Queen, where his Commission was by
' that Time sealed, for his Lieutenantship of the Army, and then took his
' Leave of her, as did other Lords, who were to accompany him.'

As the Duke came through the Council-Chamber, he took his Leave of the Earl of *Arundel*, who prayed God to be with his Grace, saying, He was sorry it was not his Chance to go with him, and bear him Company, in whose Presence, he could find in his Heart to spend his Blood, even at his Feet. The Duke, with the Marquis of *Northampton*, the Lord *Grey*, and o-thers, immediately took their Barge, and went to *Durham* Place, and to *White-*

[d] Stow's Annals, p. 610, 611.   [e] Ibid.

hall, where the fame Night, they muftered their Men ; and the next Day early, departed with about 600. As they rode through *Shoreditch*, the Duke faid to the Lord *Grey*, *The People prefs to fee us, but not one faith, God fpeed us*. The fame Day, Sir *John Gates*, and others, went after the Duke.

Fox[f] in his Account of the Duke of *Northumberland*, relates, That having his Warrant under the Great Seal, he marched againft the Lady *Mary* ; and what made moft for her, were the fhort Journies of the Duke, which by Commiffion were affigned to him, and appointed him by the Council, to the Intent that he might not feem to do any Thing, but by Warrant. So that, marching flowly on, the Lady *Mary* had Leifure to increafe her Forces ; which the Council at *London* perceiving, and that certain Noblemen ftood by her, they proclaimed her Queen.

Stow[g] gives an Account, that the Duke wrote fharply to the Council in the *Tower*, for Succours of Men, as alfo of Ammunition, but a flender Anfwer was returned him ; and from that Time forward, moft of the Council confulted how to get out of the *Tower*, and the Marquis of *Winchefter*, going out on 16 *July*, at 7 in the Evening, was fetched again to the *Tower*, about 12 o' Clock the fame Night.

The Duke of *Northumberland*[h] was advanced, as far as St. *Edmondfbury* in *Suffolk*, but his promifed Succours not coming to him, and having received from fome of the Council, Letters of their Conduct, *&c.* he returned back to *Cambridge*.

On 19 *July*, the Council affembled themfelves at *Bainard*'s Caftle, and fecretly fent Sir *John Mafon*, Clerk of the Council to the Lord Mayor, that he with the Sheriffs, Recorder, and fuch Aldermen as he liked, fhould meet them there, in an Hour. And being come, they were told they muft ride into *Cheap*, to proclaim a new Queen ; and accordingly *Garter* King of Arms proclaimed Queen *Mary*, the fame Day ; and the Earl of *Arundel*, and the Lord *Paget*, the fame Night, rode Poft to Queen *Mary*, with 30 Horfe with them.

The Duke of *Northumberland*, then at *Cambridge*, had Knowledge of it the next Day, and about 5 of the Clock the fame Night, with the Nobility, *&c.* went to the Market-Crofs in the Town[i], and himfelf proclaimed Queen *Mary*, throwing up his Cap, among others, in Token of Joy. Within an Hour after, he had Letters from the Council brought by one of the Heralds, dated at *Weftminfter* 20 *June*, in Form following[k]:

In the Name of our Sovereign Lady Mary *the Queen, to be declared to the Duke of* Northumberland, *and all others of his Band, of what Degree foever they be.*

'Y E fhall command and charge in the Queen's Highnefs's Name, the faid
'   Duke to difarm himfelf, and to ceafe all his Men of War, and to fuffer
' no Part of his Army to do any Thing contrary to Peace, and himfelf to for-
' bear Coming to this City, until the Queen's Pleafure be exprefly declared
' unto him. And if he will fhew himfelf like a good quiet Subject, we fhall
' then continue, as we have begun, as humble Suitors to our Sovereign Lady
' the Queen's Highnefs for him, and his, as for ourfelves. And if he do not,
' we will not fail to fpend our Lives, in Subduing him and his. *Item*, ye fhall
' declare the like Matter to the Marquis of *Northampton*, and all other Noble-
' men and Gentlemen, and to all Men with any of them. And ye fhall, in all
' Places where you come, notify it, if the Duke of *Northumberland* do not
' fubmit himfelf to the Queen's Highnefs, Queen *Mary*, he fhall be accepted
' as a Traitor. And all we of the Nobility, that were Counfellors to the late
' King, will, to the uttermoft Portion, perfecute him, and his, to their utter
' Confufion.

---

f Book of Martyrs, Vol. 3. p. 12, 13.   g Annals, p. 611.   h Ibid.   i Godwin's
Annals of Queen Mary, p. 272, 273.   k Stow ut fupra.

I

Signed by *Thomas* Archbiſhop of *Canterbury*, *Thomas* Biſhop of *Ely*, Chancel-- lor ; *William* Marquis of *Wincheſter*, Treaſurer ; *Henry* Duke of *Suffolk* ; the Earls of *Bedford*, *Shrewſbury*, and *Pembroke* ; *Thomas Darcy* Lord Chamberlain, *W. Peter* Secretary, *W. Cecil* 2d Secretary, with others of the Council.

On which, the Duke gave Leave to every Man to depart ; and ſoon after he was arreſted in *King's* College, by *Slegge* Serjeant at Arms ; but, other Letters coming from the Council, that all Men ſhould go each his Way, the Duke ſaid to thoſe that kept him : ' Ye do me Wrong to withdraw my Liberty, ſee ' ye not the Council's Letters without Exception, that all Men ſhould go whi- ' ther they would.'

Whereupon, they who kept him, and the other Noblemen, ſet them at Li- berty, and ſo continued they for that Night [1], and the Earl of *Warwick* (the Duke of *Northumberland*'s Son) was ready in the Morning, to have rode away ; at which Time, the Earl of *Arundel* came from the Queen to the Duke, into his Chamber, who when he ſaw him, ſaid, *For the Love of God, conſider I have done Nothing but by the Conſent of you, and all the whole Council.* My Lord (re- plied the Earl of *Arundel*) I am ſent hither by the Queen's Majeſty, and in her Name, I arreſt you. *I obey it* (ſaid the Duke) *I beſeech you my Lord* Arundel, *uſe Mercy towards me, knowing the Caſe as it is.* My Lord (anſwered the Earl) you ſhould have ſought for Mercy ſooner, I muſt do according to my Com- mandment. And thereupon committed the Charge of him, and of others, to the Guard and Gentlemen that ſtood by.

The 25th of *July* [m], the Duke, with the reſt, were brought to the *Tower* of *London*, under the Conduct of *Henry* Earl of *Arundel*, with a Body of Light Horſemen, *&c.* On *Friday* the 18th of *Auguſt*, he was arraigned [n] (a great Scaf- fold being ſet up in *Weſtminſter* Hall) with *John* Earl of *Warwick* his Son and Heir, and *William Parr* Marquis of *Northampton*, before *Thomas* Duke of *Nor- folk*, High Steward of *England*, on that Occaſion. The Duke of *Northumber- land*, with great Reverence towards the Judges, proteſted his Faith and Alle- giance to the Queen, whom he confeſſed grievouſly to have offended, and ſaid he meant not to ſpeak any Thing in Defence of his Fact, but requeſted to un- derſtand the Opinion of the Court in two Points :

' *Firſt*, Whether a Man doing any Act by the Authority of the Prince's ' Council, and by Warrant of the Great Seal of *England*, and doing Nothing ' without the ſame, might be charged with Treaſon, for any Thing, which he ' might do by Warrant thereof ?

' *Secondly*, Whether any ſuch Perſons as were equally culpable in that Crime, ' and thoſe by whoſe Letters and Commandments he was directed in all his ' Doings, might be his Judges, or paſs upon his Trial, as his Peers ?

To which was anſwered, ' That the Great Seal, which he had for his War- ' rant, was not the Seal of the lawful Queen of the Realm, nor paſſed by Au- ' thority, but the Seal of an Uſurper, and, therefore, could be no Warrant to ' him. And that, if any were as deeply to be touched in the Caſe as himſelf, ' yet, ſo long as no Attainder were of Record againſt them, they were Perſons ' able, in Law, to paſs on any Trial, and not to be challenged, but at the ' Prince's Pleaſure.' After which Anſwer, the Duke uſed few Words, but confeſſed the Indictment, by whoſe Example, the other Priſoners, arraigned with him, did the like, and thereupon had Judgment.

The Duke, on Receiving his Sentence, ſaid : *I beſeech you, my Lords, all, to be humble Suitors to the Queen's Majeſty, and to grant me four Requeſts.* Firſt,

[1] Stow ut antea.   [m] Ib. p. 612.   [n] Ibid. p. 614, & Stype's Memorials, Vol. 2. p. 21, 22.

V O L. I.   H   *That*

That I may have that Death which Noblemen have had in Times past, and not the other. Secondly, *That her Majesty will be gracious to my Children, which may, hereafter, do good Service, considering that they went by my Commandment, who am their Father, and not of their own free Wills.* Thirdly, *That I may have appointed to me some learned Man, for the Instruction and Quiet of my Conscience. . And, Fourthly, that she will send two of the Council to commune with me, to whom I will declare such Matters, as shall be expedient for her and the Commonwealth. And thus I beseech you all to pray for me.*

Monday, 21 *August* (three Days after his Conviction) was designed for the Execution of the Duke °; and, by Eight o'Clock that Morning, was got together, on *Tower-Hill,* near 10,000 People, to have seen the Execution, the Scaffold being made ready, Sand and Straw brought, and all the Men, belonging to the *Tower* Hamlet, present, as also the Waiters of the *Tower,* the Guard, and the Sheriff's Officers; likewise every Man standing in Order, with their Halberts, and Lanes made, and the Executioner there also; when, on a Sudden, they were commanded to depart.

It is not to be doubted, but this Delay of his Execution was with Design of bringing the Duke to a Recantation of his Religion, with a Promise of Pardon. And it is a further Confirmation of it, that, on the same Day, the Lord-Mayor and Aldermen were sent for to the *Tower,* with the most substantial Citizens, and divers of the Privy-council (as is observed by the Journalist living at that Time) when, in Presence of all these, Mass was said before the Duke, and the rest of the Prisoners.

The next Day, the Duke being brought to the Scaffold on *Tower-Hill* ᴾ, after putting of his Gown of crane coloured Damask, he, leaning on the East Rail, said, ' Good People, all you that be here present to see me die, though ' my Death be odious and horrible to the Flesh, yet, I pray you, judge the ' best in God's Works, for he doth all for the best. And as for me, I am a ' wretched Sinner, and have deserved to die, and most justly am condemned ' to die by Law. And yet this Act, whereof I die, was not altogether of me, ' but I was procured and induced thereunto by others; I was, I say, induced ' thereunto by others. Howbeit, God forbid that I should name any Man un-' to you, I will name no Man unto you, and, therefore, I beseech you, look ' not for it. I, for my Part, forgive all Men, and pray God also to forgive ' them. And, if I have offended any of you here, I pray you, and all the ' World, to forgive me; and, most chiefly, I desire Forgiveness of the Queen's ' Highness, whom I have most grievously offended. And I pray you all to ' witness for me, that I depart in perfect Love and Charity with all the World, ' and that you will assist me with your Prayers at the Hour of Death.' The rest of his Speech, almost in every Point, was the like as he had said in the Chapel of the *Tower,* the Day before, saving when he had made Confession of his Faith, he had these Words : ' And here I do protest unto you, good Peo-' ple, most earnestly, even from the Bottom of my Heart, that this, which I ' have spoken, is of myself, not being required, nor moved thereunto, by any ' Man, nor by any Flattery, or Hope of Life; and I take Witness of my Lord ' of *Worcester* here, mine old Friend and ghostly Father, that he found me in ' this Mind and Opinion, when he came to me; but I have declared this only ' upon mine own Mind and Affection, and for the Zeal and Love that I bear ' to my natural Country. I could, good People, rehearse much more, even ' by Experience that I have of this Evil that hath happened to this Realm by ' these Occasions; but you know I have another Thing to do, whereunto I ' must prepare me, for the Time draweth away. And now I beseech the ' Queen's Highness to forgive me mine Offences against her Majesty, whereof ' I have a singular Hope, forasmuch as she has already extended her Goodness ' and Clemency so far upon me, that whereas she might forthwith, without

---

° Stype's Memorials, Vol. 3. p. 21, 22.   ᴾ Stow p. 614, 615.

' Judgment,

' Judgment, or any further Trial, have put me to moſt vile and cruel Death,
' by Hanging, Drawing, and Quartering, foraſmuch as I was in the Field in
' Arms againſt her Majeſty. Her Highneſs, neverthelaſs, of her moſt merciful
' Goodneſs, ſuffered me to be brought to my Judgment, and to have my
' Trial by Law, where I was moſt juſtly condemned. And her Highneſs hath
' now alſo extended her Mercy and Clemency upon me, for the Manner and
' Kind of my Death. And, therefore, my Hope is, that her Grace, of her
' Goodneſs, will remit all the reſt of her Indignation and Diſpleaſure towards
' me, which I beſeech you all moſt heartily to pray for, and that it may
' pleaſe God long to preſerve her Majeſty to reign over you in much Honour and
' Felicity.'

After he had thus ſpoken, he kneeled down, ſaying to them that were about
him, I beſeech you all to bear me Witneſs, that I die in the true Catholick
Faith ; and then ſaid the Pſalms of *Miſerere* and *De Profundi*, his *Pater Noſter,*
and Six of the firſt Verſes of the Pſalm *In te Domine ſperavi*, ending with this
Verſe, *Into thy Hands, O Lord, I commend my Spirit.* And, when he had thus
ended his Prayers, the Executioner aſked him Forgiveneſs, to whom he ſaid, *I
forgive thee with all my Heart, and do thy Part without Fear.* And bowing towards the Block, he ſaid, *I have deſerved a thouſand Deaths* ; then laid his Head
on the Block, and was beheaded ; whoſe Body, with his Head, was buried in
the *Tower,* by the Body of *Edward,* Duke of *Somerſet* ; ſo that there lie,
before the high Altar in St. *Peter*'s Church, two Dukes between two Queens,
viz. between Queen *Anne,* and Queen *Catharine,* all four beheaded.

I leave it to the Reader's Judgment, whether it may not be conjectured, by
the latter Part of his Speech, that he was put in Hopes of Pardon ; for what
other Conſtruction can be put on his Words, *And, therefore, my Hope is, that
her Grace, of her Goodneſs, will remit all the reſt of her Indignation and Diſpleaſure
towards me, which I beſeech you all moſt heartily to pray for,* &c. *Thuanus* is of
the ſame Opinion, who gives this Account [q].

Moſt have written, that, being a cunning Man, and fond of Life, he did
this (meaning his Reconciling himſelf to the Popiſh Religion) in Hopes of Pardon, and that, when he looked round, and ſaw himſelf deceived, he repented
of it.

Fox, who lived in thoſe Times [r], affirms, *That the Duke had a Promiſe made
him of a Pardon (yea though his Head was upon the Block) if he would recant and
hear Maſs, and thereupon denied, in Words, that true Religion, which, before-
time, as well in King Henry the Eighth's Days, as in King Edward's, he had
oft evidently declared himſelf, both to favour and further.*

A particular Account [s] of his valiant Exploits is delivered by an Eye-witneſs.

*All theſe valliant and noble Exploytes weare attempted and atchieved by
the right honorable the Viſcount* Liſle, *High Admyrall of* England, *in the
Raigne of King* Henery *the Eighth, and after created Erl of* Warwick, *and Duke of* Northumberland, *in the Raigne of King* Edward
the Sixth.

Firſt. THE Bourding and Taking of the Admyrall of *Sluiſe,* betweene *Dover* and the *South Downes,* being but Ship to Ship, and Sir *Thomas
Seymer,* and *William Nicholles,* giving Chaſe to an other Ship.

Item, The Entering of *Edenborrow,* and the Onſett given to the Gate, he being the formoſt Man.

Item, The fyrſt Iourney to *Edenborough,* with the Landing of the Vauntgard
given him, putting the Governour and Cardinal to Flight, and then returning

[q] Thuanus's Hiſt. of his own Times, p. 444, 445.   Book of Martyrs, Vol. 3. p. 12, 13.
[s] Ex Autog. apud Penſhuſt.   [r] Ibid.

to *Leeth*, and the Entering the fame vppon the Ordinaunce at the Bridge.

The Coming Home by Land, wheare the Vauntgard, at the *Peafe*, putt to Flight the Lord *Hume*, with the Power of the Marches, *Tyndeill*, and all the Borders of *Scotland*.

The Siege of *Bullain*, wheare this Vifcount lay, then Highe Admyrall of *England*, befydes the Mount on the Eaft Syde, in the formoft Tent next the Towne, during the Siege.

The faid Admyrall received the Keyes of *Bullen*, of the Kings Maieftie, after it was rendred, and had the Keeping of the fame, after the Kings Maiefties Departure into *England*.

The Repulfe of the *Dolphins Camiafado*, given by the Admyrall at bafe *Bullen*, wheare a greate Number of *French* Men weare flaine and drowned.

The Iourney againft Mounfier *de Bies*, and the Putting him to Flight, with the Winning and Taking of his greate Artillery and Cariages.

The Entring in the Mouth of the River of *Sien*, wheare the *French* King, being that Time in Perfon, and all his Army by Sea, ready to fet foorth, but wold not fight.

The Meeting of the Galleyes betweene *Alderney* and *Garnfey*, and the Putting of them to Flight, 18 of them affayling the Admyrall alone.

The Coming of the *French* Fleete to St. *Ellens* Point, or the Eaft Syde of the *Ifle of Wight*, they being in Number 280 Sailes, befyde Galleyes, and the Yffuing out of the Admyrall with the *Englifhe* Fleete, oute of *Portefmouth* Haven, being but 48 Sayles. The Enemy fledd.

The Iourney to *Treiport*, with the Going on Land of the Admyrall, and the Burning of the whole Towne, and all the Shippes in the Haven.

The laft Iourney into *Scotland*, whear, he then being Erl of *Warwick*, was Lieutenant Generall of the whole Armye, of both Horfe and Foote, vnder the Duke of *Sommerfett*, and, in the Vauntgard, was fett vppon by Don *Lainerick* and the younge *Maxwell*; but he put the *Scotts* to Flight, and tooke a *Douglas*, and kylled many other, and loft very fewe.

The Day of Battell ftrucken vpp at *Mufkelborough*, wheare the Lord *Gray*, with the Horfmen, gave the Onfett, contrary to Apointment, and weare repulfed; but he, with the Vauntgard, Ordinaunce, and Archers, ftanding faft, had that Day the Victory, and there were flaine of the *Scottz* 7000 Perfons.

The Iourney to *Norwiche*, and the Winning of the Towne, againft the Rebells, wheare 280 of them weare flaine at the fyrft Incounter, and the Refidue, being 9 or 10,000, yeelded themfelues to the Kings Mercy.

This was drawne by Senior *Cork*, alias *Lancafter* Harald, who was with him in all thefe Exploytes.

I am not unapprifed of what has been related by Sir *John Hayward* [u], againft this Duke, and by other of our Hiftorians, who have wrote after him, taking what he has faid to be true, without Examination of the Facts. I fhall not pretend fully to vindicate him, but fhall ftate two or three Particulars, and leave the Reader to form a Judgment of his Character.

Sir *John Hayward* charges him with getting vaft Sums of Money, by defpoiling the Church of her *Chalices*, and an infinite Number of *confecrated Utenfils* of Gold and Silver, &c. Stow recites [w], that, in the Months of *April* and *May*, 7 *Edw*. VI, Commiffioners were directed through *England*, for all the Church Goods, remaining in Cathedral and Parifh Churches, *viz*. Jewels of Gold, and Silver, Croffes, Candlefticks, Cenfers, Chalices, and all other fuch like, with their ready Money, to be delivered to the Mafter of the King's Jewels, in the *Tower* of *London*; and Coapes and Veftments of Cloth of Gold, Cloth of Tiffue and Silver, to the Mafter of the King's Wardrobe in *London*. The other Coapes, Veftments, and Ornaments, to be fold, and the Money to be delivered

---

[u] Life of E. VI.   [w] Annals, p. 609.

to the King's Treasurer, Sir *Edmund Peckham*, Knight, reserving to every Church one Chalice or Cup, with Table-cloths for the Communion-board, at the Discretion of the Commissioners; which were, for *London*, the Lord-Mayor, the Bishop, the Lord Chief Justice, and others. This, it is presumed, is that which Sir *John Hayward* throws on the Duke, which no other Historian, of that Time, takes Notice of, and his Characters, in general, are inconsistent. As to the Charge, of the Duke's ordering Matters so, that the King declined in his Health, it is no Way proved; and the following Letter, which he wrote to Sir *William Cecil*, a little before his Majesty's Death, shews a Concern for his ill State of Health, and the Affairs of the Nation.

[x] ' I have receyved soche Lettres as came in your Packytt, for the which I
' hartelie thank you, wishing yt might have beyn so, as your Helth wolde
' have permytted you to have delivered them your silfe. It was styll sayde
' here, that you had but a Grudginge of an Ague; but now we heare the
' Contrary, and that you have byn thies thre or four Fytts grevously hande-
' lyd; for which I am right sorrye, trusting to God the worst ys past. Where-
' of I would be as glad as any Man, both for your own Comforte, as also for
' the Advauncement of the King's waightie Affayres. Your Companion doth
' bear out the Burdeyn with as moche Payne as any Man can do, so moche ys
' his good Will towards the Service of his Master, and his Countrie, that, of
' a great deale of Payne, he maketh litle Appearance.
' Others we have, whos Sorte you are wel acquainted withal, that nether
' ernest Zeale, or Consideration of Tyme, can skarcely awake theym out of
' theyr wonted Dreames, and smothelie wynketh all Care from theyr Harts,
' how urgent or wayghtie soever our Causes ar. Which Thinge I can so yvel
' beare, as indeed of late, but for my Duty to the State, my Harte colde
' skarsly endure the Mannour of yt, specially in thies mooste careful Daies.
' Wel, I do herewith too much trouble you, and receyvyth no Plessir with so
' often remembring the Forgetfulness or, I sholde say, the Carelesness of
' others.
' But now I will recomfort you with the joyfull Compford, which our Phy-
' sicians hath, thies two or three Mornings, revyved my Spirits withal; which
' ys, that our soveraine Lord doth begin, very joyfully, to encreafe and amende,
' they having no Doubt of the thorro Recoverye of his Highness, the rather,
' becaufe his Majesty is fully bent to follow theyr Council and Advyce. And
' thus, with my hartie Commendations, I wish you perfytt Helth. From
' *Greenewyche*, this 7th of *May*, 1553.

To my very loving Friend,   ' *Your assured loving Frende,*
  Sir *William Cycill*, Knt.

                                             ' Northumberland.'

I shall now give some Account of Sir *Andrew Dudley*, Knight, his Brother, as he shared in his Misfortunes, though not in so unfortunate an End. On 28 *October*, 1550, 3 *Edw*. VI, being then a Knight, he obtained a Grant of the Office of Keeper of the Palace of *Westminster*, vacant by the Death of Sir *Anthony Denny*, Knight [y]; and, on 17 *May*, 4 *Edw*. VI, the King granted him an Annuity of 12*l*. 13*s*. and 4*d. per Annum* for Life, in Recompence for some Houses King *Henry the Eighth* took into his Hands, belonging to the Office of Keeper of the Palace of *Westminster*. On the Death of King *Edward the Sixth*, taking Part with his Brother, in endeavouring to support the Lady *Jane* on the Throne, he was, with the Duke, committed to the *Tower*, and on 19 *August*, 1 *Mary*, was arraigned [z] at *Westminster*, and, submitting himself to the Queen's Mercy, had Judgment passed on him. However, he did not suffer Death [a]

---

[x] Strype's Memorials, Vol. 2 in Reposit. p. 161.   [y] Rymer's Fœdera, Tom. 15. p. 233,
234.   [z] Stow's Annals, p. 614.   [a] Strype's Memorials, p. 208.

with Sir *Henry Gates*, and Sir *Thomas Palmer*, on whom Sentence was pronounced at the fame Time. And having obtained his Pardon, he was delivered out of the *Tower* on 18 *October*, 1554. I do not find he was in any Employment under Queen *Elifabeth*, but died without Iffue, in 1559, 2d of Queen *Elif.* as fhould feem by the Probate of his Will, which is dated 22 of *November* that Year; but the Will [b] bears Date 21 *July*, 1556, the greateft Part whereof I have tranfcribed, and is as follows:

I, Sir *Andrewe Dudley*, Knight, beinge ficke of Bodye, but of good and perfitt Remembraunce, and confideringe that every Man is mortall, and not knowing the certeyn Tyme and Hower when it fhall pleafe Godd to call, and willinge to be in a Redyfnefs, do conftitute and make my laft Will and Teftament in Manner and Forme followinge. *Firft*, I bequeath my Soule to Almightie God, my Body to be buried at *Weftminfter*, where it fhall pleafe the Deane to beftowe; and whereas dyvers and fondrye Parfones have Goodes, Juells, and Plate of myn, and be indebted unto me in Manner and Forme followinge: That is to fay, where my Lord of *Cumberland* hath Juells, Plate, Mony, Apparell, Horffes, Wapons, and other Things, to the full Vallue of 4000 Marks and more; and whereas *Ofwald Wilkinfon* my Servaunt did receave of my Debts at *Callice*, at the Hands of my Lord *Wentworth*, Sir *Richard Cotton*, and others, the Quenes Hignes Commiffioners there, at *Guyfnes*, and other on that Side the Sea, certeyn Somes of Money, amountinge to the Vallue of 180 *l*. And whereas *James Shelley*, Gent. doth owe unto me the Some of 200 *l*. which I lent him in redy Mony; and whereas there was due to me the Some of 30 *l*. by Maifter *Duke*, at *Michaelmas* now one Yere paft, for the Rente of one Yere and a Haulfe of *Weftennmouth*, and owing unto me by *Hetferolde*, the Quenes Goldfmith, for certeyn Golde he hadd of myn, a Parcell whereof is received, and tenne Pounds which my Lorde of *Vrmond* doth owe me, which I lent him at *Guyfnes*; and 5 *l*. owing unto me by my Lord of *Weftminfter*, which I lent him at *Bulleyn*. And the yerelie Rent of feven Nobles, due unto me by the Space of thre Yeres and a Haulfe, by *Thomas Malerth*, Yoman, at *Michaelmas* nowe one Yere paft, and going out of certyn Lands and Tenements in *Surry*, called *Fredinghurft*, and other Lands, as appereth by Indentures made betwene me the faid Sir *Andrewe*, and the faid *Thomas*. I geve and bequeth all and fingular, the forefaide Plate, Juells, Apparell, Debts, Somes of Mony, and all other Things whatfoever due unto me by anythe Parfones aforefaide, unto my Nephewes *Ambrofe Dudley*, *Robert Dudley*, *Henry Dudley*, my Sifter *Jobfon*, and my Sifter *Carden*, equally (the two laft were Daughters of his Mother, by *Arthur Plantagenet*, Vifcount *L'Ifle*) to be devided amonges them; and that the Parfones aforefaide fhall pay, out of the forefaid Somes, Juells, Plate, Mony, and other the Premiffes, the Somes hereafter enfewinge: That is to fay, to my Brother *Jerom Dudley* the Some of 200 *l*. to my Nephewe *Sidney* 200 *l*. to *Robert Nowell*, of *Grayes* Inne, the Some of 100 Marks, &c. further paying my Debts, which as I remember are little above 100 *l*. and geving to the poor Folkes 10 *l*. Alfo I geve to my Ladie, my Nephewe *Ambrofe Dudley*'s Wife, 100 *l*. which I lent him in Gold, and one Gowne which I delyvered in the *Tower*, furred with Sables, by Eftimation worth 80 *l*. Alfo I geve to my Nephewe *Ambrofe Dudley*, my Nephewe *Sidney* and his Wife, my Brother *Jobfon* and his Wife, my Houfe in *Tuthill-ftreet*; and the beft of my Garments and Apparell, whatfoever they be, I bequeath to my Brother *Jobfon*, my olde Apparell to be beftowed amongs my Servaunts. The Refidue of my Goods and Debts I will they fhall ftande and be at the Order, Difcretion, and Difpofition of my Executors, my Nephewe Sir *Henry Sidney*, my Brother in Lawe Sir *Frauncis Jobfon*, and *Robert Nowell* of *Grayes* Inne, and my Overfeers my Nephewes *Ambrofe Dudley*, *Robert Dudley*, and *Henry Dudley*.

The Duke of *Northumberland* had to Wife *Jane*, Daughter and Heir of Sir *Edward Guilford*, Knight, by *Eleanor* his Wife, Sifter and Heir of *Thomas Weft*,

[b] Ex Regiftr. Chanay, Qu. 60. in Cur. Prærog. Cantuar.

Lord *La Warr.* Which Sir *Edward* [c] was Marſhal of *Calais*, Lord Warden of the *Cinque-Ports*, and Maſter of the Ordnance under King *Henry the Eighth* ; whoſe Brother Sir *Henry Guilford*, in 2 *H.* VIII, for his Valour and Conduct, under *Ferdinand* and *Iſabella*, King and Queen of *Arragon*, was honoured with an Augmentation to his Coat of Arms, *viz. On a Canton, a Pompgranate ſlipt*, being the Arms of *Granado*, and was there alſo knighted. In 4 *H.* VIII, his own Sovereign conferred on him the Honour of Knighthood, and the Year after, conſtituted him Standard-bearer of *England*, which he carried at the Siege of *Terwin.* After which he was [d] made Maſter of the Horſe to King *Henry the Eighth*, Comptroller of his Houſhold, and Knight of the Garter. Their Father, Sir *Richard Guilford*, was knighted by King *Henry the Seventh*, at *Milford Haven*, and having been inſtrumental in ſettling that Monarch on the Throne, he made him one of his Privy-Council, as alſo a Banneret, having behaved himſelf with great Bravery againſt *James* Lord *Audley*, and his *Corniſh-men*, in that Victory obtained over them at *Deptford-bridge* in *Kent.* And alſo, he was in that Reign, choſen one of the Knights of the moſt noble Order of the Garter. This Sir *Richard* was Son and Heir of Sir *John Guilford* [e], who was Comptroller of the Houſhold to King *Edward the Fourth*, and knighted at the Coronation of King *Richard the Third*, and was Son and Heir of Sir *William Guilford* of *Hempſted* in *Kent* [f], Sheriff of that County in 11 *R.* II, and Son Heir of *John de Guilford* [g], who having married *Joan*, Daughter and Heir of *William de Halden*, of *Halden* in *Kent*, brought that Mannor into the Family, on the Death of the ſaid *William de Halden* [h], who died in 50 *Edw.* III. But the Family of *Guilford* antiently wrote *Guldeford*, had been eminent in the County before, and Poſſeſſors of the Mannor of *Wickham* in *Kent* [i], but were denominated from the Lordſhip and Mannor of *Guilford*, near *Rye* in *Suſſex*, which was their antient Poſſeſſions, and bore for their Arms, *A Salteir between* 4 *Martlets Sable.*

Having ſet forth the Deſcent of the ſaid *Jane*, Dutcheſs of *Northumberland*, I ſhall now mention her Children by the Duke [k], which were 8 Sons and 5 Daughters.

1. *Henry*, killed at the Siege of *Bologne*, *An.* 35 *H.* VIII, aged 19 Years.

2. *Thomas*, who died aged two Years.

3. *John*, who had the Title of Earl of *Warwick*, in his Father's Life-time. He was made [l] one of the Knights of the Bath, at the Coronation of King *Edward the Sixth.* In 5 *Edw.* VI, he [m] accompanied the Marquis of *Northampton*, in his Legation with the Habit of the Order of the Garter, to the *French* King. In 6 *Edw.* VI, he was [n] made Maſter of the Horſe to the King, with the Fee of 100 Marks *per Ann.* after which he was choſen Knight of the moſt noble Order of the Garter. He was committed to the *Tower* with the Duke his Father, and received Sentence of Death with him ; but had his Pardon [o] from the Queen, and on 18 *Oct.* 1554, the Lord Chancellor, and divers Lords of the Council, went to the *Tower*, and delivered him, and his Brothers, from their Impriſonment. After which, he immediately ſet out to viſit his Brother-in-Law, Sir *Henry Sidney*, at his Seat in *Penſhurſt* in *Kent* [p], where he died 21 *Oct.* 1554 about Midnight ; ſo that it is probable, he came ill out of the *Tower.* He was married to *Anne*, Daughter to *Edward Seymour*, Duke of *Somerſet* ; which Match was made by the King, to reconcile that Duke, and his Father, then Earl of *Warwick* ; but he had no Iſſue by her.

4. *Ambroſe*, who was created Earl of *Warwick*, of whom I ſhall hereafter diſtinctly treat.

5. *Robert*, created Earl of *Leiceſter*, the great Favourite of Queen *Eliſabeth*, whoſe Actions I ſhall alſo hereafter relate.

[c] Harris's Hiſt of Kent, p. 263. [d] Ib. p. 440. [e] Ib. p. 431. [f] Ib. p. 426. [g] Ib, p. 263. [h] Eſc. 50. E. III. n. 45. [i] Harris p. 37. [k] Ex Stemmate apud Penſhurſt. [l] Anſtis, on Knights of the Bath, p. 50. [m] MS. ſub Effig. Julii C. 9. in Bibl. Cotton. [n] Pat. 6, E. VI, p. 5. [o] Stype ut antea, p. 208. [p] Ib. p. 202.

6. *Guilford.*

6. *Guilford*, who married the Lady *Jane Grey*, Daughter of *Henry* Duke of *Suffolk*, by *Frances*, Daughter to *Mary*, second Sister to King *Henry the Eighth*. This Marriage was the Cause of his Death, being beheaded with the Lady his Wife, who was proclaimed and crowned Queen, as before mentioned. Although they both ended their Lives so unfortunately, yet were they much regretted for their Innocence and Virtues ; but left no Issue.

7. *Henry*, who, taking to a Martial Life, was slain at the Siege of St. *Quintin's*, in the 4th Year of Queen *Mary*, unmarried.

8. *Charles*, who died aged 4 Years.

Lady *Mary* eldest Daughter, married to Sir *Henry Sidney*, Knight of the Garter, Lord Deputy of *Ireland*, and Lord President of *Wales*, from whom descended the Earls of *Leicester* of the Name of *Sidney* ; which Title became extinct in *Joseline*, the seventh Earl of *Leicester*, who died without Issue, the 7th of *July* 1743, and the only Heirs of that noble Family are *Mary* married to Sir *Brownlow Sherard* of *Lopthorp* in *Lincolnshire*, Bart. and *Elisabeth* to *William Perry* of *Turvill* Park in *Buckinghamshire*, Esq. Which Ladies are Daughters and Coheirs of the Honourable Colonel *Thomas Sidney*, the sixth Son of *Robert* Earl of *Leicester*, and elder Brother of the said Earl *Joselin*. And by Virtue of an Entail, as well as the Descent, the Family Seats at *Penshurst* Place, as also, the Mannors of *Penshurst*, *Cepham*, *Hawden*, East *Ewhurst*, West *Ewhurst*, West *Leigh*, *Ensfields*, *Ford* Place, and *Remis-leigh* ; as also, *Leicester* House in *Westminster*, with the Estates thereto belonging, did then center in them, as Joint Heirs of the Body of *Robert* Earl of *Leicester*, and are also Joint Heirs to the Barony of *Lisle*, confirmed by King *Edward the Fourth* to *Edward Grey*, and *Elisabeth Talbot* his Wife, and the Heirs of the Body of the said *Elisabeth* ; as will hereafter appear.

Margaret, second Daughter of the Duke of *Northumberland*, died, aged 10 Years.

Catharine, third Daughter, was married to *Henry Hastings*, Earl of *Huntington* [q], who died without Issue by her ; and surviving him, [r] deceased in 1620, and was buried by her Mother at *Chelsea*, *Aug.* 14.

Temperance, fourth Daughter, died, when a Year old.

Catharine, fifth Daughter, died at seven Years of Age.

The Dutchess of *Northumberland* had a melancholy Scene of it, her Husband and Son being beheaded, and the rest of her Sons under Sentence of Death, herself stripped almost of all Necessaries in Life, and turned out of her House ; and so rigid were they, as to sell the Furniture thereof, and of every Thing else they could lay Hold of. This plainly appears from the following Warrant signed by the Queen, with her Seal of Arms, within a Garter, *viz.* *France* and *England* quarterly, the *Fleuer de Lisses* being in the first Quarter [s].

Marye the Queen.

TRusty and right wel beloved, we grete you well. And where you have seised to our Use certain Stuff, Apparell, and Silkes, apperteyning to the late Duke of *Northumberland*, and presently remayning in the Custody of *Nicholas Bourman*, of our Citie of *London* Hosier ; that is to say, *First*, one Pece of Clothe of Gold, conteyning five Yardes thre Quarters. *Item*, One other Pece conteyning 11 Yardes and a Half. *Item*, One other Pece conteyning 9 Yardes and Half and Half-quarter. *Item*, A Pece of wrought Velvet colord blake. *Item*, One other Pece containing 6 Yardes and a Quarter. *Item*, In wrought Velvet colord blake, containing 11 Yardes thre Quarters half a Quarter. *Item*, One Pece of *Luke*'s Velvet, containing 6 Yards, three Quarters. *Item*, a Pece of Crimson Velvet containing 9 Yardes and a Half. *Item*, Of Purple Velvet unshorn, Half-yard. *Item*, A Payre of wide Sleaves of black Velvet embrodered with bone Lace of Gold and Silver. *Item*, Parchment

[q] Cole's Escaetr. Lib. 3. p. 200.   [r] Ex Regist. Ecclef. Chelsea.   [s] Ex Orig. apud Penshurst.

Lace

Lace of Gold and Silver in divers Parcells containing 4 Yards. *Item*, A Gown of Crimſen Capha, and a Kirtell of white Damaſk for a Child. *Item*, One old Kirtell of white Silver and Satten. *Item*, Two old caſt Kirtells, one Crimſen Velvet, and thother of Crimſen Satten. *Item*, Thre old Caſſocks two of Velvet, and one of ſtriped Satten. *Item*, Two old Taffata Frokes, one of Roſet Velvet, and the other of Crimſen Satten, ſore worne. We late you wite that, furthwith upon the Sight of thies our Lettres, being in that Behalf, your ſufficient Warrant and Diſchardge towards us, ye make Delivery of the ſame Stuff, Apparell, Silkes and every Parcell therof, unto our truſty Servaunts, *John Herle*, and *William Ryce*, or to either of them repayring unto you, for that Purpoſe. Wherof, we require you not to faile. Yeven under our Signet, at our Mannor of *Richemont*, the 26th of *Auguſt*, the firſt Yere of our Reign.

To our truſty and right wel beloved Counſaillors, Sir William Petre *and Sir* John Baker, *Knights.*

By Inquiſition taken at *Cookfield* in *Suſſex*, 6 *June* 1 & 2 *Ph. & Mar.* [t] the Jury found that ſhe was Couſin and Heir of *Thomas Weſt* Lord *la Warr*, who died without Iſſue, 25 *Sept.* 1 & 2 *Ph. & Mar. viz.* Daughter and ſole Heir of Sir *John Guldeford*, Knight, by *Eleanor* his Wife, eldeſt of the two Siſters and Coheirs of the ſaid *Thomas* Lord *La Warr*, and that Sir *Ambroſe Dudley*, Knight, was her Son and Heir, who was pardoned for Life, though not reſtored in Blood. Whereupon, the three Daughters, Coheirs of *Dorothy* ſecond Siſter and Coheir of *Thomas* Lord *la Warr*, tendered their Livery, as Heirs to the Mannor of *Stratford Tony* in *Wiltſhire*, the Mannor of *Blatchington*, and the Advowſon of the Church in the County of *Suſſex*, and Lands in *Somtynge* and *Cokeham*, in the ſame County.

She was a Lady of great Piety, Virtue, and Prudence, and by her Sollicitations, after the Marriage of the Queen with King *Philip*, ſhe obtained Pardons for her Sons, principally by the *Spaniards*, who accompanied him into *England*, as appears from her laſt Will and Teſtament, wherein ſhe expreſſes her Gratitude to them ; and being all wrote with her own Hand, without the Advice of any learned in the Laws, as ſhe herſelf ſays, I have tranſcribed it, *literatim*, being very memorable.

Here folowith my laſte Will and Teſtament, wrytten with myn owen Hande, being perfytt in Memory, in the Yere of our Lord, MDLIV.

IN the Name [u] of the Father, the Sonne, and the Holy Gooſt. *Amen.* *Firſt*, I bequeathe my Soule unto Almightie God, and my Bodye unto the Yearth, and to be buried in the Pariſhe Churche of the Houſe, where I dye, without any Solempnitie, for my Will is rather to have my Debtes paide, and my Children and Servaunts conſidered, than my Bodye that ys but Meate of Wormes ; ſo that my Charge to myn Executors is, whiche be my Sonne, Sir *Henry Sidney* the Cheffe, Sir *George Blont* the ſecond, my Couſin *Somerfield* that hath married *Thomas Maſſe*'s Siſter the third, and Mr. *Marow* of *Warwickſhire*, the fourthe : That, after I am departyd from this Worlde, I will have no Cerymony of Openyng, but, after I am cold, let me be wonde up in a Shete, and put into a Coffyn of Woode, and ſo layde into the Grounde, with ſuch Funerals, as parteyneth to the Buriall of a Corſe. And 20 Nobles to be given to the poore Houſeholders of the Pariſhe, and 40 Shillings to *Newgate* ; 40 Shillings to *Ludgate* ; 40 Shillings to the *King's-Bench*, and 40 Shillings to the *Marſhalſey*. I do comytt into the Handes of myn Executors all the hole Landes of myne Inheritaunce. As my Houſe of *Halles Owen*, with all Manner of Tenements, *&c.* in ſuch ample Maner, as I had yt in my Lyfe-time. To Thuſe and Performance of this my laſt Will, and for the Behofe of my Children, for to inheritt my Landes, after my Legacyes and Debtes paide. The

---

[t] Eſcaetr. 1 & 2 Ph. & Mar. n. 22 & 122.   [u] Ex Regiſt. Moor, qu. 36.

Quenes Highnes fhewing her Marcie, and King's Majeftie, to my three Sonnes their Pardone, that they may enjoye my Landes. I bequeath to my Son *Ambrofe Dudley* my Houfe of *Halles Owen*, and a hundreth Pound : Land unto yt, to him, and his Heirs Male. To my Sonne *Robert Dudley* I bequeath 50 Marke Lande to hym, and his Heires Male : For Defaulte of Heires Male to retorne to my Sonne *Ambrofe Dudlay*, and Heires Males. I bequeathe to my Sonne *Henry Dudley* 50 Marke Lande, out of myn Inheritaunce, as my Sonne *Robert*'s muft be, to hym and his Heires Male : For Lacke of Heires Male to retorne to my Son, *Ambros Dudley* and his Heires Males. I bequeathe to my Daughter *Katharyn Haftinges* fiftie Mark Land out of myn Landes of Inheritaunce, to her and her Heires Males ; for Lacke of Heires Males, to return to my Sonne *Ambros* and his Heires Males. If it fo chaunce, that my Lord *Haftinges* do refufe her, or fhe hym, then fhe to have this fiftie Marke Land in Fee fympyll, to her and her Heires generall, and 400 Markes in Money, leveied upon my Woodes of *Halles-Owen*, and of fuch Lande as my Will is fhal be folde, which is the Lande I had by the Deathe of my Vncle the late Lord *Lawarre*. But firfte I require myne Executors forthwithe to fe my Debtes paide, and my Servaunts difcharged, that hath in my Houfe ferved me honeftly, fence my Lord departed. I do owe to Mr. *Wafley*, Mercer of *Chepefide*, 69 *l.* 2 *s.* 8 *d.* as *Edward* of my Warderope can declare.

She then recites who fhe is further indebted to, which were only three more. She bequeaths to her Daughter, *Mary Sidney*, 200 Marks, and 200 Marks to her little Son ; but if he chance to dye, the Money to go to his Mother, and fhe chance to dye, the Money to go to her Son ; and if they both dye, to go to her Son *Sidney* ; becaufe, having no Council by her, fhe thinks the Law will give it him. She further bequeaths to her Daughter, *Mary Sidney*, her Gown of black bard Velvet, furrd with Sables, &c. and a Gown with a high Back, of fair wrought Velvet. To her Daughter *Catharine Haftinges*, a Gown of new Purple Velvet, a Summer Gown, and a Kirtle of Purple Velvet to it and Sleaves. To *Elifabeth*, Daughter of the Lord *Cobham*, a Gown of black bard Velvet furrd with Lifards, with fome Furniture therein mentioned. To Sir *Andrew Dudley*, 20 *l.* Yearly, out of her Inheritance during his Life, when he hath his Pardon, and if he marry, to make his Wife a Jointure of it, during her Life. I give to my Lord, my Hufband's Brother *Jerome Dudley*, his Board and his Aparil, as her Executors fhall think proper for him, confidering the State of him. To her Son *Ambros*'s Wife, a new Gown of plain black Velvet furrid with Lizards, and a Kirtle of black Velvet, the Ground Satten, and Sleves. To her Son *Robert Dudley*'s Wife, a Gown of wrought Velvet. To her Son *Henry Dudley*'s Wife, a Gown of black pinkt Velvet. To the Lord *John Grey*'s Wife, her Coufin, a Gown of wrought Velvet. To her Son, Sir *Henry Sidney*, the Hangings of the Gallery at *Chelfea*, that is Gold and Green, and with her Lords Arms and hers ; alfo a Chair of green wrought Velvet, with a long Cufhion, and a Foot Carpet of *Turkey* Work. She bequeaths to the Dutchefs of *Alva* her green Parot, having nothing worthy for her elfe, praying her Grace to continue a good Lady to all her Children, as fhe as has begun. To the Lord *Dondagoe Damondefay*, that is beyond the Sea, her little Book Clock, that hath the Sun, the Moon in it, &c. and her Dial, the one Leaf of it the Almanack, and on the other Side, the golden Number, in the Midft ; and with Commendations for the great Friendfhip he hath fhewed her, in making her have fo many Friends about the King's Majefty, as fhe has found. And fhe defires her Executors and Overfeers to make her humble Commendations to the Duke of *Salvan*. To the Duke of *Mathenon*, to the Lords and Gentlemen of the Privy Chamber, that did her Sons Good, befeeching them for God's Sake to continue the good Lords to her Sons, in their Needs, and her Truft is, that God will requite it to them. To her Brother Sir *Francis Jobfon*, and to her Sifter his Wife, the Verdere Hangings of her own Bed-Chamber.

She further wills to *Mary Sidney*, her Daughter, her own Nag, and her Sadle of black wrought Velvet, and her Clock again, fhe did fo much fet by, that

was

was the Lord her Fathers, praying her to keep it as a Jewel. Alſo her Son *Sidney* to have his Clock again.   She bequeaths to ſeveral of her Acquaintance ſome of her Aparel and Furniture, and Legacys to her Servants.

And yf I dye afore this my Will be thorowe fynisſhed, I ſhall deſire mine Executors to be a Mene in my Behalfe, and mine Overſeers, unto the Quenes Highneſs, and her moſt honourable Council, that this my Will, wrytten with myn owne Handes, may take Place, althoughe ytt be not made in ſuch due Forme and Order, as it ſholde have byne, and I had called to me any Man lernyd, or els of my Frends.   But, even as miche as this is by Goddes Lawe and Mannes Lawe my verie owne Lande, by my Lorde my dere Huſbandes Gifte, and confermed by the Quenes Highneſs, with ſuch Stuff and Apparell as I have.   So that my very Harte and Mynde in the beſtowinge of my Goodes and Landes, as I wolde have yt, myn owne ſelf hath done yt.   Althoughe I have not placed all Wordes in Order, but that a better Ordere with Council might have ben made, yet I praye myne Executors and Overſeers to bear with me, and to take Paynes in the Readinge of yt, for I know you ſhall have moche a doo with all, for with great Weaknes hath this my laſt Teſtament beyn wrytten, but never lackynge Memorye when I dyd wryte yt.   If none of myne Executors be nere Hande when I newly departe, the Folkes of my Houſe to burye me with ſuche Service as is in the Churche, till my Monthes Daye.   I wolde myne Executors and Overſeers, and my Houſhold Servants, and that thoſe that dwelles in *London*, have blacke Cootes, as every Man accordinge to theire Degrees.   And ſo to lett me have ſuch Service as mine Executors ſhall thinke mete for me, conſidering non of my Children ſhall inherytt the Degree I dye in.   My Will is erneſtly, and effectually (that little Solempnitie be made for me, for I had ever have a 1000 Foldes, my Debts to be paide, and the Poore to be geven unto, then anye Pompe to be ſhewed upon my wretched Carkes, that hath hadd at Tymes to moche in this World, full of all Vanities, Diſſeats, and Gilles; and who ever dothe truſt to this tranſitorie World, as I did, maye happen to have an Overthrowe, as I hadd; therefore to the Wormes will I goe as I have afore wrytten, in all Poyntes; as you will anſwer yt afore God, and you breke eny one Jott of it, your Willes hereafter may chaunce be aswell broken.   I will at my Yeres Mynde have ſuche devyne Service, as myne Executours ſhall thynke mete, and a Stone layd upon my Grave accordingly, as the Hayroldes ſhall thinke mete, with the hole Armes of Father and Mothers, upon the Stone graven, nor in no wiſe to let me be opened after I am ded. I have not loved to be very bold afore Women, moche more I wolde be lothe to come into Thandes of any lyving Man, be he Phyſician or Surgeon.   My Truſt is the Quenes Highnes will be good and gracious Ladye, ſo moche for the faythfull poor Hart, I have all borne her, althoughe yt was little in Valewe for ſuche a Perſonage; that her Highneſs will not conſente to have any Parte of my Will broken, as God will thinke ſhe doth me moſt Right in ſo doinge in this my moſt humble Sutes for my Will.   And my Sonnes all three I leave them all to the Kinges Majeſties and her Highnes behynde me.   I give Myſtres *Clarenſious* my tawny Velvet Jewell-Coffer; I give to my Lady *Pagytt* my highbacked Gowne of wrought Velvet; to my Lorde *Pagytt*, one of my black inamyled Ringes I did uſe to weare; to my Lady *Sandes*, another of them of the leſſe Sorte.   And, foraſmoch as, upon further Deliberation, I have conſidered that many Doubts and Queſtions ben lyke to ariſe upon the Force and Sufficiency of this my Will, and ſpeſially becauſe my three Sonnes, and my Brother Sir *Andrew Dudley*, ſtondyn preſently atteynted of High Treaſon, ſo as my ſaid Will cannot take Place according to my Meanyng in all Things, if I ſhould be called out of this Lif, before my ſaid Sonnes and Brother had opteyned the Kinges and the Queenes moſt gracious Pardone; therfore I do, by this my laſt Will, hooly give and bequethe to Sir *Henry Sidney*, Knight, Sir *George Blunt*, Knight, *John Somerford*, Eſq; and *Thomas Marowe*, Eſq; whom of this my Teſtament and laſt Will I make myne Executors, and to their Heyres forever, to
the

the Ufes of the fame Sir *Henry*, Sir *George*, *John Somerfeld*, and *Thomas Marowe*, and their Heires forever al my Mannors, Landes, Tenements, and Hereditaments, with Thappurtenences, wherefoever they be, trufting in their Fidelitie, that they will have fpecial Reguarde and Confideracyon to the Advauncement and Help of my Chyldren, as to them fhall feme good, according to my fpeciall Truft put in them ; and I will, that all former Clawfes, Articles, and Sentences of this my Will, beinge contrary to Thentente and Legacie laft aforefaid, other then for fuche Annuyties as before for this my laft Will ben bequeathed and paid out of any of my Landes, to any of my Servants, or to any other, fhal be voyde, any Thinge aforefaide to my Will to the contrary notwithftandinge, in Prefens of us,

　　　E. Duddeley, Anne Yorke, Henry Sydney, William Bowdon.
Probat. 23 *May* 1555.

She was buried [x] with great Solemnity on the 1ft of *Feb.* 1554, two Heralds attending with many Mourners, 6 Dozen of Torches, and 2 white Branches, and a Canopy borne over her Effigies in Wax, in a goodly Hearfe to the Church of *Chelfea*, where a Monument is erected to her Memory, on which is reprefented, in brafs Plates, her Effigies, with all her Sons and Daughters, *viz. Henry, Thomas, John, Ambrofe, Robert, Guilford, Henry,* and *Charles* ; *Mary, Margaret, Catharine, Francis,* and *Temperance* ; with this Infcription :

Here lyeth interred the Right, Noble, and Excellent Princefs, Lady *Jane Guilford,* late Dutchefs of *Northumberland,* Daughter and fole Heir of the Right Honourable Sir *Edward Guilford,* Knight, Lord Warden of the five Ports. The which Sir *Edward* was Son to the Right Honourable Sir *Richard Guilford,* fometime Knight and Companion of the moft Noble Order of the Garter ; and the faid Dutchefs was Wife to the High and Mighty Prince, *John Dudley,* late Duke of *Northumberland,* by whom fhe had Iffue eight Sons and five Daughters ; and after fhe had lived forty fix Years, fhe departed this tranfitory World, at her Mannor of *Chelfea,* the twenty fecond Day of *January,* in the fecond Year of the Reign of our Soveraign Lady *Mary the Firft,* and in the Year 1555.
On whofe Soul Jefus have Mercy.

Her eldeft furviving Son, *Ambrofe Dudley,* was attainted with his Father, the Duke of *Northumberland,* and, receiving Sentence of Death, remained Prifoner in the *Tower* [y], till the 18 *October,* 1554. He took to a Martial Life from his Youth, and, in 3 *Edw.* VI, ferved under the Command of his Father, then General of thofe Forces, fent to fupprefs the Rebels in *Norfolk* ; and, having [z] obtained a Pardon for Life, he afterwards ferved [a] at the Siege of St. *Quintins* in *Picardy.* In 4 and 5 *Phil.* and *Mary,* he was, by Act of Parliament, reftored in Blood. Which Act [b] fets forth, That, by Reafon of the Attainders of *John,* Duke of *Northumberland* the faid *Ambrofe Dudley,* and *Robert Dudley,* Knights, now remain out of all Name and Reputation, to their great Difcomfort, inward Griefe, and daily Sorrow. And forafmuch as the faid *Ambrofe* and *Robert* be, and always, ever fince the faid Attainders, have been, and always hereafter intend to be, her Highneffes true and faithful Subjects : It may, therefore, pleafe her Highnefs, *&c.* at their moft humble Petitions, for the true and faithful Service which they had done, and intend to do, during

---

[x] Strype's Memorials, Vol. 3. p. 208.　　[y] Ibid.　　[z] Cole's Efc. Lib. 2. Not. 61. A. 13.
in Bibl. Harley.　　[a] Hollinfhed, p. 1133.　　[b] An. 4 & 5 Ph. and Mar. No. 12.

their Lives ; and having already given good Proofe and Trial of their Fideli-ties, &c. it was therefore enacted, with the Assent of the Lords Spiritual and Temporal, and of the Commons, in Parliament assembled : That the said *Am-brose Dudley,* and *Robert Dudley,* Knights, the Lady *Mary Sidney,* and Lady *Catharine Hastings,* and every of them, and their Heirs, and the Heirs of every of them, from henceforth may; and shall be, by Authority of this Act; *be re-stored and inhabled in Bloud and Name, and made Heire and Heires, as well to the* said Sir John *Dudley, Knight, late Duke of* Northumberlande, *their said Father, as also to any other their Auncestor or Auncestors, Lyneall or Collaterall, in such Manner and Forme, as yf the said late Duke, their Father, or they, or any of them, had never byn attainted, and as yf no such Attayndor, or Attayndors, were, or had byn had : The Corruption of Bloud betweene the said late Duke, their Father, and your said Subjects, or any of them, or the Corruption of Bloud betwene your said Subjects, and any other their Auncestor or Auncestors, or any Acte of Parlyament, or Judgment at the Common Lawe, concerning the Attayndor of the said late Duke, their Father, or of the said Sir* Ambrose Dudley, *or of the said Sir* Robert Dudley, *or any of them; or any other Thynge, whereby the Bloud of the said late Duke, their Father, or of the said Sir* Ambrose Dudley, *or of the said Sir* Robert Dudley, *or or any of them is, shulde, or might be corrupted,* &c. And it was also enacted, That the said *Ambrose Dudley,* and *Robert Dudley,* the Lady *Mary Sidney,* and the Lady *Catharine Hastings,* and every of them, and their Heirs, &c. shall be enabled to demand, ask, have, hold, and enjoy; all such Lands, Tenements, and Hereditaments, &c. which, at any Time hereafter, shall discende, come, remayne, or revert from any their Auncestor or Auncestors, as yf the Duke, their Father, or any of them, had never byn attaynted, and as though no such Attayndor of their said late Father, or of them, or any of them, had ever byn had or made. *And that they, or any of them, and Theires of every of them, may, at all Times hereafter, use and have any Action of Suite, and make their or his Pe-digres and Conveyance in Bloud, as Heires, as well to and from their said Father, as also to any other their Auncestor or Auncestors, Lyneall or Collaterall, as yf the said late Duke, their Father, or they, or any of them, had never byn attaynted, and as yf no such Attayndor, or Attayndors, were, or had been had, the Corruption of Bloud betwene the said late Duke, their Father, and your said Subjects, or any of them, nor betwene your said Subjects, and any other their Auncestor or Auncestors, or any Acte of Parlyament, or Judgment at the Common Law, concerning the At-tayndor of the said late Duke their Father, or of the said Sir* Ambrose Dudley, *or of the said Sir* Robert Dudley, *or any of them ; or whereby the Bloud of the said late Duke, their Father, or of the said Sir* Ambrose Dudley, *or of the said Sir* Robert Dudley, *or of any of them, is, or should be corrupted, to all Intents, Con-strutions, and Purposes.*

In 1 *Elis.* he obtained [c] a Grant of the Mannor of *Kibworth-Beauchamp,* in Com. *Leicester,* to be held by the Service of Pantler to the Kings and Queens of this Realm, at their Coronation. Which Office and Mannor his Father, and other his Ancestors, Earls of *Warwick,* formerly enjoyed. In 2 *Elis.* [d] he was advanced to that great Office of Master of the Ordnance, for Life.

On *Christmas-day,* in 4 *Elis.* he had the antient Honour of his Ancestors con-ferred on him, *viz.* Baron L' Isle of *Kingston* L' *Isle* in *Berkshire,* in Consideration of his illustrious Blood, Fidelity, Valour, Prudence, and great Merits, as the Patent [e] recites. Also, the next Day, he was advanced to the Dignity of Earl of *Warwick.* The Preamble to which Patent [f] sets forth : ' The Queen, con-' sidering that the Way to increase her Royal Dignity, is by advancing Men to ' Titles of Honour, eminent for their Abilities and Valour, and of such the ' more she prefers, the brighter her Crown shines. And Sir *Ambrose Dudley,* ' Knight, Baron L' *Isle,* being lawfully descended from the illustrious and an-

[c] Pat. 1 Elis.   [d] Pat 2 Elis. p. 4   [e] Pat 4 Elis. p. 6.   [f] Ibid.

' tient Race of the Earls of *Warwick*, as also the present eldest Son of *John*,
' late Duke of *Northumberland* and Earl of *Warwick*. She, therefore, being
' willing to restore the Family, has created him Earl of *Warwick*, by girding
' him with a Sword, and placing a Cap of Honour and Circle on his Head:
' To hold to him, and the Heirs Male of his Body, with Remainder to Sir
' *Robert Dudley*, Knight, Master of the Horse to her Majesty, otherwise called
' Sir *Robert Dudley*, Knight, Brother of the said Sir *Ambrose Dudley*, Knight,
' Baron *L' Isle*, and now Earl of *Warwick*, and to the Heirs Male of the Body
' of the said Sir *Robert*, with a Grant of 20*l.* annually, out of the Fee-farm
' Rent of the Citty of *Coventry*, payable by the Sheriff and Citizens of the said
' Citty. Dated at *Westminster*, 26 *December*, in 4 *Eliz.*'

On 1 *October*, 1562, [g] he was constituted Commander and General
of all the Queen's Forces in *Normandy*, the Patent reciting, That the Queen,
for many just and necessary Causes, and by Advice of her whole Council, for
her Defence, as well as of the *French* King, who, with the Queen his Mother,
are Captives, she is proved to send a Body of armed Men into the nearest *Norman* Port to *England*; and it being necessary to send some noble, valiant, and
just Person, as their Commander, and confiding highly in the Fidelity, Prudence, Valour, and Industry, of *Ambrose*, Earl of *Warwick*, she prefers him to
the Command aforesaid.

He took Shipping at *Portsmouth* 17 *October*, but, by contrary Winds, was
twice drove back to *Dover*; so that it was the 29th of the same Month before
he landed at *Newhaven*, where he was joyfully received. *Stow* relates his Proceedings there [h], to which I refer; but he behaved himself with great Honour
and Bravery, and defended the Town from the Month of *September*, 1562, to
the 29 *July*, 1563, and had divers Skirmishes with the Enemy. At length,
being closely besieged, and *Montmorency*, Constable of *France*, sending a Trumpet to the Earl to surrender the Town, he sent Sir *Hugh Powlet* to assure him,
the *English* were prepared to suffer the last Extremities, before they would yield
up the Town without the Queen's Orders. But, there being a raging Distemper
in the Garrison, more perished by the Sickness, than the Sword, though the *English* gave the *French* a brave Repulse. Queen *Elisabeth* therefore, as *Cambden* [i]
observes, having Intelligence of this, expressed, with Tears, her Commiseration
of the sad State her People was reduced to, and, that she might no longer
expose her bravest Men, sent Orders to *Warwick*, to capitulate on honourable
Terms.

Sir *William Dethick*, Garter King of Arms in the Reign of Queen *Elis.* gives
this Account of him:

' He was sent with an Army to keep the Town of *Newhaven* in *Normandy*,
' where he had the Order of the Garter [k], sent and delivered to him from the
' Queen's Majesty, by Sir *Gilbert Dethick*, Garter King of Arms. He was an
' honourable, valiant, and friendly Man. And being there besieged by *Charles*
' *the Ninth*, King of *France*, he was forced to deliver the Town of *Newhaven*,
' because of the Plague; but standing on the Rampier at a Parley, *Contre droit*
' *d' Arms*, he was shot with a Bullet empoisoned, which consumed his Leg,
' and thereof, after he had lived several Years with great Pain and Impotency,
' endured his Leg to be sawed from his Body, and died within few Days, 20
' *February*, 1589.'

This Sir *William Dethick* had the Order of his Funeral, and he was interred
with great Pomp, in the Chapel at *Warwick*, on the 9 *April*, 1590. *Henry*,
Earl of *Huntington* (who had married his Sister) was chief Mourner. And there
attended at his Interment the Earls of *Kent*, *Bedford*, *Cumberland*, *Pembroke*,

---

[g] Pat 4 Elif. p. 2. in dorfo & Rymer. [h] Annals of Elif. p. 650, & feq. [i] Annals of Queen
Elif. in Hift. of Eng. Vol. 2, p. 392. [k] Funerals M. S. Not. 31. in Bibl. Joh. Anflis Arm.

the Lords *Dudley,* and *St. John* ; Sir *William Ruſſel,* Sir *Henry Knevet,* Sir *John Harrington,* Sir *Fulk Grevil,* Sir *Drew Drury,* and Sir *Henry Lea.*

Camden, giving an Account of his Death, ſays of him [1], *That he was a moſt excellent Perſon, and died without Iſſue.*

He married three Wives, *firſt* [m], *Anne,* Daughter and Heir of *William Whorwood,* Eſq; Attorney-general to King *Henry the Eighth,* by his firſt Wife, *Caſſandra,* Daughter of Sir *Edward Gray,* Knight ; which *Anne* [n] died on 26 *May,* 6 *Edw.* VI, and *John,* her [o] only Son, by him, died before her. Whereupon he, *ſecondly,* married *Eliſabeth,* Daughter of Sir *Gilbert Tailboys,* Knight, Siſter and ſole Heir of *George,* Lord *Tailboys,* Knight ; and, *thirdly, Anne,* Daughter to *Francis Ruſſel,* Earl of *Bedford.*

He departed this Life without Iſſue, and was buried in the Midſt of our *Lady Chapel* at *Warwick,* towards the Weſt End, where a curious Altar Monument is erected to his Memory, with his Effigies in Armour, and Mantle of an Earl lying thereon ; his Head reſting on a Mattreſs cut in Marble, his Hands conjoined in Prayer, and, at his Feet, a Bear couchant muzzled, all painted to the Life.

The Inſcription about the Sides of the Tomb is as follows :

Here, under this Tomb, lyeth the Corps of the Lord *Ambroſe Duddeley,* who, after the Deceaſſes of his elder Brethren without Yſſue, was Sonne and Heir to *John,* Duke of *Northumberland.*

To whom Queen *Elizabeth,* in the 1ſt Year of her Raigne, gave the Mannor of *Kibworth Beauchamp,* in the County of *Leyc.* to be held by the Service of being Pantler to the Kings and Queens of this Realme, at their Coronation.

Which Office and Manour his ſaid Father, and other his Anceſtors, Earls of *Warwick* held. In the ſecond Yeare of her Raigne, the ſaid Queen gave him the Office of Maſter of the Ordinance.

In the fourth Yeare of her ſaid Raigne, ſhe created him Baron *Liſle,* and Earle of *Warwick.* In the ſame Year, ſhe made him her Lievtenant General in *Normandy,* and, during the Time of his Service there, he was choſen Knight of the moſt noble Order of the Garter.

In the twelveth Year of her Raigne, the ſaid Earle, and *Edward,* Lord *Clinton,* Lord Admiral of *England,* were made Lievtenants, jointly and ſeverally, of her Majeſties Army in the North Parts,

In the thirteenth Year of her Raigne, the ſaid Queene beſtowed on him the Office of chief Butler of *England.* And, in the XVth Yeare of her Reigne, was ſworn of her Privy Councell.

Who departed this Life, without Iſſue, the XXIth Day of *February,* 1589, at *Bedford* Houſe, near the Citty of *London* ; from whence, as himſelf deſired, his Corps was conveyed and Interred in this Place.

Neare his Brother *Robert,* Earle of *Leiceſter,* and other his noble Anceſtors (which was accompliſhed by his laſt Will) and welbeloved Wife, the Lady *Anne,* Counteſſe of *Warr,* who, in further Teſtimony of her faithfull Love towards him, beſtowed this Monument, as a Remembrance of him.

John Dudley, Eſq. ſecond Sonne of *John,* Lord *Dudley,* and Knight of the Garter, married *Elizabeth,* Daughter and Heire of *John Bramſhot,* Eſquire, and had Iſſue *Edmund Duddeley.*

Edmund Duddeley, Eſquier, one of the Privy Councell to King *Henry the* 7th, married *Elizabeth,* Siſter and ſole Heire of *John Grey,* Viſcount *Liſle,* deſcended as Heire of the eldeſt Daughter, and Coheir of *Richard Beauchamp,* Earl of *Warwick,* and *Eliſabeth* his Wife, Daughter and Heire of the Lord *Berkley,* and Heire of the Lord *Lyſle* and *Ties,* and had Iſſue *John,* Duke of *Northumberland.*

---

[1] Hiſt. of Eng. Vol. 2. p. 560.   [m n o] Cole's Eſc. Lib. 2. p 14.

John, Duke of *Northumberland*, and Earle of *Warwick*, Viscount *Lisle*, and Knight of the Garter, married *Jane*, Daughter and Heir of Sir *Edward Guilford*, Knight, and *Eleanor* his Wife, Sister and Coheir of *Thomas*, Lord *la Warre*, and had Issue the said Lord *Ambrose*.

The said Lord *Ambrose Dudley* married to his first Wife *Anne*, Daughter and Coheir of *William Whorword*, Esquier, Attorney-general to King *Henry the Eighth*.

The said Lord *Ambrose* married to his 2d Wife *Elisabeth*, Daughter of Sir *Gilbert Taylbois*, Knight, Sister and sole Heir of *George*, Lord *Taylboys*.

The said Lord *Ambrose*, after he was Earl of *Warwick*, married to his third Wife the Lady *Anne*, Daughter to *Francis*, Earl of *Bedford*, Lord *Russel*, and Knight of the Garter.

His Last Will and Testament being remarkable, I shall here insert it.

IN the Name of God, *Amen*. [P] I *Ambrose*, Earl of *Warwicke*, Baron *Lisle*, Knight of the most noble Order of the Garter, Master of her Majesty's Ordinance, Chief Butler of *England*, and one of her Highness most honourable Privy Council, being of perfect Memory. Do constitute, make, and ordeyne, this my Last Will and Testament in Manner and Forme following : *First*, As a true Member of the Mistical Body of *Jesus Christ*, I do commend my Soul into the Hands of God, who, in the Person of his Son, redeemed it, hoping, and assuredly believing, to receive full Pardon and Forgiveness of all my Sins, by his Death, and to be made Pertaker of Life everlasting. And, for my Body, I reserve the same to be disposed in Christian Burial, according to the Discretion of my Executrix. And, touching my Worldly Estate, for that I have, as in Honour and good Conscience I am bound to have, a great and especial Care, that all my dewe Debts whatsoever should be well and truly paid and satisfied. And my dear and loving Wife, after my Death, in honourable Estate to be maintained, I have made one Deed indented, dated the 24th Day of this instant Month of *January*, containing a Limitation and Disposition of the Uses of divers my Fee Simple Lands, to my said dear and welbeloved Wife, *Anne*, Countess of *Warwick*, for her Advancements, upon Confidence that she will see my Debts and Legacys, by this my Will bequeathed, paid, and, for other Considerations in the said Deed expressed. I do now signify and declare hereby my Will and Meaning to be, that the said Deed shall be construed and taken of sufficient Force, to, and for, the several Uses and Purposes conteined in the same. And I do, in Confirmation thereof, by this my Will, give and devise unto the said Lady *Anne*, my Wife, all the Mannors, Lands, Tenements, and Hereditaments, in the same Deed mentioned, to have and to hold, to her and her Heirs for ever, to the Purposes in the same Deed declared, without any Condition whatsoever, upon the meer Confidence I repose in the said *Anne* my Wife, that she will perform my true Meaning therein. And, forasmuch as I rest very doubtful of the Estate of my Debts, how great and burthensome the same may grow, and be, I have therefore, in further Care of the Discharge of them (being the greatest worldly Burthen that can lye upon a Christian) by another Deed indented of Bargain and Sale, dated the 25th of this instant Month of *January*, bargained and sold, conveyed and assured, to my very good Lord, and Couzen, the Earl of *Kent*, and to others therein named, all my Fee Simple Lands, Tenements, and Hereditaments whatsoever, within the Realms of *England* and *Wales*, as by the same Deed may appear. All which my said Lands, &c. conveyed, passed, or assured, by either of the said Deeds, my full Intent, Will, and Meaning is, should be chiefly imploied for the Discharge and Satisfaction of all my Debts, and Performance of this my Will. And, after the same shall be fully and conveniently accomplished, if so be all those the same Lands, Tenements, and Hereditaments, in both those Deeds contained,

P Ex Registr. vocat. Drury, n. 75, qu. 43, in Cur. Prærog. Cantuar.

besides

befides the Mannor of *Wotton under Edge*, and the reft of the Lands, *&c.* in the fame Deeds contained, which lye and be within the County of *Gloucefter* ; and the Mannor and Caftle of *Chirk*, in the County of *Denbigh*, may, and will fuf-fice, to a full Satisfaction and Payment of all my Debts, and the Performance of this my Will. Then my Requeft and Defire is, that my faid wel beloved Wife will take fuch Order, and make fuch Conveyances by Will, or otherwife, of the faid Mannor of *Wotton under Edge*, and other Lands, in the faid County of *Gloucefter*, as the fame, after the Death of my faid Wife, may come and re-main, and be, to my right Heirs forever, chargeable with Leafes for Lives, or Years, yealding the old Rents. And, touching the Mannor and Caftle of *Chirk*, my like Defire and Requeft is (if my Debts may be fatisfied, as afore-faid) that my faid Wife will convey and affure out of the fame, 50 *l.* yearly, to Sir *Robert Sidney*, my Nephew, during his Life, and one 50 *l.* yearly to *Tho-mas Sidney*, my Nephew, during his Life, with feveral Claufes of Diftrefs. And after, to affure the faid Mannor, and Caftle, to my dearly beloved Sifter, the Lady *Catharine*, Countefs of *Huntingdon*, for Term of her natural Life, without Impeachment of Waft. And, after the Deceafe of my faid Sifter, the Inheritance of the faid Mannor, and Caftle, to be limited to my faid two Ne-phews, and the feveral Heirs of their two Bodies lawfully begotten. And, for Want of Iffue of the Body of the one, the Inheritance of the Whole to be and remain to the other, and to the Heirs of his Body. And, for Want of fuch Iffue of both their Bodies, to remain to the right Heirs of me, the faid Earl, for ever. And, if it fo happen, that the Eftate of my Debts cannot, within the Space of two Years next after my Deceafe, be fattisfied and paid, or that the faid Mannor or Caftle of *Chirk* fhall, by any Title whatfoever, be lawfully evicted from my faid Wife, or Bargains, within the Space of two Years, afore-faid, then I will and bequeath to my faid Sifter the Sume of 1000 *l.* to be paid unto her, to whomfoever fhe fhall name and appoint, within one Month next after the End of the faid two Years. And my Defire further is, that if the faid Mannor and Caftle of *Chirk* fhall be evicted lawfully from my faid Wife, or Bargains, and yet, notwithftanding, there fhall remain fufficient to pay my Debts, and to leave 100 *l.* yearly to my faid Nephews, Sir *Robert Sidney*, and *Thomas Sidney* : Then my Wife fhall affure unto my faid Nephews 100 *l.* yearly, of the Lands and Tenements, contained in the faid Deeds, if fo much will be left remaining, over and above the Payment of my Debts and Legacys, in fuch Place or Places, as fhall feem beft to the Difcretion of my faid Wife. The Eftates of the faid Sir *Robert* and *Thomas Sidney*, to be, as is appointed, in the Mannor and Caftle of *Chirk*, after the Deceafe of my faid Sifter, the Coun-tefs of *Huntingdon*. And for all the reft of the Lands, *&c.* that fhall pafs to the faid Earl of *Kent*, and others, by my fore-recited Deed of Bargain and Sale (if any do remain, after my Debts and Legacys paid, and this former Part of my Will performed) my Will is, fhall be difpofed in this Manner : *Firft*, That my Wife fhall have to her, and her Heirs, for ever, the Mannor of *Aberley*, alias *Abbotfley*, in the County of *Worcefter*, and all the Right, Title, Remainders, and Reverfion thereof; and the reft of the Lands, *&c.* by the faid Deed of Bar-gain and Sale, to the faid Earl of *Kent*, and others ; and fhall be difpofed accord-ing to the honourable Confideration and Appointment of my faid loving Wife. And whereas it has pleafed her moft excellent Majefty, of her gracious Favour and Goodnefs, to vouchfave me, as next Heir to my late dear Brother, the Earl of *Leicefter*, the Surplefage that may be made upon the Sale of the Lord-fhip of *Denbigh* (the Merchants being fattisfied their Debts and Intereft grow-ing on the fame) which, as it is a Thing in her Majefties Power to difpofe of, fo do I moft humbly befeech her, that fhe would afford my next Heirs in Blood, that is, my faid Sifter, Countefs of *Huntingdon*, and my little Neice, *Elizabeth Sidney*, the Daughter and Heir of my late Nephew, Sir *Philip Sidney*, the like gracious Favour that her Highnefs intended to my felf, that they may, by her Means, reap and have the Benefit of the fame Surplufage, and Overplufs, of the Value, which the fame, upon the Sale thereof to the beft Worth, may yeald. Concerning all my Goods, Chattels, and Moveables, whatfoever, I do give and bequeath them to my aforefaid dearly beloved Wife, whom I do ordeyn and make my fole and only Executrix, of this my Laft Will and Teftament, requiring her to have an honourable Confideration of all my Servants, according to their fpecial Deferts, and Times fpent in my Service, as, in Part, I do declare, by a Codicil, hereunto annexed. And I do inftantly intreat my very affured good Lords, the Lord *Burleigh*, Lord Treafurer of *England*, the Earl of *Cumberland*, the Earl of *Huntingdon*, to be Overfeers of this my faid Will ; befeeching them to yield their honourable and friendly Furtherance to the faid Executrix, for the better Performance of the fame : And, in Teftimony of my moft dutifull and faithfull Heart towards her moft excellent Majefty, whofe Days I inftantly befeech God to lengthen here upon Earth, to the Comfort of his Church, and this Realm, with much Happinefs ; and, after her Pilgrimage here ended, fhe may everlaftingly reign with him. I do will and bequeath to her Highnes my beft Jewell fet with an Emeravde, moft humbly befeeching her gracious Acception, notwithftanding the Bafenefs thereof ; and that it would pleafe her Highnes to continue her good Favour towards my faid Wife, whom I leave to continue her moft faithfull and devoted Servant, recommending this moft effectually, as my laft Petition to her Majefty. I do give and bequeath to my faid very good Lord, the Lord Treafurer, my Collar of Gold of the Order, and my *George* annexed thereunto. And, to the Earl of *Cumberland*, my Brooche with Diamonds, with an Aggat therein ; and, to my Lord of *Huntingdon*, my fecond beft *George* and beft Garter, and a Bafon and Ewer of Silver, of forty Pounds, at the leaft : And, to my dear Sifter, the Countefs of *Huntingdon*, a Jewell worth 500 Marks : And, to my Neefe, the Countefs of *Pembroke*, a Diamond of 50 *l.* And to my very good Lord, the Lord Chancellor, my beft *George*, with a Chain and Garter. To my Lord *Cobham*, and Lord *Grey* of *Wilton*, either of them, a *George*. To Mr. Secretary *Walfingham*, my honourable good Friend, a Bafon and Ewer of Silver of 40 *l.* And to my little Neice *Sidney*, a Jewell of 100 Marks. And to Mr. Vice-Chamberlain, a Pair of gilt Livery Potts, of 20 *l.* And to Mr. *Roger Manners*, my beft Foot-cloath, Nagg, and the beft Furniture belonging to the fame. In Witnefs whereof, I have hereunto put my Hand and Seal, the 8 and 20th Day of the Month of *January*, a Thoufand five Hundred eighty-nine, and in the 2 and 30th Year of the Queens Majefties moft profperous Reign, *A. Warwicke.* By a Codicil at the fame Time, he bequeathed to his Servants a full Years Wages, except to fuch as he left Legacyes to, which are particularly named therein.

His Countefs made her Will, as follows :

ANNE, Countefs of *Warwick*, makes her Will[a] 11 *Oct.* 1603, 1 *Jac.* I. her Body to be buried at *Cheyneys*, in the County of *Hertford*[b], without Pomp, at the Difcretion of her Executors. She wills, that all her Debts fhe owes, either in Law or Confcience, be paid with convenient Speed : Of which, fuch as are due to the King, or the late Queen *Elizabeth*, or by the late Earl of *Leicefter*, be difcharged by her Mannors, Lands, and Tenements, in the County of *Gloucefter* ; and, for that Caufe, fhe bequeaths the faid Mannors, &c. to her loving Brother, Sir *William Ruffel*, Knight, Lord *Ruffel* of *Thornhaugh*, and to Sir *Henry Cock*, and Sir *Moyle Finch*, Knights, for the Term of 1000 Years. And, concerning all her Lordfhips, Mannors, &c. fhe wills, according to the Conditions and Claufes contained in the Deeds and Writings fhe had caufed to be drawn and purpofed to perfect and finifh (God willing) with Speed. Neverthelefs, if by any Means the fame fhall not be perfected, or any Defect

Ex Regift. Hart. qu. 13. [b] It fhould have been *Buckingham.*

fhould

should be therein, she bequeaths 30 *l.* Rent Charge, *per Ann.* out of her Man-nors, *&c.* in the said County of *Gloucester*, to her loving Cozin *Oliver* Lord *St. John*, and to her loving Friends, Sir *Edmund Bowyer*, Sir *Arthur Atye*, and Sir *Thomas Fleming*, Knights, and *John Beer*, Esq; *William Holman*, and *Eustace Grubbe*, Gent. and to their Heirs and Assigns for ever, towards the Mainte-nance of 10 poor People, 4 Men and 6 Women, in an Alms-House directed to be built at *Cheyneys*, aforesaid ; and 20 *l.* more like Rent-Charge *per Ann.* pay-able for ever to the above-named Persons, and their Heirs and Assigns, out of her Mannor of *Northhaw*, in the County of *Hertford*. And she wills, that all Estates, Leases, and Grants, for Life, or Years by her, or her late Lord of *Warwick*, or both, be held and enjoyed according to their Intent and Meaning, and the Purport of the Deeds in that Behalf made. And her said Mannor of *Northhaw*, commonly called *North Hall*, and the Rectory thereof, and all her Lands, *&c.* there, or at *Cuffeley*, or elsewhere in the said County of *Hert-ford*, she bequeaths to her said dear and loving Brother, the Lord *Russel* of *Thornhaugh*, for Term of his Life, paying to his Son, her Nephew *Francis Russel*, a Rent-Charge of 50 *l. per Ann.* and, after the Decease of her said Bro-ther, to be enjoyed by his Son, her Nephew, *Francis Russel*, and the Heirs Male of his Body ; and, in Default, to the Heirs Male of the Body of the said Lord *Russel* ; and, for Want of such Issue, by her Neice the Lady *Anne Herbert*, Wife of *Henry* Lord *Herbert*, Daughter and Heir of her late Brother, *John* Lord *Russel*, deceased ; and, in Default, to her Sister, the Lady *Marga-ret*, Countess of *Cumberland*, and the Heirs of her Body ; in Default, to her Sister *Elizabeth*, Countess of *Bath*, and her Heirs ; in Default, to her Nephew, *Edward* Earl of *Bedford*, and his Heirs ; in Default, to her Cozin, *Henry* Earl of *Kent*, and his Heirs ; in Default, to *Charles Grey*, Esq; Brother of the said Earl of *Kent* ; in Default, to her Cozin *Oliver*, Lord *St. John* of *Bletsoe*, and his Heirs ; and, for Want of such Issue, to the right Heirs of her the said Countess of *Warwick* for ever. And that the Woods of her Park of *Kendal*, and her Lands, *&c.* in *Kendal*, or elsewhere, in the County of *Westmorland*, be sold by her Executors, towards the Preferment in Marriage of *Elizabeth*, Daughter of the said Lady *Herbert* ; and that one Moiety of the said Park and Lands be enjoyed by her Neice, the Lady *Herbert*, and her Heirs ; one other Quarter by her Sister the Lady *Margaret*, Countess of *Cumberland*, and her Daughter the Lady *Anne Clifford*, and the Heirs of their Bodies ; one other Quarter by her Sister *Elizabeth*, Countess of *Bath*, and her Son, *Edward Bou-cher*, Lord *Fitz-Warin*. And her Mannors of *Wotton under Edge*, *Simonds-hall*, *Arlingham*, alias *Elingham*, *Sayes*, *Cam*, and *Hinton*, in the County of *Glou-cester*, she bequeaths out of them, to *Henry Bertie*, Son of the late Lord *Wil-loughby*, deceased, 10 *l. per Ann.* during his natural Life. To her Physitian, Dr. *Wilkinson*, 20 Nobles *per Ann.* To the Lady *Catharine*, Countess of *Hun-tingdon*, during her Life, 100 *l. per Ann.* and, after her Decease, to the Lady *Elizabeth*, Countess of *Rutland*, during her Life. And afterwards, the said Mannors, *&c.* she wills to Sir *Robert Sidney*, Knight, Lord *Sidney*, and the Heirs of his Body, paying the said Annuity. And she wills, that the said Lord *Sidney*, and the Heirs of his Body, discharging, within convenient Time, all Debts, *&c.* due, as aforesaid, to the Kings Majesty, *&c.* and saving harmless her Heirs and Executors, shall have the Lease and Term of one thousand Years, in Trust for such Intent made to her said Brother, the Lord *Russel*, Sir *Henry Cock*, and Sir *Moyle Finch*, to be surrendered to him the said Lord *Sidney*, and his Heirs ; as also of the Moiety of the Mannor of *Wotton under Edge*, and of other Lands in the said Lease specified, made to her, or for her Use, by Sir *Christopher Blunte*, Knight, and his Lady the Countess of *Leicester*, for certain Years depending on her Life. She bequeaths her Lease and Term of the Par-sonage of *Hitchen*, in Com. *Hertf.* to her Brother the Lord *Russel*, as also, the Remainder of her Lease and Term in the Mannor of *Topsham*, for an Aug-mentation to the Maintenance of the 10 poor People at *Cheyneys*. She leaves her

her Jewels, Plate, &c. among her Relations; and constitutes her Brother, the Lord *Russel*, Executor, together (for his better Assistance, with *Arnold Oldisworth*, and *Richard Danford*. *Probat.* 27 *February*, 1603.

The next of the surviving Sons to the said Duke of *Northumberland*, was *Robert Dudley*, the great Favourite of Queen *Elisabeth*, who created him Earl of *Leicester*. He [a] was first made Master of the Buck-hounds for Life, by King *Edward the Sixth*, in the 4th Year of his Reign; and the Year after, was sworn one of the 6 Gentlemen of the King's Privy-Chamber.

In the 1st of Queen *Mary*, though on the Apprehending of his Father, he was also (with him) sent to the *Tower* and attainted; yet was he with his Brothers [b] released, the 18 *Oct.* 1554; and in 4 and 5 *Phil.* and *Mary*, was made [c] Master of the Ordinance, at the Siege of St. *Quintins*. And from Queen *Elisabeth*, whether for that he had shared with her in that common Fate of Imprisonment, in the Reign of her Sister, or that by Reason of their Births, in one, and the same auspicious Hour, is not easy to determine, saith *Camden* [d]; but he received from her extraordinary Favours and Benefits.

In first Year of her Reign (11 *Jan.*) he had conferred on him [e] that eminent Office of Master of the Horse, with the Fee of 100 Marks, *per Ann.* And on 20 *Dec.* following, bearing the Title of *Robert* Lord *Dudley*, Master of the Horse, was the [f] first in Commission, for compounding by Fines, with all such as were desirous of being discharged from taking the Order of Knighthood, against the Queen's Coronation, according to the Statute in that Case made and provided. And in the same Year *, 4 *June*, was installed Knight of the most Noble Order of the Garter.

In the 3d of *Elis.* he was made Constable [g] of *Windsor*-castle, and Forest of *Windsor*, and the Keeping of the great Park at *Windsor*, during Life. And increasing farther into the Esteem and Favour of the Queen, she in the 6th Year of her Reign, recommended him for an Husband to *Mary* Queen of *Scotland* [h], promising her, if she would assent thereto, she would, by Authority of Parliament, declare her to be her Heir to the Crown of *England*, if she herself should die without Issue.

But the *French*, esteeming it prejudicial to their Interests for her to marry with him, or with some other Views, offered great Advantages to the Subjects of the *Scottish* Nation, in Case they would refuse it, suggesting to them, that Queen *Elisabeth* did not at all purpose what she made Shew of. Plain it is, that having given him large Possessions, her Majesty, before the End of that Year, advanced him to the Dignity of Baron of *Denbigh*, to him and his Heirs for ever, *viz.* on 28 *Sept.* and the Day after, to that of Earl of the County of *Leicester*, in Consideration of his noble Blood, Loyalty, Valour, Prudence, and numerous Virtues; as also being lawfully descended from the illustrious and and antient Earls of *Warwick*.

Camden relates, that his Advancement to the Dignity of Earl of *Leicester*, was by some thought the better to qualify him, for his Marriage with the Queen of *Scots*, though others suspected, that this Shew of Queen *Elisabeth* was merely to try, if the Motion would be accepted, and then to marry with him herself with less Dishonour.

The Queen had before, in the 5th Year of her Reign, granted him large Possessions [k], *viz.* the Castle and Mannor of *Kennilworth*, with the Appurtenances, and *Astel* Grove, both in *Warwickshire*; the Lordships, Mannors, and Castles of *Denbigh* and *Chirk*, with other Possessions; and a Licence for transporting of Cloths, which he sold to *John Marsh*, and others the Company of Merchant Adventurers, for 6266 *l.* 13*s.* 4*d.* And, in that [l] Year, he had a Patent of the

---

[a] Pat. 4. E. VI.   [b] Stow's Annals.   [c] Strype's Mem. p. 208.   [d] Camden's Annals, p. 135.   [e] Pat. 1 Elis. p. 4.   [f] Rymer's Fœdera Tom. 15. p. 493.   * E. Tabell. in Capell. Windsor.   [g] Pat. 3 Elis. p. 5.   [h] Annals Elis.   [i] Pat. 6 Elis. p. 12. m. 13.
[k] Extracts of Grants to Rob. Earl of Leicester, MS. apud Penshurst.   [l] Ibid.

High Stewardſhip of the Univerſity of *Cambridge*, with the Fee of 4*l. per Annum*, dated 7 *Julii*, 5 *Eliſ.* and the Stewardſhip of *New Windſor*, dated 9 *September* the ſame Year. Alſo, [m] on 30 *December*, in 7 *Eliſ.* his Patent bears Date, for the Chancellorſhip of the Univerſity of *Oxford*. On 24 *January*, 8 *Eliſ.* he received the Order of St. *Michael*, with the Duke of *Norfolk*, which was conferred on them, by the Ambaſſadors of *Charles the Ninth*, King of *France*, at the Queen's Palace at *Weſtminſter* [n], and a particular Relation of his Inſtallation, is given by Mr. *Aſhmole*.

He was in much Eſtimation about that Time, for, in 7 *Eliſ.* he had a Patent of the Stewardſhip of the Biſhoprick of *Ely*, confirmed by the Dean and Chapter of that Place ; alſo the Office of Chamberlain of the County Palatine of *Cheſter*. And theſe following [o] were after conferred on him, the Stewardſhip of the Foreſt of *Snoden*, the Stewardſhip of *Reading*, the Stewardſhip of *Abingdon*, the Stewardſhip of *Harrow on the Hill*, from *Roger*, Lord *North*. The Stewardſhip of *Tewxbury*, *Cleve*, *Swell*, and *Longney*, with the Fees of 11*l. per Ann.* and the Bailifwick, with the Fees, 66*s.* and 8*d.* The Stewardſhip of *Clun*. A Patent of Maſter of the Game and Liberties, belonging to the Biſhop of *Coventry* and *Litchfield*, with Licence to muſter his Tenants, *&c.* with a Fee of 10*l. per Ann.* A Patent, from the Archbiſhop of *York*, of the High Stewardſhip of his Poſſeſſions, and Maſter of his Game, with a Fee of 10*l.* The Stewardſhip of the Church of *Norwich*, with a Fee of 10*l.* A Grant of a Rent Charge of 6*l. per Ann.* from the Biſhop of *Wincheſter* for Term of his Life, out of the Mannor of *Taunton*, and other Lands in *Somerſetſhire*, confirmed by the Dean and Chapter. The Stewardſhip of the Lands of the Archbiſhop of *Canterbury*, and a Rent Charge of 10*l. per Ann.* granted by the Dean and Chapter of *Chriſt-Church, Canterbury*. And a Patent in Reverſion of the Stewardſhip of the Lands of the Biſhop of *London*, with a Fee of 10*l. per Ann.* granted by *Edwin*, Biſhop of *London*, and a Confirmation of the ſame from the Dean and Chapter. The Stewardſhip of the Honour of *Tickhall*, with the accuſtomed Fee. The Stewardſhip of the City of *Briſtol*, with the Fee of 4*l.* alſo the Stewardſhip of the Biſhoprick, with the ſame Fee. The Stewardſhip of *Eveſham*, with the Fee of 40*s.* The Stewardſhip of the Honour of *Grafton*. He was alſo choſen High Steward of the Mannor and Hundred of *Andover*, by the Bailiffs and Burgeſſes thereof ; alſo Steward of the Town of *Great Yarmouth*, and Recorder of the Town of *Malden* in *Eſſex*.

In 14 *Eliſ.* he was conſtituted Warden of *New Foreſt*, in Com. *Southamp.* [p] the Earl of *Arundel* giving him an Aſſignment thereof, who had it from his Anceſtor, the Earl of *Arundel*, who had a Grant thereof 16 *February*, 6 *Edw.* III. The Year before, he obtained an Act of Parliament, giving him, his Heirs, Executors, and Aſſigns, full Power, Authority, *&c.* to eſtabliſh one Hoſpital, within the Town of *Warwick*, or within the Town of *Kenelworth*, in the ſame County of *Warwick*, at their Choice and Election, *for the Finding, Suſtentation, and Relief of poor, needy, and impotent People, to have a Continuance for ever. And that the ſame Hoſpital, ſo founded, ſhould be incorporated, and have a perpetual Succeſſion for ever, of ſuch Head, Members, and Numbers of Poor,* &c. *as ſhould be appointed by the ſaid Earl, his Heirs, Executors, or Aſſigns, under their Hands and Seals,* &c. *And, being ſo incorporated, ſhould have full Power,* &c. *to purchaſe and hold, to them, and to their Succeſſors, for ever, Mannors, Lands,* &c. *within any County in* England, *ſo that the ſame exceed not the yearly Value of* 200*l. above all Charges and Repriſes,* &c. *And that the ſame Hoſpital ſhould have, and enjoy for ever, ſuch a Common Seal or Seals, as the ſaid Earl,* &c. *ſhould appoint,* &c. *And ſhould be ruled, governed, ordered, directed, and viſited, by ſuch Perſon or Perſons, as ſhould be nominated by the ſaid Earl,* &c.

Whereupon the ſaid Earl, by Deed Poll of Incorporation, under his Hand and Seal, 21 *November*, 1585, 28 *Eliſ.* recited, That ſince the Making of the ſaid

---

[m] Extracts of Grants to Rob. Earl of Leiceſter, MS. apud Penſhurſt.   [n] Order of the Garter, p. 369, 370.   [o] Grants præd. apud Penſhurſt.   [p] Ibid.

VOL. I.   N   Act,

Act, he appointed a House in the Town of *Warwick* for the said Hospital, and had placed therein one Master, viz. *Ralph Griffin*, Professor of Divinity, and twelve poor Brethren, who, ever since the Making the said Act, had their Abode and Relief there, at the said Earl's Charge. *Now the said Earl calling to Remembrance, that the good and charitable Deeds and Works of* Richard Beauchamp, *Earl of* Warwick, *and other his Ancestors, being provided and intended for the Relief of the Poor within the said Town of* Warwick, *but instituted and ordained, according to the Error and superstitious Ignorance of those former Times, are abrogated and taken away. And withall, being continually mindful of the great Mercy and Goodness of Almighty God, freely bestowed upon him many Ways, and especially by the singular Bounty and Favour of his most gratious Sovereign Lady Queen* Elizabeth. And in respect thereof, by Authority of the said Statute, ordeins, establishes, and appoints an Hospital in the said Town of *Warwick*, to have Continuance for ever, for the Finding, Sustentation, and Relief *of poor, needy, and impotent Men, and especially of such as should be hereafter wounded, maimed, or hurt in the Wars, in the Service of her Majesty, her Heirs and Successors.* And did found and establish the said Hospital, to consist of one Master and 12 poor Brethren, to be called THE HOSPITAL OF ROBERT, EARL OF LEICESTER, IN WARWICK. And the said *Ralph Griffin* having lately been preferred by her Majesty, at the earnest Suit of the said Earl, to the Deanry of *Lincoln*, in the Cathedral Church of *Lincoln* : He thereupon ordeined, That *Thomas Cartwright* should be, during his Life, Master of the said Hospital, unless removed, or resigning, and, in that Case, such Person, as the Earl or his Heirs should appoint, should be Master. And did further ordein, That the 12 Persons, there named, then dwelling and abiding in the said Hospital, should be the then present 12 Brethren of the said Hospital. And that upon the Death, Resignation, Deprivation, or other lawfull Removing of any of them, *such Person or Persons, as by the said Earl or his Heir, or Heirs, after his Death,* should be named or appointed a Brother or Brethren of the said Hospital, should be the Brethren of the said Hospital for ever. And, *if the said Earl, or his Heir, or Heirs, did not,* from Time to Time, within three Months next after the said 12 Brethren, or any of them, should die, resign, be deprived, or otherwise lawfully removed from the said Hospital, then such Person and Persons, as from Time to Time, upon the Default of the said Earl and his Heirs, in Form aforesaid, should be appointed and preferred to be a Brother or Brethren, by the Bishop of *Worcester* for the Time being, and the Recorder of *Coventry* for the Time being, and the Recorder of *Warwick* for the Time being, or any two of them, under Hands and Seals, should be a Brother and Brethren of the said Hospital for ever. And he appointed the said Master and Brethren a Body Corporate and Politick, *&c.* and the Lands, Tenements, *&c.* thereof should be for ever, thereafter, ruled, governed, ordered, and directed, according to such Rules, Statutes, and Ordinances, *as were thereto annexed, or, at any Time thereafter, should be set forth,* made, devised, and established by the said Earl, by Writing or Writings under his Hand and Seal.

The said Earl, 26 *November*, 1585, also gave a Body of Ordinances, Statutes, and Rules, for the Order and Government of the said Hospital.

Whereby he appoints the Form of an Oath to be taken by the Master, That *he will govern and order that Hospital, and the Poor thereof, according to the Laws, Statutes, and Ordinances of the Founder, and not consent or agree to any Act or Thing whatsoever, whereby the good Intent of the Founder may be made frustrate* ; *but to keep, as near as he can, all the Statutes instituted by the Founder.* And afterwards appoints, that the Brethren of the said Hospital shall take an Oath, *To be obedient to the Master of the said Hospital, in all lawful and honest Things, not contrary to the Statutes and Ordinances of the Founder of the same,* &c. but, *living peaceably and quietly in this Hospital, shall, to the best of their Power, maintain and uphold the same.*

And then goes on in the following Words :

7. ' Touching the Poor of the same Hospital, we will they shall be 12 in
' Number, besides the Master. And we ordein, that such poor and impotent
' Persons,

'Perfons, not having of their own to relieve themfelves, as fhall be hereafter maim-
'ed or hurt in the Wars, in Service of the Queen's Majefty, her Heirs and Suc-
'ceffors, and efpecially fuch as fhall be under the Conduct or Leading of us or
'our Heirs, *or the Servants and Tenants of us and our Heirs, fhall be preferred*
'*before all others,* to the Places and Rooms, which fhall become void in the faid
'Hofpital.

8. '*Item,* We ordein, that none fhall be preferred to any Place or Room in
'the faid Hofpital, but fuch as fhall be born in the Counties of *Warwick* or
'*Gloucefter,* or there dwelling and abiding, by the Space of 4 or 5 Years at the
'leaft.

9. '*Item,* We will, that if there be no poor People, which have been
'maimed or hurt in the Wars, as is aforefaid, That then fuch poor and impo-
'tent Perfons, as fhall be decayed by Sicknefs, or fome other Misfortune, and
'not by their own wicked Waftfulnefs, and riotous Confuming, *and efpecial-*
'*ly the Servants and Tenants of us and our Heirs,* fhall be preferred to the Place
'and Room of a Brother in the faid Hofpital.

10. '*Item,* We ordein that the lame and maimed Soldiers, *and poor People of*
'*the Quality and Condition aforefaid, which fhall happen to be in the Towns of* War-
'wick, Kenelworth, *and* Stratford upon *Avon* in the faid County of *Warwick,*
'or in the Lordfhips of *Wotton-under-Edge,* and *Erlingham,* in the County of
'*Gloucefter,* fhall be preferred to the Places and Rooms aforefaid *before any other,*
'viz. 1ft. The Town of *Warwick.* 2dly. The Town of *Kenelworth.* 3dly.
'The Town of *Stratford* upon *Avon.* 4thly. The Lordfhip of *Wotton-under-*
'*Edge*; and 5thly, the Lordfhip of *Erlingham, alterius Vicibus*; And for De-
'fault of fuch poor and maimed People, in the Towns aforefaid, then, the
'fame poor Brethren to be taken and chofen out of any Town in the faid Coun-
'ty of *Warwick.*

'*Item,* We ordein, that fuch as fhall be admitted a poor Brother of the faid
'Hofpital, after the Death of us the faid Earl, fhall be commended by the
'Minifter and Church Wardens of the Parifh, where he was laft abiding, by
'Writing, under their Hands and Seals, to be of honeft Life and Converfa-
'tion.'

The other Articles to the 24th relate, how the Brethren fhall demean
themfelves, *&c.*

24. '*Item,* That no Perfon fhall be a Brother of this Hofpital, or enjoy any
'Part of the Living or Benefit allowed, or to be allowed, for a Brother, if he
'fhall have, any Manner of Way, any other Living, to the clear Value of 5 *l.*
'by the Year, or above. And if any hereafter fhall be, *ipfo facto,* to
'be deprived.'

The reft of the Articles, to the 32d, contain Rules for the Behaviour of the
Mafter and Brethren.

32. '*Item,* We ordein that the Bifhop of *Worcefter,* the Dean of *Worcefter,*
'and the Arch-Deacon of *Worcefter,* for the Time being, or any two of them,
'after the Death of us the faid Earl, fhall be Vifitors of the faid Hofpital, and
'that it fhall be lawful for them, or any two of them, to vifit the faid Hofpi-
'tal, at any Time, at their Pleafures, fo it be not above once in three Years,
'and to correct, punifh, and reform all Abufes and Offences to be committed
'or done by the faid Mafter and Brethren, or any of them. And to fee thofe
'our Ordinances truly executed according to the true Meaning of the fame.
'Provided always that the faid Mafter and Brethren, or any of them, fhall
'not be compelled to appear, or go, out of the Town of *Warwick,* to any
'fuch Vifitation.'

The 33d Article ordeins that thefe Statutes fhall be written in a Table, and
hang continually in the Hall of the faid Hofpital, *&c.* And the 34th ordeins
that, the Revenue of the Hofpital being divided into 4 Parts, the Mafter to
have one 4th Part, and the Brethren the reft; alfo makes Orders for letting
Leafes of the Lands, *&c.* belonging to the faid Hofpital.

Having raifed ftately and magnificent Buildings, at *Kenelworth*-Caftle, in *War-*
wickfhire,

wickſhire, and enlarged the Chaſe, Parks, *&c.* thereto belonging, ſo that the Charges thereof (as Sir *William Dugdale* [a] relates) was no leſs than 60,000 *l* he had the Honour of entertaining Queen *Eliſabeth* and her Court there, for the Space of 10 Days in *July* 1575, 17 *Eliſ.* with exceſſive Coſt, and Variety of delightful Entertainments, which are ſet forth in a *Maſk* [t] written in Proſe and Verſe, by *George Gaſcoign*, Eſq; intituled, *The Princelie Pleaſures at* Kenelworth-*Caſtle*.

Upon the Queen's firſt Entrance, appeared a floating Iſland on the large Pool there, bright blaſing with Torches, on which were clad in Silks the Lady of the Lake, and two Nimphs waiting on her, who made a Speech to the Queen in Meeter of the Antiquity and Owners of that Caſtle, which was cloſed with Cornets, and other loud Muſick. Within the Baſe-court was a noble Bridge ſet up, of 20 Feet wide, and 70 Feet long, over which the Queen paſſed ; on each Side whereof, on Poſts erected, were Preſents on them to her, by the Gods, *viz.* A Cage of wild Fowl, by *Silvanus*; divers Sorts of Fruits, by *Pomona*; of Corn, by *Ceres*; of Wine, by *Bacchus*; of Sea-Fiſh, by *Neptune*; of all Habiliments of War, by *Mars*; and of Muſical Inſtruments, by *Phœbus*.

Alſo during the ſeveral Days of her Stay, various rare Shews, and Sports were exerciſed, *viz.* In the *Chaſe*, a Savage Man with Satyrs ; Bear-baitings, Fire-works, *Italian* Tumblers, a Country Bride Ale, with running at the Quinting, and Morrice-dancing. And, that nothing might be wanting which thoſe Parts could afford, the *Coventry* Men came, and acted the antient *Play*, long ſince uſed in that City, called *Hocks Tueſday*, ſetting forth the Deſtruction of the *Danes* in King *Ethelred*'s Time, which pleaſed the Queen ſo much, that ſhe gave them a Brace of Bucks, and 5 Marks in Money, to bear the Charges of a Feaſt.

Likewiſe on the Pool, there was a *Triton* riding on a Mermaid, 18 Feet long ; as alſo *Arion* on a Dolphin, with rare Muſick. The Coſts and Expences of theſe Entertainments may be gueſt at, by the Quantity of Beer then drunk, which amounted to 320 Hogſheads of the ordinary Sort : And for the greateſt Honour thereof, Sir *Thomas Cecil*, Son and Heir to the Lord *Burghley*, Lord Treaſurer ; Sir *Henry Cobham*, Brother to the Lord *Cobham* ; Sir *Thomas Stanhope* (Anceſtor to the preſent Earls of *Cheſterfield*, *Stanhope* and *Harrington*) and Sir *Thomas Treſham*, were then knighted. And the next enſuing Year, [u] this Earl obtained a Grant of the Queen, for a weekly Market at *Kenelworth*, on the *Wedneſday*, with a Fair yearly on *Midſummer-day*.

In 1576, 19 *Eliſ. Walter Devereux*, Earl of *Eſſex*, dying in *Ireland*, [w] this Earl lay under a Suſpicion of poiſoning him, having not, long after his Death, married *Lettice* Counteſs of *Eſſex*, his Widow, who was Daughter of Sir *Francis Knolles*, Knight of the Garter. In Anſwer to this, Sir *Henry Sidney*, Lord Deputy of *Ireland*, [x] wrote to the Council of *England*, ' That he had made a dili-
' gent Enquiry into the Affair, and found, that by the Earl of *Eſſex*'s own
' Relation, it was uſual for him to fall into a bloody Flux, whenever he was
' diſturbed in Mind ; that he was by no Means apprehenſive of Poiſon, and his
' Body retained the ſame Colour in his Sickneſs, as in perfect Health ; no Spot,
' no Infection appeared, no Falling off of the Hair or Nails, and when his
' Corps was opened, there were no viſible Signs of Poiſon ſeen on him ; and
' though his Phyſicians differed in their Judgments, yet none of them adviſed
' any Manner of Application againſt the Force of Poiſon, and his Cup-bearer
' was falſly accuſed of having intermingled it with his Wine.'

In 1578, the Duke of *Anjou* preſſing for the Match that had been propoſed between him, and Queen *Eliſabeth*, and ſending over Monſ. *Simier*, a very gallant Gentlemen, attended by a large Train of *French* Nobility ; the Earl of *Leiceſter* was doubtful, whether the Marriage might not take Effect. The Earl, as it is ſaid by our Hiſtorians, had ſometime before, ſounded the Queen's Diſpoſition,

[a] Warwickſh. 2d Edit. p. 249. [t] Wood's Athenæ Oxon. Vol. p. 150. [u] Pat. 18 Eliſ. p. 6.
[w] Camd. Annals, p. 277, 278. [x] Ibid.

in choosing him for a Husband, and not receiving a favourable Answer, he abandoned all Thoughts thereof, and privately married the Countess of *Essex,* as before related. This Marriage *Simiers* discovered to the Queen, apprehending his Lordship to be the greatest Bar to the Duke's Pretensions ; and *Camden* relates, that she was so inraged thereat, that she commanded him not to stir from the Castle of *Greenwich,* designing to have committed him to the *Tower,* but was dissuaded from it, by the Earl of *Sussex.* On this (as the same Author recites) he resented it so far as it was thought he had some Intention to cause him to be murthered. And one Day, *Simiers* waiting on her Majesty in her Barge, not far from *Greenwich,* a Gun was discharged from a neighbouring Boat, and one of the Queen's Bargemen wounded through both his Arms ; this was suggested to dispatch *Simier,* but on Enquiry, it appeared to have been wholly accidental, and the Man, who had been immediately apprehended, was set at Liberty.

The Duke of *Anjou* sending an Ambassy of the greatest Nobles in *France,* into *England,* in 1581, they were received by the Queen, with all Instances of Honour ; [y] and the Earl of *Leicester* was one of the Noblemen appointed to confer with them, and that engaged for their Diversion, in [z] Justings, Barriers, and Turney ; but the People, in general, shewing great Discontent at the proposed Marriage, [a] it induced the Queen to issue her Proclamation, under a severe Penalty, that none of her Subjects should either strike or draw Weapon, within 4 Miles of *London* or the Court. And the Duke thinking his Presence might prevail more than the Oratory of his Ambassadors, who signified to him the Queen's Declination of Marriage, he came in Person to prefer his Suit ; but having tarried in *England,* the Space of three Months, and finding his Application to be ineffectual, he set out on the 6th of *February* for *Sandwich* ; the Earl of *Leicester* [b], with a Train of 100 Gentlemen, and 300 others, of inferior Sort, accompanying him to *Antwerp,* as did also the Lord *Hunsdon,* and the Lord *Charles Howard,* who had each of them 150 Followers. The Confederates of the *Low-Countries,* believing it might please the Queen, had sent over their Agents, to the Duke in *England,* to desire he would be their Protector against the *Spaniards* ; and the Queen promising him Aid, he accepted of their Proffer, [c] and on his Arrival at *Antwerp,* he with the Earl of *Leicester,* &c. who accompanied him, were entertained with great State and Solemnity, where having seen him invested in the Government of the said Provinces, *viz.* on 19 *Feb.* the *English* Nobility, with their Trains, returned to *England.*

In 1584, he prevailed on the Chief of the Nobility and Gentry of *England,* to subscribe an Association [d] by which they bound themselves to pursue unto Death, whosoever should attempt any Thing against Queen *Elisabeth.* And this by some Authors [e] is said to be in Hatred to the Queen of *Scots,* and that, a Plot being formed to set her at Liberty, he was for Making her privately away. His Aversion against the Queen of *Scots* [f] is supposed to have rose from a private View of conveying the Crown into the Family of the *Dudleys* (as *Heylin* asserts) by advancing the Earl of *Huntington* to the Throne, who had a Claim to the Crown, as being descended in a direct Line from *George* Duke of *Clarence,* and had married the Sister of the Earl of *Leicester.*

On 22 *Oct.* 27 *Elif.* being then Master of the Horse to the Queen, he was constituted Captain-General [g] of all such Forces, as do presently serve, or hereafter shall serve in the *Low-Countries,* for the Relief of the Inhabitants there. And was impowered to levy in *England,* or the Dominion of *Wales,* 500 able and sufficient Men of his Tenants and Servants to attend his Person beyond the Seas, and in his Passage thither, and returning from thence, them and every of them to imploy in his Service as he shall think convenient. Which Retainers and Followers, under his Hand and Seal, signifying the same, were during

<hr>

[y] Camden's Annals, p. 339.   [z] Stow's Annals, p. 689.   [a] Ibid.   [b] Ibid. 690.   [c] Ibid.
[d] Camden's Annals, p. 300.   [e] Johnston Rer. Britan. p 98. The Life of Mary Queen of Scots, p. 281, 288.   [f] Heylin's History of the Presbyterians, p. 272.   [g] Pat. 27 Elif. p. 2. & Rymer's Fœdera, Tom. 15. p. 799.

the Time fo imployed in his Service, to have the Queen's Protection for their Bodies, Lands, and Goods, any Law, Statute, or Reftraint to the contrary thereof in any wife notwithftanding. With a Mandate to all Juftices of Peace, Mayors, Sheriffs, &c. and all other Officers to be obedient thereto.

Before his Departure, the Queen admonifhed him to have a fpecial Regard to her Honour [h], and to attempt nothing which fhould be inconfiftent with the Imployment to which he was advanced ; and particularly fhe required him to fearch into their Method of Raifing and Falling the Value of Money, that fo the Soldiers might not receive their Pay at one Rate, and give it out at another ; and very affectionately recommended to his Care the young Noblemen of the Country, and more efpecially the Sons of the late Prince of *Orange*.

On 8 *December*, 1585, he imbarqued [i] with 50 Sail of Ships, and thofe that went with him, or made Hafte after him, were the Earls of *Oxford*, *Northumberland*, and *Effex*, the Lord *Audley*, the Lord *Willoughby*, the Lord *Sheffield*, the Lord *North*, the Lord *Borroughs*, Sir *William Ruffel*, Sir *Philip Sidney*, Sir *Robert Sidney*, Sir *Henry Stanley*, Sir *Gervafe Clifton*, Sir *Thomas Shirley*, Sir *William Pelham*, Lord Marfhal of the Field, Sir *Arthur Baffet*, Sir *Walter Walter*, with many [k] other Perfons of Diftinction. On the 10th he arrived at *Flufhing*, and with his whole Train (his Perfon being guarded by 50 Archers, bearing Bows and Arrows, 50 Halberds, and 50 Mufqueteers) were magnificently entertained by Sir *Philip Sidney*, Governor of the Town for her Majefty, by *Grave Maurice*, fecond Son to the late Prince of *Orange*, by the Queen's Ambaffador, and the States ; and all Sorts of People expreffed the greateft Joy on his Arrival. He was lodged in the Ambaffador's Houfe, and behaved with fo much Courtefy and Affability, that he gained the Affections of all who approached him.

How he further proceeded, is related by *Hollinfhed* and *Stow* ; I fhall only obferve, that he was feafted and received with the greateft Honours, and all the Inhabitants were fo overjoyed at the Arrival of the *Englifh* Succours, that they entertained the whole Army at their own private Expence, and every Citizen ftrove to go beyond his Neighbour, in all the Offices of Friendlinefs and Civility that could be fhewn to their welcome Guefts. Which Kindnefs the Earl requited, and banqueted the States, and others, all the *Chriftmas* Holidays.

On the 25 *January*, the Earl was fworn unto the States [l], and the States fworn unto the Queen, and to obey the Earl, her Lieutenant ; and, on the 6th of *February*, they publifhed a Placard, granting to him the chief Government, and abfolute Authority, over the *United Provinces*. And gave to him, befides the Authority her Majefty had given to him, ' the higheft and fupreme Command-' ment, and abfolute Authority above, and in all Matters of Warfare, both by ' Sea and Land, to execute and adminiftrate the fame, to the Refiftance of the ' Enemy, even as his Excellency fhould think moft commodious to the Prefer-' vation of thofe Countries ; and fo further, to do all fuch Things as appertain ' to the Office of a general Captain. And furthermore, we commit the Ad-' miniftration and Ufe of Policy and Juftice, over the aforefaid *United Provinces*, ' and affociated Cities and Members of the fame, into his Hands, to execute ' and adminiftrate the fame, with fuch Power and Authority, as have had, in ' Times paft, all the other Governors of thefe *Low-Countries* before him, and ' efpecially, as have been exercifed and lawfully adminiftered in the Time of ' *Charles the Fifth*, &c. We, therefore, command all Governors of Provinces ' and Cities, all Admirals, Vice-Admirals, all Officers and Soldiers, by Sea and ' Land ; and furthermore, all other Counfellors, Officers, Treafurers, Recei-' vers, Bailiffs, Burgomafters, Magiftrates, &c. of what Quality or Conditi-' on foever, to honour, refpect, and obey him, as they ought to do, &c.'

The Lord Lieutenant immediately applied himfelf to his Charge [m], and nominated Superintendants to act under him in the feveral Provinces, all of them

---

[h] Camden's Hiftory of Queen Elif. p. 326.   [i] Stow's Annals, p. 711.   [k] Hollinfhed, p. 1424, and Stow præd.   [j] Stow, p. 112.   [m] Hollinfhed, p. 1432.

Natives

Natives of the Country, and Members of the great Council ; and vifited moft of the Towns in Perfon, where he was received with the higheft Honours, and all imaginable Joy ; the *Englifh* Forces infpiring the Inhabitants with frefh Courage; which added to the Care and Sollicitude of the Prince of *Parma*, who was watchful of all Attempts made by the *Englifh*. However, General *Norris* defeated the *Spaniards* in feveral Conflicts, and the Bravery of the *Englifh* got them great Renown throughout the Provinces. General *Norris*, in his Letter from *Rawfton*, near *Grave*, on the 6th of *April*, to the Lord Lieutenant, ' That in-
' trenching himfelf within one Hour's March to *Grave*, having with him not
' above 300 Men, the Enemy attacked him with 3000, whereby his Forces
' were obliged to retreat ; but, on Hearing of their March towards him, he had
' fent for 800 *Englifh*, and meeting them about Half a Mile from their Retreat,
' he turned, and forced them to quit the Place, notwithftanding their Inequali-
' ty, and had the Killing them above an *Englifh* Mile, lofing (as he writes) a
' great Company of brave Men, and moft of their Leaders.' He concludes, that he will do the utmoft in his Power, to the Hazarding of his Life, to do his Excellency Honour and Service.

On 23 *April*, the Earl of *Leicefter*, being at *Utrecht*, kept [n] the Feaft of St. *George* in the moft honourable and magnificent Manner. The Streets of the City were ranked and fet with eight Enfigns of Burghers, richly apparelled, wearing Scarves knit like Rofes, white and red, upon their Arms, between whom, from his Lordfhip's Court, the Proceeding was on Horfeback to the Cathedral Church called the *Dome*. Firft rode the Trumpeters, in Scarlet laid with Silver-lace, founding, their Bannerols with his Lordfhip's Arms thereon difplayed. Then followed the Colonels and principal Perfons, and her Majefty's fworn Men, to the Number of forty Horfe, richly adorned with Cloth of Gold, Silver, and Silks of all Colours. After came fix Knights, four Barons, with the Council of Eftates, the Earl of *Effex*, accompanied by the Bifhop of *Cologne* Prince Elector ; and the Prince of *Portugal* rid by himfelf. Next proceeded the Captain of his Lordfhip's Guard, the Treafurer, and Comptroller of his Houfe-hold, bearing their white Staves. After whom followed two Gentlemen Ufh-ers, and Portcullis Herald in a rich Coat, embroidered with the Arms of *England*.

Then came his Lordfhip (as *Hollinfhed* faith) moft Prince-like, invefted in his Robes of the Order, guarded by the principal Burghers in the Town, who of-fered themfelves to that Service, and his own Guard, which confifted of fifty Halberds, in fcarlet Cloaks, edged with Purple and white Velvet. Being thus conducted to the Church, and paying his Reverence to her Majefty's Seat, e-rected on this Occafion, on the Right-hand, he took his Stall on the Left, which was fituate fome Degrees lower. After Prayers, and a Sermon preached by his Lordfhip's Chaplain, he proceeded to the Offering, firft for her Majefty, then for himfelf, which he performed (to ufe the Words of my Author) *with fuch Decorum and princelie Behaviour, that all generallie fpake moft honourablie of him.*

Thefe Solemnities being over, his Lordfhip returned as he came, and the Company were moft magnificently entertained at Dinner in his Excellency's Pa-lace, which was very large, and, before his Time, belonged to the Knights of *Rhodes*. The Sumptuoufnefs of the Feaft, and the Devices ufed on that Occafi-on, *&c.* may be feen in *Hollinfhed* and *Stow*.

The Honours paid to him, and the large Powers he had from the *States*, in-duced many about the Queen to think, he aimed at the Sovereignty of the Pro-vinces ; which caufed her Majefty to difpatch her Vicechamberlain to him, with an expoftulating Letter, in thefe angry Terms [o]:

' How contemptuoufly you have carried yourfelf towards us, you fhall un-
' derftand by this Meffenger, whom we fend to you for that Purpofe. We lit-

[n] Hollinfhed, p. 1433.   [o] Camden's Hift. of Queen Elif. p. 327, and Strad. de Bello Belgic. Lib. 7. p. 477.

' tle

'tle thought that one, whom we had raifed out of the Duft, and profecuted
'with fuch fingular Favour above all others, would, with fo great Contempt,
'have flighted and broken our Commands, in a Matter of fo great Confe-
'quence, and fo highly concerning us and our Honour. Whereof, though you
'have but fmall Regard, contrary to what you ought by your Allegiance, yet
'think not that we are fo carelefs of repairing it, that we can bury fo great an
'Injury in Silence and Oblivion. We therefore command you, that, all Ex-
'cufe fet apart, you do forthwith, upon your Allegiance which you owe unto
'us, whatfoever *Heneage* our Vicechamberlain fhall make known to you in
'our Name, upon Pain of further Peril.'

She alfo wrote to the States-General, 'That, to her Difgrace, and without
'her Knowledge, they had conferred the abfolute Government of the Confede-
'rate Provinces upon *Leicefter* her Subject, though fhe had abfolutely refufed
'it herfelf, &c.' She therefore advifed them 'to turn *Leicefter* out of that
'abfolute Authority, whofe Commiffion fhe had limited ; not that fhe thought
'their Caufe unworthy to be favoured, but to provide for, and fecure her own
'Honour, which fhe efteemed more dear to her than Life itfelf.'

To thefe Letters the States returned a fubmiffive Anfwer, excufed what they
had done, by the Neceffity of granting fuch an Authority to avoid Troubles
and Diffenfions, gave a fofter Senfe to the Word *Abfolute*, than was generally
meant by it, and laid before her the Inconvenience of recalling a Power they had
already given. And the Earl of *Leicefter*, at the fame Time, lamenting his hard
Fate, in having difobliged her, and, expreffing his Sorrow for it, fo wrought
on her Difpofition, that fhe overlooked the Offence, and acquiefced in the Declaration of the States. *Bentivoglio* intimates [p], as though this Step muft have
been before fecretly made known to the Queen, or the Earl of *Leicefter* would
not have accepted the Government without her private Confent. And *Strada* [q] more openly charges her Majefty with an ambitious View of feeking to add
the *Low-Countries* to her Dominions, by permitting *Leicefter* to take upon him
the Sovereignty. But this is improbable. The Provinces had been twice offered
her, by a folemn Ambaffy from the States ; her Parliament had follicited the
Acceptance, and promifed her Supplies to fupport it ; and the univerfal Inclination to fubmit to her, in Conjunction with the Forces fhe had ready to fend
over, muft have rendered all Oppofition impracticable.

It has been obferved, that *Strada* was an *Italian* Jefuit in the Pay of *Spain*,
and, confequently, the *Englifh* could expect no fair Reprefentation from him,
who hated them as Hereticks, and as Enemies. Yet he fays, the Earl of *Leicefter was fuch an abfolute Mafter of his own Temper, that he could, as he pleafed,
adapt it to any Man's Humours or Defigns.* Agreeable to this, *Mezeray* calls him
a fubtle, dextrous Courtier ; and what other Hiftorians cite, argues him to be a
Man of great Abilities, though the general Hatred and Envy of many People
fuppreffed his real Virtues, or imputed them to Artifice or Defign, which might,
however, fpring from a generous Difpofition.

The laft Mention of the Earl's Actions, this Year, was his being at *Utrecht*, and
from thence he marched to *Arnheim*, with a confiderable Force, to relieve the Befieged in *Grave* ; but after he had made himfelf Mafter of the Forts, and was
contriving in what Manner he might beft fuccour the Befieged, the Governor
fent to the Prince of *Parma*, to treat of a Surrender, who was not unwilling to
grant him any Conditions, that, this Enterprife being difpatched, he might repair to *Venlo*. Thereupon, the Garrifon marched out with their Arms and Baggage, and Colours flying. It is faid, that Van *Hemart* [r] was induced to capitulate by the Perfuafions of an Harlot, and that the Earl of *Leicefter* prefently ordered him to be apprehended, and, for an Example of Terror, caufed him,
and two other Officers concerned with him, to be put to an ignominious
Death.

[p] Hift. of the Wars of Flanders, Part 2, Lib. 4, p. 240.   [q] De Bello Belgic. Lib. 7. P. 477.
[r] Grot. de Reb. Belgic. Lib. 4. De Bello Belgic. Lib. 7, p. 488.

I

After this, the Earl of *Leicester* [s] took the ftrong Fort of *Nimeguen* on the 20 *May*, and having [t] drove the *Spaniards* out of the *Betawe*, an Ifland formed by the Rivers of *Rhine* and *Wael*, he next took the Sconce of *Barrikes-hoofe*, a Place of great Importance, which was furrendered at Difcretion. The *Englifh* were no lefs fuccefsful at *Bergenopzume*, where the Lord *Willoughby* of *Erefby* fet upon a Convoy going to *Antwerp*, feized 480 Waggons laden with Provifions, carried of 1000 Horfes, flew 200 Men, and took 400 Prifoners.

The Lord Lieutenant thinking it convenient to take a Progrefs [u] through the Country, to difpofe of every Thing to the beft Advantage ; whilft he was engaged therein, his Nephew, Sir *Philip Sidney*, and *Grave Maurice*, the Prince of *Orange*'s Son, entered *Flanders*, and took *Axel* by Surprize ; and, encouraged by that Succefs, made an Attempt upon *Gravelin*, which, upon private Notice, was to be delivered up, but the Defign mifca ried.

In the mean Time, the Lord Lieutenant [w], remaining at *Utrecht*, had Information of 500 of the Enemy being entered the City, in the Habits of Country men, with Defign to betray it ; but, a ftrict Enquiry being made after them, there were three only to be found, who were committed to Prifon.

The Duke of *Parma* laying Siege to *Reinberch*, a Town garrifoned by 1200 *Englifh*, under Colonel *Morgan*, the Earl of *Leicester* [x] ufed all Means to relieve it ; but finding his Army inferior to the Enemy, ill furnifhed with Provifions, and no Place of Retreat near at Hand, he ftrove to divert them from their Attempt, by laying Siege to one of their own Towns. He was then on the other Side of the *Rhine*, in the Province of *Overyffel*, not far from *Zutphen*, the moft confiderable Place in that Country, garrifoned by the *Spaniards*. To render the Conqueft more eafy, he determined [y] firft to take *Doefburgh* on the River *Yffel*, which would prove ferviceable in carrying on his great Defign ; and, as foon as the *Englifh* had raifed their Batteries, the Defendants demanded a Parley, and furrendered the Town to his Lordfhip, 2 *Sept.*

On 13 *Sept.* his Excellency [z] with his Army came before *Zutphen*, on the River *Yffel*, which drew the Duke of *Parma* from the Siege of *Reinberch*, and brought on an Engagement, 22 *Sept.* between great Detachments of both Armies. The *Englifh* charged them fo courageoufly, that they threw them into Diforder, and forced them to retreat ; but the Enemy returning, the Victory for a long Time, ftood doubtful. The Earl of *Effex*, General of the Horfe, the Lord *Willoughby*, the Lord *Audley*, the Lord *North*, Sir *William Ruffel*, Sir *Philip Sidney*, Sir *William Stanley*, and Sir *John Norris* greatly diftinguifhed themfelves on this Occafion. The Enemy loft a confiderable Number of their braveft Officers, and *George Creffia*, General of the *Albanois*, was taken Prifoner, after being unhorfed by the Lord *Willoughby*. But, the Duke of *Parma* coming in Order of Battle, with the reft of his Army, the Earl of *Leicester* judged the Attempt too hazardous, to venture a general Engagement, and ordered a Retreat to be founded, whereby the Enemy fent Forces and Provifions into *Zutphen*: The greateft Misfortune fuftained, in this Action, was the Lofs of Sir *Philip Sidney*, whofe exemplary Virtues gained him the univerfal Efteem of all *Europe*, and no Perfon, of any Age or Country, was more generally lamented.

The Earl of *Leicester*, however, continued the Siege, and, on the 4th of *October*, the great Fort demanded a Parley [a] ; which being granted, Count *Hollock* ftepped out to talk with them ; but, in the Midft of the Conference, as the Count was fpeaking, he was fhot through the Mouth, and took off the Jewel that hung at his Ear. To revenge this Treachery, the *Englifh* repeated their Attacks, and the fame Day made an Affault on the leffer Fort, Sword in Hand. Captain *Edward Stanley* was the 1ft, who mounted the Breach, and perhaps truer Courage was never fhewn [b]. He was oppofed by the Captain

[s] Stow's Annals, p. 718.   [t] Camden's Elif. p. 328.   [u] Grot. de Reb. Belgic. Lib. 4. & Stow's Annals.   [w] Stow. p. 733.   [x] Camden's Hift. of Q. Elif. p. 329.   [y] Stow, p. 736. [z] Ib. & p. 737.   [a] Ib. p. 738.   [b] Camd. Elif. p. 333, Stow, p. 738, 739, Strad. de Bello Belgic. p. 553.

of the Fort, who, standing alone in the Breach, aimed his Pike at his Breast, as he was entering. On which, with great Presence of Mind, laying Hold of the Pike, he strove with all his Force, to pluck him from his Post, if he refused to let go his Hold. But, finding his Strength insufficient to effect his Purpose, he suffered himself to be raised up, by his Competitor, on the Rampart; and his Soldiers following, so terrified the Garrison, with his unexpected Presence, that, deserting the Defence, as many as were able made their Escape by a back Door, and fled to *Zutphen*, leaving their Captain Prisoner. The Earl of *Leicester* knighted *Stanley* for his Courage, presented him with forty Pounds Sterling, and settled a yearly Pension on him for Life. He likewise knighted Captain *Reade*, who also shewed great Bravery on that Occasion. And the Enemy, much terrified, abandoned the great Fort the next Night. But the Earl judged it not convenient for his Army to continue any longer before *Zutphen*, till the Rigour of the Season should be abated, it being sufficiently blocked up by the Garrisons, which lay in the Towns round about it. Many Persons of Distinction of the *English* Nation having highly distinguished themselves, the Earl of *Leicester*, in Reward of their Merit, and his own Honour, conferred in his Camp the Dignity of Knight-Banneret [c], on the Earl of *Essex*, the Lord *Willoughby*, the Lord *Audley*, and the Lord *North*; and knighted Sir *Henry Goodyere*, Captain of the Guard, Sir *Henry Norris*, Sir *John Borroughs*, Sir *John Winckfield*, Sir *Roger Williams*, Sir *Robert Sidney*, Sir *Philip Butler*, Sir *Henry North*, Sir *Thomas Dennis*, Sir *William Knolles*, Sir *George Farmer*, Sir *George Digby*, Sir —— *Steward*, Sir —— *Beauford*.

On 15 *Oct.* [d] his Excellency, after Securing of *Deventry*, came to *Arnheim*, to visit his Nephew Sir *Philip Sidney*, whom he found past all Hopes of Recovery, and he died two Days after, to his infinite Regret, and was bewailed by him, with great Sorrow, shutting himself up, for a whole Day, as *Stow* relates.

On 29 *Oct.* his Excellency [e] arrived at the *Hague*, where the States-General were then assembled, who received him with Coldness, breaking out into Expostulation and Complaint, as their own Writers [f] affirm; and that, having entered on a Justification of his Proceedings, he strove to remove their supposed Misconstructions and Mistakes, and at last endeavoured to dissolve the Assembly; but not being able to bring about his Purpose, he declared his Resolution of returning into *England*, and left the Council in an angry Manner. However, as *Grotius* writes, he was afterwards brought to Temper, and told the *States*, that, by his Journey into *England*, he should be the more enabled to assist them in their Affairs, and provide a Remedy to all their Grievances.

That he sought to make Alterations in the State, and was engaged in a Design to remove the Commonalty from a Share in the Administration, is asserted by *Grotius*, who imputed it to the Haughtiness of his Temper, which could not bear to be controuled by Persons, who had been drawn from behind Shops and Counters, to make up a Part in the great Council. To effect his Purpose the more securely [g], he ingratiated himself with the Clergy, whom he easily gained over to his Interest, by a dissembled Zeal (as *Brandt* saith) for Religion, and a great Shew of pretended Piety. He frequented the Church, on all publick Days, fasted and prayed often, received the *Holy Eucharist*, and warmly expressed his Inclination to propagate the Reformation, and extirpate Popery. Whereby the Ministers were almost unanimously attached to him, and, by their Influence, he formed a considerable Party among the People.

When the Day came for his Departure, by a publick Act, he gave up the Care of the Provinces into the Hands of the Council of State [h]; but privately the same Day, by an Act of Restriction, he reserved an Authority to himself, over all Governors of Provinces, Forts, and Cities; and farther took away

[c] Stow's Annals. p. 739.   [d] Ib. & p. 740.   [e] Ib. p. 741.   [f] Bentivoglio's Hist. of the Wars of Flanders, p. 224, & Grotius de Reb. Belgic. Lib. 5.   [g] Brandt's Hist. of the Reformation in the Low-Countries, Lib. 14.   [h] Camden's Elif. p. 330.

from

from the Council of State, and the Prefidents of Provinces, their accuftomed Jurifdiction. His Lordfhip, on the 18th of *December*, took Shipping to pafs from *Dort* to *Flufhing* ; but the Ice obliged him to land, and he paffed in a Waggon for *Rotterdam*, and there imbarqued again, and on 23 *Nov.* arrived in *London*.

Whatever might be the Pretence for my Lord of *Leicefter*'s Leaving the *Low-Countries*, his Prefence in *England* [k] was very acceptable to Queen *Elifabeth*. The late Confpiracies, which had been formed, in Favour of the Queen of *Scots*, had made a deep Impreffion on her Majefty, and fhe appears to have been now refolved to difpatch her Competitor. The Difficulty lay in what Manner it fhould be done ; and fhe knew fhe could fecurely rely on Lord *Leicefter*'s Fidelity, whofe Attachment to her Perfon, and Averfion to the Queen of *Scots*, fhe had been fully convinced of, by a long Courfe of Experience. When the Matter was brought before the Council [l], his Lordfhip is faid to have delivered his Opinion, to take her off by Poifon ; but this being oppofed by Secretary *Walfingham*, who refufed to give Ear to the private Infinuations of a Court Divine, whom he had fent to draw him into a Confent, it was at laft determined to proceed againft her by an Act in 27 *Elif.* for that Purpofe, and the whole Privy-Council were conftituted her Judges.

After Sentence of Condemnation had been pronounced againft her, Queen *Elifabeth* was no lefs perplexed, in what Manner fhe fhould proceed to her Execution. She was very defirous to remove the Blame from herfelf ; and the Earl of *Leicefter*, obferving it to be her Majefty's Inclination, again advifed her to make her fecretly away. And the Queen [m] feems fo far to have come into his Sentiments, that fhe ordered her Secretaries, *Walfingham*, and *Davifon*, to write to *Fotheringay*, where the Queen was imprifoned, to have her taken off by Violence. But the Keepers declined the Office, and, a few Days after, fhe fuffered by the Hands of an Executioner.

About this Time, he [n] was conftituted Lord Chief Juftice in Eyre of all the Forefts South of *Trent* ; and, as appears from feveral Letters in the *Cabala*, was highly favoured by Queen *Elifabeth*. During his Abfence from the *Low-Countries* [o], the *Spaniards* had bribed *York*, and *Stanley*, two *Englifhmen*, whom the Earl had appointed, the firft, Governor of a Fort near *Zutphen*, and the other, of *Deventer*, to deliver thofe Places into their Hands, which, by the Treachery of *York*, fo wrought on *Stanley*, as he complied ; and the Lofs thereof gave Occafion to loud Exclamation and Complaints againft the Earl of *Leicefter* [p]. Whereupon the States-General, immediately affembling, agreed to inveft Prince *Maurice* with the full Power and Authority of Stadtholder, and Captain-General of *Holland*, *Zealand*, and *Friefland*, and to give him Command over all the Militia within the faid Provinces. And, purfuant to this Determination, they obliged all their Officers to receive a new Commiffion from him, and to take a new Oath to the States, and difcharged all Recufants whatfoever from the Service.

Queen *Elifabeth* was difpleafed with thefe Alterations in their Government, and refented the Diminution of the Earl of *Leicefter*'s Authority, as an Injury offered to herfelf ; and, thereupon, immediately fent the Lord *Buckhurft*, her Kinfman, to enquire into, and complain of the Innovations introduced in the Abfence of the Earl, and to fettle all Differences between them : And the States, in Return [q], affured her Majefty, that their late Proceedings were but provifional, and enforced through Fear of a general Revolt on the Lofs of *Deventer* ; but that, at his Lordfhip's Return, they would readily acknowledge both him and his Authority, in as ample a Manner, as if it had been granted to him at the firft. Alfo, in their Letter to the Queen, *March* the 1ft [r], they repre-

[i] Stow, p. 741.   [k] Vide Lord Buckhurft's Letter to the Earl of Leicefter in the Cabala, &c. Part 2, p. 7.   [l] Camden's Elif. p. 346.   [m] Davifon's Apology in the Appendix to the Life of Mary Queen of Scots, &c.   [n] 1 Pat. 28 Elif. p. 1.   [o] Camden's Elif. p 397.   [p] Brandt's Hift. p. 400, & feq. Bentivoglio's Wars of Fland. Lib. 4. p. 245.   [q] Lord Buckhurft's Letter to Sec. Walfingham, in Cabala, part 2. p. 14.   [r] Cabala, part 2. p. 5.

fent to her, they are infinitely forry her Majefty fhould put on any finifter Conceit of their Actions and Proceedings, which they attribute to the Practice of their Enemies, &c. And, in a Letter from the Lord *Buckhurft*, to Secretary *Walfingham* [s], it appears, ‘ They deny, they ever did any Act, or had Mean-‘ ing to touch the Honour, either of the Earl of *Leicefter*, or the *Englifh* ‘ Nation, or to prejudice the Authority of his Lordfhip, whofe fpeedy Re-‘ turn they fo earneftly defired.’

But, notwithftanding thefe outward Profeffions of Regard, they were jealous of him [t], and privately proceeded to ftraiten his Authority. And, in other Letters to the Queen, would have inferted a Claufe, to limit his Command on his Return to them, had not the Lord *Buckhurft* interpofed, and laid before them the Mifchief it would have produced from his Lordfhip's Power with her Majefty.

Thefe Proceedings were not agreeable to the Majority of the People, who were firm in the Intereft of the Earl of *Leicefter*, and threatened to be revenged of the States, if the Queen fhould take any Offence at their Alterations [u]. In *Friefland*, the Clergy offered her Majefty the Sovereignty of the *Low-Countries*, without any Reftriction, having held two Synods on the Occafion : The Synod at *Sneek* prefented a Petition to the Lord *Buckhurft*, in which they invited her Majefty to come to the Affiftance of Chrift, who threw himfelf and his Children into her Arms, and implored her Protection ; and [w] feveral other Towns protefted they would depend only on her Majefty ; alfo, the Preachers at *Amfterdam* openly inveighed againft the Magiftrates from their Pulpits, and Libels were fet up againft the States. But, as the People feemed determined to take up Arms, the Lord *Buckhurft* fignified to them, from her Majefty, that it was her Inclination to fend back the Earl of *Leicefter* to compofe their Differences, by reaffuming the Government. And this Expectation of his Lordfhip's Prefence gave a Check to their Violence, and put a further Stop to the Proceedings of the States, who had begun to introduce a new Scheme of Government [x]. Prince *Maurice* was brought to profefs all good Will and Amity to his Lordfhip, and Count *Hollock* promifed to receive him with all Honour and Friendfhip ; alfo the States-General and Council of State, both publickly and privately, affured the Lord *Buckhurft*, of all Duty and Fidelity to him.

But, before the Queen was prevailed on to give Confent to his Lordfhip's Return, fhe required [y] the Lord *Buckhurft*, by her Letter to him, to let the States know, fhe expected they fhould fend an Army into the Field, on his Arrival, of 10 or 12 thoufand Foot, and 4000 Horfe ; and, not only promife, but give Affurance, that 100000 *l.* arifing from the extraordinary Contributions, fhould be delivered in fuch feafonable Times, as might ferve to defray the Charges of the faid Army, in the Hands of fome Perfon of the Country who fhould be nominated by the Earl of *Leicefter*, to fupply the Place of Treafurer of the Army, and to be iffued out by his Lordfhip's Direction, with the Privity of the Council of State. But, this Demand not being agreeable, the Lord *Buckhurft* acquainted the Queen [z] with their Sentiments, and that, on their Non-compliance, he had fully declared to them, he had no Commiffion from her Majefty to promife his Lordfhip's Return to them.

On this, they refolved to provide for their own Security [a], and, to that End, eftablifhed new Super-intendants on their Frontiers, &c. which was oppofed by the Lord *Buckhurft*, as contrary to the 24th Article of their Contract, by which the Nomination of them was to appertain to her Majefty's Lieutenant ; yet his Oppofition met with no Effect : However, as their Perils increafed fo continually on them, there feemed no other Remedy to prevent their intire Ruin and Subverfion, but a prefent Government, attended with a Supply of

[s] Cabala, part 2. p. 14.   [t] Willis's Letters to the Earl of Leicefter and Sec. Walfingham, in Cabala, Part 2. p. 9, 32, & feq.   [u] Brandt's Hift. Lib. 14.   [w] Cabala, p. 9.   [x] Lord Buckhurft's Letter to Sec. Walfingham, in Cabala, Part 2. p. 28.   [y] Cabala, Part 2. p. 28.   [z] Ibid.   [a] Cabala, Part 2. p. 32, 33.

Men

Men and Money [b]. The Lord *Buckhurſt*, out of a Senſe of the Difficulties the States laboured under, and the Uncertainty of his Lordſhip's Return, drew up a new Scheme for the Government of the United Provinces, which very highly offended the Earl of *Leiceſter*, and ſeems to be the principal Motive of the Averſion and Hatred, he ever after expreſſed towards him.

By repeated Letters from *Oſtend*, Lord *Buckhurſt* had Information that the Enemy intended to beſiege it, or *Sluyſe*, or *Bruges*; and, if the Want of Victuals had not reſtrained them from entering on any important Deſign, the Country, in all Probability, muſt have fallen a Prey to the victorious Arms of the Duke of *Parma*. Thereupon the Lord *Buckhurſt* laid open the Miſeries to which the Provinces were reduced; and, in his Letter to the Lords of the Council, he thus expreſſed himſelf [c]:

' I Have ſo often and ſo earneſtly written for Money to relieve the poor Sol-
' diers here, and ſo plainly ſignified the great Poverty and Penury that they
' endure, with the fearful Danger that ſeemeth to approach us all, by Means of
' this woful Want of Pay, as if the ſame doth not really move; neither can I
' think that Writing will move: Yea, ſo long have I upheld theſe Provinces
' with the painted Pillars of Hope and Expectation (whom I found in a Manner
' deſperate, and, as it were, believing certainly her Majeſty would abandon
' them) as if neither Mean be eſtabliſhed how to govern their Eſtate, nor Men
' tranſported to defend the Enemy, nor Money ſent wherewith to pay the Sol-
' diers; although the wonderful Work of God by that general Famine, which
' at this preſent overſpreadeth the whole Country of our Adverſaries, doth as
' yet preſerve us from the Force and Fury of our mighty Enemy; yet have
' we certain Intelligence, that the Fruits of their Harveſt coming, which will
' be ripe and ready before the Midſt of *July*, give ſuch abundant Hope unto
' them, to miniſter all Means of Plenty for their Army, as, except it pleaſe
' God Almighty, of his merciful Goodneſs towards us, it is without Compaſs
' of Man's Reaſon to believe how it is poſſible for this Eſtate, in any Sort, to
' ſuſtain the Force and Fury of ſo reſolute and ſo potent an Enemy; for,
' when the Hopes in her Majeſty to relieve the Wants here doth once begin
' to ſink, which (be your Lordſhips moſt aſſured) hath been the only Prop
' and Foundation, whereon this State hath ſtood ſo long: If that Hope, I ſay,
' ſhall once fail or fall, ſurely, if God ſtretch not forth his Hand from Heaven
' to defend them, it is no Ways poſſible for their own Power, and theſe con-
' tracted Forces of her Majeſty, any long Time to preſerve them.'

But, before the Lord *Buckhurſt*'s Letter was received [d], the Queen's Treaſurer arrived with Money, to the great Satisfaction of his Lordſhip, and the Comfort of the diſtreſſed Soldiers. The Earl of *Leiceſter*'s Preſence was only wanting, as the States were afraid to act any Thing of themſelves, leſt it ſhould be interpreted to the Prejudice of his Lordſhip's Authority. The Queen, at laſt, became ſenſible of the Inconveniences attending any further Delay, and, after ſome fruitleſs Endeavours towards a Peace, gave Conſent to his Lordſhip's Return. Before his Departure, ſeveral Letters paſſed between him and the Miniſters of *South-Holland*, one of them as following [e]:

Gentlemen,

' T H A T I did not return ſuch an Anſwer to ſeveral of your Letters as
' you deſired and expected, was not for Wanting of good Will towards
' ſerving the Cauſe of God, and defending the poor People; but it was, becauſe
' I had not yet received her Majeſty's Reſolutions about what was farther neceſſa-
' ry to be done for the Service of your Country. But the Queen having given
' me full Directions, with regard to the Forces ſhe will ſend to your Aſſiſtance,
' and having laid her Commands upon me to return; I, therefore, poſtpo-
' ning all private Views and Conſiderations, and abandoning all thoſe Advan-

----

[b] Cabala, Part 2. p. 61, & ſeq.　　[c] Ibid. p. 36.　　[d] Ibid.　　[e] Brandt's Hiſt. Lib. 14. p. 413.

' tages, which God has beſtowed on me in this Kingdom, intend to haſten
' over, and ſatisfy the Deſires of a People, who have ſo often called for me ;
' to which the Zeal and good Inclinations of ſome have more induced me, than
' the Demerits of others, that ſuffer themſelves to be made Tools for keeping
' me back by Slanders and Detractions ; which I ſhall nevertheleſs enter into
' my Book of Oblivion, that no Harm may befall thoſe, who ſeek to do me
' ſuch Diſſervices. And, I hope, I ſhall never give the People any Cauſe to
' diminiſh their good Will and Affection for me. In the mean Time, I entreat
' you to go on in your Duty, and to admoniſh and excite thoſe under your
' Care to Peace and Vnity, to the End that they may more and more deſerve
' all the Benefits they receive. For the reſt, I refer my ſelf to my Arrival, and
' ſo I recommend you, Gentlemen, to the Protection of the Almighty.

Given at *London*,   *Your good Friend*,
    Jan. 7, O. S.
                                                    R. *Leiceſter*.

The Duke of *Parma* began the Campaign with the Siege of *Sluys*, the moſt
conſiderable Town in *Flanders*, except *Oſtend*, that remained in Poſſeſſion of the
States. He firſt attacked the Fort of *Blanchenberg*, commodious for the con-
veying Succours to the Beſieged by Land, which made little Reſiſtance, as his
Coming thither was unexpected, and no Proviſion made to oppoſe him. His
next Step was to raiſe a Fort in the Iſland of *Caſante*, to cut off all Relief by
Sea [f] : But, before he could execute his Deſign, Sir *Roger Williams*, with 5
Companies from *Bruges*, entered the Town, and ſupplied it with Proviſions and
Ammunition to hold out a conſiderable Time againſt him.

Whilſt this Town was beſieged, the Earl of *Leiceſter* [g], on the 18 *June*, was
made Lord Steward of the Queen's Houſhold ; and, ſetting Sail from *England*
25 *June*, landed in *Zealand* about the latter End of the Month. He brought [h] with
him a conſiderable Supply both of Horſe and Foot. Prince *Maurice*, and the
Deputies of the States, attended on him at *Fluſhing*, to congratulate his Return,
and left Count *Hollock* to watch the Motions of the Enemy. When they had
conferred on Raiſing the Siege, it was determined to attempt it by Sea. To
which End, they ſhipped 5000 Foot and 600 Horſe, with all neceſſary Proviſions, for the Relief of the Town. And, on the Fleet's Appearing in the Channel, the Earl of *Leiceſter* made Signs to the Beſieged, that he was come to their
Aſſiſtance : But, on Examination, finding the Channel blocked up, and the
Paſſage ſecured, he ſaw it would be in Vain to proceed that Way. For three
Days he continued in Suſpence what Step to take, and then, weighing Anchor,
he bent his Courſe towards *Oſtend*, with a Reſolution to ſuccour the beſieged by
Land. The Earl of *Leiceſter* had no ſooner landed his Forces, but he prepared
to attack the Fort of *Blanchenberg*, and, joining the whole Garriſon of *Oſtend*
to his Army, marched directly againſt it. The Loſs of it was of no leſs Conſequence to the Duke of *Parma*, than the Gaining of it would have been advantageous to the Earl; and, therefore, the Duke leaving the Siege every where well provided, he led the Remainder of his Army to the Defence of the Fort againſt his
Lordſhip. The *Engliſh* were ready to begin their Batteries, when the Duke
of *Parma* came up ; but, on Sight of the Army, they deferred their Hoſtilities,
and, after ſome Conſultation, retired to *Oſtend*, from whence they returned with
the ſame Fleet, where they had before been at Anchor not far from *Sluys*, and
the Duke of *Parma* again preſented himſelf to their View ; whereby they found
themſelves under a Neceſſity to retire again, and never more attempt to raiſe
the Siege.

The Loſs of *Sluys* renewed the Miſunderſtanding [i] between the Earl of *Lei-*
ceſter and the States, whilſt the Blame of the Action was thrown, by each Party,
on the Miſmanagement of the other. The Earl complained of the States

---

[f] Cabala, Part 2. p. 42.   [g] Stow's Ann. p. 743.   [h] Bentivoglio's Wars of Fland. Part
2. Lib. 4. p. 246.   [i] Ibid. p. 248.

Negli-

Negligence, in not making sufficient Preparations, and not restraining the 1st Attempts of the *Spaniards* against the Town. And the States, in Return, virulently inveighed against his Lordship, and imputed the whole Misfortune to his ill Conduct, and the Delay of the *English* Forces. And, this Dissatisfaction increasing, they refused to establish him in that absolute Authority, which had been conferred on him at his first Arrival.

This Diminution of his Power was so highly resented by him, that he openly expressed his Displeasure against the States [k]; and the *Dutch* Writers charge him with having entered into indirect Practices to regain it, by forming Parties in his Progress through the Country, and conversing chiefly with the Ministers and private Persons; so that they, and the common People, were so overswayed with his Appearances of Piety and his Zeal for their Interests, as to approve of all he did, and loudly exclaimed against the Proceedings of the States.

On 9 *November,* 29 *Elif.* the Queen recites [l], that, at the humble Petition of the States-General of the United Provinces in the *Low-Countries,* and being deeply affected with the Misery and Oppression of the said Provinces, she had sent *Robert* Earl of *Leicester,* as Captain-General of the Auxiliaries sent there; but, having recalled him, to be present in Council with her, she therefore constitutes *Peregrine Berty,* Lord *Willoughby,* Captain-General of her Forces there, *&c.*

Camden [m] relates, that the Earl of *Leicester,* on his Return, finding an Accusation was preparing against him by the Lord *Buckhurst,* and some other of his Enemies, for his Misconduct in the Management of Affairs in the *Low-Countries,* and that he was summoned to appear before the Council, privately implored the Queen's Protection, and earnestly besought her, ‘ Not to receive ‘ him with Disgrace upon his Return, whom, at his first Departure, she had ‘ sent out with Honour; nor bring down alive to the Grave, whom her former ‘ Goodness had raised from the Dust.’ And, that the Queen was so pacified with his Expressions of Humility and Sorrow, as to pass by the Displeasure she had conceived against him, and admit him into her former Grace and Affection. The Day, when it was expected he should have given in his Answer, he took his Place at the Council-Table; and, when the Secretary had begun to read his Accusation, he rose up and interrupted him, complaining of being injured, and declaring that his publick Commission was limited by private Instructions; and, making his Appeal to the Queen, he evaded the Accusation, and came off in Triumph: And, by his Power with her Majesty, he so far prevailed, that a Censure was past on the Lord *Buckhurst,* who was confined thereupon to his House for several Months. The Points objected to his Lordship, with his Answers, and the Replies of the Earl of *Leicester,* are in the *Cabala,* Part 2, p. 55, *& feq.*

On the Incampment at *Tilbury,* to oppose the intended Invasion of the *Spaniards,* in the memorable Year 1588 [n], the Queen committed the Charge of the Army to the Earl of *Leicester;* and, having viewed them all, she, in a set Speech, expressed her Satisfaction in their Fidelity, and her Sense of the Earl's Merit, in these Words:

‘ I myself will be your General, Judge, and Rewarder of every one of your ‘ Virtues in the Field. I know already, for your Forwardness, you have deser- ‘ ved Rewards and Crowns; and we do assure you, in the Word of a Prince, ‘ they shall be duly paid you. In the mean Time, my Lieutenant-General ‘ shall be in my Stead, than whom never Prince commanded a more noble or ‘ worthy Subject; not doubting but by your Obedience to my General, by ‘ your Concord in the Camp, and your Valour in the Field, we shall shortly ‘ have a famous Victory, over those Enemies of my God, of my Kingdoms, ‘ and of my People.’

On that memorable Overthrow of the *Spanish* Fleet, the Camp broke up, and very soon after his Lordship departed this Life. He was retiring to his

---

[k] Bentivoglio and Brandt's Hift. p. 414, 415, 416.   [l] Rymer's Fœdera, Tom. 16. p 13, 14.
[m] Hift. Q. Elif. p. 400.   [n] Stow, p. 749.

Castle at *Kenelworth*, but in his Journey thither, he was taken ill of a Feaver at *Cornbury*-Park in *Oxfordshire*, of which he died without lawful Issue on the 4th of *Sept. An.* 1588, 30 *Elis.* ° at which Time he was Lord Steward of her Majesty's Houshold, General of the Army, and Earl Marshal of *England*. And *Camden* recites that the Letters Patents were actually drawn for creating him Lord Lieutenant under the Queen, in the Government of *England* and *Ireland*, but that the Lord *Burghley*, and the Lord Chancellor *Hatton*, prevented his obtaining them, by representing to her Majesty the Danger of entrusting too great a Power in any one Man's Hands. The same Author P gives this Character of him, ' He was esteemed a most accomplished Courtier, free and bountiful to ' Soldiers and Students, a cunning Time-server, and Respecter of his own Ad-' vantages ; of a Disposition ready and apt to please ; crafty and subtle towards ' his Adversaries ; much given formerly to Women, and in his latter Days, ' doating extremely upon Marriage. But whilst he preferred Power and Great-' ness, which is subject to be envied, before solid Virtue, his detracting Emu-' lators found large Matter to speak reproachfully of him, and even when he ' was in his most flourishing Condition, spared not disgracefully to defame him ' by Libels, not without a Mixture of some Untruths.'

In a Book (which is scarce to be met with) entitled, *A Discourse uppon Usu-rye, by Way of a Dialogue,* &c. by Thomas Wilson, *Doctour of the Civill Lawes, one of the Masters of her Majesties honourable Courte of Requestes, seene and allowed, according to the Queenes Majesties Injunctions,* 1572. There is this Character of the Earl of *Leicester,* in the following Epistle to him : *

To the Right Honourable, hyghe and myghty Earle, hys most especiall and singuler deer Lord, the Lord *Robert Duddeley,* Erle of *Leycester,* Baron of *Den-bigh,* Master of the Horse to the Queenes Majestie, Knight of the noble Order of the Garter, Chauncelloure of the Vniversitie of *Oxforde,* and one of her Hyhenes most honorable Prevy Counsell : *Thomas Wilson,* Doctour of the Civil Lawes, wisheth perfite Health, with Encreafe of Honor, to Godds most holy Wil and Pleasure.

The *Stoike* Philosophers, &c. ' Thys I reache at, that where amongste a ' Nomber of Gawles and great Greefes in thys Commonweale, there spreadeth ' one especial Mischiefe, as yll, nay woorse than any Plague ; my Meaning is to ' sett all other Faultes aparte, and to disclose this one above the rest unto your ' Lordship, that by your honorable Meanes and great Aucthoritye, it may at the ' leaste bee somewhat refourmed, yf not alltogether amended or taken away. I ' do meane, that ouglie, detestable, and hurtfull Synne of Usurie, which being ' but one Grossenes of Name, caries many a Mischief linked unto it in Nature, ' the same Synne beinge nowe so rancke throughout all *Englande,* not in *London* ' onelye, that Men have alltogether forgotten free Lending, and have geven them-' selves wholye to lyve by fowle Gayning, makinge the Lone of Monye a ' Kind of Merchandize, &c.

Ibid. p. penult.-- ' Thus I have boldlye, and I trust with Godds Spirite, moved ' your Honor to loke well to your Charge and Callinge, desiring you to take ' in good Parte my good Meaninge ; for my Desire is, that my naturall Coun-' trey might bee parfite and blessed, without Daunger of Evill, or Infection of ' Mischefe, to corrupt this State, or destroy thys noble Land. And the boulder ' I am to deale thus with your Honor, before others, becaufe I have knowne ' you, and that noble Race of youre Brethren, even from theire yonge Yeares. ' And with your Honor, and that famous Erle of *Warwike* deceased, and your ' noble Brother, now Erle of *Warwike* lyvinge, I have had more familier Con-

---

° Stow, p. 750.   P History of Queen Elif. p. 416.   * The Author, *Thomas Wilson,* of an antient Family (of which the present Sir *Thomas Wilson* now of *Vckfield* in *Sussex*, Bart. is the Head) was deservedly famed for his great Learning and Eloquence, and no less conspicuous for his Know-ledge in Political Affairs, whereby he became principal Secretary of State, and of the Privy-Coun-cil to Queen *Elisabeth,* in which great Office he died, An. 1581. And it is said of him, *That he had his State among Equals, that made him not envyed ; his Observance to Superiors, that made him no Flatterer ; and his Familiarity to Inferiors, that made him not Cheap.*

I

' ference,

' ference, then with the reft ; and efpecially with your Honor (I doe thanke
' you moſt humblie therefore) I have had ſufficient Proofe of your carefull
' Mynde, even in Reading not onelye of the *Latyn*, but alſo of the *Italian*
' good and ſounde Wryters, to knowe and to underſtand the beſt uſed Governe-
' ment, and the chefe Lawes that have ben made in all Ages. And as youre
' Mynde hath bene thus godly enclyned to knowe, ſo it appeareth very well
' you have ever had a good Mynde, to put youre Knowledge in Practiſe. And
' this muſt I ſaye, that Godds Providence is greately ſhewed in thys Behalfe,
' and the Queenes Maieſties bleſſed Eſtate moſt evidently appeareth to bee the
' ſtronger, in that it hathe pleaſed her Hyhnes, to have choſen ſo ſtayed and
' ſo diſcrete a Nobleman, as you are, to deale in the Affaires of the State. For,
' I knowe, and therefore will not feare to ſaye, that you have ben next, to the
' Queenes Maieſties moſt mylde and gracious Diſpoſition, a greate Helpe and
' Meane of thys moſt calme and mercifull Governement, a Thing ſo joyful
' to all good People, as nothinge can be more ; although it hath playnely fallen
' out in Profe, that both the Queenes Mercie, and your Nature, hath ben
' greatly abuſed, *&c.*'-- And again, in the ſame Page, he adds, ' But amongſt
' all other needfull Advertiſements, I doe wiſh that your Honor, and others of
' youre Callinge, ſhoulde never at any Tyme lett ſlippe anye good Occaſion
' offered for the Welfare of *Englande*, much leſſe to be careleſſe in that greate
' Truſte which is committed unto you. And therfore, as the Maſter of a
' Shippe hath ever an Eye to keepe a righte Courſe, a Phyſicion alwayes a
' good Mynde to heale his Paciente, a Capitayne evermore a carefull Heade to
' gette the Victory, even ſo my good Lord, I pray God you may bee a fayth-
' full Counſellour to the Prince, and a watchfull Magiſtrate to the People, to the
' Advauncement of Goddes moſt holy Woorde, and for the Welfare of thys Lande.
' And ſo to care for the whole Bodie of the State, that whileſt you take the
' Defenſe of ſome one Parte, you do not leave other Parts of the State unde-
' fended, or ſmallye eſtemed. Thus yf you doe, as I pray God you maie doe, and I
᷄ hope in God, you will do no leſſe : I doe well aſſure my ſelfe that Uſurie, *&c.*'

Ffrom the Queenes Maieſties Hoſpital
 at Saincte *Katherynes*, thys twentye of
 July, 1569.

Grotius, *Strada*, and *Bentivoglio*, Writers of the Actions, and Adminiſtration of the Earl of *Leiceſter*, in the *Low-Countries*, ſhew a manifeſt Partiality,
to cover the notorious Ingratitude of their Countrymen to Queen *Eliſabeth*, and
the *Engliſh* Nation. Yet they agree that his Lordſhip was Maſter of very great
Virtues, or at leaſt ſeemed to be. And other Hiſtorians ſay of him, that he
was a very comly Perſon, of a noble and graceful Aſpect, an engaging Behaviour and courtly Addreſs, and of a Witt capable at once of entertaining agree-
bly, and deſigning deeply, which together with a Delivery and Preſence, which
had in them ſomething, at once, great and engaging, commanded Attention
and Reſpect.

He had the common Fate of Favourites, in being much aſperſed, which induced his Nephew Sir *Philip Sydney*, to anſwer the moſt virulent Libel, that
ever was publiſhed ; and not doubting but the Curious will be pleaſed to ſee
what that celebrated Perſon has ſaid of the Earl of *Leiceſter*, I ſhall here introduce it, copyed from his own Hand-writing at *Penſhurſt* Place, and atteſted
both by *Robert Sydney*, Earl of *Leiceſter*, his Brother ; and *Robert*, the 2d Earl
of *Leiceſter*, his Nephew.

The ſaid Libel was 1ſt printed in 8*vo*, 1584, in Foreign Parts, and tranſmitted by the *Engliſh* Jeſuits into this Nation, under the Title of *A Dialogue
between a Scholar, a Gentleman, and a Lawyer.* And from the Colour of the
Leaves, then uſually called, *Father Parſons's Green Coat.* The Year after
(1585) it was tranſlated into *French*, and alſo printed Abroad, under the
Title of *La Vie Abominable, Ruſes Trahiſons, Murtres, Impoſtures, Empoiſon-
nements, Paillardiſes, Atheiſmes, & autres tres iniques Converſations, due quelle*

ià Uſê, & uſe Journellement, le my Lord de Leceſtre, Machiaveliſte, contre l'Honneur de Dieu, la Majeſte de la Royne d'Angleterre, ſa Princeſſe, &c. not mentioned where printed, but in 8vo, 1585.

It was after better known by the Name of *Leiceſters Common-wealth,* being twice printed in 4*to* and 12*ves,* by that Title in 1641. And again reprinted with the Title of *Secret Memoirs of* Robert Dudley *Earl of* Leiceſter, 8*vo.* 1706. With a Preface by Dr. *James Drake,* who pretended it was printed from an old Manuſcript.

The Anſwer given to it by Sir *Philip Sydney* ſeems to have been wrote immediately after the 1ſt Publication, *An.* 1584, but I never heard of any one that has ſeen it in Print. The Manuſcript is as follows:

Of late there hath been printed a Book, in Form of Dialog, to the Defaming of the Earl of *Leſter,* full of the moſt vyle Reproches, which a Witt uſed to wicked and filthy Thoughtes can imagin. In ſuch Manner truly, that if the Autor had as well fained new Names, as he doth new Matters, a Man might well have thought his only Meaning had been, to have gyven a lyvely Picture of the uttermoſt Degree of Railing. A Thing contemtible in the Doer, as proceeding from a baſe and wretched Tong, and ſuch a Tong, as, in the Speaking, dares not ſpeak his own Name. Odious to all Eſtates, ſince no Man beares a Name, of which Name, how unfitli ſo ever to the Perſon, by an impudent Lyer, any Thing maj not be ſpokne ; by all good Laws ſharpli puniſhed, and by all civill Companies, lyke a poiſenous Serpent avoided. But to the Earl himſelf, in the Eis of any Men, who, with cleer Judgmentes, can value Thinges, a true and ſownd Honour grows out of theſe diſhonowrable Falſhods. Since he maj juſtly ſaj, as a worthy Senatour of *Rome* once in lyke Cace did, That no Man, theſe twenty Yeeres, hath born a hatefull Hart to this Eſtate, but that, at the ſame Tyme, he hath ſhewd his Enmity to this Earl ; teſtefying it herebi, that his Faith is ſo lynked to her Majeſties Service, that who goes about to undermyne the one, reſolvs withall to overthrow the other. For it is not now, firſt that evill contented, and evill mynded Perſons, before the Occaſion be rype for them, to ſhew their Hate againſt the Prince, do firſt vomitt it out againſt his Cownceilours ; naj certainly, ſo ſtale a Devyſe it is, as it is to be mervailed, that ſo fyne Witts, whoſe Inventions a fugitive Fortune hath ſharpned, and the Air of *Itali* perchawnce purified, can light uppon no gallanter Waj, then the ordinary Pretext of the very clowniſh Rebellious. And yet that this is their Plott of late, by Name, firſt to publiſh ſomthing againſt the Earl of *Leſter,* and after, when Tyme ſerved, againſt the Queenes Maieſti, by ſome of their own intercepted Diſcources, is made to manifeſt. He himſelf, in ſome Places, bringes in the Examples of *Gaveſton,* Earl of *Cornwal, Robert Vere,* Duke of *Ireland,* and *Delapool,* Duke of *Suffolk.* It is not my Purpoſe to defend them, but I would fain know, whether they that perſecuted thoſe Cownceilours, when thej had had their Will in ruining them, whether their Rage ceaſſed, before they had as well deſtroied the Kynges themſelves, *Edward,* and *Richard the Second,* and *Henry the Sixt?* The old Tale teſtefieth, that the Wolves, that mean to deſtroi the Flock, hate moſt the treweſt and valianteſt Dogges. Therefore the more the filthy Empoſtume of their wolviſh Malice breakes forth, the more undoutedli doth it rais this well deſerved Glory to the Earl, that who hates *England,* and the Queen, muſt alſo withall hate the Earl of *Leſter.*

And as for the Libell it ſelf, ſuch is it, as neither in reſpect of the Wryter, nor Matter writtne, can move, I think, the lighteſt Witts to give thereto Credditt, to the Diſcredditt of ſo worthy a Perſon. For the Wryter (whom in Truth I know not, and, loth to fail, am not willing to geſs at) ſhews yet well inough, of what Kenell he is, that dares not teſtefy his own Wrytinges, with his own Name. And which is more baſe — (if any Thing can be more baſe then a diffamatori Libeller) he counterfaites him ſelf, in all the Treatis, a Proteſtant, when any Man, with Haulf an Ey, maj eaſili ſee he is of the other

Parti; which filthi Diffimulation, if few honeft Men of that Religion will ufe, to the Helping of themfelves, of how many Carrets of Honefti is this Man, that ufeth it (as much as his poor Powr can) to the Harm of an other. And *laftli*, evident inough it is, to any Man that reedes it, what Poifon he meanes to her Maiefti, in how goldne a Cup fo ever he drefs it.

For the Matter writtne, fo full of horrible Villeinies, as no good Hart will think poffible to enter into any Creature, much lefs to be lykeli in fo noble and well known a Man as he is, oneli thus accufed to be by the railing Oratory of a fhameles Libeller. Perchawnce he had redd the Rule of that Sicophant, that one fhowld bakbyte boldli; for, tho the Byte wear healed, yet the Skar woeld remain: But fure that Scoolmafter of his woeld more conningli have carried it, leaving fom Shaddows of Good, or, at leaft, leaving out fom Evill, that his Treatis might have carried fom probable Shew of it: For as reafonable Commendation wins Beleef, and exceffive getts onli the Praifer the Tytle of a Flatterer; fo much more in this far wors Degree of Lying, it mai well rebound uppon him felf, the vyle Reproch of a Railer, but never can fink into any good Mynd. The Sufpicion of any fuch unfpeakable Mifcheevs, efpecialli it beeing everi Mans Cace, even from the Meaneft to the Hyeft, whereof we daili fee odious Examples, that even of the great Princes, the deer Riches of a good Name are fought in fuch Sort to be pickt away by fuch Night Theeves. For thorow the hole Book, what is it els, but fuch a Bundle of Railinges, as if it came from the Mouth of fom haulf drunk Skold in a Tavern, not regarding whyle Evill weare fpokne, what was fitt for the Perfon of whome the Railing was, fo the Wordes wear fitt for the Perfon of an outragious Railer. Diffimulation, Hipocrifi, Adultery, Falfhod, Trecheri, Poifon, Rebellion, Treafon, Cowardis, Atheifm, and what not, and all ftill fo uppon the Superlative, that it was no Mervail, though the good Lawier, he fpeaks of, made many a Cros to keep him from fuch a Father of Lies, and in many excellent Giftes, paffing all fhameles Skoldes, in one he paffeth him felf with an unheard of Impudence, bringing Perfons, yet alyve, to fpeak Thinges which they are reddi to depofe, uppon their Salvation, never came in their Thoughtes. Such a Gentlewoman fpake of a Matter no lefs then Treafon, belyke fhe whifpred, yet he heard her; fuch two Knightes fpake together of Thinges not fitt to call Witneffes to, yet this Affes Eares wear fo long, that he heard them. And yet fee his good Nature all this Whyle woeld never reveal them till now, for Secretcy Sake, he puts them foorth in Print; certainly fuch a Qualiti in a Railer, as I think never was heard of, to name Perfons alyve, as not oneli can, but do difprove his Falfhods, and yet, with fuch Familiarity, to name them. Without he learnd it of *Pace*, the Duke of *Norfolkes* Fool, for he, when he had ufed his Tong, as this Heir of his hath don his Pen, of the nobleft Perfons, fomtymes of the Duke him felf, the next that came fitli in his Waj, he woeld faj he had told it him, of abundance of Charity, not oneli to flawnder, but to make bate. What therefore can be faid to fuch a Man? Or who lives there, even Chrift him felf, but that fo ftinking a Breath maj blow Infami uppon? Who hath a Father, by whofe Death the Son enherits, but fuch a nameles Hiftorien maj faj his Son poifend him? Where maj two talk together, but fuch a Spirit of Revelation mai furmize thei fpake of Treafon? What neede more, or why fo much? As though I douted that any woeld build Beleef uppon fuch a durty Seat, onely when he, to borrow a little of his Inkorn, when he plais the Statift, wringing veri unlukkili fome of *Machiavels* Axiomes to ferve his Purpos then indeed; then he tryumphes. Why then the Earl of *Lefter* meanes and plots to be King him felf, but firft to rebell from the Prince to whome he is moft bownd, and of whome he oneli dependeth, and then to make the Earl of *Huntington* King, and then to putt him down, and then to make him felf. Certainli, Sir, you fhoot fair, I think no Man, that hath Witt and Power to pronownce this Word *England*, but wil piti a Sicophant fo weak in his own Faculty. But of the Earl of *Huntington*, as I think all indifferent Men will cleer him from any fuch foolifh and wikked Entent of Rebellion, fo I proteft, before the Maiefti of God, who will confound

al!

all Liers ; and before the World, to whome Effectes and Enocentcy will witnes my Trewth, That I coold never fynd, in the Earl of *Lester*, any one Motion of Inclination toward any such pretended Conceat in the Earl of *Huntington*. I saj no Wit futur, for as for the present, or for drawing it to himself, I think no Devil so wicked, nor no Idiot so simple, as to conjecture ; and yet, beeing to him as I am, I think I shold have som Air of that, which this gentle Libel maker doth so particularli and peece meal understand, and I do know the Earls of *Warwick*, of *Pembroke*, my Father, and all the rest he names there, will answer the lyke. And yet such Matters cannot be undertakne, without good Frendes, nor good Frendes be kept without knowing somthing ; but the Earles Mynd hath ever been to serve oneli and truli, setting asyde all Hopes, all Feares, his Mistris, by undouted Right Queen of *England*, and most worthi to be the Queen for her roiall Excellencies, and most worthi to be his Queen, having restored his overthrown Hows, and brought him to this Cace ; that Curs for oneli Envy bark at. And this his Mynd is not oneli (though cheefli) for Faith knitt in Conscience and Honor, nor oneli (though greatli) for Gratefulness, where al Men know how much he is bownd, but even partli for Wisdomes Sake, knowing, by all old Lessons and Examples, that, how welcom soever Treasons bee, Traitors to all wyse Princes are odious, and that, as *Mutius* answered *Tulli*, who wrote to him how he was blamed for shewing him self so constant a Frend to *Cæsar*, that he douted not, even thei that blamed him woeld rather choos such Frendes as he was, then such as thei wear. For wyse Princes well know, that these violent Discontentements arise out of the Parties wicked Humors, as in sikk Folkes, that think, wyth Change of Places, to eas their Evill, which indeed is inward, and whome, nor this Prince nor that Prince can satisfy, but such as are ledd by their Fancies, that is to sai, who leave to be Princes. But this gentle Libelmaker, becaws he woeld make an evident Proof of an unquencheable Malice, desperat Impudency and Falshod, which never knew Blushing, is not content with a hole Dictionari of Slanders uppon these Persons living, but, as if he woold rake upp the Bones of the Dead, with so apparent Falshods toucheth their Howses, as if he had been afeard, els he shoold not have been streight fownd in that wherein he so greatli labours to excell. *First*, for *Hastinges*, he saith, the Lord *Hastinges* conspyred the Death of his Maister King *Edwardes* Sons ; lett any Man but reed the excellent Treatis of Sir *Thomas Moor*, compare but his Wordes with this Libelmakers, and then judg him, if he, who in a Thing so long since printed, and, as ani Man may see by other of his Allegations of him diligentli redd, hath the Face to wryte so directli contrary, not caring, as it seemes, though a hundred thowsand fynd his Falshod, so som dosen, that never redd Sir *Thomas Moores* Wordes, mai be carried to beleeve his horrible Slawnders of a Nobleman so long ago dead. I sett down the Wordes of both, becaws, by this oneli lyveli Comparison, the Face of his Falshod mai be the better sett foorth. And who then can dout, but he that lies in a Thing, which, with one Look, is fownd a Ly, what he will do, where yet there is though as much Falshod, yet not so easi Disproof.

Now to the *Dudleis*, such is his Bownti, that, when he hath powred out all his Flood of scolding Eloquence, he saith thei are no Gentlemen, affirming, that the then Duke of *Northumberland* was not born so ; in Truth, if I shoold have studdied with my self of all Pointes of fals Invections, which a poisenous Tong coold have spitt out against that Duke, yet would it never have come into my Hed, of all other Thinges, that any Man woold have objected Want of Gentry unto him ; but this Fellow doth lyke him, who, when he had shott of all his railing Quiver, cald one Cuckold that was never married, becaws he woold not be in Debt to any one evill Word. I am a *Dudlei* in Blood, that Dukes Daughters Son, and do acknowledg, though, in all Truth, I mai justli affirm, that I am, by my Fathers Syde, of ancient, and allwaies well esteemed and welmatched Gentry, yet I do acknowledg, I sai, that my cheefest Honor is to be a *Dudlei*, and truli am glad to have Caws to set foorth the Nobility of that Blood whereof I am descended, which, but uppon so just Caws, without vain Glori,

I   coold

coold not have been uttred ; fince no Man, but this Fellow of invincible Shame-
lefnefs woold ever have cald fo palpable a Matter in Queftion.   In one Place
of his Booke, he greatli extolleth the great Nobiliti, of the Hows of *Talbot*,
and truli with good Caws, there beeing, as I think, not in *Europe* a fubject
Hows which hath joined longer Continuance of Nobiliti, with Men of greater
Service and Loialty.   And yet this Dukes own Grandmother, whofe Blood he
makes fo bafe, was a *Talbot*, Daughter and fole Heir to the Vicownt of *Lile* ; e-
ven he, the fame Man, who, when he might have faved him felf, chofe rather
manifeft Death, then to abandon his Father, that moft noble *Talbot*, Earl of
Shrewfbury, of whome the Hiftories of that Tyme make fo honorable Mention.
The Hows of *Graj* is well known ; to no Hows in *England* in great Continuance
of Honowr, and for Nomber of great Howfes fprong of it, to be matched by
none ; but, by the noble Hows of *Nevel*, his Mother was a right *Graj*, and a
fole Enheritrix of that *Graj* of the Hows of *Warwick* which ever ftrave with the
great Hows of *Arundel*, which fhoold be the firft Earl of *England* ; he was lykewife fo defcended, as that juftly the Honowr of the Hows remained cheefli uppon him, beeing the onely Heir to the eldeft Daughter, and one of the Heirs
to that famous *Beauchamp*, Earl of *Warwick*, that was Regent of *Frawnce* ; and
although *Richard Nevel*, who married the yongeft Sifter, becaws fhe was of
the hole Blood to him that was called Duke of *Warwick*, by a Point in our Law
carried away the Enheritance ; and fo alfo I know not by what Right the Tytle,
yet in Law of Herawldri and Defcentes, which doth not confider thofe Quiddi-
ties of our Law ; it is moft certain, that the Honowr of the Blood remained
uppon him cheefli who came of the eldeft Daughter. And more undoubtely is
it to be faid of the Hows of *Barklei*, which is affirmed to be defcended lineally
from a King of *Denmark*, but hath ever been one of the beft Howfes in *England*, and this Duke was the oneli Heir general to that Hows, which the Hows
of *Barklei* doth not deny ; how foever, as fomtymes it fals out between Brothers,
there be Queftion for Land between them. Many other Howfes might heerin
be mentioned, but I name thefe, becaws *England* can boaft of no nobler, and
becaws all thefe Bloods fo remained in him, that he, as Heir, might (if he had
lifted) have ufed their Armes and Name, as in old Tyme thej ufed in *England*,
and do daili, both in *Spain*, *France*, and *Itali*. So that I think, it woold feeme
as great News as if thei came from the *Indies*, that he, who by Right of Blood,
and fo accepted, was the awncienteft Vicount of *England*, Heir in Blood and
Armes to the firft or fecond Earl of *England* ; in Blood of Enheritance a *Graj*, a
Talbot, a *Beauchamp*, a *Barklei*, a ʳ *Liflaj*, fhoold be douted to be a Gentleman.
But he will fai, thefe great Honors came to him by his Mother, for thefe I do
not deny they came fo ; and that the Mother, beeing an Heir, hath been, in all
Ages and Contreis, fufficient to nobilitat, is fo manifeft, that, even from the
Roman Tyme to modern Tymes, in fuch Cace thei might, if thei lifted, and fo
oftne did ufe the Mothers Name ; and that *Auguftus Cæfar* had both Name and
Empyre of *Cæfar*, onely by his Mothers Ryght, and fo both ˢ Moderns. But
I will claim no fuch Priviledg, lett the fingular Nobiliti of his Mother nothing
avail him, if his Fathers Blood wear not, in all Refpectes, worthy to match
with hers.   If awncient, undouted, and untouched Nobility be worthi to match
with the moft noble Hows that can bee : This Hows, therefore, of *Dudlei*, which,
in Defpyte of all Shamelefnes, he fo doth deprave, is, at this Dai, a Peer, as
we tearm it, of the Realm, a Baron, and, as all *Englifh* Men know, a Lord of
the Parliament, and fo a Companion, both in Marriage, Parliament, and Tryall,
to the greateft Duke that *England* can bear ; fo hath it been ever efteemed, and
fo, in the Conftitutions of all owr Laws and Ordeineinces, it is allwaies reputed.
Dudlei Hows is fo, to this Daj, and thus it hath been Tyme out of Mynd ;
in *Harry the Fifts* Tyme, the Lord *Dudlei* was his Lord Steward, and did that
pittiful Office in bringing Home, as the cheef Mourner, his victorious Mafters
dead Boddi ; as who goes but to *Weftminfter*, in the Church maj fee. I think

ʳ Lifle.   ˢ i. e. both Name and Arms.

if we confider together the Tyme which was of *England* the moft flowrifhing, and the King he ferved, who, of all *Englifhe* Kinges, was moft puiffant, and the Office he bare, which was, in Effect, as great as an *Englifh* Subject coold have, it woold feem very ftrange; fo that Lord *Dudlei*, if he coold out of his Grave heer this Fellow make Queftion, Whether his lawfull Pofterity, from Father to Son, fhoold be Gentlemen or no? But though he oneli had been fufficient to erect Nobility to his Succeffors, bringing, as the *Romanes* tearmed it, fo noble an Image into the Hows, yet did he but receave his Nobility from his Awnceftours, who had been Lordes of that very Seignory of *Dudlej* Caftell, many Defcentes before, even from King *Richarde the Firft* Tyme; at which Tyme Sir *Richard Sutton* married the Daughter and Heir of the Lord *Dudlej*; fince which Tyme all defcended of him, as dyvers Branches there bee, left the Name of *Sutton*, and have all been called *Dudleis*, which is now above fowr hundred Yeeres fince; and both thofe Howfes, of *Sutton*, and *Dudlei*, having been before that Tyme of great Nobility; and that *Sutton* was a Man of great Honor and Eftimation, that very Match witneffeth fufficiently, it being a dainty Thing in that Tyme, that one of *Saxon* Blood, as *Suttons* Name teftefieth he was, fhoold match with fuch an Enheritryx as *Dudlei* was; the lyke Example whereof I remember none, but the great Hows of *Rabi*, who matched with *Nevell*, who of that Match, as the *Suttons* wear called *Dudleis*, fo did thei ever fince take the Name of *Nevell*; fo, as of a Hows, which, thefe 400 Yeeres, have been ftill Owners of one Seignouri, the very Place it felf, to any that fees it, witneffing; fuch as, for any that I know, in *England* none, but the noble Hows of *Stafford* hath the like, confidering the Name of the Hows, the Length of Tyme it hath been poffeft, the Goodlinefs of the Seat, with Pleafures and Roialties about it; fo, as I think, any, that will not fwear themfelves Brothers to a reprochfull Tong, will judg of his other Slawnders by this moft manifeft; fince all the World may fee he fpeakes againft his own Knowledg; for if either the Hows of *Dudlei* had been great ancientli, and now extinguifhed, or now great, and had not continewed from old Tyme, or that thei had been unentytled Gentlemen, fo as Men muft not needes have takne Knowledg of them, yet their Might have been caft fom Vail over his Untruth; but in a Hows now noble, long fince noble, with a Nobility never interrupted, feated in a Place which they have each Father and each Son continualli owned, what fhoold be faid, but that this Fellow defyres to be known; futable, having an untrew Hart, he will become it with an untrew Tong.— But perchawnce he will feem to dout, for what will not he dout, who will affirm that, which beyond all Dout is fals, whether my Great Grandfather, *Edmond Dudley*, wear of the Lord *Dudleis* Hows, or no. Certainli, he might, in Confcience and good Manners, if fo he did doubt, have made fom Diftinction between the two Howfes, and not in all Places have made fo contemtible Mention of that Name of *Dudlei*, which is born by an other Peer of the Realm; and even of Charity Sake he fhoold have beftowed fom Father uppon *Edmond Dudlei*, and not leave him not only ungentled, but fatherles. A railing Wryter extant, againft *Octavius Auguftus*, faith, his Grandfather was a Silverfmith; an other *Italien*, againft *Hu Capet*, though with moft abfurd Falfhod, faith his Father was a Butcher. Of dyvers of the beft Howfes of *England*, there have been fuch foolifh Dreames, that one was a Ferrers Son, an other a Shoomakers, an other a Milners, an other a Fidlers; foolifh Lyes, and by any that ever tafted any Antiquities, known to be fo. Yet thofe Howfes had Luk to meet with honefter Railers, for they wear not left fatherles clean, thej defcended from fome Boddi; but wee, as if we wear of *Deucalions* Brood, wear made out of Stones, have left us no Awnceftowrs from whence we are come: But, alas, good Railer, yow faw the Prooves wear cleer, and therefore, for Honefty Sake, wear contented to omitt them; for, if either their had been Difference of Name, or Difference of Armes between them; or, if though in Name and Armes thei agreed, yet, if their had been many Defcentes faln fince, the Seperating of thofe Branches (as we fee in many ancient Howfes, it fo falls

out,

out, as thei are uncertain whether came out of other) then, I fai yet, a vaillant
Railer maj venture uppon a Thing, where, becaws there is not an abfolute
Certainti, there maj bee fom Poffibiliti to efcape ; but, in this Cace, where not
oneli Name and Armes, with oneli that Difference, which acknowledgeth our
Hows to be of the yonger Brother, but fuch Neerenefs of Blood, as that *Edmond Dudleis* was no furdre of then Son to the yonger Brother of the fame Lord
Dudlei, and fo as he was to be Lord *Dudlei,* if the Lord *Dudlei* had died without Heires ; and, by the *Jerman* and *Italien* Manner, him felf was to have been
alfo called Lord *Dudlei* ; that his Father, beeing called *John Dudlei,* married to
the Daughter and Heir of *Bramfhot* in *Suffex* ; twas the oneli Defcent between
him and the Lord *Dudlei,* who was his Grandfather ; his Great Grandfather
beeing that noble Lord *Dudlei,* whome before I mentioned, and no Man need
doubt that this Wryter doth not oneli know the Trewthe hereof, but the
Proofes of this Trewth. This *John, Edmondes* Father, beeing buried at *A-
rundel* Caftell, who married *Bramfhot,* and left that Land to *Edmond,* and fo to
the Duke in *Suffex,* which, after the Duke fold, by Confifcation came to the
Crown. This Tomb any Man at *Arundel* Caftell maj fee. This *Bramfhot* Land
I name, a Thing not in the Air, but which any Man, by the ordinari Courfe of
thofe Thinges, maj foone know whether fuch Land did not fucceed unto *Edmond* from his Father. So as where is this Enheritance of Land, and Monumentes in Churches, and the Perfons them felves little more then in Mans
Memory ; truly this Libeller deferves many Thankes, that, with his impudent
Falfhod, hath given Occafion to fet down fo manifeft a Truth.

As to the *Dudleis,* he dealls much harder withall, but no Whitt trewer : But
therein I muft confes, I can not alleag his uncharitable Tryumphing uppon the
Calamities faln to that Hows, though they might well be challenged of a Wryter, of whom any Honefti wear to be expected ; but God forbid I fhoold fynd
Fault with that, fince, in all his Book, there is fcarce any one Trewth els. But
our Hows receaved fuch an Overthrow ; and hath none els in *England* done fo ?
I will not feek to wafh awaj that Difhonour with other honorable Tears. I
woold this Yland wear not fo full of fuch Examples ; and I think, indeed, this
Wryter, if he wear known, might in Confcience cleer his Awnceftowrs of any
fuch Difgraces, they were to low in the Myre to be fo thunderftrickne ; but
this I may juftly and boldli affirm, lett the laft Fault of the Duke be buried.

And, in good Faith, now I have fo far touched their, as any Man that
lift to know a Truth (if at leaft there bee any that can dout thereof) maj ftreight
be fatisfied. I do not mean to give any Mans Eis or Eares fuch a Surfett, as
by anfwering to repeat his filthy Falfhods, fo contrari to them felves, as may
well fhow how evill Lies can be built with any Uniformity. The fame Man,
in the Beginning of the Boke, was potent, to ufe his Tearm, in that the Queen
had Caws to fear him ; the fame Man, in the End thereof, fo abject, as any Man
might tread on him : The fame Man fo unfrendly, as no Man coold love him :
The fame Man fo fupported by Frendes, that Court and Contrei wear full of
them : The fame Man extreemeli weak of Boddi, and infinitly luxurious : The
fame Man a Daftard to fear any Thing : The fame Man fo ventrous, as to un-
dretake, having no more Tytle, fuch a Matter, that *Hercules* himfelf woold be
afreid to do, if he wear heer among us : In fom, in one the fame Man, all the
Faultes that in all the moft contrary humord Men in the World can remain ;
that fure, I think, he hath redd the Devills Role of Complaynetes, which he
meanes to putt up againft Mankynd, or els he coold never have been acquainted with fo many wretched Mifcheefes. But hard it wear, if every Goos Quill,
coold any Waj blott the Honour of an Earl of *Lefter,* writtne in the Hartes
of fo many Men, thorow *Europe.* Neither for me, fhall ever fo worthy a
Mans Name, be brought to bee made a Queftion, where there is oneli fuch a
nameles and fhameles Oppofer. But becaws that, thow the Wryter heerof
doft moft falfli laj Want of Gentry to my dead Awnceftowrs, I have to the
World thought good to faj a little, which, I will affure any, that lift to feek,
fhall fynd confirmed with much more. But to thee, I faj, Thow therein lieft in
thy

thy Throte ; which I will be reddi to juftefy uppon thee, in any Place of *Europe*, where thow wilt affign me a free Place of Comming, as within 3 Monthes after the Publifhing heerof, I may undreftand thy Mynd. And, as till thow haft proved this, in all Conftruction of Vertew and Honowr, all the Shame thow haft fpokne is thyne own, the right Reward of an evill tonged Shelm, as the *Jerman*, efpecialli, call fuch People. So again, in any Place, wherto thow wilt call me, provyded that the Place be fuch, as a Servant of the Queenes Majeftie have free Accefs unto ; if I do not, having my Lyfe, and Liberty, prove this uppon thee, I am content that this Ly, I have givn thee, return to my perpetual Infamy. And this which I wryte I woold fend to thyne own Handes, if I knew thee ; but I truft it can not bee intended, that he fhould be ignorant of this printed in *London*, which knows the very Whifpringes of the Prive-Chamber. I will make Dainti of no Bafenes in thee, that art, indeed, the Wryter of this Book. And, from the Date of this Wryting, emprinted and publifhed, I will three Monthes expect thyne Anfwer.

The following Indorfements are on the Original.

A Difcourfe in Defence of the Earle of *Leycefter*.

⎰ This is Sir *P. Sidney*'s Brother's Hand-
⎱ writing, *viz. Robert Sidney*, the 1ft
  Earl of *Leicefter*, of the Name of *Sidney*.

In my Uncles own Hand, worthy to be better known to the World.

⎰ This is the Hand-writing of *Robert*, 2d
⎱ E. of *Leic*. Son and Heir to the aforefaid
  Robert, and Nephew to Sir *P. Sidney*.

I fhall now proceed to give an Account of the Funeral of the Earl of *Leicefter*, &c. His Corps was removed from *Cornbury* Park to *Warwick*, where he was interred in our Ladyes Chapel, adjoining to the Quire of the Collegiate Church, and a very noble Monument is erected to his Memory with his Effigies in Armour, lying on his Back, with his Earls Coronet on his Head, and the Effigy of his Countefs lying by him, with this Infcription in Capitals,

DEO VIVENTIUM S,

Spe certa Refurgendi in Chrifto hic fitus eft illuftriffimus *Robertus Dudleyus, Johannis* Ducis Northumbriæ, Comitis Warwici, Vicecomitis Infulæ, &c. Filius quintus, Comes Leiceftriæ, Baro Denbighiæ, Ordinis tum S. Georgii, cùm S. Michaelis Eques Auratus, Reginæ *Elizabethæ* (apud quam fingulari gratia florebat) Hippocomus Regiæ Aulæ, fub inde Senefchalus, ab intimis confiliis ;

Foreftarium, Parcorum Chacearum, &c. citra

Trentam fummus Jufticiarius ; Exercitus Anglici a dicta Regina *Elizabetha* miffi in Belgio, ab Anno Mᴅʟxxxv. ad annum Mᴅʟxxxvɪɪ. Locum tenens & Capitaneus Generalis ; Provinciarum Confederatarum ibidem Gubernator generalis & Præfectus, Regnique Angliæ Locum tenens contra Philippum II, Hifpanum, numerofa claffe & exercitu Angliam Anno Mᴅʟxxxvɪɪɪ invadentem. Animam Deo fervatori reddidit, Anno falutis M.ᴅ.ʟxxxvɪɪɪ. Die quarto Septembrif. optimo & chariffimo marito Mœftiffima Uxor Leticia, Francifci Knolles ordinis S. Georgii Equitis Aurati, & Regiæ Thefaurarii filia, amoris & conjugalis fidei ergo pofuit.

He firft married, in the Reign of King *Edward the Sixth, Anne*, Daughter and Heir of Sir *John Robfart* of *Siderfton* in Com. *Norf.* Kt. Lineal Heir Male to Sir *John Robfart*, Knight of the Garter in the Reign of King *Henry the Sixth*, one of the moft valiant Commanders of his Time ; but this Lady dying on 8 *Sept.* 1560, at *Cunmore* near *Oxford*, his Lordfhip continued a Widower feveral Years ; and after having an illegitimate Son, named *Robert*, by the

Lady

Lady *Douglas Sheffield*, Widow of *John* Lord *Sheffield* ; he ' married on the 21ſt of *Sept.* 1578, at *Wanſted* in *Eſſex*, *Lettice* Daughter of Sir *Francis Knolles*, Knight of the Garter, and Widow of *Walter Devereux*, Earl of *Eſſex*, by whom he had Iſſue one Son, *Robert*, Baron of *Denbigh*, for whom an Altar Monument is erected, by that of his Father, at *Warwick*, with his Effigies lying thereon. and this Inſcription in Capitals :

> Heere reſteth the Body of the noble Imp. *Robert*, of *Dudley*, Baron of *Denbigh*, Sonne of *Robert* Erle of *Ley-ceſter*, Nephew and Heire unto *Ambroſe* Erle of *Warwicke*, Bretherne, bothe Sones of the Mightie Prince *John*, late Duke of *Northumberland* ; that was Couſin and Heire to Sir *John Grey*, Viſcont *Lyſle*, Couſin and Heire to Sir *Thomas Talbot*, Viſcont *Lyſle*, Grandſon and Heire unto the Lady *Mar-garet*, Counteſſe of *Shrewſbury*, the eldeſt Daughter and Co-heire of the Noble Erle of *Warwike*, Sir *Richard Beauchamp*, heere enterred a Childe of great Parentage, but of farre greater Hope and Towardneſs. Taken from this tranſitory unto the Everlaſtinge Life, in his tender Age at *Wanſled* in *Eſſex*, on *Sondaye* the 19 of *July*, in the Yere of our Lorde God 1584 ; beinge the 26 Yere of the happy Reigne of the moſt Vertuovs and Godly Princes Queene *Elizabethe* : And in this Place layed up emonge his Noble Aunceſtors, in aſſured Hope of the Generall Reſurrection.

On the Right Hand of the Tomb of the ſaid *Robert* Earl of *Leiceſter*, are the following Verſes in gold Capital Letters, in two Columns, on a Tablet.

Upon
The Death of the
Excellent and Pious
Lady *Lettice*, Counteſſe
of *Leyceſter*, who dyed
upon *Chriſtmas* Day in
the Morning, 1634.

1.

Look into this Vault and ſearch it well,
Much Treaſure in it lately fell ;
We all are rob'd, and all do ſay
Our Wealth was carryed this a Way.
And that the Theft might nere be found
Tis buried cloſely under Ground :
Yet if you gently ſtir the Mould,
There all our Loſs you may behold :
There you may ſee that Face, that Hand,
Which once was faireſt in the Land.
She that in her yonger Yeares,
Matcht with two great *Engliſh* Peers ;
She that, did ſupply the Warrs
With Thunder, and the Court with
    Starrs.
She that in her Youth had bene
Darling to the Mayden Quene ;
Till ſhe was content to quitt
Her Favour, for her Favourit.

2.

Whoſe gould Threed, when ſhe ſaw ſpunn,
And the Death of her brave Son,
Thought it ſafeſt to retire
From all Care and vain Deſire,
To a private Countrie Cell
Where ſhe ſpent her Dayes ſo well,
That to her the better Sort
Came as to an Holy Court.
And the Poor that lived near
Dearth nor Famine could not fear.
Whilſt ſhe lived, ſhe lived thus,
Till that God, diſpleaſed with us,
Suffered her at laſt to fall,
Not from him, but from us all.
And becauſe ſhe took Delight
Chriſts poor Members to invite,
He fully now requites her Love,
And ſends his Angels from above,
That did to Heaven her Soul convay
To ſolemniſe his own Birth-Day.

Gervas Clifton.

The Earl of *Leiceſter*'s Will being very remarkable, and wrote without any Aſſiſtance, I ſhall for the Satisfaction of the Curious, inſert a Copy of it, from

' Ex Evident. apud Penſhurſt.

the Original [u], as it expreffes the great Senfe he had of Queen *Elifabeth*'s Favours to him, and fhews his Piety and Humility, as alfo the juft Care he had for the Payment of his Debts, and Settling of his Eftate.

THIS IS THE LAST WILL AND TESTAMENT of me *Robert* Earl of *Leicefter*, her Majeftys Lievtenant General of all her Forces in the *Low-Countries*, and Governor and Captain-General of all the *United Provinces*, written with his own Hand the Firft of *Auguft* in *Middleborough* 1578. Firft I take it to be the Part of every true Chriftian, to make a true Teftimony of his Faith at all Times, and efpecially in fuch a Cafe and fuch a Time as this is. And, therefore, I do mean here faithfully to make a fhort Declaration to teftify in what Faith I do live, and depart from this World, through the Grace of my Lord and Saviour to continue me in the fame till the Seperation of this Life and Body. And fo I do acknowledge my Creation and Being, to be had and continued by the Providence of our Almighty God, the Creator of all Things both in Heaven and Earth, and do confefs, that above all Deeds, that his divine Majefty hath done for Mankind, is the Gift of his bleffed Son, Chrift Jefus, to be the Redeemer and Saviour of his People that be faithfull, by whofe only Merits and Paffion, I verily believe, and am moft affured of the Forgivenefs of all my Sinnes, be they never fo great or infinite, and that he only is the fufficient Sacrafice that hath appeafed the Wrath of his Father, and that bleffed Lamb, which innocently fuffered all Torments, to bear the bitter Burden due to us miferable Wretches, for his moft tender Compaffion over all that have Grace to believe in him. All which his Graces Goodnefs and Mercy I moft faithfully take hold on, being fo promifed by himfelf, who is the only Truth it felf, that I am the Child of Salvation ; and to be the Inheritour of his everlafting Kingdom, and to meet with him at the joyfull Day of Refurrection, with all the faithfull Children, and Saints of God. In this Faith I now live, and in this Faith I truft to change this Life, with continual Prayer to the Throne of Grace, to grant me, during this Pilgrimage of mine, a true, humble, and penitent Heart, for the due Recognition of all mine Offences, and the willing Amendment of the fame, and to fly inftantly to the fure Ankerholde my Lord and Saviour, Chrift Jefus, to whom with the Father, and the Holy Spirit, be all Honour, Glory and Dominion, forever, *Amen*. Thus being in perfect Health and Memory, and having fet down my Faith as a true Chriftian, and being uncertain of the Hour of Death, I think it my Part to fettle my worldly Matters in as good Eftate as I can, fpecially being haftily and fuddenly fent over, and likewife having very little Leafure, fince my Arrival, to get any Time for my private Buifinefs. But firft my Will is, to commit this wretched Body of mine, when it fhall pleafe God to feperate it from the Soul, to the Order of my dear Friends, that fhall be living as my Executors, and my Overfeers of this my laft Will and Teftament, and they to take fuch Order for the Burial of my Body, as they fhall think mete, always requiring that it may be done with as little Pomp or vain Expences of the World, as may be, being perfwaded that there is no more vain Expences than that is a convenient Tombe or Monument I wifh there fhould be. And, for the Place where my Body fhould lye, it is hard to appoint, and I know not how convenient it is to defire it ; but I have always wifhed, as my dear Wife doth know, and fome of my Friends, that it might be at *Warwick*, where fundry of my Anceftors doe lye, either fo, or elfe where the Queens Majefty fhall command, for as it was when it had Life, a moft faithfull, true, loving Servant unto her, fo living, and fo dead, let the Body be at her gracious Determination, if it fhall fo pleafe her. Touching my Bequefts, they cannot be great, by Reafon my Ability and Power is little, for I have not diffembled with the World my Eftate, but have lived always above any Living I had (for which I am heartily forry) leaft that, thro' my many Debts, from Time to Time, fome Men have taken Lofs by me. My Defire therefore is, and I do charge my Executors to have due Confidera-

tion,

tion, that if any Perſon ſhall juſtly after my Deceaſe make ſuch Complaint, that they may be ſatisfied as far as it ſhall be found in any Equity it is due unto them, with Advantage to them beſide. I do here appoint my moſt dear welbe-loved Wife, the Countes of *Leiceſter*, to be my ſole Executrix of this my laſt Will and Teſtament ; and do require her, for all Love between us, that ſhe will not only be content to take it upon her, but alſo to ſee it faithfully and carefully performed. And albeit there may many Imperfections be found with the Making of this Will, for that I am no Lawyer, nor have any Councel now with me to place Things in ſuch Forme as ſome are able ; yet as my true Mean-ing is I truſt to expreſs, that accordingly it may be interpreted, for I mean to make it as plain as I can. And firſt of all, before and above all Perſons, it is my Duty to remember my moſt dear, and moſt gracious Sovereign, whoſe Creature under God I have been, and who hath been a moſt bountiful, and moſt princely Miſtreſs unto me, as well in advancing me to many Honours, as in maintaining me many Ways by her Goodneſs and Liberality. And as my beſt Recompence to her moſt excellent Majeſty can be from ſo mean a Man, chiefly in Prayer to God, ſo whilſt there was any Breath in this Body, I never failed it, even as for mine own Soul. And as it was my greateſt Joy, in my Life Time, to ſerve her to her Contentation, ſo it is not unwelcome to me, being the Will of God to dye, and end this Life for her Service. And yet albeit I am not able to make any Piece of Recompence of her great Goodneſs, yet will I pre-ſume to preſent unto her a Token of an humble, faithfull Heart, as the leaſt that ever I can ſend her, and with this Prayer withall, that it may pleaſe the Almighty God, not only to make her the oldeſt Prince, that ever he gave over *England*, but to make her the Godlieſt, the Virtoueſt, and the Worthieſt in his Sight, that ever he gave over any Nation. That ſhe may indeed be a bleſſed Mother and Nurſe to this People, and Church of *England*, which the Almigh-ty God grant for his Chriſts Sake. The Token I do bequeath unto her Ma-jeſty, is the Jewel with three great Emrodes with a fair large Table Diamond in the Middeſt, without a Foyle, and ſet about with many Diamonds without Foyle, and a Roap of fayre white Pearl, to the Number ſix Hundred, to hang the ſaid Jewel at ; which Pearl and Jewel was once purpoſed for her Majeſty, againſt a Coming to *Wanſted*, but it moſt now thus be diſpoſed, which I do pray you, my dear Wife, ſee performed, and delivered to ſome of thoſe whom I ſhall hereafter nominate and appoint to be my Overſeers for her Majeſty.

Next her Majeſty I will now return to my dear Wife, and ſet down that for her, which cannot be ſo well as I would wiſh it, but ſhall be as well as I am able to make it, having always found her a faithfull, loving, and a very obe-dient, carefull Wife ; and ſo do I truſt this Will of mine ſhall find her no leſs mindfull of me being gone, then I was always of her being alive. I do give and bequeath to my ſaid dear Wife, over and beſide the Jointure I have made her, the Leaſe of *Drayton Baſſet*, freely to give and diſpoſe at her Will. *Item*, There be certain Parcels of Grounds, which I bought of the Earl of *Oxford*, being ſometime belonging to the Houſe of *Crambrooke*, and I reſerved purpoſe-ly to be joyned to the Park of *Wanſted*, as alſo the Parcel of Ground, called *Watermans*, which I bought of the L. of *Buckhurſt* ; both which I do alſo freely give and grant to my ſaid Wife forever, with the Mannor of *Wanſted*, already aſſured unto her. *Item*, I do give to my ſaid Wife, during her Life, all other Lands and Tenements, which I did purchaſe in the Lordſhip of *Wan-ſted*, beſide that is paſt by Deed, with the Houſe and Mannor, to her before. And, becauſe I do give the Houſe and Land of *Aldersbrooke*, which I bought of *Fuller* the Lawyer, to my baſe Son *Robert Dudley*, I do deſire and pray my ſaid dear Wife, that ſhe will be pleaſed to give him alſo the great Pond before the Door of the ſaid Houſe, being Parcel of the Mannor of *Wanſted*. Which Houſe and Lands of *Aldersbrooke* I do alſo grant unto my ſaid Wife, till my ſaid baſe Son ſhall accompliſh the Age of twenty Yeares. *Item*, I do give unto my ſaid dear Wife all my Goods and Leaſes whatſoever, towards the Payment

of

of my Debts, and her better Maintenance, faving fuch as I fhall hereafter, in this my Will, limit and fett down for other Vfes. *Item*, For that there is fixteen-thoufand Pounds, due by me, to the Merchants of *London*, upon Mortgage of the Lordfhips of *Denbigh*, and others, and that neither my Leafes, nor Goods, able to redeem them, and to pay other my Debts; I do give Power and Authority, by this my laft Will, to fuch as I have made Affurance already, for the fame Purpofe, as if they want Power and Authority by any fuch former Act. I do give all Power and Authority, that is poffible for me to give, either to my Executrix, and my Overfeers, jointly together, or fuch of them as fhall be living, to fell all my Lands and Leafes, with the Parfonage of *Warrington*, which I have in *Lancafhire*, and were fometimes the Lands of Sir *Thomas Butler*, Knt. and *Edward Butler*, Efq; his Son. All which Lands and Leafes I do will in any wife to be fold for the Redemption of the Lordfhips of *Denbigh*, and *Chirk*, and the Overplus thereof, to go towards the Payment of my other Debts, for the better Eafe and Reliefe of my Executrix; and for that the faid Lands of *Butlers*, were intended at the firft, by the faid *Butler*, to be given to my faid bafe Son, *Robert*, I do in Lieu thereof give unto him the faid Lordfhips of *Denbighe* and *Chirke*, &c. but after the Death of my dear Lord, and Brother, the Earl of *Warwick*, to whom, with all other my Lands, during his Life, I do give and bequeath; faving fuch as I have already granted to my faid dear Wife, in Joynture, or fhall grant unto her, by this my laft Will and Teftament. The Caftle of *Kenelworthe*, I do likewife give unto my faid Brother, with all the Parks, Chafes, and Lands, during his Life, and the Park and Padock of *Rudfine* only excepted, which I always gave unto my Wife, during her Life, the Timber Woods of all which I do referve from any Wafte (Reparations neceffary excepted) or if it fhall pleafe my Lord and Brother to build out the Gallery which I once intended, then to take fuch Timber as fhall be convenient for the fame. *Item*, I do will and give all fuch Stuff and Implements of Houfehold, as I have heretofore ftored the faid Caftle with, all to remain to the faid Caftle and Houfe, and not to be altered or removed. I do alfo give two Garnifh of filver Veffell, to remain, as the reft, to the faid Caftle, with two Bafons and Ewers of Silver gilt, with other Plate for a Cupboard, to the Value of two hundreth Pounds, over and above the former Parcelis of Veffell and Bafons and Ewers. *Item*, I do give and grant, by this my Will, the faid Caftle, and Lands belonging to the faid Caftle, and which I have purchafed to the fame: Alfo, after the Deceafe of my Lord and Brother, to my bafe Son *Robert Dudley*, as alfo the Fee Farme of *Rudfyne*. I do give alfo to my dear Wife my Houfe and Mannor of *Langley*, with all the Appurtenances, and the Ufe of all the Coppice Woods there, with the Leafe of *Whitney*, until my faid bafe Son accomplifh the Years of one and twenty; both which, after, I do give and grant to *Robert*, my bafe Son, in fuch Sort as fhall be limited unto him, with the reft of the Lands I give him. If he dye before the faid one and twenty Year, then my faid Wife to enjoy the faid Lands and Leafes during her Life. I give him alfo the Leafes of *Grafton* Pafture, after the Deceafe of my faid Wife. I doe alfo defire my good Lord and Brother, the Lands aforefaid coming to his Hands, that it will pleafe him to give fome reafonable Stipend to the *Boy*, when he comes to more Years, for his Maintenance. In the mean Time, after the Deceafe of *Gabriel Bleke*, and his Wife, I do give and grant to the faid *Robert*, all fuch Lands and Leafes, as I have conveyed unto me from the faid *Gabriel* forever; and the fame Lands, Houfes, and Leafes, to enjoy prefently after the Deceafe of the faid *Gabriel Bleke*, and his Wife, now living. I do give and grant to my faid bafe Son, alfo, after the Deceafe of my dear Wife, the Mannors of *Balfoll*, and *Long Itchington*, in the Countye of *Warwicke*, with all Appurtenances. I do likewife give and grant to my faid bafe Son, the Mannors of *Cleobury* and *Eurnewood*, after the Deceafe alfo of my faid dear Wife. *The Moyety of fuch Lands as was recovered from the Lord* Berkley, *I do leave unbeftowed; but to be imploied by my Lord and Brother upon fuch our next Heirs (for that it came by Defcent) as he fhall find living with him,* Sir

Robert Sidney, *if he live to it.* And for all thofe Things which I have granted, whereof my dear Wife hath Intereft, either during Life, or otherwife, if any mine Heirs or Affigns, fhall go about to moleft or difturb her Eftate, and fhall moleft, and any Way, difturb her from any fuch Eftate, granted to her either by Deed or Will from me ; that imediately it fhall be lawfull for her, during her Life, to enter and feize upon the Lands, that any fuch Difturber fhall prefently hold or enjoy from me, whatfoever it fhall be. *Item,* If the Lands which was *Butlers* in *Lancafhire,* cannot be fold in Sort to pay and redeem the Mortgage of *Denbigh* and *Chirk,* and to make fix or feven Thoufand Pounds more, at the leaft, towards my other Debts : Then it is my Will, that my Overfeers fhall, and my Executrix alfo, joyn with them, if fo it be needfull, to bargain and fell both thofe Lordfhips of *Denbigh* and *Chirk,* and to make the moft of it, and the Overplufs to go to the Payment of my other Debts. And then I do give and grant, by this Will, all the Lands and Leafes in *Lancafhire,* to my faid *Robert* my bafe Son, forever. And for that there is certain of my Lands, charged with Rents and Tenths to her Majefty, and that I have certain free Rents in *Wales* to as great Value or more ; my humble Requeft to her Highnefs, is, that it may pleafe her to difcharge thofe Rents from my other Lands, and to receive the other Rents in *Wales* for the fame, which is no Lofs to her Majefty at all, but as certain as the other. And where my bafe Son is young and cafual, whether thefe my Gifts fhall come unto him or no, if he dye before he be one and twenty Years old, unmarried and without Child ; then, if my Lord and Brother be living, I fhall require him to difpofe of all thofe Lands, leaving them unto him as my right and lawfull Heir. Save only, that if my faid bafe Son *Robert* fhould dye without Iffue, and that the Mannor of *Denbigh* and *Chirk* be redeemed, I do give and bequeath forever the Lordfhip of *Chirk,* to my welbeloved Son in Law the Earl of *Effex,* as alfo my Houfe in *London,* called *Leicefter* Houfe ; if the faid *Robert* my bafe Son dye without Iffue, to whom I give and grant, as other the former Lands, after the Deceafe of my dear Wife, the faid Houfe, and the Remainder, if he dye without Iffue, to my faid Lord the Earl of *Effex,* my Son in Law, and to the Heirs of his Body lawfully begotten. And where, in one Article before touching my purchafed Lands in *Wanfted,* I left my faid Lands undifpofed, but during the Life of my faid Wife : I do hereby, alfo, give and grant thofe purchafed Lands, not paffed unto her by Deed before, or not inclofed within the Park of *Wanfted,* to *Robert* my bafe Son during his Life, and to the Heirs of his Body, if he have any lawfully begotten ; otherwife if he dye without Iffue, I do give and grant thofe Lands purchafed in *Wanfted,* to the Lord of *Wanfted,* being any of the Heirs of the Body of my faid dear Wife, forever. And where I have erected an Hofpital for the Relief of certain poor Men, and do think that I have fully accomplifhed the fame, of two hundred Pounds by Year, of fufficient Land and Rent, for the Maintenance of the Mafter and poor Men, according to a Rate fet down ; if any Want be, either of Default of Rent, or other Affurance, I do give Authority, by this my Will, to my Lord and Brother the Earl of *Warwick,* to make it up out of the Mannor of *Hampton,* in *Worcefterfhire,* called *Hampton magna.* If the faid Hofpital be fully made up to the aforefaid Summe, then, the faid Mannor to come to my Brother, excepting any Eftate made to my Wife for Joynture, whereof I am here uncertain. But if it be, and the Hofpital do lack of the Value, I doubt not but fhe will be well content to fuffer my Brother to make any fuch Conveyance, which fhall not hinder her Joynture, to the Benefit of that poor Houfe. *And do hope God will fend her Life and Ability to provide fome Means to joyn fome good Deed to that Houfe, in finding fome Number of poor Women, fuch as fhall not be idle, but to be fet on Work in making Linnen Cloath, or fuch like ; a Work of good Charity it will be, and I truft it fhall not be the lefs thought on, to joyn with me, in that I have begun there : And by this Will I do give to my Hofpitall two hundredth Pounds in Money, prefently, for a Stock to relieve their Neceffitys.*

I have in *Wales* a Leafe of her Majefty of *Arnfteley* and *Cavilliock*, which Leafe I give, after my Debts paid, to my good Son in Law, the Earl of *Effex*. And I have a Fee Farm, Parcell of that, which I will fhall be imploied to the Maintenance of *two Schollars* in the *Vniverfity* College in *Oxford*, allowing each of them twenty Pounds a Year a Piece ; thofe Scholars always to be placed by my Wife during her Life ; and after, by him that fhall be left mine Heir, and fo to be at the Appointment of mine Heirs forever. This Fee Farm I know not the Name of it, but the prefent Rent is about five Pounds a Year, and worth fifty or threefcore Pounds, when the Years be out, which are above twenty, as I guefs. In the mean While, I will charge my Lord of *Effex*, with the Payment of the Schollars Stipend, and to affift his Mother about the Setling of thofe Schollars, and to fee the Leafe I fpeak of, to be confidered of for the Furtherance of this Purpofe. *Thomas Dudley*, and my Auditor, can tell you what this Thing is.

Item, I do give and bequeath to my beloved Godfon and Nephew, Sir *Robert Sidney*, Knight, my two Farms in *Kent*, of *Monfkton* and *Thornedeane*, which I hold of the Church of *Canterbury*, by Leafe for Years ; which Leafes and Years I do give unto my faid Nephew, and to enjoy them after my Debts paid. And whereas I have appointed divers Mannors and Lands to my bafe Son *Robert Dudley*, the moft whereof is after the Deceafe of my Lord and Brother the Earl of *Warwick*, and my dear Wife the Countefs of *Leicefter* ; I think good to put my faid Brother in Remembrance, *if my bafe Son fhould dye without Heirs of his Body, that, then, there may be good Confideration had of this Gentleman our Nephew Sir* Robert Sidney. For my Will is, that my faid bafe Son fhall have the State of thofe Lands thus limited, that is, during his Life, and if he have lawfull Iffue of his Body, then the fame Mannors and Lands to defcend unto them ; otherwife my Will is, that, after fuch Default, thofe Lands may defcend to Sir *Robert Sidney*, and his Heirs lawfully begotten ; and for fuch Default to the right Heirs of me and my Brother. Saving the Mannor and Lordfhip of *Chirk* and *Chirkland*, after the Deceafe of *Robert* my bafe Son without Iffue of his Body, immediately to come to my Son in Law, the Earl of *Effex*, forever ; as alfo my Houfe in *London* to him and the Heirs of his Body begotten, not hurting the State of his Mother during her Life. I do give alfo to my dear Wife my Stuff appertaining to *Wanfted*, as alfo the Moyety of the Stuff at *Leicefter* Houfe. I do defire alfo, that there may be fome Stuff provided for *Langley*. And therefore I do appoint all fuch Hangings and Stuff as I have over with me to be fent and kept at *Langley*, and there left as well for the Ufe of my Wife, as to the Owner of that Houfe after her, as alfo to leave five hundreth Pounds Worth of Veffell and Plate, to fuch as fhall be left mine Heir at her Death, to that Houfe. *Item*, that all other Plate and Jewels I give to my dear Wife, fuch Parcels excepted, as I do hereby give to my Overfeers and Friends. And for my Overfeers, I doe hereby appoint and heartily defire them, that they will for the long good Will between us, take it upon them, and to help, affift, and comfort, my dear and poor difconfolate Wife ; Sir *Chriftopher Hatton* Lord Chancellor of *England*, my loving Brother the Earl of *Warwick*, and my very good Lord and Friend the Lord *Howard* High Admiral of *England* ; trufting, that, as they will not deny my Requeft, fo they will be carefull to help my poor Wife for the Performance of this my laft Will and Teftament, who I know fhall need the good Favours and Affiftance of my good Friends, and whom I make my fole Executrix. Not doubting but they fhall find her willing every Way to the utmoft of her Power, to do all I have committed to her Charge, not thinking good to trouble any other of my Friends, but her-felf, with my hard and broken Eftate, being I know not how many Thoufand, above Twenty in Debt ; and, at this prefent, not having in the World five hundreth Pounds towards it. And the harder will her Cafe be, if I receive not fuch Debts, as are here due to me by the *States*, which I much fear ; but I have appointed Lands to be fold, and fome Leafes I leave to my Wife, to fee how all, with all that I have left her to pay my Debts, which God grant to
the

the good Sattisfaction of my Creditors. And albeit I am not fo able as willing to leave better Remembrances to their Lordfhips, yet defiring them to take a Remembrance of their faithfull Friend in good Part, I do fend them each a poor Token. To my Lord Chancellor, mine old dear Friend, I do give one of my greateft Bafons and Ewers gilt, with my beft George and Garter, not doubting, but he fhall fhortly enjoy the Wearing of it, and one of his Armors he gave me. To my dear and noble Brother I leave to him, *firft*, as dear an Affection as ever Brother bare to other. And, for a Remembrance, I fend him a Cup of Gold which my old Friend my Lord of *Pembroke* gave me, and a George, which hath the *French* Order and the *Englifh* in one, with a plain Gold Chain at it. This Token he muft keep in Remembrance, that his Brother was of both the Orders, and not only fo, but alfo almoft the oldeft of both the Orders in both the Realms. But what is this but Vanity, and too much Vanity for me now to remember them ? But my laft and beft Token to him fhall be, to prefent a faithfull Sifter and Handmaid to him, whilft you both live, which I pray God may be many Years together. To my Lord Admirall, whom I have found a moft noble Friend, a fair gilt Bafon and Ewer, with a fair Garter of ragged Staves, my beft Sword, my beft Horfe, with the fineft Furniture to him, and my faireft Piece, and Cafe of Piftolls. To my dear Sifter of *Warwick*, a fair Cup of one hundreth Marks. To my good Son in Law the Earl of *Effex*, the beft Armour I have, one my Lord Chancellor gave me, two my beft Horfes, with a George and Garter, in Hope he fhall wear it fhortly. To my dear Sifter the Countefs of *Huntingdon*, one Ring with Diamonds, and a fair little Salt of Gold. To my Lord Treafurer a faire ftanding Cup. To my Lord Chamberlaine, a George with a Chain. To my Lord *North*, a Bafon and Ewer of forty Pounds. To my Father in Law Sir *Francis Knolls*, a fair Cup. To my Brother Sir *William Knolls*, a Ring and a Horfe, with a fair Furniture and a Cafe of Piftolls. To my Brother *Francis*, I do bequeath a hundreth Pounds in Money. To Sir *Thomas Hennage*, my good old Friend, fome Jewel, or Plate of forty Pounds Value. For my Servants, I will fet down in a Bill under my Hand what I will have done for them, for I know you my Executrix fhall be hardly able to do for them, yet do I truft to fattisfie moft of them, and that you will be as good as you may be able to the reft. *Memorandum*, That wheare I made *Gooderous* a Leafe of *Woodgrange*, there be certain Things to be amended, or elfe the Leafe will be Nothing worth to him ; which Thing of *Woodgrange* I commit to your Charge and Vfe, till *Robert* do come to Years to have *Alderfbrooke*, and then my Will is, he have it ; if he dye before, then yourfelf my Wife, during your Life, to enjoy it. And I will that he have at that Time alfo *Hamefrithe*, and certain Grounds I bought for Years, of *Humins*, lying in *Barkeking*, which will ferve him for Hey at *Alderfbrooke*. All which alfo if he dye before thofe Years, to return to my Wife during her Life. Ended the fifth Day of *July*, 1587. R. *Leicefter*.

Item, I do give the Dwelling, during his Life, in *Alderfbrooke*, to *Burgane*, my Secretarie, with fo much Ground as is about it, to the yearly Value of fifty Pounds, untill he be provided of fome other Thing to as good a Value, or that my bafe Son *Robert Dudley* do place him either in the Houfe at *Highgate*, or elfewhere, to the Contentation of the faid *Burgane*, with as much and as good in Profitt as the other is. This was added by me the laft of *September*, 1587. R. *Leicefter*.

The *Probat.* bears Date, 6 *Sept.* 1588, and Adminiftration was granted to the Lady *Lettice* Countefs of *Leicefter* his Relict, and Executrix.

It may be here proper to obferve, that the Lands mentioned in his Will for the Maintenance of two Schollars at *Vniverfity* College in *Oxford*, forever ; are at *Armftrey*, and *Cavilliock*, in *South-Wales*, in the Occupation of *Valentine Hughs*, Efq. and are now lett at 140 *l. per Ann.* and the Mannors and Lands, belonging to the Hofpital at *Warwick*, are fo much increafed, fince the Death of the Founder, that the Place of a poor Brother (of which there are twelve) is now worth near 40 *l. per Ann.* each. And the Mafterfhip of the faid Hofpital, with the Living of *Hampton* in *Arden* annexed, is 250 *l. per Ann.* Which Schollars of *Vniverfity* College in *Oxford*; as alfo the *Mafter*, and Brethren of the aforefaid Hofpital, are named and appointed, by Dame *Mary Sherard*, Wife of Sir *Brownlow Sherard*, Bart. and *Elifabeth Perry*, Wife of *William Perry*, Efq. The faid Dame *Mary*, and *Elifabeth*, becoming the right Heirs of the Founder, on the Death of their Uncle *John Sidney* Earl of *Leicefter*, in 1737 [x]; and who as fuch, appointed (in the Life-time of *Joceline*, the laft Earl of *Leicefter*) the Reverend Mr. *Edward Tart*, the prefent *Mafter* thereof.

The Brethren wear the Livery of the faid Earl of *Leicefter*, and his Heirs, *viz. a blew Gown, embroidered on the Sleeve with the Bear and ragged Staff, Silver.*

Having now brought to a Period the Male Line of the *Dudley*'s, I proceed to treat of the Defcendants of Lady *Mary Dudley*, the Wife of Sir *Henry Sidney*, Knight of the Garter, and the only Child of *John* Duke of *Northumberland*, that left Iffue, in whofe Pofterity, the Rights of her Family centered.

Which, Sir *Henry Sidney*, was the only Son and Heir of Sir *William Sidney*, Knight Banneret, who being a Perfon of great Note in his Time, I fhall give fome Account of him. He was the eldeft Son and Heir of *Nicholas Sidney*, Efq; lineally defcended from Sir *William Sidney*, Knight, Chamberlain to King *Henry the Second*, with whom he came from *Anjou*. Which *Henry*, before his Acceffion to the Crown, bearing the Title of Duke of *Normandy*, and Earl of *Anjou* [y], grants and confirms to the faid *William de Sidne*, *Militi* (fo wrote in the Grant) the Mannor of *Sutton*, with the Appurtenances, to him and to his Heirs in Fee, by the Service of one Knight's Fee. *Teft. Cam. R. Com. de Clara*, and others; without any Date, fealed with the Print of a Man in Armour on Horfeback, on both Sides the Seal: Alfo, in [z] another Grant, he is wrote *Willielmus de Sidnei Camer. Dni. Reg.* whereby he gave to *Roger Sidnei*, his Son, and his Heirs, all his Lands of *Cesford*, and *Lelleford*, with the Appurtenances. *Teft. Waranio Saccavilla*, *Henr. de Neuburghe*, *&c.* without Date. Sealed with a Man in Armour on Horfeback.

In the 10th Year of King *John*, 1208 [a], Sir *Simon de Sidnei*, and *Beatrice* his Wife, on the Eve of St. *Matthew* the Apoftle, acknowledge to have received of the Abbat and Convent of *Lewes* in *Suffex*, two Marks, due from the faid Abbat at *Michaelmas* that Year. In Witnefs whereof, they have put the Seal of *William de la Mare*, their Brother. To this is appendant a round Piece of Pafte, about 2 Inches and a Half, and thereon the Print of a Man on Horfeback compleatly armed.

All our Genealogifts agree, and the Records of the Family prove, that the faid Sir *William Sidney*, Knight Banneret, was defcended from them, fo that I fhall only proceed to relate what I find memorable of him.

In 2 *Henry* VIII, being one of the Efquires of the King's Houfe (as *Stow* relates [b]) he was one of the Commanders of thofe Forces, fent under the Command of *Thomas* Lord *Darcy*, in Aid of the King of *Aragon* and *Caftile*, againft the *Moors*. And, when the Lord *Darcy* failed for *England*, obtaining Leave of him to fee the Court of *Spain*, he, with *Henry Guilford*, and *Wefton Brown*, Efqs; went to *Madrid*, where they were highly entertained by the King, who conferred the Honour of Knighthood on *Guilford*, and *Brown*; but *William Sidncie* fo excufed himfelf, as *Hollinfhed* writes, that he was not knighted [c]. And, when they had fojourned there a While, they took their Leave of the King and Queen, and returned through *France* into *England*.

In 4 *Henry* VIII, the King having prepared a Fleet to cruife on the Coaft of *France*, the Command of them was given to Sir *Anthony Oughtred*, Sir *Edward*

---

[x] Vide Writ of Mandamus iffued from the Court of King's Bench, July 7, 1742. 16 Geo. II.
[y] Ex Orig. Charta apud Penfhurft.   [z] Orig. Charta, Ibid.   [a] Ex Orig. apud Penfhurft.
[b] Chron. p. 488.   [c] Hollinfh. Chron. p. 810.

I

Ichingham [c],

Ichingham [d], and this *William Sidenie*, with Orders to join the Admiral before the *Isle of Wight* ; on which Junction, the King himself came to *Portsmouth*, to see his Navy together, and gave them a Banquet before they set Sail. And, the *French* preparing a great Fleet from *Brest*, an Engagement ensued on the 10th of *August* in the Bay of *Britany*, wherein the *French* fled. Also, in *March* following, a great Fleet being fitted out, this [e] *William Sidnei* was again one of the principal Commanders ; and had then [f] the Honour of Knighthood conferred on him, for his valiant Deportment, being in the Attempt made on Prior *John* and the *French* Fleet in the Haven of *Brest*, in which the Lord *Howard*, Lord High-Admiral, was drowned. And, before the End of that Year [g], he is wrote Sir *William Sidneie*, Knight, and commanded in the Right Wing of the Army under the Earl of *Surry*, who obtained that great Victory over the *Scots* at *Flodden* Field, when *James the Fourth*, their King, was slain ; and, for his Valour [h], was then made a Banneret. In Consideration of these Services, 20 *July*, 5 *Henry* VIII [i], the King grants to Sir *William Sidney*, Knight, an Annuity of 50 Marks *per Ann.* during his Life.

In 6 *Henry* VIII, he accompanied the Duke of *Suffolk*, the Marquis of *Dorset*, and his four Brethren, the Lord *Clinton*, Sir *Edward Nevile*, Sir *Giles Capel*, and Sir *Thomas Cheney*, to *Paris* [k], there to make Proof of their Skill in Arms, against the Dauphin of *France*, and nine other select Persons, whom he had taken for his Assistants at those solemn Justs he had proclaimed for all Comers, being Gentlemen of *Name* and *Armes*, to be performed on the Coronation of the Princess *Mary* (King *Henry the Eighth*'s Sister) then lately married to *Lewis the Twelfth*, King of *France* : Whereupon they landed at *Calais*, all in green Coats and Hoods, with Intent not to discover themselves till their Arrival at *Paris*. And, being at that grand Solemnity at the Coronation, the 5th of *November*, in the Monastery of St. *Dennis* in *France*, he was also at the Justs began on the 7th of *November*, which continued for 3 Days, wherein 300 and 5 Men of *Armes* ran five Courses with sharp Spears, and the *English* (as *Stow* and *Hollingshed* write) performed as well as the best, not only in the Justs, but also in the Turney and Barriers.

In 12 *Henry* VIII, on the Going over of the King and Queen, with great State into *France*, to the Meeting of King *Francis*, betwixt *Guisnes* and *Ardes*, and Justs being thereupon held for 14 Days, he was one [l] in the 2d Band of the *English*, at those martial Exercises.

In 15 *Henry* VIII, he was one of the principal Commanders of those Forces sent into *France*, under the Duke of *Suffolk* ; in which Year, several Places of great Strength were taken from the Enemy by the *English*, who remained in the Field till the latter End of *November*, when the Hardness of the Season induced the Duke of *Suffolk* to return to *Calais*. The King, who had prepared 6000 Men to be sent to him, was somewhat displeased at the Breaking up of his Army, without his Orders ; but, hearing (as my Author writes [n]) *the reasonable Excuses of the Duke and his Captains, he was shortly after pacified, and after remaining at* Calais *a certain Time, their Friends having asswaged the King's Displeasure, they returned, and were received in as much Favour as before.*

In 16 *Henry* VIII, before the Feast of *Christmas* [o], he was also one of those Challengers in Feats of Arms, which was proclaimed by *Windsor* Herald, and performed before the King at the *Tilt-yard* at *Greenwich*, who kept his *Christmas* there with great Mirth and princely Pastime ; but *Francis Sidneie* is mentioned in *Hollinshed*, which must be mistaken for this Sir *William Sidney*, as there was not any Person of that Name of *Francis*.

After this, I find no further Mention of him in the Reign of King *Henry the Eighth*, except that he was in Nomination [p] for one of the Knights of the Gar-

[d] Hollinsh. Chron p. 815. n. 30.　　[e] Ibid. p. 816. n. 30. a.　　[f] Nom. Equit. in Bibl. Cotton. Claudius, C. 3.　　[g] Hollinshed, p. 826, a. and Stow, p. 492.　　[h] Nom. Equit. præd.　　[i] Pat. [c] H. VIII. p. 2.　　[k] Stow's Chron. p. 496. and Hollinshed, p. 833, 834.　　[l] Stow's Annals, p. 508.　　[m] Hollinshed, p. 879. n. 60.　　[n] Ibid. p. 881. n. 40 and 50.　　[o] Ibid. p. 883.　　[p] Anstis's Regist. of the Garter, Vol. 2. p. 446, & seq.

ter, 23 *April*, 33 *Henry* VIII, and, in all succeeding Chapters of that most noble Order, in this King's Reign. Also, in 33 *Henry* VIII, the King grants to Sir *William Sydney*, Knight, and *Anne* his Wife, and his Heirs [q], the Scite of the late Monastery of *Robertsbridge*, and the Mannors of *Robertsbridge, Posingworth, Warde, Sandore, Sutton, Woodrove, Lamberherst, Vdyam, Horsemounden,* and *Maddersham,* and the Rectories of *Salehurst, Mountfield,* and *Vdymer,* in *Kent* and *Sussex.* All which were granted in Exchange with the King, for the Mannors of *Kingston upon Hull,* and *Myton,* with divers other Lands of good Value, within the Counties of *York* and *Lincoln.* And, 3 *June,* 37 *Henry* VIII [r], obtained a Grant of Free-Warren, and a Market and Fair at *Robertsbridge,* 14 *Sept.*

This Sir *William Sydney* [s] was Tutor and Chamberlain, and Steward of the Houshold to King *Edward the Sixth,* from the Time of his Birth to his Coronation. And, on the Deaths of *Henry* Duke of *Suffolk,* and the Lord *Charles Brandon* his Brother, 14 *July,* 5 *Edw.* VI, he was found to be one of their Cousins and Coheirs, and was at that Time 70 Years of Age, and, with the other Coheirs, petitioned the King, for Livery of the Lands they died seized of, *viz.* Son of *Nicholas Sydney,* Esq; by *Anne* his Wife, Daughter of Sir *William Brandon,* Knight, and Sister to Sir *William Brandon,* Knight, Father to *Charles* Duke of *Suffolk,* Father of the said *Henry* Duke of *Suffolk,* and Lord *Charles Brandon* his Brother.

Which Sir *William Brandon,* Knight, 1st named [t], married *Elisabeth,* Daughter to Sir *Robert Wingfield,* Knight, by *Elisabeth* his Wife, Daughter of Sir *Robert Gousell,* Knight, by *Elisabeth* his Wife, Daughter and Heir of Sir *John Fitz Allan,* Knight (by *Eleanor* his Wife, Daughter and Heir of *John,* Lord *Maltravers*) who was Brother of *Richard Fitz Allan,* Earl of *Arundel,* by *Eleanor* his Wife, Sister to *Henry,* the first Duke of *Lancaster* ; whose Son, *Edmund Fitz Allan,* Earl of *Arundel,* married *Alice,* Sister and Heir of *John,* Earl of *Warren,* who derived his Descent from *William,* Earl *Warren,* and of *Surry,* who had to Wife *Gundreda,* Daughter of *Baldwin,* Earl of *Flanders,* who had also another Daughter, married to *William,* Duke of *Normandy.* And the said Sir *William Brandon* also derived his Descent from the King of *Scotland,* by the Marriage of *John Fitz Allan,* Earl of *Arundel,* with *Isabel,* Daughter of *William de Albini,* Earl of *Arundel,* who was the Grandson of *William de Albini,* Earl of *Arundel,* by *Alice,* Daughter of *Alexander,* King of *Scots* : And the said *William* was the Son of *William,* Earl of *Arundel,* by *Alice,* Widow of King *Henry the First,* and Daughter of *Geffery,* Earl of *Brussels,* and Duke of *Brabant,* by his Wife, who was a Daughter of the Emperor of *Germany* the 2d. So that, by this Match with the *Brandons,* the *Sidneys* are very nobly descended.

Sir *William Sidney* married [u] *Anne,* Daughter of Sir *Hugh Pagenham,* Knight, the Relict of *Thomas Fitz William,* Son and Heir of Sir *Thomas Fitz William,* and elder Brother of *William,* Earl of *Southampton,* who died without Issue in 34 *Hen.* VIII. She died before him, in the Reign of King *Henry the Eighth,* and was buried in St. *Peter*'s Church, where a Monument, with her Effigies before a Desk, and a Book on it, was erected to her Memory. Out of her Mouth proceeds a Label, with these Words, *Sancta Trinitas, unus Deus, miserere nobis.* There is also the Figure of the Virgin *Mary,* with our Saviour on the Cross, and of two Sons, and seven Daughters. Underneath is this Inscription:

> Of your Charitie pray for the Soule of Lady *Anne* Sidney, late Wife of Sir *William Sidney,* Knight, Steward of the Right Honorable Houshold of the most high and most renowned Prince *Edward.* The which Lady *Anne* deceased the XXII Daye of *October,* in the Yere of our Lord God M. CCCCC. XLIIII. On whose Soul *Jesu* have Mercy.

q Privat. Sigill. 33 H. VIII. & ex Evident. apud Penshurst.   r Pat. 37 H. VIII. apud Penshurst.   s Philpot's Kent. p. 270. & Ex Tumulo apud Penshurst.   t Ex Stemmate apud Penshurst, deducing the Sydneys through the Brandons from William the Conqueror, &c.   u Ibid.

I

Only

Only *Henry*, the eldeſt Son, ſurvived to Maturity, and four Daughters. 1. *Mary*, wedded to Sir *William Dormer*, of *Ayſcot* in *Buckinghamſhire*, Knight, and Steward of the Honour of *Ampthill* in *Bedfordſhire* ʷ, by whom he had Iſſue two Daughters ; *Anne*, married to Sir *William Hungerford*, of *Farley* Caſtle in Com. *Wilts*, Knight, Son and Heir of *Walter*, Lord *Hungerford*, who had Iſſue by her three Daughters, his Coheirs ; *Suſan* married to *Michael Ernſey*, of *Cannings* in Com. *Wilts*, Eſq; *Lucia* to Sir *John St. John*, of *Lidiard*, in the ſame County, Anceſtor to the preſent Lord Viſcount *St. John* ; and *Jane* to Sir *John Kerne*, of the County of *Glamorgan*, Knight. The 2d Daughter of Sir *William Dormer*, was married to Don *Gomes Suares de Figuerou Cerdova*, Duke of *Feria* in *Spain*, by whom ſhe had Iſſue Don *Lorenzo de Figueroa*, Duke of *Feria*, Anceſtor to the Duke of *Feria* in *Spain*. There are Letters at *Penſhurſt*, to Sir *Henry Sidney* his Uncle, both from the Duke and Ducheſs of *Feria*, which will be publiſhed in the Collection of Letters.

2. *Lucy*, the Wife of Sir *James Harrington*, of *Exton* in *Rutlandſhire*, Knight ˣ, who had Iſſue by her three Sons, Sir *John*, Sir *Henry*, and Sir *James Harrington* ; and ſeveral Daughters. Sir *John Harrington*, the Eldeſt ʸ, was created Lord *Harrington of Exton* in the 1ſt Year of King *James the Firſt*, and had the Tuition of the Lady *Eliſabeth*, Daughter to King *James*, till her Marriage with *Frederick*, Count *Palatine* of the *Rhine* ; after which, going over with her, he died at *Wormes*, in *Germany*, 24 *Auguſt*, 1613. He left Iſſue, by *Anne* his Wife, Daughter and Heir to *Robert Kelway*, Eſq; *John*, Lord *Harrington*, who died unmarried at *Kew*, in *Surry*, 27 *February*, 161¾, and two Daughters ; *Lucy*, married to *Edward Ruſſel*, Earl of *Bedford*, but died without Iſſue by him, *An.* 1628. *Frances*, youngeſt Daughter, was married to Sir *Robert Chicheſter*, Knight of the *Bath*, who had Iſſue by her *Anne*, wedded to *Thomas*, Lord *Bruce*, Father to *Thomas*, Earl of *Aileſbury*, and dying 22 *March*, 1627, was buried at *Exton*.

Of the Daughters of Sir *James Harrington*, by *Lucy Sidney* his Wife, *Eliſabeth*, the Eldeſt, was married to Sir *Edward Montagu* of *Boughton*, in Com. *Northamp.* Knight, by whom ſhe had Iſſue ſix Sons ; *Edward*, the firſt Lord *Montagu* of *Boughton*, Anceſtor to *John*, the preſent Duke of *Montagu*. And, from Sir *Henry Montagu*, the third Son, are deſcended *Robert*, the preſent Duke of *Mancheſter*, *George*, Earl of *Hallifax*, and others. Alſo, from the ſixth Son, Sir *Sidney Montagu*, is deſcended *John*, the preſent Earl of *Sandwich*, the honourable *Edward Wortley*, Eſq; and others. *Frances*, 2d Daughter, was married to Sir *William Lee*, Knight.

Margaret, 3d Daughter, was wedded to Don *Benito Hiſpano*, of the Family of the Duke of *Fantaſgo*, in *Spain*.

Catharine, 4th Daughter, was the Wife of Sir *Edward Dimock*, Knight, Champion of *England*.

Mary, 5th Daughter, was married to Sir *Edward Wingfield*, Knight.

Mabell, 6th Daughter, was wedded to Sir *Andrew Noell*, Knight, Anceſtor to the right Honourable *Baptiſt Noel*, now Earl of *Gainſborough*.

Sarah, 7th Daughter, was the Wife of *Francis*, Lord *Haſtings*, who died in the Life-time of his Father, *Henry*, Earl of *Huntingdon*, and Anceſtor to the preſent Earl of *Huntingdon*.

Theodoſia, youngeſt Daughter, was married to *Edward* Lord *Dudley*.

Anne, 3d Daughter of Sir *William Sidney*, was married to Sir *William Fitz William*, of *Milton*, in Com. *Northamp.* Knight, Treaſurer of Wars in *Ireland*, and Lord Deputy of that Realm, in the Reign of Queen *Eliſabeth*, and had Iſſue by her Sir *William Fitz William*, Knight, Anceſtor to *John*, Earl *Fitz William*, of the Kingdom of *Ireland*, and Baron of *Milton*, in the Kingdom of *England*. Alſo three Daughters, of which *Philippa*, the 2d, was married to Sir *Thomas Coningſby*, of *Hampton* Court, in *Herefordſhire*, Knight, Anceſtor to *Margaret*, the preſent Counteſs of *Coningſby* ; and *Margaret*, the Youngeſt,

---

ʷ Ex Stemmate de Famil. Sydney, apud Penſhurſt. ˣ Ex Stemmate de Harrington, & Inſcript. Tumuli apud Exton in Com. Rutl. ʸ Pat. 1, Jac. 1, p. 14.

was wedded to *John Byron*, Efq; Son and Heir to Sir *John Byron* of *Clayton*, in the County of *Lancaster*, Knight, lineal Anceftor to *William*, now Lord *Byron*.

Frances, 4th Daughter of Sir *William Sidney*, was married to *Thomas Ratcliff*, Earl of *Suffex*, whom fhe furvived, dying at *Bermondfey*, *March* the 9th, and was buried, in great Pomp, at *Weftminfter*, the 15th of *April*, 1589, leaving no Iffue. By her laft Will, bearing Date z 6 *December* 1588 (31 *Elif.*) fhe bequeathed her Body to be buried in the Mynfter near unto the Collegiate Church of St. *Peter* in *Weftminfter*, and, if her Tomb fhould not be finifhed in her Life-time, her Executors fhould beftow 200 *l.* or more, if Need required, for the Making thereof, with her Picture in Alabafter Stone, and other Garnifhing ; and a Superfcription be engraven thereon, declaring her Name and Pedigree, and that fhe was the Wife of *Thomas*, late Earl of *Suffex*. She alfo willed that her Executors fhould purchafe a perpetual Annuity of 20 *l.* a Year, to the Ufe of a godly and learned Preacher, who for, and in her Name, fhould read two Lectures in Divinity, weekly, every Week, for ever, in the faid Church, on fuch feveral Days, as no other Sermons or Lectures were to be read there. Which Preacher to be admitted, by the Dean of the faid Church of St. *Peter* at *Weftminfter*, for the Time being. And that her Executors alfo beftow one-hundred Pounds amongft poor and godly Preachers in *London*, and the Suburbs thereof.

And alfo where, fithence the Deceafe of my faid late Lord, the Earl of *Suffex*, I have, in Devotion and Charity, purpofed to make, and erect fome goodly and Godly Monument, for the Maintenance of good Learning. And, to that Intent, have yearly gathered, and deducted out of my Revenues, fo much as conveniently I could. I do therefore now, in Accomplifhment and Performance of the fame my charitable Pretence, what, with the ready Money which I have fo yearly referved, and with a certain Portion of Plate, and other Things which I have purpofely left, Will and ordein, that my Executors fhall beftow and employ the Sume of five-thoufand Pounds, over and befides all fuch my Goods, as in this my prefent Will remain unbequeathed, for the Erection of a new Colledge, in the Univerfity of *Cambridge*, to be called the *Lady* Frances Sydney Suffex *Colledge*, and Purchafing fome competent Lands, for the Maintaining of a Mafter, and of ten Fellows, and twenty Schollars, Students there, according to the laudable Cuftom of the faid Univerfity ; if the faid 5000 *l.* and the Remainder of her Goods unbequeathed will thereunto extend. But if, by the Judgment of her Executors, it be thought not fufficient to erect and found a new College in her Name, and for the Maintenance thereof, as fhe intended, then that the faid 5000 *l.* &c. be employed for the Enlarging of *Clare* Hall, in the faid Univerfity of *Cambridge*, and for Purchafing fo much Lands, to be annexed to the faid College, or Hall, for ever, for the Maintenance of fo many Schollars there, according to the Rates, &c. then ufed, in the faid Univerfity. Which College, from thenceforth, fhall be called, Clare, *and Lady* Frances Sydney Suffex College, *or Hall*.

She bequeaths to her welbeloved Nephew, Sir *Robert Sydney*, Knight, a ftanding Tefterne of crimfon Velvet, outer Vallance and inner Vallance, and Bafes below, of crimfon Velvet, all cut with Cloth of Silver, richly embroidered in Gold, with her Arms, and five Curtains of crimfon Tafeta, ftriped with filver Lace, a Quilt of crimfon Satten, embroidered with Scollop Shells of Cloth of Silver. Alfo much other rich Furniture, therein mentioned, being in feveral Rooms. Likewife all her Plate, Jewels, &c. not bequeathed, among which was a Cup of Gold, weighing, with the Cover, 26 Ounces, with a Porcupine ftanding on the Top. Alfo a Porcupine, with a Roll of Gold, fet with Pearl, being her faid Nephews Arms and hers. She bequeaths to Sir *William Fitz William*, Knight, 200 *l.* and to her Sifter, the Lady *Fitz-William*, feveral Jewels and Furniture ; and to her Nephew, *John Fitz William*, 40 *l.* to make him a Chaine. To her Nephew, Sir *John Harrington*,

---

z Ex Regiftr. vocat. Leicefter, in Cur. Prærog, Cant. qu. 82.

and his Lady, much Furniture and Jewels. To her Niece, the Lady *Monta-gu*, a trained Gown of black Velvet, embroidered all over with broken Trees, a large Kirtle, embroidered, and a Suit of Aglets inamelled, with a Suit of Buttons, with Garnets, and Pearls of 120. And to her Nephew, *Edward Montagu*, a Suit of Hangings, of the Story of *Holifernes* and *Judith*, and much rich Furniture, in the Chamber thereto belonging ; also all her filver Plate belonging to her Cufhion Cloath, and the Plate in her Cupboard in her Bedchamber, with a Pair of gilt Andirons, with great Bowls at the Feet, like Lions Heads.

She appoints Executors, her Nephew, Sir *John Harrington*, her Coufin, Mr. *Henry Bofvil*, her welbeloved Friend, Mr. *Bond*, Dr. in Divinity, for the great Virtue fhe had always conceived in him ; her welbeloved Friend, Mr. *Robert Forth*, Dr. of the Civil Law, for the like great Virtue fhe had perceived of his fair Dealing ; her good Friend, Mr. *Gabriel Goodman*, Dr. in Divinity, for his godly and virtuous Inclination. And, for the better Execution of this her laft Will and Teftament, fhe conftitutes her honourable good Friend, the Earl of *Kent*, for the great Honour, Wifdom, Zeal in Religion and Virtue, which is noted in him, the chief and principal Executor of the fame, to whom fhe bequeaths, as a fpecial Legacy, her fair Bafon and Ewer, wrought richly with Stories enamelled, weighing 100, 60, and 17 Ounces ; and a Cup of Gold to be bought for him, to the Value of 100 *l.* And appoints her good Friend, the Lord Archbifhop of *Canterbury* Supervifor, and bequeaths to him feveral Pieces of her Plate.

The beforementioned Sir *William Sydney*, obtained in 6 *Edw.* VI, Letters Patent [a] under the Great Seal, for good Services done, in the Offices of Chamberlain, and Chief Steward of the Houfhold, to him the King, in the Lifetime of his Father, King *Henry the Eighth*, to his Death, *&c.* Of all that his Mannor of *Penfhurft*, with Lands called *Court Lands*, and *South Park*, in the Parifhes of *Penfhurft*, and *Chedingftone*, in Poffeffion of *Anthony Nevill*, Efq; The Lands, called the *Green*, before the Gate, rough Garden, and the Clofe adjoining to the Churchyard of *Penfhurft*, and divers Lands, called *Broad Meads*, and 11 Acres of Meadow in *Marchop*, late in the Tenure of Sir *Ralph Fane*, Knight, of *Felony* attainted and convicted, deceafed. And all thofe Lands, called *Hawfghfelde*, the *Hernrarie*, or lower Ground, the Horfe Pafture, and the great Conyberry Field. And all thofe Lands near the Palace of *Penfhurft*, abutting on Lands called *Cleydons*. And a Meffuage called *Well Place*, and the nether Lodge, with two Gardens. And certain Edifices and Lands, called *Martens*, *Eylond*, and *Bifhops Eylond*, late Parcel of the Park of *Penfhurft*, *Leigh*, and *Chedingftone*, containing, by Eftimation, 379 Acres. And thofe Lands called *Afhore*, late Parcel of the Park of *Penfhurft*, lying in *Penfhurft*, *Bidborough*, *Leigh*, and *Tunbridge*, containing 300 Acres ; with 26 Acres, late Parcel of the Park of *Northlands*, and divers other in *Penfhurft*, *Bidborough*, &c. particularly mentioned. And the Capital Meffuage, or Palace of *Penfhurft*, with the Park called *Northlands* Park, containing 250 Acres. Alfo all that Mannor of *Yenfelde*, alias *Enfelde*, with the Appurtenances, in the Tenure of Sir *George Harper*, Knight ; the King's Lands and Rents in *Cepham* and *Hawden*, thofe Meadows and Pafture Lands, called *Lee Park*, alias, the *North Park of* Leigh, in the Parifh of *Leigh*, containing 300 Acres. And the Advowfon and Right of Patronage of the Church and Rectory of *Cowden*, with all their Appurtenances in the faid Town and Parifhes, or Hamlets, of *Penfhurft*, *Chedingftone*, *Leigh*, *Bidborowe*, *Tunbridge*, *Spelhurft*, *Cepham*, *Hawden*, *Hever*, *Sevenocke*, and *Cowden*, or elfewhere, in the County of *Kent*, Parcel of the Poffeffion of the faid Sir *Ralph Fane*, Knight ; and Free Warren, *&c*, in the Parks aforefaid. And all Meffuages, Lands, Tenements, Commons, Woods, Reverfions, Services, Advowfions, *&c.* and Rights of Patronage of Churches, Chapels, Chanteries, Tithes, Glebes, Courts-leet, View of Frank Pledge, *&c.* Fifheries, *&c.*

[a] Pat 25, Apr. 6 E. VI, 1552, apud Penfhurft.

and all other Rights thereto belonging. And all Trees, Woods, &c. all Reverfions, Rents, and yearly Profits, &c. as fully, and in as ample Manner, as the faid Sir *Ralph Fane*, Knight, the late Duke of *Buckingham*, the late Earl of *Wiltſhire*, or any of them, or of their Anceſtors, had and enjoyed the ſame ; and as fully as the ſame came to the King, by Reaſon of the Attainder, &c. of the faid Sir *Ralph Fane*, or to his late Father, by the Attainder of the ſaid late Duke of *Buckingham*, or ought to have come. To hold to the faid Sir *William Sidney*, his Heirs and Affigns, for ever. And the King, at the ſame Time, grants to the faid Sir *William Sidney* all Goods, Chattels, Houſehold Stuff, &c. which were then, or on the 2d of *October*, or afterwards, were in, or about the faid Capital Manſion of *Penſhurſt*, or in the faid Mannor, Parks, and Premiſes, and which were late the faid Sir *Ralph Fane*'s ; to hold to the faid Sir *William Sidney*, of the King's Gift, without Account. As alſo all the Iſſues, Rents, &c. from the Time of the Attainder of the faid Sir *Ralph Fane*, *viz.* on the 27th of *January* laſt paſt.

He reſided moſtly at *Baynard*'s Caſtle, in *London*, where he made his laſt Will, bearing [b] Date the 8th of *December*, 1548, the 2d of *Edward the Sixth*, and bequeathed his Body to be buried in the Chapel of our Lady, in the North Iſle of the Collegiate Church of St. *Anthony*, in *London*, if he died in that City, or the Suburbs thereof ; but if in any other Place, that then his Body ſhould be buried in the Pariſh Church thereto belonging. By which Will it appears, that he was poſſeſſed of a great Eſtate in the Counties of *Kent*, *Suſſex*, and *Southampton*, which he left to *Henry Sidney*, his Son and Heir, whom he conſtituted his Executor, with *Thomas White*, Eſq; and orders them to give one-hundred Pounds to the Poor, at his Deceaſe, and ſix Pounds, thirteen Shillings, and four Pence Yearly, for three Years, to be diſtributed as they think proper.

A raiſed Tomb, with an Arch over it, is erected to his Memory in the Chancel of the Church of *Penſhurſt*, and thereon engraved this Inſcription :

> Here lyethe Syr *Wylliam Sydney*, Knyght and Bannorett. Sometyme Chamberlen, and after Steward to the moſte Myghte & Famous Prynce Kynge *Edward* the VIth, in the Tyme of his being Prynce, & the fuſte of that Name, being Lord of the Manner of *Penſhurſte*. Who dyed the Xth Day Of *February*, in the VIIth Yere of the Reigne of Kynge *Edward* the VIth, and in the Yere of our Lord God A M[t]. fyve Hundred fiftie & three. On whoſe Soule Ieſu have Mercy.

On the Sides of this Inſcription, are Eſcutcheons of Arms of his 4 Daughters and their Huſbands ; and, over them, is engraven Sir *William Dormer Marie Sydney*, Sir *James Harrington Lucy Sydney*, Sir *William Fitz William Anne Sydney*, Sir *Thomas Ratcliff-Suſſex Frances Sydney*.

Round the Edges of the Tomb, is

I knowe that my Redemer liveth, & that I the laſt Daye ſhall ryſe from the Yearth, & ſhall be clad againe with myne owne Skinne, & in myne owne Fleſhe I ſhall ſe God, whom I my ſelfe ſhal ſe, and myne Eyes ſhal loke upon, and none other. This Hope is layd up in my Boſome.

Henry Sydney, his only ſurviving Son, was, from his Infancy [c], bred and brought up with King *Edward the Sixth*, who treated him with great Familiarity, even as a Companion, and was many Times his Bedfellow, having the Advantage of his Father's being Chamberlain and Steward to that Prince.

On the Acceſſion of King *Edward* to the Crown, he was then reputed, for his Virtues, fine Compoſition of Body, Gallantry, and Livelineſs of Spirit, the

---

[b] Ex Regiſtr. vocat Taſh, qu. 14, in Cur Prætog. Cant.   [c] Hollinſhed's Chron. p. 1548, & Caſtrat.

moſt

moſt compleat young Gentleman in the Court [d], and for the ſingular Love, and intire Affection, that virtuous and learned Prince had ever ſhewn him, he was made one of the four principal Gentlemen of his Privy-Chamber. And ſuch Delight had he in his modeſt and ingenious Converſation and Company, as he rarely gave him Leave to be abſent from him, and drew his laſt Breath in his Arms at *Greenwich*.

On the 11th of *Oct.* 1550, he [e] was knighted, with the great *William Cecil* (after Lord *Burghley*) and *Henry Nevile*, all three of the Privy-Chamber to the Sovereign ; and, immediately after, was ſent Ambaſſador into *France*, about very important Affairs, being at that Time not fully 1 and 20 Years of Age [f], and performed his Charge with that ſingular Spirit, Wiſdom, and Dexterity, as gained him great Commendation.

In 4 *Edw*. VI, he was [g] conſtituted chief Cup-Bearer to the King for Life ; and, 21 *Feb.* that Year, obtained the [h] Office of chief Cypherer to the King for Life, with a Fee of 50 Marks *per Ann.* and Power to appoint a Deputy. Alſo, in the ſame Year, 4 *Jan.* 4 *Edw*. VI, he and Sir *Henry Gates* were [i] Challengers at Tilt and Tournay, againſt the Lord *Fitz-Walter*, and 17 others, who ran ſix Courſes before the King, and were commended for their Accompliſhments therein.

In 5 *Edw*. VI, bearing the Title of one of the Gentlemen of the Sovereign's Privy-Chamber, he [k] accompanied the Marquis of *Northampton*, in his Legation with the Habit of the Order of the Garter, *&c.* to the *French* King *Henry the Second*. After his Return, he was married to the Lady *Mary Dudley*, eldeſt Daughter of *John* Earl of *Warwick*, then Lord High-Steward of the King's moſt honourable Houſhold, and Lord-Preſident of the King's Majeſty's moſt honourable Privy-Council ; which Titles he bears in the Indenture of Covenants [l] made with Sir *William Sydney*, Knight, concerning this Marriage ; dated in *May*, 5 *Edw*. VI, whereby the ſaid Earl of *Warwick* covenants to convey, *inter alia*, the Mannor, Manſion-Houſe, and Park of *Halden* in *Kent*, to the ſaid Sir *Henry Sydney*, and the Lady *Mary Dudley* (Daughter of the ſaid Earl) and to the Heirs of their two Bodyes, Remainder to Sir *Henry Sydney*, and the Heirs of his Body.

On the 10th of *April*, in 7 *Edw*. VI, the King, in Conſideration [m] of the good, true, faithful, and acceptable Services, of his beloved Servant, Sir *Henry Sydney*, Knight, one of the 4 principal Gentlemen of his Privy-Chamber, confers on him, during Life, the Office of Chief Steward of his Manſion and Mannor of *Otford*, in the County of *Kent*, with the Gardens, Orchards, *&c.* As alſo Chief Steward of the Honour of *Otford*, and Bailiff of the Mannors of *Otford*, *Graveſend*, and *Mylton*: And, the Office of Steward of his Woods of the Honour of *Otford*, and of the great Park of *Otford*: And, of the Office of Steward of the Mannor of *Swaneſcomb*, in the ſaid County of *Kent*: Which Office *George Brook*, Knight, Lord *Cobham*, lately had for Term of his Life, by Letters Patent under the Great Seal of his Court of Augmentations and Revenues, dated at *Weſtminſter*, 18 *Jan.* 3 *Edw*. VI, and ſurrendered to the ſaid Sir *Henry Sydney*, to be cancelled in *Chancery*. And the King further grants to the ſaid Sir *Henry Sydney*, Knight, the Office of Chief Steward of his Manſion of *Knoll*, in the ſaid County of *Kent*, with all Gardens, Orchards, *&c.* thereto belonging, as alſo Chief Steward of the Park of *Knoll*, with the Herbage and Paunage, and all Woods and Underwoods, *&c.* within the Mannor of *Knoll*. And the Office of Sub-Steward of the Mannor of *Knoll*, *&c.* which Sir *Robert Southwell* held for Term of his Life, with all Advantages, Commodities, and Emoluments thereunto belonging, and all Powers to appoint Deputyes to officiate for him ; for which he was to receive, as his Wages, of Steward of the Manſion of *Otford*, 10 *d. per Diem* ; and of the Gardens and Orchards, 4 *d. per*

[d] Hollinſhed's Chron. p. 1548, & Caſtrat.   [e] Burnet's Hiſt. Reformation in King Edward's Journal.   [f] Hollinſh. præd,   [g] Pat. 4 Edw. VI. p. 1.   [h] Bill. Sign. 4 Edw. VI.   [i] King Edward's Journal, præd.   [k] Aſhmole's Order of the Garter, p. 394.   [l] Ex Orig. Cart. 5 Edw. VI. apud Penſhurſt.   [m] Ex Orig. Pat. 7 Edw. VI. apud Penſhurſt.

Diem ;

Diem ; and for Chief Steward of the Honour of *Otford*, 6 *l.* 13 *s.* 4 *d.* and for the Office of Bailiff of the Mannor of *Otford*, 2 *d. per* Day ; and for *Gravesend* and *Mylton*, 4 *d. per* Day ; and for the Office of Steward of the Woods at *Otford*, 2 *d. per* Day ; and for the Gardens and Orchards, &c. 4 *d. per* Day ; and for the Office of Steward of the great Park at *Otford*, 6 *l.* 3 *s.* 4 *d.* and for the Office of Sub-Steward of the Honour of *Otford*, with the Mannor and View of frank Pledge, Courts-Leet, and Law-Days, the Fee of 6 *l. per Ann.* and for Sub-Steward of the Mannor of *Swanescomb*, 40 *s. per Ann.* And for the Office of Chief Steward of the Mansion of *Knoll*, and all the Gardens, Orchards, &c. 60 *s.* and 10 *d. per Ann.* and for the Office of Steward of the Park of *Knoll*, 6 *l.* 1 *s.* 8 *d. per Ann.* and of the Office of Steward of the Woods and Underwoods, within the Mannors of *Knoll*, 30 *s. per Ann.* and for the Office of Steward and Sub-Steward of the Courts, and View of frank Pledge to the said Mannor of *Knoll* belonging, 60 *s. per Ann.* To which Grant, Sir *Richard Sackvyle*, Knight (Chancellor of the Court of Augmentations) was a Witness ; at *Westminster*, 10 *April*, 7 *Edw.* VI.

18 *May*, 7 *Edw.* VI, he had a Licence to retain, over and above his menial Servants, fifty Persons, Gentlemen and Yeomen, and to give them his Livery Badge or Cognizance. And that the said fifty Persons, so retained, shall be discharged, and exonerated of all Forfeitures, Losses, or Penaltyes to the King, his Heirs, and Successors, by Force of any Statute, &c. Also pardons the said Sir *Henry Sydney* all and every Trespass, Forfeiture, Penaltye, Sume or Sumes of Money owing, or whatever was by him done or perpetrated, since the 25th of *January*, in the 1st Year of his Reign.

In the same Year [o], 4 *July*, 7 *Edw.* VI, (and but three Days before the King's Death) he obtained a Grant of the Mannor and Borough of *Wotton-Basset* in *Wiltshire* ; and was undoubtedly in such Esteem with that good King, and so close an Attendant upon him, that he died in his Arms, as beforementioned ; which it may justly be presumed was a great Grief to him, who was so highly in his Favour, that, if he had lived, his eminent Abilities could not failed to have advanced him to the highest Posts and Honours.

From whence I conjecture, that his Sorrow for the King his Master induced him to retire to his Seat at *Penshurst*, whereby he was not involved in the Calamities which befel the Duke of *Northumberland*, his Father-in-Law : And it's evident, Queen *Mary* was so well satisfied with his Conduct, that she conferred on him several Marks of her Favour.

In the 1st Year of her Reign, 28 *May* [p], she grants to him the Wardship and Marriage of *Robert Pakenham* ; and, on the 8th of *November* following, by Letters Patent under the Great Seal, she [q] ratifies and confirms the several Letters Patent granted to him, and his Father, Sir *William Sydney*, by King *Edward the Sixth* ; particularly the Letters Patent of 25 *April*, 6 *Edw.* VI, to Sir *William Sydney*, then deceased, of the Mannor of *Penseherste*, &c. as also, Grants of Lands in other Counties in Fee, by Letters Patent, dated 23 *June*, 7 *Edw.* VI. Also recites other Letters Patent of 21 *Feb.* 4 *Edw.* VI, of the Office of Chief Cypherer to the said Sir *Henry Sydney*, Knight, then *Henry Sydney*, Esq; And of 3 *April*, 7 *Edw.* VI, to Sir *Henry Sydney*, Knight, one of the four Knights of his Majesty's private Chamber, and one of the principal Gentlemen of the said Chamber, of the Office of *Otter Hunter*, for Life, in Reversion. And other Letters Patents of 10 *April*, 7 *Edw.* VI, of the Office of *Keeper* of the Capital Messuage or Mansion of the Mannor of *Otford* in *Kent*, with the Appurtenances ; and of the Office of Chief Steward of the Honour of *Otford*, Bailiff of the Mannor of *Otford*, Keeper of the great Park of *Otford*, and Sub-Steward of the Honour of *Otford*, and Steward of the Mannor of *Swannescomb*, and Keeper of the Capital Messuage of *Knoll*, and of all Gardens and Orchards thereto belonging, and Keeper of the Park of *Knoll*, and of all Woods and Underwoods in the Mannor of *Knoll*, and Chief Steward of the said Mannor, to hold the said Offices for Life. All

[n] Ex Origin. apud Penshurst.   [o] Bill. Sign. 7 Edw. VI.   [p] Bill. Sign. 1 Mar.   [q] Ibid.

I

which

which Offices the Queen confirmed to the faid Sir *Henry*. Alfo recites other
Letters Patent of 22 *April*, 6 *Edw.* VI, of a Demife to the faid Sir *Henry Sidney*,
his Executors, *&c.* of the Mannor of *Marfhefelde*, *&c.* in *Glocefterfhire*, for
39 Years, at 80 *l. per Ann.* Rent: Likewife other Letters Patent of 20 *Feb.*
7 *Edw.* VI, of the Mannor of *Wefton*, with the Appurtenances in *Suffolk*, to him,
his Executors, *&c.* for 31 Years, at the Rent of 91 *l.* 7 *s.* 1 *d.* Alfo other
Letters Patent, 8 *April*, 7 *Edw.* VI, of the Park called the *Little Park* of *Otford* (then difparkt) and of all Lands, *&c.* for 30 Years, at the Rent of 20 *l.
per Ann.* Alfo other Letters Patent of 23 *April*, 7 *Edw.* VI, of the Mannor of
Tibourne, with its Appurtenances, in the County of *Middlefex*, and the Scite and
Capital Meffuage, heretofore in the Tenure of *Richard Jaquett*, *&c.* for 35 Years,
at the Rent of 16 *l.* 11 *s.* 8 *d.* all which Leafes the Queen confirmed. And, it
may be prefumed, that, the faid *Richard Jaquett* holding the faid Mannor of *Tibourne*, wherein Felons, *&c.* are now, and for Time of out Mind, have been
executed, the Name of the Executioner has corruptly been called *Jack Ketch*.

In 1 and 2 *Ph. & Mar.* (4 *May*) he [r] with *John Somerfield* obtained a
Grant of the 3d Part of the Mannor of *Hales Owen*, in Com. *Salop.*

On 28 *April*, 2 and 3 *Ph. & Mar.* he [s] was conftituted Vice-Treafurer, and
General Governor of all the King and Queen's Revenues in the Kingdom of
Ireland. He embarqued for that Kingdom, with *Thomas Ratcliff*, Lord *Fitz-
Walter*, Lord Deputy of that Realm, (who married *Frances*, his Sifter, and
was after Earl of *Suffex*) and arrived at *Dublin* on *Whitfunday*, 1556. [t] Sir *Hen-
ry Sidney*, brought over with him 25000 *l.* to provide againft the *Scots* Iflanders,
and the *Irifh* Rebels. On the 1ft of *July*, they marched to *Ulfter* againft the
Scots, and on the 18th following, defeated them, with the Lofs of 200 flain on
the Spot; in which Engagement, Sir *Henry Sidney* behaved with the greateft
Valour, killing *James Mac Connel*, one of their principal Leaders, with his own
Hand.

On 12 *Nov.* 1557 [u], Sir *Henry Sidney*, Treafurer of Wars, and Sir *Hugh
Curvin*, Lord Chancellor, were conftituted by Patent, dated at *Weftminfter*,
Lords Juftices of *Ireland*, and were fworn at *Chrift*-Church, on *Sunday* the 5th
of *December*, and Sir *John Stanley*, the Marfhal, delivered them the Sword, with
whom it was left for that Purpofe. But on the 6th of *February* following [w], Sir
Henry Sidney, by the Queen's Command, and under her Commiffion, bearing
Date the 18th of *January*, was fworn fole Lord Juftice; the King and Queen
(as is expreffed in [x] the Patent) having efpeciall Truft and Confidence in the approved Fidelity, Wifdom, and Difcretion of their trufty and wel beloved Councellor, Sir *Henry Sidney*; whereupon, he immediately attackt *Arthur O Molloy*,
Chief of *Fercalia*, then in Rebellion, and overrunning his Country made *Theo-
bald O Molloy* Governor thereof. After which by a Cefs (or Tax) in the Pale,
he furnifht the Forts of *Maryburgh*, and *Philipsburgh*, with Provifions [y]. And
on his Return to *Dublin*, made Proclamation, that no Corn fhould be carried
out of the *Englifh* Pale, which with other good Regulations, and Receiving the
Submiffion of *O Reyley*, was as much as could be performed in fo fhort Space,
to advance the *Englifh* Intereft, furrendering the Sword to *Thomas* Earl of *Suffex*, the 27th of *April*, 1558.

But the faid Earl of *Suffex*, leaving the Kingdom the fame Year [z], he rein-
ftated Sir *Henry Sidney* Lord Juftice, till his Return the 10th of *November* following.

On the 6th of *June*, in the 1ft Year of Queen *Elifabeth*, he was conftituted
Vice-Treafurer, and Treafurer of Wars in *Ireland*, and to receive the ufual Salary from the Death of Queen *Mary*, and fworn of her Privy-Council; alfo on
29 *Dec.* the fame Year, was conftituted Juftice and Governor of the Kingdom
of *Ireland*, in Confideration of the Loyalty, Wifdom, and Induftry of her be-

---

[r] Bill. Sign. 1 & 2 Ph. & Mar.   [s] Pat. 2 & 3 Ph. & Mar. p. 3. in dorfo.   [t] Cox's Hift.
of Ireland, p. 303.   [u] Ib. p 305.   [w] Ib. p. 336.   [x] Ex Origin. apud Penfhurft.
[y] Cox, p. 306, & 307.   [z] Borlace's Reduction of Ireland, p. 120, and Cox, p. 307.

loved Councellor, Sir *Henry Sydney* [a], as Queen *Elisabeth* recites in her Patent; and that she appointed him with the Advice of her Council.

In 2 *Elif.* he [b] was constituted Lord President of the Marches of *Wales*; after which, the same Year, he went over to his Government of *Ireland*, [c] where though he continued but a short Time, yet, by his prudent Demeanor, [d] he obliged *O Neal*, who had disclaimed the *English* Jurisdiction, to a Submission to her Majesty, and to continue quiet, till he resigned to the Earl of *Suffex*, who [e] took on him the Government, 30th of *August* the same Year.

In 5 *Elif.* [f] desiring his Discharge for all Disbursements he had been at on Account of his being Vice-Treasurer, and Receiver-General of the Revenues in *Ireland*, and Treasurer of Wars; the Queen, the 8th of *June*, commissions *Thomas* Earl of *Suffex*, Lord Deputy, *Hugh*, Arch-Bishop of *Dublin*, Chancellor, and others, to examine and state his Accounts; and on sufficient Proof thereof, to discharge him the said Sir *Henry Sydney*, his Heirs and Executors, against the Queen, her Heirs and Successors.

Also in the said 5 *Elif.* 1562, on the War in *France*, between the *Princes* of the *Blood* and the *Guifes*, the Queen entertaining some Jealousies that the *English* would be involved therein. And being informed that the *Guifes*, to gain *Anthony* of *Bourbon*, King of *Navar* had promised to procure him in Marriage, the Queen of *Scotts*, with the Kingdom of *England* for her Portion. Also, that through the Help of *Spain*, and Interposition of the Pope, the then Marriage of the King of *Navar*, should be dissolved, his Wife being a Heretick; for which Cause also Queen *Elisabeth* should be dispossessed of her Throne. Whereupon as *Camden* writes *, she dispatched to *France*, Sir Henry Sydney, *a Person of approved Abilities, and great Reputation, to Fathom this Business, and persuade the Heads of each Party to an Accommodation. But Things were now gone too far to admit of any Remedy; therefore* Sydney *returning out of* France, *he was immediately sent to the Queen of* Scots, *to adjourn the Interview which she had desired with the Queen of* England, *till the ensuing Year, or till the Wars of* France *were ended.*

In the same Year, *Ambrose Dudley*, Earl of *Warwick* (whose Sister Sir *Henry* had married) being elected one of the Knights of the Garter, the Queen commissions the Duke of *Norfolk* her Lieutenant to install Sir *Henry Sidney* in his Place, the Earl being beyond the Seas, on the Queen's Affairs, as the Commission sets forth; and that her Majesty, by her special Licence, had appointed Sir *Henry Sydney* to be his Deputy. And accordingly he was installed with great Magnificence; Mr. *Ashmole* having [h] observed, that the Mantle was born before him by Garter, in the same Manner as is used to Knights, personally installed, and that he also proceeded before the Alms Knights, the only Instance he had met with, when a Proxy was installed.

The Year following [i], Sir *Henry* was himself elected a Knight of that most Noble Order, with *Charles the Ninth*, the *French* King, and the Earl of *Bedford*, and was installed with them, on 14 *May*, 6 *Elif.* His Plate is in the 8th Stall in St. *George*'s Chapel at *Windsor*, wherein he is stiled, *The thrice valiant Knight, Deputy of the Realm of* Ireland, *and President of the Council in* Wales, 1564.

On 13 *Oct.* 7. *Elif.* (retaining his Place of Lord President of *Wales*) he was [k] again constituted Lord Deputy of *Ireland*, with Powers to confer all Offices in that Kingdom, except the Offices of Chancellor, Treasurer, Sub-Treasurer, Chief Justice of the *Bench*, Chief Baron of the *Exchequer*, and Master of the *Rolls*. And to present to all Ecclesiastical Benefices, *viz.* Vicaridges, Parsonages, Prebends, Chancellors, Deans, and all other Dignities whatsoever, except Arch-Bishops, and Bishops. On the 13th of *January* following [l] he land-

---

[a] Ex Origin. Pat. 1. Elif. apud Penshurst. 　 [b] Hist. Cambr. p. 400. 　 [c] Borlace præd p. 121. [d] Cox, p. 312. 　 [e] Ib. p. 313. 　 [f] Ex Origin. apud Penshurst. 　 * Hist. of Q. Elif. in Hist. of Eng. V. 2. p. 317. 　 [g] Appendix no. 53. in Ashmole's Order of the Garter. 　 [h] Regist. Garter. p. 377, 378. 　 [i] Ib. p. 324, 325. 　 [k] Ex Origin. Pat. 7 Elif. apud Penshurst. 　 [l] Cox's Hist. of Ireland, p. 317.

ed at *Dublin*, and was received with great Joy (as my Author [m] relates) being a Perfon, whofe excellent Government that Kingdom had long experienced. When he received the Sword, he made an eloquent Speech, fetting forth what a precious Thing good Government is, and how all Realms, Commonwealths, Cities, and Countries do flourifh and profper, where it's maintained.

He told them [n] alfo, ' What a continual Care the Queen's Highnefs hath had, ' and yet hath, not only for the good Guiding and Ruling of the Realm of ' *England*, but alfo of *Ireland*, which fhe earneftly defireth and wifheth to be ' preferved, as well in Peace as War. That fhe had made great Choice, from ' Time to Time, of the moft grave, wife, and experienced Councellors for the ' one, and the moft valiant, fkilful, and expert Men of Arms for the other. ' That, both in Peace and Wars, the publick State of the Commonwealth, and ' every Member therein, might be conferved, defended, and kept in Safety, ' under her Government. And, for the Performance thereof, her Majefty, ' befides the Revenues of the Crown of *Ireland*, did Yearly, far above any of her ' Progenitors, expend, of her own Coffers out of *England*, many thoufand ' Pounds. All which her exceffive Expences, and continual Cares, fhe made ' the lefs Account of, fo that her Realm and Subjects of *Ireland* might be pre- ' ferved, defended, and governed.

' That, notwithftanding her Majefty might have made better Choice of ' many others, who were better able to hold her Place in this Realm, both for ' Honour, Wifdom, and Experience, yet her Pleafure was to caft this heavy ' Charge and Burden upon him : Which he was the more unwilling to take up- ' on him, becaufe, the greater the Charge was, the more unable and weak he ' was to fuftain the fame. Neverthelefs, being in good Hope, and well promi- ' fed of her Highnefs's Favour and Countenance in his well Doings, and having his ' Confidence in them, her Highnefs's Councellors, affociated to him, to join, aid, ' and affift him in his Government, he was, and is, the more ready to take the ' Sword in Hand, in Hope that his Government fhall be to the Glory of God, ' the Honour of her Majefty, the Benefit of the Commonwealth, and Preferva- ' tion of the whole Realm.

' Clofing his Speech with his earneft Requeft to the faid Lords prefent, for ' their Aiding and Affifting him in her Majefty's Service.'

His Inftructions were figned by the Queen 5 *October*, 1565, and were to this Effect : *Firft*, That a Privy Council be named and eftablifhed, and fworn be- fore the Lord Deputy, as ufual, and he was directed to confult and advife with them, and they were to refpect and reverence his Quality, and both were to con- fpire the Good of the Realm. That Religion, and Knowledge of the Scriptures, fhould be propagated, and encouraged by Doctrine, Example, *&c.* And the Church Lands and Eftates preferved from Wafte and Alienation. That the Law be adminiftred uprightly, and infufficient Judges and Officers removed, and a Sheriff placed in every County. That the Army be kept orderly, not oppref- fing the Subject ; that Mufters be once a Month, and Enquiry made, whether the Soldiers be *Englifhmen* or not, and how paid. And that Care be taken of the Revenues of the Crown.

The Hiftorian [o] relates, that he found the Kingdom almoft ruined, by in- teftine Fewds and Diffenfions ; that the *Englifh* Pale was overrun with Thieves and Robbers ; the Countryman fo poor, he had neither Horfe, Arms, nor Vic- tuals for himfelf, and the Soldiers fo beggarly, that they could not live without oppreffing the Subject, and were grown infolent, loofe, and idle, and fufpected of the State, by their Marriage with the *Irifh*. Alfo, as to Religion, there was but fmall Appearance of it, the Churches being uncovered, and the Clergy fcattered, and fcarce the Being of a God known to thofe ignorant and barbarous People.

[m] Hooker, p. 111.   [n] Cox, p. 318.   [o] Ib. p. 319.

Thefe

These Diforders the Lord Deputy remedied as faft as poffible, but *Shane O-neal's* Rebellion was the moft troublefome to him ; and the Queen fent Sir *Francis Knolls*, her Vicechamberlain, to confer with him about his Suppreffion [P]. He arrived at *Dublin* the 7th of *May*, and they refolved the Service fhould be performed the following Winter, and that the neceffary Preparations fhould be made for it againft that Time ; the Army then not exceeding 1200 Men, until Colonel *Randolph*, with 700 Soldiers, was fent from *England* to *Derry*, and there they intrenched, till Sir *Henry Sydney* came to them.

In the Hiftory of *Ireland*, his prudent Conduct, and indefatigable Induftry, in fuppreffing *Oneal* (who was killed 2 *June*, 1567, and his Head fent to the Lord Deputy) is fully related [q], and that he returned to *Dublin* with the Applaufe of the People, and there received the Submiffion of the *O Reyles*, by Indenture, on 28 *November*. And, about the fame Time, beautified the Caftle of *Dublin* with ftately additional Buildings, which yet remain.

Camden relates [r], ' That *Ulfter* was refettled in a peaceable Condition ; but
' *Munfter* was, in the mean Time, under violent Commotions, occafioned by
' the unhappy Rivalry of two Kinfmen, the Earls of *Ormond*, and *Defmond*, who
' could not agree about the Extent of their Jurifdiction ; infomuch that the
' Matter came to a Battle near *Dromelin*, and it was argued before the Council
' Board in *England*. But, the Cafe being intricate, they were referred to the
' Lord Deputy in *Ireland*, where the Evidence and Witneffes were near at Hand.
' But as they were upon the Level, as to Power and Intereft, and had Spirits
' formed in the fame Mould, fo they refolved the Matter fhould be decided,
' not by the beft Law, but the longeft Sword. Sir *Henry Sydney* interpofed his
' Authority and Forces, but *Ormond*, willing to fet the better Face on his
' Caufe, procured the Lord Deputy to be impeached as a Favourer of *Def-*
' *mond*.'

Sir *Richard Cox* gives this Account of thofe Affairs : ' That, howfoever his
' good Services were relifhed in *Ireland*, where the Fruits of them were felt
' and perceived, yet, in *England*, they were fo little regarded, that no Men-
' tion was made of them in any of the publick Difpatches ; but, on the Con-
' trary, the publick Letters, to the Lord Deputy, were full of Reprimands and
' and fharp Reflections, on Account of the Infolencies of the Earl of *Defmond*.
' Therefore, he at length prevailed to get Licence to go for *England*, and car-
' ried with him the Earl of *Defmond*, the Baron of *Dungannon*, *O Connor Sligo*, *O*
' *Carol*, and others. When he came to *Hampton Court*, with 200 Gentlemen
' in his Train, it happened that the Queen was looking out at the Window,
' and feeing them, was furprifed thereat, until fhe was told, it was the Lord
' Deputy of *Ireland* ;' and then fhe replied [s], *It was well enough ; for he had two*
of the beft Offices of the Kingdom. And being come in, he was well received by
the Queen, but, after a While, was told by fome of the Courtiers, *That the*
Scuffle in Ulfter *was not worthy to be called a War, fince the principal Rebel*
(Shane O Neal) *was but a Beggar and an Out-law.* But the Earl of *Defmond* and
O Connor were fent to the Tower, and Sir *John* of *Defmond* was fetched from *Ire-land*, and imprifoned in the fame Place.

It has been already mentioned, that the Earl of *Ormond* impeached the Lord Deputy of being partial to the Earl of *Defmond*, though without any juft Caufe, as is explained by Sir *Henry Sydney's* Letter to Mr. Secretary *Cecil*, dated 7 *April*, 1566. The Whole fhews an uncommon Integrity, and true Honour, and will be printed in the Collection, with the Claims of thofe Earls ; but I fhall here recite one Paragraph of it :

' I affure you, Sir, I woulde withall my Harte, that you knewe and felt all
' my Thoughtes and Conceipts that I have of any Man, or any Matter, touch-
' inge the Service in this Lande (fo fimple is myne Intendement) as fenfiblie as
' I feale them my felf. I have great Caufe to rejoice, that my ill compofed

---

[P] Cox, p. 321.   [q] Ibid. p. 326.   [r] Hift. of Eng. Vol. 2, p 410.   Hooker, p. 118.

' Lettres found foe gracious Acceptation. I ment well, writte truly, an, as I
' thought. I will never unpreffid, upon my Alleageaunce, deale in the great Mat-
' ters of my Lord of *Ormounde*, untill another Chauncellor come, or fome other
' Commiffioner, out of *Englande*, to be joyned with me, for the Hearinge and
' Determyninge of that Caufe ; for, howe indifferentlye foever I fhall deale, I
' knowe it will not be thought favorably enoughe on my Lord of *Ormounds*
' Side. And I affure you, Sir, if I ferved under the cruelleft Tirant that ever
' tyranifed, and knewe him affected on the one or the other Side, in a Matter
' betweene Partie and Partie referred to my Judgement, I woulde rather offend
' his Affection, and ftand to his Mifericord, then offende myne owne Confcience,
' and ftande to Godes Judgement. Moche more I dare be boulde uprightly to
' doe, fervinge and lyvinge under fo chriftian and juft a Princes as I doe. And
' before God, Sir, this I proteft to you, that I write not this in Prejudicacion of
' my Lord of *Ormounds* Caufe, for I knowe not, nor conjecture not, but that it
' may as well fall out, on my Lord of *Ormounds* Side, as on the others ; but I
' finde that I am forejudgid of. Therefore I befeeche you, Sir, let me have
' fome other, then any yet is here, to be joyned with me, before I fhall enter
' into the Difcuffion of the Matter, as well for the finall Sentenfinge of it, with-
' out further Appeale, as for Advoidinge Infamie to my felfe.'

In another Letter to Secretary *Cecil*, dated 17 *October*, 1569, he gives the
State of the Controverfy, which the Reader will alfo find in the Collection of
Letters. And in one to him, 14 *February*, 1569, he fets forth his miferable
Condition, by being Lord Deputy.

It is to the Glory of Queen *Elifabeth*'s Reign, that fhe had the Wifdom to
diftinguifh and employ Perfons of eminent Abilities, Integrity, and Honour ;
and there cannot be a greater Inftance of it, than in her Choice of Sir *Henry
Sydney*, whofe Letters to her Majefty, to her Council, the great *Cecil, Walfingham*, and others of her Miniftry, fhew how true a Judgment he made of Men,
and of all Affairs under his Cognifance ; as well as his Piety, prudent Conduct,
and all moral Virtues, which are fully manifefted therein ; and will be a lafting
Monument of his great Worth, and a laudable Example to Pofterity. Which
Letters giving a more perfect Account of the *Irifh* Affairs, during his Government, than as yet hath been publifhed, I fhall obferve from them, what is further memorable of his Character and Conduct, as alfo from *Hollinfhed*'s Chro-
nicle, wrote by *Edmund Molineux*, Efq; his Secretary.

He was four feveral Times Lord Juftice of *Ireland*[t], and three Times, by
fpecial Commiffion, fent Lord Deputy out of *England*. In his firft Deputation,
he fuppreffed the Rebellion of *Shane O Neal*, and floored the Top of the Caftle of
Dublin with the Arch Rebel's Head. In his fecond, he fuppreffed the moft
dangerous Infurrection, begun and long continued by fome of the *Butlers*. In
the third, the Commotion of the Earl of *Clanricard*, and his two gracelefs Sons,
Shane, and *Ulick Bourke*.

Immediately after his 1ft Arrival, he caufed the old Statutes of *Coine* and *Liverie* (the antient feftering Sore of that Country) to be revived and duly executed
againft feveral Perfons of Note, who were therewith fharply touched. Whereupon followed, a long Time after, great Good to the Nation in general, and a
fpeedy Reliefe to the poor diftreffed People of that Realm. On his Advice,
the remoter Provinces were governed by Prefidents, after the Imitation of the
Marches of *Wales* ; giving his Opinion, that there could not be either a better,
or more expedite and eafie Means to reform and civilize that barbarous Country, than by Univerfal Juftice, adminiftred amongft them, whereby the Poor
might be delivered from the antient Exactions and Tyranny of their Lords, by
whom they were daily oppreffed.

He both devifed, and faw executed, the Diftribution of the *Irifh* Countries

[t] Caftrated Sheets of Hollinfhed, p. 1548, & Seq.

into Shires, whereby enfued the Currency of the Queens Writts, which before were not reguarded.   He advanced and increafed the Revenues of the Crown, by Impoft upon Wines, Compofitions with the *Irifh*, for Rents and Services, and other commendable Means ; as out of Cafualties, creating Rents certain, of 10,000 *l*. Yearly.   And intended, and would have brought a far greater Increafe, if he had not met with Oppofition, from the Chiefs there, who fpared neither Money nor Intereft, to prevent his Bringing the Kingdom to bear its own Charges, which he was fully intent upon.   He repaired the Caftle of *Dublin*, which for a long Time before was ruinous, and of no Account, filled only with mechanical Perfons, and fome of worfe Sort.   But he left it a convenient and proper Manfion, for the Governor to refide in ; and has ever fince been fo applied.

He built the Bridge of *Athlone*, over the River *Shanon*, arched it with Free ftone, ftrong Wall and Battlement, and made it of that Strength, Spacioufnefs, and Breadth, as greatly benefited the Country ; the Swiftnefs of the Stream, over which it was built, being not before paffable.   And thereby a Paffage was opened out of the *Englifh* Pale, into *Conaught*, and the Rebells more daunted and appalled, and kept in greater Awe and due Obedience, than any Policie before ufed.   He likewife began the Walling and Fortifying the Town of *Carrigfergus* in *Ulfter*, re-edified the Town of *Athenrie* in *Conaught*, and ftrengthened that of *Athlone* with Gates and other Fortifications.   Alfo laid the Foundation and Plan of the Bridge of *Catherlogh* ; made a ftrong Gaole at *Molingar*, and walled the fame with Stone, to imprifon Rebells, Thieves and other Malefactors. Likewife begun many other needfull and neceffary Works in other Places, tending to the Advancement of the Service, which he left for his Succeffors to finifh.

He found the Records of the Kingdom in an open Place, fubject to Wind, Rain, and all Weather ; and fo neglected, that they were taken for common Ufes.   Whereupon with great Care and Diligence, he caufed them to be perrufed and forted, and placed within the Caftle of *Dublin*, in a Room well boarded, with a Chimney for a Fire, fo that neither by the Moifture of the Walls, or any other Means, they could receive Prejudice.   And feveral Divifions were made, for laying them feparate ; and one of Difcretion and Skill, appointed to look after them, with an Affignment for his Labour.   He alfo caufed the Statutes and Ordinances of the Realm, which . lay hid, and hardly known (but kept in Safety) to be fearched, furveyed, and viewed, by Men of the beft Learning, Skill and Difcretion, he could felect, giving them exprefs Charge, to perufe all, and collect fo many thereof, as they fhould think neceffary, and expedient to be made publick.   Which being perufed, he caufed them to be printed, that every one might know the Laws and Statutes of his Country, and obey them.   And having, by Experience, found Defects in the Adminiftration of Juftice, by Reafon of Kindred, Affinity, Corruption, Partiality, *&c*, he earneftly applied to the Queen, and her Council, to have *Englifh* fent over to fupply the chief Places of Juftice.   And for the better Increafe of her Majefty's Revenues, he prayed the like might be fent in the Rooms of the Attorney and Sollicitor General.

He had the greateft Defire to advance the Publick Service, and efteemed all thofe who were of that Mind.   Wherefoever he fojourned, he had that gallant Behaviour and Comelinefs of Perfon, as gained him the Hearts of many, and fuch univerfal Efteem of all Sorts of People to him, that they were ever defirous of his Aboad with them.   He was a perfect Orator, having fuch Readinefs in Speech, flowing Eloquence, fweet Delivery, and excellent Memory (for he rarely forgot any Thing, he either read or heard) as he was fpecially obferved to have no Equal.   He was curious in the Stile of his Letters, or whatever he committed to Writing ; yet, when he had given Inftructions for fome Matters to be written, and brought to him to fign, which he found couched in a Manner, he did not approve of, he would not publickly difgrace

I   the

the Writer, but encouraged him to mend his Fault, willing him to remember better.

He had a fingular Gift in Difpatch of common Caufes, which induced all People to defire to have them heard before him. And to fattisfie their Humours and Affections, or more compleatly to perform the full Meafure of his Charge, and being defirous of Hearing and Helping all he could, he applied himfelf greatly thereto, fparing no Pains, but endured the utmoft Toil to difpatch them. Many were beholding to him, for as much as in him lay, he provided for all his Friends and Followers, and was fo earneft to advance their particular Suites, that he would fometimes fpeak to her Majefty about them (when he thought them deferving) or to the Council, or Chief of the Miniftry. At each Time he was fent Deputy into *Ireland*, he had a new Secretary : The firft was *Edward Waterhoufe*, who was knighted, and preferred by him, fo that he became one of her Majeftys Council in *Ireland*. The 2d was *Edward Tremaine*, Efq; whom he preferred to be one of the Clerks of the Council, Attendant on her Majefty. The 3d was *Edmund Molineux*, Efq; whom he left unprovided at his Death, grieved his Fortune was fo bad in his Decline, as to be unable to help him, often faying he had quailed under his Hands (for that was the Term he ufed) but he hoped Time, or fome good Man (in Refpect of his publick Service) would repair that he could not do.

He was, by Nature, fo tempered with Piety, Modefty, and Patience, as he feldom fhewed Heat or Anger, how great foever the Offence was. He was a fincere Friend, where he profeffed Friendfhip, and would not forfake them, but on moft juft, certain, and known Caufes, which he could not fmother, and would not hide from the Party ; and was not revengefull to any that had offended him. Being of that even Temperature and Perfection, as it was hard to judge, whether to attribute more Commendation and Praife to his Government in Time of Peace, than to his Conduct and Valour in War ; having in both been fortunate. It appears from his Letters to Queen *Elifabeth*, wrote with great Spirit, and an Indignation of all which was fordid, that he traveled through the whole Kingdom ; and the State hereof he reprefents to her Majefty, in a moft pathetick Manner, and with an ardent Defire to redrefs whatever he found grievous to the Subject. In thefe Journeys he was fometimes in Perile, but would comfort his Followers, with thefe Words, *My good Friends, and moft loving Companions.* And wherefoever he came, his principal Care was to forfee their Wants, and provide for their Neceffitys. And when it fo fell out (as fometimes it did) that he had not wherewithall to fupply them, his kind Speeches, fo fincerely, and compaffionately delivered, wrought fo much on them, that they were fully contented and fattisfied ; knowing him to be always moft upright in Juftice, and naturally inclined to help every one in Diftrefs.

He highly favoured all Men of Letters and Sciences, and greatly encouraged them, oftentimes faying, *Science was to be honoured, in whom foever it was to be found.* He would never, in publick Affemblies, Confultations, Field, or Feaft, omit any Thing that appertained to his Office or Honour. He always delighted to keep an orderly, liberal, and honourable Houfe (greatly to the Relief of the Poor) according to the Dignity of his Place and Calling. He had Steward, Treafurer, Controler, Auditor, Clerk Comptroler, Clerk of his Kitchen, and Mafter-Cook, befides ordinary Clerks, and inferior Officers, who could in their Degrees, well and fkilfully, execute their feveral Places, and knew in Honor, State, Ceremonie in Affemblies, Solemnities, and Feafts, how to ferve him as he fhould be. The Accounts of his Expences, both in his Government, and in his private Affairs, were drawn out monthly for his Perufal, which are yet at *Penfhurft*, and fhew how fplendidly he lived, and what Care he had in the Application of the publick Revenues. He had a Reguard to his Honour in all his Tranfactions, and a gratefull Mind to thofe who had fhewed any Acts of Friendfhip to him, or from whom he had received any Benefit. He made

great

great Additions to his Seat at *Penshurst*, and over the Tower into the Entrance thereof, is this Inscription :

> The most Religius and Renovned Prince, *Edward the sixt*, Kinge
> Of *England*, *France*, and *Ireland*, gave this House of *Pencester* with
> The Mannors, Landes, and Appurtenavnces there unto belonginge
> Unto his trustye, and welbeloved Servavnt, Syr *William Sydney*, Knight-
> Banneret, serving him from the tyme of his Birth, unto his
> Coronation in the Offices of Chamberlayn and Stevard of his
> Household ; in commemoration of which most worthie and famovs Kinge
> Sir *Henrye Sydney*, Knight of the most Noble Order of the Garter,
> Lord President of the Counsell, established in the Marches of
> *Wales*, Sonne and Heyer to the aforenamed Syr *William*
> Caused this Tower to be buylded, and that most excellent
> Princes Armes to be erected, *Anno Domini* 1585.

His Knowledge of Affairs in *Ireland*, was far greater than any one of his Time, as well of the natural Temper, Behaviour, and Manners of the People in general, as of each particular Province, and the whole Government : So that his Successors built on his Foundations, and framed their Designs after his Devices and Policy. His immediate Successor was *Arthur* Lord *Grey* of *Wilton*, who requested his Opinion in what Manner he should act to serve his Queen and Country. His Answer to him is in the Collection of Letters, wherein it appears, that his sole Views were to benefit, as much as in him lay, both her Majesty's Service, and the Welfare of that Kingdom. He had a perfect Knowledge of the Soil, Havens, Ports, Promontories, Necks of Land, Creeks, or whatsoever else could be known, from the North to the South, or from the East to the West ; not any Man having seen, or observed so much of that Kingdom, as he had done. His long and painful Journies over the several Provinces, and his circular Discourses thereon (as he called them) will be published in the Collection of Letters, and shew what has been asserted to be evident, and apparent.

He often invited Gentlemen of the ancient *Irish*, and reclaimed them to Civility, Comeliness in Habit, and Cleanliness in Diet, House and Lodging : Which partly, in Respect of the great Love and Affection they bore to him, and partly, of friendly Fear to offend him, many afterwards observed and followed ; so that it may justly be said, he was the first that civilised the *Irish* Nation. Amongst many other of his Excellencies, it was thought a rare Virtue in him, that, being lusty, well liked, and full-bodied, he could content Nature, and satisfy himself with so little Sleep as he did, seldom keeping his Bed above six Hours (if he was in Health) neither would he take in the Day-time any Kind of Repose. And, in his Travels, were it in Post on special Service, or otherways, he often wearied most of his Train and Company, having that Ability and strong Constitution of Body, that few could endure the continual Labour and Toil at all Times and Seasons as he could ; nor that Hardness of Diet, for the Time, as himself would do, when the Service required it : Nothing ever offended him more than Unkindness and Ingratitude, especially where he (and the World thought) he had deserved otherwise (whereof, in the Course of his Life, he had some Part) but, though he could not help shewing some Uneasiness, his Revenge was generally on himself, it went no further. In all his Concerns, his sincere, plain, and open Dealing, was ever such, that his usual Phrase was, *My Word is my woorst, and so they shall find it.* He was naturally of a pleasant Disposition, merry in Conversation with his Friends, and in Council grave, discreet, and judicious ; well read in History and Antiquities, as also in most Languages, which he attained both by Conference and Travel. And was stored with such Principles of Civil Policy and Government, as delighted and instructed those who heard him : Likewise, so friendly, courteous, and affable

to

to all his Affiftants, Collegues, and Companions, as they intirely loved, and greatly honoured him.

He had an Intention, which proceeded by Degrees, to Motion in Parliament, to have erected fome publick Schools and Nurferies of Learning, which, in Time, might have become a Univerfity; and which has fince happened.

For the better Reformation, and Civilifing of the Savagenefs of that People, he offered a large annual Revenue of his own for the Furtherance of fo good a Purpofe. But, though in the Beginning a great Appearance was fhewn to have many worthy and rich Furtherers, it ended only in Words, they failing in their Promifes. It was his hard Fortune to have his Services fubject to the Ear, and not to the Eye, whereby his noble Virtues, and Merits, were fometimes undervalued, and difregarded, and, confequently, his Services liable to Mifreport, Slander, and Calumniation; as appears from his Letters to the Queen and her Council.

He held both the chief Offices of *Ireland* and *Wales* together, and was likewife Companion of the moft noble Order of the Garter, which was as much Honour as a Subject could well have, thofe Offices being never before or fince held by any, at one and the fame Time; which caufed him fome Envy, but unjuftly; for, in Truth (as *Molineux* obferves) *in thefe Services he fpent his Youth, and his whole Life; fold his Lands, and confumed much of his Patrimony, to the Hinderance of his Pofterity, without any great Recompenfe or Reward.*

How he impaired his Health in the publick Service, is apparent from the following Cafe (amongft feveral Memorials) yet remaining in his Majefty's Office of Papers and Records of State, which being very remarkable, I have here inferted it.

Feb. 1567.
The State of Sir H. Sidneys *Bodie* *.

MY Lord Prefident, being of the Age of XXXVI Yeares, went into *Ireland* a hole Man, not towched with the Stone, and fo remaind one Yere and a Half, or there abought. And ther, after long Greif, advoided two Stones, which were verye big, and fuch as fewe Men have bene knowen to have advoided. After this, he toke his Journey into the North Parts of *Irelande*, and fo continued void of Paine and Greif, untill his Arrival in *England*, which was about VIII Weeks after. And then at *Chefter* felt the like Greif as at the firft, and fo continued in Paine untill *Chriftmas* Eve, at what Tyme being ferched with Surgeons, he advoided one other Stone, broken by the Surgion his Inftruments in divers Peeces, for that it was fo great, that otherwife it cold not have bene taken forth, for all the Peices, laied to gither, might make the Quantity of a Nutmegge. And after, for a fewe Daies, he had fome Excoriation in the Part by which it paffed, which cuered, he remaind well untill now of late, feeling himfelf troublid with the like Paine as before. And, therefore, miftruftith that fome other Stone is againe in the Bladder, for Helpe whereof he requirith our Advices, afwell for the Cuer of his prefent Eftate, as alfo for farder Direction of his Bodie, to be preferved from Breeding of the Stone, which Difeafe he fearith the more, becaufe his Father died of the fame.

The State of the Queftion conteineth the fpecial Points of Cuering and Preferving the Partie defeafed; but, becaufe both were to long to defide, we, leving the Cuer to his own Phifitians, will broch onlie Prefervacion, which chiefely doth appertaine unto our Purpofe.

Prefervation confiftith in due Order and Ufuage of Diet and Medicins, nether of the which two Things can be limitted, but by Confideration of the Partie difeafid, and the Caufes of the Difeafe.

Temperatura Corporis.] My Lord femith to have bene in his Youth of a fanguine Complexion, and of a very good Conftitution of Bodie; but now, at this

---

* MS. Ireland 1557, 1559. Lib. 5. p. 259. in his Majefty's Office of Papers and Records of State.

Prefent, by Diforder in Diet, through his Calling and Service, he feemith fomewhat changed ; and, by Reafon of groffe Feading, and fuch like, he hath verie much diftemporid divers Parts of his Bodie ; as namelie, his Hedde, his Stomack, Liver, Kidneys, and Bladder. And therby is always fubject to Diftillacions, Coughes, and other rumatick Diffeafes. And alfo the Stone of the which he moft complaineth ; and by Reafon of the great Moifture and Groffenefs of Humors, to the which his Lordfhip is now enclined, it is to be feaird, left, in Procefs of Tyme, he will be molifted allfoe with Joint Aches and Gowtes.

Locus Affectus.] The Stone in my Lord femith to take his Beginnings and Ruding in the Hollownes of the Reignes, but is increafid and perfectid in the Bladder, fo that both Parts be affectid, but the Bladder efpecially.

Caufa.]. The Caufes are groffe and flymie Fleame, with fome Collar and Hardenefs thorough Diftempature of the Parts affectid, and the natural Imbecillitie of the fame, wherby it apperith that the Conftituicion of my Lords Bodie, at this Prefent, is verie apt to breade the Ctone.

Prognoftica I.] My Lord, ever before being free from the Stone, hath, within this half Yere, advoided III Stones at two feverall Tymes, of that Quantitie, that they hardelie and painefully had Iffue, being drawen with Surgeons Inftruments ; which is a plaine Argument, that his Lordfhip is not onlie apt to engender the Stone, but alfo ftandith in great Daunger ; for, before he advoid them, they will growe to that Bignes, that they will not paffe him but by Cutting, which is not done without great Daunger, and yet maketh not perfect.

II.] The Stone in my Lord is *Morbus hereditarius*, and, therfore, unleffe he carefully follow good Counfell, he will hardely or never be perfectly cuered ; the Aptnes of Nature apperith, for that he, within a Yeare and a Half, partlie thoroughe the Default of the Country wherin he abode, partlie thoroughe the Office in the which he fervid, not being able to follow Order, bredde Stones of fo great Quantitie.

III.] The more Stones my Lord doth advoide, and the more often, the weaker the Parts affected are made, and the Difeafe more incurable, Cuftom being joynid to the naturall Difpofition ; and therfore it behoveth his Lordfhip, without Delaie, to feeke for Remedie.

IV.] Becaufe the Reines and the Bladder are affectid, the Cuer will be the harder, and likewife the Prefervacion.

V.] Whoever hath a Stone of enie Bignes, conformid ether in his Kidnes or Bladder, if he be of enie Age, can never be cuerid.

Prefervatio.

For better Prefervacion of Helth, and Efchewing of this evident Danger, which otherwife will infue, it behoveth him to call to Remembraunce this old Proverbe Νεφριλεκοι ευξεία : The Ufe of all Things muft be moderat to them that are prone to the Stone : And, therfore, he muft advoid all Exceffe, and unfeafonable Ufe, as well of Exercife, Meat, as alfo of Heate, Coldnefs, and Moifture, taking good Reguard upon what Meates he feadeth, in what Seafon, and with what Appetite, he beginnith and endeth his Meales. When, where, and how much he exercifith his Bodie ; where he makith his Abode ; when, and where, he takith his Reft, and how he yeldith to the Affects of his Minde ; but, efpecially, he muft advoid all Things which may encreafe ether Moiftnefs or Grofenefs of Humors, and feeke of the contrary Side, to drie, extenuat, and incyde all flymy Matters.

And therefore, the Place of his Aboade, muft be in Aier, nether cold, nor moift, but drie with temperat Heat, as much as may be, advoiding fpecially all Places full of Bogges, Fenns, and Marfhes, where the Winds do blow comonlie from the South, and South-weft, where Foggs, Mifts be often, and long continewe ; where the Houfes be dampiffhe, moldy, and ill favoring.

He muft exercife his Bodie moderatlie, ether by Walking or Riding, or fuch like Gefture, in the Morning (before he feadith) abroade, if the Wether be faier, but farr from all moift Places, and ftanding Waters. Within Doors, if the Aier be clowdie, mifty, or difpofed to Raine. Such Exercifes as do much heat or ftrein the Back, as Leaping, Running, Valting, Dauncing alofte, Riding Pofte, long Journeys, or uppon a fturring Horfe, Gallopping the Felde, cladd in hevie Armuer, and fuch like, are very hurtefull for the Stone. After Meat, and in the Night, Reft is holefome, fo that it paffe not Meafure, for long Sitting givith great Occafion to the Stone. After Exercife, his Lordfhip muft repofe befoer Dinner a While.

His Meates muft be of one Kind, or fuch as have like Quality or Facility of Concoction, on the which alfo, he muft feade moderatly. He muft advoid all Meates that have in them fuperfluous Moifture, which increafe groffe and fly-my Humours, or are harde to be concocted, fuch as his Lordfhip, of late, hath beene accuftomid to doe, which, whether they were of Beaft or Fowle, being never fo drie roftid, yeldid much fupperfluus Moifture, and gave prefent Matter to ingender the Stone. For the like Confiderations, his Ldfhip maie not feede much of fuch Females, the Males whereof be of themfelfs to moift. His Bred muft be made of good Wheat, well levenne, feofened, and bakid. His Drink muft be cleare, well bruid, and ftale, or good old *Gafcoine* Wine. Drink made of Wheat Malt, and Otes, is not good. All newe Wines, all thick Beare, and alfo all futtell Wines at Meates, Aqua Vitæ, or fuch like Compounds, after Meat, be verie hurtefull. The Supper muft be lefs than the Dinner.

My Lord maie not fleep between Meales, ne go to Bed within two Howers after Supper. He maie not fleape uppon his Back, ne in a Bedde of Downe, ne yet uppon or neigh the Grounde, or in the open Aier, efpecially in the Night Watching, in the Night abroad ; in the Feild greatly hurteth.

He muft not ftudie after Meates, imediatlie, nor much ocupye his Minde, but paffe the Tyme with pleafant Difports, giving himfelf to Mirth, advoiding as well Penfivenes and Cares, as Anger ; which, of all other Affections, do moft caufe the Stone. And fo in all Things, Mediocrity muft be obferved, according to the Rule of *Hippocrates*, Labor, cibus, potus, fomnus & per omnia Mediocria.

When and how his Lordfhip muft fupply the Defect of Nature, we leve to the Confideration of his Phifitian, as we do alfo the Prefcription of a moer particular Diet, and more peculiar Medifines for the Difeafe.

Yf his Lordfhip fhall kepe this Order of Diet, and furder ufe fuch Medcines, as his Phifitian fhall from Tyme to Tyme devife, as Occafion fhall offer : We doubt not, but, by the Help of God, he fhall, in Tyme, be either perfectly cuerid, or long prefervid ; and, without this exact Diet, it will be very hard, or rather impoffible, thorough the natural Imbecillity, to remove fuch Inconveniences, as his Lordfhip is like to fall into. Wherfore he muft be the more carefull in Obfervanfe of this Order here prefcribed.

He was ftrict and precife in the Obfervation of good Order, and would feldom break it in any Refpect, but on evident, known, and juft Caufe ; or, when he was over-ruled, by fuch as had his Sovereign's Power to direct and command him. Extraordinary Courfes he always utterly mifliked, efpecially when Order was perverted, or Juftice hindered ; which gained him fuch good Will every where, and even among the Officers of the Queen's Houfhold, as they often wifht he had been honoured with a White-Staff, to have been amongft them.

He was a moft endearing, kind, and loving Father to his Children, and obferving in them high Minds, and great Courage, which drew them by Degrees to Excefs in Expences, and more than an ordinary Liberality, he would fometimes fatherly advife them, That, if they meant to live in Order, they fhould ever be thoughtful whofe Sons they were, and feldom think whofe Nephews they were ; alluding to their Uncles, the Earls of *Warwick* and *Leicefter*. He was alfo an affable, courteous, conftant, and honourable Mafter to his Servants : For he would often fay, *It was an eafy Matter for them to keep him, but hard to recover his Love and Favour, if they had once loft him.* And, when any of his noble and loving Friends commended him, for Making much of his old Servants
vants

vants (for few, that came to him, ever went from him, except such as were advanced by him to better Preferments) he would pleasantly answer, *Lord, I give thee Thanks, that, of those thou gavest me, I have not lost one.*

By his Last Will and Testament [a], bearing Date, 8 *Jan.* 1581, and the *Probat* thereof 25 *May,* 1586.

He wills to his Son, *Robert Sidney,* his Mannor of *Scampton,* with the Appurtenances, in Com. *Lincoln,* to him and his Heirs Male ; in Default, to his Son, Sir *Philip Sidney.*

To his Son, *Thomas Sidney,* his Lands and Tenements, known by the Name of *Hanbecke,* alias *Hanby Grange,* late in the Tenure of *Edmond Hasylwood,* Esq; or his Assigns, and to the Heirs Male of his Body ; in Default, to *Philip Sidney,* his Heirs and Assigns for ever ; and decrees his dearly beloved Brother-in-Law, *Henry* Earl of *Huntingdon,* to take on him the Guardianship of his said Son *Thomas,* till he arrives at the Age of 21 Years, and to have all such Lands, *&c.* he had bequeathed to his said Son *Thomas,* for his Finding. And that his Son, Sir *Philip Sidney,* should have the Order, Rule, and Government of his Son, *Robert Sidney,* till he come of Age.

He bequeaths to said Son, Sir *Philip,* all his Plate, Furniture, *&c.* at *Penshurst,* and the Residue of his Estate, and constitutes him sole Executor. And appoints his Brothers, *Henry* Earl of *Huntingdon, Ambrose* Earl of *Warwick,* and *Robert* Earl of *Leicester,* Overseers ; and bequeaths to every of them, for a Remembrance, one Piece of Plate, of the Value of 25 *l.* current Money.

Sir *Fulke Grevil,* Lord *Brooke,* [b] in his Life of Sir *Philip Sidney,* gives this Character of him, ' Sir *Henry Sidney* was a Man of excellent naturall Wit, large ' Heart, sweet Conversation ; and such a Governor, as sought not to make an ' End of the State in himself, but to plant his own Ends in the Prosperity of ' his Countrey. Witnes his sound Establishments, both in *Wales,* and *Ireland,* ' where his Memory is worthily gratefull unto this Day.'

He died at *Ludlow* on the 5th of *May,* 1586, aged 57 Years, wanting a Month, and 15 Days : And the Queen, being certified thereof [c], ordered Sir *William Dethick, Garter King of Arms,* to prepare all Things appertaining to his Office, for his Funeral. Accordingly, *Garter,* and the other Heralds, coming to *Worcester,* ordered the Corpse, robed with Velvet, to be brought from *Ludlow,* which was solemnly conveyed into the Cathedral Church at *Worcester,* and there placed : And, after a Sermon preached by one of his Chaplains, the Corpse was conveyed into a Chariot covered with Velvet, hung with Escutcheons of his Arms, *&c.* And, being accompanied with Mr. *Garter,* and the other Heralds, with the principal Domesticks of the Deceased, and Officers of the Court at *Ludlow,* they proceeded on their Journey to *London,* and from thence to *Penshurst,* where, on *Tuesday* 21 *June,* 1586, he was interred in the Chancel of the Church of that Place, attended from his House, by a noble Train of Lords, Knights, Gentlemen and Ladies.

He married the Lady *Mary Dudley,* eldest Daughter of *John* Duke of *Northumberland.* As she was by [d] Descent of great Nobility, so was she, by Nature, of a large, ingenious Spirit. She survived him but a very short Time, dying in *August* following [e] ; and on the 11th of that Month, 1586, had Sepulture with him, in the Chancel at *Penshurst.* They had Issue three Sons, Sir *Philip,* Sir *Robert,* and Sir *Thomas Sidney,* and four Daughters, whereof the eldest died an Infant, as did *Margaret,* the 2d Daughter, who lies buried at *Penshurst,* near the Tomb of Sir *William Sidney,* with this Inscription in Capitals, on a plain Stone laid over her Grave :

[a] Ex Regist. Windsor, qu. 27. [b] Life of Sir Philip Sidney, p. 5. [c] Funerals of Sir William Dethick. MS. Not. A. 31. in Bibl. Joh. Anstis, Arm. [d] Sir Fulk Grevil's Life of Sir Philip Sidney, p. 5. [e] Ex Regist. Ecclef. de Penshurst.

Here

> Here lyeth *Margarete Sydney*, Daughter
> Of Syr *Henry Sydney*, Knyght, and the Lady
> *Mary* his Wyfe. Which *Margarete* departed
> This Lyfe the Yere of our Sallvation A Mᵗ.
> CCCCCLVIII, and in the fifte and fixt Yere
> Of the Reigne of Kyng *Phylyp* & Quene
> *Mary*, when fhe was one Yere and thre
> Quarters old. On whofe Soule Jhu have Mercy.

Another of his Daughters lived to near the Age of 20, but died unmarried, and lies buried in the Chancel, in the Collegiate Parifh Church of *Ludlow*, where a Monument is erected to her Memory, with this Infcription :

> Heare lyethe the Bodye of *Ambrozia Sydney* IIIIᵗʰ
> Daughter of the right honorable Syr *Henry Sydney*,
> Knight of the moft noble Order of the Garter, Lord Prefident
> Of the Counfell of *Walles, &c.* And of the Ladye *Marye*
> His Wief, Daughter of the ffamous Duke of *Northumberland*,
> Who dyed in *Ludlow* Caftell, the 22ᵗʰ of *Februarii*,
>   1574.

The only furviving Daughter was *Mary*, married to *Henry* Earl of *Pembroke*, from whom the prefent Earl is defcended. *Robert Dudley*, Earl of *Leicefter*, her Uncle, the great Favourite of Queen *Elifabeth*, made the Match for her (and paid Part of her Fortune) which Sir *Henry Sidney* acknowledges as a Favour to him, by his Letter from *Dundalk* in *Ireland*, bearing Date, 4 *Feb.* 1576, which will be printed in the Collection.

She was a moft ingenious Lady, and compofed feveral of the *Pfalms* in Verfe ; alfo tranflated, *A Difcourfe of Life and Death, written in* French, *by* Phil. Mornay. *Done into* Englifh, *by the Counteffe of* Pembroke.

> Dated, the 13 of *May*, 1590. At *Wilton.*
> At *London.* Printed for *William Ponfonby*, 1600.

Likewife, *The Tragedie of* Antonie. *Doone into* Englifh *by the Counteffe of* Pembroke.

> Imprinted at *London*, for *William Ponfonby*, 1595.
> Dated at *Ramefbury*, 26 *November*, 1590.

She lived to a very advanced Age, and died at her Houfe in *Alderfgate-ftreet*, in *London*, 25 *Sept.* 1621, and was buried in the Chancel of the Cathedral Church of *Salifbury*.

This Epitaph was alfo made on her :

> Vnderneath this fable Herfe
> Lyes the Subject of all Verfe ;
> *Sydneys* Sifter, *Pembrokes* Mother ;
> Death, ere thou has killed another
> Faire, and learn'd, and good as fhe,
> Tyme fhall throwe a Dart at thee.

> Marble Pyles let no Man rayfe
> To her Name, for after Daies.
> Some kinde Woman, borne as fhe,
> Reading this, like *Niobé*,
> Shall turne Marble, and become
> Both her Mourner, and her Tombe.

I shall now proceed to treat of Sir *Philip Sydney*, the eldeft Son and Heir of Sir *Henry*. He was born at *Penfhurft*, the 29th of *November*, 1554 [f], and had the Name of *Philip*, from King *Philip* of *Spain* (then lately married to Queen *Mary*) who was his Godfather. The celebrated Poet, *Ben. Johnfon* [g], commemorates the Place of his Birth, with thefe Lines on *Penfhurft* :

Thou haft thy Walks for Health as well as Sport ;
Thy Mount, to which the *Dryads* do refort,
Where *Pan* and *Bacchus* their high Feafts have made,
Beneath the broad Beech, and the Chefnut Shade :
That taller Tree, which of a Nut was fet
At his great Birth, where all the Mufes met.

This Tree is yet ftanding in the Park, and called *Bear's* Oak, probably alluding to one of the Cognizances of the Family. While he was very young, he was at School at *Shrewfbury* (being near to his Father, then Lord Prefident of *Wales*) and fo forward in his Learning, that, at 12 Years of Age, he fent two Letters to his Father, one in *Latin*, and the other in *French*, and how properly Sir *Henry* anfwered, will be feen in the Collection of Letters. Of his Youth, Lord *Brook* [h] obferves, That, though he lived with him, and knew him from a Child, yet he never found him other than a Man : With fuch Steadinefs of Mind, lovely and familiar Gravity, which carried Grace and Reverence far above his Years. This Eminence in Nature made his worthy Father ftile him, faith the Lord *Brook*, the Junfeen, *Lumen familiæ fuæ*. For his further Improvement, he was fent to *Chrift Church* in *Oxford* [i], where continuing till he was about 17 Years of Age, under the Tuition of Dr. *Thomas Thornton*, Canon of that Houfe ; he was, in 1572, fent to Travel : For Queen *Elifabeth*, 25 *May*, in that Year, grants her Licence [k] to her trufty and welbeloved *Philip Sydney*, Efq; to go out of *England*, into Parts beyond the Seas, with three Servants and four Horfes, &c. to remain the Space of two Years, immediately following his Departure out of the Realm, for his Attaining the Knowledge of foreign Languages.

In his Travels, the Lord *Brook* [l] relates, That, though fo young, he gained Reverence among the chief learned Men Abroad. And King *Charles the Ninth* of *France*, was fo taken with his Deportment, and extraordinary Merits, that he made him one of the Gentlemen of his Chamber. And thereupon, by his Sign Manual, and under his Seal, certified, to the Great Chamberlain of *France*, the Mafters in Ordinary of his Houfehold, and the Mafter and Comptroller of his Chamber, for Monies, &c. That confidering how great the Houfe of *Sidenay* was in *England*, and the Rank it had always held near the Perfons of the Kings and Queens, their Sovereigns, and defiring well and favourably to treat the young Sir *Philip Sidenay*, for the good and commendable Knowledge in him : He had retained and received him in the State of Gentleman in Ordinary of his Chamber, to ferve him hereafter, and to receive the Honours, Authorities, Wages, Rights, Hoftellages, Profits, and cuftomary Emoluments thereunto appertaining, during Pleafure. With Command to his faithful Councellor, and firft Gentleman of his Chamber, to take of the faid S. Baron of *Sidenay*, the ufual Oath in fuch Cafe required, &c. Willing alfo that thefe Prefents be regiftred among the Papers and Writings of his Chamber, &c. And, on the Back of the Paper, is endorfed [m] :

' We *Albert de Gondy*, Count of *Doyen*, Baron of *Reus*, Marquis of the Ifles,
' &c. of *Marly* and St. *Sarque*, Knight of the Order, Councellor of the King in
' his Privy Council, Firft Gentleman of his Chamber, Governor and Lieutenant
' General of *Metz*, and the Country of *Metfin*.' We have, this Day, received

---

[f] Wood's Athenæ. Oxon. Vol. 1. p. 182.   [g] Vide his Works, 8vo. Vol. 3, p. 177.   [h] Vide his Life, p. 6 & 7.   [i] Wood's Athenæ. Oxon. Vol. 1, p. 182.   [k] Ex Original, apud Penfhurft.   [l] Life, p. 8.   [m] Ex Origin. apud Penfhurft.

the

the S. Baron of *Sidenay* the Younger, in the State of Gentleman in Ordinary to the King, and he received and took the Oath, in such Case requisite and customary. At *Paris*, 9 *August*, 1572.

GONDY.

He was at *Paris* on the 24th of *August* [n], after he departed from *England*, on which Day was the Massacre ; but being in the House of Sir *Francis Walsingham*, the Queen's Ambassador, he received no Hurt. His Uncle, the Earl of *Leicester*, was under great Concern for him, and sent for him Home, as the underwritten to Secretary *Walsingham* shews :

' Where we understand, that the *English* Gent. who were in *Paris* at the Time
' of the Execution of the Murther, were forced [o] to retire to your House, where
' they did wisely ; for your Care of them, we and their Friends are beholding
' to you, and we think good that they be advised to return Home ; and
' namely, we desire you to procure for the Lord *Wharton*, and Mr. *Philip Sid-*
' *ney*; the Kings Licence and safe Conduct to come thence, and so we require
' you to give them true Knowledge of our Minds herein.'

Sept. 9, 1572.

Signed,   *William Burleigh, Robert Lecester,*
with others of the Privy Council.

That able Minister, who had Influence in all Countries, and had a Hand in all Affairs, did, as Lord *Brook* writes [p], confess to him, that Sir *Philip Sydney* did so overshoot him at his own Bow, as those Friends, which at first were Sir *Philip*'s, for this Secretary's Sake, within a While became so enamoured of him, as now he held them by his Son-in-Law's native Courtesy : And that Don *John* of *Austria*, Vice-roy in the *Low-Countries* for *Spain* [q], when this Gentleman was on his Travels, and came to kiss his Hand, he gave him Access at first, as in Condescension to a Youth and Stranger of Figure ; yet, after a While, when he had taken his just Altitude, he found himself so stricken with this extraordinary Planet, that the Beholders wondered to see, what ingenious Tribute the haughty Prince paid to his Worth, giving more Honour to this hopeful young Gentleman, than to the Ambassadors of mighty Princes.

He also says [r], The Prince of *Orange* protested unto him, that, if he could judge, Queen *Elisabeth* had one of the ripest and greatest Councellors of State in Sir *Philip Sydney*, at that Day, in *Europe*. To the Trial of which, he would pawn his Credit, till her Majesty had employed him. Likewise his [s] Uncle, the Earl of *Leicester*, in the End acknowledged, that by him, whilst he lived, he held up the Honour of his Authority in the *United Provinces*, and found Reason to withdraw himself from that Burden after his Death. And he further says, p. 39. Indeed he was a true Model of Worth, a Man fit for Conquest, Plantation, Reformation, or what Action soever is greatest or hardiest amongst Men ; withall, such a Lover of Mankind and Goodness, that whoever had any real Parts, in him found Comfort, Participation, and Relief, to the utmost of his Power. For, like *Zephirus*, he gave Life where-ever he blew : The Universities, Abroad and at Home, accounted him a General *Mæcenas* of Learning, dedicated their Books to him, and consulted him on every Invention, or Improvement of Knowledge. Soldiers he honoured, and they so reverenced him, as no Man thought he marched under the true Banner of *Mars*, that had not obtained *Sydney*'s Approbation. Men * of Affairs in most Parts in *Christendom* corresponded with him. But why speak I of these (saith the Lord *Brook*) with whom his own Ways and Ends did concur : *Since to descend, his Bounty was such, there was not an approved Painter, skilfull Engineer, an excellent Musician, or any other Artificer of Fame, that made not himself known to this famous Spirit, and found*

---

[n] Wood ut supra.   [o] Digs's Compleat Ambassador, p. 250.   [p] Life of Sir Ph. Sidney, p. 35.
[q] Ibid. p. 37.   [r] Life, p. 31.   [s] Ibid. p. 34.   * Which appears from a Volume of Letters in all Languages, from the most learned Men in all Countries, still remaining at Penshurst.

in

in him a true Friend without Hire ; so that he was the common Rendevous of Worth in his Time.

I shall now proceed to recite his most memorable Actions : From *Paris* he travelled through *Lorrain*, and by *Strasburgh* and *Heidelburgh*, to *Frankfort*. At the last Place he staid some Time, and became acquainted with the famous *Languet*, Minister of the Elector of *Saxony*, the greatest Prince in *Germany*, who was so taken with his Behaviour and Deportment [u], ' That he quitted his several Functi-
' ons, and became a Nurse of Knowledge to this hopeful young Gentleman, and
' without any other Hire or Motive, than their Sympathy of Affections, he ac-
' companied him in the whole Course of his three Years Travel.' In 1573 [w], he removed to *Vienna*, where he staid till *September*, and then went into *Hungary*, and from thence into *Italy*, where he continued all the Winter. Most of the Summer, 1574, he spent in *Germany* ; and the next Spring he returned by *Frankfort*, *Heidelburgh*, and *Antwerp*, Home into *England*, where he arrived about *May*, 1575.

In 1576, he was sent by the Queen [x] to *Rodolph* the Emperor, to condole the Death of *Maximilian*, being not much more than one-and-twenty Years old ; and was impowered to visit and treat with other Princes in *Germany* ; which he performed in such exquisite Order, as he exceedingly satisfied her Majesty there-in, both by his Letters and Reports, and gained himself great Credit and singular Commendation. In all Places where he took up his Abode, the following Inscription under his Arms was set up :

Illustrissimi & Generosissimi Viri
Philippi Sidnæi Angli,
Pro-regis Hiberniæ filii, Comitum Warwici
Et Leicestriæ Nepotis, Serenissimi
Reginæ Angliæ ad Cæsarem Legati.

The next Year, 1557, in coming to *England*, he saw that gallant Prince, Don *John* of *Austria*, Vice-roy in the *Low-Countries* for the King of *Spain*, and *William* Prince of *Orange*. After his Return, the same Year, I find he had some Dispute with *Thomas*, Earl of *Ormond*, on the Behalf of his Father, Sir *Henry Sydney* ; and though he was the Queen's Kinsman, and high in her Favour, Sir *Philip* could not refrain shewing his Resentment to that noble Peer, whereof *Edward Waterhouse*, Esq; in a Letter to Sir *Henry Sydney*, bearing Date from the Court at *Oatlands*, 16 *September*, 1577, relates these Particulars [y] :

' Some litell Occasions of Discurtesies have passed betwen the Erle of *Ormond*,
' and Mr. *Philip Sidney*, becaufe the Erle lately spoke unto him, and he an-
' swered not, but was in dead Silence on Purpose ; becaufe he imputeth to the
' Erle, such Practises as have bene made to alienat her Majesties Mind from
' your Lordship. But thes Contraversies are, I think, at the fardest ; for the Ex-
' pectation of my Lord Chancellors Coming, hath put all *Irish* Causes to Silence
' till he be herde ; and the Erle of *Ormond* saith, he will accept no Quarrell
' from a Gentleman that is bound by Nature to defend his Fathers Caufes, and
' who is otherwise furnishid with so mayny Vertues, as he knows Mr. *Philip* to
' be. And, on the other Side, Mr. *Philip* has gon as farr, and shewed as
' much Magnanimity, as is convenient, unless he could charge him with any
' Particularities, which I perceive he yet cannot, other then with a general De-
' fence of the Countrey Ways, wherein all the Nation here, as I think, be cul-
' pable, saving the Lord of *Donsany*, who, for ought that I hear, hath not med-
' led in the Matter, nor will not, &c.'

He was naturally of a warm and high Spirit, so jealous of his Honour and Reputation, that he could not brook the least Intrenchment on either, not even

[u] Lord Brook's Life, p. 9.   [w] Wood ut supra.   [x] Castrated Sheets of Hollinshed,
p. 1554.   [y] Ex Origin. apud Penshurst.

from

from Persons of the higheft Rank ; and much lefs from his Equals or Inferiors. As may appear in that Inftance of *Edmund Molineux*, Efq; Secretary to the Government of *Ireland*, whom he threatened with Death, if he continued to divulge any of the Letters he fent to his Father. His Letter to Mr. *Molineux* on this Topic, in *May* 1578, will be printed in the Collection, with the ingenious, refpectful, and affectionate Anfwer ; which probably produced the Reconciliation between them, that evidently occurs in their future Correfpondence.

In 1579, being neither Magiftrate nor Councellor (as Lord *Brook* writes, p. 71.) he fhewed himfelf, for feveral weighty Reafons, oppofite to the Queens Marrying with the Duke of *Anjoy*, which he addreffed to the Queen herfelf by Letter, and will be publifhed in the Collection. The Lord *Brook* takes Notice of it, and faith, that if any one fhould think it a dangerous Error, in his oppofing himfelf gainft his Sovereign's Pleafure, he muft anfwer, ' That his Worth, Truth, Fa-
' vour and Sincerity of Heart, together with his real Manner of Proceeding in
' it, were his Privileges. Becaufe his Courfe was not by Murmur among E-
' quals or Inferiors, to detract from Princes ; or by a mutinous Kind of be-
' moaning Error, to ftir up ill Affections, but by a due Addrefs of his humble
' Reafons to the Queen herfelf, to whom the Appeal was proper ; and her
' princely Heart was a Sanctuary to him. So that howfoever he feemed to ftand
' alone, yet he ftood upright, kept his Accefs to her Majefty as before ; and a
' liberal Converfation with the *French* ; reverenced amongft the Worthieft of
' them for himfelf ; and born in too ftrong a Fortification of Nature for the lefs
' Worthy to attack him, either with Queftion, Familiarity, or Scorn. In this
' Freedom, even while the greateft Spirits and Eftates feemed hood-winked, or
' blind, and the inferior Sort of Men made Captive, by Hope, Fear, or Igno-
' rance ; did he enjoy the Freedom of his Thoughts, with all Recreations wor-
' thy of them.'

And in this Freedom of Heart, being one Day at Tennis, *Edward Vere*, Earl of *Oxford*, a Peer, born great, greater by Alliance (having married a Daughter of the great *Cecil*) and Superlative in the Queens Favour, abruptly came into the *Tennis-Court*, and forgot to intreat that, which he could not legally command. And finding this Unrefpectivenefs in himfelf (though a great Lord) not refpected by Sir *Philip*, he grew to expoftulate, more roughly. The Returns of which Stile, coming to a Heart, that underftood what was due to itfelf, and what it owed to others (feemed through the Mifts of my Lords Paffions, fwoln with the Wind of his Faction then reigning) to provoke in yeelding. Whereby the lefs Amazement, or Confufion of Thoughts, he ftirred up in Sir *Philip*, the more Shadows this great Lords own Mind was poffeffed with, till at laft with Rage (which is ever ill difciplined) he commands them to depart the Court. To this Sir *Philip* cooly anfwers his Lordfhip, *That had he expreffed Defire, in milder Characters, perchance he might have lead out thofe, that he fhould now find, would not be driven out with any Scourge of Fury.* This Anfwer (like a Bellows) blowing up the Sparks, of already kindled Anger, made my Lord fcornfully call Sir *Philip*, by the Name of *Puppy*. In which Progrefs of Heat, as the Tempeft grew more and more vehement within, fo did their Hearts breathe out their Perturbations in a more loud and fhrill Accent. The *French* Commiffioners had that Day, Audience in thofe private Galleries, whofe Windows look into the *Tennis-Court*. They all inftantly drew to this Tumult, every Sort of Quarells forting well with their Humour, but efpecially this ; which Sir *Philip* perceiving, and rifing with inward Strength, by the Profpect of a mighty Faction againft him, afked my Lord with a loud Voice, that which he heard clearly enough before. Who like an Echo (that ftill multiplies by Reflections) repeated this Epithet of *Puppy*, the 2d Time. Sir *Philip* refolving, in one Anfwer to conclude, both the attentive Hearers and paffionate Actor, gave my Lord the *Lye*, impoffible as he averred to be retorted, in Refpect, all the World knowes, *Puppys are gotten by Dogs, and Children by Men.*

V O L. I.   D d   Here-

Hereupon thofe glorious Inequalities of Fortune in his Lordfhip, were put to a Kind of Paufe, by a precious Inequality of Nature in this Gentleman. So that they both ftood filent a While, like a dumb Shew in a Tragedy ; till Sir *Philip* fenfible of his own Wrong, and the foreign and factious Spirits that attended ; and yet even in this Queftion between him, and his Superior, tender to his Countrys Honour ; with fome Words of fharp Accent he led the Way abruptly out of the *Tennis-Court* ; as if fo unexpected an Accident, were not fit to be decided further in that Place. Whereof the great Lord conftruing it in a wrong Senfe, continues his Play, without any Advantage of Reputation ; as by the Standard of Humours in thofe Times it was conceived.

A Day Sir *Philip* remains in Sufpenfe, when hearing nothing of, or from this Lord, he fends a Gentleman of Worth, to awake him out of his Trance : This ftirred up a Refolution in his Lordfhip to fend Sir *Philip* a Challenge. But thefe Thoughts in the great Lord wandered fo long between Glory, Anger, and inequality of State, as the Lords of her Majefties Councel took Notice of the Differences, commanded Peace, and laboured a Reconciliation between them. Yet needlefly in one Refpect, and bootlefly in another. The great Lord being (as it fhould feem) either not hafty to adventure many Inequalities againft one, or inwardly fattisfied with the Progrefs of his own Acts : But Sir *Philip* was on the other Side confident, that he neither had, nor would lofe, or let fall any Thing of his Right. Which her Majeftys Council quickly perceiving, recommended this Work to herfelf.

The Queen, who faw that by the Lofs, or Difgrace of either, fhe could gain nothing ; prefently undertakes Sir *Philip*, and lays before him the Difference in Degree, between Earls and Gentlemen ; the Refpect Inferiors owed to their Superiors ; and the Neceffity in Princes to maintain their own Creations, as Degrees defcending between the Peoples Licentioufnefs, and the anoynted Soveraignty of Crowns; how the Gentlemans Neglect of the Nobility taught the Peafant to infult upon both. Whereunto Sir *Philip*, with fuch Reverence as became him, replyed : *Firft, That Place was never intended for Privilege to wrong, witnefs herfelf, who, how Soveraign foever fhe were, by Throne, Birth, Education, and Nature ; yet was fhe content to caft her own Affections into the fame Moulds her Subjects did, and govern all her Rights by the Laws.* Again he befought her Majefty to confider, *That although he were a great Lord, by Birth, Alliance, and Grace ; yet he was no Lord over him ; and therefore the Difference of Degrees, between free Men, could not challenge any other Homage than Precedency. And by her Fathers Act* (to make a Princely Wifdom, become the more familiar) *he inftanced the Goverment of King* Henry the Eighth, *who gave the Gentry free, and fafe appeal to his Feet, againft the Oppreffion of the Grandees ; and found it Wifdom, by the ftronger Corporation in Number, to keep down the greater in Power : Inferring elfe, that if they fhould unite, the Overgrown might be tempted, by ftill coveting more, to fall (as the Angels did) by affecting Equality with their Maker.* Thefe Truths did not difpleafe the Queen, though he did not obey her Commands.

Whereupon, the fame Year he retired from Court ; and in that Summer 1580, its conceived he wrote the eloquent and entertaining Romance, called *Arcadia*, whereof there has been printed 14 Editions ; which he dedicated to his Sifter the Countefs of *Pembroke* ; and theres a Room at *Wilton*, the lower Pannels whereof are finely painted, with Reprefentations of the Stories mentioned therein.

His noble and generous Difpofition to relieve all who were in Diftrefs, appears from feveral Inftances, as well as from his Letters ; and he was fo univerfally applauded for it, that his Fame fpread even beyond the Bounds of *Europe*. In 1580, on the Death of the King of *Portugal*, there were three Competitors for the Succeffion, which induced the *Spaniards* to poffefs themfelves of that Kingdom. Of the Competitors, only Don *Antonio* gave them any Difturbance, and he applied himfelf to Sir *Philip Sidney*, for his Affiftance. His Letter bears Date from *Tunis*, the 3d of *May*, 1581, wherein he acquaints

him

him with the State of his Affairs, and who had promiſſed him their Aid; concluding, *though many more ſhould go, if I did not ſee you in the Company, I ſhall ſay,* Numerum non habet illa ſuum. He ſtiles him his *illuſtrious Nephew,* Philip Sidney. The Letter, with a Tranſlation, will be printed in the Collection.

In 1581, the *French* Treaty of Marriage was renewed, and Sir *Philip Sidney,* [a] was among thoſe noble Gallants, that performed in the Juſts, Barriers, and Turney, for the Entertainment of the Duke of *Anjou,* and his Train. And at his Departure from *England,* in *February* the ſame Year, the Earl of *Leiceſter,* and the Chief of the *Engliſh* Court, attending him to *Antwerp,* he was [b] among them.

In 1583, *John,* Prince Palatine of the *Rhine,* being made a Knight of the Garter, gave [c] his Procuration to Sir *Philip Sydney,* to receive his Stall, and in his Name to take Poſſeſſion of it; and thereupon, he was knighted by the Soveraign at *Windſor*-Caſtle, the 13th of *January,* the Morning before he proceeded to take Poſſeſſion thereof.

In 1585, he projected an Expedition into *America,* [d] which he faſhioned to become Head of himſelf. And as the Scope of it was mixt both of Land, and Sea-Service, ſo had it accordingly diſtinct Officers, choſen by Sir *Philip,* out of the chief Perſons of thoſe Martial Times. The Project was contrived between him, and Sir *Francis Drake,* that they both ſhould equally govern, when they had left the Shoar of *England.* And while Things were providing at Home, Sir *Francis* was to bear the Name, and by the Credit of Sir *Philip,* all Particulars were to be abundantly ſupplied. But this Affair dropt, the Queen being unwilling to riſk a Perſon of his Worth, in an Imploiment ſo remote, and of ſo hazardous a Nature; and ſent her Royal Command to him delivered by a Peer of the Realm, to quit the Enterprize.

Being therefore fruſtrated in that Deſign, he was upon his Return to Court, [e] inſtantly made Lord-Governour of *Fluſhing,* with the Rammekyns, *&c.* and General of the Horſe, under his Uncle, the Earl of *Leiceſter,* in both which Charges, his Carriage teſtified to the World, Wiſdom and Valour, with Addition of Honour to his Country.

On his 1ſt Entrance into the *Low-Countries,* he contrived [f] the Surprize of *Axil* (*July* 1586) in the Execution of which, he behaved like a moſt conſummate General, reviving the antient and ſecure Diſcipline of Order and Silence in their March; and after their Entrance into the Town, placed a Band of choice Soldiers, to make a Stand in the Market-place, for Securitie to the reſt: And when the Service was done, rewarded that Obedience of Diſcipline in every one, liberally out of his own Purſe.

Alſo in the Enterpriſe, intended for the Surpriſe of *Gravelin,* he was reſolute not to hazard ſo many principal Gentlemen, with ſuch gallant Troops and Commanders, which accompanied him; yet becauſe he kept this ſteady Council in his own Boſome, there was Labouring on every Side, to obtain the Honour of that Service. To which he made this Anſwer: That his own Coming thither was to the ſame End, wherein they were now become his Rivals, and therefore aſſured them, that he would not yield any Thing to any Man, which by Right of his Place, was both due to himſelf, and conſequently Diſgrace to him to execute by others. Therefore he would never conſent to hazard them that were his Friends, where he found Reaſon to make many Doubts, and ſo little Reaſon to venture himſelf. Yet as a Commander, concluding ſomething fit to be done, equally for Obedience and Trial, he made the inferior Officers try their Fortune by Dice on a Drum-head. The Lot fell on Sir *William Brown,* his own Lievtenant, who with a choice Company, preſently departed, receiving this proviſional Caution from Sir *Philip,* that if he found Practiſe and

---

[a] Stow's Annals, p. 689. [b] Camden's Annals, in Hiſt. of Engl. Vol. 2. p. 484. [c] Aſhmole's Order of the Garter, p. 436, 438. [d] Lord Brook's Life of Sir Ph. Sidney, p. 82. & ſeq. [e] Pat. 27 Eliſ. p. 13. m. 23. [f] Stow's Annals, p. 732.

not Faith, he fhould through down his Arms and yeeld himfelf Prifoner ; pro-
tefting, that if they took him, he fhould be ranfomed ; if they broke Quarter,
his Death moft feverely revenged.

The Leader, following his Generals Commandment, difcovers the Treafon,
throws down his Arms, and is taken Prifoner ; and its agreed that Sir *Philips*
Penetration and Judgment, faved the Lives and Honour of the *Englifh* Army,
by not hazarding fo many of them in that treacherous Expedition.

His Fame and high Deferts, were now fo well known, that he [g] was in
Election for the Crown of *Poland* ; but Queen *Elifabeth* refufed to further his Ad-
vancement, not out of Emulation, but out of Fear to lofe the Jewel of her
Times.

In thofe Difcontentments, and Quarells, which naturally accompany great
Spirits in the beft governed Camps, how difcreetly did Sir *Philip* ballance the
brave *Hollock*, made Head of a Party againft his Uncle : When putting himfelf
between Indignities, offered to his Soveraign, through the Earl of *Leicefters*
Perfon ; and yet not fit for a fupreme Governours Place to ground a Duel upon ; he brought thofe paffionate Charges, which the Count *Hollock* addreffed upwards to the Earl, down by Degrees upon himfelf. Where that brave Count
found Sir *Philip*, fo fortified with Wifdom, Courage, and Truth ; befides the
ftrong Band of former Friendfhip ftanding for him in the Counts noble Nature ; that by comming to Terms of Expoftulation, there was wrought through
himfelf, if not a Kind of Unity between the Earl of *Leicefter*, and the Count
Hollock, yet at leaft a finall Surceafe of all violent Jealoufies, or factious Ex-
poftulations. ' To be fhort (fays the [h] Lord *Brook*) not in Complements and
' Art, but real Proof given of his Sufficiency above others ; in a very little
' Time his Reputation, and Authority, amongft that active People, grew fo
' faft, as it had been no hard Matter for him, with the Difadvantage of his
' Uncle, and Diftraction of Affairs in thofe Parts, to have raifed himfelf a
' Fortune there. But in the whole Courfe of his Life, he did fo conftantly
' ballance Ambition with the fafe Precepts of divine and moral Duty, as no
' Pretenfe whatfoever could have entifed him, to break through the Circle of a
' good Patriot.

In the fame Year, when that unfortunate Stand was to be made before *Zutphen*, to ftop the Iffuing out of the *Spanifh* Army ; with what Alacrity foever
he went to Actions of Honour, yet remembring upon juft Grounds the antient
Sages defcribe the worthieft Perfons to be ever beft armed, he had compleatly
put on his ; but meeting the Marfhal of the Camp lightly armed, the unfpotted
Emulation of his Heart, to venture without any Inequality, made him caft off his
Curaffies ; and fo, by the fecret Influence of Deftiny, to difarm that Part, where
he unhappily received the Wound which occafioned his Death. His Uncle, the
Earl of *Leicefter*, bemoans his hard Fate, in a Letter to Sir *Thomas Heneage*,
Captain of the Queen's Guards, dated 23 *September*, 1586 ; which being communicated to me [i], I fhall recite what is moft remarkable therein, of this moft
famous and immortal General. It begins :

Sithens my other Letters of the 20th, yt fell oute, that, Yefterday Morninge,
fome Intelligence was broughte, that the Enemy was bringing a Convoye of Victuall, garded with 3000 Horfe. There was fente out to ympeache it 200
Horfe and 300 Footemen, and a Nombre more, both Horfe and Foote, to fecond them. Among other young Men, my Nephew, Sir *Philip Sydney*, was,
and the rather, for that the Coronell *Norrice* himfelf went with the Stande of
Footemen to fecond the reft ; but the Vanguard of the Prince was marched,
and came with this Convoye, and, being a myftie Morninge, our Men fell into
the Ambufcade of Footemen, who were 3000, the mofte Mufketts, the reft
Pykes. Our Horfemen being formofte, by their Haft indeede, woulde not

[g] Wood's Athæne Oxon. Vol. 1. p. 183.   [h] Life, p. 141.   Ex Autog. penes William
Oldys de Greys Inn, Gent.

' turne,

' turne, but paffed throughe, and charged the Horfemen that flede at the Backe
' of their Footemen fo valientlie ; albeyt they were 1100 Horfe, and of the verie
' chieffe of all his Troupes, they brouke them, being not 200. Many of our
' Horfes were hurt and killed, among which was my Nephewes owne. He
' wente and changed to another, and woulde needes to the Charge again, and
' onfte pafte thofe Mufketters ; where he receyved a fore Wounde upon his
' Thighe, three Fingers above his Knee, the Bone broken quite in Peeces ; but,
' for which Chance, God did fende fuch a Daye, as I thinke was never many
' Yeres feene, fo fewe againfte fo many.'

Here the Earl proceeds, to enumerate the Commanders and other Perfons of
Diftinction in the Engagement, Colonel *Norrice* who had the Charge of the
Foot, my Lord of *Effex*, Sir *Thomas Perrot*, ' and my unfortunate *Phillip* (faies
' the Earl) with Sir *William Ruffel*, and divers Gentlemen ; and not one hurte,
' but only my Nephew. They killed four of their Enemies chief Leaders, and
' carried the valient Count *Hannibal Gonzaga* away with them upon a Horfe ; al-
' fo took Captain *George Crefier*, the principal Soldier of the Camp, and Cap-
' tain of all the *Albanez*. My Lord *Willoughbie* overthrew him at the firft En-
' counter, Horfe and Man. The Gentleman did acknowledge it himfelf. There
' is not a properer Gentleman in the Worlde towards, than this Lord *Willough-*
' *bie* is ; but I can hardly prayfe one more than another, they did all fo well ; yet
' every one had his Horfe killed or hurt. And it was thought very ftrange,
' that Sir *William Stanley*, with 300 of his Men, fhould pafs, in fpight of fo many
' Mufkets, fuch Troops of Horfe, three feveral Times, making them remove
' their Ground, and to return with no more Lofs than he did. Albeyt I muft
' fay yt was too much Lofs for me, for this young Manne, he was my greateft
' Comforte, next her Majeftie, of all the Worlde, and, if I could buy his Lieffe
' with all I have, to my Sherte I would geve yt. How God will difpofe of him
' I know not, but feare, I muft needes, greatly, the Worfte ; the Blow in fo
' dangerous a Place, and fo great ; yet did I never heare of any Manne that did
' abide the Dreffinge and Settinge his Bones better then he did : And he was
' carried afterwards in my Barge to *Arnheim*, and I heare, this Daye, he ys ftill
' of good Hearte, and comforth all aboute him as much as maye be. God of
' his Mercie graunte me his Lieffe, which I cannot but doubt of greatly. I
' was abrode that Tyme in the Fielde, givinge fome Order to fupplie that Bufi-
' nefs, which did indure almofte twoe Owres in continuall Fighte ; and metinge
' *Phillip* commynge upon his Horfebacke, not a lytle to my Greafe. But I
' woulde you had ftode by to heare his moft loyall Speeches to her Majeftie ;
' his conftant Minde to the Caufe, his lovinge Care over me, and his mofte refo-
' lute Determination for Deathe, not one Jot appalled for his Blow ; which ys the
' mofte greevous that ever I fawe with fuch a Bullet ; ryding fo a longe Myle
' and a Halfe, uppon his Horfe, ere he came to the Campe ; not ceafing to
' fpeak ftill of her Majeftie ; being glad yf his Hurte and Deathe mighte any
' Waye honour her Majeftie ; for hers he was whilefte he lyved, and Gods he
' was fure to be yf he dyed : Prayed all Men, to thinke that the Caufe was as
' well her Majeftie's as the Countrie's ; and not to be difcoraged, for you have
' feene fuch Succeffe, as maye encorage us all ; and this my Hurte is the Ordi-
' nance of God, by the Happe of the Warre. Well, I praye God, yf it be his
' Will, fave me his Lieffe ; even as well for her Majeftie's Service Sake, as for
' myne own Comforte.'

The reft of the Letter, relates to their Enemies Retreat, the Prifoners taken,
and the chief *Spaniards* who were at the Charge, with the Number of their
Forces ; the hazardous Enterprifes of the Lord *North*, who, though bruifed on
the Knee with a Mufquet-Shot, yet, leaving his Bed, haftened to this Rencounter,
one Boot on, and the other off, and went (as the Earl fays) to the Matter very
luftily, *&c.* Signed *Roberte Leycefter*.

As too much cannot be remembered with regard to Truth of this great Man ; I shall now recite what the Lord *Brook* writes [k], of his Behaviour to the Time of his most unhappy End : ' The Horse he rode upon, when he was wounded, ' was rather furiously choleric, than bravely proud, and so forced him to for- ' sake the Field, but not his Back, as the noblest and fittest Biere to carry a ' martial Commander to his Grave. In which sad Progress, passing by the rest ' of the Army, where his Uncle, the General was, and being thirsty, with Ex- ' cess of Bleeding, he called for Drink, which was presently brought him ; but, ' as he was putting the Bottle to his Mouth, he saw a poor Soldier carried along, ' who had eaten his last at the same Feast, gastly casting up his Eyes at the ' Bottle. Which Sir *Philip* perceiving, took it from his Head, and delivered it ' to the poor Man, with these Words, *Thy Necessity is yet greater than mine.* ' And, when he had pledged this poor Soldier, he was presently carried to *Arn-* ' *heim.*'

But of this it must be observed, that the Earl of *Leicester* says, in the Letter beforementioned, that, after his Wound was dressed, he was put in his Barge, and carried to *Arnheim* ; which Circumstance the Lord *Brook* might not know ; but he gives this further [l] Account, ' That the principal Chirurgions of the ' Camp attended him, with a true Zeale, compounded of Love and Reverence, ' to do him Good, and (as they thought) many Nations in him. When they ' began to dress his Wound, he, both by Way of Charge and Advice, told ' them, that while his Strength was yet entire, his Body free from Feaver, and ' his Mind able to endure, they might freely use their Art, cut and search to ' the Bottom : For, besides his Hope of Health, he would make this further ' Profit of the Pains he was to suffer, that they should bear witness, they had a ' sensible natured Man under their Hands, yet one to whom a stronger Spirit ' had given Power above himself, either to do, or to suffer. But if they should ' now neglect their Art, and renew Torments in the Declination of Nature, their ' Ignorance, or Overtenderness, would prove a Kind of Tyranny to their Friend, ' and consequently a Blemish to their Science.

' With Love and Care well mixed, they began their Cure, and continued it ' sixteen Days, not with Hope, but rather such Confidence of his Recovery, as ' the Joy of their Hearts overflowed their Discretion, and made them spread ' the Intelligence of it to the Queen, and all his noble Friends in *England*, where ' it was received, not as private, but publick good News.

' Yet there was an excellent Chirurgion of the Count *Hollock*'s, who, looking ' with no less zealous Eyes than the rest, saw and presaged more Despair. The ' Count himself lay, at the same Instant, hurt in the Throat with a Musquet- ' Shot, yet did he neglect his own Extremity to save his Friend, and, to that ' End, had sent him to Sir *Philip*. This Chirurgion returning one Day to dress ' his Master's Wound, the Count chearfully asked him how Sir *Philip* did : And ' being answered, with a heavy Countenance, that he was not well ; that wor- ' thy Prince (having more Sense of his Friend's Wounds than his own) cried out, ' *Away Villain, never see my Face again, till thou bring better News of that Man's* ' *Recovery* ; *for whose Redemption, many such as I were happily lost.*

' After the sixteenth Day was past, and the very Shoulder-bones of this deli- ' cate Patient worn through his Skin, with constant and obedient Posturing ' his Body to their Art ; he judiciously observing the Pangs his Wound stung ' him with by Fits, together with many other Symptoms of Decay, few or none ' of Recovery, began rather to submit his Body to these Artists, than any far- ' ther to believe in them. During which Suspense, he one Morning, lifting up ' the Clothes for Change and Ease of his Body, smelt some extraordinary noisome ' Savor about him, differing from Oils and Salves, as he conceived ; and, either ' out of natural Delicacy, or, at least, Care not to offend others, grew a little ' troubled with it ; which they that sat by perceiving, besought him to let them ' know what sudden Indisposition he felt : Sir *Philip* ingeniously told it, and

---

[k] Life, p. 144.   [l] Ibid. p. 145.

I   desired

‘ defired them as ingenioufly to confefs, whether they fmelt any fuch noifome
‘ Thing, or no. They all protefted againft it upon their Credits. Whence
‘ he prefently gave this fevere Doom upon himfelf, that it was inward Mortifi-
‘ cation, and a welcome Meffenger of Death.

‘ Shortly after, when the Chirurgions came to drefs him, he acquainted them
‘ with thefe piercing Intelligences, between him and his Mortality. Which
‘ though they oppofed, by Authority of Books, Pareleling of Accidents, and o-
‘ ther artificial Probabilities ; yet moved they no Alteration in him, who judg-
‘ ed too truly of his own Eftate, and from more certain Grounds, than the Va-
‘ nity of Opinion in erring Artificers could poffibly pierce into. So that after-
‘ wards, how freely foever he left his Body fubject to their Practife, and conti-
‘ nued a Patient beyond Exception ; yet did he not change his Mind ; but as ha-
‘ ving caft of all Hope, or Defire of Recoverie, made and divided that little Span
‘ of Life which was left him, in this Manner :

‘ Firft he called the Minifters unto him ; who were all excellent Men of divers
‘ Nations, and before them made fuch a Confeffion of Chriftian Faith, as no
‘ Book, but the Heart, can truly and feelingly deliver. Then defired them to
‘ accompany him in Prayer, wherein he befought Leave to lead the Affembly,
‘ in Refpect (as he faid) that the fecret Sins of his own Heart were beft known
‘ to himfelf, and, out of that true Senfe, he more properly inftructed to apply
‘ the eternal Sacrifice of our Saviour’s Paffion and Merits to him. His religi-
‘ ous Zeal prevailed with this humbly devout and afflicted Company : In which
‘ well-chofen Progrefs of his, howfoever they were all moved, and thofe fweet
‘ Motions witneffed by Sighes and Tears, ever interrupting their common Devoti-
‘ on : Yet could no Man judge in himfelf, much lefs in others, whether this Rack
‘ of heavenly Agony, whereupon they all ftood, were forced by Sorrow for him,
‘ or Admiration of him ; the Fire of this *Phenix* hardly being able, out of any
‘ Afhes, to produce his Equal, as they conceived.

‘ Here this firft Mover ftayed the Motions in every Man, by ftaying himfelf.
‘ Whether to give Reft to that frail wounded Flefh of his, unable to bear the
‘ Bent of Eternity, fo much affected, any longer ; or whether to abftract that
‘ Spirit more inwardly, and by chewing it, as it were, the Cudd of Meditation,
‘ to imprint thofe excellent Images in his Soul ; who can judge but God. Yet,
‘ in this Change, there was little or no Change in the Object. For, inftantly af-
‘ ter Prayer, he entreated this Quire of Divine Philofophers about him, to de-
‘ liver the Opinion of the antient Heathen, touching the Immortality of the Soul.
‘ Firft to fee what true Knowledge fhe retains of her own Effence out of the
‘ Light of herfelf ; then to paralelel with it the moft pregnant Authorities of the
‘ old and new Teftament ; as fupernatural Revelations, fealed up from our
‘ Flefh, for the Divine Light of Faith to reveal, and work by. Not that he
‘ wanted Inftruction or Affurance ; but becaufe this Fixing of a Lover’s Thoughts
‘ upon thofe eternal Beauties, was not only a Cheering up of his decaying Spi-
‘ rits, but, as it were, a Taking Poffeffion of that immortal Inheritance, which
‘ was given unto him by his Brotherhood in Chrift.

‘ The next Change ufed, was the Calling for his Will, which though it may
‘ feem a Defcent from Heaven to Earth again ; yet fuch was the Goodnefs of
‘ his Nature equally difperfed, into the greateft and leaft Actions of his too fhort
‘ Life, that this Will of his remains a Witnefs to the World, that thofe fweet
‘ and large, even dying Affections in him, could no more be contracted with
‘ the Narrownefs of Pain, Grief, or Sicknefs, than any Sparkle of our Immor-
‘ tality can be privately buried in the Shadow of Death.

‘ Afterwards he called for Mufick, efpecially that Song which himfelf had
‘ intitled *Lacuiffe rompue* ; partly (as I conceive by the Name) to fhew that the
‘ Glory of mortal Flefh was fhaken in him ; and, by that Mufick itfelf, to fa-
‘ fhion and enfranchife his heavenly Soul into that everlafting Harmony of An-
‘ gels, whereof thefe Concords were a Kind of terreftrial *Echo*: And, in this fupreme

‘ preme and middle Orb of Contemplations, he bleſſedly went on, within a cir
‘ cular Motion, to the End of all Fleſh.

  ‘ The laſt Scene of this Tragedy, was the Parting between the two Brothers,
‘ the Weaker ſhewing infinite Strength, in ſuppreſſing Sorrow ; the Stronger in-
‘ finite Weakneſs, in expreſſing it : So far did invaluable Worthineſs, in the dy-
‘ ing Brother, inforce the Living to deſcend beneath his own Worth, and, by
‘ abundance of childiſh Tears, bewailed the Publick in his particular Loſs : Yea
‘ ſo far was his *true Remiſſion* of Mind transformed into Ejaculation ; that Sir
‘ *Philip* (in whom all earthly Paſſion did even, as it were flaſh like Lights ready
‘ to burn out) recall thoſe Spirits together, and with a ſtrong Virtue, but weak
‘ Voice, mildly blamed him for relaxing the frail Strengths left to ſupport him,
‘ in his final Combat of Seperation at Hand. And, to ſtop this natural Torrent
‘ of Affection in both, took his Leave with theſe admoniſhing Words :’

  *Love my Memory, cheriſh my Friends ; their Faith to me may aſſure you they are
honeſt ; but, above all, govern your Will and Affections, by the Will and Word of your
Creator, in me beholding the End of this World, with all her Vanities.* And with
this Farewel, deſired the Company to lead his Brother away, and ſoon after died,
aged 32.

  Thus ſaith the noble Author, [m] ‘ You ſee how it pleaſed God to ſhew forth,
‘ and then ſuddenly withdraw this pretious Light of our Sky ; and in ſome Sort
‘ adopted Patriot of the States General. Between whom and him, there was
‘ ſuch a Simpathy of Affections ; as they honoured that exorbitant Worth in Sir
‘ *Philip* ; by which Time and Occaſion had been like enough to metamorphoſe
‘ this new Ariſtocracy of theirs, into their antient and much honoured Form of
‘ *Dukedome.* And he again applauded that univerſal Ingenuity, and proſperous
‘ Undertakings of theirs ; over which perchance he felt ſomething in his own
‘ Nature, poſſible in Time to become an elect Commander.’

  After his Death, which was [n] on the 16th of *October*, 1586, at *Arnheim*, the
States of *Zeland* became Suiters to her Majeſty, and his noble Friends, that they
might have the Honour of burying his Body, at the publick Expence of their
Government. Which Requeſt was not permitted, the Queen, in Regard to his
great Worth and Accompliſhments, giving Order for his Burial at her own Expence.

  Whereupon his Corpſe was brought from *Arnheim* to *Fluſhing* [d], and there
kept 8 Days ; from whence, on the 1ſt of *November*, he was brought to the
Sea-ſide, the *Engliſh* Garriſon, of 1200 Men, being under Arms, marching 3
and 3, the Enſigns trailing ; the Burghers of the Town following ; and his Body embarked under a triple Diſcharge of the ſmall Arms, and great Ordnance. On the [g] 8th of *November*, he was landed at the *Tower* Wharf, and after
conveyed to the *Minories* without *Aldgate*, where he lay in State for ſome Time,
till his magnificent Funeral, on the 16th of *Feb.* following, in St. *Paul*’s Cathedral, *London*, where, on a Tablet, faſtened to a Pillar, was this Inſcription :

  A briefe Epitaph upon the Death of that moſt valiant, and perfect honourable
Gentleman, Sir *Philip Sidney*, Knight, late Governor of *Fluſhing* in *Zealand*,
who received his Deaths Wound at a Battell neare *Zutphen* in *Gelderland*, the
22 Day of *September*, and died at *Arnhem* the 16 Day of *October*, 86. Whoſe
Funerals were performed, and his Body interred, within this Cathedral
Church of Saint *Paul* in *London*, the 16 Day of *February* next following, in
the Yeare of our Lord God, 1586.

[m] Lord Brook, in his Life, p. 161.   [n] Stow’s Annals, p. 730.   [o] Ibid. p. 739.
[p] Wood’s Athenæ, Oxon. Vol. 1, p. 184.

England, *Netherland*, the Heavens, and the Arts,
The Souldiers, and the World hath made fix Parts
Of noble *Sidney* ; for who will fuppofe,
That a fmall Heape of Stones can *Sidney* enclofe ?

England had his Body, for fhe it fed,
Netherland his Bloud, in her Defence fhed :
The Heavens have his Soul, the Arts have his Fame,
The Souldiers the Grief, the World his good Name.

His Burial was ordered by *Robert Cook*, *Clarencieux* King of Arms : Firft
proceeded 32 poor Men in black Gowns, according to his Age ; then Serjeants
of the Band, Fife and Drum, Enfigns trailed ; Lieutenant of Foot, Corpo-
rals, Trumpets, Guidon trailed ; Lieutenant of his Horfe, Conductors
to his Servants ; the Standard borne by a Gentleman ; his Gentlemen,
and Yeomen Servants, 60 ; Phificians and Chirurgeons, Steward of his Houfe,
Efquires, of his Kindred and Friends, 60 ; Knights of his Kindred and Friends,
12 ; the Preacher and Chaplains ; the Penon of his Arms borne ; the Horfe
for the Field, led by a Footman ; a Page riding with a broken Lance ; a barbed
Horfe led by a Footman ; a Page on Horfeback carrying a Battle-Axe, the
Head downward ; Yeomen-Ufhers to the Heralds ; the great Banner borne by
a Gentleman ; *Portcullis* bearing the gilt Spurs ; *Bluemantle* the Gauntlets ;
Rouge Dragon the Helmet and Creft ; *Richmond* the Shield of Arms ; *Somerfet*
the Coat of Arms ; *Clarencieux* King of Arms ; Gentleman-Ufher to the Corpfe ;
2 Bannerolls ; the Corpfe covered with a velvet Pall, carried by 14 Yeomen ; 2
Bannerolls following ; Sir *Robert Sidney*, chief Mourner ; Mourners Affiftants ;
4 Knights ; two Gentlemen-Ufhers to the Noblemen ; the Earls of *Huntington*,
Leicefter, *Pembroke*, and *Effex* ; Barons *Willoughby* and *North*, Supporters of the
Pall ; States of *Holland* 7 [from the 7 Provinces] in Black ; the Sword-Bearer of
London on Horfeback ; the Lord-Mayor and Aldermen on Horfeback, in their
fcarlet Gowns lined with Ermin ; the Company of Grocers in *London*, in their
Livery Gowns, 120 [Sir *Philip* being free of their Company] ; Citizens of *Lon-
don* practifed in Arms, marched 3 and 3, in the Front, the Captain, Lieutenant,
and 3 Targets ; Mufketeers 4 Ranks, Drums and Fife ; Small-Shot 20 Ranks ;
Pikes 20 Ranks ; Halberds 4 Ranks ; Chief Officers of the Field, Drums,
Fife, and Enfign ; in the Rear, Halberds 3 Ranks, Pikes 15 Ranks, Drums
and Fife, Small-Shot 15 Ranks, Mufketeers 3 Ranks, *&c.* and, when the
Corpfe were interred, they honoured him with a double Volley of Shot.

So general was the Lamentation for him, that, for many Months after, it
was [q] accounted indecent for any Gentleman of Quality, to appear at Court or
City, in any light or gaudy Apparel. King *James* honoured him with an Epi-
taph of his own Compofition : The Mufes of *Oxford*, lamenting much for his
Lofs [r], compofed Verfes to his Memory, printed in *Quarto* at *Oxon*, 1587 :
The moft ingenious Univerfity of *Cambridge*, did likewife greatly lament his
Death, in Verfes of their Compofition, publifhed by *Alex. Nevile*, one of their
Members, *Quarto*, 1587.

The Lord *Brook* hath given an excellent Character of his Will ; and, it being
not already communicated to the Publick, I fhall here infert it :

IN THE NAME OF GOD AMEN [s], I Sir *Philipp Sydney*, Knight, fore wounded in Body, but whole in Mind, all Praifes be to God, do make this my
Laft Will and Teftament, in Manner and Form following : Firft, I bequeath
my Soul to Almighty God that gave it me, and my Body to the Duft from
whence it came. *Item*, I give and bequeath, and do endow Dame *Franclucis
Sidney*, my Wife, of the one Half of all my Mannors, Lands, Tenements, Rents,
Rights, and Reverfions, with all and fingular the Appurtenances and Commo-

---

[q] Life of Sir Ph. Sydney, before his Arcadia, p. 17.   [r] Wood, præd. 185.   [s] Ex Regift.
Leiceft. qu. 57. in Cur. Prærog. Cantuar.

dityes whatfoever, for and during her natural Life only. *Item*, I give and bequeath to my Brother *Thomas Sydney*, and to the Heirs Male of his Body lawfully begotten, fo much of my Lands as is now worth yearly C *l. Englifh* Money, or may fo be lett by Year, to be affigned and fet out to him by my Brother *Robert Sydney*, fo foon as conveniently he may, after my Death ; and, if he do not fo affigne the fame, then I befeech and will, that the Right Honourable the Earl of *Huntingdon*, by himfelf, or fome other chofen by him, do it ; always excepted, that it be not affigned, out of the Mannor of *Penfhurft*, nor of any Parcel thereof. *Item*, I will, and abfolutely authorife, the Right Honourable Sir *Francis Walfingham*, and my Brother *Robert Sydney*, or either of them, to fell fo much of my Lands lying within the Countys of *Lincoln*, *Suffex*, or *Southampton*, as fhall pay all my Debts, as well thofe of my Father, deceafed, as of mine own ; befeeching them to haften the fame, and to pay the Creditors with all poffible Speed, according to that Letter of Attorney, which Sir *Francis Walfingham* already hath, fealed and fubfcribed by me to that End. Which Letter of Attorney, I do hereby confirm and ratifie, fo far forth, as concerneth for that Purpofe, to all Effect of Law. *Item*, I give and bequeath to my Brother *Robert Sydney*, and to the Heirs Males of his Body lawfully begotten, and, for Default of fuch Iffue, to my Brother *Thomas Sydney*, and to the Heirs Males of his Body lawfully begotten, all other my Lands, Tenements, Rights, Reverfions, and Commodityes whatfoever, with all and fingular their Appurtenances, together with the Reverfion and Inheritance in Fee, of all thofe Lands, with the Appurtenances, which I have before bequeathed to my Wife, during her Life natural. And the Remainder of thofe Lands which I have alfo bequeathed to my Brother *Thomas*, and to his Heirs Males, upon this Condition, that he, the faid *Robert Sydney*, or his Heirs, do well and truly pay to *Elizabeth Sydney*, my Daughter, the full and entire Sum of four thoufand Pounds of *Englifh* Money, at, or before, the Feaft of St. *Michael the Arch Angel*, which fhall be in the Year of our Lord God, one thoufand five hundred eighty and eight. And that he, or his Heirs, do alfo pay yearly fuch Annuitys, as hereafter, in this my Will, I have bequeathed to my Servants, in Confideration of their Services. Which Sum of four thoufand Pounds, fo to be paid by my faid Brother, I give unto my faid Daughter for her Portion. And pray the Right Honourable Sir *Francis Walfingham*, or the other, whom the Law fhall appoint Tutors over her, to put to the beft Behoofe, for the better Preferment of my faid Daughter, either by Purchafe of Land or Leafe, or other good and godly Ufe, but in no Cafe to let it out for any *Vfury* at all. Provided always, that if Dame *Frances Sydney*, my Wife, be now with Child with Iffue Male, and that that Iffue Male liveth, that then my Will and Bequeft to my Brother *Robert Sydney*, of my Lands, with their Appurtenances, aforefaid, be merely void to all Effect, as though it had never been ; any Claufe, Word, Sentence, or Conftruction to the Contrary, notwithftanding. And then I will and bequeath, that my Daughter, *Elizabeth Sydney*, fhall have two Parts of all my Lands before bequeathed to my Brother *Robert Sydney*, for and untill fhe, or her Tutors for her, have clearly received, or may well receive, the Sum of four thoufand Pounds, for her Portion, as aforefaid. But, if fo be my Wife be now with Child with Iffue Female, then I will, that my Brother *Robert Sydney* fhall have my Lands, to him and his Heirs Males, as before I have bequeathed, paying further to that Iffue Female, my Daughter, the Sum of one thoufand Pounds *Englifh* Money, at the Feaft of St. *Michael the Arch Angel*, which fhall be in the Year of our Lord God, one thoufand five hundred eighty and eight. Which Sum, together with the faid four thoufand Pounds, before bequeathed to *Elizabeth Sydney*, my Daughter, and by my Brother *Robert* to be paid ; I then will, to be equally divided between them, and the one to have as much as the other, in every Condition. *Item*, I will, that if my Wife be now with Child of Iffue Male, and that that Iffue Male dye without Heirs Males of his Body lawfully begotten, that then my Lands fhall revert and come to my Brother *Robert Sydney*, and to the Heirs Males of his Body lawfully begotten, as before is bequeathed.

I

Item,

Item, I give to my moſt honourable good Lord, the Earl of *Leiceſter,* one hundred Pounds, as a Token of my devowed Service, and great Love, which I have ever borne to him in all Duty. *Item,* I give to my ſingular good Lord, the Earl of *Warwick,* one hundred Pounds, as a Remembrance of my Duty and great Love to him. *Item,* I give and bequeath to my dear Siſter, the Counteſs of *Pembroke,* my beſt Jewell beſet with Diamonds. *Item,* I give and bequeath to my moſt honoured good Ladys, the Counteſs of *Huntington,* the Counteſs of *Warwick,* and the Counteſs of *Leiceſter,* every one of them a Jewell, the beſt I have. *Item,* I give and bequeath to my very good Friend, Sir *William Ruſſell,* my beſt gilted Armour. *Item,* I give and bequeath to my dear Friends, Mr. *Edward Dyer,* and Mr. *Fulke Grevell,* all my Books. *Item,* I give and bequeath to Mr. *Edward Wotton* one Fee Buck, to be taken yearly out of my Park at *Penſhurſt,* during his Life natural. *Item,* I give, grant, and bequeath to my Servants *Henry White, Henry Lyndley,* and *Griffith Madox,* ſeveral Annuitys of forty Pounds by Year, to every one of them, for and during their Lives natural; to iſſue out and go out of thoſe my Lands before bequeathed to my Brother *Robert Sydney,* and by him or his Heirs, or the Occupiers of thoſe Lands, yearly to be paid to every of them, during their Lives natural, according to the true Meaning of this my Will, any Clauſe before written to the contrary in any wiſe notwithſtanding. *Item,* I give to my Servant *Philip Jordayne,* and to his Wife, and to the longer Liver of them, one Annuity of thirty Pounds by Year, to be paid unto them by my Brother *Robert Sydney,* out of the ſaid Lands before to him bequeathed, for and during their Lives natural, and the longer Liver of them. *Item,* I give to my Servant *Adrian Molgueros* one Annuity of twenty Marks by Year, for and during his Life natural; to be paid unto him, as to the other before is ſet down. *Item,* I give and bequeath to my Servant *Stephen,* now Priſoner in *Dunkirk,* the Sum of two hundred Pounds, to be paid unto him, either there, to redeem him thence, if there be no other *Mean,* or, after his Coming out, for his better Maintenance: Beſeeching, moſt humbly, the Right Honourable the Earl of *Leiceſter,* and the Right Honourable Sir *Francis Walſingham,* to be a *Mean* for his Deliverance, to whoſe good Favour I commend the State of him, having lain ſo long in Miſery. *Item,* I give and bequeath to my Servant *Triſtram Gibbs* the Sum of twenty Pounds; and I do ſpecially commend him to the good Favour of my Brother *Robert Sydney,* and pray him, to have a favourable Care over him, and of my Servant *Philip Jordayne. Item,* I give to every Gentleman, my Servant in Ordinary, which came with me in *November* laſt to *Fluſhing,* and have, ſince that Time, waited on me, the Sum of ten Pounds; and, to every other Gentleman, my Servant in Ordinary, five Pounds. And I give to all my Yeomen, which, in *November* laſt, came with me to *Fluſhing,* and ſince have waited on me, five Pounds; and to every other my Servants now in Ordinary, three Pounds. *Item,* I give and bequeath to Dr. *James,* for his Pains taken with me in this my Hurt, the Sum of thirty Pounds. *Item,* I give to the five Surgeons, which take Pains with me, in this my Hurt, to every of them, the Sum of twenty Pounds. *Item,* I will, that my Wife cauſe three Rings to be made, and, in every of them a Diamond, to be preſented and given, one to the Right Honourable the Earl of *Huntingdon,* one other to the Right Honourable the Earl of *Pembroke,* and the third, to my very good Lady, the Counteſs of *Suſſex,* in Token of my very dutifull Love to every of them. *Item,* I give and bequeath to my moſt honoured good Father-in-Law, Sir *Francis Walſingham,* one hundred Pounds; and to that moſt honourable Lady, the Lady *Walſingham,* my good Mother-in-Law, one hundred Pounds, to beſtow in Jewells, or other Things, as pleaſeth them to wear for my Remembrance. *Item,* I give and bequeath to my Servant, *John Vvedale,* in Conſideration that he hath voluntarily releaſed unto me his Title of *Ford-Place,* which I gave him, and in Conſideration of his long and very faithfull Service to me, the Sum of five hundred Pounds *Engliſh* Money, to be paid unto him by my Executrix, immediately after my Death; and I pray the Right Honourable Sir *Francis Walſingham,* and other my very honourable good

Friends,

Friends, to favour him much for my Sake, and to let him have Accefs unto them, and their Countenances and Help in his good and honeft Caufes, when-foever he fhall need them. *Item*, I pray and befeech the Right Honourable Sir *Francis Walfingham*, to favour my Servant, *John Langford*, and to be the *Mean* to her Majefty, that he may have the Keeping of *Otford* Park, or to ufe other good *Mean*, as it pleafeth him, that my Servant may ftill enjoy the fame hereafter, as heretofore he hath done by the Grant of my Father. *Item*, I will, that my Brother *Robert Sydney* fhall alfo pay to mine Executrix, out of thofe my Lands to him bequeathed, as aforefaid, all my Legacys given by this my Will, and that fhe again pay them according to my Bequeft and Mean-ing. Or elfe I will and authorize the Right Honourable Sir *Francis Walfing-ham*, to fell fo much Lands as I have bequeathed to my Brother *Robert*, as he may, with the Sum of Money which he fhall receive for the fame, pay to mine Executrix, and fhe again, to pay them over all thofe Legacys whatfoever, which I have bequeathed, as aforefaid. *Item*, I pray mine Executrix to be good, and to give fo much Money, as to her Difcretion fhall feem good, to thofe mine old Servants, to whom by Name particularly I have given nothing to ; refer-ring it to her, as fhe fhall think good. *Item*, The reft of all my Goods, moveable and immoveable, and all my Chattels, I give and bequeath to my moft dear and loving Wife, Dame *Frances Sydney*, whom I make my fole Exe-cutrix of this my laft Will and Teftament. And I conftitute and appoint the Right Honourable the Earl of *Leicefter*, the Earl of *Huntingdon*, the Earl of *Warwick*, the Earl of *Pembroke*, and Sir *Francis Walfingham*, jointly and feve-rally, Supervifors of this my Will and Teftament : Befeeching them to have an honourable Care to fee the Things performed, according to my true Mean-ing therein contained. Given under my Hand and Seal at *Archam*, the laft Day of *September*, one thoufand five hundred eighty and fix, and in the eight and twentyeth Year of the Reign of my moft gracious Sovereign, Queen *Eliza-beth*, of *England*, &c. *Ph. Sydney.* I give and bequeath to my dear Friend, *William Hungate*, one Ring to be made for him, with my Name engra-ven in it, of twenty Pounds Vallue, for him to wear in my Remembrance. *Item*, I give to her Majefty, my moft gracious Sovereign, one Jewell, worth one hundred Pounds, which I pray Sir *Henry Goodier*, my good Coufin and Friend, to prefent to her Royal Highnefs, as a Remembrance of my moft loyal and bounden Duty to her Majefty. *Item*, I will, that a Jewell, of twenty Pounds Value, be bought and prefented in like Manner by him, to my fingular good Friend, Sir *Thomas Hennage*, in Token of my great Love unto him. Signed, fealed, and delivered to *Henry Lyndley*, the Day and Year above-faid, in the Prefenfe of Us, *William Hungate*, *John Vvedale*, *Phillippi Jordan*, *George Digby*, *Henry Goodier.*

A CODICIL to be annexed to my Will, on *Monday* the feventeenth of *October*, a thoufand five hundred eighty fix. *Firft*, I add unto my Will thefe Parts and Legacys following : I give and bequeath to Captain *Richard Harte* the yearly Annuity of ten Pounds, to iffue and go out of my Lands, before be-queathed to my Brother *Robert Sydney*, during his Life natural. *Item*, I give to Mr. *Temple* the yearly Annuity of thirty Pounds by Year, to be in like Manner paid, during his Life natural. *Item*, I give and bequeath to *Ivert*, the Bone-fetter, twenty Pounds. *Item*, I give to Mr. *Marten*, my Surgeon, twenty Pounds. *Item*, I give to *Roger*, my Apothecary, fix Pounds 13 *s.* 4 *d.* *Item*, I give to the four Surgeons, before named in my Will, *viz.* Goodridge, Kelley, *Adrian*, and *John*, every of them ten Pounds a Piece more. *Item*, I give to the Doctor, that came to me Yefterday, twenty Pounds more. *Item*, I give to my moft honourable Lord, the Earl of *Leicefter*, my beft Hangings for one Chamber, and the beft Piece of Plate I have. *Item*, I give to my beloved and much honoured Lord, the Earl of *Effex*, my beft Sword. *Item*, I give to my noble Lord, the Lord *Willoughby*, one other Sword, the beft I have. *Item*, I give to Mr. *Gifford*, Minifter, twenty Pounds. *Item*, I give to Mr. *Fountain*, the Minifter,

Minifter, twenty Pounds. *Item,* I give to my good Friends, Sir *George Digbie,* and Sir *Henry Goodere,* either of them a Ring.

  Ge. Digby. H. Goodere.   *Philip Sydney.*

Which Will was proved in the *Prerogative* Court of *Canterbury,* 19 *June,* 1589, and Adminiftration granted to the Lady *Frances,* his Relict, and Executor.

  The Authors that have given Characters of Sir *Philip Sydney,* and his Writings, are too numerous to infert; I fhall, therefore, only mention, what the learned *Camden* has [t] faid of him and his Family : ' The River *Medway* runs
' by *Penfhurft,* the Seat of the antient Family of the *Sidneys,* defcended from
' *William de Sidney,* Chamberlain to King *Henry the Second* ; of which Family,
' was *Henry Sidney,* the famous Lord Leivt. of *Ireland,* who, by the Daugh-
' ter of *John Dudley,* Duke of *Northumberland,* and Earl of *Warwick,* had *Phi-*
' *lip* and *Robert* : But *Philip* is not to be omitted without an unpardonable
' Crime ; (the great Glory of that Family, the great Hopes of Mankind, the
' moft lively Pattern of Virtue, and the Darling of the learned World) who
' hotly engaging the Enemy at *Zutphen,* in *Gelderland,* loft his Life bravely.
' This is that *Sidney,* who as Providence feems to have fent into the World to
' give the prefent Age a Specimen of the Antients ; fo did it on a fuddain, re-
' call him, and fnatch him from us, as more worthy of Heaven than Earth,
' Thus where Virtue comes to Perfection, it is gon in a Trice ; and the beft
' Things are never lafting. Reft then in Peace, O *Sidney* (if I may be allowed
' this Addrefs) we will not celebrate your Memory with Tears, but Admira-
' tion ; whatever we loved in you (as the beft of Authors, [u] fpeaks of that beft
' Governour of *Britaine*) whatever we admired in you, ftill continues ; and will
' continue in the Memories of Men, the Revolutions of Ages, and the Annals
' of Time. Many, as inglorious, and ignoble, are buried in Oblivion ; but
' *Sidney* fhall live to all Pofterity, For as the *Grecian* Poet has it, *Virtue's be-*
' *yond the Reach of Fate.*

It was 1ft propofed for him to be married to a Daughter of the famous Secretary *Cecil,* on the Recommendation of his Uncle, *Robert* Earl of *Leicefter* ; as appears from his Fathers Letter to the Secretary 14 *Feb.* 1569: But he took to Wife, *Frances,* only Daughter of the memorable Sir *Francis Walfingham,* Principal Secretary of State to Queen *Elifabeth,* by whom he left a Daughter, *Elifabeth,* born in 1585. [w] *Scipio Gentilis,* an eminent *Civilian,* wrote a *Latin* Poem, on her Nativity, entitled, *Nereus, five de Natali* Elizabethæ, *illuftrif.* Philippi Sydnæi *filiæ.* Lond. 1585. She was married to *Roger Manners,* Earl of *Rutland* ; and by Inquifition taken after her Deceafe at Eaft *Grinfted* in *Suffex,* 30th of *Oct.* in the 10th Year of King *James the Firft,* it appears that [x] fhe died without Iffue, on the 1ft of *Sept.* in the faid 10th Year of King *James* ; and that *Robert,* Vifcount *Lifle,* Lord *Sydney* of *Penfhurft,* is Uncle, and next Heir of the aforefaid *Elifabeth,* Countefs of *Rutland,* and was of the Age of 48 Years and upwards : And by her Deceafe, was Heir to the Scite, Circuit, and Precinct of the late Monaftery, or Abbey of *Roberts-bridge,* with the Mannor, *&c.* in *Suffex.* Alfo of the Mannor and Appurtenances, called *Udiam,* lying in the Parifhes of *Ewherft, Whatlington,* alias *Whatling, Sedlefcombe,* and *Salerft,* in the faid County ; and of one Houfe for Cafting of Iron in *Ewherft* aforefaid, and of divers Lands there, called *Bad-lands* : Alfo of the Mannor and divers Lands, called *Halden,* lying in *Halden, Tenterden, Bowden, Biddenden,* and *Bennendon,* in the County of *Kent.* As alfo of the Gift of the Mafter and twelve Brethren of the Hofpital, called *The Hofpital of* Robert, Earl of Leicefter, *in Warwick,*
  Which *Robert,* Lord Vifct. *Lifle,* fo mentioned in the Inquifition, to be Un-

[t] Britania in Kent, Edit. 1695. p. 191. [u] Tacitus of Agricola. [w] Wood, p. 185.
[x] Efc. 10 Jac. 2. Suffex, no. 52.

cle and Heir to the said *Elisabeth*, Countess of *Rutland*; was also, by her Decease, Heir to *Ambrose Dudley*, Earl of *Warwick*, and *Robert Dudley*, Earl of *Leicester*, being 2d Son of Sir *Henry Sydney*, Knight of the Garter, and the Lady *Mary Dudley* his Wife, Daughter of *John*, Duke of *Northumberland*, Father of the said Earls. He was [y] baptised at *Penshurst* 28 *Nov.* 1563, 6 *Elis.* And had a generous Education, both at Home and Abroad. [z] Having spent some Time in the University of *Oxford*, he, in 1578, was sent to travel, and to attain foreign Languages, as appears from a Letter of his Father, Sir *Henry Sydney*, to him, dated 24 *March* that Year, whereby we are informed that he was under the Direction of the famous Mr. *Languet*, Dr. *Lubetyus*, and Dr. *Sturmius*, at *Strasburg*; but the whole Letter is very remarkable, and will be printed in the Collections.

He took early to a Martial Life; and when his Uncle, the Earl of *Leicester*, was sent over with the Queens Forces, into the *Netherlands*, he [a] embarqued with him, on the 8th of *December*, 1585, and arrived at *Flushing*, two Days after. He [b] was in that Engagement, with his Brother Sir *Philip Sidney*, and for his Valour was knighted by the Earl of *Leicester*; on 7 *Oct.* 1586.

Queen *Elisabeth*, by Letters Patent under the great Seal, dated 28 *Jan.* 31 *Elis.* 1588, grants to her beloved and faithful Subject, Sir *Robert Sidney*, that imediately without any Probation of his Age, or Prosecution of his Inheritance, out of the Hands of the Queen, her Heirs or Successors, according to the Course of the *Chancery*, or according to the Law and Course of the Court of Wards, and Liverys, or the Law of *England*, he should enter [c] into all, and singular the Baronys, Manors, &c. of which Sir *Philip Sidney*, his Brother, were possessed, or any of the Ancestors of the said Sir *Robert Sidney*. Also on 16 *July* 1588, he was [d] constituted Lord Governour of *Flushing*, one of the Cautionary Towns in the *Netherlands*. And the same Year was sent by the Queen to the King of *Scots*, [e] to compliment him for his Respect towards her Majesty, and to return him Thanks on his Conduct in the *Spanish* Invasion; as also to acknowledge his generous and cheerfull Adherence to the common Cause, and to promise the like Assistance on her Majestys Part, should the *Spaniards* attempt to land in *Scotland*. And returned [f] with Assurances, that the King would stand firm to her Interest, and would defend and assist those of the Protestant Religion. [g] The University of *Oxford*, soon after his Return, conferred on him the Degree of M. A. And in 1593, he was sent Ambassador to the King of *France*, to recommend to him the Protestant Religion, and its Professors, and to take Care of the *English* Affairs at that Court. Where he so demeaned himself, that *R. White*, Esq; 4 *Oct.* 1595, advertises him, of Sir *Roger Williams* being come from *France*, who told him, ' That the French King, in very great ' Kindness, asked hym for you (i. e. Sir *Robert Sidney*.) and said at his Table ' many good Words of you, and willed hym, to put you in Mynd of the ' Hownd you had promised hym. Madam, in like Sort, asked very gra- ' ciously where you were. He thinkes you shall doe well to wryte to the King, ' and to her, as Occasion serves.

In 1597 (40 *Elis.* being joined in Command [h] with Sir *Francis Vere*, over those *English* Auxiliaries, which had been sent against the *Spaniards*, in Aid of Prince *Maurice* of *Nassau*, he shared in the Honour of that Victory, then obtained, at *Turnholt* in *Brabant*; when by their Conduct and Courage, 2000 *Neopolitans* and *Germans*, with their Generals, were slain. Of which Engagement, *Camden* observes, that he must leave it to the Pens of those who manage the History of the *Low-Countries*, to do Right to the Courage and Bravery of Sir *Robert Sidney*, and Sir *Francis Vere*, and to let the World know, how bravely they behaved themselves.

He was both before, and about this Time; in that Credit with the most

[y] Ex Regist. Ecclef. de Penshurst.   [z] Wood's Athenæ Oxon. Vol. 1. p. 762.   [a] Stow's Annals, p. 711.   [b] Ib. p. 738.   [c] Pat. 31 Elif. apud Penshurst.   [d] Pat. eod Ann. apud Penshurst.   [e] Camden's Annals in Hist. of Engl, Vol. 2. p. 549.   Wood ut antea.
[g] Camden's Annals, ut supra, p. 574.   [h] Ib. p. 597.

confiderable Perfons of the Court (as the Letters to him, which will be publifhed in the Colletion fhew) that the Queen was ftrongly follicited to make him
a Baron, and to confer on him, the Place of Lord Chamberlain of her Houfehold. The Earl of *Effex* (the Favourite of Queen *Elifabeth*) in the Sicknefs of
the Lord *Hunfdon,* Lord-Chamberlain, which terminated in his Death, 23 *July,*
38 *Elif.* 1596, wrote to him as follows :

Robin,

I am nott in Cafe to write largely either in Complements, or of Affaires. I do
write affetionatly to you, as I muft do ever : And wifh thatt nott my
Wordes, butt fome other reall Demonftration, might make you know how much
you are beloved of

PS. Love the Bearer, this honeft valiant
Captayne, the more for my Sake,
for I will be thankfull for yt, and
he will deferve yt.

Your trew Freind,

Effex.
20th of Febr.

Superfcribd,
To my Honorable Frind, Sir *Robert Sidney,*
Knight, L. Governour of *Ulifhing.*

Robin,

I do beleeve now that my Lord Chamberlayne will dy.   And I am refolved,
yf his Lordfhip do teake himfelf to an other World, to deale erneftly and
confedently for you,   I know Lord *Brooke* doth refolve to try both his Creditt
with the Queen, and all his Frendes in this Caufe.   But I will proteft unto
the Queen againft him, and avow, thatt I will think yt is the Reward of his
Slanders and Pratife againft me, yf the Queen fhold lay Honor upon him.
Of thefe Thinges I will geve you Accompt ; and fo, with my beft Wifhes,
I reft

You know by my Hand
that this is my Wyves
Pen and Inke.
4 *March,* 1596.

Your trew Frend,

Effex.

Superfcribed,

For my Lord Governor of
Flufhing, my very Deere
and Honorable Frend.

Notwithftanding this Affurance, the Lord *Brook* was made Lord Chamberlain,
and died in that Office.

Soon after the Earl, declining in Queen *Elifabeths* Favour, was drawn by his
Followers and Dependants into thofe extravagant Defigns, that brought his
Head to the Block.   The Friendfhip between his Lordfhip and Sir *Robert Sydney,* grew from their Services in the Warrs of the *Low-Countries,* and was ce-
mented by his Uncle *Robert Dudley,* Earl of *Leicefter,* having married the Earl
of *Effex*'s Mother, as alfo by the Intermarriage of this *Robert,* Earl of *Effex,*
with Sir *Philip Sydneys* Widow. But tho' Sir *Robert Sydney,* was at fome Meetings with his Lordfhip, and his Friends (whereof the Lord *Buckhurft*) in a Letter to him at *Flufhing* (which will be publifhed in the Colletion) mentions the
Queens Knowledge of his being at a Banquet; *&c.* and her Difpleafure thereat ;
yet he had the Wifdom to be no Ways concerned in their Intrigues.   And in
1601 (44 *Elif.*) when that unfortunate Nobleman endeavoured to raife an Infur-
retion, [1] he was fo far from being concerned therein, that he was one of the
Commanders of thofe Forces imploied againft him ; and was fent by the Lords,
to the Earl, to perfuade him to furrender.

[1] Camden, ut antea.

On

On King *James*'s Acceſſion to the Throne, he had his Patent renewed [k], as Governor of the Town of *Fluſhing* and Caſtle of *Rumekins*, *viz.* on 22 *April*, 1603. And by Letters Patent, bearing Date the 13th of *May* following [l], was advanced to the Dignity of a Baron of this Realm, by the Title of Lord *Sydney*, Baron of *Penſhurſt*, in *Kent*; in Conſideration (as the Patent imports) of his noble Deſcent; his Wiſdom and Prudence in ſeveral Negotiations; and his Conduct and Valour in the Wars in the *Low-Countries*. On which it may be obſerved, that his Aunt *Catharine*, Counteſs of *Huntington*, and his Niece, *Eliſabeth*, Counteſs of *Rutland*, were then living, and Heirs of the Body of *Edward Grey*, and *Eliſabeth Talbot* [m], who had a Patent, in 15 *Edw.* IV, to hold the Honour of Baron *L' Iſle*, to them and the Heirs of the Body of the ſaid *Eliſabeth* his Wife lawfully begotten; with Seat and Voice in Parliament, as her Anceſtors the Barons *L' Iſle* had held.

Alſo the Lord *Sydney*, on 25 *July*, the ſame Year (being the Day of the King and Queen's Coronation) was [n] made Lord Chamberlain to the Queen; who afterwards conſtituted his Lordſhip general Surveyor [o] of all her Honours, Caſtles, Lordſhips, Mannors, Woods, Lands, *&c.* within the Realm of *England*. And, the Year after, he was [p] one of the chief of the Nobility and Officers of State, that ſigned the Patent for creating *Charles*, Duke of *Albany*, Duke of *York*.

In the ſame Year (2 *Jac.* I.) the longeſt Suit, that had ever been in *Chancery*, was compromiſed between his Lordſhip and *Henry* Lord *Berkley*, by the Arbitration of Sir *Thomas Forſter*, Knight, Serjeant at Law, and Sir *Henry Montagu*, Knight, Recorder of the City of *London*; bearing Date 5 *March*, 1604, 2 *Jac.* I [q]. By the ſaid Arbitration, it was awarded, That the Borough of *Wotton*, Forrien of *Wotton*, *Wotton* Liberty, *Wotton* Mannor, and all other Villages, Pariſhes, and Hamlets, of late heretofore claimed to be within the ſuppoſed Hundred of *Wotton*, are and ought to be within the Hundred of *Berkley*, and ſo ſhall hereafter continue and be accounted of the Hundred of *Berkley*. And that there is not, nor ought to be, any ſuch Hundred of *Wotton* in the County of *Glouceſter*. And that all and every the Pariſhes, Villages, and Hamlets of *Wotton*, *Nibley*, *Cromehall*, *Huntingford*, *Bradley*, *Synwell*, *Wortely*, *Symondſall*, *Comb*, *Uley*, *Oulpen*, *Arlingham*, *Cowley*, *Cam*, *Durſley*, *Woodmancote*, and *Kingſcote*, ſuppoſed to have been within the ſaid Hundred of *Wotton*, are within the ſaid Hundred of *Berkley*. And that the Liberty and Return of Writs, *&c.* within the aforeſaid Pariſhes, do of Right belong, *&c.* to the ſaid *Henry* Lord *Berkley*, and to his Heirs.

And it is further awarded, That there is, and ought to be, a View of frank Pledge, and whatſoever to a View of frank Pledge appertaineth, of all the Reſiants and Inhabitants within the Borough of *Wotton*. And a Leete and View of frank Pledge, *&c.* within the Mannor of *Wotton* Forrein, the Towns, *&c.* of *Nibley*, *Sinwell*, *Wortley*, *Symondſall*, and *Comb* only, as appertainant and belonging to the ſaid Mannor of *Wotton*, and *Wotton* Forrein. And that the ſaid *Leet* or *Leets* ſhall for ever hereafter be uſed and enjoyed, *&c.* by the ſaid Lord *Sydney*, or the Owner or Owners thereof. And that the ſaid Lord *Berkley*, his Heirs or Aſſigns, or any Steward or Officer, *&c.* under him or them, ſhall not hereafter claim, *&c.* or take on him or them, to hold, keep, *&c.* any Leet or View of frank Pledge, within the ſaid Borough or Town of *Wotton*, or Mannor of *Wotton* Forrein, in the ſaid Villages, *&c.* of *Nibley*, *Wortley*, *Symondſale*, *Synwell*, or *Comb*, or of any Reſiants, *&c.* therein. In Witneſs whereof, to the one Part of the Indentures Tripartite, remaining with the ſaid Lord *Berkley*, the ſaid Lord *Sydney*, and the ſaid Arbitrators, ſet their Hands and Seals. And to another of the ſaid Indentures, remaining with the ſaid Lord *Sydney*, the ſaid Lord *Berkley*, and the ſaid Arbitrators, ſet their Hands and Seals. And to the 3d Part of the ſaid Indentures, remaining with the ſaid Arbitrators, as well the

[k] Rymer's Fœdera, Vol. 16. p. 501.　　[l] Pat. 1 Jac. p. 14.　　[m] Ex Rot. Cart. 15 E. IV. n. 18 in Turr.　　[n] Vincent on Brook, p. 311.　　[o] Ex Evident. apud Penſhurſt.
[p] Pat. 2 Jac. I, p. 21. m. 5.　　[q] Ex Original. apud Penſhurſt.

ſaid

faid Arbitrators, as the faid Lord *Berkley*, and Lord *Sydney*, fet their Hands and Seals.

This Law-fuit had been carried on in *Chancery* for feven Generations, from the Death of *Thomas*, Lord *Berkley*, who died on *Sunday*, the Purification of the Virgin, 3 *Hen.* V, 1415, leaving an only Daughter, *Elifabeth*, his fole Heir, married to that great Peer, *Richard Beauchamp*, Earl of *Warwick*, from whom, through the *Talbots*, *Greys*, and the *Dudleys*, the Eftate defcended to this *Robert*, Lord *Sydney*.

On the 4th of *May*, 3 *Jac.* I. he [r] was advanced to the Dignity of Vifcount *L' Ifle*. The Preamble to the Patent fets forth, That the King's moft beloved and faithful Subject, *Robert*, Lord *Sidney* of *Penfhurft*, Lord Chamberlain of his moft beloved Confort, Queen *Anne*, is fprang from the moft illuftrious Blood of the Duke of *Northumberland*, the Earls of *Warwick*, and *Leicefter*, and Vifcount *L' Ifle*. And maturely confidering the moft grateful and moft faithful Services that the faid Lord *Sydney* performed for his moft beloved Sifter, Queen *Elifabeth*, in the Wars ; as alfo his aufpicious, faithful, and prudent Embaffies to Princes in foreign Parts. Alfo his Wifdom, Valour, Dexterity, Integrity, and Fidelity fhewed to him and his Crown, he creates him Lord Vifcount *L' Ifle*, and to the Heirs Male of his Body. And, for the better Support of the Honour, grants to him and them, an Annuity of twenty Marks, iffuing out of the Counties of *Warwick* and *Leicefter*.

The King, 3 *June*, in the 5th Year of his Reign [s], grants to *Robert*, Vifcount *L' Ifle*, the Office of Steward of the Courts of his Mannors of *Timberwood*, *Raynehurft*, and *Blackmanftone*, with the Members, in *Kent*. And of *Peckham*, alias *Eaft Peckham*, *Eaft Farleigh*, and *Bexley*, in the fame County, Parcel of the Lands and Poffeffions of Sir *Thomas Wyatt*. Alfo of the Mannor of *Maydftone*, with the Appurtenances, in *Kent*, Parcel of the Lands and Poffeffions of *Reginald*, late Cardinal *Poole*. To hold by him, or fufficient Deputies, during Pleafure ; with all Fees, Allowances, *&c.*

On the 4th of *June*, 8 *Jac.* I. he [t] was, among the chief of the Nobility and Court, one of the Witneffes to the Creation of *Henry*, Prince of *Wales*.

It further appears, that, in the Year 1613, he was appointed to conduct the Princefs *Elifabeth* (married to *Frederick*, Elector *Palatine* of the *Rhine*) to the Town of *Bacharach*, in his Dominions. And made great Preparations for their Reception at his Government of *Flufhing*, where they were to land ; as is evident by Letters from Sir *John Throgmorton*, Deputy-governor, in the Collection. The Elector was fo taken with his gallant Behaviour and Deportment, as he earneftly requefted him to accompany his Highnefs, and his Confort the Princefs, to the City of *Heidelberg* ; to which Requeft he complied, and was entertained there with great Honour, and with princely Diverfions [u], mentioned by *Stow*. They landed at *Vlifhing*, 28 *April*, and the Lord Vifcount *L' Ifle* took his Leave of the Prince and Princefs, 14 *June*.

In 14 *Jac.* I, the King being follicited by the States of *Holland*, that he would be pleafed to render into their Hands, the Town of *Vlifhing* in *Zeland*, with the Caftle of *Ramekins*, and the *Brill* in *Holland*, with the Forts, *&c.* thereto belonging ; held by Way of Caution, till fuch Sums of Money, as they owed to *England*, were reimburfed, on fuch reafonable Conditions, as fhould be agreed on for the Payment of the faid Monies [w]. Thereupon, the King recommending the Confideration thereof to the Judgment of the Lords of his Privy-council ; they, after mature Deliberation and Examination of Circumftances ; and finding the Towns meerly Cautionary, wherein the King could challenge no Intereft or Property ; gave their Opinions, that it was better, on fair and advantageous Conditions, to render them, than longer to hold them at fo heavy a Charge. On which the King, 22 *May*, 14 *Jac.* I, 1616 [x], Commiffions

---

[r] Pat. 3 Jac. p. 12.   [s] Ex Evident. apud Penfhurft.   [t] Rymer's Fœdera, Vol. 16, p. 688.   [u] Annals, p. 308, & feq.   [w] Rymer's Fœdera, p. 783, 784.   [x] Ibid. 784, & feq.

and orders his right trufty and welbeloved Coufin, *Robert* Lord Vifcount *L' Ifle*, Lord-chamberlain to his moft dear Confort the Queen, and Governor of the Town of *Vlifhing* and Caftle of *Ramekins*, in his (the King's Name) to render and yield up into the Hands of the faid States of the *United Provinces* (or to fuch Perfons as fhall be by them deputed) the aforefaid Town of *Vlifhing*, &c. with all Artillery, Ammunition, &c. performing, in all Points, fuch Inftructions, as he fhould receive under the Hands of the Lords and others of his Council, concerning the Rendering up the faid Town, &c. And further commands him to difcharge all fubordinate Officers, Captains, Soldiers, &c. And thefe Letters Patent, or the Enrolment, or Exemplification thereof, fhould be his fufficient Warrant and Difcharge.

On 7 *July*, 1616, he was [y] inftalled, at *Windfor*, one of the Knights of the moft noble Order of the Garter, at which Time he was Lord-chamberlain of the Houfehold to Queen *Anne*; as appears by his Plate on the 11th Stall, yet remaining there.

On 26 *April*, 1618, 16 *Jac.* I, he [z] was commiffioned, with *Charles*, Earl of *Nottingham*, *Edward*, Earl of *Worcefter*, *Henry*, Earl of *Southampton*, *Thomas*, Earl of *Arundel*, and Earl of *Montgomery*, all Knights of the Garter, to examine the Regifters, &c. of that moft noble Order; and where any Thing fhould be found obfcure, to make it clear ; where Contrariety appeared, fitly to reconcile it. In the Preamble to the Commiffion, the King recites, That he had a fpecial Care to uphold the Dignity of the faid moft noble Order, as appeared by his Choice of noble and worthy Perfons. And, in Confideration of the Knowledge and Experience he had of the Underftanding, Wifdom, and Confidence, he repofed in the Lord Vifcount *L' Ifle*, &c. and in their Faithfulnefs and Sincerity, being Men of Honour, and Knights Companions of the faid Order, he commiffions them, as aforefaid. Accordingly the Lord Vifcount *L' Ifle*, with three of the Commiffioners, had divers Meetings, and debated feveral Things reprefented to them. And, at a Chapter held at *Whitehall*, 19 *May*, 20 *Jac.* I, they prefented to the Sovereign nine Articles, fubfcribed with their Hands, which, for the Honour of the Order, they thought neceffary to be obferved. Whereupon the King, and 12 of the Knights Companions, confirmed them on the 22d of *May* following, in a Chapter held at *Whitehall*.

In 16 *Jac.* I, by Letters Patent, bearing Date the 2d of *Auguft*, 1618, he was [a] dignified with the Title of Earl of *Leicefter*, wherein the Preamble being remarkable, I fhall infert it :

The King, &c. To all Arch Bifhops, Dukes, &c. Greeting. Wee do efteem it to be the higheft Part of Royal Dignity, by a benigne Afpect, not only to ennoble, but to advance to a higher Degree of Nobility, and to difpenfe the moft eminent Honours amongft wife and valiant Perfons. Wee, therefore, judging our Royal Crown to be as refplendant, and to fhine forth the brighter, by our Royal Attention, in promoting Men of tranfcendent Virtue and Merit, and excelling in Council, to exalted Honours, as by the Jewels with which it is adorned. Contemplating, therefore, the Nobility, Candour, and Integrity, of our welbeloved and faithful, *Robert* Vifcount *L' Ifle*, Baron *Sidney* of *Penfhurft*, Chamberlain to our moft dear Confort, Queen *Anne*, and Knight of the moft noble Order of the Garter : Who, with inceffant Labour and Vigilancy, hath, for many Years paft, always manifefted himfelf a ftout and faithful Subject, as well to our moft dear Sifter, Queen *Elifabeth*, as to us, and to this our Kingdom : And alfo calling to Mind the great Defferts of his moft worthy Father, Sir *Henry Sydney*, Knight of the moft noble Order of the Garter, Councellor to our faid Sifter, and Prefident of the Council within the Marches of *Wales*, and Deputy of her Kingdom of *Ireland* : And the noble Defcent of the faid *Robert*, Vifcount *L' Ifle*, Coufen of the late famous Earls of *Warwick* and *Leicefter*. Likewife revolving in our Mind his moft acceptable Services and true Defert,

y Ex Collect. Tho. Meller.   z Afhmole's Order of the Garter, p. 195, 196.
a Pat. 16 Jac. I, p. 11.

as well in the Office of Governour of *Flushing* in *Zeeland*; as in his Embassies *in Scotland*, *France*, and *Germany*, and other his publick Services, concerning the State of our Kingdom: All which he hath ever accomplished with great Fidelity and Dexterity. Besides his good and acceptable Services performed to our most dear Consort the Queen. Wee therefore advance the said *Robert*, Viscount *Lisle*, to be Earl of *Leicester*, &c. with a Grant to him, and his Heirs Male, of an Annuity of 20 *l. per Ann.* payable out of the Customs and Subsidies of the Port of *London*, by the Hands of the Customers, or Collectors.

In 18 *Jac.* I, 1620, he was, [b] in a special Commission, with *Edward*, Earl of *Worcester*, Lord Privy Seal, *Thomas*, Earl of *Exeter*, and others of the Privy-council, to inquire into all and singular Apostacies, in Matters of Faith, Religion, Schisms, unlawful Conventicles, tending to Schism, against the Religion and Government of the Church established.

The Offices and Titles of Honour he held, as also the Letters to him (which will be published in the Collection) wrote by Persons of the first Distinction, both in the Camp, and in the Court, demonstrate his great Worth; and in Effect, shew that he had few who were superior to him, in Abilities and Judgment, Sir *John Throgmorton*, Deputy Governor of *Flushing* (on a Dispute between him, and the Serjeant-Major) by his Letter, dated at *Flushing*, Feb. 15, 1611; says he had been a Captain, in continual Action 22 Years, and the most Part of that Time with his Lordship.

He was married in the Life-time of his Father to [c] *Barbara*, only Daughter and sole Heir of *John Gamage*, of *Coytty*, *Rhogied*, and *Lavihangel*, in the County of *Glamorgan*, Esq; Son and Heir of *John Gamage*, Esq; and *Wenlian* his Wife, [d] paternally descended from *Jestin*, Prince of *Glamorgan*, and *Morganock*, as the *Welch* Heralds assert. And the Family of the *Gamages* descended from *Pain de Gamage*, who coming over with *William the Conqueror*, had of his Gift, the Lordships now called *Gamage-hill*, in *Gloucestershire*, and *Maunsel-Gamage*, in *Herefordshire*: From whom, in lineal Descent, was *William Gamage*, who married, about the Reign of King *Edward the Second*, *Sarah*, 4th and youngest Daughter of Sir *Payne de Turbervile*, the 7th, in lineal Descent, from Sir *Payne Turbervile*; the 3d [e] of the twelve Knights, that came with *Robert Fitz Hamon*, when he conquered *Glamorganshire*, and had of his Gift, the Castle and Lordship of *Coyty*. Which Sir *Payne Turbervile*, the Father of *Sarah*, married to *William Gamage*, as aforesaid, had three other Daughters, and a Son, Sir *Richard Turbervile*, who dying without Issue, [f] entailed the Lordship of *Coyty* on the Heirs Male of Sir *Roger Berkerolls*, Knight, who had married *Catharine*, his eldest Sister; and in Default of such Issue on Sir *Richard Stackpool*, Knight, who married *Margaret*, the 2d Sister, and their Heirs Male; in Default on Sir *John de la Beer*, Knt. and *Agnes* his Wife, 3d Sister, and their Heirs Male; and for Want of such Issue, on *William Gamage* and *Sarah* his Wife, 4th and youngest Sister of the said Sir *Richard Turberville* [g]; Which Line of *Berkrolles* failed in the Heirs Male, by the said Sir *Roger*, who left an only Daughter and Heir, *Wenlian*, married to Sir *Edward Stradling*, of St. *Donats*, in Com. *Glamorg.* Knt. The Line of Sir *Richard Stackpole*, of *Pembrokeshire*, Knt. also failed in the Heirs Male; Sir *George Vernon*, of *Hadden*, in Com. *Derb.* being his Heir General, whose two Daughters, and Heirs, *Dorothy* was the Wife of Sir *John Manners*, Ancestor to the present Duke of *Rutland*; and *Margaret*, the youngest, was married to Sir *Thomas Stanley*, Knt. 2d Son of *Edward*, Earl of *Derby*. Also the Male Line of Sir *John de la Beere* failed in two Daughters and Coheirs, *Elisabeth*, the Wife of Sir *Oliver St. John*, Ancestor to the present Lord Visct. *St. John*, and ———— married to *William Basset*, of *Glamorganshire*, Esq; So that the [h] Inheritance of the Castle and Lordship of *Coyty* centered in the

---

[b] Rymer's Fœdera, Vol. 17. p. 200, & seq. [c] Ex Stemmate apud Penshurst. [d] Ibid.
[e] Powel's Hist. of Wales, p. 125, 126. [f] MS. de Famil. de Gamage apud Penshurst.
[g] Ibid. [h] MS. de Gamage præd.

Family

Family of *Gamage*, by the said Entail; and the Heir thereof, *Babara*, Countess of *Leicester*, brought that, and other Lordships, to her Husband, *Robert Sydney*, the first Earl of *Leicester* [i] : She was buried at *Penshurst*, 26 of *May*, 1621; whereupon his Lordship married, 2dly, *Sarah*, Daughter and Heir of *William Blount*, and Widow of Sir *Thomas Smith*, of *Bidborough* in *Kent*; but the Earl dyed in a few Months after his 2d Marriage, leaving no Issue by her, *viz*. at *Penshurst* 13 *July*, 1626, 2 *Car*. 1, in the 63d Year of his Age, and was there buried, the [k] 16th of the same Month. The Arms of this Earl, with several Quarterings, are impaled with his 2d Wife *Blount*'s Arms and Quarterings, in *Chidingstone* Church in *Kent*.

His Lordship had [l] Issue, by his 1st Lady, 1. Sir *William Sydney*, Knt. born at *Flushing*, who died at *Baynards* Castle in *London*, unmarried, on the 3d of *December*, early in the Morning, and was buried on the 6th of the said Month, 1612, 10 *Jac*. 1. in the Chancel of the Church at *Penshurst*.

2. *Henry Sydney*, [m] born at *Flushing*, who died young, and was there buried.

3. *Philip*, who died young. *Rowland White*, Esq; in his Letter to Sir *Robert Sydney*, dated 25 *Sept*. 1595, relates, that Mrs. *Mary*, and *Catharine Sydney*, doth much profit in their Books. Mr. *William* dances a Galliard in his Doublet and Hose, Mr. *Philip* can go alone.

4. *Robert Sydney*, his only surviving Son and Heir, who on his Father's Death, in 2 *Car*. 1, was so found by Inquisition, now in the Chapel of the Rolls.

Also eight Daughters. 1. Lady *Mary* [n] married 27 *Sept*. 1602, to Sir *Robert Wroth*, of *Durance*, in the County of *Middlesex*, Knt. The famous Poet, *Ben Johnson* [o], has several Epigrams, on this Lady *Mary Wroth*, and her Husband, Sir *Robert*; of which antient Family of *Wroth*, the present Earl of *Rochford* is the Heir, and in Possession of *Loughton-hall* in *Essex*, one of the Seats thereunto belonging. 2. Lady *Catharine*, Wife of Sir *Lewis Mansel*, Knt, and died at *Baynards-Castle* in *London*, the 8th of *May* and was brought to *Penshurst*, and buried there, the 13th of *May*, 1616. *Elisabeth*, 3d Daughter, died unmarried 1 *November* 1605. Lady *Philip*, 4th Daughter (so wrote in the Register of *Penshurst*) born 18 *August* 1594, * married to Sir *John Hobart*, eldest Son to Sir *Henry Hobart*, Bart. Lord Chief Justice of the *Common Pleas*. *Bridget*, 5th Daughter, and *Allice* 6th Daughter, are buried in the Chancel of *Penshurst* with this Inscription in Capitals:

> Here lyeth *Bridget* and *Allice Sydney*, Daughters of *Robert Sydney*, Knight, and Lord of THE House and Manor of *Penshurst*, and of Lady *Barbara* His Wife. Which *Allice*, being of THE Age of six Moneths, Died the xxv of *March Anno* 1599. And *Bridget*, of THE Age of Two Yeres And fower Moneths, Died the last of *June* the same Yeere.

Lady *Barbara*, 7th Daughter, was [p] married to *Thomas* Viscount *Strangford* of the Kingdom of *Ireland*, and of *Ostenhauger* in *Kent*; and 2dly, to Sir *Thomas Culpeper*, of St. *Stephens*, near *Canterbury*. She was baptised 22 *Dec*. 1599; the Earl of *Worcester* was her Godfather; and the Countess of *Nottingham*, and the Lady *Buckhurst*, Godmothers. *Vere*, 8th Daughter, died unmarried and was buried at *Penshurst*, 23 *July*, 1606.

Robert Earl of *Leicester*, only surviving Son and Heir, beforementioned, was born at *Baynards-Castle*, *London*. *Rowland White*, Esq; in his Letter to Sir *Robert Sydney* at *Flushing*, acquaints him, that his Lady was brought to Bed of a goodly fat Son, *Monday* 1 *Dec*. 1595, 9 of the Clock at Night; and that

---

[i] Ex Regist. Ecclef. de Penshurst.   [k] Ibid.   [l] Ibid.   [m] Vincent on Brook, p. 311, 312.   [n] Ex Regist. Ecclef. de Penshurst.   * Vide his Works, Vol. 3.   • Vincent ut antea. [p] Ex Stemmate.

there Days before, fhe was taken ill of the Meafles, was full of them, and had withall a great Cough, and gentle Feaver, and was much afflicted at his Abfence. That the Child was alfo full of the Meafles, moftly in the Face, yet fucked the Nurfe, as well as any Child could, and cried as ftrongly, fo that there was great Hopes of his Living. And by another Letter, dated 3 *Jan.* 1595, he gives him an Account, ' That his Son was chriftned on *New Years* ' Eve, by the Lord *Montjoy*, the Lord *Compton*, and the Lady *Rich* ; they ' named him *Robert*, by the Lady *Rich*'s Defire. They gave three very fair ' ftanding Bowles, all of one Fafhion, worth 20 *l.* each. There was at the ' Baptifm the Lady *Cumberland*, and her Daughter ; the Lady *Effex*, her Daugh- ' ter and Son ; the Lady *Dacres*, and her Daughter ; with many others :'

After being well grounded in Grammar-Learning, he was fent to the Univerfity of *Oxford*, where he became an induftrious Student, as appears by a Letter [q] from his Tutor to the Vifcountefs *Lifle*, his Mother, bearing Date at *Oxford*, the 11th of *April*, 1608. On leaving the Univerfity, his Father conferred on him a Company in his Regiment at *Flufhing*, [r] and after furrendered to him the Command of the faid Regiment. In 1616, he was made Knight of the Bath, at the Creation of *Charles*, Prince of *Wales* ; and bearing the Title of Lord Vifcount *Lifle*, was chofen one of the Knights for the County of *Kent*, in that Parliament, which met in the 18th Year of King *James the Firft*, [s] and one of the Knights for *Monmouthfhire*, in 21 *Jac.* 1. as alfo in the firft Parliament of King *Charles the Firft*.

In 1618, he married the Lady *Dorothy Percy*, eldeft Daughter of that great Peer, *Henry* Earl of *Northumberland*, by *Dorothy* his Wife, Daughter of *Walter Devereux* Earl of *Effex*, who was Son [t] of *Cicely Bourchier*, Sifter and Heir of *Henry Bourchier* Earl of *Effex*, Son and Heir of Sir *William Bourchier*, Vifcount *Bourchier*, Son and Heir of *William* Earl of *Effex*, by [u] *Anne* his Wife, Daughter and Heir of *Thomas* of *Woodftock*, Duke of *Gloucefter*, 6th Son of King *Edward the Third*. By Indenture, 11 *July*, 1618, 16 *Jac.* 1, his Father, then Lord Vifc. *Lifle*, [w] fettled on him, after his Marriage, and on the Lady *Dorothy* his Wife, Daughter of *Henry*, Earl of *Northumberland*, an Annuity of 200 *l. per Ann.* payable out of his Mannors of *Penfhurft, Cepham, Ensfield*, &c. And, if he fhould ceafe to enjoy the Profits of Colonel of a Regiment in the *Low-Countries*, agrees to give him 400 *l. per Ann.* more.

In 1620, being ill ufed by *James Hay*, Lord Vifcount *Doncafter* (a great Favourite of King *James*, who had married the Lady *Lucy*, his Wife's Sifter) he thought proper to refent it ; and has left, in his own Hand-writing, the Occafion thereof, as follows :

The Lord Vifcount Lifle's [x] *Relation of the Difference he had with the Lord* Doncafter, *after Earl of* Carlifle.

I Had often defyred to know of my Lord *Doncafter*, what the Reafon of his Strangnes unto me was, and hauing for that Caufe forborne his Hous for fome Time, when my Father lay at *Marblane (An.* 1620) I writt vnto him to that Purpofe (the Coppy of my Letter, and his Anfwere, I haue yet) but could neuer know of him what I had donn, or what he had bin told of me, or what he fufpected I had bin faulty in towards him ; but ftill continued an vncertain and vnequall Fafhion towards me, fometimes kinde, fometimes otherwife, with Neglect, and fometimes like a Stranger, with much Ceremony : Yet for fome Reafons (efpecially the Loue which was between our Wiues) I frequented his Hous again, defyring only an outward Familiaritie, and neuer hauing it in my Ambition to be his Bofome Freind. This continued untill his firft Returne out of *France* ; then I went to *London* to congratulat his Arriual, when I found him courteous and refpectiue, but not kinde nor fa-

[q] Ex Original. apud Penfhurft.   [r] Ex Autog.   [s] Ex Collect. Br. Willis Arm.   [t] Vincent on Brook. p. 183, 184, & 187.   [u] Rot. Fin. 7 H. V. m. 26.   [w] Ex Evident apud Penfhurft.   [x] Ex Origin. apud Penfhurft.

VOL. I.   I i   miliar

miliar to me, as I faw him to many others : Yet when I had acquainted him (out of my Refpeét vnto him) with my Purpofe to part with my Regiment, hauing no Meanes to beare the great Charges which it drewe me vnto, he offered me his Affiftance, but did Nothing at all in it, till the Night before his Departure, and then fpoke concerning that Bufinefs with my Lord of *Buckingham*, but to no Purpofe or Effeét, as I found afterwards. At his Going away, when I thought I had fome Intereft in him, I fpoke fome little Complement vnto him, offering vnto him my Seruice vpon any Occafion, wherin I might be vfefull, or feruiceable vnto him, and he gaue me only this Anfwer : *That he did much refpeét my good Parts, and was my humble Seruant.* This I thought ftrange, but yet, becaus he was then ready to take his Coach, I found it fitt to fay no more vnto him, but to obferue how he would be at his Return again. Befydes when I offered to waite vpon him to *Douer*, or fome Part of his Way, he told me, it would be too much Trouble for me, and that he would haue Nobody to go with him, but thofe that wer to go into *France* ; becaus he went in Haft ; and yet he fpoke vnto Sir *Henry Rich*, Sir *Thomas Badger*, and fome others to go with him, and had a Coach appointed in *Southwarke* to carry them, and bring them back again ; this I thinke no Man will fay, I had Reafon to take kindly. At his laft Returne, I went to fee him at *Hanworth* (2 *Auguft*) whither he came with the *French* Ambaffador, Sir *Henry Rich*, Sir *Robert Killigrew*, and fome other Company. At our Meeting I faluted him with as much Refpeét, and Gladnes of his Return, as I could exprefs. He fayd Nothing to me, but that he was glad to finde me there, and then prefently went from me to the other Company. And when I prefented him with my Fathers Seruice, and told him that he would haue waited vpon him, but that he was not able ; he fayd I am forry my Lord is fo lame.

From *Tuefday* till *Sunday* Night, he ftayd there, in all which Time, he neuer fpake Word vnto me, vnlefs it were to take an Argument out of anothers Mouth to crofs me, as he often did ; and neither vfed me as a Stranger with Ceremony, nor as a Freind with Familiarity ; but lett me be in his Hous, and fitt at his Table, without taking any Notice at all of my being there. Vpon *Sunday*, at his Going to Court, I told him I would go away next Day ; he afked me, when will your Lordfhip come again ? I told him I could not tell ; and this was our Parting at that Time : For what I meant to fay vnto him, I had no Time to do, by Reafon of much Company ; and therefore that I might a little expoftulat his Negleét of me, and the Reafon of it, I writt vnto him from *Croydon*, and defyred my Wife, to delyuer it vnto him, as fhe did (6 *Auguft*) but he fent me an Anfwer by my Groome (the Coppy of my Letter, and his, I haue ftill). In my Letter, I am fure I intended Nothing, and I thinke expreffed Nothing, but a ciuill Taking my Leaue of him, fince I was no welcome Man unto him. In his, ther were efpecially three Things, which I meant to fpeake with him, for they brought not only Difcurtecy, but Reproofe, and I thought Letters would neuer bring the Bufinefs to any End, good or bad. So hauing Occafion to go to *Petworth* (13. of *Auguft*) to waite upon my Lord of *Northumberland*, and meete my Lords of *Pembroke*, and *Mountgomery* there, I found my Lord *Doncafter* ; and there he kept his Word, That he would be a Stranger vnto me, for he neither fpake unto me, nor faluted me, neither did I to him.

The next Morning I went vp into his Chamber, I proteft vnto God, without any Defyre to quarrell with him, or to putt an Affront vpon him, as it may appeare by this. *Firft*, Becaus it was in my Lord of *Northumberlands* Houfe, whom I would not haue willingly difquieted ; and further, that I went, without any Kinde of Weapon in the World about me, into his Chamber, where he had not only Weapons, but 4 or 5 Seruants. My Defyre was, if it had bin poffible to make a quiett End between vs, and yett I muft confefs I was refolued, though it were in his own Chamber, and amongft his Men, I would neither patiently receiue ill Language, nor any other Injuries. He was fitting in his Withdrawing Chamber, within the Parloir at *Petworth*, in the Window

Window where the Table is, and his Men pulling on his Breeches and Stockings, being foued together. I came gently into the Chamber, and made a Reuerence unto him; he ftood vp vpon one Legg, and faluted me only with a ftrange Looke, as wondring to fee me there. I told him I defyred to fpeake two or three Words vnto him, but that I would attend vntill he were at Leafure, if then he were not. Then he fayd, prefently my Lord, for I haue but one Stocking to putt on, and fo he fate down again in his Chayre; and I walked vp and down the Chamber a pretty While, and fometimes looked upon a Mapp, that hang there. At the laft he rofe, and came vnto me, and we went into another Window, on the other Syde of the Chamber; his Men ftayd where they were, and might fee what was donn, but I thinke could not heare any Words, that were fpoken: Now thefe are the three Things, which I meant to fpeake of. *Firft*, he writt, that he perceiued I had taken a Refolution to be a Stranger vnto him, and his Hous, which had no other Foundation then an vnjuft Imagination of mine own Brain. In this Point, I thought to giue him Satisfaction, and to fhew that it was otherwife. *Secondly*, he prayd God I might be more conftant in this Refolution, then euer as yet he knew me in any. In this Point, indeed I expected Satisfaction, or Reafon why he fhould fay fo. *Thirdly*, he writes, that I fhoulde finde him eternally a Stranger. Of this I meant to fay fomething but not much, for I cared leaft for it. So thus I began, he ftanding with his Back to the Window, and I ftoad before him, and both bare headed. My Lord, there hath bin a little Bufinefs between your Lordfhip and me, to which I wifh there were fome End putt; (to this he anfwered Nothing, fo I proceeded) and, to that Purpofe, I come now to waite vpon you: Hauing lately receiued a Letter from your Lordfhip, wherin I finde fome Things that I thinke ftrange. Then he fayd, *What are thofe?* I anfwered, Why? *Your Lordfhip writes that yt was an vniuft Imagination of my own Braine. Now I befeech your Lordfhip to confider, that it was not fo, for many other haue obferued the fame that I haue.* Then he fayd, *My Lord, I do not vnderftand, what you meane by that Not fo.* Then I (perceiuyng his Hart was not inclined to Concord with me) anfwered, *My Lord, it is a Thing that is only in me, and no Man but myfelf can tell how it is, and therfore I muft fay, That it is not fo.* Then he, *By God, but I fay it is fo.* Then I, *Truely but I muft fay ftill it is not fo?* Then he, *Then I muft fay, you fay vntrue.* Then I, *My Lord, it is fals.* Then he, *You ly.* Upon that I gaue him a Blow on the Face, and lett my Hatt fall to haue both my Hands free, and fo we fhuffled a little; I had his Head up againft the Window, and held him by the Face, till his Men came in. Then thay pulld away my Cloke from me, and afterwards pulld me from him, but ftrooke me not. He ftood ftill with his Back to the Window, and came not neare me; and one of his Men in pulling me from him fayd, Gods Wounds, my Lord, what do you meane to do? I anfwered, *What's that to you? He hath giuen me ill Language in his own Chamber, and that hath made me do as I haue donn.* So I went towards the Doore, but moft Part backward, becaus I durft not well truft them, for they might haue donn me fome Mifchiefe behinde: When I came to the Doore, I turned to go out, and one of his Men catched me by the Breeches, and would haue pulld me back; but I gaue him a Blow backward, with my Elbow, and went out; and, as foone as euer both my Feete were ouer the Threfhold, the Doore was locked; then I mift my Hatt, but, becaus the Doore was locked, I couldnt go in to fetch it: Hard by the Doore, I mett *Peter Dodfworth*, my Lord *Percys* Man (who can wittnefs that I made no Haft down the Stayres, and that the Doore was prefently locked, and none followed me ouer the Threfhold.) I fayd to him, *Peter*, there hath happned a Difference between my Lord *Doncafter* and me, and his Men haue gotten away my Hatt, and haue locked the Doore, fo as I cant go in to recouer it; therfore, I pray thee go about, and fee if they will giue it you; fo he went, but they had no Minde to open the Doore vnto any Body, and therfore he came back without it; and, when he knocked at the Doore, Nobody would anfwer: I went into my Lord *Percys* Chamber, to whom I told what had happned:

ned : And I affuring myfelf (I proteft to God) that I was much aforehande (for I knewe I ftrooke firft, and had him at Difaduantage enough, untill his Men parted) and that therfore, perhapps he might fend vnto me, I made Haft to be gonn, becaus I would not ftay till my Lord Chamberlain and my Lord of *Moungomery* fhould know of it, who perhapps might commaund me to ftay ; fo I tolde my Lord *Percy* that I defyred to be gonn ; but, while my Horfes were making ready, he went and told all to his Father, who prefently fent for me to his Bed, and afked me what had hapned ; and I told him all, from my Lord *Doncafters* ill Vfing me at his Houfe vnto the very End.

And then he fayd my Lord *Doncafter* had told him, the Night before, of fome Vnkindnes between us, and had fhewed him my Letter, and that he meant this Morning to bring us both together, that Things might be made well again. I told him, I was forry that this had hapned vnder his Roofe ; I had no De-fyre of quarelling, but, hauing receiued the *Ly*, I thought I was forced to do as I had donn ; but befought him to pardon me, if he were difpleafed for the Dif-quieting of his Hous : Then I defyred his Lordfhip to be pleafed to lett me go away ; but he by no Meanes would fuffer me, but fayd he would rife, and go vp to my Lord *Doncafter*, to fee if he could bring vs to a Reconfiliation ; for he was very forry for this Accident, both in Refpect of the two Sifters his Daugh-ters, and our Wiues (to whom this would be a great Griefe, and occafion that they fhould not enioy one anothers Company fo much as they had) and befydes, in Refpect of himfelf, and his Sonn, who he fayd fhould not well know how to carry themfelues to us, without Exception of one Syde or other : Then I an-fwered him, *My Lord, for a Reconciliation, I thinke, it will not be, for I had Reafon to thinke, my Lord* Doncafter *loued me not before, and I am fure he loues me wors now then he did* ; but, for my Part, *I am in your Lordfhips Hous, and euery where your Seruant* ; therefore, *fince you commaund me to ftay, I will not go, but will putt myfelf into your Lordfhips Hands, to do what it fhall pleafe you to inioyne me to do :* So he thanked me very much, fayd he would prefently rife, and I went with my Lord *Percy* into his Chamber, and there I ftayd. My Lord of *Nor-thumberland* went up to my Lord *Doncafter*, and, hauing talked with him a good While, came vnto me again ; and told me, that my Lord *Doncafter* had fpoken many Words of Complement concerning me (as how much he had efteemed my good Parts, and loued my Perfon, and that, for all this Accident, he would not hinder my Fortune any Way ; that he knew I was in a State, that did more require his Lordfhips Affiftance, then that did wherin himfelf was, yet he would neuer feeke to diuert any good Inclination of his Lordfhip to help me (to which my Lord of *Northumberland* anfwered : *No, my Lord, I thinke fo, for I may do what I lift.*) Then I anfwered : Why, my Lord, if my Lord *Doncafter* require no-thing of me, I am fure I haue donn as much or more to him, then he hath donn to me, and therfore I defyre nothing of him, meaning Satisfaction ; fo he went out of the Chamber (being one of the Cloifter Chambers) and I followed him ; but, as foone as euer he was out of the Doore that goes out of the Cloifter into the Garden, he turned back to me, and beckoned to me, that I fhould not come out, but ftay within ; fo I did, and he went on : But after-wards I thought with myfelf, that it might be, he had efpyed my Lord *Doncafter* going towards the Bouling Greene ; and, indeed, it was fo : And, confidering that it was not fitt for me to ftay there, yet would not go out, becaufe my Lord of *Northumberland* had commaunded me otherwife, I fent *James*, my Lord *Percys* Barber, to defyre his Lord to do me the Fauour to come thether, as he did ; and, as foone as my Lord came, I faid thus vnto him, My Lord, your Father, hath com-maunded me to ftay in this Place, and I obey him ; but I befeech your Lordfhip to tell him, that it is much for my Difaduantage to ftay within Doores, and my Lord *Doncafter* abrode ; fo he went to his Father, and brought me Word back from him, that he would not haue me, by any Meanes, to come into the Boul-ing Greene, but that we two fhould go into the Birch Walk, as we did ; where my Lord of *Northumberland* came vnto vs, and, laying his Hand vpon me, fayd to my Lord *Percy*, *This Man will putt himfelf into my Hands, but by God my*
Lord,

Lord, my Lord Doncaſter *will not* ; and ſeemed to be angry that he would not, as I thinke he was : So he talked with his Sonn a pritty While, and then left us together again ; and by and by I deſyred my Lord *Percy* that we might go into the Bouling Greene, but, before we came into the Garden where the Roſes are, all the Lords, and the reſt of the Company, were gonn in ; ſo we followed them, and, iuſt as we were comming into the Hous, Sir *Edward Francis* whiſpered to my Lord *Percy*, who then preſently told me, that his Father had ſent to deſyre that I would not come vp with my Sword, becaus my Lord *Doncaſter*, hauing none, might take it as an Affront. Now, indeede, I had putt on mine, becaus I thought to go away, but I took it of, and deliuered it to my Lord *Percy*, who ſent it into his Chamber ; ſo we went vp into the Dining Roome, where all the Lords were, and my Lord *Doncaſter* : All of them expecting the Comming of my Lord and Lady of *Buckingham*, my Lord Treſorer, and other Company ; ſo we were a great While in the Roome together, as if there had bin no Difference ; only we ſpake not one to another. Indeede, afterwards, my Lord Chamberlaine, my Lord of *Mongomery*, Sir *Ben. Rudyer*, and I, being in the Withdrawing Chamber, my Lord of *Mongomery* ſayd to me, I pray thee, Couſin, tell me how the Buſineſs was this Day ; ſo I begann, but my Lord Chamberlaine (as if he would not haue it told to him, being a Priuy Councellour) went a little further, but I thinke he might heere what was ſayd ; ſo when I had told all, my Lord of *Mongomery* ſeemed to like very well of what I had done, ſo did alſo Sir *Ben. Rudyer* ; and this was all that paſt before Dinner ; only I made this little Obſeruation, that when all the Company (as is ſayd before) ſtayed in the great Chamber, expecting the Comming of the Lords and Ladys, Sir *George Goring* came in alone, and, as I thought, looked ſtrangely vpon me, wherby I imagined he had heard of the Buſineſs. As ſoone as he entred the Chamber, my Lord *Doncaſter* ſeiſed vpon him, tooke him into a Corner, by which, and theyr Earneſtnes, eſpecially his, I aſſured myſelf, that he made a Relation vnto him of what had paſſed ; the like he did vnto Sir *Hen. Rich*, who yet held the ſame Court Countenance, which he had uſed before, towards me. At Dinner, I ſate almoſt right againſt my Lord *Doncaſter*, but neither of us tooke Notice of the other. After Dinner, my Lord Marquis, and the other Lords, ſaid they would go to Boules ; ſo all of them, and the other Company, went down into the Bouling Greene, and I among the reſt. But there was no Bouling ; it ſeemed they had our Buſineſs in their Conſideration, for ſometimes my Lord Marquis and my Lord Chamberlain were together, talking alone ; ſometimes my Lord of *Northumberland* with them, and ſometimes my Lord *Doncaſter*, and my Lord *Mongomery*, and my Lord Treſorer ; and then changed, and went vp and down from one vnto another, I thinke for Half an Hower : All the While I ſtoode ſtill, with the Gentlemen that were there ; and my Lord *Percy*, Sir *George Goring*, Sir *Hen. Rich*, Sir *Ed. Francis*, Sir *John Leedes*, Mr. *Alford*, and ſome others at the Place where the Boules were kept. There we talked of nothing but Bouling, and Making Matches. At laſt, my Lord of *Mongomery* came to me, and ſayd thus to me, *Faith, I would there were an End of this Buſineſs :* Why (my Lord) *ſayd I, there is an End of it already, I think :* No, ſayd he, but this is not enough, and you neede not be unwilling, for you are very well ; but, ſayd I, my Lord, he goes vp and down yonder among you, and tells what he liſt, and I have not told it vnto any butt to you : Piſh, ſaid he, never feare that, for, by God, the more he ſpeakes of it, the wors it is for him. Then my Lord Chamberlaine came vnto me, and ſayd iuſt as his Brother had donn ; and I told him I would do what pleaſed him : Why, ſayd he, you are very well, what would you haue more ? You haue ſtrucken a Priuy Councellor, how the King will take that, by God I cannot tell ; and, therefore, I thinke it will be beſt for you, if there be a good End made of the Buſineſs now : Therefore, I pray, lett there be no Repitition nor Speech of being before hand : So I told him, *Well, my Lord, as pleaſe you.* Then he left his Brother and me together, and went to my Lord Marquis, and, after a few Words, they two went out of the Bouling Greene, and tooke my Lord *Doncafter* with them ; butt, I proteft, I neither knew whither they went, for I faw them not go out, but mift them prefently. When they were gonn, then my Lord of *Northumberland* came where my Lord of *Mongomery* and I were, and, taking him by the Hand, fayd, Come, will you go along with me? And my Lord of *Mongomery* pulld me with him by the Hand. Sayd I, My Lord, would you have me go? Yes (fayd he) Yet, becaus I would have thofe that were neere to marke that they carried me away, I fpoke aloud to my Lord of *Northumberland*, thus : *My Lord, doth your Lordfhip call me ? I, fayd he, pray come away* ; fo as we three went together ; he told me wherfore they went, that there might be a fayr End between us, and that Time might perhapps worke that Friendfhipp between us, which ought to be between fo neere Allyes ; and therefore, I pray make no Repitition, nor fpeake of being aforehand : Why, fayd I, my Lord, I thinke this is to little Purpofe, for no Man can make my Lord *Doncafter* loue me ; and I thinke all is donn that will be donn, for I affure myfelf, he will not meddle with me, and I find not myfelf any Thing at all aggreued, that I fhould meddle with him : Well, fayth he, for all that, pray come along : Nay, fayd I, my Lord, I will go with you, and do what you will haue me : So we went into the Birch Walk, where the other Lords were, *Buckingham*, Chamberlaine, and *Doncafter*. When we came neere them, I went and faluted my Lord Marquis, for I had not feene him a good While, and, as I thought, he faluted me with a kinde Fafhion and Countenance. Then my Lords of *Northumberland* and *Mongomery* went away, and left us four together (and then I perceiued that my Lord *Doncafter* had refufed to putt himfelf into my Lord of *Northumberlands* Hands, expecting my Lord of *Buckinghams* Comming that Day, to putt that Complement upon him, and fo had him there as his Freind ; or perhapps he fufpected Partiallity in our Father in Law). Then my Lord Marquis turning himfelf fully to me (for fo I proteft to God he did) and directing his Speech to me, he fpake a good While, and in the Beginning, like an Orator, with Amplifications ; but this, I am fure, was the Purpofe of his Speech : *How good a Thing Concord was among Men, and efpecially among Brothers, and efpecially among worthy Brothers, and therfore I am very forry for this vnfortunat Accident* ; *and therfore my Lord* Doncafter *hauing done me the Fauour to make Choyce of me, as I thinke you haue of this noble Lord* (pointing to my Lord Chamberlaine) *we both, out of Refpect to your Perfons, and the Dutys of our Places, do defyre to put an End vnto this Bufinefs, and that Time may produce the Effect that we wifh : And, therfore, I defyre you, that there may be no Repitition made, nor Speech of being afore hand.* Why, fayd my Lord *Doncafter* (vpon that) doth any one fay that he is afore hand ? (I, according as I had promifed, fayd nothing) but my Lord Chamberlaine flightly anfuered him, *No my Lord, I heare no Body fay fo.* Then I, addreffing myfelf to my Lord Marquis, fayd,

My Lord, I did for a great While much defyre my Lord Doncafters *Fauour* ; *I thinke it was his Fault that I have not ftill donn fo* ; *and, therfore, if he defyre my Frendfhipp, and my Love, I defyre his.* Then my Lord *Doncafter* fayd, *I am fo much this noble Lords Seruant* (fhewing my Lord Marquis) *that I will perform whatfoever he commaunds me, and therfore I am like enough to efteeme my Lord* Lifle *as my Freind.* Then I, turning firft to my Lord Marquis, fayd, *My Lord, I am as much your Seruant as any Man* ; *and will go as far, and do as much for your Seruice as any Man, at leaft as I am able.* Then turning to my Lord *Doncafter*, fayd I, *Like enough, my Lord, What do you mean by that ? If you bring but like enough to me, I haue but like enough for you :* Nay (fayth he) *I fay like enough, becaufe it hath not bin fo before.* (This, I confefs, I could neither vnderftand when he fpoke it, nor fince). Why then, fayd I, *Like enough be it.* And fo we all came away, and comming down, I fayd to my Lord Chamberlaine, we being alone, *Looke you, my Lord, I knew this would be all, for he will neuer loue me again* ; *and comes with his like enough.* Why, *tis no Matter* (fayd he) *a Man cannot tell what Time may do* ; *but you anfwered him with like enough too, and fo all is well* ; and this is all.

I

Since there are, as I heare, fome Things reported falfly, for they are Vil-
laines, and Lyars, whofoeuer inuented them, and fo I will prove them. They
fay, that, as he gaue me the *Ly*, he flurted vp the Sleeue of his Gownd to my
Face ; but I fweare, to my Knowledge, he ftirred it not. I fee they would fain
fay he ftrooke me firft ; but that is fo fals, as they haue not Impudence enough
to fay it ; and fure, if a Man had a Minde to ftrike, he would rather do it with
his Fift, then a Veluet Sleeue, for fo was his. Some, as I heare, do add Vil-
laine to the *Ly*, but that is fals too.

That which is moft obiected againft me, is, that I left my Cloke and Hatt
behinde me. It is true I did fo, but to that I can fay this for my felf : Firft
when I ftroke him, I lett my Hatt fall (for I fpoke with him with my Hatt in
my Hand) that I might haue both my Hands at Liberty ; likewife, my Cloke
his Seruants pulld from me, taking me from him ; and, when we were parted,
I thought neither of Cloke nor Hatt, but, being angry, I went to the Doore.
And firft they cannot fay I runn from them, for I went almoft all the Way
backward, and befydes, whill we two were alone, I am fure I made very little
Shew of Defyre to leaue him, or of Feare of him : Jf he had made me go away,
I proteft to God I fhould curs the Day of my Birth ; furthermore, I would fain
know why they fhutt the Doore fo foone after me, and would not open it again.
Nor fo much as fpeake to any that knocked, unles they thought I would come
back again to fetch my Hatt, and they were either afraid, or unwilling I fhould,
or both : Nay more, I proteft when I mift my Hatt, I would haue gonn to
fetch it, if the Doore had not bin locked, or if I had thought of it when I went
out. Neither was it Feare made me forgett it, for I faw him ftand ftill at the
Window all the While, till I was at the Doore ; but I muft confefs I was in
Paffion. Another Thing was, that my Lord of *Buckingham* fhould fay unto me,
that my Lord *Doncafter* was fo modeft, that he would not fpeake of being aforehand, and I could not ; as I am a Chriftian, he fpake no fuch Thing to me ;
if he had, why fhould my Lord *Doncafter* haue taken Hold of that which my
Lord Marquis fpoke to me (as it is written aboue) of being aforehand ? The
laft is, that I had a Knock, and the Print of a Knuckle on my Forhead ; I am
fure he had a found one upon his Cheeke, as many can wittnefs, and I proteft I
neuer faw any on my Face. Thus far his Lordfhip thought proper to leave under his own Hand, in Vindication of his Honour.

As his Lordfhip was in the Houfe of Commons in three feveral Parliaments,
till he fucceeded to the Honour of Earl of *Leicefter*, he was diftinguifhed there
for his eminent Abilities, and his Penetration and Judgment, where the Intereft
of his Country was concerned. The Obfervations he made, of Men and Affairs,
fhew his great Learning and Capacity, which are now at *Penfhurft*, in his own
Hand-writing. And I find, by his Journals and Papers, that he refided moftly
at *Penfhurft*, till he entered on the Stage of publick Bufinefs.

In 1632, he was appointed Ambaffador Extraordinary to the King of *Denmark*,
and thereupon made the ingenious *James Howell*, Efq; his Secretary, whofe Letters have been fo much efteemed, that there has been 6 Editions of them, fince
their being firft publifhed, in the Reign of King *Charles the Firft*. In one to his
Father, dated at *London*, 5 *May*, 1632 [a], he acquaints him : ' That the Earl
' of *Leicefter* is to go Ambaffador Extraordinary to the King of *Denmark*, and
' other Princes of *Germany*, to condole the late Death of *Sophia*, Queen Dowager
' of *Denmark*, our King's Grandmother. She was the Duke of *Mecklenburgh*'s
' Daughter, and her Hufband, *Chriftian the Third*, dying young, her Portion,
' which was 40,000 *l*. was reftored her, and, living a Widow 44 Years, died
' worth 2 Millions of Dollars ; fo that fhe was reputed the richeft Queen in
' *Chriftendom*. By the Conftitutions of *Denmark*, the Eftate is divifible amongft
' her Children, whereof fhe had five ; the King of *Denmark*, the Duchefs of
' *Savoy*, the Duchefs of *Brunfwick*, Queen *Anne*, and the Duchefs of *Holftein*.
' The King, being Male, is to have two Shares ; our King, and the Lady *E-*

---

[a] Howel's Letters, 7th Edit. p. 213, 216.

' *lifabeth*

' *lifabeth* is to have that which fhould have belonged to Queen *Anne* ; fo he is
' to return by the *Hague*. It pleafed my Lord of *Leicefter* to fend for me, to go
' Secretary in this Ambaffage, affuring me, that the Journey fhould tend to
' my Profit and Credit ; fo that I have accepted of it, for I hear very nobly of
' my Lord, *&c.*'

In another Letter [b] to the Earl of *Leicefter*, at *Petworth*, dated 13 *Auguft*,
1632, he informs him, That he had received 2000 *l.* in old Gold, of Sir *Paul
Pinder*, for his Lordfhip's Ufe, as alfo of Mr. *Bourla'mach*, Bills of Exchange
for 10,000 Dollars, payable at *Hamburgh*. And that his Allowance had begun,
fince the 25th of *July* laft, at eight Pounds *per Diem* ; and was to continue, till
his Return to his Majefty : That Sir *John Pennington* was appointed, to take his
Lordfhip, and his Company, on Board at *Margets* : Which being performed [c],
the Wind ftood fo fair, that they were at the Mouth of the *Elve* the *Monday*
following. In another Letter [d], he acquaints the Earl of *Rivers*, that he is returned from *Germany*, whence there came two Ambaffadors Extraordinary in one
of the Ships Royal, the Earl of *Leicefter*, and Sir *Robert Anftruther* ; *but for my
Lord of* Leicefter, *I believe there never was fo much Bufinefs difpatched in fo fhort a
Compafs of Time by any Ambaffador*, &c.

His Lordfhip has left an exact Journal of his Ambaffy, with Obfervations of
the King, and of his Court and Country, with their unpolifhed Manner of Behaviour in that Age ; which will be printed (from the Original at *Penfhurft*) in
the Collection. His Lordfhip took over with him his two eldeft Sons, and returned to *England* in lefs than three Months, arriving in *Margat* Road on *Thurfday* Night late, 29 *November*, 1632.

His Lordfhip, in 1633, had that publick Spirit and Regard to Merit, as to
prefer the learned and pious Dr. *Henry Hammond* to the Living of *Penfhurft*,
then vacant, and in his Gift. The celebrated Dr. *Fell*, Dean of *Chrift Church*,
who wrote the Life of Dr. *Hammond*. gives this [e] Account : ' In the Year 1633,
' the Reverend Dr. *Frewen*, the then Prefident of his College (afterwards Lord
' Archbifhop of *York*) gave him the Honour to fupply one of his Courfes at the
' Court ; where the Right Honourable the Earl of *Leicefter* happening to be an
' Auditor, he was fo deeply affected with the Sermon, and took fo juft a Mea-
' fure of the Merit of the Preacher thence, that the Rectory of *Penfhurft* being at
' that Time void, and in his Gift, he immediately offered him a Prefentation :
' Which being accepted, he was inducted on the 22d of *Auguft*, in the fame
' Year.' And thenceforth, from the fcholaftick Retirements of an Univerfity
Life, applied himfelf to his Minifterial Function at *Penfhurft*, where he was
diftinguifhed for his Piety, adminiftring the Sacraments, relieving the Poor,
keeping Hofpitality, reconciling Differences amongft Neighbours, vifiting the
Sick, and catechifing of Youth. The learned Author relates divers Inftances of
it, whilft he continued at *Penfhurft*, from whence he was driven, [f] about the
Middle of *July*, 1643, his Conformity to the Church becoming a Crime, and
with Difficulty he maintained himfelf there till that Time, the Committee of
the Country having fummoned him before them, and ufed their beft Arguments of Perfuafion, Threatenings, and Reproaches, to make him refign. But
he ftill went on in his regular Practice, and continued it till the Time before-
mentioned, when, an Attempt in Behalf of the King being in his Neighbourhood, it was fuppofed his Doctrine and Example had fome Influence ; and, on
the Defeat, the good Dr. was forced to withdraw himfelf, 25 *July*, early in the
Morning, in a mean Habit. This Digreffion of what happened, whilft he was
at *Penfhurft*, will not, I hope, be thought unproper, as the Dr. was fo eminent ;
and firft preferred by this Earl of *Leicefter*.

In *May*, 1636, the King fent his Lordfhip, Ambaffador Extraordinary into
France, as he writes in his Journal, and that he took with him his two eldeft

---

[b] Howel's Letters, 7th Edit. p. 217.   [c] Ibid. p. 220.   [d] Ibid. p. 227.
[e] Life of Dr. Hammond, prefixed to his Works, p. 4. & feq.   [f] Ibid. p. 8.

Sons [g]

I

Sons [g]. The King allowed his Lordſhip, during his Ambaſſy, four-hundred Pounds a Month, for his ordinary Entertainment, and extraordinary Services. His Negotiations, his Obſervations of the King of *France*, his Court, &c. will be publiſhed in the Collections. And it appears, that he lived more honoura-bly, than any foreign Miniſter at *Paris*, in the higheſt Eſteem of the King and his Miniſters.

In the Year 1639, King *Charles* (as his Lordſhip writes in his Journal) ' ſent ' for me to come out of *France*, at the Beginning of our unhappy Troubles ' and Differences with the *Scotts* : I was then in good Favour at the Court, made ' a Privy-councellor, and the King commanded me to follow him to *Yorke* ; ' which I did, but it was not Gods Will that the King ſhould follow the Ad-' vice which I gave him, to accomodate his Differences with the *Scotts, and not* ' *to make Warr, where nothing was to be gained, and much might be loſt* (which ' the World hath ſince ſeen to be very true). The King then commanded me ' to return into *France*, in the ſame Quality of Ambaſſador Extraordinary, ' and there to ſtay till further Order from him : So I returned to *Lon-*' *don.*

' During my Abode there, a Marriage was concluded between my eldeſt ' Daughter, *Dorothy Sydney*, and the Lord *Spencer*, which was conſummated at ' *Penſherſt*, 20 *July*, 1639. Being to return to *France*, as I did in *Auguſt* the ' ſame Year, I took my Son *Robin Sydney* with me, who was then about 13 ' Yeare old : My Wife was to follow me thether, which ſhe did, with my new ' Son-in-Law, and my Daughter, his Wife, and arrived at *Paris* much about ' *Michalmas* ; her two eldeſt unmarried Daughters, *Lucy*, and *Anne Sydney*, alſo ' came thither with her, and the others were left at *Penſherſt*, with a Gentle-' woman their Governeſs, Siſter to Sir *Dodmore Cotton*, being very young, the ' Eldeſt about 10 Years old.

' In *May* 1641, I came into *England* by the Kings ſpeciall Commandment, ' and the Death of my Lord of *Strafford* hapning at that Time, the King to ' performe his Promiſes often made unto me, to employ and advance me fur-' ther in his Affaires, declared me Governor of *Ireland*, at the Councell Table, ' and ſoon after gave me Commiſſion under the great Seal of *England*, to be ' Lord-Lievtenant of *Ireland* ; but it pleaſed God, that, which ſhould have ' bin for my Good, became unto me an Occaſion of Falling, though not by ' my Fault, as I can make it appear to any juſt and reaſonable Man.

' Notwithſtanding this Deſignation of me to that great Employment, the ' King commanded me to returne into *France*, to finiſh my Ambaſſage there, ' and to come into *England*, towards the Winter, to meete him in *London*, at ' his Returne out of *Scotland*, whether his Majeſtye was to go, as he did in *Au-*' *guſt* ; and that then I ſhould receive my full Diſpatch and Inſtructions for that ' Goverment.

' In *Auguſt* that ſame Year 1641, I returned into *France*, and having there ' diſpatched my Buſineſs, both for the Kings Service, and my own private Af-' faires, I took my Leave of that King and Court ; and, bringing away my ' Wife and Family, we arrived at *London*, about the 5 or 6 of *October* that ' Year. And, at my Coming away, the *French* King gave me a Jewell, va-' lewed at 1200 *l.* and the Queen of *France* gave my Wife another Jewell, va-' lewed at 600 Pounds, but hardly worth ſo much *.

VOL. I. L l ' All

---

[g] Letters of Privy Seal, at Penſhurſt.   * The King of *France* wrote to all his Lievts, com-manding them to ſhew his Lordſhip in his Return to *England*, thro' their reſpective Juriſdictions, all the Favour, Grace, and Aſſiſtance, that he ſhould require. And in his Letter to King *Charles* ex-preſſes, ' The Care, the Wiſdom, and Affection, with which the Earl of *Leiceſter* had always car-' ried himſelf during his Embaſſy, for maintaining the good Underſtanding and Correſpondence be-' tween both Crowns, which had given him perpetual Satisfaction and Contentment ; and was one ' Motive, why he would have deſired his Continuance longer at his Court, as he the King of *Eng-*' *land* declared in his Letters, had not an Opportunity offered to employ him otherways ; that he ' could not let him depart without theſe Tokens of his Affections, his Behaviour, during his Stay, ' having been moſt agreeable to him.' But ſince it was, for ſo conſiderable a Charge as that of

Lieu-

' All that Winter I ftayd at *London*, till 25 *July* 1642, when on fome Bufi-
' nefs I came to *Penfeherft*, with the Earls of *Northumberland*, *Pembroke*, and
' much other Company. The Troubles increafing in the Kingdom, which
' was now divided into the Kings Quarters, and the Parliaments Quarters,
' from *Wales* I could not receive my Rents, after our *Lady-Day* 1643, which
' was in the Kings Quarters. But I found Meanes by the Way of *Briftol*, to
' get Part of my Rents for three half Yeares, though not all my fayd Rents.'

By an Order figned 20th of *July* 1642, by *H. Manchefter*, *W. Say* and *Seale*,
and *E. Newburgh*, Commiffioners of his Majeftys Treafury, his Lordfhips Allowance for 400 *l.* per Month, during his Ambaffy into *France*, was ftated, to
the 25th of *November*, 1641, on which Day he returned into his Majeftys Prefence ; and 3033 *l.* 6 *s.* 8 *d.* was then ordered to be paid to him. And 333 *l.*
6 *s.* 8 *d.* was remaining in Arrear. It further appears, that the Lords and
Commons, 19 *Dec.* 1642, ordered his Ldfhip, ten Pounds, *per Diem*, as General of the Army in *Ireland*. And the Lords Juftices of *Ireland*, *John Borlace*,
and *Henry Tichborne*, ordered Sir *Adam Loftus*, Knight, Vice-Treafurer, and
Treafurer of Warrs in *Ireland*, to pay out of fuch his Majeftys Treafure, as remained in his Cuftody, to their very good Lord, *Robert* Earl of *Leicefter*, 100 *l.*
a Month for his Lordfhips Diet ; 59 *l.* 6 *d.* per Day, for his Lordfhips Reti-
new of 50 Horfemen ; 3000 *l.* per *Ann.* in Lieu of *Ceffe* ; an Allowance of 235 *l.*
per *Ann.* in Lieu of 235 Beeves, formerly paid out of the County of *Cavan*.
And an Allowance of 240 *l.* per *Ann.* likewife formerly allowed out of the
Tyths of *Dunboyne*.

In *June* 1644, his Lordfhip came from *Oxford* to *London*, and fo to *Penfhurft*, and fent for his Son, *Robert Sydney*, out of *France*, as he writes in his
Journal.

His Eftate, whilft he was with the King, being liable to Sequeftration, the
Countefs of *Leicefter*, by her Brother the Earl of *Northumberland*'s Intereft, got
it taken of, and on that Occafion, fent the following Memorial to the Parliament:

Whereas a Sequeftracion of the Eftate of the Right Honorable the Earle
of *Leicefters*, in the Countie of *Kent*, is intended by the Comittee in that
Countie, in Purfuance of the Ordinances of Parliament, of the Firft of *Aprill*,
and the Nineteenth of *Auguft* laft, in that Countie : The Right Honorable, the Counteffe of *Leicefter*, hauing Notice thereof, doth on the Behalf of the faid Earle her Hufband, affert, That the Earle of *Leicefter* is
not a notorious Delinquent nor Papift ; that he hath not voluntarily or will-
fully abfented himfelf from the ufuall Place of his Abode. But hauing
his Majefties Comiffion to be Lord Lieutenant of *Ireland*, and General of his
Majefties Armie there, did, with the Leaue, and by the Directions of both
Houfes of Parliament, depart from the Cittie of *London*, towards *Dublin* in *Ireland*, about the Beginning of *November* laft, and vfed all Diligence to repayre
thither, by the Way of *Chefter* ; but before his Lordfhip could fhip himfelf
and his Family at *Chefter*, he was comanded by his Majeftie to returne thence
to *Oxford*, and there to attend his Majefties further Difpatch ; that his Lordfhip, before his Comming from *Chefter*, acquainted the Parliament with the Comand his Majeftie had laid vpon him, and attended their Anfwere neere a
Moneths Space ; that afterwards, upon a fecond Command of his Majeftie, he
did repaire to *Oxford*, and attended his Majeftie for his Difpatch, which he hath
moft earneftly follicited euer fince ; and as foone as he can receiue the fame, he
will haften to his Charge in *Ireland*, with all Expedition ; that during the Time
of his Lordfhips continuing at *Oxford*, where he yet remayneth by his Majefties Comand, he hath not done any Thing, which may be called an Offence to
the Parliament.

And therefore the Counteffe of *Leicefter*, conceiuing the Earle not to be con-

Lieutenant of *Ireland*, he could more eafily bear it. Dated at *Amyens*. 4. *Oct.* (N. S.) 1641.
Signed *Louis*.

cerned

cerned in that Ordinance, defireth that the Committee for Sequeftracions in *Kent* will either leaue the faid Earles Lands, and other Eftate, free from Sequeftration, or certifie to the Comittee of Lords and Comons in Parliament, vpon what Grounds they proceed for the Sequeftracion, to the End they may giue fuch further Order therein, as they in their Wifdomes fhall thinke meete.

Whereupon the following Order was made :

XI. October 1643. *At the Comittee of Lords and Comons for Sequeftracion of Delinquents Eftates.*

VPON Perufall of the Certificat of the Comittee of *Kent*, and the Reafons inclofed, no Caufe appears to this Comittee of Lords and Comons, for the Sequeftracion of the Earle of *Leicefters* Eftate, and therefore, they think fit, and order, that the Sequeftracion and Stay thereof, already made, be difcharged.

Jo .Wylde.

Notwithftanding this Order, when his Lordfhip came to his Seat at *Penfhurft*, he was under fome Difficulties on Account of the Sequeftration of his Eftate, as appears by the following Letter from his Son, *Algernon Sydney* :

My Lord,

I attended the laft Weeke upon the Committee of Sequeftrations, but they did not fit. I had fome Expectation that they would this Day ; but the Painted Chamber is taken up this Afternoone, by the Commiffioners, for the Tryall of the King. I have fpoken with diuers, concerning your Lordfhips Bufineffe, and find them all of Opinion, it cannot be denied. The only Difficulty is in getting a Comittee to fit, for all Mens Braines are foe full of the great Bufineffe, that they will not giue themfelues Leaue to think of any other. The Propofition of the Caualiers, for the Sauing of the King, doth not obtaine foe much as a Hearing. This Day they are againe to be fent out of Towne, by Order of the Houfe of Commons, to the Generall. The Lords fate Yefterday, paffed the Ordinances for Mony, for the Army, and Navy ; and are now very feafonably paffing an Ordinance to make it Treafon, for any King to make Warre upon the Parliament, and haue defired a Conference with the Houfe of Commons, to know, wheather thoes Votes, that goe under theire Names, afferting all iuft Power to be originally in the People themfelues, to be the Reprefentatiue of the People, and that to the Validity of any Law, paffed by them, neither the Affent of King nor Lords is neceffary, weare paffed by them. I think, that if the Houfe of Commons had not bin very hafty in turning the Ordinance, for the Kings Tryall, into an Act of theire owne, and contented themfelues with theire owne Power, the Lords are now in a Temper to haue giuen theire Affent, if they had receiued a fecond Meffage from us. My Lord of *Northumberland*, I think, intends to comme to the Houfe ; our Admirall hath not bin theire yet ; he is foe fick as not to comme thither, but takes Liberty to goe to any other Places ; he is in great Uncertainty, and knowes not yet which Party to ioyne with. I will endeauour, if it be poffible, to get your Lordfhips Bufineffe heard this Weeke ; Mr. *Windham* hath promifed me to be theare ; Mr. *Hales* excufeth himfelf, he neuer hauing practifed theare. My Brother *Robert*, I heare, is made Lieutenant Colonell to my Lord of *Oxford*, old *Berinton* being dead, which is the Caufe wee doe not fee him hear. I am

Leicefter Houfe, *Jan.* the 10, 1648.   *Your Lordfhips.*

I am in great Haft called away, fo that I cannot write to my Lady. I defire your Lordfhip to tell hir that I will be at the Comittee the next Weeke, if fhe thinks that my being theare will be any Wayes feruiceable to her Ladyfhip.

This

This Letter, relating to the Sequeftration of his Eftate, I thought proper to infert here ; but the other Letters of that famous Perfon, which are very memorable, will be publifhed in the Collection.

In *June* 1649, on the Recommendation of the Earl of *Northumberland*, the Parliament placed the Duke of *Gloucefter*, and Princefs *Elifabeth*, with the Countefs of *Leicefter*, allowing for them 3000 *l. per Ann.* and for 10 or 11 Servants, which they brought with them ; and they continued at *Penfhurft*, till the latter End of *Auguft* 1650 ; where there is yet remaining two Pictures of the Duke ; one with a Black behind him in the Royal Livery.

The Parliament, 13 *June*, 1649 [a], ordered the Earl and Countefs of *Leicefter*, to take Care that no other Ceremony be ufed to the King's Children, than is ufed to Noblemens Children of this Nation. However, they were treated with fuch Regard, both by the Earl and his Countefs, that the Princefs *Elifabeth*, dying foon after her Removal from *Penfhurft*, left, at her Deceafe, to the Countefs of *Leicefter*, a Jewel, in Recompence for the Care and Refpect fhewn to her. But this Bequeft was the Caufe of great Trouble, both to the Earl and his Countefs, and was not finally adjufted till after the Reftoration of King *Charles the Second*, as appears by the following Certificate, under the Earl of *Leicefter*'s Hand [b].

15 *May*, 1660.

The chief and moft neceffary Papers, concerning the Diamond Jewell, and the Necklace of Perle, which the Princeffe left with me, and difpofed of by her Will, are in the Hands of the Officers of the *Exchequer*, hauing bin brought thether, and remained there euer fince the Informafions putt into that Court againft me and my Wife, in the Name of the Atturney Generall, for the Lord Protector, becaufe no Iudgment was giuen in the Caufe by the Court, as the Hearing thereof in *Eafter* Terme, as I remember, 1659 ; or, if they were taken from the faid Officers, they are with Mr. *Robert Raworth* a Counfeller of *Grayes Inne*.

LEYCESTER.

The Proceedings, relating to the Jewels, were not determined till the Year 1659, when the Earl was obliged to deliver them ; and, the Cafe being remarkable, the Curious may be defirous of the Particulars.

Mr. *Lovel*, who is mentioned in the Earl of *Clarendon*'s Hiftory of the Rebellion, for his Integrity, and other Qualifications, as being Tutor to the Duke of *Gloucefter*, &c. was with the Princefs when fhe died, and figned the following Teftimonial :

Memorandum, That on, or aboute the fixt Day of *September*, Anno Dominj 1650, the Princeffe *Elizabeth* lying ficke, but being of perfect Vnderftanding and Memory, did declare, in the Prefence and Hearing of me *Richard Lovell*, concerneing certaine Jewells of hers, which then were in the Cuftodye of the Earle of *Leycefter*, That her former Will fhould ftand ; only fhe appoynted, that the Neckelace of Perle (by her formerly willed to her Sifter the Princeffe of *Orange)* or the Worth thereof, fhold be to her Brother, the Duke of *Glocefter*, in Cafe he fhold haue Neede thereof, which fhe left to the Confideration and Iudgment of the faid Earle of *Leycefter*, into whofe Cuftodie and Poffeffion fhe had voluntarily deliuered the fame.

And that the faid Earle of *Leycefter* fhold haue, and detaine the Jewell of Diamonds, which fhe had alfoe voluntarily deliuered vnto him.

Some other little Things alfoe the Princeffe faid fhe had left with my Lady of *Sunderland*, which fhe gaue to her, in Cafe fhe fhold dye. In Witnes whereof, I haue herevnto fet my Hand, the 5th Day of *October*, Anno Dominj 1650.

RIC. LOVELL.

---

[a] Whitlock's Memorials, p. 349.   [b] Ex Autog. apud Penfhurft.

The following Cafe [c] was delivered to *Oliver Cromwell,* Protector, which fhews the Proceedings thereon.

Concerneing the Jewells depofited by the late Princeffe Elizabeth, *one of the late Kings Children, with the Earle of* Leycefter, *and her Difpofeall thereof.*

In *Aug.* 1650.] T H E faid Lady depofited with the Earle of *Leycefter* 2 of her Jewells, the one her Necklace of Pearle, and thother her Jewell of Diamants.

With this Defire, that his Lordfhip wold be pleafed to take the Care and Cuftody of them, vntill fuch Tyme as fhe fhold, by a Lettre, or fome other fure Token, defire his Lordfhip to returne them to her.

Soone after, and whyles fhe remayned in his Lordfhips Houfe, fhe gave his Lordfhip Directions how fhe wold have them difpofed of, in Cafe fhe fhold die.

6 *September,* 1650.] The faid Lady, being remoued to the *Ifle of Wight,* and lyeing vpon her Death Bed, did then declare, before credible Wittneffes, that her former Will, concerning the faid 2 Jewells, fhold ftand, with this Alteration, that her Brother, the Duke of *Glocefter,* fhold haue her Necklace of Pearle, or the Value thereof. And that the Earle of *Leycefter* fhold haue, and detayne to himfelfe and his Wife, her Diamant Jewell, which fhe had formerly deliuered into his Cuftody, and died.

22 *November,* 1651.] The Counteffe of *Leycefter* obtayned her Letters of Adminiftration, with the Words of the deceafed Ladies Will and Mind, formed into a Nuncupative Will, annexed therevnto, approued before the then Judge of the Prerogatiue Courte, vnder the Seale of their Office belonging therevnto, which now remaines, with other Papers, in Mr. *Scobells* Cuftody, Clarke to the late Parliament.

And thus ftands the Earle of *Leycefters* Clame to the Diamant Jewell, in Right of himfelfe and his Wife, their Intereft therein being infeparable.

26 *January,* 1649.] An Act of Parliament is publifhed, declareing the Goods and Perfonall Eftate of the late King, Queen, and Prince, to be forfeited by their feuerall Delinquences, and expofeing them to Sale, for Payment of their Debts, and noe otherwife.

This Act extending only to the Sale of the faid late King, Queen, and Princes Goods, and Perfonall Eftate, the faid Earle and Counteffe conceiued themfelves not comprehended therein, or concerned to make any Difcouery of the faid Jewells foe difpofed of as aforefaid.

17 *July,* 1651.] But almoft 12 Monethes after the Death of the faid Lady, and her Gift of the faid Jewells, as aforefaid, an additionall Acte was publifhed for Sale of the late King, Queen, and Princes Goods, as before, with this Claufe in the very Clofe thereof, *viz.* That the Goods and Perfonall Eftate of, or belonging to any Child or Children of the late King and Queen, bee, and are hereby declared to be within the Intent and Meaneing of this and the former Acte, as if the fame had beene particulerly named, to all Intents and Purpofes.

In this Acte, the faid Earle and Counteffe conceiued themfelues concerned, to make Difcouery of the faid Jewells vnto the Truftees appoynted by the faid Acte, within the Tyme prefcribed by the fame, to efcape the Penalty thereof, which was done accordingly ; and withall, the faid Earle made Clame to the Necklace of Pearle, in Right of the Duke of *Glocefter,* and to the Diamant Jewell, in Right of himfelfe and his Counteffe. And produced vnto them the Lettres of Adminiftration, obtayned by the Counteffe of *Leycefter,* with the faid Ladyes Will, vnder the Seale of the Prerogatiue Court.

And afterwards had feuerall Debates with the faid Truftees, concerning his faid Clame to, and Intereft in the faid Jewells ; but they being not fatisfied therewith, nor admitting his Claime thereof :

23 *December*, 1651.] Ordered the said Earle of *Leycester* forthwith to pay vnto the Treasurers, in the said Acts named, the Sume of 2000 *l*. within 7 Dayes after the Date thereof.

The Countesse of *Leycester* herevpon made her Addres to the Parliament by Petition, to take the Iustnes of her Ladyship Clame into Confideration, and to giue Order therein.

8 *January*, 1651.] The Parliament, upon Reading of the said Petition, ordered, That the Petition be referred to the Comittee, for remoueing Obstructions in the Sale of the late King, Queen, and Princes Goods, to examine the Busines, and to state the Matter of Fact, and to reporte it to the Houfe for their farther Confideration. And the Trustees, in the meane Tyme, forbeare all Proceedings concerning the Jewells, mentioned in the Petition.

Shortly after, the said Comittee examined the Busines, before whom diverse Witnesses were produced, on the Behalfe of the said Earle and Countesse, who proued :

1. That the said Jewell of Diamants was giuen to the said Lady, by the late Prince of *Orange*, and soe neuer belonged to the late King, Queen, Prince, or Crowne of *England* ; but her Interest therein, and Power of dispofeing thereof, was euer cleerely in, and of her selfe.

2. That she was aboue 14 Yeares of Age, at the Tyme that she dispofed thereof, as by her Will ; and soe had a legall Capacity, in and of herselfe, to dispofe thereof.

3. That she did dispofe thereof, as by the Will is declared.

4. That she was of found Mynd and perfecte Memory, at the Tyme of such her Dispofeall thereof.

And likewise heard the Clame on the Behalfe of the said Trustees, and ordered a Reporte thereof to be made to the Houfe, but neuer had any Oportunity to make the same, and the Parliament is now diffolued.

2 *May*, 1652.] Since which Diffolution, *the said Trustees haue renewed their Demand of the said Jewell of Diamants*, neglecting the Order of Parliament of 8 *January*, 1651, aforesaid.

3 *May*, 1652.] To this the Earle caufed Returne to be made, and the said Order of Parliament to be deliuered vnto them.

But they regarded it not, declareing that they conceiued they had now againe the same Power to proceed againste the said Earle, for not Deliuering the said Jewell, as if the said Order had neuer beene made, and that they adhere to their former Order, of the 23 *December*, 1651.

Herevpon, the Earle addressed himselfe to the General, in whose Care it now rests to doe his Lordship Justice in the said Jewell.

Observations vpon the Earle and Countesses Tytle to the said Jewell.

1. That this Jewell was giuen to the deceased Ladie, by the late Prince of *Orange*, and soe it was her owne, not the late Kings, Queens, or Princes, nor the Crownes.

2. That, it being soe her owne, she had an abfolute Power and Capacity in her selfe, to dispofe thereof.

3. That she did dispofe thereof, as by her Will, in Prefence of credible Witnesses.

4. That she was about 14 Yeares of Age when she gaue the same, as by her said Will, and at her Death.

5. That she was of found Mynd and Memory, at the Tyme of such her said Gift.

All which was duelie proued and manifested, before the Comittee for remoueing Obstructions.

Obſervations vpon the Caſe, as to the ſaid 2 *Acts of Parliament.*

1. That the ſaid Acts do declare the late King, Queen, and Princes Goods only, and none elſe, to be forfeited for their ſeuerall Delinquencies.

But the ſaid deceaſed Lady was neuer yet declared a Delinquent.

2. That, therefore, the ſaid King, Queen, and Princes Goods are expoſed to Sale, for Payment of their Debts, as by the ſaid Acts, not others Debts.

The ſaid Lady owed no Debts that yet haue beene hearde of.

3. That the firſt Acte, for Sale of the ſaid late King, Queen, and Princes. Goods, was publiſhed 26 *January*, 1649, and extended only to the Goods of the late King, Queen, and Princes, and no others.

4. That an additionall Acte was publiſhed 17 *July*, 1651, aboue 2 Yeares after, entitled, An additionall Acte for Sale of the late King, Queen, and Princes Goods, &c. Perſonall Eſtate, and no otherwiſe, ſaueing that, in the Cloſe thereof, the Goods and Perſonall Eſtate of any Child, or Children, of the late King and Queens, are hereby declared to be comprehended within that and the former Acte, as if they had beene particularly named therein.

Without declaring the deceaſed Lady guilty of any Cryme, by which ſhe might forfeite what was her owne.

But as if it were meant only for the Recouery of the ſaid Jewell, from the ſaid Earle and Counteſſe, to whom ſhe had giuen the ſame, as aforeſaid.

And as if it were intended thereby, that the Innocent ſhold be puniſhed equally with the Guilty.

It appears from his Lordſhip's Journal, the Letters ſent to him; and other Authorities; that from the Time of his leaving the King, and retiring to *Penſhurſt*, he never ſtirred from that Seat, but took to a ſtudious Courſe of Life, and has left, in Manuſcript, Eſſays on divers Subjects. When the Reſtoration of the Royal Family drew near, the Earl of *Northumberland* ſent to him to take his Place in the Houſe of Peers, without any Oath, or Engagement. Upon which, his Lordſhip came to Town, and concurred in thoſe Votes for the Return of the King and the Royal Family. How he was received, is related in his Journal, as follows:

' *Tueſday*, 29 *May*, 1660, King *Charles the Second* made his Entry into *Lon-*
' *don*, and paſſed to *Whytehall*, where the Houſe of Peeres, and Houſe of Com-
' mons, ſeverally, met, and ſaluted his Majeſtye, and wellcomed him with
' Orations by their Speakers, the Earl of *Mancheſter* of the one, *pro tempore*,
' and Sir *Harbottle Grimſton*, of the other. I ſaluted his Majeſtye among the
' reſt, and kiſſed his Hand; but there was ſo great Diſorder and Confuſion,
' that the King ſcarce knew, or took particular Notice of any Body.

' *Thurſday*, 31 *May*, a Meſſenger came to my Houſe, and warned me to
' come to *Whytehall*; the like he did to the Earl of *Northumberland*. We
' went together, not knowing for what; and, having ſtayed a Whyle in the
' Kings Withdrawing Chamber, we were called into the Councell Chamber,
' and there, contrary to his and my Expectation, we were ſworn Privy Coun-
' cellors, as was likewiſe the Earl of *Mancheſter*, and others, that, and the next
' Day.

' Having attended the Parliament till it was adjourned, 13 *Sept.* 1660; and
' afterward, the King and Councel: My Health and Buſineſs requiring it, I in-
' tended to go into the Country; and, *Friday* 12 *Oct.* 1660, after the King and
' Councel was riſen, I went to the King, and ſayd, Sir, *I have not the Vanity*
' *to thinke that your Majeſtye will miſſe me, or take Notice of my Abſence; but,*
' *having the Honor to be your Servant, I thought it would not agree with my Duty*
' *to go from hence, without your Leave and Permiſſion, which I beſeech your Ma-*
' *jeſtye to grant, that I may go into the Country for my Health.* The King, with
' a favourable and ſmiling Countenance, ſayd, *With all my Heart; but how long*
' *will you ſtay.* Sir, ſayd I, *To myſelf I have propoſed to ſtay a good Whyle, un-*
' *leſs your Majeſtye command the contrary.* Whether do you go, ſayd the King
' ſtill with a ſmiling Countenance). Sir, ſayd I, *to my Houſe* in Kent. *Well*,

' ſayd

' fayd the King, *And when will you come again?* Sir, fayd I, *It is for my Health*
' *that I go; but, if your Majeftyes Service require it, I fhall not confider either my Health*
' *or Life itfelf, but will be where you pleafe to command me.* I thank you, fayd the
' King, *but, for the prefent, I have no Occafion to ftay you: I wifh you a good*
' *Journey.* I pray God to blefs your Majeftye, fayd I, *with Health, long Life, and*
' *all Happinefs.* I thank you, fayd the King again, with the fame favourable
' Countenance; and gave me his Hand, which I kneeling down, kiffed, and fo
' came from him; who ftayed to let me fay more to him, if I would. The
' like favourable Entertainment he gave me, the firft Time alfo (which I had
' forgotten) in the Councell Chamber, when I was fworn; for he came to me,
' and gave me many gracious Expreffions of his Favour, and more than ordi-
' nary good Opinion and Efteem.'

As his Lordfhip came heartily into the King's Reftoration, fo was he for
eftablifhing his Majefty on the Throne by neceffary Laws. In the Seffion of the
Parliament beforementioned, he made this Speech [a], on Taking the Oath of Allegiance:

' Your Lordfhips appointed *Thurfday* for the Time, when all the Lords
' fhould take the Oath of Allegiance; and, I hope, all have taken it, or will
' take it. And, though therein I differ from the Opinion of a noble Lord [the
' Lord *Roberts*] I conceive that your Lordfhips take that Oath as Peers of
' *England*, and Members of this Houfe; not as Subjects only; for, I think,
' that whatfoever is communicable to, or required of any Sort of Men, and of
' every Man of that Sort, and of none elfe; is required of them, as they are of
' that Sort. But the Taking this Oath is by your Lordfhips required of eve-
' ry one of your Lordfhips, and of none elfe here: Therefore, it is required,
' as you are Peers: But, whether the Peers take it as Peers, or otherwife, it
' is not material; but, that the Peers take it, I think, is very reafonable. And
' though a noble Lord of the Barons Bench [the Lord *Wharton*] feemed the
' other Day very tender in impofing the Taking this Oath, upon the Peers,
' leaft, for the not Taking of it (as I underftood him) any one of your Lord-
' fhips fhould be deprived of his Seffion here, which is his Inheritance: I am
' of another Opinion, for though I grant and acknowledge that Seffions in this
' Houfe is the Inheritance of every one of your Lordfhips; yet your Lordfhips
' I am fure remember, from whence you have that Inheritance; from the King:
' And, certainly, for that Inheritance, we owe this Expreffion of Gratitude
' and Fidelity to the King that gives it us. And, befides, as Seffions in this
' Houfe is the Inheritance of your Lordfhips, fo our Allegiance is the Kings
' Inheritance: And, if one muft be (of which I fee no Neceffity) it were better to
' difinherite one, or more private Men, then the King; nay, my Lords, the Fide-
' lity of the Kings Subjects, *and of your Lordfhips, the beft of his Subjects*, is the
' Kings beft Inheritance. For his Majeftyes Dignity and Power, and the Security
' of both, exifts in the Fidelity of his Subjects. And the Deftruction of his Ma-
' jeftyes Dignity and Power, comes from the Default of the Fidelity of his Sub-
' jects; as by fad Experience we have lately feen. And truly, my Lord, I am
' of Opinion, that not only all your Lordfhips, but every Subject ought to take
' this Oath, to affure the King of their Fidelity. And I know not why any one
' fhould have Seffion and Vote in this Houfe, or Benefit of the *Kings Protection*,
' or any *Being* in *England*, that will not take it. Therefore I humbly move,
' ' *That every Peer or Perfon, that hath Right of Seffion, in this Houfe, from*
' *thefe illuftrious Princes that fit there* [Dukes of *York* and *Gloucefter*] *even to me,*
' *the unworthieft of all this noble Affembly, or to the youngeft Baron that is come, or*
' *that fhall come into this Houfe, be obliged, by a certain Time fett, to take this*
' *Oath; or not to have Vote or Seffion in this Houfe.*

After fome Paufe (none anfwering his Lordfhip) he faid, ' I think it the
' Order of this Houfe, *That if any Peer make a Motion, and no other Peer fpeak*
' *againft it, it ought to be ordered.* This I defire may be done. If there be
' any Oppofition, and the Queftion be put, I defire to have my Diffent entered

---

[a] Ex Origin. apud Penfhurft.

' before

' before the Queſtion be put, in caſe that the Queſtion ſhould be carried
' in the Negative.'

Alſo, on the Debate on the Act for Veſting the Power of the Militia
in the King, his Lordſhip argued ſtrenuouſly for it.   Among other Inſtances,
he ſayd, ' The Perſons in the County of *Kent*, where I have a poor Dwelling,
' there are ſome noble and wealthy Perſons, Commiſſioners in this Act ; but,
' as I have heard, there are others of very low Condition, and vile Affections ;
' inſomuch that, the *Quorum* being but five, one more might make up a *Quo-*
' *rum*, of thoſe that condemn'd the King to Death ; as *Liveſey, Dixwell,* and
' *Say*, who, I think, are in the Liſt, and others as bad as they.   No Perſon
' is excepted.   The Peers wronged, as Lord *Roberts* ſaid, and great Inequality
' uſed in the Aſſeſſments, *&c.*'   Whereof his Lordſhip mentioned ſeveral
Particulars ; and moved, ' That no Commiſſioner, or Commiſſioned Officer,
' ſhall exerciſe any the Powers or Authorityes contained in the Act, *&c.* untill
' he, in the Preſence of five, or more of the ſaid Commiſſioners, ſhall firſt ac-
' knowledge in theſe Words following : *I do acknowledge and declare, that the*
' *War undertaken by both Houſes of Parliament in their Defence, againſt the Forces*
' *raiſed in the Name of the late King, was not Juſt and Lawfull : And that Ma-*
' *giſtracy, and Miniſtry, are the Ordinances of God.*'

From the King's Reception of his Lordſhip, and his great Services and
Loſſes, it is highly probable he might have been imployed in the Adminiſtration, if he had deſired it ; the Earl of *Clarendon*, Lord Chancellor, being very
much his Friend, as is evident by the Correſpondence between them (which
will be publiſhed in the Collection) and General *Monk*, Duke of *Albemarle*, had
been preferred by him, to be his Lieutenant-Colonel, and had ſerved under
the Lord Viſcount *Liſle*, his Son.   But it appears from his Lordſhip's Papers
and Letters, that he choſe a retired Life, and very ſeldom came to Town ;
and not at all in his latter Years.   His Proxy in the Houſe of Peers he left
with *Algernon* Earl of *Northumberland*, whoſe Siſter he had married ; and the
Letters, that paſſed between them, ſhewed ſuch a Sympathy in Affections, and
ſincere and faithful Friendſhip, as is hardly to be paralleled.

The Earl of *Clarendon* profeſſing the greateſt Regard to his Lordſhip
he ſent to him the following Relation, 29 *Auguſt*, 1661, on his Promiſe to
intereſt himſelf, that his Arrears in *Ireland* ſhould be paid him ; and, containing ſome remarkable Paſſages, I ſhall here inſert it from his own Hand-
writing.

Copye of a Relation concerning my Arreres in Ireland, *with a Copye of the
late Kings Letter to me,* 29 Nov. 1642, *and a Copye of the ſayd Kings
Letter to the Marquis of* Ormond, 14 Jan. 1643, *for the Payment of
my Arreres.*

IN *Aprill* 1641, it pleaſed the late King, of bleſſed Memorie, to ſend for the
Earle of *Leyceſter* to come into *England* out of *France*, where hee was then,
and had bin, during five Yeres before (*viz.* from *May* 1636) Ambaſſador Extraordinary for his Majeſtie to the *French* King.   Soone after the Earle of *Leyceſ-
ters* Arrivall at *London*, and very few Dayes after the Death of the Earle of *Strafford, viz.* 19 *May*, 1641, it pleaſed his gratious Majeſtie, at the Councell
Board, to declare his Intention, to conferre vpon the Earle of *Leyceſter*, the Government of his Majeſties Kingdome of *Irland* ; and accordingly granted his Comiſſion vnder the Great Seale of *England*, bearing Date the 14th of *June*, 1641, in
the 17 Yeare of his Majeſties Reigne, to the Earle of *Leyceſter*, to bee his Majeſties Lieutenant Generall and Generall Governour of his Majeſties ſayd Kingdome, and Generall of his Majeſties Army and Forces then preſent and future,
with all Authorities, Stipends, *&c.* belonging and perteyning to the ſayd Office,
during his Majeſties Pleaſure, as by the ſayd Comiſſion it may appeare.   In
July, the next Moneth of the ſame Yere, the King ſent the Earle of *Leyceſter*
back into *France*, to finiſh ſome Negotiations there concerning his Majeſties

Service ; comanding him to returne into *England* againe, by the Time that his Majeſtie himſelf ſhould bee returnd out of *Scotland*, whether his Majeſtie did then ſhortly intend to goe, as hee did in *Auguſt* following ; and that then the Earle *Leyceſter* ſhould receiue his Majeſties further Comandments for the Government of *Ireland*. In Obedience to his Majeſties Orders, the Earle of *Leyceſter* (haueing ſent many Servants, and much of his Goods, out of *France* into *Ireland*, by Sea) came into *England* in *October* of the ſame Yeare. And, in *November* following, the Earle of *Leyceſter* attended the King at his Majeſties Returne out of *Scotland*, expecting his Diſpatch to goe into *Ireland*. But, in Regard that a great Rebellion was then raiſed, and the Rebells had poſſeſſed themſelves of the greateſt Part of that Kingdome, it pleaſed the King to deferre the Sending of the Earle of *Leyceſter* thither, vntill ſuch Supplyes were provided, as were neceſſary for the Proſecuting of that Warr, and Reducing the Rebells to their due Obedience ; to which End, it pleaſed the King earneſtly to recomend to the Parliament, then ſitting at *Weſtminſter*, the Managing of the Affaires of that Kingdome, coniuring them to provide all Things neceſſary for that Service. The Troubles then growing high betweene the King and Parliament, the King departed from *London* in *January* 1641 ; but comanded the Earle of *Leyceſter* to attend the Parliament, to haſten the Supplyes for *Ireland*, according to his Majeſties Deſire, often times ſignifyed to the Parliament : But the Earle of *Leyceſter* could procure no Money of the Parliament, for the Satiſfying of the Souldiers in *Ireland*, that Money which was raiſed of the Adventurers, and otherwaies, being converted to other Vſes. Att the laſt, the Parliament having aſſured the Earle of *Leyceſter*, that 55000 *l.* ſhould bee forthwith ſent into *Ireland* ; and the King hauing comanded him to waite vpon his Majeſtie, to receiue his full Diſpatch for *Ireland*, in *July*, 1642, the Earle of *Leyceſter* went to *Yorke*, where the King then was, and there attended, as likewiſe all the While that his Majeſtie was at *Nottingham*, and as farre as *Stafford* : But, hearing that the Parliament had ſtopd the Money deſigned for *Ireland*, as aforeſayd, the Earle of *Leyceſter* (having ſent a great Part of his Traine of Servants and Horſes to *Cheſter*, to ſtay for him there, and leaueing another Parte thereof at *Lichfeild*, to ſtay for him there alſo) with his Majeſties Knowledge and Approbation : He returned to *London* about the End of *September*, to ſollicite the Supplyes of Money, and other neceſſary Proviſions, for his Majeſties Service in *Ireland* ; but not prevailing in his Solicitations, and chooſing rather to goe empty, then not goe at all, the Earle of *Leyceſter* took his Iourney towards *Ireland* ; but, falling ſick by the Way, hee had much adoe to gett to *Cheſter*, where he continued very ſick ſome Parte of *November* and *December*. Nevertheles, hee omitted not to give Order for the Providing of Veſſells to tranſport his Traine into *Ireland*, as likewiſe for his owne more decent Paſſing the Sea (having the Honour to bee the Kings Lieutenant). At his Setting forth from *London*, hee had written to the then Lords Juſtices in *Ireland*, to ſend over Captaine *Barkly* with the Kings Pinnace, which hee then comanded. The Earle of *Leyceſter* (having provided Veſſells ready at *Leerpoole*, and in *Cheſter* Water, for the Tranſportacion of his Goods, Servants, and Horſes, which were many ; and Captaine *Berkly* comeing to him at *Cheſter*, to tell him that the Pinnace was at *Beaumorrys*) prepared himſelf for his Iourney, though in *December*, the worſt Time of the Yeare. And, intending to depart from *Cheſter* to *Beaumorrys*, hee receiued the Kings Order the 8th of *December*, ſigned by his Majeſtie, and dated the 29th *Novemb.* comanding him to repaire in Perſon to his Majeſtie then at *Oxford* ; the Copy whereof follows :

Charles R.

RIght truſty and right welbeloved Cozen and Councellor, Wee greete you well. Wee haue with Sorrow vnderſtood of your Sicknes, and are much troubled that ſuch Indiſpoſition of Health is ſtill vpon you, as renders you vnable, as yet, to vndergoe your Paſſage by Sea into *Ireland* : And, ſince you are ſtill remaining on this Side, Wee haue thought good to adviſe with you before your

your Departure, vpon fome Affaires much importing the Good of Vs, and Our Service : Wherefore, Our Pleafure is, that, as foone as your Health will permitt, you repaire to Vs in Perfon, when Wee fhall communicate to you the Bufines for which Wee fend for you. In the meane Time, Wee wifh you may fpeedily recover your perfeët Health. Given at our Court at *Oxon.* 29 *November* 1642.

The Earle of *Leycefter* would faine have ferv'd the King in the Government of *Ireland,* to which his Majeftie had defigned him ; and therefore hee tooke the Boldnes to write vnto the King by his Secretary, whom hee fent expreffely, hoping that his Majeftie, vpon further Confideracion, might bee pleafed to change his Mind : But, his Majeftie being refolu'd to the Contrary, the Earle of *Leycefter* receiued a fecond Order at *Chefter,* 17 *December,* from Mr. Secretary *Nicholas,* by his Majefties Comand, confirming the former. In Obedience to which, the Earle of *Leycefter* went from *Chefter,* about the End of *December,* and at *Worcefter* mett with a third Order from Mr. Secretary *Nicholas,* fignifying, that the King expeéted him at *Oxford* ; where the Earle of *Leycefter* arrived about the 8 or 9 of *January,* 1642-3, and was gratioufly receiued by his Majeftie. Many Moneths hee attended at *Oxford,* in Hope and Expeétacion that it would pleafe the King to fend him into *Ireland,* and preffed his Difpatch with as much Earneftnes, as might confift with his Dutie and Reverence to his Majeftie, to whom hee often reprefented the hard Condicion wherein hee was, being obleigd to keepe a great Traine of Servants and Horfes at *Dublyn,* another at *Chefter,* and another at *Oxford,* to the Mainteyning of which, hee recciued nothing out of *Ireland,* nor from his Majeftie. To which, it pleafed the King to giue very gratious Returnes, with Promifes of Recompence and Satisfaétion. But, after a long Attendance at *Oxford,* from the Begining of *January* 1642-3, to the End of *November* 1643, it pleafed the King to determine the Earle of *Leycefters* Comiffion, and to conferre the Government of *Ireland* vpon the Marquis of *Ormond* ; yet his Majeftie was fo gratious, as to tell the Earle of *Leycefter* divers Times, that hee did it not for any Difpleafure to him, or Diftruft of him, but that the Neceffitie of his Affaires requiring a Peere in *Ireland,* obleiged him to make that Change ; and that, for the Earle of *Leycefters* full Contentment, hee would beftow vpon him fome other Office nearer his Perfon (and named one or two) with a Penfion of 2000 *l.* a Yeare, and Payment of all the Arreares due vnto the Earle of *Leycefter,* from his feverall Entertainements in *Ireland* ; in Performance whereof, it pleafed his Majeftie to write his gratious Letter to the Marquis of *Ormond,* the Copy whereof follows :

Charles R.

R Ight trufty, *&c.* Whereas wee formerly difigned our right trufty, *&c.* the Earle of *Leycefter* to bee our Lieutenant Generall, *&c.* of *Ireland* (of whofe Fidelitie and Affeétion to our Service, though wee were well perfwaded ; yet finding it fitt to place that great Charge and Truft in your felf, who had performed vnto vs fo many eminent Services) on the 29 of *November* laft, wee determined his Comiffion : Whereupon our fayd Coufin having reprefented vnto vs the feverall Particulars granted by vs vnto him, and praying Payment of his feverall Entertainments : Accordingly, Wee haue thought fitt to recomend the fame in an efpeciall Manner vnto you, to caufe Payment to bee made vnto him, or his Affignes, with all convenient Speed, of all Arreares growne due vnto him, as our Leiutenant Generall, Generall Gouernor, and Generall of our Army from the 20th of *June* 1641 (being the Day of the Date of his Comiffion) to the 29th of *November* laft, which was ye Day, that wee declared to the fayd Earle, that wee had appointed another Governour there. And becaufe the Accounts thereof (and of his fequent Prefeures) are not as yet calculated (which wee require you to give Order to one of our Auditors to performe) wee doe hereby particularly direét to bee forthwith paid vnto his Affignes, the Sume of one thoufand Pounds, as Parte of his aforefaid Arreares, it being to difcharge his Debts in that Kingdome, and to enable him

to

to bring away his Servants and Goods from thence. But, out of that thousand Pounds, wee intend not any Defalcacion shall bee made for Oates or other Provisions issued out of our Stores in that Kingdome; hee representing to vs, that those Provisions did not cost vs any Thing, but were Parte of the Provisions layd vp especially for his owne Vse. Our further Pleasure is, that the Troope of Horse, consisting of 110, and Foote Company of 100, of our old standing Army, and which wee gaue to the sayd Earle, shall stand and remaine, and that they bee neither dissolued nor reduced to any lesse Number, then as they are entred vpon the List of our Army, nor bee disposed of to any Person whatsoever without his Consent; the Arreares and growing Entertainements of both which, our Pleasure is, shall be from Time to Time paid vnto him, and Warrants of full Pay accordingly orderd on that Behalf. Our further Pleasure also is, That the Regiment of Foote which he raised by our Authoritie, and sent over into that our Kingdome, and his Company in the sayd Regiment, remaine likewise to him, and bee not otherwise disposed of till our further Pleasure signifyed. And whereas the sayd Earle hath desired Allowance for Waggons, as all other Officers of our Army, according to their Qualities have had: Wee recomend the same to your Consideracion to give him Satisfaction therein. And whereas (though hee transported not himself) a great Part of his Family was sent over by him, and his Attendance of vs in severall Places of this Kingdome was no lesse chargeable to him, then if hee had gone over himself: And therefore hath besought vs, to allow him the same Proporcion of Money, as the Earle of *Strafford* (then Viscount *Wentworth*) was allow'd for his Transportacion, when hee went first over to bee Governour of that Kingdome. Wee are pleased and require that you cause the same to bee audited and allowd him; and that, his Arreares and growing Entertainements vpon all these Particulars being calculated, you acquaint vs therewith by one of our Secretaries: Wee intending that the sayd Earle, shall in his Payments, in such Manner, receiue the Fruite of theis our Letters, as may best stand with the other important Services in that our Kingdome. And for so doing, &c. given, &c. Oxon. 14 *Jan.* 1643.

But this Letter and Order hath bin ineffectuall; only 1000 *l.* or Part thereof, according to the sayd Letter, was paid at *Dublin* for the Discharge of some Debts, and to bring away the Earl of *Leycesters* Traine from thence. Neither hath the Earl of *Leycester* receiued any Recompence or Satisfaction according to his late Majestys gratious Intentions and Promises, but hath bin constrained to part with 1000 *l.* a Yeare Land, to discharge Parte of those Debts wherewith those Lands were charged in the Time, and by Reason of his Imployments; besides other Debts of the same Kinde yet remaining, charged vpon his Estate; and besides the Losse of his Plate and Goods at *Chester*, and *Beaumorrys*, to the Value of 3000 *l.* at the least. So as having serued the late King many Years faithfully, and to his Majesties Satisfaction, as hee hath bin many Times pleased to acknowledge.

The Earl of *Leycester* is impaired in his Fortune, to the Value of many thousand Pounds, since hee had the Honour to be in his Majesties Employments. And the King, since his happy Returne into *England*, having set forth his gratious Declaration, for the Satisfying of those Officers that had Comissions for Employments in *Ireland*, before the Yeare 1649, the Earl of *Leycester* conceiueing, and being advised by his Freinds, that hee was comprehended therein, made his Claime knowne to the Comissioners in *Ireland*; but they would not admitt the sayd Claime, as hee is informed, for two Reasons: 1. Because (as they conceiue) his Majesties Declaration, and Instructions, comprehend not the Generall Officers, or, as they call them, Staff Officers. To which it may bee answered, that there seemes to bee but little Reason, that the superiour Officers should bee excluded, when the inferiour Officers are included. 2. Because the Earl of *Leycester* hath not bin, nor serued Personally in *Ireland*, which is acknowledged; but yet to that also it may be sayd, That, all the Time of the Duration of his Comission, hee was in the Kings Employments and Service, and by his Majesties jefties fpeciall Comandment, attending his own Royall Perfon. But it is conceiued, that thefe Anfwers will not preuaile, without further Order and Authoritie from his Majeftie. It is therefore humbly defired, that the King will bee gracioufly pleafed to fignifie his Pleafure to the Lords Juftices, or to the Comiffioners, or to whom, and in what Manner his Majeftie fhall thinke fitr, that the Earl of *Leycefters* Accounts fhall bee ftated with all convenient Expedition, and his Arreares fatisfyed, in Regard of his great Expences, and Loffes, in the Time of his being employed in the late Kings Service ; and according to the Intention of his fayd Majeftie, expreffed in the Letter aforementioned, and the Earl of *Leycefter* fhall ever pray for his Majefties long Life and Happynes.

Among others of the Royal Family, that came over to congratulate the Reftoration of the King, was *Elifabeth*, Queen of *Bohemia*, his Majefty's Aunt, and only furviving Daughter of King *James the Firft* ; the happy Mother of a Proteftant Heir to thefe Kingdoms, the Princefs *Sophia*, from whom our moft gracious Sovereign is lineally defcended, and, as Heir to her, inherits his Crown. She had been married to the Elector *Palatine*, on *February* the 14th, 1612 ; and having been out of *England* 49 Years, and furvived all the Misfortunes of her Family, came now to her native Country to die in Peace, arriving at *London May* 17, 1661. She was for fome Time at *Drewry*-Houfe, with the Earl of *Craven* ; but being too clofe there, King *Charles the Second* wrote the following Letter to the Earl of *Leicefter*, which was delivered to him at *Penfhurft* by Dr. *Frafer*, her Phifician [a].

Whithall, 28 *Jan.* 1662.

MY Lord *Lefefter*, I fend this Bearer, Dr. *Frafer*, to defire a Curtofy of you in the Behalfe of the Queene of *Bohemia*. He will tell you the Particulars, and the Reafon of it. I fhall only add, that, in doing of it, you will oblige

Your affectionate Frinde,

Charles R.

Whereunto, his Lordfhip returned this Anfwer [b], by the fame Bearer.

S I R,

TO the Honor that I have even now received by thofe Lines which it hath pleafed your Majeftye to write unto me, by Doctor *Frafer*, it is not in my Power to make any proportionable Return : That which comes neareft to it, and all that I can do, is to prefent unto your Majeftye the fincere Profeffion of a perfect and ready Obedience to all your Commandments ; and that my poore Houfe, my felf, and whatfoever I may call mine, are, and fhall ever be at your Majeftyes Service : For there is nothing that I defire, or fhall fo much endeavour, as to give your Majeftye a full Affurance of my being, in all Humility,

Your Majeftyes moft faithfull and

30 *January*, 166½,
from *Penfhurft*.

moft obedient Subject and Servant,

L E Y C E S T E R.

His Lordfhip, immediately after, fent his Steward to Dr. *Frafer*, with the following Letter [c].

S I R,

ACcording to your Direction, I have fent this Bearer to receive from you the Commands of the Queene of *Bohemia*, concerning my Houfe, if it pleafe her Majefty to make Ufe of it. I confefs that I was in a Streight, but

[a] Ex Origin. apud Penfhurft.   [b] Ibid.   [c] Ibid.

you may be my Witnefs, that I quickly refolved thereupon. Before your Coming hether, I had no Defyre nor Intention to let my Houfe ; for, as old as I am, I do a little confider my innocent Pleafure, and I think that a pretty pleafant Place. I confider my Health and the Ayre of the Houfe. I confider my little privat Bufinefs, and the convenient Scituation of the Houfe for it.   I confider the Honor of wayting on the King fometimes, when his Majeftye will give me Leave ; and the Nearnes of the Houfe to the Kings Pallace. But, above all, I confider my Duty and Obedience to the Kings Commandment : And, next to that, I confider the Opportunity of contributing fomewhat to the Service of the Queen of *Bohemia*, whofe humble Servant I am, and have bin thefe many Yeares. And I fhall think it a great Happinefs to me, if the Ayre of my Houfe may contribute to the Recovery of her Health, or that I my felf may be any Way ferviceable to her Majeftye. And I heartily wifh, that your Art and Care may be fo directed and affifted, by the Bleffing of God, as to reftore her Majeftye to her perfect Health again. This is all the Trouble, that at this Time fhall.be given you by

Your humble Servant,

Penfhurft,
4 *Feb.* 1661.   LEYCESTER.

The Bearer will propofe fome few Things, which I prefume will not be thought unreafonable.

Afterwards the Earl of *Craven* made the following Requeft to his Lordfhip, by Letter :

My Lord,

IN Perfuite of your Refpect to the Kings Defires, and your Complaifance to the Queen of *Bohemia*, whome your Lordfhip has profeffed alwaies foe much to honour : Shee enjoyes att prefent the Benefitt of *Leicefter* Howfe ; and that your Lordfhip fhould not beleeve that there is leffe Entertainment on her Majefties Part, or of thofe who are intrufted to ferve her, the two Hundred Pounds, which was required by Mr. *Spencer*, as advanced for three Months Lonage, has bin payd him. The which, I hope, will induce your Lordfhip to add to your former Orders, for the better Convenience of the Queenes Ladies, fome Roomes, that may be fpared, from the neceffarie Putting afide of your Goods. Your Lordfhip is of a Race, to have a greater Reguard to the Accomodation of that Sex ; and I am confident when you are informed, that as yett they have none at all ; not fo much as to lodg them with any reafonable Fittingnefs, becoming either theire Perfons or Conditions : Your Lordfhip will give Command for that which may pull an.Obligation uppon you, and the Queene theire Miftreffe, without any Inconveniencing the Propertie of thofe Goods you referve a part. There are fome other Things, which Mr. *Spencer* and I have difcourfed ; which, according as your Lordfhipp fhall relifh, I fhould be glad to receive your Reply unto ; to the Intent that I may be juft to all. And your Lordfhipp may be confident, that, what Agreement foever may be made, there fhall be ever a like Punctuallitie in mee, to performe itt. And has the Queene has commanded mee to affeure your Lordfhipp of her continued Affection towards you, foe you may be confident that fhee will never proceede otherwaies then in that Way, for ought fhe may ftand in Neede of your Kindnes to her : And your Lordfhipp may pleafe to reley uppon mee, to ferve you according as you fhall pleafe to lett me know, what may be moft agreeable to your Mynd, either concerning your Howfe, or ought elfe : For truly, my Lord, I have a greate Defference for you ; and fhall ever approve my felf to bee

My LORD,
Your Lordfhipps moft faithfull,
affectionate humble Servant,

the 8th of *Februarie*
166½.

CRAVEN.

To

To this the Earl of *Leicefter* returned the following Anfwer:

My Lord,

I Am obliged to your Lordfhip for your good Opinion of me, and I verily beleeve that I fhall not forfit it by Want of Reverence to the Queene of *Bohemia*, or of Civility to her Ladyes. And if it had been known, that the uppermoft Roomes, or Garrets, could have been ufefull to them, my Servant *Spencer* would not have propofed the Refervation of them for any Ufe of mine: But they were thought unferviceable to Perfons of that Condition, and fit only to keep fuch Pictures, Furniture, *&c.* as were not worthy to be left in the Queenes Sight, nor theyr Ufe offerd to her Majeftyes Service: But now I hope the Ladyes are as well accomodated, as they can be in that little Houfe; which was not built for a Levie, but only for a privat Family. I appointed *Gilbert Spencer* to returne unto your Lordfhip the Reply which you required of me, concerning fome other Particularityes: And I am perfwaded, that your Lordfhip hath received it as reafonable; and therefore agreeable to your Judgment; and if your Lordfhip be pleafed to direct me, how I may, in any other Thing, render me acceptable to the Queene, you will do me a great Favour: As alfo, wherin I may, better then in Words, give you reall Teftimonyes of my being

Your Lordfhips moft humble

and affectionat Servant,

L E Y C E T E R.

The Queen lived but a very little Time in his Lordfhip's Houfe; for fhe departed this Life in it, the 13th of *February*, 166½; and thereupon his Lordfhip wrote a very elegant Letter to the Earl of *Northumberland*, condoling her Departure; which will be printed in the Collection. But the following Letter to the Earl of *Craven*, I fhall here infert:

My Lord,

T H E Advantage you have had of me, in the Occafions and Opportunityes of expreffing your Devotion to the Servis of the excellent Queen, lately deceafed, tempteth me to acknowledge your Lordfhip, more then my felf, her Servant: But, that being an Honor I cannot allow to any Body, I know not how to determine the Contention, or fupprefs my Emulation better, then by congratulating your Merit and good Services, and lamenting my own Want of both; which makes me inferior to your Lordfhip in that Competition, as alfo in every other Thing.

To fo much of the Letter, which your Lordfhip did me the Favour to write unto me, as conteined Bufines, or fomwhat like it; my Anfwer was firft hindred by my prefent Indifpofition, and then prevented by the fad Event, which hapned foone after I received it; but, for the Civility of it, I muft thinke my felf ftill indebted to you, even after I have returned my humble Thanks for it, with the Prefentation of my earneft Defyer, to be efteemed by you, as I am,

Your Lordfhips moft humble

Penfhurft,
26 Mar. 1662.   *and affectionat Servant,*

L E Y C E S T E R.

His Lordfhip, for fome Time before his Death, had a very ill State of Health, and was altogether refident at *Penfhurft* Place; where, by a regular and abftemious Way of Living, he furvived till the 2d of *November*, 1677, when he departed this Life, aged eighty-one Years and eleven Months. The Countefs his Wife died before him, on the 19th of *Auguft*, 1659, and was buried in the Chancel of *Penfhurft*, the 23d of the fame Month [d], where the Earl had alfo a Sepulture, on the 8th of *November*, 1677.

[d] Ex Regiftr. Eccl. de Penfhurft.

The

The Countess was distinguished for her good Sense, fine Breeding, and excellent Oeconomy. Her Letters, which are wrote with great Spirit, give some Account of the Intrigues of the Court of King *Charles the First*, and will be published in the Collection. The Earl of *Leicester*'s Letters contain the Occurrences of his Times, wherein are many Particulars not hitherto known ; and the Correspondence he kept with the most considerable Persons, then living, shew the great Value and Esteem they had of him ; as well as his great Learning, and Application in all Affairs he was concerned in. There are two Volumes of his Lordship's Letters, relating to his Negotiations, in his Majesty's Office of Papers and Records, for Business of State ; which I have examined, and such of them have been transcribed, as were wanting of what he had preserved ; and will be printed in the Collection.

I shall now add the Characters given of him. *Borlace*, in his Reduction of *Ireland*, p. 222, gives this Account of the Earl of *Leicester* : ' On the Removal of
' the Earl of *Strafford*, in 1641, he was nominated Lord Lieutenant of *Ireland*,
' a Person acceptable on all Accounts, having never been engaged in the publick
' Current of the Times, a Virtue very remarkable ; but often employed on the
' noblest Embassies Abroad and at Home ; whereby he was a fit Instrument to
' serve his Prince in so eminent an Employment (on the Loss of such a Minister
' of State as the Earl of *Strafford*) who by his Knowledge in Martial Affairs,
' and other his great Abilities, would have been, no Doubt, abundantly capa-
' ble to have reduced the *Irish* to a due Obedience. But though he had sent
' over Servants, and much Furniture into *Ireland*, and lay a long Time at *Ches-*
' *ter* for a Dispatch, he yet never came there, much to the Regret of many that
' wished well to that Service.'

Sir *William Temple* [e], in his Miscellanies, gives this Character of him, *That he was a Person of great Learning and Observation, as well as of Truth* ; of which he relates some remarkable Particulars.

The Earl of *Clarendon* [f] recites, ' That he was a Man of great Parts, very
' conversant in Books, and much addicted to the Mathematicks, and tho' he
' had been a Soldier, and commanded a Regiment in the Service of the States
' of the *United Provinces*, and was afterwards imployed in several Ambassies, as
' in *Denmark*, and in *France*, was in Truth, rather a speculative, than a prac-
' tical Man, and expected a greater Certitude in the Consultation of Business,
' than the Business of this World is capable of : Which Temper proved very
' ill-convenient to him, through the Course of his Life. He was after the
' Death of the Earl of *Strafford*, by the concurrent Kindness of both the King
' and Queen, called from his Ambassy in *France*, to be Lieutenant of the
' Kingdom of *Ireland* ; but in a very short Time after, unhappily lost that
' Kindness and Esteem : And being, about the Time of the King's coming to
' *Oxford*, ready to embark at *Chester*, for the Execution of his Charge, he was
' required to attend his Majesty, for farther Instructions, at *Oxford* ; where he
' remained ; and though he was of the Council, and sometimes present, he
' desired not to have any Part in the Business ; and lay under many Reproaches
' and Jealousies, that he deserved not : For he was a Man of Honour and Fi-
' delity to the King, and his greatest Misfortunes proceeded from the Stagger-
' ing and Irresolution in his Nature.'

The Earl of *Clarendon* further relates, [g] that the Earl of *Leicester* was the only Peer at *Oxford*, who followed the King, that refused to sign a Letter from the Peers on his Majesty's Behalf, to the Council in *Scotland*. The Earl's Reasons, for not Signing that Letter, are already mentioned, with an Account of his Conduct, from his being Lord Lieutenant of *Ireland*, to the Time he quitted the King's Service. So that I leave it to the Judgment of the impartial Reader, how just the Accusation may be, *of a Staggering and Irresolution in his Nature.* But his Letters, which are to be published in the Collection, will

[e] Vide his Works, Vol. I. p. 276.   [f] Hist. of the Rebell. 8vo. Vol. III. p. 201.
[g] Hist. of the Rebell. 8vo. Vol. III. p. 411, 412.

clearly

clearly evince, that he was of a humane Difpofition, well grounded in his Principles, and fteady to the Eftablifhed Church, and Monarchical Confti-tution.

The noble Author himfelf, [h] feems to be confcious, that the Earl of *Leicef-ter* was not well ufed, delivering his Thoughts, why he refufed to fign the Letter before mentioned, in thefe Words : ' Whether he had not yet digefted, ' his late Depofal from the Lieutenancy of *Ireland*, to which the Marquis of ' *Ormond* was deputed, and thought the Difobligation of it not capable of a ' Reparation, or whether he thought the King's Fortune defperate, and refolved ' not to facrifice himfelf, to any popular Difpleafure ; and not to provoke the ' Parliament farther than by not concurring with them ; or whether he had it ' then in his Purpofe to be found in their Quarters, as fhortly after he was, ' did in the End pofitively refufe to fubfcribe the Letter, and thereby was ' the Occafion of a Mifchief, he did not intend. For both their Majefties, in ' their fecret Purpofe, had defigned him to fucceed the Marquis of *Hertford*, ' in the Government of the Prince : For which he would have been very pro-' per ; but upon this fo affected a Difcovery of a Nature, and Mind, liable to ' no Kind of Compliance, the King could not profecute his Purpofe ; and fo ' the Government of that hopeful and excellent Prince was committed to the ' Earl of *Berkfhire*, for no other Reafon, but becaufe he had a Mind to it, be-' ing moft unfit for that Province.'

As I have perufed his Lordfhip's Letters, Journals, and Mifcellanies, &c. as well as thofe Letters wrote to him, which he kept in exact Order, mark-ing the Time, he received them, and explaining the Cyphers therein ; they fuffi-ciently fhew, he was efteemed by Perfons of all Ranks, and Profeffions. And I think it will appear, that there was not a Nobleman of more Virtue, and Learning, truer Honour, or founder Judgment, in his Time. He was well read in the Claf-ficks, and fpoke elegant *Latin, French, Italian*, and *Spanifh* ; fo that he purchafed moft of the curious Books in thofe Languages, publifhed whilft he was Abroad on his Ambaffies ; and feveral learned Men made him Prefents of their Works. He was induftrious in fearching into the Interefts of the feveral Kingdoms and State of *Europe* ; and no lefs ftudious of the Nature and Conftitution of his own Coun-try, than in the Religion profeffed therein ; his Obfervations in his Ambaffies, and on Political Goverment, with feveral Effays on divine and moral Subjects, in his own Hand-writing, are yet remaining at *Penfhurft* Place, the Seat of the Family. His Leaving the King at *Oxford* could not juftly be imputed to any Thought of com-plying with the Parliament, and his Going into their Quarters proceeded from his Houfes, and Eftate, being under their Jurifdiction ; and he had followed the King, till he was reduced to the greateft Neceffity. It is apparent, that he went to *Chefter*, in order to go over to *Ireland*, at a Time there was very little Provifion made for his acting offenfively againft the *Irifh* Rebels ; yet under all Difadvantages, he was determined to embark for that Kingdom ; but fal-ling dangeroufly ill, it was impoffible to effect it till his Recovery, and then he was commanded to attend the King at *Oxford*, where he found the Marquis of *Ormond* had procured for himfelf the Government of *Ireland*. It is likewife certain, that he never was of the Parliament Faction, and *Oliver Cromwell* ex-acted annual Engagements from him under his Hand, not to oppofe the Com-monwealth. The clofe Intereft of his Son, the Lord *L' Ifle*, with that Party, might be fome Means of their fuffering his Lordfhip to live quietly ; yet it appears that both the Lord *L' Ifle*, and his Brother, *Algernon Sydney*, who had been fent over to *Ireland* by his Lordfhip ; were on their Return from thence (the King having charged them to come directly to him) taken into Cuftody by the Parliament, on their Landing in *Lancafhire*, whereby they could not comply with his Majefty's Command, who being therewith offended,

---

[h] Hift. of the Rebellion, p. 412.

they then engaged with the Army. King *Charles the Second*, on his Reftoration, had thofe Sentiments of the Earl of *Leicefter's* Principles, and Honour,
that he received him very gracioufly, and two Days after his triumphant Entry,
through his City of *London*, he was fworn of his Privy-Council, with the Earl
of *Manchefter*, and others, who had contributed to his Settlement on the
Throne, as already mentioned. He was truly a moft indulgent Hufband, tender Father, generous Friend, and a ftrict Obferver of all moral Virtues.

His Lordfhip's laft Will and Teftament, bears Date * the 28th of *Sept.* 1665,
which, with neceffary Alterations, he confirmed by feveral Codicils; the laft
whereof is dated the 6th of *April*, 1675. He therein bequeaths to his Daughter *Dorothy*, Countefs Dowager of *Sunderland*, one-hundred Pounds; and to his
Daughter the Lady *Lucy Pelham*, one-hundred Pounds, to buy each of them
a Ring; to be paid by his Executors, within a Month, or fooner, after his
Deceafe.

He bequeaths to his eldeft Son, *Philip* Lord Vifcount *Lifle*, all his Books, Papers,
and Globes, in his Library, Evidence-Houfe, and Study, in his Manfion of *Penfhurft*
in the County of *Kent*; and in his Study and Evidence-Houfe, in his Meffuage
called *Leicefter* Houfe, in the County of *Middlefex*; with all his Books in other Places: The faid Books, &c. to be ufed by his faid Son Vifcount *Lifle*, during his
Life; and after his Deceafe, to remain to his Grandchild *Robert Sidney*, his eldeft
Son, for his Ufe, during his Life; and after to remain from one Heir to another, *That is to fay, to every of them, who, for the Time being, fhall hold and en-*
joy his Mannors, Lands, and Tenements, by Virtue of, and attending to the Inden-
tures of Settlement thereof. And defires and requires his faid Son *Lifle*, and his
Grandfon, and thofe Heirs to whom he has given his Books, &c. as aforefaid,
to carefully preferve the fame, for the Benefit of thofe that fhall fucceed them,
as he had done in his Time, and largely increafed them.

He gives to his Son *Henry Sidney* all his Plate, Silver Difhes, &c. marked
with his late dear Wife's Arms only: And all the Jewels, Medals, Cabinets,
Pictures, Books, and other Things which were his faid Wife's; and which fhe
gave to his faid Son *Henry*, with his Confent. And he bequeaths to his faid
Son *Henry Sidney* the Diamond Jewel, which the Princefs *Elifabeth*, Daughter
of the late King, by her Will, gave to himfelf and his Wife, *as a Teftimony*
of her being well fattisfied, with the Entertainment and Service, which fhe received
in my Houfe, whilft fhe lived therein, by Order and Direction of the then Parlia-
ment. Alfo all the Money or Lands due unto him, in Satisfaction for his
Allowances and Entertainments, as Lord Lieutenant of *Ireland*, and General of
the Army there, and as Colonel and Captain of Horfe and Foot, by Commiffion under the great Seal of *England*, dated in the Month of *June*, 1641.

He gives to his Son *Robert Sidney* all his Money due to him on a Judgment
which he obtained in the Court of *Common-Pleas*, againft *Thomas Buckley*, Efq.
commonly called Lord *Buckley*. Alfo to his Sons *Robert*, and *Henry Sidney*,
equally between them, all Money due to him from the late King for his Allowance, as being Lord Ambaffador Extraordinary from his Majefty to the King
of *France*, as appears from the then Lords Commiffioners of the Treafury,
and alfo by Warrant of the now Lord Treafurer, for the Payment thereof.

He makes and ordains the Earl of *Sunderland*, his Son *Henry Sidney*, and Sir
John Pelham, Bart. his Executors; and gives to them all his ready Money,
Mortgages, and other his Perfonal Eftate, not before given, towards the Per-
formance of his Will.

And whereas, upon the Conclufion of the Marriage of his Son *Philip* Lord
Vifcount *Lifle*, he did by Indentures bearing Date, 16 *May* 24 *Car.* I. fettle
his Mannors, Lands, and Tenements on Sir *John Temple*, Knight; *Hugh Potter*
and *Thomas Dorral*, Efqrs; *Miles Smith*, and *Thomas Elliot*, Gent. his Truftees;
by which he had Power by any Deed or Writing under his Hand or Seal, or
by his laft Will, to nominate and appoint fuch Perfon or Perfons, as he fhould

* Ex Regiftr. in Cur. Prærog. Cantuar.

think

think fit to hold *Leicefter* Houfe, and the Eftate there, for 99 Years; he charges the fame with 4000 *l.* payable by his faid Son, the Lord Vifcount *Lifle,* in two Years, to his Executors, for the Ufe of his younger Sons *Robert* and *Henry Sidney.* Alfo, by the faid Indentures, one and twenty thoufand Pounds being limited and appointed to be raifed and paid, out of the Mannors, Lands, *&c.* in the faid Indentures fpecified for the Ufes therein expreffed: He, by feveral Codicils to his Will annexed, on Alterations which happened by Deaths, *&c.* leaves his whole Perfonal Eftate to his youngeft Son *Henry Sidney,* except 5000 *l.* that he bequeaths to his 2d Son *Algernon.*

His Lordfhip had Iffue, by the Lady *Dorothy Percy* his Wife, fix Sons, whereof four furvived to Maturity, *Philip, Algernon, Robert,* and *Henry,* of whom I fhall diftinctly treat; alfo nine Daughters.

1. Lady *Dorothy,* highly celebrated by the famous *Waller,* for her excellent Beauty and Virtues[a], married 11th *July* 1639, at *Penfhurft,* to *Henry* Lord *Spencer,* after created Earl of *Sunderland,* and by him had Iffue *Robert* Earl of *Sunderland,* Grandfather to *Charles* the prefent Duke of *Marlborough,* and the honourable *John Spencer,* Efq. and others. She 2dly (after living a confiderable Time a Widow) married[b] on the 8th of *July,* 1652, *Robert Smythe* of *Sutton* at *Hone,* and *Bounds* in *Kent,* Efq. Son and Heir of Sir *John Smythe,* Knight (by *Ifabella* his Wife, Daughter of *Robert Rich,* firft Earl of *Warwick*) Son and Heir of Sir *Thomas Smythe,* Uncle of *Thomas Smythe* created Vifcount *Strangford,* who had to Wife *Barbara* Daughter of *Robert Sidney,* the 1ft Earl of *Leicefter.* The Countefs of *Sunderland,* by her 2d Marriage, had Iffue *Robert Smythe,* Efq. Governor of *Dover* Caftle; who, by *Catharine* his Wife Daughter of *William Stafford,* of *Blatherwick* in *Northamptonfhire,* Efq. had Iffue *Henry,* Father of *Sidney-Stafford Smythe* of *Bounds* in *Kent,* Efq. the prefent Judge of the Marfhal's Court, who married *Sarah,* eldeft Daughter of Sir *Charles Farnaby* of *Kippington* in *Kent,* Bart.

2. *Lucy,* chriftened at *Penfhurft, March* 7th, 1623[c], and buried there *Feb.* 23, 1624.

3. Lady *Lucy,* chriftened at *Penfhurft, July* 7th, 1625, and married there, 20 *Jan.* 1647, to *John Pelham,* Efq. Son and Heir to Sir *Thomas Pelham,* Bart. by whom fhe had Iffue *Thomas* Lord *Pelham,* Father of his Grace, *Thomas* Duke of *Newcaftle,* Principal Secretary of State to his Majefty; and of the Right Honourable *Henry Pelham,* 1ft Commiffioner of the Treafury, Chancellor of the Exchequer, and of the Privy Council to his Majefty. And *Elizabeth* her eldeft Daughter was married to the Honourable *Edward Montagu,* Efq. who had Iffue by him *George* late Earl of *Hallifax,* Father of the prefent Earl.

4. Lady *Anne,* who took to her Hufband (without the Confent of her Father) the Revd. Mr. *Jofeph Cart,* his Chaplain, and had Iffue by him a Son, *Sidney Cart,* and two Daughters, who all died very young, and were buried at *Leigh* in *Kent,* where their Father was Rector.

5. Lady *Mary,* chriftened at *Penfhurft, Nov.* 3, 1629, who was buried there, the 4th of *June* 1648, unmarried.

6. Lady *Frances,* chriftened at *Penfhurft,* 18 *Dec.* 1630, and buried there, the 3d of *October,* 1651, unmarried.

7. Lady *Ifabella,* chriftened at *Penfhurft,* 30 *Sept.* 1634, and married there, 22 *Auguft* 1650, to *Philip Smythe* Lord Vifcount *Strangford,* and died without Iffue by him.

8. Lady *Elizabeth,* who died unmarried, and was buried at *Penfhurft,* 7 *Oct.* 1650.

9. Lady *Diana,* who alfo died unmarried, and was buried at *Penfhurft,* the 23d of *June,* 1670.

---

[a] Ex Regiftr. Ecclef. de Penfhurft.   [b] Ibid.   [c] Ex Regiftr. Ecclef. de Penfhurft.

I fhall

I shall now proceed to treat of *Philip* the eldest Son of *Robert* Earl of *Leicester*. He had a liberal Education, and from his Youth had been trained up in Legantine Affairs, attending on his Father to *Denmark*, and after in the *French* Court. He had a Troop of Horse under his Uncle, the Earl of *Northumberland*, General of the Forces, sent by King *Charles the First*, against the *Scots*; and after his Father, the Earl of *Leicester*, was made Lord Lieutenant of *Ireland*, he had the Command of a Regiment of Horse, and with his Brother *Algernon*, Captain in the same Regiment, went over to that Kingdom, and did good Service against the *Irish* Rebels.

Before his Return from *Ireland*, with his Brother *Algernon Sidney*; the King ordered them on their Allegiance to come to *Oxford*, which the Parliament hearing of, sent into *Lancashire*, where they landed, and had them taken into Custody. The King, thinking this was by their own Management, was greatly offended with them; and thereupon they entered into the Measures of the Parliament. And the [d] Lord Viscount *Lisle*, in 1644, had 1000 *l.* allowed him for his Services in *Ireland*.

On 21 *Jan.* 1645, they [e] voted *Philip* Lord Viscount *Lisle* to be General Governor of the Kingdom of *Ireland*; and, on the 31st of the same Month, came to a Resolution [f], that the Committee of both Kingdoms receive from the Lord *Lisle* his Propositions touching *Ireland*. Also, on 16 *Feb.* following, voted [g] him an Allowance of 1200 *l.* a Month for his Salary.

On 13 *May*, 1646, the Commons sent an Ordinance to the Lords [h], to enable the Lord *Lisle*, Lieutenant of *Ireland*, to raise 6000 Foot, and 850 Horse, to be sent to that Kingdom.

Dec. 22, 1646, the Lord Viscount *Lisle* [i] delivered Proposals to the Parliament, for Supplies and Money to carry on the Wars in *Ireland*, and that he was ready to go over thither in Person. His Lordship landed at *Cork*, the Beginning of *March*, and immediately sent a Detachment into the Rebels Country, which did good Service there, as *Whitlock* writes [k].

Whilst he was in *Ireland*, the House voted, 6 *March*, 1646, that 7 Regiments of Foot, 3000 Horse, and 1200 Dragoons, out of the Army in *England* should be sent to that Kingdom; all Places in *England* being reduced to the Obedience of the Parliament; but, *Cromwell* having ambitious Designs in View, this Order had no Effect.

The Year after, the Commons having [l] voted Major General *Skippon* to be Field Marshal of *Ireland*, the Lord *Lisle* thought it an Infringement on his Power; and sent Letters to the Parliament, which were received, 13 *April*, 1647 [m], giving therein an Account, that he was ready to take the Field, and would do all the Service he could, but, at the same Time, expressed his Willingness to return, if they were not satisfied with his Conduct.

On the 21st of *April* following [n], the House of Commons received an Account from the Council War in *Ireland*, that the Soldiers were in great Want there; and that the Lord Viscount *Lisle* was very careful to get Supplies for them, and to do them Service. But, whilst the House was imployed, how to send Part of the Army to *Ireland* (the King being in Custody) and many being unwilling to go there, as *Whitlock* writes [o], the Lord *L'Isle* returned from thence, 27 *April*, 1647. And, on the 7th of *May*, reporting to the House the State of Affairs in *Ireland* [p], his Lordship, with his Brother Colonel *Algernon Sidney*, and Sir *John Temple*, had the Thanks of the Commons, for their good Services in *Ireland*.

For the Trial of the King, the Lord Viscount *L'Isle* [q] was nominated one of his Judges, but refused to act, and did not once come among them, retiring to *Penshurst*, as the Earl of *Leicester* has observed in his Journal.

---

[d] Whitlock's Memorials, p. 87.　　[e] Ibid. p. 194.　　[f] p. 196.　　[g] Ibid. p. 198.　　[h] p. 210.
[i] p. 235.　　[k] p. 243.　　[l] p. 246.　　[m] p. 247.　　[n] p. 248.　　[o] Ibid.　　[p] p. 249.
[q] Dugdale's View of the Troubles in Eng. p. 367.

After

After the cruel Murder of the King, the Parliament proceeding to form their Commonwealth, voted, 14 *Feb.* 1648, a Council of State, confifting of 38; and [p], thereupon, nominated the Lord Vifcount *L'Ifle* to be one of that Number, with the Earls of *Pembroke*, *Salifbury*, *Mulgrave*, and *Denbigh*, and the Lord *Grey* of *Groby*, *&c.* Alfo, in 1649, fome Alterations being made in the Council of State, he was then again nominated [q], with the Earls of *Salifbury*, *Denbigh*, *&c.* His Lorfhip's Letters to the Earl of *Leicefter* his Father (which will be publifhed in the Collection) difclofe many fecret Paffages of thofe Times.

In 1652, he was nominated, to go Ambaffador Extraordinary from the Commonwealth of *England*, to the Queen of *Sweden*, but never went.

In 1653 [r], on *Oliver Cromwell's* being proclaimed Lord Protector, he was one of his Council of 21 Perfons; and, on his Going in State to the Parliament [s], the Lord Vifcount *L'Ifle*, General *Montagu* (after Earl *Sandwich*) and *Whitlock*, ftood with drawn Swords by the Earl of *Warwick*, who carried the Sword of State before the Protector. His Lordfhip was alfo [t] one of his Houfe of Lords, fummoned by Writ, 11th of *December*, 1657. And his Name was [u] to the Proclamation of *Richard Cromwell*, the Protector's Son, 3 *Sept.* 1658; but, when he refigned, the Lord Vifcount *L'Ifle* concerned himfelf no farther in publick Affairs.

After the Reftoration of King *Charles the Second*, his [w] Lordfhip obtained a general Pardon, bearing Date the 30th of *Oct.* 1660, 12 *Car.* II; and, during his Father's Lime-time, refided at *Shene*, near *Richmond* in *Surry*, where he entertained himfelf with fome of the greateft Wits of the Age.

Sir *William Temple* addreffes feveral Letters to him there, with fine Compliments; and I have heard it well attefted, that he fet a-part one Day in the Week for Entertainment of Men of Letters.

In 1677, he fucceeded his Father, and became Earl of *Leicefter*, but always declined being concerned in publick Affairs. Neverthelefs, I have been informed by thofe who knew his Lordfhip, that King *Charles the Second* confulted him in private on Affairs of State; yet he could never be brought to accept of any Employment at Court.

On King *William's* Acceffion to the Throne, he retained the fame Sentiments as to publick Bufinefs; and dying at *Leicefter-Houfe* in *London*, the 6th of *March*, 1696-7, aged more than 80 Years, was buried with his Anceftors at *Penfhurft*, the 17th of the fame Month.

He married [x], on the 19th of *May*, 1645, the Lady *Catharine*, Daughter of *William Cecil*, Earl of *Salifbury*, and of his Wife, *Catharine Howard*, youngeft Daughter of *Thomas* Earl of *Suffolk*; by whom he had Iffue two Sons, *Robert*, his Succeffor, and *Algernon*, and two Daughters, *Dorothy*, and *Elifabeth*, born 13th of *Auguft*, 1652. The youngeft Son, *Algernon* [y], died young, and was buried at *Penfhurft*, the 10th *June*, 1648; and the youngeft Daughter, *Elifabeth*, died alfo young; but the eldeft Daughter was married to *Thomas Cheek*, Efq; 2d Son of Sir *Thomas Cheek*, of *Pirgo*, in the County of *Effex*, Knight. The Lady, their Mother, died at the Age of 24 Years, in *Northumberland-Houfe*, *London* [z], on the 18th of *Auguft*, 1652, being 5 Days after fhe was delivered of her youngeft Daughter, *Elifabeth*, and was buried the 22d of *Auguft*, in the Chancel of the Church of *Penfhurft*, belonging to the Family.

I fhall now proceed to treat of *Algernon*, the 2d Son of *Robert* Earl of *Leicefter*. His noble Father was careful in giving him a learned Education; and, in 1632, when he went Ambaffador to *Denmark*, took him with him; as alfo, when he was Ambaffador in *France*.

The Countefs his Mother, in a Letter to the Earl at *Paris*, dated 10 *Nov.* 1636, acquaints his Lordfhip, *That fhe hears him much commended by all that come from thence, for a huge deal of Wit, and much Sweetnefs of Nature.*

---

[p] Whitlock, p. 376.   [q] Ibid p. 425.   [r] Rapin's Hift. of Engl. 8vo, Vol. 13. p. 95.   [s] Whitlock's Memorials. p. 661, 662.   [t] Ibid. p. 665.   [u] p. 675.   [w] Ex Orig. apud Penfhurft. [x] Journal of the Earl of Leicefter.   [y] Ex Regift. Ecclef. de Penfhurft.   [z] Journal, at antea.

On the Breaking out of the Rebellion in *Ireland*, he had a Commiffion for a Troop of Horfe in his Father's Regiment, and went over with his Brother, the Lord Vifcount *L'Ifle*, into that Kingdom, where he behaved very gallantly againft the Rebels.

In 1643, he had the King's Permiffion to come to *England*; and the Earl of *Leicefter* gave him this Licence [a] :

By the Lord Lieutenant Generall of Ireland.

WHereas his Majefty is gratioufly pleafed to giue Permiffion vnto *Algernon Sidney*, Captayne of a Troope of Horfe for his Majeftyes Service in *Ireland*, to be abfent from the fayd Troope, and to come ouer into *England*. Thefe are to will and require you, that you forbeare Impofing any Cheque vpon him and the fix Horfes allowed to him, in his Entertaynment from his Majefty, during the Space of fower Monthes next to come. Whereof you may not fayle. And, for fo doing, this fhal be a fufficient Warrant. Given at *Oxford*, the 22th of *June*, 1643.

To Sir *Robert King*, Knight,   *Leycefter*.
or his Deputy or Deputys.

But, landing in *Lancafhire*, he was, by Order of Parliament, brought in Cuftody to *London*, where he was prevailed on to take a Command under them; and [b] 2000 *l.* was ordered him for his Arrears. The Order of the Houfe of Commons was as follows :

Die Jovis vlt. Augufti 1643.

A Letter [c] was read from the Committee att *Liverpoole* and *Manchefter*, and an intercepted Letter, there taken from Captayne *Sidney*, newly come out of *Ireland*, to *Orlando Bridgman* at *Chefter*, of his Intencions to goe to the Kinge, were read :

Ordered,

That a Letter bee written to the Deputy Leiutenants and Committees in the Countie of *Lancafter*, to fend vpp in fafe Cuftody the Lord *Lifle*, Captayne *Sidney*, and Sir *Richard Grinville*, guarded with a ftrong Convoy : And that the Committees and Deputie Leiutenants in the Counties betwixt this and *Lancafhire*, refpectively, doe appointe a good Convoy with the faid Perfons, through their feveral Counties, and that a Stay bee made of all their Goods and Armes, till this Howfe take further Order. And Mr. *Afhurft* is to prepare this Letter, and to write the fame accordingly.

H. *Elfynge*, Cler. Parl. d. Com.

Mr. Afhurft's Letter.

Gentlemen,

THE Houfe of Commons doth take fpeciall Notice of your great Care and Diligence in Staying and Securing the Perfons and Goods of fuch, who, at this Time, come out of *Ireland* ; for which, they haue commanded mee to giue you Thankes, and to affure you, that they will euer haue a tender Regard to you and your County, who, vpon all Occafions, haue fhewed fo much Faithfulnes and Zeale to the Publike.

For the Particulars in your laft Letter, I am to acquaint you, that it is their Pleafure, that the Perfons of the Lord *Lifle*, Captaine *Sidney*, and Sir *Richard Greenvill* bee fent vp with a ftrong Convoy, according to the Direccions in the inclofed Order. And that all their Goods and Armes bee depofited into fafe Hands, vntill the Houfe take further Order. This being all that I haue in Charge, I fhall only adde, that I am

September 5,   *Your, &c.*
1643.

[a] Ex Orig. apud Penfhurft.   [b] Whitlock's Memorials, p. 237.   [c] Ex Autog. apud Penfhurft.

Another

Another Letter was fent by the Speaker, to Sir *William Brereton* [d], as follows:

SIR,

AMongft the many Euidences of your Care and Zeale to the Publike, the Houfe hath taken fpeciall Notice of your often reprefenting to them their Danger, by the frequent Comeing ouer either of the Rebells, or other Soldiers, out of *Ireland*, at this Tyme; and, for Prevencion of that Mifcheife, haue paffed this inclofed Ordinance, which they hope you will make good Vfe of. For the Perfons of the Lord *Lifle*, Captaine *Sidney*, and Sir *Richard Greenvill*, they haue fent their Direccions to *Liuerpoole*, that they bee brought vp hither to *London* with a fafe Convoy, where in they doubt not of your beft Affiftance. And, vpon this Occafion, I am to affure you, and thofe worthy Gentlemen of your Country, that ioyne with you, That, as the Houfe haue obferved Gods great Goodneffe in preferuing you in fo many Dangers, and profpering you in fo many difficult Vndertakings, fo they haue taken fpeciall Notice of the great Courage, Care, and vnwearyed Paines, which haue beene manifefted, not only in your owne Defence, but in your ready Affiftance of all neighbouring Counties. And haue commaunded me to giue you Thankes, and defire you, in their Names, to do the like to all the Gentlemen in your Country, with you, who haue deferued fo well of the Comon Wealth. And, as they affure them felues, that you will make Vfe of your Chiefe Comaund with a great deale of Wifdome and Tendernefs towards thofe worthy Gentlemen, fo they hope that all thofe Gentlemen will haue the like Refpect to you: And both labour in a Bond of Loue to preferue Vnity, as your greateft Strength, and to auoyd Diuifion, as a certaine Ruine to your Country; which wee know you ftudy to preferue. And this being all I haue in Comaund (only to affure you, that as the Houfe hath euer heretofore, fo they will euer, hereafter, bee ready to afford you all Suplies and Affiftance in their Power) I fhall only adde, that I am, *SIR*,

September 5, 1643.   *Your affured loving Freind,*

Wm. Lenthall.

The Earl of *Manchefter*, Serjeant-Major-General of the feveral Counties of *Effex*, *Norfolk*, *Suffolk*, *Hertford*, *Cambridge*, *Huntingdon*, and *Lincoln*, conftitutes, 10 *May*, 1644, *Algernon Sydney*, Captain of a Troop of Horfe, within his own Regiment, confifting of one hundred, to be raifed for the Defence of the King, Parliament, and Kingdom [e]. And Sir *Thomas Fairfax*, Knight, Commander in Chief of all the Forces, raifed for the Defence of the Kingdom, conftitutes him Colonel of a Regiment of Horfe, raifed, and to be raifed, for the Service aforefaid. Dated the 2d of *April*, 1645.

Alfo, *Philip*, Lord Vifcount *L'Ifle*, Lieutenant-General of the Kingdom of *Ireland*, and General of the Forces there, by the Power and Authority to him given, by an Order of the Lords and Commons of *England*, in Parliament affembled, bearing Date the fixth Day of *July* laft paft, [f] conftitutes and appoints *Algernon Sydney*, Colonel of a Regiment of Horfe, to ferve in this prefent Expedition for *Ireland*, &c.

It appears by the Earl of *Leicefter*'s Journal, that he was Leiutenant-General of the Horfe in *Ireland*, and Governor of *Dublin*; and that before he went into that Kingdom, he had the Goverment of *Chichefter*, and was in the Battles of *York*, and other Places. Alfo, that on the 8th of *April*, 1647, early in the Morning, the Houfe of Commons being then thin, and few of my Sons Friends prefent (faith the Earl) 'it was moved by Mr. *Glyn* the Recorder, that Colonel ' *Jones*, fhould be made Governor of *Dublin* in Chief, and not Deputy-Gover- ' nor to *Algernon Sydney*, pretending that *Jones* would not go, unlefs he might

[d] Ex Autog. apud Penfhurft.   [e] Ex Orig. apud Penfhurft.   [f] Ex Orig. apud Penfhurft.

' be Governor : Which was not true, *Jones* having accepted of the Place of Depu-
' ty-Governor from the Committee at *Derby*-houfe ; who had alfo appointed the
' Lord *L' Ifle*, to commiffion his Brother *Algernon* to be Governor of *Dublin*,
' which he had done before they went into *Munfter*. This Motion of the Recor-
' der, was feconded by old Sir *Henry Vane*, who pretended, that his Confcience
' moved him to be of Opinion, that fince the Houfe had thought proper to re-
' call the Lord *L' Ifle*, it was not fitt to let his Brother, *Algernon Sydney*, remain
' Governor of fo important a Place as *Dublin*. Sir *William Armyn*, and others,
' oppofed this Motion, alledging, if they had ufed one Brother ill, they ought
' not to do Injuftice to the other, who had fo well deferved of them. But it
' was carried againft him, and the Goverment was conferred on *Jones*. After
' which Refolution, it was moved, *That fome Recompence might be given to* Alger-
' non Sydney, *according to his Merit*, to which the Houfe affented without Op-
' pofition'. And *Whitlock* [g] writes, that, on 27 *April* 1647, Colonel *Sydney* had
the Thanks of the Houfe for his good Services in *Ireland* ; and [*] was afterwards
made Governor of *Dover*.

He was, by Inclination and Principle, fo grounded in his Opinion for a Commonwealth, that when *Cromwell* had affumed the Goverment, he refufed to act
under him ; or his Son *Richard Cromwell* who fucceeded him in the Protec-
torfhip : During which Time he lived retired at *Penfhurft*, and other Places,
when it is conceived he began to write his *Difcourfes on Goverment*. But on the
Refignation of *Richard*, and the Reftoration of the long Parliament, and their
Speaker *Lenthall* ; they, on the 7th of *May* 1659, having voted a Declaration
to fecure the Liberty and Property of the People, both as Men and Chriftians,
without a fingle Perfon, King, or Houfe of Peers, he then came into their
Meafures. Whereupon on 13 *May* following, [h] he was named, by that Parliament, one of the Council of State, with the Lord *Fairfax*, Sir *Anthony Afhley
Cooper*, Sir *Horatio Townfhend*, Sir *Henry Vane*, *Whitlock*, and others.

On 5 *June*, 1659, he was nominated, with Sir *Robert Honywood*, and *Whitlock*, to go Commiffioners to mediate a Peace between the Kings of *Sweden* and
Denmark. *Whitlock* recites, [i] that he was not willing to undertake this Service,
efpecially being joined with thofe who would expect Precedency of him, and he
knew well the over-ruling Temper, and Height of Colonel *Sidney*, and therefore endeavoured to excufe himfelf by Reafon of his old Age and Infirmities.
Whereupon the Council at length gave him Leave to ftay in *England*, fo that
only Colonel *Sydney*, and Sir *Robert Honywood*, went on that Ambaffy, which
was not ended on the Reftoration of King *Charles the Second*.

His Letters to his Father, the Earl of *Leicefter*, give a full Account of his
Negotiations there, and are very curious and remarkable. It further appears,
that the King would not fuffer him to return to *England*, and thereupon he
travelled through *Germany* to *Bruffels*, where he refided for fome Time, and
from thence went to *France*, [k] having the following Licence from the *French*
King :

To all Governours and our Lieutenants-Generall, *&c.* Greeting, Mr. *Sydney*,
Son to the Earl of *Leicefter*, having defired, notwithftanding the War againft *England*, that he might change his Place of Abode from *Germany*, to go to *Montpellier*, to which we having affented : We Command you to let him pafs freely
through your feverall Jurifdictions, with his Domefticks, to *Montpellier*, without Interruption, and to fhew him all the Favour, and aid him as far as you
can. Given at our Caftle of *Vincennes*, 3 *Aug.* 1663.

Signed Louis.

He afterwards travelled into *Italy*, and made his Abode at *Rome*. His Obfervations on the Courts, and Manners of the Countries he paft through, more
particularly of the Cardinals and People of Diftinction at *Rome*, are very learned
and entertaining ; and will be publifhed in the Collection of Letters, *&c.*

---

[g] Memorials, p. 249. [*] Ib. p. 463. [h] Whitlock, p. 679. [i] Ib. p. 681. [k] From the Original.

It does not appear, that he had acted farther, than several who had been preferred by King *Charles the Second* ; it being certain, that though he was nominated one of the Judges of his Royal Father, he had no Concern in his Murther ; so that he was hardly used, in being forced to forsake his Country. But the Earl of *Leicester,* shewing a Desire of seeing him before he died, and *Robert* Earl of *Sunderland,* his Lordship's Grandson, being in Favour with King *Charles the Second,* he obtained his Majesty's Leave for his Return, in 1677 ; [1] as also his Pardon.

On the 13th of *November,* 1677, he was at *Penshurst,* and then [m] gave a Discharge to the Executors of his Father's Will (*Robert,* Earl of *Sunderland* ; *Henry Sydney,* Esq; his Brother, and Sir *John Pelham,* Bart.) for the Legacy left him therein, of 5000, and 100 *l.*

As he joined with those that opposed the Measures of the Court, the King took great Offence at it, which in the End proved fatal to him.

In 1678, he stood Candidate for Member of Parliament for *Guilford,* but the Court opposing, he lost his Election. I find among his Papers, at *Penshurst* Place, the following Account.

Algernoon Sidney, *Esq; his Case concerning the Election for the Towne of* Guilford *in* Surry.

BEfore the Election, Colonell *Sidney* went to the Mayor, and acquainted him of his Intentions to stand for the Towne of *Guilford,* and desired him to acquaint the Corporation therewith ; to which the Mayor answered, that both himselfe and they were engaged to Mr. *Delmahoy,* and that it was the Custome of the Towne, for the Electors to vote as the Magistrates (who were the Mayor and Aldermen) did.

Colonell *Sidney* informed the Mayor, that he heard Mr. *Delmahoy's* Party had given out, that he was incapable of being chosen a Burgesse for that Towne, because he was no Ffreeman ; to prevent which Objection, he did tender himselfe to him, and desire he might be made Free of the Towne of *Guilford* ; to which the Mayor answered, it did not depend upon him, but upon the rest of the Majestrates, and that he would propose it to them, and returne the Colonell their Answer, which he never did.

Vpon the Day of Election, the Colonell went againe and renewed his Desire of being made Free of the Towne ; to which the Mayor answered as before, but never returned the Colonell any Answer.

The Mayor, upon the Colonells Goeing to him, which was the *Fryday* Seavennight before the Election, desired to know when the Election would be ; to which the Mayor replyed, *Ffryday* next, or *Munday* Seavennight ; and withall promised, whatever Day it was, that the Colonell should have timely Notice thereof. Upon which, on the *Thursday* after, the Colonell came downe Part of the Way, but hearing the Pole for the County was not over (which ended not till *Fryday* Morning) did not come to *Guilford* till *Fryday,* expecting the Election to be on *Munday,* as before agreed. But the other Party, hearing the Colonell was come, prevailed with the Mayor, at past 12 a Clock on *Fryday,* to proclaime the Election the next Day at 9, which was Markett Day, and never knowne before.

At the Time of the Election, and after the Precept read, the Recorder asked who stood, and being answered (amongst the rest of the Competitors) Colonell *Sidney,* he asked if he was a Freeman ; and being answered no ; he, in the Court Howse, where the Election was, openly declared before the Electors, he could not be chosen, although he had the Plurality of Voices ; so as many of those, that were for the Colonell, refused to pole, and others, that were for him, would give no Voice upon the Account of what the Recorder said.

---

[1] Rapin's Hist. of Eng. 8vo. Vol. XIV, p. 334.   [m] Ex Autog. apud Penshurst.

Severall of those, that would have poled for the Colonell, were laughed at and affronted, and refused their Pole, because they did not pronounce the Colonell's Name right.

They refused severall that had Voice to be poled for the Colonell, and admitted severall that had not, for Mr. *Delmahoy*; as Almsmen, and others, that received the Charity of the Corporation.

Severall that would have voted for the Colonell, were threatened, that, if they did not vote for Mr. *Delmahoy*, they should not receive the Benefitt that others did of a considerable Revenue that belongs to the Towne, and perticulerly the Landlord of the *Crowne-Inne*, where the Lord *Longford* owed a considerable Sume of Money (Three-hundred Pounds and upwards) upon the Account of the Election of Knights of the Shire; that if he voted for the Colonell, and not for *Delmahoy*, he should never be paid, or at least not in a long Time; in which Matter the whole Towne were almost concerned, and in Probability the same Argument might be used to many of them, as well as to the Man of the *Crowne*.

One Mr. *Penn*, a Quaker, appearing for the Colonell, was called into the Court, and hindred from encouraging such as were for the Colonell, and told by the Recorder he was a Jesuite (in Affront to the Colonell) to whom the Recorder would have tendred Oathes (at that Time contrary to Law) and at last the Mayor turned him out of the Court, and forbid him to appeare amongst the Colonell's Party, to the great Discouragement of them; and more perticulerly to such as were of the same Perswasion with Mr. *Penn*; amongst which Party, the Colonell had severall Voices.

Mr. *Penn*, therein mentioned, was the famous Sir *William Penn*, who appears to be greatly in his Interest, by the following Letters to him.

1st, 1st Month, '79.

Deare Friend,

I Hope you gott all well Home, as I by Gods Goodness haue done. I reflected vpon the Way of Things past at *Guildford*, and that which occurs to me, as reasonable, is this: That so soon as the Articles or Exceptions are digested, show them to Serjeant *Maynard*, and gett his Opinion of the Matter; Sir *Francis Winington*, or *Wallope*, haue been used in those Occasions too. Thou must haue Councel before the Committee, and to advise first vpon the Reason of an Address or Petition, with them, in my Opinion, is not imprudent, but very fitting. If they say, that, the Conjuncture considerd; thy Qualifications, and Alliance, and his Ungratefulness to the House, they beleive all may amount to an unfair Election; then I offer to waite presently vpon the Duke of *Buckingham*, Earl of *Shaftsbury*, Lord *Essex*, Lord *Halifax*, Lord *Hollis*, Lord *Gray*, &c. to use their utmost Interest in reversing this Business. This may be done in five Dayes, and I was not willing to stay till I come, which will be with the first. Remember the Nonresidents on their Side, as *Legg*, &c. I left Order with all our Interest to bestirr themselues, and watch; and transmitt an Account to thee dayly. I bless God I found all well at Home. I hope the Disapointment so strainge (140 Pole Men as we thought last Night considerd) does not moue thee; thou (as thy Frends) had a conscientious Regard to *England*; and to be putt aside, by such base Ways, is really a Suffering for Righteousness; thou hast embarqu't thy selfe with them, that seek, and love, and chuse the best Thing; and Number is not Weight with thee. I hope it is retrieveable, for to me it looks not a fair and clear Election. Forgett not, that Soldiers were made free 3 Weeks agoe, in Prospect of the Choice (and, by the Way, they went, we may guess, for *Delmahoy's* Sake) and thy selfe so often putt by, a Thing not refused to one of thy Condition. Of the Lower House, the Lord *Cavendish*, and especially Lord *Russell*, Sir *Jo. Coventry*, *Powell*, *Saychevrill*, *Williams*, *Lee*, *Clergis*, *Boskowen*,

Boſkowen, Titus. Men, ſome able, ſome hott, and fitt to be neerly engaged in the Knowledge of theſe Things. 'Tis late, I am weary, and hope to
ſee thee quickly. Farewell.

Thy faithfull Friend,

W I L L I A M P E N N.

It appears, that the Colonel did not think it proper to purſue his Claim. And,
that Parliament, which met at *Weſtminſter* in *March* following, being diſſolved,
Mr. *Penn* ſent the following Letter to him :

Wiſton, 29th 5th Month, 79.

I Am now at Sir *John Faggs,* where I and my Relations dined. I haue preſſed
the Point with what Dilligence and Force I coulde ; and to ſay true, Sir *John
Fagg* has been a moſt zealous, and, he beleiues, a ſuccefsfull Friend to thee. But,
vpon a ſerious Conſideration of the Matter, it is agreed that thou comſt down
with all Speed ; but that thou takeſt *Hall-land* in thy Way, and bringeſt Sir
John Pelham with thee, which he ought the leſs to ſcruple, becauſe his haueing no Intereſt, can be no Objection to his Appearing with thee ; the common-
eſt Civility, that can be, is all deſired. The Burrough has kindled at thy Name,
and takes it well ; if Sir *John Temple* may be credited, he aſſures me it is very
likely ; he is at Work dayly. An other, one *Parſons,* treats to Day. But for
thee, as well as him ſelfe, and moſtly makes his Men for thee, and perhaps
will be perſwaded, if you two carry it not, to bequeath his Intereſt to thee, and
then Captain *Goreing* is thy Collegue ; and indeed this I wiſh, both to make the
Thing the eaſier, and to prevent Offence. Sir *John Pelham* ſent me Word, he
heard that his Brother, *Henry Sidney,* would be propoſed to that Burrough, or
already was, and, till he was ſure to the Contrary, it would not be decent for him
to appear ; of that thou canſt beſt inform him. That Day you come to *Bramber,* Sir *John Fagg* will meet you both ; and that Night you may lye at *Wiſton,* and then, when thou pleaſeſt, with us at *Worminghurſt.* Sir *John Temple*
has that Opinion of thy good Reaſons to perſwade, as well as Quality to influence the Electors, that, with what is and will be done, the Buſineſs will proſper ; which, with my true good Wiſhes that it may be ſo, is all at preſent,
from

Thy true Friend,

W. P E N N.

Sir *John Fagg* ſalutes thee:

The Colonel was not choſe, the Intereſt being before made by Sir *John Pelham,* for his Brother, *Henry Sidney* (after Earl of *Romney*) who was elected, and
ſat in Parliament for *Bramber,* as will hereafter be related.

In 1683, he was accuſed of being concerned in the *Ryehouſe* Plot ; and, after the Lord *Ruſſel* had been examined, he was next brought before the King
and Council [n]. He was ſo wiſe to ſay, he would make the beſt Defence he
could, if they had any Proof againſt him ; but he would not fortify their Evidence by any Thing he ſhould ſay : So that his Examination was very ſhort ;
and, there being no [o] Sort of Evidence againſt him, his Commitment was againſt
Law ; for he was [p] not taken up directly as a Plotter, but for a Republican and
Fanatick.

He lay ſome Time in the *Tower,* and was brought thence by *Habeas Corpus,*
on the 7th of *November,* 1683, to the *King's Bench* Bar, where he was arraigned
on an Indictment of High Treaſon [q]. To which he pleaded not Guilty, and
deſired a Fortnight's Time for preparing Evidence ; which being granted, he
came to his Trial on the 21ſt of *November,* and was found Guilty.

[n] Burnet's Hiſt. of his own Times, Vol. 1, p. 548. [o] Ibid. [p] Hiſt. of Engl. Vol. 3,
p. 403. [q] Ibid.

A Ju-

A Jury was returned [r], confisting, for the moft Part, of very mean Perfons, and thofe tried beforehand how tractable they would be, and, fome of them not being Freeholders, he excepted to them. But *Jefferies*, Lord Chief Juftice, told him, that had been overruled in the Lord *Ruffel*'s Cafe, and could not be allowed to him. This was one of his bold Strains, as Bifhop *Burnet* writes, for the Lord *Ruffel*'s Jury confifted of Citizens, on his being tried in *London*, and in that Cafe it was cuftomary. But this Trial was in *Middlefex*, where it had always been allowed to challenge the Jury, whether they were Freeholders or not.

Four Witneffes were produced againft him, *Rumfey, Weft, Keeling*, and the Lord *Howard* of *Efcrick*. The three firft gave a particular Account of the Plot, but faid nothing directly againft the Prifoner ; only they faid they heard of a Council of Six, and that he was one of them. Yet even in that they contradicted one another ; *Rumfey* fwearing he had it from *Weft* ; and *Weft* fwearing that he had it from him ; which was not obferved till the Trial came out. If it had been obferved fooner [s], it is thought *Jefferies* would have ordered it to be ftruck out, as he did all that *Sidney* had objected on the Point of the Jury, becaufe they were not Freeholders.

The Lord *Howard* depofed (as before at the Trial of the Lord *Ruffel*) ' That, ' after the Earl of *Shaftfbury*'s Flight, the chief Perfons concerned in the Con- ' fpiracy, in his Time, began to confider, they had gone fo far, that it would ' be unfafe for them to make a Retreat ; and that in fo great an Affair, confift- ' ing of fo many Particulars, it would be neceffary to have fome felect Council ; ' and that therefore they refolved to erect a Cabal among themfelves, which u- ' fually confifted of fix Perfons, the Duke of *Monmouth*, the Earl of *Effex*, the ' Lord *Ruffel*, Colonel *Sidney*, Mr. *Hamden*, Junior, and the Deponent ; and ' this was about the Middle of *January* laft. They met at Mr. *Hamden*'s Houfe, ' where it was agreed, their proper Province was to take Care of the Infurrecti- ' on : That the chief Things they debated were, *Whether that Infurrection fhould* ' *begin firft in* London, *or in the Country ; then what Counties or Towns were fitteft,* ' *and moft ready for Action : Then what Arms were to be got, and how to be difpofed :* ' *Then that it was neceffary to have a common Bank of twenty-five or thirty-thoufand* ' *Pounds, to anfwer the Occafions of fuch an Undertaking :* But that the greateft ' Point was, *to order it fo, as to draw in* Scotland *into a Confent with them* ; be- ' caufe it was requifite, that all Kinds of Diverfion fhould be given to the King's ' Forces. That, about ten Days after, every one of the fame Perfons met a- ' gain, at the Lord *Ruffel*'s Houfe : That they then came to a Refolution of ' fending to the Earl of *Argyle*, to fettle a Correfpondence with him, and that ' a Meffenger fhould be difpatched into *Scotland*, to invite fome *Scotchmen* hi- ' ther, who beft underftood the State of *Scotland* ; to give an Account of it. ' That the Perfons determined to be fent for, were Sir *John Cockram*, the Lord ' *Melvil*, and one of the Name of *Campbel* : That Colonel *Sidney* was intrufted ' to take Care of a Meffenger ; and he told the Deponent, he had fent *Aaron* ' *Smith* : Then they agreed not to meet again, till the Return of the Meffenger : ' That all this Debate at the Lord *Ruffell*'s, went without Contradiction, all ' there prefent giving their Confent : That, as for Raifing Money, every one ' was to think of raifing it in fuch Way, as it might be collected without giving ' Caufe of Jealoufy : That, after this, the Deponent met no more with them ; ' but when he returned out of the Country, he was informed, that *Aaron Smith* ' was come back, and that Sir *John Cockram* was alfo come to Town.'

To all this Colonel *Sidney* objected : *Firft*, The great Improbability of Erect- ing a Council of *Six* ; and that Perfons, fo little knowing one another, fhould prefently fall into fo great and intimate a Friendfhip. As to the Duke of *Mon- mouth*, he faid, he never fpoke with him above three Times in his Life ; one Time was when Lord *Howard* brought him to his Houfe, and cozened them both ; telling the Duke, the Colonel had invited him, and the Colonel, that the Duke invited himself ; and neither of them was true.   He said the Lord *Howard* was too infamous by his Life, and the many Perjuries not to be denied, to be credited, and took Notice of his varying in his Evidence, with Refpect to the Lord *Ruffel* and him.   He alledged the Lord *Howard*'s Indigence, and his Owing him Money, which Debt might probably be cancelled by his Conviction. He proved, by the Teftimonies of the Earl of *Clare*, the Earl of *Anglefey*, of Mr. *Philip* and Mr. *Edward Howard*, Dr. *Burnet*, Mr. *Ducas*, and Mr. *Blake*, that the Lord *Howard* had confeffed, *That he could not get his Pardon, untill he had done fome other Jobbs ; untill he was paft the Drudgery of Swearing.*

But what was moft urged and aggravated againft him (as only the Lord *How-ard*'s Evidence made any Thing againft him) was a Manufcript found in his Clofet among his Papers, in Anfwer to a Book wrote by Sir *Robert Filmer*, in-titled *Patriarcha*, wherein he endeavoured to prove the Divine Right of Mo-narchy, on the eldeft Son's fucceeding to the Authority of the Father ; infinua-ting thereby, that the Kings of *England* were invefted with abfolute and un-limited Power.   By the Manufcript it appeared, that Colonel *Sidney*, in Anfwer to this, afferted, that Princes had their Power from the People, with Reftrictions and Limitations ; and that they were liable to the Juftice of the People, if they abufed their Power to the Prejudice of the Subjects, and againft eftablifhed Laws. This, by an *Innuendo*, was faid to be an Evidence to prove, that he was in a Plot againft the King's Life.   And it was infifted on, that this ought to ftand as a fecond Witnefs.

As to the Manufcript, the Colonel faid, it was not proved to be wrote by him, and that a Similitude of Hands was not a legal Proof in Capital Charges, though it was in Civil Matters.   That whatever was in thofe Papers, were his own private Thoughts, and Speculations of Government, never communicated to any, and that it had been wrote fome Years ago.   So that it could not be pretended to be a Proof of a late Plot.   That the Manufcript was not finifhed ; fo it could not be known how it would end :   That the fiftieth Part of it was not produced, nor the Tenth of that offered to be read.   *Jefferies*, the Chief Juftice, interrupted him very rudely, probably to put him in a Paffion, to which he was fubject ; but he maintained his Temper to Admiration.   The Sollicitor-general aggravated his Writings, as a Proof of his Intentions, pretend-ing it was an Overt-Act, for he faid *Scribere eft agere* [t].   *Jefferies* delivered it as Law, and faid that all the Judges were of the fame Mind :   That if there were two Witneffes, the one to the Treafon, the other only to a Circumftance, fuch as the Buying of a Knife ; thefe made the two Witneffes, which the Statute required in Cafes of Treafon.   With thefe wretched Subtilties, and pofitive Directions from the Bench, the Jury (which all agree had been packed) were induced to bring him in Guilty.   This was the firft Precedent, that any Perfon loft his Life on an Indictment of High Treafon, for Writing any Thing, without Publifhing it.   The Lord Chief Juftice *Jefferies* fhewed fuch great Partiality, that he told the Jury [u], *The Prifoner was born a Traytor.*   But, from what has been already related, his Anceftors had eminently ferved the Crown, and their Coun-try.

The learned Sir *John Hawles* has well remarked, ' He *was merely talked to* ' *Death*, under the Notion of a Commonwealth's Man ; and found guilty by a ' Jury who were not much more proper Judges in the Cafe, than they would ' have been, if what he had wrote had been done by him in *Syriack* or *Arabick*.' And that it was obfervable, ' the Indictment againft him was never prefented ' to the Grand Jury, before they came into the Hall, and yet they found it immedi-' ately.   The greateft Part of the Evidence (as it was in my Lord *Ruffel*'s Cafe) ' was only Hear-fay, *&c.*'

When he was brought into Court to receive Sentence, he then repeated his Objections to the Evidence againft him [w], in which Judge *Withins* interrupted

---

[t] Burnet, p. 572.   [u] Hift. of Engl. Vol. 3. p. 404.   [w] Burnet, Ibid.

him, and by a ſtrange Indecency gave him the *Lie* in open Court ; which he bore patiently. His Execution was reſpited for three Weeks, the Trial being univerſally cried out upon, as a Piece of moſt enormous Injuſtice. He ſent to Lord *Hallifax* (after Marquis of *Hallifax*) who was his Nephew (having married Lady *Dorothy Spencer*, Daughter of *Henry*, Earl of *Sunderland*, by Lady *Dorothy* his Wife, Daughter of *Robert Sydney*, Earl of *Leiceſter*) the Heads, and main Points of his Defence ; deſiring he would lay it before the King. Which Lord *Hallifax* performed, praying his Majeſty to review the whole Matter. Where-upon ˣ *Jefferies* told the King, in his furious Way, that *Sidney muſt die, or he muſt die.* When all Application failed, and he ſaw the Warrant for his Execution, he expreſſed no Concern at it : And the Change that was in his Temper a-mazed all that went to him. He told the Sheriffs that brought the Warrant, he would not expoſtulate upon any Thing on his own Account (for the World was now nothing to him) but he deſired they would conſider how guilty they were of his Blood, who had not returned a fair Jury, but one packed, and as they were directed by the King's Sollicitor : He ſpoke this to them, not for his own Sake, but for their Sake ʸ. One of the Sheriffs was ſtruck with this, and wept.

He wrote a long Vindication of himſelf, which Biſhop *Burnet* ſays he read, and that he ſummed up the Subſtance of it in the Paper he gave to the Sheriffs ; and, ſuſpecting they might ſuppreſs it, he gave a Copy of it to a Friend. It was a Fortnight before it was printed, though the Speeches of thoſe, who died for the Popiſh Plot, were publiſhed the very next Day : And it would not have been ſuffered to have been printed, but that written Copies were daily diſperſed. He met Death with an Unconcernedneſs, that became one who had ſet up *Marcus Brutus* for his Pattern. He was but a very few Minutes on the Scaffold on *Tower Hill* ; he ſpoke little, and prayed very ſhort, and his Head was cut off at one Blow, on the 7th of *December*, 1683, aged about 61. The next Day, he was ᶻ buried with his Anceſtors at *Penſhurſt*, viz. 8 *December*, 1683.

The Paper, he delivered to the Sheriffs, ſets forth his Innocence, and the un-natural Treatment he had undergone, in ſuch pathetick Terms, and ſtrong Reaſoning, that it would be Injuſtice to his Memory, to leave it out here. He thus begins :

Men, Brethren, and Fathers ; Friends, Countrymen, and Strangers.

IT may be expected that I ſhould now ſay ſome great Matters unto you ; but the Rigour of the Seaſon, and the Infirmities of my Age, increaſed by a cloſe Impriſonment of five Months, do not permit me.

Moreover, we live in an Age that makes Truth paſs for Treaſon : I dare not ſay any Thing contrary unto it, and the Ears of thoſe who are about me will probably be found too tender to hear it. My Trial and Condemnation doth ſufficiently evidence this.

Weſt, Rumſey, and *Keyling,* who were brought to prove the Plot, ſaid no more of me, than that they knew me not ; and ſome others, equally unknown to me, had uſed my Name, and that of ſome others, to give a little Reputation to their Deſigns. The Lord *Howard* is too infamous by his Life, and the many Perjuries not to be denied, or rather ſworn by himſelf, to deſerve Mention ; and, being a ſingle Witneſs, would be of no Value, though he had been of unblemiſhed Credit, or had not ſeen and confeſſed that the Crimes committed by him would be pardoned, only for Committing more ; and even the Pardon promiſed could not be obtained, till the Drudgery of Swearing was over.

This being laid aſide, the whole Matter is reduced to the Papers ſaid to be found in my Cloſet by the King's Officers, without any other Proof of their being written by me, than what is taken from Suppoſitions upon the Similitude

---

ˣ Burnet, p. 572.   ʸ Burnet ut antea.   ᶻ Ex Regiſt. Ecclef. de Penſhurſt.

of

of an Hand that is eafily counterfeited, and which hath been lately declared, in the Lady *Car*'s Cafe, to be no lawful Evidence in Criminal Caufes.

But, if I had been feen to write them, the Matter would not be much altered. They plainly appear to relate to a large Treatife, written long fince, in Anfwer to *Filmer*'s Book, which, by all intelligent Men, is thought to be grounded upon wicked Principles, equally pernicious to Magiftrates and People.

If he might publifh to the World his Opinion, that all Men are born under a Neceffity derived from the Laws of God, and Nature, to fubmit to an abfolute kingly Government, which could be reftrained by no Law, or Oath ; and that he that has the Power, whether he came to it by Creation, Election, Inheritance, Ufurpation, or any other Way, had the Right ; and none muft oppofe his Will ; but the Perfons and Eftates of his Subjects muft indifpenfably be fubject unto it ; I know not why I might not have publifhed my Opinion to the contrary, without the Breach of any Law I have yet known.

I might, as freely as he, publickly have declared my Thoughts, and the Reafons upon which they were grounded ; and I am perfuaded to believe, that God had left Nations to the Liberty of fetting up fuch Governments as beft pleafed themfelves.

That Magiftrates were fet up for the Good of Nations ; not Nations, for the Honour and Glory of Magiftrates.

That the Right and Power of Magiftrates, in every Country, was that which the Laws of that Country made it to be.

That thofe Laws were to be obferved, and the Oaths taken by them, having the Force of a Contract between Magiftrate and People, could not be violated without Danger of diffolving the whole Fabrick.

That Ufurpation could give no Right, and the moft dangerous of all Enemies to Kings, were they, who, raifing their Power to an exorbitant Height, allowed to Ufurpers all the Rights belonging unto it.

That fuch Ufurpations being feldom compaffed without the Slaughter of the reigning Perfon, or Family, the worft of all Villanies was thereby rewarded with the moft glorious Privileges.

That, if fuch Doctrines were received, they would ftir up Men to the Deftruction of Princes, with more Violence, than all the Paffions that have hitherto raged in the Hearts of the moft Unruly.

That none could be fafe, if fuch a Reward were propofed to any, that could deftroy them.

That few would be fo gentle as to fpare even the beft, if, by their Deftruction, a wild Ufurper could become God's Anointed ; and, by the moft execrable Wickednefs, inveft himfelf with that Divine Character.

This is the Scope of the whole Treatife : The Writer gives fuch Reafons as at prefent did occur unto him, to prove it. This feems to agree with the Doctrines of the moft reverenced Authors of all Times, Nations, and Religions. The beft and wifeft of Kings, have ever acknowledged it. The prefent King of *France* has declared, that Kings have that happy Want of Power, that they can do nothing contrary to the Laws of their Country ; and grounds his Quarrel with the King of *Spain*, *Anno* 1667, upon that Principle. King *James*, in his Speech to the Parliament, *Anno* 1603, doth in the higheft Degree affert it : The Scripture feems to declare it.

If, neverthelefs, the Writer was miftaken, he might have been refuted by Law, Reafon, and Scripture ; and no Man, for fuch Matters, was ever otherwife punifhed, than by being made to fee his Error ; and it has not (as I think) been ever known, that they had been referred to the Judgment of a Jury, compofed of Men utterly unable to comprehend them.

But there was little of this in my Cafe ; the Extravagance of my Profecutors goes higher : The abovementioned Treatife was never finifhed, nor could be in many Years ; and, moft probably, would never have been. So much as is of it, was written long fince, never reviewed nor fhewn to any Man ; and the

fiftieth

fiftieth Part of it was not produced, and not the Tenth of that offered to be read. That which was never known to those who are said to have conspired with me, was said to be intended to stir up the People, in Prosecution of the Designs of those Conspirators.

When nothing of particular Application to Time, Place, or Person, could be found in it (as has ever been done by those who endeavoured to raise Insurrections) all was supplied by *Innuendo's*.

Whatsoever is said of the Expulsion of *Tarquin*, the Insurrection against *Nero*, the Slaughter of *Caligula*, or *Domitian*, the Translation of the Crown of *France* from *Moroveus* his Race to *Pepin*, and from his Descendents to *Hugh Capet*, and the like ; was applied, by *Innuendo*, to the King.

They have not considered, that, if such Acts of State be not good, there is not a King in the World, that has any Title to the Crown he wears ; nor can have any, unless he could deduce his Pedigree from the eldest Son of *Noah*; and shew, that the Succession had still continued in the eldest, of the eldest Line ; and been so deduced to him.

Every one may see, what Advantage this would be to all Kings of the World ; and whether, that failing, it were not better for them to acknowledge, they had received their Crowns by the Consent of willing Nations ; or, to have no better Title to them, than Usurpation and Violence ; which, by the same Ways, may be taken from them.

But I was long since told, that I must die, or the Plot must die.

Left the Means of destroying the best Protestants in *England* should fail, the Bench must be filled with such, as had been Blemishes to the Bar.

None but such as these would have advised with the King's Council, of the Means of bringing a Man to Death ; suffered a Jury to be packt by the King's Sollicitors, and the Under-sheriff ; admit of Jurymen who are not Freeholders ; receive such Evidence as is abovementioned ; refuse a Copy of an Indictment, or suffer the Statute of 46 *Edw*. III, to be read, that doth expresly enact, *It should in no Case be denied to any Man, upon any Occasion whatsoever* ; over-rule the most important Points of the Law without Hearing. And whereas the Statute, 25 *Edw*. III, upon which they said I should be tried, doth reserve to the Parliament all Constructions to be made in Points of Treason ; they could assume to themselves, not only a Power to make Constructions, but such Constructions, as neither agree with Law, Reason, or common Sense.

By these Means I am brought to this Place. The Lord forgive these Practices, and avert the Evils that threaten the Nation from them.

The Lord sanctify these my Sufferings unto me ; and, though I fall as a Sacrifice to Idols, suffer not Idolatry to be established in this Land. Bless thy People, and save them. Defend thy own Cause, and defend those that defend it. Stir up such as are faint; direct those that are willing ; confirm those that waver ; give Wisdom and Integrity unto all. Order all Things so, as may most redound to thine own Glory. Grant that I may die glorifying thee for all thy Mercies, and that, at the last, thou hast permitted me to be singled out, as a Witness of thy Truth ; and even by the Confession of my Opposers, for that *Old Cause*, in which I was from my Youth engaged, and for which thou hast often, and wonderfully declared thyself.

On the Revolution, such Regard was had to his Innocence, and Justice to his Memory, that the Parliament made it one of their 1st Acts to repeal his Attainder, *viz*. 13 *Feb*. 1688, 1 *W*. & *M*. whereof the Preamble, *&c*. is in these Words [a] :

' Whereas, *Algernoone Sydney*, Esq; in the Term of St. *Michael*, in the five
' and thirtieth Year of the Reign of our late Soveraign Lord, King *Charles the*
' *Second*, in the Court of *King's-Bench* at *Westminster*, by Means of an illegal
' Return of Jurors, and by Denial of his lawfull Challenges to divers of them,

[a] Ex Cop. de Orig. apud Penshurst.

' for Want of Freehold, and, without fufficient legal Evidence, of any Trea-
' fons committed by him ; there being at that Time produced a Paper found
' in the Clofet of the faid *Algernoon*, fuppofed to be his Hand-writing, which
' which was not proved by the Teftimony of any one Witnefs, to be written by
' him ; but the Jury was directed to believe it, by comparing it with other
' Writings of the faid *Algernoon :* And, befides that Paper fo produced, there
' was but one fingle Witnefs, to prove any Matter againft the faid *Algernoon :*
' And, by a partial and unjuft Conftruction of the Statute, declaring what was
' his Treafon, was moft unjuftly and wrongfully convicted, and attainted, and
' afterwards executed for high Treafon. May it therefore pleafe your moft
' excellent Majefties, at the humble Petition and Requeft of the Right Honour-
' able *Philip* Earl of *Leicefter*, Brother and Heir of the faid *Algernoon Sydney*,
' and of the Right Honourable *Henry* Vifcount *Sydney*, of *Sheppey*, the other
' Brother of the faid *Algernoon*, That it be Declared and Enacted, *&c.* That
' the faid Conviction and Attainder be repealed, reverfed, *&c.* And, to the
' End, that Right be done to the Memory of the faid *Algernoon Sydney*, de-
' ceafed, Be it further Enacted, That all Records and Proceedings, relating to
' the faid Attainder, be wholly cancelled, and taken off the File, or otherwife
' defaced and obliterated, to the Intent that the fame may not be vifible in af-
' ter Ages : And, that the Records and Proceedings, relating to the faid Con-
' viction, Judgment, and Attainder, in the Court of *King's-Bench*, now re-
' maining, fhall and be forthwith brought into the faid Court, this prefent
' *Eafter* Term, and then and there taken off the File and cancelled.'

His *Difcourfes on Government* were publifhed on the Revolution ; but there are
yet at *Penfhurft*, in his Hand-writing, Treatifes in *Latin*, and *Italian* ; as alfo, an
Effay on Virtuous Love, in *Englifh*.

The 3d Son *Robert*, [b] baptized at *Penfhurft*, *Sept.* 19, 1626, was a fine Gentleman both in Perfon and Addrefs. The Countefs of *Leicefter* his Mother in a
Letter, dated at *Penfhurft*, to the Earl her Hufband at *Paris*, gives him a
very great Character, being then about 12 Years of Age ; which Letter, being
remarkable, will be publifhed in the Collection.

In 1639, the Earl his Father coming into *England*, and returning to his Ambaffy in *France*, in *Auguft*, the fame Year, he took with him this *Robert
Sydney*, then about 13 Years old, as his Lordfhip writes in his Journal ; and
that, having learned there all his Exercifes very well, he fent him from thence
to *Holland* about *Michaelmas*, 1644. It appears by a Letter from Lieutenant
William Carne, to the Earl of *Leicefter*, dated *May* 12, 1643, that his Lordfhip,
before that Time, had procured him a Company in the Service of the States-
General ; and another Letter of his Brother *Algernon Sidney*, dated 10 *Jan.*
1648, gives an Account to his Father that he was made Lieutenant-Colonel of
a Regiment there ; which, on the Breaking out of the War with the *Dutch*,
was fent for to *England*, and is yet fubfifting, and called the *Holland* Regiment.
The Commiffion of King *Charles* the 2d, to this Colonel *Robert Sidney*, bears
Date 31 *May* 1665. He died unmarried [c], and was buried at *Penfhurft*, *Aug.*
12, 1668.

The 4th and youngeft furviving Son, was *Henry Sydney*, who, for his great
Abilities and Merits, was advanced to the Honour of Earl of *Romney*. He was
born at *Paris*, *An.* 1641, during his Father's Ambaffy at the *French* Court,
and was brought over to *England*, with the Countefs his Mother in *October*,
the fame Year, as the Earl writes in his Journal. He was, from his Youth,
much favoured and beloved, as well by his Father, as his Mother, who, on her
Death-bed, recommended the Care of him in an efpecial Manner to the Earl.
Who by a Codicil to his Will, bearing Date the 5th of *April*, 1675, left to
him and his Heirs for ever the Mannor and Eftate of *Long-Itchington* in *Warwickfhire* ; as alfo by his faid Will, twenty-five Thoufand Pounds, charged on

[b] Ex Regiftr. Eccl. de Penfhurft.   [c] Ibid.

his Eſtate in *Leiceſter* Fields, &c. And his Mother, on her Deceaſe, left him an Annuity of 200 *l. per Ann.* for the Term of 21 Years, purchaſed in *Dec.* 1653, of Sir *Edward Radcliffe*, of the County of *Cumberland*, in the Name of *Ant. Hinton*, in Truſt for her Uſe; alſo an Annuity of 100 *l. per Ann.* during the Life of *Dorothy* Counteſs Dowager of *Sunderland*; alſo Lands and Tenements in *Blackets* and *Bixley* in *Kent*, which ſhe had purchaſed in her own Name for the Sum of 5800 *l.* He had a very liberal Education, and, in his Father's Life-time, took to a Military Life. In 1685, *Ariſtotle's Rhetorick, or the true Grounds and Principles of Oratory*, was dedicated to him, with this Title,

To the Honourable Colonel *Henry Sidney*, Ambaſſador Extraordinary, from his late Sacred Majeſty, to the States of *Holland*.

He had the Command of a Regiment in 1678, as his Warrant to *Lemuel Kingdom*, Eſq. Paymaſter of his Majeſty's Land Forces, to pay 3240 *l.* for Cloathing it, ſhews. It appears from Sir *William Temple*'s Memoirs, that *Robert* Earl of *Sunderland* (Grandfather to the preſent Duke of *Marlborough*) repoſed an entire Confidence in Colonel *Sidney*, who was his Uncle, though they were about the ſame Age. Upon the new Conſtitution of the Council, *An.* 1679 [d], Mr. *Sidney* was ſent by the Earl of *Sunderland* to Sir *William Temple*, to bring him over to his Intereſt; and Sir *William* acknowledges [e], that at the Earl of *Sunderland*'s, and Mr. *Sidney*'s Preſſing of him, to ſuffer ſeveral ſmall Things he had written, to be printed under the Title of *Miſcellanea*, he conſented thereto; they thinking that he, who had ſuch a Part in the King's Affairs, ought to ſtand as well as he could with the Houſe of Commons; and that, by the Publication, they would ſee, he was not a Man of the dangerous Principles pretended; and that he might aſſure the whole World, of his being Author of no Books, that had not his Name.

On the 7th of *July* 1675 [f], he obtained from his Majeſty a Grant during Life (on the Surrender of *Sidney Godolphin*, Eſq.) of the Office, Of *Gentleman and Maſter of the Robes*, for the Providing of Robes, Apparel, and other Neceſſaries, for the Uſe of the King, his Heirs and Succeſſors. And to receive 5000 *l. per An.* out of the Exchequer, payable half-yearly, *to the End, Proviſions, incident to the Place, may be paid more Huſband-like, and bought cheap.* The 1ſt Payment to commence from *Lady-Day* laſt paſt; of which 4500 *l.* to be for the Maintenance of the Charges incident to the ſaid Place; and to be accounted for, Annually. And the other 500 *l.* to remain to the ſaid *Henry Sidney*, Eſq. *in Lieu of the ordinary Fees and Vailes, upon the Meaſures and Poundage of the Payment of Moneys, heretofore taken by the Officer in that Place.* But if it ſhould be neceſſary to expend more, than the ſaid Sum of 4500 *l.* that then, on the Delivery of his Account, he ſhould receive the full Charge of what he had ſo laid out.

On the 15 *July* following, 1679, [g] he kiſſed his Majeſty's Hand, and took his Leave of him, on his Going Envoy Extraordinary to the States-General. The Prince of *Orange* had then projected an Alliance againſt *France*, and moſt of the *German* Princes were much diſpoſed to come into it. Biſhop *Burnet* writes [h], that the Earl of *Sunderland* entered into a particular Confidence with the Prince of *Orange*, which he managed by his Uncle Mr. *Sidney*, who was Envoy to *Holland* in the Year 1679: In which Ambaſſy, Mr. *Sidney* ſo ingratiated himſelf with the Prince, as to have the higheſt Meaſure of his Truſt and Favour, that any *Engliſhman* ever had. Sir *William Temple* [i] obſerves, That ' Mr. *Sidney* ſending over a Memorial, given him by the Penſioner *Fagel*, re- ' preſenting the ſad Conſequences Abroad of his Majeſty's not Agreeing with ' his Parliaments; the Danger of his Allies, and of the Proteſtant Religion; ' and thereupon, though not directly, yet ſeeming to wiſh, that the King would ' not break with them, though it were even on the Point of the Bill of Exclu-

[d] Memoirs, Part 3. in Sir Wm. Temple's Works, p. 336. [e] Ib. p. 738. [f] Ex Origin. Patent. apud Penſhurſt. [g] Ex Autog. apud Penſhurſt. [h] Hiſt. of his own Times, p. 479. 673, 674. [i] Memoirs, Part 3. in his Works, Vol. 1. p. 355.

' ſion.

' fion. This being believed a Thing directed and advised from hence by Lord
' *Sunderland*, as a Matter that would be of Weight to induce the King to pass
' the Bill ; and also his Voting in the Lord's House, not only against the
' King's Mind, but against his express Command, was the Cause of the Earl's
' Remove from the Secretary's Office, and the Council.

Mr. *Sidney* was also recalled from *Holland*, and returned in *June* 1680[k]; for,
on the 20th of *May* that Year, the Lords of the Admiralty sent Orders to
Captain *Fausby*, Commander of the *Henrietta* Yatcht, to be at the *Brill* in *Holland*,
the 28th of *May*, where being arrived, he should attend 8 Days for
Henry Sidney, Esq. his Majesty's Envoy Extraordinary to the States-General (in
Case he should not happen to be on the Place at his Arrival) and receive him
on Board, together with his Baggage, Company, and Servants, and to transport
him, or them, into the River of *Thames*, as high as *Greenwich*.

In the Parliament, that met at *Westminster*, the 21st of *October*, 1680[l], he
was one of the Members for *Bramber* in *Sussex*; and, in that Session, were
warm Debates on the Bill of Exclusion of *James* Duke of *York*. Mr. *Sidney*[m]
spoke and voted for it. And on the sudden Dismission of the Grand Jury,
by the Judges, when a Bill was presented against the Duke of *York*, as a Popish
Recusant, which occasioned the House of Commons to examine into the
Matter ; Mr. *Sidney*, towards the Close of the Debate, made this Speech[n] :

Mr. Speaker, ' I would beg Leave to observe to you, because I think it
' may be necessary to be considered by your Committee, what an Opinion was
' given not long since by some of these Judges about Printing ; which was
' that Printing of News might be prohibited by Law ; and accordingly, a Pro-
' clamation issued out. I will not take on me to censure the Opinion, as il-
' legal, but leave it to your further Consideration. But I remember there was
' a Consultation held by the Judges a little before ; and they gave their Opini-
' on, that they knew not any Way to prevent Printing by Law ; because the
' Act for that Purpose was expired. Upon which some Judges were put out,
' and new ones put in ; and then this other Opinion was given. These Things
' are worthy of a serious Examination. For if Treasurers may raise Money,
' by Shutting up the Exchequer, Borrowing of the Bankers, or Retrenchments ;
' and the Judges make new Laws, by an ill Construction, or an ill Execution
' of the old ones : I conclude that Parliaments will soon be found useless ; and
' the Liberty of the People, an Inconvenience to the Government. And there-
' fore, I think Sir, you have been well moved to pass your Censure on some
' of these illegal Proceedings by a Vote ; and refer the farther Consideration to
' a Committee.'

Sir *Francis Winnington* spoke on the same Side, and then the House came to
these Resolutions :

Resolved, That the Discharging of a Grand Jury by any Judge, before the
End of the Term, Assizes, or Sessions, while Matters are under their Consideration, and not presented, is arbitrary, illegal, destructive to publick Justice,
a manifest Violation of his Oath, and is a Means to subvert the fundamental
Laws of this Kingdom.

Resolved, That a Committee be appointed to examine the Proceedings of
the Judges in *Westminster-Hall*, and report the same, with their Opinion, to
this House.

On King *James's* Coronation, 23 *April* 1685, being Gentleman and Master
of the Robes, he attended on his Majesty, and the Crown, being too big for
his Head, was often in a tottering Condition. Whereupon Mr. *Henry Sidney*,
supporting it once with his Hand, pleasantly said to the King[o], *This is not the
first Time our Family hath supported the Crown.*

---

[k] Ex Autog. apud Penshurst.   [l] List of Parliament in Chamberlain's State of England
[m] Rapin's Hist. of Eng. 8vo. Vol. 14, p. 268.   [n] Proceedings of the House of Commons, Vol.
1, p 459.   [o] Rapin's Hist. of Eng. 8vo. Vol. 15, p. 8.

The unjuft Proceedings, againft his Brother, could not but be frefh in his Memory ; and though the Earl of *Sunderland*, his Nephew, was prime Minifter ; yet he had fo ftrong an Attachment to the Religion and Liberties of his Coun-try ; and withal too much Honour to enter into the Meafures of that bigotted Monarch. Which joined to that particular Confidence the Prince of *Orange* was well known, over *England*, to repofe in him at this Time (as Bifhop *Bur-net* writes) [p] was the Caufe that all, who defired to recommend themfelves to the Prince, did it through his Hands. He was fo apprehenfive of the Dangers, this might caft him in, that he travelled almoft a Year round *Italy*. But Mat-ters ripening in *England*, towards a Revolution, he returned to *Holland* ; and, by the Prince's own Order, the Conduct of the whole Defign [q] was chiefly depofited with him : And all the Tranfactions of that grand Affair centered in him.

He was particularly zealous in the Interefts of the Prince of *Orange*, and fo de-firous to free his Country from Popifh Tyranny, that before he went out of *England*, he difpofed of his whole Fortune there, to ferve him ; which was ve-ry great for a younger Son, as I have before obferved.

He had [r] the Command of a Regiment, on the Expedition of the Prince in-to *England* ; was one whom he principally confulted after his Landing, and con-tinued in the Efteem and Confidence of King *William*, whilft he lived. The Day after the Proclamation of King *William* and Queen *Mary*, he [s] was ap-pointed, by their Majefties, one of their moft Honourable Privy-Council ; and made one of the Gentlemen of the Kings Bed-chamber, with the Duke of *Or-mond*, the Earl of *Oxford*, the Lord Vifcount *Mordaunt* (after Earl of *Peter-borough*) the Lord *Lumley* (after Earl of *Scarbrough*) and the Lord *Churchil*, af-ter Duke of *Marlborough*. Alfo [t] was conftituted, 16 *March* 168$\frac{8}{9}$, Colonel of his Majefty's Regiment of Foot-Guards.

On 9 *April* following, 1 *Will. & Mar.* 1689, he [u] was advanced to the Digni-ties of Baron of *Milton*, and of Vifcount *Sydney*, of *Sheppey* in *Kent*. The Pre-amble to the Patent fets forth, ' That the Royal Dignity in nothing fhines ' more, than when Honours are conferred on Perfons, whofe fplendid Birth, ' heroick Actions, and fteady Loyalty, Induftry and Merits, recommend ' them. Therefore, their Majeftys, in their firft Creation of Peers, deter-' mined, that the renowned *Henry Sidney*, Brother of the Earl of *Leicefter*, ' fhould have Place among them. Being defcended from the moft antient and ' illuftrious Family of the *Sidneys*, and by his Mother from the *Percy*'s. And ' whofe great Uncles, *Robert* [*Dudley*] Earl of *Leicefter*, and *Philip Sidney*, fhined ' bright in the *Dutch* Wars, the one being chief Governor of the *United Pro-' vinces*, and the other, the great Ornament of his Family, and of the Age ' he lived in, to his immortal Glory. And as the faid *Henry Sidney* had, hi-' therto, not only fupported the Honour of his Birth, but alfo increafed it in ' War, both by Land and Sea ; as well as by his political and prudent Nego-' tiations, wherein with no lefs Glory, he difcharged his Ambaffy to the States ' of *Holland*. Whereas alfo his firm Loyalty, to Us, and the Kingdom of *Eng-' land*, being as confpicuous, as his Labour, and Trouble in our Service ; more ' efpecially in the great Care and Diftinction he fhewed in Treaties, for the ' Prefervation of his Country in the late Expedition, wherein he difpofed all ' Things fo happily, for the *Englifh* Intereft, as redounds to his great Glory. ' And when he was made by Us one of our Council, and rewarded by Us, with ' a Place among the Chief of our Army ; in him appeared all the Qualities of ' a brave General. In Confideration whereof, and ferioufly revolving in our ' Mind, in what Manner We fhould be grateful, and fhew the Value of his ' Merits, We have determined that he fhall be imployed in the Adminiftration

[p] Hift. of his own Times, p. 763, 764,　　[q] Ibid.　　[r] Diary of K. William's Expedition, p. 68.　　[s] Hift. of Eng. Vol. III. p. 550.　　[t] Succeffion of Colonels of his Majeftys Forces, p. 8. [u] Ex Orig. Pat. 1 W. & M. apud Penfhurft.

' of the high Affairs of the Kingdom, and be in the Number of the first of
' thofe to be made Peers by Us. Know, *&c.*

Whereupon he attended at their Majefties Coronation the 11th of *April* 1689;
and on the ʷ firft of *Oct.* following, was conftituted Lord Lieutenant of the
County of *Kent*, and of the City of *Canterbury.* Alfo on the 3d of the fame
Month and Year ˣ was conftituted Vice-Admiral, and Commiffary of the County of *Kent*, and the Ports thereof, with all Powers *&c.* thereto belonging.

His Lordfhip attended on King *William* in *Ireland*; and before the Battle of
the *Boyne*, his Majefty held a Confultation and long Difcourfe, with the Prince
of *Denmark*, Duke *Schomberg*, Duke of *Ormond* ʸ, Lord Vifcount *Sidney*, and
other chief Officers, on their Obfervations of the Enemy. Whereupon his Lordfhip having given Proofs of his Conduct, and Valour, in the Victory then obtained; as alfo at the Siege of *Limerick*, where he commanded in the Trenches,
as Major-General, ᶻ and took a ftrong Redoubt by Affault: Therefore, in
Confideration of his Services, he was conftituted with *Thomas Coningsby*, Efq;
Lords Juftices of *Ireland*, on his Majefty's Leaving that Kingdom, *Sept.* 5, 1690.

It appears by Letters, fent to the King, which were delivered by his Lordfhip immediately after the Battle of the *Boyne*, that on the Defertion of *Dublin*,
by King *James*'s Forces, the Proteftants were in the utmoft Confternation, fearing the Plundering of the City. On the faid Defertion, *Longford*, *Rofs*, *William King*, *S. Lymerick*, *Thomas Newcomen*, *Edward Rofcarrick*, *Anthony Medenns*,
and *Dud. Loftus*, met, and defired the honourable *Robert Fitz-Gerald*, to take
on him, and execute the Office of Governor of the faid City and Caftle till his
Majefty's Pleafure fhould be known. Whereupon the two following Letters
were delivered to the King by his Lordfhip:

Royall Sir,

SINCE your Majefties happy Succefs, near *Drogheda*, the late King, about
4 a Clock in the Morning, took Horfe, and went as we hear, and believe,
towards *Munfter*, having affembled a fmall Council laft Night about 11 a Clock.
My Lord *Tyrconnell*, General *Laufon*, and the other Grandees of the Army,
came to Town late in the Morning; the remaining Forces, which we compute
with thofe then in the Citty to be about 5000 Men, having been in Armes, but
never willing to unite or make a fighting Body. Since then, the moft eminent in
the Army, both the Lord Chancellors, the Chancellor of the *Exchequer*, and all
the Popifh Judges, with the Mayor, and many of the moft remarkable Citizens,
of that Religion, have left the Citty; which is now by the Flight of the
Governor, and his Deputy, abfolutely in your Majefties Difpofe, and, by
the Bleffing of God, in perfect Peace and Quietnefs; and the Keys of the
Citty and Caftle in the Hands of Mr. *Fitz-Gerald*, who is ready, with feveral Thoufands of your Majefties Subjects, with great Joy to lay them at your
Majefties Feet, whofe Prefence is much longed for and defired; and the rather,
becaufe there is none now in Armes here, but the few Gentry and fome Citizens, who do, with all their Endeavors, take Care to preferve this Place for your
Majefties Service, who are

Your Majefties ... dutifull and

obedient Subjects,

Fitz-Gerald,

Bishop Lymerick,

and others.

July 3d, 2 a Clock
in the Morning.

ʷ Ex Orig. Pat. 1. W. & M. apud Penfhurft.   ˣ Pat. 1 W. & Mar. ut antea.   ʸ Hift. of
Eng. Vol. III. p. 598.   ᶻ Ibid, p. 605.

Dublin Caſtle, *July* 3d, 1690, *Thurſday* at 8 in the Morning.

Royall Sir,

SINCE our laſt, wee preſume to acquaint you with our Condition, and with what further Advances wee have made : Wee have put a few Proteſtants here into the beſt Poſture of Defence wee can, but are not able to preſerve our ſelves without the Aſſiſtance of your Majeſties Arms. Wee therefore moſt humbly beſeech your Majeſtie, ſpeedily to ſend ſuch Forces, as to your Majeſtie ſhall ſeem meet, for the Preſervation of this Citty, and the Inhabitants of it ; for wee are certainly informed, that the Army, which have deſerted this Place, are withdrawn no further then the *Naas* (which is within 12 Miles of this Citty) and wee fear the Unrulineſs of the Rabble, leaſt wee ſhould not be able to contain them within the Bounds of their Duty.

Since the Writing of the above, wee are informed, that, within 6 Miles of this Citty, there is a conſiderable Body of Horſe and Foot remaining, who wee are told are upon their Return to this City ; and there are three Ships come into this Harbour, commanded by Capt. *Dover*, and have landed ſome of their Men, who are all the Forces we have in Town, except ſome few Gentry and Citizens. Wee are

Your Majeſties moſt humble

Subjeĉts and Servants,

Fitz-Gerald, Meath,

Lymerick, *and ſeveral others.*

His Lordſhip made but a ſhort Stay in *Ireland*, returning to *England*, in *December* following ; for his Majeſty knowing his eminent Abilities, and having had Experience of his Fidelity, was pleaſed not long after to recall him from being one of the Lords Juſtices of *Ireland*, and to conſtitute him one of his Principal Secretaries of State ; for which Office he took the [a] uſual Oath at the Council Board the 12th of *December* 1690. And on the 8th of *January* following he had the King's [b] Warrant, to the Commiſſioners of the Treaſury, and Chancellor of the *Exchequer*, for the Payment of the yearly Sum of 1850 *l.* the accuſtomed Salary, for the Execution thereof, payable by 462 *l.* 10 *s.* a Quarter, without Accompt. To which, [c] on the 10th of the ſame Month, 100 *l. per Ann.* more was added. And his Majeſty, taking further into Conſideration his great Services, was pleaſed to grant him ſeveral Eſtates in *Ireland*, forfeited by thoſe who were in the Rebellion againſt him, in that Kingdom.

In the Preamble to one of the Grants, it ſets forth, in Conſideration of the many faithful and great Services, performed unto their ſaid Majeſties, by the ſaid *Henry*, Lord Viſcount *Sidney*, as well in their Kingdom of *England*, as of *Ireland*, while he ſerved in the Army, where the King was perſonally engaged in the War there. And afterwards as one of the Juſtices of the ſaid Kingdom of *Ireland*, during which Time he had expreſſed a conſtant and more particular Zeal for, and hath been greatly concerned in the preſent Settlement of the ſaid Kingdom of *Ireland*.

The Affairs of *Ireland* were immediately under his Lordſhip ; and Addreſſes were made to him, from moſt Perſons who had any Concerns in that Kingdom. There are Letters fom the Lord *Coningſby* (after Earl of *Coningſby*) whereof I ſhall inſert the following, as it ſhews his Attachment to him :

Dublin, Nov. the 7th, 1691.

My Deareſt Lord,

I Haue incloſed ſent your Lordſhip a Breuiat of the Bill for Diſpoſing of *Iriſh* Eſtates, intended to be paſt laſt Seſſions ; with ſome Notes in the Margent.

---

[a] Hiſt. of Eng. Vol. III, p. 610.   [b] Ex Origin. apud Penſhurſt.   [c] Pat. 2 W. & M.

By all Means, my Lord, dont lett his Majeftye be complemented out of fome Intereft in the Eftats heer; which he will moft certainly be, if he firft paffes this Act, and leaues his Proportion to be fett out afterwards.

I can't yett gett a Copye of the Outlaws, it is foe longe, there being aboue 3000 Names.

Pray, my Lord, dont forgett the Affair of the Farthings; it will be very well worth your While, and I hear the Duke of *Ormond* is putting in for it; I fhould be troubled to diliuer all thofe Materialls, I haue foe carefully faued, into any other Hands.

I long to hear how the Settlement of this Country is like to goe on. I dont defire to haue any Share in't, but for their Majeftyes Seruis, and I confefs upon that Account I am uneafye, knowing that the future Wellfare of it depends up-on the Meafures now taken; and if they fhould proceed from the Sugeftions of the *Irifh* with you, I know them foe well; but efpecially the Characters of fuch who are moft likely to be confulted; that I can't but fear the Confequences.

I hope your Lordfhip will honor me with an Anfwer to fome Particulars in my laft Letters. I am for ever and ever,

My Deareft Lord,

Your Lordfhips moft obedient and

moft humble Servant,

Tho. Coningsby.

Sir *Richard Cox* (after Lord Chancellor of *Ireland*) alfo fent his Lordfhip the following particular Relation of what had been done in *Ireland*:

Dublin, 8 *October,* 1691.

My moft Honourd Lord,

NOW that I have layd afide the Sword, and have again refumed the Gowne, I hope I fhall find Leifure to give you a full and perfect Account of this War, and particularly of this Campagne, which has been exceeding troublefome, and no lefs glorious. It was opened in a happy Houre, and the cheap and fpeedy Reduction of *Ballymore* was a propitious Omen of the great Succefs that was to follow. The Paffing the *Shenin*, and the Takeing of *Ath-lone* in the Face of the *Irifh* Army, was an Action hardly equalld in Hiftory; it was an Attempt foe dareing, that nothing but Succefs could determine, whe-ther it fhould be reputed Rafh or Brave. As for the Battle of *Aghrim*, there was nothing more ftrange in it, then that the Enemy made a braver Refiftance then they were wont. To which, neverthelefle, they were encouraged by the Scitu-ation of the Place, and the Strength of their Retrenchments. And after all, they found more Security in the Darknefs of the Night, then either in their For-tifications or their Valour. Soe that, if the Battle had begun two Hours fooner, that Day had made an End of the War. And as it was, their Loffe was exceed-ing great, *viz.* 1 Generall, 3 Major Generalls, 7 Brigadeers, 22 Collonels, 17 Leivtenant Collonells, and ten Majors, and about 7000 private Souldiers.

The Confequence of this great Victory was the Surrender of *Galway*. And, now that *Limrick* is likewife in our Hands, you may not onely conclude that this War is at an End, but alfo, that, if Matters be well handled, there can never be an *Irifh* Rebellion in this Kingdom any more.

Nor doe I doubt but that this Affair will be well managed, for I am fure that nothing is more true, then that the Rebells generally hate our King above all Mankind, as one that has diffapointed them of the faireft Hopes that ever they had. And therefore they will be allways hankering after their Prince of *Wales,* in whom all their Hopes are fixd, and whofe Intereft centers with their own in the Subverfion of the prefent Goverment. Nor is their Hatred lefs implacable

to

to the *English*, as appears by the barbarous Murders they daily comitt ; and is yet more manifeſt by ſome Inſtances which I ſend you in a ſeperate Paper, rather then interupt the Series of this. And therefore I conclude, that the King and Kingdom of *England* can have no Security, but in the Impotence of this rebellious Generation ; and that therefore they will weaken them all they can, by Methods honeſt and diſcreet, without makeing it a War of Religion, or giveing any juſt Diſtaſt to the Confederates.

But, leaveing the Politicks to Stateſmen, my Buſineſs is to proceed as an Hiſtorian, and give you an Account of my Goverment at *Cork.* Where my Freinds feared I ſhould be ſhipwrackt, being to ſayle betwixt *Scylla* and *Charibdis*, the Army and the Enemy. But haveing Credit with the Generall, and uſeing it modeſtly, I ſoon got rid of ſuch of the Army as were moſt troubleſome, and kept a ſtrict Correſpondence with the reſt, and often borrowed Money for them in their Diſtreſs, and did them all other good Offices that I could ; ſoe that I had a good Underſtanding, or rather a Freindſhip on that Side. And as for the Enemy, I uſd them like Nettles, and ſqueezd them (I mean their vagabond Partyes) ſoe hard, that they could ſeldom ſting. Haveing, as I beleeve, killd and hangd not leſs then 3000 of them, whilſt I ſtaid in the County of *Cork.* And taken from them, in Cattle and Plunder, at leaſt to the Value of 12000 *l.* which you will eaſily beleeve, when you know that I divided 380 *l.* between one Troop (Collonell *Townſends*) in the Begining of *Auguſt.* After which Collonell *Beecher* and the Weſtern Gentlemen got a Prey worth 3000 *l.* beſides ſeveral other leſſer Preys, taken by ſmall Partyes, that are not taken Notice of.

I ſhould not be juſt to my ſelf, if I did not let you know, that, tho I could have had what Share I pleaſd of theſe Preys, yet I never took to the Value of ſix Pence ; for my Heart was in the Cauſe, and I was ſoe well pleaſd to have the Service done, that I quitted all to the Encouragement of the Men, who both wanted and deſervd it.

What I have to add is, that tho the Militia, in the beſt of Times, conſiſted but of 26 Troops, and 16 Companyes, I have brought them to 36 Troops in ſix Regiments, and 26 Companyes in three Regiments of Foot ; ſoe that I have kept a Fronteer 80 Mile long, from *Tallow* to *Sherkin* ; and have ſupplyed two and twenty Gariſons, and ſent 1000 Men to the Camp, who had the Honour to guard the Paſs at *Killaloo*, whilſt the Artillery was marching from *Connaught* ; and afterwards, being poſted at *Annahbeg*, had the good Fortune to reſcue 200 Proteſtants, and 46 good Horſes, out of an Iſland within a Mile of *Limrick.*

But I ſhould have mentiond, that tho at laſt we had but two Regiments of the Army, *viz. Churchills* and *Haſtings*, left in the County of *Cork*, yet the Army ſometimes by themſelves, and ſometimes with the Help of the Militia, did keep thoſe important Poſts of *Fformoy* and *Ballymacgooly* all the Summer. And did many good Services againſt the Common Enemy, and in generall agreed better with the Militia, then at firſt I expected they would.

But that which you will moſt wonder at, is, that all this did not coſt the County of *Cork* above 1200 *l.* nor did I looſe above ſix or eight Men in all the Expeditions that I orderd : You have already had an Account of ſome Loſſe we ſuffered in *May*, when Major *Culliford* went to *Newmarket* ; and of a greater Loſs, when Capt. *Barry* went to *Caſtletowne*; but, theſe Sallyes being made without my Privity, I doe not place to my Account ; and if I did, both Loſſes did not exceed 30 Men of the Militia, now that the Priſoners are returnd.

Nevertheleſs I was not without Enemyes ; but they were ſuch as neither contributed Purſe nor Perſon to the Cauſe, any more than they were forced. And of this Sort there were ſome on the Grand Jury, who, I beleeve, came on Purpoſe to doe Miſchief. But, haveing Right and Authority on my Side, I found it no difficult Matter to baffle ſome, and convert others. Soe that the Country Buſineſs was done, and they, of their own Accord, preſented me the encloſed Addreſs, to which you will not find the Names either of Captain *Mills*, or

Robert

Robert Mead ; tho they were both upon the Jury. But I have tyred you with this tedious Scroll, and therefore will onely add that I am ever,

My L O R D,

Your moſt obliged and

moſt obedient Servant,

R I C H A R D C O X.

To the Right Honorable Richard Cox, *Eſq; one of the Lords Juſtices of Aſſize for the Province of* Munſter, *and Governor of the County of* Cork, *and County of the Citty of* Corke.

WE the Grand Jury of the County of *Corke,* being ſenſible of your Lord-ſhips Zeale and Dilligence in their Majeſtyes Service, and the Benefit this County has received by your Induſtry and Conduct, in the Time of its greateſt Danger ; and the great Succeſs which it has pleaſed God to give your Endeavours for our Preſervation, doe think our ſelves obliged, in the Name of the whole County, to return your Lordſhip our humble and hearty Thanks for the indefatigable Pains you have taken in our Affairs, and the affectionate Con-cerne, which you have in all your Actions manifeſted for us. And we make it our humble Requeſt, That your Lordſhip would be pleaſed to continue among us, if it may ſtand with your Convenience ; and if not, that you would depute ſuch of the Commiſſioners of Array, to manage this County in your Abſence, as may follow and obſerve your Meaſures, in Hopes they may be bleſſed with the ſame Succeſs. And as we ſhall allways be forward to ſerve your Lordſhip in any Thing within our Power ; foe we pray your Lordſhip, wherever you are, to perſevere in the ſame Affection and Concerne for this County, which will all-ways acknowledge it ſelf in the higheſt Degree obliged to you, as we are in par-ticular, who are,

May it pleaſe your Lordſhip,

Your Lordſhips moſt humble Servants,

Jo. Gibbins,	Connor Callahan,	Dig. Foulk,
Robert White,	Hen. Rice,	Richard Newman,
J. Mountford,	John Watkins,	Richard Travers,
Samuell Hoſkins,	Matthew Deane,	War St. Leger,
William Taylor,	John Travers,	Robert Sanders.

On the 4th of *May* [d], 3 *Will.* and *Mar.* (being then Secretary of State) his Lord-ſhip had a Patent, conſtituting him Lord Warden of the *Cinque Ports,* Conſtable of *Dover* Caſtle, and Chancellor, and Admiral of the *Cinque Ports,* and the Members of the ſame, with all Wages, Fees, Profits, *&c.* in as ample Manner as *William Cobham,* Knight, Lord *Cobham,* deceaſed, or *Henry Cobham,* Lord *Cobham,* *Henry,* Earl of *Northampton, Edward,* Lord *Zouch, George,* Duke of *Bucking-ham,* or *James,* late Duke of *Richmond* and *Lenox,* deceaſed, or *James,* late Duke of *York,* had or enjoyed.

His Lordſhip, in a very grand Manner, was ſworn into the Office on *Breden-ſtone* Hill near *Dover* [e], where he arrived the latter End of *May,* 1694 ; and on the firſt of *June,* being attended by all the Officers of the *Cinque Ports,* the Chancellor of the Ports made him a congratulatory Speech, expreſſing the great Satisfaction the Ports had, in having him for their Warden, *&c.* opening to him the Rights and Privileges of the ſaid Ports, and concluded with a Recommen-dation of them to his Lordſhip's Protection. This great Poſt he held to his Death ; after which it was conferred on Prince *George* of *Denmark* ; and his im-

---

[d] Pat. 3 W. & M. apud Penſhurſt.   [e] Harris's Hiſt. of Kent, p. 482, 483.

mediate Predeceſſor was *James*, Duke of *York*, who did not fill up the ſame when he came to the Crown.

On Delivery of the Seal of Secretary of State to his Majeſty, 3 *March*, he was conſtituted [f], on the 28th of the ſame Month, 4 *Will.* III, Lord Lieutenant-general, and General-governor of the Kingdom of *Ireland*, and General of the Forces there.

Whilſt he was preparing to go for *Ireland*, and the King being beyond the Seas, Sir *Rowland Gwin*, Treaſurer of their Majeſties Chamber, having reflected on his Lordſhip's Integrity and Honour, he was cited before her Majeſty in Council, to ſhew what Ground he had for his Aſperſions. And not being able to make good his Accuſation, he was turned out of his Place, and this Order in Council, from the Court at *Whitehall*, was publiſhed *April* 7, 1692 :

' A Complaint having been made by the Lord Viſcount *Sidney*, Lord Lieu-
' tenant of *Ireland*, againſt Sir *Rowland Gwin*, for Words ſpoken on the 21ſt,
' or 22d Day of *March* laſt by him, reflecting upon his Lordſhip, as if he had
' taken Money for Diſpoſing of Places in *Ireland* ; and Sir *Rowland Gwin* having
' been required by her Majeſty, to ſhew what Grounds he had for ſpeaking the
' ſaid Words,' (for doing whereof, he had Time given him to this Day). And now being called in and heard ; and not being able to make out the ſaid Matter, or to ſhew any Ground for ſpeaking the ſaid Words : Her Majeſty thereupon, in Council, was pleaſed to declare, *That the ſaid Words were groundleſs and ſcandalous ; and that her Majeſty was fully ſatisfied of the Falſhood of the ſame.*

His Lordſhip landed at *Dublin* the 5th of *Auguſt*, 1692, and, having received the Sword from the Lords Juſtices, the Lord Chancellor made a ſhort Speech to him to this Effect [g] :

' That it being uſual, on ſuch Occaſions, to give his Excellency an exact Ac-
' count of the Condition and Affairs of the Kingdom ; they now thought it
' wholly unneceſſary, being ſenſible his Lordſhip was thoroughly acquainted
' therewith.
' That their Majeſties could not have fixed on a Perſon, more to the Mind,
' and general Satisfaction of the Kingdom, than his Excellency ; and that they
' were in Hopes, the Work which was ſo ſucceſsfully begun, in bringing the
' Nation out of the Ruin it was involved, into an entire Peace, whereunto his
' Excellency had been the greateſt Contributor ; they did not doubt, but it
' would now be fully perfected.'

On his Return from *Ireland*, he was conſtituted [h], 28 *July*, 5 *Will.* III. Maſter-general of the Ordinance, Armour, and Habiliments of War, to officiate by himſelf, or ſufficient Deputies, with all Authorities, Privileges, Wages, Fees, Perquiſites, &c. as *George*, late Lord *Dartmouth*, *Frederick*, late Duke of *Schomberg*, or any other, had enjoyed. Likewiſe, on the 20th of *November*, 1693, in the ſame 5th Year of his Majeſty, the King [i] conſtitutes *his right truſty and welbeloved Councellor*, Henry, *Viſcount* Sydney, *Maſter-general of his Ordnance*, &c. Colonel of his firſt Regiment of Foot Guards, and Captain of a Company in the ſaid Regiment. It was then vacant by the Death of the beforementioned Duke of *Schomberg* (who was killed at the Battle of *Martaglia* in *Italy*) and his Lordſhip was continued in the Command of the ſaid Regiment till his Deceaſe ; when he was ſucceeded by *John*, Duke of *Marlborough*, whoſe glorious Victories over the *French* has made his Memory immortal.

The King had ſuch particular Confidence in his Lordſhip, that, about this Time ; and indeed whilſt his Majeſty lived, he was, by all Ranks of People, thought to be his Prime Miniſter. And by Letters Patent, bearing Date 24 *May*, 6 *Will.* III [k], was created Earl of *Romney*, in the County of *Kent*.

[f] Pat. 4 W. III, apud Penſhurſt.   [g] Hiſt. of Eng. Vol. 3. p. 661.   [h] Pat. 5 W. III, apud Penſhurſt.   [i] Ex Origin. apud Penſhurſt.   [k] Pat. 6 W. III, apud Penſhurſt.

The

The Preamble recites, That the Virtues of the *Sydneys*, known for many Years, shine more and more in his welbeloved and faithful Councellor, *Henry*, Vifcount *Sydney*, whom, for his apparent Merits, he had ranked amongft the Vifcounts of his Realm. And confidering with what Wifdom, Loyalty, and Valour, he had difcharged the Places committed to his Truft, when he was of his Privy-council, of his Chamber, Secretary of State in *England*, Lord Lieutenant of *Ireland*, Warden of the *Cinque Ports*, and Conftable of *Dover* Caftle, Lord Lieutenant of *Kent*, Mafter of the Ordnance, and Colonel and Commander of his Regiment of Guards; therefore nothing was more equitable, than to promote him to a higher Degree of Honour.

And the King at the *Hague*, 24 *October*, 1694, in the fixth Year of his Reign, repofing efpecial Truft and Confidence in the Loyalty, Courage, and Experience in Military Affairs of his welbeloved Councellor, *Henry*, Earl of *Romney*, Mafter-general of his Ordnance, conftitutes him Lieutenant-general of his Forces.

In the fame Year, his Lordfhip [1] was commiffioned, with *John Glover* (by whofe Infight, Difcovery had been made) to inquire into all Prizes taken in *Guinea*, or Parts under the *African* Company, whereof the King's Moiety was not accounted for; and obtained a Grant thereof. Alfo, 20 *March*, 7 *W*. III [m], had the like Commiffion, and Grant, of the feveral Prizes taken, and carried into *Jamaica*, *Barbados*, *New-England*, *Virginia*, or other his Majefty's Colonies, in the *Weft-Indies*.

On the 22d of *April*, 1697, his Majefty leaving the Kingdom [n], he was declared one of the Lords Juftices for the Adminiftration of the Government during his Abfence. And, in this Year, was fo vigilant for the Safety of the Kingdom, that he ordered a Survey to be taken of the Fortifications of *Portfmouth*, the Harbour, *&c.* when the following Report was made:

Sir Martin Beckman's *Report concerning the prefent Condition of* Portfmouth, *the* Point, Blockhoufe-Point, *the* Dock, Portbridge, *and* Gofport [o].

I Have, purfuant to my Order from the Honourable the Ordnance Board, bearing Date the 31ft of *March*, and the Memorialls of the 28th of *March*, and 1ft of *Aprill* laft, furvey'd, and taken Notice of fuch Repairs as is moft neceffary to be done at the refpective Places here above mencioned. *Portfmouth* is in that ill Condicion, that, if not timely taken Care of, it will demollifh it felfe. The Earthworke doth not founder in the Moat from the Superficies of the Ramparts, as is reported, but it finks within the Ramparts, and boyles up under the Foundation in the Moat, and the Faceing falls inward in the Ramparts, and in fome Places it fwells out at the Bottome, and even the ftone Wall or Scarpe it felfe; foe that the Lieutenant Governor, Colonel *Gibfon*, has been obliged to caufe the Cannon, in fome Places, to be drawne back from the Plattformes or Batterys, as efpecially at *Gays*, and *Towne-Mount* Baftions; the Reafon of this is, That the Foundacions are not well fecured, and not deep enough by 10 Foot, and the Scarpe of Stone have noe Counterforts, which make the Weight of the Ramparts prefs out of the ftone Wall. To fpeak in fhort, the whole Place is extreamly ill proporcioned, and the Profile worfe of all. The Parrapets have noe Height nor Thicknefs as it ought to have, of which I have often told the late King *Charles*, and King *James*; but all what the late Engineer, Sir *Bernard de Gomme*, was pleafed to doe; was approved off, as from an Oracle.

And I kept from having any Thing to doe with the Fortifications, till I fucceeded him; and then the Fortificacions was laid afide, and the Army by Land, and the Fleet, was accounted the Walls of *England*, *&c.*

[1] Pat. 6 W. III. apud Penfhurft. [m] Pat. 7 W. III. [n] Hift. of Eng. Vol. 3. p. 734.
[o] Ex Autog. apud Penfhurft.

Portfbridge ought to be repaired ; and the Rivulet from Sea to Sea, to be foe fecured, that noe Paffage may be there, but thro' the Fort ; as fheweth my Defigne hereto annexed.

Blockhoufe-Point, and the Point at *Portfmouth*, ought alfoe to be at leaft foe fecured, as I have fett downe in the Eftimate.

Colonel *Gibfon* fhewed me a Place 200 Paces from the old Worke att *Block-houfe Point*, where the Sea went over twice the laft Winter, for 100 and more Paces in Length, which made the Banke flatt, and lower by 3 Foot, then it was ; which, I fear, if the Sea works a Paffage there, it will fill up the whole Harbour where the Men of Warr rydes, and foe utterly fpoyle that famous Port, if not fecured. The Bank or Neck of Land is about 60 Foot over from Sea to Sea, at high Water or Spring Tydes.

The Dock at *Portfmouth* is in noe Manner of Defence, the flight Works, that were in Haft made there, are all ruined, and can be noe lefs, for the prefent, done to it, then what I have fet downe for its Repaire in the Eftimate.

I have allfoe taken Notice of the Works at *Gofport* in the Eftimate ; tho' it is not mencioned in my Order ; yet I thought it neceffary to be done ; for who-ever is Mafter of that Place, is as much Mafter of the Harbour, as *Portfmouth* is. I have only defigned the Graft to be at prefent but 30 Foot wider then now it is, and fecured with Pallizadoes, and a double Barrack for 150 Men, or 3 Companys.

23d June, 1697.

On 16 *July*, 1698, he [p] was again conftituted one of the Lords Juftices of the Kingdom, during his Majefty's Stay beyond the Seas ; and, on the 18th of *Auguft* the fame Year, he authorifed Sir *Richard Cox*, Knight, one of the Judges of the Kingdom of *Ireland*, *Charles Deering* of *Dublin*, in the faid King-dom, Efq; *James Allet*, Efq; and *Thomas Carter*, Efq; of *Dublin*, aforefaid ; to contract and agree with all and every of his Tenants of the Kingdom of *Ireland* (being Proteftants) and others (being Proteftants) for Selling, Affuring, and Conveying to them, and their Heirs, any Part or Parts of his faid Lands, *&c.* for the beft Price or Prices they could get for the fame, rendering yearly to him, his Heirs and Affigns, not lefs than one third Part, of the feveral and refpective yearly Values or Rents, due and payable to him, out of the refpective Lands, *&c.* fo to be fold. And, on fuch Contract or Agreement, *&c.* made, and the Receipt of the refpective Sums, *&c.* in his Name, and for his fole Ufe and Benefit, to convey and affure to them, their Heirs and Affigns, all fuch Lands, *&c.*

Whereupon they made feveral Contracts and Agreements, as Letters and Pa-pers now at *Penfhurft* fhew. It is probable, his Lordfhip was then apprifed of the Intention of the Houfe of Commons, to refume the *Irifh* Forfeitures. For, in 1699, Commiffioners having been appointed by the Houfe of Commons, to inquire and take an Account of the forfeited Eftates in *Ireland*, they gave an Account, That the Earl of *Romney*, in Confideration of Services done, had three Grants of 49517 Acres : The Earl of *Albemarle* two Grants of 108,620 Acres in Poffeffion and Reverfion ; and *William Bentinck* Lord *Woodftock*, 135,820 Acres of Land, *&c.* And, the Commons bringing in a Bill to apply all the forfeited Eftates to the Ufe of the Publick [q], their Proceedings were ill relifhed at Court : On which the Houfe waiting on the King with an Addrefs relating thereto, his Majefty returned this Anfwer :

' *Gentlemen*,
' I was not only led by Inclination, but thought myfelf obliged in Juftice,
' to reward thofe who had ferved well ; and particularly in the Reduction of
' *Ireland*, out of the Eftates forfeited to me, by the Rebellion there,' *&c.*
Which being reported to the Houfe, they refolved [r], *That whofoever advifed*

---

[p] Hift. of Eng. Vol. 3. p. 755.   [q] Hift. of Eng. præd. p. 771, 772.   [r] Ibid. p. 773.

I

it,

it, had ufed his utmoft Endeavors **to** *create a Mifunderftanding and Jealoufie, between the King and his People.*

However, the Commons, believing the Bill would be rejected by the Lords, tacked it to the Land-Tax Bill, which created fuch warm Debates in Conferences; that the King, to prevent a Rupture between them, thought it proper to intereft himfelf therein : So that their Lordfhips gave their Concurrence to it.

It doth not appear, either by the Journals of Parliament, or the Accounts of thofe Times; that the Earl of *Romney*, notwithftanding his Grants, interefted himfelf, fo as to draw an Odium on him, or the Difpleafure of the Houfe of Commons : Who, indeed, had fuch a Regard to his Services and Merits, that his Grants were excepted out of the Act for the Refumption of them. And they had the better Opinion of him, as he was not concerned in the Treaty of Partition.

By the Duke of *Shrewfbury*'s Warrant ˢ, 30 *April*, in the 12th Year of his Majefty's Reign, directed to the Houfe-keeper of the Palace of *Hampton-Court*, he fignified his Majefty's Pleafure, to deliver to the Earl of *Romney* the Keys and Poffeffion of three Rooms over the King's Apartment there, which lye next to the Mafter of the Robes, and were formerly appointed for the Earl of *Jerfey*. By which it is evident, his Majefty was defirous of having his Lordfhip near to him. And, on the 24th Day of *June*, 1700, the Earl of *Jerfey* ᵗ certifies, that, in Obedience to his Majefty's Warrant, he had fworn *Henry* Earl of *Romney*, into the Place and Quality of Groom of the Stole to his Majefty, in the Room of *William* Earl of *Portland*; to hold, *&c.* with all Rights, Profits, *&c.* as the faid Earl of *Portland*, or any other Groom of the Stole, enjoyed the fame.

Whereupon the Earl of *Jerfey* ᵘ, by his Warrant, 24 *December*, 12 *W.* III. directed *Henry Lowman*, Efq; Houfe-keeper and Wardrobe-keeper of his Majefty's Palace at *Kenfington*, to deliver to the Earl of *Romney* the Keys and Poffeffion of the Rooms and Offices at *Kenfington*, formerly belonging to the Earl of *Portland*. Alfo, on 23 *April*, 13 *W.* III, he had the King's Warrant to the Commiffioners of the Treafury ; reciting, That *Edward* Earl of *Jerfey*, Chamberlain of his Houfhold, by Warrant under his Royal Sign Manual, had, in Obedience thereto, on the 24th of *June* laft paft, 1700, fworn and admitted *Henry* Earl of *Romney*, into the Place of Groom of the Stole, and firft Gentleman of his Bed-chamber, in the Room of *William* Earl of *Portland*. His Will and Pleafure therefore is, That they pay, or caufe to be paid, out of the Treafure applicable to the Ufe of the Civil Government, to the faid *Henry* Earl of *Romney*, or his Affigns, the annual Sum of two-thoufand Pounds, to commence from the faid 24th of *June* laft paft. The firft Payment to be made for three Quarters, which became due at the faid 24th of *June*, and the fubfequent Payments, as they fhall thenceforth quarterly become due.

After this, I find his Lordfhip's Titles thus ranked ʷ, ' *Henry* Earl of *Rom-* ' *ney*, Vifcount *Sidney* of *Sheppey*, and Baron of *Milton* in the County of *Kent*, ' Lord Lieutenant of the fame, and of the City of *Canterbury*, Vice-Admiral ' of the fame, Lord Warden of the *Cinque-Ports*, Conftable of *Dover* Caftle, ' Mafter of the *Ordinance*, Lieutenant-General of his Majefty's Forces, Colonel ' of his Majefty's own Regiment of Foot-Guards, one of the Lords of his Ma- ' jefty's moft honourable Privy-Council, Groom of the Stole, and firft Gen- ' tleman of his Majefty's Bed-Chamber.' Which great Offices evidently fhew, that he was in the utmoft Favour of King *William* ; and, by feveral Addreffes to his Lordfhip yet remaining at *Penfhurft*, it further appears, that he was reputed to have the firft Direction of Affairs in the Government.

On the Acceffion of Queen *Anne*, her Majefty, 22 *June*, in the firft Year of her Reign ˣ, renewed his Patent for the Office of *Cuftos Rotulorum* of the County

ˢ Ex Orig. apud Penfhurft. ᵗ Ex Orig. ᵘ Ex Orig. ʷ Ex Evident. apud Penfhurft.
ˣ Ex Orig. Pat. 1 Q. Anne.
V O L. I. Y y of

of *Kent*, which had been granted to him by King *William* (as it is recited) 26th of *September*, in the first Year of his Reign. Also ʸ, on 29 *July* following, was constituted Lord-Lieutenant of the County of *Kent*, and of the City and County of *Canterbury*, which he had held from the 3d of *October*, in the 1st Year of King *William* and Queen *Mary*. And, in both Patents, he is stiled of the Privy-Council to her Majesty Queen *Anne*.

On the ᶻ 25th of *August*, in the said first Year of the Queen, he obtained of her Majesty, by Privy-seal, 1860 Ounces of Plate, belonging to the late King *William*, that had been delivered into the Jewel Office. Wherein it is recited, that King *William* ordained, amongst the Rules established for the Office of Groom of the Stole and first Gentleman of the Bed-chamber to his Royal Person: That all his Chamber Plate, Utensils, and Goods, which should be in the Custody of his Pages, or any other belonging to his Bed-chamber at the Time of his Death, should be to the only Use and Benefit of the said Groom of the Stole for the Time being. And whereas *Edward Yardley*, Esq; of the Jewel Office, had certified, That there had been delivered to the Pages of the Bed-chamber and Back-stairs 2250 Ounces of gilt and white Plate, of which 1860 Ounces had been, since the Decease of the King, brought back to the Jewel Office, and the other 390 Ounces certified to be lost in *Flanders*: The Queen grants, for her and her Successors, the said Plate to the said Earl of *Romney*.

His Lordship's Place of Lord Warden of the *Cinque Ports*, the Queen conferred on his Royal Highness Prince *George* of *Denmark*; and that of Master of the Ordnance on his Grace *John* Duke of *Marlborough*: But the Command of the First Regiment of Foot Guards his Lordship held to the Time of his Decease, the Duke not succeeding thereto till 25 *April*, 1704.

And the Queen, in Consideration of his Lordship's Services, granted to him a Pension of 1200 *l. per Annum*; of which there was unpaid of the said Pension at his Lordship's Decease three Quarters of a Year, *viz.* 900 *l.* And there was likewise due at his Decease one Year's Patent Fee, as Master of the Ordinance, *viz.* from *Midsummer* 1701, to *Midsummer* 1702, amounting to 175 *l.* 18 *s.* 4 *d.* all which the Honourable *John Sidney*, Esq; his Nephew and Executor, received.

His Lordship, by his Last Will and Testament, bearing Date the 12th of *April*, 1699, and a Codicil, dated 21 *July*, 1702, desires to be buried decently, according to his Quality, in the Parish where he should happen to die: And bequeaths to the Poor of the Parish of St. *Martin*'s in the Fields, in the County of *Middlesex*, the Sum of 150 *l.* To the Poor of *Penshurst* in the County of *Kent*, 150 *l.* and to the Poor of *Leigh* in the said County, 150 *l.*

He bequeaths all his Honours, Castles, Mannors, Messuages, Lands, Tenements, &c. to his Nephew *John Sidney*, second Son of the Earl of *Leicester*, and to the Heirs Males of his Body; and, for Want of such Issue, to his Nephew *Thomas Sidney*, Brother to the said *John*, and the Heirs Males of his Body, and for Want of such Issue, to his right Heirs for ever.

And whereas King *William*, by his Letters Patents of Lease, dated the 31st of *August*, in the 9th Year of his Reign, granted to him, for the Term of 31 Years, his Majesty's Palace called the *Queen's House*, in *East Greenwich* in the County of *Kent*, and his Park there called *Greenwich Park*, and several Parcels of Land there, Part of the Places called the *Old Tiltyard*, and the *Queen's Gardens*, and other Hereditaments; under a Proviso and Agreement, that his Majesty may resume the same, on Payment of so much Money, as he, his Executors, Administrators, and Assigns, should expend on the Premises, not exceeding 5000 *l.* And whereas his said Majesty had, by other Letters Patent, granted to him several Offices, Fees, Perquisites, &c. relating to the *Queen's House*, and *Greenwich Park*, and Mannor of *East Greenwich*, and other Mannors and Hereditaments of his said Majesty: He gives and bequeaths to his said Ne-

ʸ Ex Pat. 29 Jul. 1 Q. Anne, apud Penshurst.   ᶻ Privat. Sigil. 1 Q. Anne.

I

phew

phew *John Sidney* the said *Queen's House*, *Greenwich Park*, &c. and all other the Premises in or by the said Letters Patents granted, *&c.*

He bequeaths to his Nephew *Thomas Pelham*, all his Cabinets, and all that shall be in them at his Decease, except the Writings of the several Estates he had bequeathed, or any Notes, Bonds, Securities, or other Writings relating to Money: And to his Nephew *Henry Pelham* of *Lewes* in *Sussex*, Esq; all his Plate and Furniture in his House in St. *James's* Square, except his Pictures, which he bequeaths to his Nephew *John Sidney.*

He bequeaths to his Nephew the Earl of *Leicester* all his Books; and desires the same may be placed and kept at *Penshurst*, for the Use of his Lordship, and those who shall succeed him in that Seat. And further bequeaths to him the Clock which was his late Majesty's.

He bequeaths to his Nephew *Thomas Sidney*, the Sum of 1000 *l.* and to the Earl of *Sunderland*, the Diamond Ring which was given him by his late Majesty King *William*, when he was Prince of *Orange.*

He constitutes Executors, his Nephews *Thomas Pelham*, *Henry Pelham*, and *John Sidney*; and leaves to their Discretion the Expences relating to his Funeral and Interment, and Mournings on Occasion of his Death. And whatever remains of his Personal Estate, after his Debts, Legacies, and Expences, relating to their Executorship and Trusts, be fully satisfied and discharged, shall be vested in them for the Purchase of Lands and Hereditaments; which, together with his real Estate not devised, shall be settled to the Use of his said Nephew *John Sidney*, and the Heirs Males of his Body, and, for Want of such Issue, to his said Nephew *Thomas Sidney*, and the Heirs Males of his Body, and, for Want of such Issue, to his right Heirs for ever.

[a] His Lordship died of the Small Pox, unmarried, at his House in St. *James's* Square, on the 8th of *April*, 1704; and on the 18th of the same Month was buried in the Chancel of St. *James's* Church, *Westminster*, where a Monument is erected to his Memory, near the Communion Table, with this Inscription:

> To the Memory of the Right Honourable
> *Henry Sidney*, Earl of *Romney*, Viscount *Sidney*
> of *Sheppey*, and Baron of *Milton* in the
> County of *Kent*,
> Lord Warden of the *Cynque* Ports, Constable of *Dover-*
> Castle, Master General of the Ordnance, and sometime
> Lord Lieutenant of *Ireland.*
> Lieutenant General of the Forces of His late Majestie King *William*
> the 3d, First Lord of His Bed-chamber, and one of the Lords of His
> Most Honourable Privy Council, and also Privy Councellor to Her
> Present Majestie Queen *Anne*,
> Who dy'd *April* the 8th, *Anno Dom.* 1704, in the 63d Year of his Life,
> and was here inter'd.
> The Honourable *John Sidney*, second Son of his Nephew
> *Robert* Earl of *Leicester*,
> Dedicated this as a lasting Monument of his
> Gratitude and Affection.

He was graceful in his Person, and of a sweet and affable Disposition: Of great Humanity, and very benevolent to all in Distress. He lived in the highest Splendor, in a most generous and hospitable Manner, so that few envied him the Favour of his Royal Master. It is also much to his Honour, that, tho' he was at the Head of Affairs for so many Years, and tho' several of the King's Ministers had fallen under the Displeasure of the House of Commons, he was never charged by them with Corruption, or Avarice, or Errors in his Administration. And, considering the Estate he inherited, he left it not at all improved.

[a] Ex Registr. Eccl. S. Jac. Westmon.

I now

I now return to *Robert* Earl of *Leicester*, eldest Son and Heir, and Successor to *Philip* Earl of *Leicester*. Which *Robert*, in his Father's Life-time, was summoned to Parliament among the Barons by Writ, 11 *July*, 1689, 1 *W.* & *M.* by the Title of *Robert Sydney* of *Penshurst*, Knt. [b] ; and the same Day was introduced in his Robes, between the Lord *De la War*, and the Lord *Osulston*, and placed on the Barons Bench. And voted as a Baron, till he succeeded his Father in the Earldom of *Leicester*, *Anno* 1697.

His Lordship married *Elisabeth*, only Daughter to *John Egerton* Earl of *Bridgwater*, by his Wife the Lady *Elisabeth Cavendish*, Daughter of *William* Duke of *Newcastle*, by whom he had Issue 15 Children, whereof 9 died young, and 4 Sons and 2 Daughters survived him.

His Lordship made his Will on the 14th of *December*, 12 W. III. *An.* 1700 ; Wherein [c] he gave to the Poor of the Parish of St. *Anne*'s, *Westminster*, 50 *l.* To the Poor of the Parish of *Penshurst*, 50 *l.* To the Poor of the Parish of *Leigh* in Kent, 40 *l.* He constitutes his loving Brother-in-Law, the Honourable *Charles Egerton*, Esq, Sir *Henry Monson*, Bart. and *Thomas Bromfield*, his Executors. And appoints his honoured Uncle, *Henry* Earl of *Romney*, Guardian of all his Sons, under the Age of 21 Years, at the Time of his Death ; and of their Estates, during their respective Minorities. And the Lady *Elisabeth*, Countess of *Leicester*, his Wife, during her Widowhood, and Sir *Henry Monson*, and the Survivors of them, Guardians of his Daughters, the Lady *Elisabeth* and Lady *Catharine*, during their Minorities.

He died on the 10th of *November*, 1702, and was buried at *Penshurst* the 23d of *November* following, where a sumptuous Monument of white Marble is erected to his Memory, in the Chancel of the Church. The Cornish is composed of 7 Cherubs, whereof two are supporting an Earl's Coronet, and on the Top are two Porcupines (the antient Crest of the *Sidneys*) with these Inscriptions underneath in gilt Letters :

ROBERT SIDNEY

The eldest Son. He had Wit Judgment
and Beauty to so great a Degree that daily
increased the surprising Admiration
Of all that knew him.
He died in 1680
the 6th Year of his Age.

FRANCES SIDNEY

The 4th Daughter, in all Respects a
perfect Copy of her eldest Brother.
So that she was all
that could be wished.
She died in 1692
the 6th year of her Age.

In the Middle, are two Angels supporting an Urn ; on each Side of them two grey Marble Pillars. And below them are two Oval Compartments of white Marble, with these Inscriptions in black Letters :

To the Dear Memory
Of ROBERT SYDNEY Earl
Of *Leicester*, Viscount *Lisle*,
Baron *Sydney* of *Penshurst*, 4th Earl of this Family.
He married the Lady ELIZABETH
EGERTON, Daughter to the Earl of *Bridgwater*,
with whom he lived 30 happy years, had 15 Children, of
which 9 died young, whose Figures are plac'd here.

[b] Journal Dom. Procer. 1 W. & Mar.   [c] Ex Regist. Horn. qu. 200. in Cur. Prærog. Cantuar.

I

Robert the eldeſt Son, the 2d, and 6 Daughters buried in this Place.
6 ſurvivd him, whereof 4 were Sons, and 2 Daughters.
His Perſon was Gracefull and Beautifull; his Mind truly
Noble & Great.   Of a quick Wit, good Judgment, A Sweet
Temper and pleaſing Converſation.   He had an Honeſt Heart,
A gratefull & generous Spirit ; and upon all Occaſions
ever ſtrictly Juſt and Good.
A faithfull Freind, the beſt of Huſbands. A moſt kind
& tender Father.   A true lover of the Intereſt of his
Country, and the Church of *England.*
He died in the 53d Year of his Age, the 10th of *November*
1702, & was buried under this Monument.
Which in true Affection to his lov'd Memory
is erected by his diſconſolate
Afflicted Wife.

On the other Oval Compartment is this Inſcription ;

To the Memory
of ELIZABETH Counteſs of
LEICESTER, the happy and only Wife
of her dear Lord ROBERT Earle of
LEICESTER, whoſe Death ſhe ſurvived 7
tedious Years, having loſt in him her better
life. The Affection and ſollicitude for her Children
which was conſtantly very great for all,
forced her a little into the World, and not
wholly giving up her ſelf to what was
moſt agreable to her, luling her ſelf in
her infinite ſorrow.   The great deſire of her
life was, to make a good Wife, and a good
Mother ; and did ſo.   She died in the 57th
year of her Age, in 1709, and is buried
under here, in the ſame Vault, with
Her dear Lord.
Theſe Inſcriptions are here plac'd
by her own Directions.

Their two Daughters, were Lady *Elizabeth,* born the 31ſt of *May,* 1681, married
to Sir *Harcourt Maſters,* Knt. one of the Aldermen of *London,* and, dying without Iſſue by him *March* 23, 172⅞, was buried at *Penſhurſt* the 1ſt of *April* following.   And Lady *Catharine,* born 21ſt of *Auguſt,* 1685, married to *William*
Barker of the *Inner Temple,* Eſq; and was buried at *Penſhurſt,* 29 *Sept.* 1722,
leaving Iſſue a Daughter, chriſtened *Sidney,* who died unmarried *An.* 1736, and
was buried at St. *Anne's, Weſtminſter.*

d The eldeſt ſurviving Son *Philip,* born the 8th of *July,* 1676, was elected
one of the Knights of the Shire for the County of *Kent,* to that Parliament
which met at *Weſtminſter* 22d *Nov.* 1695; and, in 1702, ſucceeding his Father,
was Earl of *Leiceſter.*

He married *Anne,* one of the Daughters and Coheirs of Sir *Robert Reeves* of
Thwates, in *Com. Suff.* Bart. by *Mary* his Wife, Siſter of *Richard* the firſt Lord
Onſlow, by whom he had Iſſue a Son and a Daughter, who died before they
were a Year old, and were buried at St. *Anne's, Weſtminſter.*

His Lordſhip made e his Will 20th *June,* 1704, in the 3d Year of Queen
Anne : And bequeathed to his Siſter-in-Law, Madam *Mary Reeve,* his Diamond
Ring, his *Turky* Stone Ring, ſet with Diamonds, and his Hair Ring, ſet with

---

d Ex Collect. Br. Willis, Arm.   e Ex Regiſt. Gee, qu. 103.

Diamonds. And, after Legacies to his Servants, he bequeaths *all the Reſt and Reſidue of his Goods, Chattels, Monies, Plate, Debts and Eſtate whatſoever, after his Debts ſhall be paid, Legacies ſatisfied, and Funeral Expences diſcharged*, to his loving Wife *Anne*, Counteſs of *Leiceſter*, whom he appoints his ſole Executrix.

His Lordſhip departed this Life on the 24th of *July*, 1705, and was buried at *Penſhurſt* the 4th of *Auguſt* following ; but, leaving no Iſſue, his Honours and Eſtate devolved on his Brother *John*, the 2d ſurviving Son of *Robert* Earl of *Leiceſter*.

Which *John* Earl of *Leiceſter* (born 14 *Feb.* 16⅞) being under the Guardianſhip of his Uncle, *Henry* Earl of *Romney*, he preferred him firſt to be an Enſign, in his Majeſties own Regiment of Foot-Guards, whereof the Earl had the Command. And ſerving under King *William* in *Flanders*, he was promoted to a Company in the ſame Regiment, with the Rank of a Lieutenant-Colonel. In the Reign of Queen *Anne*, he ſerved under *John*, Duke of *Marlborough*, and very much diſtinguiſhed himſelf, in the famous Battle of *Hockſtet*, where Marſhal *Tallard*, the *French* General, was taken Priſoner. And the ſame Year, the Earl of *Romney* dying, he made him his Heir.

In 1705, on his Brother's Deceaſe he became Earl of *Leiceſter*, on which he ſurrendered his Command in the Army to his Brother, Colonel *Thomas Sidney*.

During the Remainder of the Queens Reign, he had no Imploiment at Court ; but on the Acceſſion of our late Sovereign to the Throne, he was made one of the Lords of his Bedchamber, and conſtituted Lord Warden of the *Cinque-Ports*, and Governor of *Dover* Caſtle in 1717.

In 1725, on the Erection of that Degree of Knighthood of the *Order of the Bath*, into a regular Military Order for ever, he was choſe one of the Knights Companions of the ſaid Order, with other Lords, and Perſons of high Degree, who were inſtalled with great Solemnity in King *Henry the Seventh*'s Chapel, in the Abbey of *Weſtminſter*. Alſo the ſame Year, was conſtituted Captain of the Yeomen of the Guards to his Majeſty.

On the Acceſſion of our preſent Sovereign, he was continued in his Poſt of Captain of the Yeomen of the Guards, and appointed Lord-Lieutenant of the County of *Kent*. And ſurrendering his Place of Captain of the Yeomen of the Guard ; he was, on the 24th of *November*, 1731, declared Conſtable of the *Tower* of *London*, and at the ſame Time ſworn of his Majeſties moſt honourable Privy-Council. His Lordſhip died unmarried on the 27th of *Sept.* 1727, and was buried at *Penſhurſt*, with his Anceſtors, the 11th of *October* following.

The next in Succeſſion was the honourable *Thomas Sidney*, Eſq; 3d ſurviving Son of *Robert* Earl of *Leiceſter* ; which *Thomas* was born the 27th of *November* 1683, and ſucceeding his Brother *John*, Earl of *Leiceſter*, in his Command in the 1ſt Regiment of Foot Guards, ſerved under the Duke of *Marlborough*, till he quitted the Service the latter End of the Reign of Queen *Anne*. On the Acceſſion of our late Sovereign, he was conſtituted Colonel of the Royal *Iriſh* Regiment of Dragoons ; and dying in the Life-time of Earl *John*, his Brother, on the 27th of *January*, 172⅘, was buried at *Penſhurſt*, the 15th of *February* following. He married *Mary*, youngeſt of the two Daughters and Coheirs of Sir *Robert Reeves*, Bart. before mentioned, by whom he left two Daughters, his Coheirs, *Mary*, married in 1738 to Sir *Brownlow Sherard*, Bart. and *Elizabeth*, alſo married the ſame Year to *William Perry*, Eſq; Which Ladies, by the Death of *Joceline*, 7th Earl of *Leiceſter* (the youngeſt ſurviving Son of *Robert* Earl of *Leiceſter*) who died at *Penſhurſt* Place, *July* 7, 1743, without Iſſue, are the ſole Heirs of this noble Family, as alſo Heirs to the Barony of *Liſle*, firſt treated of (through the *Beauchamps*, *Talbots*, *De Greys*, and *Dudleys*, Earls of *Warwick* and *Leiceſter*, Viſcounts and Barons *Liſle* ;) who had Summons to Parliament, in the Reign of King *Edward the Second* ; and in ſucceeding Times (as I have ſhewn) has been confirmed by divers Letters Patent.

And

And since their Accession to the Estate, there is erected in the Chancel of *Penshurst* (near the Monument of Sir *William Sydney*) a handsome Tomb of white Marble, with a grey Marble Pyramid, against which, are the Crests and Supporters of the Family, curiously engraved, as also an Escutcheon of 80 Coats of Arms (the Quarterings of the Family) finely painted; with the Motto, *Quo Fata Vocant.*

Under the Pyramid, Supporters, *&c.* is this Inscription in black Letters:

To the Memory
of the most Noble Lord, PHILIP SIDNEY, the 5th Earl
of *Leicester*, Viscount *Lisle*, and Lord *Sidney* of *Penshurst*,
Son and Heir of *Robert*, the 4th Earl of *Leicester*, here interred,
who was Son and Heir of *Philip* Earl of *Leicester*, Son and Heir
of *Robert* Earl of *Leicester*, Son and Heir of Sir *Robert Sidney*,
Knight, created Earl of *Leicester*, by King JAMES *the first*;
which last named *Robert* Earl of *Leicester*,
was Nephew and heir of *Ambrose Dudley*,
and *Robert Dudley*, Brethren,
Earls of *Warwick* and of *Leicester*,
Sons of the high and mighty Prince, JOHN DUDLEY, Duke
of *Northumberland*,
whose Grandson and Heir, the said Earl *Robert Sidney*,
was, after the Deaths of his said Uncles, his Aunt *Catharine*,
Countess of *Huntington*, and his Niece *Elizabeth*, Countess
of *Rutland*, who all died without Issue:
Which Duke of *Northumberland* was Son and Heir of
Elizabeth Grey, Viscountess *Lisle*, Daughter and sole Heir of
Edward Grey, and *Elizabeth Talbot* his Wife,
Created Baron *Lisle*, to them and the heirs of their Bodies
Issuing for ever, by Patent, 15th of *Edw. the 4th.*

PHILIP, the 5th Earl of *Leicester*, married *Anne*, eldest
Daughter and Coheir of Sir *Robert Reeves*, of *Thwaits*, in the
County of *Suffolk*, Bart.
by whom he had a Son, and one Daughter, who all died in the
first Year of their Ages; and his Lordship departing this Life on
the 24th of *July*, 1705, was succeeded by *John* his Brother and Heir.

JOHN, the 6th Earl of *Leicester*, was Cosin and heir of
Henry Sidney, Earl of *Romney*, and one of the Lords of the
Bed-chamber, and Lord Warden of the *Cinque-Ports*, and
Governour of *Dover*-Castle, and chose one of the Knights
Companions of the most Honourable order of the Bath, in the Reign
of King *George the first*, and under King *George the second*
he was Captain of the Yeomen of the Guard, Constable of the
Tower of *London*,
Lord Lievtenant of the County of *Kent*, and one of his
Majestys most Honourable Privy Council; who deceasing unmarried
on the 27th of *Sept.* 1737,
his Nieces *Mary*, and *Elizabeth Sidney*, Daughters and
heirs of his Brother, the Honourable *Thomas Sidney*,
third surviveing Son of *Robert*, the 4th
Earl of *Leicester*,
became his Joint-heirs,
and Legal Representative.

THOMAS

THOMAS SIDNEY, their Father, married *Mary*, youngeſt Daughter, and after the Death of her Siſter, *Anne*, Counteſs of *Leiceſter*, without Iſſue, Sole heir of Sir ROBERT REEVES, Bart. which *Thomas*, dying on the 27th of *January*, 1728-9. was here interred, as was alſo the ſaid *Mary* his Widow.

Joceline, the 7th Earl of *Leiceſter*, youngeſt Brother, and heir Male of Earl *John*, died without Iſſue, on the 6th of *July*, 1743, and alſo lyes here interred with his Brethren, in whom the Title of Earl of *Leiceſter* expired; ſo that the aforeſaid *Mary* and *Elizabeth* his Nieces, are his Heirs, and alſo the only heirs of their Noble Anceſtors abovementioned, of whom *Mary* the eldeſt, is the Wife of Sir BROWNLOW SHERARD of *Lopthorp* in *Lincolnſhire*, Bart. and *Elizabeth* of WILLIAM PERRY, of *Turvile*-Park in *Bucks*, Eſq. who erected this Monument in the Year 1743.

F I N I S.

THE

I N D E X.

Darcy,

I

SYDNEY,

LETTERS

LETTERS

AND

MEMORIALS of STATE.

Collections made by Sir *Henry Sydney*, Knight of the Garter, Lord Prefident of the Marches of *Wales*. *Touchinge the Antiquitie, Aucthoritie,
and Jurifdiccion of the Lord Prefident and Councell of the Marches of
Wales ; and touching the Aucthoritie of the Lord Prefident, when he hath
not been in Place with the Councell.*

T H E Lorde Prefident and Counfail of the Domynion and Pryncipallitie of *Wales*, and the Marches of the fame, were eftablifhed in the
Tyme of Kinge *Edward the IIIIth*, and everfythens, untill the Making of the Statutes of *An.* 27, 30, 33, 34, and 35 of *Hen.* VIII. had
Contynuance. Who, before that Time, by Commiffions and Inftruccions from
the King, harde and determyned Caufes arrifing within that Pryncipallitie, as
alfo in the County of *Worcefter*, and other *Englifh* Shires adjoining. And have,
fince the Making of thofe Statutes, by Commiffion and Inftruccion, likewife
hard and determyned Caufes ; taking the Benefitt of that Statute in further
Strengthnyng of their Aucthoritie. And thereby the hole Countrey of *Wales*
have ben, by the Goverment of the fame Lord Prefident and Counfaill, fythens
the Eftablifhment of the fame, brought from their difobedient, barbarous, and
(as may be termed) lawles Incivilitie, to the civill and obedient Eftate they now
remayne. And all the *Englifh* Counties, bordering thereon, brought to be af-
frayed from fuch Spoyles and Felonyes, as the *Welfh*, before that Tyme, ufually
by invading their Borders, annoyed them with.

By the Statute of *An.* 27 *Hen.* VIII, the Domynion, Countrey, and Prynci-
palitie of *Wales*, and divers Marches, were divided into xii Shires ; whereof viii
were antient Counties, and iiii new made Counties. And the Statutes, *An.* 31,
33, 34, and 35 *Hen.* VIII, are Recitalls, and Declarations of that Statute, *viz.*
That there fhalbe, and remayn a Lord Prefident and Counfaill, *&c.* with all
Officers and Incidents, *&c.* in Manner and Forme, as it had been before that
Tyme ufed and accuftomed. And for the better Strengthnyng the Aucthoritie
of the Lord Prefident and Counfaill (to deale in Caufes as may be gathered) it
followeth in the Statute, *An.* 34 and 35 *Hen.* VIII.

Item, That there fhalbe and remayne a Prefidente and Councell in the faid
Domynion and Principalitie of *Wales*, and the Marches of the fame, with all
Officers, Clercks, and Incidents to the fame, in Maner and Forme, as hath
been heretofore vfed and accuftomed ; which Prefident and Councell fhall have
Power and Authoritie to heare and determine, by theire Wifdomes and Difcrea-
çions, fuch Caufes and Matters, as be, or hereafter fhalbe affigned to them, by
the Kings Majeftie, as heretofore hath been accuftomed and vfed.

Vpon thefe Wordes, it is thoughte that the Authoritie and Jurifdiccion of the faid Lord Prefident and Councell, doth principally confift in the Hearinge and Determinacion of Caufes and Matters, by theire Wifdomes and Difcreacions, to them by her Majeftie affigned, as heretofore hath been accuftomed and vfed.

Nowe, to make Declaracion, what hath been affigned by the Prince, in formour Tyme, to the faid Lord Prefident and Councell, thefe be the Wordes:

A°. 17, *H.* VIII.] Inftruccions geven by the Kings Highnes, and figned with his gracious Hande, to the right reuerend Father in God the Bifhopp of *Excefter*, Prefident of Councell, with his deareft Daughter the Princeffe; the Lord *Dudley*, Chamberlayne, the Lord *Ferrers*, Stuard of Howfhould, Sir *Iohn Porte*, Knight, Juftice; and fo namynge the reft, *&c.* whom his Highnes, of fpeciall Truft and Confidence, hath appoynted to be Counfailours, attendaunt vpon the Perfon of his deareft Daughter the Princeffe, and alfo Comiffioners in the Parties of *Wales*, and Marches of the fame, for Execucion of the Matters hereafter mencioned.

Firft, In afmuch as by Reafon of the longe Abfence of any Prince makinge continnuall Refidence eyther in the Principalitie of *Wales*, or in the Marches of the fame: The good Order, Quiet, and Tranquillitie of the Countrey there about, hath greatly been altred and fubuerted, and the due Adminiftracion of Iuftice, by Meanes of fondry Contrarieties, hethervnto hindred and neglected. And for that alfo it fhould be greatly to the Damaige and Hurt of the Kings lovinge Subiects in the faid Principalitie and Marches, which myght fynde themfelves greaved or offended, to repaire for makinge and exhibitinge theire Complaynts before the Kings moft honorable Councell, or to purfue theire Accions and Quarrells in the Kings ordinary Courts, kept at his Pallace of *Weftminfter*. And to Thentent further, that the faid Countreyes may hereafter be reduced vnto the priftine and found good Eftate and Order, due Juftice adminiftred, poore Mens Caufes rightfully redreffed, Offendours and Malefactours to be punifhed, good Men condignly cherifhed and rewarded, and alfo the Parties there about, by Meane of good Hofpitallitie, refrefhed. The Kings Highnes therefore, by mature Deliberacion and fubftanciall Advife of his Councell, hath determyned to fend, at this Tyme, his deareft, beft beloved, and only Daughtour, the Princeffe, accompanyed and eftablifhed with an honourable, fadd, difcreate, and experte Councell, to refide and remayne in the Marches of *Wales*, and the Parties thereabouts, whom his Highnes hath fufficiently furnifhed with ample Comiffions and Aucthoritie, afwell for Thadminiftracion of Juftice, as for all other Things requifite and expedient to be done concerninge the Premiffes; that is to fay, a Comiffion of Oier, and Determiner; another for Thadminiftracion of Juftice, and Deficion of Caufes, Greeves, and Complaynts, to be made betweene Partie and Partie; and fo proceeding with like Remembraunce of the reft of theire Comiffions, concludeth in this Sorte. All which the Kings fpeciall Truft and Confidence is, they will duely, truely, and effectually execute, accordinge to the Purporte and Tenor of the fame: For the better Performance whereof, and of all other Things which may concerne the Premiffes, certeyne Articles be devifed by his Highnes to be obferved, kept, and fulfilled by the faid Councell, as followeth:

Of thefe Inftruccions and Articles, there is an ould Parchement Booke remayninge in Thoffice of the Clerck of the Councell there at this prefente, which is delivered to the right Honorable Sir *Henrie Sydney*, of the noble Order of the Guarter, Knighte, Lord Prefident of the fame Councell, to be fhewed by the faid Lord Prefident, for Mayntenaunce and Defence of the Jurifdiccion and Aucthoritie aforefaid, where the faid Sir *Henrie* hath been Lord Prefident, from *Anno fecundo* of the Queens Majeftie, that nowe is, hethervnto.

The

The Lord Prefident and Councell aforefaid being thus eftablifhed, to have Continuaunce, are to be directed by her Maiefties Inftruccions, as heretofore hath been accuftomed.

It appereth by theefe ould Inftruccions recived, and by diuerfe other Orders, Rules, and Remembraunces, what Caufes the faid Lord Prefident and Councell have, and might have taken into theire Audience, by Reafon of theire Inftruccions and Comiffions, before the Statute for theire Eftablifhment, as aforefaid.

It appereth alfo, that the Meaninge of the Prince was ; that, for fuch Caufes that did aryfe within this Comiffion, the fame fhould be heard and determined before the faid Lord Prefident and Councell, and not at his Courts at *Weftminfter* ; for Prouff whereof,

The ould Inftruccions aforefaid.

A Letter from the Lord Chancelour of *England*, to Bufhopp *Sampfon*, Lord Prefident, commending the Heareinge of a Caufe, beinge within this Comiffion.

Another Lettre from Sir *John Gaige*, Chancelor of the Duchie of *Lancafter*, to Bifhopp *Sampfon*, Lord Prefident, to the like Effecte.

The Lord Prefident and Councell are fworen to the Performance of her Majefties Inftruccions, by the which receiving theire Direccion for the Hearinge of Caufes, as aforefaid, they have been accuftomed to receave the Complaynts of fuch Perfons, as fhall fynde them felfes greeved to be vexed in her Majefties Courts at *Weftminfter*, for Matters by her Majeftie appointed to be heard and determined before the faid Lord Prefident and Councell.

A Lettre from Bufhopp *Sampfon*, Lord Prefident, Sir *Roberte Townfhend*, Juftice, and others of the Councell to the Lord Chancelor of *England*, declaring that the Writ of *Certiorari* hath not been allowed in this Courte, from any the Kings Courts at *Weftminfter*.

That the Juftices of Affifes in theire Circuit within this Comiffion, have conformed them felfes to the Proceedings of the faid Lord Prefident and Councell ; may appeare by feuerall Lettres, to be fhewed in the Tyme of Juftice *Morvyn*, and Juftice *Portman*.

That the Lord Prefident and Councell fhall geve Direccion to the Shireff and Juftices of Peace, of each County within this Comiffion, for the Seruice of the Prince to them fignified, from her Majeftie or the Lords of the Councell.

Seuerall Lettres from the Lords of the Councell from Tyme to Tyme extant.

That the Lord Prefident and Councell fhall certefie the Elleccion of Shireffs for *Wales*, and afterwards, by *Dedimus Poteftatem*, to receave theire Recognifances and Othes, may appere by the Statute.

Lettres from the Lord Chancelor of *England* to Bufhopp *Sampfon*, Lord Prefident, fheweth fome what therof.

The Lord Prefident beinge within the Realme, and from the Place where the Councell make Abode, is to geave Direction to the reft of the Councell, and to be made Pertaker of Matters of Importance, as the Heade of the Body of the Councell ; and his Affent to be hadd to the Proceedings in Matters of Importaunce, may appere by feuerall Orders taken in *An.* 2, 3, and 4to of Kinge *Edward*, before the faid Lord Prefident and Councell ; fome whereof beringe Date at *Shrewefbury*, fome at *Worcefter*, fome at *Ludlow*, and fubfcribed by *John*, Earle of *Warwick*, then Lord Prefident ; in Teftemony of his Affent to that which was done by the reft of the Councell in his Abfence : He that nowe fupplyeth Thoffice of Clerck of the Councell, then feringe vnder Mr. *Evans*, deceaffed, that was then Clerck of the Councell, brought thefe Orders to *Bufhops Hatfield*, to the faid Lord Prefident, and procured his Hand to the fame, as may appere.

The feuerall Lettres, and Mynuts of Lettres, betweene Bufhopp *Heath*, Lord Prefident, then beinge at *London*, and the Councell then beinge in the Comiffion, fhewe, that he, then beinge Lord Prefident, gave Direccion to the reft of the Councell, althoughe he was abfent from the Place.

Touchinge

Touchinge the Diett and Order of the Howſhould, and what Allowaunce hath been, and howe the ſame hath been encreaſed, and vpon Conſideracions, and in whoſe Tymes; is to be knowen by the Inſtruccions from Tyme to Tyme; whereof ſome Remembraunces are preſently deliuered, as remayne in Thoffice of Clerck of the Councell.

Alſo, touchinge the Fines, and the Diſpoſicion thereof, the Inſtruccions from Tyme to Tyme ſerve as Warrant for the ſame. There is a Recorde, for the Payment of certayne Fees, to be made by this Councell, to certayne Gentlemen of the Comiſſion for the Princes Servis; but whether the ſame were to be payed out of the Diett, or Fynes, is not certeignly knowen.

Remembrances [b] *of principall Matters, in the Inſtruccions ſent down with Prynces* Mary, *for Prouſs of the Cauſes and Lymitts aſſigned to the Coun-ſaill in the Marches of* Wales. *An.* 17 H. VIII.

APpointement of the Prynces Counſaill and Comiſſioners, in the Parts of *Wales*, and the Marches of the ſame, for Execucion of the Matters men-cioned in the Inſtruccions　　　　　　　　　　　　　　　　　　　*Fol.* 2

The Cauſe why Matters within the Marches ſhalbe determyned by the Coun-ſaill there　　　　　　　　　　　　　　　　　　　　　　　　　　*Fol. Eod.*

The Princes, with her Counſaill, to reſyde and remayne in the Marches of *Wales*, and the Parts thereabouts　　　　　　　　　　　　　　　　*Fol. Eod.*

The Authoritie of the Counſaill by Comiſſions　　　　　　　　　　*Fol. Eod.*

The Tenor of their Comiſſions　　　　　　　　　　　　　　　　　*Fol.* 3

The principall Cauſe of eſtablyſhing of the Counſaill in the Marches for the Admyniſtracion of Juſtice　　　　　　　　　　　　　　　　　　　*Fol.* 6

The Princes fyrſt Arryvall at *Thornebury*, in the Countie of *Glouceſter*, and af-ter her Houſe there ſetled, to proceade to the Execucion of the Comiſſion of *Oier* and *Terminer*　　　　　　　　　　　　　　　　　　　　　　*Fol. Eod.*

Vpon Bills at the Sute of the Partie, Proces to be made at the Sute of the Plaintiefs, with all reaſonable Speed, retornable at a convenient Day enſuyng; and thervpon the Defendants to anſwer, and the Plaintiefs to reply *vſq; ad exi-tum*, as by theyr Diſcreacionsſhal be thought reaſonable, ſo that Juſtice be had and myniſtred, *&c.*　　　　　　　　　　　　　　　　　　　　　　*Fol.* 7

1. Twoe of the Comiſſioners to ſitt at euery Seſſions of the Peas, to be holden in euery of the Counties of their Comiſſion　　　　　　　　*Fol.* 8

2. The Counſaill, or iiij of them, to determyne Matters for Title of Landes　　　　　　　　　　　　　　　　　　　　　　　　　　　*Fol. Eod.*

3. The Counſaill to take into theyr Audience, and into theyr Rule and De-termynacions by theyr Diſcreacions, all Cauſes of Sutes, and other Variaunces and Debates depending, or growing in any of the Shires, Counties, or other Places, of any of theyr Comiſſion　　　　　　　　　　　　　　　*Fol. Eod.*

4. In which ſaid Cauſes, yf any of the Parties comytt any Contempt, Reſiſ-tance, or Diſobedience, either of there Apparaunce, or contrarie to the Mediacion, Direccion, or Determynacion, to be made or decreed, by the ſayd Counſaillours, *&c.* Attachement to be adwarded againſt hym, and ſent vp to the Privie Counſaill; or ells to be deteyned in Ward, vntill the Kings Pleaſure knowne, or that the ſaid Perſon aſſent and agree to the Decree and Determi-nacion of the ſaid Counſaill, and accordingly, indede, to execute and performe the ſame　　　　　　　　　　　　　　　　　　　　　　　　　*Fol.* 9

If any Perſon complayne to the Counſaill of any Wrong done to them, the Defendants ſhalbe ſent for by Proces, and yf they diſobey, Attachement to be adwarded, and vpon Apparaunce, Order to be taken as ſhall ſtand with ryght and good Conſcience.

[b] Ex Autog. apud Penſhurſt.

The

The Comiſſioners ſhall take Bandes of all and ſinguler Gentlemen, and Noble-men, within the Lymitts of their Comiſſion, that they ſhall not maynteyne any Matter, nor be confederat againſt the Lawe *Fol.* 10

The Counſaill ſhall dailie attende to the Reading of Bills put to them, and to anſwer them ; and theyr Anſwers ſhalbe endorced by the Clerk of the Coun-ſaill, excepte greate Cauſes, touching the Kings Realme ; or his Lordſhips lett it 11

5. The Counſaill, within the Precynct of their Comiſſions, to compound with all Offendors, for all Forfectures of Obligacions and Recognizances 15

Conſideracion to be taken, to a Matter within the Towne of *Beawdeley*, which is nowe annexed to the Countie of *Worceſter*, by the Statute of An. 34, & 35, *H.* VIII. *Eod.*

6. The Counſaill to compound and make Fynes with all Maner of outlawed Perſons, nowe being within the Precynct of theyr Comiſſion 16

An Account c *of what Money was annually allowed to the Couwnſell and Commiſſioners, in the Marches of* Wales, *An.* 3 *Edw.* VI.

THE whole Some of Money, by the Kings Ma-jeſtie, allowed to his Comiſſioners in the Marches of *Wales*, aſwell towards and for the Diet ; as for all other Chardges there arryſing, admounteth yearly to } viiiC,lxxvi *l.* xv *s.* vi *d.*

Payed by the Quarter (that is to ſaie) at euery Payment } CCxviij *l.* xviij *s.* x *d.* ob.

Fees of the Comiſſioners thereof paied.

Sir *Thomas Bromley*, Knight, *per Ann:*	xiij *l.*	vi *s.*	viij *d.*
Sir *John Pakyngton*, Knight, *per Ann.*	x *l.*		
Sir *Rice Maunxell*, Knight, *per Ann.*	x *l.*		
Sir *Thomas Holcroft*, Knight, *per Ann:*	x *l.*		
David Brooke, Sergeant at Lawe, *per Ann.*	vj *l.*	xiij *s.*	iiij *d.*
Sir *John Priſe*, Knight, *per Ann.*	xiij *l.*	vj *s.*	viij *d.*
Sir *Adam Mytton*, Knight, *per Ann.*	vj *l.*	xiij *s.*	iiij *d.*
Richard Haſſall, Eſquier, *per Ann.*	vj *l.*	xiij *s.*	iiij *d.*
George Willoughby, Eſquier, *per Ann.*	xiij *l.*	vj *s.*	viij *d.*
Richard Germyn, Eſquier, *per Ann.*	v *l.*		

Sum total is lxxxxv *l.*

Twoe Meſſengiers, *per Ann.* xl *s.* a peece iiij *l.*

William Armerer, for keaping the Kings Highnes Armor at *Ludlowe, per Ann.* } ix *l.* ij *s.* vj *d.*

William Auſty, for Solliciting of the Comiſſioners Cauſes aboue at *London, per Ann.* } v *l.*

For the Receipte and Portaige of the Diet-money, *per Ann.* } v *l.*

The Treaſurer of the Kings Majeſties Chamber, for making ſpeedie Payment of the ſaid Diet-money and in good Money, *per Ann.* } v *l.*

The Clerke of the ſaid Treaſaurer, *per Ann.* xxvj *s.* viij *d.*

The Porter there, *per Ann.* ij *s.* viij *d.*

Sum total is xxix *l.* xi *s.* x *d.*

c Ex Autog. apud Penſhurſt.

Officers Waiges.

The Stuard of the Houfhold, *per Ann.*	iiij *l.*
The twoe Cooks, xl *s. per Ann.* a Peece	iiij *l.*
Twoe Laborers of the Kitchyn, xx *s.* a Peece, *per Ann.*	xl *s.*
The Butler, *per Ann.*	xl *s.*
The Panter, *per Ann.*	xl *s.*
The Yoman of the Celler, *per Ann.*	xl *s.*
The Cater, *per Ann.*	xl *s.*
The Almner, *per Ann.*	xx *s.*
The vnder Breuer, *per Ann.*	xx *s.*

Sum total is xx *l.*

And it hath been vfed to allowe out of the Groffe Some aboue remembered, towards the Diet of the faid Comiffioners, weekly (that is to faie) for all Victualls, Fuell, and Implements of Houfhold   xiij *l.*   vi *s.*   viij *d.*

And alfo to allowe towards fforeyn Expences (that is to faie) for Rewardes, Carraiges, and all other Chargies not before remembred, *per Ann.*   C Marks.

Sir Henry Sydney *to the* [d] *Lords and others of the Queens Highnefs (Queen* Mary) *moft honourable Privie Counfaill.*

MYN humble Duetie to your Right Honorable Lordfhips. Like as I have in myn other Letters of the laft Defpeche from hence, amongeft the generall Aduertifements of the State, prefent of this Realme, made mencion of the Wants and Neade we have here of Artillary, Municion, and other Habillyments for the Warre : So nowe haue thought it expedient to addreffe vnto your Honors this Berar *Thomas Elyot*, Mr. Gunner here ; toguether with the Proporcion herin enclofed, touching the Supply of the faid Wants. And haue iudged it no leffe mete to requier the Complement therin expreffed, both to the Refournyture of fuche Things as we ar vtterly deftitute (with which no Service can be done) ; as alfo to be in Stoare and a Readynes for all Events to come ; Ihan thought the faid Berar, for the prefent, moft fitt to be fent for the chofing, trying, and forting of the Things nowe requyred in this Proporcion : Whofe Knowledge with long Experience and paynfull Practife here, in Things belonging to his Feate, with Honefty, Fidelitie, and Difcrecion, may in this Exployte alfo ferue to great Purpofe. And whear, in this Proporcion, your Lordfhip may thinke ftraunge the Demaunde of fower Thoufand of Leade : It may pleas the fame tunderftonde, a great Part therof to be ment for and towarde the Covering of a certein Tower within the Caftle of *Dublin*, whofe Rowf was taken down by my Lord of *Suffex*, and a Platfourme thereon made ; and theruppon a Cannon planted, to the great Force of that the Queenes Maiefties Piece, and Terror of thevill difpofed Sort : So as, if the fame be not in Tyme couered agayn, it wilbe the fynall Decaye of that Tower ; befide the Loffe we haue in the meane, of the neither Rowmes there, for the Beftowing of Poweder, and other Munycions wherof (being as it is) we can lay there nothing. And whear likewife it may be thought by your Wifdomes, that the Fawcions and Fawconnetts, mencioned in the faid Proporcion, fholde be here to fmall Purpofe : It is neuertheles thought here very convenient to haue fome of them ; both when Occafion fholde require (as perhappes it might come to paffe herafter, for Repreffing of great Attempts, the Nomber of Souldiors decreafing) the fame to ferue for the Felde, convenient to be aried; or ells vppon any fodeyn Landing, or Doubt of Landing of Enemyes, to be eafely drawen forth for Repulfe of fuche Hoftilitie: Where alfo there remeyneth here, difperfed in fondry Places of this Realme, certein groffe and huge Pieces of Ordennances, the Note wherof this Berar fhall exhibit and make further Declaracion therin to your Honnors; for that the fame both lacking their Cariadge, and alfo ferving here to fmall Purpofe, but rather ftande in perill of taking away, if foreyn Enemyes fholde here arryve; it may pleafe your difcrete Wifdomes to confider the fame, and (fo feaming good unto you) to take Order for the Conveighaunce therof from hens thither at Tyme and in Sort convenient. I thought it my Part, for the good Lykelyhood of good and neceffary Purpofe, to remember the faid Fawconnes and Fawconnetts, remitting the Nomber to your honorable Difcrecions, befeching your Lordfhips, weighing Thimportaunce of the neceffary Fourniture, to tender Thexpedicion of the faid Berar; and further to haue Confideracion to fupplye his Lacke of curraunt Moneye, wherof we cannot here get the half for our Moneye; being one the greteft Extremytie we fynde; and namely, when for vrgent Occafions (as at this Tyme one) fome ar to be fent thither from hens, befides thunyuerfall Smart growing euery weys therby: It may therfore pleas your Honnors, as well to ponder this State of owers, as alfo for Thinftaunt to caufe this Man to be conveniently fournifhed with Money for his Expences, comyng and going, and for the Cariage, Conveighaunce, and Tranfportacion of this his Chardge. Requiring further, that it may pleafe your Lordfhips to repofe firme Credit in his Trueth, of long Tyme tried, and to his Iudgement and Difcrecion in the Choyfe and Sorting of the Things, wherto his Knowledge (beft of any other we haue) doth ferue. And, laftly, to haue your honorable Refpects towardes the Man for his long Seruice, well and worthely beftowed here, meriting to haue Favour in his honeft and refonnable Caufes and Purfuits. So humbly taking my Leaue. At *Dublin*, this xiiiith of *Aprill*, 1559.

Your honorable Lordfhips at Comaundement,

H. Sydney.

Queen Elifabeth *to Sir* Henry Sydney [e], *on the Quarell between* Thomas *Earl of* Ormond, *and the Earl of* Defmond, *Anno* 1565.

Harry,

IF our partiall fhlendar Managing of the contentious Quarrell betwine the two *Irifche* Irells, did not make the Way to caufe thes Lines to paffe my Hande, this Geboureft fhuld hardly have cumbered your Yees; but, warned by my formar Fault, and dreading worfar Hap to come, I rede you, take good hede that the good Subjects loft State be fo revenged, that I here not the reft be won to a right By-way to brede more Traytors Stoks, and fo the Gole is gone. Make fome Difference twixt tried, juft, and falfe Frinde. Let the good Servis of well Defarvers be never rewarded with Los. Let ther Thank be fuche as may incorege mo Strivars for the like. Suffer not that *Defmonds* deninge Dedes, far wide from promifed Workes, make you truft to other Pleage, than ether him felfe or *Ibon*, for Gaige: He hathe fo well performed his *Inglefche* Vowes, that I warne you truft him no longer than you fee one of them. *Prometheus* let me be, and *Prometheus* hathe bine myne to long. I pray God your olde ftrainge Shepe late (as you fay) retorned in to Fold, wore not her wolly Garment upon her wolvy Bak. You knowe a Kingdome knowes no Kindered, *Si violandum jus regnandi caufa.* A Strength to harme is perilous, in the Hande of an ambitious Hed. Wher Myght is mixt with Wit, ther is to good an Accord in a Goverment. Effayes be oft dangerous, fpetially whan the

[e] *Ex Origin. apud Penfhurft.*

Cupberar

Cupberar hathe receved fuche a Prefarvatif, as, what met fo ever betide the Drinkars Draught, the Carier takes no Baine therby. Belive not, thogh the fwere that they can be ful found, whofe Parents foght the Rule that the full fayne would have. I warrant you, thei wyll never be accufed of Baftardy; you wer to blame to lay it to ther Charge, they will treace the Steps that others have pafed befor. If I had not efpied, thogh very late, *Leger de main*, ufed in thes Cafes, I had never plaid my Part. No, if I did not fe the Balances holde awry, I had never my felfe come into the Wayhous. I hope I fhall have fo good a Couftumer of you, that all under Officers fhall do ther Duty a-monge you. If aught have bine amys at Home, I wyll pache, thogh I cannot hole it. Let us not, nor no more do you confult fo longe, as til Advis come to late to the Givers: Whare than fhall we wifche the Dedes, while all was fpent in Wordes; a Fole to late be wares, whan all the Perrell is paft. If we ftill advife, we fhall never do; thus are we ever knitting a Knot, never tied; yea, and if our Webbe be framed with rotten Hurdells, whan our Lome is welny done, our Worke is new to begin. God fend the Wever true Prentiffes again, and let them be Denizins, I pray you, if the be not Sitecins; and fuche to as your anciants Aldermen, that have, or now dwell in your official Place, have had beft Caufe to comende ther good Behaviour. Let this Memoriall be only committed to *Vulcanes* bafe Keping. Without any longer Abode, than the Leafure of the Reding therof, yea, and with no Mention made therof to any other Wight. I charge you, as I may comande you. Seme not to have had but Secretaries Letters from me.

Your lovinge Maiftres,

ELIZABETH *R.*

Sir Henry Sydney [f] *to his Son* Philip Sydney, *at School at* Shrewfbury, *An.* 1566. 9 Eliz. *then being of the Age of* XII *Years.*

I Have reaceaved too Letters from you, one written in *Latine*, the other in *French*; which I take in good parte, and will yow to exercife that Practife of Learninge often: For that will ftand yow in mofte fteade, in that Profeffion of Lyf that yow are born to live in. And, fince this ys my firft Letter that ever I did write to yow, I will not, that yt be all emptie of fome Advyfes, which my naturall Care of yow provokethe me to wifhe you to folowe, as Documents to yow, in this your tendre Age. Let your firft Actyon be, the Lyfting up of your Mynd to Almighty God, by harty Prayer, and felyngly dyfgeft the Woords you fpeake in Prayer, with contynuall Medi-tation, and Thinkinge of him to whom you praye, and of the Matter for which you praye. And ufe this as an ordinarye, at, and at an ordynarye Hower. Whereby the Time yt felf will put yow in Remembraunce to doe that, which yow are accuftomed to doe. In that Tyme apply your Study to to fuche Houres as your difcrete Maifter dothe affign yow, earneftlye; and the Time (I knowe) he will fo lymitt, as fhalbe both fufficient for your Learninge, and faf for your Health. And mark the Sens, and the Matter, of that yow reade, as well as the Woordes. So fhall yow bothe enrieche your Tonge with Woordes, and your Wytte with Matter; and Judgment will growe as Yeares growyth in you. Be humble and obedient to your Mafter, for unles yow frame your felfe to obey others; yea, and feale in your felfe, what Obedience ys; yow fhall never be able to teache others how to obey yow. Be curteefe of Gefture, and affable to all Men, with Diverfitee of Reverence, accordinge to the Dignitie of the Perfon. Ther ys nothinge, that wynneth fo muche with fo lytell Coft. Ufe moderate Dyet, fo as, after your Meate, yow may find your

Wytte freſher, and not duller, and your Body more lyvely, and not more heavye. Seldome drinke Wine, and yet ſometime doe, leaſt, beinge enforced to drinke upon the ſodayne, yow ſhould find yourſelfe inflamed. Vſe Exer-ciſe of Bodye, but ſuche as ys without Peryll of your Yointes or Bones. It will encreaſe your Force, and enlardge your Breathe. Delight to be cleanly, as well in all Partes of your Bodye, as in your Garments. It ſhall make yow gratefull in yche Company, and otherwiſe lothſome. Give your ſelf to be merye, for yow degenerate from yowr Father, yf you find not yowr ſelf moſt able in Wytte and Bodye, to doe any Thinge, when yow be moſt mery : But let your Myrthe be ever void of all Scurilitee, and bitinge Woords to any Man, for an Wound given by a Woorde, is oftentimes harder to be cured, then that which is given with the Swerd. Be you rather a Herer, and Bearer away of other Mens Talke, then a Begynner or Procurer of Speeche, otherwiſe yow ſhalbe counted to delight to heare your ſelf ſpeake. Yf you heare a wiſe Sentence, or an apt Phraſe, commytte yt to your Memorye, with reſpecte of the Circumſtaunce, when yow ſhall ſpeake yt. Let never Othe be hard to come out of your Mouthe, nor Word of Rybaudrye ; deteſt yt in others, ſo ſhall Cuſtome make to your ſelf a Lawe againſt hit in your ſelf. Be modeſt in yche Aſſemble, and rather be rebuked of light Felowes, for Meden lyke Shamefaſtnes, then of your ſad Frends for pearte Boldnes. Thinke upon every Woorde that yow will ſpeake, before yow utter hit, and remembre how Nature hathe rampared up (as yt were) the Tonge, with Teeth, Lippes, yea, and Here with out the Lippes, and all betokeninge Raynes, or Bridles, for the looſe Uſe of that Membre. Above all Thinges tell no Untruthe, no not in Tri-fels. The Cuſtome of hit is naughte, and let it not ſatiſie yow, that, for a Time, the Hearers take yt for a Truthe; for after yt wilbe knowen as yt is, to your Shame ; for ther cannot be a greater Reproche to a Gentellman, then to be accounted a Lyare. Study and endevour your ſelf to be vertuouſly occupied. So ſhall you make ſuch an Habite of well doinge in yow, that yow ſhall not knowe howe to do Evell, thoughe you wold. Remember, my Sonne, the noble Blood yow are deſcended of, by your Mothers Side ; and thinke that only, by vertuous Lyf and good Action, yow may be an Ornament to that illuſtre Famylie ; and otherwiſe, throughe Vice and Slouthe, you ſhalbe counted *labes generis*, one of the greateſt Curſes, that can happen to Man. Well (my litell *Philippe*) this is ynough for me, and to muche I fear for yow. But, yf I ſhall finde that this light Meale of Diſgeſtione nouriſhe any thinge the weake Sto-make of your yonge Capacitie, I will, as I find the ſame growe ſtronger, fead yt with toefer Foode.

Your lovinge Father, ſo long as you lyve in the Feare of God,

H. Sydney.

ⁱ Sir Henry Sydney, *Lord Deputy of* Ireland, *to Mr. Secretary* Cecill.

ALbeit my Lettres of Yeſterdaies Date (as I take it) weare not gone at the Arryvall of *William Peirs* here this Morninge : Yet I thought good to lett them paſſe, and accompany them with this other of myne, in Ainſwere of yours received by him. For, I aſſure you, Sir, I woulde, with all my Harte, that you knewe and felt all my Thoughtes and Conceiptes, that I have of any Man, or any Matter touchinge the Service in this Lande (ſo ſimple is myne Intende-ment) as ſenſiblie I feale them my ſelf. I have greate Cauſe to reioice, that my ill compoſed Lettres founde ſoe gratious Acceptacion. I ment well, writte tru-ly, an as I thought. I will neuer, vnpreſſid, vppon my Alleageaunce, deale in the great Matters of my Lord of *Ormounde*, vntill an other Chauncellor come, or ſome other Commiſſioner out of *Englaunde*, to be ioyned with me, for the

Heareinge and Determyninge of that Caufe ; for, howe indifferently foeuer I fhall deale, I know it will not be thought favorably enoughe on my Lord of *Ormoundes* Side. And, I affure you, Sir, if I ferved vnder the cruelliſt Tirant that ever tyranifed, and knewe him affeted on the one or the other Side, in a Matter betweene Partie and Partie referred to my Iudgement, I woulde rather offende his Affection, and ftande to his Mifericord, than offende myne owne Confcience, and ftande to Godes Iudgment. Moche more I dare be boulde vprightly to doe, feruinge and lyvinge vnder foe Chriftian and Iuſt a Princes as I doe : And, before God, Sir, this I proteſt to you, that I write not this in Preiudicacion of my Lord of *Ormoundes* Caufe, for I know not, nor coniecture, but that it may as well fall owt on my Lord of *Ormoundes* Side, as on the others; but I finde that I am foreiudgid of. Therefore, I befeeche you, Sir, let me have fome other, then any yet is here, to be ioyned with me, before I fhall enter into the Diffcuffion of the Matter, as well for the finall Sentenſinge of it, without further Appeale, as for advoidinge Infamie to my felf.

I pity Mr. *Stukeley*, as you doe, and nowe he repairethe into *Englande* ; he hoped here to have fetled, beinge well allied to dyvers Noble Men here, and in great Towardnes to mary the Earle of *Worcesters* Sifter.

If any Good come of the Intelligence of *Oneills* Intendement, *Stukeley* is to be thanked for it. And for the Weight of th' Office which I recommended him to, only by my particuler Lettres to you, my Lord of *Penbrooke*, and my Lord of *Leicefter*, from all which I had before received very favorable Lettres in his Behalf. Suche it is as heretofore, and no longer agoe, then in my Lorde *Lenardes* Governement, the Marfhall of his Hall was Marfhall of the Armie. And the Office was, and is, of the Deputies Gifte. The Bargaine for the Lande, as in my other Lettres I writte, was made betweene *Bagnall* and him, before I knewe of it : And, that beinge his, I knowe noe Man, if the Queene wolde have Peace withe *Oneill*, that better coulde pleafe him, nor no Man, if her Highnes woulde have Warre, that more woulde annoy him ; and this moved me to confent to it, and yet I nether defier it, nor perfwade it. I fpare particulerly to wright, howe to make this intended Warre on *Oneill*, till the Arryvall of Mr. Vicechamberlaine ; for that my Opynion then may carrie withe it Refolution of vs bothe, and others ; but for the Tyme, what Yeare foever, the Queene will beginne this Warre : Yt muſt be begonne aboute the middeſt of *September*, and not to be looked to be ended, before *Midfomer* followinge. In which Tyme, by the Grace of God, if the Warre be dilligently followed, he may be fubdued to Order, killed, or an other eftablifhed in his Place, whereby the Queen fhalbe in good Sewerty to have Service of that Countrey at Pleafure, where nowe fhe hathe none. Her Landes, Rightes, and Dueties, due to her by others, and now detayned from her by him. And Peace and Quiet emonge her People, where there is nowe nothinge but Warre and Diftruccion, and foche a Subiection as may be equall in Obedience withe the beſt of the *Irifhe*. But if her Highnes meane foche a totall Extirpacion of him, and his, foe as there fhall neuer be *Oneill* more ; and either to bringe the People to the iuſt Rule of *Englifhe* Lawe, or to banifhe them quite, and vnpeople the Soile, by Inducement of Collonies, *hoc aliud eſt*, but yet optable and fezible, but with moche more Charge and Tyme : For then looke for noe founde Freindfhippe at anye original *Irifhes* Hande, for eche will thinke that his Staffe ſtandethe next to that Dore. And withall, the Conqueſt of *Leix*, and *Offaully*, is to be remembred, which I am fuer hathe coſt the Queene, and this Countrey, more then woulde purchafe fo moche Rent, tenne Tymes tolde, in *Englande*. Good Mr. Secretary, let me knowe her Majefties Pleafure, in the Choice of theis Proceedinges, which will expedite a Refolution of our Confultacion, and fhorten our Difcours of the fame.

Who foeuer fhal be Chauncellor here, and have no other Lyving here, but 500 *l.* yerelie for his Office. Yf his Lyvinge be not the greater in *Englande*, he fhall eyther lyve here like a Mifer, or come Home a Begger, as I am lyke to doe. I write plainelie that whiche I knowe certainelye.

Yf ever there be Faulte founde for Partiality in Sir *Warhame Sentleger*, let it be my Faulte, afwell as his ; he hathe alreadie done good Service to the gret Quiet of the Countye of *Waterforde* ; doubtles, he is an honeft and a fufficyent Man. O, Sir, I never promifed that the Countrey fhoulde beare the Charge of the Counfell in *Mounfter* ; I doe not, nor never I will doe, any Thinge ells but my true Service, and the Imployment of my vttermoft Indeavor ; nor I wot not whie it fhoulde be looked for in *Mounfter*, which was never had in *Walles*, nor the Northe of *Englande :* Let my Difcourfes be confidered, and conie&ture of the Succes. I intend to plant withe Reafon, and water withe Iuf- tice ; but God muft give the Increafe.

I befeeche you, Sir, remember the Order for the Starre-Chamber, and War- raunt for Leade.

I perceive it is thought, that I am a Staie of Sir *Nicholas Arnoldes* Aboade here. Oh the Mallice of Man. Sir, I never ftaied him, favinge, at my firfte Comminge, he tolde me, that if he might ftaie one Monethe, or fomewhat more, he woulde make Declaracion of juft Checke, and Controllmente, to the Queenes Advantage, of a great Maffe of Money. I required him, that he woulde make Speede, the rather for that I had no Au&thoritie to make out Warraunte, but accordinge to his Controllmente, and Checke : He faide he woulde, but yet I have it not ; but nowe he faiethe, I fhall. Three Monethes are paft, and more, in which Tyme, fuer he hathe beene litell idell ; I have callid vppon him dai- ly for it, or to goe away, and leave the reft, to give it me, and yet I ftaie him (as they faie). Yt is faide, that I fought this Office. My Declara&ion thereof I at large have written, in my Lettres to the Lordes of the Counfell, which I befeeche you, Sir, as I maie have Caufe to think you love me, fpeake of pub- lickley. Yt is faide alfo, that I have been an evill Speaker of the Erle of *Suf- fex.* God deeme me to die without Confcience, or Confeffion of Synne, if ever I fpake worfe of him, then I have done to you ; and fpare not you to fpeak, to my Condemnacion, the worft that I have faide of him to you. I write not this to flatter him, foe farre fourthe as he is my Foe : But that Evill come to me and myne, I pray God, that I wifhe to him. My Wief returnethe you freindly Commendacions, multyplied by Millions on her Parte, bothe to your felf and to my Lady. And now I befeeche you, Sir, remember that I have paf- fed three Monethes of my three Yeres Peregrination, in this Purgatory, the vt- termoft Tyme promifed by her 'Majeftie of my Service here. But if the Daies might be fhortned for the 'Ele&t Sake, happy weare I. And thus with my harty Commendacions to you, and to my Lady your Wief, I wifhe you both a longe happie' Lief. In Haft, this xvijth of *Aprill*, 1566.

your affured to commaund,

H. Sydney.

P. S. I muft be in the Confines of *Oneills* Countrey, the lafte of this Monethe, to parle withe him ; or ells he will do Hurte, before I fhall be rea- die to offende.

Sir Henry Sydney, *to Mr. Secretary* Cecill.

S I R,

ALbe it, I have lytle to faye vnto you at this Tyme, that hath not beene ymparted by me to Mr. Vicechamberlaine, whofe Wifdom, Dilligence, and Habilytie, to conceyve the State of this Countrey, might excufe me to write any Thinge particulerlie of the fame. Yet lyke as, before his Com- minge, my Lettres of the viijth of *Marche*, dire&ted to the Right Honorable the Earle of *Leicefter*, and emparted withe the Queenes Majeftie, and the hole Counfaile, did premonifhe you of the Perill ymynent to this Eftate ; foe have I thoughte it my Part, vpon foche other Occurrentes, as fall out vpon *Oneilles*
Pra&tizes,

Practizes, to let you vnderſtand what he hathe done, ſince our late Diſpatche of *William Peirs.*

Maguier, the Capten of *Fermanaughe*, hathe beene of late invadid by *Oneill*, and totally expulſed owte of his Countrey; who beinge not able to withſtande the Force of his Enemye, fled into *Oreileighs* Countrey, his near Kinſman, for Succour, bringinge with him the Nomber of 5000 Kyne, beſides other Studde and Goodes, whiche was immediately taken from him by *Oreylleighs* Sonnes, Servaunts to *Oneill.* He, vpon Reſpect never to violate his Fidellitie and Obedyence to her Majeſtie, is with ſome Difficultie eſcaped from thence, and hathe preſented himſelf before me to ymplore her Majeſties Juſtice and Comyſſeration towardes him. His Brother, beinge nowe become *Oneilles* Servaunte, is poſſeſſed by him of the mors Part of that Countrey: All which *Maguyer* himſelf might have poſſeſſed with all Quietnes, if he woulde but have conſented to have bent his Freindſhippe to *Oneill*, and to that Point, to have alienated his Obedience from her Majeſtie. You ſee nowe, by this Expulſion of *Maguyer*, one Degree towardes the Tyranizing over the reſt; ſuſpected by me in all my former Lettres. And to this there is come to my Knowledge, by the Report of a Servaunt of myne owne, one *Dowglas*, an *Engliſhe Scott* (whom I ſent latelye into *Scotlande*, for my neceſſary Proviſions of Jacks, Sculles, and ſoche like) that *Oneil* hathe had a Gentleman of his Countrey, remayninge a good While withe the Earle of *Argile*; which Earle, at my Mans beinge at *Edenboroughe*, brought him thither to the Courte, where he had good Entertainement, duringe his Aboade.

The Erle, as my Man vnderſtode, hath confeſſed himſelf to be moche beholdinge to *Shane*, in that he offered him Releif here, in the Tyme of his Baniſhment; for which Cauſe he ſaiethe he meanithe to viſite him this Sommer. *Oneill* havinge nowe learned, that a Man of myne hathe diſcovered his Mans beinge withe th'Erle of *Arguile*, at the Courte, hathe excuſed to me, by an honeſt and grave Gentleman, Mr. Juſtice *Doudall*, that the Cauſe of his Servaunts Repaire to the Courte, was, for that th'Erle was deſirous to ſhewe the monſtrous Glybbe, which he ware vpon his Heade; and that otherwiſe he ſent him, but vpon ordynary Meſſage, in Reſpecte of the Allyance betwene them. All this confirmethe my Opynion of ſome great Confederacye and Combynacion of the *Skotte* and *Shane.* And, therefore, to you I vtter it, requiringe you to way the Circomſtances, and to declare this to the Queenes moſt excellent Majeſtie, who if ſhe provide not for theis Miſcheifes in Tyme, muſt look for none other Yſſue herein, then happened to *Callayes*, in the Raigne of her Highnes Siſter, Queene *Marie.* And havinge made a Choice of you, to reveale theis Thinges, bothe becauſe you doe conceive the Daunger of the Practice, the vtter Maime and Diſhonor, that ſhould enſue to her Majeſtie, if any other ſhoulde ſubdue or tyraniſe this Realme: I doubt not but you will earneſtly ioyne with Mr. Vicechamberlaine, for a ſpedie and a neceſſary Reſolucion in theis great Cauſes of Ymportaunce, concerning the Chaſteſinge of *Oneill*, before he growe more ſtronge and perillous; and ſoe, withe my moſt harty Thanks, for the Friendſhips which I daily fynde at your Hands, I bid you as my ſelf Farewell. Ffrom *Killmayneham*, the ixth of *June*, 1566.

Your aſſured, lovinge Freinde,

H. Sydney.

Sir Henry Sydney's *Letter to Mr. Secretary* Cecill, *ſent by Sir* William Fitz-William.

S I R,

I AM moſt hartely glad to here of your Recovery, which Almightie God parfectly confyrme, and longe contynue. I reaceved the Queenes and yours, of the xiiijth of the laſt, the xvth of this preſent; Coppies of the Queenes

weare

weare to common, for here weare dyvers, before the Arryvall of the Orygi-
nall; the Interpretacion and Amplification, by the Bringers whereof, was
foche as I feare, will, and hathe done more Hurt to the comon Quiet
of this Countrey, then the Procurer of the Lettre, or any one Man wilbe
able to doe Good; for wheareas Coine and Lyvery was foe extinguifhed, as it
was noe wheare harde of, in the Countyes of *Waterford* and *Kilkenny*, and foche
a Confidence and Corage conceved of all Hands, that it fhoulde neuer be put in
Vfe againe, but that the Queene, of her Juftice and Pity of fo many Thou-
fandes of her oppreffed Subiectes, woulde fee the auncyent Lawes of this her
Realme, nowe revyued, to be obayed. It is nowe bruted by fome of theis Coppy
Carryers, that I am commaunded, by that Lettre, to fuffer Coyne and Lyvery
to contynue, to the vnfpeakeable Greif of all the Honeft and Grave; and to
the great Reioyfinge of the Light and Lewde; and moft of all, to the Derogation of the Authoritye of Lawe; for that fyve feverall Parliamentes have made
the Takeinge of it Felony, and fome one Treafon, or ells my Memorye failethe
me. For my Difcreditt I force not, for I truft, before this Tyme, her Highnes is refolued to revoke me, accordinge to my humble and earneft Suite made,
afwell by my Lettres fent by *Peirs*, as my Suite by Mr. Vicechamberlaine; and
doubtles, Sir, moche better, and more for the Queenes Service it fhalbe, to revoke me, then to kepe me in Difcreditt, as nowe I am, beinge dyrected by a
pryvate Mans Parfwacion, grounded vpon a bare Reporte, in Matters of Waight,
publicke, and concernynge the vnyverfall State of the Realme. And I affure
you, Sir, there was of the Earle of *Ormounds* faithfull, difcreete, and well trufted Followers, that of themfelues lamented to me that Parte of the Lettre, fayinge that *Olypher Grace* only procured my Lord of *Ormound* to move the
Queene foe to write; for my Parte I am content to be fcilent in it, and in anye
Thinge of mine owne Invencion, and will invent noe more; vppon Truft that I
am alreadie revoked. But, if the Countrey finde Offenders in it accordinge to
Lawe, doubtles I will not hinder the Lawe, it is againft my Oathe. All other
Thinges materiall in the Lettre weare done before the Receipt of it, as the For-
biddinge of the Commyffioners in *Mounfter* to deale in any Matters betwene the
Earles, before the Earle of *Ormoundes* Retorne; and the Difcharge of the Lord
of *Dunboine* from any Captenery in the County of *Tipporary*, which, inclufiue, is
done by takeinge away Coyne and Lyvery; and foe dothe it from the Erle of
Ormounde the Captenery of the County of *Kilkenny*, which I thinke wone Coyne
and Lyvery foe great a Patronage. Of this Lettre I would make larger Anfwere, weare I not in Hope to vnderftand of my Revocation from this myferable and accurfed Iland, by the next Eaft Wynd. If I be conftrayned, with Confirmation of any Continuance to tarry here any longer, I will write more largely of this and other Matters. In the meane Tyme, Sir, procure Regarde, with
Execution, to be had to this Countrey, accordinge to former Devyfes and Adver-
tifments, and I pray you, Sir, acquaint your felf withe that which I did nowe
write to my Lord of *Leceifter*, and perfwade her Maieftie, and the Lordes of
her Councell, to confider it, and to provide with Spede for this Countrey. If
they doe not, if I have any Iudgement, we fhall fee as evill an Event of *Irelande*, as (with wofull Memory) we may remember of *Callaies*. I can doe no
more but fpeake and wryte; on there Charge be it that may doe. Howe I
have delt withe your Cofen *Bryan FitzWilliam*, I leave to his Report. Suerly
I have delt in my Confcience truly with the Queene, and yet freindly withe him.
I befeeche you, Sir, be good to this Bringar, my Brother *Fitz-William*. In
my Confcience he is a true Man in all his Seruice and Charges to the Queenes
Maieftie; what fryuolous Obiections weare made againfte him, by *Brymyngiam*,
for a huge Debt, of late written of againft him to Mr. Vicechamberlaine, you
may vnderftande, by other of them, or by the Informer, *Brymyngiam*. Doubtles I durfte be bound, vpon Forfeite of all my Lande, that he hathe not wittingly
deceaved the Queene in nothinge; and for his Checks, I doe not thinke that the
Queene fhall gaine moche aboue that which he hathe ever confeffed. In Det

fure I thinke he is, and yet farre from that Somme which hath beene reported. He hathe deferved well, which is not to be forgotten, if it weare but one Dayes Service : In which he faued the Honor of our Nation in this Lande, and the Lyves of as many *Englifhe* Men as weare on Foote that Daie in the Feilde. I pray you, Sir, freinde him, for in Trothe he is honeft. *Oneill* fortefyethe ftronglie, the Caftells wone of *Odonell* and *Maguier*. The Earle of *Arguile* wilbe withe him in *July* next ; he hathe fled all his Cattell beneathe *Armaughe* farre. I fend you herewith the Depofition of certaine Parfons, toucheing a Prodige of late feene in *Couley*, in this Realme ; doubtles there was foche a Thinge feene. I have no more, but befeechinge Almightie God to bles you, and yours, with a longe happy Lief, I take my Leaue of you. From *Kilmaynham*, in Hafte, as may appeare by the Writinge of it, this xxiiiith of *June*, 1566.

Your affured Freinde to commaunde,

H. Sydney.

PS. I pray you, Sir, commende me moft hartely, and my Wief, to my Lady *Bacon*, and to my Lady, your Wief.

Sir Henry Sydney *to* Robert Dudley, *Earl of* Leicefter, *fent by Sir* Nicholas Arnold.

My deareft Lorde,

SINCE this Gentleman, Sir *Nicholas Arnolde*, dothe now repaire into *Eng-lande*, to render Accompt of his longe and painefull Service, leaft my Science might be an Argument of my Condemnacion of him, I thought good to accompany him with theis my Lettres, certyfinge your Lordfhip, by the fame, that I finde he hathe beene a mervelous painefull Man, and very dilligent in Enquiry for the Queenes Advantage, and in proceadinge in the fame more feuere, then I woulde have wifhed him, or would have beene my felf in femblable Service ; but he fayethe he followed his Inftruccions. Doubtles the Thinges whiche he did deale in, are very darke and intricate, by Reafon of the longe Tyme paffed without Accompt. And he greatly impeached, for Lacke of an Auditor, as I take it. In Trothe, what will fall out of it, I cannot faye, but I feare he hathe written too affirmatively vppon *Brymyngehams* Informacion : It is reported by fome of his Adverfaries, that he fhold trivmphe greatly vppon a Lettre, fuppofed to be fent him lately from your Lordfhip, as thoughe, by the fame, he fhold be encouraged to procead more vehemently againft the Erle of *Suffex*, and to make his Aboad longer here, then ells he woulde. And that he fhoulde vfe this Bravery, either by fheweinge this Lettre, or by Speach to me and to others. My Lord, I beleeue the Hole of this to be vntrue ; and, for fo moche as concernethe my felfe, I affure your Lordfhip is a ftarke Lie ; for albeit he hathe fhewed me, as I beleue, all the Lettres your Lordfhip hathe fent him, fince myne Arryvall here, and a good many fent before, yet in none of them is there any foche Matter conteined ; neither yet did he to me, or, to my Knowledge, to eny other, of any Lettre fent by your Lordfhip, make any foche Bravery, or like Conftruccion, as is reported.

My deareft Lord and Brother, without any Refpecte of me, or any brother-like Loue borne me by you ; but even for our naturall Countrees Caufe (where-vnto, of late, not a litell to your farre fpreadinge Fame, you fhewe your felf moft willingly to put to your indefatigable and moche helpinge Hande) helpe to revoke me from this Regiment, for, beinge not credited, this Realme will ruin vnder my Rule, haply to my Shame ; but vndoubtedly to *Englandes* Harme. Yea and will vnder any Man, whom the Queene fhall fende, thoughe he have the Force of *Hercules*, the Magnanimity of *Cæfar*, the Dillygence of *Alexander*, and the Eloquence of *Tully* : Her Highnefs withdrawinge her gracious Counte-naunce. Yea if it be but thought, that her Highnes hathe not a refolute and vnremoveable Lykeinge of him ; as for noe Tale fhe will direct him to faile by

I

any

any other Compas then his owne. His Shippe of Regiment, who so ever he be, shall soner rushe on a Rocke, then rest in a Haven. I write not this, as thoughe I thought Governours here could not erre, and soe erre, as they should be revoked. For I knowe and confesse, that any one may soe erre, yea, without any evill Intent to her Highnes Crowne or Countrie, as it shalbe convenyent and necessary to revoke him ; but let it be done then withe Spede. Yea if it be but conceived, that he be insufficyent to governe here, I meane of the Soveraigne, or Magistrates, retire him, and send a newe Man to the Helme. *Episcoparum eius accipiat alter :* Soe as my Counsaile is (and you shall fynde it the soundest) that the Governours Contynuaunce here, and his Countenaunce there, be concurrent and correlative. For, while her Highnes will emploie any Man here, all the Countenaunce, all the Creditt, all the Commendacion, yea and most absolute Truste that may be, is litell enoughe. Cause once Appearinge to withdrawe that Opynion, withdrawe him to, if it be possible, even in that Instaunt. Of this I woulde write more largely, and more partyculerly, and to the Queenes Maiestie, and to all my Lords, weare it not, that my many Lettres in this Forme already written, togeather withe sondry Arguments of my crased Credit there, did put me in Hope of a speedy Redemtion from this my misereable Thraldome. A Resolucion of which, my Hope, my derest Lord, procure me with Speede : I have no more, but *Sub vmbra alarum tuarum protegat me Deus.* In Haste I take my Leave of your Lordship, wishinge to the same present increasinge, and immortall Felycitie. From *Kilmaynham,* the xxviiith of *June,* 1566.

Your Lordships bounden, faste,

and obedient Brother,

H. Sydney.

PS. I assure your Lordship, I doe knowe that Sir *Nicholas Arnold* hathe spente, above all his Enterteignement, 500 *l.* Sterlinge in this Realme. I meane he hathe spent so moche in this Realme.

Sir Henry Sydney, *to* Robert *Earl of* Leicester, *sent by the Archbishop and Primate of* Ardmaghe.

My derest Lord,

I Have long forborne to send any Advertysementes into *England,* because, since the first Daie of this Monthe, I have beene howerly in Expectacion for Newes from thence, and especially for the Supplie of Men and Money necessary for the Extirpacion of the Tyraint and Traytor *Shane Oneill.* And albeit this Bearer, my Lord Prymate, havinge seene, and, I suppose, noted the Actions of the Rebell, can sufficiently report and testifie the Insolency of him : Yet have I thought good to advertise to your Lordship thus moche of his Doinges. About the xxvith of this laste Monethe, I was certainely informed, that he would fourthwith repaire to the Borders with his hole Force to invade the *Englishe* Pale ; wheather he came indeede, and therein confirmed my Opynion in my former Lettres to the Queenes Maiestie, wherein I iudged, that, after the Begyninge of *August,* he woulde breake out into Warre. His Comynge knowen, yt was thought mete, that I, likewise, withe a convenyent Force, shoulde repaire to *Dundalke,* whiche Force gathered thoroughe the Willingnes of the People within twoe Daies, I repaired thether withe the Garrison, and the Countrey People, to the Nomber (as I suppose) 1500 Footemen, and six hundreth Horsemen ; and, in the meane Season, receved Lettres of him of dyvers Effecte, some humbly vrgeinge a Parlyament, and others full of Insolency, refusinge to be any Subiecte to those that shoulde kepe or assiste his Servaunt *Maguyer* (as he tearmed him). Notwithstandinge, beinge advertised that he had taken an Othe to give vs Battell, if we issued out of *Dundalke,* I marched forthe to the Hill Foote wheare he incamped, and there

contynued

contynued till the Eveninge, without any Matter offered, favinge fmale Skir-myfhes. The next Daie, likewife, we went agayne to the Mouthe of his Paartis, and thoroughe the greateft. All which Tyme he kept himfelf in his Faft-nes, without offeringe any Fight, favinge withe a fewe Horfemen, and cer-tayne Kearne, whereof Part weare flayne; on our Part none hurte, favinge one of the Earle of *Kildares* Gentlemen wounded, with a *Scottifhe* Arrowe, and the Earle himfelf, with defperate Followinge of a Horfeman into a Pace, fhot throughe his Sloppe of his Hofe with a Callyver, but not hurt. At our Retorne to *Dundalke*, yt was thought meete that neceffary Force fhoulde be lefte to de-fende the Townes, and that the reft fhoulde repaire, fome being therevnto con-ftrayned thoroughe the Want of Victualls. Within twoe Daies after my De-parture thence, *Oneill* made a Rode into the Pale, and for Lacke of due Ob-fervation of my former Commaundements (wherein the People were willed to ftripe their Houfes) he burned certaine Villages in the Border, whereof the cheif was the *Haggard*. The next Day he repaired to *Dundalke*, and befeiged that Towne, wheare I had lefte the Soldiers vnder the Leadinge of Captayne *Bryan Fitz Williams*. The Towne was, of it felf, fo ruynous, as it was fkarfe gardable; and, befides, of foe great Circuite, that it offered no fmall Difad-vauntage to the Defendaunts. The *Irifhe* entred the Towne, but had foch a Welcome, as the Traytor lofte there of his Gentlemen fo many, as, I was cre-deblie enformed, there weare feventene of there Countrey Horfelytters filled with deade Courfes, and fent to be buried at *Ardmaghe*; befides thofe that he buryed neire the Towne, which, as fome of them have confeffed, weare about the Nomber of a hundreth. Thofe, that weare flayne within the Walles, doe nowe garnifhe the Gates withe there Heades. But foche was the Repulfe, as he coulde not procuer any more of his Men to followe the Enterprice. And fuer, my Lord, it was manfully and honorably defended. From thence he departed towardes *Carlingforde*, where he made a Shewe, as thoughe he would have at-tempted that Towne. Nevertheles, he did nothinge, but departed withe Speede to the fardeft Parte of *Vlfter*, to treate withe the *Scottes* to have Affiftaunce of them. I am certaynly informed, that he offered to them of *Kintier* all *Clande-boy*, all the geld Kyne of his Cuntrey; to delyver *Soreleboye*, and to give them Pledge and Affuraunce for his Fidelytie towards them. But I, feareinge this before hand, have fo temporyfed withe the Capteine of *Kintier Sorley* his Bro-ther, that they have vtterly refufed his Requeftes, as I am certainely advertyfed, and, without Hope of Ayde and Releif from thence, he is nowe returned a-gaine to the Borders.

To avoyde alfoe that Practice that he might make in *Connaught*, I late-ly fent for the Earle of *Clanrycarde*, and Mr. *William Ewter*, vpon whofe Factions all the inteftine Warres in *Connaght* hathe growen; they bothe re-payred vnto me this lafte Weeke to *Dublyn*, vttred their Greife the one againft the other, had the fame ordered and determyned, and the Freindfhipe compound-ed by folemne Oathe and Profeffion; on which they bothe departed fatisfyed, promifinge Ayde, and themfelves in Perfons, withe all the Lords of that Pro-vince, to ferve her Maieftie this Iorney, and to come vpon *Oneill* thoroughe *Tyreconell*. And, lyke as I am made beleive, that Mr. *William* hathe never heretofore repaired to any Governour, foe have I noted in him that Conformy-tie and Shewe of Conftancy, that I have not founde in any other of his Sorte. For, albeit th'Erle of *Thomonde*, very rafhely and vndutyfully (as I here) hathe invaded his Countrie in his Abfence, and wounded twoe of his Brethren: Yet, afer his Departure from me, heareinge of this, he fent me Worde, that, thoughe it weare an Iniury able to difcourage him, yet woulde he not breake any Parte of his Promife made to me on the Behalf of the Q. Maieftie. My Lord, I thinke my felf not a lytell bounde to God for this newe compounded Amytye, by which Meanes I ftand affured of good Obedyence throughe the moft Part of that Province of *Connaught*. But lyke as herein I fynde myfelf well fatif-fied, and hope alfo, that I have foe temporyfed with the *Scottes*, as they will not be haftely allured to ioyne with the Rebell: Soe when I have Regard to

I

the

the Doinge in *Mounſter*, I finde there great Cauſe to doubt Diſquiett; for as, in my laſt Letter by *Finche*, I partly touched the Deſparacion of *Deſmonde*. So nowe have I not only founde great Arguments of his Wilfulnes by ſoche Things as I have lerned from Sir *Warham Seintleger*, but alſoe feare ſome ill Effectes of his late Doings in thoſe Parts: For this I learne for certaine, that he is retyred into the County of *Kerry*, and hathe ſpoyled the Lord *Fitzmoryce*, and one other of his Name, beinge his owne Kynſman, and there remaynethe with a Band of twoe thouſande Men. He giveth fourthe alſoe to his Freindes, which cometh to my Eares, that Promiſe is broken withe him in *England*, and the Articles infringed taken betwene him, and the Earle of *Ormounde*. And even this Daie I received Letters from the Portryſs and Soveraigne of *Clominell*, that th'Erle threatnethe to diſtrene of them for Rente, which th'Erle of *Ormondes* Offycer hath already taken. Sir *Moryce Fitzgarold* alſoe doubtethe his Invaſions, into which Riotts and Rowts yf he hedlonge fall, and ſoe into the Forfeyture of the Bandes acknowledged, your Lordſhip may iudge howe farre from Reformacion thoſe Partes wilbe. For Preventinge whereof, I have omytted noe Pointe of Lenytie or Perſwacion, nether to charge him vpon his Duty and Allegiaunce, neither to remember what he is lyke to be, nor what he ought to be, eſpeacially in this perilous Tyme. I have partly thus touched to your Lordſhip the preſente Condicion of *Ulſter*, *Connaught*, and *Mounſter*.

The fourthe Parte I fynde ſoe lovinge, conformable, and dutyfull, as in all *Leinſter*, I ſee not a Thing ſomoche to be hated amongs honeſt Men, as the Ingratitude of him whom your Lordſhip ſomoche commended, I meane, Sir *Edmounde Butler*, who bothe vnnaturally and diſhonorably hathe procured Letters to me from the Queenes moſt excellent Maieſtie, heavie and bitter to ſo inocent a Mynde as (I thanke God) I beare; wherein it apperethe, that for a Matter of xvj *d*, he ſtode indicted, and ſhoulde be arrayned, and therefore was I commaunded not to ſuffer his Lief or Lybertie to be touched. And althoughe I have partly heretofore, upon the Speache that ſoche a Lettre ſhoulde come, offered my Excuſe to the Lordes of the Counſaile: Yet am I not ſatiſfyed, till I make your Lordſhip iudge of my Dealings towards him, which I proteſt, before God, weare theſe: After that th'Erle of *Kildare*, the Viſcounts of *Baltinglas* and *Mountgarrett*, the Barons of *Delvin* and *Upperoſſerye*, Sir *Edmond Butler*, and Sir *Barnabye Fitz-Patricke*, and others, were indicted, Sir *Edmonde* was the firſte that brought it to my Knowlege, who added further, that he ſhoulde by and by take his Triall, if the Iudge weare not commaunded to ſtay his Proceadinge. Wherevpon I wrote ymmediatly to the Cheif Iuſtice, not to proceade; wherevnto he obayed. The next Day, metinge withe Sir *Edmonde*, I tolde him the Daunger, offeringe to him the Q. Maieſties Pardon, which he accepted, and had it not to himſelf onely, but, I ſuppoſe, to the Nomber of a hundrethe Raſcalls of his Servaunts and Followers. After this, I gave him bothe Countenaunce and Creditt, moved thereto bothe by our olde Acquaintance, Education, and Service of the moſt vertuous Prince, the Kinge then our Maſter; and alſoe thoroughe the Commendacion of your Lordſhips earneſt Lettres, which I ſhewed vnto him, to declare your Lordſhips Favour and Devotion, and thereby the Encreaſe of my Goodwill and Obligacion of Freindſhippe. After all which Actions, and when I had of ſpeaciall Affection paide vnto him the full of his Entertainment, which no one of this Garriſon can ſaye in Effect: I receved this Fruite of my well ſowen Seede, which provethe the Inſuffyciency of my Iudgment, to overweene of him that hathe ſoe well requyted me. Your Lordſhip may now iudge of my Dealinges, and wheather my Seuerytie have myniſtred Cauſe of Offence, or my Lenytie or Remyſſines have not beene the greater Faultes. I ſaye this, but to declare my ſelf as I am, and not as I am reported, and yet able (I thanke God) to forgive the worſte Deſert of myne Enymie. I humblye take my Leave. At *Drogheda*, the xixth of *Auguſt*, 1566. *Your moſt bounden Brother*,

H. Sydney.

To *Queen* Elizabeth [h].

A Lbeit in my Letters of the laſt of *Februarie*, addreſſed unto your moſtᵉ
excellent Maieſtie from the Cittie of *Waterforde*, I partely advertiſed your
Highneſs of my begon Journey into *Mounſter* ; yet, ſince my Return from the
ſame, I thought good to ſignifie to your Highenes more amply of that Parte
(at that Time briefelie touched) and of my Proceedinge and Finiſhinge of the
ſame Jorney. It may therefore pleaſe your Highenes to underſtande, that I departed from this your Maieſties Howſe, at *Kylmayneham*, the 27th of *Januarie*,
and traveiled into *Leix* (now called the *Queenes Countie*) where I cauſed (afore
certeyn Commiſſioners, whome I had to attende upon me) a Seſſion to be held.
Where there was ſuche Obedience ſhewed and uſed, aſwell of the Soldiers and
Engliſh there lately planted, as of the *Iriſherie* there inhabitinge ; as, conſidering the Infancy of anny good Order in that Countrie, was meerveyled at by as
manny as ſawe it ; and ſo was alſo the great Encreaſe of Tillage, that thoroughe Quiet was there ſeene. There were executed ſundry Malefactors ; and
ſo quieting particuleer Contentions between Partie and Partie, I left that Countrie, in good and better Order then I founde it, and departed to *Killkennye*.
There alſo I cauſed a Seſſion to be held, but ſuche Reformacion, Obedience,
with Quiet and Encreſe of Welth, appered there, and yet dothe contynew ; as
were harde, upon Report, to ſeeme credible to your Maieſtie ; for that the miſerable Eſtate of the ſame before, was utterlie unknowen unto your Highenes.
For unto me that ſaw both, the Amendment thereof ſeamed to exceade Reaſon.
In this Place there were ſome Malefactors executed, and *Peers*, the youngeſt
Brother of the Erle of *Ormounde* (for the violent Breaking of a Goale, and Enlarging of certayne Priſoners, committed for Felony) beinge indicted for the
ſame, was at the Barre arraigned, who confeſſed the Indictment, and humbly
ſubmitted himſelf to your Maieſties Mercy ; on whome I cauſed no Judgement
to be geven, in Conſideration of his yonge Yeares, and his reverent and penitent Behavyour. And ſo leaving that Countrie in ſuch Quiet, Welth, and Joye,
as they have not ben in better thies xxtie Yeares : I departed to the Baron of
Upper Oſſories, whoſe Countrie I found in indifferent good Order, ſavinge ſomewhat moleſted by certeyn Outelawes of the ſame Countrie Breede, mayneteyned
in the Erle of *Ormounds* Countrie, as manifeſtly appered ; of whome, by the
good and diligent Service of *Edward Butler*, Brother to the Erle of *Ormounde*,
there were two of the moſt Notable afterwards apprehended, who I ymediately
cauſed to be executed. This bred ſuche a Terror amonges the reſt of the Malefactors in that Countrie, as imediatelie they made Sewte to the Baron, to be reconciled to him, and that he woulde becom a Sewter to me, that they mighte
be received to your Maieſties Protection. Wherin following his Opinion, who
moſte was annoyed by them, I condeſcended thereunto ; and ſince have not herd
one Complaynte from thenſe, but here, that there contynueth verie good Quiet
there. I founde alſo there, that the yonger Sonnes of the Baron of *Upper Oſſerie*, were verie evill Doers upon the Countie of *Kilkenny*, and the Landes of the
Erle of *Ormounde*. Whereupon I apprehended two of them, namelie, *Florence*
and *Geofrey*, whome I ſtill detaine in Priſon, meaning to proceade with them
with ſuche Severitie, as ſhall ſeeme convenient. Since the Apprehenſion of
whome, there hath growen no ſmall Quiet in thoſe Quarters. But ſurelie it
will never be throughelie well, till the ſame be made *Shier Grounde*, and your
Highenes Writte currante there, as in your other Countyes. From thence I departed to *Ely*, called *Ocarrolls* Countrie. Which Countrie I founde very well
inhabited, and himſelf, for civill and bountifull Entertayninge me, for Obedience and Conformity, ſuch a one, as I never founde the like of anny of the
Iriſherye. He is moſt deſirous to take his Lands of your Maieſtie, and to hold
the ſame, in Chief, of your Highenes, and in Leiue of *Bonnonghr*, for fower-

[h] From the Original MS. Ireland, 1557, 1559, Lib. 5. page 1. in his Majeſty's Office of Papers,
and Records for Buſineſs of State.

I

fcore Galloglas, for fix Weekes, to be paide but once in feaven Yeares (as he fathe) but oftener demanded, and had of late Yeares; he offered to yelde unto your Highenes, Yerelie, one hundred Markes. To one hundred Poundes I have allreadye brought him; and think I fhall be able (if your Highenes Pleafure be, that I fhall proceede with him) to perfwade him to the Payment of two hundred Markes. In my Opinion, this is a good Bargayne for your Maieftie; nevertheles, leaving the fame to your Highenes good Confideracion, I onelie defire your Refolucion herin, and that with Speede. He defireth alfoe that he might have fome Title of Nobilitie, as to be called a Baron, wherin I can fee no Hurte to com to your Highenes Service, but rather Good. His eldeft Brother was fo, and had his Eftate, bothe of his Lande and Dignitie, geven to him, and to his Heires Males. whofe Sonne died without Iffue, and fo the Title extinguifhed; and the Capteynerye of the Countrie, according to the *Yrifhe* Cuftome, devoluted to this Man. I counfeile this Manner of Dealinge with him the rather, for that his eldeft Sonne is a yonge Man of vearie greate Hope, of muche Honeftie, and manny good Partes, nerelie addicted to the *Englifh* Order. I can fay this of him the more certaynelie, for that he hath ben my Boy and Man thies tenne Yeares. From thence I departed, and traveiled over *Ikerwyn*, called *Omagher* his Countrie, which, in Effecte, I founde all wafte, and uninhabited (as the Lorde of the Countrie faide) partely by the Outelawes of *Upper Offorye*, before named, and partelie by the Exceffes comitted by the Erle of *Ormoundes* yonger Brethern; but, fince my Departing thence, I have not herde any one Complaynt, either out of *Ely*, or out of that Countrie; and came into the Countie of *Tipperarrye*; in which Countie, lodginge in five foundrie Placies, I fpente fouretene or fifteene Dayes, endevoringe my felf, to the uttermofte of my Power, for the Reformacion of the infinete Diforders which there I founde generallie, and in Manner wholie growinge amonges themfelfes, in efpecial, on the Contencion of the Erle of *Ormound* and the Baron of *Donboyne*, for a Captaynery of a thirde Parte of the fame Countye; and the Injuries and Revengs committed, for the Enioyinge and Poffeffing of the fame. Wherin, albeit the Baron of *Donboyne* may alleage fom auncyent Prefcription, and alfo fhewe fom Allowaunce of fundrie Governors therunto. Yet, in my Opinion, he hath not Title juftifiable to allowe the fame, and accordingelye I have geven Sentence in it. One other fpeciall Caufe of no fmall Myfchief in that Countrie, was the unnaturall Contencion between the two Brethern, the Baron of *Donboyn* and *Piers,* and the great Mallice betweene their two Wifes. Who, mayneteyninge their Sonns and Followers, to comitte Iniuries and Revengies dayly the one upon the other, for the mofte Parte fpoiled the whole Countrie rounde aboute them. One other Caufe of the Spoile of that Countrye, was the exceffive Traynes of Horfemen and Footemen, led and kepte there by the yonger Brethern of the Erle of *Ormounde,* who rather confumed, then defended the Goodes of the poore Countrie. I alfo founde that theire Neighbours had been fomewhat noifom to them, namely *Mac Bryan Ogonaughe,* and the *White Knighte.* Whome if I could have com by, by Order, I woulde have orderlie ponnyfhed, and caufed them to have made Sattisfaction; whome for that I coulde not in fuch Sorte have, by Meane of their Difobediience, and the Maynetenaunce of the Erle of *Defmond,* I fo plaged them by Force, Fier, and Sworde, as fince that Tyme I have not herde, but that they doe leffe anoye their Neighbors, and, at the lefte, I am fure they be leffe able then they were. I founde alfo, that the Erle of *Defmonde,* in Perfon, had done fome Hurte in that Countie, namelie, by Taking of a great Pray from the Mannor of *Killfhelau*; yet far from that in Quantity, which as I here your Maieftie has ben enformed of. And alfo, that the fame Erle procured a great Spoile to be taken from *Oliver Grace* his Landes in *Ormounde*; for which his Doinges, howe he hath fped, your Majeftie hereafter, by thies my Lettres, may vnderftand. But doubtles, Madam, the greateft Caufe of all other Mifchief in that Countie, is *the Infufficiency to govern* of them that have the Rule under the Erle of *Ormounde*; in whom there appered, manifeftlie, to wante both Juftice,

Judgement,

Judgement, and Stoutenes to execute. Of the two First, there was some of them manifestlie detected before me; and of the Third (Lack of Stoutenes I mean) to execute that which they ought. I also did see manifest Argumente, for that they being willed by me to bringe certayne of the *Okenides* (a great Sirname in that Countrie, who are, and ought to be naturall Followers and Sewters to the Erle of *Ormoundes* Courte) to answere to suche Matter, as was to be objected against them; and likewise certayn of the *Bourckes*, dwellinge within the same Countries: The Erles Officers affirmed resolutelie, they were not able to doe it. Whereupon I, using the Service of thirtie or fortie of my Horsemen, did fetche them all in, and made them pay well for their Contumacie, and detayned them untill suche Tyme as they had entered into Bonde, and delivered of their best Pledgs for Performaunce of the same, that they would be henceforward true Subjects to your Majestie, and humble and obedient Sewtors to that Courte. Which was suche an Acte for the Credite therof, as, by the Testimony of all the Erles Officers, had not ben done by his Grandfathers, his Fathers, or his owne Dayes. But it maye like your Majestie, if you will have that Countrie free from the Annoyaunce of their Neighbours, your Majestie must plante (as I have often wrytten) Justice to be residente in those Quarters. For while Sir *Warham Senteleger* there still remayned (whose Revocation, by all the Honest that I coulde speak withall, in the whole Province of *Mounster*, was not a little lamented) there was no soche Outrage committed, nor, I dare say, had ben neither in *Kylshelau*, nor upon *Oliver Grace*, if he had there remayned. Or if your Highenes will loke to have that Countrie kepte in good Order, either must your Majestie resume *those Liberties*, which the Queene your Sister granted to the Erle of *Ormounde*, or ells must the Erle appointe more upright, diligent, and sufficient Officers, then those I founde. He hath there a Royall Signory, as anny Subject that I knowe in *Christendome* hath; but so misgovernened, as it is too greate a Pittie to beholde it. Whereof I would write nothing to your Majestie, were it not, that the good and evill Estate of the rest of your Majesties Countrey, not under his Jurisdiction, but unto the same adjoyninge, is unseperatly lincked with it (as it being out of Order) the rest cannot be kepte in Order or Quiet. Thies Innormities in that Countie, I conceyve not onlie of myne owne Experience, throughe som Dilgience I used travelinge there; but by the Affirmacion and Testimonie of all, or the most Parte of the honest Men, dwellinge in the three incorporate Townes of the same Countie, namelie, *Clonmell*, *Cashell*, and *Fedart*, who agreeing with that, which I my self by Veiw conceyved, witnessed unto me the unmeasurable Tracte of Lande nowe waste and uninhabited, which, of late Yeares, was well tilled and pastured. The Depopulacion of so many of your Higheneffes Subjects, partelie by Slaughter, partelie by Bannyshement, and a great Nomber thoroughe Famyn; as it was too lamentable to here or behold, with the Subversion of so many Villages, Ruyn of Churches, and Vacancy of anny Kinds of Ministeries in the same, as anny Christian woulde lament to here it or see it; and yet Suffrance of most detestable Idolatrie, used to an Idoll, called the *Hollie Crosse*, wherunto there is no small Confluence of People daielie resorting. The Prophanacion also of the Cathedral Churches, partelie growing for Want of Bushopps, is a Thinge not a litle to be bemoned. The honest Men also of thies three proper and well walled Townes signified unto me (agreing in that, which in Effecte I sawe) that they were as People beseaged, and readie in Effecte, without Redresse, either to famyshe within the Walles, or whollie to abandon the Placies, for all Trade and Commerse was berefte them; for neither durste the People of the Countrie bring anny Thinge in unto them, neither yet durst they yssue out of their Walles, to buye anny Thinge in the Countrie, but that, both of the one and the other, there were often tymes spoiled, and many Times killed.

Madam, this is a Matter of no small Moment and Consequence; for thies Townes (not onelie thies now in Speeche) but all other, wheresoever they be in this Realm, are your Highenes Fortes and Garrisons, and yet they cost you nothing the kepeing of them, but rather render unto you Service and Rente.

I

They

They are in Effecte the onelie Monumentes of Obedience, and Nurceries of Civilitie in this Countrie, to the Overthrowe of which, all the tiranous Potentates, and licensious Subjects of this your Realm, applie their uttermoft Endevor, as the onelie Obftacles againfte their outeragious Devifies. I foughte to have com by the actuall Malefactors, fupported and mayneteyned by the forenamed Gentlemen ; but I coulde in Effecte com by none, fo obftinate and difobediente I founde the Heddes of them. Whereupon I affeffed heavy Fynes uppon the Baron of *Donboyn,* and *Piers Butler,* his Brother, for the Contempte. And comitted them both to Warde, and their Wifes, with a Baftarde Sonne of the Lord of *Donboynes.* All which I prefentlie doe detayne in the Caftell of *Dublyn,* and will doe, untill they fhall procure the Bringinge of fuche their lewde Followers, Deftroyers of that Countrie ; unleffe your Majeftie commande me to the Contrarie ; which if you doe at anny Mannes Sewte, *Actum eft de hac Republica.* I wanted not Caufe to have done the like with Sir *Edmond Butler,* and *Patrick Shurlock,* and fuerlie would have don it, if I coulde have founde, in the whole Countie, anny able Man of Countenaunce to have taken the Charge of the Governaunce therof, albeit there was a greate Nomber of fuche that were demanded of them. While I was in that Countie, namelie of *Fedarte,* fitting in publick Place, *Patrick Shurlock* openlie appeached the Baron of *Donboyn* of Highe Treafon to your Majefties Perfon, the Baron beinge prefente. Whiche *Shurlock* beinge queftioned withall, touching the Particularitie of the Treafon, for that I knewe the Baron of *Donboyn* never fawe your mofte Royall Perfon, nor came nere the fame : Being more fharpelie ftirred with that Tearm (of Treafon againfte your Perfon, then if the Woordes had ben more generall) queftioned with him of the fame. Who made this Conftruction of his Speeche, *That, if Mayntenance of proclaymed Rebells, Murderers, and Burners of Corn, and Howfes, were Treafon to your Perfon, then he had to accufe him of Treafon.* The Baron denied the fame, and defyed his Accufer ; humblie cravinge at my Handes Trial, either by the Lawes of the Realm, or by the Lawe of Armes. I offered the Accufer the Advocacye of your Highenes Atturney, and other your Majefties Counceill lerned in the Lawes : Which at that Tyme he thought not good to employe, alleadginge that the Place was not fitte. Which I fuppofed he had done, for that that Towne was oute of the Erles Libertie, being well contented to deferre the fame for your Majefties more Advantage, till my Comyng to *Clonmell,* a Place within his Libertie, and there eftefones remembred *Shurlock* of it ; but fince that Tyme I have herd no more of that Matter. Ever fithens the Baron hath remayned in Warde, affirmynge, that, if that Appeall and Apprehencion had not ben, no Malefactors dependinge upon him, but fhoulde have ben brought to their due Triall, who, heringe of his Apprehencion, ymediatelie fledde. Being at *Fedart* alfo, upon an Indictement, was arraigned *Edward Butler,* Brother to the Erle of *Ormounde,* who, albeit he was by Jurie quitte of the Indictement, yet was the fame no fmall Comforte to the honeft Afflicted, and no fmall Terror to the Wicked and Difordered. Seing then I coulde not have broughte unto me anny of the Malefactors by Proclamacion, I charged as manny, as had anny idle Perfon dependinge upon them, by a Day certayne to bringe them in, and either comitte them to Goale, or enter into Bond for their good Behavyor. I alfo granted unto fundrie, Power to execute the Martiall Lawe, and lefte Authoritie with Sir *Edmund Butler,* and *Patrick Shurlock,* to levie and entertayne Men, to profequute the Outelawes, and fuche as no Man woulde anfwere for. I have herde, that, fince that Tyme, fom have ben executed ; and litle Speeche of the refte, but, in Effecte, vniverfallie quiet, fince my beinge there.

From that Countie I paffed to the Cittie of *Waterforde* ; where I was in fuche honorable Manner receaved and enterteyned, as mighte better have ben thoughte worthy gracious Acceptacion, if it had ben done to your mofte Princelie Majeftie, then to be loked for of fo meane a Subjecte as I am. To this Cittie I fent for the Lordes, Gentlemen, and Freeholders of that Countie, who, for the mofte Parte of that Callinge, came unto me ; for there be not manny in the fame Shier. And it well appeared, that they had not forgotten the good Obedience, which they had ben taught to obferve by Sir *Warham Scintleger*, and the other Commiffioners during the Tyme of their Abode there. And yet fomewhat reverted from that good Eftate they were lefte in at their Revocacion. And are readie, accordinge to the Parable of the Scripture, to playe the Parte of the *Wafshed Swyne*, in returninge to her foule Puddle. Vnleffe Contynuaunce of Juftice emonges them detayne them from it. By thies Gentlemen and Freeholders, or, at leaft, by the graveste and fubftauncialeft of them, I underftode that Countie to be muche molefted by certeyn diforderd Perfons, by Surname *Powers*: All which were wounte to depende upon the Lord *Power*, as their Hed and Capteyne. Which difordered Men, for that they mighte no longer be mayntenyed by the comen Rankes of this comen Welthe, called *Coyne* and *Liverie*, comitted fome Outragies and Difobediencies, as it mighte feeme of Purpofe, to Thende theire Lorde and Capteyne might be reftored to their wonted Exactions, and they to their accuftomed Idlenes and Ravyn. But that Devife prevailed not; for callinge the Lord *Power* unto me, and charginge him with heavy Tearmes to bring in thoife Malefactors, for fom of which he before was bounde, and gevinge him Daye to doe the fame; at whiche Day, for that he brought not in fuche as were to my Contentacion, and fuche as I well knewe he was able: Albeit he brought me two taken by him (whome, in the Way of good Speede, I comitted to the Gallowes) I bounde the fame Lord *Power*, by a certeyne Day, to yelde himfelf Prifoner in the Caftell of *Dublin*, which he obferved, and where he yet remayneth. This Cittie of *Waterforde* muche florifsheth; and, I fuppofe, was never in better Eftate fince it was buylded, the People therof beinge verye civill, and, for this Countrie, full of Induftrie; the Countie, albeit muche amended within thies 12 Monethes, yet, in Effecte, much wafte and defolate. The Apprehencion of the Lord *Power*, hathe greatlie animated the Honeft, and abaifhed the Wicked. And I gevinge Auctoritie, to the Sheriff of that Countie, being an *Englifhe* Man borne, and a righte honefte and welthie Citezen of that Cittie, to profequute thoife forenamed Outelawes; doe underftande from hym that he hath apprehended fom of them, and the reit he hath forced to fubmitte themfelves, craving Pardon for Thinges pafte, and offering Seurtie for their good Behavyor hereafter. Wherbie it may appeare unto your Majeftie, that *Coyne* and *Liverie* was no neceffarie Defence for the Countrie, but a nedeles Myfchief to the fame; a Mayntenaunce of the Tyranye of the Greate, and the Idlenes of the Inferior.

From *Waterforde* I went to *Dungarvan*, and finde that Place, in my Opinion, worthy Repayre and Entertaynement, for fundrie Refpectes. Then did I enter into the Poffeffions of Sir *Maurice Fitz Gerald*, betweene whome and the Erle of *Defmond*, and their Aunceftors, as your Majeftie hath herde, hath ben longe Contencion. But, doubtleffe, I find that Gentleman lefte evill of the reft, that be of any Power, and fuche a one, as if he were not urged to ufe Revenge in his owne Caufes, for Wante of Juftice refidente nere hym, he would live in a verie good and well ordered Manner. For the Grieffes betweene the Erle and him, touchinge Spoiles and other Hurtes, for that it refted upon Proofes, by Confent of bothe Parties, there were Commiffioners appointed to examine the fame; and for the Erles Titell and Clayme, for Service, or his Lande, the Erle, as it feemed, not thinkinge me indifferente to here the Matter, and alleadginge Wante of his learned Counfeill, he alfo beinge Pleyntiff, comenced no Action againfte him. And foe they bothe being bounde for Obfervacion of the Peace, I lefte both their Caufies, and that Countie, and arrived at *Youghall*, the firfte Towne of the Countie of *Corke*. A verie propper Towne, and an indifferent good Haven, and the Towne in no evill Cafe, and yet of late muche decayed, by reafon of foundry Spoiles made upon them by Pirates upon the Sea; and no leffe annoyed by feverall Lande Lordes of the Countrie, all under the Rule of the Erle of *Defmond*.

At this Towne, the Erle havinge ben with me at *Waterfourde* before, met me; where we entered into the Debatinge of the Caufies between him and the Erle

of

of *Ormounde*, of the Particuler wherof I meane not to troble your Majeftie with anny Difcours; but fhall deferre the fame to the Reporte of anny, that fhall lifte to fpeake or write therof; truftinge, that, if I fhalbe therin accufed, as heretofore, unjuftelie, in the Erle of *Ormoundes* Caufies, I have ben, I fhall finde at your Majefties Hands, gracious Sufpence, untill I may be herde. Onelie it may pleafe your Highnes to underftande touchinge their Affaires, that when I did diffende, accordinge to the Orders taken in *Englande*, to examine who was in the Poffeffion of *Kilfhelau*, and other Mannours in Controverfie, at the Tyme of the Skirmyfh betweene the two Erles; and founde, after longe Debatinge, bothe in myne owne Judgement, and in the Opinion of all the refte, that the Poffeffion was in the Erle of *Ormounde*, at the Tyme of the Fray making; I accordingelie pronounced, awarded, and ordered the fame. Wherat the Erle of *Defmond* did not a little fturr, and fell into fom difallowable Heates and Paffions, which were not fuffred to goe with him; but was well taughte to underftaunde bothe his Deutie to your Majeftie, and his Obedience to your Lawes; and Reverence, that he oughte to fuche as fate by your Auctoritie. Albeit I could not blame him to be fomwhat quicke at the Matter; for that that Judgment, touchinge the Poffeffion, induced him to be within the Reache of *twentie Thoufande Poundes* unto your Highenes. I alfoe founde oute, duringe the Tyme of my beinge there, and had it confeffed; that he procured the Spoilinge of *Oliver Grace*; wherbye alfo, as I take it, he hath incurred the Forfeiture of the fame Bonde. From this Tyme forwarde, nor never fince, founde I anny Willingnes in the Erle of *Defmonde*, to com to anny Conformitie or good Order, but alwayes waywarde, and unwillinge to doe anny Thinge at my Appointmente, that mighte further the Weale of the Countrie, or your Majefties Service: Your Name no more reverenced, nor Letters of Commaundement obeyed, with in anny Place within his Rule, then it would be in the Kingdome of *Fraunce*. He femed ftill defirous to be gone; to prevente which, albeit unwittinge unto hym, I appointed a fecret Guard to attende upon him. He hindered as manny as he coulde from comynge to me, which prevailed in none (his own Followers excepte, wherof no one came of anny Accompte) favinge onelie in the Erle of *Clancarre* and Sir *Owen Ofulivan*, otherwife called *Ofulivan beare*: Unto whome, as I was crediblie enformed, he writte, that they fhoulde not com at me. I thoughte good, notwithftanding all this, to temporife with him, expectinge that which after hapened; that I fhould finde fome more apparante and weightie Caufe then yet he had manifefted. The Lordes and principall Gentlemen of all the Countie of *Cork* (thoife two forenamed onlie excepted) came unto me, namelie, the Vicounte *Barrye*, the Lord *Roche*, the Lord *Courcy*, Sir *Donaghe Mac Carty*, Capteyn of *Carbery*, otherwife called *Mac Carty Reaghe*, Sir *Dermot Mac Carty*, Capteyn of *Mufkry*, *Barry Oge*, *Richard Cordon*, and *Barret*. All which are the greateft, and, in deede, verie greate Poffeffioners in that County; and are, or ought to be, free Subjectes, owinge imediate Service to your Majeftie and your Crowne Imperiall. Neverthelefs, fo injured and exacted upon by him, as, in Effecte, they are or were becom his *Thralls* or *Slaves*. All which, with open Mouthe, and helde upp Handes to Heaven, cried out for Juftice, and that it might pleafe your Majeftie to caufe your Name to be knowen emonges them, with Reverence, and your Lawes obeyed; offeringe to fubmitte them felves, Lief, Landes, and Goodes, to the fame. Befides all thies Lordes and Gentlemens Poffeffions; the Erle of *Defmonde* enjoyeth under his Rule, or rather Tiranny, the thirde Parte of this great Countie, which, I affure your Majeftie, I knowe to be greater then all *Yorkfhire*. In all whiche his Limittes, neither is your Name reverenced, or your Lawes obeyed. Neither dare anny Sheriff execute anny Parte of his Office therein. And yet injuriouflie helde by him, by the Reporte of the Inhabitauntes, having not anny Thinge to fhewe for the fame, but by Prefcription, as he termeth it. In this Countie is one Cittie, and two Townes, namelie, the Cittie of *Cork*, and the Townes of *Youghall*, and *Kynfale*; all

which

which be walled, and Placies of great Momente for your Majesties Service; as before of the Townes in the Countie of *Tipperarry* I writte; and all thies greatlie empayred, and in the highe Way of utter Ruyn, if your Majestie, by speadie Redresse, and Ministringe of Justice, doe not prevent it. This Myschief groweth not onelie by the Abuse of the Lande Lordes, though greatlie by the same (who are easie to be reformed, the Erle of *Desmond* once well corrected) but partelie, yea, and verie muche, by the Trade of *Spanyardes* to that Coaste. Where they find suche Commoditie of Havens (as, in deede, I thinke in all *Europe*, in so short a Tracte of Grounde, there is not so manny good to be founde) and are nowe growen into suche an Acquayntaunce with the People, as not onlie they doe yerelie take from thence an incredible Quantity of Fishe, which mighte be turned to the Use and Benefitte of your Subjectes; but also eche Thinge ells of anny Price, which your Countrie here breadeth; as, Hide, Tallow, Fell, Wooll, and Floxe, Fleshe, and Yarne. All which were wonte to be sold at the forenamed Townes; and thereby they were maynteyned and enriched; and nowe, for Want of the same, not a litle empayred, and the People thereof enforced, for the Mayntenance of that littell Trade which is lefte with them, to use the same for readie Monney. Wherbie all the Treasure your Highenes sendeth, is yssued out of this Realm; and so will it be, thoughe your Majestie sent as muche as *Englande* bredeth. This Myschief is no Waye to be helped, but by ministring of Justice, and planting som civill People upon thoise barbarous Placies. And, moste gracious Soveraigne, this Matter is worthie deliberate Consideracion and spedy Redresse, or ells I confesse my self to have no Judgement; for, if I were Kinge *Phillippes* Man, and that he mighte attende it, and did intende it, I am perswaded that it were possible with three Thowsaund Men, and twentie Thowsaund Pounde of Monney, either to dispossesse your Majestie of all *Mounster*, and *Connaght*, or to enforce your Highenes to employe the Service of twentie Thowsaund Men, and the Charges of two hundred Thowsaund Poundes to recover it and defend it. It shall therefore, in my symple Opinion, behove your Majestie to take Care for the Conservacion of thiese your Townes; for the Losse of them would be the Losse of this your Countrie.

As touchinge the Estate of the whole Countie, for so muche as I sawe of it; havinge travailed from *Youghall* to *Cork*, from *Cork* to *Kinsale*, and from thence to the uttermost Boundes of it towardes *Limerick*; like as I never was in a more pleasaunt Countrey in all my Life: So never sawe I a more waste and desolate Lande, no, not in the Confynes of other Countries, where actuall Warre hath contynuallie ben kepte, by the greatest Princies of *Christendome*; and there herde I suche lamentable Cryes and dolefull Complayntes, made by that small Remayne of poor People which yet are lefte. Who hardelie escaping the Furie of the Sworde, and Fire of their outeragious Neighbours, or the Famyn with the same, which their extorcious Lordes hath driven them unto, either by taking their Goodes from them, or by spending the same by their extorte Taking of *Coyne* and *Liverie*; make Demonstracion of the miserable Estate of that Countrie. Besides this, suche horrible and lamentable Spectacles there are to beholde, as the Burninge of Villages, the Ruyn of Churches, the Wastinge of suche as have ben good Townes and Castells: Yea, the Veiw of the Bones and Sculles of the ded Subjectes, who, partelie by Murder, partelie by Famyn, have died in the Feelds; as, in Troth, hardelie any Christian with drie Eies could beholde. Not longe before my Arrivall there, it was crediblie reported, that a principall Servaunt of the Erle of *Desmond*, after that he had burnt sundrie Villages, and destroyed a greate Peice of a Countrie, there were certeyn poor Women sought to have ben recerved; but to late, yet so sone after the horrible Facte comitted, as their Children were felte and seene to sturre in the Bodies of their dead Mothers. And yet did the same Erle lodge and banckett, in the Howse of the same Murderer his Servaunte, after the Facte comitted. Suerlie there was never People that lived in more Miserie, then they do, nor, as it shulde seeme, of worfe Myndes, for Matrimonie emongs them is no more regarded, in Effect, then Conjunction betwene unreafonable Beaftes. Perjurie, Robberie, and Murder, counted alloweable. Finallie, I cannot finde that they make any Confcience of Synne, and, doubtleffe, I doubte whether they chriften their Children or no ; for neither finde I Place where it fhulde be don, nor anny Perfone able to enftructe them in the Rules of a Chriftian ; or, if they were taughte, I fee no Grace in them to follow it ; and, when they dye, I cannot fee they make anny Accompte of the Woorlde to com.

And for that I have thus overtedioullie written to your Majeftie, of this Countrie : It fhall pleafe your Majeftie to underftaunde, that I founde the like of the whole Countie of *Lymerick,* and the Countrie of *Tomonde* (thoroughe which I traveiled) as well for Defolacion, Wafte, and Ruyns of the Countrie ; as alfo for the Lacke of Reverence to your Name, Obedience to your Lawes, and evill Difpofition of the People. Namelie, where the Erle pretendeth any Rule, being the Half of that Countie, the Whole being but a verie fmall Shire : Savinge the Lord *Roches* Countrie, in the Countie of *Cork,* and a fmall Porcion of Land, about *Killmallock,* in the Countie of *Lymerick,* are well inha-. bited. Nowe to returne to the Erle of *Defmound,* whome I ftill ledde with me, he daielie being defirous to be gonne, and from Tyme to Tyme blowing out Wourdes of evill Digeftion : That he would not put downe his idell Men, nor leave his Coyne and Liverie, but kepe his Galloglas ; and where as he had, in Tymes paft, one Man, he would have five (and yet would bring no one to me) not doubting, before it were *Mydfomer-day,* he would have five Thowfaunde Men a foote at once ; and for his Sake, leadinge ftill with me, all the fore-named Noblemen, and Gentlemen, and meeting alfo by the Waye the Lord *Fitz Morrice,* a Baron of the Countie of *Kerry,* whome at the firfte I doubted to be of the Erle of *Defmonds* Faction, but neverthelefs, founde him faithefull and affured to your Majeftie ; came with them, in my Trayne to *Killmallock,* a good Towne, and indifferentlie well walled. Where I was no foner arrived, but that I was by foundry advertifed, that all the Countries adjoining, and rounde aboute farre and nere, which were at the Devotion of the Erle of *Def-mounde,* were in an Uprore, and readie to goe to Armes : And fendinge oute Spiall, the rather to be advertifed of the Truthe, founde undoubtedlie true, that fo it was ; and then foundinge all the Noblemen, and Gentlemen, beforenamed, and findinge them faithefull and affured to your Majeftie : Albeit unarmed, and unaccompanied, for that I had not made anny of them privie to my Inten-cion ; and tryeing alfo the Difpofition of Sir *John* of *Defmonde,* the Erles Bro-ther, whome I found a readie, and an humble Subjecte, to ferve your Ma-jeftie, where it againft his owne Brother, or whoefover ells. Albeit he femed muche perplexed, for Fear of the Overthrowe of the Howfe, and troubled in na-turall Affection, towardes his naturall Brother. Nevertheles, moft readie to anny Service, that by me he fhould be employed unto. He confeffed unto me, that fuche Nombers of Men were in Armes, but to what Ende he knewe not. I alfo examyned the Busfhopp of *Lymerick,* who was fuppofed to be an erneft Freende to the Erle, and one lefte in fpeciall Trufte by his Father : Who con-feffed that fuche Men were gathered, and muche he myflyked the fame, but knewe nothing of the Caufe. I caufed alfo of his neareft Servauntes to be ex-amyned, who all confeffed, that fuch Men were affembled, but to what Ende, they were ignoraunte. And I alfo founde by fuche Meanes, by dealinge with him, as he hymfelfe confeffed the Affemblie of thoife Men ; whereupon, I callinge unto me, afwell thoife of your Majefties Counfeill there, as the Com-miffioners, and the Lords and Gentlemen, beforenamed, and alfo the principall Men of that Towne of *Killmallock,* of which Towne the Erle claymed to have no fmall Superioritie ; and unjuftlie, as it femethe to me, receiveth a yerelie Tri-bute from them ; fent for the Erle to com unto me, and there, in Publique, charged him with that Sturre and Levy of Men, which he denied not : Then burdeninge him with grevous and weightie Woordes, for his rafhe and difloiall

Doinges therein ; he humblinge hymſelfe upon his Knees, confeſſed that he had ſo donne, as in Reſpect of levienge the Men, without Intendement of Evill (as he ſaide). Whereupon, I aſked hym, why he had levied anny ſuche Nomber ; he aunſwered me, for no evill Intente, but onelie that I had demaunded of hym his baſe Brother, *Thomas Macybryne Ogonoghe,* and the *White Knighte,* and others ; and that he could not tell howe otherwiſe to have them, then by publiſhing an Aſſemblie of his People ; generallie he ſhould have them to com in Companye, as Leaders of the reſte ; whereby, ſaide he, I ſhoulde have Comoditie to have taken them. Why (ſaide I) you have ben ever a Sewter to departe from me, ſince my Comyng from *Youghall,* and this Daye you have ben three ſundrie Tymes in my Lodginge, to move me to departe to my Ladie your Wief, as it were in Poſt to the ſame Towne (and in deede, his Wief was delivered of a Doughter, not longe before) and your Waye is, in Effecte, directlie South to *Youghall,* and myne almoſte Northe to *Lymerick.* Thies Men, whome I have demaunded at your Handes, be the Leaders of your Companye, being ſixe Hundred at the leaſt, and all in the Waye betweene me and *Lymerick.* You knowe, I have not, in the Whole, two Hundred Men in my Companye ; howe may it be thoughte that you beinge gonne awaye clene contrarie to that which I entended to holde, I being accompanied with ſo ſmall a Nomber, that ſuche woulde either preſent themſelves, or that I were able, if they would not, by Force to apprehende them ? He, ſtill reſtinge upon his Knees, offered, that if I liſted, I ſhould ſee them all, or I ſhould ſee none, if I would. I uſing ſome roughe and rigorous Tearmes, ſaide unto him, that I woulde neither bidde him to have them there, nor forbidd him ; but this I tolde him, that on to Morrow, according to my former Intendement, I woulde goe to *Lymerick* at the ſame Hower, and paſſe the ſame Way, that I had purpoſed, and if that he, or anny of his, durſte offer any Kinde of Bravery to me, or anny of myne, albeit I was not, as he well knewe, two Hundred Men, I badde him doe what he or they durſt, aſſuring, him by the Waye, that if any Outerage were offered, he ſhoulde be the firſte that ſhoulde dye for it. Hereupon he ſemed humble and ſilente, and therewith *I committed him to Warde,* where he hath ever ſince remayned : I leading him with me, from thence to *Lymerick,* and from *Lymerick* to *Gallwaye,* and ſo to the Caſtell of *Dublyn,* where he yet remayneth. But Madam, this I am bounde in Conſcience to ſaye, and in the ſoundeſt Fidelitie, that I can conceive to your Majeſtie, I proteſt, that in myne Opinion, he did not this upon anny trayterous Mynde to your Perſon, Crowne or Dignitie, nor yet of Will to hurte or apprehende me ; but onelie, as I take it, to ſhewe that he were able, if he woulde, to deliver himſelfe oute of my Handes ; and if it had com to that Paſſe, whether he, ſo accompanied, had ben able, though he would, to have appeaſed their Furie, whome he was not able before to bring unto me, or no, I muche doubte. At Adventure, oute I went, at the Hower, and in the Waye before determyned, leadinge with me the Companye before ſpecyfied, together with Eighte or Nyneſcore of well appointed Footemen, whiche that Towne of *Killmallock* offred me ; and ſo marched towardes *Lymerick,* and in the Midwaye, there mette me three Hundred well appointed Footemen, of the Cittie of *Lymerick,* ſent me at the Busſhopps Motion, upon ſixe Howres Warninge. This partlie I write, to th'Ende your Majeſtie ſhould have Reguarde to thies your Townes. They are your onlie Force, that your Majeſtie hath to truſt to, oute of the *Engliſh* Pale of this your Realme.

Hereupon, with the Advice of ſuche of your Counſeill as were with me, I combyned all the forenamed Lords and Gentlemen in faithefull Love and Amytie, confirmed by their Promes, and ſolempne Othes, which in all Semblance, they ſhewed faithefullie to kepe. They all ſemynge deiſirous that Sir *John* of *Deſmounde* ſhoulde be Chief in Commiſſion emonges them, I accordingelie addreſſed unto hym and them, together with one learned in the Lawes, *Andrewe Skydye,* and *Henry Davells,* an olde Soldier in this Lande, and

I   an an honeſt, diſcreete Gentlemen, Comiſſioned for the Governinge of thoiſe three Shieres of *Corke, Lymerick,* and *Kerry,* and ſo returned them from me at *Lymerick* ; ſince which Tyme I have ben, and daielie am crediblie advertiſed, that thoiſe Counties doe remayn in verie good Quiet ; eche honeſt, and diſcreete Man, muche rejoyſing at the Withdrawing of the Erle from thoiſe Partes.

And nowe, moſte gracious Soveraign, if it ſeeme more honorable for your Maieſtie, to have hym thus apprehended, as it were in the Myddes of his Kyngedom, and as a Captive openlie conveyed oute of the ſame, and ſo to be broughte thoroughe all the reſte of *Tomonde* and *Connoughe,* to the Terror of all other of his Sorte, or to have ben taken in the *Engliſhe* Pale, when he came to the Service of your Highenes: As it ſemeth your Highenes was perſwaded I ſhould have don, and, as it is written hither, that I was comaunded to have don ; thoughe I never receved from your Majeſtie anny to that Effect. And if alſo it nowe appere unto your Highenes, more advantageous, that I temporiſed with him, untill ſuch Tyme as he not onelie hath incurred the Forfeiture of twentie thowſande Pounde, but hath alſo comitted ſuche an Error, as is at the leaſte juſtelie ponnyſheable, with Impryſonment at your Pleaſure, and grevous Fine. Then to have taken hym, onelie to have anſwered the Complaynte of anny perticular Man. Yf, I ſay, that this my Manner of Proceedinge ſeeme more honorable and more beneficiall to your Majeſtie, I humblie beſeche the ſame, no longer to kepe me in Office here, then your Majeſtie dothe thinck, that I (that actuallie and contynuallie am occupyed in the Managinge of the Affaires of this your Countrie, and perſonallie ſee and here howe Thinges dothe paſſe) can better decerne howe and when to execute that, that perteyneth to your Service, then anny there, whoeſoever he be, beinge but enformed by Reportes, and thoiſe often tymes but ſiniſterlie made. Nowe it reſteth for your Highenes to reſolve what you will doe with this Erle, as firſte, whether yowe will have hym into *Englande,* or that he remayne here. The Example wilbe muche more terrible, if he be ſent for into *England.* And, for my Parte, I woulde be very well contented to be diſburdened of the Charge of him, becauſe I muſt be ſo occupied in your Majeſties Service, as I muche doubte the ſafe Keping of him. Then your Highnes hath to reſolve howe further you will proceede with him ; for albeit, as before I write, I cannot condempne him of anny trayterous Intente towardes your Majeſtie, yet is his Act ſo ponnyſheable and fyneable, as therbie the Matter, being well handeled, may growe in Effecte the Reformacion of all *Mounſter.* Yf your Majeſtie will deale with him there, you muſte have ſome of this Countrie thither, to enforme againſt him, and of thoiſe none meter, then *Lucas Dillon,* your Majeſties Atturney, and *Nicholas White.* Yf your Highenes will have him delte with all here, it ſhalbe verie neceſſarie that your Majeſtie ſende hither ſome one quick and ſtowte Man learned in the Lawes ; who, both for Judgement and Sinceritie, may be repoſed upon for the Advauncemente of your Majeſties Service, and the Benefit of the Countrie. Albeit, I aſſure your Highenes, that I founde both Sir *Thomas Cuſak, Lucas Dillon,* your ſaid Atturney, *Edwarde Fitz Symons,* and *Nicolas White* (all learned in the Lawes, all which, alſoe, I had with me in the Journey) as fervente in your Majeſties Cauſe and the Countrie, and as voide of Affection towardes him, as I coulde wiſhe anny Men to be. This Good, at the leaſte, will growe by this Facte, that there may juſtelie be taken from him his ſuppoſed Liberties. Which Abuſe of Liberties, aſwell in him, as in others, is the verie Roote of all the Diſorders in *Mounſter.* In this weightie and great Matter, I moſte humblie deſire your Majeſtie, that I may have imediate and undelayed Anſwers and Reſolucion.

And nowe to the State of the Countrie agayne. I founde the Cittie of *Lymerick* ſo empayred in Welth, ſince I laſt ſawe it in the Queene your Siſters Dayes, as was ſtraunge to me to beholde, muche by the Diſorder of the Erle of *Deſmound,* whoiſe Countrie joyneth unto it upon the Sowthe Side, but more by the greate Spoiles comitted, and ſuffered to be comitted, by the Erle of

Thomond,

Tomond, their next Neighbor, upon the North Side, whoſe Lacke of Diſcretion and Inſufficiency to governe, is ſuche, as, if I could have founde anny one *loiall* and reaſonable Man in his Countrie, I woulde not onelie have withdrawen him from Ruling there, but, for a Nomber of Spoiles juſtely approved againſt hym, would have comitted him to Priſon.

The *Obrines,* of *Tomond,* came not at me, as it is ſuppoſed, by the Perſwacion of the Erle of *Deſmound.* In what Caſe this Country was, I wrote before; all waſte and deſolate thoroughe 'whiche I paſſed, and lodged one Night with *Oſhanghenes,* whome I found a verie obediente, loiall, and civil Man, and moſte deſirous to holde his Land imediatlie of your Majeſtie, and to be delivered of the Exactions of both the Erles of *Clanricarde,* and *Tomonde.* His Countrie is rich, plentifull, and well ordered, but verie ſmall. I promiſed him to be a Sewter to your Highenes, that it would pleaſe yowe ſo to accept it. His Father was in *England,* and there by the Kinge, your Majeſties moſt noble Father, made Knighte, and had Lettres Patentes of his Countrie, in whoſe Behalf nowe I meane ſhortlie to ſend a Bill readie drawen, to Thend he may, by Acte of Parliamente, be reſumed to your Majeſtie, and exempted from the reſte.

From thence I wente to your Highenes Towne of *Galliwaye,* the State wherof I found rather to reſemble a Towne of Warre, fronteringe upon an Enemye, then a civill Towne in a Countrie under one Soveraigne. They watche their Walles mightelie, and garde their Gates daielie with armed Men. They complayned muche of the Warres of *Mac William Ewter,* and *Oſlartye,* againſte the Erle of *Clanrycarde,* but, moſt of all, of the Diſorder of the Erle of *Clanrycardes* two Sonnes, whiche he hath by two Wives, and bothe alive, and thies two yonge Boyes in the Lief of thir Father, yet likelie long to live, doe ſtrive who ſhalbe their Fathers Heire, and, in the ſame Strife, comitte no ſmall Spoiles and Damage to the Countrie. Whereupon, I tooke bothe the Sonnes, and carried them awaye with me, and here I doe detayne them. To this Towne of *Galliwaye,* came to me *O Donell,* ſhewinge himſelfe moſte willinge and readie, to accompliſh all Thinges, that his Brother, in his Lief Tyme, had covenaunted with me for the Service of your Majeſtie, and did deſire that he might have his Countrie by Letters Patentes, which I graunted him, and accordingelie have ſent it unto him. There came alſo unto me *Oconnor Sligo,* of whome, and his Greatenes and Diſpoſition, I wrote to your Majeſty at large, in my Lettres ſent by Mr. *Gilbert.* He is deiſirous to holde his Countrey imediatelie of your Majeſtie; but, in anny wiſe, he will into *Englande* to ſee your moſt Royall Perſon, and there to receive not onlie his Countrey, but, as he termeth it, Regeneration at your Majeſties Hand: And I meane ſhortlie to ſend him to your Highenes. From thence I traveiled thoroughe a greate and an aunciente Towne in *Connoghe,* called *Anrye,* where I was offered a pytyfull and lamentable Preſente, namelie, the Keyes of the Towne, not as to receive them of me agayne, as all other accuſtomablye doe, but for me ſtill to kepe, or otherwiſe diſpoſe at my Pleaſure, in aſmuche as they were ſo impoveriſhed, by the Extortion of the Lordes aboute them, as they were no longer able to kepe that Towne. The Towne is large and well walled, and it appereth by Matter of Record, there hath ben in it three hundred good Howſeholders, and, ſince I knewe this Land, there was twentie, and nowe I finde but fower, and they poor, and, as I write, readie to leave the Place. The Crye and Lamentacion of the poor People was greate and pityefull, and nothinge but thus, *Succor, Succor, Succor.* The Erle of *Clanricarde* coulde not denye, but that he helde a hevie Hande over them. For which I ordered him to make them ſom Recompence, and bounde him not to exacte upon them hereafter; whereunto he willingelie conſented. As this Towne, for Lacke of Juſtice, is, in a Manner, totally deſtroyed, ſo will the reſt of your Highenes Townes be, if with Speede you plant not Juſtice emonges them. From thence I traveiled thoroughe *Clanrycarde,* and founde the Countrie in good Quiet, univerſallie well tilled and

manured,

manured, and was at two of the Erles Howfes vearie honorablye entertayned. From whence, paffing thoroughe the *Okellies* Countrie, I came to your Majefties Howfe of *Athelone*, and fo toke my next Waie to this your Majefties Howfe of *Kyllmayneham*, where I arrived the xvith of this *Aprill*. So as I was oute, in the Whole, eleven Weeks and two Days. Which Journey, as it was the longeft, and the mofte paynefull that ever I made, fo I trufte it will prove honorable to your Majeftie, and advantagious to the Countrie.

Albeit, in this my overtedious Letter, I have touched unto your Highenes, fundrie Myfchiefes, in theis two Prouinces of *Mounfter* and *Connought*, yet have I not hitherto fpoken of the greateft of all other ; which is, that there is not one Man in them fufficientlie qualified for the Reformacion thereof ; but that in the beft, fuche Imperfection is to be founde, as he is not worthie to have the onlie, or the chief Charge, for the Reformacion of his owne Jurifdiction ; much leffe of the Whole. For the Erle of *Ormound* being abfente, and not loked for to returne in anny fhorte Tyme, as it is thoughte here, hathe no one *Agente*, as far as I can perceive, fufficient to governe fuche a *Seigniorie*, as he hathe in *Mounfter*. The Erle of *Defmound*, a Man bothe voide of Judgement to go-vern, and Will to be rewled. The Erle of *Clancarre*, I fuppofe, willinge enoughe to be ruled, but wanteth Force and Credite to rule. The Erle of *Tomond*, the mofte unperfecte of all the reft ; hath neither Witte of himfelf to govern, nor Grace or Capacitie to learn of others. The Erle of *Clanricarde*, equall in all good Partes with the beft of his Cote of this Countrie Breede, bothe of good Judgment to rule, and alfo of himfelf of greate Humblenes to obey your Majeftie and your Lawes ; is yet fo over ruled by a putative Wife, whome he nowe kepeth, as ofte Tymes, when he beft intended, fhe forceth hym to doe worfte. Hereby Madam, if I have anny Judgement, your Majeftie may ea-felie perceive there is no Waye for Reformacion of thies two Provinces, but by planting Juftice by Prefident and Counfeills, in eche of them ; but, if that cowardlie Policy be ftill allowed of, to kepe them in contynuall Diffention, for feare, lefte, thoroughe their Quiet, might follow I wot not what. Then myne Advice unto your Majeftie, bothe is, and fhalbe, to withdrawe me, and all Charge here. In myne Opinion, as little difhonorable were it, totallie to abandon it, as wonte Obedience to fome to govern it. And fo farr hath that Pollicie (or rather Lacke of Pollicie) in keping Diffention emonges them prevailed, as nowe, albeit, all that are alive, woulde becom honeft, and live in Quiet. Yet are there not lefte alive in thoife two Provincies, the xxth Perfon neceffarie to in-habite the fame. And fo I conclude, for thoife, that, as they were never in Me-morie of Man in wourfe Cafe then nowe they be, fo were they never in more Forwardenes to Reformacion, yf it pleafe your Majeftie to goe thoroughe with it ; befeachinge your Majeftie to call to your Remembraunce, that this was myne Opinion half a Yeare before I came hither. And, having been nowe a Yeare and half, I have contynuallie written of the fame, and yet nothinge don for the Accomplifhing thereof. For better Staye of which Countries of *Connaght* and *Tomonde*, and for Orderinge of their Griefes, which be manny ; I have re-folved to fend thither, forthwith, Sir *Thomas Cufak*, whome I, for his Experi-ence, Paynefullnes, and Willingnes, have Caufe to like, and recomend above the refte. And, therefore, defire your Majeftie, by fome fewe comfortable Wordes of good Acceptacion of his Diligence, to encorage him, and, by his Example, others to applie themfelves to your Majefties Service, who, perhapes, are now leffe diligent, in that they fee when they deferve well, and I report well, and they not ignoraunt of my Comendacion ; they yet receive from your Highe-nes no Significacion of your good Acceptinge of the fame.

As towchinge all *Leinfter* and *Methe*, I dare affirme, upon my Credite, unto your Majeftie, afwell for the *Englifh* Pale, and the Juftice therof : It was ne-ver, in the Memorie of the oldeft Man that nowe liveth, in greater Quiet and Obedience ; nor, for this Time of Yere, a Garrifon beinge kepte here, all Manner of Thinges better cheape. And fo well was the *Englifh* Pale garded in myne Abfence, chieflie by the diligente and paynefull Service of the Erle of

Kildare, who, for the moſte Parte, did continuallie reſide upon the Borders, as I cannot here, that there was the Vallue of one Cowe, by Force or Stelthe, taken out of the ſame : A Caſe here, ſo rare, as is not ſpoken of withoute greate Admiracion ; ſuch, and ſo many Incurſions and Invaſions were made into the Rebells Countrie. Duringe the ſame Tyme, as he *(O Neal)* is nowe driven to the Wooddes, and allmoſte not herd of where he is. Daielie Spoiles and Prayes taken from him, to the Enrichinge of your Higheneſſes Subjectes, and Empoveriſhing of hym. His principall People alreadie either comen from hym, or in Comynge ; namelie, all the *Ohanlons,* *Mac Mahon,* and all his Followers ; *Maginnes* dayelie ſewing to be received ; and of the beſt Gentlemen of his Surname, alreadie comen from hym. Which *Maginnes* I yet holde of, becauſe I have ben informed, that he hath ſoundrie Tymes ſpoken ſlanderouſlie of your Royall Perſon. *Tirloghe Lenoghe* ſheweth himſelf a devote Subjecte to your Highenes, daielie Embruynge himſelf in the Bloud of the Rebbells Followers. All *Clandyboy* is whollie at your Majeſties Devotion. The *Glynes,* the *Arde,* the *Duffryn,* and *Lacale,* are nowe poſſeſſed by the righte and aunciente Owners, and readie at your Majeſties Comaundmente. All *Tireconnell,* together with *Ochanes* Countrie, under the Governement of *Richarde Ochane,* in quiet Obedience to your Majeſtie, and daielie dothe Annoyaunce to the Rebbells. In *Farmanaghe,* the Rebell hath no Footinge, the Capteyn therof, *Maguier,* being a devote Subjecte to your Majeſtie : So as the Rebell is, nowe as it were, cowped in *Tirone,* neither dare he ſhewe himſelf in the Playnes therof, being ſo oft diſtreſſed by your Soldiers, by their daielie Incurſſions ; his Cattaill do, by greate Nombers, dailie ſtarve and dye in the Wooddes, in which, God willinge, ere it be long, he himſelf ſhall be well hunted. But, alas Madam, howe can your Highenes thinke that I can attende that, your martiall Service, when aſwell for the Providinge and Furniſhing of it, as alſo for Governinge in all other Civill Cauſies, there is none, in Effecte, to comaund or execute, but my ſelf ; for aſwell in all martiall Matters, either by Sea or by Lande, or Proviſion for Victuells, or Orderinge, or Diſpoſinge of the ſame ; muſte paſſe all myne own Hande. I am alſo charged with your Higheneſſes Treaſure, to my no ſmall Burden and Perill. What Aſſiſtances in Counſeill I have, God knoweth, and your Highenes, to your Loſſe, in Thende you will feele. Your Chauncelor is nowe, in a Manner, bothe ſpecheles and ſenceles. The Maſter of the *Rolles* ; a verie ſick and a weke Man, ſo as that Court is nowe, in Effecte, utterlie vacante. The ſame Maſter of the *Rolles,* being alſo Chauncelor of your *Exchequier,* and the Chief Baron therof, being bothe ſick and impotente, are forced to be abſente from that Courte. So as therby not onlie Sewtors be verie evill ſatiſfied, but God knoweth, howe your Revenues and Finnances are there ordered. And I partelie ſee how you looſe, and yet cannot amende it, for Lack of Tyme, and other greater Matters. The Chief Juſtice of your Highenes *Benche,* an olde Man, and evill able with that Diligence to attende that Place, that were convenient. The Chief Juſtice of the *Comon Pleas,* a Man much ſpente in Yeares, and decayed both in Senſe and Bodie, ſo as I am no ſoner returned from anny Jorney, and can unwrappe my ſelf anny one Hower, out of martiall Actions and Deviſies, but that Cauſies of all thies Courtes, by Swarmes, flye in unto me, to the greate Confoundinge of my Memorie, and Hindraunce of your Service ; and that in ſuch Sort, as of Neceſſitie ſomewhatt I muſte doe, or ells intollerable Evill would enſewe. And, to my further and greateſt Diſcomforte, there can no Advertiſemente com from hence, be it from never ſo ſlighte an Informer, or never ſoe untrewe ; but that, before I be herde, the ſame is accepted, to my great Diſadvauntage. All whiche tendethe not onelie to my greate Grief, Decaye of Helthe, Quiet, and Subſtaunce ; but alſo to the Hinderaunce of your Majeſties Service, Prejudice of the Countrie, and waſtfull Conſumption of your Treaſure. For Redreſſe wherof, ſince I have ſo oft written, and finde by the comforteles Silence in the ſame uſed, that your Highenes hath ſo little Compaſſion, either of your ſelf, or of

me ;

me ; that I proteft to God, I will write no more after this, of thies Matters ;
but referre them to Allmightie Goddes Direction, to whome for my felf I praye,
that if I have not more fpedie, or more comfortable Relief, then hitherto I
have had, that yt may pleafe him, either by fhorte Lief to deliver me, or by
fom grevous Sicknes to excufe me, from this miferable and thaunkleffe Service.
And for your mofte excellent Majeftie, with bowed Knees, and proftrate Bodie,
I pray to his Devine Majeftie, to fende you longe and perfecte Joyfullnes in
this Woorlde, and after, immortall Felicitie. At *Killmayneham*, the xxth of
Aprill 1567.

Your Majefties moft humble

and obedient Servaunt,

H. Sydney.

Queen Elizabeth, *for Sir* Geo. Stanley, *fent to Sir* Henry Sydney.

WHeareas Sir *George Stanley*, Knight, late Marfhall of our Army, in that
our Realme of *Ireland*, hathe bene charged by Way of Informacion,
given by *William Brymyngham*, which hathe bene, by our Order, confidered by
our Pryvey Counfell, and by them, vppon Conference, thought meete : That of
the Some of MMccxviii *l.* x *s.* iv *d. Irifhe*, feminge to be due vnto the faide
Sir *George Stanley*, by a Declaracion of Accompt fent from thence, and figned
by *Gabriell Crofte*, late Auditor there, and *Mathewe Kinge*, alfo late Clarke of
the *Checque* ; there ought to be ftayed and defalked the Some of MDccc.xcii *l.*
xiiii. *s.* iiii *d. ob. Irifhe*, for certaine particuler Matters, obiected by the faide
Brymyngham, and denyed by the faide Sir *George Stanley*, as by a particuler
Writinge, herewith fent vnto you ; which hathe bene collected by our faide
Counfell, vntill the Matters of the faide Allegations may be there further tryed
and determyned, as already there hathe beene by our Counfell allowed to him,
and paide, the Some of CC.xliv *l.* vi *s.* xi *d. ob.* as in the Paper included is conteyned. Forafmoche as the Tryall of thefe Matters are moft meteft to be
harde and determyned in that our Realme of *Ireland*, and not well in any other
Place, as fhall appeare unto you, vppon the Confideracion of the Nature of the
Obiections and Ainfwers thereto : We will and require you, that, vpon the Repaire thither vnto you of the faide Sir *George Stanley*, with thefe our Lettres,
or any other fufficyently auctoryfed for him, to caufe the Matters conteyned in
the fame Scedule, wherevpon the Controverfy fhall by the fame feme to aryfe,
to be examyned by all convenyent and reafonable good Meanes, for the Under-
derftandinge of the Truthe, without any vnneceffary Delay. And therevpon
to give Order, that vpon the Paye claymed, and to be payd to the faide Sir
George Stanley, for him and his Bande, that which fhall appeare due vnto him,
of the faide Some of MDccc.xcii *l.* xiiii *s.* iiii *d. ob. Irifhe*, may be allowed, and
the reft difallowed and faved to vs vppon his Pay. And that alfo, in the Order
of his Paie, it may be well forfene, that the Sommes of Money, which fhalbe
due by him, or his Band, to the Country, there may be by him payde ; and in
the Ende, if the Condicions, conteyned in his Bonde there, fhalbe by him performed, then his Bonde to be delyvered to him. In all which Proceadinge,
we thinke it mete and reafonable, that all good Expedicion be vfed, afwell for
the Triall of his Allegations made againft *Brymynghams* Informacions, as for
his redye Payment, confideringe he hathe of longe Tyme remayned here, followinge this his Suite, and hitherto hathe not had Expedicion thereof, partly by
Reafon of other Affaires, wherewith our Counfell hath byne occupied, which
had the Hereinge thereof, and partly for the Diffyculty of the Matter it felf.
And for the doinge hereof, if you fhall not, as you cannot well, attende the
particuler Difcuffion thereof : We woulde have you for advoydinge of Delay,
appointe the fame to fome other of our Counfell, that may be thought in foche.

I Caufes

Caufes acquainted, and alfo indifferent towardes Sir *George Stanley*, whom we wifhe, in all reafonable Caufes, to have favourable Order, becaufe we knowe noe other Thinge by him, but that he hathe ferved, as your felf hathe by your Letters well teftified, allwayes as a forwarde, painefull, and obedient Gentleman. And becaufe he hath here had Graunte to receive, at our *Efchequer*, the Somme of CCxliiii *l.* vi *s.* xi *d. ob.* as allowed due to him, aboue all Cheques : You fhall take Order, that for any Claufe in his Bond there remayninge, the fame be not preiudiciall vnto him. Yeoven, *&c.* the xiith of *Auguft*, 1567.

[a] *Sir* Warham Sent Leger *to Sir* Henry Sydney.

Myne humble Dutie don unto your Lordfhip,

IT may pleafe you to underftand, that upon *Sunday* laft, beinge the 13 of this Monthe, a Brother of Sir *Dermot Mc. Teigs*, called *Cormucke*, came to me to *Cork*, having ben with the Erle of *Clancarty*, *James Fitz Moris*, *Mc. Do-noughe*, and the reft of the *Irifhry* of the Southweft Partes, at their Parliament, that they helde ; from whome he underftode the whoel Effect of their Affembly, which as he creadably enformeth me, was for the fuer Fyrmyng of them felves together, to refift all your Lordfhips good Devices. And withall to fend Meffingers to the Kynge of *Spaigne*, for Aid to help them, in this their lewde Enterprice. And for a Proof, that they minde fuche Matters ; I am by the faid *Cormuck*, as alfo by others, credably enformed, that thefe vile Traitours have difpatched into *Spaigne*, to be Practitioners in their Villanye. The Bus-fhoppe of *Rofs* in *Carbury*, the popeft Traitour in *Ireland*, and alfo the ufurped Busfhoppe of *Caisfhell*, who thofe Traitors aforenamed ufed, as thoughe he weare a God. And great Goffeppry paffed betwene him and them, which is the great-eft Confirmation of Frendfhippe, that paffeth betwene this *Irifh* People.

Thefe two Divelifhe Prelats, be, by *James Fitz Morris*, conveighed into *Ker-ry* in the Erle of *Defmonds* Liberties ; where either of them be fhipped, or ells fhalbe, when they departe this Land ; either they be gon, or the next Wynde that ferveth they goe. This Mifchief is to be prevented in Tyme. In my poore Opinion, it were very requifit, the Queens Majeftie were forthwith adver-tifed herof, and that her Highnes may prefentlie, with all the Speede that may be, fend hether thofe well mynded Gentlemen, that intend to adventure their Lyves and Lyvings in thefe Partes. Which don, her Majefty fhall not only be afeured to have theife Traitors Devices prevented ; but with all, enjoy to her felfe good Revenue, and have this Cuntrey thoroughly refourmed ; towards the which, as I doubte not but your Lordfhip will be a Furdearer of this good Offer, wherin her Highnes fhall ftand in good Suerty, and receive good Bene-fit, you will with Expedicion procure their Comyng ; and if her Majefty, to-wards this good Attempte, bare thofe Gentlemens Charges, the firft Yeare, to-wards their better Encouragement, it were, in my fymple Judgment, a Some of Money as well beftowed, as was any Money in *Ireland*, this forty Yere. If there fhoulde happen Wars betwene her Highnes and the *Spanifhe* Kynge, it were greate Daunger to this Realme, to have thefe Southweft Partes unguard-ed ; and chiefly confideringe, what Liking the People of thefe Partes of the Country have to the *Spanifhe* Nation, by their deyly Trafacking together. The Comyng hether of thofe Gentlemen, with fuch Force, as they will bring with them, preventeth all their Mifchiefs, and as I faid before, refourmeth this Country ; and therefore, my good Lord, ageyn let me be bolde to befeche you to be erneft with the Queens Majefty, for the Setting furth of this good At-tempte. Thus muche I thought it my Duty to advertyfe unto your Lord-fhip, as alfo my poor Oppynion for the preventing of the Mifchiefs before written, and refourmyng this Country ; wherin if I take upon me to meddle

---

[a] Ireland. 1557. 1559, Lib. 5. p. 419, in his Majeftys Office of Papers and Recordes of State.

further then becometh me, I humbly crave Pardon, as one that myndeth well. So I humbly take my Leve. From *Cork*, this 14 *February* 1568.

Your Lordſhips evermore to comaund,

Warhame Sentleger.

Sir Henry Sydney, *to* Edward Clinton, *Earl of* Lincoln, *Lord High Admiral of* England.

My very good Lord,

I Receyved your Lettre of the laſt of *Ffebruary*, the xiiiith of this Inſtant, whereby I vnderſtand of the poore Gifte, it pleaſed your Lordſhip, to take in good Parte at my Handes, ſo as I muſt thanke your Lordſhip for that Curteſie ; beinge farre vnequall in Goodnes, vnto that I wiſhed him. And, as if I had one, coulde thinke him worthely beſtowed on your Lordſhip, ſyndinge my ſelf alwaies moche beholdinge vnto the ſame, for your contynuall Favors towardes me. And, for that I knowe not wheather your Lordſhip have of late receyved any Newes of the Doinges here, I thinke good to make a brief Reherſall of the ſame.

On the 19 Daye of *February* laſt, a Nomber of *Scotts*, of iiiiC, and odde, intendinge (as it was ſaide) to creat a newe Lorde of *Clandeboye*, not farre from *Knockfargus*, ment, vnder that Pretence, to enter a Woodde, nere *Caſtell Reagh*, which is not moche diſtant from the ſaide *Knockfargus*, to take away the Pray from thence ; whereof Capten *Peirs*, havinge Knowledge, iſſued out of *Knockfargus* in the Night, with vi ſcore Footemen, and lx Horſemen, marchinge towardes the ſaide Woodde, whether he commynge before Day, lay cloſe with his Company, and anone the *Iriſhe* Streinght, according to their former Purpoſe, came and gathered the Pray together, out of the Woode, and drave them a longe Myle, before Capten *Peirs* iſſued out, hopeing they had byne ſafe, and paſt all Daunger. But ymmediately, *Peirs* withe his Footemen compaſſinge them on Way, the Horſemen ſett vpon them, where by Overvaliantnes, and great Courauge, not able to ſtaye himſelf from th'Execution of his Service. One *Richarde Hunt*, a ſinguler Soldior of Name, with a Pellet, ſhotte into the Hedde, by *Owen Mac Gillaſpicke*, Cheifetaine of the *Scottes*, was ſtroken deade ; and twoe other Horſemen, their Horſes ſlayne vnder them, and they ſoe farre before their Company, as they had noe Reſcue, weare likewiſe ſlayne, beinge all that of our Company did periſhe. In which Tyme of Skirmiſhe, Capten *Piers* came on the other Syde of them, they beinge gotten over a Bogge, and forſaken their Pray, and ſo as the Horſmen could not come to them, and gave them a luſty Charge ; where they ſhewed ſoche Valiauntnes, wheather the over Nomber of theirs, to our Handefull, or the Vauntage of their Ground, encouraged them the rather, or not, I knowe not ; but the lyke Stoutnes, duringe ſo longe Tyme, was neuer ſeene emonge their Nacion, nor at that Tyme looked for by our Companie. In ſomoche as, by their haſtie Cominge on our Men, the Harquebuſſiers, diſchargeinge in there Boſomes, woulde not ſhrinke, but preſſed emongs them ſoe feirſlie as they, once diſchargeing, had noe Leiſure to charge agayne, but weare dryven to their Swordes ; and had not the Pikes and Holberdes bene, there had beene an evill a doe emongs our Soldiors, for Captaine *Piers* his Enſigne was torne in Titters, with very Fingers of the Enymies. The Medle contynued ſoe longe, and ſoe buſie, as he was not there, that had not his Hands full that Day ; and the Victory, on eyther Side, hanginge a great While doubtfull, it pleaſed God of his great Goodnes in th'Ende, to give the *Engliſhmen* the Vpphand, wheare weare dyvers hurte withe the *Scottiſhe* Arrowes, but none preſently ſlayne, nor deade thereof ſince, but one. And of the *Iriſhe* there was founde deade, as in one Quarrey, iiC and xv Bodies, beſides thoſe that weare ſlaine by the Horſemen, in the Flieinge awaie, and the Kearne that followed them twoe Dayes after, foe as it is judged the odde only efcaped not. So as thofe Partes, Thanks be to God, be very well quieted by this Meanes ; emongs whome, Mr. *Gillafpicke*, aforefaide, withe dyvers other of the chief Captaines, and Gentlemen of Name, weare lykewife flayne : And this, my good Lord, I thought to advertife you, as the onlye Newes of this wicked Countrey. And fo with my moft humble Commendacions to your good Lordfhip, reftinge allwaies at your Commaundement, prayinge for your Lordfhips longe and profperous Lyfe and Eftate, I take my Leave. From *Dublyn*, this of *Marche*, 1568, *&c.*

H. Sydney.

Sir Henry Sydney *to the Duke of* Feria, *in* Spain.

It may pleafe your Excellency,

I Wolde be gladde to fhowe fome greater Argument of my Loue and Dewtie towardes you, then by often Writinge, efpecially when my Lettres cary with them Caufe of Supplicacion, to the Trouble of your felffe. Neuertheleffe, fuche is the prefent Occafion, by the Defire which this Berer, Mr. *Verney*, hathe to trauell into thofe Countries, which are vnder the Septer of the moft Catholike Kinge, as I can not leaue him deftitute of my Commendacion to your Excellency. And this geuethe him no fmale Aduantage, that he is here defcended of an Howfe of a greate Honor ; and the Maner of his Liffe, hitherto, hathe promifed a Continewance of the Vertu of his Auncefters. Yt may therfore like you the rather, by your good Worde to the Catholike Kinge, to further him in his Trauell into *Naples*. And, if he fhall defire of your Excellencie to remaine any While in your Seruice there, my humble Defire is, that he may receaue your Furtherance to the Viceroy of the fame. And fo remayninge alwaife at your Deuocion, as the fmaleft Member of your Howfe, that couetethe dailie to doe you all the Honor he can. I humble take my Leaue. From the Courte at *Grenewiche*, redie to returne to my Gouuernement in *Irelande*, the laft of *Aprill*, 1568.

Your Graces Vncle to comaunde, as

Your Seruant,

H. Sydney.

Sir Henry Sydney *to* Robert, *Earl of* Leicefter, *fent by* Dowglas.

My dereft Lorde,

I Coulde not come foe neire your fayer and auncyent Caftell of *Killingwoorth*, as my Way led me to doe, and leave it vnfeene ; but thither I went, where the Entertainemente that my Cofin *Thomas Blunt*, and other your Servauntes gave me, fhewed their Civilitie, and that they knewe me to be your Lordfhips welbeloved Brother. There met me my Lord *Barkeley*, Sir *Foulke Grivell*, and *John Stanhope*. Sir *Giles Poole*, and *Thomas Throkmorton*, of *Glocefterfhire*, came thether with me. I woulde not hunt, but fifhe I did, and tooke an Hundrethe good Breames at a Draught, which I appointed to be kept for you, till your Lordfhips Comminge. I was neuer more in Love withe an olde Houfe, nor never newe Worke coulde better be beftowed, then that which you have done. I have appointed, *Saluo meliori Judicio*, where your Chappel fhall ftande. In the voide Roome, by *Cæfars* Tower, or agreably with the ftately Buildinge of the Houfe, to fill vp a Part of the Roome betweene *John* of *Gaunts* Buildinge, and the Porters Lodge ; whiche Chappell, if you will get me Home this next Springe, I and *Coxe*, at our owne proper Cofts and Charges, will be bounde to begynne and fynifh, within one Yeare, in fayer, decent, and durable Maner. In my Way towarde this Towne, I met this Bringer, my Man *Dowglas*, whom your

Lordfhip

Lordſhip put to me, whome I have of late (as ſundry Tymes by paſt) employed in *Scotlande*, to founde the Practiſes of them there for *Irelande*. He hathe brought me Intelligence of their Gatheringe, and Mynde to invade *Irelande*, and Suppocicion of the Earle of *Arguiles* doble Dealing, albeit he brought me Lettres to the Contrary. I vnderſtande by him, of a newe Leage betweene Therle and *Doneill Gorme*, pretendinge to be Soveraigne of the Iles ; there Forces are great, beinge ioyned. I have ſent the Earle of *Argiles* Lettre to Mr. Secretary, and the Letter of *Peirs* and *Malbie* ; by which you may vnderſtande the good Quiet of all the Quarters vnder their Rules, and the good Readynes the Shippinge is in, havinge good Fortune to mete with the *Scotts* in their Paſſage. I beſeche your Lordſhip, queſtion with this Fellowe, and then ſignyfie to the Queen my ſimple Opynion as followethe : *Firſt*, That her Highenes write to the Earle of *Arguile*, in ſoche pryncelyke Forme, as may ſeme beſt to her grave Wiſdome, that he kepe at Home thoſe idell *Scotts* ; for he maye do it if he will. This may be a Meane, whereby her Majeſtie may ſave a great Deale of Treaſuer, which otherwiſe ſhe muſt ſpende in Wageinge of Soldiors, for kepeinge her Countrey from their Vſurpacion. *Secondlie*, That I will not beſtowe any of the Treaſure, nowe appointed, for Building and Raſſinge of Soldiors to that Vſe, if they doe get in, but in proſecutinge of them ; I meane not withe any farder Charge then nowe her Highnes is at ; for they ſhall not wynter betweene the Sea, *Loughe foile*, *Strangforde*, and the *Engliſhe* Pale, if I be able to kepe the Feilde. *Thirdly*, That her Highnes will diſpatche Counſells into *Mounſter* and *Connaught*, for, as faſt as I ſhall mende *Vlſter*, they will marre, if there be noe Aucthoritie reſident emonge them. *Fourthlye*, That her Majeſtie write to the Juſtices there, that they be vigillaunt for the well Governeinge of the *Engliſhe* Pale, and dilligent to ſee me furnyſhed of my Wantes. If this be done, I have good Hope of Reformacion ; without this, I looke for none. Albeit, as you ſee by this, I intende to make Choice of the worſte Parte to my ſelf. I pray you, my Lorde, let this Bringer reaceve comfortable Wordes of you ; I have founde him faithfull ; it was he that brought in the *Scotts* that killed *Shane Oneill*. I have noe more, but that I have beene three Daies troubled withe my Diſeaſe : God helpe me, and ſende your Lordſhip a longe, happy, and mery Life. In Haſte and Payne, from *Saloppe*, this viijth of *Auguſt*, 1568.

Your Lordſhips aſſured Brother

to commaunde,

H. Sydney.

Sir Henry Sydney *to Mr. Secretary* Cecill, *ſent by* Dowglas.

IT may pleaſe you, Sir, to be advertyſed, that, in my Waie towarde this Towne, I mett withe this Bringer, a Man of myne, whome, not longe ſince, I ſent into *Scotlande*, as ofte heretofore I have done, to vnderſtand what was intended by them to *Irelande*. I have ever founde him faithfull, true of his Report (thoughe a *Scott*) and dilligent. He brought me a Lettre from the Erle of *Argile*, whiche I ſende you here incloſed. I ſende you alſoe Lettres from *Peirs* and *Malbie*, which beinge read, I praye you ſende me agayne. I thought good to ſende the Fellowe to you, to Th'ende he might open his Intelligence by Mouthe, with whom, if your Healthe ſerve you, I pray you interrogate ; the Points of his Intelligence moſt worthie Conſideracion, in my Opynion, are theis : The doble Dealinge of the Earle of *Argile*, his Confederacion with *Donill Gorme*, his auncyent Ennymie, nowe pretendinge to be Soveraigne of the Iles ; the Aſſembly of the *Scottes* ; and the Contribucion and Aſſiſtance of the Erle of *Caſshells*, and other lowe Land Lords. I beſeeche you, Sir, move the Queene, that withe Speede ſhe addreſſe her Counſells into *Mounſter*, and *Connaught*, without whiche, all will to Wracke there, while I ſhall goe about to

mende

mende fomewhat in *Vlſter*. That comfortable Lettres be written to the Juſtices, to looke well to the Governement of the *Engliſhe* Pale, and that they be dilligent to furniſhe me of my Wants. And to ſignyfie to her Majeſtie, that if the *Scotts* doe arryve, that I thinke it not convenyent to beſtowe any of the Treaſure, whiche I nowe carry over, ether in Buildinge or Raſſinge of Soldiors, but in profecutinge them. That her Highnes write her princely, and earneſt Lettres, to the Earle of *Arguile*, and others of that Nacion. That I have Letters to Sir *Richard Bulkeley*, Conſtable of *Beaumorryce*, *Hearley*, Conſtable of *Conwaye*, *Edwarde Harbert*, of *Mountgomery*, and *Hurleſton*, of *Cheſter*, to receaue foch *Iriſhe* Prifoners, or Pledges, as I ſhall fende thether, or to any of them. A Lettre of Favor to Sir *Brean Mac Phelim Bacco*. I befeeche you, Sir, remember the Vicount *Hereford*, you wot what I meane. The *Scottes*, and I, will not, God willinge, winter betwene *Longefoile* and *Strangforde*, but fome ſhall fmart for it. I truſt you fee I make not Choice of the eaſieſt Parte for my felf. I pray you haſte Capten *Gilbert* to me, withe as moche Speede as withe his Helthe he may. I have bene three Dayes fore trobled withe my Difeafe. I have no more, but moſt hartely I recommende vnto you my Wief, my felf, and my Boie; and I befeeche you recommend me humbly to my Ladie, your Wief, my Ladye *Bacon*, and my Lorde *Keper*. God guide you all withe his Holy Spirite, and bleſſe you withe a long, happy, and helthfull Lief. From *Saloppe*, this viijth of *Auguſt*, 1568.

Yours, aſſured and bounden.

H. Sydney.

You may fee by *Peirs* his Letter, what Readynes the Shippinge is in, to mete withe the *Scotts*.

Queen Elifabeth *to the Earl of* Argyle; *a Copy whereof was fent to Sir* Henry Sydney.

ALthoughe we vnderſtand, from our Deputy of our Realme of *Ireland*, Sir *Henry Sydney*, Knight of our Order, that vpon foche Lettres and Meſſage, as he lately receued from you, your good Meaninge to ſtaye, as moche as in you ſhall lye, the difordered Refort and Hauntinge of certen evill difpofed Peoplee, of the *Ilands*, and *Kentyre*, into the Northe Partes of our Realme of *Ireland*, there to invade and fpoile our good Subiects; and that you are the more earneſtly mynded thus to doe, in Refpect of the Goodwill we beare to the Queen of *Scottes*, your Soveraigne; for which your Goodwill we cannot but thanke you, and commend your good Dexterity, in being adverfe to foche barbarous rude People. Yet, forafmuche as otherwife we heare, that, at this prefent, the Heads of the faide People have aſſembled great Nombers, and made and levyed great Taxes of Victuall, and that partly in foche Countries as you have Charge of, and in other Places, where Th'erle of *Caſſells*, and foche like, as are nowe ioyned withe you in Freindſhippe, have to commaund: We have thought good thus plainly to write vnto you, that if thefe Reports ſhall prove true, and that any Nombers ſhall refort into our faide Realme, beinge in this Sort ayded and releeved vnder your Rule, we doubt not but they ſhall fynde fmall Advantage of their Comminge, or Intentions to annoy our Realme. And for your Parte, we ſhall make leſſe Accompt of foche Goodwill, as in Apparaunce you have pretended, bothe heretofore, and lately towardes us. And on the other Part, if your Doings ſhall accorde with your Lettres to our Deputy, you ſhall not faile, but fynde vs alwayes redie to acquite your Goodwill at all Tymes. And in this Sort we have thought beſt to write as plainlye as we meane, whiche in all Caufes proveth beſt. At *Eſton*, the xiiijth of *Auguſt*, 1568.

The Earl of Argyle's *Anſwer to Queen* Elifabeth.

Pleafe your Highnes,

I Reaceved your Majeſties Lettres at *Glaſſgo*, the xxijth Daye of *Auguſt*, perceueinge thereby, it is come to your Knowlege, my laſte Writinge fent to the Deputie of *Ireland*; whereof pleaſethe your Highnes to give me Thankes.

Conforme to my former Wrytinge written to him. My Mind was, and is to doe whatfoeuer might doe your Highnes Pleafure, foe farre as lyethe in my Power, in all Thinges that is vnder my Charge, or all others that I may refonably ftaye, from troublinga of your Highnes Country, or Liege. And that moft fpeacially, in Hope your Highnes will fet forwardes the Queenes Majeftie, my Soveraigne, to her Aucthority Ryal, and Suppreffinge of her vnnaturall and difobedient Subiectes; conforme to your Highnes Promife made to her Grace, whiche, I doubte not, but your Majeftie will doe, in Refpect of your princely Honor, and that my Soveraigne is foe nere of Blood to your Highnes. And where your Majeftie writethe, that there is great Nombers of People levied in my Bounds, and my Lord of *Caffels*, who is my Freinde, to invade your Majeftie Lieges in the Realme of *Irelande*; I affure, on my Honor, that your Majeftie fhall not fynd the Reportes to bee true, nor yet fhall doe nothinge that maye be offenfive to your Majeftie, you ftandinge good Freinde to my Soveraigne. But fhall doe your Highnes all the Honour and Service that lyethe in my Power, next her Grace, whom to I owe my Obedyence and Service. Thus makeinge my humble Commendacions of Service, committe your Majeftie to the Protection of th'eternall God, 24 of *Auguft*, 1568.

Your, &c.

Argyle.

Sir Henry Sydney *to Mr. Secretary* Cecill.

S I R,

IN my Lettre of myne owne Hand, I remember I noted vnto you (in fpeakinge of *Edward Butler*) a Servaunt of myne, of great Familiarytie withe him, and of Truft about my felf. At whofe earneft Peticion to travell the feconde Tyme to *Edward Butler*, and to make Proof what he coulde do by Perfwafion to bringe him hither, I lycenced him to departe, and is now retourned from him this Morning; after the Enfealinge of my other Letters, he declarethe, that he founde him in the County of *Tipporary*, nere *Durlees*, withe 1000 Men in his Company, his Brother Sir *Edmond* within twoe Miles of him, accompanid withe fo many, but in freindly Manner, without offeringe Violence one to the other. My Man vfed what Perfwacion he thought mete for his Repaier vnto me, alleadginge my Care of him in Tymes pafte, my Love to him for the prefent, his Education in my Houfe, the Honor of his Race, my good Inclynation to remyt his Fault, vpon Submiffion, and his owne Miferye, which woulde followe, if he fhoulde be proclaymed a Rebell. He anfweared in fome Things as thoughe he had a Difpofition to come, favinge that his Brother Sir *Edmond* was (as he faide) redy to cut his Men in Peces, as fone as they fhoulde departe: He alleadged the Hatred of his Brother, the Earle, towardes him; his owne Defertes to be foche, as he coulde looke for no Favour. Lately the Apprehenfion of Sir *John* of *Defmond*, who if for litle or nothinge was fent to the *Tower*: Howe fhall I (quoth he) prefume of Favour, that have thefe People aboute me, and fo many redy to complaine, if they fhoulde be defeuered. In Th'end, my Man procured a Conference betwene the twoe Brothers; they met, and had longe Speache togeather. Sir *Edmond* offered him very refonablie, in many Points, and defired to fpeake withe him in fecret. But to that *Edward* ainfwered, Your fecret Conference, Brother, hathe brought me to this Mifcheif, and therefore what you lifte to faye, fpeake openly. In Th'ende, they departed without any Conclufion; my Man ftill accompanid *Edward*, and, in Th'ende, departed from him, with this Determynacion, That he wolde neuer come at me without a Pardon, or a Protection; and with any of thefe I coulde bringe *Tirlaugh Lenagh* to *Dublin*, and could have done *Shane Oncill*, I fuppofe, when he was in the Cheif of his Pride. By theis Things, Sir, ye may gather his Difpofition, the Neceffitie of the Erles Comminge, who felethe the moft Smart of any other. The Amafednes of the People in thofe Parts, and the Feare to complayne, thoughe withe theis twoe great Companies they be, in a Manner, eaten vp. Nevertheles I am credibly enformed, that the whole Country is made to beleue by foche as come out of *England*, that all, vnder the Rule of my Lord of *Ormound*, are exempted from my Authority; and that this is the principall Caufe why they feeke for no Redreffe here. Sir, you knowe beft my Difpofition to be rid, not only from that, but from the reft, wherein I will bleffe every Inftrument that fhall furder my Reuocacion; and, fixinge my chief Hope vpon your felf, I leave to trouble you, this viiith of *November*, 1568.

Your bounden and affured to commaunde,

H. Sydney.

To the Same.

S I R,

AS this Bearer was redy to imbarke, Capteyne *Gilbert* arryved here, withe Lettres from the Queenes Majeftie, and other from your felfe. Thofe from her Highnes concerned the Earle of *Defmonde*, that Order might be taken for his Lyvinges, whereof Parte to ainfwere his great Dett to her Majeftie, and Parte to fupport his owne Charges there, and the Relief of the Counteffe here; wherin I will, withall convenyent Speede, trauell, to fett fome Order, accordinge to her Highnes Direction. But, if any Thinge procuer any Certainety of that Revenue, it will be the Refidence of a Prefident in *Mounfter*, whereof I here nowe fome Towardnes. At whofe Arryvall I fynde it moft expedyent that I repaire thether; whiche I cannot doe, vnles I be furnifhed with the Corne, whereof I wrote in my other Lettres by *Paule*. The Haft, as I faide, of this Bearer, and myne owne ill Hap to ufe Phificke, at this Inftant, is the Caufe that I defier to be excufed to her Highnes, that I write not more at Leingth in therles Caufes. But chieflie I confeffe it an Iniury to my felf, that I write not to you of myne owne Hande, in Ainfwere of your moft lovinge and kynde Lettres; which give me more Comforte, then euer I looked to enioye in this Governement. But in this Error you muft not only forgive me, for your owne Particuler, but alfoe excufe me to my Wief, to whome I have no Tyme to faie eny Thinge fince *Gilberts* Arryvall. The Comminge of him, and the Departure of *Sackford*, beinge, as it weare, in one Moment, otherwife I woulde haue craued Pardon for my longe Silence to you bothe, and woulde have alleadged, that I might iuftly foe doe, in thofe remot Parts of *Vlfter*, wheare nether Tyme, Place, nor Occafion, ferved for the Difpatche of any Meffinger. My other Lettres declare my Devocion to *Thomas Stukeley*, your poore repentaunt Follower; I am fuer from his Harte, for otherwife he coulde not enioye my good Countenance; but fince I nowe fee, that her Majeftie cannot allowe of his Service, I muft be forie for his Vndoinge, and ceafe my Suite; nether will I otherwife, then with all humble Reverence, challenge that whiche I might clayme by my Patent, and that whiche the Deputies here have alwaies difpofed; but make my Will her Majefties Will, in that Pointe: Nevertheles, as I thinke *Nicholas White* very able to execute the Office of Senefhall of *Wexford*, beinge a quiet Country, where no martiall Force is vfed, nor is greatly nedefull; fo if, within his Graunte, the Captentrye of *Laughlin*, the *Cavenanghtes*, and the Leadinge of Soldiers be conteyned, I cannot counfell that he is fitt for that Charge; otherwife I allowe of him, for his Iudgement, Honefty, and good Service. And he cannot want my affured Freindfhipe, when he findethe any Tafte of your Favour and good Opynion. And the fame I faie, for your Commendacions of Capten *Gilbert*, to whome I am as I have bene, unlefs your Lettre have encreafed my former Love to the Party. And foe wifhing that Mr. *White*, in his Lettres,

I

tres, weare exemptid from thofe Captenries, and martiall Matters, I ende withe my moft effectuall Commendacions. At *Dublin*, in Hafte, this xiiijth of *November*, 1568.

Your bounden and affured to commaund,

H. Sydney.

To the Same.

S I R,

AFTER the Fynifhinge of my other Lettres, and before the Shippinge paft out of this Haven, here arryved from *Corke* Sir *Wharham Sentleger* ; and, vppon Conferrence withe him of the Eftate of thofe Parts, I fynde not only all his former Reports confirmed concerninge the vndutyfull Behaviour of the Earle of *Clancarre*, but lately *Spanifhe* Shippes weare with him, and made fecret Combynacion with him to retorne agayne before *Criftmas* ; leavinge already in his Hande 1000 Targetts at the leafte, and a far greater Nomber of Sworde Blade Hargabuferie, and other Weapons : Befides, there is contynuall Meffage betweene the Northe and the Earle, and lyke Intercourfe betweene him and thofe that be in Armes in *Kilkenny* and *Tipporary*. His Followers give fourthe his Intendment, to be Kinge of the Southe Parte of this Realme. And I fynde good Proof, by Lettres from her Majefties good Subiects of thofe Parts, that Sir *Warhame* hathe bene the greateft Staye, without whom and *Greinvile*, they fuppofe the moft of the *Irifhrie* had revolted. And, forafmoche as I fee his Difpofition altogeather bent to be an Inftrument to ferve her Majeftie there, and that vpon his owne Charges, I will retorne him within thefe twoe Dayes withe foche Direction, as I fhall fynde meteft for the prefent Occafion : You may nowe call to Remembraunce my former Opynion touching this new Earle, made of an olde Rebell, andlyke enoughe to prove the moft dangerous Man, that, in our Memory, hathe bene in this Countrey, being beft affifted withe the Service of the *Mac Swynes*, and other mercenarye Soldiors, and lyeinge moft aptlie for forrin Affiftaunce of any other ; havinge a Nomber of good Havens at his Devotion, and thofe not without many Galleis, and other convenyent Shipping : And, fince the Tyme that I directed my Lettres vnto him for the Delyverie of the Lord *Fitzmarrice*, he kepethe him in more Dureffe then at any Tyme before my Sendinge : For thefe Caufes, Sir, I think it nedefull, that the *Spanifhe* Ambaffadoure of *Spaine* be talked with ; that the Prefident be haftned to come hither furnifhed with Money, and fome Force, till thefe Occafions be taken awaye. That the Corne for whiche I write, may forthwithe be fent to *Corke*. That *Sackforde* be retorned withe Speede. And if the Brute be true, that *William Wynter* is by her Majeftie already fent vnto the Seas, that he be dyrected to plie fome Tyme to the Southe of this Realme about *Baltymore*, to vifite thefe *Spanifhe* Practifers, becaufe I cannot well fpare the Shipinge here already, from attending the *Scottes* vpon the Coafte of *Vlfter*. This is all that prefently I think mete to be fpoken, favinge to befeche you to imparte thus moche to her Majeftie, in whofe Service I will extende the vttermoft of my Travell, bothe of Bodye and Mynde. And fo preparinge on *Mondaye* next to beginne a Iourney, and in it to vifite all *Leinfter*, I ende withe my hartie Comendacions. At the Caftell of *Dublin*, this xviith of *November*, 1568.

Your, &c.

H. Sydney.

To the Same.

ON the xvth of this prefent, I receyved yours of the 5 of the fame, fent me by my Brother *Fitzwilliam*; and doe truft, thoughe not in full Satisfaction of my Negligence pafte, yet in Excufe of fome Parte of the fame, before the Receipt of theis, others of myne by *Thomas Sackforde* are come to your Handes.

I receyved twoe Writings, conteyninge Rates for Prefidentes and Councells for this Realme; which I fende you herewithe againe, accompanid withe a thirde of myne own, not moche differinge from one of yours, whereby my Opynion may by you, (if it foe like you) be manyfefted to her Highnes, and others, at your Difcrefion; affirminge, and that vpon Knowlege, that no Eftate of a Councell can be placed to reduce ether of thefe Provinces to perfect Obedience, withe leffe Charge then in myne is fett downe; and howe the fame fhalbe borne (if it fo pleafe the Queene) by it apperethe alfoe; by which, if I have not mifcaft the Rates (as happely I have, for I my felf was the beft Auditor that was at the doinge of it) the Surplus of my Rate aboue the meaner Rate, fent by you, fhalbe borne, and her Highnefs noe more charged then prefently fhe is, and accordinge to the meaner Rate : Doubtles no Man lyvinge is able to ferue in ether of the Places : Then addinge the Charges of the fruteles Commiffiòners that from Tyme to Tyme muft be fent thither, and of Neceffitie; for els all woulde to Havocke, and the Revenue of her Lands nowe vtterly lofte, which doubtles, in fewe Years, will growe to a great Matter, with the Fynes that for Chearge of Bondes, and other Contempts, wilbe levied. I verily believe that, in a fhort Tyme, the Governement of thofe twoe Provinces will ftande her Majeftie in litell or nothinge.

Nowe if it be obiected, that I might have raffed fo many Soldiors as nowe I offer, albeit not foe imployed as in *Mounfter* and *Connaught*; to that I ainfwere, I coulde not, for that of Neceffitie I muft have to ainfwere foche fodaine Ventes as from Tyme to Tyme occurrethe, and to convey Commiffioners thither; for that ofte Tymes, by the Way, there is more Perill then in the Place whither they goe. And this I thinke fuffycyent, or, at the leafte, it is as moche as I can prefently devife to diffolue your dutifull and naturall Perplexitie betweene the Sparinge of the Queenes Treafure, and Advauncenge this Countryes common Weale. *Tirlanghe Lenanghe* is hunted on every Side, as by *Odonnell*, *Maguyre*, and them of *Clandeboye*; he feketh dayly to come to me, but not foe fimply, as in God I hope to make him. *Edward* and *Peirs Butler* are withe me, the firft in curteoufe Warde. My dere Sir *William*, get me Refolution for the Northe of this Lande, for, if her Highnes will not goe thoroughe withe the Plantenge of it, this next Springe (accordinge as I wrote by *Sackforde)* I can faue her Majeftie 5000 *l.* a Yeare, and have a large Rent promyfed; but I will not be bounde for Payment of it, nor I councell not to holde that Courfe.

I moft hartely thanke you for your curteous Vifitation of my Wief; I pray you fometyme harken of our Boye, and be workeinge howe to get Home the Father. I have no more, but withe my moft harty Commendacions to your felf, my Ladye, and my fweete Juell your Daughter, I wifhe you all afwell as I woulde my felf. From *Maryboroughe*, this lafte of *November*, 1568.

Yours bounden and affured,

H. Sydney.

P O S T C R I P T.

S I R,

Since the Writinge of my other Lettre herewith fent, I called to Rembraunce howe nedefull it is that the Prefidents be here at a Tyme certayne;

foe

foe as neither by there over foone Comminge, nedeles Charge, fhoulde be fpent, nor by their ouerlonge Taryinge, Tyme fhoulde be lofte. By the Ende of *Februarye* the Parliament will ende, and they muft foe be here as they may be redy to goe forwarde withe me, by the Begynninge of *Marche*, for by the vth of *Aprill* I muft be in the Northe, or ells it will not be well. I pray you be curious in this, and for him of *Mounfter*, let him come with Coyne and Money, or ells he weare as good to tary at Home: Even nowe am I advertifed from Capten *Peirs*, that certen of Capten *Malbies* Northen Horfemen; named Ratleges (*Malbie* being in the *Englifhe* Pale) have murdered *Ranuell.* *Og Mac Alifter Caraghe*, in Revenge of a particular Fude betweene them and him, for the Slaughter of twoe of their Bretheren, in deede evill killed by him and his Men; his Brother *Alexander* came in, in the Daie of his Buriall, whoe, findinge that it grew upon a particuler Quarrell, contented himfelf; and foe he, with all the reft, (thoughe in fome Sufpicion) remayne in Quiett and Obedyence. There weare xii of that Surname of the Confpiracie, whereof three are taken, and one alredy hanged in Chaines by *Peirfs*; the Doinge was evill, but the Deede good. This Daye I receved this Letter, fent me by the Attorney of this Realme, and addreffed to him by the Widowe Lady of *Dunboyne*, Mother to the Queenes Warde, nowe in *Englande*; I beleeue euery Thinge therein conteyned as if I fawe it, foe credybly am I aduertifed of it. It is to lamentable to vnderftande the pityfull and nedeles Calamytie that the Queenes Majefties good and obedient Subjects fuffer, only by the Extorcion of the Earle of *Ormonds* Followers, and his Bretheren, in thofe Quarters, in Mayntenaance of *Coyne* and *Lyvery*, and his abufed Liberty, whiche is to me a *Noli me tangere, quia,* &c. For the Honor of God, Charitie, and Knighthood Sake, be good to the Widowe and Infant, and move the Queene eyther to charge my Lord of *Ormond*, or vs to fee it amended. I pray you haften fome Money to me, written as before, and Year, as before.

Sir Henry Sydney *to Mr.* Secretary Cecill.

S I R,

VPPON the firft Metinge of the Earle of *Ormonde* and me at *Lymericke*, I reaceued a Letter from the Queenes Majeftie, very largelie in his Favour, the Coppie whereof I fende you here inclofed. And becaufe it ftandethe upon many Parts, whereof fome be very mete and allowable, fome to be refpited and well confidered of, and other extreme dangerous (in myne Opynion) bothe for the State, and for my felf, without Affiftaunce to deale in: I am bolde not only to crave your Advife, but alfoe that I may have a Countermande either not to deale in it, or to procede by the Opynion of the whole Counfell, and the Letter foe to be endorfed to us all.

The firft conteyninge his Right to the Prize Wynes of *Youghall*, and *Kinfale*, pronounced by the Judges in *England*, I knowe duly to apertayne vnto him: And therefore, accordinge to the Tenor of her Majefties Commandement, the Receyvors of the Wynes by Sequeftracion, fhalbe fourthwith appointed to ainfwere the Profitts to foche as the Earle fhall affigne; and this I thinke very iufte and requifite.

The fecond for Reftitution to the Earle of *Ormonde*, and his Tenaunts, by *Defmonde*, and his Followers, femethe very ftraunge. The Booke thereof, as I heare, amountethe to aboue fiftie Thoufande Poundes; and the Demands of *Defmonde* againft the Earle are accompted to be littel leffe, whereof no Mention is made. If this fhoulde be reftored, all the Cattell and Houfholde Stuffe in *Mounfter* (the Corporations excepted) are not worthe it; if the Landes be delyvered in Pledge, all *Defmondes* whole Inheritance, beinge reafonablie furveyed, will not ainfwere this 50000 *l.* thefe fortie Yeres to come. If then it be neceffary, and not perilous to the State, that the Earle of *Ormond*, be not only Earle of *Ormonde* and *Offerie*, and Countye Palautyne of *Tip-*

porarye,

porarye, but alfoe Earle of *Defmonde*, and Lorde of the Lybertye of *Kiery*, I woulde gladly be refolued. And then what Hope is lefte for *Defmonde*, and the Counteffe to lyve; what Order for the Recoverie of 20000 *l.* forfeited to her Majeftie? And when *Dias*, the *Portugeffe*, fhalbe reftored to foche Somes as are awarded to him, I knowe not. But hereof I doubt not, that where, by my late Arryvall in *Mounfter*, I withdrewe half the Force of *James Fitzmorrice*, by encourageinge Sir *Thomas* of *Defmonde*, the Earles Brother, and many other of his Kinfmen, to ferue her Majeftie; that affone as they fhall fynde the Earle of *Ormonde*, there auncyent Ennemye, to be poffeffed of the others Inheritaunce, they will not only dangerouflie revolte, but all the Countrye withe them, that have fufteyned Hurte by the *Butlers*, and their Followers; whereof, I thinke, duringe the Contencions betweene the Earles, all *Monfter* tafted. And, wheather it be now feafonable to make Warrs with foe great a People, is a feconde Queftion.

The thirde that he be free, and exempted from all Ceffes, and Impofitions, upon his owne Landes. The Subfidies excepted, femethe no great Matter, and is indeede the leffe, becaufe the Burdens, layed by Ceffe upon the Pale, is not often extended to the Counties of *Kilkenny* and *Tipporary*. But the Earle hathe dyvers Lyvings within the Pale it felf; and this Claufe caufethe others of the Nobilitie, to looke for like Privilege. And Yefterdaye they made Peticion vnto me for it, iudginge and affirminge, that there Services had well deferued thus moche Favour; and therefore hoped I woulde have Confideracion of them, whome the Refpect in that Article touched as moche, as the Earle of *Ormonde*, or any other. I woulde be therefore refolued, wheather the Example be good, to have the Nobilitie exempted, for their great Portions, and the Ceffes, taken here by the Prerogative Royall, to be laide vpon the Sholders of a fewe Men, who beare already as great a Pack as they can fufteyne.

The fourthe to provide Victualls at her Majefties Prices, in Apperaunce no great Matter, and extenuated and made leffe by this, that it is granted but for a Tyme, and that to be lymitted by me. Sir, I will ainfwere this by Example. At my late beinge in *Connaught*, I eftablifhed there the Prefident Sir *Edward Fitton*, who, before my Iorney, exhibited certain Peticions to be confidered by the Counfell; emongs which one was to like Effect, to provide Victualls as the Governor dothe. For my Parte, knowinge the principall Place that he helde within that Province, I thought it reafonable, that, as farre as his Commiffion extended, he fhoulde have Liberty to provide Victualles at like Rates; but, comminge in Queftion before the whole Councell, they concluded thus: That they had but one Queene, and her Majeftie had but one Deputie, and he fhoulde have the Prerogative, and none other. And foe the Lord Prefident refufed of his Peticion. Therefore it woulde be confidered, wheather that is fitt to be graunted to the Earle, which was denyed to a principall Officer, and for her Majefties Houfholde, in *Connaught*, or not: And wheare it is alleadged, that other have the like, that cannot be prouid; and therefore I iudge that this hathe proceeded of wronge Enformacion.

In the vth, it is thought mete to be provided by Parliament, that Eftates fhoulde ceaffe, *&c.* In this I will not hinder any Bill that he fhall put vpp, but many Gentlemen that have Landes of his in the *Englifhe* Pale, in Fee farme, and otherwife, thinke themfelues narowly touched in this, and, therefore, I iudge, the Bill will hardly paffe; but, if it paffe not, I knowe not howe to compell them; but fure, as farre as Juftice will extende, I will favorably proceede, and will treate withe the reft, if they be brought vnto me; wherein he fhall have any ordynary Proceffe or Commaundement for their Aparaunce; but if they doe not confent in all Points to his Lordfhips Likeinge, haveinge Lawe on their Side, I cannot vfe compulfary Meanes to wreft Juftice, nor, I hope, it is not required in my Place.

The vjth and vijth, conteyne his Peticion for *Langhlin*, and his Recompence for the fame; wherein his Titell fhalbe examyned, and the Examinacion, withe

I

my Opynion of that whiche he defirethe in Recompence, certyfied to her Ma-
jeftie ; but if his Lordfhip meane to challenge the Queenes Majefties Houfe of
Langhlin ; which I gather by this, that it is alledged, that it was builded in his
Mynorytie : I mervell howe he can intitle himfelf to a Houfe of Religion by
Inheritance ; if he meane the olde Caftell in *Langhlen* Towne, I beleue (and fo
I am credibly enformed) that there was no newe Increafe of Buildinge there
thefe 100 Yeares. And, therefore, it fhalbe the more exactly examyned and
advertyfed. And thus boulde, not only to crave your Opynion, but her High-
nes full Refolucion in thefe Thinges, or ells that it may be referred to others,
afwell as my felf, I bidde you moft hartely Farewell. At *Dublin*, the xvijth of
October, 1569.

Your, &c.

H. Sydney.

To Mr. Secretary Cecill.

IF there remayned any reioyfinge Humours in me, the former Parte of your
Lettre of the 25 of the lafte, which, togeather with an other of the 28 of
the fame, I receued the 12 of this prefent, weare fuffycient not a litell to comforte me. But I affure you, I have felt Myfery without Releif fo longe, as I
remaine foe fenfeles, as I thinke nothinge can reviue me ; noe fcantly Redemption from this my Servitude, aboue all worldly Things moft hevieft to me. I
dare affyrme, there is no Servaunt in *Chriftendome*, that indurethe greater Toile
of Mynde and Bodie then I doe, nor that with fo litell Affiftaunce weldith fo
weightie Matters, and metethe withe fo many and variable Accidents ; and, albeit the Hapines of the Event excedethe farre ordynary Expectacion, yet as, in
the Proceadinge, I found litell Comforte or Confideracion : So, in the Ende,
I finde leffe Thanke, or good Acceptacion ; herewith I have foche a Familier of
Penury, as I thinke neuer none endured as a Prince Deputie ; What fhoulde I in
particuler dilate it, when I am forced to borrowe, yea almoft to begge for my
Dynner ? Howe then dothe my Servaunts, howe then my Soldiors, but moft of
all, howe dothe the poore Countrey, which hathe borne all, without receyvinge
any Thinge, theis tenne Yeres paft ? Suerly ftarvinge, ripe, abandon the Countrey, and leave it waft ; with this I am, I thanke my good Happe, hated of all
here ; of the Nobility, for depofinge their Tyranny ; of the Merchaunt, for
that, by my Perfwafion, he hathe fo farre trufted the Soldiors, as not receyvinge
his Money is become Bankerupt (and indede fo are fome) of the Gentleman,
for that he cannot get his Rent of his Tenaunts, thoroughe theire Kepeinge of
the Soldiours ; the Hufbandmen cry out of me, and will doe no Worke, for
that they are neuer paide for fo long Beareinge the Soldiors : The Soldiors have
twife refufed to goe to the Feilde, for that the Horfman is not able to fhoe his
Horfe, nor the Footeman to bie a Paier of Shoes to his Feete ; and when I punifhe one of them for any Offence, done to the Hufbandman, the reft are redye
to mutyne ; and in deede, for the moft Parte, Hunger enforceth them to doe
that which they doe, and fteale awaye my Soldiors doe every Daye. What
Affiftaunce I have to eafe me in all this, God knowethe ; what I want I feele ;
in efpeaciall my Lord Chauncelor, nowe lame of the Gowte, and Mr. *Agard*
almoft ftarke deafe : In Fyne, I have not a Man of the Counfell, of any Action
in Effecte, but *Cufacke* and *Bagnall* ; and God knowethe, withe what Digeftiues
I recyve out of them ; iudge. To eafe thefe, none knowethe fo well as you ; but,
howe my Lettres are allowed there, God knoweth ; it femethe it is not mete
for me to vnderftand, for I had neuer Anfwere of any I wrote fince *Auguft*, by
Owen Moore. And, to knitt the Knotte of this Sacke of Sorrowes, I feele daily
Increafe of Decaye in Helthe, and yet not halfe faft ynoughe ; for, if I weare
ftarke blinde, or ftarke lame, withe Quietnes of Mynde, I fhoulde holde my
felf excufed, in not doinge that, which nowe, without Thanke, I doe. But, Oh
Lorde, why ranefacke I thus theis tender Woundes, fpeacially in your Prefence,

since

since by good Proof I finde, that you be confentible and conpatible with me ; well, I will noe more of this nowe, for I feare I have done to moche ; yet fomewhat, I confeffe, I am eafed by openinge this my Greif. Nowe for our Particulers, and for our Children ; I am forie that you finde Coldenes any where in Proceadinge, where foche good Likeinge apered in the Beginninge ; but, for my Parte, I never was more redye to perfecte that Matter, then prefently I am ; affuringe you, for my Parte, if I might have the greateft Princes Daughter in *Chriftendome* for him, the Matche fpoken of betwene vs on my Parte fhold not be broken. Articles, I confeffe, I receued, figned, as I remember, by my Lord of *Leicefter* and you, and well allowed by me ; but wheare they be God knowethe, for *Waterhoufe* is weaned from me, and *John Thomas* is ficke ; the Paper I cannot fynde, but this for Trothe, Sir, I was neuer more ioyous of the Matche then nowe I am ; but howe, and whiche Waye, never conferre withe me while I am here, without fpeciall Direction, for I nether can care, nor confider, while I here dwell, for Wief, Childe, or my felf *. Remember the Queenes Profitte, afwell by Increafinge her Revenues, as Savinge a thoufand Pownds a Monethe in Soldiours Wages. I pray you commend me moft hartely to my Lady, and to our Daughter *Anne*. God bleffe you all. From the Caftell of *Dublyn*, this 24 of *February*, 1569.

Yours affured to commaunde,

H. Sydney.

Orders ᵃ *taken by the Queenes mooft excellent Majeftie, with the Aduife of hir Counfell, in the Caufes of the Erles of* Ormond, *and* Defmond ; *and by hir Majeftie, in Writyng, as followeth ; declared and notefyed to both the Erles.*

FURST it is ordered by her Majeftie, that the fayd Erles fhall proceed in the Chauncery in *Irelande*, by Bill and Aunfwer, to an Iffue concernyng all Matters in Queftion betweene them ; afwell for any Lands, Tenements, Offices, or other Hereditaments ; as alfo for all Manner of Slaughters, Ryots, Frayes, vnlaufull Affemblies, Breaches of the Queenes Majefties Peace, Spoylers and Deteynours of Goods, Cattells, or Men ; and for all Maner of Offenfes and Trefpaffes, don by one againft the other, or committed againft the Queenes Majefties Lawes of the Land there ; and thus, without any dilatory Plees, or Delayes, other then fuch as the Lord Deputye and Chauncellour there fhall allowe of.

2. *Item*, It is furder ordered, that, after Iffue ioynd, as aforfayde, and after Advertifement therof, from the Lord Depute and Counfail there, vnto the Queenes Majeftie ; fuch and fo many Commiffions fhalbe awarded, vnder the Great Seale of *Englande*, to fuch Perfons, and in fuch Forme, as, after Advife from the fayd Lord Depute and Counfaill, it fhall pleas her Majeftie to graunt, for the Tryall of the fayd Iffues ; which Commiffions, with their Certeficats, fhalbe retourned, firft to the Lord Depute and Counfaill in *Irelande*, and by them fhalbe opened, and well confydered ; and thereupon the fame fhal be retourned to her Majeftie, with the Opinion and Advife of the fayd Lord Depute and Counfaill, vppon the Certificat of the fayd Commiffions, or Commiffioners, fo as her Majeftie maye tak fuch Order, as the Iuftice of the Caufes fhall require, vpon the due Examination and full Vnderftanding of the fame, by Thadvife of her Counfailes, both in *Englande* and *Irelande*.

3. *Item*, It is ordered further, that the Profits and Revenues of the Price Wynes of the Ports of *Yoghall* and *Kenfale*, fhalbe, from Tyme to Tyme, receved and taken, by fuch indifferent Perfons, as the Lord Depute and the Counfaill there fhall appoint, vntil fuch Tyme as the Queenes Majeftie fhall,

---

* This related to his Son, Sir *Philip Sydney*.   ᵃ Ex Autog. apud Penfhurft.

by Order vnder the Great Seal, determyn, to whom, of Right, the fame Profits do belong. And that fufficient Bond be taken, by the Lord Depute and Counfaill, of the Perfons fo appointed to aunfwer the fame truely, accordinge as by the Queenes Highnes Order it fhalbe declared, the Right of the fame to apperteyn.

4. *Item,* It is alfo ordered, that all Maner of Lands, Tenements, and Hereditaments, wherof the Erle of *Ormonde* was in quiet Poffeffion, before the Fray comitted, and made between him and Therle of *Defmond,* in the Demefnes in the County of *Waterford,* the Firft of *February* laft paft, fhall remayn in Poffeffion of the fayd Erle of *Ormond,* without Trouble or Vexation of the fayd Erle of *Defmond,* vntil fuch Tyme as Order be taken, by the Quenes Majeftie as aforefayd ; or vntil the fayd Erle of *Defmond* hath recovered the fame, by the ordinary Courfe of the Lawes of the Realm of *Irlande.*

5. *Item,* It is alfo ordered, that all Maner of Lands, Tenements, and Hereditaments, wherof the fayd Erle of *Defmond* was in quiet Poffeffion, before the fayd Fraye comitted, and made betwene him and the fayd Erle of *Ormond,* in the Demefnes, in the County of *Waterford,* the Furft of *February,* fhall remayn in the Poffeffion of the fayd Erle of *Defmond,* without Trouble or Vexation of the fayd Erle of *Ormond* ; vntil fuch Tyme as Order be taken by the Quenes Majeftie, as is aforefayd, or vntil the fayd Erle of *Ormond* hath recovered the fame by the ordinary Courfe of the Lawes of the Realm of *Irlande.*

6. *Item,* It is alfo ordered, that fuch of the Lands and Hereditaments of either of the fayd Erles, as fhall appere to the Lord Depute and Counfaill, vpon Examination by them to be made, to haue ben in doubtfull, and not in quiet Poffeffion, at the Tyme of the fayd Fray, fhall remayn and be in the Poffeffion of fuch indifferent Perfons, as the Lord Depute and Counfaill fhall name, without Let or Difturbance of either of the fayd Erles, vntil fuch Tyme as the Quenes Highnes fhall take Order as aforfayd, or vntil fuch Tyme as one of the fayd Erles fhall recovor the fame againft the other by thordinary Courfe of the Laws there. And that Bonds be taken of the Perfons, fo to be named, for the Aunfwering of the Profits which they fhall receve of the fayd Lands, to fuch, as by the fayd Recoverey or Order, they fhall apperteyn.

7. *Item,* It is furder ordered, that the fayd Erle of *Ormond,* and his Servants, and Folowers fhall kepe the Quenes Majefties Peas againft the fayd Erle of *Defmond,* his Servaunts and Folowers ; and that likewife the fayd Erle of *Defmond,* his Servaunts and Folowers, fhall kepe the Quenes Majefties Peace againft the fayd Erle of *Ormond,* his Servaunts, and Folowers, vntil it fhalbe otherwife ordered by her Majeftie.

8. *Item,* Forafmochas vpon Examination of the great Diforder committed in the forfayd Fraye, betwixt the fayd two Erles, in open Feld, with Men armed, both on Horfeback and on Fote, by Reafon of the Contraryete, appering afwell in the Aunfwere of the fayd Erles, being therewith chardged, as in the Teftimony of fum Perfons examined theruppon in *Irlande,* and fent hither in Writting, it hath not fully appered whether both the fayd Erles haue ben gilty of the fayd Difordre and Conflict as they haue been chardged, or wherwith they hath ben mooft gilty therof ; but that a further Tryall of the Trouth therof is to be made by Commiffion in *Irlande :* Her Majeftie, notwithftanding, perceiving plainly, that her Peas was evidently broken by the fayd Conflict and Fraye, and fundry of her People therin flayne, and that both the fayd Erles did fight in open Felde, although that the one chardgeth the other with the Begynnyng ; hath thought meet for Punifhement therof, and doth order, That either of the fayd Erles fhall yeld to her Majeftie in the Name of Fine, as a Knowledg of the Breach of Peas, the Somme of   thoufand Pounds, to be taken of the Profits of their Goodds and Lands, within the fame Realm of *Irlande,* to her Majefties Vfe. And yet, nevertheles, if, vppon Examination and Certificat to be made of the fame, her Majeftie fhall iudge that one of them did therin offende, and that the other was not gilty

of the Offenfe, or was not fo much in Faulte as the other; that the Party judged gilty fhall pay the Fyne afore affeffed; and the other fhall, either be acquited, or, according to the Quantitie of the Offence, moderated in the Payment of the fayd Fyne.

9. *Item,* Where both the fayd Erles be indebted to the Queenes Majeftie in diuers great Summes of Moneye, afwell vppon Prefts and Loanes made vnto them by her Majeftie, as for Rents and other Duetyes due to her Majeftie: It is ordered by her Majeftie, that the fayd Erles, after their Arryval in *Irlande,* fhalbe called to Accompt, and fhall mak Payment of all fuch as fhall appear to be due Debt in fuch Sort and Manner, as her Lord Depute and Counfaill fhall order and decree, mooft for Thadvantage of her Majeftie, according to the Neceffite of her Service.

10. *Item,* It is ordered, that the fayd Erle of *Ormonde* fhall, within twenty Dayes next after his Repayr in to *Irlande,* delivre to the Lord Depute and Counfail a Bill in Writting, conteyning the Names of all fuch Perfons as he fhalbe able to chardg with any Treafon, Murdre, Felonnye, or other notable Offence againft the Peace, and whom Therle of *Defmond,* or any by his Commaundement, or Confent, doth maynteyn in his Countrey: Whereupon the fayd Depute and Counfaill fhall giue Knowledge to the fayd Erle of *Defmonde,* and him fhall chardge to caufe all the fame Perfons, or fo many of them, as the Lord Depute and Counfaill fhall think meet, to be apprehended and produced to aunfwer to fuch Offence, as, by Order of Lawe, they ought to be; which Chardge and Commaundemente, the fayd Erle of *Defmonde* fhall, to his vttermooft, obferue and kepe in fuch Manner, as the fayd Lord Depute and Counfaill fhall prefcribe.

11. *Item,* It is alfo ordered, that the fayd Erle of *Defmonde* fhall, within twenty Days next after his Repayr in to *Irlande,* delivre to the Lord Depute and Counfaill a Bill in Writting, conteyning the Names of all fuch Perfons as he fhalbe able to chardge with any Treafon, Murdre, Fellonnye, or other notable Offence againft the Peas, and whom the Erle of *Ormonde,* or any by his Commaundment, or Confent, doth maynteyn in his Countrey: Wheruppon the fayd Lord Depute and Counfaill fhall giue Knowledge to the fayd Erle of *Ormonde,* and him fhall chardge, to caufe all the fame Perfons, or fo many of them as the Lord Depute and Counfaill fhall think meet, to be apprehended and produced to aunfwer to fuch Offence, as by Order of Lawe they ought to be; which Chardge and Commaundmente, the fayd Erle of *Ormonde* fhall, to his vttermooft, obferue and kepe in fuch Manner, as the fayd Lord Depute and Counfaill fhall prefcribe.

12. *Item,* It is alfo ordered, that the Lord Depute and Counfaill fhall here and determyn as manny of the Controuerfies before remembred, concerning Goods and Cattells, or the Deteynors of them, or of any Perfon or Perfons imprifoned, in fuch Sort and Manner as fhalbe thought to them meeteft, for the Service of her Majeftie: And for fuch of the fame Controverfyes as fhalbe thought not meet or neceffary to be determyned by the fayd Depute and Counfaill, that the fame fhalbe remitted to the Order of her Majeftie, vppon Retourn of the Commiffioners aboue mentioned. And, whatfoeuer Orders the Depute and the Counfaill fhall take in the Matters mentioned in this Article, the fame fhalbe as good and effectual, and taken and accepted, as though the fame was exprefly prefcribed and ordered by her Majeftie; any Thing before remembred, to the Contrary, notwithftanding.

13. *Item,* It is furder ordered, that the fayd Erle of *Ormonde* fhall, within twenty Days next after his Repayr in to *Irlande,* put in fuch fufficient Pledges to the Lord Depute, for the Parformance of any of the Things, which, by Recognifance, bearing Date the xxijth Day of *Nouembre* laft paft, he is, or fhalbe bound to performe, as the fayd Lord Depute and Counfaill fhall think meete; and the fame fhall deteyn or alter, or fully delyuer, and put to Liberte, as fhall feme to the fayd Lord Depute and Counfaill neceffary for the Service of her Majeftie, and Contynuance of her Peas in that Realm.

14. *Item,*

14. *Item*, It is likewife ordered, That the fayd Erle of *Defmonde* fhall, within twenty Dayes next after his Repayr in to *Irlande*, put in fuch fufficient Pledges to the faid Lord Depute, for the Performance of any of the Things, which, by Recognifance, bearing Date as in the aforefayd, the xxijth Day of *Nouembre* laft paft, he is, or fhalbe, bound to perform, as the fayd Lord Depute and Counfaill fhall think meet ; and the fame fhall deteyn or alter, or fully delyuer, and putt to Liberte, as fhall feme to the fayd Lord Depute and Counfaill neceffary for the Service of her Majeftie, and Contynuance of her Peas in that Realm. In Witnes wherof, We have caufed our Great Seale of *Englande* to be putt to thefe Prefents, being figned with our owne Hands. Geven at our Pallace at *Weftminfter*, the xxiijth Day of *December*, 1565, the viijth Yere of our Reigne.

The Submiffion of Therle of Ormonde.

WHERE I have byn charged, before your moft honorable Lordfhips, of late, with Thaffembling of a Force of Men in warlike Maner ; and that I have carried the fame Men with me, from myne owne Countrey in to the Countie of *Waterforde*, and there did kill a grete Nomber of Therle of *Defmonds* Men ; whereupon I dyd than declare the Caufes of my Affembling of thofe Men, and my other Doings, that I was than charged withall, to be fuche as my Aunceftours, and other noble Men of the Realme of *Irlande* heretofore, for their owne Defenfe, and for the Defenfe of the Subjeðts adioyning to them, have, Tyme out of Mynde, vfed to do ; and that, without Doing thereof vpon fuche Occafions, as the faid Erle of *Defmond* then dyd minifter, the noble Houfes of that Realme could not have had Contynuance hitherto ; neither can they have Contynuance hereafter, fo long as any Subieðt there fhalbe permitted to levie, vnlaufully, any Force offenfive ; and that the Force I levied was, forft, for the Defenfe of myne owne Countrey ; and, being affembled, went, at Sir *Moryces* Requeft, in to his Contrey, to bring away his Cattell, vnder my Garde, in to myne owne Countrey ; and travelling quietly within a Myle of Sir *Moryces* Houfe, in the high Way, Therle of *Defmond*, accompanned with a grete Number of proclaimed Traitours, and *Ierifhe* Rebells (whom I had Commaundement and Auðtoritie, from the Governour, to profecute with Force and Severitie) fet vpon me, as appereth by Depoficions ; fo as I was driven, for Savegard of my felf, and my Company, to comit fome Slaughter vpon his Men, and the faid Traitours and Rebells ; which I thought, by the Lawes and Cuftomes of the Realme of *Irlande*, I might have don, for the Defenfe of my felf and others, the Quenes Majefties Subieðts, and the Refifting of any Perfon, that woold attempt any fuche vnlewfull Force, as Therle of *Defmonde* than did attempt ; vpon whiche my Declaracion, your Lordfhips favorably did advife me to confider well, whether I myght iuftefie my Doings by the Lawes, as I thought I myght, and fo woold ftand in Law againft her Majeftie, in the Iuftefieng of my Doings, or fubmit my felf to her Highnes Order. Wherunto I than affured, and fo now do, that I will never ftand in Law againft my moft dere and dread Sovereine Lady, in that, or any other Mater, but do heer moft humbly fubmit my felf to be ordered by her Majeftie, according to her moft gracious Pleafure and Commaundement ; humbly befeching your good Lordfhips, therwith, to perceyve that my Defire of your Lordfhips, to confider of the Lawes and Cuftomes of *Irlande* than, was not foe, that I dyd, or do feeke to iuftefie my felf therby, but for that, my Offence might, vpon your favorable Confideracion of them, appere to you to be no worfe than it was : I meane, not ment of Malyce, by an offenfive Invafion, but rather of a good Zeale, in Defenfe of her Majefties good and *Englifshe* Subieðts, vnlawfully invaded.

Thomas Ormond and *Offery.*

The Submiſſion of the Erle of Deſmonde *to the Quenes moſt excellent Majeſtie.*

WHERE, by the honorable Eſtates of the Quenes Majeſties moſt honorable Pryvie Counſell there, are obiected and layde to the Charge of me *Garret*, Erle of *Deſmonde*, diverſe and ſundry Treaſons, Murders, Burnings, and other criminall Offences, againſt the Quenes moſt excellent Majeſtie, her Lawes, Crowne, and Dignytie : I, the ſaide Erle of *Deſmonde*, do moſt humbly, lowly, and obediently, ſubmytt my ſelf, my Life, Landes, and Goodes, to my ſaide ſovereign Ladye, *Elizabeth*, by the Grace of God, Quene of *England*, *Fraunce*, and *Irelande*, Defendour of the Faythe, &c. to be ordered and directid by her Majeſties Determynacion and Iudgement, in all and ſinguler the ſayde Offences ſo layde to my Charge, ſince I receyved the Benefyte of her Majeſties moſt gracious Pardon. Wherein I do moſt humbly beſeche her Clemency, to ſtande my good and gracious Ladye ; and, with lyke Humylytie, I beſeche her Excellency to graunt vnto me, as to the reſt of her good and faythfull Subiects, the ordinary Courſe of her Graces common Lawes, for the Tryall of ſuche Tytle or Eſtate of Inheritaunce, as ys, or may be in Demaunde, betwene anye other of her Majeſties Subiects and me, who am, and wilbe for ever, lyke as hereby I do acknowledge my ſelf, her Majeſties humble, faythefull, loving, duetyfull, and obedyent Subiect. In Wytneſſe whereof, to be bothe faythefully ment, effectually ſpoken, and to be confirmed and approved with my Deedes and Fydelytye hereafter, I haue herevnto ſubſcribed my Name, and ſett my Seale, the xijth Daye of *September*, 1565, and in the vijth Yere of her Majeſties moſt proſperous Reign.

Gerrat Deſmond.

A Formular [a] *of Inſtructions and Orders, for the Eſtabliſhyng of a Counſell in* Munſter, *with a Lord Preſident to govern the ſame.*

THE Lorde Deputy and Counſell *of the Realm*, hauinge ſuche Care as becommith *them*, for the vniuerſall good Gouermente of this her Majeſties Realm ; and finding that the remote Parts thereof haue of longe Time, by Lack of Juſtice, and Adminiſtracion of Lawes, continued in greate Diſorders : And that, vppon good Conſultacion herein of longe Time had, no Menes can be fownde more meete, to reduce the ſame to Order, for the Honor and Seruice of Allmighty God, for Obedience to the Queenes Majeſtie, for the Recouerie and Conſeruacion of comon Peace and Tranquilitie, and finally, for to breede and eſtabliſhe all good Ciuilitie, then to haue Juſtice indifferently applied and adminiſtrid to all States and Sortes of People, haue, for that Purpoſe, certified the ſame to the Queenes moſte excellente Majeſtie ; who hauinge no leſſe princelye and naturall Regarde to her ſaide vniuerſall Realm, and to the People thereof, then even to her Realm of *Englande* : And beinge deſierous, that the Knowledge of Allmightie God, and the good Fruits of Juſtice, ſhoulde be equally diſtributid throughe all Partes of her ſaide Realm, hathe (withowte Regarde had to anye Charge of Expence of yerelie Somes of Money) geven Commaundement *to her ſaid Lorde Deputie and Counſell of her Realm, accordinge to their Aduiſes*, to erecte and eſtabliſhe, by her Commiſſion, ſpeciall Counſelles in ſondry remote Partes of her ſaid Realm, with honourable Stipends and Entertainmentes : Wherevppon, by her Majeſties Aucthoritie and gracious Conſente, the Lorde Deputie and Counſell have, in her Name, deuiſed, orderd, and eſtabliſhid, in the Portion of the Realm, which is commonlie callid *Munſter*, a Counſell of a convenient Nombre of Parſons of the thre Eſtates, in the ſame Partes. *And, becauſe the ſame Counſellours ſhall haue an ordinarie Continuance, for Reſorte of*

---

[a] Ex Autog. apud Penſhurſt.

her

her Subiects, Suites, and Complaints. *Her Majeftie hath, by Aduife of her faid Deputie and Counfell,* determinid to haue one fpeciall Parfon, beinge knowne meete, not onlie for Wifedom and Loue of Juftice, but allfo by Birth indifferente, and free from all Partyalitie towardes the People of the fame *Countrey,* to be the Chief and Heade of the fame Counfell, and to be namid the Lorde Prefidente of her Majefties Counfell eftablifhed in *Monfter.* In whiche Place and Roome, her Majeftie, *by like Aduife of her faid Deputie and Counfell of her faid Realm,* hathe, vppon Knowledge had of the Wifedome, Habilitie, and Dexteritie, in her righte truftie and welbelouid Seruant, *Sir* John Perrot, *Knighte, borne in her Majefties Realm of* England, *in the Countye of* Penbroke, appointid, nominatid, and placid the faid Sir *John Perrot* to be the Lorde Prefidente of the faid Counfell : To whom her Majeftie hathe, by Commiffion, vnder her greate Seale of *Irelande,* geuen Aucthoritie, with fuche others, as he, by the faid Commiffion, appointid to be of her faid Counfell, to rule and govern the faid Countrey and People. And for the further Inftruction of the faid Lorde Prefident and Counfell, in Thexecution of the faid Commiffion, the faid Lorde Deputie *and Counfell,* by Aucthoritie which *they* haue from her Majeftie, will and commaund the faid Lorde Prefidente and Counfell, fo eftablifhed by her Majefties Commiffion, to directe their Doinges, in all Maner of Thinges, to the befte of their Power, accordinge to theis Inftructions followinge :

1. Firfte the faid Lorde Prefidente fhall, att all Times, when he fhall thinck meete, for the Service of the Queenes Majeftie, call together all fuche as be, or that hereafter fhalbe appointid to be of that Counfell ; and fhall with the Aduife of fuche of the Counfell, as fhalbe by their Inftructions appointid to affifte him with Counfell, by Lettres, and Precepts, commaund all, and every Parfon of the faid Counfell, at all convenient Times, to do fuche Things as fhalbe meete, for the Service of the Queenes Majeftie, in Adminiftracion of Juftice, and Maintenaunce of the fame, amongefte all her Subiects, refidinge, or cominge into the Partes of the Jurifdiction of the faid Commiffion ; and in his Commaundements and Directions to the faid Counfell, he fhall haue fuche Regarde to their Eftates, Vocations, and other Condicions, as the Credites, and feuerall Eftimacions of the fame Counfailors, maie be in their due Actions, and well Doings, prefervid and mainteinid for the Furtheraunce of her Majefties Seruice.

2. And on the other Parte, her Majeftie willethe, chargethe, and commaundith, that all, and everie of her Majefties faid Counfailors, fhall exhibite and vfe, to the faid Queenes Prefidente, all fuche Honor, Reuerence, and Obedience, as to their Dueties appperteinith, and as to the Parfon hauinge the principall Place in the Counfell is due ; and fhall receaue and execute, in fuche Sorte, all the Precepts and Commaundements to them to be addreffed in anie Proceffe, to be done, or feruid in her Majefties Name, and fhall geue, at all Times, fuche Aduife and Counfell, as apperteinith to the Dueties of truftie Servaunts and Counfailors to her Majeftie, and accordinge to their corporall Othe.

3. And to the Intente the faid Lorde Prefidente, thus eftablifhed for the aboue recitid Purpofes, maie be furnifhid with fuche Nombre of Affiftants and Counfailors, as be of fuche Experience, Difcretion, and Power, as maie be thoughte meete to haue the Name of her Majefties Counfailors there : The faid Lord Deputie and Counfell, vppon good Aduifement and Deliberacion haue elected theis Parfons (whofe Names enfew hereafter) to be her Highenes Counfailors, joynid in the faid Counfell, with the faid Lorde Prefidente, in the Province, Counties, and Countreis, *above reherfid,* viz. *The mofte Reuerend Father in God,* E. *Archbuſſhhoppe of* Casfhell : *The Right Honorable* Thomas, *Erle of* Ormond *and* Offerie ; the Righte Honorable *Connor,* Earle of *Thomond ; Donalde,* Earle of *Clancarre ;* the Righte Reverend Fathers in God, the Busfhoppes of *Waterforde, Corke,* and *Lymericke,* &c.

4. *Her Majeftie alfo, by the Aduife of the faid Lorde Deputie and Counfell, dothe ordein and appointe* Thomas Burgate, *to exercife the Office of Clerke of the Signet and Counfell.*

5. And becaufe it fhalbe conueniente, that fome Nombre fhalbe continuallie abidinge with the faid Lorde Prefidente, or fuche as fhall fupply his Place, with whome he maie confulte, in heringe fuche Matters as maie be exhibitid vnto him, for the better Expedition of the fame: The faid Lorde Deputie and Counfaile, by theis Prefents, dothe ordein, that *James Dowdall,* and *Nicolas Walfhe,* beinge of fpeciall Trufte, appointid to be of the faid Counfell, fhall geue their continuall Attendance at the faid Counfell, and fhall not departe at anie Time with out the fpeciall Licenfe of the faid Lorde Prefidente. *Likewife,* Tho. Burgat, *who fhalbe Clerke of the Counfell and Signet, fhall make the like Attendance vppon the faid Lorde Prefidente and Counfell.*

6. And the faid Lorde Deputie and Counfell haue thoughte fitte, by the Affent of the Queenes Majeftie, that the faid Lorde Prefidente fhall haue, in Confideracion of his continuall Attendance, and great Paines to be taken in that Office, the Waiges and Intertainment of one hundrid thirtye thre Poundes, five Shillings, eighte Pence, *Sterlinge,* by the Yere for him felf; and for that the Countreis aforefaid beinge in fuche Diforder, and the People in the faim, in fuche Difobedience, as prefentlie they are; whereby it fhalbe needefull for him to have continuallie aboute him fome competent Nombre of Souldiers, whereby his Decrees and Orders iuftly taken, and made, the more effeactually maie be executed: It is confiderid and orderid by the Lorde Deputy and Counfell, that the faide Lorde Prefident fhall haue the Choice, Leadinge, and Enterteynment of xxxtie Parfons, beinge Horfemen, at nine Pence *Irifhe* by the Daie; xxtie Footemen at eight Pence *Irifhe,* by the Daie; and two Shillings by the Daie, for a pettye Captein; and for a Trompetor and Guydon, *it maie be allowed as the Lord Deputie of the Realm fhall think meete*; the Enterteyment and daily Waiges of all whiche Officers, and martiall Men, fhalbe taken and deductid out of the Paie appointid for the Queenes Majefties ordinarie Garrifon, refident in this Realm of *Ireland.*

Prouided allwaies, that the faid Lorde Prefident fhall, at the furfte Entry, geue in the Names of all, and everie the forefaid Souldiors, to the Clerk of the *Check,* to be entrid in his Booke, and from Tyme to Time, fhall certefie the Deathes and Alteracions of the fame to the Lorde Deputy, and Clerk of the *Check,* in convenient Time, as the fame maie reafonably be done, hauinge Regarde to the Diftance of the Place, and as other Captaines of the Army are bounde to doo.

7. *Item,* The faid *Juftice* fhall haue for his Stipende, yerely, one hundrid Pounds, *Sterlinge*; and the Affiftante or fecundarie Juftice, one hundrid Marks, *Sterlinge*; and the faid Clerk of the Counfell, twentie Pounds, *Sterlinge.*

All whiche Stipendes and Wages fhalbe paied quarterly by the Handes of the Threfurer at Warres, or Vicethrefurer here of this Realm of *Irelande*; and if the faid Juftice, or Affiftante, and fecundarie Juftice, fhall departe owte of the Limites of the Commiffion aforefaid, without the fpeciall Licenfe of the faide Lorde Prefident, or hauinge Leave, fhall tary longer owte, then the Time grauntid them, without reafonable Caufe of Excufe, the faid Lorde Prefident fhall deduct and defalk, owte of their faid feuerall Enterteynments, fo muche as the Wages of fo manie Daies doth amounte vnto, to th'Ufe of her Majeftie, towardes her other Charges to be extraordinarily fufteinid, in Thexecution of this Commiffion, at the Difcretion of the faid Lorde Prefident.

8. *Item,* For the further Reputacion and Honor of the fame Office, the faid Lorde Prefident fhall appointe fome one difcrete and comly Parfonage, which fhall continuallie attende vppon him as Sergeant at Armes; and fhall beare before him the Mafe of the Queenes Majefties Armes, in fuche Manner as the Sergeant at Armes dothe beare the Mafe before the Prefident in *Wales.* Whiche Sergeant maie, at all Times, be fente by the faid Lorde Prefident and Counfell,

for

for the Apprehending and Bringinge yn of any difobedient or contemptuous Parfon ; receavinge of every fuche Parfon, beinge of the Degree of a Gentleman, fo comonly knowen, and havynge yerely Lyvelyhode by anie Meanes of tenn Poundes, for his Arrefte, ten Shillinges ; and for the Arrefte of everie other Parfon, five Shillings eighte Pence ; and fix Shillings eighte Pence for everie Daies Travell, and not aboue ; he fhall allfo haue his Diets in the Howfeholde of the faid Lord Prefident, and towards his Maintenaunce, *if Neede fo fhall require*, the ordinarie Wages of one of the xxxtie Horfemen ; and forafmuche as there mufte be of Neceffitie one Officer, to whom all Offendors and Malefactors are to be committid, duringe the Time of their Imprifonement ; it is thoughte meete, that the faid Lorde Prefident fhall appointe one Porter to haue Charge of the Gaole, who fhall haue his Diets in the Howfholde of the faid Lorde Prefident, and be accomptid as one of the xxtie Footemen, and receave the Wages due for the fame, and allfo fuche other Profits, vppon everie Prifoner as enfuithe, *viz.* For the Entrie of everie Prifoner, fo to him committid, hauinge Lyvelyhode of ten Pounds by the Yere, iii *s.* iiii *d.* and xii *d.* by the Daie for his Diets, duringe his Abode in Prifon ; and for everie other Parfon of inferior Condicion, ii *s.* for his Entry, and fix Pence by the Daie for his Diet.

9. *Item*, The faide Lorde Prefident fhall not remaine owte of the Counties and Countreis abouefaid, at anie one Time, without the fpeciall Licenfe of the Queenes Deputie and Counfell, or other Governor of the Realm, for the Time beinge, aboue the Space of fix Daies, fauinge that, becaufe the Habitacion of the faid Sir *John Perrott*, now Prefident, is in the Countie of *Penbroke*, beinge the nexte Parte of *Wales*, oppofite againfte the Parties of *Monfter*, and thereby the Paffage by Sea but fhorte, it fhall be leefull for him, vntill our Deputie of our Realm fhall finde it meete once in the Yere to repaier over into his Native Countrey, and for that Purpofe, to be abfente from his Chardge, one Monthe, and no more, excepte our Licenfe obteinid for the fame.

10. *Item*, The faide Lorde Prefident and Counfell fhall (if Oportunitie maye ferue) monthely advertife vs, the Lorde Deputie and Counfell here, of the State of the Countrey within their Commiffion, or oftener, if theie fhall fe Caufe.

11. And wheare the faid Lorde Prefident and Counfell fhall haue, by their Commiffion, fufficient Aucthoritie to here and determin, by their Difcretions, all Manner of Complaints, within any Parte of the Province of *Monfter*, as well yildable as Franchife ; yet they fhall haue good Regarde, that excepte great Neceffitie, or other Matter of Confcience, conceavid vppon the Complainte, fhall moue them ; they fhall not hinder nor impeache the good Courfe and Vfage of the common Lawes of the Realm ; but fhall, to their Power, further Thexecution thereof ; nor fhall, without evident and neceffarie Caufe, interrupte fuche Liberties and Franchefies, as haue lefull Commencement and Continuance by the Warrants of the Lawe, otherwife then wheare any fpeciall Complainte fhalbe made vnto them of anie manifefte Wronge or Delaie of Iuftice, done or vfid by the Owners, Officers, or Minifters of the faid Franchefes or Liberties ; in which Cafes the faid Lord Prefident and Counfell fhall examin the faid Defalts fo alledgid by Waie of Complainte, to be committed in the faid Franchefes, and fhall fende for the Officers againfte whom Complaint fhall be made. And, findinge the fame to be trew, they fhall not only here and determyn the particuler and principall Caufes of the Parties Complaints, but fhall alfo refourm and punifhe, accordinge to their Difcretion, the Defalts of the faid Owners or Minifters of the faid Liberties. And if the Matter fhall fo ferue, they fhall caufe due Informacion to be made to *the Lorde Deputie of this Realm*, of the Abufes of the faide Franchefes and Liberties, fo as the fame maie be, by our Order, accordinge to the Lawes tried, and vppon iufte Caufes the Liberties refumid into the Queenes Majefties Hands.

And wheare, amongefte other Liberties reclaimid and clengid in certen Places in *Monfter*, the Earle of *Ormonde* hathe chalengid, by Graunte of Charter, to haue Regalities, and other Liberties, in the Countie of *Tipperary :* And likewife

I

wife the Earle of *Defmond* hathe chalengid to haue Regalities in the Countie of *Kirry*: Forafmuche as heretofore, vppon fome Queftions moued herein in *Englande* before her Majeftie, and her Pryvy Counfel, wherevnto the Chief Juftices of her Majefties *Benche* and *Comon* Pleas were all called, there was fhewed, and not difalowed, a fpeciall Graunt made by the Queene *Marie*, in the fourthe Yere of her Reigne, by her Majefties Lettres Patents vnder the Greate Seale of *England*, to the faid Erle of *Ormond*, to haue to him and the Heirs Males of the Bodie of the late Erle his Grandfather, of the Regalities, Knyghtes Fees, and other Liberties, in the faid Countie of *Tipperary*, excepting fower Plees, that is to fay, of Burninge, Ravefshynge, and Threafure founde, and the Profitt termed in the faid Charter *De Croccis*, in the faid Countie, all which are fpecially refervid to the Crown owte of the faid Graunte made to the faid Erle ; and, at the fame Time, no Graunt or Charter was fhewed, nor anie other leefull Title, for the Liberties claimid by the Earle of *Defmond* in the Countie of *Kirry* : The faid Lord Prefident and Counfell fhall not otherwife intermeddle to impeache the faid Jurifdiction and Libertie of the Countie of *Tipperary*, then in fuche neceffarie Caufes of Complaints made to them, as in the Claufe nexte afore in this Article, towchinge the Vfinge of generall Franchefes and Liberties, is fpeciallie mentionid, or in the forefaid fowr Cafes, which be allfo fpeciallie exceptid in the faid Graunt made to the faid Earle of *Ormond* ; excepte the faid Regalities and Liberties fhalbe hereafter fownde by evell Vfage, Abufage, Non-vfage, or other leefull Caufe, duelie forfeitid, and fo fhall be for that Caufe refumid : And for the other pretended Liberties of the faid Countie of *Kirry*, confidering no Title is fhewed by fome Warranty, the faid Lord Prefident and Counfell fhall heare, order, and determin all Manner of Caufes within the faid Countie, in like Manner as they fhall or maie, in anie other Places within the Jurifdiction of this Commiffion, hauing no Manner of leefull Franchefes to the contrary, vntill further fufficient Matter fhalbe fhewed and allowed by Order of Law, for the Warrantie of the faid pretendid Liberties againft her Majeftie.

12. *Item,* Wheare the faid Lord Prefident and Counfell, *toogeether with fuche other Commiffioners as the Lorde Deputie and Counfell fhall appoint,* fhall haue Commiffion, Power, and Aucthoritie, by Letters Patents under the Greate Seale of this Realm of *Ireland*, of Oyer, Determinor, and Gaole Deliuerie, in as large and ample Manner as anie fuche Commiffion or Aucthoritie is grauntid to anie Commiffioners for that Purpofe within the Realmes of *England* or *Ireland*: The faid Lord Deputie and Counfell do earneftlie requier and charge the faid Lord Prefident and Counfell, that he and they do often and diligently, feverely and juftly, fitte, here, and determin, by Vertue of the fame, fuche Caufes as fhalbe broughte before them in fuch feuerall Places, as befte may agree with the Neceffitie of the Caufe, and the Commoditie of the People.

13. *Item,* Wheare allfo the faid Lord Prefident *and Counfell, or two of them at the leafte, whereof the Lord Prefident to be one,* hathe full Power and Aucthoritie, by Letters Patents vnder the Greate Seale of this Realm, to execute the Martiall Lawe, when Neceffitie fhall require, in as large and ample Manner as to anie other it hath been accuftomid to be grauntid within this Realm of *Ireland* : The faid Lorde Prefident *and Counfell* fhall haue good Regarde thereto, that no Vfe be of the Martiall Lawe, but wheare mere Neceffitie fhall require ; for the Exercife thereof is only to be allowed wheare other ordinarie Adminiftracion of Juftice by Law cannot affume Place ; forefeinge allwaies, that no Party hauinge *five Pounds* of free Holde, or Goods to the Valew of *fortie Pounds,* fhall be tried by the Order of the Martiall Lawe, but by Order of the Comon Law ; and yet, if Neceffitie, for Service and Terror to others, fhall at anie Time require to execute the Martiall Law vppon any one Parfon or more, beinge of greater Valew in Landes or Goodes, then aboue is expreffed, the Prefident, in fuche fpeciall Cafes, may vfe his Difcretion, and thereof, and of the Caufes that moued him, fhall make us the Lord Deputie *of the Realm* pryvy.

I

14. *Item*, It is and fhalbe lawfull for the Lorde Prefident and Counfell, or to anie two of them, whereof the Lord Prefident to be one, to profecute and oppreffe anie Rebell or Rebelles with Sworde and with Fier; and, for the doinge of the fame, to levye in warlike Manner and Array, and with the fame to marche fuche and fo many of the Queenes Highneffes Subiects, as to his Difcretion fhall feme convenient; and if that any Caftell, Pile, or Howfe, be with Force kepte againfte them; it fhall be lawfull for the faid Lord Prefident and Counfell, or two of them, whereof the Lord Prefident to be one, to bringe before any fuche Caftell, Pile, or Howfe, fo to be kepte againfte them, any of the Queenes Majefties Ordennance and greate Artillery, remayninge within the Limites of their Commiffion; and with the fame, or by anie other Meanes or Engine, any fuche Caftell, Pyle, or Howfe, to batter, myne, and overthrow, as to their Difcretions fhall feeme befte; ftrayghtly charging and commaunding all Archbufhoppes, Earles, Bufhoppes, Vicounts, Barons, Banorets, Knightes, Maiors, Sheriefs, Juftices and Minifters of the Peace, and all other Gentlemen, and Comers, beinge her Majefties Subiects, to helpe, ayde, and affifte the faid Lorde Prefident and Counfell in fuche Sorte, and at fuche Time, as by the Lorde Prefident and Counfell, or two of them, whereof the Lord Prefident to be one, they fhalbe commaunded, vppon fuche Paines, as, for the Nature and Qualitie of the Defalts, fhalbe thoughte meete to the Lord Prefident and Counfell to limite and affeffe.

15. And it is ordred by the faid Lord Deputie and Counfell, that if any Parfon complain to the faid Lord Prefident and Counfell, and that they fhall think their Complaints worthy the Hearing, that the Parfons, fo complainid vppon, fhall be fent for, by a Lettre miffiue vnder the Queenes Signet, to appere before the Lord Prefident and Counfell, at a Daie and Place by them to be appointid, there to anfweare to fuche Thinges as fhalbe laied to their Charge, and further to be ordred, as fhall ftand with Righte, Juftice, Equitie, and Confcience. And, for Lack of Apparance vppon fuche Lettres, they fhall fende for the Lettres of Allegeance, Proclamacions, or any other Proceffe to be made, directid, or awardid by their Difcreffions, to the Sherief, Conftable, or other Minifter, whereby the Partie complainid vppon maie be callid to come to his Anfweare, as apperteinithe. And if, by the Obftinacy of the Partie complainid vppon, the Cafe fo require, to fequefter his or their Landes or Goodes, or either of them, by their Difcreffions : And furthermore, if in Cafe any Parfon, hauing Habitacion or Dwelling on any Landes or Tenements, by Leafe or otherwife, within the Limits of the Commiffion aforefaid, fhall, by Covin, Fraude, or Deceipte, or otherwife, abfent him felf or goo owte of the Limites of the faid Commiffion : That then Lettres Miffiues, figned with the Queenes Signet, fhalbe deliuered at his Howfe, Landes, or Tenements, and the Coppies of the fame fhall be lefte there ; fo that by mofte Likelyhode the fame may come to his Knowledge, beinge fo fent for; and if within a certein Time after, to be limittid by their Difcretions, the Parfon or Parfons fo fent for will make Defalte of Apparance : The faid Lord Prefident and Counfell, or anie two of them, whereof the Lord Prefident to be one, fhall afwell proceede to other Proceffes, as to the Hering and Determininge of the Matter or Cafe in Variance, accordinge to the Lawes, Statuts, and Ordenaunces made therein, or otherwife, at their Difcretions.

16. And in Cafe any Lettres Miffiue be addreffid from the Lord Prefident and Counfell, or to any Parfon or Parfons, of what Eftate or Degree foever they be, to appere before them at a Daie appointid, the fame Lettres beinge deliuered to him, or otherwife lefte at his or their Howfe, as is above fpecified ; the faid Lord Prefident and Counfell, or any two of them, whereof the faid Lord Prefident to be one, fhall caufe him or them, fo contemninge or difobeyinge, to be punifhid by Imprifonment and reafonable Fine, or fhall otherwife proceede, accordinge to their Difcretions ; in which faid Caufes if anie of the Parties commit anie Refiftaunce or Difobedience, either of their Apparance, or contrary to the Commaundements, Direction, Decree, and De-

terminacion, made or to be made and decreed by the faid Lord Prefident and Counfell, that they the faid Lord Prefident and Counfell, or any two of them, whereof
the Lord Prefident to be one, fhall or may comaunde the Sherief, Maior, Sergeant at Armes, Cunftable, Bailief, or other Officer or Minifter, to whome it
fhall appertein, to attache everie Parfon fo offendinge, contemninge, and dif-
obeying, and to fend him or them to the Lord Deputy in Warde, together
with Certificate of his Contempte and Difobedience ; or ells by their Difcrecions
to caufe the Parties fo attachid to be committid to Warde, there to remain in
fafe Cuftodie untill the Time the Pleafure of the faid Lord Deputie and Counfell be knowen in the Premiffes ; or that the fame Parfon, or Parfons, affent,
fulfill, and agree to the Determinacion of the faid Lord Prefident and Counfell,
or any two of them, whereof the Lord Prefident to be one.

17. And the faide Lorde Prefident and Counfell, *according to their Commiffion,* fhall
have Power and Aucthoritie, by theife Prefents, diligently to here, determyn, and
trye all, and all Manner of Extortions, Maintenance, Imbraceries, and Oppreffions, Confpiracies, Refcues, Efcapes, Corruptions, Falfhodes, and all
other evell Doinges, Defalts and Mifdemeanors of all Sheriefes, Juftices of
Peace, Maiors, Souueraynes, Portryves, Bailiefs, Stewards, Lieutenants,
Exchetors, Coroners, Gaolers, Clerks, and other Officers and Minifters of
Juftice, and their Deputies, afwell in all the Counties and Countreis within the
Province of *Mounfter,* aforefaid, and within the fuppofed Liberties of *Tipperary* and *Kirry,* as in all Cities and other Townes Corporate within the Limites
of their faide Commiffion, of what Degree foeuer they be, and punifhe the
fame accordinge to the Qualitie and Quantitie of their Offence, by their Difcretions, leavinge neuertheles, to the Lords and Owners of all leefull Liberties,
fuche Profits as they may leefully claime.

18. And it fhalbe lawfull for the faid Lord Prefident and Counfell, or any
three of them, whereof the Lord Prefident to be one, to conceave, make, and
caufe to be proclaimid in her Highnes Name, and as they fhall thinck good,
any Thinge or Matter tendinge to the better Order of her Majefties Subiects,
within the Precincte of their Commiffion, and the Repreffinge of Malefactors
and Mifdoers, after fuche Tenour and Forme as they fhall thinck convenient ;
and to punnifhe the Offenders there by there Difcretions, *fo the fame be not repugnant to the common Lawes and Statuts of the Realm.*

19. And allfo the faid Lord Deputy and Counfell haue thoughte meete that
the faid Lord Prefident and Counfell, or any three of them, whereof the faid
Lord Prefident to be one, fhall and maye compound, vppon reafonable Caufes
by their Difcretions, with any Parfon, for all Forfeitures growing, or comminge,
or that fhall grow or come, afwell by all and finguler penall Statuts, as allfo
of Obligations and Recognizances taken, made, or acknowledged, before the
faid Lord Prefident or Counfell, or any of them, within the Limits of their
Aucthorities and Commiffion, for Apparance, or for the Peace, or good
Aberinge, or by Reafon of any penall Statute whatfoeuer they be, made or to
be made : And, allfo, fhall haue Aucthoritie to ceffe reafonable Fynes for anye
Offence, whereof any Parfon fhall happen to be convictid before the faid
Lord Prefident and Counfell ; and fuche Somes of Money as fhall growe or
come, by Reafon of anie fuche Compofitions or Fines, they fhall caufe it to be
entrid into a Book, fubfcribed with the Hand of the Lord Prefident and Counfell, or two of them at the leafte, whereof the Lord Prefident to be one, to
Thintent the Queenes Majeftie maie be anfwerid of the fame accordingly. And,
allfo, upon fuche Compofitions made of Fyne or Fines, fet as aforefaid, fhall
haue Aucthoritie to cancell and make voyde all fuche Obligacions and Bands.

20. And allfo the faid Lord Prefident fhall caufe, as muche as in him lieth,
all Writts or Proceffes, *or Letters miffive,* fent, or to be fent, to any Parfon or
Parfons inhabitinge or beinge within the Precinct of his Commiffion, *from the
Lord Deputie,* owte of the *Kings Benche, Chauncery,* or *Exchequer,* or any other
Coorte of Recorde, diligently to be obfervid and effectually to be obeyid, ac-
cordinge to the Tennor of the fame ; and, if he fhall find Negligence, Slacknes,

or

or willfull Omiffion in any Officer, or other Minifter, to whom the Deliuerie or Servinge of fuche Proceffes dothe appertein, he fhall punnifhe the fame feverely, according to the Greatenes and Qualitie of the Offence.

21. And it fhalbe lawfull for the faid Lord Prefident and Counfell, or any three of them, whereof the Lord Prefident to be one, after Examinacion in the Caufes neceffarie, vppon vehement Sufpicion and Prefumption of anye greate Offence in anie Partie committid, againfte the Queenes Majeftie, to put the fame Partie fo fufpectid to Tortures, as they fhall think convenient, and as the Caufe fhall require. And allfo to refpite Judgment of Deathe vppon anie Parfon convicted or attaintid before him and the Counfell, for any Treafon, Murder, or anie other Fellony. Or, after Judgement geven, to ftaie Execution, vntill fuche Time as he fhall certefy vs, the Lord Deputy and Counfell, of his Doings and Confideracion of the fame, and receave Anfweare thereof from vs. Provided allwaies, that the fame Certificat be made to vs, the Lord Deputie and Counfell, within the Space of xx Daies after any fuche Thinge is done.

22. Allfo, if anie Inquefte within the Precincte of their Commiffion, within Liberties or withowte, being fworn and chargid vppon Triall of anie Fellon, Murderer, or anie like Offendor whatfoeuer he be, hauinge good and pregnant Evidence for fufficient Proof of the Matter, whereof the faid Offendor fhalbe accufid, indytid, arraynid, do vtterly acquite fuch Offendor, contrary to the faid Evidence, That then the faid Lord Prefident and Counfell, or anie two of them, whereof the faid Prefident to be one, fhall examin fuche Periuries, afwell by Depofition of Witneffes, as by all other Kinde of Proffs by their Difcretions. And, if the faid Enqueftes be convicte thereof before the faid Lord Prefident and Counfell, or three of them at the leafte, whereof the Lord Prefident to be one, the faid Lord Prefident and Counfell may, and fhall, proceede to the Punnifhment of fuche Offence by Fine, Imprifonment, Wearinge of Paper, or Standinge on the Pillory, as by their Difcretion fhall feeme meete.

23. Allfo, the faid Lord Deputie and Counfell earneftly requireth, and ftraightly chargeth the faid Lord Prefident and Counfell, that they, at all Times, and in all Places, wheare any greate Affemblie fhalbe made before them, to perfwade the People by all good Meanes and Waies to them feeminge good, and efpeciallie by their own Examples, in obferuinge all Orders for Dyvine Seruice, and other Things appertayninge to Chriftian Religion; and to embrace, follow, and devoutly to obferue the Order and Seruice of the Churche, eftablifhid in the Realm by Parliamente, or otherwife by leefull Aucthority. And earneftly to call vppon and admonifhe all Busfhoppes and Ordinaries within the Precincte of their Commiffion, diligently, fervently, and often to do the fame. And if the Lord Prefident and Counfell fhall find them necligent, vnhable, or vnwilling to do the fame, That then they fhall aduertife the Lord Deputie and Counfell thereof, and they fhall call earneftly vppon the Busfhoppes, feverely to proceede, accordinge to the Cenfures of the Churche, againfte all notorious Advoterers, and fuche, as, without lawfull Devorce, do leave their Wiues, or that, whilefte their leefull Wief lyveth, do marry with any other. And the Sentence, pronuncid by the Busfhopp or Ordinary vppon fuche Offendor, the faid Lord Prefident and Counfell fhall endevor them felves to the vttermofte, that they conveniently maye, to caufe the fame Sentence to be put in Execution according to the Lawes. And, if they fhall finde the Ordinary flack or remiffe in his Duetye, and not doinge according to his Office, they fhall punnifhe, or caufe to be punnifhid, the fame Busfhopp or Ordinarie, accordinge to their Difcretions.

24. Allfo, the Lord Prefident and Counfell fhall examin the Decaye of all Parifhe Churches, and throughe whofe Defalte the fame be decayed, and to proceede to the Procuringe or Inforcing of fuche as oughte to repayer any Churche or Churches, with all convenient Speede, according to their Difcretions. And in Cafes wheare her Majeftie fhalbe (after due and aduifid Inquificion) fownde, by Reafon of her Poffeffions, bownd to repayer the fame Churches : In thofe Cafes, Aduertifement fhalbe geven to vs the Deputie *of*

I *the*

the Realm : Or, if they fhall knowe of any that fhall fpoyle, robbe, or deface any Churche, they fhall, with all Severitie, proceede to the Punnifhment of the Offendors, accordinge to the Lawes, Statuts, and Ordenances of this Realm, or accordinge to their Difcretions.

They fhall allfoe affifte and defend all Archbufhoppes, Bufhoppes, and all other Ecclefiafticall Minifters in the Miniftery of their Function, and in the quiet Poffeffing of their Lands, Rents, Tenements, and Hereditaments ; and fhall punnifhe the Withholders, Intruders, or Vfurpers of the fame, accordinge to their Difcretions, and the Qualitie of the Offence. They fhall allfo geue earnefte Charge for the Obferuacion of all Lawes, Statuts, and Ordenances made, or to be made, for the Benifite of the Common Wealthe, and Punnifhement of Malefactors ; and in, efpecially, the Statute of Hue and Crye, for Nyghte Watches, and for Weights and Meafures, to be diligently confidered, and feuerely put in Execution.

25. Allfo, the faid Lord Prefident fhall haue and retain one Chaplein or Minifter, that fhall and can preache and reede the Homylies ; who fhall be allowed his Diets in the Howfhold of the faid Lord Prefident ; and fhall receaue the Enterteynment of *one of the Horfemen affignid to the Prefident* ; to whom the Lord Prefident fhall caufe due Reuerence to be given, in Refpect of the Office that he fhall haue for the Seruice of God.

26. Allfo, the faid Lord Deputie and Counfell will, that the faid Lord Prefident and Counfell, or two of them at the leafte, whereof the Lord Prefident to be one, fhall endevor them felves to execute, afwell all and all Manner of Statuts of this Realm, Proclamacions, and other Ordenances, as to punnifhe the Tranfgreffors of the fame, according to the Statuts, Ordenances, and Proclamacions, and to do and execute all other Lawes and Statuts of this Realm ; and to levy, or caufe to be levyed, all and all Manner of Forfeitures conteynid in the fame, according to the Order limitid by the fame Lawes ; and, if Caufe fo require, fhall compound for reafonable Caufes, for all and finguler fuche Forfeitures and Paines, by their Difcretions, hauinge therein Regarde not to deminifhe the Fines fpecially limitid by the Lawes, without greate Neceffitie of the Pouerty of the Parties be ioynid with the Repentance and Difpoficion of Amendment in the Partie : For, otherwife, it is perilous to geue Example in weakenninge the iufte Terror of good Lawes.

27. Allfo, the Lord Prefident and Counfell, or two of them, whereof the faid Lord Prefident to be one, fhall and maie affeffe and taxe Cofts and Damages, afwell to the Plaintief as to the Defendant, and fhall awarde Executions for their Doinges, Decrees, and Orders ; and fhall punnifhe the Breakers of the fame, being Parties therevnto, by their Difcretions.

28. And the faid Lord Prefident and Counfell fhall, immediatly vppon their Repare to fome convenient Place, where they meane to refyde within the Lymites of their Commiffion, appoint three or fowre honefte and fufficient Men to be Clerks or Atturneys to that Counfell, for the makinge of Billes, Ainfweares, and Proceffes, for all Manner of Suters ; and, therein, not to multiply fuch Officers, leafte allfo they be Occafion to multiply vnneceffary Suites ; and fome truftie wife Parfons, to examin Witneffes between Partie and Partie, which, of Neceffitie, would be chofen with good Aduife : Forefeinge exprefslye and charitably, that no exceffiue Fees be by anie of them taken of the Subiects ; but that their Fees be affeffid by the Lord Prefident and Counfell, and the fame faier written vppon a Table, and fixed vp in fome publike Place wheare the fame may be feene and vnderftood of all Suters : And that, in the Beginninge, the fame Fees may appere, and be meane and reafonable : So as, in no wife, the Profecution of Relief, by Way of Juftice, be not fo chargeable, as the poore oppreffid Sorte of Subiects be thereby difcoragid to make their Complaints.

29. And, becaufe it fhall be convenient that a Regeftre be dulye kept for all the Doings, Orders, Decrees, and Proceedinges, which from Time to Time fhall paffe by the faid Lord Prefident and Counfell : The Lord Deputy and Counfells

Pleafher

Pleafher is, That the Clerk of the faid Counfell, for the Time being, hauing reafonable Allowance for the fame of the Parties hauing thereby any Interefte, fhall diligently execute and perform this Charge, without any further Expenfes, then fhalbe efpecially directed vnto him by the faid Lord Prefident, to be fufteined by her Majefties Subiects, for Entris of Articles and Orders.

30. And, alfo, the faid Lord Deputie and Counfell haue thought it conuenient, that there fhall be one honefte and fufficient appointed, to be Clerk and Receavor of the Fines, at the Nominacion of the faid Lord Prefident ; who fhall diligently and orderly keepe a Booke of all fuch Fines as fhall be taxed vppon any Parfon. The Fine to be enterid by the Hand of the faid Lord Prefident, and fhall haue full Power to fend out Proceffes for any Perfon vppon whome any fuche Fine fhall be fo ceffid ; and to receive all fuche Fines ; and, in everie *Michaellmas* Terme, thereof to make a true and parfecte Account before the Barons, and other Officers of the Queenes Majefties *Exchequer*, for the Time beinge ; to Thende, *the Lord Deputie and Councell, in the faid Realm of* Ireland, [may be afferteinid what Fines haue been acquirid to the Queenes Majeftie, and howe the fame haue ben employed. Prouided allwaies, and it fhall be lawfull for the faid Lord Prefident and Counfell, to imploye, of the faid Fines, reafonable Sommes for Reward of Meffengers, and Repairinge the Queenes Caftells and Howfes, and in Buyldinge or Reedifyinge of Gaoles in eache Countie, within the Precinct of their Commiffion, where, by Lawes of the Realm, no other Parfons are thereto bound and chargeable ; and, allfo, for furnifhing of neceffarie Vtenfills *only* for the Howfehold, as to the faid Lord Prefident and Counfell, or any two of them, whereof the Lord Prefident to be one, fhall feeme needfull and convenient. In all which, the faid Lord Prefident fhall haue Regard to moderate thofe Allowances, as, of the Fines affeffid and levyed, the Queenes Majeftie may be anfwerid fome yerely reafonable Sommes towardes her great Charges, in Maintenaunce of this Counfell, the fame beinge to the Crown of *England* a new Charge. And any Warrant fignid by the faid Lord Prefident, and any *one* of the Counfell, for any fuche Some or Somes, fhall be a fufficient Difcharge to the faid Clerk or Receavor of the faid Fines, for the Iffuinge of the faid Somes. And the faid Clerk or Receavor fhall haue full Power for the Sendinge owte of Proceffe againfte any Parfon, vppon whome any fuche Fine fhall be ceffid, and to haue his Proceffe *gratis* from the Clerk of the Signet ; and he to haue his Diets in the Howfe of the faid Lord Prefident, and to be accomptid one of the Nombre of his Horfemen, and to receaue the Wages and Enterteinment due for the fame.

31. Allfo, the faid Lorde Deputie and Counfell haue thoughte good, that there be a Signet, grauen with the Queenes Majefties Armes, vnder a Crown Imperiall, which allwaies fhall remain in the Cuftodie of the Clerke of the Counfell, who fhall figne, with the fame, all Proceffes, whiche fhall be fent from the faid Lorde Prefident and Counfell. In the vpper Margent of every of whiche Proceffe fhall be written, *By the Lorde Prefident and Counfaill of* Monfter. And the Clerke of the Signet fhall not take, for the Wrightinge and Sealing of everie fuch Proceffe, aboue 'the Some of   and for fuche as fhall be allowed by the Lorde Prefident, or any of the Counfell, *in forma Pauperis*, Priveledge or Refpect of Service, nothing.

32. Allfo the faid Lorde Deputie and Counfell have thought meete, there fhalbe a continuall Howfhold kepte, within the Precincte and Limits of the Commiffion aforefaid, in fuche Place, as to the Lorde Prefident fhall feeme mofte convenient ; all Seruants neceffarie for whiche Howfhold, fhall be at the Nomination of the faid Lorde Prefident ; in which Howfe eche Counfailor bounde to continuall Attendance, and attendinge, fhall be allowed to haue two Seruants, and the Clerk of that Counfell one, and every other Counfailor, beinge either fent for, or coming for any needefull Bufines, for the Queene or Countrey, fhall be allowed, duringe his Abode there, one Seruant ; and, for the more honorable Maintenaunce of the faid Howfehold, there fhall be allowed vnto the faid Lorde Prefident and Counfell after the Rate of tenn Pounds, *Sterling*,

by the Weeke, only to be imployed vppon the Table Charges of the faid
Howfhold, half yerely to be receavyd at the Hands of the Vicethreaforer, and
generall Receavor of the Queenes Majefties Revenues of this Realm ; for Paiment of which, there fhall remayn in the Hands of the faid Vicethreaforer (who
allfo is Threaforer for the Warres) a Warrant dormant, whereby the faid
Vicethreaforer fhall be aucthorifid to paie, to the faid Lorde Prefidente, one
half Yeres Allowance allwaies before Hande, towardes the makinge of his neceffarie Prouifion, out of the Revenu ; or if he fhall not haue fufficient Threafher, than owte of any other Threafher.　And the faid Lorde Prefident fhall
nominate and appointe one difcreete and fufficient Man, to be Steward, or
Clerke of the fame Howfholde, who fhall weekely write, and fome the Charges
thereof, and the fame allfo fhall weekely prefent to the faid Lorde Prefidente
and Counfell, to be confiderid. And at the Yeares Ende, the fame totally fom-
mid and fignid, beinge allowid by the faid Lorde Prefident, and two of the
Counfell, fhall delyver to the Officers of the Queenes Majefties *Exchequer*, to
remayn there of Recorde.

33. And, becaufe her Majeftie meanithe principallye to benefite her Subiects,
not only with the Fruits of Juftice, but with the Deliuerie of them from all
vnneceffarie Burdens :　The Lorde Prefident and Counfell fhall forefee, that
no Manner of extraordinarie or exceffive Charge be put and layde vppon any
Parfon, againfte their own Willes or Agreements, by finding or fufteininge of
any Horfeman, or Footeman, or Horfe-boye, or Horfe, belonging to the faid
Lorde Prefident, or any of the faid Counfell, or of anie belonging to them.
And in like Manner, fhall fee, that the Subiects be not oppreffid with the like
by any other, contrarie to the Lawes of the Realm, for fuche Caufes prouided :
*Neuertheles, confideringe the Seafon of the Yere is paffid, wherein the Prefident fhould
haue made Prouifion for him felf, and the Counfell attending with him, afwell for
the Prouifion of their Howfe, as for their Horfemen, vntill the Fruits of the Earthe
may be gatherid, this nexte Sommer ; it feemeth meete, that there may be fome reafonable Rate and Taxe fet vppon the Countrey, by the Aduife of the Deputie and Counfell of that Realm, for the Relief of the faid Prefident and Counfell vppon reafonable
Prices, afwell for the Maintenance of their Howfeholde, as for their Horfemen and
Seruants.*

34. *Item,* Confideringe the Queenes Majeftie hathe Title and Right to no
fmall Quantitie of Poffeffion within *Monfter*, afwell of the auncient Reuenue of
the Crown, and of other Seignories deuoluid to the Crown, as allfo of the dif-
foluid Monafteries, and other Howfes of Religion, the which are not duely anfwerid to her Majeftie as Reafon woulde :　The faid Lorde Prefident and Counfell fhall, from Time to Time, imploye their Labors by all good Difcretions to
procure, that her Majefties Officers, or Farmors, appointid for that Purpofe,
may peaceably and fullie, from Time to Tyme, poffeffe and receaue the Profitts
of the fame :

And the faid Lorde Deputie and Counfells further Pleafher is, that the faid
Lorde Prefident fhall minifter vnto every Counfailor in that Commiffion, being
not allreadie fworne of her Highnes Counfell in *Irelande*, afwell the Othe
prouided in the Statute, for Swearinge of Officers, as allfo this hereafter men-
cionid.

You fhall fweare, to the uttermofte of your Power, Will, and Conninge, you
fhall be true and faithfull to the Quenes Majeftie, our Soueraigne Ladie, and
to her Heires and Succeffors.

You fhall not know nor heere anie Thing, that may, in any wife, be preiudicial to her Highnes, or the Comon Wealthe, Peace and Quiet of this her Highnes Realm ; but you fhall, with all Diligence, reueale and difclofe the fame to
her Highnes, or to fuche other Parfon or Parfons of her Majefties Priuie Counfell in *Ireland*, as you fhall think may, and will foonefte conuaie and bring it
to her Highnes Knowledge.

You fhall ferue her Maieftie truly and fathfully in the Roome and Place of
one of her Majefties Counfell.

You

You fhall in all Things, that be mouid, treatid, and debatid, in any Counfell, faithfully and truely declare your Minde and Opinion according to your Harte and Confcience, in no wife forbearing fo to do, for any Manner of Refpecte of Fauor, Meede, Dreade, Difpleafure, or Corruption.

You fhall faithfully and vprightly, to the befte of your Power, caufe Juftice to be duelie and indifferently miniftrid to the Queenes Majefties Subjectes, that fhall haue Caufe to fue for the fame, according to Equitie and Order of Lawes.

Finally, you fhalbe vigilant, diligent, and circumfpecte in all your Doinges and Proceedinges, towching the Quenes Majeftie, and her Affaires.

All which Pointes and Articles before expreffid, with all other Articles fignid with the Handes of the Lorde Deputie and Counfell of this Realme, and deliuerid to me, the Lorde Prefident of her Highnes Counfell, eftablifhid in theis Partes, you fhall fathfully obferue, keepe, and fullfill, to the vttermofte of your Power, Witt, Will, and Conning ; fo helpe you God, and the Contents of this Booke.

xiiij *Decembris*
1570.   *Examynid by me,*
A°. 13 *Elizabeth. Reg.*

                                        W. Cecill.

An Order to the Sheriff and Juftices of the Peace of the County of Monmouth.
ª Apud Ludlow 9 Martij, An. Reg. Elizabeth, &c. 15, 1572.

THE Quenes Majeftie having appointed her right truftie and welbeloved Sir *Henry Sydney*, of the noble Order of the Garter, Knyght, to the Office of Lord Prefident of her Highnes Counfail in the Marches of *Wales* : In the which Office, though the faid Sir *Henry* hath contynued for many Yeers paft ; and nevertheles, of fome Years of that his Contynuance of Lord Prefident as aforefaid, hath ben occupyed, by her Graces Appointment, in other Service of her Majefties, within the Realm of *Ireland*, as Lord Deputy there. And, reteyring of late to the Place of Service of the faid Office of Lord Prefident, hath found the Countrey in reafonable good State, faving only the Countie of *Monmouth*. The which, at Tymes, whereof, partely for Want of the Feare of God, and partely for Lack of good Order, or dutifull Reverence and Obedience to the Lawes, have growen to fuch Libertie and Infolencie, as they have not left any Infolencie or Offence unatempted : So many Murders, Manflaughters, Robberyes Theftes ; fuch Fighting and Quarelling, and manifold Offences ; that no Country, within the Commiffion aforefaid, is fo much mifliked. The Contynuance and Increafe whereof, femeth to growe by the Default of the Shieriff and Juftices of Pees, in Refpect of Favour, fhewn one towards the others Officers, Servants, and Reteiners ; wherebie, in maintenyng of Matters, one Gentleman or other fhalbecome a Partie, what Offence foever the fame fhalbe. Whereof the faid Lord Prefident, being hartely fory, not only to fee, but alfo to know, of fo manifold Diforders, in a Countrey fo apt for Civilitie and Quietnes ; intendeth very fhortely, with the Affiftance of her Majefties Counfaill aforefaid, in Perfon to travail amongeft them, to lern and try out the principall Caufes, that worketh the Effect of thefe Diforders : And fo having Notice, by Degrees, of the Favourers and Furtherers of the fame, intendeth to fett down fuch Order of Chaftifement, in publique Sort, as fhalbe thought mete Reward for their Defertes. Neverthelefs, the faid Lord Prefident and Counfaill, chieffly defyring Reformacion of that which is amiffe. Wherbie, fuch as are in Aucthoritie within that Countie, for Defectes of due Perfueverance of Service, though may not, of mere Neceffitie, be called to Accompt in that Behaulf ; have thought good, in the mean Tyme, of the purpofed Repayr aforefaid, to put them in Remembraunce of the Premifes, to Thend they

---

ª Ex Autog. apud Penfhurft.

may rather have Regarde to their Credit and Charge, and the common Quiet of theire Country. It is therefore ordered, by the faid Lord Prefident and Counfaill, that a Letter, reherfing the Premifes, be directed to the Sheriff, and Juftices of the Pees, of the faid Countie of *Monmouth*, commanding them to have Confideracion of theife Thinges, in fuch diligent Sort, as may be anfwerable to the Truft in them repofed ; bending their fole Study and Induftry to the Performaunce of the Pees, the common Quiet of the Countrey, and Doing of Juftice. And, for that Purpofe, to affemble themfelfes together, and confulting, by what Meanes, good Order and Quietnes may be beft contynued ; and to devide themfelfes into viii, x, or xii Parties, more or leffe, as to their Difcreacions ; having Regarde to the Quarter of the Shier, and Number of them felfs, as fhall feeme moft convenient ; befides theire generall Care, that every particular Member may give diligent Hede, within the Lymytts appointed to them, for Prefervation of Quietnes and good Order : Shewing good Examples of Reformacion in themfelfes, wherein it were not amiffe, that the Order, heretofore prefcribed to them, for appointing Overfeers of good Rule, in every Parifh, were eftfoon put in Execucion. With no leffe Perfeveraunce to Thexecution of the Lawes againft Vagabonds, idle Perfons, Loyterers, and fuch as can not yeld Accompt of their Way of Living, within the Compaffe of the Lawe, lately provided in that Behaulf. The Statutes againft Alehoufe-keepers, whether they be more in Number then needeth, or the Places of their Habitations, convenient or inconvenient, is fpecially to be remembred ; with the Statutes of Reteyners, Hue and Cry, and for Keeping of good and fubftantiall Watches in Places convenient, at the Tymes appointed by the Lawes. And for the advoyding of the fundry and manifold Theftes there lately committed ; the Order heretofore fett down, that the Bucher, or fuch as killed any Cattell, to caufe the Hide and Hides therof to be openly fhewed in the Market, or before the Overfeers of the Parifh, before the Sale therof, fheweth alfo to good Purpofe to be remembred. Commanding them further, that as foon as any Offenders, for Murder, Felony, or Offences, fhalbe taken, the faid Juftices of the Pees fhall caufe the Matter to be forthwith examined, and Certificat thereof made imediatelie, to the faid Prefident and Counfaill : To the Intent, that they thereupon may proceed to the Punifhment of the Offenders, as the Cafe requirethe. And, finally, that the faid Sheriff, and Juftices of the Pees, fhall mete and confult together, at the leaft, ones every Moneth, and more often, as Occafions may require ; conferring amongeft them felfes, upon the Statute of the perticuler Partes of the Shier ; and taking fuch Order for all Mifdoers, as to their Wyfdomes may feeme requifit. Signifying, the xxth of *April* next, of their holding Seffions ; as alfo from Tyme to Tyme, to the faid Lord Prefident and Counfaill, the State of their Country, and their Proceedings in this Bufinefs ; as they tender the Service of her Majeftie, and will for the Contrary anfwer at their Perill.

Concerning the County of Worcefter [b].

AFTER our hartie Comendacions : Whereas a certen Controverfie is of late rifen, touchinge the Juryfdiccion of the Lord Prefident, and hir Majefties Counfell, in the Marches of *Wales*, by fekinge to fubdue the Cittie and Countie of *Worcefter* out of the fame, to the Derogation of hir Majefties Prerogative, and her Heighnes Authoritie, eftablifhed in thofe Parts ; which Thinge hathe ben practifed by one *Wilde*, who hathe ben encouraged therto by Thadvife of certen Lawiers, who haue, to that Effect, fubfcribed a Booke, which we fende you herein enclofed : We have thought good to requier you to confider afwell thereof, as of the Statute made for Theftablifhement of the faide Counfell, together with fuche Comiffions and Inftruccions, as are graunted to the Prefidents in that Behalf. And further, to enforme your felfes, bothe by

---

[b] Ex Autog. apud Penfhurft.

foche

foche as fhall repaire vnto you from the Lord Prefident, as alfo the faid *Wilde* him felf, what eche Partie hathe to faie therein : And, therevpon, to returne vnto us your Anfwer what the Lawe is therein ; and in what Sorte it fhalbe requifite to proceade for Redreffe of the faid Diforder, as may be for hir Majefties Honour, and the Benefitt of the Realme. And fo fare ye hartely well. From *Hampton* Courte, the xxiiijth of *February*, 1573.

Your loving Freinds,

W. Burghley,	E. Lincoln,	
A. Warwick,	F. Bedford,	Thomas Smith.
F. Walfingham,	Thomas Suffex,	

To Mr. Attorney and Solliciter Generall, and to either of them.

Vera Copia,

Robert Bele.

Grenewiche, viij *Martij,* 1573.

UPON a Supplicacion and Submiffion, exhibited by *Roberte Wilde,* of the Cittie of *Worcefter,* Gent. late comytted to the Cuftodie of the Knyght Marifhall, yt was ordered, that he fholde be releafed, vpon his Band to be taken to hir Majefties Vfe, in ij C *l.* that he fholde make his Repaire before their Lordfhips, at foche Tymes hereafter, as he fholde be reafonablie warned. And alfo appere before them the firft Daie of the next Terme. And touchinge the Matter in Controuerfie, betwene the Lord Prefident and the Counfell, in the Marches of *Wales,* and him, touchinge the Exemption of this Cittie and County of *Worcefter* from the Jurifdiccion of the faid Councell ; the faide *Wilde* fhall not attempte or do any Thinge therein, in the meane Seafon, to the Derogacion and Preiudice of the fame, but fubmitt him felf and ftand to foche Order, as fhalbe by their Lordfhips, with the Advife of her Majefties learned Counfel, taken therein.

Grenewiche, xiiijth *Martij,* 1573.] The Lord Prefident of hir Majefties Counfell, in the Marches of *Wales,* was fent for in, and required, by their Lordfhips, to give Order, that *Roberte Wilde,* of the Cittie of *Worcefter,* Gent. fhould be releafed, as aforefaid.

Edward Waterhous, *Efq; to Sir* Henry Sydney.

It may pleafe your Lordfhip,

I Have forborne long to difcharge my Duety to your Lordfhip, at left by writing to acknowledge the Benifits I have received, and to make Accompt of the Succeffe of our Northerne Journey : But, becaufe your Lordfhips Deferts towards me are allwaies before me, it perfuadith me, that your Lordfhip, knowing that I hate Ingratitude, will allwaies judge of the Intereft you have in me ; and fo hold me excufid, howfoever I feme ether negligent or forgetfull.

In the other Matter, that concernith our Procedings in *Irland* ; there are comme thence fo maynie Apoftates ; and fo maynie of thofe *Welch,* and fuch as maie commodiouflie bringe the Certainty to your Lordfhips Eares ; as it is not worth the Repiticion on my Part : Neverthelefs the Effect is this, That Lack of good Forfight, in Provifion of Bedding, and other Neceffaries for the commen Soldier, have bredd Difeafes in maynie ; and, in other, fuch a Lothing of the Place, as they chufe rather here to be hangid for Vagabounds, thenn to endure the Hardnes of this Winter Warre.

At my Comming over, I prefentid here to the Lords above xx Articles, on the Behalf of the Erle, fomme of them tending to the Increafe of the Quenes

Charge, for neceſſary Fortificacion, and Remediing of the Decaies of the Armie ; and the reſt, ſuch as, in common Opinionn of all the Bord, were meet to be grauntid : Yet, having now travailid ſix Weakes for my Diſpatch, I fynd no Reſolucion to eny of thoſe Peticions.

Which Slacknes is excuſid, by the Looſenes of *Deſmond*, and with their Care to meet with his Rebellion, wherein they travell ſo farre Southward, as they have loſt the Sight of the North Pole.

Thes *Iriſhe* Cauſes, now in Queſtion, have brought all Governours, meet for the Deputacion, to be conſiderid of ; emongs which your Lordſhip is namid. The Plotts appointid, for Reformacion of *Ireland*, are divers ; ſomme thinking it meet, that the Deputy there do remaine. And that a Liuetenant, or a Generall, over the Armies, be ſent with ſuch Aucthority, as Therle of *Penbroke* had in *Picardie*, in Queene *Maries* Daies : Who, after he had appeaſed all Sturrs, might retorne, and leve the Deputy to governe. Other have a Deviſe, to have the Provinces of *Munſter*, *Ulſter*, and *Connoughe*, under particuler Regimen, diſtinct from the Controulment of the Deputy ; which, as they ſay, ſhuld breade a certaine vertuus Envie in thes Monarches, who ſhuld do her Majeſty beſt Service. Other Deviſes alſo ther be, which be more perilus ; as to have the Sword put into the Hands of the *Iriſhe* Lords. I mene Lords of *Ireland*, as Therlis of *Ormond* and *Kildare* ; and the Deputy only to manage Cauſes of Juſtyce and Lawe : But all thes prevaill not ; and, thoughe much hath beine ſaid againſt the Plott laid by your Lordſhip, yet it is likely, that that Courſe, namely of Preſidency, ſhall proceede.

Since my Comming, I have urgid a Sewt to maynie of the Lords, and moſt eſpecially in Writing to my Lord of *Leceſter*, to this End, that, if the Deputy now there muſt contynew, then that he be aſſiſted with a private Army ; and that he be directly commaunded to enter *Ulſter* with Force ; and that his Actions may be ſuch hereafter, as may concurre with the Erle of *Eſſex*, in ſuch Sort, as both their Doings do ſeeme to tend to one Ende.

Secondly, That emongs ſuch, as are now namid to the Government, the Erle of *Eſſex* be thought uppon, whoſe Expenſes being above that, that eny Subject is hable to beare, might be eaſid with the Entertainment of the Deputacion ; whereby the Quene ſhuld ſeme to countenance the Warr, and ſhewe a Meaninnge, to go thorough with that which is begon ; wherunto I added ſuch Reaſons, as his Frends here have collectid.

Laſtly, concludid, That if her Majeſty ment to purſue the Cours in *Ulſter*, and that Therle ſhall remayne ther ; that then they wold conſider of ſome Mann of Experience and Knowledge, wherof ther weer but two ; the one, of that Greatneſs about her Majeſtie [the Earl of *Leiceſter*] as he nether cold be ſparid from the Affaires of the Realme, nor wold be entreatid to accept ſo great Travell ; wherby, of Neceſſyty, we were drivenn to the other, whom the Cuntrey did above all Menn deſier. Whoſe Succeſſe againſt *Shane Oneall* hath bine a Terrour to the Northern Rebells, whoſe Experience of the hole Goverment was able to make a ſhort Warre, and with as eaſy Conditions for the Prince, as eny other ; who being alſo well affectid to Therle of *Eſſex*, and to the Cauſe which he had in Hande, was likelie to ſettell his and the Gentlemens Feet fyrm. And, becauſe I ſhuld not ſeeme to wade in Cloudes, I namid my Lord Preſident of *Wales*.

I know, my Lord, that I ſhall be ſo farre of from deſerving Thanks of your Lordſhip, as I looke for ſome Rebuke for my Eaſſenes ; but ſeur I am, it canne do you no Hurt ; for the Queene ſhall vewe it, and therby, at leſt, muſt think vppon your former Service. Neuertheles, by this, or eny other Meane, your Lordſhip ſhall be ſought by her Majeſtie, directly or indirectly. I humbly beſeach you not to ſtand vppon Condicions, for your owne privat or perticuler Comodity, ſo as you be furniſhed meet for the Service. For as you ſhall deſerve well of all *England*, and all *Ireland*, ſo moſt eſſpecially of the Erle of *Eſſex*. And, if the Quenes Majeſtie be not good vnto you, be good

vnto

vnto your felf ; for that your Lordfhip knoweth you may do, if you lift.
And fo meaning neuer to offend you herafter by Silence, I comytt your Lordfhip to the Tuicion of God. At the Court, this 17 of *December*, 1573.

Your Lordfhips bounden,

during Lief,

Superfcribed, Ed. Waterhous.

To the right honorable my finguler good Lord,
  Sir *Henry Sydney*, Knyght of the Order, and Lord
  Prefident of *Wales*.

To Sir William Fitz William, *Lord Deputy of* Ireland, *and to the Earl
of* Effex.

By the Queene.

RIGHT truftie and welbelovid, and right truftie and right welbeloued
Cofen, we grete you well. We have at good Leingth confidered of the
Matter propounded by you our Cofin of *Effex*, for the Enterprice to reduce
the Province of *Vlfter* to our Obedience, by yeldinge to the Maintenaunce of a
Garrifon there, with the yerely Charge of xxvi thoufand Pounds for twoe
Yeres, and by grauntinge to expende thirteene thoufand Pounds in fortefyinge
of certaine Places there within the fame twoe Yeres. In which Matter we
thinke it mete to imparte iointly to you twoe our Opinion and Determination :
Firft, thoughe you the Erle, firft have by your feuerall Lettres, and nowe alfoe
by the Declaration of *Nicholas Malbie*, labored to make this Enterprice appere feizible and honorable, and, in the Ende, alfo profitable ; and you, the
Deputie, with fome others of our Counfell there, have, by your Lettres, recomended the fame Enterprice ; yet we cannot but thinke the Matter doubtfull,
wheather the Effect that is pretended may certenly followe, confideringe we
here not of every Thinge of Moment in every Part of *Vlfter*, anfwearable to
the Charge that hathe beene borne by vs, and fome Parte by you the Earle,
almoft thefe two Yeres : Nether doe we fee it made manyfefte but coniectu-
rall, when the twoe Yeres fhalbe at an Ende, that there fhalbe good and affured
Means, firft, to beare foche a Garrifon as fhalbe neceffary to continewe there
afterwards, which, we thinke, muft nedes be more then v C, which we
thinke to fmale a Number by your Plotte lymitted ; and next alfoe to make
fome Recompence of our great Charges, which in Certeinty, muft be fpent
theies two Yeres, over and aboue many vncertene accidente Charges not nowe
thought of. Befides this, we alfoe finde it not expreffed by any Aduertifment from thence, that admittinge to have the Numbers of twoe Thoufande
to be maintayned by vs for the Charge of the whole Realme, as you the
Earle did firft, in your Lettres of *October*, fuppofe to be fuffycient ; and that
owt of theis there might be M CCC employed as a contynuall Garrifon for
this Enterprice of *Vlfter* for twoe Yeres. Howe we may thinke or iudge
the reft of *Irelande* fhoulde be governed and kept, if, out of that Number of
twoe Thoufande, the Number of a Thoufand three hundrethe fhoulde be
taken, and alwaies for the Space of theis two Yeres contynued in *Vlfter*, and
not be ferviceable towardes the Pacyfyinge of eny fodaine Tumults in the
other Parts of that Realme. And by reafon of thofe Difficulties and Vncer-
taineties, with foch like, we have forborne the longer to refolue what to
doe, or not to doe herein ; for indede, as we cannot but greatly allowe the
noble Mynde of you the Earle, to offer your Service in fo painefull and hafar-
dous a Place, and muft neds thinke it a great Honnor and Shuertie vnto vs
and our Crowne, yea, in Tyme to come alfoe profitable, if the Succeffe

I

might

might followe, which in your Offers is promifed : So woulde we be lothe to enter and continewe foch an exceffive Charge, as this is intended, and to adventure both your Perfon, and many of our Subiects, in this Service, without more manyfeft and certaine Apparaunce of the Succeffe ; and alſoe withowt Determinacion aforehand that our Army fhoulde not exceede the faide Number of twoe Thoufand, afwell for the reft of that Realme as for *Vlfter*. And therefore not meaninge to reiect this your Offer, but very willinge to yelde therevnto, we have thought good to let you bothe vnderftand, that for this Enterprice to be well achieuid with the Number by you the Earle required. We thinke the beft Means to have our whole Charge not to excede the faide Number of twoe Thoufand ; befides certaine Kearne and Pioners, in your firft Plotte mencioned, fhalbe, that you bothe doe enter into theis particuler Confideracions followinge.

First ; Forafmoche as in all the reft of *Irelande*, befides *Vlfter*, there is, at this Tyme, no notable Troble nor Apparaunce, as you the Deputie do wright ; and that we can be content, only for the Refpecte of *Vlfter*, to contynewe the Charge of twoe Thoufande, which otherwaies we meane not, nor fee Caufe why ; it is to be iudged, in all good Probabilitie, that xiii C, or fome fewe more or leffe of the faid Number of twoe Thoufand, ought and may be imployed in *Vlfter* ; and the reft of the Realme ftaied in Quietnes, wherein it is, only withe the reft of the Nombers, beinge about vii C ; havinge thereto, at the Commandement of you the Deputie, the Forces of all other good Subiects. And yet neuertheles alfo, if foch Neceffitie fhoulde require for a fhorte Seafon, we fee not, but you, our Cofen of *Effex*, might foe ftaye the Parts of *Vlfter*, as owt of your Forces you might yelde to the Lord Deputy fome fuffycient Aide, for fome fmale Tyme to ferve the Stayinge of any Sturre that may be imagined, in any other Part owt of *Vlfter*.

Secondly ; It is to be confidered, that to this may be aded, to make the fame more probable, that you the Deputy, in refpect to furder this Enterprice of *Vlfter*, without any frequent Callinge for Aide of Numbers from the Service of *Vlfter*, may doe well for your felf, and foe alfoe caufe all other our Minifters, to forbeare from all Meanes of open Force to irritate eny of the Captains of the *Irifhe* in other Parts, or other the Lords owt of the *Englifhe* Pale, to move any notable Diforder againfte our State ; but to permitte them, without Innovacions, to contynewe as they nowe doe, and have donne in former Tymes of vniuerfall Quietnes.

And theis Things thus well confidered by you both, and concurringe with one Intencion for our Service, as we have Caufe to hope that you will, with a mutuall Aidinge one of the other : There is here, by vs and our Counfell (whofe Advife we have herein vfed) a manifeft Likelihod conceved, that, of the Numbers of twoe Thoufand, to be mainetayned by vs, there may be xiii C well fpared for *Vlfter*, and the Remayne to ferue for the Realme.

And befides that alfo, becaufe we have more Caufe to doubt of the Succeffe, as it is promifed with thofe Numbers in *Vlfter*, then to haue the reft of the Realme ftayed withe the Remayne :

It is here thought very neceffarie, that you, the Deputy, fhoulde, at fundry Tymes requifit for that Purpofe, give Order of fome Hoftinges for Carriage and Victuallinge of the Places wheare the Fortificacions fhalbe, vntill the fame may be brought into Defence.

Laftlye ; It is here alfo thought, that, theis twoe Thoufande beinge at the Commaundement of you twoe, it may be your mutuall Affent affentid, that fometyme for the Releif of the Bandes, that fhalbe appointed for *Vlfter*, fome of the other Bandes may be fent thether ; and fome of thofe in *Vlfter*, for there Releif, placed in there Roomes. And foe, by foche Relief and Changinge, they of *Vlfter* may the better indure the Service.

And thus, havinge fhewed to you bothe, as you fee, firft fome Doubtes that have lingered vs from Refolucion, and next foche Opynion, as we have conceived howe ; with the Charge of the reft of the twoe Thoufande that fhall not be imployed in *Vlſter*, you, our Deputye, may ſo ſtaie the reſt of our Realme in Quietnes, as our Coſen of *Eſſex* may haue the Uſe of the Number by him required: We require you both well to conſider hereof, and to ioyne your good Wills towards this Enterpriſe, withe a Determynacion, that ether of you ſhall, in Caſes neceſſary, aide the other, with a principall Reſpecte to the whole Realme.

And if you ſhall reſolue ſoe to doe, then we doe aſſent to the Maintenance of the ſaid Charge of twoe Thouſand, and doe will and authoriſe you bothe, to procede herein, requiringe you our Deputy, havinge the Authoritie of the whole Realme, ſo to contynewe in the Care thereof, and to ayde and aſſiſte our Coſen of *Eſſex* in this Enterpriſe, as Cauſe ſhall require from Tyme to Tyme. And becauſe you our Coſen of *Eſſex* did, at the Beginninge, require, beſides the Number of xiii C, foure hundrethe Kearne, and one hundrethe Pyoners; we can be content withe the Chardge of the ſaide Kearne and Pioners, ſo that the Charges of the Kearne exceede not the Wages of iii *d. per Diem* a Perſon, as is allowed in other Partes of the Realme: And where his Motion was to have the Wages of our Garriſon in *Vlſter* to be *Starlinge* Pay, we cannot aſſent thereto, neather for Examples Sake, nor yet for the Charge thereof; nether do we thinke it ſo nedefull, ſeing there ſhalbe a Staple of Victuall provided for the ſame, as is in the reſt of our Realme. And yet if you ſhall thinke it mete to rewarde ſome that may have Nede, as it may be thought the Horſmen, we think that you may reſonably requier, within a ſmale Tyme after your Entry: For the two firſt Yeres, that ſome Ceſſe or Relief be given and contributed to the Amendment of there Wages by the *Iriſhrie*, whom you ſhall defend from the Tyranny of *Oneill* and the *Scotts*; and we ſee not, but, to eaſe vs alſoe of ſome further Charge in other Thinges, you may reaſonablie require and obtaine of the ſaid *Iriſhe* ſome reaſonable Releif. Of whiche Thinges howe to require the ſame for our Service, and without Offence, Tyme ſhall teache you beſt howe to obtaine the ſame.

Nowe haue we alſo to charge you bothe, with that we thinke neather of you have had Care of, vnneceſſary Charges; for you, the Deputie, ſeme to contynewe in Charge under your Pay, the Number of xviii C. l*ti*. and you, the Earle, have in Charge vnder you xii C xci, both whiche Numbers make iii M clxi. of which Numbers, if it be trewe that they contynue ſoe in Charge, we haue great Marvell by what Warrant ſo many were firſt taken in, or are contynued in Paie. Nether can we imagin for what Service ſo many ſhoulde be taken or thus contynued. For you the Deputy knowe, that, when you had Iorney to make againſt the *Deſmonds*, xix C weare thought ſufficient. And you the Earle, as before in this Lettre is mencioned, did not require for the Matter of *Vlſter*, but xiii C, beſides Kearne, and C Laborers, nor, for the whole Realme, thovght any more nedeful then ii M. And now, havinge no Trouble in all *Irelande*, as you the Deputie do wryght, do contynue us in Charge iii M Men. A Matter that ſuer we cannot endure to be burdoind withall. And therefore we charge and commaunde you bothe, with all poſſible Speade, thoughe you make Meanes to borrowe Money for the Purpoſe, to diſcharge owt of your Pay, ſo many and of ſoche Sorte as may be beſt ſpared, ſo as no moe remaine then this our Lettre we doe aſſent ſhall remain, if the Enterpriſe of *Vlſter* ſhall goe forwarde. And, if you twoe ſhall accorde to proceade with our Enterpriſe of *Vlſter*, in Sorte as before we have mentioned, then we charge you bothe ſoe to aſſent. And, namely, we charge you our Deputy, havinge the Charge of our whole Realme, that noe moe be contynued in our Paye then xv or xvj C Soldiors for the whole Realme. For the Orderinge whereof, we require you ſoe to conferre withe the reſt of our Counſell, that aſmoche therein may be donne as reaſonably may be deviſed. And yet, thoughe the Enterpriſe of *Vlſter* take noe Place, as our Coſen of *Eſſex* ment it, we thinke it good that ſome convenient Force be lefte at *Knockfargus*, and ells wheare in *Clandeboye*, and ſome alſo nere the *Newrie*, for Staie of thoſe Partes, in as

good

good Quiet as refonably may be requifite, as in like Cafes heretofore hathé bene vfed.

And wheare we prefcribe you to difcharge out of our Paye fo many, as noe more remaine, then we have determined, whether the Enterprife of *Vlfter* take Effect or noe : Our Meaninge is not that, with our Charge or Treafure, eny be paide, but foche as haue bene entered in to Wages, by either of you bothe, by Vertue of our Warraunt. For if fo many be in Wages, as by the Auditors Book is mencioned, dyvers are there in Wages and Allowaunce, without our Warrant or Knowledge. And where we feeme here to wright fome Wordes as in Care the Enterprife of *Vlfter* might not peraduenture take Effect ; yet, fuerly, we doe not thinke but you bothe will fo confider of the Matter, as except you can fee more there, then we, or our Counfell, can fee here, the Enterprice, which hetherto hathe bene foe coftly to vs, fhall not by any of your Defaults, nowe quaile and come to nothinge. Geven vnder our Signet, at our Mannor of *Richmond*, the 15 of *Marche* 1574, in the 17 Yere of our Raigne.

> *To our truftie and welbeloued Sir* William Fitz-William, *Knight, our Deputy, in our Realme of* Ireland ; *and to our right trufty and right welbeloued Cofin, the Earle of* Effex.

The Right Honorable Thomas Sackvil *Lord* Buckhurft, *to* Sir Henry Sydney.

My Lord,

I Truft your Lordfhip will pardon me, in that I have not (as, indede, poffibly I cold not) attend to make ane Meting, for Thend of this Varians betwixt your Lordfhip and me ; and now being this Day alfo fo wrapt in Bufynes, as I can not by any Menes be a Seurtier, I thought to wryte thes few to your Lordfhip, and therin to affertain you ; that, becaus our Meting with the Mafter of the *Rols*, and Mr. *Henfias* Meting, wilbe fo uncertein : That, therefore, what Time fo ever you fhall like to appoint, I will come to the *Rols*, and there your Lordfhip and I, as good Neybors and Frends, will, if we can, compound the Caus of our felves. If we can not, we will both pray the Mafter of the *Rols*, as indifferent, as I know he is, to perfwade him to the Right, that ftands in the Wrong. And thus, I dout not, but ther fhalbe a good End to both our Contentacions : Your Lordfhip not feking that which is not yours ; nor I, in any Sort, mening to detein from you your ouen. This 23 *May*, 1574.

All yeurs to comand,

T. Buckehurft.

Superfcribed,

To the Right Honorable and my very
good Frend, Sir *Harry Sidney*, Knight,
Lord Prefident of *Wales*.

The Lady Mary Sydney, *to* Edmond Molineux, *Efq*; *Secretary to Sir* Henry Sydney.

M OLENOX, in dyuers Letters from my Lord, his Lordfhipe wryghts I fhould receue Wourd from you, how his Befynes goeth forward at the Courght, but yet I heare nothinge from you. I fent Letters, acordinge to my Lords Requeft, to my Lords my Brothers, and to Mr. *Dyer*, by *Barnes* my Servant, bearinge Daet, the xxiiij of the laft Mounth ; which I wild him very erneftly, myght, in Mafter *Dyers* Abfens, be deliuered vnto you ; and fo I alfo dyrected them, that you myght keap them tyll Mr. *Dyers* Cominge thether, who I am fuer will not longe be from thens, yf, er longe before this Tyme,

I

he

he be not thear al redy. I would be glad to hear, that fome good Refolution wer towards for my Lord, eather for an honorable Voyadge or a contentfull A-boud at Home ; I pray wryght by this Bearer, what you kno of hit ; and in all your Proceadings in my Lords Cawfis, take the wyfe, noble Mr. *Dyers* frendely Counfell, who I kno douth moft dearly tender my Lords Honor, and well Dowing, as mouche as a faythfull Frend may do. For my none Part, I canot aduyfe you to no better Coors, then my Lord hath written to his Frends ; but yf that go not fo faft forward as hit fhould, or you do wifhe ; as ill as I am in Health, or able to travaill, I would infors my fealf, in good Tyme, to be at the Courght, to ftand my dear Lord in what Steed, my Duty and beinge thear with her Maiefty, and my Frends, myght do ; thearfor, I pray you, wryght at lardge by this Bearer, *Gilbart*, who of Porpofe I fend to Mr. *Dyer*, and you, to the fame Ende, to hear from you bouthe ; and fo, for this Tyme, I leue you. From *Chifwyke*, this Fyrft of *September*, 1574.

Your affured Miftris, to do you

enny Good I cann,

M. Sydney.

I pray inquyre for Miftris *Edmonds*, of the Pryuy Chamber, and offer to fend her Letters at enny Tyme to me, and make my moft hartye Comenda-tions vnto her ; and alfo to Myftris *Skudamore*, of the Priuy Chamber ; and lern of them the good and profperus Health of her Majefty, and wryght to me thearof, and tell them, I would wryght to them, but I haue nothinge to tell them, but of my vnrecouerd, vnhealthfull Carcas. Pray alfo go often in my Name, to inquyer how my deare Brothers do, and the moft vertufe Lady of *Warwyke* ; good Mr. *Dyer*, in whom I fynd a fetled good Opinion of you, hath had fome Taulk with me, of you, confefninge your oneft Hart, and good Will towards me ; which yf I fynd accordingly, you fhall alfo fynd me no les thankfull, and redy to fteed you, with my beft Abylytye.

Matthew, *Archbifhop of* Canterbury, *to Sir* Henry Sydney.

WHeareas I purpofed to your Lordfhip one of my poore Bookes of *Thomas Walfinghams* Storie, *&c.* latelie fett owte ; the rather, for that I knowe your Lordfhip to loue Antiquities ; foe I fende you, by this Bearer, one ; and if you will lett mee haue the Sight of fum Bookes, that you haue, perad-venture, I maie enlarge them, or, by fum Comparifon, amende thofe that I haue in Hande, by Diuerfitie of Copies ; and foe maie the Worlde enioye fum Comoditie by vs, in fuch rare Bookes. And if that your Lordfhip will ef-fectuouflie fende to mee the Bookes, which you haue at Home in your Howfe : I maie further vnto you fum other Booke, that I haue of late caufed to be printed, meate for your Knowledge. And thus I bid you hartely well to fare as my felf. From my Howfe at *Lambith*, this Firft of *December*, 1574.

Your Lordfhips lovinge Frende.

Matthue Cantuar.

* *The Earle of* Effex *Lettre, in Ainfwere to her Majefties, iointly adreffed to the Lord Deputy and him.*

It may pleafe your moft excellent Majeftie,

I Have fene a Lettre figned by your Majeftie, dated the xvth of *Marche*, and endorfed to my Lord Deputy and me, in Ainfwere of the Matter propound-ed by me, for the Reducinge of the Province of *Vlfter* to your Majefties Obedience :

* Ex Autog. apud Penfhurft.

Obedience : In whiche Lettre, your Majestie semethe so well to fauour that Enterprice, as you have bountifully granted all soche Peticions as I thought mete
to demaunde for your Service ; namely, for the Numbers of Men to be mainetayned in *Vlster*, and for the Charges of the Buildings, and every other Thinge,
savinge the *Sterlinge* Pay ; wherein, neuertheless, your Majestie had a principall
Consideracion, to have had the Horsemen holpen with Cesse of the *Irishe*, and
the Foatebands reliued sometyme in the Pale, whiles others, that should serue
vnder my Lord Deputy, might supply there Places. Theis Graces and Fauors
proceadinge of my Suite (thoughe most necessary for your Honor, Profitt, and
Suerty of this State) doe give me Cause to yeld to your Majestie my humble
Thankes, and to increase my Zeale and Duty to serue your Majestie for euer.
But, althoughe this Lettre of your Majestie was in theis Points comfortable to
me, yet was it no Warraunt to me for my Proceadinge in the Enterprise,
without the Assent of my Lord Deputy, and that his Lordship shoulde tye
himself to a Nomber certaine, to be maintayned in other Parts of the Realme.
The Choise therefore of Proceadinge, or not Proceadinge, beinge in your
Deputy, and not in me, his Lordship hathe resolued, for soche Reasons as I
thinke he will open to your Majestie, that this Enterprice shall cease, and your
Army to be rassed to the Nomber appointed in your Majesties saide Lettre.
And, althoughe this Conclusion is grevous vnto me, after your Majesties
Consent obtained, and soche Assurednes that my Plott might in euery Pointe be
well accomplished ; yet, vppon Knowledge of my Lord Deputies Pleasure in
this Behalf, I have, as Reason is, delyvered to his Lordship all the Soldiors vnder me in *Vlster*, to be rassed, but not before I had vsed some Perswasion to
him, to make some of the Counsailors here privie in so weightie a Case : Or,
that I might procede withe some Hostinge, to establishe the Countrey, and
bringe *Tirlanghe* to Order : Or, that it woulde please him to take Th'execution
of the Plotte vppon him, and I to serue privately vnder him : Or, as he
would himself : And, havinge nowe noe longer Soldiers over whome to governe, I haue also resigned the Government of *Vlster*, havinge, I trust, the Testimony of his Lordship, and all your good Subiects here, that, duringe my
Remayninge in that Office, I have, withe your Force, and my owne Industry,
kept your Pale Northward from Invasion, your *Englishe* Subiects from Slaughter or Losse, and the *Irishe*, soche as weare well inclyned, from Tyranny of
the Rebell ; yea, and euen the Rebell himself, in Feare of his vtter Overthrowe, as might appeare by his contynuall Suite for Peace. Theis Things, in
soe daungerous a Tyme, as when Armes weare in Manner vniuersally taken
in *Mounster* and *Connaught*, and some Parts of *Leinster*, was thought here to be
good Seruice ; and soe, I doe assure my self, your Majestie dothe accept it. In
the first Parte of your Majesties Lettre, you semed to doubt that vC Men,
after twoe Yeres, and the Townes builded, should not be hable to defende
those Townes, and kepe the Country obedient ; but, as I knowe, iiC Footemen
are enoughe for the Wardes : Soe 300 Horse distributed, as my Plott appointed, woulde alwaies have serued to have kept them in all Duty and Subiection.
In the same Parte of your Lettre, your Majestie takethe Holde of my Wordes
written to the Lords in *October*, to deminishe your Nombers to ijM of all Sorts.
Yt may please you therefore to consider of my Wordes, which weare these :
And I see noe Reason, but if her Majestie kepe 2000 Soldiors (without which,
Obedience or Profitt will not be had of *Irishe* or *Englishe* in *Yreland*) why 1300
of them shoulde not, for the most Parte, reside in *Vlster*. This was, and
is still my Opynion ; and, I hope, cannot be construed but theis Soldiers weare
ment *Englishe* Bandes, and not to be extended towardes Officers or Kearne,
which are nether at Commandement, nor can be emploied but in their
Charges. Besides, I neuer tooke vpon me to sett downe my Opynion for the
Government of the whole Realme, whearewithe I nether had to doe, nor, with
your Fauour, will have to doe, but only of my Charge ; and, therefore, I
trust my Wordes have not procured this great Dyminishment of your Majesties
Armye.

Armye. But nowe I will faye directly, that which before I fpake coniecturally, that ijM *Englifhe* Soldiors vnder Bands, well mayntained, wilbe enoughe to governe all the whole Realme of *Yreland*, and to make all that be Rebells, or that be of the *Irifhe* Faccions to quake, and either to be good Subiects, or to feeme good Subiects. In the latter Parte of your Majefties faide Lettre, you fynde Faulte withe the Nombers kept vnder me, commandinge none more to be paide with your Treafure, then are warraunted from your Majeftie ; wherevnto I thinke good to ainfwere, that I have entertayned, for the Defence of all *Vlfter*, no more then I had for *Clandeboy*, except thirty Horfemen *Irifhe*, vnder the Baron of *Dungannon*, whom it behoued your Majeftie to aide and countenance, and foche Bandes of Kerne as weare neceffary for your Service. For, in *Clandeboy*, I had CC Horfe, and vjC Footmen. I had Cth allowed for the Sea, whereof I have vfed but 50. I had Cth Pyoners, whereof I vfed but 50 ; and nowe, latelie, but thirty ; and, for all theis, I truft I had your Majefties Warraunt. Indeede, vpon the Deathe of Sir *Thomas Smythes* Sonne, I gave Mr. *Moore*, your Majefties Pencioner, fome Countenance in the *Ardes*, by a few Men in Wages, and after maintayned a Warde in his Houfe, when he was flaine ; and in this, and whatfoeuer ells, in foche likeCafes, I have done, I truft to fhewe good Reafon, to moue me to doe it for your Majefties Service. And nowe, I muft confeffe, and neuer before, that your Charge is vtterly lofte fince Th'enterprife is diffolued ; and I dare avowe, that, if Th'enterprice had gonne forward, the Money, whiche you have fpent, had beene the beft imployed, that euer your Majeftie fpent in *Ireland*, and is nowe the worft. Which, I feare, will fhortly appeare ; for the *Irifhe*, heare, have nowe Reafon neuer to looke for Reformacion, and neuer to truft to your Majefties Proteccion, but to combyne themfelues. For their commen Obiection is (efpeacially they of *Tyrconnell*) that they are alwaies lefte without Defence, and to their Shiftes. For fo *Odonell* termed it to me, who is nowe in open Warre, by my Meanes, againft *Tirlanghe*, and muft, in dede, be left to Extremitie. I fende your Majeftie his Lettres, and foche as I receued out of *Scotland*, declaringe the Comminge of the *Scotts*. Their reftethe nowe, that I make my Proteftacion, that I am noe Waye confentinge, or doe allowe of this Goinge Backe of your Northern Service. And fuer, fince there hathe not bene at any Tyme any Default in me, but haue ben called from Th'enterprice of *Clandeboy*, to the Defence of the whole Province of *Vlfter*, wherein I have ferued your Majeftie without Entertainement, paynefully and truly to your Honour, Suerty of this State, and Defence of your Subiects : I miftruft not, but your Maieftie will, bothe of your Juftice and Bounty, gracioufly confider of my intollerable Charges paft ; and, aboue all Things, retayne me in your Majefties good Opynion, as your humble Servaunt, devoted and moft affectionnat to ferve your Majeftie. And, beinge nowe altogeather pryvate, I doe defier your Majefties good Lycenfe foe to lyve in a Corner of *Vlfter*, which I hyer for my Money ; wheare, thoughe I paffe my Tyme fomewhat obfcurely (a Lief, my Cafe confidered, fitteft for me) yet fhall it not be without fome Staye in theis Parts, and Comforte to foche as hoped to be ridde from the Tyranny of Rebells. And fo, prayinge for your Majefties happy Raigne, with a longe helthfull Lief, I humbly ende at *Dublin*, this Laft of *Marche*, 1575.

* The Earle of Effex to the Lords of the Councell.

My good Lordes,

I Have of late feene a Lettre figned by the Queenes Majeftie, and iointly endorfed to my Lord Deputy and me, concerning myne Enterprice in the Province of *Vlfter* ; which, althoughe it carry a Shewe of a prefent Proceadinge therin, and of a Confent to all my Peticions, yet hathe it brought forthe none other Effectes, but the prefent Difcharge of all that ferue vnder me, and a finall Difolvinge of my Enterprice : Whereunto, what Ainfwere I have made to her

Majeſtie, may appeare vnto you, by the Copy of my Lettres herein encloſed. And, althoughe it become me to ſtande contented with any Thinge that her Majeſtie ſhall ſignifie to be her Will, yet, when I compare this Concluſion to the Courſe that hathe beene taken with me ſince my Comminge heather, I cannot but thinke the Dealinge verie ſtraunge. Firſt, I can, with the good Likeinge of all your Lordſhips, and withe the Allowance of the Councell here, ſoe as, by the Conſents of bothe Realmes, I tooke my Iorney, the Matter beinge firſt thoroughlie debated, and ſoe digeſted, as thoughe no Scruple ſhoulde at any Time arryſe. I had not bene here three Monethes, but that it was given forthe, that the Contynuance of Th'enterprice was in Queſtion, and in that Staie hathe it remayned euer ſince, till nowe, that, in all Apparaunce, the Proceadinge therein is agreed vppon, and all my Peticions graunted; and yet the ſame Lettre, that ſo dothe aſſure me of all this gracious Fauour, is a Warraunt to my Lord Deputy (as he takethe it) to overthrowe the Hole. My Lords, I humbly deſier you to conſider well of this Matter: Yt is ſomewhat to me (thoughe litell to others) that my Houſe ſhoulde be overthrowen, with ſufferinge me to runne my ſelf out of Brethe with Expences. It is more, that, in the Worde of the Queene, I have, as it weare, vndone, abuſed, and bewitched, with faire Promiſes, *Odonell, Mac Mahon,* and all others that pretende to be good Subiectes in *Vlſter.* It is moſt, that the Queenes Majeſtie ſhall adventure this Eſtate, or ells ſubdue Rebellion withe intollerable Charge. For will not all Partes of this Realme take Holde of this Diſſolucion? Or can any in *Vlſter,* or in any Parte of the Realme, hope of Defence hereafter? But, to retorne to my owne Eſtate, let my Lief here, my good Lords, be examyned by the ſtraighteſt Commiſſioners that may be ſent, I truſte, in examyninge my Faultes, they will alleage this for the Cheif, that I have vnſeaſonably tolde a plaine, probable, honorable, and effectuall Way howe to doe the Countrey Good. For, of the reſt, they can ſay nothing of me, but wytnes my Miſery by Plage, Famyn, Sicknes, contynuall Toile, and contynuall Wantes of Men, Money, Carriages, Victualls, and all Thinges mete for great Attempts: And, if any of theis have growen by my Defalt, then condemne me in the Whole. I pray you, my Lords, pardon my Earneſtnes; I thinke I have Reaſon, that am thus amaſed withe an overſodden Warninge, that muſt take a Diſcharge, before I am made acquainted withe the Matter. I thinke it had been a better Courſe, that I might have had Tyme to haue made ſome profitable Peace withe *Tyrlanghe,* which hathe bene ſought at my Handes, and not, at one Inſtant, to looſe my Travaile, my Money, my Creditt, and, with the ſame, hazard the Honor of her Majeſtie, and of the Realme of *England.* I truſt, my Lords, my plaine Dealinge ſhall not doe me Hurte with you; for my owne Parte, a ſolitary Lief is beſt for a diſgraced Parſon; but, becauſe there is none of you but hathe profeſſed Fauour towardes me, and ſome of your Lordſhips are mixt withe me in Blood and Alliaunce, I crave of you all, that, as I have entred into this Action with your good Likeings and Advices, ſo nowe, the Failinge beinge noe Way to be laide vpon me, you will all be Meanes for me to her Majeſtie to deale well withe me for my Charge, as in Honor, Conſcience, and Juſtice you ſhall thinke good. And ſo comyttinge my ſelf, and my Poſterity, to her Majeſties Fauour, and your Perſwacion in this Point, I comitt your Lordſhips to God, and humbly take my Leave. At *Dublin,* this xxixth of *Marche,* 1575.

Sir Francis Walſingham *to Sir* Henry Sydney.

My verry good Lord,

THE Erle of *Leyceſter* and I have taken uppon us, without your Knowledg or Privytye, knowing the Suffytyencye of this Bearer [Capt. *Malbie*] every Waye to perſwade her Majeſtye to make Choyce of him, to governe under you in *Connawghe,* with ſuch Tytle and Allowance, as to your Lordſhip

ſhall

shall be thowght convenient. And suerly, yf his Fortune answered to his Val-lewe, I knowe him not in this Lande more fytt to beare the Tytle of Presy-dent then he. Yf he lyved in any other Cuntrye then this, where martyall Men presently beare no Pryce, he shoulde not have ben so longe kept under Foote. I doe but loose Tyme to commende him unto your Lordship, being so well knowen unto you as he is. And, to geve Testimonye of the Affecti-on he bearethe towardes you, and how myche he honorethe you, were also but a fruteles Labor. My chefe Request is unto your Lordship (howesoever you deale with him towching Tytle) to deale frendely and favourably with him, towching his Interteynement, bothe, for that I knowe he will deserve well ; as, also, for that his poore Estate shall so require. I hope you shall repent no Frend-ship you shall shewe him, for sooche a worthye Instrument can not be to derely interteyned. And so, assuringe my selfe of your honorable Dealyng towardes him, as one whom I love derely ; and, therefor, will repute any Frendeship, shewed unto him, bestowed on my selfe ; I commyt you to Gods good Keep-yng. At *London,* the 15th of *Maye,* 1575.

Your Lordships assured Frende,

Fra. Walsyngham.

Sir Henry Sydney *to Queen* Elizabeth.

May it please your most excellent Majestie,

I Have received your Highnes Lettres, dated at *Woodstocke,* the Seconde of this present *September,* by the which, your Pleasure is, to knowe my Opini-on towchinge twoe of the Earle of *Essexs* Demaunds ; wherein, as I am most humblye to thanke your Majestie, that you will not resolve of any Thinge that may tende to the Alteracion of that you formerlye concluded with me, for my Chardge of Governement vnder you in this Realme, without my selfe, so long as it shall please your Majestie to imploy me heere : So, of the Earle, I must say, that he is so noble and woorthye a Personage, and so forwarde in all his Actions, and complete a Gentleman, wherein he may either advaunce your Honnor or Service, as you may take Comforte, to have in Store so rare a Subiecte, who hath nothinge in greater Regarde, then to shewe hymselfe souch a one in dede, as the commen Fame reportethe hym ; which hath bene no more in Troth, then his due Deserts, and painefull Travells, in the hardest Partes of this miserable Countrie, have deserved. For his Sute to have three hundered Men in Pay duringe his Liffe, your Majestie may do verie well, in myne Opi-nion, to graunte hym his Demaunde ; for, by that Meanes, he shall be incourag-ed, the rather, to thinke, that his Service past is neither least vnremembred, nor he altogether vnrewarded : And the Border of the *Englishe* Pale (by the Layenge, and Imployment of theise Men in *Ferney,* and those Confynes) moche strengthened and defended : But yet I wold wishe, that the same were graunted from your Majestie, with this Condicion, that one Hundered of theim should be at the Deputies Direction, for the Service of *Vlster,* where they should remayne, and not be removed, but when vrgent Necessitie of Service should so re-quyre to be imployd for the Defence of the Borders of *Connaught,* or the *Eng-lyshe* Pale, and not els where : Twoe Hundered of theim, whereof one Hunde-red of Horsemen, and one hundered Footemen, to remayne in *Ferney,* or *Mac Guise* Ilande, where the Earle shall thinke most requisite and necessarie for his best Commoditie, to imploy theim in those Partes, and those yet to be viewed and mustered by the Direction of the Governor. And theise three hundered Men, thus distributed, may convenientlye be graunted without Encrease of your further Chardge, whereof, as a Councellor to your Majestie, it behoveth me to have dewe Regarde. Towchinge his other Demaunde for *Mac Guyse* Ilande, your Majestie may esteme, that you have made a good Purchase for your selfe, to have foche a Tenaunt, who, befides Obedience (which is rather to be defiered, then generallye looked for in thofe Partes) may, in Tyme, by Buyldinge, Plantinge, and Setlinge there, drawe foche a Confent, and Lykinge of others, to fanfye his Neighborhoode, as Benifitt may growe to your Coffers, Honnor to your Realme, and Safetye to maney of your good Subiects. And thus, Maddame, havinge in the one, and the other, declared myne Opinion, accordinge to your Majefties Commaundment, I humblye fubmitt my felfe to your gratious Refolution; which, I hoope, fhalbe to the Satisfienge of the Earle, to whom, I finde alreadie, you are moft gratioullye difpofed: And I, for my Parte, wifhe as moche Honnor, as may happ, to fo woorthie a Subiect, and pray God bleffe your Majeftie with a moft happie and profperous Reigne. From *Drogheda*, the xxviijth of *September*, 1575.

Your Majefties moft bounden humble

Subiect and Servaunt,

H. Sydney.

Sir Henry Sydney, *to* William Cecil *Lord* Burghley, *Lord High Treafurer of* England.

My verie good Lord,

SITH my Arryvall here, I received Lettres from her Majeftie verye favorablye written, in fomme Allowance of the Earle of *Effexs* Demaundes; whereunto I have affented, as farre in all Pointes, as convenientlye and reafonablye I might, to the Satisfienge of the Earle. And, for that the Payment of thofe Men, that are to be appointed vnder his Chardge (if her Majeftie fhall confirme his Graunte) are to be iffued out of that Affignacion allotted vnto me for this Governement: I am the more ftreightened, and therefore muft hufband the reft, in foche Sorte (if I can) as, at the Yeares Ende, I fall not fhorte of my Accompte, as heretofore I have donne. And, therefore, I pray your Lordfhip, be mindfull that Promiffe may be kept, with me, and affigne me fomme Place, where certeinelye I fhall receive my Porcion at my Day for my Quarterage: For, otherwife, I fhall not be able, either to kepe Promiffe withe hym, nor ferve myne owne Tourne, which I would be lothe fhould fo fall owte, fince I have vndertaken the Chardge: And, therefore, my good Lord, effectuallye remember me, as I hope you will. For the State of this Countrey, I finde it fo generallye infected, as I can fkarce fynde a fafe Place to put my Head in; and this Towne it felfe is not free from Infection, for, within theife twoe Dayes, dyvers are dead of the Plague. I am nowe vpon my Iorney towards *Caricfergus*. God fende me good Speede, for the Northe is farre out of Order, as your Lordfhip fhall perceive by my Lettres fent to the Lords of the Council. And thus, havinge no more to write, but my humble Thankes, for your Lordfhips accuftomed Favor and Pleafure beftowed vpon me, I take my Leave. From *Drogheda*, the xxviijth of *September*, 1575.

Your Lordfhips lovinge Freinde to

commaunde,

H. Sydney.

Sir Henry Sydney, *to the Lords of her Majeftys Council.*

My Duetie humblye remembred, to your good Lordfhips,

MAY it pleafe you to be advertized, that I arryved, and landed at the *Skerries*, the viith of this Prefent, in the Morninge, being brought with a calme Wether, and faire Paffage, till the Pointe of ftrikinge Sayle, where it

grewe

grewe fomewhat ftormye ; yet, I thanke God, without Daunger in Landinge, though fome of my Trayne, that were imbarked with me at the fame Tyme, in other Veffells (by Reafon of the Storme which devided vs) were landed at an other Creke, ij Dayes after me. And, at my Comminge, I founde the Infection of the Plauge, fo generallye difperfed, and fpeciallye thorough the *Englifhe* Pale, as hardlye I could finde a Place clere to fettle in, without Daunger of Infeccion ; the Soldiours, foche as were apointed to be caffed, remayned ftill vndifcharged at my Comminge : And, as I learne by Conference withe the Threaforer, the Treafure, appointed for their Difchardge, will fall owte rather fhorter, then any remayne left, to be imployed for the Defrayment of other Debts ; fo that for their full Difchardge and Imbarkemente (beinge thorough their Infolencye verye greivous, and bourdenous to the Countrie, and cried owte vpon, with a generall Complaynte) I affigned theim of myne owne, by Way of Warraunt, an Hundered Crownes, *Sterlinge*. The *Irifhrey* in *Vlfter* growe verye infolent, and of foche Force and Head, as Capteine *Selbie*, and *Bawmfoorde*, Clarcke of the *Checke*, coming from *Knockfergus*, with fyvetie Horffemen in Companie, were fett vpon and chafed by the *Irifhrey* ij or iij Tymes by the Way, and hardlye efcaped without Daunger of Takinge : The xvjth of this Prefent, for my *Biene venum*, to welcome me into the Countrie, *Sorley Boy*, with his Companie came to *Knockfergus*, there to make the Pray of the Towne, and gave fo proude an Affault, as they flewe Capten *Baker*, and his Lieutenaunt, and fortie of his Bande, befides Townefmen and others ; dyvers hurte and maymed, the Perticularities whereof your Lordfhips fhall perceive by the inclofed. And al be it, by the Courage and Valor of the reft of the Captens, and Souldiours of that Garrifon, the Pray was refkued ; yet the Towne fo diftreffed, they remayne fo doubtfull, and in contynuall Feare, that I, for their Relieffe, have entended and appointed a Iorney thetherwardes, with as moche Spede and Expedicion as may be. And by theife Attempts your Lordfhips may fee, howe prowd the *Scott* is growen, fo that either to dawnt theim, or banifhe theim totallye, for annoyenge thofe Partes, that Force is to little, that I am hable to maynteine, with the Affignacion appointed me, but onelye by Way of Pacificacion and Practiffe ; havinge fo maney nedefull Places els where in the Realme, to difperfe the Soldiors for her Majefties Service : Yet am I lothe, in any Sorte, to confent to the Encreafe of her Highnes furder Charge, for any Accident, that hathe happened, or I truft fhall happen, duringe my Governement vnder her Majeftie here : Nevertheles, as a Forewarninge, I write thus to your Lordfhips : That if any Thinge fhould fall owte hereafter, by the *Scotts*, contrarie to your Expeccacions (as I will do my beft Indevor, there fhall not, accordinge as I have vndertaken, and promifed her Majeftie) I may be the rather holden blameles, and excufed, havinge written to your Lordfhips the Certeintie of Things, as they ftande nowe ; and the Lykelyehoode of the Sequell to followe hereafter, except the fame by good Forefight may be prevented in Tyme. For the State of the reft of the Countrey in what Sorte it is, the Tyme beinge fo fhorte, fince myne Arryvall, and the Infeccion fo great, as I have not ftirred farre Abroade, I can fay little, for that in Trothe I could not fynde any apt Place fafelye to gooe vnto. And therefore, for the prefent (befeachinge your Lordfhips to take Knowledge of that I have written to her Majeftie, towchinge the Earl of *Effexs* Demaunds) I humblye take my Leave. From *Drogheda*, the xxviijth of *September*, 1575.

Your Lordfhips lovinge Friende to

commaunde.

Sir Henry Sydney *to the Lords of the Council.*

My verye good Lords,

ALbeit, in my laſt Lettres, I made mention vnto your Honnors, of the Want of Treaſure remayninge in the Treaſorers Handes, for the Payment of ſoche Souldiors, as were caſſed by your Appointements ; whereby, out of that Porcion aſſigned vnto me, I was fayne, by Way of Warraunt, to allowe theim, for Tranſportacion, a hundered Crownes *Sterlinge :* And, this Day, paſſed an other Warraunt, for lyke Purpoſe, from me, to vnburthen the Countrie, that makes Exclamacion againſt theim. I thought rather, my Lords, and ſo was your Lordſhips Expeċtacions, that, the Men, your Lordſhips willed to be diſchardged, beinge caſſed and paied, the Remayne ſhould be imployed for the Defrayment of other Chardges. But, findinge none to remayne at all, but iſſu-inge owt of myne owne for thoſe Purpoſes, my Brother, *Fytz Williams,* could not receive Money, in any Sorte, for his Tranſportacion, and other Chardgies ; but enforced to make other Meanes, by Way of Borrowinge, to diſpatch hym ſelfe hence ; whereof I thought good to advertiſe your Lordſhips, that, for his Payments, he might fynde the more Favor, as I beſeache your Lordſhips he may. And even ſo I humblye take my Leave of your good Lordſhips (beinge this Day reddye to ſett forwarde on my Iorney towardes *Knockfergus.*) From *Termondfacan,* the vth of *Oċtober,* 1575.

Your Lordſhips lovinge Freinde

humblye to commaunde,

H. Sydney.

Sir Francis Walſyngham, *Secretary of State, to Sir* Henry Sydney, *Lord Deputy of* Ireland.

My very good Lord,

I Was gladd to underſtande, by the Earl of *Eſſexs* Letters, that your Lord-ſhip and he is growen to ſo good a Concluſyon, towching his Demawndes ; wherby his Lordſhip ſeamethe to be greatly ſatysfyed with your frendely Deal-yng towardes him. Suche here as doe wyſhe generally well unto that State, and partycularly to your ſelves, doe deſyre nothing more, then the Contynewaunce of good Lyking and ſownde Frendeſhip betwene you. And therfor, good my Lord, lett your Eares be cloſed ageynſt Tale Bearers, who make their Proffyt of Dyſſentyon. That Natyon, as I learne, is cunnyng in that Profeſſyon ; and, therfor, yt behovethe your Lordſhips, bothe to be verry ċyrcumſpeċt in that Behalfe. I praye God, that peſtylent Humor receyve no Nouryſhement from hence. When I fawle into Conſyderatyon of the Sowndenes of bothe your Judgements, then doe I ſhake of all Feare ; but, when I caule to Mynde the curſed Deſtynye of that Ilande, I can not put of all Dredd. I hope your owne Wyſdomes, the Caulynge on eny of your Frendes here, and the good Miniſters abowt you there, wyll prevent the Mallyce of ſuche, as ſhall ſeeke any Waye to ſlander you.

The Sendyng over of your Aſſyſtaunts, I am not unmyndefull therof. Him whom you cheflye deſſyre, I meane Sir *W. Dreurye,* wyll not fayle at the Tyme by you appoynted, yf God let yt not, or her Majeſty. Mr. *Rockebye,* without ſome Impreſt at your Lordſhips Handes, to forniſhe him of ſooche Neceſſaryes, as the Place he is appoynted for requyre (having not the Meanes otherwyſe to furniſhe him ſelfe) ſhall be forced to refuſe the ſame, thorowghe Diſabylity : When I conſyder the Woorthynes of the Man, howe hardely ſuche are, where-of his Integryte is to be ſownde ; and howe great Neade that Place hathe of ſuche as are : I cannot but wyſhe your Lordſhip, to ſtrayne your ſelfe as muche as you maye, to ſupplye his Wants. And, ſo leavyng further to troble your
Lordſhip,

Lordſhip, I moſt humbly take my Leave. At my Howſe at *Odiam*, the xxd of *Octobre*, 1575.

Your Lordſhips aſſured Frend,

Francis Walſyngham.

Sir Henry Sydney *to the Lords of the Council.*

MY humble Duetie remembred vnto your honorable good Lordſhips: After I had leaft Order for the Pale, appointinge the Lords and Gentlemen, of the beſt Accompt, Diſcreacion, and Iudgement, in Commiſſion, to ſee to the Defence and Quiet of the Countrie, I ſett forwardes in my Iorney towardes *Knockfergus*, the vth of *October* laſt ; and takinge with me iiij C Footemen, and 200 Horſſe, of the Forces of her Majeſties Armye ; I was accompanied withe the Barons of *Lowth* and *Dungannon*, Sir *Nicolas Bagnoll*, the Marſhall, Sir *Edward Fitton*, the Threaſorer, Sir *Lucas Dillon*, the Cheife Baron, *John Chaloner*, her Majeſties Secretorye, and *Jaques Wingefield*, Maſter of the Ordenaunce ; and, in this Sorte, paſſinge from *Drogheda* to *Dundalke*, and thence to the *Newrie*, I found ſoche good Pollecye and Order in the Countries where the Marſhall dwellethe ; his Landes ſo well manured, his Tenaunts ſo cheriſhed and mainteined, the Towne ſo well planted with Inhabitaunts, and encreaſed in Bewtye and Buyldinge, as he is moch to be commended ; aſwell that he vſeth his Tenaunts to lyve ſo welthilye vnder hym, as his owne Bountie and large Hoſpitallitie, and Howſekepinge, ſo able and willinge to geve Enterteinment to ſo maney, and cheifely to all thoſe that have Occaſion to travell to or froe Northwardes, his Howſe lyenge in the open high Way to their Paſſage.

The *Fews*, the Countrie of *Phelim Roos* Sonnes, and *Orerye*, the *Chanlons* Countrye, I found in extreme Diſorder ; not onelye for vniverſall Waſt of theim ſelves, but for the intollerable Annoyaunces and Spoyles of their Neighbours in both Borders, as well *Engliſhe* as *Iriſhe*. The Landes of bothe which Countries were geven, by her Majeſtie, by Indenture, to *Chatterton*, who nowe remayneth there in *Englande*, I ſuppoſe halſe diſmayed, of the vntowarde Succeſſe of this Enterpriſe, and the little Poſſibilitie he findethe, either in hym ſelfe or his Parteners, to do any Good, but waſt theim ſelves, and ſett vpp ther Reſtes of Vndoinge, before they bringe any Thinge to goode Effecte. The Nomber of the Natyves of the *Foyle* are ſo many, the Reckninge ſo ſmall alreadye, of *Engliſhe* Enhabitaunts, and the Liklyhoode of Encreaſe leſſe ; ſince theſe fower Yeares Space they have enioyed their Graunte, they have not donne any Thinge woorthe the Remembraunce ; no Fortificacion to Effecte made, not one Man yet wonne, to retorne to theim, either in Knowledge, Service, or Tenauncye : They are to paye Rent to her Majeſtie, by Covenaunt, at *Michelmas* next, after the Rate of xx *s.* the Ploughland, and ſett downe, plant, and enhabite, before the Ende of the Yeare of oure Lorde 1579, otherwiſe their States by Covenauntes are determined : In both the latter, I found that great Vnlyklyhoode, and almoſt Impoſſibilitie, to be brought to paſſe by theim and their Parteners, that I dealt withe *Chattertons* Brother, whome I founde here ; and moch pittienge both hym and his Caſe, and the wilfull Conſuminge of their Goodes (to ſo manifeſt a Loſſe, and Imparinge of theim ſelves, and theire Patrimonyes) that I offered to be a Meane for Compoſicion ; which he refuzed, and told me, that he coulde not deale in the Matter alone, without his Brother. And one the other Side, the *Chanlons* beinge ſent for, to come vnto me, vpon Protection, they refuzed to come, for that they feared, and ſo they anſweared the Meſſenger, that I would compell theim to Compoſicion with *Chatterton*, which they ſaied they would neuer yeeld vnto. So that I neither finde Meanes to agree theim, nor ſee in *Chatterton*, and his Parteners, any Lykelyhoode, or Poſſibilitie, to do Good for theim ſelves. Therefore if her Majeſtie would, in ſome Sort, reaſonablye compound with theim, for their Graunte, the Countrie would growe moche quieter, and their Neighbors welthier, and the

old

old Inhabitaunts (as I thinke) will yeeld her Majeſtie yearelye, to becomme Tenaunts to her of hir Countrie, twoe hundered Poundes by the Yeare, and an ordenary Ryſinge out of Horſſemen and Footemen.

Next I came to *Evaugh*, or *Mac Denneſſe* Countrie, which is not yet recovered, but feeleth ſtill the heavye Burden of former Spoyles, and impeached with preſent ill Neighborhoode, and ſpeciallye of thoſe twoe Countries before remembred ; and the worſſe planted, manured, and inhabited, for that he is not ſure of it by any certeine Eſtate ; and therefore deſiereth, by Peticion (which here incloſed I ſend your Lordſhips) that he may have it confirmed vnto hym from her Majeſtie. He hathe, ſince the firſt Tyme I brought hym out of Subieċtion to *Oneill*, remayned a conſtant and aſſured good Subieċte, growen civill and verye traċtable, accompanied me this Iorney hym ſelfe, and his Force, with that Forwardnes to ſerve her Majeſtie, as there wanted no Token of good Will, wherein he might expreſſe any Note of aſſured Fidellitie and Obedience.

From thence I came to *Kinnaliartie*, or *Mac Cartains* Countrie, which I found all deſolate and waſt, full of Thieves, Outlawes, and vnreclaymed People ; none of the old Owners dare occupie the Lande, becawſe it hath pleaſed her Majeſtie to beſtowe the Countrie vpon Capten *Nicolas Malbye*, tied, neverthele ſſe, to ſoch Obſervacion of Covenaunt and Condicion, as *Chatterton* had his. Al be it I could wiſhe *Malbie* a farre better good Torne, both in Creditt and Commoditie, then that Countrie is, or can be to hym (for ſo I thinke hym worthie) yet for that I ſee there is no Poſſibilitie in hym to do any Good, but to ſpoyle and wearye hym ſelfe, and bourden his Freindes, and make the Countrie waſt, and altogether abandoned of Inhabitaunts : I would wiſhe that ſome reaſonable Recompence were offered hym for his good Contentment, and that the Quene ſhould reſume the Landes into her owne Handes, and then Proffitt of Rent and Service would be made of it, where nowe no Beniſitt arryſeth at all to *Malbye*, nor none ells ; but contrariewiſe, beinge held as it is, breadethe moche Trouble and Inconvenience to the good Neighbourhoode, and commen Quiet and Securitie of the Countrie.

Leavinge that Countrie, I paſſed thoroughe *Lecale*, which is my Lord of *Kildares* Landes, and there found dyvers verye honeſt Freholders ; but moche of the Countrie waſt, but nowe on the mendinge Hand, and far the better ſince the Earle of *Eſſex* had it, and that by his Plantinge of Tenauntes, and Placinge of Soldiours ; ſo that it doth verye well defende it ſelfe.

The *Dufferen*, or *Whites* Countrie, I found all waſt and deſolate, vſed as they of *Clandeboy* liſt. The Owner of it is a proper young Man, and well diſpoſed, but I feare vnhable to do any Good on it, either for the Publike or his owne Particular. In the Streights of this Countrie, *Neill Mac Brian Ertough*, made Capten of *Clandeboy* by the Earle of *Eſſex*, ſhewed his Force, and refuzed, though, vpon Proteċtion, to come to me, yet that Day he offered me no Skirmiſhe.

From thence paſſinge into the *Ardes*, I found that Countrie moche impoveriſhed, but in good Hope of Recoverie, for that there are maney Freholders of *Engliſhe* Race, of auntient Habitacion there ; and moche the better I hope it wilbe, thorough Sir *Thomas Smythes* Pollecye and Purſſe. And nowe moche quieter, for that I have taken into Proteccion one *Edmound Savage*, alias *Ferderough Mac Seneſhall*, who before, by Reaſon of ſome hard Dealeinge vſed towardes hym (which he alleadged vnto me in Particularitie, the better to collor his Faulte) ioyned to his owne naturall Diſpoſition to Vnquietnes and Stirre ; he both attempted hym ſelfe, and procured others, greatlye to annoy the honeſt and quiet Inhabitaunts, and to burne and deſtroy that that they had, and to make their Landes waſt and vnproffitable. In the Confynes of this Countrie (as I take it) I was offered Skirmiſhe by *Mac Neill Brian Ertaugh*, at my Paſſage over the Water at *Belfaſt* ; which I cawſed to be anſwered, and paſſed over without Loſſe of Man or Horſſe ; yet, by Reaſon of the Tydes extraordinarie Retorne, oure Horſies ſwamme, and the Footemen, in the Paſſage, waded verye depe.

The

The Countrye of *Clandeboy* I found vtterlye difinhabited. The Capten refuzed to have Conference with me, and anfwered, that *Con Mac Neill Oge* was Captene, and not he (who, beinge apointed to be delyvered to the Marfhall by Negligence of his Kepers, made an Efcape in his Comminge from *Dublin*, where before he remayned Prifonner.) The Towne of *Knockfergus* I found moche decaied and impoverifhed ; no Ploughes goinge at all, where before were maney, and great Stoare of Kyne and Cattle, belonginge to the Towne, nowe fewe or none leaft ; Churches and Howfies, favinge Caftells, burned ; the Inhabitaunts fled, not above fixe Howfeholders, of any Countenaunce, leaft remayninge ; fo that their miferable State, and fervile Feare, was to be pittied ; yet they fo comforted to heare of her Majefties gratious Difpoficion, to wall their Towne (whereby they affured theim felves of Saffetye and quiett Dwellinge heareafter) as that Hope hath, and doth procure, and drawe, dyvers to teforte and buyld there ; which, when it fhalbe donne, the Townefmen will multiplye in Number, and therebye will followe an Encreafe of an yearelye growinge Revenue to her Majeftie.

The *Glynnes* and *Rowte* I found poffeffed by the *Scottes,* and nowe governed by *Sorley Boy.* The Countrie full of Corne and Cattle, and the *Scott* verye hawtie and prowd, by Reafon of the late Victories he hath had againft oure Men, fyndinge the Bafenes of their Couragies : Notwithftandinge, he made Meanes to have Treatie with me ; yet great Diffidence I fawe in hym (as is vniverfallye in all the reft) to truft they are fo pulled backe by their Followers : I dealt with hym by Commiffioners, who concluded with hym for Abftinence from Armes for a Tyme, till his Peticions were confidered, and refolved vpon, by her Majeftie : The Copie whereof I here with fend vnto your Lordfhips.

The Forte of the *Raghlines* I cawfed to be abandoned, for that I fawe little Purpofe, for the prefent, to kepe it ; and fo fmall Commoditie to fo great a Chardge to her Majeftie, being a Place fo difficult to be victualled, they within the Piece havinge no frefhe Water to relieve theim ; which, with great Daunger to theim felves, they are forced to fetche Abroade. The Souldiours I caufed to be brought thence being 40 in Number, they confeffed, that, in this fmall Tyme of their Contynuance there, they were driven to kill their Horfies, and eat theim, and to feede on theim and young Coltes Flefhe one Moneth before they came away ; foche Extremitie they endured for Victualls. It is a Piece verye eafie to be wonne agayne at any Tyme, but very chardgeous and hard to be held.

In my Retorne thorough *Kilwarlen*, *Cormocke Oneill*, Capten of the Countrey (made by the Earle of *Effex*) came vnto me, and fubmitted hym felfe, and was my Guyde ; he defiereth to heve the Countrie of her Majeftie, and offereth Rent and Service for it : But the Man is of fmale Wealth and Habilitie, and the Countrie very pore and defolate.

Leaving that Countrie I came to *Kilultagh*, which I found ritch and plentifull (after the Manner of theife Countries ;) the Captain prowd and infolent ; he would not come at me, nor I had not apt Seafon to vifitt hym as I would ; but he fhalbe taught his Good, before it be longe ; I will not remayne in his Debt.

After my Retorne to the *Newrie*, I went to vifitt the Fort upon the *Blackwater* ; all the Tract of the Ground, betwixt the Forte and the *Newrye*, is vnder the Rule of the Baron of *Dungannon*, and, in Effecte, all waft. *Armache* Churche all downe ; the Towne miferable ; the Fort imperfecte, not worth the Chardge of the Kepinge, if their be peaceable Proceading ; the Bridge and Gate to garde it not halfe reared ; but I have taken Order it fhalbe finifhed, and verye neceffarye it is to be kept, if forceable Proceadinge be entended.

At my Retorne from the Fort to *Armache*, *T. Oneills* Wife came vnto me ; fhe is one verye well fpoken, of great Modeftye, good Nurture, Parentage, and Difpoficion ; fhe was Aunte to the Earle of *Arguyle* that laft was, and lykewife to hym that nowe is ; and a great Defier fhe hath to have her Hufband

band lyve lyke a good Subiecte, and to have hym nobilitated. The next Day followinge *T. Oneill* came hym selfe simplye, without Pleadge, Promis, or Hostage, and taried with me twoe Dayes, vsinge hym selfe with soche Subiection and Reverence, and reposinge soch Confidence and Trust in me, as, in all his Speaches, he referred hym selfe to be adiudged, directed, and satified by me. The first Petitions he presented, were reiected, becawse he demaunded as ample an Estate and Rule, as others of his Surname heretofore have had. His humble Submission, in his latter Petitions, accepted, and herewith sent to your Lordships, he saied he would send his Man to solicite her Majestie and your Lordships Resolucions for theim : When he cometh, I beseache your Lordships he may be gratiouslye vsed ; and, if your Lordships thinke it convenient to rewarde hym, I pray you, that I may knowe what you have bestowed vpon hym.

Mac Mason came to me lykewise to *Armache* ; he offereth duetifull Obedience and Fidellitie, and sheweth no small Ioy and Comfort, to be delyvered from *Oneills* Servitude ; he hateth to be in Bondage to hym, he hath to moche felt his Tirrannie ; and therefore, if he may obteine to be delyvered, he will yeeld Rent and Service largelye to her Majestie, to hold his Landes of her.

For *Ferney*, I have donne nothinge, for that I exspecte my Lord of *Essexs* Resolution, and he the Quenes, as I take it.

Where *Sorley Boy* nowe enioyethe the Occupacion of the *Glinnes*, which rather of Right seameth should descende to *James Mac Donells* Sonne, his elder Brother, and not to be transferred to hym as hys owne Right : The Ladye *Oneill* desiereth to have it by Graunt from her Majestie for her second Sonne, who will sweare, to be her Majesties liedge Man, and a dutifulle Subiect to her ; dwell vpon it hym selfe, and yeeld Rent and Service as moche as her Majestie shall reasonablye demaund, and defend the same against *Sorley* and his.

Thus, my Lords, havinge sett downe vnto you in what State I found *Vlster* in this my late Iorney, I am not variable and discentinge from that I was wont to say ; which is, that if forceable Subiection, which I lyke better then any other Proceadinge, be best allowed, I will rather hold that Course, so that I may be assured to be supplied with readye Money, and I knowe I can do it as good cheape as none better. And surelye the Plott my Lord of *Essex* sett downe for Reformacion of that Province to reduce the Subiecte to Obedience, and her Maiestie to have Proffitt of her owne, was the trewe Plott and best Way in dede ; well meant by his Lordship, and a Matter fecible, and in a short Tyme to be donne. But it is no Subiectes Enterprise, a Princes Pursse and Power must do it, as I have heretofore at large discoursed ; and, if her Majestie lyke not of that, but will have a peaceable Reformacion : My Opinion is, that she graunt *T. Oneills* Petitions, savinge that I would wishe, that *Mac Guier* and *Mac Mason* were exempted from hym. How be it, though in gratious Tearmes, I would they should be denied hym absolutelye, and hym selfe to be nobilitated by the Title of Earl of *Clanoneill*, duringe his Lyffe ; whiche, consideringe his Age, wounded and imperfect Boddye, his ill Diet, and contynuall Surfett, he cannot be of longe Lyffe ; and her Majestie hath good Presidents of the like Proceadinges : First, in her gratious Fathers Tyme, of famous Memorie, the Creacion of the Earle of *Clanrickarde*, of the Surname of *Mac William* ; and, in her Majesties owne Tyme, she created *Mac Carte More* Earle of *Clancarre*. The Takinge from *T. Oneill* all theise Capteines of Countries, that heretofore have depended vpon hym and the Prediceffors of his Surname, as of their cheife Lorde, and contentinge hym with this Title of Earle, and his Issue made, ever after, to be Barons of some one Place ; it wilbe the Discipation of his Force and Strength, Encrease of Revenue and Service to her Majestie, that theise Lordes and Capteines of Countries hold absolutelye of her, and none els. And, by this Meanes, it will, in one halfe an Age, come to passe, that his Succession and Posteritie shall not be of Power to do any Harme, that may not easilye be resisted ; which will breade a great Quiet in

the

the Northe, which Countrie heretofore hath, from Tyme to Tyme, bene fo troublefome.

Touchinge *Sorley Boyes* Peticions for the *Rowte*, I would wifhe it fhould be flatlye denied hym, for that he hath no Right to it at all ; his Vfurpacion and Enioyenge of it grew, by Reafon he, to whome the Captenrie of the Countrie belonged, was a diffolute and lofe Fellowe, feeble both of Witt and Force, not hable to defende the Countrie : And the Freholders, defierous to be protected and fhielded, by one mightier in Power and Pollecye, contented theim felves to imbrace the *Scott.* Howe be it, there are nowe, of the Iffue of the right Proprietaries, Men hable, with a little Healpe, to kepe the *Scotts* out of it, or at leaft for beinge moch better by it. And, in this Pointe, her Majeftie (if it fo pleafe your Lordfhips) is to be remembred to write to the Regent of *Scotland* effectuallye, that he geve Order to kepe the *Scottes* at Home, who, from that Region, and, namelye, the out Ifles, fwarmme daylye hether, to the great Annoyaunce of the North Parte of this Realme. To the *Glinnes* he hath an apparaunt Title. I knowe no Man, of this Countrie Birthe, to clayme it, or care for it, but the Surname of the *Scottes* ; therefore I wifhe they had it, yeeldinge a convenient Rent and Service.

Mac Genneffe hath alreadie humblye fought to have his Countrey immediatlye of her Majeftie, and to pay Rent, Royaltie, and Service for the fame ; I have promifed and vndertaken to get it for hym. The Rent referved vpon thofe Landes fhalbe at the leaft one hundered Poundes by the Yeare, befides Service of Horfemen and Footemen. My earneft Defier therefore to your Lordfhips is, that, in refpect of his Loyaltie, Cyvillitie, and ftayed Conftanncye, it would pleafe her Majeftie to geve me Power to create hym Baron of *Evaugh.* The Example would be good, and a good Inducement to others of his Sorte, by the lyke Service, to hope of the lyke Rewarde that he hath, to the Honnor and Creditt of their Pofteritie ; and therefore this Requeft, for his Nobilitacion, may not, in my Opinion, well be denied hym.

That it would pleafe your Lordfhips lykewife to have in Remembraunce, that the Grauntes, made to *Chatterton* and *Malbye*, may prefentlye be revoked ; which Grauntes, thorough their Inhabilities, to performe Covenauntes with her Majeftie, will of theim felves become voyd, within fewe Yeares ; and yet, in the meane Tyme, beinge not revoked, are foch Stayes and Impediments to the Quiet of the Countrie, and her Majefties Service in thofe Partes, as without that, nothinge can perfectlye be donne ; which, if it fhall pleafe her Majeftie to affent vnto, and give Order, the fame be fpedilye done, it fhalbe moche avayable to her Highnes, both in Honnor and Proffitt to graunte me full Power, afwell for the Lettinge and Grauntinge of thofe twoe Countries to the olde Inhabitants, as all the reft of the Landes in *Vlfter* to be lett, referving Rent and Service to her Majeftie ; and this donne, I dare vndertake the Revenue, growinge to her Majeftie in her Province of *Vlfter*, by Refervation of Rent, and Service, fhalbe able to mainteine neceffarie Garrifons, to kepe and defend *Vlfter* from all Annoyaunces, the Refiftaunce of Forreines and Buyldinges only excepted.

Amongeft other Matters for *Vlfter*, I am humblye to pray your Lordfhips, to be Remembrauncers to her Majeftie, for the Benevolence of her Almes, towardes the Buylding of the Churche of *Armache*, whereby better Enterteinement for the Deputye and his Traine will growe, when he hath Occafion to repaier thether ; the laft Money for that Purpofe, beinge twoe hundered Poundes, was reftored againe by the Prymate to Sir *William Danfell*, as the Primate affirmed ; which if it pleafe her Majeftie, it may be redelyvered, or a larger Somme graunted, I will fee it proffitablye beftowed ; it wilbe Occafion I hope of more Buyldinge, Reforte, and Confluence of People and Inhabitaunts thether, whiche were verye neceffarye fhould be, the Place beinge, for dyvers Refpectes, fo commodious for Service as it is.

I humblye befeache your Lordfhips lykewife to geve Order, that my Money for the next Quarter, payable the Firft of *Januarye* next, by Affignacion

and

and Compoſicion from her Majeſtie, may be foorthwith delyvered to this Bearer, my Servaunt, *John Giffoorde*, this firſt Quarter havinge bene alreadye ſo hard with me, by Reaſon of my Preparacion, and Furniſhinge for this Place, and Tranſportacion; painge and makinge Proviſion of Victualls, for the Findinge of the Garriſon for the moſte Parte of the Yeare to come; delyveringe large Impreſts for Buyldinge, Money laied out by me, for ſavinge the Queenes Chardgies, in Painge of the Soldiours diſchardged, which I neded not : The twoe thowſand Poundes out of my Quarterage, which was impreſted vnto me aforehand, I beſtowed fullye in *England*, before my Comminge over ; all whiche Chardgies, laied together, makes me in greater Want, and the rather to preſſe your Lordſhips, I may be preſentlye holpen, which I hope you will geve Order I be.

I humblye thanke your Lordſhips, for your honorable Remembraunces of me, to be ſupplied with the Healpe of Sir *William Drewries* Service, for her Majeſtie here ; he is ſo gratefull and welcome a Man vnto me, as any of his Ranke and Place in *England* could be. I knowe his Valor and Worthines, and what Eſtimation is held of hym of the beſt, which he hath well deſerved ; none you could have ſent, whoſe Companye I have more deſiered, nor whoſe Preſence in Comminge ſhalbe better welcome, then he ſhall ; and therefore, eft ſones, I humblye thanke your Lordſhips for hym.

Vpon the Conſideracion of the Soldiours Enterteinement here, I finde howe difficult and hard a Matter it is, for the Footeman to lyve vpon his Pay, beinge but vi *d*. a Day, painge for his Piece, Pouder, and Armor, Victualls, and all other neceſſarie Things he nedeth to be furniſhed of, being as deare here, for the moſt Parte, as in the midſt of *Cheapeſide* : And if it be ſo hard for the Footeman to mainteine hym ſelfe with the Wagies of his Pay ; I can ſee no Poſſibilitie howe the Horſſeman can do it, who hath the onelye Enterteinement of vi *d. ob. qr.* the Day, to fynde hym ſelfe, his Horſſe, Hackney, and Boy ; and therfore, to make theim lyve more contentedlye, then nowe they do, I feare I muſt be enforced to encreaſe their Wagies, and to contynue ſo maney the fewer in Nomber ; whiche I would gladlye do, by your Lordſhips good Allowauncies and Conſentes, leaſt after my Tyme, it may be ſaied, I have brought in this Innovacion and Deviſe of myne owne, to the Encreaſe of her Majeſties Chardge, which loth I would, ſhould be laied vpon me, to beare ſo heavye a Burden alone. But, therefore, deſier your Lordſhips, vpon the well Wainge, and your wonted diſcreate and grave Conſideracions had of the Matter, to ioyne and concurre with me in Opinion, if youer Lordſhips ſhall finde it ſo expediente.

Harrye Oneill, Shanes Sonne, was comitted to the Caſtell of *Dublin*, as a Pleadge for his Fathers Debt ; he hath remayned there a great Whyle, to a Charge to her Majeſtie, and nothinge to be had out of hym, though, dyvers and ſondrie Tymes, Meanes hath bene made for it : I would therefore be glad to knowe your Lordſhips Reſolucions for his Deteininge or Enlardginge, or what ells your Lordſhips would wiſhe I ſhould do in it.

And thus humblye beſeachinge your good Lordſhips, to imparte vnto her Majeſtie either the whole Effecte thereof (if you thinke it ſo neceſſarye) or ſoche Partes thereof, as to your grave Iudgementes and Adviſes it ſhall ſeme convenient, humblye cravinge her Majeſties Reſolucion in thoſe ſpetiall Pointes I write of ; I take my Leave of your good Lordſhips. From *Mellefount*, niere *Drogheda*, the xvth of *November*, 1575.

Your honorable Lordſhips aſſured lovinge

Freinde humblye to commaunde.

Sir

Sir Henry Sydney *to the Lords of the Councell.*

My verie good Lords,

MY Duetie moſt humblye remembred to your honorable Lordſhips, ſince my laſt Lettres, wherein I made Reporte of the Eſtate of *Vlſter,* and in the ſame omitted (as I thinke) to write of *Odonnell,* Lorde of *Tirconnell,* and *Mac Guyer,* Lord of *Farmanaugh,* who write humblye vnto me, lyve welthful-lye, and denye not to paye Rente and Service to her Majeſtie (ſo as they may be diſchardged from the Exaction of others.) I have paſſed, and gonne through the whole *Englyſhe* Pale, conteininge the greateſt and beſt Parte of the Pro-vinces of *Myethe* and *Leynſter,* and of the ſame have had Conferrence, withe the principall Parſonadgies and Gentlemen, aſwell *Englyſhe* as *Iriſhe,* of the State of thoſe two Countries. In lyke Sorte as I meane (before I ceſſe to travell in Iorney as I do) to viſitt the moſt and chiefeſt Partes of everye Province with-in this Realme. And yet, before I enter to perticuler Diſcourſe of any other Parte, I muſt retorne backe to the Province of *Vlſter,* and ſpeake of the Cown-ty of *Lowthe,* beinge a Percell of the *Engliſhe* Pale, which I finde greatlye im-poveriſhed, through the contynuall Concourſe of Soldiors, paſſing twoe and fro the North, and beſides the ill Neighborhood of the Men of *Ferney,* the *Fuze,* and *Orrerie,* mentioned in my former Reporte of *Vlſter.* The good Townes of *Carlingfoorde, Dundalke,* and *Ardie,* are extremelye impoveriſhed, and onelye the Towne of *Drogheda* in better State ; which was more amended, and encreaſ-ed in Wealthe, thoroughe the great Exſpenſies of the Earle of *Eſſex,* who lay and contynued there moche, and, duringe his Abode, verye bountifullye, and honorablye, ſpent in the ſame : Howe be it, the reſt of the Countrie, in great Confidence of ſpedie Recoverie, for the Gentlemen are willinge to obey, and for-warde to ſerve ; and the rather, for the good Inclynation I fynde of my Lord of *Lowthe,* who is one both well geven, and forwarde (as it ſeameth) to execute any Thinge comitted vnto hym. The good Neighborhood of the Marſhall, who governeth thoſe vnder his Rule, without doinge of Harme, but rather, by their Labors and Travells, Procurers of Amytie, freindlye Societie, and Quiet to their Neighbors : So that onely *Ferney* is the Gapp open to the Hurte of the reſt, which I beſeache your Lordſhips, to haſten my Lord of *Eſſex* to take Or-der in, as the Occaſion of his Stay in Reſolution to place ſome one Man, to take the Chardge of the Countrie, breede not further Trouble, then in ſhort Tyme is to be recovered.

And thus to begynne with *Myethe,* I fynde the ſame curſelye ſcorched on the out Syde, aſwell by the Incurſions of the *Ochonnors* and *Omoloyes,* whyle they were in open Rebellion, as oppreſſed by theim, ſince they were protected ; not yet recovered nor reformed, but in verye good Way to be (the Noblemen and Gentlemen of the ſame performing, in their Doings, that whiche francklye they have offered ;) and a great deale the better it is, for the good Neighborhod and iuſt Dealinge of *Oreilye,* whoſe Countrie, for that it is in the Province of *Connaught,* for the Preſent I write the leſſe of hym and of it ; yet, for that he confyneth with this Countrey, and it very well vſed by hym, I thought good thus moche to touch of hym and it, as of the juſteſt *Iriſhman,* and the beſt ruled *Iriſhe* Countrie, by an *Iriſhman,* that is in all *Ireland.*

The moſt of the Barronnies, of the Borders of *Weſtmeithe,* are ſore ſpoyled, and made waſt, by the aforenamed Rebells, as *Fertulaughe,* or *Terrills* Countrie : The Barronie of *Ferbill,* called *Darcies* Countrie, ſometyme, and nowe, held of the Earle of *Kildare* ; *Dillons* Countrie, *Daltons,* and *Delamore.* Theiſe, and dyvers others, as the *Brawney, Yrin,* or *Obriens* Countrie, were made Barron-nies of *Weſtmeithe,* when the ſame was firſt made a Shire ; and, in the Tyme of my laſt Governement here, I added *Kinnelliaugh,* or *Magoghegans* Countrie, the *Caulderie,* or *Mac Sawles* Countrie, *Clancolman,* or *Omolaghlins* Countrie, to be lykewiſe Members and Percells of the ſaide Countie : In theiſe *Iriſhe* Countries, the Writt yet hath had no perfect Currencie ; but, God willinge, it shall have : Whereunto the Lords of the same have willinglye agreed, and most humblye desiered to take their Landes of the Quene, yeldinge for the same both Rent and Service. *Fircall*, or *Omoloies* Countrie, *Mounteregan*, or the *Foxes* Countrie, together withe the rest before remembred, are all wasted, and extremelye impoverished, by the Rebells aforenamed (*Magoghegan* or *Maccoghlans* Countrie onelye excepted) but I hoope well of the speedie Reformation of this Countrie, a great deale the rather, thoroughe the good Hope I conceive of the Service of my Lord of *Delvin*, whome I fynde actyve, and of good Discreation.   There ioyneth vnto this the *Annalye*, a Countrie by me heretofore made the Countie of *Longfoorde*, beinge a Percell of the Province of *Connaught*, the Lordes of the same beinge of twoe Lynagies, though of one Surname ; they were with me, and proved, by good Testimonie, that they were good Neighbours, both to *Westmeithe*, and the rest of the Pale ; and lyved nowe in farre better Order, and greater Wealthe, amounge theim selves, then they did, before they were made Shyre Grounde ; they confesse to be in Arrerage for their Rent, for all, or most of the Yeares since I departed, which they willinglye agreed to pay speedilye, and in convenient Tyme.   And thus moche for the State of the Province and Countries of *Myeth*.

In the Province of *Leynster*, first I fynde the Borders of the Countie of *Dublin* greatlye annoyed, almost by Night Stealthes, and some Daylight Bodraggs, cheifelye fathered vpon one *Feugh Mac Hugh Mac Shane*, of the Surname of the *Birnes*, but vnder his Father, Owner and Fermor of sondrie Landes aparte from theim : The Father was with me without Protection, but the Sonne lyveth a loofe ; yet without Hurte, for any Thinge I heare since myne Arryvall ; but, my Circuite once finished, I intend to attend hym somewhat nerer, then hetherto I have donne.   The Countye of *Kildare* is extremelye impoverished, and in especiall the Earle of *Kildares* Lordshippes and Landes ; which, in a great Parte, are wasted, partlye by the last named loose People, partlye and cheifelye by the *Omores*, aswell in their Rebellion, as since they were vnder Protection ; and in one Barronnie of the said Countye, called *Carberie*, it was constantlye affirmed vnto me, by old *Henrye Cowley*, with Teares in his Eyes, that that Barronnie was three thowsand Poundes in worsse Case, then it was the last Tyme before I was there with hym.   The Countye of *Caterlaugh* is more then halfe wast, aswell by the aforenamed Outlawes of all Sortes, as partlye by the Inhabitaunts of *Kilkennye*, the *Cavannaughes*, and some other of their owne Soyle, lyvynge vnder Sir *Edmound Butler* ; and some Doubt I have of the good Order of that Quarter, for that Sir *Peter Carewe* is latelye departed this Woorld, and the Land left to a younge Gentleman his Kinsman : For the Countye of *Weixfoorde*, it is constantlye affirmed, both publykelye and pryvatelye, by *Thomas Masterson*, and maney other principall Gentlemen, that, if it were devided into twoe Partes, the one of theim is vtterlye wasted ; most by theim of the Countye of *Kilkennie*, partlye by some of theim selves, and moch by the *Cavannaughes*, lyvinge in the woorse Order, for that their Captens, *Englishmen*, agree no better, which is moche to be pittied ; but hardlye it wilbe redressed, it is so innate, after they be once placed heere.   For the *Irishe* Countries, on the East Syde of *Leynster*, being vnder the Rule of Mr. *Agard*, as the *Otooles*, and *Obirnes* Countrie, I finde they are in verye good Order, except *Hugh Mac Shanes* Sonne, whom before I remembred.   And here, my Lords, least I should forget it, I cannot but lament the Lacke of Mr. *Agarde* so longe from hence ; suerlye the Losse of a thowsand Pound should not so moche have grieved me, as the Wanting of hym hathe troubled me.   The *Kinshelaugh* is devided into three Linagies, but originallye all *Cavannaughes*, nowe vnder the Order of *Thomas Masterson*, who (in myne Opinion) is a good Servaunt, both for the Quene and Countrie ; for he hathe brought the People to good Order, and made them obedient and willinge to pay that Rent, which I heretofore brought theim to ; and, though moch in Arrere, yet pay it they will and shall.   The *Omurroes*, an other Race of the

Cavannaughes,

Cavannaughes, are, vnder the Rule of one *Richard Synott*, in indifferent good Order, obedient, and fhall pay their Rent and Service, afwell that in Arryre, as that fhall growe due hereafter. That Race of the *Cavannaughes*, that dwell about *Fernes*, by the good Pollecye and Rule of *Thomas Mafterfon*, Conftable of the fame, are willinge and reddye to yeeld all Rents and Services, due to her Majeftie ; and thus moche for the *Irifhrey* in *Eaft Leynfter*.

On the Weft Syde lyethe the Countries of *Offalye*, or *Occhonnors* Countrie, *Leax*, or *Omores* Countrie, *Upper Offerie*, or *Mac Gill Patricks* Countrie, *Irregan*, or *Odonnes* Countrie ; the twoe firft were fhired by the Names of *Kinges* and *Queenes* Counties. And, in the Tyme of my Lord of *Suffexs* Governement, graunted in Fee Ferme, with good Refervacions, to fondrie Tenaunts, whereof the greateft Parte then were mere *Englyfhe* ; and nowe bothe Countries are moche fpoyled and wafted, by the Race and Offspringe of the old natyve Inhabiters, whiche growe great, and increafe in Nomber ; and the *Englifh* Tenaunts decay, both in Force and Wealthe, not of Abilitie to anfwere their Rents and Services, but let their Landes to *Irifhe* Tenauntes : They are daylie fo fpoyled and burned, the Chardgies they have bene at, and their daylie Exfpenfes they be at, to defende theim felves, fo weakenethe theim, as their State is to be pittied ; twoe hundered Men, at the leaft, in the Princes Pay, lye there, to defende theim. The Revenue of both the Countries countervayle not the xxth Parte of the Chardge : So that the Purchafe of that Plott is, and hath bene vearie deare, yet nowe not to be geven over in any wife ; for, God willinge, it fhalbe recovered and mainteined ; but this may be an Example, howe the lyke hereafter is attempted, confideringe the Chardge is fo greate, and the Honnor and Proffitt fo fmall, to wynne Landes from the *Irifhrey* fo dearlye, as theife twoe Countries have ben to the Crowne. *Rorie Oge* hath that Poffeffion, and Settling Place, in the *Quenes* Countye, whether the Tenaunts will or noe, as he occupieth what he lifteth, and wafteth what he will. *Gefshell*, in the *Kings* Countye, is verye neceffarie to be had of the Earle of *Kildare* ; it is a Matter of Confequence for her Majefties Service in that Countye, and therefore it were verie neceffarie, he were dealt effectuallye with to departe withall. Duringe the Tyme of my beinge at the Forte at *Maribrough*, the Earle of *Clanrickard* came vnto me, not unfent for, but verye humblye and loyallye offered his Service ; what and howe I fynd of hym, I will more at lardge writte to your Lordfhips, when I fhall come to *Connaught*, where he is. *Upper Offerie* is fo well governed and defended, by the Valor and Wifedome of the Baron that nowe is (for the old Man, whome before the Cawfe of the greateft Diforder of that Countrie grewe, God hath taken, I hope, to his mercyfull Favor) as, favinge for Suertie of good Order here after in Succeffion, it made no Matter, if the Countrie were never fhired, nor her Majefties Writt otherwife curraunt then it is ; fo humblye he kepeth all his People fubiect to Obedience and good Order ; and yet vnited to fome Shire it fhalbe, and the Baron hym felfe verye well agreeinge to yeeld both Fyne, Rent, and Service, as other Countries, latelye brought to foch Frame, doe and fhall do. *Irregan*, or *Odonnes* Countrie, in good Cafe ; the Lord of it a valiant and honeft Man, after this Countrie Manner : And here I thought fitt to remember likewife *Elye*, or *Occarrolls* Countrie, though the fame be of the Province of *Mounfter*, yet adioyninge in Lande and Neighborhoode to the Countries before named.

The laft of this Province, in this my Accompt, is the Countye of *Kilkennye*, which I finde in verye bad Cafe, yet by maney due Circumftaunces proved, to be the Sincke and Receptacle of innumerable Cattell and Goodes ftolen, out of maney other Countries ; but vndonne by their owne idle Men, and partlye by Harboringe of protected Rebells ; which yet was done by Order, and for the Avoydinge of a greater, or, at the leaft, a more prefent Mifcheife : Here *Rorie Oge* came vnto me vpon the Earle of *Ormounds* Woorde, and, in the Cathedrall Churche of *Kilkennye*, fubmitted hym felf, repenting (as he faid) his former Fawltes, and promifinge, hereafter, to lyve in better Sorte (for woorffe, then

he

he hath ben, he cannot be) for, by hym and his, the greateſt Spoyles and Diſorders have been comitted vpon the *Quenes* Countye and the Pale. I accepted hym vpon Entreatye, and Triall of Amendement till my Retorne, and both leſſoned hym and threatned hym for his former Fawltes; ſo that I ſtand in ſomme Hope, he will lyve more orderlye and quietlye, then he hath donne, renouncing that aſpiringe Imagination of Tytle to the Countrie ; which, if he do not, and content hym ſelfe with ſoch a Portion of Freehold, as I ſhall allot, and thinke mete for hym, he ſhall be the firſt, that will repent the Matche, for he ſhall forgooe Lyffe, Land, and all, otherwiſe I will ſayle moche of my Purpoſe; for ſo I have geven hym Warninge, and will kepe Touche with hym, if I can. At this Towne like wiſe, the Earle of *Ormound* feaſted and entreated me very honorablye, and accompanied me to this Cittye, very courteouſlye, where I was received with all Shewes and Tokens of Gladnes and Pompe, aſwell vpon the Water, as the Lande ; preſented withe the beſt Commodities they had, with Ceremonie of their Thankefulnes and good Wills, as true Pledges of their Obedience to her Majeſtie, and her Governor. I could not paſſe over in vnthankefull Scylence, but thought it expedient to recorde the ſame to your Lordſhips ; that, hereafter, in their reaſonable Sutes, their Cittie may the rather fynde both Thankes and Favor at your Handes. In paſſinge through the Counties and Countries, I have heretofore ſpoken of, to your Lordſhips, I left eche of theim, before my Departure from theim, vnder Governement and Garde for the moſt Parte, accordinge to their owne Deviſes, which they thought wold be moſt for their Safetyes and Commodities, till my Retorne ; ſomme I left to theim ſelves, and the Garde of their owne Borders, as they deſiered ; yet, with Authoritie ſufficient, to levye Force amongeſt theim ſelves, if Nede ſo requyred : Some other Places I left well garded withe the Garriſon, and other ſufficient Strength of their owne, for ſuche was their Deſier ; and ſo, by Conference with theim of their States, it ſemed beſt and lykelyeſt to me. I placed the Baron of *Vpper Oſſerie* Lieutenante of the *Kinges* and *Quenes* Counties, and divers *Iriſh* Countries adioyninge : The lyke Authoritie I left with the Earle of *Ormounde*, of the twoe Counties of *Kylkennye* and *Typperarie* : So that I fynde in all the Places, I have yet paſſed, the People remayne in good Confydence, beinge ſo provided for, and garded as they be, to remayne in good Quiett till my Retorne.

My Lords, at my Comminge over, becawſe I founde the Garriſon was vtterlye vnprouided of Victuall, for the Yere followinge, I cawſed an Aſſemblye of the Countrie, and Agreement for a Ceſſe ; which, after maney Debaytings amongſt vs, and Opinions of eche Man harde, I found generallye by them all, or, at the leaſt, by the greater, and wiſer Sorte of theim : That, to be exempted henceforthe, and not to be chardged with any ſoche Impoſitions, for the Victuallinge of the Garriſon, they wold more willinglye yeelde a certeine yerely Rent, out of every Ploughland, to be a Perpetuitie to her Majeſtie, and her Poſteritie : So they might on the other Syde be aſſured, vppon what Accydent ſo ever happen, to be diſchardged of the Ceſſe, and Victuallinge of the Soldiors (they have of late growen ſo burdenous to theim.) My Demaund was, but for the Victuallinge of a Thowſand of all Sortes, aſwell Horſemen as Footemen : And, to be diſchardged of theim, their wilbe made an Encreaſe of Rent to her Majeſtie, towardes the Victuallinge of that Thowſande, the Somme of twoe thowſand Pounde by the Yere, after the *Engliſhe* Accompte, if the ſame may be brought to paſſe ; as theire is Likelyhoode, if the Matter be well proceaded in, it will be. But, becawſe it may ſeme an Innovation, and that loath I were, to enter into a Matter of ſoch Conſequence alone, but aſſiſted from you, I humbly deſier your Lordſhips Reſolutions herein ; which, when the ſame ſhall, at your good Pleaſures, be ſignified vnto me, I will then ſhewe your Lordſhips myne Opinion, and further Advice, whiche Way the ſame may be beſt wrought for an Aſſurance to her Majeſtie of her yerelye Encreaſe of Rent, and beſt Contentement, and Satisfaction to the Countrie, both which I wiſhe were obſerved and donne. And the Way is, for the Preſent, that if you lyke

of

of the Overture, that her Majeftie write to the Countrie, and promiffe theim Fredome of their Landes, if that Increafe of Rent be graunted towardes the Victuallinge of the Garrifon.

Nowe, beinge reddye to departe hence, I fett forwardes towardes *Corcke*, where, God willinge, I meane to be before *Chriftmas*: Sir *Lucas Dillon*, Mr. *John Challoner*, *Jaques Wingeffeild*, the Mafter of the Ordenaunce, and *Launcelott Alfforde*, the Surveior, accompanienge me thether. Sir *Lucas Dillon* hath well affifted me, as well in the late Northeren Iorney, as in this; his Travell and Paynes have bene greate; and furelye, for his greate Care, to quiet and bring the Countrie to better Frame, he deferveth great Prayfe and Thanks, which I befeache your Lordfhips, in your next Lettres, he may have from you. And thus, to drawe to an Ende, fearinge I have rather overmoche weried your Lordfhips with my Tedioufnes, I have twoe fpeciall Requeftes to make; the one is, to haften away my Money, fent for by my Servaunt, *John Gefforde*; the other is, to difpatche Mr. *Agarde* thence; the firft beinge the Stringe to my Bowe, the other the beft Marke Man I have. And, even fo with my hartie Prayer, and well Wifhinge to God, to profper and preferve you all, to your honorable Contentementes, I humblye take my Leave. From *Waterfforde*, the xvjth of *December*, 1575.

Your honorable Lordfhips affured loving

Freinde to commaunde,

H. Sydney.

Sir Francis Walfingham *to Sir* Henry Sydney.

My very good Lord,

HER Majeftys Pleafure is, that I fhoold fende unto you the inclofed Note, conteyning certeyn pryncypall Poyntes of your Inftructyons, to the Ende you may render an Accompt what hathe ben don in the fame: Unto fome of the feyd Poyntes, I knowe ther can be gyven no preffent Awntfwer, for that your Lordfhip hathe had neythor Tyme nor Leyfure to confyder in fooche Sorte of them, as that you can give any full Awntfwer therunto.

I am fuer yt hathe ben bruited in *Irelande*, that her Majeftye meaneth not to contynewe her Allowaunce of the xx Thoufande Pownde agreed on; as alfo, that fhe doothe not lyke of the Erectying of Prefydents: Which Brute may greatly hynder her Majeftys Servyce, and can not but greatly difcorage your Lordfhip to fee us waver; and to dowbt of the Succeffe of your Proceadyngs before any Tryall made of the fame.

But this is no newe Fault, thowghe yt be a moft dangerowfe Fawlte. Trewe yt is, as yt is bruted abrode, that her Majefty hathe no Affectyon to contynewe the Charges agreed on; and yet for that my Lords are of Opynion, that her Majefty uppon a Soddeyne, withowt any Tryall made, fhoold not breake of the Matter: She feamethe to yelde to a Yeares Tryall: And yet dothe fhe lycke, that Sir *Wyllyam Drurye* fhoold have his Alloweaunce, from the Tyme he hathe ben in a Readynes to come over; having ben furcharged withe bothe Horfe and Men provyded for this Servyce: Wheruppon I feare he wyll refufe to goe; efpetyally, feing no more affeured Determynatyon of his Imployement ther, with that Contynewaunce, that might be for the Advauncement of her Servyce, and his owne Credyt. Befydes, he confyderethe howe chargeable yt woold be for him to goe thither, and then, within a fewe Monethes after, to be revoked; fo that I cannot affure you of his Determynatyon herein. Neyther can your Lordfhip yelde any effectuall Tryall of your Determynatyon for the Redreffe of that Contrye; where as you fhall lacke fyt Men to execute that which by you ys fet downe.

I knowe not whether I may afcrybe thefe Impedyments unto the Irrefolutyon of this Tyme, or to the curfed Deftenye of that Contrye; being not or-

deyned

deyned to receyve any Good of any Determynatyon agreed on for the Reformatyon therof.

I had almoſt forgotten to tell your Lordſhip, Mr. *Agar* and I were forced
(uppon the Caulyng in Queſtyon, whether the Charges agreed on weare to be
contynewed) to ſett downe the incloſed Plott I ſende you; whereby yt myght
appeare unto her Majeſty, how profytably her Treaſure ſhoold be imployed,
which, by my Lords [of the Councell] wear verry well allowed of; and not
otherwiſe myſlyked by her Majeſty, but in reſpect of the Charges.

Towching Mr. *Agars* Commyng over, whos Aſſyſtaunce you ſeme greatlye to
deſyre, I refer the Declaratyon of his Staye to his owne Letter.

I have dealt with her Majeſty, to have had Mr. *Gerrard* ſent over as Chancelor in that Realme; but I fynde her not dyſpoſed therunto: For that ſhe
thinkethe he may not be well ſpared, in the Place where he nowe ſerveth. And
ſo having ſcrybled unto you, that which I thinke fyt to be imparted unto your
Lordſhip, I commyt you to Gods good Keeping. At *Hampton Coorte*, the
xxviiith of *Januarye*, 1575.

Your Lordſhips aſſured Freind,

Fra. Walſyngham.

Propoſitions for the Chardges of Irland.

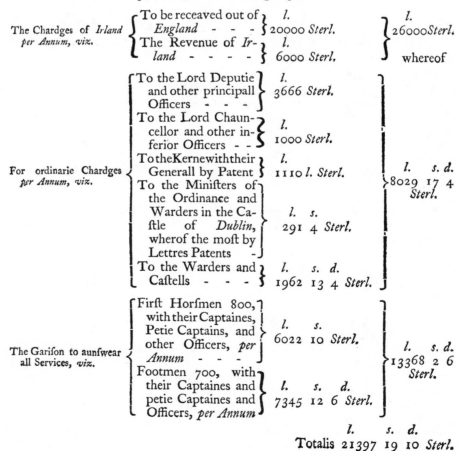

The Chardges of *Irland per Annum*, viz. — To be receaved out of *England* — — — 20000 *l.* *Sterl.* / The Revenue of *Irland* — — — 6000 *l.* *Sterl.* } 26000 *l. Sterl.* whereof

For ordinarie Chardges *per Annum*, viz.
- To the Lord Deputie and other principall Officers — — — 3666 *l. Sterl.*
- To the Lord Chauncellor and other inferior Officers — — 1000 *l. Sterl.*
- To the Kerne with their Generall by Patent — 1110 *l. Sterl.*
- To the Miniſters of the Ordinance and Warders in the Caſtle of *Dublin*, wherof the moſt by Lettres Patents — 291 *l.* 4 *s. Sterl.*
- To the Warders and Caſtells — — — 1962 *l.* 13 *s.* 4 *d. Sterl.*

} 8029 *l.* 17 *s.* 4 *d. Sterl.*

The Gariſon to aunſwear all Services, viz.
- Firſt Horſmen 800, with their Captaines, Petie Captaines, and other Officers, *per Annum* — — — 6022 *l.* 10 *s. Sterl.*
- Footmen 700, with their Captaines and petie Captaines and Officers, *per Annum* 7345 *l.* 12 *s.* 6 *d. Sterl.*

} 13368 *l.* 2 *s.* 6 *d. Sterl.*

Totalis 21397 *l.* 19 *s.* 10 *d. Sterl.*

The

Other ordinarie and extraordinarie Chardges to be borne of the Some aforesaid, *viz.*

The Towne of *Knockfergus* to be walled, and the Peeres buylded.

The decaied Bridge of *Dundalke* to be newe made.

Rofcomon to be reedified.

A Houfe to be builded in *Athenrie* for the Prefident of *Connaughe.*

A Bridge of Stone at *Lurtmiche* to be made.

A Bridge befide given to be made.

The Fort in the *Queenes Countie* to be repaired and made fit for the Lord Deputie to lie at.

The Bridge of *Langhlin* to be repaired.

All the Queenes Majefties Houfes to be maintayned and repaired.

The Allowance and Fees of the Prefidents and their Affociats in *Munfter* and *Connaghe* to be borne; the Victellers Wages and Loffes of Victells rered, with all other Kinde of extraordinarie Charges; his Attendant of the Counfell traveling with the Lord Deputie in Iorneis, and divers other like.

How the Forces and Garifons of 1260 is to be imploied, *viz.*

In the Northe and at the *Ferney* under the Conduct of the Earle of *Effex*, Horfmen - - -	100
Footmen ther - -	250
In *Monfter* Horfmen -	100
Footmen ther - -	200
In *Connaghe* Horfmen	100
Footmen ther - -	200
For the Garde of the *Englifhe* Pale, the Reforming of *Eft Linfter*, and the Expulfing of the difordered *Omoores* and *Otomores*, and to attend everie Suddaine - - - -	250

The Commoditie licklie to infue by the Planting of Prefidents in Mounfter *and* Connaghe, *&c.*

Imprimis, The Townes dutifullie affected to her Majeftie fhall be preferved from the Oppreffing of their cruell Neighbours.

The well difpofed in the Province, whom her Majeftie in Honnor is bound to defend agenft the Tirannie of their Oppreffors, fhall be protected.

The evill Difpofed in the *Englifhe* Pale, as *Omoores, Ochomores, Cavenaghes*, and fuche like, having Refuge to the faid Province, fhall be brideled.

Her Majefties Write fhall have Currencie within the faid Province, and fhe acknowledged onlie Souueraigne; and fuche reduced to yelde due Obedience, that partlie ftande in vndutifull Termes with her Majeftie, to her great Difhonor.

Her Majefties Revenus, now poffeffed by Vfurpers or Concealers, fhall be recovered and aunfwered.

The faid Realme, by Planting this civill Kinde of Governement, will be within fewe Yeres fo peopled, as they fhall be hable to make Heade agenft fuche forraine Princes as have anie Intelligences within that Realme.

I

And

And, if annie fhall oppofe him felf agenſt the Placing of the faid Prefidents, they fhall be fuppreffed, without annie Supplie to be had out of this Realme, either of Men or Monie.

The Townes by this Couerfe being defended from their Oppreffiers, the well difpofed Subiects protected, her Majefties Revenues in thes Provinces ain-fweared, the evill Difpofed in the *Englifhe* Pale brideled, and her Writt having Currencie, her Majeſtie, within the Space of twoe or three Yeres, fhall not be yearlie charged with above 20000 *l.* for *Irland,* vnleffe it be to withſtand forrain Invaſions.

Sir Henry Sydney *to* Robert Dudley, *Earl of* Leiceſter.

My Dereſt Lord,

I Receved not your Letter of the 25 of *November*, untyll the 24 of thys *January*, by *James Prefcot*, who was feven Tymes at the Sea, and put bak agayn, befere he could recover thys Coſt.

I truſt I have fatysfyed your Lordfhip with my Wrytyng, and others by my Procurement, fent by *Pakenham*, touchyng the fals and malycyus Brute of the Earl of *Effex* Poyfonyng. If not, what you wyll have moore doon, fhall be doon. I am fory I here not how you lyke of that I have doon, and the more, for that I am advertyfed of *Pagnaneys* Arryvall theare. I would not have douted to have made *Knell* to have retracted his inconfyderat and foolifh Speech and Wrytyng; but God hath prevented me, by Taking hym away, dying of the fame Dyfeafe that the Earl dyd; whych, moſt certaynly, was free from any Poyfon, and a meere Flux; a Dyfeafe apropryated to thys Cuntry, and whearof thear dyed many in the later Part of the laſt Year, and fum out of myne one Houfehold; and yet fre from any Sufpycyon of Poyfon.

And for my Lord of *Ormundys* Caufes, I umbly befych your Lordfhip be my Paune, that I wyll do hym Juſtyce as indyferently and fpeedyly as I wyll to any Man, confyderyng the Caufe and neceffary Cyrcomſtances incydent to the fame; but for Love, and lovyng Offyces, I will do as I fynd Caufe. I I craue no thyng at hys Hand, but that which he owyth to the Queene, and that whych her great Lyberalyte, befyde naturall Duty, byndyth him to. And, if he will have of me that I ow hym not, as he hathe had, he can not wyn yt by croffyng me, as I heere he dooth in the Court; and as I have Caufe to deme he dooth in thys Cuntre. In fyne, my Lord, I am redy to accord with hym: But, my moſt dere Lord and Brother, be you upon your Kepyng for him, for, if *Effex* had lyved, you fhould have found hym as vyolent an Enemy, as his Hart, Power, and Cunyng, would have farved hym to have byn; and for that their Mallyce, I take God to record, I could brooke nother of them bothe.

Your Lordfhvppys later wrytten Letter I received, the fame Day I dyd the firſt, together with one from my Lord of *Penbrooke* to your Lordfhyp; by both whych I fynd, to my excedyng great Confort, the Lykleod of a Maryage betwyne his Lordfhyp and my Doghter, whych great Honor to me, my mean Lynuage and Kyn, I attrybute to my Match in your noble Houfe; for whych I acknoleg my felf bound to honor and farve the fame, to the utter-moſt of my Pouer; yea, fo joyfully have I at Hart, that my dere Chyldys fo happy an Advancement as thys ys, as, in Troth, I would ly a Year in clofe Pryfon, rather than yt fhould breake. But, alas! my dereſt Lord, myne Abylyte anfwereth not my harty Defyer. I am poore; myne Eſtate, as well in Lyvelod and Moveable, is not unknown to your Lordfhyp, whych wantyth mutch to make me able to equall that, whych I knowe my Lord of *Penbrook* may have. Twoo Thoufand *l.* I confes I have bequethed her, whych your Lordfhyp knowyth I myght better fpare her whan I wear dead, than one Thoufand lyvyng; and, in Troth, my Lord, I have yt not, but borro yt I muſt, and fo I wyll: And, if your Lordfhypp wyll get me Leave, that I may feede my Eyes wyth that joyfull Syght of thear Couplyng, I wyll gyve her a

Cup

Cup worth fyve Hundryth *l.* Good, my Lord, bear wyth my Poverty, for, if I had it, lyttell would I regard any Sum of Money, but wyllyngly would gyve it, proteftyng before the Almyghty God, that if he, and all the Powers on Earth, would geve me my Choyfe for a Hufband for her, I would choofe the Earl of *Penbrooke.* I wryte to my Lord of *Penbrook*, whych hearwyth I fend your Lordfhyp ; and thus I end, in anfwering your moft welcom and honorable Letter, wyth my harty Prayer to Almyghty God to perfect your Lordfhypps good Wurk, and requyte you for the fame ; for I am not able. For my felf, I am in great Dyfpayre to obteyne the Fee Farme of my fmall Leafes ; whych grywyth me more for the Dyfcredyt, duryng myne one Tyme, than the Lak of the Gayn to my Succeffyon, be yt as God wyll.

I fynd by dyvers Meanys, that thear ys great Expectacyon of my wyfhyng her Majeftyes Treafure apoynted for the Sarvyce of this Cuntre ; and, in Troth, no Man lyvyng would fayner noyryfh yt than I ; and, in Proof thearof, I wyll abate one Thoufand *l.* of the Quartereg du the Laft of *March*, fo as I may have the other fouer Thoufand du, than delyvered to the Treaforers Affigne, together wyth that du the Laft of *December* laft ; and, if I can, I wyll abate every Quarter one Thoufand *l.* The actuall Rebellyon of the *Clanrykcardynes*, the *O Conners* and *O Mores*, the Sumys of Money delyvered in Dyfcharg of thofe Soldyarys, which weare of my Lord of *Effex* Regyment, and the great Sumys imprefted in the Begynnyng of my Charge, well confydered ; it may and will appear a good Offer ; and, I pray your Lordfhypp, let yt have your favorable Recommendatyon.

Now, my dereft Lord, I have a Sute unto you for a neceffary and honeft Sarvant of myne, *Hercules Raynsford*, who hys Father, and whole Lynnage, are devote Folloers to your Lordfhyp, and Famely. My Sute ys, that whear as, by Compofytyon wyth *James Wyngfeld*, he is Coneftable of the Caftell of *Dublyn*, and thearin both paynfully and carefully farveth, that it would pleafe your Lordfhyp, to obteyne yt for hym duryng hys Lyfe. Truly, my Lord, lyke as you fhould bynd the poore gentyll Man, and all his honeft Freyndys, alwayes to farve you, for your Bounty doon to hym ; fo fhall I take yt as a great Mercye doon to my felf : For truly I have found hym a faythfull and profytable Sarvant, and befyde, he hath marryed a good and an old Sarvant of my Wyfes. Good my Lord, fend *Phyllip* to me ; thear was never Father had more Neede of hys Soon, than I have of hym. Ons agayn, good my Lord, let me have hym.

For the Eftate of thys Cuntre, it may pleafe you to geve Credyt to *Prefcot.*

I am now, evyn now, deadly wery of Wrytyng, and therfore I end, prayeng to the Almyghty to bles you, wyth all your noble Hartys Defyres. From *Dundalk* thys 4 of *February*, 1576.

Your moft affured Brother at

Superfcribed,   *Commandment,*

To the Right Honorable, and my   H. Sydney.
   very good Lord and Brother,
   the Earle of *Leycefter*, Knight of
   the Noble Order of the Garter.
      Att the Courte.

Sir Henry Sydney *to the Lords of the Council in* England.

My verie good Lords,

MY Duetie moft humblye remembred to your Lordfhips, lyke as from *Waterforde*, of the xvth of *December* laft, I writt vnto your Lordfhips of my paffinge thorough *Meith*, and *Leinfter*, and in what Cafe I left the *Englifh*

Pale and the *Irifhe* Lordfhipps of the fame, garded and defended till my Re-torne, from whence I am fundrie Tymes advertized, of the good Contynu-aunce of the Quiet of the Countrie; which hath bene a great deale the better ftayed, thorough the Dilligence, Pollecye, and carefull Service of my Lord of *Vpper Offerie*, whome I left my Liuetenaunt of the *Kings* and *Quenes* Coun-ties: So it may lyke the fame (my Expedicion nowe ended in theife Partes, and I reddye to paffe into an other Province) to vnderftand of my Procedinge in this Province of *Mounfter*.

The Day I departed from *Waterfforde*, I lodged that Night at *Corragmore*, the Howfe that the Lord *Power* is Baron of; where I was fo vfed, and with fouch Plentie and good Order enterteined (as addinge to it the Quiet of all the Countrie adioyninge, by the People called *Power* Countrie, for that that Surname hath bene fince the Beginninge of *Englifhe* Mens Plantinge Inhabi-taunts there) it may be well compared with the beft ordered Countrie in the *Englifh* Pale; whereby a manifeft and moft certeine Proffe may be conceived, what Benifitt rifeth both to the Prince, meane Lorde, and inferior Subiecte, by Suppreffinge of *Coyne* and *Lyverie*; for nowe they are both willing and able to beare, and pay any reafonable Subfidie towardes the Findinge and Enter-teinement of Soldiours, and Cyvill Minifters of the Lawes, that I will impofe vpon theim. And the Lord of the Countrie, though he be in Scope of Ground a farre leffe Territorie then his Neighbor is, yet he lyveth in Shewe farre more honorably and plentifullye then he or any other, what foever he be, of his Callinge, that lyueth in that Province. And al be it the Soyle, for the moft Parte, of it felfe, is very barren; yet is there not any Gentleman or Free-holder in that Countrie, but may make more of an Acre of Lande there, then they have of three in the Countye of *Kilkennye*, the next Countye confininge on the one Syde (where the Soyle is verye good) or in the *Decies*, the Lord-fhip next adioyninge one the other Syde; and this was openlye fpoken before me, and affirmed by credible Perfonnes, havinge Lande in bothe; and this was yeelded for the Reafon, for that they fuffer no idle Men in the one, and are oppreffed with theim in the other. The next Countrie adioyninge to this is the *Decies*, whereof Sir *James Fytz Gerrald* is cheife Lord; his Brother was Vicount of the fame, who beinge the firft created, and dyenge without lawfull Iffue Male, his Lands (though not his Title) defcended to this Gentleman, who is one of bad Governement; and fo it well appearethe; for, beinge left by his Brother, and other Freinds, verie ritche, is fince moche fpent, and almoft no better then a Bankerupte, his Landes beinge verye great; I am fure in Quan-titie fower Tymes as moche as my Lord *Powers* is, and yet made fo waft, as it is not hable to finde competent Foode for a meane Famelye, in good Order: Yet are there harbored and lyve more idle Vaccabonndes, then good Cattle breed. The reft of that Countye is either in meane Gentlemens Handes (who have had longe Contynuance of Auntiente and Dwellinge there) or ells in Citti-zins Hands of *Waterffoord*, by Purchace or Morgage, had by theim of the meane Gentlemen; but all defierous of Cyvill Reformacion, willinge to obey and beare for their Portions.

From thence I came to *Dungarvan* Caftle, where I lodged three Nights; thither the Earle of *Defmound* came vnto me, and verie humblye offered me any Service that he was able to do her Majeftie. That Towne of late is moche decaied by the Rebellion of *James Fytzmorris*, and his graceles Followers; but in great Hope of Amendement by the dilligent Travell of *Henry Dauells*, Conftable of the Caftle there, who vfeth all earneft Endevor, for the Punifh-inge of Malefactors, and to fee good Order kept in thofe Quarters; and truelye, my Lord, he is a rare Man, for his Painefulnes, upright freindlye Dealinge, and Bountie of Minde everye Way. Wherefore I befeache your Lordfhips, that he may in fome Sorte vnderftand from fome of you, that I have written well of hym; which will not onely be a Memorie of Rewarde for hym, for that which is paft, but alfo henceforth an Encouragement to hym to proceede in his commendable well Doinge.

I

I paſſed from *Dungarvan* to Sir *John* of *Deſmounds*, leavinge *Youghall*, for that they were not (as they proteſted) hable to receyve me, and my Traine, by Reaſon of their Spoyles, donne vpon theim, and their People, in the Tyme of the Rebellion of *James Fytzmorris*, and ſo, paſſinge out of the Countye of *Waterſoord*, entred the Countye of *Corck* ; and from Sir *Johns* came to the Lord *Barries*, and the xxiijth of *December* laſt, arryved at the Cittye of *Corck*, where I was received with all Ioyfulnes, Tokens, and Shewes, the beſt they could expreſſe of their duetifull Thanks Gevinge to her Majeſtie ; they received willinglye my *Engliſhe* Footemen and Galloglas, lodged and enterteined theim, during my Abode there (which was ſixe Weekes) without Grudginge or Complainte, either of Towneſmen, or of Souldiors. The Towneſmen receivinge, in reddie Money, the one Halfe of the Soldiors Wagies, for his Boarde, Fier, and Lodginge ; wherewith he held hym ſelfe verye well ſatisfied, and the Souldiours, in lyke Manner, well contented to geve it. The good Eſtate, and Floriſhinge of that Cittie, well approveth the good Effects of reſident Authoritie amongſt theim, for it is ſo amended, as in ſo fewe Yeares, I have ſeldome ſeen any Towne ; and out of Doubt, if Miniſtracion of Juſtice be contynued, it will daylie multiplie in People, and amplifye in Buyldinge. I was, for the Tyme of my Contynuaunce there, verie honorablye attended on, and accompanied by the Earles of *Deſmound*, *Thomound*, and *Clancarre*, the Biſſhopps of *Caſſhell* and *Corck*, and the Electe of *Roſſe Carberye*, the Vicounts of *Barrye* and *Roche*, the Barons of *Curſey*, *Lixnawe*, *Dunboyne*, *Power*, *Barrie Oge*, and *Lowth*, who onlye to doe me Honor, came oute of the *Engliſh* Pale to that Cittye, and did great Good amongſt great ones ; for beinge of this Countrye Birthe, and of their Language, and well underſtandinge their Condicions and Manners, did by Example of hym ſelfe, beinge but a meane Man of Landes in Reſpect of their large Patrimonies and Lyvinge, both at Home and Abroade, lyve more orderlye and more commendablye, then they did, or were hable to do ; which did moche perſwade theim to leave their Barbarietie, and to be aſhamed of their wilfull Miſerie. There were, beſides they above remembred, dyvers of the *Iriſhrie*, not yet nobilitated, the Lord of *Carberie*, called Sir *Donell Mac Cartye*, and the Lord of *Muſkery*, called Sir *Cormock Mac Teige Mac Cartye* ; neither of theiſe but, in Reſpecte of their Territories, were able to be a Vicounte ; and truelye, I wiſhe theim bothe to be made Baronnes ; for they be both good Subiects, and in eſpeciall the latter ; who for his Obedience to hir Majeſtie, and her Lawes, and Diſpoſition to Civilitie, is the rareſt Man, that ever was borne in the *Iriſhrie* ; but of hym I intende to write ſpeciallye, erre it be longe, for truelye he is a ſpeciall Man. There came to me alſo Sir *Owen Oſulyvant*, and the Sonne and Heire of *Oſulyvan More*, the Father not beinge able to come, by Reaſon of his great Yeares and Impotencye ; Sir *William Occarroll*, of *Ely Occarroll*, and *Mac Donogho* ; never a one of theiſe, but for his Landes, might paſſe in the Ranke of a Baron, either in *Irelande* or *England*. There were in lyke Manner with me, of the *Iriſhrye*, *Okyne* and *Mac Fynnen*, the Sonnes or Heyres, as they would have theim, of *Mac Auuley* and *Occhallahan* ; the olde Men not beinge able to come, by Reaſon of extreme Age, and Infirmitie ; *Omahon*, and *Odriſcoll*, ech of theſe have Land enough, withe good Order to lyve lyke a Knight either here, or there. There were with me, that diſcended of *Engliſhe* Race, Sir *Morris Fytzgarrold*, Brother to the Vicounte *Decies* ; Sir *Thibald Butler*, whoſe Vncle and Cozen Germaine were Baronnes of the *Cayre*, whoſe Lands he lawfullye, and iuſtlye, enjoyethe and better deſerveth that Title of Honnor, then any of theim ever did ; for whome I entende more ſpeciallye to write, for truelye, for his Deſerte, he is worthie any Commendacion. Sir *Thomas*, Sir *John*, and Sir *James* of *Deſmound*, Bretheren to the Earle, were continuallye with me, and a Nomber of other Gentlemen, whoſe Names I omitt to repete here, leſt they ſhould be tedious to be redd by your Lordſhips : There came to me alſo maney of the ruyned Relicks of the auntient *Ingliſh* Inhabitaunts of this Province, as the *Arundells*, *Rocheſordes*, *Barretts*, *Flemings*, *Lombardes*, *Tirries*, and maney other ; whoſe

Aunceſtors

Aunceftors (as it may appeare) by Monuments, afwell in Writinge, as of Buyldinge, were able, and did lyve lyke Gentlemen, and Knights ; fome of theim, and nowe all in Miferye, either bannifhed from their owne, or oppreffed vpon their owne. *Laftlye*, there came to me fyve Bretheren, and the Sonnes of twoe other Bretheren of one Lynage, all Captaines of Galloglas, called *Mac Swynes*, who although I place them laft of the reft, yet are they of as moche Confequence as any of the reft ; for of foche Creditt, and Force, were they growen vnto (though they were no Lordes of Landes theim felves) as they would make of the greateft Lordes of the Province, both in Feare of theim, and gladd of their Freindfhipp ; and the better to furnifhe the Bewtye and Fillinge of the Cittye, all theife principall Lordes had with theim their Wyves, duringe all the *Chriftmas*, who trewlye kept verye honorable, at leaft verye plentifull Howfies ; and to be briefe, maney Wydowe Ladies were there alfo, who erft had bene Wyves to Earles and others of good Note and Accompte.

And nowe my Lords havinge towched in this firft Parte of my Lettre of my Receivinge at *Corcke*, and the great Affemblie there, to attende, and accompanie me ; it may pleafe your Lordfhips in fome fewe, to vnderftand the reaft, what this Companie for their Perticuler did, and I, withe the Affiftaunce of foche, as I named in my former Lettres, together withe Mr. *Dowdall* and Mr. *Walfhe* (whome I found Commiffioners in this Province) what we did. And for theim, they feamed in all Apparaunce generallye to lothe their vile and barbarous Manner of Life ; they offered all Feaultye, Homage, and Service to her Majeftie, and Crowne for ever, and I dare well vndertake, there is never a one of the above named but (if her Highnes will) fhall performe it at *Weftminfter* ; foch as do not alreadie yeld Rente and Service, moft humblye defier, after Surrender made, to hold their Landes of her Highnes, her Heyres, and Succeffors, and to yeelde both Rente and Service : They did agree to delyver in the Names of their idle Men, and then to anfwer for theim, and if any were founde vnbooked, to be vfed as a Felon or Vaccabounde, according to his Defert ; they affented that this fhould be proclaymed, and were prefent at it theim felves, and, for a Performaunce of the fame, they offered to me the Choyce of any, belonginge vnto theim, to remayne as Hoftage for theim. Nexte the Some of my Doings, with the Affiftaunce withe me, was this in Effecte : I cawfed daylie Seffions to be helde, in that Cittye, from the Morrowe after *Twelve Day*, till the Laft of *Januarii*, in which appeared verye honeft and good Juries, founde and good Triall made by theim, a Nomber of Civill Cawfies determined and ended, and above xxiiij notable Malefactors condempned, and executed : *Condon* or *Canton* of *Armon* attainted, and adiudged to die (yet ftaied from Execucion) but his Landes (which are greate) are by the Meanes of his Attayndor efcheted to hir Majeftie. A younger Sonne of the Vicounte *Roches* was indited, arraigned, and condempned to dye, but ftaied from Execucion, for (as the Worlde goeth here) his Faulte was verye fmall : So moche hath bene donne, I dare affirme to your Lordfhips, at this Tyme, in this Province, for Recoverye of the Quenes decayed Rents, and imbefeled Landes, as hath not bene donne in the Memorie of Man ; but hereof I will not write perticulerlye at this Tyme, till that which hath bene donne, in my whole Iorney, be collected and put together, which will not be till *Aprill* next. In the meane Tyme, I affure your Lordfhips, her Highnes hath foche a Servaunt of *Launcelott Alford*, her Surveior here, as both for his Dexteritie, Dilligence, and Stowtnes, in her Service, I never mett with his Matche in this Lande : I doubt not, but you fhall finde the Iffue of his Travell greatlye to her Highnes Advauntage ; in the meane Tyme, if your Lordfhips do incourage hym, with your honorable Lettres, it wilbe to hym in Lieu of great Rewarde.

I was prefent at the Readinge and Publifhinge of the Proclamacion before fpoken of, and it feamed, that, with great Ioye and Gladnes (as moch as might be well expreffed by Countenaunce) the fame was received of the moft, yea of the Nobilitie theim felves (whome it moft touched) with earneft and affured

I   Promiffe,

Promiſſe, that it ſhould be followed.)   For the better Performaunce whereof, they have offered, and I have taken ſufficient Pledgies of everye one of theim, of any Regarde, and namelye of the *Mac Swynes* (Abroade not a little perillous to this Province.)

I have alſo entred into Conſideracion, howe I might beſt, in ſome reaſonable Sorte, ſatisfie the Lordes with ſome conveniente and certeine Revenue, in Stede of their extorcious and tyrannicall Exactions, and finde theim, in this Pointe, ſome what tractable and pliaunt, to be reduced to accepte Certainetie : Howe be it, the Matter in handlinge is ſomewhat toughe (for Extorcion, though it be, or extorciouſlye vſed that they do) yet is the ſame ſomewhat in Particula-rities, and, by different Deviſes, to be redreſſed ; which I truſt your Lordſhips ſhall here of, to be digeſted before it be longe, and ſoch Order taken, as ſhall be to the Gayne of the Proprietarie, Honnor, Proffitt, and Suertye, to the Quenes Countrie, and Succeſſors of theim that nowe lyve.

For the laſt Pointe of my Doings in *Corcke*, I hope I have layd ſoch a Plott, as the Province ſhall beare 50 Horſſemen, and 100 Footemen, of her Majeſties *Engliſhe* Souldiours, contynuallie, if forreine Invaſion impeache not the Deviſe ; and finde theim both Victuall and Wagies, and daylye pay theim their Enter-teinements.   This Plott is to beginne at *Maij Day* next ; and none will impugne this, but it ſhall take Place, if it be not a great one or twoe ; neyther ſhall they be able to reſiſt it, if they finde not Countenaunce and Maintenaunce there.   I hope, my Lords, that this will prove a good, beneficiall, and acceptable Ser-vice for the Quene.

And thus havinge left the Cittye of *Corck*, the Firſt of this Moneth, I lodged twoe Nights by the Waye hitherwardes, at my Lord *Roches*, where I and all my Trayne were verie largelye and bountifullye enterteyned : And, paſſinge from thence, I entred into the Countye of *Lymericke*, and ſo lodged one Night in the Towne of *Kilmallock*, which was lamentablye ſpoyled and bourned, by that vyle Trator and Rebell, *James Fytzmorris* ; but ſo ſpedilye agayne reedified, as ſuerelye it is not almoſt to be credited, but by the conſtant Reporte of theim that knewe it, and ſawe it then, and nowe have pervſed and ſene it againe ; for, where there was not one Roffe nor Flower lefte vnbourned, fewe or no Howſes, within the Wall, are nowe vncovered ; wherebye the Beniſitte and good Fruite of *Engliſhe* Lawes, and Forces, moſt ſenciblye is felt ; without which, the People confeſſe theim ſelves, they would for ever have abandoned that Place, and ſought ſome other Habitacion ; and the lyke Deſolacion be-come of that Towne, as may be ſene by Ruynes of maney other within this Lande, whome *Iriſh* Rebells have ſuppreſſed, and, *Engliſhe* Forces and Governe-ment faylinge, were never ſince reſtored.

From thence I came to this Cittie, the iiijth of this Preſent, accompanied withe the Earle of *Deſmound*, the Biſshoppes of *Caſshell* and *Corck*, my Lord of *Lowth*, and ſome others of the Nobilitie, dyvers Knights and principall Gentle-men of the Countrie ; where I was received with farre greater Pompe, then ei-ther I my ſelfe have heretofore had, or ſawe yeelded to any other in this Lande ; for which, leſt I ſhould ſeme leſſe thankefull to this Cittye, or to *Corck*, then I was to *Waterford*, I humblye beſeache your Lordſhips to beſtowe your favo-rable Lettres on theim both ; for truelye, my Lords, they are Peices of great Regarde, and greatelye ſhall their Willingneſs (to ſerve the Governor here) ad-vaunce the Seruice of oure Sovereigne.

Since my Entrie into this Countye, all the principall Gentlemen of the ſame, and lykewiſe thoſe that dwell in the Lordſhipps adioyninge, and yet doubtfull whether they be of this Countye or noe, by Reaſon ſome Chalendge, of late, hath bene made in the Matter, which, as yet, is not fullye determined, repayred vnto me ; as namelye the *Bourckes, Lacyes, Sappells, Purcells*, the *Red Roche*, and dyverſe other originall *Ingliſhe* ; diverſe alſo of the Lords of the *Iriſhrey*, as *Omoleyan, Mac Brien Ogonough, Mac Brien Arra, Obrien* of *Arloc*, whiche do inhabete the Southſide of *Shenon*, and maney other of Note, originall *Iriſhe*, all lamentinge the Spoyle and Waſt of the Countrie.   And, in Trothe, waſted they be, and therefore crave, that they may have the Forces of their meane Lordes fuppreffed, and that they may be equallye ceffed to beare an *Inglifhe* Force, and to have *Englifhe* Lawes planted amongeft theim, and *Englifhe* Sheriffs to execute thofe Lawes, and to furrender their Landes to her Majeftie (as maney as may, and have not donne alredie) and herein, God willinge, fome Payne fhalbe taken, and I hope foch Rent and Service either created or renewed to her Majeftie, as hath not theife maney Yeares ; which, I hope, fhalbe to her Highnes Likinge, and your Lordfhips, and I truft the fame fhall not be longe in doinge, my Iourney once finifhed.

Hether to this Towne the Earle of *Ormounde* came vnto me, and freindlye accompanied me fyve or fixe Dayes ; and likewife my Lord of *Vpperoffery*, who made Reporte of the vniuerfall Quiett and good State of the Pale, wherein his Service, and great Travell taken therein, is worthye Note, for fuerlye he defer-vethe right well in his Chardge. Lykewife, bothe the Earles of *Clanrickards* Sonnes, *Vllick* and *John Burck* (who, not maney Yeares paft) were moft execrable evell Doers (but fince pardoned) and I licenzed theim both to departe, but with Condicion, that they fhould mete me againe at *Galway.* To this Place came to me, and alfo contynuethe with me the Earle of *Thomound*, and all the principall Gentlemen of his Surname, beinge niere Kinfmen, yet extreme Ennimies. Twoe Lordes of *Thomound*, called *Mac Nemarroes*, came lykewife vnto me, lamentinge the Ruyne and Waft of their Countrie ; and ruyned they are in dede, cravinge to have the Execucion of *Englifhe* Lawes, and to have *Englifhe* Sheriffs planted amongeft theim : But for the *Briens*, and their Coun-trie, al be it the fame be a Parcell of this Province, yet, for that I meane to lay it to the Governement of *Connaught*, as I did at the firft ; and for that I love rather to write to your Lordfhippes, after I have feen that I have hard of that Countrie, then of any Reporte, I will therefore deferre to write more largely of that, in my Difcourfe of *Connaught*, which, God willinge, I will difpatche vnto your Lordfhips, by the Beginninge of *April* next. For the State of this Cittye, althoughe the fame have bene moche hindered by the late Rebellion, yet it re-maynethe in indifferent good Cafe ; and Juftice beinge once vniverfallye minif-tred within the Realme, and quiet Trade from forraine Partes, it will fpedi-lye growe ritche ; and thus motche for the State of this Cittie and Coun-trie.

Twoe other Countries there are in this Province, namelye, *Kerrye* and *Typpe-rarye*, of which twoe I cannot write moche, for that I thinke the Quene hath little to do there, hir Writt not beinge allowed currentlye in theim ; but thus moche I coniecture, and, in myne Opinion, affirme, and fo do others of great Experience too, that, fo longe as any Subiecte hath any Jurifdiction *Pallantyne*, in either of theim bothe, there will hardly be any founde and perfect Reformaci-on in *Mounfter*, for vndoubtedlye they are no fmall Impediments to it. The principall Gentlemen of eche Countye hath bene withe me, and fome Parte of their Greiffe I have vnderftand by their owne Relacions ; and thus I ende for the Province of *Mounfter*, wherein I finde great Towardnes of Reformacion, as may appeare by this my Difcourfe, and great Lykelyhoode that the fame fhall beare the Chardge incydent to the fame ; for if the Countrie pay the Men of Warre, as I doubt not, but they fhall, by Degrees, be wonne, and brought to do it ; then I am affured, that the certeine Revenue of *Mounfter*, and the cafu-all Commodities, will anfwere the Chardge of the Prefident, and all Minifters apointed for Cyvill Governement, neceffarie to affift hym. But, this Province beinge nowe in this Towardenes to be reformed, I thinke it fhould be thought, that I, for Gaine Sake or Glorye, or happelye for bothe, fhould be vnwillinge that any fhould deale in Governement here but my felfe. But truelye, my Lords, I proteft vnto you it is not fo ; for, as I was the firft that either devifed or planted any refident Governement here, fo am I ftill of Opinion, that, without that, this Countrie will never remayne quiet, neither good and peaceable for the People, nor profitable to the Prince ; for foche Effectes finde I, fince my laft Repayre into theife Partes, of their Services that remayned here, as I dare affirme, that, if Mr. *Perrott* had contynued till my Arryvall, and mainteined the Courfe ftill, he helde, while he was heare, I fhould have found *Mounfter* afwell as I left *Wales.* And Mr. *Agarde,* confideringe the Impediments he founde (which Mr. *Perrot* left not) did as moche as might be ; and fo have twoe Gentlemen of this Countrie Birthe, *Iames Dowdall* and *Nicholas Walfhe,* both Profeffors of the Lawe, and remayninge here, fince the Revocacion of Mr. *Agarde,* have donne as moche, as was to be looked for, of Men of their Qualitie, wantinge Men of Warre, and Force, to execute their Orders, Arrefts, and Decrees, and have deferved Thanks for their Travells, which hartelye I befeache your Lordfhips they may receive by your comfortable Lettres. And, my Lords, in my fimple Opinion, *Mounfter* never needed, at any Tyme, more, then at this prefent, to have a difcreate and active Governor, to be contynuallye refident in it ; for theife People are, for the moft Parte, all Papifts, and that in the malitiouft Degree, *Et nouarum rerum cupidi,* delighteth in Ravyn and lycentious Liffe, though the fame be voyde of Proffitt, Suertie, or Pleafure, to any but theim felves. *Iames Fitzmorris* lyethe in *St. Maloes,* and kepeth a great Porte, hym felfe and Familye well apparelled, and full of Money ; he hath oft Intelligence from *Rome,* and oute of *Spaine* ; not moche Relieffe from the *Frenche* Kinge, as I can perceive, yet oft vifited by Men of good Countenaunce. Thus moche I knowe of certeine Reporte, by fpecyall of myne owne from thence. The Man futtle, malitious, and hardye, a Papift in Extremitie, and well eftemed, and of good Credit emongft the People. If he come, and be not wholye dealt with all at the firft (as with oute an *Englifh* Commaunder I knowe he fhall not) all the loofe People of this Province will flocke vnto hym : Yea the Lordes, though they would do their beft, fhall not be able to kepe theim from hym. So as if he come, and in Shewe and Apparaunce lyke a Man of Warre (as I knowe he will) and that I be in the Northe, as, God willinge, I will be, at *Carickfergus,* before *Midfommer* Day, he may take and do what he will with *Kinfale, Corck, Youghall, Kilmallock,* and happelye this Cittye too, before I fhalbe able to come to the Refkewe thereof. Haften therefore, my good Lords, hym that fhall take the Chardge here, in the Quene and Countries Behalfe ; I crave it, and the onelye Man, that I hope you will fende, is Sir *William Drewrye* ; and, if my ioyfull Likinge of hym may any Thinge quicken hym hetherwardes, then I proteft vnto your Lordfhips, that he lyveth not, that I knowe wold accept that Place, that I would be fo glad fhould have it, as Sir *William Drewrye* ; for I knowe he wilbe for the Safetie of the Countrie, Honnor and Proffitt of the Quene, and Comforte of my felfe, and to my felfe, as I may fay with *Dauid, Inueni hominem fecundum Cor meum* ; this I truft fhall fuffice for a Refolution irrevocable by me, both touchinge the Man and the Matter, for the Plantinge of refidente Governement in *Mounfter.*

The like, I knowe in Effecte, is as neceffarie for *Connaught,* for after I have bene amongeft theim, and fomewhat tafted their Humors, I doubt not, but that I fhall have Occafion to write as earneftlye of it, as I nowe do for this, and fo confequentlye to have a Chauncelor, for the whole Realme ; the Lacke, and Loffe, for Want of a good one (fitt for that Place) is foche, and the fame fo well knowen to your Lordfhips, as I can impute it to nothinge more, but to the fatall Curffe of this Countrie ; that a Greife fo great, a Remedye fo eafye to be had, fhould fo longe be defferred, fpeciallye, fince it is fo moche to the Quenes Chardge, who paieth three hundered Poundes a Yere, to the Keper of the great Seale (ever fince the Deathe of Mr. *Wefton,* late Lorde Chauncelor) who never fittethe in Courte, to order and decree Cawfies, nor dothe any Thing ells, incydent to the Office of a Chauncelor, but onelye kepethe the Seal. I once heard, that Mr. *Rookebye* was reddye to imbarke hetherward, to have fupplied that Office, whereof I was hartelye glad ; and fince I harde, that Mr. *William Gerrard* was apointed to it ; yf it be fo, I befeach your Lordfhips, haften hym away, for, if he be not here, before the Beginninge of the next

Tearme,

Tearme, it will be yll for the Quene, and worffe for the Countrie; I have had longe Experience of hym, having had his Affiftaunce in *Wales*, nowe xvj Yeares, and knowe hym to be verye honeft and dilligent, and of great Dexteritie, and Readines, in a Courte of that Nature; and if my Judgment be any Thinge, he is a Man of good Sufficiencye for the Office, and therefore, once againe, I humblye befeache your Lordfhips, to haften hym hether.

One Thinge I had almoft forgotten, which was difcovered to me at *Corcke*, certeine Peices of counterfeited Coyne of *Spanifhe* Stampes were brought to me, vttered from Hand to Hand: I fifted the Matter, till I found it oute, and was geven to vnderftand, that it was made in a Caftle of the Earle of *Ormoundes*, in his Libertie in the Countye of *Typperarye*; thither I fent, the Parties were found, taken, and brought to me, with Stampes, and fome of their Money Potts for Meltinge, Stuffe for Myntinge, and other Inftruments. The Parties, that were taken, were but twoe, the Mafter and the Servaunte, bothe *Englifh men*, borne in the Northe; the Mafter a Gentleman (as he fayeth) and is called *Harrifon*, and moche delighted (as he confeffeth) a long Tyme in Alcumiftical Practizes, his Man an excellent Artizan in fondrie Occupacions; the Facte they confeffe, and the rather, for that they are perfwaded, it is not Felonye and Treafon by the Lawe of this Lande; and fo they affirmed, they were induced to thinke, by fome of the beft Lawiers in *Englande*; and the lyke is affirmed to me, by fome of that Profeffion here, though in dede I be geven to vnderftande that the Facte is Treafon, by others of better Truft aboute me, as namelye Sir *Lucas Dillon*. And this Perfwafion makes theim the bolder, bothe to vtter more, and prefume further vpon the Creditt of their Freindes to helpe theim; which their Prefumption, I fuppofe, will cawfe greater Matter to fall oute, and be difcovered of their Confederats (if any be) and that maketh me, having theim faft in Holde, not to haften to vfe Extremitie, or Punifhement towards theim, but to attende, what Tyme will bringe out; yf the Matter be tryed here, by the ordinarie Courfe of Lawe, it muft be tryed before my Lord of *Ormoundes* Officers, for that the Offence was committed within his Libertie, or ells he will thinke hym felfe moche wronged, and his Graunte infringed. Since their Apprehenfion there arryved a Barke att *Waterforde*, which brought theym certeine Stuffe, Potts, and Inftruments, which I have cawfed to be ftaied, and the Partie that brought it; certeine Peices lykewife of *Englifhe* Counterfeites were found in thofe Quarters, with People fo fimple, as are not to be fufpected to be fawltie for the Makinge of theim; and as I was thus farre forwarde, myndinge to have made my Difpatche, and to have fent theife Advertizements to your Lordfhips; my Servaunt, *John Gifforde*, arryved here, who brought me Lettres from your Honors, dated at *Hampton Courte*, the xxiiiith of the Laft, in Anfwere of myne, of the iiiith of *November*, and the xvith of *December*; for the which I humblye thanke your Lordfhips. And firft, for the Queftion you move, touchinge my Sute for *Mac Genneffe*, wherein you defier more fullye to vnderftand my Meaninge, whether it be meant, that he fhall have the Captenrie by Inheritaunce, and the Lande he holdeth prefentlye, as his owne Freeholde, leavinge the reft to other Freholders, or ells to have the Capteinrye of the Whole. Wherein, although I am, and ever have bene of Opinion, and holde the fame for an infallible Principle, that the Difcipacion of the great Lordes and their Countries, by good Diftribucion into maney Handes, is a founde Way of Proceadinge to the perfecte Reformacion of this vnhappie and curfed Eftate; fo the Attemptinge of it is as perillous, and breadethe foch a Nomber of Inconveniences as will hardlye be cured, excepte that Courfe be contynued, and followed with Effecte; and herein I am to note, and remember to your Lordfhips, my Lord of *Effex* Plott, for Reformacion of the Northe, which in dede, of all other, is the beft, and fureft Foundacion to buylde on, and truelye his Lordfhip, highlye to be commended in it, both for the Worthines of the Enterprife, as for his great Valor, and Nobilitie of Mynde, ioyned to that great Travell, Payne, and Penurie he indured in fo barraine and harde a Soyle:

But

But if that Enterprife by her Majeftie be not purfued, but let fall, which, for a Tyme, is to be mainteined by Treafure and Force, and, for a Tyme, the People kept in Obedience, by Violence and Compulcion : What better Meane is there to make the Lordes of the Countries to applye to Obedience, then to affure then, of their owne they pretende, and to perfwade theim, that her Majeftie meaneth to maynteine theim, and not to difturbe theim in their Poffeffions ; and then, if Obedience and Rente may be had (fince Temporifacion, and not Force, muft be vfed) me feamethe in my fimple Opinion, vnder your Lordfhips Reformacion, better to take fomme Rente, and Service, then to for goe it, fince a better Compoficion, and more Affurednes, cannot be had of theim, except there be at Hande prefent Force to fubdue theim. And for thofe Landes *Mac Genneffe* nowe enioyethe, and by his Occupacion, pretendethe Title vnto, the Landes are her Majefties, and geven her by Acte of Parliament, fo that, the Lands beinge in hir Gift, fhe may make hym what Eftate pleafethe her, and referve to hir felfe, what pleafethe hir ; befides, if fhe wold difpoffeffe hym, and place an other, I knowe not of that Countrie Birthe, that will dwell there any one, that is able to do her Highnes better Service, or of greater Loyaltie, then he is. And for that it is obiected, that the Rente is fmall in Refpecte of the Greatnes, and Quantitie of the Soyle, fince *Chanlons* Countrie, beinge a leffe Scope of Grounde and Territorie, is valued at a greater Rente ; I anfwer in that, that the Qualitie of the Perfonnes are not lyke, the one beinge in all his Practizes, and Actions, an open and profeffed Ennemye, and the other hath contynued a duetyfull Subiecte, fince the Overthrowe of *Shane Oneill,* fo that, in that Refpecte, more Confideracion, in Reafon, is to be had to the one, then Regarde to the other ; the one for his Deferte is worthie to be cherifhed, the other for his Difobedience fharpelye to be corrected ; and this Diverfitie I put betwene the Qualitie of the one, and the lewde Behaviour of the other, wherein I fubmitt my felfe to your Lordfhips grave and honorable Iudgements.

I humblye thanke your Lordfhips, that it will pleafe you to have in Remembraunce to deale with *Chatterton* and *Malbye* ; and, becawfe at *Maij* Day commonlye, the *Irifhe* Capteines and Lordes vfe to bargaine and compounde with their Tennaunts, which Tyme nowe approchethe, I am the bolder eft fones, to renue the Matter to your Honnors, fo, that your Refolucions therein knowen, I may take Order accordinglye.

For *Terelaugh Lynaughes* Requefts, I yeelde your Lordfhips myne humble Thankes, that you have fo gratioufleye confidered both of hym and theim. And, accordinge to your Lordfhips Directions in that Pointe, I will conclude the beft Bargaine for her Majeftie that I can ; but, becawfe his Agent is not yet retorned, and that I cannot have his Warrant drawen, nor any Thinge convenientlye donne in it, before I come to *Dublin,* I will not trouble your Lordfhips any further for hym, nor in this, till I comme thether, but to lett your Lordfhips vnderftand that the Articles youer Lordfhips fent me, poftilled with your Opinions, I thinke they were miftaken ; for I received the Copie of the Treatie betwixt the Earle of *Effex* and hym, and not your Lordfhips Refolucions in thofe Articles I prefented vnto you for his Cawfies. And thus, recommendinge vnto your good Lordfhips this Bearer, my Servaunt, *John Gifford,* whome I have expreffelye fent to attende vpon your Lordfhips Pleafures, for Order for the Receipte of my Quarterage, due the Laft of *Marche* next, to be brought over by hym, who hathe myne Acquittaunce to delyver for the fame, where he fhalbe directed to receive it ; I humblye take my Leave, fearinge I have weried your Lordfhips with my long and tedious Reporte of my pleafureleffe Travell and Toyle in this Province. From *Lymericke,* the 27 of *Februarij,* 1575.

Your honorable Lordfhips affured lovinge
Freinde, humblye to commaund,

H. Sydney

Sir Henry Sydney, *to* William Cecil *Lord* Burghley, *Lord High Treafurer of* England.

My verie good Lord,

FOR that I heare of fome Bruites of an old Miflyke and Mutteringe in the *Englifhe* Pale, after their wonted Manner of Repininge, for the Payment of the Ceffe which is nowe impofed vpon them (as the Cuftomes ever hath bene) towardes the Victuallinge of her Majefties Garrifon : And that it is not vnlike, but that this fecreate Flame will torne, in the Ende, to fome open Fier, if it be not preuented, and fo burft out into greivous Complainte to fomme one or other for Redreffe, and moft lyke, as I thinke, to be brought by Writinge, or Reporte, to your Lordfhips Eares : I thought good, therefore, by Prevencion aforehande, to acquainte your Lordfhip with this Note here enclofed, to the Ende your Lordfhip may feelinglye perceive, both what the Countrie anfwereth in Ceffe to the Soldiour in all Kindes, and what I fhall be forced further to provide for there, out of myne owne Purffe, to fupplye this Chardge of Victuallinge ; which this Bearer, if it will pleafe your Lordfhip to heare hym, I hope will fo fullye fatisfye your Lordfhip by Perticulers, and Degrees of the Whole, as you can defier in any Pointe. And the Matter of Ceffe, my Lord, is of that Confequence, as it muft be ftoucke in, and not yeelded vnto by any Meanes to the Countrie, nor they put in any Comforte to fhake of this Yoke and Burden. It is her Majefties Intereft, and may be, in fhorte Tyme, and good Proceadinge in the Matter, reduced to a certeine yerely Rent, and wil be hereafter fomme Healpe towardes the Alleviattinge of her Majefties bourdenous Chardge of Victuallinge ; which the Soldiour may not beare vpon the Allowance of his Wagies, nor her Majeftie at a greater Chardge to enterteine the Soldiour, then fhe is alreadye ; but the Countrie (as they have alwayes hetherto accuftomed and vfed) muft beare the Chardge of fome Ceffe, or ells certeine Rent (I hope) wilbe levied of them in Lieu of it. But your Lordfhip may perceive, by this, my harde Cafe at my firft Entringe, howe farre this Burthen of Victuallinge is lyke to tourne to my Difadvantage, except I be moch holpen therein, by fkilfull, good, and carefull Minifters, to take vp and provyde all Things in the beft Places of Plentie, where the fame may be fpared, to my moft Profitt and Commoditie ; and yet I looke (be the Matter never fo fkilfullye, well, and carefully delt in by myne Officer) to be a greate Loofer, I finde the Chardge lyeth alreadye fo heavie vpon me. And thus, not beinge fatisfied with my felfe, before I had difcovered vnto you my Bourden, and Greiffe, wherein, when Occafion fhall ferve, I pray your honorable and freindlye Healpe and Affiftaunce, I take my Leave. From *Galway, Marche* 1575.

A Copie of the Note fpecified to be inclofed.

A Proportion of Victualls for Furnifhinge of one hundred and xij Allowances for one whole Yere, *viz.*	Wheate ——— vijC xxviij Pecks.
	Dredge Malt — M iiijC lxvj Pecks.
	Beiffes ——— iiijC xlviij.

A Proportion of Victualls for Furnifhing of 1120 Allowances nowe to be provided for the Tyme aforefaied, *viz.*	Wheate ——— viijM lx Pecks.
	Dredge Malt — xvjM cxx Pecks.
	Beiffes ——— vM lxxvj.

Whereoff

Ceaffed in viij feverall Counties, *viz.*	Wheate ——— M M M Peckes.
	Dredge Malt — iiijM Peckes.
	Beiffes ——— MM.

Off

The which Ceaffe will not be anfwered, *viz.*

In { Wheate and Malte —— Beiffes —— } MM Peckes. iiijC.

And fo

The Ceaffe aforefaied amounteth vnto in the Whole, *viz.* } In { Grayne —— vM Peckes. Beiffes —— iM vjC.

And, therefore,

The Lord Deputie is to provide for the better Parte of the aforefaied Nombre, *viz.* } In { Grayne —— xixM Peckes. Beiffes —— iijM iiijC lxxvj.

Furthermore, if the Inhabitaunts be earneft Sutors to compounde, and delyver Money in Lieu of the Grayne, and Beiffes before fpecified, that then there is no more demaunded of theim, then foch Rates and Prifes as the Markett yeeldeth ; the which is, *viz.* v *s. Sterling* the Pecke of Grayne of eche Kynde, and xx *s. Sterling* for everye Beiffe.

The Rates as the Soldiors be victualled withe in Money, and the Loffe whiche groweth thereof, *viz.* { And if the Soldiour be compounded with for Money to be delyvered vnto theim monethly for their Victuals, then they receive ix *s.* iiij *d. Sterling, le* Piece, *per Menfem,* and do anfwere to her Majeftie but vij *s. Sterling.* So that it may playnelye apeare, her Majeftie doth lofe, for everie Allowance fo delyvered, ij *s.* iiij *d. Sterling per Menfem* ; and *per Annum,* for every Allowance, xxx *s.* iiij *d. Sterling,* which amounteth vnto in the Whole, for iM Cxx Allowannces, } iM iiC xcviij *l.* xiij *s.* iiij *d. Sterling.*

Sir Henry Sydney, *and the Lords of the Councell in* Ireland, *to the Lords of the Councell in* England.

Oure verie good Lords,

OURE Dueties humblye remembred to your honorable Lordfhips : This Bearer, Sir *Nicholas Bagnoll,* Marfhall of her Majefties Armye of this Realme, hath, fince the Recontynuance in his Office and Service here, fo well deferved, as we have good Cawfe to lyke well of hym, and have alwayes founde great Dexteritie, Care, and good Indevour in hym, to anfwere his Chardge fo fullye, as we could not have wifhed a better and more fufficient Man to execute any Thinge, that was either commaunded hym to do, or that was incydent to his Place : He hath, befides, bene a great Stay to thofe Partes where he dwellethe, a bountifull Howfekeper, and a reddye and willing Hoft, to receive any of Accompte, that paffed by him, lienge in the open, and reddye Paffage, to all thofe that have Occafion to repaier to the Northe, either twoe or frooe : He hath beftowed largelye in Buyldinge, enlarged the Towne where he dwellethe, both with Bewtie of Buyldinge and Wealthe, and a great Stay and good Example to his Neighbours, in thofe rude and vncyvill Partes, to induce theim to Conformitie and Order : So that we fynde hym foch a neceffarie Cowncellor and Servaunt to her Majeftie, as his Prefence hence cannot

I

longe

longe be fpared, without Preiudice to her Highnes Service : And, therefore, we are humble Sutors to your Lordfhips (recommendinge foch his perticuler Sutes, as he hath to prefer to your Honnors) afwell to ftand his good Lords in theim, as to difpatch hym thence, with that good Speede, as convenientlye you may, for that he is fo neceffarie a Man for this Service, as he may not longe be abfent from his Chardge. And, even fo, we humblye take oure Leaves. From her Majefties Caftle of *Athlone,* of *Marche,* 1576.

Your good Lordfhips affured lovinge

Freindes to commaund,

H. Sydney, *&c.*

Thomas, *Earl of* Ormond, *to Sir* Henry Sydney.

My veray good Lorde,

YOUR Lettre of the Firft of this Moneth I receaved Yefterday, with Acopie of your Lettre to my Lorde of *Vpperofforrie,* therinclofed : Rendring your Lordfhip my humble Thanckes, for that it pleafed youe to command him to reftore my Tenaunts Goodes of *Teampollmore,* and to haue his Brother *Florence* fourthcomming, to appere before your Lordfhip in *Dublin,* to make Aunfwer to that Outradge commytted by him. And, wheare your Lordfhip hath willed me to fend my Mann and Tenant, *Redmond Morres,* to my Lord of *Vpperofforye,* to be remayning with him as Prifoner, for fuch Demandes as he hath againft him (yf he haue any) or els to bind him to appere before youe : I wold (not offending your Lordfhipp) thinck fowle Skorne to fend him, or any other of my Tenants and Servaunts dweling within my Libertie, or Rule, vnto my Lord of *Vpperofferie,* to be vfed at his Difcreffion ; but, yf he haue any Demand againft the faid *Redmond,* he fhalbe fourthcoming at your Commaundement, to aunfwer before your Lordfhip : So as youe nede not appoint my Lord of *Vpperoffory* to bind him to appeare before you, vnles myne owne Credite be lefs with you then I haue deferved. Thus, humblie praing your Lordfhip not to referr the Hearing or Determynacion of my Caufes from your felf, to thofe that offer me thefe Iniuries in Spoyling my Tenants, I commytt you to the Tuicion of God. From *Waterford,* the viijth of *Apriell,* 1576.

Your Lordfhips Brother to command,

Thomas Ormonde.

My Lord, your felf have requyred me to vfe Playnes in fhowing my Grefe to you, in anye Thing whear in I might think you dèlt vnkindlye with me, as in this I partly do, having my Servant referred to my Lord of *Vpperofforye.* Som other Caws ther is (if hit be true alfo) which I omitt to wryte till my felf fe you ; in the mean Tyme, fufpend Creadit, and think the beft, fo fhall you be leaft defeaved.

The Earl of Ormond *to Sir* Henry Sydney.

My veray good Lord,

I Receued a Lettre this prefent Day, being the 14. of *Aprill,* from youe, wherein hit pleafeth youe to accept my Dealing in Thexamyning of *Moris Crome* ; trulye, the Enformer might haue vfed a better Office, then fo rafhlye to enforme an Vntroth to you ; but for Cutting of thofe, that anoye the County of *Waterford,* bothe borne in the fame, afwell as elfwhere, I haue made a better Ryddance of evell Members, then he is to hir Majeftie : I wyfhe him to do well, and to carry a Confideracion of his Honefty, for any Thing fhall paffe to youe

from

from him. His Sarvis to my felf, afore I put him to her Majeftie, maketh me alfo wyfhe him to deale vprightly. I am nowe to lett your Lordfhip know of the ill Dealing of my Lord of *Upper Offoryes* Brother, called *Kallagh*, who toke a Plowgh of *Garrans*, from a Towne of *Richard Shethes* called *Aghoure*, and left a Hufbandman for dead, the 12 of this Month. Another Brother of his, called *Tirrelagh*, came to a Towne of myne, with a Nombre of Kerne, and there forfably toke Meate within thies thre Nights, being the Day afore (as I am enformed) lyeng in Ambofhe, to wourke fome Villeinye in the Countre. My Lord, he ftill kepith from me the Poffeffion of my Caftell of *Dorowe*. *Donell Mac Shanes* Caftell he ftill kepeth alfo, notwithftanding your Lordfhips Lettres for Deliuery thereof to *Donell*; dyvers brave Speches paft from him, as I heare, which I omitt to write; and truly, my Lord, weare hit not for fom Refpeds, I cowld not well beare to receave fo many Iniuryes as I do. Whereof I humbly pray your Lordfhip I may have prefent Remedy, and fo to Gods Guyding I committ you. At *Kilkenny*, this 14th of *Aprill*, 1576.

Your Lordfhips Brother to command,

Thomas Ormonde and Offory.

This is donn fins the late Spoyll committed vpon my Mann *Redmond Morer.*

Thomas *Earl of* Ormond, *to Sir* Henry Sydney.

My veray good Lord,

I Vnderftand by your Lettres fent to the Sherif of the Countie of *Kilkenny*, that Complaint hath bene of late made to youe, by the Barron of *Vpper Offorye*, of divers Robories, and Spoiles, taken by fumm of this Countrye, from thofe of *Offorye* (as he faid) wherevppon, Yefterday, there was a Meting betwene the Barron, and the Sherif, vppon the Borders of bothe Countries. Where (being defirous to vnderftand, if there were any Caufe of Complaint of the Barons Side) I rod my felf, and founde the chefe Caufe of his Complaint, to be onely, for that the Sherifes Men, by my Commandment, toke certaine Victuals of Men of *Offory*, carreinge the fame away without my Licence, having before (after that your Lordfhip comitted the Chardg of this Country to me) Corne growing to be fcarce, and the People out of all Hope to be releued out of *Englande*, comandid that none fhold carry any out of the Countrye, vppon Paine of Punifhment, and Forfetinge the fame. And meaning to procede further in hering of the Complaints of bothe Sides, my Lord of *Upper Offory*, being chardgid by *Richard Shethe*, for Staing of fumm Victuals bought in *Offory*, by a Man of his, and requiring Reftitucion of a Plow taken from him by the Barrons Brother, he in a great Radg ons or twift gave Mr. *Shethe* the Lye; and thother anfwering him, that, faving his Honnor, he was as trewe as he, the Barron, after fum hott trethning Words in his Anger, departid prefently; which Kynde of Dealing I thought good to aduife your Lordfhip, wifhing that the Barron may be warnid by your Lordfhip to vfe herafter to give better Langadg to fuche as be Gentlemen of honeft Behavior, feking but Iuftice. Thus I humbly take my Leave. From *Kilkenny*, the xviith of *Aprill* 1576.

Your Lordfhips affured Brother to

command,

Thomas Ormonde and Offory.

I do fend vnto you fuch *Frenfh* Newes as wear fent me owt of *Ingland*: My Lord *Howard* and Mr. Secretary *Walfingham* are fent to the King with Thorder. I know your Lordfhip hath more Newes then I, yeat, for Promes Sake, I fend you thefe; your Lordfhip hathe wrytten to me to fend to you fom Menn to apear (as I ges) vpon my Lord of *Vpperofforys* Enformafion. What they are, or whofe Men I know not, nether is hit wrytten in your Lordfhips Letter; two are myne awne Servants, who I woll fe fhalbe forth comming to awnfwer at your Pleafur.

Sir Henry Sydney *to the Lords of the Councell.*

My verie good Lords,

I Firft moft humblye crave Pardon of your moft honorable Lordfhips, that I have not, with more Dilligence, addreffed this my fowerth and laft Provintiall Difcourfe, namelye of *Connaught*; by the which, and the other three before fent vnto you, you may perceive, howe I have occupied my felfe and fpent theife vi Monethes, fince I arryved here, in which I have viewed, and almoft circuled this whole Realme, on everye Syde: But the Cawfe of my Deferringe proceaded, partlye that I exfpected, from Tyme to Tyme, the Arryvall of Mr. *Agarde*, whofe Miffe hath bene no fmall Mayme to me; in this my Travell, and alfo for that I looked to have received fomewhatt from or by *Gefforde*, wherebye I might have bene occafioned more fullye to write to your Lordfhips. But where I looked for Satisfaction, I found Sorrowe, for by Lettres of the laft Paffadge, arryvinge here the xxiiijth of this Prefent, I vnderftoode of his Death, not a little to my Greiffe; for he was to me a kynde Kinfman, and a faythfull fufficient Servant, for whofe Death I feele equall Paffion, and as great Torment of Mynde, as for the Death of a naturall Chylde; but foch are the Accydents of this Woorld, and Croffes to put vs in Mynde, what we are. But to retorne to my Matter, I remember, that in my laft Difcourffe of *Mounfter*, I omitted to write of my beinge at *Kinfale*, where I contynued three Dayes, and went to the old Head, vj Myles diftaunt, beyonde the Towne, which is one of the forticableft Places that ever I came in; and for the Towne, al be it I founde it moche decaied, in Refpect of that I knewe it, by Reafon of the longe and great Vnquietnes of the Countrey; yet, thoroughe the Contynuance of Juftice, and *Englifhe* Governement niere theim, it holdeth his owne well enoughe, and is on the mendinge Hande, the People honeft and obedient; a Caftle they had vpon their Peere, which was all ruyned, and the Peere it felfe greatlye decaied; and theife were the onelye Defence and Garde for their Shippinge, afwell agaynft the Force of the Piratt, as the Furie of the Sea: They prayed fomme Ayde of the Quene, towards the Reedifienge of the fame; and fomme I graunted theim, but in foch Order, with their owne Confents, as they fhall fynde, vpon their owne Cofts, all Manner of Stuffe, Victualls, and Labor, till that Somme of Money, which I gave theim, be onelye exfpended in the Defrayenge of the Wages of Artificers about that Woorke, fo as, with a fmall Chardge to the Quene, I hope a great Woorke fhalbe donne, for the Common Wealth; and I vnderftande it is verye well forwarde alreadie, and I truft fhalbe finifhed this Sommer.

After my laft Difpatche made at *Lymericke*, and fent to your Lordfhips by *Gifford*, I departed thence the 27 of *Februarij*, and fo entered into *Thomounde*, attended on by the Earle of *Thomounde*, Sir *Donell Obrien*, *Teige Mac Murrogh*, *Teige Mac Conohor*, *Tirelagh*, the Earles Brother, and *Donogho Mac Murrogh*; all theife are Gentlemen of one Surname, called *Obriens*, and yet no one of theim Freinde to an other, and fometymes they have ben named Kings of *Lymericke*. Theife are the greateft Doers, and onelye Vndoers, of their owne Countrey and Neighbours, yet fo niere Kinfmen, as they difcended of one Graundfather. I had alfo with me the twoe *Mac Nemarroghes*, by vs called the *Eaft* and *Weft Mac Nemarroghes*, cheife Gentlemen of that Countrey, which, if it were in Quiet, they might lyve lyke principall Knights in *Englande*. There was alfo with me in Companie the twoe Land Lordes of the *Mac Mahons* of *Thomound* and *Olaghlande*: Theife three are Captens and Lordes of large Territories; together with theife were maney other Gentlemen Freholders, and others of meaner Sorte of that Countrie; but, amongeft them all, I could not finde one difcended

of

of *Englishe* Race, yet was that Countrie once the Lord *Clares* of *Englande*, and moft Parte of it poffeffed by *Englishemen*; all theife, and maney more, complayninge vpon the *Obryens*, and eche of theim vpon other, for the Ruyne of their Countrey; and truelye in foch Defolation and Waft it is, as, if they were not a People of more fpare Dyett then other are, both of Fleafhe, Breade, and Drincke made of Corne, it were not poffible that a Soyle, fo wafted, could fufteine theim, and yet maney they are not in Nomber.

I lodged the firft Night, after I left *Lymericke*, in a diffolved Frierie of the Quenes, called *Coyne*, where, by the Earle and Countrey, I was well provided for: The Night followinge, I rather encamped, then lodged, in the ruyned See of the Bifhopp of *Kilmakogh*, where I and my Companie had bad Fare, and woorffe Harbor: Here the Earle of *Clanrickarde* mett me, in verye comelye and cyvill Manner, but immediatly departed from me. The next Day agayne he met me, and fo paffinge into *Oshaghnes* Countrie, where *Thomounde*, beinge of *Mounfter*, confineth with *Connaught*, I came, the fame Day, to *Galway*, where I was to their Powers verie honorablye received and enterteined. And beinge there, as fone as I could gett all theim of *Thomounde* vnto me, havinge lycenzed maney of theim before, to repaier to their Howfies, for their better Furnifhinge to attende me: I entred into Confideracion of their Troubles, Greives, and Loffes, complayned on to me by theim; wherein I founde Plentie of Murder, Rape, Burninge, and Sacraledge, and, befides, foch Spoyle of Goodes and Cattell, as in Nomber might be compted infinite, and in Quantitie vnmeafurable; and in deede, the whole Countrey not able to anfwere a Quarter of that which was affirmed to be loft amongft theim; and yet, by the great Travell of Sir *Lucas Dillon*, who examined everye perticaler Matter, as it was booked, reduced the fame to a reafonable and certeine Quantitie, which the Parties theim felves were dryven to confeffe to be true, and fo, by their owne Confents, Commiffioners apointed, to take the Proffes, and to fee the Goodes reftored to the Loofers. And finding in this Examinacion, that the mutuall Hurtes and Revenges, donne betwixt the Earle and *Teige Mac Murrogh*, was one great Cawfe of the Ruyne of the Countrey: I committed theim bothe, and, after twyfe or thryfe publike Dealinge in their Cawfes, I bounde theim, by Bondes, in great Sommes, to abandon their Countrey, during my Pleafure, as well in Sorte to reftraine theim, as to binde theim to performe foche Orders, as I tooke with theim; whiche they have humblye fubmitted theim felves vnto, and, fince that, obedientlye obferved the fame; and, at that Tyme, I tooke the Earles Brother, and ftill deteine hym in Iron, and *Teige Mac Conoghor* I deteined likewife, vntill he had delyvered a fufficient Hoftage for his good Behaviour. I made Sir *Donell Obrien* Sheriffe of the Shire, and apointed fome other of the Countrie Birthe to be Sergeaunts, Ceffors, and other meane Officers in that Countye; Men that were no evell Doers, and foche, in Effecte, as were vnapeached of any, or complayned of by any: The Countrie yeelded by generall Confent, to be at the Chardge of a Provoft Marfhall of myne Apointement, and geve him Enterteinement both of Wagies and Foode, for hym felfe, xij Horffemen, and xxiiij Footemen; for that the Countrie fwarmed of idle Men, and, by this Meanes, they thought beft to fuppreffe theim. Duringe my Abode at *Galway*, dyvers notorious Malefactors were brought in and executed, and more have bene fince. Commiffioners they were defierous to have to comme amongft theim, and, accordinge to their Defier, I fent theim. *Laftlye*, for that I founde, and proved before theim, the verie Roote and Origine of their Ruyne, was the vncerteine Graunte, and vnftable Poffeffion of their Landes, wherevpon grewe their Warres: I brought theim to agree to furrender all their Landes into the Quenes Handes, for forfeyted I proved it alreadye: So that they affented, that, when foever I wold fende for theim, they wold comme and furrender their Landes, and take it of her Highnes agayne, and yeelde bothe Rent and Service; and hereof I have good Confidence to make a good Reckninge for the Quene. And thus moche for *Thomounde*, a Lymme of *Mounfter*, but in my laft Governement here adnexed to the Prefidenty of *Connaught*, by the Name of the Countye of *Clare*.

I devided

I devided *Connaught* (befides the *Eaft Breanie* or *Oreilies*, and the *Annalye* or *Offerralls* Countrie) into fower Counties ; namelye *Sligo*, which was a Parte of nether *Connaught*, and *Maio*, which was an other Parte of the fame : *Galway*, which was called *Upper Connaught*, and *Roffecommen*, which was called the *Playnes* of *Connaught*.

Out of the Countye of *Sligo* I had nothing but Lettres, but thofe humblye written from *Ochonnor*, affirminge, that he durft not come, for Feare of the Warres, hapned betwene *Odonnell*, and *Con* his Nephewe ; but lewd and malitious Tales rather made hym afrayd, as I take it. He hath vnder his Tyrannie *O Doud*, twoe *Mac Donoghes*, twoe *Ohares*, and *Agare*, and yet he hym felfe trybutarie to *Odonnell*. They be all Men of great Landes, and they fhall not chufe, but yeelde, bothe Rent and Service, to the Crowne ; all, but *Ochonnor* hym felfe, have offered it, and he, to be difchardged of *Odonnell*, will moft willinglye do it ; I loke daylie for *Orwarcke*, whofe Countrie, called *Weft Breanye*, is alfo a Porcion of this Countie, with whome I doubt not but to conclude for a good Rente and Service for the Quene : This Countye, or thefe Countries, are well enhabited, and ritche, and more haunted with Straungers, then I wifhe it were, vnles the Quene were better anfwered of her Cuftome ; and thus moche for the Countye of *Sligo*.

Out of the Countye of *Maio*, came to me to *Galway* firft feaven principall Men of the *Clandonells*, for everye of theire feaven Linagies one, of that Surname, and enhabitinge that Countye, all, by Profeffion, mercenarie Soldiers, by the Name of *Galloglas* ; they are verie ftronge, and moche of the Wealth of the Countrie is vnder theim ; they are able to goe where they will, and, withe the Countenaunce of any meane Lorde of Force, to make Warre with the greateft. Theife humblye fubmitted theim felves, and their feverall Linagies, to her Majeftie, proteftinge, by Othe, and byndinge theim felves by Endenture and Hoftage, never to ferve any, but with Allowaunce of the Governor. Troth it is, I was enformed by dyvers Advertifements, that *Mac William Ewghter* wold not come to me ; and therefore I drewe this Plott, that I wan his cheife Force from hym, in getting theife *Clandonells* : But it fell out otherwife in the Ende, for *Mac William* verye willinglye came hym felfe ; and moche the rather, by the good Perfwafions and Meanes of the Deane of *Chrift Churche*, one of this Counfell, whome I fent into *Connaught*, when I went in *Mounfter*, onelye to founde the Difpoficion of the Potentates, and great ones of that Province ; and therein he did good Service, and furelye fo is he well able, both for his owne Skill, and the Creditt that others repofe in hym ; if it pleafe your Lordfhips to beftowe a thankefull Lettre vpon hym, it will be verie comfortable to the olde Man, which I humblye befeache your Lordfhips to doe. I founde *Mac William* verie fencible, though wantinge the *Englifhe* Tongue, yet vnderftandinge the *Lattin* ; a Lover of Quiet and Civylitie, defierous to holde his Landes of the Quene, and fuppreffe *Irifh* Extorcion, and to expulfe the *Scotts*, who fwarme in thofe Quarters, and in deede have almoft fuppreffed theim ; in fome Proffe whereof, he taried with me moft of the Tyme I remayned at *Galway*, and thence went with me to *Athlone*, and departed not till I went from thence, where verie reverentlye, by Othe, he fhewed his Feaultye, and did his Homage, as humblye byndinge hym felfe, afwell by Othe as Indenture, ever hereafter to holde his Landes of her Majeftie, and her Crowne, and to pay yerelye twoe hundered and fyvetie Markes *Sterlinge*, and to fynde twoe hundered Soldiors, Horffemen and Footemen, for twoe Monethes by the Yere, and to geve theim Foode in that Proporcion, as I truft, in Tyme, fhall fuffice bothe for their Meate and Wagies. In one of his Peticions exhibited vnto me, he humblye befought (doubtinge that I wold have taken away the Bonnaught from the *Clandonells*, which they have of him and his Countrie) that they might (with drawinge it from hym) holde it of the Quene. This Devife was vnderhande practized by me, and they, verie glade of this Overture made by hym, humblye defiered to hold it of her Majeftie ; and fo, by Indenture paffed betwixt the Galloglas and the Quene, they prefentlye doe. This, my Lords, is an Entraunce of no fmall Confequence, bothe

bothe for the Reducinge of the Countrie to her Majesties Obedience, and no small Increase may be made besides to her Commoditie, and the Augmentacion of her Revenue. He received his Countrie at my Handes, by Way of Seneschallshipp, which he thankefullye accepted. The Order of Knighthoode I bestowed vpon hym, whereof he semed verie ioyous; and some other little Triffles I gave hym, as Tokens betwene hym and me, wherewith verie well satisfied he departed: This is all I thought necessarie to write of *Mac William,* savinge that he was desierous I shoulde sende thether an *Englishe* Sheriffe, as I have lykewise donne in all the other Counties within that Province, which, of late, hath bene omitted: *Mac William* protested he wold obey hym I sent, and geve hym Findinge for a sufficient Strength of Men on Horssebacke and Foote; which I accomplished accordinge to his Desier, and sent one with hym. Surelye, my Lords, he is well wonne, for he is a great Man; his Lande lyeth a longe the West North West Coast of this Realme, wherein he hathe maney goodly Havens, and is a Lorde in Territorie of three Tymes so moche Lande, as the Earle of *Clanrickarde* is. He brought with him all his Bretheren, *Mac Phillippin,* who in Surname is a *Bourke,* as he is; and, besides theim, a great Nomber of Owners of Landes and Castells, lienge in the same Countrey: *Omaylle* came lykewise with hym, who is an originall *Irishe* Man, stronge in Galleys and Seamen; he earnestlye sued to hold of the Quene, and to pay her Rent and Service. At that Instant were also with me *Mac Phaten,* of *Englishe* Surname, *Barrett*; *Mac Ivylye,* of *Englishe* Surname, *Staunton*; *Mac Jordan* of the lyke *Dexter, Mac Custelo* of the lyke *Nangle, Mac Morris,* of *English* Surname, *Prendergast*; and theise v shewe Matter of some Recorde and Creditt, that they have not onelye bene *Englishe,* which everye Man confesseth, but also Lordes and Barons in Parliament, as they theim selves affirme; and suerlye they have Landes sufficient for Barons, if they might weeld their owne quietlye; but so bare, barbarous Barons are they nowe, as they v have not three Hackneys to carrye theim and their Trayne Home. There were with me maney more of lower Degree, and no deeper of Wealth, as the Cheife of *Clanandros,* and *Mac Thomyn*; both they, and maney more *Barretts, Cusackes, Lynches,* and of sundrie *Englishe* Surnames, nowe degenerate, and all lamentinge their Devastacion, and with one Consent crienge for Justice and *Englishe* Governement, in so miserable (and yet magnanimous) Manner, as it wold make an *English* Harte to feele Compassion with theim; and thus for the Countye of *Maio.*

Touchinge the Countye of *Galway*; first, I finde the Towne of *Galway* moche decaied, both in Nomber of expert sage Men of Yeares, and younge Men of Warre, in respect of that I have seene; which great Decay hath growen thorough the horrible Spoyle donne vpon theim, by the Sonnes of the Earle of *Clanrickarde,* in so moche as it was evidentlye proved before me, that fiftie Howseholders of that Towne doe nowe enhabite vnder *Mac William Croghter.* And it seameth, they have not onelye lost their Wealth, but with it their Wittes and Hartes; surelye it may well seme they were in Pointe to have geven vp all, and almost to have forgotten that they received any Corporacion of the Crowne; but I trust they are nowe revived, and I hope on the mendinge Hande. Duringe myne Aboade there, the Earle of *Clanrickarde* contynuallye attended on me, and so did the Earle of *Thomounde,* the Archbishopp of *Tweom,* the Bishopps of *Clanfert* and *Kilmagkogh,* and the Baron of *Athenrie,* by Surname *Breminghme,* as poore a Baron as lyveth, and yet agreed on to be the auntientest Baron in this Lande; *Oflahertye, Okelley,* and maney of their Surnames, which are verye great; *Omadden,* and all of any Accompt of that Surname, *Onaughton,* and maney other pettie Lordes and Capteines of Countries, all were with me, confessinge that they ought Service, cravinge that they might hold their Landes immediatlye of her Highnes: Theise are the principall of this Countye, savinge soche as be of my Lord of *Clanrickards* Sute or Surname, as *Oheyne,* originall *Irishe,* and in old Tyme verye great, nowe meane: *Mac Cough, Mac Hubbert, Mac Davye, Mac Edmound, Mac Redmounde*; all theise *Burks,* and many more, but all holdinge of the Earl of

Clanrickarde

Clanrickarde (by due Service, fayeth he) but thorough Oppreffion, fay they, but all longinge for Reformation crye for *Englifhe* Governement and wold fayne hold of the Quene, and her Crowne : Maney other there were, who, for Shamefaftnes, durft not fhewe their Faces, for that they had bene Partetakers with the Earles Sonnes in their moft horrible Rebellion. Theife twoe hopeles Sonnes came into the Churche of *Galway* on a *Sonday*, at publike Service, their lamentablye craved their Pardon, and moft humblie fubmitted theim felves, confeffinge their Fawlt ; and, one of theim fimplye renouncinge his Protection, the other came in of him felfe, without Protection. I fayed as I thought good to theim, reprehended theim, committed theim to my Marfhall, lead them away, and have theim here Prifonners in this Caftle of *Dublin* ; whereat the People comforted greatelye, and were rowfed in Hartes and Mindes to fee this Example of Juftice.

After I had remayned in *Galway* three whole Weeks, I departed from thence the xxiith of *Marche*, and paffed thorough *Athenrie*, the moft wofull Spectacle that ever I looked on in any of the Quenes Dominions, totally burned, Colledge, Parrifhe Churche, and all that was there, by the Earles Sonnes ; yet the Mother of one of theim was buried in the Churche : I toke Order for the Reedifinge of the Towne, and the Woorke is begonne ; and I have taxed for the Satisfienge of the old Inhabitaunts indifferently vpon that Countrie, weyenge the Abilities of eche Perfon, and the Qualitie of their Fawlte, as I thought moft reafonable ; which fhalbe confirmed and ratefied by Order of Commiffioners authorized vnder the Greate Seale, accordinge to the Meaninge of her Majefties Lettre graunted to theim of *Athenrie*, and the Somme of this Taxation amounteth to twoe Thowfand Pounde ; and I doubt not to levye it, and the rather, for that the Earle is entred into Band of v M *l.* to fee afwell this performed, as the firft Order taken at *Lymericke* agaynft his Sonnes, in my Prediceffors Tyme. I have cut the Towne almoft into two equal Partes, it beinge before full as bigge, with a faier high Wall, as the Towne of *Callyce*. I tooke from the Earle, the better to anfwere the Expectation of the People, twoe principall Caftells and Keys of Strength ; the one called the Caftle of *Bellaneflowe*, which ftandeth betwixt *Galway* and *Athenrie* ; the other called *Clare*, and feated betwixt *Galway* and *Mac William Ewghters* Countrie ; and, by this Kind of Proceadinge, havinge greatlye fatisfield the old Inhabitaunts of *Athenrie* ; I went thence with the Earle of *Clanrickarde*, and was verye honorablye enterteined with hym. The next Night I lodged in the *Kellies* Countrie, and the Night followinge in the Caftle of *Roffecommen :* The Countrie is indifferentlye manured, by reafon of the Earle of *Clanrickards* Force, whofe Freindes and Followers farewell, the reft goe to Wracke. The Bisfhop of *Meith* came to me to *Galway*, who affifted me verie well in my Service there ; but of hym I fhall have Occafion to write more amplye to your Lordfhips, when I fhall touche the *Englifhe* Pale ; and thus for the Countye of *Galway*.

I ftayed at *Roffecommen* but a Night, both for that I had apointed Provifion at *Athlone*, which is in the fame Countye ; as alfo, for that I found nothinge there layed in to furnifhe me withall, and therefore willed the Affemblie to be at *Athlone* ; yet, duringe my Abode at *Roffecommen*, *Ochonnor Donne* came vnto me, whofe Aunceftor, they fay, was fometymes called Kinge of *Connaught*. The Caftle of *Roffecommen* I tooke from hym in my former Governement, whofe Aunceftors poffeffed the fame the Contynuance of C xl Yeares, and never came into *Englifh* Men Handes : Vnder his Rule there are *Obyrne* and *Offlun. Ochonnor Roe* came not at me, for Feare I wold make hym make Recompence for Hurtes donne in the Rebellion Tyme ; under hym is *Oflanigan,* but I can have theim when I will, and make theim bothe Arme in Arme beare and drawe, with their Fellowes. *Mac Dermod* was with me, and one vnder hym called *Mac Manus* ; theife People, and fome more pettie Lordes, enhabite the Playnes of *Connaught,* and are all deftroyed by the *Scotts* cheifelye. The Countrie is large, and of excellent Soyle ; the beft, and all the reft Beggars,

I

defierous

defierous to be delyvered from the Tyrrannie of their ftronger Neighboures they all craue to be fubiected to the *Englifh* Governement. A Nomber of perticular Cawfies were ended duringe my beinge at *Athlone*, where I remayned ix Dayes, in which Tyme was executed a notable Rebell of the *Burks*, whome I cawfed to be apprehended in the Countye of *Galway* ; and, by Order of Lawe, (for Burninge comitted by hym in *Weftmeithe*) he was indyted, atteinted, and executed as a Traytor, (whofe Landes I have cawfed to be feifed to her Majefties Vfe) ; and thus moche for the Countye of *Roffecommen*.

I look daylie for *Ochonnor Sligo*, *Orwarcke*, and *Odonnell* and *Con Odonnell*, his Nephewe, and doubt not but fo to agree with theim, as the *Scottes* fhalbe fone banifhed out of that Prouince of *Connaught*. I do not remember any more Partes of the fame vnfpoken of, favinge the *Annalye* or *Offerralls* Countrie, and *Eaft Brenie* or *Oreilies* Countrie : For the firft, they all came to me in verye duetifull and orderlye Sorte, and attended vpon me, duringe myne Aboade in the Countyes of *Roffecommen* and *Weftmeithe* ; yeelded to any Reafon, and, in their owne Countrie, willinglie imbraced the Currencye of the Quenes Writt. At my beinge at *Athlone*, I fent Commiffioners thether to hold Ceffiones ; where good Service was donne by the Countrie, and due Juftice miniftred by the Commiffioners. This Countrie was made Shire Grounde by me, by the Name of the Countye of *Longforde*, and the cheiffe Lordes are bound to pay CC Markes by the Yeare of Encreafe of Revenue ; whereof al be it they were in Arrere for iiii or v Yeares, yet, immediatlye vpon my Demaunde, they paied Parte, and tooke fhort Dayes for Payment of the reft ; and, by the Grace of God, by the Example of theife, the reft fhall followe. From the *Eaft Brenye* or *Oreileys* Countrey, I received all duetifull Offices that reafonablye were to be looked for ; and the Capten of the Countrie is a verye honeft Man, but olde, very impotent, and bedred ; he cannot lyve but a Whyle, by all Likelyhoode ; his Death will brede great Trouble, if, in due Tyme, the fame be not looked to : The Competitors for his Place will hazard the Deftruction of their Countrie theim felves, and their Neighbors : What I fhall do in it, I cannot tell yet, but I meane to diffypate it into more Captenries then one, if I can ; every Way, I doubt not, but it fhall yeeld both Rent and Service to the Crowne, in larger Proportion then ever it did.

By this Tyme I feare I have weried all your Lordfhips with this my tedious Difcourffe of the Particularities of *Connaught*, yet moft humbly I pray the fame, geve Readinge or Hearinge to the reft. In generall, as the Countrie is thus in greate Miferie thoroughe the fainte Proceedinge of Juftice, whyle it was emongft theim, and the totall Withholdinge it fo long from theim fence ; for the which, of verie Compaffion of their Woe, and at the earneft Sute and Crye almoft of theim all, I left amonge theim *Thomas le Straunge*, and *Thomas Dillon*, learned in the Lawes, to be their Commiffioners to determyne Controverfyes amongft them ; and left lykewife *Robarte Damporte*, Provoft Marfhall, to apprehende and execute the Thieves and Deftroyers of the Countrie : They of *Connaught* are willinge (or at leaft fhall not chufe to beare) as maney Men of Warre, as fhalbe neceffary for Suppreffion of any Rebell or Outlawe in that Province. The Quenes Revenue reviued, and that withe cafuall Revenues, will groe niere to beare the Chardge of the Cyvill Magiftracye : In fyne, I am moche deceived, if *Connaught* may not be made to beare his owne Chardges within one Yere and a halffe, fo as a Prefident and Counfell be fent thether to recyde amongeft theim.

And for as moche as I am advertized, that my Lord of *Effex* is minded to come agayme to this Realme, and to beftowe fome more of his Tyme here, I knowe no Man halffe fo fitt as he, if he might be entreated and wonne, to take it upon hym ; and great Pittie it were (in myne Opinion) that fo noble and gallaunt a Sprite, and fo hable a Boddye as he hath, fhould lyve vpon fo fmall a Portion, as he hath here, or a private Lyffe, from publike Function ; I knowe he is held of the People of this Countrey, both in honorable and dreadfull Tearmes ; the good Partes, and rare Vertues, that are in that Noble

Man,

Man, I knowe I nede not to expreſſe to your Lordſhips, for that the ſame are better to be iudged of by you then me ; therefore I will leave to ſpeake of hym any further, but write for the Countrie and my ſelfe, aſſuringe your Lordſhips, my Opinion is, if he come, and be placed in publyke Authoritie, as Preſident with the Counſell in *Connaught*, it will imprinte in their Myndes ſoch a Reſolution of the Quene to reforme theim to their Benefitt, and her Obedience, as I beleve they will fall proſtrate vnder his Feet: For my ſelfe, I ſhall be moſt ioyous of hym, and thinke that I am moche honored by the Companye of ſo noble a Perſonadge, and will ſo imparte with hym, as, without her Majeſties further Chardge, then preſentlye ſhe is contented to be at, he ſhalbe made able to lyve honorablye there ; and ſo his Lordſhip and Sir *William Druerie* ioyninge together, as I doubt nothinge but they will, and, as twoe good Wheeles, holding up the Sowth and Weſt Endes of this Realmes Axeltree : I will ſo deale, I hope, with the Eaſt, and Northe, as the Wayne of *Ireland* ſhall bring Harveſt merelye Home, within very fewe Yeres, thoughe not to *Englands* Gayne, yet without *Englands* Chardge. If I cannot, nor by good Entreatye poſſiblye may not, have the Earle of *Eſſex*, lett me have an other, confeſſinge vnto your Lordſhips, that, if I may not have hym, I am reſolved to be a Sutor for an other. But, if I ſhall have none at all, then looke that the Bodye of the Reformacion of this Realme ſhalbe conveyd as a Carte, that goeth upon one Wheele. And thus moche for *Connaught*, and myne Opynion for the Governement of it ; wherein, I truſt, I ſhewe ſmall Reſpect, either to my ſinguler Ambition or Proffitt.

I departed from *Athlone* the Second of *Aprill*, and lodged by the Way at *Mac Le Straunges, Mollingar*, my Lord of *Delvins*, my Lord Biſhopp of *Meithe, Lawrence Dallahides*, and ſo the xiiiith of the ſame I arryved in this Cittye of *Dublin*, beinge the firſt Entrie I made into it, ſince I landed laſt in *Irelande*, which was the xiith of *September* paſt. By the Way, as I went, Ceſſions were held in the Counties of *Weſtmeithe, Lowthe, Longfforde, Meithe*, and *Kildare*, very good Service donne, and great Obedience ſhewed ; yea, and in myne Abſence I could not almoſt have wisſhed for better Service to be donne, then I found donne of all Handes, that I put in Truſt, aſwell of this as of that Countrey Birthe, and in eſpeciall of my Lord Bisſhopp of *Meathe*, whome I hartelye pray your Lordſhips to thanke in lovinge Manner ; and let the Direction be to his Lordſhip, and to ſoche as I ioyned with him in Commiſſion in myne Abſence, for Gardinge of the Borders of the Pale. I write not to your Honnors the Names of eche particuler Verletts that hath died ſince I arryved, aſwell by the ordenarie Courſſe of the Lawe, the Marſhall Lawe, as flat Fightinge with theim, when they would take Foode, without the Goodwill of the Gever ; for I thinke it no Stuffe woorthie the Lodginge of my Lettres with to your Lordſhips : But I do aſſure you, the Nomber of theim is great, and ſomme of the beſt, and the reſt tremble, for moſt Parte ; they fight for their Dinner ; and maney of theim looſe their Hedds before they be ſerved with their Supper. Downe they goe in everye Corner, and downe they ſhall goe, God willinge, if her Majeſtie will countenaunce me, and your Lordſhips will comforte me and ſoche as I ſhall ſet a Woorke. And thus your Lordſhips hathe by this, and my other three Reportes of my Travell in this Lande, ever ſince the xiith of *September* laſt, vntill the xiiiith of this Preſent, and ſo to doe I meane : During this Yeare, you ſhall here from Tyme to Tyme, wherein, as I hope, you fynde I have not bene idle hetherto ; ſo I truſt hereafter, in the reſt, I will not be ill occupied.

Nowe, my Lords, I feare I have over tyered your Lordſhips with my Woords ſimply conceived, and badlye delyvered ; yet humblye I beſeache the ſame, that you will reade and marke this my fewe Heddes followinge, for the generall Reformation and chardgeles Kepinge of *Irelande* hereafter, which, in Troth, I find feaſible, and with great Confidence hope, to ſee within fewe Yeares brought to paſſe.

I   The

The Hedds are thefe.

The firft is, the Churche nowe fo fpoyled, afwell by the Ruine of the Temples, as the Difcipacion and Imbeafelinge of the Patrimonye, and moft of all, for Want of fufficient Minifters; as fo deformed and over thrown a Churche there is not, I am fure, in any Region where Chrift is profeffed; and prepofterous it feameth to me, to begin Reformacion of the Pollitique Parte, and to neglecte the Religious. The Meane to amend this is eafye, in my Opinion, whereof I have, at fome Length, written to the Quenes Majeftie, and wisfhe that it might pleafe your Lordfhips to acquainte you with that Lettre, and, if you lyke my Device, to further the fame.

The fecond is, an Army muft contynuallye be maynteined heere; and let this be a Maxime with your Lordfhips indifputable, That a Garrifon of 300 Horfemen, and 700 Footemen, may contynuallye be kept here, without any great Chardge to *Englande*, or ells my Aymé fayleth me more, then ever it did in any Thinge hetherto, towchinge the Governement of *Ireland*. This Chardge nowe muft be reared by the newe Rents of the *Irifhrie*, and by an Alteracion of the old Burthen of the *Englifhe* Pale; for though the *Irifhrie* be nowe mollified and malleable, fo that you may have of theim, what reafonablye you will axe; but yet, never without an Armye. The *Englifhe* Pale fhall not be fo moch bourdened, as now it is, in Quantitie of the Chardge, though haplye fomme particuler Men made to beare more indifferentlye with their Neighbours then nowe they dooe; and this will be the woorft Stone in all the Wall, to be well couched; and yet, by the Grace of God, it fhalbe well enough; and with this Nomber of 1000 complete in Garrifon, I will vndertake to kepe *Ireland* in Quiett, and to appeafe all Accydents and Cyvill Stirre, that may ryfe in any Parte, with in the Countrie, by Practife, Rebellion, or otherwife (Strangers and forreine Invafions onelye excepted.) But nowe, me thinke, you will afke me, *Quo modo*, this is to be donne, for in that is all the Hardnes. I could expreffe what I thinke in it, though tediouflye: For, of it, I have had Conference with the Wifeft here; but, becawfe I finde foche an Vnifon in their Opinions, with my Devife, and fo little Abilitie of Contradiction, it maketh me the more miftruft the fame; for hetherto there is nothinge conceived, but of myne owne Invention, no Perrill forefeene, but by myne owne Prevention, nor nothinge in Wisfhinge refolved on, but myne owne Iudgmente; and, findinge foch Imperfection in my felfe, as I do, it maketh me doubt that my Foundacion might be vnfounde, to beare fo great a Woorcke, and fo both Coft and Labor might be loft: Wherefore, if it fo lyke your Lordfhips, I hartelye wisfhe, that it might pleafe her Majeftie to fende hether fower wife Perfonagies, whereof one well acquainted with the Courfe of that grave and moft honorable Counfell, as it might be Mr. *Tremayne*; twoe ftoute and well learned Lawyers, as ij of theife three, *viz.* the Mafter of the *Rolls*, the Attorney Generall, and Mr. *Bell*: Somme one difcreate Countrie Gentleman, as Sir *Edwarde Mountague*; that were able to argue what might be reaped out of a good Soyle quietlye poffeffed: With the Affiftaunce of theife my Harte ferveth me, within the Space of fixe Monethes, to create the Quene a Revenue, fufficient to fynde the Nombre of Soldiers above written. Theife Affiftaunts I wold have here, by the Middft of *September* next; and, although I intende, in the meane Tyme, to whele and torne about, as farre as *Killmallocke* Sowthweftwarde, and *Knockfergus* Northwarde; yet, by that Tyme, I meane to be here agayne. And, by this my Dealinge, I truft your Lordfhips doth fynde, that I am neither greedye of fecreate gotten Gayne, nor vnwillinge to perticipate, with others, publyke deferved Prayfe; but, I perceive, I am fo long on my fecond Hed, that I had almoft forgotten the thirde, *viz.*

That it wold pleafe her Majeftie to fend hether three Lawyers, whereof twoe to be Cheife Juftices of the Principall and Common Benches, and one to be an Attorney Generall of this Realme; this is fo neceffarie, that, if I fhould write a whole Quier of Paper onelye of this Pointe, I were not able to expreffe the Neceffitie of it : But, in fewe Termes, this I affure your Lordfhips, there is none here fo mete for thofe Places, as is to be wifhed, onelye Sir *Lucas Dillon* excepted, who is Cheife Baron. And thus, craving Pardon that I have fo long held you in the Readinge of fo large and tedious a Lettre, I humblye take my Leave, befeaching God, longe in moch Honnor, quiet Dayes, and Happines, to preferve you all. From the Caftle of *Dublin*, the xxviijth of *Aprill*, 1576.

Your honorable Lordfhips affured loving

Freinde to commaunde,

H. Sydney.

Sir Henry Sydney *to* Sir Francis Walfingham, *Secretary of State.*

S I R,

ACcordinge to the Note you fent me enclofed in your Lettres of the xxiiijth of *Januarij* laft, towchinge the Anfweringe of certeine Pointes collected out of her Majefties Inftructions, you fhall vnderftande, that, vpon Receipt of the fame, foorthwith, as fone as I could convenientlye have the Officers vnto me, and namelye, the Auditor, who knoweth moft, and to whofe Office it apperteinethe to vnderftande the State of her Majefties Debts here : I willed hym, accordinglye, to make vp a perfect Booke of all thofe Recknings, both what was dewe by her Majeftie, to whome, and for what Cawfe. His Anfwere was, That al beit, amongft his other Travells and Encombrances, that was his principall and cheife Care, to make a perfect Booke thereof, to be fent and prefented to the Lords ; yet, that he could not do it poffiblye, before he had finifhed the Treaforers Accompte ; which Accompte, he affirmethe, he can not perfectlye goe thoroughe withall, before foche Tyme, as certeine of the Capteins Bills, which were paied in the *Efchequer* there, be retorned hither : Of all which Bills, the Threaforers Deputie hath a Note in what Sorte to receive the fame there. For Delyverie whereof, my Lord Treaforer is to be moved to geve Order to the Tellors, to redelyver thofe Billes backe to the faied Threaforers Deputie, takinge a Bill of his Hande, confeffinge the Receipt of the faied Bills : For otherwife, if he have theim not to fhewe, fomme of the Capteins (without Sight of thofe Bills) will denye Receipt of their Payment.

And, towchinge the Revenues, what Diminucion or Encreafe hath bene made of late Yeres ; the Auditor faieth, that that Woorke is in Hande, but not yet finifhed : Neither (as he fayeth) can he perfectlye ende it, before foch Tyme as the Threaforers Accompte be perfected.

Concerning her Majefties Landes in *Leix* and *Offalye*, I am not yet refolved what Manner of Warraunt it were beft to devife to encreafe her Majefties Rent, and gett her Tenaunts. For, firft, to have meere *Irifh* were verie perrillous ; and of others of this Countrie Birthe fewe there be, that I knowe, of Wealthe, that will be Fermors there. And foch of that Countrie Birthe, as are neadie, and have no Wealthe, I thinke theim not the fitteft Tenaunts heere. And, to procure any thence of Wealthe and Subftaunce, to take Landes, and to plant, and inhabite thofe twoe Countries, I fuppofe it will be a verie harde Reckninge, to bring to paffe ; in fo moche that the Cafe ftandeth thus, in Effecte, hitherto, for thofe twoe Countries, as her Majeftie may be at Choife, whether fhe will geve theim Wagies and Enterteinement to fynde her Lande, or ells her Lande to fynde theim Wagies and Enterteinement ; for I will vndertake for every Pennye fhe receiveth in Rent for Land there, fhee geveth Wagies xij *d.* to kepe that Lande : Yet I will never confent, that the Countrie fhould be habandoned in any Sorte, for helde it fhalbe ; but onelye, herebye to note vnto you by the Way, what a deare Purchafe this is, and hath

bene

I

bene to the Crowne; and, by the Exfample of this, you may iudge of the reft, that are of this Nature.

Towchinge the Lettinge of the *Knight of the Valley*, and the *White Knights* Landes, what hath bene confidered of, and donne therein, and in the lyke Cafe, I referre you to the Reporte of *Launcelot Alfordes* Booke, which herewith I fende you, whofe Travell and Dilligence in this my laft Iorney, and the good Effecte that (I doubt not) will followe of his Travell, I cannot leave neither vnremembred nor vnrecommended vnto you; and pray you, that he may bothe vnderftande from you, and other of the Lords, that his Travell is well accepted, which wilbe both an Encouragement and Comforte vnto him, for trewlye he hath well deferved no fmall Commendacion.

Concerninge the Remayne of the Victualls, I founde none, but that I bought of the Victualler; for it was his owne Store, and not the Quenes, for he tooke the Victuallinge at her Majefties Handes by Compoficion.

For the Advertifement of the Nombers of her Majefties Garrifon in ordenarie Wagies, and in what Places they ferve, the Clarcke of the Checke hath of late (as he enformeth me) fent you a perfect Booke thereof. And nowe, lykewife, I have cawfed hym to engroffe an other, which Courffe, he fhall holde halfe yearelye, that her Majeftie may vnderftand the State of her Armie : The Booke you fhall herewith receive.

Howe this halffe Yeres Affignacion from thence, and the Revenues heere have bene expended, the Auditor hath made a Collection of it, and, in a perticular Booke, made Declaracion thereof; whiche Booke, together with theife, fhalbe delyvered vnto youer Hands. And thus, havinge breifelye yet fufficientlye (I hope) and as fullye as I could for the Prefent, anfwered the Articles you requyred to be advertized, of apperteininge to the principall Pointes, of her Majefties Inftructions delyvered vnto me, which I pray you imparte withe the Lords, with my moft hartye Thankes for youer honorable, courteous, and freindlye Partes towardes me, and my Cawfes, I bid you Farewell. From *Dublin*, the xxviijth of *Aprill*, 1576.

Your affured lovinge Freinde.

H. Sydney.

P O S T S C R I P T.

SIR,

My Nephewe, *Henrye Harrington*, obteined, at her Majefties Handes, a Leafe in Reverfion, of xxx *l*. by the Yere, for the Terme of xxj^{tie} Yeres; by Warraunt whereof, certeine Percells he paffed, in the Tyme of the Governement of my Brother, Sir *William Fitz-William*; and fome Percells he hath yet to paffe, wherein he hath defiered my Furtheraunce, which I wold gladlye graunt hym : But becawfe the Lettre, fent from her Majeftie to my Brother, is not warrantable to me, being fpeciallye addreffed to hym, and to none other Governor, as commonlye Lettres of that Nature, are : My Nephewe, therefore, prayeth you, and fo do I likewife, for hym, entreate you, that the Lettre may be eft fones renewed, and made warrantable, and fo retorned backe, that he may have the full Benifitt of her Majefties Graunte perfected by me. The Copie of the Lettre he obtained I heere with fende you. *Dublin*, xxviij *Aprill*, 1576.

Your, &c.

H. Sydney.

SIR,

Sir Henry Sydney *to Queen* Elifabeth.

May it pleafe your moft excellent Majeftie,

I Have in fower feverall Difcourffies, addreffed vnto the Lordes of your Highnes moft honorable Councell, certified theim howe I founde this your Highnes Realme, at myne Arryval into the fame ; and what I have feene, and
vnderftand by my Travell theife fixe laft Monethes, in whiche I have paffid
thorough eche Province, and have bene almoft in eche Countye thereof : The
whiche I would not fende to your moft excellent Majeftie, immediatlye to be
reade by the fame ; leaft they fhould have feamed to tedious, partelye thorough
the Quantitie of the Matter, but cheifely thoroughe the bad Delyvery thereof,
by my Pen ; not doubtinge but your Majeftie is by this Tyme advertized of the
materiall Pointes conteined in theim.

And nowe, moft deare Miftres, and moft honored Sovereigne, I folye addreffe to you, as to the onelye Sovereigne Salve Gever, to this your fore and
ficke Realme ; the lamentable Eftate of the moft noble and principall Lym
thereof, the Churche I meane, as fowle, deformed, and as cruellye crufhed, as
any other Parte thereof ; by your onelye gratious and relygious Order to be
cured, or at leaft amended : I would not have beleved, had I not, for a great
Parte, viewed the fame, thoroughout the whole Realme, and was advertized of
the perticuler Eftate of ech Churche, in the Bifhoppricke of *Meithe* (beinge the
beft inhabited Countrie of all this Realme) by the honeft, zealous, and learned
Bifhopp of the fame, Mr. *Hugh Bradye*, a godlye Minifter for the Gofpell,
and a good Sarvaunt to your Highnes, who went from Churche to Churche
hym felfe, and found, that there are within his Dioces 224 Parifhe Churches,
of which Nomber 105 are impropriated to fondrie Poffeffions, nowe of your
Highnes, and all leafed out for Yeares, or in Fee Farme, to feverall Farmors,
and great Gayne reaped out of theim above the Rent, which your Majeftie
receivethe ; no Parfon, or Vicar, refident vpon any of theim, and a verye fimple, or foarye Curat, for the moft Parte, apointed to ferve theim ; amonge which
Nomber of Curatts, onelye Eightene were founde able to fpeake *Englifhe* ; the
reft *Irifhe* Preifts, or rather *Irifhe* Roges, havinge verye little *Lattin*, leffe
Learninge, or Cyvilitie : All theife lyve vpon the bare Alterages (as they tearme
theim) which God knoweth are verye fmall, and were wont to lyve vpon the
Gayne of Maffes, Dirges, Shryvings and foch lyke Tromperye, goodlye abo-
lifhed by your Majeftie : No one Howfe ftandinge for any of theim to dwell in.
In maney Places, the very Walles of the Churches doune ; verye fewe Chaun-
cells covered, Wyndowes and Dores ruyned, or fpoyled : There are 52 other
Parifhe Churches in the fame Dioces, who have Viccars indued vpon theim,
better ferved and maynteined then the other, yet but badlye. There are 52
Parifhe Churches more, Refidue of the firft Nomber of 224, which perteine to
dyvers perticuler Lordes, and thefe though in better Eftate, then the reft commonlye are, yet farre from well. If this be the Eftate of the Churche, in the
beft peopled Dyoces, and beft governed Countrie, of this your Realme (as in
Troth it is) : Eafye it is for your Majeftie to coniecture, in what Cafe the reft
is, where little or no Reformation, either of Religion or Manners, hath yet
bene planted, and contynued amonge theime ; yea, fo prophane and heathen-
nifhe are fome Partes of this your Countrie becomme, as it hath bene preached
publikelye before me, that the Sacrament of Baptifme is not vfed amonge
theim, and trewlye I beleve it : If I fhould write vnto your Majeftie, what
Spoyle hath bene, and is of the Archbifhoppricks, whereof there are fower,
and of Bifhoppricks, whereof there are above 30, partelye by the Prelatts theim
felves, partelye by the Potentates, their noyfome Neighbors, I fhould make
too longe a Lybell of this my Lettre ; but your Majeftie may beleve it, that
vppon the Face of the Earthe, where Chrift is profeffed, there is not a Churche
in fo myferable a Cafe : The Miferye of whiche confiftethe in thiefe 3 Particulars,

the

the Ruyne of the verye Temples theim felves ; the Want of good My-nifters to ferve in theim, when they fhalbe reedified ; competent Lyvinge for the Minifters beinge well chofen. For the firft, let it lyke your moft gratious Majeftie to write earneftlye to me, and to whome els, it may beft pleafe you, to examyne in whome the Fault is, that the Churches are fo ruynous ; if it be founde in the Countrie or Fermors, to compell theim fpedilye to goe about the Amendement of theim ; if the Fawlt, for the Churches of your Highnes Inhe-ritaunce, be not in the Fermors, nor they bound to repaier theim (and the moft ruyned of theim are foche as are of your Poffeffion) it may lyke you, to graunt Warraunt that fome Porcion may yerelye, of the Revenue of everye Par-fonadge, be beftowed on the Churche of the fame.

For the *fecond* and *third* ; which is that good Minifters mought be founde to occupie the Places, and they made able to lyve in theim ; in Choyce of which Minifters, for the remote Places, where the *Englifh* Tounge is not vnderftood, it is moft neceffarie, that foche be chofen, as can fpeake *Irifhe*, for whiche Searche would be made firft, and fpedilye, in your owne Vniverfities ; and any found there well affected in Religion, and well conditioned befide, they would be fent hether animated by your Majeftie ; yea though it were fomewhat to your Highnes Chardge ; and on Perrill of my Liffe, you fhall fynde it retorned with Gayne, before three Yeres be expired : If there be no foche there, or not inough (for I wifh tene or twelve at the leaft) to be fent, who might be placed in Offices of Dignitie in the Churche, in remote Places of this Realme then do I wifhe, (but this moft humblye vnder your Highnes Correction,) that you would write to the Regent of *Scotlande,* where, as I learne, there are ma-ney of the Reformed Churche, that are of this Language, that he would prefer to your Highnes fo maney, as fhall feme good to you to demaunde, of ho-neft, zelous, and learned Men, and that could fpeake this Language ; and though for a Whyle your Majeftie were at fome Chardge, it were well beftowed, for, in fhorte Tyme, theire owne Preferments would be able to fuffice theim ; and in the meane Tyme, Thowfands would be gayned to Chrift, that nowe are loft, or left at the woorft : And for the Minifterie of the Churches of the *Eng-lifhe* Pale of your owne Inheritaunce, be contented, moft vertuous Quene, that fome convenient Porcion for a Minifter may be allowed to hym, out of the Fermors Rents ; it will not be moch Loffe to you, in your Revenue, but Gayne otherwife ineftimable, and yet the Decay of your Rent but for a While ; for, the Yeares once expired of the Leafes alreadye graunted, there is no Doubt, but that to be graunted to the Churche wilbe recovered with Encreafe.

I wifhe, and moft humblye befeache your Majeftie, that there may be three or fower, grave, learned, and venerable Parfonagies of the Clergye there, be fent hether, who in fhort Space, being here, would cenfiblye perceive the Inor-mityes of this overthrowene Churche, and eafelye prefcribe Orders, for the Re-paier and Vpholdinge of the fame, whiche I hope, God would confirme ; and I fynde no Difficultie, but that your Officer here might execute the fame ; cawfe the Bisfhopps of that your Realme, to vndertake this Apoftelfhipp, and that vpon their owne Chardgies : They be ritche enoughe, and if either they be thankefull to your Majeftie, for your immence Bountye donne to theim, or zealous to increafe the Chriftian Flocke, they will not refufe this honorable and religious Travell ; and I will vndertake their Guydinge and Gardinge honorablye, and fafelye from Place to Place : The great Defier that I have, to have foche from thence, is, for that I hope to fynde theim, not onelye grave in Iudge-ment, but voyd of Affection.

I moft humblye befeache your Majeftie to accept theife my rude Lettres, as Fygures of a zealous Mynde for Reformation of this your Churche and Coun-trie ; wherein me thinketh I woorke waywardlye, when the latter is preferred before the former. Whan I had thus come to an Ende of this my evill fcriblid Lettre, and beheld the illegiable Lynes, and ragged Lettres of myne owne ftaggering Hand, I was afhamed to fuffer the fame to be fent to your Majef-tie, but made my Man to write it out agayne ; for whiche I moft humblye crave Pardon, as for the reft of this my tedious Peticion. And thus, from the Bottome of my Harte, wisfhing to your Majeftie the longe Contynuaunce of your moft profperous and godlye Reigne over vs, your moft happie Subiectes; as a moft faythfull and obedient Servaunt, I recommend myfelf, and Service, to your moft excellent Majeftie. From your Highnes Caftell of *Dublin*, this xxviiith of *Aprill*, 1576.

Your Majefties faythfull, humble, and

obediaunt Servaunt,

H. Sydney.

The Dutchefs of Feria, *in* Spain, *to her Vncle,* Sir Henry Sydney.

THE Bearer hereof, the Bifhoppe of *Emly*, paffinge by this Court, hath diuers Tymes vifited me, and, nowe defirous to repaire Home to his Countrey, hath required my Commendation to you for him; that ye will, the rather for my Sake, in his needefull Occafions there, fauor and defende him; which I do the more willinglie, becaufe I take him to be very quiett, and alwaies fpekethe great Honor of you, of your Bountie, Pietie, and Clemencie. Wherefore I fhalbe right gladde, that you do finde him the fame, and that he vnderftande his Doinge hereof, to be as gratefull to you, as it hath ben to me; befekinge you that ye will take him for fo recommended; and to vouchefafe him your lawfull and fauorable Protection. Our Lorde alwaies preferue you. From *Madrid*, the xiij of *June*, 1576.

Your lovynge Nes,

during Lyfe,

The Duches of *Feria*.

Sir Henry Sydney *to the Lords of the Councell in* England.

Right honorable, and my verie good Lords,

SINCE my laft Difcourffe of *Connaught*, written the xxviijth of *Aprill* laft, and fent by my Servaunt, *Henrye Catelyn*, I have, greatlye to my Difcontentment, remayned in this Cittie, chiefeliye expectinge the Arryvall of the newe elected Chaunceler of this Realme, and the Prefident for *Mounfter*; of the firft I have harde fomewhat, that he will be at the Waterfyde fhortlye; of the other nothinge, before this Day that he is prefentlye arryved. I hoped alfo to have received, by this Tyme, either Refolution from her Majeftie, or comfortable Advife from your Lordfhips, concerninge the Repaier of the fpoyled Churche of this Lande, and the Governement of *Connaught*, befeachinge your Lordfhips, that, for the latter, you will have fome Regarde to myne Advife, fo longe at it fhall pleafe her Majeftie to imploy me in the Governement of this Countrie: I looked lykewife for Mr. *Waterhowfe*, who, by Reafon of fome extreme Sicknes, hathe ftaied over longe at *Chefter*, and nowe, this Day likewife, arryved, with a Recckninge of my Quarterage dewe the Firft of *Aprill* laft. I cannot but complayne, and lament to your Lordfhips, the great Loffe of Tyme here growen, both thorough this longe Staye of the Threafure, and other Delayes there. For if the Chauncellor and Prefident, before named, had bene here by the Middft of *Aprill* laft, as I defiered, and was promifed they fhould have bene, I could have placed the Chauncellor in his Courte, and the *Englifhe* Pale; travelled thorough *Eaft Leinfter*, the Counties of *Kilkennie* and *Typperarie* (in fome Partes of which there hath bene, and is great Diforder) have fettled the Prefident in the Prefence of all the Nobles of his Province, and a Multitude of others in the principall Cittie of his Iurifdiction, and my felfe, by this Tyme, have bene at, or verye niere *Caricksfergus*: The Delay of whiche hath alreadye

alreadye bred this ; that in *Mounster* fome of the Potentates are fallen to their olde extorcious Abufes, contrarie to their Othe and Covenaunt. In *Vlfter*, *Con Mac Neill Oge* is combined with the *Scotts*, his auntient Ennimies. Thus your Lordfhips may fee, how fone the Sowtherne lyke the Dogge, the Northern lyke the Hogge, mentioned in the moft Holye Booke, are readye to revolte to their innate and corrupt Vyletie ; yet have I held as good Handes over theim as I coulde, being reftrayned in Boddye from the one, and not furnifhed with a fufficient Hedd for the other ; fo, as vntill now, I remayned vnrefolved, by whether Pointe of the Compas I had to wende firft. My Lordes, I feare to offend you with maney Woords, but thees as I doe, Zeale enforceth me to write : I am comme hether to woorke, or, at leaft, to fee Woorke donne, and not to be idle ; but I could not have from thence foche Artificers and Stuffe, before nowe, for the neceffarie Furnifhinge of the Woorke, as this Lande breedeth not : But nowe that fome Treafure, and the Prefident are comme, I will loefe no more Tyme, but on with Spede in my Iorney, for the Setlinge of the Prefident in his Province ; and I truft you will holde me, and my poore Laborers vnder me, for the meane Tyme, excufed ; though wee, to oure little Gayne, the Quenes leffe Proffitt, and the Countries left Good of all, fpende oure Wagies. I fynde, in my Conceipt, moche more to write of this Tenor, but, fearinge that I have contynued the fame to longe, will ceaffe therein ; moft humblye befeachinge your Lordfhips, withe all Spede to expedite that, which I have alreadye written for ; fpeciallye Magiftrates, and Money to be fent by this Bringer, *James Prefcott* ; it is due to me the laft of this Monethe : And I pray your Lordfhips, give ftreight Commaundement, that it come intirelye to me ; if this be not donne, that Money be foorthwith fent, I fhall not be able to hold my Courfe to the North, but, at my Retorne backe, remayne ftill at *Dublin*, a Place of more Delectacion, then any other in this Realme, and where I finde Health and Happines ennough for *Irelande* to yeelde me ; and yet I loth it, for that I knowe I do not the Quene that Service, that, by beinge in other Partes of the Realme, I might doe.

And yet, my Lords, leaft you fhould thinke that I have bene altogether idle, fince myne Arryvall in this Cittie, it may pleafe you to vnderftande, in Parte, what I have donne : There came vnto me thether, fhortlye after *Eafter*, *Owrycke*, *O Donnell*, *Con Odonnell*, his Nephewe and Enemye, *Ochonnor Sligagh*, of the principall of the *Okellies* ; and all theife for Matter of great Confequence, to be ordered betwene the State and theim, and lykewife betwixt one an other of theim felves. And firft for *Owrycke*, I found hym the proudeft Man that ever I dealt with in *Irelande*, and vfinge hym thereafter, told hym, that, as he was the Quenes Subiecte, and ought to holde his Lande of her, fo he fhould behave hym felfe in Obedience as a Subiecte, and for his Lande yeeld both Rent and Service, or els I wold place an other in the fame : He faied he wold be a gcod Subiecte, as alwayes his Aunceftors had bene, and fpake verye moch Good of theim and hym felfe, and wold pay foch Rent and Service for his Countrie, as was agreed vpon betwene the Governor and his Father, and alleadged, that he had a Patent at his Howfe for his Lande ; I anfwered hym (as in dede it was true) that I was ignoraunt thereof, but, vpon Searche, I founde the fame entred in the eldeft Councell Booke that ever was made here, in the xxxiijth Yere of Kinge *Henrie the Eight* ; Sir *Anthonye Sentleger* beinge then Deputie ; by which he bounde hym felfe to pay to the Kinge **xx** *l. Irifh* Yerelye, with the Service of fome Horffemen and Footemen, as by the fame apearethe ; of which nether his Father, nor he, ever paied any Thinge, and that he confeffed, offeringe to compound for the Arreragies, and to contynue that Rent and Service ; whiche I made Light of, and lighter of the former Compoficion, and wold not agree vnder three hundered Markes *Sterlinge* Yerelye. Befides Service, and Findinge of Men of Warre, he offered fixefkore Poundes *Sterlinge* ; all which I refuzed, left, he beinge fo great a Man, as he is reputed to be, an overlight Compoficion with hym might be a Prefident of great Hindraunce to the Quene, in compoundinge with others, afwell in *Connaught* as *Vlfter*. Finallye, he humblye

defiered

defiered that there might be fent into his Countrie, difcreate and indifferent Commiffioners, to viewe his Countrie, and to certifie trewlye the Waft and Barrannes thereof, and therevpon to take Order, and not before : Herevpon we agreed, and that to be donne in *Auguft* next, favinge that he requyred to have certeine pettie Lordes, dwellinge vnder or niere hym (of Duetie his Tributaries fayeth he, vniuftlye oppreffed by hym fay they) to yeeld hym his accuftomed Exactions, namelye, the twoe *Mac Granells*, *Omolindye*, *Mac Glaugh*, *Keneloghan*, *Collofluyn*, *Mac Cahelrewe*, *Obirne*, *Mac Ternan*, and *Mac Amarrowe*. But I would not graunte theim hym, and yet he departed fatisfied, and fince hath both wrytten and fent to me, verye humblye, that I fhall finde hym more obedient in his owne Countrey, then I did in this Cittie ; and thus moche for *Owricke*.

I founde *Odonnell* verie humble and tractable, defierous to be accompted in the Nomber of her Highnes good Subiects ; I put hym in Remembraunce of the Compoficion taken betwene his Brother and me, when I, thorough the Quenes Force, reftored his Brother to his Countrie, beinge banifhed by *Shane Oneill* ; at what Tyme, he agreed for ever to bynde his Countrie to yelde to the Crowne of *Englande* ij C Markes *Sterlinge*, or iij C Bieves, befides Findinge of Men of Warre, both Horffemen and Footemen. He would fayne have forgotten it, faienge it was never afked of hym fince ; but I helped his Memorie, and proved that he him felfe confented to it ; and as a Wittnes, and feconde Perfon of the Countrey, affirmed the Inftrument ; at laft he yeelded, defieringe reafonable Dayes, for Payment of the Arreragies, and indented, by Writinge and Othe, to yeelde accordinge to the former Agreement. And whereas he, and his Aunceftors, have had a Rent of iij C Markes Yerelye out of *Occhonnor Sligaghs* Countrie, fabuloufly chalenged to have bene paied, ever fince St. *Patricks* Dayes, but probablye averred on both Sides, it hath bene taken for theife fower or fyve Difcents by the *Odonnells* (but never without Vyolence alledged *Ochonnor*) and fo I thinke *Odonnell* agreed, in the Ende, to ftay Exactinge of it, vntill I had fent Commiffioners to examyne his Clayme, and the others Deniall ; and, vpon their Certificatt, I to take Order, and this to be donne in *Auguft* next ; which Order, I hope, will fall out to be foche, as the Quenes Majeftie fhalbe entituled to the Rent and Service from theim bothe. *Occhonnor* compounded in *Englande* to geve an hundered Markes Yerelye, to be difchardged of *Odonnell*, and fo hath his Countrey graunted hym, vnder the Great Seale of *England* ; but, if I can clenlye difchardge hym from *Odonnell*, he fhall pay better. He defiered me to conftitute a Sheriffe in his Countrie, wifshinge rather a Forriner, then any of the Soyles Brede, which I graunted, and fent one with Commiffion. I have great Confidence, that this *Ochonnor*, who is the fame that I brought into *England*, will prove a goode Subiecte. Betwene *O Donnell* and *Con*, thus I agreed ; that *Con* fhould have a Caftle, called the *Leiffer*, withe the Territorie to the fame belonginge, whiche he, by his Force and Sleight, furprifed from *Odonnell*, fince his Efcape, and foche other Landes, as the principall Gentlemen of that Countrie will allott hym, and to be declared Heire apparant to the Countrey, and prefentlye to enioye all Commodities incydent to the feconde Perfon of the fame : And thus as they came hether mortall Enimies, in all Apparaunce, and good Semblaunce, they departed hence goode Freindes ; and yet their Freindfhippe not foche, and fo entire, but that as I could, fo yet I can, receive woorthe a thowfand Poundes of eiether of theim foever I will permitt to fuppreffe the other ; but that I deemed neither allowable in Confcyence, nor profitable for Quene nor Countrie. Thus moch for the *Odonnells* and *Occhonnor*.

The *Okellies*, and I are agreed, and Articles of the fame drawne betwene vs, to be perfected at *Michelmas* Terme next ; from which Terme, for ever, they fhall pay for their Countrie, in Rent and Service, better then fyve hundered Markes Yerelye. Duringe my Contynuaunce here, there have come vnto me the Lord *Fytzmorris* of *Kerrye*, *Mac Cartye Reough* of *Carberie*, *Mac Nemarrough* of *Thomound*, and a Number of others from the moft remote Partes of this Realme ; and

and all to feeke Juftice. It is to be reioyced at that they fo doe, but to moche to be lamented, that they have it not nerer to theim. The *Englifhe* Pale, I dare affirme, was never, in Memorie of Man, in better Eftate, favinge for Dearthe of Victuall, which indede, at this Prefent, is verye extreme. The Rebells and Outlawes never in greater Feare, of which Kinde of People, what by Commiffion, ordenarie and extraordenarie, and by Slaughter, in Defence of the poore Hufbandmen, fince my Arryvall, there hath died above fowre hundred Men.

I moft humblye befeache your Lordfhips, geve once a Readinge and Hearing to my Lettres ; it may be, that maney Woordes in theim may feme fuperfluous to your Honnors ; but it cannot be, but that fome in theim are more materiall, then, as it feameth to me, your Lordfhips efteme theim. In *November* laft I writt to your Lordfhips of *Vlfter*, and, in the fame, wifshed the Revocacion of the Graunts made to *Chatterton* and *Malbye*. I was promifed it fhould be donne, but nothinge is donne, and it is the Midft of *June* ; I am to goe thether this Sommer. The *Chattertons* are there, and there they wraftle and woorke, and goe to the Woorffe ; trewlye they are to be pittied, for they be tall and honeft Gentlemen, and have loft, in that Enterprife, all that ever they have, and all that any Boddye els would truft theim withe, and their Bloude and Lyms too. I knowe their Contynuaunce there wilbe an Obftacle to any Proceadinge for the Quenes Proffitt. In that my Difcourffe of *Vlfter*, I made fpeciall Requeft to your Lordfhips for *T. Oneill* to be created Earle of *Clanoneill*, and his Sonne to be Baron of . And lykewife I recommended to your honorable Lordfhips Sir *Hugh Mac Genneffe*, to be created Baron of *Evaugh* ; which Requefts, (as I tooke it) your Lordfhips allowed of (as I gather) by your Lettres of the xxiiijth of *Januarii* laft ; wherevpon I put theim in Comforte of your Lordfhips honorable Intencions towardes theim for their Advancements. And for as moche as they are daylie in Expectancie to receive theife Titles and Tokens of Honnor from her Majeftie (as I have enterteined theim by Promiffe, that they fhall do) I befeache your Lordfhips to be Mediators to her Majeftie, that Warraunt may be fent by me, either by Lettres Patents, or privat Lettre, figned by her Majeftie, of Authoritie and Power to create theim. And withall, that it wold pleafe her Majeftie, of her further Grace and princelye Bountye, to beftowe the Robes, Inveftiture, and Ornaments of Honnor vpon theim ; which, I may affure your Lordfhips, they will accept more humblye and thankefullye, then if her Highnes fhoulde endowe theim with large Poffeffions and Terretories : The Matter is not great, yet of fo great Confequence to theim, as they thinke they have received nothinge without that.

In an other I writt to have Affiftaunce in Counfell of fome from thence, and that but for a Whyle, and to have Perfonagies fent, apt to fupplie the Places of bothe the Juftices, and the Attorney Generall ; which if I have, I doubt not, but to bringe the fyve Shires of the *Englifhe* Pale, to geve to the Crowne of *Englande*, for ever, 2000 *l. Sterlinge* a Yere, to be difbourdened of the Souldiors ; I hold me within my Boundes, and althoughe abfolutelye I affure it not, yet, vpon probable Arguments, and with great Confidence, I coniecture it, and I am affured, the Wifeft in this Lande are of myne Opinion. That donne, there is no Doubt, but that the other Counties, and remote Provinces, will beare a fufficient Garrifon, to fuppreffe the Infolencye of the Natyves of the Soyle, and the Revenue will beare all Cyvill Chardges ; and thus may *Irelande*, that longe hath bene bourdenous to *Engeland*, become beneficiall. In the fame, or in an other, I writte for a Prefident for *Connaught*, which Place, if my Lord of *Effex* will not take, then do I befeache you, that my firft Choyce may holde, which is for Sir *Edwarde Mountagewe* : And fuerelye, my Lords, whofoever hath not, of hym felffe, the Countenaunce and Creditt of a good Knight in *Englande*, is not fitt for that Place here ; and, fince I am in Speache of *Connaught*, I will move your Lordfhips of a Matter I verye latelye knewe ; which is, that the Quene hath latelye geven the Kepinge of the Howfe of *Athlone*, with the Appurtenaunces, to Sir *Edwarde Fitton*, dutinge her Majefties Pleafure : Trewelye I take no Exception to the Gentleman, for wee are good Freindes, but yet I thought foch a Thinge as that fhould not have paffed, without my Privetie ; but, vpon your Refolution for *Connaught*, reuoked it muft be, for, if a Prefident be fent, he, of Neceffitie, muft have it ; if not, but that I muft rule *Connaught*, as nowe I doe by a iorneyinge Juftice and a Marfhall, then I muft, for the moft Parte, be there my felfe ; fo, everye Way, that Patent muft be called in, which, I befeache your Lordfhips, may be foorthwithe. I feare I have weried your Lordfhips ; for, if you be halfe as werye with Readinge of this, as I was with Writinge the Coppie, you will thinke your felves tyred enough for one Day. Thus, prayenge the Almightie to bleffe you all with longe Happines in this Woorld, and eternallye after, I take my Leave, this xvjth of *June*, 1576. From the Caftle of *Dublin*.

Your honorable Lordfhips affured

lovinge Freinde to commaunde,

H. Sydney.

Thomas, *Earl of* Ormond, *to* Sir Henry Sidney.

My veray good Lord,

I Am afhamed to bear the Iniuryes often offered to me by the Baron of *Vpperofforye*. This laft Day, his Servants fpoyled my Tenants Dwelling in *Gawle*, of 300 Kyne and Garrans, at leaft. He never made me pryvye to his Demaund (if anye) he pretended : And, if anye of thofe he fpoyled be by him charged for anye Thing, I will vndertake they fhalbe forthcomming to awnfwer him. My Lord, I pray you lett not this, my kinde Cofynn, vfe to fpoyle me at his Wyll ; you know well inough, I cowld (if I thoght you wold not miflyke of hit) make him repent his Quarreling with me. Truely, if my Lord of *Vpperoffory* did not prefume to moche vpon your Fauor, he wold not deale in this Sort with me. I pray you, my Lord, if you do favor me anye Thing, let the World fe that you miflyk of him for thefe Parts, and wryte your Comaundment to him for Reftitufion of my Tenants Goods prefentlye. So committing your Lordfhip to God, I leave. At *Kilkenye*, the 21 of *Iunij*, 1576.

Your Lordfhips Brother to commaund,

Thomas Ormonde Offory.

Thomas, *Earl of* Ormond, *to* Sir Henry Sydney.

My veray good Lord,

I Receavid two Lettres from your Lordfhip ; thone by Mr. *Davels*, wherin you requirid me to mete you at *Waterford* the xth of the next Moneth, where I will, God willing, waite on you : Thother, towching a Pray, fuppofid by my Lord of *Vpperofforye*, to have ben taken by *Foulk Grace* from the *Kings* Country, and certaine Gerrans taken by *James Oig*, from my Lord. In your Lordfhips Letter, dated the 24 of *June*, fent by Mr. *Sherlock*, you aplye the Words of my Letter fent by Mr. *Sherlock*, in wors Sort then I ether wrote, or ment them, as may apear by hit felf : For I nether wrote you did animate my Lord of *Vpperoffory*, nor that you delt one Way in Aparance, and another Way in Secret and Vnderhand betuene vs, as your Lordfhips Letter porporteth. But my Words wear thefe, as I remember, That, if he did not prefume to moche vpon your Fauor, he wold not haue delt with me as he did. In Wryting this moche vpon Grefe of fo great an Iniurye don me (I hope) I have nether forgotten my Duety to your Place, nor in Frendfhip and good Wyll to

your

your felf, overfhott me fo far, as your Lordfhip femed to take hit, but performed with Playnes, that which your felf wylled me to vfe to you vpon anye
Occafions offered vnto me ; as, vpon this Iniury my Lord of *Vpperoffory* hathe
don, I wrote. If this my Playnes miflyke your Lordfhip, pardon hit, I pray
you, for I vfe hit to thofe I beft loue, and in good Wyll to your felf, not in-
feryor to your Brother *Barnabe*, thogh he cann vfe fweter Words. My Lord,
if, vpon the Going to *Dubling* of my Cofyn *Florence*, you wrote for anye Man
of myne, that I did not fend, I am defeaved ; and, if I awnfwered not your
Letters, I woll acknowledg my felf worthy Blame. He of whome he toke the
Pray fhalbe, as I wrote, forth comminge, if pleas you, now at *Waterford* ;
fo fhall any other, being my Servants. I had a Man flayn Yeafter Night in the
Abay of *Lex*, a tall Gentleman ; by whome, as yeat, I cannot fartenly enform
your Lordfhip, but bad Neghborhod I finde ; whiche, by your Meanes, I hope,
fhalbe amended. Sir *Iohn* of *Defmond* hathe taken, of late, a Caftle, called
the *Grenane*, in *Conaght*, Parcell of my Feefarm, holden of her Maieftye ; I
befech your Lordfhip, command him to deliuer hit to me, or to wayt on you
at *Waterford*, to fhow why he kepeth hit. I am, by thefe fondry Occafions,
dryven moch to troble your Lordfhip, which I am fory for.

I will troble your good Lordfhip no longer with thefe Caufes, till I waite
on you my felf, and fo to Gods Guiding I comitt you. From *Kilkeny*, the
xxviijth of *June*, 1576.

Your Lordfhips affured Brother to command,

Thomas Ormonde Offory.

Sir Henry Sydney *to the Lords of the Counfell in* England.

Right honorable, and my verie good Lords,

I Havinge to longe as me thought, and lothefomelye as I felt, remayned in
Dublin expecting the Comminge of the Lord Chauncellor for this Realme ;
and Lord Prefident for *Mounfter* : Vpon the Arryvall of the Lord Chauncellor, which was the xxiiith of *June* laft, I, together with Sir *William Druerye*,
departed from *Dublin*, the xxvith of the fame, and havinge apointed my Iorney, and intendinge to have paffed thorough *Eaft Leinfter*, and the Countye of
Weixfoorde, to the Cittie of *Waterffoorde*, where I purpofed to have fettled hym
Prefident for that Province, and had for that Purpofe fommoned all the Nobilitie and Potentates, of the fame, to mete me there. Beinge a Dayes Iorney in
my Way thetherwardes, and my Cariage and Provifion, more then one other
Dayes Travell before me ; I was overtaken with Lettres, fraught full of Feare,
fent from the Bifthop of *Meithe*, whome I had left in the Confynes of *Meithe*,
and *Connaught*, for Orderinge of Matters that might arryfe, betwene Partye
and Partye ; lykewife from the Mayor and other perticuler Men of *Galway*, well
affected to the State, and from dyvers other the Quenes good Subiectes, as well
of that Countries, as of the Birthe of this, all cryenge oute, with tremblinge
Tearmes, and lamentable Reportes, that the Earl of *Clanrickards* Sonns, not
without manifeft Confent of their Father, and probablye by Councell of hym,
were in the Night ftolen over the Ryver of *Shenon*, and there caft away their
Englifhe Habitt, and Apparrel, and put on their wonted *Irifh* Weede ; fent to
all their Freindes to come to theim with their Forces, folicited *Scottes*, and other
lofe mercynarie People to ferve theim ; had bene at *Athenrye*, and there facked
thofe fewe poore Howfies, whiche were buylded, fince their late Burninge of
the Towne ; fett the newe Gates of the fame on Fier (which I cawfed to be
buylt, for the better Force and Strength of the Towne, for the Defence of the
Inhabitaunts from Iniurye of the Ennimie, or foddeine Oppreffion) beat away
the Mafons, and other Laborers (which were woorkinge on the Wall, apointed
by me to be made in *Aprill* laft, and nowe in good Forwardnes) and fought
for

for the Stones, wherevpon the Armes were cut, to have broken theim; fwearinge, that none foche fhould ftande in any Wall there; and beinge certified further, that daylye they multiplied in Nomber and Force, in foch Sorte, as if they were not fpedilye refifted (which would not be donne, without myne owne Prefence) not ohelye all the honeft and beft Sorte of that Province fhould be fpoyled; but that the Rebells might, and would do what Mifcheiffe they lifted els where, and the Towne of *Galway* feared Surprifall by Scale, or Famyn by Affiedge. Theife Advertifements I received on *Tuefday* in the Afternoone, and prefentlye I refolved to alter my former intended Iorney, and to addreffe me hetherwarde, and fo came to *Dublin* the fame Night; foche Expedicion I vfed, beinge accompanied with my Lord of *Lowthe*, the Prefident of *Mounfter*, Sir *Lucas Dillon*, and the Mafter of the Ordinaunce, that on *Friday* longe before None I arryved here; and in Trothe, my Lords, founde all theife Reportes trewe, and fent Mr. *Agarde* immediatlye into *Eaft Leinfter*, to prevent the Vnquietnes that thorough theife Occafions might happen there, who fo fubftaunciallye, fpedilye, and foundlye dealt therein; as he not onely left Quietnes there, but brought away *Feaugh Mac Hugh Mac Shane*, the onelye Man to be doubted to make any Trouble or Commotion within his Rule, duringe his Abfence, and within fyve Dayes after, he him felfe came vnto me hether, the vth of this Prefent. I gave Order that my Forces, afwell of the Armye, as of the Countrie, fhould fpedilye followe me, which they moft willinglye and forwardlye did; and the Brute was no foner blowen Abroade of my beinge here (which, in Dede, neither the Rebells dowted, nor the honeft Subjects looked for, with foch Expedicion) but the trayterous Boyes, with their loofe Rafcall and Kerne, and verye fewe other of any Accompte that remayned with theim, came away to the Mointeines: The principall Gentlemen of their Fathers Countrie left theim, and either came or fent to me, offeringe me Loyaltye and Service; all their Freindes els, and foche as they moft prefumed vpon, fayled theim, and offered me lykewife their Service with Fidelitie: Their Father writt to me, faintlye excufinge hym felfe for their Efcape, confeffinge, that he was in Companye with theim, one whole Night, before they paffed over the *Shenon*, in *Mac Coughlans* Howfe, and after in the Howfe of *Vllicke*, his eldeft Sonne, one of the twoe Rebells; proteftinge that he was innocent in the Matter, and not, of Knowledge or Confent, of their Rebellion; and defiered to fpeake with me, fo as he might have Protection, for fafe and free Comminge to me, Remayninge with me, and Departinge from me; which feamed to me an Argument, and fome Manifeftacion in it felfe, of a guyltie Confcyence, and that he doubted his owne Cawfe. Nevertheles, Protection I fent hym in the Ende, but with this Condicion, that before he fhould receive it, he fhould delyver the Poffeffion of his Caftell of *Ballylough Reough*, to the Commiffioners, to be garded, or otherwife vfed, as I fhould lyke beft; and if he would not fo dooe, abfolutelye without Condicion, that then they fhould proclayme both hym and his Sonnes Rebelles, befige the Caftell, and feaze his Goodes, and fpedilye advertife me of their Proceadinge; for by reafon my great Artillerye was in fome Diforder, I could not be there fo fone, as otherwife I would have bene; for I knewe the Place to be ftronge of it felfe, well furnifhed with Victuall, and Munition, and thoroughlye manned. The Commiffioners, I fent to receive the Place, were the Lorde of *Lowthe*, *Thomas le Straunge*, *Henrye Harrington*, and Capten *Collier*, with 150 Horffe, and 300 Footemen; but it feemed the Earle was daunted before their Comminge, for immediatlye, vpon the firft Conference with hym, and Difclofinge of their Commiffion, he delyvered his Howfe to theim whole and entire as it was, without removinge of Munition, Vittayll, or other Goodes, or Moveables, that he had remayninge there, and fo received at their Handes the Protection I fent him; and they, levinge Capten *Collier* withe a Warde in the Caftell, brought hym and the reft of the Bandes and Companies to me, to this Caftell of *Athlone*: And, for that I would make fhort Woorke, I admitted him immediatlye to comme to me, where verie humblye vpon his Knees, he befought Pardon and Grace, for hym felfe, and his twoe Sonnes; I vfed hym

bitterlye

bitterlye ennough, and fo I thought it beft. And demaundinge of hym, what was the Cawfe, he, and his Sonnes, made this vnnaturall Stirre and Commotion ; he anfwered by Proteftacion and Othe, that he knewe no other Cawfe, but that they alleadged foche a heavie Bourden was laied vpon theim, for a Contribucion, towardes the Reedifienge of the Towne of *Athenrye,* as they, and their Followers, were not hable to pay ; which by Order was paffed from her Majefty and your Lordfhips thence, and brought to me, by the Agents of that poore defolate Towne, with expreffe Commaundement to me, that that Order fhoulde be put in Execucion ; and yet nothinge thereof was levied vpon the Countrie, and foche Taxacion as was made to have bene levied, was allowed by their owne Confents ; and in Somme, when I received no other Anfwere from hym, this was my Con- clufion, that I had not to thinke of hym, but as of a guyltie Man, fo demed by his Doinge and Writinge, before, and nowe, confirmed by his cravinge Pro- tection ; and more then the Benifitt thereof, Parte whereof he had alreadye re- ceived, in beinge brought fafe to me, and the reft I would performe, for his lyke Tarienge with me, and Departinge from me, fo the fame were within three Dayes, and more then that I would not promyfe hym. He departed from me penfyve, and hevyelye perplexed, not knowinge what Refolucion to make with hym felfe, and fo remayned doubtfull, a Day or twoe, till Yefterday being *Sondaye,* and the viijth of this *Julye,* after Service donne, in the Parrifhe Churche of this Towne, he came thether vnto me, and there before fondrie noble Men of this Countrie Birth, fixe of the Counfell, and a Multitude befide ; he, in moft lowlye Man- ner vppon his Knees, thanked me, that I in Safetye had fuffered hym to come to me, and openlye in that Affemblye, with verye good Woordes, and lowlye and reverend Speaches, renounced his Protection, and befought Mercye, and Grace, as may appeare by the Coppie of his Submiffion, which herewithe I fende your Lordfhips.

And nowe, my Lords, I dare affirme, I have recovered as good a Pledge as I loft ; for, in fteede of twoe beggerlye baftard Boyes, I have their Father, an Earle, and all his Caftells, yea, Men, and Followers of any Accompte, and all this in leffe then one Weeks Woorke. The Caftell of *Ballyloughreough,* that I have taken from the Earle, is diftant hence xxiiij^tie Myles, and from *Galway* xiiij^en, and almoft the reddye and high Paffage, and Bridge, betwixt bothe. It ftandeth in the Strength and Harte of *Clanrickarde,* and is foch a Place, as may kepe all the Countrie round about in Feare and Subiection : It is diftant from the lamentable ruined Town of *Athenrie,* onelye feaven Myles, and the fame ftandeth in the Midway betwixt *Galway* and it ; and it feamethe, that that kindled their Spite the more, to have any foche Towne where Obedience and Civilitie is profeffed fo niere theim. My Lords, I am perfwaded, if the Quene will but take that which Lawe will geve her, and that which in Polle- cye, Confcyence, and Honnor, fhe may do, fhe fhall, by this Accydent, make her Majeftie a greater Maiftres in *Connaught,* and fo confequentlye in all *Ire- land,* then ever any of her Prediceffors for theife 300 Yeares were : Marye, howe in particuler, I fpare, for a Whyle, to fignifie my Opinion, vntill I fee further of theife mifbegotten Brattes, whome I hope, ere it be longe, to have either quicke in Prifon, dead in the Field, or banifhed the whole Lande. But, when I have donne, if your Lordfhips be fo flowe in fendinge one to recyde in Go- vernement in this Province, as you have bene, bothe for *Mounfter,* and this hetherto ; or not fende one fo quallified, as in my former Lettre I writt, I fhall but trindle *Syfiphus* Stone, and bringe it to the Brymme of the Bancke, and then forced to torne both Head and Hande, and fo, haplye, breake either Backe or Necke ; but that is the leaft Matter. In the meane Tyme, the Quene fhall loofe both Honnor and Treafure, and her People lacke both Diftribucion of Juftice amonge theim, Suretye of their Lyves, and Savinge of their Goodes. Good my Lords, lett me here from you, or procure me Leave to comme over to you. I knowe my Delyverie by Penne is tedious, it may pleafe you there- fore to heare me : This is the fowrth of whiche I have yet received no An- fwere ; the firft by *Gifford,* the fecond by *Catlyn,* the third by *Prefcott,* and this fowrth by *John Cockram.* In this my Expedicion into *Connaught,* I finde howe neceſſarie it is, that this Caſtell be the ſimple Poſſeſſion of the Governor of this Countrie, and therefore humbly beſeache your Lordſhips, that, accordinge to my former Lettres, the Graunt made to Mr. *Fitton* may be revoked ; it is but *Durante beneplacito:* And, if it ſeme not ſo good to you, I pray you ſo advertiſe me, and looke for leſſe good Service at my Hande in this Province.

Though, by this Accydent, I was forced to alter my Courſſe, from the Eaſt, to goe by the Weſt into the Sowthe, yet, God willinge, I wilbe there, and intend to be at *Galway* the xiijth of this Preſent, and at *Lymericke* before the xxiiijth, and yet, at *Carickffergus,* in the Northe, before *Michelmas:* I truſt, my Man *Preſcot,* before this Tyme, hath received his Money, due for me, the Laſt of the laſt Monethe : If I have it not by the Laſt of this Monethe, I have no Foote to move towarde the Northe this Yeare. I have no more, but Almightye God ſende your Lordſhips as pleaſaunt a Progreſſe from the Beginninge to the Ende, as I have had a painefull hetherto ; a happy Progreſſion in all your Proceadings, and Heavens Comforte and Bliſſe at the Ende. In Haſt, from the Quenes Caſtell of *Athlone,* this ixth of *July,* 1576.

Your Lordſhips humble and aſſured

to commaunde,

H. Sydney.

The Copie off the Earle of Clanrickards Submiſſion, as followeth:

WHere vpon this your Honnors Expedicion into theiſe Partes of *Connaught,* to ſuppreſſe the Rebellion, and trayterous Attempts of *Vllicke* and *Iohn Bourke,* the moſt ingrate and wicked Sonnes of me, *Richard,* Earle of *Clanrickard* ; I was ſo far foorth perplexed for myne owne Misfortune, and daungerous Eſtate, that I durſt not repaier vnto your Lordſhips Preſence, without your Honors Graunt of Protection to comme ſafe, remayne with you ſafe, and to departe at my Will and Pleaſure. And nowe that I am ſafelye commen vnto your Honnors Preſence, callinge to Remembrance her Majeſties manifolde moſt gratious Mercyes, whereof I, of all others, have moſt often and bountifullye taſted : Here, I do moſt freelye and voluntarilye renownce, and geve over, the full whole Benifitt and Priveledge of the ſaied Protection ; and, in Teſtimonie thereof, I do here ſimplye ſubmitt my ſelfe vnto your Honnor, to be ordered by your Lordſhip in all my Cawſies, and Accions, as if I had never made Peticion, nor your Lordſhip graunted vnto me the ſaied Protection. And I humblye beſeache your Lordſhip, and all other that be here preſent, to teſtifie with me, that this is my plaine Meaninge and Entent ; which I take God to wittnes, I doo francklye and frelye, in reſpecte of my bounden Duetie. In Wittnes whereof, I have hereunto, in your Preſence, ſubſcribed my Name, the eight Day of *Julye,* 1576, and in the eighteneth Yere of the Reigne of oure moſt dread Sovereigne Ladie, Quene *Elizabethe,* Quene of *England, Fraunce,* and *Ireland,* Defendor of the Fayth, *&c.*

Preſent at this Submiſſion   *R. Clanrickard.*
    theiſe followinge :

P. Lowthe,

W. Drewrie

       Ed. Fitton, Lucas Dillon,

Fraunces Agarde,

      Jo. Garvey.

Sir

Sir Francis Walſyngham, *Secretary of State,* to *Sir* Henry Sydney.

My very good Lord,

BY your Letters of the 20th of *June,* I fynde your Lordſhip doth make very good Acceptatyon of my ſundrye Letters, wrytten unto you : For the which, I have juſt Cauſe to thanke you, for that the moſt Part of them were in Recommendatyon of my Frendes, and whom yt pleaſed her Majeſty to imploye ther in her Servyce under your Lordſhip. From whom I have receyved ſo good Teſtimonye of your moſt honorable and frendely Dealyng towardes them, as I have Cauſe to thinke my ſelf greatly bounde unto you therfor. Bothe Sir *W. Dreurye,* and Mr. *Waterhowſe,* have, by ther ſundrye Letters, deſyered me to thanke your Lordſhip for the ſame. I hope you ſhall fynde them ſo good Inſtruments under you, for the Advancement of her Majeſtys Service, as neyther of you ſhall have Cauſe to fore thinke any Favor you beſtowe on them, nor I, in that I have been a Furtherer towardes ther Imployement. I perceyve, by your Lordſhips Letters, the good Diſpoſytyon you have to uſe the Earle of *Eſſex* well, whoe, I doe aſſure my ſelfe, wyll recompence the ſame, by well Deſervyng any Kyndnes and Favour he ſhall receyve at your Handes. Before his Departure hence, I dyd laye before him the Inconvenience that would enſue, as well for the publycke Servyce, as his owne pryvat, in Caſe ther ſhoold not be good Agrement betwen you : Whoe proteſted unto me, that, thowghe he hopethe to receyve at your Handes all kynde Dealyng, yet, in Caſe you ſhoold myniſter unto him very hard Meaſure, he would ſwallowe up any Injurye, rather then breake out into any Diſagreement : So that I hope, conſyderyng bothe your reſolute Determynatyons, to contynewe good Frendeſhip betwene you : Neyther *Yngliſhe* nor *Iryſhe* Mallyce, or Practyce, ſhall ſeparat you. For other Matters that concernethe the Governement of that Realme, ſo amply have my Lords wrytten unto you, in Awntſwear of the ſundrye Poynts, conteyned in dyvers of your Letters, as I ſhall not neade to ſaye any Thinge. Glad I am, to ſee your Lordſhip write ſo confydently, towching the Hope you have to dyſburden ſhortly, this Crowne, of the intollerable Charges that that Realme puttethe yt unto. I feare that thes newe upſprunge Trobles in *Connaugh* will greatly impeache your former Deſygnes : And yet ther may enſue great Good therof : For hardely can good Herbage proſper, emongeſt evyll and unprofytable Weedes: For yf the Grownde of the Conſpiracye may be by you decyphered, and the Authors therof (of what Qualyte ſoever they be) receyve ther dewe Deſerte ; ytt is the only, and reddye Waye, to reforme *Irelande.* Your great Dylygence uſed in repeyring towardes *Connaughe,* imediatly upon the Newſe of the Erls Sunnes Revolte, is verry well allowed of. We are in great Exſpectation of the Yſſue of thes Trobles, and have ſome Cauſe to doubt they are muche greater, then hetherto they appeare ; for we heare, that one *Angwys,* and Mr. *Connell,* of the *Scottiſhe* Iſles, hath in a Readynes nyne Score Gallyes, for the Tranſportyng of Men, as we take yt, for *Ireland* ; thowghe the Erle of *Darbye,* whoe dyd fyrſt geve Notyce of the ſayd Preparatyon, fearethe ſomewhat to be attempted, in his lyttle Kyngedom of *Man.*

As Tyme ſhall ſerve, I wyll neyther be unmyndefull of the Archebyſſhop of *Dublin,* nor of the other two Byſſhops, *Roſcarburye* and *Ardaghe,* whom your Lordſhip dothe recommende unto me.

Here, at Home, we lyve in Securytye, as we weare wonte, growndyng owre Quyetnes uppon others Harmes. And ſoe having preſently more good Wyll, then Leyſure to wryte, I ende ; beſeching God to bleſſe your Lordſhips

†

ſhips

fhips Governement, with mofte happye and profperoufe Succeffe. At St. Jamefs, the 17th of *Julye*, 1576.

Your Lordfhips to

commaunde,

Fra. Walfyngham.

Sir Francis Walfyngham *to* Edward Waterhoufe, *Efq;*

My good Mr. Ned,

I Have yeelded unto my Lord Deputye my moft hartye Thankes, for his well Ufyng of you, for that I knowe you wyll well deferve. I am forrye for the newe Trobles lately broken out in that Contrye : I have great Caufe to fufpect that yt receyvethe fome Nourysfhement from hence. And, by Proffe, you fhall fynde this Confpyracye generall thorowghe owt *Irelande.* Yet, the Matter being well looked to in the Begininge, which I percevye is the Deputyes Determinatyon, ther may followe great Good therof.

Yf I had a Cypher, I would wryte fome Thing unto you, that I dare not commyt to Letter. I praye you, therfor, fend me one. And fo God keepe you. At St. *Jamefs*, the 17 *Julye*, *A.* 1576.

Your affured Frend,

Fra. Walfyngham.

Superfcribed,
To his lovinge Frend, Mr. *Edward Waterhowfe.*

Sir Francis Walfyngham, *Secretary of State, to Sir* Henry Sydney.

A FTER my hartie Commendacions to your Lordfhip, whereas, by a Lettre of yours, written about *Eafter* laft, you fignified vnto me, that the Beftowinge of th'Office of the Clerkfhip of the Fynes in the Marches of *Wales* was in your Difpoficion, by Vertue of your Prefidentfhippe there, I haue therevppon hethervnto ftayd the Sute which Mr. *Wigmore* made for the faid Office ; though I perceauid in her Majeftie an Inclinacion to graunte the fame vnto him. And now the Gentleman, being defirous to obteyne your Lordfhips Fauor for his Preferment to that Office, hath earneftly craued my Lettres of Recommendacion vnto you vn his Behalf : Which, confideringe Thinclinacion her Majeftie had to do him Good, and the Hope I haue that he will cary him felf very honeftly in th'Execucion therof, I could not denye vnto him, prayinge you to ftand his good Lord herein. Wherby, as I am perfwaded, you fhall affuredly, and for euer, bynde vnto you, a yonge Gentleman, willinge and apt to do you and the Countrie he lyueth in good Seruice. And fo alwayes commending your Lordfhip to God, I take my Leaue. From the Courte at St. *James*, the xxth of *July*, 1576.

Your Lordfhips affured Frinde,

Fra. Walfyngham.

Sir Francis Walfynham *to Sir* Henry Sydney.

My verey good Lord,

Y T is no fmaule Comforte unto your pryvat Frendes, to fee you have fo good Souccefte in your Proceadynges ther, as your verry Ennemyes can not but commende you. How her Majeftie dothe allowe therof, you fhall to your Comforte underftande by my Lords of the Councells Letters. All honeft Men,

I

that

that wyfhe well unto you and to the Reformatyon of that Realme, are of Oppinion, that, as you have ufed Celeryte in quenchyng the Fyer ther lately kyndeled, fo you fhoold profecute the fame with all Severyte. For as lyght Remedyes, for grevouffe and dayngerowfe Dyfeafes, doe rather hurte then cure ; fo fuerly, in the curynge of foche a dyfeafed State as that is, it is a les Offence to offende in the Ufe of overmyche Severyte, then in the contrary. Therfor feing you have Authoryte fuffytyent, and that owre Eares (under Hande) are overmyche open unto *Iryfhe* Advertycements, tendyng to the Contynewance of the dyfordered Governement of that Contrye : Your Lordfhip fhall doe well to execute, fyrft, that which fhall feeme unto you to apperteyne to Juftyce, and to the Removing of the corrupt Membres of that State ; without receyvyng Dyrectyons from hence, and then to advertyfe often of your Proceadyngs. Your Lordfhip lackethe no good Frendes here to ftande with you in your good Caufes, efpecially feing, emongft other Thinges, the End and Scope of your Servyce, is to fpare the Treafure of this Realme, and to make *Ireland* to bear her owne Charges. Yt may be, your Lordfhip may receyve fome wronge Informatyon, touching my late Dealyng in the Reformatyon of the Diforders of *Wales* ; only I fhall defyre you to referve an Eare for me, and then I doubt not but to fatysfye you. And fo I moft humbly take my Leave. At *Whytehawle* the 24th of *Julye,* 1576.

Your Lordfhips affuredly to

command,

Fra. Walfyngham.

Thomas *Earl of* Ormond *to Sir* Henry Sydney.

BEING comm this Day hether, not dowbtinge, by your Lordfhips and Cownfels Order, to have receaved of my Lord of *Vpperofforye* the Caftle and Lands of *Dorowy* ; as I rode to the Bridge to go over to the Hows, 2 of his Men, one named *Nicholas Brenane,* and another called *Donell in Shain,* his Sarvant, met me at the Bridge End, and told me, the Ward that wear in the Hows wold fhote at me if I did enter the Bridge, and that I fhold not have the Poffeffion of the Hows deliuered vnto me. Althogh I was lothe to receave fuche a Flowt, I have thoght good to vfe my accoftomed Pafiens, and forebear to vfe Force, prayeng your Lordfhip to direct your Commandment to the Sherif of the Cownty of *Kilkeney,* to put me in prefent Poffeffion of the fame. The Mill Stones and Irons of my Mill are taken away, fins this Order was by your Lordfhip taken. I hope your Lordfhip will confyder of my Lord of *Vpperofforyes* Dealing hearin as becommeth. So prayeng to know your Lordfhips Pleafur with Speed, I comitt you to God. From *Dorow,* this 13 of *Auguft,* 1576.

Your Lordfhips Brother to command,

Thomas Ormonde Offory.

Sir Henry Sydney *to the Lords of the Councell in* England.

My verie good Lords,

MY Dewtie moft humblye remembred to your honorable Lordfhips, fince the Writinge of my laft, dated at *Athlone* the ixth of *Julye,* and fent by my Servaunt, *John Cockram,* wherein I advertized your Lordfhips of the Committinge of the Earle of *Clanrickarde,* who remayneth nowe clofe Prifoner in this Caftell : The Poffeffion I had of the Caftells of his Countrie, and namely of *Ballylough Reough* ; and that his Sonnes were forfaken of all their Streingth, and fledd to the Mounteines : I departed towardes *Galway,* where after I had made fome fewe Dayes Aboade, comforted the Townfemen, who ftood moche difmaied and fearefull of their State, and to be furprifed ; and taken Pledges of all the Gentlemen of Note, and Free Holders of the Countrie ; and namelye, thofe of *Clanrickarde*. I paffed thence thorough *Thomounde* to *Lymericke*, fetled the Prefident, left him in his Chardge, accompanied and attended vpon withe the Nobilitie of that Province, and dyvers other Gentlemen of Accompte towardes *Cork*, where he remaynethe : Whileft I yet remayned at *Lymericke*, I had fomme Intelligence of a great Confluence of *Scottes* arryved in the Northe, and of greater Nombers expected to comme thence owt of *Scotlande*, and Preparacion of Shippinge and Boates for their Tranfportacion, who were (as it was affirmed unto me af-furedlye) practized withall to ioyne withe Therle of *Clanrickards* Sonnes.   At the firft I gave not fo full Credit to the Matter, till it was eft fones confirmed, and nowe in deed fo fallen owte ; fo that it feameth, by the Sequell, that this Devife hath bene longe in Hatchinge, and fomme further Matter bothe Forren and at Home, then yet hath bene difcovered ; for, fince my Departure thence, theife *Scottes* are comme into *Connaught*, to the Nomber of twoe Thowfand at the leaft : They are ioyned with the Earles Sonnes ; fpoyle and waft the Countrie, and it cannot be intended otherwife, but they doo as moche Harme and Mifcheiffe as they can :   And although I heare not yet that any of the Gentlemen of the Countrie, whofe Pledges I have taken, are ioyned with theim, or any other of Accompte do followe theim but Stragglers, and idle mafterles Men, nor any Place or Holde taken by theim that I tooke when I was there : Yet theire Power is fo greate, as the Force of the Countrie is not hable any Wayes to refift, nor make Head againft theim before my Comminge, which I prepare to doe with all the Spede and Dilligence I can affemble and gather my Forces together ; and intend, God willinge, to be amongft theim my felfe within thefe x Dayes. I leaft there, at my Comminge awaye, for the Garde of the Countrie, *Tho. le Straunge*, with l^{tie} Horffe, and Capten *Collier*, with a Bande of one Hundered Footemen ; planted theim in *Ballilowgh Reough*, which, as I learne, is either al-readye befiedged, or at leaft readye to be : But the Place is tenable, and cannot be wonne, if their Victualls hold out, which, if they wante, it is ther owne Fawlt, for there was enough left to fuffice theim, both Corne, Wyne and Flefhe. All the other Partes of the Realme, thankd be God, are in good peaceable State, and I nowe almoft in Readines to advance towards *Connaught*, to repreffe the Sturres there ; and doubt not, God willinge, fhortlye fo to doe, and to make that Province as quiet as the other Partes of the Realme are, except this Enter-prife have further Backinge, then yet can plainelye be decyphred. And even fo, prayenge the Almightie longe and profperouflye to preferve your good Lordfhips, in all Honnor and Happines, I humbly take my Leave. From the *Queenes Caftell* of *Dublin* the xvth of *Auguft*, 1576.

Your Lordfhips humble and affured

to commaund,

H. Sydney.

P S. I yeelde your Lordfhips, in the dutifulft and lowlieft Manner I can, my humble and harty Thanks for the honorable Confideracion you have had of me in myne Abfence for the Matters of *Wales*, which, erre it be longe, your Lord-fhips fhall here from me in more ample Manner, towchinge the Particularities and Pointes of thofe Cawfies.

The Earl of Ormond to Sir Henry Sydney.

My veray good Lord,

I Receavid a Lettre from youe of the ixth of *Auguft*, which came to me the xviiith of the fame ; wherby your Lordfhip requirid that I fhold give Co-miffion to my Brother *Edward* to levye Men at his Choife, within the Countryes of *Kilkeny* and *Tipperarie*, to make Heade againft the Rebels, till I could put my felf in Areadinefs. Howe thefe may be furnifhed, with him, and others providid
after,

after, to fett forth, I knowe not; but, yf he can provide Men, he fhall not want my Furtheraunce. An other Lettre of your Lordfhip, of the xith of the fame, I receavid the xixth therof, wherin were enclofid certaine Lettres to thofe vnder me, to be in Areadynes the xxiiiith of *Auguft*. I wrote prefently to the Fre-holders of both thofe Countryes to mete me, who I knowe are badly furnifhid for Sarvice: Till I confer with them, I can not certifie your Lordfhip howe fone they fhalbe ready, nor howe long they fhalbe able to victuaill them felves; but this is the worft Tyme of the Yeare, for that their old Corne is holye fpent, and the newe, not as yet able to be cutt. So committinge your good Lordfhipp to Godds Guiding, I take my Leave. From the *Carricke* the xxth of *Auguft*, 1576.

Your Lordfhips Brother to commaund,

Thomas Ormonde, Offory.

I wrote to your Lordfhip, how my Lord of *Vpperoffory* kept the Caftle at *Doro* Bridge from me, whearof I receaved no Awnfwer; I pray your Lordfhip com-mand him to deliuer hit; or, if he do not, command the Sherif of the Cownty of *Kilkenye* to put me in Poffeffion of hit.

The Earl of Ormond *to Sir* Henry Sydney.

My ueray good Lord,

HIT pleafed you, at my Sute the other Day, goinge from *Caftle Dermot*, to alow of my Frend, Mr. *Richard Aylward*, to be fecond Iuftice in *Mown-fter*, of which your Lordfhips Goodnes to him I gave him to vnderftand; your Lordfhip then requyred, that I wold procure my Lord Prefedent of *Mownfters* Letter, declaring his Acfeptance of him, whofe Confent, as I told you, I had afore I moved hit to you. Now vnderftanding, that fom other is erneft for the fame, I thought good to put your Lordfhip in Remembrance of this moche paffed, and humbly pray you to beftow the Office vpon him, according to the good Opinyon I did finde you held of him, when I moved this Sute vnto you. So comitting your Lordfhip to Gods Guyding, I humbly take Leave. At *Ka-rick*, this Laft of *Awguft*, 1576.

Your Lordfhips Brother to commaund,

Thomas Ormonde, Offory.

I did pray the Mafter of the *Rolls* to put your Lordfhip in Remembrans of this Matter, knowing ther wear fom others, Sutors for hit.

Sir Henry Sydney *to Queen* Elifabeth.

May it pleafe your moft excellent Majeftie,

TO vnderftande, that, of late, it hath pleafed Almightie God to call to his Mercye the Bifhopp of *Offorie*, and fo the Rome of that Sea is becomme voyde, and to be nowe by your Highnes conferred. I have therefore thought it my Duetie, moved in Zeale for the Reformacion of the Countrie, and Good of the People, humblye to befeache your Majeftie, that good Care were hadd, that that Churche might be fupplied with a fitt Man, and foche a Perfon, as is acquainted withe the Language and Manners of this Countrey People, might be promoted to fuccede in the Place; of which Nomber I humblye recommende vnto your excellent Majeftie Mr. *Davye Cleere*, one that hath bene long bred, and brought vp in the Vniverfitie of *Oxforde*, a Mafter of Arte of a good Con-tynuaunce, a Man eftemed not meanelye learned, befides well geven in Religi-on, and of a modeft, difcreete Governement, and commendable Converfacion, beinge a Man fpeciallye noted vnto me, by the good Reporte of the Lord Arch-bifhop of *Dublin*, for his Sufficiencye to the Place, with a verie earneft Defier, that

that (the fame beinge the Place of a Suffragan vnder him) the faid *Cleire* might be preferred vnto it. The Bifshoppricke is but a meane Lyvinge, yet a fufficient Findinge for an honeft Man. And, becawfe the foner the Place fhalbe full of an hable Man (foch a one for his Integritie as this Man is eftemed) the greater Fruite will therebye growe to the Churche, Honnor to your Majeftie, and no fmall Hope to be conceived of Good to the People; whereof, as it becommeth me (havinge the principall Chardge of this Realme vnder your Majeftie) I have a fpeciall Care. I write not onelye to your Majeftie in this Cafe, by a Reporte of others, but partlye by Knowledge and Experience I have had of the Man my felfe. And therefore am the more defierous, that your Majeftie fhould gratiouflye allowe of my Commendacion and Choife, and geve Order for his Admiffion and Confecracion, when it fhalbe your Majefties Pleafure to fignifie the fame. And even fo, with my moft earneft and humble hartie Praier to the Almightye, longe and happilie to preferve your Highnes, to reigne over vs, your Majefties humble and obedient Subiects, to our ineftimable Comforts, I humblye take my Leave. From your Majefties Caftle of *Athlone*, the iiijth of *Septembre*, 1576.

Your Majefties moft humble,

faythfull, and obedient Sarvaunt,

H. Sydney.

The Earl of Ormond *to Sir* Henry Sydney.

My veray good Lord,

I Recevid two Lettres from youe; thone of the xvth of *Auguft*, towching *Durro*, came to me the vth of *Septembre*, wherin your Lordfhip wrote, that my Lord of *Vpper Offory* affirmith, that he was, and is redy to deliuer me the Poffeffion of either Houfe or Lande, which was the Bufshops, in *Durro* (being that which your Lordfhip orderid to me.) I require onely the Benefut of your Order; and if I do not fufficiently prove, that the Caftell, at the Bridg Fote, which he kepeth, is Parcell of the Bufshops Land in *Durro*, I will forfeat 500 *l.* I wold hit might pleafe your Lordfhip to give him leffe Credit in this Caufe; he doth but abvfe you with Vntroth, fekinge to detaine my Right. Thother of your Lordfhips Lettres, of the xxxth of *Auguft*, came to me this Day, wherin you willid me to com to the *Skanyn* Side with xxj Dayes Victuaill; I will not faile to be there, God willing, with as convenient Spede as I may, and woll fett forward herehence a *Saturday* next. So wifhing to your Lordfhip all good Succeffe, I moft humbly take my Leave. From *Kilkeny*, the vjth of *Septembre*, 1576.

Your Lordfhips Brother to commaund,

Thomas Ormond, Offory.

Sins my being benethe the *Baro* with my Lord Cancellor, I have had a Toche of the lofe Difeas, that trobleth manye in this Land, and (God willing) hit fhall not lett my Travell at this Tyme.

Sir Henrye Sydney *to the Lords of the Councell.*

My verie good Lords,

M Y Duetie humblye remembred to your honorable Lordfhips. I have received your Lettres, dated at *Weftminfter* the xxiijth of *Julye* laft (which, by Reafon of contrarie Windes and Wether, ftaied on that Side, and came not to my Handes, before the xixth of this prefent *September*) for the which I yeeld to your Lordfhips my humble Thankes, for the honorable Allowance of my fmall Expedicion (foch as it was) made towardes this Province, when the fecrete Fier of this Rebellion was firft in kindlinge; wherein, al be it (I thanke God) my my Travells had, by the fpedie Prevencion of the Tyme, the better Succeffe and lyke Hoope to be conceived by that Iorney of the reddier Quenchinge of the Flame, that it burfte no further owte, then it hath fpred it felfe alreadye, and then was vnder Hande in coverte Woorkinge; yet I never efteemed my good Will and Dilligence in the Service, what foever it was, woorthie fo gratious Acceptacion, as it pleafethe your Lordfhips to geve of it; for the which, eftfones I render vnto you all my moft humble Thanks.

Since my Retorne to this Province, which was immediatlye after the Writtinge of my laft, fent vnto you by Mr. *Bowes*; I have bene ftill occupied, as prefentlye I am, in a Kinde of an actuall Warre, and contynuall Searche for the Rebells; fometymes difperfinge one Parte of my Forces into one Parte of the Countrey, and fometymes into an other, as I was directed by the beft Intelligence where theire Haunte was. But the hollowe Hartes of the Inhabitaunts, and the fecrete Lurkinge of the Rebells, is foche, and hath bene yet hetherto, as I have had no great Hand vpon theim, though I have at fondrie Tymes flayne of their Men, taken their Pray, and fomme of their beft and ftrongeft Holdes from theim. And where, in the Tyme of the Fathers Governement of the Countrie, they cried out of the Sonnes Oppreffions, and their contynuall Extorcions, and Vyolence vfed vpon the poore People; and daylie Complainte was made vnto me againft theim, yet nowe they are fo tender harted (as it feameth) over theim, whether it be for the Hate they beare to vs, and the Governement, or the fecreate Love they beare to the Rebells, or bothe, I knowe not; but loth they are to difcover theim where they are, or to ferve vpon theim actuallye in any Sorte, more then they are by Force and Vyolence compelled vnto; fo that this Service is not vnlike to be drawen, into a greater Lengthe, afore the Rebells be thoroughly rooted out, then if there were any true Zeale, or Love in the Inhabitaunts to the Service, it could be. The *Scottes*, when they vnderftoode of my Approche niere the Confines of *Mac William Ewghters* Countrie, where they were then in Campe, fodeinlye they difperfed their Companies, and moft of theim fledd into the Rowte in the Noorthe, and fome remayne ftill in this Province, but fo fcattered, as I cannot yet light vpon theim in Troupes; which if I doe, I hope to make an Ende of the Matter, but if I cannot, whyles I fhall remayne here, by Reafon of their often Flittinge from Place to Place, in foch fecrete Sorte, as I cannot have trewe Intelligence of theim, and where they lurcke: I will appointe the Execucion of that I fhall leave vndone to Mr. *Malbie*, who I hope will fhortlye perfect the Matter. And I purpofe my felf, within fewe Dayes, to march into *Mac William Ewghters* Countrie, and fo into *Sligo*; firft to fettle *Mac William*, who in this Rebellion is the onelye Man of Power in *Connaught*, that hath fhewed hym felfe loyall, and donne beft Service vpon the Rebells; and after I have ftrengthened and placed hym, and repofleffed hym of his Caftells and Holdes, that in theife Sturres have bene taken from hym; vifited *Occhonnor Sligo*, and *Orwoorke*, in their owne Countries, and founded theim, whether I may ftande affured of their Loyaltie, or fufpect their Goodwills and Diffemblinge, and ordered my Forces to lye here or there, accordinge as I fhall fynde their Difpoficions bent to Good or Ill; I meane my felfe to retorne towardes *Dublin*: And the rather, for that I finde that Sufficiency in Mr. *Malbye* everye Way, as I thinke my felfe verie well affifted by hym, in the Service of this Province, being a Man of that Ripenes in Iudgement, and of that Difcreation in Governement, of that Painefullnes for Marfhall Service, and in all fo complete, as I am to render your Lordfhips moft humble Thanks for hym, and doubt not, but that he will prove fo apt an Inftrument, to frame the rude barbarous People of this Province to Obedience, and Civilitie, partlye by Force, and fomewhat by Perfwafion; and cheifelye by the Taft of the Fruites, and Benifitts of Juftice, to be indifferentlye applied to the Curinge of their old feftred Sores, as they will in a Whyle be brought to deteft the Loathfomnes of their former Lyves and Diforders, and imbrace foche wholefome Orders, for Reformacion of theim felves, and the Countrie, as fhalbe devifed for theim. Which will in Tyme, I hope, prove to the great Good and Comforte of the

People, and Honnor and Proffitt to her Majeftie, which is the onelye Marke I cheifelye fhote at, and hope, erre it be longe, with Gods Healpe, to hit it, or els I fhall far miffe of myne Ayme. For the reft I have to write, touchinge the Anfwere of the particuler Pointes of your Lordfhips Lettres, and fo confequent-lye for the State of the Chardge of the Realme for the whole Yere; and for the Matters of *Wales*, wherein I am by your Lordfhips Lettres directed to con-ferre with my Lord Chauncellor, which I cannot convenientlye doo, before my Retorne to *Dublin*, and therefore crave Pardon till then. I meane, God will-inge, to fett downe the Pointes to your Lordfhips at Lengthe, and fo, for the meane Tyme, beinge not a little weried with the toylefome Travall of this weri-fome Iorney, in tracinge and fearchinge the Rebells from Place to Place, and the ill Succeffe I have to light vpon theim. I humblye take my Leave of your good Lordfhips, with my hartie Praier to God, to profper all your honorable Pro-ceadings, to your noble Harts Defiers. From *Galway*, the xxth of *September*, 1576.

> *Your honorable Lordfhips affured,*
>
> *lovinge Freinde to commaunde,*
>
> H. Sydney.

The Cafe of Thomas, *Erle of* Ormond *and* Offorie, *tutchinge Prife Wynes of* Irelande.

KINGE *Edwarde the Third*, by his Lettres Patentes, dated at *Weftminfter quinto die Junij*, in the xlvj Yere of his Raigne, graunted vnto *James But-ler*, then Erle of *Ormonde*, and Theires Males of his Bodie, amonges other Thinges, the Prife Wynes of *Youghell, Kinfaile*, and of all other Portes and Havens of *Ireland*. And after Kinge *Philip* and Quene *Mary* (recytinge the faid Graunte made by Kinge *Edwarde the Thirde*) by theire Lettres Patentes, bear-inge Date at *Weftminfter*, the xjth of *Marche*, in the thirde and fourthe Yeres of their Raignes, graunted the faid Prife Wynes, amonges other Thinges, vnto the faid *Thomas*, nowe Erle of *Ormond* and *Offorie*, and to the Heires Males of his Bodie: And for Lake of fuche Yffve, to the Heires Males of the Bodie of his Graundefather, *Piers Butler*; which Grauntes are all generall, and make no Excepcion of the Prife Wines of Strangers, more then of Denizins. By Force of which Graunte of Kinge *Edwarde the Thirde*, the faid *James*, Erle of *Ormonde*, and his Heires Males of his Body, received Prife Wines, afwell of Straungers, as of Denizins, in the Portes of *Waterforde, Lymericke, Youghell, Kinfale*, and other Portes of the Weft Partes of *Irelande*, that had not their Prife Wines to them felves by former Grauntes: And the faid Erle of *Ormonde* nowe receivethe the faid Prife Wynes, in the faid Portes and Havens of the Wefte, in licke Ma-ner, afwell of Straungers, as of Denizins, by Force of the faid Grauntes; but the Citizens of *Dublin*, and the Inhabitaunts of the Towne of *Drogheda*, clayme, that all Marchauntes Straungers, commenge withe any Wynes to theire Portes, have vfed, Tyme out of Minde, to pay no Prife Wynes, and that alwaies theie have bene difcharged of fuch Prife Wynes.

And alfo theie allege Accompoficion to have bene made by Kinge *Edwarde the Firfte*, with Marchaunte Straungers comenge to the Realme of *Irelande*, whereby he did releafe his Prife Wynes; and, for Prooffe of that Compoficion, fhewed fourth the Copies of certaine Memorandumes of the *Exchequer* of *Ire-land*, makeing Mencion, by Way of Reherfall, of fuch Acompoficion; in fomme whereof, is recited what Cuftomes thofe Marchaunts Straungers fhould pay for Silkes, Scarlettes, Clothe in Graine, and Clothes, and Thinges to be caried by theim owte of the Realme.

And alfo there alledge a Recorde, *Termino Pafche Anno* xxj *Ric. Secundi*; by whiche it apperethe, that a Commiffion was directed to one *Roger Mauclefild*, by whiche he was made the Kinges Collector, to receave and gather **xx** *s.* of everie

† Tonne

Tonne of Wyne ; for whiche, Prifadge fhoulde be due at the Hauen of the Citie of *Dublin*, in any Shipp thither commenge, and to receive ij *s.* of every Tonne of Wynes of Marchauntes Straungers, in any Shipp thither commenge.

Alfo they have an other Recorde, in *primo* of Kinge *Henrie the iiij*th, teſtifienge a Commiſſion, by him to be awarded to *Hughe Frangton*, comaundinge him to enquire, by the Othe of lawefull Men of the Towne and Viſinage of *Drogheda*, what Sommes of Mony for priſeable Wynes, for which xx *s.* was dewe vnto the Kinge of euery Tonne, as alſo for thoſe priſeable Wynes of Straungers, that yelded ij *s.* of everie Tonne, have bene received and leuied, by one *Gotwham in Annis* xxj *et* xxij of *Ric. the Seconde.*

And theie ſhewe further Arecord of a Plee and Judgment vpon an Informacion, brought in the *Exchequer* of *Ireland*, *Anno v. Henrici Quartie*, againſte one *Gulliam de Glauſter*, Burges and Marchaunte of *Burdeux*, for a Cuſtome of ij *s.* of everie Tonne, of xxxiij Tonnes and Apipe, of *Gaſconn* Wynes, diſcharged by hym in the Haven of *Dublin* ; which *Gulliam*, for Aunſwer to the ſaid Informacion, ſaid, that he ſold the ſaid Wines, at *Burdeux*, vnto one *John* of *London*, a Citizen of *Dwblin*, who, by the Lawe, ought to pay Priſe Wynes, and not ij *s.* of everie Tonne without that ; that the Propertie of the ſaid Wynes was in him, after the ſaid Sale ; and the Kinges Sergeante maintened the Propertie of the ſaid Wines to have bene in the ſaid *Gulliam*, when theie were diſcharged at *Dwblin*. And ſo beinge at Iſſue vpon the Propertie of the ſaid Wynes, a Jurie of the Citie of *Dwblin* tried the Propertie of the ſaid Wines to have bene in the ſaid *Gulliam* ; wherevpon he was charged to pay ij *s.* for everie Tonne of the ſame ; vpon which Recorde and Judgement, they do gather, that Straungers ſhoulde pay no Priſe Wynes, but ij *s.* Cuſtome out of everie Tonne.

And alſo theie alledge a Decree, geven at the *Starre Chambre*, in *Englande*, againſte *Pieres*, Erle of *Ormonde*, in *Anno* xix^{no} *Henrici Octaui*, whereby yt was decreed, that the Citie of *Dwblin* ſhould pay no other Priſe Wynes, then theie vſed, or were accuſtomed to pay, vntill the ſaid Erle have ſhewed better Evidences, and Title, to prowe his Right to the ſame. All which Allegations, we of the Queenes Maieſties lerned Councell in the Lawe, whoſe Names be vnder written, havinge ſeene and pervſed, do thinke thereof, as followeth :

Furſte, As to the Preſcription, we thinke it not to be good, for that it is in the Negatiue.

Alſo, for that Priſe Wynes are an aunciente Prerogative of the Crowne, a-gainſt whiche Preſcripcion cane not lye.

And alſo, for that the ſame Preſcripcion hathe bene interruptede, in the Tyme of Kinge *Edwarde the Thirde*, by his Writte : And, in the Time of Kinge *Edward the Fourthe*, by his Lettres Patentes, and lickewiſe by Acte of Parliament, as the ſaid Erle, by Recordes, and other Evidences, hathe ſhewed vnto vs, as more largelie hereafter followethe.

Secondelie, As the ſaid Compoſicion, and generally to all the reſt of the Recordes by them alledged, the ſaid Erle hathe ſhewed vnto vs the ſaid Write, directed by Kinge *Edwarde the Thirde*, vnder his Greate Seale, in *Anno* xxix ^{no} of his Raigne, to the Iuſtice of *Irelande*, declaringe that he was enformed, that Marchauntes, aſwell Denizins of that Lande of *Irelande*, as Straungers, refuſed to pay his Priſes, of Righte due, of the Wynes brought to the ſaid Lande ; and willinge that theie ſhoulde be compellede to pay the ſame Prices, and in that Writte did ſet fourthe the Maner how Priſe Wynes ſhoulde be taken of the Wynes commenge to that Lande ; like wiſe he hathe ſhewed vnto vs, that, in the Tyme of Kinge *Edward the iiij*th, *Anno ſecundo* of his Raigne, Thoffice of Highe Butlerſhipp of *Irelande* was graunted to one Sir *William Welles*, Knighte, by Lettres Patentes, for Terme of his Lief ; in whiche his Patent it apeereth, that he ſhoulde have, by his ſaid Office, the Priſinge of Wynes ; which ſaid

Office,

Office, and his said Title of Prisadge of Wynes, was allowed, by Decree in the *Chauncerie* of *Irelande*, in the Yere aforesaid, whereof he shewed vs Arecord vnder Seale.

Also he hath shewed vs, that, in *Anno tertio* of the same Kinge, the said Office and Title of Sir *William Welles*, and also the Writ of Kinge *Edward the Thirde*, so by hym made in *Anno* xxix^no of his Raigne, were confirmed by Act of Parliament in *Irelande* ; licke wise he hath shewed vs, that the said Office was so graunted vnto the said Sir *William Welles*, duringe the Tyme that *John*, then Erle of *Ormond*, was attainted, for Takinge the Parte of Kinge *Henrie the Sixt.* Which Erle of *Ormonde* was after, in the Tyme of the same Kinge *Edward the Fourthe*, restored to his Blodde, and after had the Office aforesaid, accordinge to his former Title.

Vpon all whiche the Erles Allegations, we thinke suerlie, that the said Composicion, *tempore Edwardi Primi*, yf yt did extend to *Irelande*, as it is dowtefull whether it did, or not, yet beinge made but to endure at the Kings Pleasure, and beinge revocable at his Will, was in deede, by the said Writt of Kinge *Edward the Thirde*, revoked and vndone, and so were the said Prise Wynes of Straungers annexed againe to the Crowne, and beinge so annexed, were graunted to the said Erles Auncestoure, *James*, Erle of *Ormond*, by the said Kinge *Edward the Thirde*, *Anno* xlvj° of his Raigne ; and, after the same Sorte, was the same Revocation of the said Composicion contynued, by the said Lettres Patentes of Kinge *Edwarde the Fourthe* to the said Sir *William Welles*, and, by the said Acte of Parliamente in his Tyme, so as the said Erle, by his said Lettres Patentes, of all Prise Wynes, graunted in *Anno* xlvj^to of the same King *Edward the Thirde*, beinge after confirmed vnto the said nowe Erle, in the Tyme of Kinge *Philipp* and Queene *Mary*, as ys aboue said, may verie well take the auncient and due Prise Wynes, accordinge to the said Writte of Kinge *Edward the Thirde* ; and that, aswell in the said Citie of *Dwblin*, and the Towne of *Drogheda*, as in all the Residue of the said Cities and Townes in the West Partes of *Irelande* ; all which quietelie yeld, and have alwayes vsed quietlye to yeld the same to the said Erle, and his Auncestors, as the said Erle hathe declared vnto vs, and hath shewed vnto vs good Proof of a greate Parte thereof.

Moreover, whereas it appereth, in somme of the said Recordes, alledged by the said Citizens of *Dwblin*, that the said Straungers, in Consideracion of the said Composicion of ij *s.* a Tonne, shoulde yeld dyverse Custtomes for Scarletts, and other Marchaundises, by them to be caried out of the Realme, of which Marchaundises, the best (as Silkes, Skarlettes, Clothes in Grain, Kersies, and all other Clothes speceified in the said Recorde) ar not, nor never were to be had in *Irelande* (as the said Erle hathe enformed vs) and the Custtomes of the Residewe which ar there to be hadd, as Hiddes, Skinnes, Tallow, Waix, courfe Wolle, and suche licke, are but of small Value, in Respecte of the rest, as he also hath declared vnto vs.

Therefore it seemeth, that vpon good Reason the said Composicion was revoked in *Ireland*, and yet remaineth good in *England*, duringe the Queenes Pleasure, and not otherwise.

Also as vnto the Recordes in xxi *Ricardi* ij^di and *Primo Henrici* iiij^ti, it seemethe, that the said Commissions were wrongefully graunted, for that the said Erle of *Ormond* having the said Office of Butleradge (as appereth) the said Prise Wynes and all Dueties therefore apperteined of Right to him ; and then could not the Kinge, of Right, graunte any Commission for the Gatheringe of any suche Duties, or for any Inquirie towtchinge any Gatheringe thereof.

Therefore it seemethe, the said Commissions yssueinge out vnduely were graunted vpon some wronge Suggestion, duringe the Minoritie, Imprisonament, or some Trouble of some Erle of *Ormonde* ; and the later of them in the Time of Kinge *Henrie the iiij*, might be graunted, rather to enquire of the evill Doinges of the said *James Gotenham*, then any Way to entitle the Prince : And so the said Recordes, as we thinke, are no Proof against the Erle. Then as to the

I

Recorde

Recorde of the Informacion in v^to *Henrici quarti*, that maketh rather for Therle, for yt apereth by the Verdict, that the faid *Guilliam* was Owner of the Wynes; and that, to difcharge himfelf of the ii *s.* demaunded, he alledged the Propertie to be in a Citizen of *Dublin*; which had bene averie evell Polici if ii *s.* alon hade bene due, for by that Meanes Prifadge fhould have bene due cliearly by the Citizen for the faid Wyne; whiche Prife Wynes *Guilliam* fhould have lofte by the Seifer thereof, although he hadd difcharged himfelf of the ii *s.* in the Ton. Wherevpon it may be well gathered, that there was not only demaunded of him Prifadge, but alfo the ii *s.* in the Tonne; and therefore he took that Way to eafe himfelf of the ii *s.*

Laftlie; As vnto the Order in *Sterre Chambre,* the fame maketh nothinge againft Therle, for that Order, as we are enformed, was not taken for Marchantes Straungers, but only, as it feemeth, for the Citizens of *Dublin,* that theie fhould pay no other Prife Wynes then theie were accuftomed to pay, vntill better Matter were fhewed, which Decree the Erle faythe he obferveth; for the Citizens (as he faythe) do and alwayes fythens paid theire accuftomable Prifadge, and neither more nor leffe.

The Opinion of the Attorney General and Sollicitor General, in England, *on the Erle of* Ormondes *Cafe, towchinge the Prife Wynes of* Londoners.

THE faide Erle, by Vertue of his Office of Highe Butlerfhippe of *Irelande,* whereof he ys feafed in Fee Taile, ys to haue all the Prife Wynes in all the Portes and Creekes of *Irelande*; where vpon he came, by his Atturney, into a Shippe in the Haven of *Dublin,* to feife the faide Prife Wynes, of whiche Shippe, and of the Wynes therein, one *Roger Winftone* faide he was Owner: But the faide *Roger* faide further, that he was a Merchaunte and Free Man of the Citye of *London*; and that all fuche Merchaunts and Free Men of the fame Citye, ought to be and alwaies haue bene free from the Paymente of anye Prife Wynes, in all the Quenes Maiefties Cities, Townes, and Havens, within her Realmes and Domynions, bothe by Prefcripcion and alfo by Charter; and theire Charter being vewed, ys to this Effecte (as appereth by theire owne Certificate) that ys to faye, that the Citizens of *London* fhalbe quyte of all Prifadge of Wyne. But this *Roger Winftone,* albe yt he be a Free Man of *London,* as he hym felfe faithe, yet ys not he any Citizen of *London,* for that he ys not any Dweller in *London,* nor beareth Scott nor Lotte, nor haithe anye Houfe within the fame Citye, as the faide Erle faithe; whiche Cafe beinge feene and confidered of by vs, of the Quenes Maiefties Councell lerned in the Lawe, we thinke, that yf the Cafe be fo, then the faide *Roger Winftone* ys not to be difchardged, but muft yelde the faide Prifadge of Wyne; for none are to take Holde of the faide Charter but Citizens of *London*; and we thinke none to be Citizens but fuch as dwelle in *London,* and haue Houfes there, wherein they abide and dwelle, at the leafte fomme Parte of the Yere: And yf a Man, tothende to take Holde of this Charter, will paye Scotte and Lotte, althoughe he be not an Inhabitaunte in Forme aforefaid, yet can he not be counted anye Citifen, for that he dothe not inhabite, as ys aforefaide: And yf anye Free Man of *London* fhulde haue all the Libertyes that Citizens can haue, the Quene then fhulde be defraudet of a greate Parte of her Cuftomes and Proffitts in *Irelande,* by the Multitudes of poore Men of *Irelande,* who are Free Men of dyvers meane Crafts in *London,* as the faide Erle enformeth vs: And as to the Prefcripcion, we thinke the fame not to be good, as we haue faide in the faide Erles other Cafe, of Pryfadge of Wynes of Merchaunts Straungers, in *Dublin* and *Drogheda.*

G. Gerrard.
Tho. Bromley.

Hereafter enſueth the Names of ſuch as the Erle of Ormonde *and* Oſſorie, *now at his Goeinge into* Englande, *doth appointe to take Charge of the Countie of* Kilkenie, *in his Abſence; with a Note of their ſeverall Charge. Which Countie the ſaid Erle doth devid into ſeverall Partes, as followeth:*

FIRST from *Dobins* Houſe to the } *Pires Fitz Edmonde* and Mr. *Deane.*
 Blake Water ——— ———
From *Blake Water* to *Currigge* — *Daton* and *Galle.*
In the Baronies of *Knocketoffer* and } *Walter Waylſh* and *Fraunces Lovell.*
Kelles, John Tobins Lande and *Fleddy* lie }
In *Silloleghe,* that from *Lahenegapoll* } Mr. *Sweteman* and *Richard Oge Co-*
to *Benetes* Bridge ——— ——— } *merſord.*
From *Craumneghe Duffe* to the Water } Mr. *Grace* and Mr. *Shartall.*
of *Owtney* ——— ———
Infaſagh, Gluvley, Faſaghdeynyne and } *Donell Mac Shane* and *Phillippe Grace.*
Iddonghe —— —— ——
In the Baronie of *Gawrone* — Mr. *Blanſhvill* and *Cluttvell.*
In *Buttleres* Woode *Fearon Oram* and } *Pires Butler* and *Edmond Guldey.*
Monkes Land —— —— ——

Hereafter enſueth certaine Inſtruƈtions tutching the Charge geven them and others.

FIRST, that the ſaid Erles Deputie, my Lord Vicount of *Mountgarret,* and the Sherif of the Countie for the Time beinge, Aſſiſtaunt vnto him, ſhall have Authoritie, over and aboue thoſe eight Quarters, to remove and puniſhe ſuch of thoſe Gentlemen as ſhalbe ſlake or neglegent in executinge their Charge.

Item, That the ſaid Gentlemen ſhall have full Power and Authoritie to apprehind and puniſh all Vagabondes and idle Perſones remainenge within their Charge, by Impriſonment, or other Waies, at their Diſcrecions.

Item, That the ſaid Gentelmen ſhall cauſe ſuch Gentlemen, dwellinge within their ſeverall Charge, to booke their Men, and to delyver a Copie of thoſe Bookes to the Erles Deputie, and to the Sherif; and that it ſhalbe lewefull for them to fine any that ſhall refuſe ſo to do in ſixe Pounde xiii *s.* iiii *d.*

Item, That all ſuch Idellmen or Gentlemen, as ſhalbe founde vnbooked, may be taken and comitted to her Majeſties commen Goale, there to remain till the next Ceſſions.

Item, Any Borderer that ſhall have his Goodes taken from him, and followes the Traƈt to any of thoſe Quarters, and ſhall ſhewe the ſame to anye the Gentlemen, or other dwellinge within the ſame; that the Townes within the ſaid Quarter wher the Traƈte is followed, ſhall aunſwer the Goods ſo taken and followed, if the Dwellers within the ſame do not put the Traƈte from them; ſo as the Capteines of the Borders doe vſe the like of their Side.

Item, Vpon any the like Occaſion of Traƈte lefte in any of thoſe Quarters, or vpon any Robberie, Murder, or Stelth to be comitted, that all the Gentelmen and Idellmen of that Quarter ſhalbe aunſwerable and attendant at the firſt Crie vpon their Captein in their beſt defenſible Maner, vpon Pain of Impriſonmente, to every one makinge Default, and to be fined everie Time vi *s.* viij *d.* and ſo preſentlie to followe the Traƈte, and apprehend the Offenders.

Item, That in everie Quarter th'aforeſaid Gentlemen having Charge be allowed vi Horſemen and xii Footemen, to be ceſſed vpon Landes ceſſable within the Quarters nightlie.

Item, That the ſaid Gentlemen of the eight Quarters, with all their Force, vpon Warninge geven them, ſhalbe attendant vpon the Erles Deputie, the Lord

Mountgarret, and the Sherif of the Countie as Affiftant vnto him, upon Paine of Imprifonmente, and to be fined for everie Default in xl *s*.

Item, The faid Erles Deputie, the Lord *Mountgarret*, and the Sherif as Affiftant vnto him, fhall have Commiffion to ceffe their Men in any Place within the Countie of *Kilkenie*, as often as any of theme fhall have Occafion of Service; and to do all other Thinges as if the faid Erle were prefent.

Item, For the better Bannifhinge of Idellmen owt of that Countie, that the faid Erles Deputie, the Lord *Mountgarret*, and the Sheriff, as his Affiftant, fhall have Comiffion to parle with Rebelles, and, for the better Reformation of the Countrie, to graunt Protection for eight Daies.

Item, To get Pledges of everie Gentleman that fhalbe thought to have any Traine or Companie in the Countrie, lyvinge in Difcorde.

Item, That the faid Comiffioners fhall not fuffer any Caftelles or Fortes, or any other Faftnes to be made, by any vpon the Borders of the Countrie, without efpeciall Leave of the faid Erle, vnles it be thought to be for her Majefties Service, and the Welth of the Countrie.

My Lord *Mountgarret*, and Sherif of the Countie of *Kilkenie*, take care to fee the Countrie well defended, and gouerned accordinge to the Inftructions before written : And according as you fhall receive further Direction from my Lord Deputie. From *Denmore* the Laft of *September*, 1576.

Your lovinge Cofine,

Thomas Ormonde *and* Offory.

Apud Ludlowe *viceffimo primo Die* Octobris *Anno Regni* Elizabethe *Dei Gracia* Anglie, Frauncie, & Hibernie, *Regine Fidei Defenforis, &c. decimo Nono* 1576.

WHereas the Quenes Majefties Counfaill in the Marches of *Wales* are given to vnderftand, that there are fondrye lighte, lewde, defperate, and difordered Perfones, dwelling and inhabiting within fondrye the Countyes of *Wales*, and the Marches of the fame, that dailye weare, carrye, and beare dyvers and fondrye Kyndes of Municion, Armure, and Weapones, as Lyvery Coates, Shurtes of Male, quilt Dublettes, Sculles, quilte Hattes, and Cappes, *Mores* Pickes, Gleyves, longe Staves, Billes of vnlefull Sies, Swordes, Bucklers, and other Weapones, defencive and invafive, vnto divers Fayres, Markettes, Churches, Seffions, Courtes, and other Places of Affembley, in Affraye and Terror of the Quenes Highnes Subiectes, wherby divers Affaultes, Affrayes, Hurtes, Woundes, Murders, and Manflaughters, hathe bin don, perpetrated, and comitted, whiche this Counfaill conceave the rather to groweby the Incowragement of the vnlefull Weapons and Armor, and by the vnlefull Reteyning of Servaunts, and giving Liveries, contrary to the Queenes Majefties Lawes and Statutes, in that Cafe made and provided. And albeit, fondrye Proclamacions have bin directed from this Counfaill, vnto the Officers of the feverall Counties vndermencioned, that all, and all Manner of Perfons, fhold laye afide their Armor, Municion, and unlefull Weapones, and to weare, beare, or carrye the fame : Yet, they having fmale Care or Regarde therunto, in meare Derogacion and Contempte of the Lawes and Statutes, doe weare, beare, and carrye the fame Weapones, and Armur, facing and bracing the Queenes Highnes quiet, loving Subiects, and to their greate grevous Comitting diuers Outraiges and Diforders, to the Imbolding and Incurraigment of Mallefactors. And where, alfoe, this Counfaill are given to vnderftand, that there are dyvers Sheriffes that have fold theire Offices of Vnder Sheriffes, Shere Clerkes, Bailiffs, Gailors, and Vnder Officers, and have had and receaved for the fame nce fmale Somes of Monye ; by Meane wherof, manifold Briberies, Exaccions,

Comithers,

Comithers, Extorcions, and other Iniuries and Wronges have bin alſo perpetrated and comitted, and the cheeffeſt, meetieſt, and honeſt Freholders,
keapte from Apparaunces at Seſſiones ; and the meaneſt Sorte that are not hable to give Rewarde, and have left Care of their Othes, or are otherwiſe vn-
ableſt to ſerve, are compelled to ſerve, whereby Fellonies and Malefactors eſcape
vnponiſhed, to their greate Incorraigment and Bouldneſs, and the Hindraunce
of Juſtice and Detierment of the Common Wealthe ; and for that this Counſaill are given in Chardge and Comaundement, from her Highnes, and her moſt
honorable Pryvey Counſaill, to have a ſpeciall Eye, Care, and Regarde vnto
the Official Comiſſioners, Chauncellers, and other Spirituall Officers ; by Meanes
of whoſe Negligence in doing their Duties and Offices, incontynent Living
dothe muche abounde, and abhominable Inceeſt and Advlterye creapt in, and
muche frequented in thes Days. And where alſoe vncharitable Exceſſe of V-
ſarye and vnlefull Games ys much vſed, Artillarye and Shoting whiche was
provided for the Defence of the Realme lefte aſide, many Allhowſes, and Tip-
pling Howſes, not leſullye lycenſed nor bounden, keapt and muche haunted ;
Foreſtalling, Regrating, Buing and Silling of Cattelles out of Fayer and Markett dailye vſed, and the Statute of Drovers not dulye put in Execucion, wherby the Price of Cattelles is greatly enhauncid, and pryvellye conveyed and
ſtollen from Place to Place, whiche will tende to the Impoueriſhment and Vndoing of her Majeſties Subiectes, and Encreaſſe of Offendors, if the ſame ſhold
nott in Time be prevented and loked vnto, and the Offendors poniſhed, according to the Order of the Lawe. And, allthoughe there hathe byn ſpeciall
Informacion given vnto this Counſaill of the ſaid Miſdemenors and Diſorders,
and vehement Preſumpcions againſt diuers Perſons ; yett they meane not to
ſend for eny of the Perſons ſuppoſed to be Offendors, before they be truly aduertiſed, and vnderſtand ſome probable Matter againſt theim, of the ſaid Offence.
And, thervpon, to take Order for their Poniſhment, that the ſame maye be a Terror to others not to comytt the like. And for that this Counſaill having made
Choiſe of the Perſons vndernamed, for their Dexterities, Knowlaidges, Wiſdomes,
and Vpprightnes, thinke good to putt them in Remembrance, that they have
a carefull Eye and Regarde vnto the Premiſſes, that neither for Affeccion, nor Curruption, they wincke at any of the ſaid Offences or Offendors,
nor yet for Malice nor Diſpleaſure, to vexe or troble eny innocent Perſone, nor eny Manns Fault, but vprightly, circumſpectlye, and dilligentlye
enquier and trye out the Offences, and Offendors. It is therefore conſidered and ordered, that ſeverall Letters be directed vnto the Gentlemen
vndernamed, of the ſeverall Counties vndermencioned, or any twoe of them,
whereof *Richard Vaughan*, Eſquire, the Quenes Highnes Solicitor attending
this Counſaill, to be one, mencioning the Premiſſes, comaunding them aſwell
within Libertyes as without, by all the Wayes and Meanes they canne, aſwell
by Examinacion of Wittneſſes vpon theire Othes, as otherwiſe, to learne and
trye out aſwell who are, have bin, or ſhalbe, in the mean Time, of the Retorne of thes Letters, the Wearers, Carriers, or Bearers, of eny Municion, Armor, or Weapones, and the Time certaine of the wearing, carreing, and bearing
of the ſaid Municion, Armor, or Weapones, and vnto what Churche, Fayor,
Market, Seſſions, Corte, or other Place of Aſſemblie, prohibited by eny Lawe
or Statute : And what Goodes, Cattelles, Mony, Corne, or any other Thing,
any Officer or Officers, ſpirituall or temporall, or any other Perſone or Perſones,
have levied, or gathered, by Way of Comither, Exaccion, Extorcion, or Bry-
bery, whoe hawe offended againſt the Statute of Retainers, and wherein, with
the certaine Manor thereof, the Statute of wnlefull Games, the Statute of Artillary ; whoe are the Keaperes of Tipling Howſes, and alle Howſes without
Licences, unlefull Droving, Regrating, Forſtalling, Buing and Selling of Cattell
without Licens and whither eny were boughte out of Fayor and Markett ; whoe
were the Buyers thereof : Alſoe to enquier of all incontinent Living, Inceſt, and
Adultory

Adultory and Fornicacion, and whoe have offendid againſt the Statute of Vſerie, when, and at what Time, howe, and by what Meanes ; and for howe much Mony, upon what Bargaine and Contracte, and the certaine Maner therof ; what Aſſaults, Affrayes, Murders, Manſlaughters, Felonies and Miſdemenors have bin committed, ſithens the Quenes Highnes laſt, free, and generall Pardon, with the Names, Surnames, and Dwelling Places of the ſaid Offendors, and the Manor and Circumſtance therof, and the Sayinges and Depoſicions of the Wittneſſes in that Behaulf, to putt in Writing, together with the Preſentments, their hole Doinges, Knowledges and Proceadinges in the Premiſſes ; And ſuche as they ſhall finde culpable in enye of the Offences to bynde by ſeverall Obligacions in **x** *l.* apeece, with ſufficient Suretyes vnto the Quenes Maieſtie, for their perſonal Apparaunce before this Counſaill furthwithe ; and, at their Apparaunce nott to depart without Lycencs of this Counſaill : And Incaſe they, or eny of them, refuſe to enter into the ſaid Band, then to comytt him or them ſoe refuſing into Warde, there to remaine vntill he or they ſhalbe conformable to enter into the ſaid Band, and of ſuch Committment (if eny be) together withe ſuche Bandes, and Depoſicions, as they ſhall have taken touching the Premiſſes, from Time to Time, to certifye the ſaid Counſaill, in the meane Time of the xixth Daye of *Octobor* next ; and then to certifye their whole Proceadinges the ſame Daye, *&c.* Requiring further by the ſaid Lettres, all Sheriffs, Maiors, Bailiffes, Conſtables, and all other Officers and Miniſters, the Quenes loving and obedient Subiects, to be aiding, aſſiſting and helpeing the ſaid Comiſſioners, and euery of them, in due Execution of the Premiſſes, from Time to Time, as ofte as nede ſhall requier, as they tender her Majeſties Service. And will for the contrary, anſwere at their Perilles.

S A L O P P.

Roberte Pigott, Eſq;
Roberte Eaton, Eſq;
Frauncis Blunt, Eſq;
Richard Vaughan, Eſq; the Quenes Highnes Solicitor.
Richard Jones,
Frauncis Smalman, } fower of the Attornies of this Corte.
David Lloyd,
Richard Evanes,
Hughe Lloid, Gent.
John Vaughan of *Clone,* Gent.
Andrewe Blonuden, Gent.

W O R C E S T E R.

Sir *John Litletonn,* Knight, one of this Counſaill.
Frauncis Welſhe, Eſq
John Follyott, Eſq;
Edmond Cowles, Eſq;
Richard Vaughan, Eſq; the Quenes Maieſties Solicitor.
William Gomond, Gent. one of the Attornies of this Corte.

G L O U C E S T E R.

Sir *Nichollas Arnold,* Knt. } twoe of this Counſaill.
Richard Pates, Eſq;
Thomas Smithe of *Campdenn,* Eſq;
Richard Vaughan, Eſq; the Quenes Highnes Solicitor.

Harry Cadogann, Gent. one of the Attornies of this Corte.
Roger Morgann, one of the Clerkes of the fame Corte.

MONMOTHE.

Thomas Morgann, Efq;
William John ap Proger, Efq;
Richard Vaughan, Efq; the Quenes Majefties Solicitor.
Dauid Thomas, } Gent. twoe of the Attornies of this Corte.
HarryCadogann, }
Roger Morgan, Gent. one of the Clerckes of the fame Corte.

HEREFORD.

Sir *John Huband,* Knighte, one of this Counfaill.
Richard Seborne, Efq;
Frauncis Blont, Efq;
Richard Vaughan, Efq; the Quenes Highnes Solicitor.
William Gromond.
Dauid Thomas. } Gent. three of the Attornies of this Corte.
Humffrey Haworthe. }

GLAMORGAN.

Edmond Morgann, Efq;
Thomas Lewis, Efq;
Leizon Priefe, Efq;
William Jenkines, Efq;
Miles Button, Efq;
Richard Vaughan, Efq; the Quenes Majefties Solicitor.
Harry Cadogann, one of the Attornies of this Corte.
Roger Morgan, one of the Clerkes of the fame Corte.

RADNOR.

John Priefe, of *Mynaughtye,* Efq;
Richard Vaughan, Efq; the Quenes Highnes Solicitor.
Owen Powell Phellipp, Efq;
Morgann Meredithe, Efq;
John Wen, the Younger, Gent.
Rees Johnes, of *Knighton,* Gent.

FLINT.

John Griffithe, Efq;
Richard Vaughan, Efq; the Quenes Majefties Solicitor
Thomas Kinafton, Efq;
Dauid Johnes, Gent. one of the Attornies of this Corte.
John Davies, } Gent. ij° of the Attornies of this Corte,
Elles ap Elles, }
William Thomas, Gent.

DENBIGH.

The Busfhopp of St. *Affaphe,* one of this Counfaill.
Elles Priefe, Efq; one of this Counfaill.
John Priefe Efq; the Quenes Highnes Attorney.
Richard Vaughan, Efq; her Majefties Solicitor.

Foulke Lloyd, Efq;
Robert Turbridge, Efq;
Moris Kiffin, Efq;
Ellis Abellis,
Jenkin Meredithe, } Gent. ijᵒ of the Attorneis of this Corte.
William Lloyd, Gent.

MOUNTGOMERY.

Edward Herbert, Efq;
Richard Vaughan, Efq; the Quenes Majefties Solicitor.
Dauid Lloyd Jenkin, Efq;
Jenkin Meredithe,
Morgan Glin, } Gent. ijᵒ of the Attornies of this Corte.
Dauid Moris, Gent.
Owen Johnes, Gent.

MEREIONITH.

Ellis Priefe, Efq; one of this Counfaill.
Richard Vaughan, Efq; the Quenes Highnes Solicitor.
Rees Hughes, Efq;
John Owen, Efq;
Owen Wyn, Efq;
Robert Owen, Gent.

CANERVON.

The Busfhopp of *Bangor,* one of this Counfaill.
Richard Vaughann, Efq; the Quenes Highnes Solicitor.
John Griffith, of *Lyen,* Efq;
Richard Mofton, Efq;
Thomas Maderenn, Efq;
Roland Pulafone, Efq;

ANGLIZEY.

Richard Vaughann, Efq; the Quenes Highnes Solicitor.
William Lewis, Efq;
Owen Wooddes, Efq;
Richard White, Efq;
Rowland Meredith, Efq;
Rowland Buckley, Efq;
Rowland Kemick, Gent.

CARDIGAN.

Richard Vaughann, Efq; the Quenes Highnes Solicitor.
John Lloyd, of *Kilgwin,* Efq;
John Steadman, Efq;
Rees Dauid Jenkin, Efq;
Morgan Lloid, Efq;
John Thomas ap Engnonn, Gent.
Rees Johnes, of *Knighton,* Gent.

PEMBROK.

Sir *John Parrot,* Knighte, one of this Counfaill.
Richard Vaughann, the Quenes Majefties Solicitor.

John

John Barlow, Efq;
Thomas Revell, Efq;
Albon Stepneth, Efq;
John Thomas ap Ergnon, Gent.

CARMARTHIN.

Richard Vaughann, the Quenes Highnes Solicitor.
John Davies, of *Carmarthin*, Efq;
Griffith Vaughan, of *Trimfurne*, Efq;
Griffith Dunn, Efq;
William Penrin, Gent.
John Thomas ap Engnon, Gent.

BRECOC.

Richard Vaughan, the Quenes Sollicitor.
John Games, Efq;
William Vaughan, Efq;
Water Proffes, Gent. } ij° of the Attorneys of this Corte.
Dauid Thomas,
Rychard Morgan, Gent. one of the Clerks here, *exum.* per *Ri. Vaughan.*

Sir Henry Sydney *to Mr. Secretary* Walfyngham, *concerning the Reports of the Earl of* Effex's *Death.*

S I R,

IMmediatlye vpon my Retorne out of *Connaught* to this Cittie, which was the xiijth of this prefent *October*, and knowinge of the Deathe of the Earle of *Effex*, which I did not certeinely, till I came within xxxth Myles of this Toune, and that his Boddye was gonne to be buried at *Carmerthen*. And hearinge befides, that Lettres had ben fent over, afwell before his Deathe, as after, that he died of Poyfon, I thought good to examyne the Matter as farre as I could learne, and certifie you, to the Ende you might imparte the fame to the Lords, and both fatisfie theim therein, and all others, whome it might pleafe you to participate the fame vnto, and wold beleve the Trothe. For, in Trothe, there was no Apparaunce or Cawfe of Sufpicion, that could be gathered that he died of Poifon. For the Manner of his Difeafe was this : A Fluxe tooke hym on the *Thurfeday* at Night, beinge the xxxth of *Auguft* laft paft, in his owne Howfe, where he had that Day both fupped and dined ; the Day followinge he ridd to the Archbifhopp of *Dublins*, and there fupped and lodged ; the next Morning followinge he ridd to the Vicount of *Baltinglas*, and there did lye one Night, and from thence retorned backe to this Cittie : All theife Dayes he traveled haftelye, fedd three Tymes a Day, without findinge any Fault, either thorough Inflammation of his Boddye, or Alteracion of Taft ; but often he wold complaine of Greiffe in his Bellye, and fometymes fay, that he had never hartie Grieffe of Mynde, but that a Fluxe wold accompanie the fame. After he retorned from this Iorney, he grewe from Day to Day ficker and ficker, an havinge an *Irifhe* Phificion fente to hym by the Earle of *Ormounde*, Doctor *Trevor*, an *Oxford* Man, and my Phificion, Mr. *Chaloner*, Secretarie of this State, and not vnlearned in Phificke, and one that often, for Goodwill, geveth Counfell to his Freinds in Cafes of Sicknes ; and one Mr. *Knell*, an honeft Preacher in this Cittie, and a Chaplayne of his owne, and a Proffeffor of Phificke, contynuallye with hym, they never miniftred any Thinge to hym againft Poyfon. The *Irifhe* Phyficion affirmed before good Wittnes, that he was not poyfoned ; what the other do fay of that Matter, by their owne Writtings, which herewithe I fende you, you fhall perceive. And

drawinge

drawinge towards his Ende, beinge fpeciallye afked by the Archbifhopp of *Dublin*, whether he thought that he was poyfoned or no, conftantlye affirmed, that he thought he was not; nor that he felt in hym felfe any Cawfe, why he fhould coniecture fo to be: In his Sicknes his Coullor rather bettered then impayred, no Heare of his Boddye fhead, no Nayle altered, nor Tooth loofed, nor any Parte of his Skinne blemifhed. And when he was opened, it could not appeare, that any Intrall within his Body, at any Tyme, had bene enfected with any Poyfon. And yet I finde a Brute there was, that he was poyfoned, and that arrofe by fome Woordes fpoken by hym felfe, and yet not originallye at the firft conceived of hymfelfe, as it is thought by the wifeft here, and thofe that were contynuallye about hym: But one that was verye niere hym at that Tyme, and whome he entirelye trufted, feinge hym in extreme Payne, with Fluxe and Gripings in his Bellye, by Reafon of the fame, faied to hym, By the Maffe, my Lord, you are poyfoned; wherevpon the Yeoman of his Seller, was prefentlye fent for to hym and myldlye and lovinglye he queftioned with hym, fayenge, that he fent not for hym, to burden hym but to excufe hym. The Fellowe conftantlye anfwered, that if he had taken any Hurte by his Wyne, he was guiltie of it, for my Lord (faieth he) fince you gave me Warninge in *Englande*, to be carefull of your Drincke, you have drouncke none, but it paffed my Handes. Then it was bruted, that the boyled Water, which he contynually drouncke with his Wyne, fhould be made of Water, wherein Flaxe or Hempe fhould be ftiped, which the Yeoman of his Seller flatlye denied, affirminge the Water which, he always boyled for hym, was perfect good. Then it was imputed to the Sugar; he anfwered, he could get no better at the Stewards Hands, and faier though it were not, yet wholefome ennoughe, or els it had bene lykelye, that a great maney fhould have had a fhrewed Toorne; for my Howfeholde and maney more have occupied of the fame, almoft this Twelfemonethes. The Phificions wer afked, what they thought, that thei fpake doubtfullye, fainge it might be that he was poyfoned, alleadginge that this Thinge or that Thinge might poyfon hym, fince they never gave him Medecine for it; they conftantlye affirme, that they never thought it, but for Arguments Sake, and partlye to pleafe the Earle. He had twoe Gentlewomen that Night at Supper with hym, that the Difeafe tooke hym, and they comminge after to vifitt hym, and he hearinge that they wer troubled with fome Loofenes, faied, that he feared that they and he had tafted of one Drugge, and his Page (who was gonne with his Boddye over, before I retorned.) The Women vpon his Woordes were afrayed, but never ficke, and be in as good State of Healthe, as they were before they fupped with hym. Vpon Sufpicion of his beinge poyfoned, Mr. *Knell* (as it was told me) gave hym fondrie Tymes, of Vnicornes Horne, vpon which fometymes he vomited, as at other Tymes he did, when he tooke it not. Thus I have delyvered vnto you, as moche as I can learne of the Sicknes and Deathe of this noble Peere, whome I left when I left *Dublin*, in all Apparaunce, a luftie, ftronge, and pleafaunt Man; and before I retorned, his Breathe was out of his Boddye, and his Boddye out of this Countrey, and vndoubtedlye his Soule in Heaven; for in my Liffe I never harde of a Man to dye, in foche Perfectnes; he was ficke xx or xxj Dayes, and moft of thofe Dayes tormented with Paings intollerable, but in all that Tyme, and all that Torture, he was never harde fpeake an idle or angrye Woorde: After hee yeelded to dye, he defiered moche to have his Freindes come to hym, and to a byde with hym, which they did of fondrie Sortes, vnto whome he fhewed foche Arguments of hartie Repentaunce of his Liffe paffed, fo found Charitie with all the Worlde, foch Affuraunce to be Partaker, of the Ioyes of Heaven, thorough the Meritts of Chrifts Paffion; foch a ioyfull Defier, fpedilye to be diffolved, and to enioye the fame, whiche he would fometymes fay, That it pleafed the Almightie, to reveale vnto hym, that he fhould be Partaker of (as was to the exceding Admiracion of all that harde it.) He had contynuallye about hym Folkes of fondrie Degrees, as Men of the Clergie, Gentlemen, Gentlewomen, Cittizins, and Servaunts, vnto all which he would vfe fo godlye Exhortacions, and grave Admonicions, and that fo aptlye,

for

for the Perfones he fpake vnto, as in all his Liffe, he never feamed to be Halfe
fo wife, learned, nor eloquent, nor of fo good Memorie, as at his Deathe. He
forgott not to fende weightie Warnings to fomme of his abfent Freinds by Meffage. Oft tymes, when greivous Pangs, had dryven hym out of Slombers, he
wold make foche Shewe of Comforte in Spirite, and expreffe it with foche
Woordes, as maney about hym thought, he fawe, and harde fome Heavenlye
Voyce and Vifion. Maney Tymes after bitter Pangs, he wold with cherefui
Countenaunce crye, Corage, Corage, I have fought a good Fight, and thus ought
everye true Soldiour to dooe, that fighteth vnder the Standdard of his Capten,
and Patrone, *Jefus Chrift*. About a Leven of the Clocke before None, on the
xxiith of *Septembre*, withe the Name of Jefus, iffuenge out of his Mouthe, he
left to fpeake any more, and fhortlye after, lifting vp his Hand, to the Name of
Jefus, when he could not fpeake it hym felfe ; he ceafed to move any more, but
fwetelye, and mildlye, his Goft departed, by all Chriftians to be hooped,
into Heavenlye Bliffe. The Almightie graunt, that all Profeffinge Chrift, in their
Liffe, may at their Deathe, make foche Teftimonie of Chriftianitie, as this noble Earle did. And thus endinge my tedious Lettre, with the dolefull (and yet
comfortable) Ende of this noble Man, I wifhe you, from the Bottome of my
Harte, good Liffe, and longe ; and the Ioy of Heaven at the Ende. From the
Caftell of *Dublin*, this xxth of *October*, 1576.

Your affured lovinge Freinde,

H. Sydney.

Sir Henry Sydney *to Mr. Secretary* Walfingham.

S I R,

WHereas, the Bifhoppricke of *Ardagh* is nowe voyde, and at her Majefties
Difpoficion, by Reafon of the Deathe of *Pattericke Mac Mahon* the late
incumbent, and for that it is not convenient, that that See fhould be longe deftitute of a fpritual Paftor to fuccede in the Place, the rather for that, by good
Teachinge, and Doctrine, the People might be drawen, firft to knowe their Dueties to God, and next their Obedience to their Prince and cyvell Order. I have
thought fitt (partelye vpon myne owne Knowledge of Sir *John Petitt,*Clarcke, and
partelye vpon the good Reporte I have harde of the Man by others, that affirme vnto me, that afwell for his Sufficientcye in Learninge, and good Example of Lyffe, and honeftie of Manners, he is one mete for that Rome) to preferre hym, therefore to your Recommendacion to her Majeftie. And, for that
bothe the Lyvinge is verye meane, when it is whole, and entire, and yet the
fame by the late Incumbent, moche difcypate, leafed, and aliened to foch Perfonnes, as hardlye it is to be recovered againe to the Poffeffion of the Churche, except fomme Man, who bothe by his Pollecye, and fomewhat by his Strength in
Freindfhippe, and Countenaunce in the Countrie, be fubftitute in the Place ; I have
the rather geven my full Allowance of this Man, who afwell for that he is defcended
of *Englifhe* Race, and fpeakethe the Languadge, as alfo for that he is well alied in
Freindes, whofe Landes and Lyvings adioyne to the Poffeffions of this Bifhoppricke. So that if it fo like her Highnes, to nominate him to the Place, I knowe
not any one Man of this Countrie Birthe, that will accept the Name of fo great
a Dignitie, with fo fmall Commoditie as this Bifhoppricke hath belonginge vnto it ; fo fitt a Perfon for the Place as he is. And therefore, for that the Lyvinge
is fo meane, he defiereth that he may have the little he nowe enioyethe, and
dwelleth vpon, beinge called the Perfonage of *Pierfton*, in the Bifhoppricke
of *Meithe*, which is not extended in Valewe above fower Poundes *Sterling*, by
the Yere, by Way of *Commendam*, annexed to the Bifhoppricke, which beinge
a Thinge of no greater a Valewe ; I thought it not amiffe to fatisfye hym therein, the rather, therebye to encourage hym, to take the other Chardge vpon hym,
which I hope he will well fupplye.: He hath bene allowed by the Bifhopps here,
for his Sufficiencye, and fo commended vnto me from theim : And even fo

I

prayinge

prayinge you to furder the Cawfe to her Majeftie, that I may with convenient Spede receive her gratious Pleafure for hym, I bid you farewell. From the Caftell of *Dublin* the xxviijth of *October*, 1576.

Your affured lovinge Friende,

H. Sydney.

Sir Henry Sydney *to the Lords of the Councell, with his Opinion for Reformation of the Diforders in the Marches of* Wales.

My duetie humblye remembred to your moft honorable Lordfhips,

I firft humblye crave Pardon, that I have not before this Tyme, anfwered your honorable Lettres, concerninge the Reformacion of the Abufes creapt in of late, into the Courte of the Marches ; which in Parte, the infinite Toyle of this Lande, forced me to pretermitt, and partlye the Hope I had, that I fhould foner have finifhed my Iorney in *Connaught*, then it fell oute I did, which made me over fhoote the Tyme, lymitted by your Lordfhips Lettres. And next I moft humblye thanke your Lordfhips for the honorable Refpecte it well apeareth you have of me ; that it pleafeth the fame to knowe myne Opinion, in Alteracion of Orders, perteininge to that Courte (where I have ferved as principall Officer, nowe almoft xvij Yeares) before you will confirme or allowe theim.

And if I had ben harde, when certeine newe Councellors were admitted into that Courte, fince my departinge ; I suppofe that Howfe fhould not have bene fo chardged, as nowe it is ; the Countrie afwell ferved, and your Lordfhips leffe encombred. I have fith my retorne hither, accordinge to your good Advifes, conferred withe the Lord Chauncelor of this Realme, touchinge the State of this Cawfe, wherein we agree ; and trewlye my Lords, I ever found him the fufficienteft Man, both for Judgement and Dilligence, that ever I knewe attende that Howfe, and no fmall mayme, hath that Governement by the miffe of hym, which if it be not fubftantiallye fupplied (then for ought I heare yet it is) it is to be doubted, that the Credit, and good Service of that Howfe, will fall to Ruyne, which were greate Pittie ; for befide the greate Dammage, that infinite poore Subiects fhould finde, by takinge away the Redreffe of their Wrongs, and the Releiffe of their Greives (that withe Expedicion they finde there) which if that Councell were not, they fhould either reft with their Harmes at Home, or feeke their Healpe a farre of, at the Chauncerye, or Courte of Requefts ; and the Terror, which the longe contynued Severitie of that Howfe, holdeth the bafe People of that Countrie in, in reftrayninge theim from robbinge and killinge one another ; it were in myne Opinion, no fmall flackinge of the Reignes of Regiment of the whole Realme, either to diffolve that Howfe, or to fuffer it to be vnfurnifhed, with fufficient Men to Iudge and Commaunde. And omitting as a Thinge nedeles, any Argument to prove what Obedience, Love, and loyall Fear, a Refident, and contynuall Miniftracion of Juftice, with a Reprefentation of fome Parte of the Majeftie of the Prince, printeth in the Hartes of the Subiects, I will onelye remember your Lordfhips of the happie Succeffe, as I think iuftlye to be attributed to the Service of that Howfe ; which is, that fince the eftablifhinge thereof, that is now niere iiij C. Yeres agooe, there nevar beganne Rebellion, within the whole Precinct of that Dominion, nor in any Parte thereof, which lacketh little of a whole third Parte of *Englande* ; nor it hath bene feldome feen, nor harde of, that maney People of the fame, affifted Rebellion, els where begonne ; and that in eche Sovereignes Reigne, fince that Tyme, there hath bene Rebellion in one Parte of the Realme, or other, your Lordfhips knoweth well enough. I nede not ftande to prove it ; and therefore leavinge that to your good Difcreacions, I will proceede to declare myne Opinion of the Booke nowe fent me by your Lordfhips, which I, and my Lord Chauncelor, have delyberatlye confidered of, and do verye well allowe of the Rules, and Orders fett downe ; favinge in the Article, mentioninge what Cawfies fhalbe admitted to be harde in that Courte, and apointeth certeine, not to be received, vnles the Bills for the fame, be figned by three feverall Counfellors of that Counfell ; my fimple Opinion is, that one Counfellors Hand, fo it be not his that hath the

Proffit

Proffit of the Signett, is fufficient, withe the Prefident or Viceprefident, and in the Abfence of theim bothe, any two other of that Councell.

The lyke Diforders as thofe, for which theife feame, and in dede are good Remedies, have oft Tymes ben founde, and corrected in that Courte, and yet thorough Crafte, and Covetoufnes of the Minifters of the fame, have fecreatlye creapt in agayne ; as about xv Yeres paft, foch Diforders were complayned of to me, as nowe are to your Lordfhips, and therevpon (a great Deale the better by the Advife of Mr. *Gerrard*) Orders verye lyke theife, were fett downe, for Reformacion thereof, well lyked by the reft of that Councell, as it feamed, publifhed, and fomme of theim in publike Places fixed to the Ende, both Minifter of the Courte and Countrieman, might the better knowe what their Duetie was. That whole Yeare it pleafed her Majeftie, to imploy my fimple Service, in *Fraunce, Scotland*, and *Newhaven*, at *Porchmouth* for *Newhaven*, and at the Courte ; all which Tyme Mr. *Gerrard* was my Viceprefident ; for fo had I Power at that Tyme byInftructions, to make Choyce of any of that Counfell, to fupplie my Place in myne Abfence, which Order was altered in an other Tyme of my Abfencye ; in all which Tyme, there was no foche Complainte, nor Cawfe of Complainte, miniftred to my Knowledge : In other Tymes of my Imployment, out of that Place, others occupied the fame ; in which Tyme I fuppofe thofe good Ordinaunces, devifed, and executed, to fuppreffe foche Diforders (as both in that Courte, and in everye other Courte will fpringe) were neglected ; whereof, if Complainte had beenne eftfones made duringe myne Abode there, I durft have vndertaken the Reformacion thereof, without troublinge her Majeftie, or your good Lordfhips. Whyle I attended there, the Howfe was cleane out of Debt, and Money fufficient alwayes, in the Receivor of the Fynes Handes, to pay all that was due : And, befides, I am well affured, I cawfed to be layd out, for the Makinge of the Conduits of Water, for *Beawdley*, and *Ludlowe*, the Repaier of thofe twoe Howfies, and other her Majefties Howfies, above a thoufand Poundes. When I retorned out of this Realme, I found the Howfe twelve hundred Poundes in Debt, and no Reparacion donne ; no, nor that finifhed, which, at my Departinge, I left halfe donne. While I attended there laft, the Howfe recovered well, fo as though not out of Debt, yet moch leffe in Debt I left it, then I found it ; and nowe is it fo farre behinde Hande, as not onelye olde Bills of Counfellors cannot be paied, which they have foreborne a longe Tyme, but daylie growinge Chardges for the Howfe, as for Fuell, Cariage, and foch other neceffarie Incydents to Howfeholde, as the Howfe cannot be mainteined without, are left vnpaied ; fo moche to my Burden, as were it not for fomme Provifion, that by myne owne Pollecye I have made, I were not able to kepe the Howfe, confideringe the Dearth of all Things, with the Allowance I have, though the fame be verye honorable. And, my Lords, fince it hath pleafed you fo honorablye to vfe me, as to fende for my Opinion in the Reformacion of the Diforders alreadye creapt in, or lyke enough to growe in that Courte, I am emboldened to write thus moche to your Lordfhips, That the beft Way to reforme that, which is alreadye in Diforder, and to kepe it in good Eftate after, is to mainteyne there, a difcreate and bold Gentleman to be principall Officer ; who, for foch Infolent Actes, as fometymes doth and will happen, will feverelye rebuke, and punifhe the proudeft of theim ; and that he have a willing Mynde, and an hable Boddye to take Payne, whereof he fhall finde in that Office Cawfe enough, foche a one was Bifhopp *Rowland Lee*, as it apearethe, afwell by the honorable Fame, that yet foundeth of hym, for the great Reformacion he made in that Countrie, as by maney vndoubted Teftimonies of an eftablifhed Obedience he held the People in. And here I have good Occafion, though, in Trothe, nothinge meaninge the Difadvantage of Sir *Andrewe Corbett*, to befeache your Lordfhips, to thinke of fomme one, more able to take Paine, in that Place, then he is, as I finde fpeciallye by his owne Lettres : It is nowe a Yere, very niere, that he writt to me at good Length, of his Infirmitie ; and by Reafon thereof, his great Defier to be difcarged of that Office, prainge my Healpe and Furtheraunce to her Majeftie, and to your Lordfhips, for the fame : And

† now

now again, not a Fortnight fince, I received an other Lettre from hym of lyke Effecte, expreffinge the Contynuance and Increafe of his Infirmities and Weri-fomenefs of that Place. Wherefore, I humblye befeache your Lordfhips, to have favorable, and fpedie Confideracion of bothe. For, as it is of Importaunce, in Refpecte of the Publike, that an hable Man be placed there, fo were it great Pittie, in Refpecte of the Gentlemans owne Particular, that he fhould be tyed to a Place, where he found hym felfe vnhable to difchardge the Office belong-inge to the fame; and, therefore, once again, I befeache your Lordfhips have fpeedie Regarde to this: I will not take vpon me the Nominacion of any, but leave the fame to your Lordfhips Confideration, and her Highnes Choyce.

The fecond Perfon there, which alwayes hitherto hath bene the Juftice of the Countye Palatyne of *Chefter*, muft put on a Minde to refyde for the moft Parte with the Councell, for fo did *Englefield*, *Hare*, *Silyayard*, *Townefend*, *Pollard*, and *Wooddes*; who, befides their Dexteritie to expedite Sutes, were, for their Gravetie, and Iudgement in the Lawe, demed woorthy to occupie a Place vpon the Benche in any Courte in *Englande*; and, when any of thefe attended that Counfell, as continuallye, for the moft Parte, they did, light Cawfes were pre-fently hard and ordered, afwell out of Tearme Tyme, as in Tearmes, and Matters of more Weight, were determined in the Tearmes, when alwayes the Benche was furnifhed with Men of foche Gravetie, and Iudgement in the Lawe, as the Ianglinge Barifters wold not, nor durft not lye of the Lawe, nor over longe clamper in any bad Cawfe of their Clyents; as fince, and yet, as I heare they doe, to the great Loffe of Tyme, and to the Drivinge of the Su-tors, to needeles and intollerable Chardge. And, more over, the Juftice of one of the other three Circuits, alwayes, in Tearmes, attended there; and fo doe I wifhe, that nowe they might be willed to doe, namelye, Mr. *Bromley*, or Mr. *Phetiplace:* And then was the Benche well able to over rule the Barre. But I have fene it farre otherwife, for I have maney Tymes, as me thought, felt the Barre fo farre to ftronge for the Benche (which hathe hapned, for the moft Parte, in the Abfence of the Juftice, and the Want of his Affiftaunce) as I have, confideringe myne owne Ignoraunce in the Lawes, deferred Iudge-ment after to longe Pleadinge, vntill I was better affifted; and, I feare, the Benche is not moche the ftronger for theim that were laft made of the fame: But I knowe the Howfe moche bourdened by theim; and, if the Counfellors Stipendarie by the Yeare, who ought, as they are lymitted by the Inftruccions, and were heretofore accuftomed, to geve contynuall Attendaunce there, be not enforced to remayne there, more than they doe: But that the Counfellors enterteined by the Day, contynue there, to furnifh the Howfe for Want of theim, there muft be fome other Meane devifed for Payment of their Fees, then by the Fynes of that Courte, for fure they will not ftretch vnto it, vn-les more neceffarie Allowancies be left vnpaied; for which Cawfe, I gave Mr. *William Gerrarde*, nowe Lorde Chauncelor here, a hundered Marks a Yere out of the Fynes, which is not paft halfe fo moche, as one of theim nowe hath, according to the Allowaunce by the Day, for which he gave, in Effecte, con-tynuall Attendaunce there. And the Benche beinge thus furnifhed, the Craft or Corrupcion of the Attorneys, will eafelye be prevented, or reformed; and, in dede, the Nomber nowe is to great of theim, fo as if the fame were reduced to a fmaller Nomber, it were better, and all they to be vnder one Man, who might be anfwerable for all their Doings, it were the fureft Way, both for the Honnor of that Courte, and Benifitt of the Subiecte. And, if it might like your Lordfhips to allowe one of my Choyce to that Office, I fhould thinke my felfe greatlye bounde vnto you for the fame: It is *Edmound Molyneuxe*, a Gen-tlemen of woorfhipfull Parentage, not vnknowen, I fuppofe, to moft of your Lordfhips, and to me, by a good many Yeres Service, as my Secretarie bothe there, and here, well proved to be honeft, dilligent, and circumfpecte; I be-feache your Lordfhips, therefore, fhewe your Favor to hym, that he may be affigned to the Place: And, in the Patent that fhall paffe from her Majeftie for the Erection of this Office, I pray your Lordfhips, that Mr. *Fowke Grivel* may be joyned with hym, and placed in the Patent before hym, for that my Servaunt moſt earneſtlye deſireth he ſhould ſo be, if it may ſo ſtand with your Lordſhips good Allowaunceis.

By this my over tedious Diſcourſe, your Lordſhips may vnderſtand my Opinion, aſwell of the Booke you ſent me to conſider of, as howe that Howſe of the Courte of the Marches, may be honorablye mainteined, to the Honnor of the Quene, Commoditie of the Subieƈte in particuler, and vniverſall Quiet of a great Part of that Realme, which I moſt humblye beſeache your honorable Lordſhips, with like Favor, to accept, as you vſed in ſendinge the other, and then ſhall I acknowledge, that I have received a double Grace from you, of whome I humblye take my Leave, this xijth of *November,* 1576.

Your Lordſhips to be commaunded,

H. Sydney.

A Memoriall ſent from Sir Francis Walſyngham, *by* James Preſon, *Gent. Servant to my Lord Deputy.*

1. INprimis, to let my Lord vnderſtande howe it was loked for heere, that he ſhould have ſpared ſome Parte of the ordynarye Allowaunce he hath from hence this Yeere; which, being not performed, doth geve his Enemies Cawſe to Diſgrace his Service, who do not conſider that the vnloked for Trobles of that Realm, is the Cawſe of the Contynuaunce of that Charge.

2. That my Lord ſhould avoide all Occaſyons which may breede Troubles, in reſpeƈt, thereby, to avoide Charge.

3. That I thinke it neceſſarye there ſhoulde be ſome profeƈt Friendſhip betweene hym and Therle of *Ormonde,* which cannot be, onles he carry his Affection indifferently betweene the ſaid Erle, and the Lord of *Vpper Oſſerye.*

4. That it were convenient, for the better Satysfaƈtion of Therle, his Lordſhip ſhoulde allowe him ſome ſuche Porcion of Enterteynment, as he alloweth to the Lord of *Vpper Oſſery.*

5. That Therle hath promeſed me to doe any Thing that may deſerve the Lord Deputies Favour, whom I have aſſured that he ſhoulde be well dealt with all by my ſaide Lord Deputye.

6. That I may receyve Aunſware from my Lord Deputy vnto the Erle of *Ormonds* Requeſts conteyned in his Lettre, whereof I ſend his Lordſhip a Copie.

7. That by ſecret Lettres ſent owt of *Irelande,* it is advertized, that there was never ſo extreme Ympoſicions laide vppon the *Engliſhe* Pale, as are preſently; and that the Souldiors, notwithſtanding the due Payment that is made them, are Burdeners vnto the Contrey.

8. That his Lordſhip graunteth many Pardons, which bredeth Boldnes in thoſe that are evill affeƈted to offende.

9. That his Lordſhip ſend over Aunſwere to ſuche Points of his Inſtruƈtions as remayn yet vnaunſwared.

10. That I thinke it not good to move for a new Treaſurer, vntill ſuche Tyme as hir Majeſty may ſee ſome Part of hir Charge demyniſhed.

11. That I will do what ſhall lye in me, to make good Freindſhip betwene Therle of *Leiceſter* and Erle of *Ormonde.*

Fra. Walſyngham.

Towchinge the Diſpatche of the Bisſhoppes to commende *Welſhe,* if *Cleire* be not allowed of.

Towchinge the Graunte of Coneſtabellſhippe of *Arklow,* duringe Pleaſure.

The Earl of Ormond *to Sir* Francis Walfyngham.

S I R,

I Have thought good to fend you my Lord Deputyes owne Order : I affure you, there is nothing put in Execucion thereof, notwithftanding my feverall Lettres requiring the fame.

Only 3 other Things I have willed my Mann to geve you a Noate of, which be thies : That I may have Execucion vpon an Order paft to me by Sir *William Fitzwilliam*, and the Counfell, for Price Wynes, to be paide by Straungers. That my Lord of *Vpper Offery*, his Tennants, and Followers, may comm to Seffions, as the reft within the County of *Kylkenny* doe. That my Lord will do them Iuftice with Favor and Expedicion, that have the Charge of my Contrey and Tenants in myn Abfence here ; is all I require ; and fo to God I commyt you. The 12 of *November*, 1576.

Your very affured Freinde,

Thomas Ormonde.

Edward Waterhous, *Efq; to Sir* Henry Sydney.

May it pleafe your Lordfhip,

THE Funeralls of the Erle of *Effex* have bene deferred 'till now that they be appointed to be honorably fynifhed at *Carmarthen* the 24th of this Month. I have forborne to wright to your Lordfhip, fince my Arrivall in this Realme, becaufe I wold give free Scope to all Men to utter their Opinions concerning my Behaviour hear in fuch Caufes as I had to deale in ; and I doubt not, but you have herd enough of it ; but, if eny Reports have come unto your Lordfhips Eares, that in the Caufes of my Lord of *Effex*, I have delt indirectly, I affure your Lordfhip, they have done me Wrong ; for, as I have juftifyed hym and his Doings againft all the World, without Refpect of Feare or Favour, fo have I been free from malitius Thoughts, and have quenched all Sparkes that might kindell eny newe Fier, in thefe Caufes, which I hope be buried in Oblivion, wherein I ftand to the Report of Sir *Phillip Sydney*, above enie other.

The State of the Erle of *Effex* being beft knowen to my felf, doth require my Travell for a Tyme in his Caufes ; but my Burden cannot be great, when every Man puttith to his helping Hande. Her Majefty has beftowed uppon the yong Erle his Mariage, and all his Fathers Rules in *Wales*, and promifeth the Remiffion of his Debt. The Lords do generally favour and furder hym ; fome for the Truft repofed, fome for Love to the Father, other for Affinity with the Child, and fome for other Caufes. And all thes Lords that wifhe well to the Children, and, I fuppofe, all the beft Sort of the *Englifhe* Lords befides, doe expect what will become of the Treaty betwene Mr. *Phillip*, and my Lady *Penelope*. Truly, my Lord, I muft faie to your Lordfhip, as I have faid to my Lord of *Lecefter*, and Mr. *Phillip*, the Breaking of from this Match, if the Default be on your Parts, will turne to more Difhonour, then can be repaired with eny other Mariage in *England*. And, I proteft unto your Lordfhip, I do not think that their is at this Day fo ftrong a Man in *England* of Freinds, as the litell Erle of *Effex*, nor eny Man more lamented then his Father, fince the Deth of King *Edward*.

In fuch Things as my Service might furder your Lordfhips Affairs, I have not bene filent fince my Commyng into *Englande* ; and *James Prefcott* will enforme your Lordfhip of the Place where I mynd for the moft Parte to be Refident, fo long as your Lordfhip fhall allowe of myne Abfence ; which, I hope, fhalbe at my Choice, fince I maye do your Honour Service herein, and there fhall live but an idell Lief, without Credit or Hability, to pleafe your Lord-

fhip.

fhip. And, for the Tyme of my Continuance in thes Parts, I humbly pray your Lordfhip, that my Penfion may be paid me by fuch, from Tyme to Tyme, as have the Conduction of the Treafurer. All other Things I repofe upon the Report of this Bearer, Mr. *Prefcott*, who is exceding well thought of, by fuch as are beft hable to finde your Caufes heer. And fo wisfhing rather that my Duty to your Lordfhip, were difcovered by others, then utterid by my felf, I humbly leave you. At *Chartly*, the 14th of *November*, 1576.

Your Lorfhips moft bounden,

and at Commaundement,

Ed. Watèrhous.

Sir Henry Sydney *to the Lords of the Councill in* England.

My humble Dewtie remembred to your honorable Lordfhips,

SINCE the Receipt of your Lordfhips Lettres of the xiijth of *Julye* laft, fent by my Servaunt *Henrie Catlyn*, amongeft other Things, your Lordfhips thought it mete that I fhould deale with *Chatterton* beinge nowe here, and fall to fome Agreement and Compoficion with hym for the Revocacion of the Graunte paffed vnto hym from her Majeftie of the *Ohanlons* Countrie : And, becawfe the Matter is of foch Weight and grave Confideracion for me to deale in, and that (as I take it) I have not fufficient Warrant, by your Lettres, abfolutelye to compound the Matter my felfe, I thought it convenient, as well to fatiffie your Lordfhips Expectacions, as his earneft Defier, to fignifie vnto your Lordfhips, howe farre I have proceeded with him ; and, withall, to yeeld my Opinion, what I thinke of the Matter. Firft, vpon oure Conference, I laid before hym, howe vnpoffible a Matter it was for hym to do any Good in his Enterprife, and that he daylie wafted and fpoyled hym felf more and more, without any Hope of Recovery, or Likelyhood to do Good in that he went about. And, although there was fome Hôpe to have bene conceived duringe the Tyme the Êrle of *Effex* Enterprife was on Foote, that Good might have come of that he tooke in Hand, to'expulfe and fubdue the *Ohanlons*, and to reduce the Countrie of the *Fuze* and *Arrerie*, to yelde hym Commoditie ; yet, after the Earle had once geven over his Enterprife, there was no Reafon for hym any longer to contynue his, or to hope that it could take any good Effecte. And, in trothe, my Lords, the poore Gentleman hath vtterly vndonne hym felfe in Wraftlinge with theim, and hath nothinge left to maynteine hym to lyve on ; and his Brother likewife, an honeft valiant Gentleman, wounded and mayned in the Service, and loft and fpent all that ever he hath : So that I fynde their Cafe is too lamentable, and *Chatterton* to be in her Majefties Mercy and Grace, in fome Sorte to be confidered of. The Countrie, although it be large and longe, yet is it altogether waft, neither Howfe, Pile, nor Caftell left ftanding in it, but onely one little foorie Forte, pitched of Soddes and Turves, that he buylt there for his Streingth and Defence. I cannot, as yet, bringe the Inhabitaunts to offer above threefkore Pound Rent by the Yeare, but I will make it more, if I can ; and humblye pray your Lordfhips to be a Meanes to her Majeftie, that *Chatterton* may have fome Recompence for his Stay to lyve by : And the firft Degree is, that he may be protected for his Boddye, that he may not be troubled for foch Debts as he owethe, which (as he fayeth) by Reafon of this Enterprife are growen greate, and to fondrie Perfons : And next, that he may have fomme Meane to lyve either by Inheritance, Fee Ferme, or long Leafe, for that he hath nothinge left, nor Meane to gett any Thinge, that I can learne, but by her Majefties Benevolence, which I befeach your Lordfhips may be extended towards hym, by Way of Permutation and Exchaunge. And, if her Majeftie will voutchfafe to beftowe vpon hym lx *l.* by the Yeare in fome Sorte to lyve by, and better his Countenaunce withall,

there

there can be no Loſſe in that Bargain for her Majeſtie. I will make her Majeſties Profitt greater, of that he will ſurrender againe into her Handes, if I can. And even ſo humbly recommendinge hym to your Lordſhips favorable Conſideracion of his poore Eſtate, I take my Leave. From *Tryme*, the xxvijth of *November*, 1576.

Your honorable Lordſhips aſſured lovinge

Freinde to commaund,

H. Sydney.

The Earl of Ormond to Sir Henry Sydney.

My veray good Lord,

HAving appointed my Frend *Richard Hethe* to deale in my Cauſes, and the Cauſes of my Tenants, in myn Abſence, I haue thought good to pray your Lordſhip, that it may pleaſe youe to do him Iuſtice againſt ſuche as he ſhall complaine on, and to ſhewe him your lawfull Favor in all his reaſonable Cawſes ; for trewely he is honeſt, I dare vndertake. And ſo referring him to your Lordſhip, I take my Leave, wisſhing to you all good Succeſſe. From the Court, the ixth of *Januarij*, 1576.

Your Lordſhips louing Brother,

Thomas Ormonde, Oſſory.

My Lord, I am geven to vnderſtand by my Wyfe, and others, that a Brother of my Lord of *Vpperoſſoryes*, with a Son of *Odwyns*, haue ſpoyled my Lands, which *Donell Mac Shane* holdeth of me : This beinge true, I pray your Lordſhip to caws preſent Reſtituſion to be made, and ſo to poniſh the Offenders, as other ill diſpoſed may take Example therby.

Porcell is alſo ſpoyled, to whome I pray you ſtand a good Lord for Reſtituſion of his Goods alſo.

Sir Henry Sydney to the Lords of the Counſell.

My humble Dutie remembred to your honorable Lordſhips,

SInce the Writinge of my Lettres, of the xxth of *September* laſt, dated from *Galway*, I ſtill remayned in Expectacion of ſome Anſwer from thence to ſomme of my former Lettres, which came not vnto me, before the xxiijth of this preſent *Januarye*, and the ſame brought me by my Servaunt *James Preſcott*, whoſe Negligence therein, as I cannot iuſtlye condempne, but lay the Fault (as in Troth) it was, to the Contrarietie of the Wyndes, and Vntowardenes of the Weather, which would not ſuffer hym to paſſe, though maney Tymes he enforced the Mariners, to take the Seas ; yet, nevertheleſſe, he was ſtill beaten backe, by Storme, or contrarie Wynde, ſo that, in ſtainge to heare, I have bene to longe ſcylent, to write, whereof I humblye crave Pardon of your good Lordſhips. And as in thoſe my Lettres ſent from *Galway*, I ſpake then of my Proceadings in *Connaught*, what I had donne alreadye in Purſute of thoſe Rebells, and what I entended to dooe before my Departure thence : So conſequentlye after my Diſpatche made to your Lordſhips thence ; the Day followinge, I went to *Athenrye*, ſo to the *Shrughor*, and into *Mac William Eughtors* Countrie ; and within a Day or twoes Remove, came to the Caſtell of *Ibarrye*, which before I had cawſed to beſiedged by certaine Companyes I had diſperſed from me before, to lye in that Countrie, and to make Hed againſt the *Scotts*, who were reported to lye, not paſt fyve, or vj. Myles from the Place of this Siedge, and had gathered together all the Pray of the Countrie (as it was reported.) The Caſtle was noted to be a verye ſtronge

Place, and harde to be wonne by Affault, without great Slaughter, and Loffe of Men : Att my Cominge thether, the Mother of twoe of the principall Gentlemen, that were in the Warde of the Caftle, and Sonnes to one *Edward Bourck* (who was fent from the Earle of *Clanrickards* Sonnes, to enterteine the *Scotts*, to come into *Connaught*, to the Ayde of thofe Rebells) made humble Sute vnto me, that fhe might fpeake with her Sonnes ; and firft fhe entreated for their Lyves, that I wold graunte theim Pardon, which I would not in any Sort affent vnto, except they would prefentlye yeelde the Caftell into my Handes, and fimplye fubmitt theim felves, their Lyves, Landes, and Goodes to my Devocion ; and affured her, that fince I was comme thether, I would not departe thence, and leave the Place, before I had wonne it. She thought the Condicions verye harde ; neverthelefle fhe tendring moche her Sonnes Lyves, went to them by Lycence from me, and put them in fo harde Hope to obteine Mercye, but vpon thefe Condicions, as the Miferie of their State, made theim to hazarde the Extremitie of Fortune, and fo privelye at a Spike Hole, on the Backfide, and in the mayne Wall of the Caftell (which duringe the Parley, they had wrought fomewhat wider) and made Paffadge to lett downe a Man by Devife, into the Ditche, betwixt the twye Light, and Settinge of the Watche, the Warde ftale away, and efcaped with their Lyves.

Hether came to me *Mac William Eughter*, whome after I had fomewhat rebuked, that I beinge commen thether into thofe Partes, cheifelye for his Defence, and to repoffeffe and fettle hym in his Countrie, in as good State as he was before, that he had nether come, nor fent vnto me, before that Tyme. He excufed hym felfe verye modeftlye and wifelye, alleadginge, that after he vnderftoode, my Force was entred into the Countrie, whereof the *Scotts* ftoode moche in Doubt ; he gathered his Strength, and People together, and foorthwith gave a Chardge vpon the *Scotts*, and cried *Bowes, Bowes*, which Voyce fo foddeinely geven (and they thinkinge it in dede to be true) it ftricke foche a Terror, into the amafed Myndes of the beggerlye *Scotts*, as they leaft all the Pray behynde theim, and faved theim felves, by flyenge and ronninge away. I delyvered to hym the Caftle I had taken, to kepe it to her Majefties Vfe, and all the Caftells and Piles befides he was difpoffeffed of ; fettled hym quietlye in his owne, with foch Credit and Countenaunce, as I hope he fhalbe hable, to mainteine hym felfe in Defpite of all his Ennemies, that fhall hereafter attempt any Thinge againft hym.

From this Place I meant to have gonne to *Sligo*, but by Reafon, of the extreme Raignes, that fell in foch Aboundaunce, the Water of the *Moy*, which I muft nedes paffe, was ryfen fo high, and fo moche increafed, as havinge no Boates, I could not by any Meanes paffe either my Horffemen or Footemen over, without to great Daunger. And befides, the Soldiours were fo over toyled, and weried, what with contynuall Marchinge, Fowlenes of Wether, and Wayes, weete Lodgings, after their Marche, and maney of theim beinge feeble and ficke, as they could have hardlye indured, to have performed, this Iorney, but I fhould have bene forced to have left maney of theim behynde me. And with all, for that *Occonnor Sligo* came vnto me thither, the *Clandonells*, and all the reft of that Countrie, either of any Accompte, Force, or Power. And alfo, for that I was crediblye advertized, and founde the Reporte true, that the *Scotts* were fled the Countrie, and had left *Vllick Bourck* ; and he hymfelfe likewife fled to the Mounteines of *Sleuartye*, to his Brother *Shane* : And moreover for that alfo *Orwarck* fent vnto me, to mete me, where I would apointe hym, I thought the Iorney leffe neceffary for this Tyme, havinge in Effecte donne as moche with their Prefences, beinge all together with me, as if I fhould have gonne to *Sligo*, to have founde hym there. And, therefore fhortninge my Iorney, I retorned Homewardes, by the Playnes of *Connaught* towardes *Dublin*, and left Sir *Nicolas Malbye*, poffeffed of the Howfies of *Roffecommen* and *Athlone*, and all the Earles Howfies in *Clanrickard*, befides twoe Bandes of Footemen, and Capten *Daniells* Companye of Horffemen, two Hundred of the *Clandonells* of *Leinfter* (beinge her Majefties Galloglas) with a hundred Kerne, all to be at the Directien of the Collonell, over and befides his owne Companye, being xxxtie Horffemen, and xxtie Footemen, and gave hym Order and Commiffion, to take *Bonnaught* ; and fpendinge

for

for the Findinge of the Galloglas, vpon foche Countries, and Lordes, as had not yet compounded with her Majeftie for their Landes ; and fo leavinge hym fufficient Authoritie, and Power, for the Governement of the Province, I departed thence, and arryved at *Dublin*, the xiijth of *October*. And vndoubtedlye my Lords, foche a fufficient Man I fynde of Sir *Nicolas Malbye*, for the Service of *Connaught*, fo forwardes, valiaunt, wife and refolute, fo hable a Boddye to endure Paynes, and fo patient in this hard Seafon, to bear any Travell, and his Succeffe fo happie, in lightinge vupon the Rebells, and diftreffinge theim, as I am humblye to thanke your Lordfhips, for your Choyce of fo fitt a Man to the Place ; and muft confeffe (as Things have fallen oute fince) your Lordfhips have donne better for me, then I devifed for my felfe. Howe be it, the Hope of the Earles Inlardgement, is fo daylye gaped for, as it is the onelye Cawfe of the Contynuance of the Warres there, which Hope if it were once cleane taken away, the People of that Countrie, as they are, of their owne Difpocions, the moft amenable, and tractableft People of *Ireland :* So would they yeeld to as moche Obedience, and frame theim felves, to that Order of Cyvill Governement ; as eafye it would be to rule theim (without any great Force contynuallye refident amongft theim) and fasfhion and make them to do, what you woulde reafonablye commaunde theim. And in Trothe the Earles Cawfe, fawlethe oute againft hym, everye Day fowler and fowler, as bothe by his owne Confeffion and the Depoficion of others (which fhortlye fhalbe fent vnto your Lordfhips) it will plainlye and evidentlye apeare vnto you ; at which Tyme, I meane lykewife to fende a Bill drawen for his Atteyndor by Parliament, if he be not found a Baftarde, as it is thought he may be, and then he may be tried by a Jewrye of common Perfons. And his Sonnes Warres and his, once fuppreffed, which by this Meanes will be donne, there is no Doubt, but the Revenue of *Connaught*, will in fhort Space beare the Chardge of *Connaught*.

The Province of *Mounfter* is vniverfallye quiet, as yet, but the Prefident findeth fomme Stubburnes of *Thomound*, in not obeyinge foch Orders, as be taken againft hym, and fomme Wilfulnes of *Defmound*, that will not be withdrawen from his wonted Exactions, and foche a generall Repininge thorough out to beare Ceffe, not with out fomme Intelligence, or as it is rather to be fufpected Confpiracie, with theim of the *Englifh* Pale. Howe be it the Lord Prefident is fo carefull in his Chardge, fo watchfull of their Doings, and fo dilligent to fearche out their Intencions, and prevent their Driftes, and fo vpright a Iufticer in Cyvill Cawfies, and fo readye for Martiall Service, if they fhould ftarte oute, as he holdeth theim in a great Securitie of Quiet. And fuerlye, my Lords, if the Ceffe, that they fo moch kicke at, might be once converted to a certeine Subfedie (as, in a fmall Contynuaunce of Tyme, it wilbe no harde Cafe to bringe to paffe, without any great Greiffe to the Subiecte) there is no Doubt, but that the Revenue of that Province would do more, then beare the Chardge of the fame : And therefore I finde no Reafon, but that the Thinge beinge fo eafye a Burthen to the Countrie, in Sorte as it may be impofed, and fo great a Savinge to the Quene ; but fome Devife fhould be vfed, it were put in Execucion.

The *Englifh* Pale is, in all Partes, verye quiet, fo that, in the Memorie of Man, never Winter paffed over, with leffe Loffe, and fewer Stealthes, and Bodraggs, then this hath donne.

The poore Subiecte enioyeth his owne without Feare, he is nether oppreffed by his ritche Neighbour, nor fpoyled of his noyfome Ennemie, but lyveth fafe, and in Securitie, without Daunger. The onelye Gawle of the Pale, for this Prefent, is the wilfull Repininge at the Ceffe, which is ftirred vp, by certeine bufye hedded Lawyers, and mifcontented Gentlemen, who in dede beare not theim felves the Burden of it, but the Fermors and Hufbandmen, who willinglye wold contribute towarde it, if the Gentlemen wold fuffer theim ; in fo moche as the Countie of *Meith*, beinge twife as bigge as any other Countie of the *Englifh* Pale, hath offered to geve fyve Marke *Sterlinge* out of everye Ploughland,

which

which is not above ij *d. Sterlinge* out of everye Acree ; and yet, if the fame were vniuerfall over *Leinſter* and *Meith*, it would amounte above 5000 Markes *Sterlinge* by the Yeare. And yet, in this Accompte, all auntient Fredomes ſhall remayne and contynue free ſtill : The Repiners, from whome theiſe newe Freedomes are nowe taken, and to whome the ſame were firſt graunted, in Reſpecte of Service to be donne by theim at generall Hoſtings, it was a Mocke-rye to ſee, what ſoarye Service thoſe Men they ſet forth, either did, or for their Traeyninge, or Abilitie, were hable to do for their Fredomes ; ſo that the Quene loſt both ordenarye and extraordenarye Subſidie. The Conſideracion whereof moved me to call the Statute in Queſtion, wherebye they challendge theiſe newe Freedomes and Exempcions ; and the Statute beinge ſeene and ſkanned vpon, it was founde that they could not iuſtlye any longer clayme any Fredomes by Force of the ſaied Statute, and ſo adiudged both by my Lord Chauncellor, and Sir *Lucas Dillon :* None of the reſt profeſſinge the Lawes, willinglye agreed to that Iudgement, and yet not any of theim all, hable, in Learninge nor Reaſon, to mainteine probable Argument to the Contrarie. And leaſt this Name of Ceſſe, beinge not an vſuall Woorde there, might ſeme to carrye ſome ſecreate Miſterye in the Terme, beinge miſconceived : May it pleaſe your Lordſhips therefore to conceive, that Ceſſe is nothinge ells but a Prerogatyve of the Prince, and an Agrement and Conſent, by the Nobilitie and Counſell, to impoſe vpon the Countrie a certeine Proporcion of Victuall of all Kindes, to be delyvered, and iſſued, at a reaſonable Rate, and, as it is commenlye tearmed, the Quenes Price : So that the Ryſinge and Fallinge of the Prices of Victualls, and Achates, and the Seaſonablenes of the Tymes, diere or cheape, makes the Matter eaſier or heavier to the Subiecte ; for when the Cowe was commenlye ſolde for viij or ix *s. Sterlinge,* the Pecke of Wheate at ij *s.* viij *d.* or iij *s.* the Pecke, and the Mutton at xij *d.* and ſo of the reſt, after the lyke Prices, this Burden was not fealt ; but ſoch an Agrement betwixt the Soldiour and Countrie Man, and ſo deſierous and lovinge one of an other, as there was no Repininge, but ſo wel-come was the Geſt to the Hoſt, as their was ever Greiffe and Sadnes, at their De-partinge, eche from other. And nowe although as moche be paied, as ever was in Rate, yet the Price growinge hier, and the Inſolencye of the Soldiour more then it was wont to be, in exactinge of Money vpon the poore Fermors, and ſometymes eſcapinge vncorrected for the ſame (which happneth as ſeldome as never, if they be complayned vpon) provoketh this Kickinge and Spurringe, at Ceſſe. Att the Beginninge when they found theim ſelves greived at this Bur-den, they exhibited their Complainte by Supplicacion vnto me, and the Coun-ſell, which we received verye willinglye, and I offered my ſelfe to ioyne with theim in Adviſe, if any Way might be thought of to eaſe their Greives, and not any further to chardge the Quene ; for the Soldiour could not pay above the Rate he did for his Victuall, and yet of Neceſſitie he muſt be found at that Price, except they would vndertake to defende theim ſelves, and lyve without the Soldiour. My Lord Chauncellor afterwardes tooke greate Travell to ſett downe their Device, and had both the Gentlemen of the Countrie and Victu-allers before hym, harde their Obiections, and the Victuallers Anſwers. And what he did in this Matter, and what he found, I referre to his Certificat and Reporte ; yet the Wilfulneſs of ſomme of the Gentlemen is ſoche, as not ſatiſ-fied withe anye Thinge I can doo, or invent for their Goode, doo combine and conſpire to lay their Purſes together, and to complayne of Ceſſe, and of me and my Governement. And therefore for the Firſte, myne Opinion is, that your Lordſhips mightlye mainteyne it, with your grave Cenſure, for without that, or Subſidie in Liewe of that, her Majeſtie ſhall never reare a Revenue to beare the Chardge of the neceſſarie Defence of this Countrie : And for the other, what ſo-ever they ſhall ſay of me, or my Governement, I ſhall crave no more, but that I may be harde, before I be condempned. The poore Mans Burthen, whom I ſeeke moſt to eaſe, by Reaſon of the Revocacion of theiſe newe Freedomes, beare a farre more eaſye Chardge, ſince ſomme of the Gentlemen, their Neighbours,

contribute

contribute with theim more, then heretofore they did : They are glad and thankefull for it, though others repyne, and spurne at that, which they cannot in any Sorte remedie, as longe as they are not hable to defende and maynteine their owne, without the Ayde and Healpe of a Garrison to reside amongest theim. It was avowched vnto me, in a generall Speach by the Countrie, that their was paied ix *l.* out of everye Plowghland for Cesse ; I offered to dischardge theim for fowre Markes ; and this is the harde Hand and ill Will I beare to the Countrie, and therefore your Lordships may see what iust Cawse they have to complayne.

I have sent your Lordships, herewith, the State of the Chardge of the whole Yeare, begonne the First of *October,* 1575, and ended the Last of *September,* 1576, and cawsed the Auditor to make a perfecte Booke and Collection of the same ; and although I have somewhat exceded my Promyse, for this Yeares Chardge, the same hath growen cheifely by Payments and Imprests, I made out of my Assignacion for Matters growen dewe, before the Tyme I entred Governemente ; yet, for vrgent Cawsies, and savinge her Majestie further Chardge, and to disbourden the Countrie of the Extorcions and Oppressions of the Soldiours, that remayned dischardged, and not paied, I cawsed to be issued oute, as may appeare more playnelye, by a Booke of Perticularities and Rates, set downe, and signed by Mr. Threasorer and the Auditor, which herewith I send to your Lordships ; of which Somme so disbourced for Things dewe before my Tyme, a-mountinge, in the Whole, to xv M. 2 C. lxiij *l.* iij *s.* viij *d. Sterlinge.* I am humblye to crave Allowaunce and Consideracion at her Majesties Handes : Besides the large Imprest delyvered, by Order there vnknowen to me, or without my Privetye here, and some entred into Enterteinement so longe before their Comminge hether, and neverthelesse the whole Chardge contynued here, for the Service of the Countrie, as though no soche Allowaunce had bene graunted there, which grewe, in the Ende, to a double Chardge to the Quene. Moreover, this vnloked for Broyle and Stirre in *Connaught,* which drewe some extraordenarye Exspence and Increase of her Majesties depe Chardge, that otherwise I meant to have bestowed in necessarie Reparacions, Fortificacions, and Buyldings, for Necessitie, Strength, and Defence of the Countrie ; so that, if theise extraordenarye Payments and Accidents had not happned, I had bene as farre vnder my Bondes, as nowe I have exceded theim ; neither is it to be hoped for, or expected by any Possibilitie, that, this next Yeare, her Majesties Chardge can be lessened, theise Winters Warrs having bene allreadye so chardgeable : But as my principall Care and Travell cheifelye tendethe to cut of her Majesties great Chardge, and encrease her Highnes Revenue, both certeine and casuall, as moch daylye as I can, and possiblye may devise to doe, and to bringe eche Province to defraye his owne Chardge, and beare his owne Burthen : So, to make a more sound Foundacion and Entraunce thereunto, I have, bothe in *Mounster* and *Connaught,* made Composicions with dyvers Lordes and Potentates of *Irishe* Countries, for a certeine annuall Rent and Service to be answered to her Majestie, as may apeare by a Booke of a perticuler Rentall, sent to Mr. Secretarye *Walsinghame,* to be imparted to your Lordships. And although it may be, that the Payments of the *Irish* Lords, accordinge to their Composicions with her Majestie, will not be at all Tymes so duelye observed, as amongst the cyviller Sorte, wherebye there may be a Certeintie sett downe of their Payments, by Recorde in the Surveior and Auditors Bookes, for the Lesseninge of her Majesties Chardge ; yet if Iustice may be contynued amoungst theim, and not pulled away from theim, I doubt not, within twoe or three Yeares, to make that as certeine a Rent and Revenue to the Crowne, as the *English* Pale yeldeth any. And therefore I hope your Lordships will consider, in the meane Tyme, that Things cannot be donne vpon the Soddeine, and looke for certeine and checker Payment at their Handes, as sone as Promise and Covenaunt is past their Mouthes, but waye those Sorts of People in their Kindes, who must be trayned by Degrees, and wonne by lyttle and lyttle to knowe their Dueties, even as the Tree bringethe forth his Fruite, and the Grounde yeldeth his Encreafe of Grayne, not forthwith, but in due Seafon, and Contynaunce of Tyme, which muft be obferved in theim. So in lyke Sorte, in managinge of theife Things, Tyme muft be had, and what Travell and Pollecye may do therein, I hope I fhall performe to the good Lykinge of her Majeftie and your Lordfhips. There is befides, for the Reducinge of *Mounfter* and *Connaught* to more Plyantnes, and Aptnes to yeeld Obedience, and imbrace Iuftice and Cyvilitie, feverall Commiffions devifed (wherein the Commiffioners take Travell) to apointe a Certeintie betwixt the Lorde and Tenaunt, that the Lorde may knowe what he fhould demaunde, and the Tenaunt what he fhould pay, to the Ende to abolifhe all *Irifhe* Extorcions, and vniuft Cuftomes amongft theim : Whiche Commiffions have bene verye well proceded in, by the great Care and Dilligence of the Lord Prefident of *Mounfter*, and brought, in a Manner, to verye good Effeéte in that Province. I lykewife fende vnto your Lordfhips, herewithe, the Booke of the State of the Armye, and alfo a Booke of all foche Fees as are due to the Patenties, whereof, as may appeare to your Lordfhips, fome have bene longe vnpaied. I humblye befeache your Lordfhips to have fpedie and gratious Confideracion of their Payments, that Money may be fent over hether, to difchardge that Debt ; it wilbe greatlye to their Satisfaccions and Comforts, if, by your Order, foch fpeciall Care be had of theim in Tyme. For, if they fhould expeéte their Payments to be made out of the Arreragies, as they are brought in, that will not be in a longe Tyme, and as the fame comethe in, it muft he imployd for the Payment of old Debts, due for Viétualls taken vpp, for Wagies of Artificers, Laborers, and Stuffe taken by Commiffion for Buyldings, for Wagies of Stipendaries, and other Extraordenaries, fit to be anfwered of thofe Arreragies ; and therefore I humblye pray your Lordfhips, have fpedie and gratious Confideracion of the Payment of the Patenties.

In my Memorialls for *Connaught*, I leaft vnremembred to your Lordfhips the good Service donne by *Thomas Le Straunge*, and Capten *William Collyer*, whome I leaft in the Entervall, betwixt my firft Iorney into *Connaught*, and the Settlinge Sir *Nicolas Malbye* Collonell there, to have in myne Abfence the principall Rule of that Province ; and beinge placed by me at *Ballyloughreough*, a principall Howfe of the Earle of *Clanrickardes*, they manfullye and valyauntlye defended bothe the Caftle and the Towne ; fo that they beinge befiedged, with twoe thowfand *Scottes* and *Irifh*, brought thether by the Earles Sonnes, to difpoffeffe theim of the Hold, they fhewed foch Pollecye and Valor, in manninge of their Walles, and other Places of Strength and Defence, as they preferved the Towne, beinge verye large, that no one Howfe or Cotage perifhed in it. And beinge in Nomber but one Hundered Footemen, and Fiffetye Horfemen at the moft, they manfully, fondrie Tymes, iffued out vpon the Ennemye, and, at Tymes, flewe fixe principall Captenes and Gentlemen of Note and Accompte amongft theim, and feaven Skore more of their Men and Soldiors, without Loffe of any one Man, in all thofe hote Skirmifhes. I humblye therefore befeache your Lordfhips that they may receive your Lordfhips Lettres and Thankes, in Token of fome good Allowance of their Service, which will be no fmall Ioy and Comforte vnto theim, to finde that Teftimonye of your Lordfhips Favors, which, in Troth, they have verye well deferved.

Some Hurte hath hapned of late in the *Kinges Countye*, by the foddeine Startinge out of the *Occonnors*, growen cheifely by the vnadvifed and negligent Dealinge of fomme put in Truft, who to haftelye gevinge Credite to the Othes of the Outlawes, difmiffed the Gard of the Countrie, whereof infued the Burninge of fome Ricks of Corne, and a fewe Cottagies, but nothinge fo moche as, I fuppofe, hath bene advertized over.

And where the Booke of Arreragies of the Quenes Debtes, which hath bene and is contynued, from Yeare to Yeare, and in Apparaunce and Bulke fheweth no fmale Matter ; fo that great Hope hath bene conceived, of longe Tyme, to bringe in a great Porcion thereof towardes the Anfweringe of her Maiefties

owne

owne Debts, growen due here. For as moch as the Parties, vpon whome thofe Arreragies are contynued, are either for the moft Parte dead, flayne, or in fo miferable and poor Eftate, as they are not in Cafe to anfwere theire Dewe, reftinge in Debt vpon theim in any Sorte. And therefore, for that the fame might more playnelye appeare to her Majeftie, which are fperate, and which are defperate Debtes, your Lordfhips fhould do well, in myne Opinion, to write expreffelye to the Auditor and Surveior, to certifie your Lordfhips the State of the faid Arreragies, and which Debts be fperate, and which be defperate, and to yeelde you the beft Reafons, why the Booke is contynued in Sorte as it is: And lykewife (for that fomme more Proffitt might growe to her Majeftie from the Parties or their Affignies, that owe the faid Arreragies, if they might once gather Hope, that any reafonable Order might, in the Ende, be taken with theim, and not vtterlye driven to difpaire of their Eftates) to graunt me, and her Majefties Counfell here, a generall Commiffion to compounde with theim att oure Difcreacions, to the moft Advantadge that may be to her Majeftie; wherein I hope to make more Commoditie to her Highnes then nowe (in Sorte, as the Cafe ftandeth) is any Wayes to be hoped from at foche Debtors Handes; for where there is nothinge (they fay) the Quene muft loofe her Right.

I intende, God willinge, within fewe Dayes, to repaier towardes the Northe, and there to deale with *T. Oneill*, whome I have fent for to mete me at the *Newrye*, whether when he fhall comme, I will compounde the beft Bargayne I can for her Majeftie, and likewife conclude with *Mac Genneffe*, and others of the *Irifh* Lordes in thofe Partes, and certifie your Lordfhips of my Proceadings with theim.

I will fhortlye fend over Bills for the Parliament, and then I will fhewe my fimple Advice, for Lettres for the Subfidye, which I differre till I be better informed of the Conclufion of theife Coniurates, who are yet in Hatchinge of their Devifes. I may not omitt to make knowen to your Lordfhips the Worthines of the Lord Chauncellor, as the beft belyked Man that ever was knowen to fitt in his Place, and, in deede, the beft worthie for his Dilligence, Iudgement, and Dexteritie. And becawfe I pittie the daylye Toyle he taketh, without Affiftaunce to his Lykinge and Contentacion, and feare, that the Contynuaunce will hazarde his weake fickelye Boddye: I am therefore to put your Lordfhips in Remembraunce of the fpedy Sendinge over of twoe learned Perfons, the one to fupplye the Place of a Iuftice, the other to be her Majefties Attorney here; it hath bene my fpeciall Sute maney Tymes to your Lordfhips: I befeache you therefore nowe, effectually remember it, that they may be apointed and fent hether with that Speede that convenientlye may be.

And nowe fearinge I have over weried your Lordfhips with my Tedioufnes of Diverfity of Matter, ill cowched, and put together, I will ende with fome fpeciall Requeftes to your Lordfhips: Firft, your good Acceptaunce and Allowaunce of my Lettres for the Courte of the Marches and Marche Cawfes, and your Anfwere vnto me vpon theim, towchinge the Points and Perticularities, whiche before this I looked for. Next I crave, by your Lordfhips Mediacions, to knowe her Majefties Refolucion in the Lykinge or Diflykinge of thofe Perfons I recommended of late to her Majeftie, to be placed in the Romes of Bifshoppes heare, as namelye, for *Offery*, *Ardawgh*, and *Roffe* in *Carberye*. And, laftlye, for that, by reafon of theife Winters Warres in *Connaught*, Supplye of Money muft fpedilye be had, to furnifhe thofe neceffarie Turnes of Service, which may not, without apparaunt Loffe and Hinderaunce, be omitted: I therefore humblye befeache your Lordfhips to take prefent Order, that afwell foch Money as is due alreadye the Firft of *January* prefent, as that whiche fhalbe due the Laft of *Marche* next, may be prefentlye delyvered to the Threaforer, or his Factor there, to be fpedilye convayed hether vnto me. And even fo, withe my hartie Prayers for you all, and humble

Duetie

Duetie remembred to your good Lordſhips, I take my Leave. From *Dublin*, the xxviith of *Januarye*, 1576.

Your honorable Lordſhips aſſured lovinge

Freinde to commaund,

H. Sydney.

Sir Henry Sydney *to Mr. Secretary* Walſyngham.

S I R,

I Have received your Lettre of the xvith of *November* laſt, the xxiijth of this *January* preſent, browght by my Servaunt *James Preſcott*. And like-wiſe ſene ſoch Notes and Memorialls as you delyvered to hym, to be imparted vnto me, and harde and vnderſtand from hym, what you gave hym further in Chardge to ſay vnto me, vpon ech perticuler Pointe, for the which I hartelye thanke you. And muſt deſire you, for the Preſente, to hold me excuſed, that I anſwere not the ſame with myne owne Hand, partlye for that I am impe-dited by Multitude and Varietie of Matters, and thorough Urgencye of Buſynes flittinge from Place to Place ; and beſides myne owne illegible Lettres and ſtag-gering Hand, wherein I finde ſoche Infirmitie, in the Weeldinge of my Pen, as it is very painefull for me to write. And withall, for that I meane very ſhortlye to write agayne, with myne owne Hand, vnto you at lardge, I deſire you, for this Tyme, excuſe me in this, and to expecte and accept that. And, firſt, I thanke you with all my Harte, that you take it thankefullye, any Thinge I have donne for Sir *Nicolas Malbye*, or Mr. *Waterhowſe*, which I thinke verye well beſtowed vpon theim, and wilbe no leſſe willinge nor readie hereafter to pleaſure any of your Freindes, you ſhall recommende vnto me, in the beſt and freindlieſt Sorte I can, in lyke Manner as I will make bold with you for myne.

And towchinge the Pointes conteined in the Earle of *Ormounds* Lettre, wherein firſt he deſierethe to have an Execucion of an Order paſt by Sir *William Fitz William*, for Pryce Wynes to be paied by Straungers : I wold be glad therein, or in any Thinge els, to ſatisfie the Earle ; but the Matter beinge of ſoch Weight, and for that neither his Lordſhip, nor any of his Aunceſtors, have at any Tyme had Poſſeſſion of Price Wynes of Straungers, in the Havons of *Dublin* and *Drogheda*. And alſo, for that the Cittie of *Dublin*, and the Towne of *Drogheda*, againſt whome he would have the Order maynteined, thinke theim ſelves greatly intereſſed, that they ſhould be condempned by an Order, and never called vnto it : And do offer, that if the Attorney and So-licitor, whoſe Opinions have bene alreadye certified of the Cawſe, or any twoe Iudges of *England*, not *arbitrablye, but iudiciallye, will affirme* (after their Coun-ſell be harde, who they wilbe reddye to ſend over at any Tyme) that the Earle ought to have Price Wynes upon Straungers ; they will never ſtande in Tryall of the Matter any further, but yeelde to the Earle. But that an Order, taken agaynſt one Straunger, ſhould conclude all Straungers, they thinke therein, that they ſhould be too hardlye dealt with all. Theiſe Reſpectes moved me, that I did not ratefie the Order, beinge not ſatisfied in Conſcyence of Therles Right. Nevertheleſſe, what I have donne to maynteyne the Order, and what Cawſe the Earle hathe to complayne for any Thinge I have donne therein to his Preiudice, I referre the Declaracion of the whole State of the Cawſe, and my Proceedings therein, to the Lorde Chauncellor, to whome I committed the Hearinge of the Matter.

To the Seconde, That my Lord of *Vpperoſſerye*, his Tenaunts and Followers, may come to Seſſions, as the reſt of the Countye of *Kilkennye* : It may like you to vnderſtand, that this Iorney beinge ended for Conference with *T. Oneill*, I have not onelye reſolved to make *Vpperoſſerye* Shire Grounde ; but all the

other

other Membres, and Lymes of *Leynſter* ; ſo that therein the Earle may be ſatisfied.

For the Thirde, That I ſhould deale favourablye in his Abſence with ſoch as he leaſt to take the Chardge of his Countrie and Tenaunts, what I have donne, and in what Sorte I have dealt with theim, aſwell in particuler as generall, for Confirmacion of their Authoritie he leaft them; as alſo in the renuewinge or grauntinge any other Commiſſion or Authoritie, they have requyred at my Handes ; I referre my Dealings with theim, and Vſage of them to their owne Reportes : And would wisſhe, that his Lordſhip ſhould deale no leſſe freindlye with me there, nor I do with his heare ; then theiſe Matters could breede no Queſtion betwixt us.

For the Order he writethe was not put in Execucion, if his Lordſhip meaneth that Order, which was taken for the *Dorowghe* : I do not remember, he made any further Demaunde, but to have the Poſſeſſion of that, which was graunted vnto his Lordſhip from the Biſhop of *Oſſerye*, and confirmed after by the Deane and Chapter ; and that was ordered he ſhould have : And I was moche offended with my Lord of *Vpperoſſerie*, as the Earles Agents can teſtifie, that he would ſtand in it, againſt the Earle. The Poſſeſſion of that he had, or at the leaſt might have had. But I ſee nowe, which I vnderſtood not then, neither was their any for the Earle, that ever acquainted me withall : A Pyle buylt by my Lord of *Vpperoſſeries* Father, which the Earle claymeth, as Percell of the Biſhopps Landes, and ſo conteined in his Graunte, which my Lord of *Vpperoſſerie* deniethe : There is an old ruynous Howſe called *Bisſhopps Courte*, that hath neither Dore, nor Wyndowe, good Flower, nor Rowſfe, and lies open on all Sides, for the which I had thought the Contencion had bene, and for the Landes belonging vnto it : This Pyle the Earle nowe challengethe, ſtandeth on the other Side of the Water, and the Streame runninge betwixt ; ſo that it is to be enquyred of by Commiſſion, and by Verdict of the Freeholders of the Countrie, whether it hath bene at any Tyme taken, and reputed a Parcell of the Biſhopps Landes, or noe. And if it be founde to have bene, I ſhalbe as willinge the Earle ſhould have it as the other ; but this was not then, browght in Queſtion before, which ſince hath bene opened.

And where you ſay, that it is looked for, that I ſhould ſpare ſomme of the ordenarye Allowance from thence this Yeare ; and by Reaſon that this is not performed, Holde is taken (by ſomme that neither wiſh moch Good to my ſelfe, nor yet to the Service) to my Diſadvantadge. I hope you will (as I perceive by your Notes you do) conſider the Cawſe of the Contynuance of this Chardge. But theiſe Troubles of *Connaught* beinge ended, which dependeth for the cheife Pointe, as I have written to the Lords, on the Hope of the Earle of *Clanrickards* Inlargement ; which Hope beinge once cut of, I doubt not then but *Connaught* wilbe quiet. And vntill that Tyme that *Connaught* be ſettled, Sparinge of Treaſure thence, more then Spendinge above my Porcion, is not to be loked for ; or vntill the Relieffe and Encreaſe of her Majeſties Revenue, for the Diſchardge of Ceſſe, be agreed vpon : That donne and made vniverſall, fowre Thouſand Pounde may be ſpared, from *Michelmas* next forwarde yearelye, and perhapps more, wherein I will travell to my vttermoſt.

That I ſhould avoyde all Occaſions which might breede Trowbles, in reſpecte therebye to avoyde Chardge. Sir, I have ever loved and ſought to ſettle a peaceable Governement, and all my Plotts and Deviſes have tended vnto that cheifley ; and if I have bene either by Wilfulnes and Diſobedience of ſomme, or by ſecreate Practiſe of others, croſſed in this Courſe, the Occaſion hath not at any Tyme growen from me ; neither can I deviſe to followe a better Rule therein, then I have donne.

For the Confirmacion of the Freindſhipp betwixt the Earle of *Ormounde* and me, I wold be verye glad of it ; neither, on my Parte, have I geven the Earle any Occaſion of Diſcontentment : But what he hath deſiered at my Handes that I could do, he hath had it ; he never aſked me Pardon for any, that I denied hym ; he never deſiered me to ſtay Pardon from any, that I have refuzed him : Thoſe that he recommended to Offices of Chardge, I have accepted and placed: Thofe he wold have difchardged, I have difplaced; and all other Tokens of Favor and freindlye Goodwill, I have fhewed hym: But for my Affection, that is not in my Power fo to rule, as I can place it where I am directed, but fome one Man I fhall affecte more then an other: There be fecreat Inftincts in thofe Cafes, which will not be repreffed; yet, in Matters of Iuftice, I have and will beare my felfe fo indifferent betwixt my Lord of *Ormounde*, and my Lord of *Vpper Offerie*, as Right fhall onlye prevayle, without Paffion or Affection more to one, then to an other.

For the Allowaunce of Enterteinement to the Earle, of fome fuch Porcion as is allowed to the Baron of *Vpper Offerye*, I meane this Service nowe in Action, againft the *Omorres* and *Occonnors*, beinge finifhed, to allowe neither the one, nor the other, any Enterteinement at all; but fave that and what I can befides, for the Leffeninge of her Majefties Chardge, which is called on daylye, and looked for at my Handes.

Touchinge the fecreat Lettres advertized hence, that there was never fo extreme Impoficions laied vpon the *Englifhe* Pale, and that the Soldiour, notwithftandinge his Payment is bourdenous to the Countrie. I affure you, Sir, that the Ceffe and Bourthen vpon the Pale, is no greater nowe then it was wont to be; neither is the Outrage of the Soldiour foche, as there is any iuft Cawfe to complayne againft him. For I have not onelye by expreffe Proclamacion reftrayned the Soldiour from all Infolencyes and Exactions, vpon extreme Payne for everye Offence he fhall committ, but animated the Countrie Man to complayne vpon the Soldiour, if he paffe the prefcript Order and Rule I have apoynted him; wherevpon fome Complaynts have bene brought vnto me, which, in Shewe, feemed greate at the Beginninge, and fo by Complaynte they were made; but, in the Ende, when they have bene duely examined, nothinge materiall hath bene iuftified and proved. And truelye, Sir, I am carefull to do the Countrie Good, and to prevent and take away from theim all Cawfies of Griefe and Complainte, but fome bufye hedded Lawyers, and difcontented Gentlemen, that are towched with the Loffe of their newe Freedomes: They are Procurers of theife Complaintes, more for Clamor, then for any Cryme, or iuft Cawfe of Greife they have.

For that it is faied I graunte maney Pardons, which breedeth Boldnes in thofe that are apte to offende: I never graunted fewer then nowe I do, nether graunt I any at all, but either at the fpeciall Sute of the Lord Prefident of *Mounfter*, the Collonell of *Connaught*, or at the Requeft of fomme other that hath fpeciall Chardge vnder me. The Cawfe they fue for theim, and that I graunte theim, is, for the better Quiet of the Countrie, and for Service Sake; other Refpecte moveth me not: For if he that hath bene an Outlawe, or other notorious Offendor, will nowe, vpon the Obteyninge of his Pardon, put in fubftancyall Suerties, hencefoorth to lyve obedientlye, and duetifully, and apear at all Seffions and Sifes, and anfwere in Iuftice to every Mans Demaunde (for all the Pardons I graunte have that expreffe Provifo) Good commeth to the Commen Wealthe, and Safetye to the Subiecte, by Grauntinge of foch Pardons. And therefore you may conceive by this, howe apt they be to complayne if they could finde Matter.

Concerninge the Anfwere to foch Pointes of my Inftructions as remayne yet vnanfwered, I have herewith fent vnto you, to be imparted to the Lords, the Booke of the whole Chardge for the laft Yeare; and an other Booke of the State of the Armye; the third a Rentall for *Mounfter* and *Connaught*; and the fowerth of the Fees dewe to the Patenties; fo that, as I take it, I have therein anfwered fully my Inftructions.

And where I wrote vnto you longe fince for *Cornelius Obreino* to be preferred to the Bifhoprick of *Roffe* in *Carberie*, Sir *John Petit* to *Ardagh*, and Mr. *David Cleire* to be Bifhop of *Offerye*, I am eftfones to put you in Remembraunce of theim; and pray you to procure me her Majefties Refolucion and Anfwere for theim, as fone as convenientlye you may. And for the laft, if in Cafe it be fo, that he be not thought worthye of the Place, but that I am croffed in my

Choyfe

Choyfe of hym ; and yet, in Troth, whatfoever is reported of hym, I affure you, he is a very honeft and fufficient Man, and a Devyne and not a Civilian : Neverthelefe, if it fhall not fo ftande with her Maiefties Pleafure, to allowe of my Recommendacion of *Cleire*; then, I pray you, commend Mr. *Walfhe* vnto the Place, who is a very godlye and well learned Preacher, and foch a one as for his Modeftie, Learninge, and other commendable Vertues, is verye worthye of that or a better Place.

And where I have bene earneftlye in Hand with Mr. *Agarde* for the Wallinge of *Arcklowe*, which he hathe halfe promifed, and wold vndertake to doe, if he might have a Patent onely duringe Pleafure of the Conftablefhipp of the Caftell : For as moche as the Wallinge of the faied Towne, ftandinge in the Harte of a wylde Countrie, wold be a Meanes both to replenifhe the Towne with People, and to drawe maney Artifans, and other mecanicall Perfons, to dwell there, when they may be affured to remayne in Saffetye within Walles. And lykewife a great Cawfe of Increafe of Obedience and Civilitie in the Countrie, befides the Working of foch Commodities within the Towne, which are now tranfported over thence, for Lacke of foch People to be fet on Woorke, to the great Hyndraunce and Preiudice of the Common Wealthe. I pray you therefore, for the common Benifitt of the Countrie, to procure Mr. *Agarde* a Patent of the faied Conftablefhipp ; it will encourage hym the rather to take vpon hym the Woorke.

The reft off this Lettre finifhed and written with my Lords owne Hand, and fo fent away.

Sir Henry Sydney *to Mr. Secretary* Walfyngham.

S I R,

I Received a Lettre from you, dated from *Readinge*, and written on the Behalfe of a Freinde of yours, who, as it feameth, hath bene an earneft Sutor unto you, to obteine for hym Lycence from her Majeftie, to tranfporte over certeine Packes of Yarne out of this Countrie. And becawfe the Matter might carrie a better Teftimonie of my Goodwill and Allowaunce of the Sute (if that were brought in Queftion, or fhould neede to be fhewed hereafter) you requyred my Lettre vnto you, to that Effecte, which I have not prefentlye written as you defiered, becawfe I wold be lothe to deftroy a Creature of my Makinge, and an Invencion of myne owne, which I devifed for the Benifitt of the Commen Wealthe, that the People might be fett on Worke, and that the Commodities might be wrought within the Realme, and not to be tranfported hence rawe and vnwrought, as they were accuftomed ; which, if it wold pleafe you to looke into, and pervfe the Statute, (it is in Printe) you fhall more playnelye perceive the Grounde, wherevpon that Statute was made. If therefore I fhould nowe be the firft Breaker of that I procured to be made, for the Good of this poore Countrie, and that doe of my felfe, without Confent of others, in a Thinge that may do fo great a Hindraunce to the Commen Wealthe, and no Commoditie to the Sovereigne, I fhould not well allowe of myne owne Doings ; If nowe fince Mr. *Hattons* Lycence is expired, the Grauntinge whereof was thought to be no Benifitt to the Countrye, I fhould be a Meanes to further an other Lycence of the fame Nature : Yet becawfe I would be lothe to denye you for any Freinde you write for any Thinge I might do : I wold wifhe you to write your Lettre to me, and the Counfell here, to call fome of the Marchaunts of the Porte Townes before vs, and to examyne the Matter of the Commoditie or Difcommoditie of foche a Lycence, and certifie you what we finde by Conference with theim, and oure Opinions, what we thinke of the Grauntinge of it, wherein, if convenientlye, I may freinde you without to great Preiudice to others (the Quantitie not being great) you fhall fynde howe

reddie

reddie I wilbe to pleafure your Freinde for your Sake. And even fo I bid you Farewell. From *Mellefont* the xxxth of *January*, 1576.

Your affured loving Freinde,

H. Sydney.

Sir Henry Sydney *to the Lords of the Counfell.*

My verye good Lords,

MY humble Duetye remembred to your honorable Lordfhips: After I was comme hether to deal in Cawfes of the North, I received Lettres fent vnto me, by an expreffe Meffenger from the Archbifhopp of *Dublin*, to defier Lycence of me, to repaier into *England*, with fomme Note and Teftimonie from me, what I had found of hym here. And al be it the Motion femed to me at the firft to be verye fodden: Yet confideringe the Manner of his Writinge, and the Conveyinge of his Meaninge, proceded from fomme depe Conceipt of a perplexed Mynde, and a forowfull Harte, for fomme Matter that touched hym niere (as it femed) I could not denye hym fo reafonable a Requeft, but graunted hym Leave to departe, with this Teftimonie, that I have found hym reddye to comme to me at all Tymes, when I had Occafion to vfe his Affiftaunce for her Majefties Service, and verye willinge to fett forwarde any Thinge, that might either concerne the publike Benifitt, or Quiet, of the Countrie, or her Majefties Honnor or Proffit; befides a Man well geven, and zelous in Religion, dilligent in Preachinge, and no Nigarde in Hofpitallitie, but a great Relyver of his poore Neighbours, and by his good Behaviour, and Dealinge, gayned both Love and Creditt, amongft thofe with whome he hath bene converfant; and caried hym felfe in that Reputacion in the Worlde, as I have not knowen hym at any Tyme, either detected or fufpected of any notorious, or publike Crime. And thus moche I thought good to declare to your Lofdfhips of hym, and that I have not had Cawfe at any Tyme, to thinke otherwayes of hym, but as of a found Councellor to the Quene, and good Minifter to this Countrey and Common Wealthe. And even fo, befeaching your Lordfhips favorable Acceptacion of hym, and in his Peticions (if he have any) to ftand his good Lords: I humblye take my Leave. From the *Newrye* the xiith of *Februarye*, 1576.

Your good Lordfhips affured lovinge

Freinde to commaund,

H. Sydney.

Sir Henry Sydney *to Queen* Elizabeth.

May it pleafe your moft excellent Majeftie,

BEinge here at the *Newrie*, for Cawfies of Conference with *T. Oneill*, and to deale in the Matters of the Northe: I received Lettres from Tharchbifhopp of *Dublin*, not conceived (as it femed to me) by the Phrafe of his Writinge, without fome great Perplexitie of Minde, and inwarde Sorrowe, and Greife of Harte; and made earneft Sute vnto me, to geve hym Lycence for a Tyme, to repaier over to your Majefties Prefence, with fome Teftimonie from me, what I have found of hym here; and although it may like your Majeftie, the Motion femed to me verye fodden; yet waying the Earneftnes of his Demaunde, thought his Occafion greate, and therefore lyke as I helde it expedient, to geve hym Lycence to departe, and not to deteine hym here: So I fuppofed it convenient thus farre to witnefs of hym, that I have ever founde hym reddye to comme when I had Occafion to call hym, to ferve your Majeftie; and in debatinge of Cawfies, an vpright, and found Councellor to the State, and

I   one

one willinge to advaunce and fett forwarde any Service, that might concerne either your Honnor or Benifitt, or the commen Quiet of the Countrie : Befides, I have found hym dilligent in the Woorkes of his Vocacion, zelous, and intire in Religion, a good Preacher, and one that as often occupied the Pulpitt, as any one of his Callinge, that I have harde in this Land ; not fpare in Hofpitallitie, and fo generally hath behaved hym felfe in the Woorld, as I have not knowen hym either detected or fufpected of any notorious or publike Offence, but a Man that hath fimply walked in the Feare of God (for any Thinge I knowe) and gayned Love and Creditt amongft thofe, with whome he hath bene moft converfaunt. And thus having expreffed that I thinke and fynde of hym, I humblye pray your Majeftie, to ftande his gratious Sovereigne, befeachinge the Almightie longe and happelye to preferve your Majeftie to rule and reigne over vs, to your noble Hartes Defier, and to our ineftimable Comforts. I moft humblye take my Leave. From the *Newrye* the xijth of *Februarye*, 1576.

Your Majefties moft humble and obedient

Subiect and Servaunt,

H. Sydney

Sir Henry Sydney *to Mr. Secretary* Walfyngham.

SIR,

WHereas of late certeine Agents, from the Marchaunt Straungers, of the *Lowe Countries*, have bene Sutors vnto me, that they might obteine my Allowaunce, and good Confent, to have fome convenient Place, within this Realme, affigned vnto theim, where they might remayne and dwell in Saffetye togethers, in the Exercyfe of their Religion, and be incorporated with certeine Freedomes, Privelidgies and Liberties, according to a Booke of Peticions they exhibited vnto me ; I havinge withe the Advife of her Majefties Counfell, my Affiftaunts here, had Confideracion of their Sute, and wayenge howe neceffarie, and expediente it is, to have this Countrie more plentifullye peopled, and efpeciallye ftored, with mecanicall and handye Craftes Men (whereof nowe there is to great Want and Scarcetie) for the Woorkinge of the Commodities, within the Lande ; and likewife the rather, both to allure, and teache the Natyves of the Soyle, to be more induftrious, and to learne to fett theim felves a Woorke, wherebye fo lardge Commoditie wold growe to the Countrie, Beniffit to her Majeftie in the Encreafe of her Cuftome, and otherwayfe, in Licenfinge the Straungers to refide and dwell here amongft theim : I have therefore affented to dyvers of their Peticions, and put theim in Comforte, that they fhalbe both lovinglye receaved, countenanced by my Authoritie, and lykewife enioy foch Lyberties and Favor, as, in good Difcreacion, I can graunte theim. And for as moche as in their Removinge thence, to comme hither, they are to bringe over with theim, both Money to fett their Artifans and handye Craftes Men on Woorke, Howfehold Stuffe, and other Vtenfilles and Neceffaries (fuch as in Removinge of Howfeholds is accuftomed) which they cannot doe, but they fhall encurre Penaltie and Daunger of Lawe, and Forfeyture of foch Things as they fhall tranfporte and carrye over, without fpeciall Lycence and Favor. I pray you extende your freindlye Goodwill towardes theim, and the Advauncement of fo good a Plott intended, for the Benifitt of this Realme, as to procure theim a Pafporte, and Lycence, for the Tranfportacion of their Money, Howfehold Stuffe, Vtenfills, and other their Neceffaries and Commodities, that they may not be ftayed in their Comminge over, but may have fre Paffage, paienge either no Cuftome, at all, or ells fo reafonable a Rate for Cuftome, as they may not be difcouraged of this their Adventure, at the Beginninge, which I hope in Tyme to come will torne to no fmall Commoditie to bothe the Realmes, if this Enterprife may be well favored and countenaunced : For it is a Thinge I have longe wiſhed, and fought for, to have this Countrie ſtored of Men of their Sorte (whereof there is in all Places of this Realme ſo great Want) : Their Factor, *Godfray Slabbard*, alias *Cotten*, will attende vpon you, for this Difpatche. I pray you both favor, and further hym in his reaſonable Requeſts, the rather to haſten hym, with his Companye hitherwards, which I exſpecte at this next Springe. And even ſo I bid you hartelye Farewell. From *Dublin*,   1576.

Your aſſured lovinge Freinde,

H. Sydney.

Sir Henry Sydney *to Queen* Elizabeth.

May it pleaſe your moſt excellent Majeſtie,

THE Bearer hereof, Sir *Cormocke Mac Teige Mac Cartye*, hath deſiered Lycence to repaire over, to doe his Dutie to your Highnes ; whiche he is drawen to dooe, ſo moche the more, with an erneſt Deſier, for that he and his Aunceſtors have ſo maney Yeares bene accompted loyall and duetifull Subiectes to the Crowne of *England*, and received Lettres from their Sovereignes, enriched with that worthie Blaſon and Title (which auntient Teſtimonies he kepes, as the rareſt Jewells, and deareſt Treaſure he hathe) and yet hetherto nether he, nor any of his Aunceſtors, have atteined to that Felicitie, to have ſeene their Sovereignes ; affirminge, that he hym ſelfe ſhould be the firſt, that hath donne it, and therebye accompteth his Life, and State, ſo moche the more happier, then theirs was. And in Trothe, Madame, as he is not inferiour to any of theim, nether in honeſt Qualities of the Mynde, nor Happines in Fortune, and Eſtimacion amongſt his Equalls ; yet in this Pointe he thinkethe him ſelfe farre to have exceded theim all, that he may have Acceſſe to his Princes Preſence, and beholde his deare Sovereigne, to his Ioy, and Comforte. His next Requeſt is, that he may ſurrender his Landes into your Handes, and take theim agayne of your Majeſtie, and yeld you Rente and Service ; and laſt, that your Majeſtie will hold hym, in thoſe Tearmes of your gratious Favor, as one of the dutiefulſt, lowlieſt, and humble Subiecte, your Majeſtie hath of his Trayninge and Breadinge of all thoſe Partes ; for ſo I found hym at my beinge there, and placed him Sheriffee in the Countye of *Corcke*, and had that Service at his Handes, and that Readines to anſwere, that I commaunded and directed hym vnto ; as I never held my ſelfe better ſatisfied of any Man of his Sorte, then of hym. I gave hym by the Hande to Sir *William Drewrie*, the Preſident of the Province, where he dwellethe, who hath founde ſo good Effecte of his Travell in your Majeſties Service, as he hath moſt ſpeciallye and earneſtlye recommended hym vnto me, nowe at the Leavinge of his Chardge of Sherifewicke, as the onelye odd Man he founde of this Countrie Birthe in *Mounſter*, reddie to performe and execute that, that apperteined to his Office. I therefore humblye befeache your Majeſtie, let hym fynde youer gratious Acceptacion of his Service paſt, to his Comforte, and Encouragement of that to comme ; for aſſuredlye he deſervethe to be moche cheriſhed and made of, as a good Inſtrument of your Majeſties Service, in the middeſt of thoſe rude, and barbarous People, where Civilitie, and good Governement, and Taſt of your Lawes, is but in her tender Infancye, and by Degrees to be hoped daylye to growe, to more Ripenes and Perfection, whiche I befeache God proſper your Hignes, that you may ſe complete, and perfect, in your moſt gratious and happie Reigne, to your immortall Fame, and perpetuall Memorie, to your Poſteritie. And even ſo I moſt humblye take my Leave. From your Majeſties Caſtle of *Dublin*, the   of *Marche*, 1576.

Your Majeſties moſt bounden humble

Subiecte and Servaunte,

H. Sydney.

Sir

Sir Henry Sydney *to the Lords of the Councell.*

May it pleafe your good Lordfhips,

THE Bringer hereof, Sir *Cormocke Mac Teige Mac Cartye,* havinge nowe ended his Chardge of Sherivaltie in the Countye of *Corcke* (where I placed hym) greatlye to his Commendacion, as may appeare by a Lettre fent me from the Lord Prefident of that Province, the Copie whereof I herewith fende your Lordfhips, is nowe defierous to have Lycence to repaier thither, to do his Duetie to her Majeftie, and to furrender his Landes into her Handes, and to take theim agayne of her Highnes, and yeeld her Rent and Service. Younge *Ocaloghan* accompanieth hym thither lykewife, for that Purpofe, to furrender his Landes, and to hold theim agayne of her Majeftie, vpon the lyke Condicions ; he is Heire to his Grandfather, who is fo aged and impotent a Man, as he hath geven vp, both the whole Chardge of his Countrie into his Handes, and affured his Landes vnto hym, beinge, by lawfull Difcent, his next Heyre in Bloud. Off the firft I have written in fomme of my former Lettres to your Lordfhips, that I found him, for his Obedience to her Majeftie, and her Lawes, and Difpoficion to Civilitie, the rareft Man, that ever I found was borne in the *Irifhrey,* and therefore I told your Lordfhips, I entended to write more fpeciallye of hym, as of a fpeciall Man, and trewlye fo I finde of hym, to be a fpeciall Man in deede : For his good Endevours, and Forwardnes in the Advauncement of her Majefties Service, geve me daylye new Occafion to encreafe my good Opinion and Lykinge of hym everye Way. And therefore, I humblye befeache your Lordfhips, let hym fynde thankefull Acceptacion of his Service at your Handes, and foche fpeedie Furtheraunce and Favor in his honeft Sutes, as he may be encouraged to hold on the good Courfe he hath begonne, whiche vndoubtedlye he will doe, in doublinge his former Defertes, if, by your comfortable Speaches, he may receive good Countenaunce and Thankes, for that he hath donne alreadye. He is one defierous to have Iuftice planted, and Civillytie imbrafed in his Countrie, and cravethe the due Correction of Offendors, and that they may be made of that Enclyne to Reformacion, and feeke to obey her Majefties Lawes. And his playne Talke expreffethe his honeft Mynde, for he cannot difguyfe his Meaninge ; his Territorie is greate, and, in maney Commodities and Pleafures, aboundant ; he is defierous onelye to depende of the Crowne of *England,* as he and his Aunceftors have donne, and to be well thought of by your Lordfhips, for his Loyaltie and Service. And even fo humblye recommendinge hym, and his Cawfe, to your Lordfhips grave Confideracions, I humblye take my Leave. From the Caftle of *Dublin,* the .... of *Marche,* 1576.

Your honorable Lordfhips affured

lovinge Freinde to commaund,

H. Sydney.

Sir Henry Sydney *to his Son,* *Sir* Philip Sydney.

Phillipp,

I Have recommended this Bearer, Sir *Cormocke Mac Teige Mac Cartye,* afwell by my Lettres to her Majeftie, as to the Lords, as one, that for his longe Fidellitie, and duetifull Behaviour, and Forwardnes to advaunce her Majefties Service, is to be cherifhed and made of. I would have you make hym knowen to my Lords, your Vnckles, and to other your Freindes in the Courte, as a fpeciall Man of this Countrie Birthe ; and his Trayninge and Breadinge vpp. His Comminge over is to doe his Duetie to her Majeftie, to furrender his Landes into her Majefties Handes, and to holde theim agayne of her, in yeeldinge her Rent and Service. He is not the beft Courtier, for his Bringinge vpp hath bene fomewhat homelye, but his plaine Talke will well expreffe his honeft

Mynde,

Mynde, which he beareth to the *Englifhe* Governement ; and defierous he is of an vniverfall Reformacion of this Countrie, vnder the moft happie Reigne of her Majeftie ; he is one, that in Hand and Harte, much honoreth me, and I have ever founde him iuft of his Woorde, and forwarde in her Majefties Service. I recommende hym vnto you as my good Freinde, and a fpeciall Man ; acquainte hym, countenaunce hym, and further hym, as moche as you can. And fo prayinge God to bleffe you, and make you his contynuall Servaunt, I bid you Farewell. From the Caftle of *Dublin*, the   of *Marche*, 1576.

Your lovinge naturall Father,

H. Sydney.

Sir Henry Sydney *to the Lords of the Councell.*

My verye good Lords,

MY humble Duetie remembred to your honorable Lordfhips. After I had finifhed, and fent away my laft Difpatche, addreffed to your Lordfhips, from *Dublin*, the xxvijth of *January* laft, I fet forwardes immediatlye towardes the Northe, and went as farre as the *Newrye*, of Intencion to fpeake with *Tirelaugh Lynaugh*, to conclude with hym the beft Bargayne I could for her Majeftie, vnto whome I had written afore, to come to me thither. He humbly, by Lettres (after he hard I was come) excufed hym felfe vnto me, he could not repaier vnto me, partlye for that (as he alleadged) he was ficke and weake, and fo not hable, with out Daunger of fome apparaunt Perrill, to travell fo farre : And fomewhat he deferred longer (as it femed) for that he defiered, and made Shewe, as it were by newe Treatie to have larger Condicions at her Majefties Handes, then formerlye was concluded, betwene hym and me, together with Encreafe of Territorie and Fee : But I found at length, it was but all Delay he went about, for he yeelded fo moche to the fayre Speaches, and lewd Counfell of his Wyffe, as he would not come : Whofe Defigne is (and if it might take Place) to make her younger Sonnes, fhe had by *James Mac Conell* (her eldeft Sonne beinge alreadye provided for in *Scotland*) Starcke in *Ireland* (for that is her Tearme) and therefore ftayethe her Hufband all that lyethe in her, that he fhould not yeeld to that Conformitie, as of hym felfe he was apt ennough, and enclyned vnto : Leaft if he fhould, her Plot for her younger Sonnes, would be quite overthrowen. For fhe fuppofethe, that if he kepe hym felfe a Loofe, and in Tearmes, as he dothe, the *Scotts* fhall gett the better Footinge here, and foche a Plantinge and Setlinge in the Northe, by Contynuaunce of Tyme (as hard and difficult it wilbe to fupplant theim hereafter) for fhe fayeth fhe is not here, in Refpecte of her felfe, but for the Benifitt of her Sonnes, and the Wealth and Good of her Countrie : And for a more cleire Manifeftacion and Note, that fhe was the onelye Lett of her Hufbands Comminge vnto me to the *Newrye*, it appearethe in this, that he beinge at *Carigfergus*, defierous to be made free of the Towne, and fo readye to take the Othe of his Freedome, fhe with held hym, and would not fuffer hym to do it ; for (fayeth fhe) you have not bene yet with my Lord Deputie, you knowe not what Ende you fhall have in your Cawfies with hym. And therefore I would not have you take the Oth, and knowe not howe you fhalbe able to kepe it. But *Piers* reported vnto me, that vpon fomme private Conference *Terelaugh* had with hym, he told hym in fecreate Sorte, that if I would come downe, and make Warre vpon the *Scotts*, and do one Dayes Service vpon theim, that in deede they might feele my Forces, to make theim ftoope. He would put away his Wiffe, and do his beft, to chafe, and expulfe all the *Scotts* out of *Ireland :* Yet mofte of his Strength confiftethe by the *Scottes*, for he is not beloved, but rather hated of his owne Followers ; and without *Scotts* he is verye weake, and eafye to be dealt with : And therefore I would wifhe her Majeftie fhuld write to the Regent of *Scotland* (as formerlye I have

written

written to her Majeftie, or to your Lordfhips) that for the better Prefervacion of the Amytie, and Neybourhoode, betwixt her Majeftie and the Kinge his Mafter, and their Dominions and Subiects, that he would, either by Lettre of Reftrainte, or els by publique Edicte, forbid, afwell thofe of the meane Lande, as thofe of the out Ilandes, to comme hither : Vndoubtedlye, my Lords, it would make the Northe, eafier to be governed, the People more quiet and o-bedient, and yeeld more both in Rent and Service to her Majeftie, then without that they can be brought vnto. *Terelaugh* folicited and intreated me, at my Departinge from the *Newrye*, that the former Agreement he made with me at *Armach*, in *November* 1575, might be ratefied, which (by Reafon I was pre-fentlye drawen thence, by other Occafions) I rather yeelded vnto. But in Trothe I fynde he is eafye ennough to be fubdued, what by Reafon of his old Yeares (which rather covet Reft, and more willinglye followe Quiet) his Infirmitie of Brayne and Boddye, geven to large Exceffe and daylye Surffeit, and a Bullet or twoe in his Boddye, whereof he is not yet delyvered : So as if the reft of the Provinces were once fettled, it were no hard Cafe to frame hym to do what I would, and to make hym little or great as I lift my felfe. Duringe the Tyme of my Aboade at the *Newrye*, I concluded Agrement with *Mac Mahon*, who co-venaunteth to yeeld her Majeftie in Rent 250 Bieves Yearelye, and a Laborer out of everye Howfe, when Occafion of Service fhall requyre, and the Ryfinge out to all Hoftings and Iorneys, xij Horfemen, and xxiiij^{tie} Kerne ; the Booke and Draught of which Agrement, concluded betwixt *Mac Mahon* and me, I fende to Mr. Secretarye, to be imparted to your Lordfhips. I lykewife entred into Speache with fome other of the Lords of that Province, who are defierous to make lyke Compoficions with her Majeftie as he hath donne. And I doubt not, if other more neceffarie Occafions of Service, with drawe me not thence, but that I might freelye, without other Troubles and Impediments, fpende but one Sommer there, to make all *Vlfter* pay, certeine and good Tribuite to the Quene. But one Difficultie I finde, which geveth no fmall Impedimente in this Service, afwell in that Province as in others, which is, that I am reftreyned ab-folutlye to make Compoficion and Agreement with the *Irifhrye*, when they make offer of Surrender vnto me ; but that by Way of Mediacion, I muft firft certifie their Offers, and then expecte the Retorne of your Lordfhips Anfweres : And the *Irifhmen* thinke the Tyme fo longe, if they be deferred, and not ac-cepted at the firft, when they fhall make offer, as they imagyne, that there is no found Dealinge meante towardes theim ; and that this Deferringe importethe no leffe, but that they fhall never have that which they feeke for at her Majefties Handes, and that maketh maney of theim to forbeare to comme vnto me, which otherwife would, yea, vpon their Knees, offer the Surrender of their Landes withall their Hartes. And therefore neceffarie it were in my fimple Opinion (favinge your Lordfhips better Reformacions) for the Advauncement of her Majefties Service, and the Difbourden of her Chardge, and the Increafe of her Revenues, that I, and others with me here, fhould henceforth have abfolute Commiffion fent vs, to deale without foche Circumftaunce and Ceremonie, and compounde with the *Irifhrye* (I fpeake it, my Lords, for her Majefties Service) and then I would not doubt, but to make a fpedye, and beneficiall Bargayne for her Majeftie, and do a good Service to the State, and woorke no fmall Quiet to the Countrie : For all do not offer to furrender vpp their Landes, and take the fame againe by *Englifhe* Tenure ; but fomme of theim to furrender their Landes, and take it agayne at her Majefties Handes, to hold accordinge to the Cuftome of the Countrie. For where there are maney Pretendors, and collaterall Com-petitors to the Lande there, if the Lande fhould difcende by *Englifh* Tenure to the eldeft Chylde, the Striffe amongft the Competitors, would never be ftinte, as longe as any of the Competitors were alyve : Experience hath taught it fo maney Tymes, and in fo maney Places, as I fynde rather Hurte then Good groweth of thofe Mannor of Surrendors. But contrarye wife, where there are fewe or no Competitors at all, and the Lorde that furrendereth hath fufficient and hable Iſſue of his owne, there to extinguiſhe all Debate, the *Engliſh* Tenure (in myne Opinion) is the beſt : So that in theiſe Grauntes, a great Regarde muſt be had, and no generall Rule can be ſett downe in the Caſe, but the Thinge to be governed from Tyme to Tyme in good Diſcreacion, as Occaſion ſhall fall oute.

Mounſter, Thankes be to God, contynueth in good Quiet ; moch the rather thorough the good, and pollitique Governement of Sir *William Drewrye*, Lord Preſident there, whoſe vpright Juſtice, ioyned to his great Dilligence, Dexteritie and Travell, to heare Greiſſes and Complaintes, and ſo ſpedilye to redreſſe theim (as he dothe) his Severitie and Terror to the worſt Sorte, in the Execucion of her Majeſties Lawes vpon theim, and Courteſye and Bountye to thoſe that deſerve it, kepethe the Countrie in good Obedience, Cyvillitie, and Order : Somme Frowardenes he hath founde of late in the Earle of *Deſmounde*, to yeeld to beare Ceſſe : Yet Fearefulnes in hym with all (as it ſeameth) to moche to offend hym, or the State, he is commen in to the Preſident, and delyvered in his Men, that were demaunded (which before he denied) being in deede notorious Malefactors, and Breders of Vnquiet. His Brother, Sir *John*, is committed for Conferrence he had with *Shane Bourke*, and a Combinacion ſuſpected to have bene concluded betwixt theim, for the Maintenaunce of *Shanes* Rebellion, Sir *John* promiſſinge to ſupplye *Shane* with Ayde out of *Mounſter*, and ſo perſwadinge hym to hold oute. He hath an Intencion to put away his owne Wyffe, and to matche in Marriage with *Shanes* Siſter, who was *Orwacks* Wiffe, and of late forſaken by hym. The Intelligence (as I heare) betwixt *James Fytzmorice* and the Rebells, and their Complices, is ſtill nouriſhed ; Lettres ſent, and Meſſagies curraunt betwixt theim, in Hope to have Force by *James* his Meanes thence, to invade here, as *James* promiſeth by Lettres, for too maney there be, that carrie vnſounde Myndes, partlye for Religion, partlye for that by Reaſon of the reſident and ſettled Authoritie there, they are bridled and reſtrayned daylye more, and more, from their wonted, and innate Tirrannies, which they are loth to forgoe.

I may not forgett to recommende to your Lordſhips, the great Travell and daylye Toyles of Sir *Nicholas Malbye* in *Connaught*, who thorough his contynuall Paynes, and infinite Labors, in the moſt harde Seaſon of the Yeare, hath ſo broken the Harts, and daunted the Courages of the Rebells, as moſt of their Followers of any Accompte, have vtterlye forſaken theim. The one Brother left the other, ſo that nowe they are ſo weake brought, as the onelye Hope of their Fathers Enlardgement holdeth theim vpp, which if it were once determined, the inteſtine Warrs of this Countrie were ſone finiſhed, and without that, neither quiet Obedience nor Increaſe of Revenue are to be loked for there. And therefore I meane to procede withe the Earle, accordinge to Lawe, for the longer the Matter is deferred, the more Harme, and Perrill, will enſue, both to the Quiet of that Countrie, and the State of the Realme ; for he is ſo ill a Member (ſavinge your Lordſhips Reformacions) to be kept any longer : And the Preſervacion of hym, and the Hope conceived of hym, doth not onelye infecte the Province of *Connaught*, but all the Members and Provinces adioyninge ; yea, and I feare the whole Realme too. I have therefore thought it expediente (to the Ende the Manner of this diſguyſed Dealings, and his ſubtill and Rebellious Intencions and Practizes, may the better appeare to your Lordſhips, to iudge of his Deſerts) to ſende to Mr. Secretarye, to be imparted to your Lordſhips, aſwell the Accuſacions that are layed againſt hym, as the Examinacions, and Depoſicions that are taken of hym, and his Anſweres to the ſame, both at large, and by Way of Abbreviate, for your Lordſhips more Eaſies (if you ſo like) to viewe, and pervſe theim.

Rorie Oge Omore, and *Cormocke Mac Cormocke Oconnor*, accompanied not with above 140 Men and Boyes, on the Third of this Monethe, bourned betwene vij or viij C. thatched Howſies, in a Markett Towne, called the *Naas* ; they had not one Horſeman, nor one Shot with theim ; they ranne thorough the Towne, beinge open, like Haggs and Furies of Hell, with Flakes of Fier faſtened on

Pooles

Pooles End's, and so fiered the lowe thatched Howsies; and beinge a great windie Night, one Howse tooke Fier of an other in a Moment; they tarried not halfe an Howre in the Towne, neither stoode they, vpon killinge or spoylinge of any. There was above fyve hundered Mennes Boddies in the Towne, manlyke enough in Apparaunce, but nether Manfull, nor Wakefull, as it seamed, for they confesse they were all aslepe in their Bedds, after they had filled theim selves, and surfeyted vpon their Patrone Day; which Day is celebrated for the most Parte, of the People of this Countrie Birthe, with Glottonye and Idollatrye as farre as they dare. They had nether Watche, nor Gate shutt, and if they had had, yet the Towne is open on all Sides of it selfe; but this makethe a good Proffe, and playne Declaracion, what good Champions theise People are, for the Defence of a Frontier, where no Soldiours are planted to defende theim; yet howe vnwillinge to beare any Chardge towardes the Maintenaunce of theim. Howe be it, I hope erre it be longe, so to devise to healpe theim, as the Towne shalbe better, then ever it would have bene, if it had not bene bourned. Theise Rebells, *Moores,* and *Occonnors,* exceede not the Nomber of one hundred fightinge Men, nor of that Companie, not above sowre able to leade to anie Exploite; so moche of late hath their principall Men ben bereft theim, by the great Dilligene, Pollecye, and Payne Takinge of my Lord of *Vpper Osserie,* Mr. *Cosbye, Harpoole,* and *Owen Mac Huge.*

In my last I touched somewhat at length to your Lordships, the great Repininge at the Cesse, that is made by certeine Gentlemen of the Pale, whose Fredomes, by Order and Proclamacion, are of late taken from them; and in Troth the Bourden is great, as the Prices and Rates of Things are nowe; but since I came first Governor to the Lande, the Prices that are geven nowe, are as moche as the Things were woorthe then in Value, to be sold in the Markett, so that the Rysinge and Fallinge of Prices, is the greatest Matter, that maketh the Bourden of Cesse hevier or lighter to the People. But I entende to make it generallye more easye, by makinge it more indifferent. The Gentlemens Resistaunce is onelye for their owne Particuler, which nether furthereth Service, nor benifitteth the Common Wealth. The poore Fermors and Tenaunts, who beare the Bourden in deede, are verye desierous to geve fyve Marke out of a Ploughland, to be easied of the rest, which if it may be reduced, generallye, in the whole Pale, it will amounte to 2500 *l. Sterlinge* by the Yeare, which is a good Encrease of Revenue to her Majestie, and therefore not easylye to be forgonne, except her Majestie will beare the Chardge of Victuall for the Souldior, at the Rates he nowe payeth, or els encrease his Wagies; for he may pay no more for his Victuallinge out of his Enterteinement then nowe he dothe. My Lord Chauncelor hath in publike Place, both learnedlye, discretelye, wiselye, and stowtelye dealt in the Matter of Cesse (a Thinge as it seameth moch kicked againft) and rather lyke a Councellor at the Barre, then a Iudge vpon the Benche, argued, and defended the Cawse for the Quene against all the Impugners, and proved evidentlye, both by the auntient Lawes, Statutes, and Customes of this Realme, the Contynuaunce of the lyke Chardges, from Tyme to Tyme had ben, and the Princes Prerogatyve to impose it. And here, my good Lords, Occasion offereth me to speake, and withall to lament vnto your Lordships, the Weakenes of the Quenes learned Counsell here, the feble Assistaunce my Lord Chauncelor had by theim that Day, who in the Debatinge of the Case of Cesse, beinge twoe Howres at the least, stoode all the Whyle still and mute, and laied the Bourden vpon hym alone. And therefore I eftsones beseache your Lordships (as maney Tymes I have donne afore) to sende twoe learned Lawyers hither, one to supplye the Place of Cheife Justice, the other of her Majesties Attorney. They will gayne her Majestie more, to the Proffitt of her Cofers, and the Creditt of the State, when soch Cawsies, or the like, came in Question in one Dayes Service, then their Fees and Enterteinements will amounte vnto in a Yere. I beseache your Lordships therefore once more, thinke of it, and make Choyce of somme, and lett theim be spedilye sent hither. My Lord Chauncellor

I

is not able, confidering his weake and feeble Boddye, to endure the lyke Payne and Toyle he hath donne hetherto. And, my Lords, he is to be thanked by your Lordſhips Lettres for that which is paſt, for trewlye he hathe verye well deſerved it. And ſo is lykewiſe the Lorde Preſident of *Mounſter*, and *Sir Nicholas Malbye*, who in their Places and Rankes, do her Majeſtie honorable, and moſt acceptable Service; and ſoch Aſſiſtaunce I have at their Handes, for the Governement of thoſe Provinces, they have in Chardge, as I hope in ſhort Space, to decreaſe her Majeſties Chardge there, and to encreaſe her Commodities here. And ſo to conclude, for the Matter of Ceſſe, I heare greivous Complainte is made of it there, and moche ſett downe againſt it, and I ſpeciallye complayned of, for it; my Advice, and Perſwaſion is, to your Lordſhips, that no Gripp be looſed of the Quenes Poſſeſſions, till I may anſwere their Oppoſicions.

In my laſt vnto your Lordſhips, amongeſt other Things, I beſought your Lordſhips to knowe her Majeſties Pleaſure, and Reſolucion, touchinge the Nominacion of the Biſſhopps, to the Biſſhoppricks I wrote for, as namelye *Roſſe* in *Carberye*, *Ardaugh*, and *Oſſorye*; to the laſt I recommended, as ſpeciallye, and effectuallye as I could to her Majeſtie, Mr. *David Cleire*, a Man both of good Learninge, good Diſcreacion, and good Fame; and I gage it to your Lordſhips, vpon my Creditt, that he is the fitteſt Man, to be Biſſhopp for that Place, in all Reſpects that may be named vnto it. I beſeache you therefore, procure me her Majeſties Anſwere for hym, and lykewiſe for thoſe Particulers I writ of for *Wales*.

And even ſo beſeachinge God, longe and happelye to preſerve you all to the Service of her Majeſtie, the Good of the Countrie, and Comforte to your ſelves, I humblye take my Leave. From the Caſtle of *Dublin*, the xvijth of *March*, 1576.

Your honorable Lordſhips aſſured lovinge

Frende to commaunde,

H. Sydney.

Edward Waterhows, *Eſq;* to *Sir* Henry Sydney.

It may pleaſe your Lordſhip,

UPPON the Arrivall of Mr. *Gifford*, with your laſt Letters, Mr. *Philip Sidney*, and he, brought them to my Lord of *Eſſex*, and deliverid ſuch farder Credence as you commytted to Mr. *Gifforde*; both which did ſo concurre in expreſſing the great Good-will conceyved by your Lordſhip towards hym; and as he then to them, and ſince mannie Tymes to me, hath utterid honorable Speaches of you, wytniſſing both his thankfull Acceptacion and willing Mynd to requite your Lordſhip with mutual Frendſhip. And, laſtly, it hath confirmid hym in Opinion of ſpedy Departure towards you, and followith his Diſpatch with the greater Diligence. Yt ſemith that your Letters to the Lordes were not agreable to the Erle of *Leiceſters* Mynde, whereby he took Occaſion of miſliking Mr. *Giffords* Diſpatch, and ſomewhat of Offence againſt you, as though your Lordſhip had not made it apparent enough to her Majeſty, or the Lords, that you erneſtly wiſhid the Erles Return. And it ſemed his Lordſhip wold have had you to have made ſomme particular Offer to the Erle of *Eſſex* or to his Friends. But your Lordſhip did much better, and farre more agreeable to my Lord of *Eſſex*'s Mynd, who underſtanding of my Lord of *Leceſters* Conceyt, did forthwith ſatisfy his Lordſhip of your moſt freindly and effectual Dealing. Seming better to like of this Cours, then of eny other, wherwith my Lord of *Leceſter* is now exceeding well ſatisfied.

Your Lordſhips modeſt Maner of Writing, as in Baſſhfulnes, to offer eny Thing that might be refuſed, did move the Erle of *Eſſex* to anſwer Mr. *Philip* your Sonne (whom he by Adoption callith his) in this Sorte. That as he ſtill reteineth his

† firſt

firſt Opinion, that in Matters of his Recompence, and tending in ſome Things to a State of Enheritaunce ; and in other Things to a Perpetuitie during Lief, he would not accept eny ſuch Matter, but ymediatlie from a Prince. So in ſuch Things as were temperall, and not perpetuall ; but uppon Pleaſure and remove-able ; he thought them moſt meet to proceed from the Governor, and a Dero-gacion to that State to accept them otherwiſe : And therfore proteſted, that in ſuch Things he wold be as ſcrupulus to receive them here, as he is reſolute, never to receyve the other there. So (as my Lord) you may ſuppreſſe that Opinion in your ſelf, that Diſdeine might follow of your Offers, or Preſumtion imputed to you for them, when you ſee how the Erle is affeċtid, to do Honour to your ſelf, aſwell as to your Place. Nevertheleſſe it is a ſingular Vertue in your Lord-ſhip, that ſitting in the Chaire of your Soveraign, you will yet looke backe to your owne Eſtate, and think uppon a Difference betwene the Erle and your ſelf. And your niceſt Freinds, and amongſt them my Lord of *Leceſter,* doth much allow of your Judgement and Temperaunce in that Point.

I referre to the Erles owne Letters, the Declaracion of your Intencion : But I find that your curteus Letter hath geven Noriſhement to the Sparks of good Will, that were before no more then kindelid. As I ſee it now groweſh to a Flame, I will never hereafter ſuſpeċt Diſagrement, unleſſe it be in a frendly Contraverſie, who ſhall deſerve beſt of other : Wherin perhaps your Lordſhip may be of-fendid, becauſe you ſhall hardely faſten eny Thing of hym, but ſuch as be ne-there diſcomodius to your ſelf, nor repugnant to the Cours of your Governe-ment. And herin their muſt be exceeding good Handeling, or els you ſhall finde hym more willing to followe his privat Cauſes, and to accompanie your Lordſhip privatelie in all your Journeies, then to deall in Thaffaires of the State in enie publique Aċtion.

In this, and in all other Cauſes, that may concerne you bothe, I feele mine owne Diſpoſition to do you both Service, if God had ordeinid my Returne with his Lordſhip : But finding his Eſtate to be ſuch, as he hath not the Diſpoſing of eny Part of her Majeſtys Purſe (by whome her own Servants ought to lyve) and finding in my ſelf a Deſier, rather to live meanlie of a litell here, then to be chargeable to his Lordſhip there (to whome even for Conſcience Sake I would not be burdenous) I have reſolvid to yelde to Quietneſſe, to prevent that which Yeares wold ſhortly of Neceſſiti, oblige me to: So as I referr to Mr. *Agard* and Mr. *Mably,* the Confirmacion and Maintenance of that Unity, betwixt your Lordſhip and this noble Erle, which, in my Hart, I have ever wiſhid, and which no honeſt Man will corrupt, or impugne.

And now ſomewhat to myne owne Particuler, eſpecially that may concerne my Credit, with your Lordſhip. I heare that I have been uncurteuſly dealt withall, namelie, by Mr. *Edward Moore,* who, in a great Aſſembly, when a Cauſe was publiquely herde before you, betweene the Viſcount of *Gormanſtoun,* and *Thomas Flemyng* ; and the Viſcount challenging *Flemyng* for his ſworne Sar-vaunt ; ſuch a Sarvaunt (quod Mr. *Moore*) as *Ed. Waterhowſe* was to your Lord-ſhip. My Lord, as I can never forget, what a Maſter you were to me ; ſo I truſt, that your Lordſhip will ever remember the duetifull Devotion of my Ser-vice to you. I know you had, and have maynie more ſufficient : But Mr. *Moore* might judge, that your extraordinary Favour then unto me, procedid of ſom-what ; if he aſcribe nothing to Defeċt in me, but altogether to your owne Liking and Affeċtion : Yet he might have forborne for your Sake, to have ſlandered me openly ; but uppon Condition that your Lordſhip will in as publique a Place bring hym to charge me with ill Demeanure towards you, I wold yet breake my Determinacion, and upon my own Charges repair unto your Lordſhip to have this Matter duely tried.

I ſpeake not this of eny Policy, for I nether ſue for eny Thing, nor looke for eny Thing by eny Mans Favour, but only wold advoid this Note of Ingratitude towards your Lordſhip, that Mr. *Moore* hath publiquelie laid uppon me. I will con-clude only with this, that if your Lordſhip, by enie ſpedy Diſpatch, doe write eny thing hether concerning the Erle of *Eſſex,* let it not be in eny particuler Offer, but in Generallity, perfuading his fpedy Retorne, for fuch Caufes as you think moft convenient in Reafon : And fo affuring your Lordfhip, of all good Will from the Erle, and of all duetefull Offices, from Mr. *Malby*, I humbly ende ; reftinge fuch towardes you, as you have heirtofore judgid ; and not as Mr. *Moore* laborith to perfuade. At the Courte the xxith of *March*, 1575 *.

> *Your Lordfhips moft bounden and*
>
> *at Commandement,*
>
> Ed. Waterhows.

Orders fett downe by the Queenes mofte excellent Majeftie, with th' Advice of her Previe Counfell, for the Direction and Reformacion of her Highnes Courte in the Marches of Wales, An. 1576.

WHeareas of late Yeares, greate and fondrie Abufes and Diforders are crept into the Courte of the Marches of *Wales*, thorough Lacke of Care in fuche inferior Minifters, to whome the Reformacion thereof did apperteigne, wherebie Juftice hathe lackt his due Execution, and the Inhabitaunts dwelling within that Province haue bene fundrie Waies moft grevouflie molefted and vexed : As alfo by long Delaie of Sutes and newe Exactions of Fees greatlie impouerifhed, whearbie that Courte (which at the Begening was erected for the Eafe and Relief of the faid Inhabitaunts) is nowe become vnto them, thorough theis newe crept in Abufes, moft grevous and intollerable, whereof her Majeftie being aduertized, like a good and gracious Princeffe tendring nothing more then the good Government and well Vfadge of her Subiects by due Execution of Juftice, caufed the Lords and others of her Previe Counfell to enter into Confideracion howe the faide Abufes might be removed, and her Subiects relieued, whoe therevppon after dilligent Pervfing of fuch former Orders as weare latelie fent vppe by the Vice Prefident and Counfell there, and Conference had with the Juftice of Affife and others of the Counfell of that Province, did fett downe the Orders following, which her Highnes Pleafure is, fhalbe dulie and inviolably obferved.

Th' orders concerning the Courte.

1. FIRST, it is ordered that everie Man that by Proces is called before the Court, fhall not be compelled to anfwere till the thirde Courte, accompting the firft Court of the Daie of his Apparaunce for one ; at which thirde Courte if the Defendant appeare not and take vp his Bill or the Copie thereof, to make his Anfwere, then a Contempt fhall paffe out againft him at the fourthe Court, vppon *Affidauit* made.

2. *Item*, If the Defendant doe appeare the thirde Court, he fhall haue three Courts after, or a Daie and a half to afke Councell, and to make his Anfwere at his Perill : Wherevppon, the Plaintif (if Replication be requifett, and the Parties not at Iffue vppon the Anfwere) fhall haue twoo Daies after the Bringing in of the Anfwere, to take out the Copie of the fame, and to confulte with his Counfell and to make his Replicacion : And like Tyme the Defendaunt fhall haue for making his Reioynder (if the Iffue be not perfite before).

3. *Item*, For everie Daie that the Plaintife or Defendaunt fhalbe letted for Lacke of fuche Pleading, the Partie making fuch Defaulte fhall yelde to the other Partie xij *d*, and if there be more than one of a Side, he fhall yelde to everie one xij *d* for everie Daie : And if it be a Gentleman having Servaunts with him, after his Degree that is fo limitted, the fame to be thereafter confidered

---

* This Letter fhould have come in the Year before.

by this Counfell, the other to be ordinarelie taxed according to this Order, without trobling the Court therewith.

4. *Item,* If the Plaintif do not fetch foorthe the Coppie of Thanfwere to replie within one Daie after the Bringing in of the Defendaunts Anfwere, the Defendant then to be difmiffed with his Cofts, and that to be no leffe then xij *d.* everie Daie, for everie Defendaunt, in Comming, Going, and Tarying, over and befides th'ordinarie Chardges of the Courte ; except alwaies Matters of Land, wherein the Courte being moved, fhall graunt longer Tyme to pleade, as the Confideracions alledged by the Parties fhall require. And although the Tyme aboue limitted be the longeft Tyme, that Men maie not except in perfonall Caufes for Bringing in of their Plees, yet that fhalbe no Reftraint, for any Man that will, for his owne Expedicion, bring in his Anfwere or Plea, rather before the Daie.

5. *Item,* If the Plaintif make anie Departure from the Matter of his Bill in anie his Pleading, that the Defendaunt vppon Difclofing of the fame, fhall be difmiffed with his Cofts. Moreover, all Iffues fhalbe fett foorth according to the Pleading by bothe Parties Counfell (if bothe do affent thereunto) or els the fame fhalbe fett foorth by the Courte, and none otherwife.

6. *Item,* That no Man of Councell, after the Books be once at a perfite Iffue, fhall either charge the Parties, or moleft the Court with fuperfluous Pledings, at his Perill; to be confidered by the Councell vpon Difclofing of the fame.

7. *Item,* All Maters of the Court from henceforth, fhalbe called, ruled, and ordred by Booke of Affignements, in Order as they be affigned, without Refpeet of anie Perfon, except the Councell, for Confideracions, fhall call fome other Matter.

8. *Item,* For the leffe Trobling of the Counfell, all Witneffes, all Seruers of Proces, and fuch as come to excufe Mens Apparaunces, fhalbe brought out of the Courte before anie one of the Councell, fomewhat before the Court, to take their Othes.

9. *Item,* No Books or Originalls of the Court fhalbe deliuered to anie Man, from henceforth out of the Office, but onlie the Copie or Copies of the fame, in fuch Sorte as is appoineted by Th'inftructions.

10. *Item,* Witnefes brought into the Court, afwell for the Queene as for the Parties, fhalbe examined with all Speede; at the leaft in twoo Daies after they be fworne, except the Nombre of them be fuch, as a longer Tyme fhalbe thought requifett by the Iudgment of the Court : And that no Man being of Counfell with either of bothe Parties, or their Atturnies, fhalbe at Th'examinacion of them, nor fhalbe admitted to the Sight of their Depoficions, before they be publifhed by the Court.

For the Minifters of the faide Courte.

ITEM, It is ordered that the Clarcke that maketh anie Bill to be exhibited to the faide Lord Prefident and Counfell, fhall fubfcribe the fame Bill with his owne Hand.

Item, The faid Bill fhall conteigne the Name, Sirname, Dwelling Place, the Towne or Parrifh and Countie wheare the Plaintif named in the faide Bill dothe inhabite : And whither the faid Plaintif be prefent at Thexhibiting of the faid Bill, or not.

Item, It fhall conteigne the Name, Sirname, Dwelling Place, Towne, Parrifh and Countie, wheare the Defendauntes named in the fame Bill doe inhabite, and fo enfuinglie in eny Order.

Item, The Clerck that writeth anie Bill, Anfwere, Replication, or fuch other; and fpeciallie the Order; fhall write the fame faire, without anie Rafing, Interlyning, or Blotting.

Item,

Item, It is ordered, That the Clercke of the Counfell fhall haue for the Supplie of his Office the Nombre of twelve Clerks, to be allowed vnto him by the Lord Prefident, or Viceprefident for the Tyme being, of which Nombre, the faid Clerke fhall haue Libertie hereafter vppon Occafion to chaunge anie, and to putte other in their Places, and fhall not haue nor retaine anie more in Nombre, to write and fupplie in his Office, but onlie the Nombre fo to him affigned.

And it is ordered, that the fame his Clerks, for Meyntynaunce of their Living, fhall haue Libertie to make Bills and Anfweres concerning all fuche Caufes (Titles excepted) as their Capacities can extend vnto, of all Matters determinable in this Courte.

And that they fhall haue Libertie to ferve out Proces ; but that they, nor anie of theim, fhall enterprife or prefume to move Caufes in Courte, or fpeake as Attorney for anie Perfon; or to putt his Hand to anie Order of Contynuance, except in Tyme of Vacation ; nor fhall exact nor take for their Doings, anie more Somme or Somes of Monie, then the Fees allowed for the Making of anie fuche Bills and Anfweres.

And it is likewife ordered, That all the faid Vnder Clarks nowe allowed, and hereafter to be allowed and reteined by the Clerks of the Counfell, fhalbe fworne before one of the fame Counfell, as well to obferue and keepe the Points before fpecified : As fafelie to keepe, and well to vfe the Records and Books of the Courte, during the Tyme they fhall haue anie of theim in their Keping and Chardge, and fhall do their Indeuour to write and make their Bookes and Copies faire and legible.

And it is ordered, That the Clercke of the Counfell in all Things (corporall Punifhment excepted) fhall anfwere for all their Clerks afore mencioned, and paie fuche Fyne and Charge as hereafter fhalbe affeffed (if anie be) for Th'offences and Mifdemeanors in Courte of anie his faid Clercks.

Item, It is ordered, That the Attorneis which fhalbe allowed, nor anie of theim, fhall haue anie more Clercks to write theire Books and Caufes of the Courte, but onlie one a Peece, of whome they fhall make Choife. And fhall have Libertie hereafter, vppon the Death, either Preferment or Mifliking of anie their Clercks, to putte others in their Places, fo as they doe write faire, and be fuche as this Counfell fhall haue no iufte Caufe to miflike of, and fhall prefent his and their Names to the faid Clerke of the Counfell, to be regiftered.

And it is ordered, That all and everie the faid Atturneis Clerks fhalbe fworne before one of this Counfell, afwell for his good Behauiour towards the Courte and Counfell, as that he and they fhall trulie and vprightlie deale concerning anie Matter in Courte, and fhall make nor preferre anie Bill, Informacion, or other Writing, to be exhibited in this Courte, but fuche as whereunto their Mafters Hands fhalbe fubfcribed.

And it is ordered, That the faid Atturneis, and every of them, fhall anfwere for everie their faid Clerks, except in corporall Punifhment, and paie fuche Fine and Chardge as fhalbe affeffed (if anie be) for enie their Faults and Offences.

And wheare the Atturneis are increafed to the Nombre of foure and twentie, which heretofore haue bene thought more then needefull, It is ordered, That they fhalbe reduced prefentlie by the Viceprefident, and twoo fuche as fhalbe appoincted by him, to the Nombre of eightene ; and after, if anie die or departe, then none to be admitted, vntill they fhall come to the Nombre of xij, which faide Nombre of xij they fhall not in anie wife after exceade.

And for afmuch as the Framing and Perufing of Bookes and Pleadings in Matters of Weighte, dothe chieflie apperteigne to the Counfellors at the Barre ; and that it is requifett they fhoulde haue convenient Tyme and Oppertunitie for that Purpofe, where bie they maie be the riper to open the Caufes for the better Inftructions of the Courte, to induce theim to proceade to founde Iudgement. And it is requifett the fame Counfaillors fhoulde be harde in Mocions

touching

touching Infufficiencie of Pleadings, Wager of Lawe, for Evidence, and for Stallacions of Poffeffions ; which commonlie are moued amongeft other Rules in the After Noone.

It is therefore confidered and ordered, That henceforth, in every Terme, the faid Counfellors fhall have to theim allowed the After Noone of twoo Daies in everie Weeke, *viz. Tewfdaie* and *Friday,* to make their Mocions, and move their Rules, for th'onlie Caufes aforefaide, and to be heard without Difturbaunce or Interruption of the Attorneis. And that the fame Atturneis, in all other Daies of the Weeke in the After Noones, fhall haue Libertie, likewife, to move their Rules for all other Matters, without Interruption of the Counfellors.

What Matters fhalbe hearde in Court.

FIRST, that hereafter no Sutes in the Nature of Replevie, Debte without Specialtie, Detynue, Accord vppon the Cafe, or Accompt, fhalbe hearafter receiued in this Courte, vnleffe the Bill thereof, be figned by three of their Counfell at the leaft refident, wheare the Seale apperteyning to this Courte fhalbe. And of the fame three, the Lord Prefident, or the Viceprefident, to be, if they be there refident at that Tyme, and in the Abfence of theim, and either of theim, then one of the Quorum appointed by Th'inftructions to be one of thofe, which fhoulde figne fuche Bill or Bills.

And alfo if Complaint be made for Trefpaffe, or wrongfull Entring or Difturbing of the Freehoulde, or of the Poffeffion of anie Fermor, for Yeares or at Will, within anie of the twelve Shires of *Wales, viz. Flint, Denbigh, Mountgomerie, Merioneth, Carnarvon, Anglezey, Cardigan, Brecknocke, Glamorgan, Radnor, Carmerthen* and *Pembroke* ; and furmife he is not of Habilitie to trie the Common Lawe, in the Countrie wheare the Wrong was comitted, and therefore for Inequalitie praieth to be hearde in that Courte : No Proces to be graunted vppon anie fuch Bill, except the Complaint be firft exhibited to the Juftice of Affife within that Countie, wheare the Caufe of fuch Sute arifeth, and he, by Lettres or other Note of Allowaunce, recommend the Hearing of the fame for that Caufe, to this Councell.

And alfo if anie Complaint be exhibited concerning forceable Entrie, or forceable Withholding of Lands, the Surmife to be tranfverfed, afwell as the Title, and the fame to be hearde before the Title. And if the Surmife of the Force be not directlie proued in fuche Sorte and Manner, or to like Effect as it is fett downe by the Complaint, then the Matter with full Cofts, to the Defendant to be difmiffed, and the Title not to be hearde.

Item, That no Title of Copieholde Land be hearde, except againft the Quene, without manifeft Teftimonie, that the Complaynaunt cannot haue indifferent Triall in the Queenes Courte.

Item, That no Bill of Complaint be *preferred,* conteyning anie Title of Freholde, Copieholde, Eftate for Yeares, or at Will, except the fame be drawen by a Counfellor learned, and his Name fubfcribed. And that the like Order be obferued, touching Anfweres to be made to fuche Bills.

Alfo, if the Order paffe with the Defendaunt by Difmiffion, or otherwife, that then he by himfelf, or his Atturney, exhibite his Bill of Cofts, what the fame hath bene fince the Begenning of his Sute, and the fame to be allowed to him by the Difcreacion of the Courte, the greater Coftes efpeciallie when it maie be proved, or appeare the Sute was profecuted without Title. And if the Order paffe with the Complaynaunt, then Cofts to be for him in like Manner affeffed.

If anie Councellor, Attornies, or Clerks, doe imbefell or convey out of Waie, anie of the Bookes of the Courte ; or after the fame be figned by anie of the Councell, doe alter or chaunge the fame, by rafinge, adding, or diminifhing ; the fame Perfon to be punifhed by Fine or Imprifonment, and vtterlie debarred

red from all Attendaunce and Service, in anie Place, Rome, or Office, belonging to the Courte.

Item, If anie Perfon preferre anie Bill to be figned, and alledg in his Bill, the Partie to be prefent, knowing him to be abfent ; to be hereafter excluded from making of Bills.

Item, That no Councellor be permitted to pleade at the Barre, except he haue ben Vtterbarrifter in Courte for five Yeare Standing at the leaft, and the fame Counfellor of fuche Standing, to be allowed or difallowed by the Lord Prefident, or Vicepreſident, according to his honeft Behauior.

And everie one hereafter to be admittted Councellor, Atturney, or Clercke, fhall take the Othe of the Supremacie to be miniftred vnto theim openlie in Courte, by fome of the Councell of this Courte.

If it be dulie proued, that anie Councellor, Atturnie, or Clerke attending, profecute anie Caufe, before the Councell, in the Behalf of anie other, having Affuraunce or Promife of the Thing fued for, or anie Parte thereof ; befids Fine and Imprifonment, to be excluded for ever from fuch Place of Service or Rome, as he vfed before. The like Order for fuch as fhall take anie Somme or Sommes of Monie, and for the fame affure the Client to haue Order to paffe with him, and the like Order with all fuche, having Fee certein appointed either for making Billes, Proceffe, Indorcements, Examination of Witneffes, or other Execution of their Office, as fhall for the Thexecuting thereof exact more or greater Fees.

Item, That no Proces be graunted for Thappearaunce of anie before this Councell, except the Value thereof exceade fortie Shillings.

Item, If anie Surmife be made that the Value of the Thing fued for, exceade fortie Shillings, and then, vppon Profe, it falleth oute to be vnder the Value of xl *s.* then vppon the Hearing, the Plaintif to paie the Defendaunts Cofts, and in Confideracion of his falfe Surmife (although the Matter fall oute vppon Examinacion with the Plaintif) yet the Defendaunt to be difmiffed.

The Fees of the Courte.

The Office of the Clercke of the Counfell.	FIRST, For the Making of everie Bill or Informacion, if it be by him made and not otherwife — viij *d.*
	Item, Everie Indorcement vppon a Comiffion by Confents or Placarde — ij *d.*
	Item, Everie Warrant for Proceffe — ij *d.*
	Item, Everie originall Order — iiij *d.*
	Item, The Copie of Th'ordre with Contynuance — iiij *d.*
	Item, For the finall Ordre — iiij *d.*
	Item, For everie Band and for the Warrant thereof — xij *d.*
	Item, The Recording of Apparaunce for everie Perfon, fo it be vppon Band and not otherwife — ij *d.*
	Item, The Coppie of everie Bill, Anfwere, the reft of the Pleading and Witnes — iiij *d.*
	Item, The Copie of Evidences, and for Exemplificacions, according to the Quantitie of the Bufines
	Item, The Search of everie Recorde within the Yeare — iiij *d.*
	Item, For Regiftring of everie finall Order of the Partie, for whome the Order paffeth — iiij *d.*
	And if it paffe by Confents, either of theim, ij *d.* — iiij *d.*

All

All which Fees fhalbe to him allowed, in Cafe the faid Billes, Orders, &c. being aboue limitted, fhall be by him, or his Clerks, made without putting the Subiect to doble Chardges.

Clerke Examiners Office.	*Firft*, The Examinacion of everie Witneffe and other Parfon examined	xij *d.*
	Item, For the Copie of everie Depoficion and Examinacion	vj *d.*
Fees for Attorneis and other Clercks.	In everie Mattere the Atturnies Fees, one with another, for one whole Terme, and not for everie Retorn	ij *s.*
	Item, The Making the Bill, and everie other Pleading to him that maketh it, and fo as the fewter be not doble charged	viij *d.*
Councellors Fees.	The Counfellor for the Penning of everie Bill, drawen by an other, and Subfcribing the fame, for one whole Terme	iij *s.* iiij *d.*
	Item, Everie Councellor for to be of Councell, for his Interteignment for one Terme onlie, to the Fees of v *s.* and no more	v *s.*
The Secretarie and Clerke of the Signetts Fees.	*Firft*, for everie Lettre at the Sute of the Partie	viij *d.*
	Item, For everie Placarde	ij *s.*
	Item, For everie Exemplification to the Secretary for the Seale	iij *s.* iiij *d.*
Fees appointed to the Solicitor.	*Firft*, for Recording Thapparaunce of everie Perfon appearing vppon Informacion of Treafon, Murder, or Fellonie	ij *d.*
	Item, For the Coppies of Examinacions in the faide Caufes	iiij *d.*
	Item, For the Searche thereof, the Recorde being founde	ij *d.*
	Item, For the Drawing everie Originall for Difchardge or Bailment of everie Perfon, appearing to be examined for Appearaunce againe, or otherwife in the fame Caufes	iiij *d.*
	Item, For Making of every Obligacion for the Queenes Majefties Vfe in the Caufes aforefaid	viij *d.*
	Item, For the Coppies of Minuts of everie of the fame Obligacions	iiij *d.*
	Item, For the Making of Informacions, for Forfeiture of anie of the faid Obligations taken, or to be taken to the Queenes Majefties Vfe, for or concerning anie Perfon or Perfons accufed of anie of the faid Offences, at the Sute of anie Partie	xij *d.*
The Porters Fees.	*Firft*, To take and receive, as th'ordinarie Fee, of eny Perfon comitted for a fingle Contempte, ij *s.* vj *d.* and not aboue, except for his Diett	ij *s.* vj *d.*

The Porters Fees.

Item, Of everie Perſon of a Degree of an Eſquier, or aboue, comitted for Offence, to weare Irons ; for the Comitment ii *s.* vj *d.* and for Diſchardge of the Irons (if he ſeeke to be diſcharged) the Some of ij *s.* vj *d.* — — — v *s.*

Item, For Commitments in the Cauſes next aforeſaide, vnder the Degree of an Eſquire, ij *s.* vj *d.* — — — ij *s.* vj *d.*

Item, For the Diett at the Choice of twoo Tables, the one at viij *d.* the Meale — viii *d.*

Item, The other at vj *d.* the Meale —— vj *d.*

For the Porters Lodge.

Firſt, That everie Perſon comitted to the Chardge of the Porter, ſhalbe their deteigned as a Priſoner, according to the Qualitie of Th'offence, and not to departe out of the Circuite of the Porters Lodge without ſpeciall Licence of this Counſell, and to take and receive of theim ſuch Fees as hereafter enſueth.

Firſt, For Treaſon, Murder, or Felonie, to be deteyned in Irons during the Counſells Pleaſure, and not to departe out of the Circuite of the Porters Lodge.

Item, All Perſons comitted for Contempts or anie Miſdemeanors or Offences, wheare the Queene to haue a Fine for the ſame ; they likewiſe to be deteigned in Priſon without Sufferance to go Abroade, except by the ſpeciall Licence of this Councell.

Item, To take and receive as their ordinarie Fee of everie Perſon comited for a ſingle Contempt ii *s.* vi *d.* and not aboue except for Diett.

Item, To take and reteine of everie Perſon, being of the Degree of an Eſquier and aboue, and comitted for anie Offence, for the which he is to weare Irones, to take for his Comittment ii *s.* vi *d.* And of every Perſon being comitted, as is aforeſaid, and vnder the Degree nf an Eſquier ii *s.* vi *d.* for his Fee.

Item, It is further ordered, that the Porter ſhall continewallie haue in a Redines for the Interteignement of Priſoners, twoo Tables for Diett, to be in this Sorte kept ; *viz.* The beſt and firſt Table at viii *d.* the Meale, the ſecond at vi *d.* the Meale, and the ſame to be with Meate and Drincke ſo furniſhed as the Parties maie, according to their Paiment, haue therein competent and convenient. And the Partie comitted, to chooſe at his Comittment, at which of thoſe Tables he will remaine. And if he faile to make Paiment of his Fees of Comittment, the Daie following his Committment, and th'ordinary Charge of his Diett after everie Weeks Ende, then the Porter to take Bands for the due Paiment thereof.

Item, It is further ordered, that if anie Perſon be comitted to remaine in Warde vntill he ſhall paie the Quenes Majeſtie anie Some for a Fine, or to anie Perſon anie Somme of Monie to the ſame Partie by this Counſell ordred, or for the not Accompliſhing of anie Order taken by this Counſell, and ſhall not conforme him to performe the Order, diſchardge the Fine, and make Paiment to the Parties, within one Moneth after the Tyme of his Comitment ; then the Porter, at the Ende of the ſaid Moneth, to give Knowledge to the Counſell thereof, to th'end Order therevppon maie be taken, that the Partie be removed to *Wigmore,* or ſuche other Place as this Counſell ſhall thincke meete.

And when anie Perſon is or ſhalbe comitted to Warde, there to remaine vntill he ſhall paie Fine or other Debts to the Queene, or any Some of Monie for Coſts, or other Cauſe to the Partie ; to detaine him as a Priſoner in Manner aforeſaid, vntill the Atturnie of the Partie, and the Clerck of the Fines, by a Note in Writing, ſubſcribed by their Names vppon the Copie of the Submiſſion, ſhall

acknowledge

acknowledge to haue reteined the said Some, wherein he is chargeable aswell to the Queene as to the Partie.

Sir Francis Walsyngham *to Sir* Henry Sydney.

My very good Lord,

THOS that departed out of *Ireland*, to complayne of the Cesse, are alreadie arryued here for the same Purpos, notwithstanding you maie assure your self that the Matter shalbe so handled as your Authoritie shall receaue no Preiudice therebie ; and yet yf their Griefes appeare to be such as maie seeme to requyer some Easement, th'one shalbe in such Sorte remedied as th'other shall no whitte be empayred.

My Lord of *Ormond* hearing that there is Advauntage taken against such her Majesties Tenants, as fayle in Payment of ther Rent at the Daies limited, desyred me to wryte vnto your Lordship to deale fauorablie with him in that Behalf, in Case any of his Vndertenants of such Things as he farmeth of her Majestie do negligentlie faile in Payment, wherein he promiseth, that whereas heretofore they haue ben perhaps negligent, they shall hereafter prepare to paie at their Daie. Further he desyred me that for such Monie as shalbe delyuered to your Lordship there by this Bearer his Servaunte, yt would please you to write your Letters to the Lord Thresorer, to make Payment of the lyke Somme here vnto his Lordship, out of such Portyon of the Allotement as shalbe dewe at *Midsommer* Quarter. And so I commit your Lordship to God. From *Leycester* Howse, the viijth of *Aprill*, 1577.

Your Lordships assured Frind,

Fra. Walsyngham.

Sir Francis Walsyngham *to Sir* Henry Sydney.

My verie good Lord,

THIS poore Gentleman, *Peter Carye,* thoughe he have hir Majesties Lettres written vnto you for some Provision of Livynge to bee assigned him in *Ireland*, yet dyd he also verie earnestly crave at my Handes, some fewe Lynes to your Lordship in his Recommendation : Which, for that I have heard so good Report of his Honestie and faythfull Service, whereof the Marckes apparant on his Bodie make good Demonstration to all the World, I could in no wyse denye him. And therefore most hartelye praye you, bothe in that hir Majestie writethe of for him, and also in anie other Matter you may, to stand his good Lord : Wherby as you shall greatly comfort the poore Man, so shall you, no Doubt, encourage all other poore Souldiers in that Realme the more willingly to aduenture them selfes in anie Service, seeynge by this Mans Exaample, that the same shall not bee vnrewarded. And so humbly committynge your Lordship to God, I take my Leave. From my Howse in *London* the xviijth of *Aprill*, 1577.

Your Lordships to commaund,

Fra. Walsyngham.

ª *Sir* Francis Walsyngham *to his Cosen* Edward Moore.

AFTER my hartye Commendacions, yt is very latelie come to my Knowledge, that some Controuersies haue happened betwin your Sonne in Lawe, *Edward Brabazon,* and you, especiallie about a Bill, signed by the late Lorde Deputye, vppon a Warraunt directed from her Majestie, to him ; which Bill

ª **Ex Origin. apud Penshurst.**

or Fiat hath ben taken by you, out of Th'office of the *Hamper*, and deteyned ftill vppon the Mifliking of the Partie. The Loffe whervnto yt feemeth that the yong Gentlemen is dryuen, by the Stay of his Graunte, hath procured him, as I thinke, to reueale his Cafe and to feeke Remedye of yt; wherein, albeyt he hath vfed much Temperaunce, as loth to invey againft him, that hath maried his Mother; yet hath yt not ben fo fecreatlie handled but that yt is come to the Knowledge of fuch as are very hable, and as I doubt, exceeding willing to profecute Matter of mifliking againft you; and I haue heard the Faulte fo agrauated, as though by Lawe yt weare a Thing moft daingerous. Whervppon, willing to take the Deffence of your honeft Caufes, vppon me, I fent for *Brabazon*, and do fynd that he is more vrged to complaine, then willing of him felfe, yf he might otherwies haue the Matter compounded. And therfore having receauid his Promis to ftaye for a Tyme, I haue thought yt good to wifhe you to fatiffie him fome Way, otherwies I fynd yt will not be fufficient to faye that fome Parcell of your Lyvings weare conteyned in the Graunte, or by any fuch Meanes to excufe your Doings, but that yt wilbe conftrued, and I feare, punifhed as a greater Contempt then you are ware of; for nether can her Majeftie like that her Hand fhould be abufed, or the Signature of her Deputye in that Place fo contemptuouflie dealt withall; which in Refpect of your felf I frindlie tell you, hoping you will in Tyme prevent yt, and fo do bid you hartelie Fare well. From *Leycefter* Howfe the   of *Aprill*, 1577.

Your loving Coufin and Frend,

Fra. Walfynham.

Sir Henry Sydney *to the Lords of the Council in* England.

Right honorable and my verie good Lords,

I Defire you will advertize me, by your Lordfhips Lettres, whether, to what Place, and to whome to fende for the Men. And lykewife Order wold be geven to the Captens and Soldiors, to comme when I fende for theim; my Defier is to have this Nomber levied in, *Sowth Wales* and *North Wales*, and the *Englifhe* Shires within the Prefidencye there. It is moft requifite lykewife in myne Opinion (if it fo lyke your Honnors) that a Maffe of Munition convenient for foch a Nomber, or more, fhould be fent; and that to remayne in Store vnfpent, except this Occafion fall out, and her Majeftie fhalbe duelye anfwered agayne of that Proporcion fhe fendethe hither, at the Mafter of the Ordenaunce Handes, except the fame fhould chaunce to be fpent in Refiftinge this Invafion; and without Money and Municion, beinge the Forces and Synewes of Warre, nothinge is to be hoped can be done, for the Repulfinge of any forreine Power. And for that I daylye heare by Intelligence the Confirmacion of theife Advertizements of forreine Invafion, both what Preparacion is made, and what Nomber of Men are appointed, and in what Arreadines they are to fett forwarde, and that their full Intencion is to arryve in fomme one Haven or other, towarde the Weft of this Lande, before Harveft next. I befeache your Lordfhips thinke of the Weightines of the Cawfe, the Honnor of the Quene, and Safetie of the Realme, and you cannot be fo carefull to forefee, and prevent the Daunger that may enfue; for the Townes, for the mofte Parte, in thofe Partes are all fo weake (*Lymericke* onelye excepted) which is fomewhat gardable, that it is almoft impoffible to kepe the Forreiners out, if they fhould attempt to comme: And therefore neceffarie it were to have fome Shippinge to be prepared and rigged vp, and fent Abroade to fcower the Seas, and to be in a Readines to watche, and attende vpon *James Fitzmorris* Comminge; the rather to prevent this Attempt intended by hym againft this Realme. For the hollowe Hartes and Difpoficions both of the Lords theim felves, and the popular Sorte are fo altogether geven to Papiftrie, and apt to Innovacions, and Chaunges, as I dare not in any Sorte truft to their Forces. And therefore, my Lords, I humblye befeache you once againe, have more fpeciall Care of me, that both, Money,

1   Municion,

Municion, and Shippinge be prefentlye fent, and Soldiours levied, and put in Readines to come hither, when I fende for theim. And although the Nomber of a Thowfand be but fewe ; yet beinge well forted and chofen, I will venter my felfe with that Nomber with foch Bandes and Companies, as I have alreadye heare.

There have bene afore you, as I heare, *Barnabye Scurlocke* and his Companions, who repine at her Majefties Prerogatyve for Ceffe. They be bad Inftruments for her Majefties Service, and fo your Lordfhips fhall fynde theim ; and by their lewd Perfwafions maney Men be drawen, to refift the Yeeldinge of Ceffe, hopinge daylye of the Comforts and good Succeffe theife their Agents fhall fynde there. For *Scurlocke*, before his Departure hence, threatned a Gentleman called *Garrot Wefley*, beinge Sheriffe of one of the principalleft, and beft Countie within the Pale, that if he fhould diftreine or levye any Ceffe, either for the Vfe of the Garrifon, or Provifion of my Howfehold, for any Speache, Commaundement, Proceffe, or any other Thinge, that I fhould fend hym for that Purpofe, that he would endite hym of Treafon. This beinge vttered by a Man of that Apparaunce and Creditt, he feamethe to carrye in the Countrie, hath wrought foch an Opinion amongft the common Sorte, as maney refuze to pay Ceffe, which otherwayes moft willinglye would have donne it. The Punifhinge of hym for this his vndecent, and vnduetifull Speache, will bringe maney to more Pliantnes, and due Obedience. I fpeake it, my Lords, duetifullye, and without Paffion or Affeccion any Wayes to the Man. And his Fellowe, *Richard Newtervill*, is as feditious, and mutinous a Perfon, as this Realme hath any, who although he hath had all his Lyvinge and Preferment by the Quene, doth yet more fecreate Hurte with his Practizes, in fowinge Difcorde, and Difcention, devifinge Matters daylye to complayne vpon, and never fatisfied with any Anfwere ; a common Proctor, and Promoter of any Cawfe, that may either hynder her Majeftie in Benifitt, difquiett the Countrie or trouble the State : As he doth more Harme where he commeth, and breede more Vnquiet and Difcontentment amonge the People, then any one Man hath donne in this Realme theife maney Yeares. And the better to allure others to beleve hym, and to drawe theim to followe his Devifes, he fticketh not to reporte, and fo geveth it foorth, that this Nobleman, and that Nobleman be of the fame Mynde he is of, yea and that he hath their Lettres to fhewe : So that onelye by his Lewdnes, Vntrothes, and Mifreportes, he gayneth his beft Creditt amongft the Multitude, who maketh hym a Piller of their Common Wealthe. The fevere and due Correction of hym will woorcke foch good Effecte, and procure foch Obedience in this Countrie, as no one Thinge more, for he is one of the cheife Poftes thei fticke to. And if he onelye, that bad Fellowe, *Newtervill*, had not bene the Impediment, by his Practizes and lewd Perfwafions in the Countrie, I would not have doubted, but afore this Tyme to have created vnto her Majeftie, in this Converfion of Ceffe, ten thowfand Markes of yearelye Revenue. Of *Burnell* I will fay little, but wifhe he had bene better occupied, for he is a Man well fpoken and towardlye enough otherwayes, if he would have applied hym felfe to his Profeffion, and followed his Clyents Cawfies, and not fo bufilye have medled with her Majefties Prerogatyve, which is not lymitted by *Magna Charta*, nor found in *Littletous* Tenures, nor written in the Bookes of Affifes ; but regiftred in the Remembraunces of her Majefties *Efchequer*, and remayne in the Rolles of Recordes of the *Tower*, as her Majefties Threafure. It were good therefore he were taught to knowe it better, if he have not yet learned fo farre. And for the Ceffe, it is the Quenes Right, it is her Royaltie, verye longe and of Auntientye contynued, and found to have had a Beinge, by the Name of *Ceffe* and *Ceffor*, in the auntienft Rolles of Lawes, that are extant in this Lande ; the Impugners thereof are the more feverelye to be dealt withall, which I referre to your Lordfhips grave, wife, and honorable Confideracions. And if this Manner of bearinge of Ceffe, might be converted into an annual Rent, wherebye the Soldiour might in fome Sorte be waged, and borne, and her Majeftie eafed of fomme Chardgies,

the

the Plott were good, and foch a one as I cannot buyld vpon a better. And therefore, my Lords, it is to be ftocke in, and mainteined, and not fuffered any Wayes to goe to the Ground, for it is her Majefties Prerogatyve and Enheritaunce, and may not be geven away. And for that it may be thought moft lykelye, that the Enformers againft me there, will fuggeft to her Majeftie and your Lordfhips, that my hard Dealinge with theim, in not yeelding theim contented and good Anfwers, hath bene the Cawfe of theire Complayninge there to your Lordfhips, to feeke Redreffe at your Handes; becawfe they founde fo lyttle Comforte at myne : I humblye pray your Lordfhips to write to the Councell here, to certifie your Lordfhips the Manner of the Proceadinge for the Ceffe, and their Opinion of it. And even fo befeachinge God, to profper you and all your honorable Proceadings, I humblye take my Leave. From *Kilmaynghame*, the xvth of *Maij*, 1577.

Your honorable Lordfhips affured lovinge

Freinde humblye to commaunde,

H. Sydney.

Sir Henry Sydney *to Queen* Elizabeth.

I N the lowlieft Manner I can, I moft humblye befeache youer moft excellent Majeftie, to pardon me that I have fo feldome written to your Highnes : So bad a Delyverie of my Minde I have by Pen, and fo illeagible it is when I do it my felfe, as I rather thought it neceffarye for me, to addreffe that which I had to write to the Lordes of your Majefties Councell, and to pray theim to relate the fame to your Highnes, then convenient to trouble your felfe with it. But nowe hearinge from fome of my private Freindes there, that I am complayned of to youer Majeftie, do prefume in Defence of my felfe, to write thus rudelye. As I am enformed theyr Complainte is for that they are chardged with *Ceffe*, and annoyed with Diforder of the Soldiours : And for that your Majeftie may the better knowe, what that *Ceffe* is, it may like the fame to vnderftand, that it is a Quantitie of Vittell, and a Prifage fett vpon the fame, neceffarie for foch Soldiers as here youer Majeftie is contented, to be at Chardge with for their Defence, and of fo moche as is thought competent for the Expence of your Deputies Howfe, fo farre vnder the Valewe, as it goethe betwene Partye and Partye, as the Soldiour may lyve of his Wagies, and your Highnes Officer of his Enterteinement ; and this to be taxed by your Highnes Deputie, and your Councell here eftablifhed, callinge to theim the Nobilitie adioyninge. The which your Highnes Price (as nowe it is) excedeth the Value of thofe Thinges fo prifed, till of verye late Yeares that the fame was woorth in the Markett. The Maffe of this for the moft Parte hath alwayes bene layed vpon fyve *Englifhe* Shires, and certeine *Irifhe* Countries adioyninge, and the fame diftributed accordinge to the Nomber of the Ploughlandes into which the fame Shires are devided : And accordinge to this accuftomed and longe contynued Order, I for this Yeare proceaded at the wonted Tyme, and vfed lyke Summons, as in lyke Cafes had bene donne, and a greater Affemblye was at the fame, then often Tymes hath bene fene in femblable Cawfies; but when the Proporcion was fene, al be it fo ftreightlye allowed, as neither by Skill of Baker, Boutcher, or other Victualler, leffe could be apointed then was demaunded, and by the moft agreed vpon to be delyvered : And although I was content to take but for the one Halfe of the Nomber of the Soldiours that your Majeftie geveth Wagies to, yet lokinge vpon the Prices of all Things, as nowe they be valued and fold, fo farre excedinge your Highnes Price, which the Soldiors may not exceede, vnles your Majeftie will encreafe their Wagies, to youer Highnes vnreafonable, and intollerable Chardge, the Loffe feamed fo great vnto theim as the Burden was not to be borne : Affirminge that the Chardge of eche Ploughland came to above

† x *l.*

x *l.* yea fomme faied xij *l.* and in dede as the Prices of all Things prefently are, I found theim to be verie niere viij *l.* For Eafe of whiche, by makinge the Burden to be borne more vniverfallye, and fo more indifferentlye, I by Procla-macion diffolved all Fredomes, that had not had their Contynuaunce Tyme out of Memorye of Man, whereof they were maney, the moft by a Statute, pre-tendinge therebye an Encreafe of Militarye Men, which God knoweth, and I fometyme have proved, are little woorth ; which Statute was but for x Yeares, and thofe Yeares expired, maney by fpetiall Favor of me, and other Governors, were graunted to fondrie Parfonnes. And al be it I knewe this was for the Com-mon Wealthe, and for the Eafe of the greateft Nomber : Yet hereat did dyvers, namelye thofe that nowe are in *England*, and fome other who had their Fredomes fuppreffed by Proclamacion grevouflye repyne, ftill cryenge out that they were fo pore, they were not able to beare any Burden any longar. It was proved they bare nothinge, and that they had as moche as ever their Aunceftors had ; but it was the bafe Tenaunt that bare the Bourden, who for the more Parte lyved more wretchedlye vnder his covetous and gredye Landlorde, havinge Freedome, than maney did contributinge with the Chardge of the Soldiour : Yet this not fatisfi-enge theim, but ftill exclayminge of the Greatnes of their Burden and Loffe, I offered to acquite theim for fyve Markes vpon the Plowghland, whereof in thofe fyve Shires (*Meith* alwayes accompted for ij) and fo are fixe Divifions, I beleve may be found at the leaft 700 Plowghlandes, which after the Rate of fyve Markes vpon a Plowghland, dothe amounte to 2840 *l. Sterlinge* Yearelye, befide your accuftomed Subfidie, which is 13 *s.* 4 *d.* out of eche. Than deneid they flatlye, that they would agree to any Ceffe, alleadginge that it was Will, and contrarye bothe to Reafon and Lawe to impofe any Chardge vpon theim without Parlia-ment or Ground Councell. It was proved before theim, and that by the moft auntient, and credible Recordes, that are in the Realme, that in all Ages, from the xjth of *Henrie the iiijth* to this Tyme, which is above 160 Yeares, there hath bene ftill from Tyme to Tyme, as Occafion moved, Chardgies impofed, and fometyme by Name of *Ceffe* and *Ceffor*, and fometyme by other Names, and not alwayes by Parliament, but oftner by the Governor and Councell, and foche of the Nobilitie as beinge fent for did comme, which made that Ground Coun-cell they fpeake of : And of this Opinion for a Ground Councell, are the auntienft, and the learnedft in the Lawe of this Countrie Birthe. Finallye they faied they were *Englifhe* and free Subieftes, and if they could not have Remedye at my Handes, they would feeke it at your Majefties ; I anfweared theim, I found that your Highnes and Progenitors had had it, I found you in Poffeffion of it, and I would have it, vntill I knewe your Majefties Pleafure to the Contrarye. They de-fiered me I wold write in their Favor : That I denied, vnleffe they would fhewe me, what they would fhue for ; they defiered me to geve theim Leave to goe over, I told theim I would not forbid theim to goe.

The other Complainte (as I heare) that they make is, that I beare to moche withe the Infolencye of the Soldiore ; which I proteft before God, and will prove before your Majeftie, or whome your Highnes will appointe, I do not, but do punifhe feverelye when I fynd any Matter proved againft a Soldiour, whiche fel-dome or never I do, but when the Soldiour is appointed (thorough the Wilfulnes, of the People thereunto animated by the Landlord, to affift the Sheriffe or other Officer) to levye that which is apointed for the Soldiours : It muft be confeffed, that Soldiours are no Angells, nor yet amonge Men the harmeleft Creatures. But this I dare avowe, that there is not in *Chriftendome* a Garrifon, not remayninge in a clofed Towne, that doth leffe Hurte to the Countrie where they do remayne, than the Soldiours of *Ireland* do, to the good Subieftes of the fame. Thus moche, for fo moche as I yet learne I am complayned of, and if there be any more, I hope to myne owne Difchardge, and your Highnes Satisfaccion, being hard, I fhall cleare my felfe ; vntill which Tyme I do moft humblye crave your Ma-jefties gratious Sufpence.

I knowe they will inculke into your Highnes moft gratious and readye Eares, to heare the Greiffe of your Subiectes Povertye. But if I were their faythfull Advocate, knowinge theim as I do, I could not tell howe to make Demonftracion thereof and fpeake truelye. Their Land was never more vniverfallye tilled, nor fuller of Cattle then prefentlye. Their Citties and Townes more populous than ever in Memorye of Man. Their Howfies fo farre excedinge their Aunceftors, that they may be thought rather, to be an other and a newe People, then Defcendentes of the old. In beftowing of their Children, a Gentleman I have knowen of this Age, geve more then three Baronnes in Tymes paft. In Plate and all other Furniture of their Howfies, in Apparrell of theim felves, Wyues and Children, there is as great Odds, betwene prefent Ages People, and their Prediceffors, as in *England* is betwene a Yeoman and a good Squier. Befide the Nomber trebled of their Sonnes, Kinsfolke, and Freinds nowe by theim kept in the Vniverfities, and at the Studdye of the Lawe of the Realme, to that whiche their Elders kept, and eche one they have ftandeth theim in treble the Chardge that one ftoode the others in before ; and there be fomme principall Gentlemen, that have their Sonnes in *Lovayne, Doll, Rome,* and other Places, where your Majeftie is rather hated, then honored in, and it is to be fuppofed not without their Chardiges. And as deare as all Things are, they fare more delicatelye, and chardgeouflye then ever they did. And me thinke it fhould little impoverifhe the People to fell now for a Pounde, which, in Memory of Man, was not woorth an Noble, as longe as in Quantitie, regardinge Vnfeafonablenes of the Tyme and other Accydents, they have as before Tyme they were wont to have ; onelye their Greiffe is, that your Majeftie (though for their owne Defence, without which they fhould have nothinge left with theim) fhould have any Thinge vnder the Price, a privat Perfon would geve theim. They are not able, they fay, to geve to youer Majeftie ether Stuffe or Money for Fyndinge your Soldiours. But to furnifhe that Triumuirat, now fent to fuppreffe your Majefties Prerogatyve, they can make above 1000 *l.* if they have gathered fo muche as they made their Reckninge for, whereof I wifhe it would pleafe your Majeftie to geve Order, that they may be examined. And of their owne Eftates, in refpect of their Parentage ; firft for *Scurlocke,* I am fure he hath purchafed more, and buylded more, then ever his Father, Graundfather, or all his Surname ever did ; and his cheife Creditt and Meane to gett this, was by beinge Attorney to your Sifter and your felfe, from which Office, for his Negligence and Wilfulnes, in the Tyme of my Lord of *Suffex* Governement, he was difplaced : Since which Tyme (as he might) he never ceafed to impugne *Inglifh* Governement, and in efpetiall your Majefties Prerogatyve. *Nettervill* is the younger Sonne of a meane and fecond Juftice of one of the Benches, borne to nothinge, and yet onelye by your Majefties Bountye lyveth in better Countenaunce, then ever his Father did, or his elder Brother doth ; and not withftandinge that all he hath, he holdeth of your Highnes in Effecte, yet is he (your facred Majeftie not offended with fo bad a Tearme as his Lewdnes deferveth) as feditious a Varlett, and as great an Impugner of *Englifh* Governement, as any this Land bearethe. *Burnells* Father is alyve, and an old Man ; but neither in Youth nor Age lyved, or was able to lyve, in halfe that Apparaunce that this Man dothe. He thirfteth earneftlye, to fee the *Englifhe* Governement with drawen from hence : But, for ought I knowe, he is the leaft vnhoneft of the three. By theife, it may pleafe your Majeftie to iudge of the reft ; I do not meane for Mallice, but for Wealthe and happie Eftate, which, in dede, is vniverfall, as farre as your Authoritie is extended, favinge the verye bafe Tenaunt who lyveth miferablye, and not fo moche for any Burden of the Soldiour, as thorough the Gredines of his covetous Landlord, for no where lyve they more wretchedlye, then where the Land is freed from the Soldiors.

And thus moche, my moft gratious Sovereigne Miftreffe, which I feare will feame to moche to your Majeftie, I have written of the Eftate of the *Englifhe* Pale in this Realme (as they tearme it) what I have donne, and what they

practice,

practice ; which is a vniverfall Confpiracye to denye any Supportacion for your Majefties Armye, without which, as I have often faied, neither you fhall be obeyed, nor the good People vnoppreffed. If their Practize and Standinge in this Matter had not bene, all *Mounfter* (the Lyberties of the Earles of *Ormound* and *Defmound* onelye excepted) had concented to yeeld an annuall Rent out of their Lands for their Defence ; as the Vicount *Barrye* and *Mac Cartye Reough* alreadye have donne ; the firft 150 *l.* the other 250 *l. Sterlinge*, by the Yeare : Theife twoe make not a fixth Parte of *Mounfter.* So the twoe Lybertyes of *Tipperarie* and *Kerrie* fubmittinge to the fame Contribucion, as I knowe no Reafon why they fhould not ; *Mounfter* wilbe woorth in newe encreafed Rent, befide the old and the Impoft, 3000 *l.* yearelye. And as *Mounfter* had donne, there is no Doubt, all the reft of the remote or vnreclaymed Partes of the Realme would have donne ; and as confidentlye as I can conceive of any Thinge which fenfiblye by Sight or Feeling I have not, fo probablye am I perfwaded, that if *Nettervill* had not bene, I had before this Tyme affured your Majeftie of above 10000 Markes of Encreafe of Revenue yearelye, more then I found you poffeft of. For I held a ftreighter Hand in the Matter of Ceffe, the rather to bringe theim to a certeine Rent for the Releafe of the fame. *Nettervill* geveth it forth, that he was animated to do that he hath donne, by fomme of the greateft of this Countrey Birthe. Nowe for that your Majeftie hath to do in this Countrey, this is my fimple Opinion, your Highnes muft refolve without Intervall, continuallye to kepe an Armye here. If you do not, Madame, though no Boddie comme to take *Ireland* from you, it will be geven from you and your Crowne for ever, and 20000 *l.* Spendinge, with three Monethes Settlinge by any forreine Prince of Force, will coft you and your Countries 200000 *l.* before they be expulfed : This Armye wilbe fome what chardgeous, which Chardge, as I have often faied and written, if it pleafe your Majeftie to take that, which by your Lawes and iuft Prerogatyve you may and ought to have in this Land ; fuppreffe the abufed Priveledgies of your Subiectes, wyll, to be Sovereigne in dede, and not in Title onelye. Finallye, do but animate me and your Councell here, to proceade iuftlye, and lawfullye, without Refpect of Parfon, who ever he be ; and that your Majeftie will mainteine vs, as I have faied often, fo fay I nowe agayne, that I fee no Cawfe to the Contrarye, but that *Ireland* may, and fhall in fhort Tyme, yeeld Revenue ennough to wage a fufficient Garrifon, befide the Chardgies of Cyvill Magiftrates. I meane one thowfand Soldiours to fuppreffe any Infolencye of the Natyves of this Realme : Whereunto dyvers Things for your Advantage muft be donne yet not begonne, in efpetiall a Mynt ; and in this I defier to knowe your Majefties Pleafure, howe in generall you lyke of it ; which, if your Majeftie doth, I will in particuler fett downe my fimple Devige, howe the fame I truft fhall torne to your Highnes Benifitt and Commoditie of your People. But in theife myne Offers Making, I am not a lyttle terrefied, by a Speache which your Highnes Chauncellor told me, he hard your Majeftie fay ; which was, that I promifed, at the three Yeares Ende, you fhould not nede, to be at any more Chardge for *Ireland,* than *Ireland* would yeeld ; and yet the fame reformed, and kept in Order, and everye Yeare fome Chardgies to be diminifhed. God knoweth beft, my intirelye revered Mayftreffe, from what Mynde any of my Offers hath proceaded. But if your Majeftie will fay that I fo offered, I will not agayne fay it ; but rather then I will hazard your Highnes Difpleafure, at the three Yeares Ende, whereof halfe the Tyme is paft, in a Matter fubiect to fo maney Accidentes, as that is, I will rather afd prefentlye, do proftrate my Lyffe and Landes before the Feete of your Highnes, to take what you lift for my Proffer fo inconfideratlye made, and howe your Majeftie conceivethe, and what the fame expectethe of me herein, I moft humbly befeach your moft gratious Majeftie, with Speede let me be advertized, for till then I fhall not with that Comforte, and Cherefulnes, proceede in your Highnes Service, as for the fame, and Animatinge of others, is neceffary I fhould.

Even as I was thus farre writinge this my tedious Letter to your Majeſtie, I received Advertizements from ſondrye Places, in Confirmacion of ſuch as before I did, aſwell out of *England*, as out of *Fraunce*, and from thence not onelye, from ſpetiall Spiall there mainteined to attend vpon *James Fitzmerrice*; but from ſondrie honeſt Marchauntes, your Majeſties faythfull and lovinge Subieétes, and lykewiſe by Reporte of ſome verye vehementlye ſuſpeéted to be ſent into this Land from hym, whereof ſome are apprehended, and have ſent out Searche for others. That *James* is in Readines with Force to invade this your Realme. It is ſaied he bringeth with hym 4000 Shott, and dyvers principall Gentlemen of *Fraunce*. It is certeine, that he is retorned from *Rome*, where he was Princelyke enterteined: He retorned not without a good Maſſe of Treaſure: He lyveth nowe in *Fraunce* chardgeouſlye. All my Advertizements I have imparted to this Bringer, Mr. *Waterhowſe*, your Highnes Servaunt, who can and will delyver the ſame to your Majeſtie, or your Councell, as it may pleaſe you to commaund hym. Madame, I have great Cawſe to miſtruſt the Fidellitie of the greateſt Nomber of the People of this Countrie Birthe, of all Degrees; they be Papiſts, as I may well tearme theim, Boddye and Soule. For not onelye in Matter of Religion they be *Romiſhe*, but for Government they wiſhe Chaunge, and to be vnder a Prince of their owne Superſticion. Since your Highnes Reign, the Papiſts never ſhewed ſoch Boldnes as nowe they do; the Perticulers I leave to this Bringars Reporte. I moſt humblye beſeache your Majeſtie to geve expreſſe Chardge to put Force in Reddynes, to reſiſt this imminent Force, intended againſt your Countrie, and Furniture for the ſame Force to ſerve with. The Nomber I deſier is twoe thowſand Footemen furniſhed, whereof the moſt Parte Shott; a large Maſſe of Powder, Lead, Matche, and Peeces, with Pikes and ſhort Weapon, and 20000 *l*. to mainteine that Warre. If that Invaſion happen, your Majeſtie hathe to conſider, whether it be not requiſite to man forth ſome Parte of your Navye; in my ſimple Opinion it were. He cometh with 14 Sayles, as I am advertized. But if there were but three of your Majeſties, and thoſe but of a mean Sorte, with this I have alreadye, I hope, if they mett with theim, they would make theim repent their Comminge hether; and though they came ſomewhat to late, and after they were landed, yet, if they light on their Shippes, I do truſt in Almightye God, they ſhall pay dearelye for their Landinge, before they recover agayne newe Shippinge. Your Threſure and Munition may lye ſafe, vntouched in your Officers Cuſtodye, as a dead Threaſure, not to be iſſued, but for that Service onelye. If this Advertiſement had not comme, I had, notwithſtandinge ſome actuall Rebellion preſentlye here, diminiſhed your Highnes Chardge in your Garriſon of above one thowſand Poundes a Yeare, which I nowe contynue with Encreaſe, by as muche as the Manninge and Vittellinge yoûr Highnes Shippe cometh to, beſide other great Chardge for Spiall and Meſſengers, Fortificacions, and other Extraordenaryes pertcininge to the ſame Service. Which I moſt humblye beſeache your Majeſtie gratiouſlye to allowe, and to pardon me, that I remember your Majeſtie, howe, in your Siſters Tyme, *Calles*, the Jewell and Honnor of *England*, was loſt for Lacke of Force in Readines. Though the Kepinge of this be ſomewhat burdenous, yet would the Greiffe for the Loſſe of it, be more inſupportable; the Recoverye farre more chardgeous; and, if it were not recovered, the Diſhonor irreparable.

Moſt deare Sovereigne, in the Beginninge of this my rude and evell digeſted Lettre, as their was Cawſe, I beſaught your Majeſtie to pardone me for ſo ſeldome Writinge to the ſame; and nowe have I greater Cawſe: And ſo do I beſeache your Highnes for Encombringe the ſame, with ſo many ill written Lynes, which I had once donne with myne owne Hand; but when I beheld theim, they ſeamed to me ſo evell favored, as I thought theim not worthy to comme into your Sight, but made theim to be written out agayne, by one that can better do it then I.

And thus, prayinge the Almightie God to contynewe with Encreafe your Majefties Felicitie, with a greater Nomber of Yeares then ever Prince reigned in this World, and to crowne you after with a celeftiall Diademe, I moft humblye kiffe the Feete of your facred Majeftie. From your Highnes Howfe of *Kilmaynghame,* the xxth of *Maij,* 1577.

Your Majefties moft humble and

obedient Servaunt,

H. Sydney.

Inftructions and Memorialls geven by Sir Henry Sydney, *Knight of the noble Order, and Deputie of* Ireland, *&c. to Mr.* Edward Waterhowfe, *being fent to her Majeftie and the Lords, for the State and Cawfies of this Realme, the xxth of* Maij, 1577.

1. FIRST to delyver my Lettres to her Majeftie, the Lords, and other my perticuler Freindes, and to prefent my humble Service, Duetye, Thankes, and Commendacions, with the reft of other freindlye Ceremonies, and Accomplements, feverallye to eche in their Degrees, as Courfe of Speache, and Framinge of Tyme, will geve you Leave.

2. Next to imparte to her Majeftie and the Lordes, when you fhall have Acceffe vnto theim, or be demaunded of theim, the peaceable and quiet State of this Countrie, vnder my Governement for the prefent, and the great Lykelyhood of the Contynuaunce thereof (if the fame be not impeached by forreine Attempts) and to encreafe and growe daylye to more Aptnes and Pliauntnes of Reformacion, and to fhewe that the People frame theim felves daylye to be more menable, and better geven to imbrace Civillitie, by the Meanes of the Plantinge of Juftice, vniverfallye amongeft theim, and fpeciallye in the remoter Partes, who of late have tafted the Sweetenes and Fruites of Lawe and Juftice ; and therefore the rather defier, to furrender the old States they have in their Landes, to take the fame againe of her Majeftie, and yeeld her Rent and Service.

3. To reporte what Intelligencies I receive out of *Fraunce,* and dyvers other Places, beinge daylye put in Mynde, frefhe and frefhe of the Intencion, and Preparacion made againft this Realme, by the futtle Devifes and Practizes of *James Fytzmorris,* and his Confederates ; howe imminent the Daunger is at Hand, and what hollowe Hartes, bothe the Lordes and People beare to this Governement, that generallye all the Realme is addicted to Papiftrye ; howe weake the Townes be, to kepe out Forreiners, and howe feeblye and howe weakelye I fhalbe affifted by this Countrey People, if I fhould be driven to vfe their Healpes, and howe little I have Cawfe to truft to their Forces.

4. To folicite with all Care, Erneftnes and Dilligence you can, to have a Maffe of Threafure, fent prefentlye over hither to wage and enterteine Souldiours ; to have lykewife a Maffe of Munition to be fent foorth with, to lye in Stoare to be imployed, if Neade fhall requyre, as a dead Threafure; to have fome Shippinge rigged, prepared, and fet forth to the Seas, afwell to fkowre the Coaft, and diftreffe Pirates, as to refift the Entringe of forreine Force, all that poffiblye they may : Solicite alfo to have twoe thowfand Men, at the leaft, well forted, appointed, and in Areadynes at the Waterfide, to be in Order to comme when I fend, and to procure Lettres to me, from the Lords, to knowe where I fhall haue theim, and other Letters to be fent into the Countrie, to commaund the Captens and Souldiours to comme, when I fende, vpon an Howers Warninge. And you may fignifie to their Lordfhips that my Defier is, to have one Thowfand of the Men levied and taken vp in *South Wales,* and *North Wales,* and the other *Englifh* Shires, vnder my Governement there ; and the other Thowfand neere the Sea Side, in foche Places, as their Lordfhips thinke meteft.

5. To declare the extraordenarie Expenſes, I nowe defray, aſwell to kepe and enterteine more Souldiours, then otherwiſe I would do, or neceſſarie it were, for the Leſſeninge of her Majeſties Chardgies, and Savinge of her Threaſure, I ſhould do ; what Chardgies I am at to enterteine Mariners, and Sea Men, what for Fortificacion, what for Pyoners, and Laborers, and dyvers other extraordinarie Wayes, which nowe would have bene ſpared, if the Feare of forreine Attempts were not ; and therefore ſolicite with all Care and Dilligence, that in Reſpecte of any extraordenarye Chardgies, by Reaſon of theiſe vnlooked for, and extraordenarie Occaſions of forreine Attempts, that my next Quarterage be encreaſed one thowſand Poundes at the leaſt, and the ſame preſentlye to be ſent me, by Mr. Threaſorer, or his Agent.

6. To procure me Warraunt, from her Majeſtie, to my Lord Threaſorer, for the Payment of M.DCClxiii *l.* iii *s.* viii *d. Sterlinge,* iſſued and layed out by me, out of myne owne Aſſignacion, for Thinges due before my Tyme, and Acceptacion of this Chardge and Governement ; which Somme was promiſed me (as I take it) ſhould preſentlye have bene paied, by ſpeciall Lettres from the Lords.

7. Not to forgett to deſcypher the Deviſes and lewd Practizes of *Barnabye Scurlocke, Richard Newtervill, Burnell,* and their Aſſociates, and to declare what Diſcontentment and Mutynye, they have before their Departure hence ſowen, and diſperſed amongſt the People, by their privey Whiſperings, and bad and vnſounde Perſwaſions ; what Comforte the Countrey conceiveth of good Succeſſe by theim, that they, by their Repininge at the Ceſſe, and the Diſputinge of her Majeſties Prerogatyve, have ſett both *Mounſter,* and all the reſt of the Realme on Goge, and made theim ſtartle and draw backe at the Matter ; and namelye that bad Fellowe, *Newtervill,* hath bene the ſole, and onlye Occaſion of the Hyndraunce of her Majeſtie, in this Converſion of Ceſſe, into Certeinetye of Rent, tenne thowſand Markes at the leaſt. That he may therefore, for this Reſpecte, and his other lewd, preſumptuous, arrogant, and vnduetifull Dealings to me, the State, and Governement, be more ſeverelye dealt with all, above the reſt, for Examples Sake ; and his Companions to fynde as little Favor for their Preſumption, and bold Attempt, againſt me, and the Government, as in Reaſon, Equitie, and Honnor, may any Wayes be ſhewed theim. For aſſuredlye the Correccion, and due Puniſſhment of theim, wilbe ſoch a Preparatyve for the Amendement of the reſt of the malitious, mutinous, and ſtubborne Sorte here, as it will make theim have apt Boddies, to receive wholeſome Medicyne for the Reformacion of theim ſelves, and the Countrie, and learne theim both to be more wiſe, and adviſed hereafter, howe to yeeld to the lewd Counſells, and Perſwaſions, of ſo malitious Perſwaders, and vnſound Councellors, as the Enformers be, though in their owne Conceite, and the Opinion of the People, they are reputed wiſe, and Fathers of the Common Wealth, or els at leaſt would make Showe ſo to be.

8. Not to omitt to declare to the Lords, and namelye to my Lord of *Leyceſter,* my Lord Threaſorer, and Mr. Secretorye *Walſynghame,* to what Boldnes and Inſolencye, ſomme of the Gentlemen and Freeholders of the Pale, thorough this Lybertie are growen vnto, in ſo moche as they were not afrayd, to prefere an Enditement of Treaſon againſt me, and moſt of the Counſell, for Takinge of Ceſſe, and that in no meaner Place, then in the *Kings Benche,* and ſhewe theim the Bill of Enditement.

9. To remember, to delyver to Mr. Secretorye, the Copies of ſoch Intelligencies, of forreine Advertizements, as I gave you, and to ſhewe my Lord of *Slanes* Letters, both to my Lord of *Leyceſter,* to hym, and the Lords.

10. To ſolicite to have Warraunte from her Majeſtie to me, for the Admiſſion and Conſecration of the three Biſſhops, I have ſo often and perticulerlye written of, both to Mr. Secretorye, and the Lords, as namelye *David Cleire* to be Biſſhopp of *Oſſerie, John Petit* to be Biſſhop of *Ardaugh,* and *Cornelius Obreion,* Biſſhop of *Roſſe* in *Carberye.*

I

11. To folicite Mr. Secretorie for the Preferment of the Bill, to her Majefties gratious Signature, for my Sonne, *Robert Sydney*, and *Edmound Molyneuxe*, to have the Framinge and Makinge, of all originall Bills, and Making out of all Orders for Proceffe of Apparaunce. The Lords have bene acquainted with the Sute, by my Lettres vnto them of late ; and namelye my Lord of *Leycefter*, and Mr. Secretorye more perticulerlye ; and longe agoe it was commended to the Lords, by my Lettres, to have paffed in the Name of *Fowke Grivell*, and *Molyneuxe*. But, becawfe *Fowke Grivell* is fpedd fo well alreadye, of the Reverfions of twoe of the beft Offices in that Courte, whereof I am glad, I have therefore in his Steede named my Sonne *Robert*, to be ioyned with *Molyneuxe* ; I would therefore have you earneftlye, dilligentlye, and carefullye folicite it. And for the better Furtheraunce, and Expedicion in the Sute, you fhall do well to entreate my Lord Threaforers good Will and Confent, for that he hath heretofore, as it is thought, not bene the beft affected vnto it. But you may nowe refolve his Lordfhip of my good Lykinge, full Confent, and Allowaunce of the Matter, that it fhould goe forwarde, and take Place.

12. Solicite me a fpedie Anfwere touchinge my Lorde of *Clanrickards* Cafe, and procure to be fent thence the Manner, Order, and Proceffe, that is vfed for Tryall of Noblemen, for here is no Prefident thereof to be found.

13. You muft tell my Lord Treaforer and Mr. Secretorie *Walfinghame*, that, at their Inftaunce and fpeciall Recommendacion of Doctor *Hector*, and his Cawfies, that I am and wilbe as carefull to do hym Good, as I can any Wayes devife to do ; and for that Purpofe I will prefentlye write to the Lord Prefident in the Matter ; but the Tyme is verye vnapt for the prefent, to enter into Cawfies of that Nature. That the Spoyle and Diforder was committed within *Defmounds* Liberties, and the Matter not ordered and decreed fo autentikelye againft *Defmounde*, as any faft Hold may be gathered vpon that Order to recover the Debt. And you may add withall, howe hardlye any Money is got out of *Defmounds* Handes, and howe careleffe he is to anfwere his Credit, or pay any Debt, and nowe fpeciallye, fince he hath his Sonne out of *England*, which was the beft and moft affured Pledge of his Loyaltie, and framed hym to fome Shewe of Obedience, and that his Sendinge hether was without my Knowledge or Confent. Howe be it I will deale as effectuallye as I can, and more precifely then if it were myne owne Cafe, when the Doctor fhall appointe hereafter any Agent or Factor here, to followe the Matter for hym.

14. To remember to fhewe the Lettre the Bifhopp of *Meithe* fent me touchinge the Friers of the *Novan*, and reporte the Intelligences I delyvered you of the Synode at *Armache*.

15. To folicite to have a Commiffion to compounde for the Arreragies which the Lords, by their Lettres vnto me, dated in *Marche* laft, promifed that they would be a Meanes to her Majeftie I fhould have.

16. To folicite to have this Proporcion of Municion fent, and delyvered here, by fomme of the Officers of the Ordenaunce, or by fomme other of Truft, her Majeftie fhall apointe to remayne as a dead Treafure in the Mafter of the Ordenaunce Chardge to her Majefties Vfe, and not to be imployed to any other Service, but onelye to refift the Invafion intended, and forreine Attemptes, *viz.*

Fyve Laft of Corne Powder.
One Laft of Serpentyne Powder.
Sixe Fodder of Lead.
Matche xxxiij M. Weight.
Bowes iiij C.
Sheffes of Arrowes xij C.
Strings fyftie Groffe.
Pykes iij C.
Blacke Bills, v C.
Halberds, CC.
Turkey Murions, CC.

Corceletts

Corceletts complete of the beſt Mold, CC.
Spades and Shovells, xx Dozen.
Pick Axes, CC.
Hedging Billes, C.
Reapinge Hookes, CC.
Coyles of Handrope, M Weight.
Ginne Ropes, CC Weight.

17. You muſt tell the Lords and Mr. Secretorie, in my Excuſe, that where in their Lettres, I made Requeſt for M Men onely, and in her Majeſties for ij M. it proceaded of this, that for as moche as from Day to Day, I received freſher and freſher Advertizements of theſe forreine Attempts, I thought it verye neceſſarie to crave a greater Supplye, the better to be hable, if Nede be, to reſiſt the Invaſion.

18. To declare to Mr. Secretorie *Walſinghame*, that that I wrote vnto you touchinge the Plott of the Reformacion, he hath by his Lettres remembred me of, and tell hym, that the Foundacion of that I have cheifely to buyld vpon, is the vniverſall Converſion of the Ceſſe into an annuall Rent, whereunto I pray hym put his healping Hand.

Theiſe be the principall Matters and Heddes I have nowe for the preſent to delyver you, which I pray and requyre you ſolicite and followe from Pointe to Pointe acordingly. And if any Thinge ſhall either be farther demaunded of you, or ſhall happ vpon Occaſion to fall in Conſideracion and Debate by her Ma-jeſtice or the Lords, touhinge either myne owne Perticuler, or generallye of the State and Governement here, which I have neither in private Speache imparted vnto you, nor expreſſed in theiſe Memorialls and Notes; you may therein ac-cordinge to the Tyme, Place, and your beſt Diſcreacion, ſatisfie their Demaundes for the preſent as you can, and advertiſe me with Spede, what you have ſaied or donne therein, to the End if Nede requyre, I may from Tyme to Tyme ſupplye you with further Matter and Enſtruccion.

H. Sydney.

Spetiall Notes for Mr. Waterhowſe *to remember at the Courte, which were omitted in my Lords Inſtruccions,* xxj° Maii, 1577. *viz.*

FIRST, if Occaſion fall out, to ſend over Men to reſiſt the forreine Inva-ſion intended by *James Fytzmorris* and the *Frenche,* that the Captens and Soldiours, that are to be levied in *Sowth Wales,* and the Weſt Partes of *England,* may be ſent and appointed to land at *Waterfford* ; and thoſe of *North Wales* and the Shyres adioininge, to be ſent to *Dublin.*

2. A Maſſe of Victuall to be provided and ſent with the Soldiours, aſwell for thoſe that direct their Courſe to *Waterfford,* as thoſe that ſhall comme to *Dublin,* and namelye Corne, for that the ſame is not in any Sorte to be had or found here, and ſome Proporcion would lykewiſe be ſent of Cheeſe, Butter, and ſoch other lyke groſſe Proviſions, for that thoſe Kinds are both ſkarce to be had, and at exceſſyve Prices to be bought.

3. To recommend Sir *Nicholas Malbye,* and his Service in *Connaught,* which my Lord hath in Parte touched in my Lord Threaſorers Lettres, and to declare what Lykelihood there is, if this Courſe be held thorough *Connaught,* that *Con-naught* will ſhortlye be brought to beare *Connaughts* Chardge.

4. To declare the Order taken with my Lord *Mountgarrett,* and the great Preſumptions, that are gathered againſt hym, to be an Aydor, Succorer, and Relyver of detected and proclaymed Rebells.

5. To ſhewe my Lord of *Leyceſter* the Originall or Copie of the S of 14 Lettre, written by Way of Warraunt and Commaundement to my Lord 11 of 4 ; and pray his Lordſhip to note the Manner of the Signature.

✝

6. To prefent my moft humble Dewtie, Service, and Thanks to Mr. Secretorie *Walfinghame*, to whome, for his fondrie Favors, and perfect Tokens of Good-will, I confeffe my felf at all Tymes to have bene moft bovnd. And befeache hym to excufe me, that I nowe do not this by Lettre my felfe vnto hym, and that all this Whyle hetherto I have omitted to do it. Which hath not proceaded (you may affure hym) either for Lacke of Remembraunce of Dewtie, or Forgetfulnes of that which I have found at his Handes, but that fome other Rule hath made me fcylent, which henceforth I will not be.

7. To aske foch Planks as *William Fofter* left upon the *Tower* Wharffe ; they were forgotten by hym, as it fhould feame, for Want of Cariage: It would do well you fhould demaunde of *Fofter* what is becomme of theim.

8. My Lord hath written to my Lord Threaforer, that he thinketh it the beft Courfe for Doctor *Hector*, that hee make *James Gold*, her Majefties Attorney in the Province of *Mounfter*, to be his Agent, for the Followinge of his Cawfe againft the Earl of *Defmounde*, for he is the apteft and moft fufficient Man to do it. And what my Freindfhipp may any Ways ftand hym in fteade, he fhalbe fure of it.

E. Molyneuse.

A Declaracion howe and in what Manner the Towne of the Newrie, *in the Realme of* Irelande, *maye be fortified by the Queenes Majeftie, without her Highnes Chardge, by the Trayvell of Sir* Nicholas Bagenall, *her Highnes Marfhall of* Ireland, *to Thadvauncement and Eftablifhment of the peafible Government of the North Parts of the Realme. With Sir* Henry Sydneys *Notes.*

FIRST, where the faid *Nicholas* hath erected and buylded a Caftle and Towne vpon the Ryver of *Carlingford*, beinge one of the leaft Havens in the Land, at a Place cawled the *Newry :* He fynding by good Reafons and Experience the faid Caftle and Towne to be the veary Occafions and Grownds wherby, in fo fhort a Tyme, his Tenaunts and Neighbours, not only be growen to great Cyvylytye of Lyef, but alfo do geave theym felves altogether to get their Lyvings by the Manuraunce of the Grownde, and the Noble Men and Gentlemen neere vnto him, do vfe and governe theym felvs in farre more quyet and orderly Sort then before the faid Fortificacions they were accuftomed to do. The which Towne beinge allready trentched and fortified with a Rampier of Earth ; fo is it further to be confidered, that if the fame Towne were fo walled with Stone, as Marchaunts, and other of good Habillities, might perfwade theym felfs to lyve there in good Saeffty with there Shipps and Goods ; then it were no Dowbt nor Queftion, but both Towne and Countrye, in veary fhort Tyme, wold become of fuche Force and Strength, as her Maieftie fhold not need to be at any Chardge in defending the Partes of the Northe, but fhold allwayfe have of theym felves great Strength and Force of Men there, to ferue her Highnes as they fhalbe cornaunded.

The faid Sir *Nicholas* maketh Offer vnto her Maieftie, vnder the Condicions hereafter expreffed, that he will, at his awne Cofts, walle the faid Towne with Stone, hable and fufficient to defend Thennymie, and to buylde two or three Churches, a Jayle, a Court Howfe for Thaffemblie of the People, and Keeping of Lawe Dayes, and a Stone Bridge over the Ryver, which, by Eftymacion, wilbe x or xj Arches, the Accomplifhment of which Workes will ftand him, by all Judgement, in fowrty Thowfand Pownds at the leaft.

In Confideracion of the Premiffes, and that he may be the better enhabled to finifhe the faid Worke, his Sute and Petition is as enfueth, *viz.*

Firft, That yt will pleafe her Maieftie to graunte vnto the faid Towne a Sentuary, that her Maiefties Subiects, and others, maye freely, for certeyne Yeres, lyve there under the Protections and Government of the faid Sir

Nicholas, and his Heires or Affigns, notwithftanding any Offences by theym comytted, Treafon, Myfprifon of Treafon, Petty Treafon, Wilfull Murther, Robbing by the Highe Waye, Burglaries and Rapes onlye excepted; with further Privifho, that fuche Perfons as be broken or fhall breake, cawled Banckerupts, fhall aryve at the faid Towne of *Newry,* or to any Parte of the Lands adioyninge therevnto, there Names to be recorded; and the faid Sir *Nicholas,* and his Heirs, to do his and their Endeavours, everye Waye, to cawfe theym to anfweare the Creadytors, as their Habillities fhalbe founde hable. ' For ' no Rape, Felony, or other Trefpafs, but for one Year, and that but for his ' Parfon; and for Det abfolutely for one Year; and after that for vii Yeares; fo ' as within that one Year the Detter put in fuffycyent Surety to pay the Det at ' feven Yeares End.'

Item, Further, it maye pleafe her Maieftie to graunte, that yt maye be lawfull for the faid Towne to traffacte withall Nations, afweil in Warre as in Peace, in as ample Sorte and Manner, as *Garney* or *Jerfey* dothe. ' To dangerous and ' to evyll a Prefydent for me to move.'

Item, It may pleafe her Maieftie to allowe him vnder his Leading iij C Soldiars of her Highnes ordynary Garrifon there, duringe fuch Tyme as the faid Walle of the faid Towne, Bridge, Jayle, and Churches, be in Buyldinge, with Provifo, that ij C of the faid iij C Soldiars fhalbe at the Lord Deputies Appoinctment, at all Hoftings, if Neceffytie of the Cawfe fhall fo requyre. ' I cannot agree to thys.'

Item, It may alfo pleafe her Maieftie to graunte him the Lone of certeyne Braffe Peeces, with Allowance of Shott and Powder for Defence of the Haven of the faid Towne, during the Tyme of the faid Fortificacions and Buyldings. ' The Lone of the Peecys I agre to without Chardge of Powder or ' Shot.'

Item, It maye likewife pleafe her Maieftie to encorporate the faid Towne of the *Newrie,* and to graunt vnto the fame every Weeke a *Thurfdaye* Markett; and every Yere two Fayers, to contynewe as a Free Mart, every of theym, for feaven Dayes at the feverall Tymes.

Item, It maye alfo pleafe her Majeftie, for the better Enhabling of the faid Sir *Nicholas* to fynifhe the faid Worke, to joyne his Sonne *Henrye Bagenall* in Patent with him in his Office of Marfhall, which by Gods Grace fhall turne to the Advauncement of your Majefties Service, and Peace of that Countrye. The Creadytt wherof fhall gayne great Furtherance to his Worke, and much enhable the faid Sir *Nicholas,* to brynge the fame with the more Expedicion to good Ende, whereby your Majeftie fhall, amongeft all Pofteritie, obteyne a moft honorable and perpetuall Fame; for the doinge wherof will to the World moft evydently the fame, to be the moft benyficiall Acte to the Furtherans of the Common Wealth, and Advauncement of Gods Glorie, that hath bin donne in that Lande by any Prynce this iiij C Yeres. ' I wyllingly will further thys.'

Laftly, Where the faid Sir *Nicholas* hath feruyd your Majeftie as Cheiff Comyffioner in the Province of *Vlfter* xj Yeres, and hetherto hath not had any ordinary Allowaunce for the fame, affuring him felf, that thofe whome hath bin Lord Deputies, and the whole Realme, will faye that his Chardges and Expences therin, hath not bin inferior to either the Prefydents of *Connaught* or *Mounfter:* He humblie befecheth your Majeftie, that if he be thought a fytt Perfonne to contynewe the faid Chardge, then he maye have fomme convenyent Allowaunce to him affigned for Thexecucion therof. ' I agre to thys with all my Hart, the ' Graunt to be *Durante bene Placito.*'

And your Majefties faid humble Servant, according to his bownden Dewtie, fhall daylie praye to Almightie God for the longe and profperous Contyneuaunce of your Majefties Raigne.

My

My good Knyght,

'YOU may fe by thys I have not forgotten you, yet haply not fo largely
'   graunted as you would ; but indeed as largely as I can yet concent to.
'Uppon Conferens it is poffible that we may alter fum Thyng. At *Kilmaynham*
'thys 21 *May*, 1577.'

Your faft Freynd,

H. Sydney.

Edward Waterhous, *Efq*; to Sir Henry Sydney.

It may pleafe your Lordfhip,

I Write vnto you from *Hilbrie*, at my Landing there on *Wednifday* Night the
22th of *May*. The *Sondaie* following being *Whitfonday*, I deliuerid your
Letters at the Court erly in the Morning ; Mr. Secretary having perufid his, and
conferrid with me, had Spech with my Lord of *Lecefter*. And vppon Deliuery of
the reft of my Lettres, and Euidence to the Lords, they grewe to a Confultacion
towchinge the *French* Advertifements, wherof Sir *William Drury* had fent them a
Copy the Daie before my Comyng ; vppon Reading wherof, albeit (the Stat of
Fraunce confiderid) it was thought impoffible that any Attempt cold be made by
theim this Year : Yet when their Lordfhips had confiderid farder the dailie Confirmacion of this Newes in *Irland*, the open Difcords that the Papifts make of theim
felfs, the Soliciting of the *Irifhe*, or fuch as comm from the Traitor ; the Sinode
appointid at *Armaugh*, the Combinacion of *John Burk*, and Sir *John of Defmounde*,
and the Obftinacy of thofe of the Pale : In Conclufion it was refolvid by theim,
and by good Perfuacion confirmid by her Majeftie, that your Lordfhip fhall
prefently have fyve thoufaund Pounds for this next Quarter, and tenne thoufaund
Pounds for a dead Maffe not to be broken, but for this Extremity. Two thoufaund Men fhall be put in Readines in the Counties of *Somerfett*, *Devon*, *Corne-
wall* ; and within your Lordfhips Commiffion of *Wales*, feuerall Provifions to be
made for theim of Corne, Buttor, and Cheefe ; but not before you giue a newe
Alarme.

Three gallant Shipps goe prefently to the Sea, the *Lyon*, the *Swiftefuer*, and
the *Dreadnought* ; and your Proportion of Municion with fomme Encreafe fhalbe
prefently fent you. If your Mafter of the Ordnaunce had not fett downe a miferable Proportion, your Lordfhip fhuld haue had a Roiall Provifion to haue remainid
in Store with you, for their was appointid by the noble Erle of *Warwick*, xv Laft
of Pouder, and all Things anfwerable, but Mr. *Wingfields* Note marred
all.

Hir Majeftie angry at the firft, when Money was demaundid, faid, that
Henry Sidney did allwaies feek to put her to Charge ; but when the Lord of *Lecefter* had perfuaded, that the Money was not to be broken but vppon thes forren Matters, and that it was all one to haue Treafure and Municion ether there or
heere ; her Highnes confented to all.

Your Lordfhip fhall do well, vppon Receipt of the Counfelles Lettres, which
fhalbe prefently fent you with thes Things, to geue them a generall Letter of
effectuall Thanks, that they haue with fuch Expedicion refoluid vppon your Releif, and particularly to my Lord Threaforer, my Lord Chamberlain, &c. for to
my Lord of *Lecefter* I know you will do, and in deed his Lordfhips Care of your
Caufes, extraordinary in it felf, deferues the higheft of Frendfhip. I haue not feen
him fo cairfull of you at enie Tyme.

Vppon *Wednifday* laft, the Erles of *Lecefter*, and *Warwick*, went to *Killingworth*,
and from thence to *Buckftons*, and fo as it is thought to *Wilton*, to the Lord of
Penbroke, who with his Lady went towards *Wiltfheir*, vppon the fame Day that
the Erles departed towards *Killingworth*.

†

Mr.

Mr. *Phillip Sidney* is retornid into *Flaunders*, and there ftaieth, as I heare, to chriften the Prince of *Oraunges* Childe. He is looked for heere within tenne Daies ; but he paffed his Journey with Honur and good Opinions, both Abrode and at Home, and is helthfull for ought that I can lerne.

My Lord of *Ormound* findith him felf grevid with the Ouerburdening of his Tennaunts of *Rathvilly* by the holding *Kerns*, which he faith hath fpoiled his Tennaunts in that County ; wherevppon I tooke Occafion to declare vnto him, that they had not done eny Thing but that which Sir *William Fitz William* had done the like ; I declarid the hole Circumftance, and how *Hary Davells*, and he had teftified the Receipt of the *Kern* Money in Sir *William Fytz Williams* Daies : I told him farder, it was for the Securitie of the hole Sheire, and the Sparing of his Lordfhip (being not made free by the Queins Letter) that had bene an Iniury to the reft of the County, becaufe the Burden fhuld not haue bene vnequally car- ried and more laid vppon them then of Right ought. He faid to that Matter, your own Concordate had made it free, and your Profeffion of good Will to him did banifhe Miftruft that he fhold haue bene fo vnkindly vfid in his Abfence. I tooke a Copy of the Words of the Concordatum, which I fend your Lordfhip enclofid. *Laftly*, I anfwered that you had diffolued all Feudores, faving fuch as were auncient, and I faid your Lordfhip had Caufe to think Vnkindnes in him, that he wold animate *Nettervile*, and his Companions, to complayne of *Seffe*, and told him *Nettervilles* Speaches to my Lord of *Slane*. And my Lord of *Slanes* Caws to dif- prove *Newtervilis* Reports, that it might not take Roote in the Lordfhip. To that he protefted, that he never wrot of eny fuch Matter, and that if *Nettervile* wold advow it, he wold prove him a lieing Varlet ; I faid the Erle of *Defmond* left to his Difcrecion, to deliver or not to deliver the Complaints he made to her Majefty, which he alfo refufed with Othes. That he fawe not the Lettre, nether knewe the Contents, till her Majefty had red it. And fo we departed ; but truly, my Lord, in Refpect of the Concordatum I wold it had not been.

The Triumvirat are ftill clofe Prifoners ; the Reafing of Rent vppon the Vicount *Barry*, with the Increafe of the Revenue in *Connoght*, be generally liked ; and great Hope conceyvid of a large Revenue if that Cours be followid ; yet all Men be not refoluid that the *Seffe* may be in Equity fo converted, but rather mainteyned as a Prerogative for the Prince for the Releif of the Army, to be to the People ether more or leffe burdenus, as the Number of Soldiers fhalbe neceffary, mayny or fewe. I found the Mark whereat thes Words weir fhott, and faid that I was fuer the laft *Seffe* was demandid but for V Hundred Soldiers, and leffer then that Number cold not be mainteynid in the moft quiet Tymes hereafter. It was an- fwered, that the Ceffe of the Army ought to be laid vppon the *Irifhe*; I faid to her Majefty, if fhe wold compell them forceably. But if her Highnes had now xv C Soldiours, and laid but the third Part of the *Seffe* vppon the Pale, I thoght it fauorable Dealing.

Mayny are Suters here for the Leading of the newe Bands, if they be levied ; but I haue overthrowen their Sewtes, for it is reafonable your Lordfhip chufe your owne Captens and Officers, wherin howfoeuer you fhall be procuered to chufe for privat Refpects, I hope your Lordfhip will confider that your owne Safety, and the State ftandith vppon the good Choice of your Menn of Warre. And when your Requeft was opened by my Lord of *Leicefter*, for one of Suf- ficiency to commaund vnder you, the Lords did excedingly well like of your Care in that Matter, and mayny were namid ; emongft which your old Follower, *N. Errington*, was appointed to direct the Artillary.

Laftly, my Lord, let me remember your Lordfhip, that you live emongft a difcontentid People ; your Patent is to governe accordinge to your owne Difcre- tion ; if in this ticle Tyme they will be held with Lenity, it is the beft Cours ; but if that will not fatisfy, if your Lordfhip laie as mainy by the Healis, as you doubt will obftinatly perfuade the People, or encline to Rebellion, it will be al- lowid in you for Wifdom. God fend your Lordfhip that Honor that your

i

felf wifsheth of that Service, and fo I humbly leave you at *London, primo Junij,* 1577.

Your Lordfhips, &c.

Edward Waterhous.

Sir Francis Walfyngham *to Sir* Henry Sydney.

My verie good Lord,

BEcaufe your Lordfhip fhall vnderftande fufficientlie by the generall Lettre from my Lords, what Order is taken for the neceffarie Defence of that Realme againft the pretended Danger, I will not trouble youe with ouer many Lynes more, then to certefie your Lordfhip of one Poynt which is left vnanfwered in the fame, and concernethe the Payment of the 1660 *l.* 3 *s.* 8 *d.* iffued and laide out by your Lordfhip for Things due before your Entrance and Takinge the Gouerment vppon youe. Her Majeftie beinge moued therin, hath made Stey therof, vntill fhee maye fee Thaccoumpts, which her Highnes looked fhoulde haue ben fent ouer at *Midfomer* next, and is difpleafed that they are deferred vntill *Michelmas*; wherefore I haue written vnto Mr. *Genifon*, giuinge him to vnderftande of the faide her Majefties Difpleafure conceiued, and willinge him to fee they be ended with all Dilligence; for, by Reafon of the Want of the Vewe of thofe Accoumpts, there is Stey made of Payment to diuers, which her Majefty woulde willinglie fhoulde be fatisfied if fhee might, as Reafon is, vnderftande her owne State.

Now touchinge your Lordfhips perticuler, I am to impart vnto you the Returne of the yonge Gentleman, Mr. *Sidney*, your Sonne, whofe Meffage verie fufficientlie performed, and the Relatinge therof, is no leffe gratfullye received, and well liked of her Majeftie, then the honorable Opinion he hathe left behinde him, with all the Princes with whome he had to negotiate, hathe left a moft fweet Savor and gratfull Remembraunce of his Name in thofe Parts. The Gentleman hathe given no fmall Arguments of great Hope, the Fruits wherof I doubt not but your Lordfhip fhall reape, as the Benefitts of the good Parts which ar in him, and wherof he hathe given fome Taft in this Voyage, is to redounde to more then your Lordfhip and him felf. There hathe not ben any Gentleman, I am fure thefe many Yeres, that hathe gon throughe fo honorable a Charge with as great Comendacions as he: In Confideracion wherof, I could not but comunicate this Part of my Joy with your Lordfhip, beinge no leffe a Refrefhinge vnto me, in thefe my troublefome Bufinefs, then the Soile is to the chafed Stagge. And fo wifhinge the Increafe of his good Parts, to your Lordfhips Comfort, and the Seruice of her Majeftie and his Countrie, I humblie take my Leave. From the Court at *Grenwich*, this xth of *June*, 1577.

Your Lordfhips affured Frend,

Francis Walfyngham.

Edward Waterhowfe *to Sir* Henry Sydney.

It may pleafe your Lordfhip,

THE Things that may minifter you the greateft Comfort is, that Mr. *Sidney* is returnid fafe into *England*, with great good Acceptacion of his Seruice at her Majefties Hands; allowed of by all the Lords to have bene handled with great Judgement and Difcretion, and hath bene honorid Abrode in all the Princes Courts with much extraordinary Favour. The Emperour gave him a great Chaine, the Princeffe of *Orange* another with a fair Jewell. The reft I will leave to Mr. Secretary his Report, and to Mr. *Phillips* owne Letters. God bleffid him fo, that nether Man, Boy, or Horffe failid him, or was fick in this Journey; only *Folke Grevill* had an Ague in his Returne at *Rochefter.*

I am emploied Weſtward to prepare the 2000 Men, and to furniſh them with Victuall, according to the Proportion namid in the Counſells Letters; where I think I ſhall ſpend 2 or 3 Monthes, without any Allowance for eny Thing, that yet I know; for all is ſett heere uppon good Huſbandry. Your Lordſhips Men and Victualls, ſhall be in Redines. I have erneſtly ſolicyted Mr. Secretary, for the Dett of MDClxiii *l.* iii *s.* viii *d.* for which a Pryvy Seall hath bene longe made, and I perceyve by my Lord Threſorer he hath great good Will to pleaſe your Lordſhip; not only with that, but with Empreſts uppon Captors Billes, for which you wrote to him to uſe his Freindſhip: But both by him and Mr. Secretary, I perceyve that the Queene is bent uppon a generall Anſwere, both for that, and all Docquits; and the Threſorours Billis due to others, that ſhe will pay nothing, 'till Mr. Auditour hath certified, what ſhe owith in *Ireland*: But if it cannot be gotten, then I think the next Way is, that if this *French* Invaſion proceede not, that Mr. Secretary do hearafter procuer you a Warrant, to pay yourſelf out of the 10,000 *l.* now ſent; for all that is once paſt will be forgotten, and ſo more eaſyly optainid then out of Thexchequer here: But I humbly beſeach your Lordſhip haſten Mr. Auditors Certificat. I have written playnly to him in this Matter.

I ſuppoſe your Promoters ſhall ſhortly optain that Favour to have the Liberty of the Fleet without Reſours of *Iriſh* unto thes, and ſomwhat I think will be done for a ſmale Cure of the *Seſſe*, wherof your Lordſhip ſhall heare more as ſoone as it comith in Queſtion: Your Warrant for Conſecration of Biſſhops will be ſhortly ſent you, and the Sewt for Mr. *R. Sydney* and Mr. *Molineux* hath bene movid to her Majeſty, wherunto ſhe anſwerid that your Lordſhip did erneſtly perſwade her, that ſhe ſhold not make any ſuch Innovation in the Marches: But it is not receyvid as eny abſolute Anſwer, but ſhall again be movid to her Majeſty as ſone as commodiuſly it may be.

I ſuppoſe a Forme of Arraignments, will be ſent you for Nobility: But when I moved for the Erle of *Clanricards* Caſe, I was willed to forbeare a While. It was not good to have to many Irons in the Fire at once; Tyme wold worke Things at better Leiſure; but the Attorney and Solicitour have appointid to ſend me the hole Cours of the Arraignment of a Peere.

Thes be all the Particulers, that beſids the Matter conteynid in your Letters, from the Lords and Mr. Secretary, I thought good to move them of at this Tyme; only this I think, that if you call not uppon Aide from thence, they will be cold enough here. If good Collour were to ſend the Men over, I wold then treate with your Lordſhip, for as it wold prevent the Miſcheif which you feare, ſo wold it breake all Competitions, *&c.* Your Lordſhip knoweth my Meaning: And ſo to the Lord I commytt you, reſting ever faythfully at your Lordſhips Commandment.

x *Junij,* 1577.

Ed. Waterhows.

Sir *Francis* Walſynham *to Sir* Henry Sydney.

My verry good Lord,

FYndyng the Erle of *Ormonde* greatly diſcontented, as well for Impoſyng a Ceſſe uppon his Tenants of the Countye of *Caterloe* (being exempt as they are by a Concordate ſygned by your Lordſhips Hande) as alſo for the Commyttyng of the Lord *Mongarret,* I ſowght to ſatyſfyce him as well as I coold, wyſſhing him to ſtaye from ſeekyng Redreſſe here, untyll he might receyve your Lordſhips Awntſwer; wherunto his Lordſhip hath yeelded, and therfor I ſhall deſyre your Lordſhip, to deale in ſooche Sorte towardes him, in thes Poyntes, as he may have no juſt Cauſe of Offence. Whatſoever Reporte hathe ben made unto your Lordſhip, of my Lords Dealynges here towardes you, I am right well aſſured, that he hathe don no evyll Offyces, notwithſtandyng the Injuryes he conceyvethe he hathe receyved at your Lordſhips Handes: For the Matter of *Ceſſe,* ſeing by her Majeſtys eſpecyall Grawnte his Lande in the County of *Caterloe* is

†

exempt;

exempt ; in my Opinion (not knowing what may be awntfwered) yt feamethe he hathe ben hardely dealt withall. And as for the Commyttyng the Lord *Mongarret*, being accufed by one that hathe not ben the beft affected towardes him, and the Matters as yt thowght, eyther not verry great, or not well proved ; he thinkethe, that the Commyttyng of him growethe uppon fome Dyfpofytion to deface him by the Perfwatyon of fooche as are his Enemyes about your Lordfhip. Of thefe his Greeves, he defyered me to advertyce your Lordfhip, and to requeft you, that he, his Family and Tenants, may be otherwyfe dealt withall, for that otherwyfe he fhall be forced to have Recourfe to fooche Remedyes, as fhall be good for neyther of you. I can not, but ftyll be of Opynion, that yt is moft neceffarye for him that fhall governe *Irelande*, to have the Erle of *Ormonde* a Frende ; for that the Gentleman is bothe wyfe, valyant, and ould ; hath Credyt heere, both with her Majeftye, and the great Parfonages of this Coorte ; and being an Ennemy, fhall be able as well ther, as here, to croffe any Governor ther. And therfor good my Lord, let no lyght Caufes drawe you, to doe any Thing that may mynifter any juft Caufe of Offence. Yf you fynde any Caufe of Myflyke, eyther pryvat or publycke, charge him with all roundely as becommethe the Authoryte of the Place you houlde. And in Cafe he fhall not yelde to Reformatyon, then may you proceade the more feverely ageynft him. Thus your Lordfhip feethe, that I am bownde to imparte my Opynyon unto you, which I prefume you wyll accept in frendely Parte. And fo I commyt you to God. At *Greenwich*, 11th *June*, 1577.

Your Lordfhips affured Frende,

Superfcribed,

Fra. Walfyngham.

To the right honnorable Sir *Henry Sydney*, Knight of the Th'Order, Lord Deputye of her Majeftyes Realme of *Ireland*.

James *Lord Regent of* Scotland *to* Sir Henry Sydney.

After my richt hertie Commendaciones to your gude Lordfhip,

ANE honeft Man of the Toun of *Air*, namid *Dauid Colthird*, quha vfes the Trade of Merchandice at *Dublin* and otheres Partes thair in *Irland*, hes certane his Guids ftayed in *Dublin*, the Perfonis in quhais Handes the fame remanys, pretending the fame to be arreftit for certaine Cuftumes dew to haue been payed be the faid *Dauid* ; howbeit he affermis that he hes alwayes trewly and thankfullie payed all Cuftumes that he aucht, and wold repairis him felf to fatiffie and anfher for all Thing that iuftly may be layed to his Charge. Before I will hertly requeft and pray your Lordfhip the Premiffes confiderit, that you will fhaw your fauorable Guidwill toward this honeft Man, in furthering him to haue expedite Iuftife agains the Withalders of his Guidis, incaife thay refuife to do him Reafoun and Mefour with Beniuolence ; quherein ye fhall do me gude Pleafher, quhilk I falbe verie willing to acquite, quhen any of the Q. Majeftie her Souerains Subiects may happin to haue awd in this Cuntrie at your Recommendatioun. And fa I commit your Lordfhip in the Protectioun of the Almightie Chrift. *Edinburgh* the xx Day of *Junij*, 1577.

Your Lordfhips verey affured Freind.

James Regient.

Sir Henry Sydney, *and the Council of* Ireland, *to the Council in* England.

Oure verye good Lords,

OURE Dueties humblye remembred vnto your honorable Lordfhips, we have received (greatlye to oure Comforte and Contentacions) your Lordfhips honorable Lettres, dated from *Grenewitche*, the xiiijth of the Laft, the
xxvijth

xxvijth of the fame: For the which, we render vnto your Lordſhips our moſt humble Thanks for the honorable and freindlye Conſideracion you have had of oure Creditts, and the Countenaunce of this State, which well apeareth vnto vs, in the Manner of your moſt grave and wiſe Proceadings with *Barnabye Scurlocke,* and his twoe Companions: Who beinge more wilfullye bent, then wiſly adviſed, and ſtirred (as it ſhould ſeme) vpon an Humor to pleaſe the Multitude, and ſomewhat to power out their owne Malice, which they had ſo longe conceived againſt vs, and the State; beinge covered, neverthelefs, vnder the Shadowe of their well Meaninge and good Intention, to eaſe the heavye Burthen impoſed (by longe Ceſſe) vpon the Countrie, would not be difſuaded by any good Meanes we could vſe vnto theim, from the Enterpriſe they had taken in Hande; but nedes they repaier over to complaine of oure grevous and hard Dealinge towards theim, to your Lordſhips. And nowe having received at your Honnors Handes (to your owne iuſt Prayſes) the dewe Rewarde of their Deſerts, we thought it expedient, beinge led by ſo good and grave a Preſident, accordinge to her Majeſties Direction (whereunto your honorable Lettres referred vs) to ſende not onelye for thoſe Lords and Gentlemen that ſubſcribed the Lettres ſent vnto her Majeſtie and you, but alſo in Diſcreacion for ſome others, whoſe diſguiſed and cunninge Manner of Dealinge, we had heard of before by Report, beinge Men ſpeciallye noted vnto vs, to be cheife Counſellors, Ringleaders, and Procurers of the late Embaſſage ſent to your Lordſhips. And when all theiſe (thus beinge ſent for by oure Lettres) came before vs, havinge firſt Occaſion to deale withe theim, touchinge their Claime of Fredome from Ceſſe; found generallye in theim all, by the Manner of theyer Anſwers to oure Demaundes, an arrogant, and wilfull Kinde of Repininge at her Majeſties Prerogatyve for Ceſſe, affirminge boldly, in *playne Speache,* without any Stickinge, that no Ceſſe could be impoſed but by Parliament, or graund Councell, and what ſoever was otherwiſe ſet downe by vs, was againſt Lawe: Wherevpon we grewe by Degrees from one Matter to another, over longe to be repeted by Diſcourſe of Lettre; yet ſo neceſſarie to be known to your Lordſhips, as an vndowbted Argument of their Stubbornes and Arrogauncye, that what Greife and Bourthen ſo ever they complayne of to your Lordſhips, we could never yet finde hetherto any ſounde Towardnes or Diſpoſition in any one of theim to conferre with vs, vpon any good Deviſe, how to leſſen the Chargde of Ceſſe, and make the Bourden more eaſie vnto theim, and her Majeſtie to be at no greater Chardge in Victuallinge the Soldiour, then nowe ſhe is at; otherwiſe then in this Sorte, to have the Ceſſe totallye taken away, and referred to their Conſideracions, what they thought good and expedient to be donne therein at the next Aſſemblye of Parliament: Though (we muſt confeſſe) that ſomme fewe of theim, ſince the Tyme of their Reſtrainte of Lybertie (the better to diſſemble their furder Intencions) have of late made ſomme Manner of Mocion, to comme to Conference, but ſo coldlye, and ſo farre from the Matter, that is expected at their Handes, as their Mocion is rather to be compted no Mocion at all. And therefore we ſtay to growe to any Reſolucion in this Matter of Ceſſe with theim, before we ſhall vnderſtand your Lordſhips Opinions, as by your Lettres you have ſignified vnto vs we ſhould do, which we deſier ſpedilye to have from you, and cheifelye for this, becawſe we finde this Manner of Metinge with their Arrogancye and Stubbornes, hath framed the Tyme better nowe then of late it hath been, to deale vpon ſome good Deviſe, for her Majeſties beſt Commoditie. And ſurelye, my Lords, as longe as a Garriſon muſt be mainteined here, for their Defence (with out the which, they cannot lyve and defend theim ſelves) ſomewhat muſt be contributed out of every Plough Lande, or rather rathed vpon every Acre, towardes the Victuallinge and Mainteininge of the Soldiour; otherwiſe her Majeſtie muſt nedes encreaſe her Pay, which we as Counſellors will not adviſe. And, my Lords, as longe as Ceſſe remayneth, there muſt be vnder Officers, and Miniſters of Neceſſity appointed, to levye and gather the ſame, whoſe Diſorders although when they ſhalbe knowen and complayned of,

may

may be duelye corrected by vs, yet hardlye or never fo totallye taken away, or
fo prevented by any Devife we can fet downe or devife, as they fhall not happen at all.   In the Entervall betwixt the Committment of theife wilfull Gal-
launts, and the Writinge of theife oure Lettres to your Lordfhips, by the
Proceadinge, and Dealinge, that fomme of vs had with theim, we had good
Cawfe to note, that they were bent in the Ende, to a certeine Kynde of more
arrogant Wilfulnes, and ftubborne Stoutnes, then they were before, refuzinge to
yeelde to any Acknowledgment of their Offence, or to do as they ought
(and we looked for) by Way of Submiffion, confeffe their Error, in impugninge her Maiefties Prerogative (although vpon their fecond Examinacions taken, everye of theim acknowledged both the one and the other) and mervayl-
inge whereof this foddeine Alteracion fhould growe ; founde in the Ende, that
this newe Habit of Chaunge and Encouragement, did growe thence, from
fomme of their Companions, that were committed there by your Lordfhips :
And makinge dilligent Searche, amongft other Things, we found a Lettre fent
from *Richard Nettervill* to the Lord *Howthe*, which carried foche Matter in
their Conceipts, as made theim all to alter their former Opinions ; and becawfe the Manner of his Writinge feameth to vs fomewhat obfcure, conteininge no good Meaninge, touchinge your Lordfhips Manner of Proceadinge
withe theim (as we take it) we have therefore thought good, to fende the Lettre enclofed to your Lordfhips, to the Ende, that if it feme fo expedient to
your grave Wifedomes, *Nettervill* may be called to explayne his Meaninge, and
make Conftruction of his Writinge.   And even fo with oure moft humble,
and duetifull Thanks, and Thanks agayne to your Lordfhips for the honorable
and freindlye Care you have had both of vs, oure Creditts, and this poore
disjoynted State, enclyninge nowe (we hope) to fome better Reformacion by
the Correccion of this wilfuller Sorte.   We humblye take oure Leaves.   From
Dublin, the xxth of *June*, 1577.

Your honorable Lordfhips affured

loving Freinds humblye to commaunde,

H. Sydney, &c.

Sir Henry Sydney, and the Council in Ireland, to Queen Elizabeth.

Moft gratious Sovereigne;

OURE Dueties moft humblye remembred to your Majeftie, we have, in
oure lowlieft and moft humble Manner, received your Highnes gratious
Lettres, dated from *Grenewitche*, the xiiijth of the Laft, and by the fame perceive the Manner of your Majefties moft wife, grave, and princelye Proceadings withe *Barnabye Scurlocke, Richarde Nettervill*, and *Henrie Burnell*, fent
hence withe Lettres and Enftructions, from fomme of the Lords and other
Gentlemen of the Pale, to your royall Majeftie, and the Lords of your Majefties honorable Privey Counfell attendinge vpon your Perfon.   And as we are
in oure moft humble Manner, to acknowledge oure bounden Dueties to your
Highnes, that afwell in Refpecte of their iuft Faults and due Deferts, for their
Arrogancye and Prefumption in impugninge your royall Prerogatyve to take
Ceffe, you have committed theim.   As alfo for the iuft Prefervacion of oure
Creditts, who (as they affirme) in impofinge of the Ceffe without Parliament,
have done contrarie to your Highnes Lawes, and the auntient Cuftomes and
Statuts of this Realme : So we are on the other Side to crave your Highnes
Pardon, for that we committed theim not of oure owne Authorities vpon their
bold Prefumption in fo publicke a Place, and in fo open and plaine Speaches
to impugne your Prerogatyve, which oure remiffe Dealinge in oure humble
Excufes, we muft fay, proceeded of the Care we had in all oure Proceedings,
from the firft to the laft, with all device and mild Meanes, to winne theim to

theyr Duties, and due Acknowledginge and Confeſſion of their groſſe Faultes, and palpable Errors ; leavinge to your moſt gratious Iudgement, what Hold thoſe Perſons would have taken, to have troubled your Highnes with Complainte of oure Proceadings, had we, as iuſtlye they deſerved, puniſhed theim ; who impudentlye in thoſe Lettres abaſſhed not, to ſurmiſe to your Highnes, that they had not Redreſſe vpon Complainte exhibited to vs, although we (with Regarde to have ſaved the great Expences, wherewithe by this Iorney they chardge your Majeſties Subiects) graunted to enter with theim in Conference vpon any good Deviſe, howe your Highnes beinge at no greater Chardge, with Victualinge the Soldiour, the Countrie might be eaſied of the heavie Bourthen, wherewith they were ſo greatlye greived : Whereunto they vtterlye refuſed otherwiſe to be holpen or healpe theim ſelves, except we ſhould have conſented, to cut of the whole Ceſſe, and leave all Contribucion to your Majeſtie, to their Wills in Parliament. So that we conceived, had we then puniſhed theim, they would have bruted into the Eares of the common Sorte, that we went aboute rather, by Authoritie and with Severitie, to ſuppreſſe theim in a rightfull Cawſe (as they bare theim ſelves, and others in Hande) then by good Reaſon and ſounde Argument to convince theim or perſwade theim ; and as it were ſo to reſtrayne and tye theim, as they ſhould not have Lybertie to have Acceſſe to your princelye Preſence, to ſhewe their Greives, and ſue for their Remedie. Theiſe, with other lyke Reaſons of no leſſe Weight, led vs, moſt gratious Sovereigne, to geve theim the larger Reines of Lybertie, and not to vſe that Curbe of ſharpe Severitie vnto theim, that they had well deſerved. For which Fault, wee humblye crave Pardon at your Majeſties Hands. Oure Proceadings withe the reſt of the Furtherers of this Sute, hath bene in this Sorte ; we ſent aſwell for theim that ſubſcribed the Lettre, that *Scurlocke* and the reſt brought to your Majeſtie, as for dyvers others, that were noted and knowen to vs, to be the cheife Doers and Perſuaders of the People, to reſiſt and impugne the Ceſſe. At their Comminge before vs, we founde theim all as obſtinate in Speache, and wilfull in Conceipts, as they were before, without Relentinge, or Shewe of Repentaunce for their former Faultes, but inſiſtinge and mainteininge their late Error, that by Lawe the Ceſſe could not be impoſed. And therefore, accordinge to your Majeſties expreſſe Commaundement, we committed theim all. Somme of theim ſince hath made humble Submiſſion, and Acknowledgement of their Faults to your Majeſtie, the Copie whereof, with further Notes of oure Proceadings withe the reſt, we have imparted to the Lords in oure Lettres, to be declared by theim to your Majeſtie, at your moſt gratious Pleaſure, becawſe we would not in theiſe be to tedious vnto your ſelfe. To thoſe that have ſubmitted theim ſelves, and others that duetifullye have ſought the ſame at oure Hands, we have declared the great Commiſeracion your Highnes hath of their Greives, what open Eares you have to heare theim, and readie Hands to healpe theim, and what ells your Highnes hath commaunded vs to ſay vnto theim for the Ceſſe, in as large Manner as was fitt to be told theim ; who moſt humblye and duetifullye acknowledge your princelye Bountye and Mercye extended towardes theim. And this, Madame, beinge the Somme of oure Proceadings hitherto with the Impugners of your royall Prerogatyve, we thought it oure Dueties to advertize the ſame to your Highnes. And ſo moſt humblye proſtrate vpon oure Knees (beſeachinge the Almightie longe and hapelye to proſper and preſerve your Highnes to reigne over vs, to the ineſtimable Ioy and Comforte of vs, and all your faythfull good Subiectes) we moſt humblye take oure Leaves. From *Dublin,* the xxth of *June,* 1577.

Your Majeſties moſt bounden and

obedient Subiects and Servaunts,

H. Sydney, *&c.*

Edward

Edward Waterhous *to Sir* Henry Sydney.

It maie pleafe your Lordfhip,

AS I wrote in my laft Letters, fo it is comme to paffe, that I am appointid to remaine here, to embarque fuch Soldiers as you fhall direct to be fent vnto you out of thes Wefterne Counties, and *Southwales* ; for which I prepare Victualles for vij Daies, to ferve the Tranfportacion of 1600, and Wheat and Malt, &c. for xxj Daies, for the full Number of 2000. Before my Going, I was condicionid with, that if the Journey went not forward, the hole Provifion muft light in my Neck, for the Queene wold be no Lofer ; and rather then the Service fhuld haue failid, I was content to accept the Condicions. This makith me verie fcrupulus in my Provifions, and therfore I befeache your Lordfhip to giue me fomme Watchword, whether you meane to vfe the hole Number, or eny Parte of theim, to Thend I may be in fome Certainty what to doe.

My Dewty to your Lordfhip doth alfo conftraine me to defier you not to doe eny Thing in the Calling over of thes Men, but by a generall Confent and Concordaunce of the hole Counfell of *Irland*, vnder their Hands ; for if of your felf you fholde extraordinaryly encreafe her Majefties Charge, and no forraine Invafion followe, then it maie be ill taken, that fuch caufeles Expenfes fhold growe : On the other Side, if having now abfolut Auctority in your felf to commaund more Aide, your Lordfhip fhold not vfe them, and that Invafion fhold followe, then I know not what will be obiectid to fuch Hafard of the Eftate. And therefore I humbly praie your Lordfhip (if you be not plainely di-rectid by the Counfells Lettres) to doe nothing in this Matter, but by generall Confent of the hole Bourde, though I knowe by your Letters Patents, you may governe according to your Difcretion.

My Lord of *Lecefter* was not retornid to the Court at my Comming from thence, but fent for in Refpect of the Ambaffadors that weare then come to *London* from the Emperour, from *Fraunce*, and from Don *John*, whofe Ambaf-fadour the Vifcount of *Gaunt*, was honorably accompanied, having in his Traine 120 Perfons, wherof 50 Chaines of Gold, as I was enformid by theim that fawe hym ; but the Caufes of thes Ambaffages, and their Entertaigne-ments, I referre to Mr. *Phillips* Letters, or rather to his Report, if he holde his Determinacion to vifit your Lordfhip. And fo depending altogether vppon your Refolucion for thes Matters of my Provifions, I humbly take my Leave. At *Briftowe*, the 26 of *June*, 1577.

Your Lordfhips moft bounden,

Edward Waterhous.

Sir Francis Walfyngham *to Sir* Henry Sydney.

YOUR Lordfhips thankfull Acceptacion of my plaine Manner of Wri-tinge, will make me the bolder to continewe the like Courfe. I am forie, that ther fhould be giuen out here fuche lewde Brutes of a generall Difcontent-ment in that Realme ; and yet, as appeareth by your Lordfhips Lettre, ther is not that Mifcontentment ther, as is giuen out. Notwithftandinge, your Lord-fhip may perceaue by her Majefties Lettre, ther hath bene fome certaine Infor-mation giuen to her in that Behalfe, which makethe her to write fomewhat of-fenfiuely at this Prefent (a Matter that cannot but bringe vnto your Lordfhip fome Greefe) yet I doubt not but your Lordfhip, beinge fo acquainted with her Majefties Difpofition as you are (which is not to dwell longe in Difpleafure) and beinge withall able to yeld good Accompte of your Doings, as I conceaue by your Lordfhips faid Lettres, you fhall haue the leffe Caufe to be moued therwith. I moued her Majeftie, that it would haue pleafed her that you might haue fent ouer Mr. *Agar*, to haue giuen her full Information of the Eftate of

†   that

that Countrie, and of your Proceedings in the Matter of the Ceffe, which feemeth to be the verie Ground of the faid Mifcontentment. But her Majeftie doubtinge that you may ill fpare fo good an Affiftante, will not confente therto as yet. Touchinge the Eafyinge of the Burden of the Ceffe, what my Lords Opinion is therof you may perceaue by their Lettres. This Daye her Majefties Shipps departe towards your Coafts, wher is ordered they fhall continewe vntill the latter Ende of the next Monethe, vnleft ther fhall fall out fome more Caufe then prefentlye appearethe, either for ther longer Staye, or fpeedier Returne : Duringe the Tyme of their Aboade vppon that Coafte, they are appoynted to yelde to your Direction. The Advertifements which we receaue out of *Fraunce*, of *La Roches* Preparacions, confiftethe rather in Generallitys then Particularitys. I fuppofe, that duringe the Tyme of the Aboade of her Majefties Shipps in that Coafte, they will not be over hafty to attempt any Thinge. I fend your Lordfhip here enclofed a Confeffion of *Calleys*, the notable Pyrate, of fuche Speaches as paffed betwixte *Soliuano Beere* and certaine *Frenche* Capitaines, touchinge the *Frenche* Kings Difpofition of attemptinge fomewhat in that Realme, by the which your Lordfhip may perceave wher they meante to lande. Touchinge th' Allowaunce of the 1600 *l.* wherof you are put in Comforte by my Lords Lettres, the fame beinge difburfed to fo good a Purpofe, as it was : Her Majeftie can not otherwife be perfuaded to allowe it ; then out of the Allotement of the 20000 *l.* whiche fhee is verie lothe to continewe. And yet confideringe, that the Impofition of the Ploughelande, which your Lordfhip intended, is not like to take Place : I fee no Reafon of any Abatement, vnleft her Majeftie fhould withdrawe the Prefidents, whervnto I fee her fomewhat enclyned. And furely, lookinge into her Difpofition (as I do) if the Prefidents were to be planted, I doubt whether I fhould giue my Confent thervnto. If Reformation of Contries might be had without Charge, *Irlande* fhould not remaine in that broken State that it doth. And fo havinge nothinge els prefentelye to write vnto you, I committe you to Gods good Keepinge. From the Courte at *Richemonde*, the xxth of *Julye*, 1577.

Your Lordfhips affured Frende,

Fra. Walfyngham.

At the Clofing of this Letter, her Majefty being advertyfed from her Ambaffador, refident in *Fraunce*, that the Earl of *Weftmoerlande* fhold be privatly repayred into *Irelande* about fome Practice ; and thoughe fhe fyndethe yt a Matter vnlikely, yet her Pleafure is, that your Lordfhip fhall, in fome fecreat Sorte, ufe fome apt Inftruments in the Difcoverye, whether he be there or not ; and in Cafe he be ther, to feeke all the Wayes you may, for the Apprehenfyon of him. The lyke Charge fhe hathe wylled me to gyve unto the Prefydent of *Monfter* ; for that it is thought he is retyred into thofe Partes, in Cafe yt be trewe that he fhoold be com thither.

To Mr. Secretary Walfingham, *from* John Calis, July, 1577.

May it pleafe your Honor,

TO vnderftand and to forefee, that *Solivan Beere*, of *Beere.* Haven in *Irland*, do not practife any Treafon towards her Majeftie in *Irland* ; for that the faid *Solyvan* declarid to me, in his Caftell at *Berehaven*, being in familier Talke with him of *James Fitzmorice*, that the faid *James*, and a Nomber of *Frenchemen*, determinid to come to *Berehaven* to lande there, if he had but Pilotts to conduct him thither. And all perfwadid with me to ioyne with theim in their Practife, and to be their Guyde, and promiffed me many large Offres and Gifts. Whervnto I anfwerid him, I wold not confent or ioyne with any Rebell againft the Queenes Majeftie, but hopid of her Mercy in Tyme to come. And in *Marche* laft paft, my Happe was to meete with a *Frenche* Man, being my felf ryding at an Ancre in *Thorbay*, one of theim called Capten *Mollonde*, and one

I

John

John Grawth, a Mafter of *St. Mallowes* ; the fame Mr. *Mollonde,* being of my old Acquaintaunce, came Aboord my Shippe, and there did breake with me concerning the Coafts of *Irland,* and afked what Harboroughes wer beft on that Coaft. Wherto I anfwerid him, that *Cork* and *Kynfale* wer the beft Havens in *Irland.* And afkid me further, whether *Berehaven* and the *Dyngell* wer not a good Place to land Men on. Then I afked him why he did demaund thofe Queftions of me. He faid then, if I wold go over into *France* with him, I fhuld not neede to feare the Queene of *England* for any Offence I had done againft her. And that the Kinge his Mafter wold pardon me for any Thing I had done againft him, or any of his Nation. And wold gyue threethowfand Crownes to become his Subiect, and be fworne his Man, and alfo a yerely Fee duringe my Lief. Then I afked him to what Ende he wold have me fo to doo. Becaufe the Kinge his Mafter did fhortly meane to haue fome Seruice to be done on the Coaft of *Irlande,* and did want Pylots for the Purpofe. Then I anfwerid him, that what foever fhuld become of me, I wold never be fworne to any forrayne Prince. Then he faid, I fhuld never haue the lyke Preferment offred me in *England,* as I might haue in *France.* And thervpon he went his Wayes ; and I made fmall Accompt of him or of his Offeres.

Sir Henry Sydney *to* Edward Waterhoufe, *Efq;*

Mr. *Waterhowfe,*

FOR that I vnderftande that you have made a Provifion of a good Quanti-tie and Maffe of Victuall for the Findinge and Victualinge of fuche Nom-ber of Souldiors as are in Arredines to be tranfported thence for Thaffiftance of the Service heere againft foren Invacion : I hartely and moft erneftlie pray you that notwithftandinge thofe Souldiors comme not prefentlie over : For lothe I wold be in any Sorte to encreafe her Majefties Charge but vpon evident Growndes and verie vrgent Matter : Yet that you wold take prefent Order to fende over that Maffe of Victuall that you have provided to be in Arredines to ainfwere every Event whatfoever might happen : For the Want and Scarcetie of thofe Kindes (is fuche heere) as namely of Malt, Wheets, Bifket, Butter, Cheife ; as upon a foden non is to behad in Quantitie, what Care and Diligence ever be vfed. And therfore as you tender the Service or honor me, or wold have me conceive well of your good Endevour and Travell, applie with Speede to fende me that Proporcion of thofe Kindes I have before remembered : (As for Bief I fhall I hoope provide for heere as muche as fhalbe neceffarie) the one Half to be delivered at *Waterforde,* the other at *Dublin:* I have alredie cawfed Garners and Stoorehowfes to be taken vp ; and Minifters to attende at bothe the Portes, to fee to the Difchberginge and Vnloodinge of the faid Provifions. And therfore I pray you haften them away to be embarked and fent hither with all the Speede you can : For the Service erneftly requirethe that Stoore fhowld be at Hande and in Arredines, of thofe Thinges whereof this Countrie hathe fo greate Want. And even fo not dowtinge but that you will heerin carefully provide that Thinges be done with Speede. I bid you Farewell. From *Caftell-Diermot,* the xxvjth of *July,* 1577.

Your lovinge Frende,

H. Sydney.

Edward Waterhous *to Sir* Henry Sydney.

It maie pleafe your Lordfhip,

I Have receivid by the Waie of *Waterford,* a Letter of yours datid at *Caftell-Dermot* the 20th of *July,* wherin your Lordfhip doth direct me to goe to the Court. And therfore I prepare to go thether upon *Monday* next, and there (till I fhall receive fome Inftructions from your Lordfhip) to follow the Opinion of Mr. *Phillip Sidney*, or in his Abfence, to do that which in Difcretion I fhall think convenient.

I do leave here a Proportion of Victualls for the Tranfportation of the Soldiers appointed for *Irland*, and to feed them there, for a Moneth; but if they be not fhortly emploied, then muft I make Sale of Parte of it, or els it is like to torne to Loffe. So as the Care of this Provifion muft of Neceffity drawe me hether again, in the Beginning of the next Moneth.

Your Lordfhip maie think that the Victualling was no Occupation fit for me, and I confeffe myfelf apter for other Things: But if I had refufed it, when no Man els was to accept it, I beleeve there had bene lefs Hafte in levieng of Soldiers, or fetting forth of the Navy: And it is conceyvid, that if eny Thing do divert the Enterprize of *James Fitz-Maurice* for this Yere, it is the Knowledge of Preparacion of Soldiers and Provifions of Victualls, which is given forth to be in farre more Abundance, then is in deed ether prepared, or ment. For howfoever your Lordfhips Frends, have countenaunfed this Matter, with Men, Munition, Money and Victualls: Your Lordfhip is nevertheles to think, that nothing paffith without Difficulty, that may concerne the Service in *Irland*. And if your Abfence from the Court, have given your Enemies any Advantage, I am excufable by this, that I have not bene idell: And I doubt not, but at my Retorne thether, to untwyne all, that they have twifted: And fo with my moft humble Thanks for your Lordfhips favourable Acceptacion of my Service, and for your honourable Dealing with my Dwarfe, your Purfevant. I humbly take my Leave at *Briftoll*, the 2d of *Auguft*, 1577.

Your Lordfhips old Servant,

moft bounden,

Ed. Waterhows.

I write to your Lordfhip foe lamentable Newes, that the Lord Chiefe Baron, and Mr. Sargeant *Barham* Juftices of Affife, for *Gloucefterfhire*, and one Mr. *Stevens* and another Lawyer of this Contrey, with 10 or 12 Jurats are all fodenly dead. Mr. *Phetipace* in great Daunger, the Caufe unknown. In *Oxford* a Defeafe is grown, being neither the Plague nor Swett, but as wors as eny of them; for which yet no Phifyck can be founde.

Sir Francis Walfyngham *to Sir* Henry Sydney.

My verie good Lord,

THIS Gentellman Mr. *Thomas Dillon*, coming hither commended from your Lordfhip, I could do no leffe at this his Returne, but recommende him vnto you againe. Whofe Succeffe in his Suts here, thoughe it have not ben anfwerable to his Expectacion, yet as him felfe can beft declare vnto you, ther wanted not in me the beft I could do for the Obtayninge his full Defyre: As I meane ther fhalbe neuer any Defecte in me, to doe the like for any that bringeth with him your Lordfhips Commendacion. Alfo I am to let you vnderftande, that my Lords have not long fince receaved Lettres from Sir *William Drurye*, wherin he anfwereth the Complaynte and Obiections made by the Erle of *Defmonde*, againft him for fome Matter of Ceffe, and Provifion taken for his Houfe, wher withall their Lordfhips reft fo well fatiffied, as that they iudge the faid Complainte to be caufeleffe, and be more confirmed that the generall Murmure againft Ceffe proceedeth rather of Practife, then any iuft Greefe. Laft of all, your Lordfhip may vnderftande that *Scurlocke*, *Nettervill*, and *Burnell* fince their Submiffion made here, by Reafon of the Sickenes of the Plague, which is in the *Fleete*, where they were Prifoners, are enlarged vppon good Bands to remayne ether in the Citye, or within ten Miles therof, vntill further Order be taken with them; and that it

is

is meante, they fhall not come into *Irelande* to make their Submiffion in like Manner there, vntill my Lords here may firft heare fomewhat more herof from your Lordfhip. And fo humblie commendinge your Lordfhip to God, I take my Leave. From the Court at *Richemonde*, the ixth of *Auguft*, 1577.

Your Lordfhips affured Frende to

commaunde,

Fra. Walfyngham.

Sir Francis Walfyngham *to Sir* Henry Sidney.

After my hartie Commendacions vnto your Lordfhip;

I Am willed by her Majeftie to fignifie vnto you, that wheras longe Tyme fince, to witt the Laft of *June* in the xith Yeare of her Raigne, fhe writt her Lettres vnto you on the Behalfe of the Erle of *Ormonde*, lettinge you to vnderftande that her Pleafure was, that his Lordfhips Lands within that Realme, fhould be exempted from all Ceffes and Impofitions (the Subfidie due vnto her onlie excepted) in Refpecte that he fhold forbear from thenceforth the Exactinge of Coyne and Lyverie vfually taken before by him, and his Auncefters, vppon the faid Lands. Whervppon a *Concordatum* was made to that Effecte by your Lordfhip, and the Counfell there, which fhee hath feene. And beinge enformed that, notwithftanding her faid Pleafure fignified vnto you in that Behalfe, you have lately impofed Ceffe vppon his Lands : Her Pleafure is that you fhould advertife the Caufe of your fo Doinge, and in the meane Tyme hath required me in her Name to lett you knowe, that her Will is, your Lordfhip do forbeare to laye any Manner of Tallages, Taxes, Charges, Ceffes or Impofitions vppon any his Lands or Mannors, wherfoeuer they be within that Realme (accordinge to the Meaninge of the faid *Concordatum*) the Subfidye onlie except, vntill her Pleafure to the Contrarie fhalbe to you ether by her owne Lettres, or otherwife made knowen, after fhe fhall have had due Confideracion of fuche Caufes, as have moved you, contrarie to the Tenor of her Lettres, to impofe the faid Ceffe. And fo I committ your Lordfhip to God. From the Courte at *Richemonde*, the ixth of *Auguft*, 1577.

Your Lordfhips affured Frende to

commaunde,

Fra. Walfyngham.

Sir Francis Walfyngham *to the Lord Prefident of* Munfter.

S I R,

THEIS are to fignify vnto you, that her Maieftie beinge geven to vnderftande that *La Roche*, who hath ben heretofore faid to make Preparacions in *Britanny* for *Ireland*, is now at a Place of the faid Country called *Vannes*, with a Force of fiften hondreth Men, fower Gallions, and dyverfe other Veffells ; her Highnes doubtinge the wourfe, and fekeinge to provid in Tyme for the Meetinge with fuch Inconvenience and Perill as may growe thereof to her Realme of *Irelande*, by a foddaine Surprice, hath geven Order, that where her Shippes were appointed to contynue aboute the Coafte of her faid Realme, but till the xiijth or xiiijth of the next Moneth, they fhall nowe contynue there vntill the Ende of the fame ; and to that Purpofe there are Victualles provided at *Briftoll*, to be from thence fhipped to *Waterford*, where Mr. *John Winter*, her Highnes Viceadmirale of the faid Shippes, is to receive the fame, as by this inclofed Lettre of my Lords vnto him, he may vnderftande more at large. And therefore her Maiefties Pleafure is, that fo foone as the faid Lettre fhall come to your Handes, you do advertife Mr. *Winter* of it by fome Meffinger, in cafe he be not at *Waterforde*, to Thend he may come and receive

receive his Victualles there. And fo with my very harty Commendacions, I bid you Farewell. From the Courte at *Richemond*, the xxth of *Auguſt*, 1577.

Your affured Frend,

F. Walſingham.

Edward Waterhous *to Sir* Henry Sydney.

It may pleaſe your Lordſhip,

BECAUSE the Lords of her Maiefties Pryvy Counfell do judge, that the Continuaunce of the Ships at Sea will be a great Sewerty againſt Invaſion there, if eny be intendid. It is thought requiſite, that the Ships ſhold be revictuallid vppon the Sea, or at *Waterford*, for iij Weakes longer, wherof their is Order geven to Mr. *Baiſſh* to fend a Maffe from *Briſtoll* with all Speed, to be tranſportid to *Waterford*; their ether to be deliuerid to Mr. *G. Winter*, or yf the Shippis be not vppon that Coaſt, then to be deliuerid their to the Surveior of the Victualls for *Irland*, by the Lords Direction, and according to an Indenture that comith with the Victualls; and therfore the Lords do expect, that in the Abſence of Mr. *Winter*, your Lordſhip will cauſe the Victualler of *Irland*, or his Deputy, by your Auctority, to gyve his Bill to Mr. *Baiſſh*, for the Receipt of the fame Proviſion; and for the better Ordering of it, Mr. *Baiſſh*, vppon Report of me and *John Bland*, hathe made Choiſe of *James Brinklowe*, to cary the fame to *Waterford*. I haue fent by the Way of *Cheſter*, other Letters to your Lordſhip concerning your Affaires at Court. And fo do humbly take my Leave at *London*, the 20th of *Auguſt*, 1577.

Your Lordſhips humbly at Commandment,

Ed. Waterhous.

Sir Henry Sydney *to* Queen Elizabeth.

I Received the Lettres of your moſt excellent Maieſtie, geven at *Greenwitche* the xvijth of the laſt *Julye*, the viith of this preſent *Auguſt*: Beinge thus farre Northwards in this your Realme, with Intention to have gonne furder into the Province of *Vlſter*, for the Setlinge of Quiet amonge the Potentates and People of the fame Province, and to encreaſe Revenue to your Highnes in the fame. But with Greife and great Difcomforte I ſtay that my Jorney, not for that I have any Doubt fufficientlye to ſatisfie your Maieſtie in ech Pointe, the fame feameth to be offended with me in (had I convenient Tyme, and were I in convenient Place.) And for the Doinge thereof, I will, with as moch Spede as I can, retorne to *Dublin*, where, after Informacion and Confideracion of fome Things conteined in your Maiefties Lettre (which poſſibly I cannot do here) I will, God willinge, addreffe vnto your Highnes fome foche Perſonadgies fo well inſtructed, as I truſt ſhall thoroughlye ſatisfie your Highnes in eche Particuler conteined in your faid Lettre; and alſo advertize the fame of fondrie other Matters concerninge your Eſtate here, afwell in Suertye as Proffitt, whom al be it for Parliament Cawſies I meant to have ſent to your Maieſtie, as fone as the Coppies of the Actes of Parliament had bene readye; yet for this ſpeciall Purpofe, I will nowe haſten theim, to preſent theim ſelves to your Majeſties Preſence. But, in the mean Tyme, I reſt perplexed, and in no ſmall Sorrowe, for that it feameth to me, your Highnes, by the Inſtigation of myne Ennimies, Adverſaries to your Prerogative and Proffitt, hath condemned me vnhard; for Eafe of which my troubled Mynde, I foorthwith write theiſe fewe bad ſcribled Lynes: Moſt humblye cravinge by the fame, the Sufpence of your Highnes Conceipt againſt me, untill they, (whome I entende to fend to your Maieſtie with Lettres, may more at lardge declare

declare from me, and the reſt of your Councell here, then I can here write theim) ſhall arryve there, which, God willinge (Wynd and Wether ſervinge) ſhalbe before the xxvth of the next Moneth.   By which I do aſſure my ſelfe, that it ſhall manifeſtlye apeare to your Maieſtie, that I have not impoſed more vpon the People of the *Engliſh* Pale, either for my Howſehold, or your Garriſon, then is neceſſarye, nor chardged theim ſo moche as heretofore they have bene ; albeit conſideringe the Price, farre excedinge that which hath bene in Tymes paſt, the Burden ſeameth farre greater, though the Quantitie in Stuffe be not ſo moch, whiche, if it do comme to viij *d.* vpon a Ploughland (as haply, as they priſe their Wares at this preſent, it commeth to little leſſe) I thinke, and ſo I hope your Maieſtie will judge, that I offered theim no ſmall Eaſe, when I accepted their willinge Offer of fyve Marks vpon a Ploughland.   And my Truſt is, that your Maieſtie will conceive that I wrought for the Wealth of your People in generall, when I diſſolved ſo many Freedomes as I did, whereby the Burden was the lighter to the Bearers, and whereat the great Ones repyned : For had not that bene, your Hignes ſhould never have hard of this ſuppoſed Lamentacion of the Poore : And that which was impoſed is not yet levied (and therefore the leſſe Cawſe to find theim ſelves greived) and ſome Parte wholye remitted.

And for Alienatinge your Subiectes Hartes from their loyall Obedience to your Maieſtie by this, I never ſawe Lykelyhood of it, nor wilfull Refuzall to pay the rebated Porcion, vntill they were by theim in *England,* and other their Sectaries, encouraged that they ſhould yeeld nothing at all.

And if any have bruted that I have taken the whole Realme in Ferme (as I think ſome there be that hath) it is ſoch as impugneth *Engliſh* Governement that ſo hath bruted it, for it never came out of my Mouth, nor any borne on that Side of the Sea to my Knowledge.

If I have ſpent more for my firſt Yeares Chardge then your Maieſtie hath hetherto determined to iſſue out of your Threaſure there, beſides your Revenue here, whereof you ſhalbe trewlye certified (God willinge) the next Moneth ; as the ſame hath growen by the Payment of ſoche Things as were due before my Tyme, as in diſchardinge Soldiers, painge for their Tranſportacion and other Neceſſaries, and thereby ſavinge your Maieſtie ſome daylye growinge Chardge, which otherwiſe would have bene ſpent ; as in my former Lettres I have at lardge ſignified vnto the Lords : So I am humblye to praye Allowaunce and Payment thereof, ſubmittinge my ſelfe to your Maieſties Miſericord ; and yet with this Confidence, that you ſhall ſee ſoch an Encreaſe of Revenue, as your Majeſtie ſhall not thinke the Pourchace over prized.

I am well aſſured your Highnes old Revenue was never better anſwered, then it hath bene theiſe two Yeares, ſince I ſerved your Maieſtie here, although haply it fall not out ſo moche, by reaſon the Wyne of the Impoſt, riſeth not ſo great thorough the ſmall Trade of Coynes in theiſe troubleſome Yeares. But of the Eſtate of your Revenue, and Encreaſe of the ſame (for of any Decay I do not thinke, that I ſhall have any Cawſe to write, if greater Fault be not in other inferiour Miniſters) God willinge, your Highnes ſhalbe trewlye certified the next Moneth : And alſo what the whole Ceſſe levied ſince my preſent Governement here commeth vnto, aſwell in Quaintye (as niere as I can certeinelye) as in Price, with as good Conſideracion, as I and the reſt of the Councell here can valewe it at : But of what your Maieſtie is therebye diſbourdened, I thinke I ſhall certifie nothinge, ſavinge this, that if your Maieſtie had not had that Contribucion, your Highnes muſt have geven greater Wagies, or have enterteined fewer Soldiers.

Sir *William Drewrye* ſhould not have lacked any Forces that I had to ſend hym vpon his owne Requeſt, al be it your Maieſtie therein had not remembred me to do my Duetye : For in Troth he ſerveth your Majeſtie there honorablye and effectually.

The laſt Clauſe in your Majeſties Lettre, I am not poſſiblye able to anſwere preſentlye, but I will by my next : The *Moores,* and *Occonnors,* have donne moche Hurte, and more it is poſſible they will do ; and in ſo open a Countrie, where your good Subiects inhabite they may do, if there were a thowfand Men more for the Garde of it then there is, and being fo freinded by their Neighbors as they are: But as they have fpoyled fome of your good Subiects of their Goodes, fo have your good Subiects and Soldiors bereft 150 of theim and their Followers (at the leaft) of their Lyves, fince their laft Revolt and Rebellion.

Thus endinge as I began, with my moft humble Peticion to your Maieftie, to ftay from any Mifconceipt of me, vntill I may more fullye anfwere your Highnes Lettre, then prefentlye I can, and addreffe foch Certificat to your Maieftie, as in this Place I cannot; I moft humbly ende this my Lettre, prayinge the Almightie to bleffe your Maieftie with longer and happier Yeares, then ever Prince had, and after with eternall Glorie. From the *Newrie* the of *Auguft*, 1577.

Your Maiefties moft humble and

obedient Servaunt,

H. Sydney.

Sir Henry Sydney *to the Lords of the Council in* England.

Right Honorable and my very good Lords,

I Have received your Lordfhipps Lettres fent by *Colman*, my Lord Prefident of *Mounfters* Servaunt, moft comfortable and welcome vnto me, in the Refpecte of your Lordfhips good and grave Allowaunce of my Proceadings with thofe Lords and Gentlemen, that fo wilfullye withftand, and fo obftinatlye contynue and perfever in denienge her Maiefties Royall Prerogatyve to impofe Ceffe, vpon any Occafion of Neceffitie, except the fame be donne by Parliament. And although at the Beginninge, the Lords and Gentlemen committed, could well have framed theim felves (as I fuppofe) after the Taft of fower or fyve Dayes Imprifonment, humblye to have fubmitted theim felves, and, in lowlye Manner, by Way of Submiffion, to have acknowledged their groffe Errors, ignoraunt Wilfulnes, and former Offences againft her Maiefties Prerogatyve and the State, were it not that they had bene animated by fome of their Freindes out of *England*, and (as I take it) of fome of the beft Sorte of this Countrie Birth. Nowe they are growen to that deepe Degree of Induratnes, and contynue fo malitiouffly bent, to perfever in their former Obftinacye, and indutifull Wilfulnes, as havinge fent vnto me, at my late Retorne by *Dublin*, the Forme of a Peticion, onely to pray for their Enlardgement (not remembringe in the fame either any former Fault committed by theim, or acknowledging any Kinde of Submiffion) which Peticion, for that the fame was not fubfcribed with any Hand, I refuzed to allowe and accept from theim: And they afterwardes beinge requyred, that if it were their Acte to fett to their Hands to the fame, with one Voyce and vniforme Confent (and yet confeffeinge it to be their Acte) flatlye denied to do it. Whereby I can gather none other Thinge nor Lykelyhood, but that they are daylye encouraged thus to do by fomme that beare theim felves over bold of her Maiefties Favor, at whofe Handes, fomme of theim fay, they looke and expecte for Anfwer, and not from me; for that the Cawfe is in Debate before her Highnes, and fo I reputed a Partie in the Matter, and not a competent Judge.

I perceive my Lords, that maney Matters be engrieved againft me by myne Ennimies, and maney Thinges obiected againft my Manner of Governement and Proceading here, as partlye to my no fmall Greife and inwarde Sorrowe of Mynde, I vnderftoode by her Majefties owne Lettres; in fo moche as beinge here thus farre Northwarde in my Iorney, myndinge to have made a Vifitacion of the greateft Parte of *Vlfter*; upon the Receipt of thofe Lettres from her Majeftie, I torned my Courfe, and haftened my felfe towardes *Dublin*, to the Ende more fullye to anfwere to eche perticuler Pointe conteined in her Highnes faied Lettres, I hope to her Majefties full Satisfaccion and good Lykinge, and your honorable Contentments. As lykewife to conferre and confider of foch Platts and Devifes for the Matter of Ceffe, as your Lordfhips fent me in Packett with your Lettres. And to addreffe vnto you for that Purpofe, fome foch grave, difcreate, and wife Perfonadores, as I hope your Lordfhips, both for their Callings, Reputacions; and Creditts, will geve both a readie Eare, and foch Beliefe, as the Nature and Qualitie of the Matters they are to entreate of, for her Majefties Service; and this State requyre ; and in the meane Tyme I doubt not, but you will fufpend your Opinions, and Conceites, either to dif-allowe or condemme my Doings. They fhall come plainelye and fullye in-ftructed, afwell of the Nature and Cawfe of the Ceffe; and the Effectes there-of, as of the Proporcions and Kinds fet downe for eche Perticuler ; what hath bene taken by others before my Tyme, what in my Tyme hath bene impofed and ceffed, what thereof hath bene levied; and what is in Arrere behynd, and not paied ; what eche Countye bearethe; what the fame amounteth vnto vpon a Ploughland, in Kynd and Proporcion ; difgefted into fo playne and manifeft a Forme, and delyvered in foch Manner, as the full Boddye and State of the whole Matter fhall at Eye and Viewe appeare to your Lordfhips; howe I have bene mif-reported, and what Drifts privat Malice, and wilful Obftinacye put together, hath devifed againft me. And thus in the meane Tyme hopinge, and even fo befeachinge your Lordfhips to way foch Things; as hetherto have bene obiected againft me by myne Ennimies, in no Conftruccion to the Preiudice or Difad-vantadge either of me or the Matter, till you fhall receive my further An fwere to eche Pointe fett downe by her Majeftie; which God willinge (Wynd and Wether fervinge) fhalbe before the xxvth of the next Monethe. In the Meane, I humbly take my Leave, befeachinge the Almightie longe and hape-lye to profper and preferve your Lordfhips, in all your honorable Actions and grave Counfells, for the Honnor of her Majeftie; and the Benifitt and Wealth of her duetifull good Subiectes. From the *Newrie*, the   of *Auguft*, 1577.

Your honnorable Lordfhips affured

lovinge Freinde to commaunde;

H. Sydney.

Sir Henry Sydney *to* Robert Dudley *Earl of* Leicefter.

My deareft Lord;

BEING thus farre Northwarde in this Realme, with Entencion to have gonne as farre as the Sea would geve me Leave, I received her Maje-fties Lettres by a Man of my Lord Prefidents in *Mounfter* ; whereby, to my hartie Greiffe and vnfpeakeable Sorrowe, I fynd her Highnes offended with me, by the Informacion of my Ennemies (Adverfaries and Impugners of her Profftt and Prerogative) fpeciallye for a Ceffe, or a Taxe; impofed by me vpon the *Englifh* Pale, fince my laft Governement here, and for the difor-derly Diftribucion and Levienge of the fame. I perceive alfo by Lettres from others, of the fame Paffage, that neither my Lettres; for that they were formed by my felfe onelye, nor any my Agents, thorough their Infufficiencye, hath fo fatisfied the Lords, as by their Reporte her Majeftie might be induced to thinke well of my Doings in her Service. I am forye that I trufted any that fo badlye delyvered, or fo fayntlye were able to anfwere in thofe Matters which they feamed fo ripelye to conceive, and fo thoroughlye to vnderftand at their Departinge from me. What fo ever I write fhalbe found trewe, be it tried by what Meanes it fhall beft lyke her Majeftie and the Lords. Well; this cawfed me to cut of my Iorney almoft in the Beginninge of the fame, whereby there wilbe leffe Good donne this Yeare in this Province, then there was good Hope fhould have bene donne ; and I do retorne to *Dublin* after a fewe Days (in which I hope

hope to have fomme of the greateft of this Province with me) with whome (albeit not fo well as if I had gonne furder) I truft yet to take fome Order for the good Quiet thereof. And at *Dublin* have I appointed an Affemblye of the whole Councell of this Realme, and then by theim fhalbe collected and exa- myned, of what Contynuaunce the Ceffe hath bene, of what Neceffitie and Va- lewe, and howe the fame is taxed, levied, and iffued ; and I truft, with playne and true Explanacion of eache neceffarye Circumftaunce dependinge vpon the fame : And with this I will fend twoe of this Councell, I truft, fufficientlye in- ftructed, not onely in that Matter, but in fondrye others of Confequence, afwell for the Common Wealthe, as for the Proffit and Dignitie of the Crowne. I will alfo fend with theim an Officer of my Howfehold, who, vpon my Creditt, is an honeft Man ; and he fhall make fo fimple and fubftantial Declaracion of my Receipts and Expences, as I truft fhalbe to the Contentacion of her Majeftie, the Satisfaccion of your Lordfhip, and the Shame of my Ennemies : This fhalbe donne, and, God willinge (Wynd and Wether fervinge) fhalbe with you before the Laft of the next Monethe.

I fynd it is thought in me a hard Dealinge, that I demaunded fyve Marks vpon a Ploweland, to difchardge theim of all Manner of Ceffe ; I have often written it to her Majeftie, and to you, and to Mr. Secretorye, and nowe agayne do : That it feameth to me to abfurd, that fyve Marks fhould be thought over bourdenous, when it fhould difchardge theim of that which they faied ftoode theim in x *l.* And the Lords feamed to me, that I had made an evell Bargayne at fo bafe a Price, to difpence with her Highnes Prerogative. And I proteft to God, and as you take me to be a Chriftiane, or honeft, I do knowe it, that the People moft willinglye would have confented to it, had not the Lords for- bidden theim : Yea, and when they were committed, were reddye with one Voyce to cry out vpon theim, for that they ftoode with me in it.

And that Rebellion, or at leaft Alienation of the Peoples Myndes, were lyke ennough by the fame to arrife. My Lord, I do beleve, for farre the greateft Nomber of the Inhabitaunts of the *Englifhe* Pale, her Highnes hath as trewe and faythfull Subiectes, as any fhe hathe fubiecte to her Crowne ; and foch as if the great Ones would have theim (for without theim, they will never rebell) would not once ftirre againft the Quenes royall Eftate ; but if they and their factious Sectaries would, they, and as maney as would take their Parte, dare not, as longe as there is an Armye here ; and rather, in my fimple Judge- ment, this Kind of Bearinge with their Infolencye and Arrogancye, is a great Alluraunce to the People, rather to refpecte and followe their meane Land Lordes Will, then the Sovereignes iuft Demaunde ; and if I have any Judge- ment, this hath ben, is, and wilbe the Deftruction of *Ireland.*

I am condempned there, I finde, for Lacke of Pollecye, in that in this bro- ken Tyme, and Doubt of forreine Invafion, I fhould committ foche Parfon- adges, as I deteine in the Caftell. My Lord, I am the Quenes principall Of- ficer here, and have Cawfe to vnderftand, as well as an other, of the Eftate of this Countrie, and Humor of People of the fame, and fo whyle I am in Of- fice, ought to be credited as fone as an other ; and this is my Opinion, if *James Fitzmorrize* were to land to Morrowe next, I had rather a good maney of theim nowe in the Caftell, fhould ftill remayne then be Abroade.

I heare I have maney Accufacions obiected againft me ; I would fayne knowe whether from maney or one, and who he or they be, and that the Mat- ters may be reduced to Hedds fent to me, and I truft I will anfwere theim.

I have often written for the Triall of the Earle of *Clanrickarde* ; I can gett no Anfwere ; if her Majeftie will none of it, for ought I can perceive, it were beft for her Majeftie to geve over any Chardge out of *England*, and to leave the Rule and Ravyne of the Countrie to theim felves.

It is bruited here, that I am to be reuoked, and that fpedilye ; the Brute doth no good ; but if it be intended, the fooner the better, for the Quene, and for my felfe. I atteft to God, I had rather have *Harrye Refwycks* Office in *Killing- woorthe*, then Sir *Harrye Sidneys* in *Kilmaynghame.*

I

My deareſt Lord, I did not thinke to have entered into theiſe Particulers, vntill I had ſent over the intended Commiſſioners above written (which, as is written, ſhalbe the next Monthe, God willinge) but when I was entered in, I ran on I feare to farre, at leaſt ſo farre, I am ſure, as is to your Payne in Readinge; and moche more ſhould have bene, if after I had penned it, I had not made my Man to write it out agayne; for ſo maney Eſcapes paſſed me in double Writinge of Woordes, yea, and Lynes, and Raſinge agayne (through vnquiet Accidents) as the Letter ſemed to fowle to be ſent you.

My deareſt Lord, ſende to me forthwith, and contynue your brotherlyke Care of me; you ſhall fynd me honeſt, and wel willinge to deſerve well, and I hope to have bene no evell Servaunt. And ſo I take my Leave. Ouer Lord bleſſe you with contynuall and eternall Comforte. From the *Newrye*, the of *Auguſt*, 1577.

Your Lordſhips bounden and moſt

aſſured Brother,

H. Sydney.

Sir Henry Sydney *to Mr. Secretary* Walſingham.

S I R,

I Have by this Diſpatche brought by *Colman*, the Lord Preſident of *Mounſters* Servaunt, received three Lettres from you, one touching ſoche Writings as you ſent me in the blacke Boxe, concerninge Sir *John* of *Deſmound*, which you received of my Brother Sir *William Fitzwilliams*; an other to haſten the Auditor to make vp his Accompts, which have bene ſo longe expected there; and the laſt of ſoch Reports and Informacions, as have bene made to her Majeſtie agaynſt me, and my Manner of Government here, whereof her Highnes writt ſo offenſivelye vnto me. And, al be it, you geve me comfortable and freindlye Adviſe, not to diſquiet or diſcourage my ſelfe, with her Highnes ſharpe Manner of Writinge, for that her Majeſtie cannot dwell longe in Diſpleaſure: Yet you may conceive it cannot be any ſmall Griefe and Torment of Mynde vnto me, that her Majeſtie carieth ſo open an Eare, and geveth ſo eaſie a Creditt to myne Ennemies, that I may ſuſpecte my ſelfe to be halfe condempned in Opinion and Conceipt before I be harde. How be it, for your ſpeciall Freindſhipp towards me, in that and all other Things, I finde my ſelfe moche beholding vnto you, and pray you to contynue the lyke vnto me ſtill, for the which, I will not forget to be thankefull. And even ſo I bid you farewell. From the *Newrye*, the of *Auguſt*, 1577.

Your aſſured loving Freinde,

H. Sydney.

Edward Waterhows, *Eſq;* to Sir Henry Sydney.

It maie pleaſe your Lordſhip,

U P P O N Receipt of your Letters latelie at *Briſtoll*, I committed thoſe Doings to myne Agents there; and according to your Lordſhips Commaundement, I repaired to the Court, taking *Wilton* in my Way, aſwell to do my Duty to the Counteſſe of *Pembrook*, as to have ſome Speach with Mr. *Phillip* concerning your Lordſhips Affaires; and to underſtand his Advice, what Cours he wold have me to take in your Lordſhips Buſines. Who, becauſ he found ſuch dailie Alterations in Court, cold adviſe me none otherwiſe, but to referre me in Diſcretion to do as I ſawe Cauſe: And therefore leving there the Erle, the Counteſſe, Mr. *Phillip*, Mr. *Robert Sydney*, and your litell Coſin *Mountagu*, all in Helth; and the Erle, in all Appearaunce, as duetifull to you, as Mr. *Phillip.* I arrivid at the Court uppon *Wednesday* last at *Richemont,* where the Erle of *Lecester* was newly retornid from his House in *Waltam* Forest. When I had reportid to him in what Estat I had left my Prouisions at *Bristoll,* I declarid that I was now come to follow your Lordships Causes, and praid his Direction, and what Cours he wold have me take. His Lordship told me, that within a fewe Daies before, the *Irishe* Prisoners in the *Fleete* were inlarged, uppon Infection in the Prison, and that he wold have farder Conference with me abought the Causes, having then no Leisure. From thence I attendid Mr. Secretary, by whom I lernid that *Barnabe Skurlock,* and his Fellowes, imediatly after their Enlargement, cam to the Court without praing eny Licence ; for which rashe Parte (the Infection and their Offence considerid) Mr. Secretary gave them such a Wellcom, as they retornid in Post, in some Fere to be presently again committid : But it is lookid for that both they, and their Adherents, will shortly renue their Petition for Release of *Sesse* ; abought which Matter it is like your Lordship shall shortly have some Direction, at the Arrivall of your newe Judges, who nowe beginne to prepare for their Journey.

It semith some Practice hath beene attemptid, since myne Absence, for your Repair Home, under such Collours, as caried no Disgrace to your Lordship : But I perceive the Scope was to have translated the Government, as most judge, to your last Predecessor ; but that Things are not like to happen now, before your selfe shall importunatly seeke it.

The Letters that cam latelie out of *Mounster,* give great Occasion of Mislike of the Erle of *Desmounde,* which comparid with the Arrogancy of such as be imprisonnid in the Castell of *Dublin,* who as it is said make a Sport of their Restraint ; and considering also the apparent Discontentacion of some *Irland* Courteors, it cannot be but your Lordship shall very shortly see some End of thos Contencions. Which in Reason I thinke must be in some Extremity, ether in a precice Maintenance of the Prerogatyve, or els in an over liberall Remission of the *Sesse* ; for our *Irland* People are farr from eny Meane.

Some of your Frends think, that their is not enough said in her Majestyes Behalf, for the Maintenance of *Sesse* ; and some blame yourself and your Agents heere ; but they be suche as knowe not *Irlande* ; and for myne own Part, I think it sufficient to say, that ether her Majestye must mainteyne it, as she found yt uncertaine, or as it is now devisid by your Lordship, to bring it to a Certainty, for the Inhabling of her Officers, Soldiers, and Relief of her own Charges, or els she must increase their Wages, and content her self with continuall Expence of Blood and Treasure, or commyt it to *Irishe* Governement. And with a farder Answer then this I will not beat my Brains, though if they shold wade in Particularityes with me, I were an ill Scholler, yf after xii Yeirs Experience, I shold not be hable to give the Reason for your Doings.

At my Comminge now to *London,* I find a Letter of *John Cockcrans* unto me, with two Billes of your Lordships inclosid, the one of 3001 *l.* the other of 1600 *l.* wherin I have alredy movid Mr. Secretary, who will once again be a Meane to her Majestye, protesting to do his best : But he saith the *Irishe* Marchaunt uppon the last Pryvy Seale, delt verie ill both with him and you, or els had the 1600 *l.* bene paid. He hath taken newe Notes of me of those Billes, and of all such Sewtes, as your Lordship hath otherwise commended ; namelie for Mr. *Mollineux, George Arglas,* and other Matters conceyvid uppon your Lordships Lettres, to all which I hope, uppon some good and spedy Answer ; and howsoever it take Successe, I humbly beseach your Lordship to think of me, as of a carefull Solicitor of all your Causes ; and truly, Sir, Mr. Secretary is your constant Frend, in great Assurance of Amity with my Lord of *Lecester* ; which two, do take uppon them the Protection of all your Affaires, and therfore you cannot be to thankfull unto them ; and if in your Lordships Letters you seme to take such Knowledge from me, it may enhable me to do you the more effectuall Service.

I did Yesterday send Letters to your Lordship by the Way of *Waterford,* declaring that her Majestie, for Revictualling her Ships at Sea, had sent a Masse of

Victualls from *Briſtoll* to *Waterford*, and if the Shipps be not uppon that Coaſt, then the Victualls to be delivered to the Surveyour of the Victualls for *Irland*, to be iſſuid out at your Diſcrecion : They be ſent in Charge of *James Bricklow*, who is to receyve a Bill, ether from Mr. *Winter*, if the Ships be there, or from Mr. *Woodford*, if they be abſent.

Your Lordſhip may do well to ſend him to *Waterford*, to ſee the Victualls landid, and well orderid ; which is a Proportion for 700 Men, ſerving in the Ships for 21 Dayes.

God ſend your Lordſhip Helth, Honour, and Contentacion, and ſo I committ you to his Protection. At *London*, the 21ſt of *Auguſt*, 1577.

Uppon a Practice made by Don *John*, to overthrowe the States, they are all uterly revoltid, and have poſſeſſed them ſelfs of *Antwerp* Caſtell, and all the Holds in the *Lowe Countries*. The *Spaniards* are comming back into *Flanders* : *Moundiagon*, and *Julie*, are come alredy ; the moſt of the reſt did never paſſe the *Alpes*. Great Trobles are like to grow there ; all do now depend uppon the Prince of *Orange*. The Duke of *Aſcot* ran from Don *John*, and had lyke to have left his Hed behind for Haſt.

There is no late Newes come out of *Fraunce* ; but that *Jereſey* and *Gerneſey* be in Fere ; and then ther is as good Reaſon for your Lordſhip to looke for your *Frenche* Geſts in *Irland*. *La Roch* is certainly in Armes with 1500 Shott. *James Fitz Maurice* is not knowen to be in *France*.

Your Lordſhips faithfully,

Edward Waterhows.

Edward Waterhows, *Eſq;* to *Sir* Henry Sydney.

My ſingular good Lord,

AFter the Arrivall of Mr. *Briſket* heere, their was ſome Staie made in the Delivery of your Letters, by Meanes of the Abſence of Mr. *Phillip Sydney*, at whoſe Going the Pacquet was deliverid, and not red by her Majeſtie till two Daies after, becauſe her Majeſtie hath not bene very well diſpoſid in Body ſince her Going to this Houſe at *Otlande* ; but vppon the Vewe of the Lettre, ſhe did generally like well of the Contents ; and by Mr. Secretary I perceive, that an expreſſe Meſſanger ſhall ſhortly be ſent from her Highnes to your Lordſhip. Your Frends here do very well allow of the Coming of my Lord Chauncellor, and Mr. *Agarde*, and have, I think, written erneſtly to your Lordſhip for theim ; and truly my Opinion is, that if they comme together, it ſhall ſhortly work you a good and an honorable Reſolucion. And although my Lord Chauncellor can of him ſelf deale verie ſufficiently in your Cauſes, yet their be mayny (and namely her Majeſty) that will much more leane to Mr. *Agards* Experience and Judgement, then to eny one Man that ſervith in that State, and therfore if they comme together, you may aſſuredly hope of honorable Succeſs. Mr. Secretary made me to frame Mr. *Malbyes* Compoſition for *Connoght*, into a plainer Maner, for her Majeſty to vnderſtand, and will take a Tyme to enforme her Majeſty how her Charges in that Province are eaſed, and make that an Example to induce her to the reſte. But the noble Men of *Irland*, which be here, wold faine furder ſome Deviſe, that all of them ſhuld be free from all Burdens. And this Day the Erle of *Thomounde*, in the Chamber of Preſence, began to diſcours how he wold wynne the Queene CCCC *l.* a Yer clearly, when now ſhe ſpendith a Thowſaund. I deſierid to know how ; but he hath taken Daies, wherein he ſaith he will tell me all ; but the Deviſe is, that *Mounſter* and *Connoght* ſhuld be in *Statu quo prius*, without eny Preſident ; Perhaps ſome other Mens Deviſes ſhall be putt into his Mowthe, and ſo he made an Inſtrument ; but after nyne Daies we ſhall leave wondring at his Wiſdom, for he is no Chaungeling.

Your Lordſhip comittid vnto me two Papers of Truſt, the one a Letter from my Lord of *Slane*, the other a Warraunt for *Seſſe*. I ſervid them both to

ſuch

fuch as you comaundid me, and to Mr. Secretary, becaufe I wold haue hym know the Humor of the Man ; and after I deliuerid that Warraunt where you willid me.

I will again remember your Lordfhip to ftrengthen my Lord Chauncellor, with the Coming of Mr. *Agard.* Both are thoght to be well chofen, but the one without the other fhall not deale to your Expeċtacion. And fo I humbly leave your Lordfhip to the Proteċtion of God. At the Court, the vth of *September*, 1577.

Your Lordfhips moſt bounden

Ed. Waterhows.

Sir Henry Sydney, *and the Council of* Ireland, *to the Lords of the Councell in* England.

Oure very good Lords,

OURE humble Duetyes remembred to your honorable Lordfhips. Beinge carefull as becommeth vs of the good Quiet of this Countrie, and the Prefervacion of the fame from Daunger, to be furprifed by any forreine Invafion, as moche as in vs lyeth, have thought good, vpon foch Advertizements, as we received thence, takinge Knowledge by a Lettre, fent from Mr. Secretorie *Walfinghame,* dated at the Courte at *Richmound* the xxth of this laſt *Auguſt,* and addreſſed to Sir *William Drewrye,* Lord Prefident of *Mounſter,* to aſſemble oure felves, and fall into Confideracion of the Matter : For the Lettre conteined that her Majeſtie was advertized, that *La Roche* is at a Place in *Bretteine,* called *Vannes,* with a Force of xv C. Men, iiij Gallions, and dyvers other Veſſels, and thought that he prepareth hetherwardes. An other Lettre we received lykewife from *George Winter,* the Viceadmirall here, of Advertizements that he had received from your Lordſhips commaundinge hym, that he ſhould prefentlye imploy hym felfe betwene this Land and the Coaſts of *Fraunce,* for the Metinge withe *La Roche* and *James Fitzmorrice.* And although we were verye doubtfull, notwithſtanding theife Advertizementes, to refolve to fende for any Force thence, confideringe the Tenor of the Lettres we received from your Lordſhips, bearinge Date the ixth of *June* laſt, expreſſinge your Pleafures, amongeſt other Things, that notwithſtanding ij M. Men were in a Readyneſs apointed to come at any Tyme, when we ſhould think convenient for Occafion of Service to fende for theim, without either Warraunt or furder Direccion from her Majeſtie, or your Lordſhips ; yet that you conceived that Opinion of vs, that without apparaunt Cawfe, and imminent Daunger, we would not call for theim, fince foch a Nomber could not be imployed without great Encreafe of her Majeſties Chardgies, and fome Bourden to her Highnes good Subieċtes, in the Counties where they ſhould be levied. We yet wayinge foch due Circumſtauncies, as in a Cawfe of foche Importaunce is requifite, thought it better, in Refpeċte of our Duetyes, and the Care we have to prevent any Mifcheife that might be vpon the Soddeine attempted, to conclude amongſt oure felves, that the Forces apointed there to refiſt this forreine Invafion ſhould be fent for ; and withall, at the fame Inſtant, to advertize your Lordſhips, what we had donne ; to the Ende, that if any Perrill and Daunger ſhould fall out, and we beinge forewarned by Advertizements from thence of the fame, ſhould not in Tyme provide Remedye, we might of oure Negligencies be iuſtlye condempned ; fo that we are nowe to crave your Lordſhips Aydes, and Advifes in the Matter, that if your Lordſhips ſhall thinke convenient, either vpon theife Advertizements that we have received, or any others that fince you be advertized of, that the Men be fent ; that then there be no Staye, but that they may comme, accordinge to our Lettres addreſſed in that Behalfe ; otherwayes your Lordſhips to make Stay of theim, or as maney of theim, as to your grave Wifdomes and Confideracions (wayinge the Neceſſitie and Importaunce of the Cawfe) fhall feme beſt, and moſt agreable for her Majeſties Service. Prayinge your Lordſhips nevertheleffe, that if Stay be made

nowe

nowe for this Tyme; yet that the Order may ftande, your Lordfhips alreadie have taken for their Comminge, when I the Deputie fhall fend at any Tyme hereafter vpon iuft Occafion for theim, leaft if that Rule vpon this Accydent fhould be broken, and an other newe prefcribed, the Service might fayle vpon the Soddeine, if any forreine Invafion fhould be attempted, whereof we befeache your Lordfhips to have due Confideracion. And even fo we humblye take our Leaves of your good Lordfhips. From the Caftell of *Dublin*, the vth of *September*, 1577.

Your honorable Lordfhips affured lovinge

Freinds humblye to commaund,

H. Sydney, *&c.*

Sir Henry Sydney *to the Vice Prefident, and Council of the Marches of* Wales.

AFter my verye hartye Commendacions, by Lettres written vnto you from the Lords of her Majefties honorable Privye Counfell, bearinge Date at *Grenewitche* the vth of *June* laft, you were directed to put in Areadynefs, with all Expedicion, in the Shires vnder your Commiffion, to be fent vnto me hether, one thowfand Soldiors, at foche Tyme as you fhould receive Order from me in that Behalfe, and not expect any other or further Warraunt, either from her Majeftie or their Lordfhips for the fame : And you were lykewife furder directed by the fame Lettres, that everye Hundered of the faied Soldiors to be fent hether, fhould be compofed of lx Calyvers, or Harquebufe Shott, withe their Murrions or Burgonetts, Swordes and Daggers, xx^{tie} Pikes, and xx^{tie} Bills or Halberds, with Corfeletts, and other Furniture as apperteinethe, in foch Sorte as by a former Lettre from her Majeftie directed to me, when I was there prefent amoungeft you vpon lyke Occafion of Service was apointed to be donne ; and you alfo by the fame Lettres put in Mynd, that accordinge to my Plott you fhould make your Divifions, afwell for the Nombers of Men to be borne vpon every Shire, as for the Choyce of the Capteins, *viz.* thofe CC. that are to be leuied in *Gloucefterfhire, Worcefterfhire,* and *Hereffordfhire,* to be vnder the Leadinge of *Thomas Throckmorton.* Thofe 200 to be levied in *Monmowth, Brecknocke,* and *Glamorgan,* to be vnder the Leadinge of Sir *William Morgan* of *Penycoyd.* Thofe 200 to be levied in *Carmerthen, Penbrooke, Cardigan,* and *Radnor,* to be vnder the Leadinge of Mr. *Deveraux,* Brother to the late Earle of *Effex.* And fo theife 600 oute of *Sowthwalles,* with their Capteins and Proporcion of Victualls, to be ordered by you to be imbarqued at *Briftoll,* and tranfported to *Waterford,* and there to attende and receive Direceion from me. Further, thofe 200 to be leuied in *Merioneth, Mountgomerye,* and *Sallopp,* to be at the Direccion and Leadinge of *Richard Corbett,* or *Lacon* of *Willey.* Thofe 200 to be levied at *Flint, Denbighe, Carnarvan,* and *Anglefey,* to be at the Leadinge of *John Salifberye* of *Reeke :* And fo thofe 400 of *Northwales,* with their Capteins and Provicion of Victualls, to be ordered to be imbarqued at *Chefter,* and landed at *Dublin.* And for that by Order from the Lords, afwell Conducte and Coate Money is apointed for the Soldiors, as the Maiors of *Chefter* and *Briftoll* directed, to provide for the Lodginge and Victuallinge of theim duringe the Tyme of their Aboade in thofe Partes, expectinge Wynde and Wether : I truft that vpon the Receipt hereof, that, without furder Delay, you will geve Order for the Sendinge of the Men, furnifhed and forted as afore, to imbarque as fone as the firft Wynde and Weather will ferve ; the more fpedilye to prevent the Preparacion and Invafion intended by the *Frenche :* Who, as I am advertized, are nowe prepared in *Breitteine,* and readye to imbarque and take Shipping towards theife Coafts, for the Annoyaunce and Difturbaunce of the Quiet of this Realme. And al be it in this fo weightie an Action of Service, I have no Cawfe to doubt ; but in Refpecte of the Importaunce of the Matter, you will vfe all Dilligence and

Expedicion to fee theife Nombers of Soldiors fet forwards : Yet I hope, that partlye in Regarde they are fent to ferve vnder me, who have borne the principall Office of Chardge there amongeft you, nowe almoft theife xviij Yeares ; you wilbe more readye both to fett the Matter forwards, and likewife the Soldiors theim felves to be more readye and willinge to comme. And even fo requiringe you, on her Majefties Behalfe, to vfe all Dilligence to fee theim fpedilye fet forwards, and prepared hetherwards, I bid you Farewell. From the Caftell of *Dublin* the vth of *September*, 1577.

Your affured lovinge Freinde,

H. Sydney.

Sir Henry Sydney *to the Sheriffe, Juftices of the Peace, and Commiffioners of the Muflers in the County of* Devon.

AFter my hartie Commendacions. Whereas by Lettres addreffed vnto you from the Lords of her Majefties honorable Privey Counfell, bearinge Date at *Grenewitche* the vth of *June* laft, you were willed to put in a Readines the Nomber of 400 able and furnifhed Men of that Countrie, forted with Weapon in that Order, as by the faied Lettres may apeare vnto you ; and thofe Men to be ftill in a Readines to be imployed for the Service of *Ireland*, at all Tymes when you fhould receive Order from me to fend theim over, and not to expecte either any other or furder Warraunt from her Majeftie, or the Lords in that Behalfe. I therefore, in her Majefties Name, earneftlye and effectuallye requier you prefentlye, vpon Sight hereof, to affemble thofe 400 Soldiors, and put theim in Order foorthwith, as fone as the firft Wynde and Wether will ferve to imbarque theim felves at *Barneft able*, beinge the fitteft Place for the Tranfportacion of theim to *Waterford*. And likewife I am to put you in Remembraunce, that vpon fome Conference amongft your felves, you make Choyce of fome fpeciall Perfon, who may have the Chardge of the Conductinge of the faied Men to *Waterford*, expreffelye chardginge hym to have Care for the Prefervinge of the Soldiors Furniture, to the Ende they may be the better able to do her Majeftie Service when they fhall arryve here. And for that Order is taken by the Lord Threaforer, both for a convenient Proporcion of Victualls, Coate, and Conducte Money, and Chardge for the Tranfportacion of the Soldiours, to be delyvered vnto foch Perfonnes, as fhalbe by you authorized to receive the fame : I hope there fhalbe no Stay, but that they fhalbe prefentlye fent over with the firft Wynde and Wether that fhall ferve for their Tranfportacion, the more fpedilye to prevent the Invafion intended by the *Frenche*, who, as I am advertized, are nowe prepared in *Breitteine*, and reddye to imbarque and take Shippinge towards theife Coaltes, for the Difturbaunce of the good Quiet and Tranquillitie of this Realme. And therefore I doubt not, but accordinge to your wonted Wifedomes and approved Difcreacions, you will have Care of fo weightye a Cawfe, as the Neceffitie and Importaunce of the Service requyrethe, which in her Majefties Behalfe I eftfones requyre and chardge you to do. And even fo I bid you hartelye Farewell. From the Caftell of *Dublin*, the vth of *September*, 1577.

Your lovinge Freinde,

H. Sydney.

The Lords of the Council in Ireland *to Queen* Elizabeth.

Moft gratious Sovereigne,

WHereas the Right Honorable your Highnes Deputye of this your Realme [*Sir Henry Sydney.*] hath fignified vnto vs your gratious Pleafure, that we fhould once every Yeare at the leaft advertize your Highnes, of the Eftate

of

of this your Countrie, the Quiet or Difquiet of the fame ; and fo confequent-
lye, of the Diforders (if any were) and the Cawfe thereof ; which were Letts to
good Governement ; and therevpon to fett downt oure Opinions, not onelye of
the Meanes to reforme foch Diforders, but alfo to devife fome Way to dimi-
nifhe the great Chardge, your Highnes doth, and hath fufteined theife maney
Yeares, for the Good of this People and Countrie.

It may lyke your Highnes vpon Relacion made vnto vs, by your Majefties
Deputye, after the Ende of his longe Iorney into all the Provinces, the firft
Yeare after his Arryvall, that the Lords, and Cheifeteynes of all the *Irifhery*,
had fubmitted theim felves vnto your Highnes, with foch Offers and Compoficions, to hold their Lands and Countries of your Highnes ; yeelding foche
Rent, and Service, as was thought by vs, a good Encreafe of your Highnes Revenue, with further Declaracion of your Majefties moft gratious Intencion fpedilye to fende vnto vs Prefidentes and Juftices, to be refident in thofe remote Places,
that he had vifited ; and a Chauncellor and Juftices, to ferve within the Pale :
We comfortablye lyved with Hope in fewe Yeares to have tafted of the Fruite
of that your Highnes moft gratious Intente, to the Good of this Realme, and
the Benifitt of your poore obedient People, which we all acknowledge, is the
fole and onelye Way, to cure and remedie the longe feftered Cankers, which
for fo maney Yeares hath had Contynuaunce, and fore greived this Eftate. For
when Juftice and refident Authoritie fhalbe pulled away, or difcontynued in
thofe remote Partes, your Majeftie wilbe acknowledged (in oure Opinions) but
onely by Title and Name, and not in Dede and Effecte ; fo moche Cuftome and
Tyrannye hath prevayled, as in moft Places the great ones, without Controle-
ment or Refiftaunce, would expecte to poffeffe yours, and their owne. But
moft gratious Sovereigne, in this ioyfull Tyme (we fay) of quiet and comfortable Hope of Reliefe : In the Moneth of *June* the Yeare paft, vpon the Landinge of your Majefties Chauncellor, and Prefident, a Rebellion (confpired by
the Earle of *Clanrickard*, in *May* before, to drawe Force of *Scotts* into *Connaught*)
was by the faied Earle hym felfe then actuallye put in Execucion, as we have
moft apparauntlye perceived by fondrie Examinacions alreadye taken, whatfoever be faied or enformed of the Fathers fevere Dealinge againft the Sonnes.
Which trayterous Rebellion, your Highnes faied Deputye (moft worthy therein
of finguler Commendacion for his Dilligence and Expedicion) fo daunted in the
verye Beginninge, as the Forces and Healpes, which the Rebell expected, were
cutt of for that Tyme, the Fortefienge of the Caftells and Holdes they were in
Hand withall fodenlye ftayed, and their Trenchinge and Wallinge prevented :
But yet this Rebellion not altogether fo totallye fubdued, but that the Dreggs,
and Remaynes that the Earle had leaft in the Harts of the People, that he
had gathered, was foche, as they helde Sir *Nicolas Malbye* (your Highnes
Collonell there) fo occupied, as vntill almoft *Eafter* laft, he had fmall Tyme to
fee Juftice delyvered, or to deale withe the Countrie for Contribucion, towards
the Supportinge of your Majefties great Chardgies of that Province : The Manner of which Confpiracye of Rebellion ftretched it felfe (as we are perfwaded)
by fondrie Braunches into *Mounfter*, with Determinacion to hold your Deputie
and Prefidents, in bothe the Provinces, fo occupied in Armes, as they fhould
not greatlye trouble Courtes with *Englifhe* Juftice, of thofe Confpirattors abhor-
red and hated, expectinge (as may be gathered) fome greater Force from forreine Partes, to have wrought this Yeare the lyke, that the laft yeelded. For
this apeareth by the Confeffion of Sir *John* of *Defmound*, that fith the Earle was
committed, his Sonnes, and their Force, beinge not yet fubdued, but remayninge armed in the Fieldes, Mediacion and Entreatie was made for the Conclufion of a Mariage between *Marie Bourcke*, the Earles Daughter, and the faid Sir
John, although he have a nother Wife lyvinge, and fhe another Hufband. And
further it apeared by Examinacion, that he received feverall Lettres from *John
Bourcke*, and *Marie* ; and as it is by others affirmed (although collorably by
hym denied) he fecretelye met, and had Conference with *John Bourcke*, who

I   fhewed ſhewed hym Lettres of Advertizements of *James Fitz Morrice* Invaſion, as it were in Vaunte of the Likehode of ſome forreine Invaſion, and Healpe the rather to ſturre hym to take his Parte : And as Rebells and rebellious Hartes, are eaſely knitt to ioyne together in Miſcheiſe, ſo *Connor Mac Cormocke Oconnor,* and *Rorie Oge Omore,* contrarye to their Othes, Submiſſions, and Promiſes (hopinge for Ayde out of *Connaught*) beganne to gather of their Freindes and Confederates, out of ſeverall Places, to the Nomber of a hundred Swoordes or thereaboutes, and ſo to revolte ; who vpon a ſoddeine, at one Inſtant on *Chriſtmas Eve* laſt, burnt dyvers Haggardes and poor Mens Cottagies of the *Kings* Countye to the Valewe, as was reported vnto vs, by the Teſtimonye of the Sheriffe, and others of the beſt Creditt and Accompt in the Countrie, of twoe hundered Poundes. And after Takinge ſome Encouragement by the Succeſſe they had in this, with ſome greater Force of ſoche as they have gathered, came to the Towne of the *Naas* by the Night, and bourned to the Nomber of Seavenſcore thatched Howſies, or thereabowtes : And likewiſe, ſince that Tyme they have bourned a great Parte of *Laughlin,* and donne ſome other Harmes and Spoyles vpon the Borders of the Pale. And not withſtandinge your Majeſties Force contynually followed theim in Chaſe, who have cut of the greateſt Nomber of thoſe, who firſt were aſſembled, and of the beſt of theim, as we have received Vnderſtandinge by good Certificat ; yet ſoch is their Maintenaunce in the Counties adioyninge to *Leix,* and their Watche and Spiall ſo good, with the Healpe of their Faſtnes, Bogges, and Woodes, as ſtill they be oute. Vnto whoſe Daunger, Captein *Harrington,* and *Alexander Coſbye,* overmoch creditinge ſome ſuttle Promiſes and Othes, as we be enformed, have of late, thorough their owne Follies, caſt theim ſelves.

Theiſe Conſpiracies and ſoch lyke, may be eaſilye deviſed and caſt out as Letts to hynder your Highnes moſt gratious Determinacion and Procedinge to ſettle Juſtice ; but as the firſt that beganne theiſe Rebellions, and their greateſt Force are well ſubdued, ſo we miſtruſt not, but very ſpedilye to ſee *Rorie* and *Connor* of no Force to be accompted of ; which donne, we may then boldlye ſignifye vnto your Highnes that the People within your Pale, were not of longe Tyme, more apt to be framed to good Order and imbrace Juſtice, then at this Preſent.

The State of the Northe, and the Towardnes of good Quiet there, is ſoche, as of longe Tyme hath not bene better ; for *Tirlaugh Lynaugh* hath come in, to your Highnes Deputie, and after his Comminge, ſimplye, without Pledge, Proteccion, or Hoſtage, ſhewed ſoch Tokens and Notes of Duetye and Obedience, as the Troubles of thoſe Partes are not to be feared as before ; which if they ſhould bruſt out by Meanes of the Inſolencye, and Pride of the *Scotts,* *Tirlaugh* is to be framed, as an Inſtrument and Scourge for theim, to conteine theim in the Bonds of Obedience.

And, moſt gratious Sovereigne, the Benifitt that hath riſen by this laſt Yeares Travell of your Highnes Preſident in *Munſter,* and Collonell in *Connaught,* notwithſtandinge the actuall Rebellion in the one Place, and the Shewe of Miſlyke in the other, is an Argument to vs, what would have growen therebye to your Maieſtie, had not the Rebellion in *Connaught* bene ; or if the Earle of *Deſmound* had, in all Pointes, ſhewed ſoch willinge Diſpoſicion to obey and lyve vnder the Rule of Juſtice, as he might have donne, as the Note delyvered by the ſaied Preſident and Collonell to your Hignes Deputye ; and, as we vnderſtand, certified to your Maieſtie, will declare. And therefore, for the preſent, we paſſe it over ; but onely to remember your Maieſtie of what Force reſyent Authoritie is, if the ſame be contynued ; and what Increaſe both of Obedience and Revenue, will therebye grow yerelye to your Maieſtie, to the Deminiſhinge and Decreaſinge of the great Chardge your Highnes nowe ſuſteyneth. And like as we muſt confeſſe vnto your Maieſtie, that the People within the Pale are over moche blemiſhed with the Spottes of the *Iriſhry* ; and that the ſondrie good Lawes from Age

†

to

to Age, devifed to wype out thofe Staynes, have rather bene hid and not knowen, then duelye executed : So are we to be befeache your Highnes of the Contynuaunce of that your gratious Care, to fend Juftices to put thofe and other nedefull Lawes fitt to paffe at this next Parliament for the State of the Realme, in due Execucion. And becawfe both by the feverall and longe Jorneys, which your Maiefties Chauncellor hath taken in this Land, he hath fene the feverall Exaccions, Extorfions, and *Irifh* Impoficions, which decayeth the Poore, and hyndereth Juftice : And by his like Search into the Parliament Rolles, and Rolles of Accompt, hath fene into the Governement of this Eftate in Tymes paft ; and therefore the beft able not onlye to acquainte your Maieftie with what he hath conceived touchinge the fame ; but alfo a Man, for his Judgement and Skill, fit to conferre with foche as your Hignes fhall pleafe to apointe, touchinge theife newe Lawes that are to paffe this next Parliament. Therefore we have vpon Confideracion of foch Perfons, as we thought meteft to repaier to your Maiefties Prefence, with Advertizements, made fpeciall Choyce of hym, and accordinge to former Prefidentes, when, vpon foch like Occafions, the Chauncellors of this Land, have bene fent thether, we have taken Order for the faulfe Vfinge and Cuftodie of your Majefties Seale ; whereunto, as vpon our Mocion, he hath willinglye affented : So we humbly befeache your Maieftie, that he be not deteined there longe, but that he may be retorned to his Chardge agayne withe convenient Spede. For we affure your Highnes fithence his firft Landinge, his Diligence in his Office, readye Difpatch of Cawfies and Sutors, and Care of this Eftate, deferveth Commendacion. And were it not for the verie Neceffitie of this prefent Service, ill could we have affented to have fpared hym. And for the Matter of Ceffe, where with the Country feameth more nowe to find theim felves greived then before, we are of this Opinion ; that other Order and Courfe would be taken, then hath bene, to take and receive the Countries yearelye Yeldinge to eafe your Maiefties great Chardge, duringe the Tyme that Neceffitie enforceth a Garrifon to be kept. And do thinke it verye expedient, that they of the Countrey fhould fall to fome certeine Compoficion, that a certeine Somme might yearelye be yeelded ought of everye Ploughland, and by fomme of the beft Callinge, put in Affuraunce, to be delyvered at Dayes ; for, as it is nowe, and for dyvers Yeares hath bene, the Exaccions and Diforders of the Gatherers of the Ceffe, hath greatly oppreffed the Poore. And if it hath bene reported to your Highnes, that your Deputye hath vfed other Manner and Order, in the fettinge downe of the Ceffe, for the twoe Yeares paft, in Quantitye for the Garrifon or his Howfe, otherwife then was before vfed, we affure your Maieftie the fame is vntrewe ; for he imitated the commen Order vfed heretofore, by callinge the Counfell and Nobilitie together, and layenge the Impoficion, which in Quantitie was leffe for the Garrifon then had bene laied before. His Motion to the Countrie ftill was, to conferre vpon fomme other Manner of Devife to victuall the Soldior, your Maieftie at no greater Chardge, and he would affent thereunto ; offeringe theim openlye a Contentment in hym for their Eafe, to receive fyve Marks of the Plowelande, and to difchardge theim of all Ceffes. And becawfe the Lord Chauncellor was prefent, and can certifie your Maieftie fullye and particularlye, of the Manner and Order of the fetting downe of the Ceffe this laft Yeare, and of your faied Deputies and oure Proceadings therein. The Offers made to thofe travellinge vp withe Complainte : The Withftandinge of your Highnes Royall Prerogatyve in fome Pointes, by dyvers the Lordes, Knights, and Gentlemen within the Pale, and oure Committinge of theim, and their Enlardgment vpon their Submiffion. Therefore we, to avoyde Troublinge your Highnes with tedious Writinge, leave the Whole to his Report, and pretermit the fpeciall Recitall thereof, craving your Maiefties Pardon, for that we have fo longe, with this oure rude and longe Difcourfe, troubled your Maieftie, whome we befeache the Almightie longe and happelye to profper and preferve, to the ineftimable Comforte of your Hignes humble Subiects, and the Confufion and Overthrowe of your

Ennemies. We moft humblye take oure Leave. From *Dublin* the xijth of *September*, 1577.

Your Maiefties moft humble, obedient, and

faythfull Subieƈtes,

H. Sydney, &c.

Sir Henry Sydney *to* Queen Elizabeth, *fent by the Lord Chancellor.*

Moft gratious Sovereigne,

AFTER the Writinge of my laft Lettres vnto your Maieftie, dated from the *Newrie* in *Auguft* laft ; I hafted hetherwards to fynde both more convenient Tyme, and apter Place, more fullye to informe my felfe of thofe Things, wherein your Maieftie requyred to be anfwered ; which there, as I writt vnto your Maieftie, I could not fo commodiouflye do. And duringe the Tyme of my Aboade there, *Tirlaugh Lenaugh* came vnto me in humble and duetiefull Manner, fhewinge foch Tokens of Obedience and Loyaltie, as greater could not be found in a Subieƈte (farre above his Trayninge) offeringe to do foche Service vpon the *Scotts*, or any others where I fhould direƈte hym, as the lyke Offer hath not bene made vnto me, by any of his Sorte, fince my Governement. And his fimple and playne Manner of Proceadinge was foche, as cominge thether cheifelye to feeke Juftice at my Hands, and Redreffe of foch Iniuries as had bene offered hym, he exhibited his Peticions in Writinge, wherein, and in all the reft of his Proceadings, I found hym fo conformable to Reafon, and fo yelding to Order, as greater Conformitie I have not found at any Tyme in any *Irifhman*. He remayned with me there fome fewe Dayes, while his Cawfies were in Hand, without Hoftage, Pledge, or Proteccion ; and, in the Ende, delyvered me a Lettre addreffed to your Maieftie from hym, and befaught me, that I would accompanye the fame, with my Commendacions to your Highnes ; which, in Trothe, Madame, I thinke he hath very well deferved. His Peticions be, to be created into Degree of Honnor, and that his Sonne may be made Baron, and he to have fome Enterteinement and Stipend from your Maieftie, foch as you fhall thinke hym worthy of, to inhable hym the better to ferve againft the *Scott*, or any other Rebell, where he fhall be direƈted by the Governor : And for better Profe of his Loyaltie and Fidellitie, he hath, fince his Departing from me, made a Iorney vpon the *Scottes*, and killed *Sorley Boyes* Sonne and his Brother ; fo that I am to crave your Maiefties Anfwere and Refolucion for hym. And for that his Wife hath bene an Inftrument, and cheife Counfellor, to frame hym to this Order of Obedience, and duetifull Manner of Proceadinge, I humbly befeach your Maieftie to beftowe a Garment vpon her, as a Token of your Favor, which Mr. *Marfhall* telleth me, your Maieftie did geve Order for, at his beinge there, who was a Sutor for it on her Behalfe ; who, afwell in this as in dyvers other good Offices, in managinge thofe Northern Cawfies, where I have apointed hym Cheife in Chardge ; hath for his Care, Travell, and Dilligence, to fettle good Order and Quiet in thofe Partes, deferved great Commendacion and Thanks, which I befeache your Maieftie, by fome comfortable Lettre to beftowe vpon hym.

After my Comming hether, beinge perplexed with no fmall Greife and Sorrowe conceaved of the hard Phrafe of your Maiefties Lettre, I fell to the Confideracion with my felf, howe I might beft fatisfie your Maieftes Expectacion towchinge the material Pointes of the fame ; which, I thought, I could not fo plaineley fet downe in Writinge, were it never be fo large a Difcowrfe (to tedious for your Highnes to reade) but havinge there foche Ennemies to me, and Adverfaries to your Prerogatyve and Proffitt, they would impugne (as they have donne) as moche as lay in theim any thinge I fhould write. And therefore I thought beft, the Matters beinge of foch Gravetie and Weight, havinge no Boddye to refolve your Maieftie

ieftie, nor the Lords, in Cawfies of Doubt which arife maney Tymes ; and to anfwere the Objections that are made againft the Defectes of this Governement ; to fend fome expreffe Man over to your Maieftie, chofen by the Affent of your Counfell here, who fhould be of Sufficiencye to do the fame : And for that Purpofe have chofen, by a generall Confent of the Boorde, your Chauncellor, beinge a Man of that Gravetie, Wifedome, Staiednefs, and Experience, as I hope fhalbe fufficientlye hable to anfwere your Maieftie in that you fhall demaunde of hym ; to whome I befeache your Maieftie to geve fyrm Creditt, who repayreth fullye inftructed for the Matter of the Ceffe. Firft, for the Beginninge of it ; then of the Cawfe and Contynuance of the fame ; the Neceffitie to have it ; and the reft of the Circumftauncies and Incydents to that Matter : Next, what Ceffe, fince my laft Acceptacion of this Governement, hath bene levied for the Vfe of the Garrifon, or taken vp ; for the Provifion of my Howfehold, both for the Quantitie and the Manner ; the Kinds and Proporcions in every Sorte ; vpon what Countries the fame is laied ; what hath bene paide thereof, and what remayneth vnanfwered ; and, to make the Matter more evident and plaine to your Maiefties Viewe, I have cawfed one of my fpeciall Officers of Howfehold, to attend vpon hym with my Howfehold Booke ; to the Ende your Maieftie may fee (or foch whome it fhall pleafe your Maieftie to apointe) what hath bene received, what hath bene beftowed, and thereby perceive in what Sorte I have bene mifreported. And, moft gratious Ladie, I had thought I had rather deferved large Thanks, that have had this Care of the Countrie, that where the Countrie afore was chardged with the Victuallinge of a thowfand Soldiors, I demaunded Victuallinge onelye for 500 ; and as fcant a Proporcion is demaunded for thofe 500, as in any reafonable Confideracion may be : So that the Grevaunce is not in the Quantitie but in the Price, which lyeth not in me to healpe. For a Cowe that was wont heretofore to be fold for vj s. is nowe worth xx s. and fo after the lyke Rate in other Things ; and the Soldiour may not have a leffe Proportion in Fode then he was wont to have ; for he eateth nowe as he was wont to do, and thereof he may not be moch fcanted : So that except your Maieftie will increafe the Soldiors Pay, I cannot fee howe to eafe the Countrie more then I have donne. And in fome other Mens Tymes (as apeareth by the Counfell Bookes) there hath bene a greater Ceffe layed for the Kepinge onely of twoe Fortes, then is nowe demaunded for the whole Garrifon ; and yet fomme Soldiors lay vpon the Countrie ftill, and no Fault found withall, nor Complainte made : But my hard Happ is otherwayes, which difcourageth me to ferve, when I feare I am condempned, before I be hard, and myne Ennemies hard and believed. And touchinge the Alienacion of your Maiefties Subiects Hartes, by any newe Impoficion layed vpon theim, me feameth this may hardlye be conftrewed a good Cawfe or Grounde, when I offer to difchardge theim for fyve Markes a Ploughland, where they complayned that they were chardged with viii l. vpon a Ploughland ; neither is this any hard Kinde of Dealing with the Countrie, where the Bourden lay but vpon a fewe, to eafe theim the more, to make it more vniverfall (as I have donne) and a greater Nomber to beare the Bourden. And albeit fome fewe of the Lords, who are willfullye and malitioullye bent, repyne and kicke that their newe Freedomes are touched (wherein lyeth the Gall of all this fecreat Greife) yet others there be of the Nobilitie that lyke of my Devife and Diftribucion ; and proteft in their owne Names, and the Names of the poorer Sorte, there was never a more gratefull and plaufible Matter offered for the Eafe of the Countrie. But what foever I devife or do, of fomme I perceive it is ill taken, and I flaundered ; and the Greife of the Countrey made great, although it be leffe in my Tyme, both for the Garrifon and my Howfehold, then it hath bene in former Tymes before me, whatfoever Reporte be made to the contrarie.

And, moft gratious Sovereigne, the late Grauntinge of a generall Fredome to the Earle of *Ormound,* is the Cawfe either of the Decreafe of fome Parte of your Ayde and Subfidie of Contribucion for Service, or ells wilbe a greater

Bourden

Bourden to the Subiecte, then in Reafon they fhould or wold be willinge to bear ; for in Equitie that cannot be impofed vpon theim, which his Landes fhould beare ; for therein were Oppreffion, and no Equalitie in Diftribucion ; fo that your Maieftie onely is to beare the Loffe. And howe can you expect fo great an Encreafe of your Revenue, when your Highnes is fo greate an Ennimye to your owne Proffitt, and geve it forth both by Woorde and otherwayes, as fome reporte that your Maieftie will have no Ceffe ? For the Example of this wilbe a Prefident and Encouragement to others, to fue for the lyke Immunities at your Hands, which, if you fhould graunte, it wold be a Decreafe of that, which, in Tyme, would growe to be a certeine Revenue : And, if your Maieftie fhould not graunte the fame, it might happelye be a Cawfe of Difcontentment : For the reft of his Ranke (as it is to be fuppofed) will attempt to obteine the like Favour at your Highnes Hands as he hath donne.

And theife People here are fo incouraged and comforted of late from thence, by fome your Maieftie geveth Countenaunce vnto, and foch Reportes brought hether of their Proceadings and the favorable Eare you enclyne to heare theim, and healp theim ; as maketh both fome of the Nobilitie and common Sorte to be more willful and obftinate, then otherwife they would be ; and, on the other Side, the flender Backinge of me in your Services, difcourageth me altogether either to attempt or do any Thinge with Comforte or Conceipt of good Lykinge ; for Bruites flye hether, that I fhalbe revoked, and that your Maieftie hath conceived Difpleafure againft me ; and you knowe what Service is to be expected, and howe the People wilbe inclyned, when they fhall fufpecte your Maieftie is offended with me, and that I am in Difgrace with you. And, Madame, theife Bruites do no Good ; if they be trewe (it be determined I fhalbe revoked) I humblye befeache your Maieftie that I may knowe your gratious Pleafure ; if it be not fo, it were good in the refpect of Thadvauncement of your Service, that thefe Bruites were fuppreffed. But when I looke into the Services that I have donne, the Care and Travell that I have taken, and the found Confcyence I beare, that I have ferved you faythfullye, trewlye and profitably ; I cannot but lament with Sorrowe of Harte, and Greife of Mynde, to receive foch fharpe and bitter Lettres from your Maieftie, which fo moch have perplexed me both Bodye and Mynde fince I received theim, as I fhall finde no Comforte till your Maieftie be fullye enformed, and thoroughlye fatisfied, howe I have bene mifreported vnto you ; and they that fo have enformed you, receive the iuft Rewarde of their Vntrothes.

And where your Highnes hath conceived that I have not fo well vfed your Threafure, or extended the fame fo farre as to your Benifitt I might have donne : For your Maiefties better Satisfaccion therein, I have cawfed a breife Abftract to be made of the Number of youer Garrifon, the Placeis where they ferve, the Pay they have, and the Neceffitie to vfe and imploye theim, and the Chardge to victuall theim, befides your Pay ; to be confidered, fearched, and tried, by whome it fhall pleafe your Maieftie to appointe.

And for the Increafe or Decreafe of your Revenue, the Auditor vpon the Endinge of his Accomptes (which, I hope, wilbe fhortlye) he will reduce the fame to a certeine Somme ; fo that I doubt not, but your Maieftie fhall rather finde an Encreafe, then Decreafe of Revenue, whatfoever it hath pleafed fome others to fay to the contrarie.

And nowe, moft redoubted Sovereigne, havinge fullye and plainelye anfwered (as I take it) the Pointes of your Maiefties Lettre in foch Sorte, as in ech Perticuler I will ftand to my Iuftificacion ; if this (for the which I fhalbe moft hartelye foarye) fhall not fatisfie your Maieftie, I humblye befeache your Highnes, that the fame may ftand with your gratious Pleafure, that I my felfe may come to anfwere myne owne Matters, and to prove vnto you that to be trewe which I have faied, to the Difprofe of theim, whofoever have informed you to the contrarie ; moft lowlye upon my Knees prayinge the Almightie to bleffe your Maieftie with longe and happie Life, Obedience of your Subiecles, and Triumphe

over

over your Ennemies. From your Highnes Caftell of *Dublin*, the xvth of *September*, 1577.

Your Maiefties moft humble and

obedient Sarvaünt,

H. Sydney.

Sir Henry Sydney *to the Lords of the Council in* England, *fent by the Lord Chancellor.*

My very good Lords,

MY Dewtye humblye remembred to your good Lordfhips. Together with your Lordfhips Lettres of the xxth of *July* laft, brought by *Colman*, the Lord Prefident of *Mounfters* Servaunt, I received iij Plotts; one of the Greives of the Pale with Anfweres thereto by Poftills; a nother a Way howe to eafe the Grieves of the Ceffe impofed vpon the Pale for the Deputies Howfe; the third conteyned certeine Wayes of Victuallinge of an Armye of a thowfand Men, whereby the Pale may be fomewhat eafed. All theife Plotts beinge confidered of by me and the Counfell, and long Confultacion had howe to eafe the Countrie (whereof we have a fpeciall Care) to take away all vnneceffarie Grevauncies, and Impoficions, without Hyndraunce of the Service. We firft called the Captens vnto vs, and imparted vnto theim that Parte of the Plott that concerned theim felves; whereunto they made Anfwere in Writinge, which I delyvered vnto the Lord Chauncellor, to be prefented vnto your Lordfhips; whereby you fhall perceive, afwell the Impoffibilitie the Soldiour fhould lyve vpon that Condicion of Victuallinge offered vnto hym by that Plott, as alfo in Parte difcover the heavye Loade laied vpon the Countrie, that are forced to victuall the Soldior at fo bafe a Rate; which, in Troth, is no fmall Bourden vnto theim. For Things growinge daylye to higher Prices, the Countrey is fore greived, and the State of the Soldiour not in any Sorte amended, who is forced maney Tymes, in his Travellinge, to pay his whole Dayes Wages for his Victuallinge, and fometymes his Dayes Wagies for one Meale; foche is the Dearth of all Things here, in fo moche as the Queftion beinge afked at the Boorde, it was affirmed by fomme of the Lords of the Countrey, that the Countrie could not aforde to beare the Soldiour better cheape then vj *d.* a Meale: So that I fhalbe forced to be a Sutor vnto your Lordfhips, to be a Meane to her Majeftie for the Eafe of the Countrey, and the Increafe of the Soldiors Pay, who affuredlye is not able to lyve of his Enterteinement, except the fame may be increafed. The other twoe Plotts were lykewife debated and confidered of, and Anfwere made vnto theim to eche perticuler Pointe, which I referre to the Lord Chauncellors Reporte, to whome, I befeache your Lordfhips, afwell in theife Matters of Ceffe, as in other Things he hath to delyver vnto you from me and the Boorde, to geve full Creditt. And, my Lords, for myne owne Perticuler, I am to render vnto your Lordfhips my humble Thanks, that it pleafeth your Lordfhips fo well to allowe of the Courfe of my Proceadings with thofe Lords, Knights, and Gentlemen, that fo vnduetifullye fhewed theim felves Impugners of the Ceffe, and her Majefties Prerogatyve, who of late were by me and the Borde inlardged vpon their Submiffion: They made faier Shewe in Woordes, and expreffed moch Duetiefulnes in Writinge, as may apeare by the Copye of their Submiffion, which the Lord Chauncellor hath to fhewe vnto your Lordfhips: But howe farre that differed from their inward Conceite and Meaninge, they fhortlye after made Demonftracion to the World; for beinge called (as the Cuftome is) to fett downe a Ceffe for the Victuallinge of the Garrifon and my Howfehold for this next Yeare, and requyred to ioyne with me, and the Counfell, in Devife howe the Countrie might be beft eafed of the Bourden of Ceffe laied vpon theim, refufed either to enter into Confideracion with vs of the Matter, or to put their Handes to the Booke of oure Agreement ; alleadging, that the Cawſe was afore her Majeſtie, and that they had there Agents there, and that they expected Reſolucion from her Highnes for thoſe Matters of Ceſſe and Chardge to be impoſed vpon the Countrie, which otherwiſe, they thought, except the ſame were either expreſſely ſignified from her Highnes, or ells agreed vpon and concluded by Parliament, they ought not to beare. Of whoſe Refuzall, I thought good to make your Lordſhips acquainted, referringe the reſt of the Circumſtauncies and Incydents to the Reference of my Lord Chauncellor, who was preſent, and a Witnes of all their Proceadinge, how, and what Manner, and by what Courſe and Degrees the ſame paſſed. And even ſo, with the humble Remembrance of my Dewtye to your Lordſhips, I take my Leave. From her Majeſties Caſtell of *Dublin,* the xvth of *September,* 1577.

Your honorable Lordſhips aſſured loving

Freinde humblye to commaund.

H. Sydney.

Inſtruccions geven by the Lord Deputie and Counſell, to William Gerrard, *Eſq; Lord Chauncellor of this Realme, beinge expreſſely choſen and ſent to her Majeſtie and the Lords, from vs, to entreate of Cawſies of this State, and to anſwere ſoch Accuſacions and Obieccions as her Majeſtie and the Lords have bene informed of, by ſoch Perſons and there Agents, as have of late ſevered theim ſelves from oure Fellowſhip, and oppoſed theim ſelves againſt the Governement. Dated at* Dublin, *the xvth of* September, 1577.

1. FIRST, you ſhall with all good Dilligence make youer Repaier to the Courte, and delyver ſoch Lettres as we have ſent to her Majeſtie, and the Lords, and preſent oure humble Services, Dueties, Thanks, and Commendacions to ech in their perticuler Degrees, as the Courſe of Speach, and the Framinge of Tyme, will geve you Leave.

2. Next, you ſhall imparte to her Majeſtie, or to ſoch of the Lords to whome you ſhall have Acceſſe, the State of this Countrie, and perticulerlye the State of every Province, according to the Effecte and Tenor of oure Lettres, from Pointe to Pointe, with ſoch furder Inlargement or Addicion (not diſcentinge or diſagreenge from oure ſaied Lettres and Inſtruccions) touchinge eche ſeverall Matter you ſhalbe demaunded of, or by movinge of Queſtions from her Majeſtie, or her Counſell, you ſhalbe vrged vnto, to the Ende, both her Majeſtie and they may vnderſtand the full State of all Things concerninge the Quiet or Diſquiet of this Realme, as niere as you can expreſſe or delyver the ſame vnto theim.

3. You ſhall declare vnto her Majeſtie, or the Lords, from vs, that for the Reformacion of this Realme, there is nothinge ſo neceſſarye as the Plantinge of Preſidents and Counſells, or ſome ſoch lyke reſident Authoritie, in the remoter Partes of the Realme. And the better to induce the Matter, you ſhall ſhewe the Fruites thereof by all due Circumſtauncies, that her Majeſtie may felinglye perceive, both the Increaſe of Obedience in her People, and Augmentacion of Revenue to her Cofers, growing towards the Maintenaunce of her Chardge in thoſe remoter Provinces.

4. You ſhall alſo put her Majeſtie and the Lords in Remembrance, that the Delyveringe of Juſtice vniverſallye thorough the Realme, is the ſole and onelye Meanes to reforme this diſioynted State, and barbarous Countrie, and howe glad the common and poorer Sorte are to imbrace it, and that none but the great Ones vnderhand repine at it : And what Sweetnes her good Subiects feele, by the Benifitt of her Majeſties Lawes adminiſtred vnto theim, wherebye

they

they are nowe of late Yeares, not onelye delyvered from the Exaccions and Oppreſſions of their Lordes, who tirranned over theim, but alſo lyve in Hope of more Eaſe and greater Wealth from Day to Day (if the Courſe of Juſtice may duelye take Place) and be planted amoungſt theim.

5. You ſhall declare how wilfullye maney of the noble Men of the Pale, as namelye, the Viſcount of *Baltinglas*, the Barons of *Deluyn, Trymleſton*, and *Howth*, are bent to oppoſe theim ſelves againſt the State, howe loth they were to make any Submiſſion ; which, although it carried Apparaunce in Writinge and Shewe of Words, to be verye duetifull, and from the Harte, yet within fewe Dayes after beinge called, as in former Tymes they had bene accuſtomed, to yeeld their Conſents to lay downe a Ceſſe for the Victuallinge of the Garriſon, and the Deputies Howſehold, refuzed to put their Hands to the Counſell Booke, alleadginge that the Cawſe was afore her Majeſtie, and that they expected Reſolucion from her Majeſtie, for thoſe Matters of Ceſſe and Chardge to be impoſed vpon the Countrie, which otherwiſe they thought, except the ſame were either expreſſelye ſignified from her High-nes, or ells agreed vpon and concluded by Parliament, they ought not to beare : You ſhall move therefore, that they be ſpeciallye ſent for over to yeeld their Opinions there of Lykinge or Diſlyking of the Matter. For the Example in puniſhinge of theim, will brede both a great Honnor to the State, and a Con-tentment and Quiet to the Countrie. For that their Wilfulnes, if the ſame be borne withall, and not gayne ſaied by Authoritie, will make a generall Diſcon-tentment and Mutinye amongſt the People, whoſe Opinions depend moſt vp-on their Lordſhips Wills, to be framed in any Sorte that they liſt to direct theim.

6. You ſhall furder declare vnto her Majeſtie, and the Lords, howe maney Wayes and Deviſes we vſed to eaſe the People of their Greives and Bourden of Ceſſe (which, in Troth, is heavy) and howe maney Tymes we offered to have ioyned with the Lords in Adviſe for Redreſſe of the Matter, which they from Tyme to Tyme refuzed to do.

7. You ſhall furder declare, that there is no iuſt Cawſe offered of the Alie-nacion of the Peoples Hartes, by Meanes of any newe Greivauncies or Impoſi-cions laied vpon theim ; for that neither the Ceſſe for the Garriſon, nor the De-puties Howſehold is ſo great, as in other Governors Tymes the ſame hath bene, wherein you are to remember ſoch Notes and Memorialls, as be collect-ed out of the Councell Books touching thoſe Matters.

8. You ſhall alſo make known to her Majeſtie the State of her Revenue, and that the ſame hath neither bene neglected, either duelye to be called for, or yet remayneth vnanſwered, as her Majeſtie is informed ; but rather, of late, there hath bene a good Increaſe of the ſame.

9. To remember to the Lords, that the Quarterage aſſigned for the Service of this Countrie, due the Firſt of *October* next, may be delyvered to the Threa-ſorer, or his Agent, to be preſentlye ſent hether ; and to move that the Threaſure that is here alreadye, may remayne as a dead Maſſe to anſwere the Events of any foreine Invaſion, if Nede ſhall ſo requyre.

10. You ſhall declare to the Lords, what Hurte and Hinderaunce to her Majeſties Service, the Bruites do that are brought over ; firſt, that I, the De-putie, ſhalbe revoked, which, if it be ſo determined, I would be glad to knowe it, that I may direct my Courſe accordinge ; and if it be not ſo, it were good with Spede to ſuppreſſe thoſe Brutes, for they increaſe Miſlyke and Diſcon-tentment in the People. They ſay furder, that her Majeſtie will have no Ceſſe, and that I, the Deputie, have taken the Land to Ferme ; which, although it be no newe Thinge, that Deputies have bene placed by Patent to governe the Land, ſometymes for x Years, ſometymes for vj Yeares, and ſometymes for more, and ſometymes for leſſe ; and have had, by Compoſicion, all the Revenues, beſides other Allowauncies yeelded vnto theim ; yet no ſoch Rumor nor Bruite hath bene rayſed, as is nowe, for the Settinge and Takinge of the Land to Ferme ; wherebye it may evidentlye appeare, howe farre the Diſpoſicions

then,

then, be different from the Difpoficions nowe; and that Malice, and not Matter, are the Ground of all theife Vntrothes, and lewd Reportfe.

11. You fhall fay furder, that where it is reported, that I, the Deputie, paffe all Things by myne owne Mynde contrarie to the Courfe of other Deputies, who did never any Matter of Confequence, without prefent Advertizinge the Prince, and fome other principall Counfellors: That it will therefore pleafe their Lordfhips to call to their Remembraunce, what longe and large Lettres, I have written vnto theim, from Tyme to Tyme of my Proceadings in this Service; and that I have fet downe, from Pointe to Pointe, my Plottes, Iorneys, and other Devifes, in fo moch as I have rather bene afrayed, that I have over weried, and troubled their Lordfhips, with twoe tedious and longe Difcourfes in thofe Matters, then in any Sorte (as I take it) left vntold, and not certified any neceffarie Matter, concerninge the Service, wherewith it had bene expedient to have made her Majeftie, or their Lordfhips acquainted.

12. You fhall declare vnto the Lords, the great Hope that is conceived of the Reformacion of thofe twoe Provinces of *Mounfter* and *Connaught*, and what Likelyhoode we fee, by the Effectes and Fruites of this Yeares Service, that thofe Provinces wilbe in fhort Tyme brought to beare their owne Chardges, fo that her Majeftie, for a Tyme, may be perfwaded and wonne to be at fomme Chardge, as prefentlye fhe is at, for the Countenaunce and Maintenaunce of thofe twoe Authorities; otherwife if fhe will none of it, to advertize her Pleafure, that thofe twoe States may be diffolved, and her Majeftie thereby to be eafed of that Chardge, which we, as Councellors to her Majeftie, would not advife for the Honnor of the Realme, and Good of the People, fhould be donne.

13. The like Reafon would be yeelded for *Vlfter*, and the Hope we conceive by the Conformitie we fynde in *Tirlaugh Lenaugh*, as may in Parte appeare by the late Service he attempted againft the *Scottes*, which you may declare.

14. And where it is alleadged, that I, the Deputie, goe about to impofe and lay a newe Kinde of Ceffe vpon the Countrie; and that confideringe the Ceffe of it felfe (as is alleadged) is but a Thinge cafuall and voluntarie to bynd theim and their Inheritors, to a Thinge Royall, and of Perpetuitie, were in it felfe iniuft, and in Refpect of the Tyme, néither in Equitie to be borne, nor in Pollecye to be allowed. You may declare to the Lords, that my Meaninge was not, neither had I any Intencion to chardge the Countrie with any newe Kinde of Ceffe, or Impoficion, except they will tearme this newe to make a Converfion of the Ceffe into Money, and thereby to creat her Majeftie a Rent, in which Manner of my Proceadinge, I thought rather, I fhould have deferved great Thanks, both of her Majeftie and the Countrie; firft to have created her a certeine Rent, and then to have difchardged the Countrie of a Chardge, which they alleadged was viij *l.* vpon a Ploughland, to fyve Marke vpon a Ploughland; if this be Iniuftice or voyd of Equitie, or, in Refpect of the Tyme, of Pollecye, I the Deputie referre the Confideracion of the fame, to their Lordfhips grave Iudgements.

15. For the Matter of the Ceffe, generall and perticuler, and what hath bene impofed vpon the Earle of *Kildares* Land, by Reafon of the Diffolvinge of the newe Fredomes, and what Proffer I the Deputie made for my Stable, and what Devife I fett downe to difbourden the Countrie of the Kepinge of my Horfe, and Horfeboyes, which (as they alleadge) is a Chardge to theim of 660 *l.* at the leaft, and I offered to difcharge theim for leffe then Halfe the Money, and that from henceforth they fhould not be troubled hereafter, with Horfe or Horfeboy, which they refuzed to accept. The Fermors alleadginge, that they durft not enter into any Compoficion at all, were the fame never fo reafonable, for Feare to offend their Landlordes.

16. You fhall declare vnto the Lords, that if her Majeftie be refolved to take away Ceffe totally, and thinke it not convenient, that her Deputie fhould have Allowaunce of the Ceffe, for the Provicion of his Howfehold; if it fhall pleafe her Majeftie to geve me that Allowaunce, that other Deputies have had, that

I

have

have not had Ceſſe, *viz. Sterlinge* Pay for me, and my Companie, where nowe I have but *Iriſh* Pay, and ſoch other Benefits, for Commoditie and Proviſion of my Howſehold, as other Deputies have had, when they had no Ceſſe ; although the Priſes of all Things, be farre dearer nowe, then they were then, I will yet be very well ſatiſſied, and aſſent to ſubmitt my ſelfe to that Order, and not de-maund any Ceſſe for me, or my Howſehold, duringe the Tyme it ſhall pleaſe her Majeſtie I ſhall contynue in this Governement.

17. Touchinge the auntient Lawes, which you, by your Travell, and dilli-gent Search, have found out in the Records of the Rolls, we leave thoſe to your Diſcreacion, to be recommended, inlardged, corrected, or amended, as you ſhall thinke expedient for the Tyme. Wherein you ſhall do well to have ſomme Conference, with ſomme of her Majeſties learned Counſell there, and others of Gravetie and Experience ; ſo that havinge agreed vpon a Forme, the ſame may be ſent hether, to be ingroſſed, and paſſed vnder the Seale, to be ſent thi-ther, as in ſoch Caſes of Actes of Parliament is commenlye vſed ; wherein we requyre you to vſe all Dilligence, that they, with the reſt, may paſſe at the next Parliament.

18. To remember to procure to be ſent thence, the Manner and Order of the Proceſſe, that is vſed for the Triall of Noblemen, for here is no Preſident of it to be found, if Nede ſhould requyre.

19. Theiſe be the principall Matters, we have nowe for the preſent to dely-ver you, which we pray and requyre you, to obſerve from Pointe to Pointe accordinglye. And if any Thinge ſhalbe furder demaunded, touchinge the Governement here, her Majeſties Honnor, the Good of the Common Wealth, or the Defence and Quiet of the Countrie, which we have neither by Lettre nor theiſe our Inſtruccions imparted vnto you. You ſhall therein, according to the Tyme, Place, and your grave Iudgement and Diſcreacion, ſatiſſye their Demaundes, concerninge thoſe Pointes for the preſent, as you can ; and advertize vs with Spede, what you have ſaied or donne therein ; to the Ende, we may (if Neade ſo requyre) ſupply you with furder Order, Matter, and Inſtruction.

Edward Waterhows, *Eſq; to Sir* Henry Sydney.

My good Lord,

I Hope ſhortlie to optaine your Paiment of 1660 *l.* but if I ſhold make Mo-tion for the other Bill of 3000 *l.* it wold be thought that *Irland* were a very happy Clymat : Yet to Mr. Secretary I have movid the Matter, and gueſſed at the Maner of your coming by it ; namely that you have borrowed Billes of the ſeverall Captens, drewe vppon their Intertaignments, and ſo the Uſe of the Mo-ney, and not the Principall yours : But Mr. *Phillip* and I do reſolve to op-tain the Firſt, before we move the Second.

For Newes, there is arrived in *England*, the Marques of *Avery*, Brother to the Duke of *Aſcott :* He cometh towardes the Court with a great Traine, and his Errand, as 'tis thought, to ſolycit from the States, Amity and Furniture to their Wants : They have wholly rejected the *Spaniſhe* Governement, and reſerve the Forts of *Antwerp*, and *Ghent*, and other Places of Importance. Don *John* gatherith Force : His *Spaniards* are againe vppon Retorne, and the Power of *France* expected to his Aide.

In *France*, it is thought that generall Peace is concluded, vppon Articles that are like to hold. The Proteſtants ſo weake as they will refuſe nothing ; and *French* Practices beginn to ſhowe them ſelfs agenſt her Majeſtys State, every where. Therfore your Lordſhip hath done very wiſely, to diſburden yourſelf of the Care of Calling for Aide of Men to aſſiſt you, and to lay it vppon the Counſell heere, who have now ſtaied the Soldiers you ſent for ; and you are, in my Opinion, very honorably diſcharged.

The only Courtier heere, is the Erle of *Toomond :* He hath exhibitid a Sup-plicacion, wherin he hath had ſomme of my Help in noriſhing of a vaine

Humour. He alleagith the great Honour and Auctority of his Aunceftors, the *Obrines*, for a thowfaund Yeares on both Sides of *Shenyn*. The Submiffion of his Father to *Henry the 8th*, and the Yelding of certain of his Libertyes to the King for a Tyme, wherof he now praieth Reftitucion. He requireth in Effect the Government of fuch, on the other Side of *Shenyn*, as his Anceftors had; as *Okennedy*, with *Ibrine Ara*, in *Ibrine Ogonough*, and fome other in *Ormond*. He alleadgith the Palatynes of *Ormond*, and *Defmond*: And lookith for like Libertyes in *Toomond*. He praieth all the Abbey Lands, the Cuftom of the Havens, the Bounds thereof, the Gallogles, the Allowing of all Surnames within his Countrey ; and *laftlye*, that if her Majeftie would have their Lands to go by Deffent, and not after the *Irifhe* Cuftom ; then that all Freeholders may hold of him, by the fame Tenure he holdeth of her Majeftie. *Ecce Rex gloriæ* ; but you are beholden to his Lordfhip ; for my Lord of *Lecefter* telleth me, he hath offrid my Lord of *Ibrecan*, to be matchid with fome of my Lords Bludde, to affure him the Intereft of your Howfe.

This Supplicacion hath not yet had his dewe Hearing ; but it is commaunded to be written out in Articles, that the Lords may adde Codicills to every Braunch of his Peticion. So referring all other Matters to my other Letters, I humbly end. At the Court of *Otlands*, the xvth of *September*, 1577.

Your Lordfkips moft bounden,

dewring Lief,

Ed. Waterhows.

Sir Francis Walfyngham *to Sir* Henry Sydney.

My very good Lord,

I Haue received your Pacquet, fent by one *White* your Servaunt, who in his Repaire to the Courte left thefe Lettres, that were directed to your Vice-prefident in the Marches of *Wales*, wherby it is iudged, that the Counfell there are preparinge for the Men to be put in Redines. But for afmuche as her Majeftie heareth no Likelihod of the Comminge of the *Frenche*, a Staye is made of thofe Men for a Tyme, and all your other Lettres retayned, till further Order fhall be taken heere. I am forye to fee your Lordfhips Mynde wounded by heapinge one Affliction vppon an other. But as in that Cafe of your Nephewe *Harrington*, I heare litle Speache vttered, that might concerne either you, or the Gentellman, favinge that he is reported to have dealt overe careleffely in gevinge ouer muche Truft to thofe that can not have fkill of Faithe keepinge : So in the Matter of her Majefties Difpleafure, I do rather iudge the Bitternes of her Letters to have proceeded of fome Paffion for the Tyme, then of any grounded Conceipte of ill Opinion, or Diflikinge of you. For Confirmacion wherof, I hope your Lordfhip fhall fhortlie vnderftande fome Significacion and Apparaunce of her Majefties good Favor. For wee that are heere do note, that when her Highnes hath fometymes preffed the Mynde of her Subiecte with Greife, fhee hath not deferred to raife him vpp againe with gracious and favourable Dealinge ; which Experience muft ferve your Lordfhip for a Perfuafion, not to make your felfe vnapt for her Majefties Service, ether by harde Interpretacion of your Doings heere, or by the vnhappy Accidents that may fall out there.

The Arrivall of my Lord Chauncellor is dayly looked for ; but when her Majeftie was moved for Mr. *Agard*, fhee anfweared, that fhee wold not leave you fo naked of Advice, as to fpare them both at one Inftant ; fo as I wifhe my Lord Chauncellor to be the more fullye inftructed. And fithence her Majeftie cannot be brought to fuche a Charge, as is convenient to be beftowed vppon *Irelande* ; and is above all Things to regarde her Eftate heere, and the Greatnes of her Neighbours on all Syds, that nowe ftande but in ticle Termes : I

fuppofe

suppose it muſt fall out, that in Steede of Force, we muſt vſe Perſuaſion, and ſee howe farre the Lords, and the reſt of *Ireland,* may be drawen to contribute for a Tyme towards her Majeſties Charge; and accordinge thervnto, and the yearely Stipende that her Majeſtie will allote, ſo to pilote the Gouernement with the Contentacion of the Subiects, till better Opportunitye ſhalbe offred. But this I deliuer as myne owne Opinion, beinge nowe in Expectacion of that which the Lord Chauncellor ſhall bringe, which may perhapps breed another Iudgement in mee. And thus redy to further any good Deſignement, that ſhall come from you for the State, or that which I may by the Office of a Frende in your owne Perticuler, I bid your Lordſhip Farewell moſt hartelye. From the Court at *Oteland,* the xvth of *September,* 1577.

Your Lordſhips aſſured Frend,

Fra. Walſyngham.

Edward Waterhows, *Eſq; to Sir* Henry Sydney.

It maie pleaſe your Lordſhip,

SOME litell Occaſions of Diſcourteſies have paſſid betwen the Erle of Or-mond and Mr. *Phelip Sidney,* becauſe the Erle lately ſpake unto him, and he aunſwerid not, but was in dead Silens of Purpoſe, becauſe he imputith to the Erle, ſuch Practiſes as have bene made to alienat her Majeſtyes Mynd from your Lordſhip. But thes Contraverſies are I thinke at the fardeſt; for Thexpectacion of my Lord Chancellours Commyng, hath put all *Iriſhe* Cauſes to Silence, till he be herde; and Therle of *Ormond* ſaith he will accept no Quarrells from a Gentilman that is bound by Nature to defend his Fathers Cauſes; and who is otherwiſe furniſhed with ſo many Vertues, as he knowes Mr. *Phillip* to be; and on the other Side Mr. *Phillip* hath gon as farre, and ſhewid as much Magnanimity as is convenient: Unleſſe he cold charge him with eny Particularieties, which I perceive he yet cannot, other then with a generall Defence of the Countrey Cauſes, wherin all the Nacion here, as I thinke, be culpable, ſaving the Lord *Donſany,* who, for ought I hear, hath not medlid in the Matter, nor will not.

Somme Spech is ſodenly growen here, that your Lordſhip deſirith much to be diſchargid of the Governement, whereat I thinke the Miſlikers of your Cours will rejoyce. And therefore, my Lord, howſoever your Lordſhip determineth, I do not wiſhe that you ſhold apparently ſerve any ſuch Entendment, leſt it be gathered, that you ſee Impoſſibility to doe Good; but rather fortefy your Plat, and requier the Queene to back it, which if ſhe will doe, ſhe muſt reape Gaine, and you Honour: And if ſhe will not, then the Fault is not yours, and ſo in Equity you are (if you be revokid) to be revokid with Honour: And when your Enemies ſee you will not be weried with their Practiſes, they will make you a Binding of Gold, or els all com abought under your Lee, and ſeeke a Reconſiliacion. I hope you ſhall have a good Iſſue of my Lord Chancellours Travell, and Mr. *Agards,* if he com; and in the meane Seaſon, I will ſolicyt Mr. Secretary, and do the uttermoſt of my Service to your Lordſhip.

I have written to Mr. *Molineux* of ſome Particularitys, wherof I am ſure, he will enforme your Lordſhip; and ſo with myne humble Dewty I take my Leave. At the Court at *Otlands,* the 16th of *September,* 1577.

Your Lordſhips moſt bounden,

during Lief,

Ed. Waterhows.

Sir

Sir Francis Walſingham *to Sir* Henry Sydney.

My very good Lords,

ACcording to your Lordſhips long Deſier, to haue a ſufficient Man ſent to be her Majeſties Attorney Generall there, at length her Majeſtie hath reſoluid and determyned vppon this Bearer, Mr. *Snagge,* whom ſhe hath commended vnto you by her particular Lettre. And although the Diſcontinuance, by this Meanes, of his Study and Practice here, doth bring with yt many Diſcommodityes, and therfore might moue him to be ſlowe in conſenting to enter into this fruyteles Iournye, yf he had cheefe Regard to his owne Particular; yet the Dutye that he oweth to her Majeſtie and his Countrye, with th' Aſſuraunce that he conceaueth, by my Promis and otherwayes, of your Lordſhips good Fauor, doth make him leaue all other Reſpects, and willinglie to dedicat him ſelf to that Seruice; for the which I thinke him a Man ſo well choſen, both for Iudgement, and bould Spirit to countenaunce ſuch of her Majeſties Cauſes as ſhall eome to his Handling, as hardlie all the Howſes of Court could yeld his like; which maie argue vnto your Lordſhip the great Care had of your Requeſts, and of the Reducing of the State there, eſpeciallie the Revenue to be more certenlie aunſwered. For your owne Parte, I tell him that he is happye to ſerve vnder your Lordſhip, whos Fauor ſhall alwayes accompanye his Trauell in her Majeſties Cauſes, and whos Recommendacion he cannot want at the Tyme of his hoped Returne. So as he going nowe with a full Mynd to do to her Majeſtie his vttermoſt Seruice, and to do your Lordſhip Honnor, ſhall, I hope, fynd all Things to proceade from you to his full Contentacion, and to the Encouragement of others that ſhall ſucceede him; and ſo I leaue, having committed him whollie to your Fauor and Direction. At the Corte at *Oteland,* not very well enioying my Healthe, this xxjth of *September,* 1577.

Your Lordſhips aſſured Frind

to commaunde,

Fra. Walſyngham.

Edward Waterhows, *Eſq; to Sir* Henry Sydney.

It may pleaſe your Lordſhip,

I Hope Mr. *Whitten* will wright to your Lordſhip what Entertainment he hath found at the Secretaries Hands. I had rather he did it then I; but uppon the Veiw that I have had of Mr. *Whittens* Notes, I dare warrant you an honorable End of that Buſines; and I find my Lord Threaſuror very well effectid to your Cawſes. And I have optainid that at my Lord Chauncellors Coming, your Lordſhips Matters ſhall have preſent Hearing: And I think that to the *Ceſs* Rates, Mr. *Philip,* Mr. *Whitten,* and I, ſhalbe called to aſſiſt him. Before the Arrival of Mr. *Whitten,* Mr. *Philip* had gatherid a Collection of all the Articlis, which have bene enviouſly objectid to your Goverment, wherunto he hath fraimid an Anſwer in Way of Diſcours, the moſt excellently (if I have eny Judgement) that ever I red in my Lief; the Subſtance wherof is now approvid in your Letters, and Notes, by Mr. *Whitten.* But let no Man compare with Mr. *Philips* Pen. I know he will ſend it your Lordſhip, and when you read it, you ſhall have more Cauſe to praye God for him, then to impute Affection to me, in this my Opinion of him.

I humbly thank your Lordſhip for your honorable Letter, which I received by Mr. *Whitten.* It ſemith you hold the olde Opinion of me, which you ſhall never have Cauſe to change, unleſſe it be from good to better, in all Things that may torne to your Honor or Service; wherof I hope the Succeſs of your Cauſes ſhall make Demonſtration. Yet I find that I have not bene free from

envious

envious Perfecution, that have fought to make your Lordfhip conceive ieloufly
of me. For Mr. *Agard,* my beft Friend, doth in Manner charge me, with af-
fedtyng Faintnes in fpeaking my Confcience ; but God knowith my Heart, and
what Mynd I beare towards you, both as to my Mafter, and to my good Lord.
Which doble Bond might perfuade the ill difpofid ; fince I have never fhewid
my felf fearfull to honour my Friends : But to conclude, my Lord, I am not
utterly without Credit here, which I will ftretch to the uttermoft, to do you
Service. Affuring your Lordfhip, that whenfoever I fhall finde you condemne
me in your Opinion, I will give over the Worlde, and lede a moft privat and
folitary Lief. And fo humbly praing you to pardon me, I take my Leave,
oppreffid with Greif. At *Windefor* Caftell, the Laft of *September,* 1577.

Your Lordfhips moft bounden,

My Lord Treafurer, and Mr. Secretary, do
very well like of Mr. *Whitten.* I affure my felf   Ed. Waterhows.
his Comming will be to great Purpofe.

Sir Henry Sydney *to the Lords of the Council in* England.

My verye good Lords,

MY Dewtye humblye remembred to your honorable Lordfhips. Not longe
after the Departure of the Lord Chauncelor, who went hence fullye
inftrudted, as I fuppofe, in all foch Things as concerned either her Majefties
perticuler Service, or this Eftate : The firft Accydent worthye Note that hapned, was the Death of my deare Freinde, Mr. *Agarde,* whome it pleafed
God to take to his Mercye, the xjth of *Odtober,* wherebye her Majeftie hath
not onelye loft a faythfull Servaunt and good Counfellor, but the Countrie an
expert wife Man, and a rare Jewell ; and I the Want of fuch an Affiftaunt and
faythfull Freinde, as almoft (for the Service of this Countrie) a greater Loffe
could not in any Sorte have chaunced vnto me.

I touched to your Lordfhips in my Laft, of the hard Accydent that had
hapned to my Nephewe Capten *Harrington,* who fince that Tyme is delyvered,
and taken out of his Ennimies Handes, after maney Attemptes and Proffers
made by Treatie for hym, which were fpiced with that Pollecye, to allure the
Rebell better to bite at the Baite, that all Things almoft he requyred, were a-
greed vnto ; till at length, by a Draught that *Robert Harpoll* drewe, he was in-
trapped, who came to the Caben in the Woode where he lay, about twd
Howres afore Day, havinge with hym in his Companye, *Parker,* Capten
Furres Lieutenaunte, and fiftye Soldiours of that Band, befett the Place, tooke
Capten *Harrington, Alexander Cofbye,* and the reft that were Prifonners there
from hym, killed all in the Howfe, fave onelye *Rorie* hym felfe, and one
other, who by Reafon of the Darkenes of the Night, and the Gredines of the
Soldiours, eche Man to wynne Creditt, *Rorie* efcaped away, beinge once fmitten
downe (as they reported) and beinge fo niere thruft together, by Reafon of the
Narrowenes of the Place, he crept from amongeft theim into the Thickett, beinge not paft twoe Yardes of, and fo faved hym felfe from any further Daunger. In the Intervall, betwixt *Harpools* Comminge vnto the Howfe, and the
Breakinge open of the Doores vpon the Rebells, *Rorie* hearinge a foddeine
Noyce, and fufpedtinge he was betraied, put on a refolute and defperate Mynde
to do fome Mifcheife, and geffinge at the Place where Capten *Harrington* lay
(the Howfe being darcke, and without Light) gave hym in a Moment dyvers
Woundes, though none deadlye or Mayme vnto hym, fave onelye the Loffe
of his little Finger on the left Hand. In the Howfe there were found dyvers
Lettres fent from *Shane Bourcke,* and other Rebells, to *Rorie,* to animate hym
to contynue in his Rebellion, promifinge hym both Ayde of Men, and Supplye
of other Neceffaries, to kindle hym the more to perfevere in his wicked Intencions. And *Rorie,* as it fhould feme, ftill reteininge fixed in his Mynde,
what Reproche and Difcreditt he had received by Lofinge of his Prifonners in

that Sorte, privelye affemblinge his Freinds on everye Side, and havinge Ayde out of *Connaught* from *Shane Bourcke*, and Affiftaunce from fomme other of his Neighbours, who feme to carrye the Face of good Subjects, fayinge that the Cawfe of his Affemblinge of theim, was to take a Pray in the Countie of *Kildare*, came foddeinelye vnto *Caterlaugh*, the viijth Day of this prefent *November*, an Hower before Day, the Towne being large and greate, and the Walles ruined and downe in maney Places, entered and bourned moft of the thatched Howfies, fome fewe Ricks of Corne, and committed a fewe other Spoyles, without any further Harme doinge ; but retyred hym felfe, and, in his Marche away, *Robert Harpooll*, with halfe a Score of Horffemen, chardged vpon theim in the Ford, and there killed a xvij or xviij of his Men. And this is the Somme, afwell of the one Accydent as the other, howfoever the fame may be there increafed by Reporte.

Off late, the Gentlemen of the Countrey have bene earneft Sutors vnto me, to yeld fome yerelye certeine Contribucion to her Majeftie, to be freed of Ceffe, which I have accepted, beinge after the Rate of five Marke vpon the Plough Land ; which, al be it hetherto, rather for Wilfulnes (expectinge Anfwere of their Agents from thence) then vpon any Grounde of Reafon they obftinately ftode in with me ; yet remembringe howe moche the Poore were eafied, and theim felves benifited by this Compoficion, they fought the fame earneftlye at my Handes. And although the beft and apteft Seafon of the Yeare was alreadye paft for Provifion, and that moft Things were growen to higher Prifes then they were before, and they havinge fo maney Tymes refuzed all good Conformitie, yet foch is and hath bene ever my hard Dealinge with the Countrie, that I confented, for the Benifitt and Eafe of the poore Men, to accept the Offer for the five Shyres of the Pale, which the People, with humble Thankes, and great Reioyfinge, have received at my Handes, as a large Favor and Grace : Yet, nevertheleffe, if this Converfion may be brought to be vniverfall, the fame will growe to a great Increafe of Revenue to her Highnes, fufficient to wage and enterteine 300 Soldiours, without further Supplye of her Majefties Chardge, if fhe her felfe be not the Impediment. And in this Pointe I muft remember to your Lordfhips, the good Service of Sir *Nicholas Malbye*, who hath almoft reduced the whole Province of *Connaught* vnder his Chardge, to growe to Compoficion with her Majeftie, to be difbourdened of Ceffe, of whofe Travell fomme foche as her Majeftie hath freed of late, take Benifitt ; fo that where neither their Father nor Graund Father, ever received, at any Tyme heretofore, Proffitt of thofe Lands in *Connaught*, by Way of certeine and annuall Rent, nowe they receive an yerelye Benifitt of Revenue in Money, makinge their Commoditie of other Mens Travells, wherebye fo moche Revenue is pulled away from her Majeftie by their Fredomes, which otherwayes, if foch generall Fredomes had not bene graunted, would have accrewed vnto her Majefties owne Coffers, towardes the Difbourdeninge of her Chardgies in that Province ; which the Counfell there have maney Tymes touched vnto me, in their Lettres by Way of Complainte, for that her Majeftie therebye loofeth her certeine Revenue, which fhe muft otherwife fupplye out of her Coffers ; for when the Earle of *Ormounde* fhalbe freed onelye, and other Lordes bourdened (Perees as he is) they will finde theim felves grieved ; for either her Majeftie muft lofe it, or they beare it, wherein is no Equalitie. And for that Sir *Nicholas Malbye* hath, fince the Tyme he hath bene imploied in that Chardge (wherein he hath fo well deferved) fpent a farre larger Porcion then hath any Wayes bene allowed vnto hym, whereby he is growen depelye in Debt, and come moche behinde hande : I humblye befeache your Lordfhips, that afwell in Refpect of that, as in Confideracion of his good Deferte, and former Service paft, to be Interceffors to the Quene, that it would pleafe her Majeftie to beftowe vpon hym fome large Token of her Bountye and Favor, to enable hym the better hereafter to lyve, wherebye bothe he and his, may be daylye bounde with thankefull Minds, and cherefull Hartes, to ferve her Majeftie and her Pofteritie for ever. What he hath donne in his laft Iorney in *Connaught*, both with

†

Orwoorcke,

Orwoorcke, Occonnor Sligo, Odonnell, and the *Scottes,* I referre the fame to the Reporte of his owne Lettres and Difcourfe, which, as I take it, by this Paffage he fendeth vnto your Lordfhips.

And where your Lordfhips have longe looked to have fomme Certificat from the Auditor of the State of her Majefties Debtes, and of the Arreragies due to her Majeftie in this Realme; the Auditor nowe hath finifhed the Booke, whiche herewith I fend vnto your Lordfhips: And alfo I have cawfed hym to make Certificate afwell of the Threafure fent from thence for theife twoe Yeares paft, as of the State of the Revenue here, howe the fame hath bene iffued and expended by my Direccion; wherevpon I am to crave of your Lordfhip to geve Order that foch Money as is due vnto my felfe, as Money layed out by me for the Savinge of her Majefties growinge Chardgies, for Things due before my laft Acceptacion of this Governement, that the fame may be prefently paied, which, by your Lordfhips Lettre of the Date of the   of *Marche,* 1576. I was put in Comforte long erre this it fhould have bene: And fuerlye, the Want thereof hath, in the meane Tyme, bene a heavye Burthen vnto me, which I effectuallye pray youer Lordfhips to confider of.

I have apointed for Extirpinge of the Rebell *Rorie Oge,* and the *Occonnores* and *Omores,* his Confederates, a generall Hoftinge, to begin the Firft of the next Moneth, and hope, on all Sides, fo to hedge theim in, as fomme one or other of the Companye (in foch Streigthes as I fhall apointe theim to lye) fhall light upon theim. And although I have to deale with a flyenge Foe, and one that dare not abyde my Comminge, to fhewe hym felfe in the Field; yet fo maney Starting Holes and Muffetts he hath to fly vnto, and foch Ayde and Succor of fomme of his Neighbours, as I fhall not fo eafilye light vpon hym, but onelye by good Guydinge; yet fomme of his beft and principall Followers I daylye cut of, and pare his Winges by little and little as I can; for I will neither fpare Travell nor Chardgies to make fome good Ende of this Service, and to fettle her Majeftie in the quiett Poffeffion of thofe two Countries, *Leix* and *Offalye;* I meane, by the totall Extirpacion of thofe Rebells, which have coft the Crowne of *Englande,* I fuppofe, from the firft to the laft, at leaft twoe hundered thowfand Poundes.

The Bills of Parliament are nowe in a Readynes to be fent away by the next Paffadge. Mr. *Snagge,* nowe her Majefties Attorney here, hath taken fomme Paynes to confider of theim: I fynd hym a Man well learned, fufficient, ftoute and well fpoken, an Inftrument of good Service for her Majeftie, and foch a one as is carefull to redreffe by Wifdome, and good Difcreacion, foch Errors as he fyndeth in her Majefties Courts here. So that by his Prefence I finde my felfe well affifted, and humblye thanke your Lordfhips for the Sendinge of hym vnto me, and more of his Sorte are nedefull, which, I hope, your Lordfhips will not forgett when Tyme ferveth to fend. And even fo I humblye take my Leave of your good Lordfhips. From the Caftell of *Dublin,* the xxvjth of *November,* 1577.

Your honorable Lordfhips affured loving Freinde

humblye to commaund,

H. Sydney.

Sir Henry Sydney *to Queen* Elizabeth.

May it pleafe your moft excellent Maieftie,

I, With the Affiftaunce of your Majefties Counfell here, have of late had fomme Confideracion amongeft oure felves of fomme Lawes to be devifed, neceffarie to paffe here at the next Parliament, for the Good and Benifitt of this rude Countrie, whereof I (though vnworthy) next to your Maieftie, have the principall Chardge; and for that Purpofe have cawfed certeine beneficiall

and

and neceſſarie Bills to be drawen ; and as the Manner and Vſage of this State is, have willed the ſame to be put vnder your Great Seale here, and by youer Chauncellor (to whome I have thought good to ſende theim) to be preferred and preſented by him vnto your ſacred Majeſtie, beſeachinge your Majeſties good Allowaunce of theim, and that they may be with convenient Spede retorned agayne, with Commiſſion vnder your Highnes Great Seale there vnto me, to the Ende that at the next Parliament they may be enacted and eſtabliſhed for Lawes : They wilbe, moſt gracious Sovereigne, I hope, beneficiall for youer Realme and Subiects, honorable and profitable for youer ſelfe, and an Increaſe of Revenue to youer Crowne. And therefore I moſt humblye beſeach your Majeſtie, that after the ſaied Billes ſhalbe conſidered of, and gratiouſle allowed by your Highnes, they may, together with your Chauncellor (whoſe Preſence here for your Majeſties Service, and the good Eaſe of your Highnes Subiects, may ill be ſpared longe) be ſpeadilye retorned hither.

Your gratious Lettre of the Laſt of *October*, I received the vth of this preſent *December*, moſt comfortable to me, and your Counſell here, that it hath pleaſed your Majeſty ſo juditiouſlye, gravelye, wiſelye, carefullye, and gratiouſlye, to proceade in theiſe Cawſes of Complainte againſt me, your Counſell, and Governement here, in cawſinge thoſe Matters (ſlaunderouſlye, and impudentlye, reported to your Majeſty for Trothes) to be ſo duelye examined, thoroughlye hard, and after ſo gravelye ſentenzed ; for this Courſe of ſo gratious, honnorable, and iuſt Proceadinge, will make your Highnes to be both better loved and feared, your Prerogatyve regarded, your Commoditie increaſed, your Lawes better obſerved ; and me your Officer, and the reſt of your Counſell here, with better Duetye, in ſoch Things as we ſhall directe (for the Advauncement of your Majeſties Service) obeyed. That Courſe your Majeſtie hath ſett downe and preſcribed for my Direccion, to proceade with the Offendors, ſhalbe followed : How be it (by reaſon that I am nowe ſettinge forwarde in Iorney againſt the Rebell *Rorie Ogie*, and his Confederates the *Omores*, and *Occonnors*, who contynue and increaſe in their wicked Inſolencies and Lewdnes) ſomme of thoſe Gentlemen, before the Receipt of your Highnes Lettre, I had apointed to attend vpon me this Jorney ; and ſomme of the reſt (beinge of the beſt Sorte) I had ordered to kepe and defend the Countrey in myne Abſence : So that I cannot convenientlye deale with any of theim, before my Retorne, and this Iorney ended ; at which Tyme, God willinge, I meane to proceade with theim, in Sorte as your Majeſtie hath commaunded. And I doubt not, but the iuſt Proceadinge with theim, wilbe ſoch an Example, to the reſt, that feele in Conceipt, that they theim ſelves are to be touched with the like Fault, by conſentinge with the reſt, in thoſe Accuſacions and vntrewe Reportes (at which yet it ſeameth ſomme of theim bluſhe not, though there be iuſt Cawſe why) that both they and their Sequell, will ever hereafter more duetifullye and obedientlye feare and reverence you, and youer Authoritie here. And this is all that for the preſent I can anſwere to your Majeſties moſt gratious and comfortable Lettre ; for the which lowlye, upon my Knes, I render vnto your Highnes my moſt humble Thanks.

And whereas your Majeſties Servaunt, Mr. *Edward Waterhowſe*, havinge Pencion here for Tearme of Lyfe, hath bene of late, and yet is imployed there in your Maieſties Affayres, and is not tyed to any Attendaunce in this Realme, by any ordenarie Office or Place here, but compelled by an Infirmitie of the Stone to reſorte maney Tymes for Phiſicke into *England* : It may pleaſe your Majeſtie to graunte vnto hym your gratious Lettres for his Warraunt of Abſence abſolutelye, wherebye I am perſwaded your Majeſtie may imploy his Service there, to as good Purpoſe as here, though in both, in myne Opinion, he may be profitablye vſed. And even ſo beſeachinge the Almightie to bleſſe your Majeſtie, to the Comforte of your ſaythfull Subjects, with a

long

long and moſt happie Raigne over vs, I moſt humblye take my Leave. From the Caſtell of *Dublin*, the xith of *December*, 1577.

Your Maieſties moſt faythfull bounden

Subieċt and Servaunt,

H. Sydney.

Mr. *Secretary* Walſyngham *to* Sir Henry Sydney.

My very good Lord,

I Haue receauid Commaundement this Daye from her Majeſtie, to admoniſhe you of ſuch Advertiſments as her Highnes vnderſtandeth, both out of *Fraunce* and *Portugall*; namelie, that the trayterous Deſines of *James Fitzmorrice* are agayn reviued; and, as yt is thought, ſo farre hath his Perſwaſion prevayled with other Princes, as yt is very likely that ſomewhat ſhall ſhortlie be attempted in *Ireland* by forreygn Invaſion. And becauſe, by all Conieċture, ſome Praċtiſe is like to be firſt in *Mounſter*, for Strengthening of the Confederats, her Majeſties Pleaſure is, that both you and the Lord Preſident there (as admoniſhed ſecretly from you) haue an Eye vnto yt, howe beſt to meete with thes Praċtiſers, eſpecially if *James* ſhould land in privat Manner, for Conference with *Deſmond*, or any other, as yt may faule out, becauſe he is (as you may perceaue by th'incloaſed Aduertiſments) on the Seas; vppon which Manner of privat Landing, yt is thought that ſome Perſons in *Mounſter*, to be well choſen for that Purpos, might, for a good Reward, be wonne ether to ſlaye or intrappe him, and ſo to diſapoint the whole Enterpriſe. And albeyt her Majeſtie, vppon any perfeċt Reporte, and aſſured Likelyhood, of a forceable Landing of Straungers, will give Order to haue Men put in a Readines to be ſent from hence to the Reliefe of her Subieċts; and is alſo of Opinion, that you may ſo order her Forces there as may kepe the Invaders from doing any great Hurte till that Reliefe come from hence; whereof her Highnes is not voyde of provydent Care: Yet leaſt other Princes, her Neighbours, may take Pleaſure, by Rumors, to put her to Chardge, as vppon like Bruites raiſed heretofore, they haue latelie don, ſhe forbeareth to enter into any preſent chargeable Preparacion; till ſhe ſeeth more Apparaunce of the Euill intendid; hoping, that your Lordſhips Vigilancy may prevent any Daihger to that State, with ſeaſonnable Intelligence to be geven to her from thence: And, in the meane While, yt weare good your Lordſhip had a ſpeciall Eye to the Cittie of *Limerick*; leaſt yt ſhould vppon the ſoddeyn be ſurpriſed, being a Place of greateſt Importaunce, both for Strength, Scituacion, and the Commoditye of the Haven. And this being the Subſtaunce of all that I haue at this Tyme to ſaie, I referre yt to your Lordſhips good Conſideracion and Wiſdom; and ſo do commit you to the Lord. At *Hampton* Courte, the xviiith of *January*, 1577.

Your Lordſhips aſſurid Frind,

Fra. Walſyngham.

The incloſed Adviſes I have received.

By *Lettres from* Liſbona, *of the* xth *of* December.

J A M E S *Fitzmorice* came to this Courte from *Rome* in *June* laſt, and had Acceſſe vnto the King, but receauid no great Countenaunce of him in outward Shewe; he departed from hence the xvijth of the laſt, with an *Iriſh* Frier, latelie made Buſhop in *Spaine*, in a *French* Shippe of three ſcore and tenne Tunnes, and caryed with him one hundreth Souldiers well appointed, beſides two hundreth ſpare Harquebuſes, with their Furniture and other Municions;

nicions; he pretended to go to *Morlais*, in *Britanny*, to fetche his Wyfe from thence, but we are in Truth advertifed that he is gon into *Ireland.*

There is a Brute fpread, that *Stukelie* fhould be come hether, and that he doth as yet keepe him felf cloafe.

This King maketh great Preparacions by Sea, and fome do thinke yt is for fome Enterprife to be made in *Africa*, but the Certentie of his intended Purpos is not yet knowen.

Paris, 8 Jan. 1577.

YT is confirmed vnto me of euerye Syde, that *Strozzy La Roche*, *Lanfarq*, *Langreau*, and others, proceede in theire Preparacions of Men, Shipps, and Municions, with Pretence to go to the *Weft Indes*, or (as fome faye) to *Molind* in *Affrique*, but in deed to make fome Attempt vppon *Irelande,* as others of good Iudgment do imagine; to which Purpofe they are faide to haue fecreat Intelligence, afwell with *Fitzmorice*, as with the Earle of *Weftmorlande*, or els to be in Readines againft the Openinge of the Warre in this Realme, and then to make fome Exploict againft *Rochell*, and the Ifle of *Reth*. *La Roche* is a *Guyfarde*, and a Man of no Habilitie to beare the Chardge of any great Enterpryfe, and yet he makethe Accoumpt to beftowe in thefe Preparacions 200000 Francks, which may feeme to proue that this Iorney is furthered by fome great Perfonages.

Sir Francis Walfyngham *to Sir* Henry Sydney.

My verry good Lord,

HER Majeftye uppon the fyrft Knowledge, howe fare your Lordfhip had exceaded the Proportion agreed on, was greatly moved withall; not withowt fome Offence ageynft thos that were Fortherers of you unto that Place you nowe hould. Somewhat fhe is appeafed, notwithftanding in Refpect of the Charges, which fhe is perfwaded wyll not be leffened under your Governement, I fynde her dyfpofed to revoke you, whereof I thowght good to geve your Lordfhipp fomme fecret Notyce: Yt is meant, that the Cullor of your Revocatyon fhall be to confer abowt fomme Plotte for the Deminifhing the fayd Charges, and to fatisfye her, towching the Exceeding of the Proportion allotted unto you. Your Frends here are not unmyndfull, afwell for her owne Servyce, as for your Credyt, to fhewe her Majeftye howe neceffarye yt is for her to caule you Home, with fome Marke of her Favor; eyther by Nobylytatyon, or Grawnting your Sute, or bothe; wherin my Fellowe, Mr. Secretary *Wylfon*, hath dealt moft frendely towardes your Lordfhip. What will be the Yffue, though I dare not put you into two good Hope; for that we are fubject to change; yet I truft ther wyll be fomewhat don to your Contentement. The Warrant for the xvi *l.* I truft to get dyfpathed owt of Hande.

Within a Daye, or twayne, we meane to dyfpathe hence towardes your Lordfhip, her Majeftyes full Intentyon, towchyng the Eafyng of that Cuntrey of *Ceffe*, *Barnell*, and *Nettarvyll*. And fo in the meane Tyme I commyt you to Gods good Protection. At *Hampton* Coorte, the 20th of *Januarye*, 1577.

Your Lordfhips affured Frend,

Fra. Walfyngham.

Mr. Secretary Walfyngham *to Sir* Henry Sydney.

After my hartye Commendacions,

HER Majeftie having feen the Bookes of your Accompts you latelie fent over, refteth fome what better fatisfied in that Behalfe then heretofore fhe hath ben, though fhe do partlie find it ftrainge, that the Chardges of that Realm fhould

fhould this Yeare haue fo muche exceeded the ordinary Proporcion allowed for the fame. You maye do well, with as much Expedicion as you can, to perfect the Refidue of your Accompts yet vnfinifhed, and to fend the fame hether, for the better Satisfaction both of her Majeftie, and fome others, that thinke you do of purpos vfe Delayes in the Matter, to prolonge the Beneffit of your Enterteynement; and thus I bid you hartelie Farewell. From *Hampton* Courte, the 21th of *January,* 1577.

Your loving Frind,

Fra. Walfyngham.

Mr. Secretary Walfyngham *to Sir* Henry Sydney.

My verie good Lord,

BY Reafon of the Care and Bufineffe that prefently occupiethe vs here, throughe the late ill Accident in the *Lowe Contries,* whereof wee receaved Aduertifement but this Mornyng, I can not write vnto you fo at Length as otherwife I would: And therefore defyre your Lordfhip to accept in good Part theife fewe Lynes, wherby I referre you to this Bearer, Mr. *Waterhowfe,* whoe fhall, and is able to enforme you throughly, bothe of the fayd Accident, and of all others, bothe forayne and domefticall Matters. And fo moft hartely commendyng your Lordfhip to God, I take my Leave. *Hampton* Court, the Fourthe of *Februarye,* 1577.

Your Lordfhips verie loving and

affured Frend to commaund,

Fra. Walfyngham.

Sir Henry Sydney *to Queen* Elizabeth.

May it pleafe your moft excellent Majeftie,

NOT longe after the Retorne from my Iorney made vpon the Rebells, the *Omores* and *Occonnors;* whereof I have written at fome Length to the Lords, to be reported by theim, when it fhall beft like to your Highnes. I firft, according to the Direccion of your gratious Lettres, bearinge Date at *Windfor* the Laft of *October,* fent for *Barnabie Scurlocke,* and laied before hym your Majefties grave Senfure vpon hym and his Companions, and declared that your Majeftie had nowe, vpon the Difclofinge of the Matter before you, by your Highnes Chauncellor, and their Vntrothes, Difguyfings, and flaunderous Reportes, by good Matter and dewe Proffe by hym overthrowen, converted your princely Compaffion into a trewe Iudgement, and therefore had fett downe Order for his Punifhment. He feamed at the Beginninge fomewhat more for his Reputacions Sake, then vpon any good Matter he had to produce, to iuftifie hym felfe, and would have vfed fome Perfwafion, that his Intencion and Meaninge was not to attempt any Matter againft the State and Governement, but onelye to fhewe to your Majeftie, by humble Peticion, the Countries Greives, which were fo bourdenous vnto theim (as he faied) as they could no longer indure theim. He was anfwered at full to all that he could fay, and fharply reprehended for his Fault, Follye, and Prefumpcion, and fo in fyne, committed to the Caftell of *Dublin.* Within fewe Dayes after his Committment, the Lords and Gentlemen of the Pale, both foch of theim as had formerly at the Affemblye of the Ceffe laft agreed vpon, publikelye refuzed to fubfcribe to the fame, as accuftomablye heretofore at other Tymes they had donne, as other principall Perfons and Men of Note, foch as were before committed by me for the Impugninge of the Ceffe, were fommoned to apeare before me and your Counfell; and, when they came, after fome Admonicion geven theim of their former Faultes, and put in Minde of their Dueties, they were demaunded whether they were of the fame Mynde they were

of

of before, or noe ; which was, whether it was againſt your Majeſties Lawes, and the auntient Vſage of this Realme, in Cafes of Neceſſitie, to impoſe a Ceſſe and Contribucion for the Victuallinge of your Garriſon, and your Deputies Howſehold, without Callinge of a Parliament, or graund Counſell ; and, if they were not, whether they could be contented to ſubſcribe to a Submiſſion and Acknowledgement of their Fault, and in Writinge to allowe of the Ceſſe, and of the Cuſtome vſed in that Behalfe. To which Demaund they would not make any direct Anſwere, vſinge maney Excuſes, and Evaſions ; but relyenge moſt vpon this Pointe, that they had their Agents in *England* with your Majeſtie, from whome they expected Anſwere. And my Lord of *Delvin*, who was their Mouth, carried the Matter in ſoch doubtfull Tearmes, as he would ſtill leave the Ceſſe as a Matter of Debate, and Queſtion. It was told him, that the Matter was not nowe any more in Queſtion, but growen to a perfect Reſolucion, and iudged by your Majeſties moſt wiſe and grave Senſure, as they ſhould perceive by your Majeſties Lettre, which was read vnto theim. In the Ende, after longe Debate, they deſiered Reſpitt of Tyme to conſider of the Matter for iij or iiij Dayes, expectinge (as it ſhould ſeame) Newes from their Agents thence in the meane Tyme, for that the Wynd ſerved well for ſoch a Paſſage. I told theim, it was a ſpeciall Pointe of Favor to geve theim that Scope of Lybertie, and therefore I would be adviſed ; and that Afternone, at ij of the Clocke, I would tell theim howe longe Reſpitt I would geve theim. So at oure Metinge, when they were before me, I aſked theim what Mynde then they were of, for I had reſolved to geve theim no further Tyme of Breathinge ; if they would ſubmitt, ſay ſo ; if they would not, tell me their Mynds flatly, and then I would proceade accordingly. When they ſawe that that Courſe was held on with theim, they promiſed the Morrowe after to ſubmitt, which Reſpitt of Tyme was geven theim. In the Morninge, they delyvered in a Submiſſion, ſubſcribed with all their Hands (the Copie whereof I hearewith ſend to your Majeſtie) which beinge miſlyked by me, and your Counſell here, I told theim the Defects I found in it, and ſhewed theim, if they would make no other but that, it was not ſoch a Satisfaccion as your Majeſtie loked for at their Handes ; nor I knewe not howe (in the Diſchardge of my Duetie to your Majeſtie) I could accept or allowe of. They ſaied they could make no other. I told theim your Majeſties Attorney ſhould frame theim an other, and a-pointed theim to comme to hym the next Day in the Morninge, at vij of the Clocke : At what Tyme the Baron of *Delvin* came vnto hym, and his Vnckle *Nicolas Nugent*, the ſecond Baron of your *Eſchequer*, vpon whome moſt of the reſt ſeamed to depend ; and there, after they had viewed and reviewed, the Forme the Attorney had drawen, they deſiered to have it with theim, to conſider of it with better Adviſe, which was yelded vnto ; and after they had a full Day and a Night debated the Matter amongeſt theim ſelves, they brought it agayne vnto hym, and framed an other of their owne (the Copie whereof I likewiſe herewith ſend to your Majeſtie) which beinge alſo miſlyked of, they were moved to ſubſcribe to that, which the Attorney had drawen, which was tempered in ſo good Woordes, and myld Tearmes (as your Majeſties Meaninge and Direccion reverently obſerved) their was nothinge conteined neither in Woorde nor Subſtance of Matter, but that every duetifull Subiect ought to ſubſcribe vnto, if he would not ſtand in Tearmes with his Prince, and be carried and led away, more by wilfull Paſſion, than Ground of good Reaſon. That notwithſtandinge they ſtode in flat Tearmes of Refuzall to ſubſcribe vnto it, alleadginge that they had good Cawſe that moved theim ſo to doe : When they were demaunded what it was, they ſaied that they had received Intelligence from their Agents, that they were vpon an Agrement and Compoſicion with your Majeſtie, and deſiered their Aſſents and Hands thereunto ; and therefore loth they would be to do a Thinge that ſhould be ſo preiudiciall to theim ſelves and their Poſteritie, beinge fore warned before what was donne there. I proteſted vnto theim (as in Troth I might) that I had received no ſoch Advertizements, and therefore willed theim not to deceive theim ſelves : How be it,

it, they ftill infifted in their obftinate Wilfulnes. I gave theim Refpitt till the
next Morninge to be advifed, and willed them not to engreive one Fault with
an other, and fo to provoke your Majefties iuft Indignacion towards theim,
who was fo well inclyned to do theim Good ; which, if they did, the Bourthen
would be to heavye for theim to beare. I dealt with theim together, and
likewife dealt with theim feverally aparte ; firft with the meaner, then with
the better Sorte ; with the Learned by theim felves, and the Simple by theim
felves ; but all were framed to one Bent. The moft Parte of their Anfweres
was, what the Lords would do, they would followe ; they were but Inferiors,
and therefore they would do as their Betters did : They ftoode moft vpon my
Lord of *Delvin*, who feamed to be the cheife Ring Leader. When I fawe they
were fo vntractable, that neither faire Meanes, nor Perfwafions, nor fharpe
Speache, nor Threats, could wynne theim to do that becamme theim : And
that *Miffett, Flemminge*, and *Barnaby Scurlock*, one of their principall Agents,
had fubfcribed the Submiffion (the Doubble whereof I hearewith fend to your
Majeftie) I, by the Advife of your Majefties Counfell here, thought good to
committ theim till your Majefties Pleafure were further knowen ; and, within
a Day, or Day after, called theim before vs agayne, and, for Examples Sake,
and the greater Terror to others hereafter, impofed Fynes vpon eche of theim :
The cheifeft of theim, and thofe that in dede feme moft wilfully bent to refift
the Ceffe, have received Benifitt from your Highnes and your Crowne ; and one
of theim is of your Fee at this Day, which was told theim by your Attorney ;
who, afwell in this, as in any Thinge els, that either is incydent to his Place,
or concerneth your Majeftie in Honnor or Proffitt, is a good Inftrument, and
a dilligent, carefull, and readye Man. His Affiftaunce is a great Ayde vnto me,
in any Thinge that apperteineth to youer Service, or his Profeffion.

I feare, Maddame, I have bene in this Pointe over tedious to your Majeftie ;
but I humbly pray Pardon, for that fo longe a Matter cannot be delyvered in
fewe Woordes, nor the Thinge well conceived, but by Declaracion of fome
Circumftance, which I have in as fewe conteined as I could. There refteth yet
vntold fomewhat concerninge myne owne Perticuler, whereunto I muft humbly crave your Majeftie to enclyne a gratious Eare : The Matter is, moft revered
Sovereigne, that I heare (not a little to my Greife and great Difcomforte) that
your Highnes hath denied to figne your Warraunt, for the Payment of three
Thowfand and one Pounde, that is dewe vnto me vpon certeine Bills ; fuppofinge that thofe Bills were gayned by me, or, at the leaft, very eafely come
by, and procured. I am forry (my moft dere Sovereigne) that my hard Happ
is foch, fo to be condempned without Cawfe, or fufpected without Deferte ;
and for Tryall of the Troth, would to God it whuld pleafe your Majeftie, to
apointe Commiffioners, or fomme others of Truft, to examyne the Matter, and
reporte what they fynde to youer Highnes : It would then plainely and trewly appeare vnto you, that I have bene mifreported to your Majeftie, for that
I have never a Bill, for the which my Specialty lieth not, and I indebted for ;
and God knoweth, that all that I gayne, is but Tyme ; for I dewly pay for
every Bill, and none comme to me frelye without Payment : And thofe Bills I
fought onelye, not to enriche my felfe (as fome that envie me feme to geve
forth) but (without my to great Loffe) to inable me the better to pay my
Lord of *Penbroke* the Mariage Money I ought hym for my Daughter ; which
Bills, amount but to one Pounde more then the Money I have, and muft pay
hym. And moft facred Sovereigne, that Things fhould be taken in that Senfe,
or fo hardly conftrued againft me by your Majeftie, is no fmall Greife and Torment of my Mynde vnto me, which cannot be removed from me, before in
my rightfull Cawfe, I be cleared in your Majefties Conceipt and thought of,
as I deferve for my Service.

An other Matter I hear of likewife, which is an equall Greife vnto me with
the firft, and that is, that youer Highnes hath refuzed to graunte me the Fee
Ferme of thofe fmall Things I my felfe have an Eftate of for maney more
Yeares (for fome of thofe Percells I fue for) then I am by Courfe of Nature

likely to lyve : So that for myne owne Tyme, there can growe no further Co-moditie vnto me by the havinge of theim, then I have alreadye : How be it, I had a Defier in that Sute, to have donne fomewhat for my Children and Pofte-ritie ; but I fhall leave theim to the World to provide for theim felves as they can, and content my felfe (fince it fo liketh your Majeftie) with that my Father left me, and fubmitt my felfe to your Majefties gratious Mifericord, for I am not to ftand in Tearmes with your Highnes in any Thinge, but with all Hu-militie, fubiect my felfe, and all my Cawfies, to your princely Pleafure and Will, as fhalbe moft agreable to your felfe.

And, moft gratious Sovereigne, one other Matter there is, which moft of all importeth me at this Tyme, and that is, that the laft Yeare, by Reafon of the frequent Reportes and Bruites fo maney Wayes confirmed vnto me, and from fo maney dyvers Places brought, and from thence likewife fignified vnto me by maney Lettres from fomme of your Majefties honorable Privey Counfell, of the Intencion and Practize of that Archrebell *James Fitzmorrice*, to bringe in forreine Power to invade this your Realme, I was neceffarily forced, both for better Safety of your Realme, and Honnor of your State, to prevent all daungerous Occafions and Events that might in fo broken a Tyme have hapned to enterteine moe Bands and Companies, and a greater Force both of Horffemen and Fotemen, then otherwife I would have donne ; to make Fortificacion in fondrie Places, to wage Spiall both Abroade and at Home, to have in Hold Marriners and Sea Men, and to imploy other extraordenarie Chardgies, which might well have bene fpared, if this Accydent had not bene ; but fince it is fo, that in your High-nes Service this hath bene iffued and fpent, and could not in Honnor or good Pollecye have bene faved in your Cofers : And that by this Occafion onely, my fecond Yeares Chardgies have farre furmounted my former Yeares Expenfe (as I feare, contrarie to your Majefties Expectacion) that it would therefore pleafe your Majeftie to way the Cawfe, and the Neceffitie that moved the fame ; accordinglye, and gratiouflye to confider of my humble Peticion for Allowaunce of foche Sommes of Money, as fo have bene expended, which, in Qualitie and Kinde (if it fhall like your Majeftie to viewe theim) fhall appeare vnto your Highnes by the Accompt laft fent over by your Auditor, and delyvered to the Lords of your honorable Privey Counfell ; wherein, and in all I have befids (moveable and vn-moveable Goodes or Landes, proftrate at your facred Fete) I fubmitt my felfe to your Majefties Mifericorde, to take what you will. And withall, in all Hu-militie, put you in Remembraunce, that when your Majeftie fhall enter into Confideracion howe moch I have in yearly Rent and Commoditie encreafed your Revenue, and what great Likelyhoodes and good Teftimonies there be of the daylie Increafe of more, and Augmentacion of youer Proffitt, the Purchafe is not diere, nor the Chardges greate, in Refpecte of foche a Benifitt. And even fo befeaching the Almightie, longe and haply to contynue youre moft godly and profperous Reigne over vs, youer moft happie Subiects, vnder fo vertuous and bleffed a Sovereigne, I ende. From your Majefties Caftell of *Dublin*, the xiijth of *Februarye*, 1578.

Your Majefties moft bounden humble

Subiect and Servaunt,

H. Sydney.

Thomas *Earl of* Ormonds *Demand againft* Terrelagh Mac Brien.

To the Right Honorable the Lord Deputie,

SHEWETH to your honorable good Lordfhip, *Thomas* Earle of *Ormond* and *Offerie*, that wheare he was feifed, as of his lawfull Inheritaunce of the Cantred Landes and Territorie of *Arrae*, the Certaintie and certaine Name of the Landes whereof appeareth herevnder written ; and that by meane Con-veighaunce from King *Henry the Second*, ones King of *England*, and Conqueror

of

of this Realme, to certaine Perſons which lawfullie conveighed the ſame, emongeſt other Parcells to the ſaid Earles Aunceſtours, whoſe Heire he is; which accordinglie enioyed the ſame, and died ſucceſſively ſeiſed, thone after thother, of the ſaid *Arrae*; diſpoſing, entayling, and otherwiſe conveighing, occupying, vſing and enioying the ſame, as their other Lands, Freholds, and Inheritances. So it is, Right Honorable, that one *Tirrelagh O Brien*, of *Caſtleton*, Gent. of his mere Wrong, clayming Intreſt in the ſaid Cantred and Landes, as eldeſt of his Blood, dwelling within the ſaid Territorie; and by Vſurpacion vſed by certaine of the *Mac Briens* of the ſaid Countrie, in the Tyme of Civill Warres and Diſcenſion in *England* and *Ireland*, have diſſeiſed your Suppliant of the ſaid Cantred Territorie and Lands, contrarie to all Right and Equitie. The Premiſſes conſidered, may it pleaſe your Honnor to compell the ſaid *Tirrelagh*, (being preſent within the Citie of *Limericke*) to mak inde-layd Aunſwer therevnto; and your ſaid Suppliant ſhall pray, *&c.*

> *Pullice, Caſtelton, Bealenahe, Knockannenen, Caſtelgeard, Moneroo, Oghell, Carrigtogher, Crennagh, Coneboy, Ballyee, Kilcolman, Carrig-maden, Curriggeal, Boreſtleboy, Kilkrenan, Dirre, Currigweler, Dromon*, with all other Townes and Lands, with their Appurtenances in *Arrae*.

Apud Lymeric xiiiith Februarii, 1577.

Day is geven peremptorie to *Mac Brien*, to anſwere to this Bill, before the vith Day of the next *Eaſter* Terme: And lykewiſe to the Plantif to amend his Bill, in the meane Time, if he think ſo convenient.

H. Sydney.

Edmund Molyneux *to the Archbiſhop of* Dublin, *with his Anſwer.*

My verie good Lord,

BECAWSE I am deſirows in this Matter for the Chancellorſhippe, to deale for that which appertainethe to my ſelf, ſimpellie, plainly, and na-kedlie, and to avoid (as niere as I cowld) either Condempnacion, or Suſpect on either Side, carienge an equall Frendſhippe to yow bothe. At my Returne Home Yeſterday, I cawſed all my Preſidents and Formes of Preſentacions to be reviewed, and finde moſt of them to have theſe Words: *Reverendiſſimo in Chriſto Patri ac Domino Adamo miſeratione Divina, Dublinienſi Archiepiſcopo, Hibernieque Primati, ac Cuſtodi magni Sigilli noſtri, Regni noſtri Hibernie, ſive ejus in abſentia Vicario ſuo in Spiritualibus Generali, aut Officiali principali, ſeu cuicumque alteri Judici in hac parte, poteſtatem & auƈthoritatem ſufficientem habenti ſalutem.*

And, my Lord, becawſe I find this a commen Forme, and (as I take it) doithe neither hinder nor further the Right and Titell on either Side, being of no greater Effeƈt and Efficacie, indeed, then the Law withowt them doithe geve to every Man: I thowght it good to acquaint yowr Lordſhip with all, before I inſert the Wordes in the *Fiant*; becawſe lothe I wold be in any Sorte to geve yowr Lordſhip the leaſt Occaſion of Offence; and yet, as niere as I cowld, to provide for mine owne Saffetie. And even ſo prainge your Lordſhips Anſwere, I humbly take my Leave. From the Caſtell of *Dublin* the xvith of *Februarye*, 1577.

> *Your good Lordſhips aſſured to*
>
> *commaunde,*
>
> Edm. Molyneux.

P. S. The Diſpatche of the *Fiant* from me ſtandethe only upon yowr Lord-ſhips Aunſwere; otherwaiſe it is preſſed to be ſent away, and browght to your Lordſhip to the Seale.

Good Mr. *Mollineux,* Let the Words be only to me, and to my Officers, for fo Mr. Attorney thowght meete, and yowrfelfe affented to the fame Yefterday.

Adam Dublin.

Sir Francis Walfyngham *to Sir* Henry Sydney.

My very good Lord,

THE cheefeft Caufis why her Maieftie at this prefent hath fent for you to come to her Prefence, are two ; as you may perceave by her Heighnes Letters; thone that fhe defireth to conferre with your Lordfhip, by the removing of the Greefes and eafing the Burthens, whereof the Subiects of that Countrye do complayne ; and thother, that marveylinge very much, and finding great Faulte that, contrary to her owne Expectacion, and the Hope fhe was put into by others, the ordinary Chardges of that Realme are nothing diminifhed ; her Heighnes would underftand from your owne Mouth the Caufe wheruppon the fame doth growe ; being borne in Hand by fome here, who haue fet downe a Plotte of the Matter, that the Realm of *Ireland* may be peaceablie governed, all Occafions of Greefes and Mifcontentement remouid, and Thinconvenience of forrein Practifes met withall, with half the Chardge your Lordfhip doth demaund, as at your Comming hether you may perceave more at large.

The Warraunt for your Quarterage Monney I haue mouid her Majeftie for, but as yet can get no Aunfwer therein. This is as much as I haue to fay vnto your Lordfhip at this prefent. And fo I commit you to God. From *London* the xxviith of *February,* 1577.

Your Lordfhips affured Frind,

Fra. Walfyngham.

By the Reafon of my Abfence, your Lordfhips Letters dyrected to her Majeftie, were delyvered by my Fellowe, Mr. Secretarye *Wylfon* ; and therfor I can not let you underftande, how her Majeftie was moved to have Confyderatyon of your Greaves conteyned in your fayd Letters. Affure your felfe, that there hathe not lacked earneft Sollycytatyon by your Frendes, to have drawne her to have yelded fomme Satysfactyon; but the Tyme is harde, and was never more owt of Seafon. And therefor, withowt your Lordfhips owne Sollycytation, no Good wyll be don. Yet fometymes, when I have layde before her your Decaye of Lyvelyhood, by the Burden of her Servyce, her Highnefs hathe ben moved to Commyferatyon, thowghe the Affects thereof cood not take Place. It is not yet refolved whoe fhall fuccede you : The Speeche goethe of the Lord *Graye*; but untyll her Majeftie hath Conference with your Lordfhip, I fee fhe wyll growe to no Refolutyon.

Sir Henry Sydney *to the Lords of the Council in* England.

MY humble Dewtie remembred to your honorable Lordfhips. After I had made my laft Difpatche, and fent away the Billes for Parliament Cawfies to her Majeftie (whereof I befeach your Lordfhips there may be fpedie Retorne) and taken Order for the better Setlinge of the *Birns,* and *Tooles,* my Neighbours at Home ; I made my Repaier prefentlye to the Borders of the *Kinge* and *Quenes* Counties, to mete with the Infolencie of the Rebells, the *Occonnors* and *Omores,* who were, fince the Takinge of Capten *Harrington,* fo increafed both in Streintgh and Pryde, and growen to foch vnduetifull Tearmes, as they were not any longer for the Honnor and Creditt of the State to be indured ; but either by Devife or Force to be forthwith fuppreffed : For which Purpofe, I affembled Parte of the Ryfinge out, apointed for the generall Hoftinge, which, from the Beginninge of *June* laft, had bene from Tyme to Tyme differred, and not diffolved ; devidinge the fame into three Partes, ech

I   to to ferve their Torne for fortie Dayes, to contynue the Iorney the longer, if Occafion fo requyered : And likewife fent for *Nicolas Bagnall*, the Marfhall, to take the Chardge of the Service in myne Abfence, for the Profecution of the Rebell, makinge hym my Lieutenaunt of *Leinfter* and *Meithe*; apointinge the Lord Prefident of *Mounfter*, with his Chardge, to lye vpon the Confynes of the Province vnder his Rule next adioyninge to the Rebell ; and on the other Syde affigned Sir *Nicholas Malbye* to remayne with the greateft Parte of his Force vpon the Frontier of *Connaught*, where he might beft annoy, and lie moft aptlye to ftopp the Rebells Paffage. I my felfe fpent fome Tyme in takinge Pledgies of the *O Dempfies*, and other doubtfull Neighbours vpon that Border, gevinge Direccion to the Marfhall what I would have donne in myne Abfence, and forted my Iorney in that Sorte, that on *Chriftmas Even* I came to *Kilkennye*, Sir *Lucas Dillon* onely accompanienge me thether: And beinge enformed both before and after my Comminge thither, that the fpedieft and beft Way to fuppreffe the Rebell, was to plague his Mainteiners (whereof that Towne and Countie were to moch noted to be faultie) I fell to fomme exacte Examinacion of the Matter, and found in dede that trewe which had bene reported vnto me, both that the mecanicall and meane Sorte, and fomme of the principall and beft Sorte of the Towne, had, from Tyme to Tyme, relyved the Rebell both with Victualls, and all other Neceffaries, for Fedinge and Defence, and the Countrie, in like Sorte, to be the Retreite and Sinke to receive the Rebelles Goodes, fofter their Children, mainteine their Wyves, and in any other Sorte they could, from Tyme to Tyme to relyve and healpe them : And makinge further Profe of the Matter, fewe would comme vnto me with out Protection, and amongeft the reft of the beft Sorte, thofe that had fpeciall Rule and Chardge of the principall Howfies and Caftells of the Earle of *Ormoundes*, refufed to come at me, as namelye *Fowke Grace*, Conftable of *Rofcrey*, who denied to admitt the Prefident to enter into the Howfe before he had graunted hym Proteccion. *Owen Mac Donagh*, *Oge Okenedye* of *Ballyhagh*, and *Ferderrough Mac Edmound*, *Purcell* of *Potellrath* (one of the faied Earles Mannors) and Capten of his *Kerne*; eche of theife three laft, to amend the Matter, and in Token of the great Hate they bare to the Rebells, foftered everie one of theim one of *Rories* Childeren, which was both dewlye proved, and confeffed, in the Ende, by theim felves : Whereby I note both where the cheife Maintenaunce is, and howe hard it is to fuppreffe the Rebell, as long as he fyndeth foch Comforte and Succor of foch principall Men, who fhould rather both for their Dewties, Place, and Callings, feeke to deftroy and not to preferve foch an vndewtifull and an vnnaturall Broode. And (as I take it) hardly they durft do it, if the Matter were taken fo niere at Harte as outwarde Shewe is made, and is pretended, were not fome vnderhand Dealinge and Winkinge at the Matter, by theim whome they ferve. Nowe after I had had this Taft of theife principall Men, I fell into Confideracion howe to found the reft, and, by degrees, found daylie more Matter, and Cawfe of more vehement Sufpicion ; fo that both in the Towne and Countye, I cawfed every Day fome one or other to be apprehended, and found found and iuft Matter to chardge theim to bringe theim to their Triall. I therefore apointed a Ceffions to be held, the fame to beginne the Day next after the *Twelfth Day*, which contynued a Fortnight ; and in that Tyme, and both before and after, there was foch Plentie of Accufacions, and good Matter produced, as, I fuppofe, if the Seffions fhould have held till *Eafter*, the Commiffioners fhould not have wanted Stuffe and good Matter to have wrought on, if they would have hard all that would have bene verified of that Towne, Countie, and *Offerie*, for Maintenaunce of the Rebells. But foch Parcialitie and affectionate Dealings were found in the Juries, as were the Matter never fo playne and evident, the Evidence never fo full and apparaunte, if it touched any of their Freindes, and namely, any of the Conftables, Tenauntes or Servaunts of the Earle of *Ormounds*, no Inditement would be found, no, though the Partie made Submiffion and confeffed the Fault: And, on the other Syde, if the Matter touched any of *Offerie*, were the Evidence never fo weake, the

Proffe never fo flender, the Jurie would fynd it : Which, when the Commiffioners reported vnto me, what Slacknes and Partialitie they found one Way, and what Want of Indifferencie on the other, in that which fo moch touched her Majefties Service, I willed theim to take Recognizances of the Juries, to apeare here in the Caftell Chamber, and likewife to cawfe the Prifonners to be brought ; where, I hope, they fhall better heare of their Proceadings, and learne better hereafter what is their Dewties in the Quenes Cawfies.

Duringe the Tyme of my beinge at *Kilkennye*, the Earle of *Thomound* came vnto me, and brought me Lettres afwell from her Majeftie as from your Lordfhips ; but he was either fo curious or negligent, or both, in carrienge of theim, as he delyvered theim vnto me open, and the Seales broken vp ; I told hym fomewhat roundlye, and in plaine Tearmes, that I was not wont to receive Lettres from her Majeftie and youer Lordfhips in that Manner. He would have excufed the Matter vpon the Negligence of his Servaunt, and faied he had Copies of the Lettres hym felfe, fo that he neded not to breake theim open, knowinge the Matter they conteined ; which Anfwere fatisfied me not, but I referred hym for further Order in his Cawfies hither, where I will with fome Advife confider of the Nature and Qualitie of his Demaunds, and deale with hym for his Grauntes, as I may in beft Sorte for her Majefties Service, and his reafonable Reliefe, according as her Majeftie hath directed me.

A Day or twoe before my Comminge from *Kilkennye*, the Earle of *Defmound* came likewife vnto me, for whome I expreffely fent for by Meffadge and Lettre, for that I herd he had refuzed to comme to the Lord Prefident, being fondry Tymes fent for by hym, and befids, had of his owne Authoritie, without Warraunt or Commiffion from me, gathered together a Rabble of lewd and vnruly Followers, which he harried with hym vp and downe, eatinge and fpendinge the Countrie ; fo that if the Matter had bene any longer fuffered, confidering the Mans Humor, and howe fone he may be drawen by lewd and vnfound Counfell to runne hedlonge to forgett hym felfe, great Harme might have bene like to have enfewed by his Diforder : I thought good therefore, after he was comme vnto me, to chardge hym with the Matter, which in fomme Sorte he confeffed, alleadginge for his beft Excufe, that he was dryven to affemble this Companie for Feare of the Prefident : I demaunded of hym what Cawfe of Feare he had geven hym ; he could alleadge no probable and good Matter, but fome Conceite of his owne, and Reporte that was brought hym of fomme Intencion the Prefident had to ftaye hym. I reprehended hym fharply of his Follye, and the better to prevent all further Inconvenience, confideringe the Waveringe and Doubtfulnes of the Tyme, I cawfed the Prefident and hym to comme together, and reconciled theim, and made theim Freinds in as good Sorte as I could (who before would not fpeake the one to the other) the Earle promifinge, prefently vpon his Retourne, to difperfe his Companies, and to obey the Prefident as her Majefties principall Officer of that Province, and to comme vnto hym at any Tyme, when he fhould be fent for ; which if he performe (as I hope, and he protefteth he will) it will fave her Majeftie a great Chardge, which otherwife neceffarilye fhould have bene imployed, to have made the Earle the better to have knowen hym felfe, and to do that which in Refpect of Duetie he ought to her Majefties Officer, for the Countenaunce and Credit of the Place, which the Lord Prefident (as became hym for her Majefties Honnor) ftoode moche vpon. And this I may affure your Lordfhips, that if I had not devifed and wrought the Earles Comminge vnto me as I did, which by my Iorney to *Kilkennye* I procured : The Earles Follie would not have bene vnlike to have coft her Majeftie tenne thowfand Markes, before he would have bene thoroughly reclaymed, holdinge on that daungerous and vnadvifed Courfe he beganne, which by Degrees I hope I have brought hym from, and eafed her Majeftie of that Chardge. When the Earle went from me, I fent a Man of fpeciall Truft and Creditt with hym, to obferve the Manner of his Proceadinge, and to reporte vnto me the Courfe he held when he came Home into his Countrie, who accompanied hym as farre as *Kerrie*, and told me at his Retorne,

torne, that duringe the Tyme the Prefident and he were together, which was ij
Dayes Iorney, lodginge and fedinge both in one Howfe ; Therle vfed hym felfe
as orderly and reverentlye to the Prefident, as became hym every Way, and
after his Comminge Home, tooke Order forthwith for the Difperfinge of moft of
his Companie, and gave it out in every Place where he came, that he ment no
Harme to the State, nor wold be Author of any Diforder, nor countenaunce any
in their ill Intencions, if there were any foch Dealings ; and that he was and ever
wold be a trewe Subiect, obedient and duetifull to her Majeftie and the Governor, and wold fo contynue, and geve good Teftimonie of it, duringe his Liffe.
And, my Lords, I hold hym the leaft daungeroufe Man of iiij or v of thofe
that are next hym in Right and Succeffion (if he were gonne) and eafieft to be
dealt withall.   So that be it for the Doubt of the Attempt of the Rebell, *James
Fitzmorrice* his Kinfman, if he fhould come in, and he ioyne with hym, or in
Refpect of his Harme otherwaife, which he could do, if he fhould growe ill
difpofed hym felfe, I fuppofe there is leaft Daunger in hym of any of the reft,
and foneft may be mett withall, and cut of, beinge foch an impotent and weake
Boddye, as neither can he gett vp on Horfebacke, but that he is holpen and lift
vp ; neither when he is on Horfebacke, can of hym felfe a light downe without
Healpe ; and therefore, in myne Opinion, the leffe to be feared or doubted, if he
would forgett hym felfe, as I hope nowe he will not.

The State of the Countrie, Thanks be to God, is in good Quiet : *Vlfter* at no
Tyme quieter (fave that which of late hath hapned betwixt *T. Oneill* and *O-
donneill*, for Killinge of *T. Oneills* Sonne ; wherevpon there had bene like, for this
Matter, fome Brawle to fall out betwixt theim, but that I fuppreffed the fame
in dewe Tyme, wherein I muft note to your Lordfhips, the great Conformitie I
fynde in *Oneill*, that would not feeke his Right, but by Order from me : And in
both, this I obferved, that neither the one nor the other feeketh to enterteine
Scotts, or to make their owne Revenges, but both defier and fue to me for Ayde
of *Englifh* Forces ; and for the Matter, referre theim felves to ftand to myne Order : So that *Vlfter* is a good Neighbor to the Pale, no Complainte of Bodragge
or Stealth made by theim fince my Departure, but honeft Neighborhoode, without Oppreffion either on the one Syde or the other.   *Connaught* and *Mounfter*
in like Sorte quiet and obedient, gladd to imbrace Juftice, and feeke their owne
by Lawe without Oppreffion.   The onely Gaull is this Rebell of *Leinfter*, which
I hope, erre it be longe, to make her Majeftie and your Lordfhips a good Accompt of, for I waft hym and kill of his Men daylye, and I affure your Lordfhips, there was never Rebell better followed.   I befeach your Lordfhips haften
hither the Lord Chauncellor, whofe Abfence may ill be fpared longe, for the
Difpatche of poore Mens Cawfes, wherein he hath that Facillitie and Dexteritie,
as to his great Commendacion, and the Parties no little Contentment, he endeth
infinite Cawfes, which till his Retorne ly ftill in the Derke, and are not ended and
determined, expecting his Comminge.

In like Manner I befeache you geve Order for my Quarterage, to be dewe
the Firft of *Aprill* next ; for that by Reafon of the Advertizements, afwell of
that I have from thence, as from fondry other Partes, of the Practife of the
Archtraytor, *James Fitzmorrice*, as that the Rebell, *Rorie Oge*, is ftill on Foote,
I am enforced to vfe Money, and to imploy no fmall extraordenarie Chardge,
which otherwife, if that were not, might well be fpared, and her Majefty difbourdened of that Expence, as I hope fhortly fhe fhall, whereof above all other
Things I have a fpeciall Care.   I gave Order, vpon the Receipt of your Lordfhips firft Lettres, touchinge *Hix* the Pirate, that he fhould be prefently fent
thether.   My Lord Prefident promifed he would do it, fo that I hope, erre this,
he be arryved and delyvered in Saufety to your Lordfhips, for fo he hath written vnto me he fhould be.   My Lords, it feameth by foch Lettres I received of
late thence from fomme of your Lordfhips, and other my Freindes, that I am
not onely greatly blamed, but almoft generally condempned, that I advertize no
oftner foch Occurrents as happen here, fince there is fo good Stoare of others, whofe
Dilligence

Dilligence wanteth not, from Tyme to Tyme, to enriche you with Reportes, which if they would do as trewly, as they indevor to frame malitioufly, I fhould have as great Cawfe to thanke theim for their Paines and Prevencions, as I have nowe to condemne theim both of their Malice and Follies, and your Lordfhips have no iuft Occafion to thinke I am to flowe in my Advertizements : And yet in Trothe, as I love not to write of every Accident, or fleight Matter that hapneth, fo I hope I leave no Matter of Weight vnadvertized, but as the State of Things be from Tyme to Tyme, make trewe Reporte and Relacion to your Lordfhips, what foever other Men vntrewly devife by their Newes to flaunder my Governement.

Touching *George Wynters* lewd Dealinge, and vntrewe Reportes of me, who would cover his owne Faultes vnder the Shaddowe of my Authoritie ; I am afhamed of his Impudencye, but I hope, ere this you have difcovered fo moche of the Man, by his owne Contradiccions and Confeffions, as I nede not fay any more of hym, but God make hym more honeft. I willed my Lord Prefident to anfwere the Contents of your Lordfhips laft Lettres (the Copie whereof, with the Scedule I received from your Lordfhips inclofed, I fent hym) and defiered hym, afwell for your Lordfhips better Satisfaccions, as for his owne Difchardge and Creditt, to make a full Declaracion what had paffed betwixt *George Wynter* and hym, from Point to Pointe, as I hope he hath donne. And for myne owne Parte, as I neither fawe hym nor dealt with hym, but referred the whole State of the Cawfe to my Lord Prefident, and others of good Creditt and Truft, I apointed in Commiffion for the Matter, as namely her Majefties Eafcheator Generall, *Henry Davells*, *Peter Sherlocke*, and *Piers Aylward*, all fubftauntiall and difcreate Men ; the twoe laft, the one the Maior of *Waterfford* that was the laft Yeare, the other the Maior this Yeare : So I efteme the Difcourtefie and Wronge he offered me the greater, that fo vntrewly would report of mee, for he dealt fo ftraungely with me, as he would not let me have fo moche as one hundred Hydes for my ready Money, which I defiered for the Provifion of my Howfehold, and fent an expreffe Meffenger with Money for theim ; nor yet fo moch as geve me a Perrot, which I hard fay he had in the Shipp he tooke, although he were intreated by my Man to beftowe her vpon me. And thus fearinge I have bene over tedious to your good Lordfhips, for the which I crave Pardon, I humbly take my Leave. From her Majefties Caftle of *Dublin*, the   of *Februarye*, 1577.

Your honorable Lordfhips affured lovinge

Freinde, humblye to commaunde,

H. Sydney.

Mr. *Secretary* Walfyngham *to Sir* Henry Sydney.

My very good Lord,

HER Majeftie having nowe written her Lettre vnto your Lordfhip for your Repaire hether to her Prefence, for fomuch as the Impoficion of the Ceffe hath, as you knowe, breadd fome Mifliking of you there ; I wifhe that, for the Prefervacion of your Credit and Reputacion, you would take fome Order before your Comming, to leaue a generall Contentment and Satisfaction in the Myndes of the Subiects of that Countrie, wherein ye fhall do her Majeftie acceptable Service, and winne vnto your felf a great good Name. And for that the fame can no Way fo aptlie be perfourmid, as by putting in Execucion the Plotte fet downe by their Agents there, which, with my Lords of the Counfells Lettres, you fhall receaue ; I cannot but aduife your Lordfhip to yeld to the Allowing therof. Towching the noble Men and Gentlemen, long fithens committed for Impugning of the Ceffe, though their Offence therein hath ben great, yet would I wifhe your Lordfhip, in Refpect of the Reafons alreadie mencioned, to deale with theim as fauorablie as you maie ; following therein th' Example of her

Majeftie,

Majeſtie, who in her Gouernement, vppon like Occaſions of Offence, chooſeth rather to vſe Mercie, then to proſecute the ſame with Seueritie ; and the rather, for that in theis troubleſom Tymes a generall Diſcontentement of the Subieets of that Land maie prove of moſt daingerous Conſequence ; which Aduice I do geue vnto your Lordſhip, as your very Frind, being ſuch in deede as I would followe my ſelf, yf I weare in your Place. And ſo for this Tyme I commit your Lord-ſhip to God. From *Grenwich,* the xxiijth of *Marche,* 1577.

Your Lordſhips aſſurid Frind,

Fra. Walſyngham.

Thomas Wylſon, *Eſq; Secretary of State to Sir* Henry Sydney [a].

I Have ever had a wel diſpoſed Mynde towardes your Lordſhip, and the Howſe with the whyche you have matched. This good Wyl contynueth ſtil, and ſhal not fayle ſo longe as Life laſteth. Then I beeing thus affeeted, maye bolde-lie deale with your Lordſhip, for your own Welfayre, and uſe Freedome, by Ad-vertiſements, without Offence. It is towlde me, that grevouſe Exaetions are uſed under your Governement, after a verie ſtraunge Maner, and ſome Countries more charged then others, eaven of a Stomake Accuſations, deviſed upon light Cauſes ; and ſome verie hardche uſed, becauſe they wyl not profeſſe Thynges as they are requyred, although the Parties them ſelfes bee vtterlie ignorant, and in-nocent of the ſame. It maye be, that muche of this is untrew, and yet it maye bee alſo, that ſomewhat is trew, without your Knowlege. The Countrie where you governe, is apte to complayne, and your honorable Dealinge for the Matter of *Seſſe,* maye perhaps offende ſome, that woulde lothelie contribute by Force of Law, for the Advancement of her Majeſties Service. I knowe not the Trewthe of Thynges, but I would wyſhe that your Lordſhip were blameleſſe, and your Officers, under yow, voyde of Corruption ; that yow may geave good Accounte of the Talent committed to your Charge, with a cleare Concience upon your Re-tourne. And greate Pitie it were, that her Highnes Prerogative, which is ſacred, and verie honorable, beeinge wel uſed, ſhoulde be a Colour, or Pretexte, to ſerve private Gayne, without publyke Profite. Mr. *Newterfylde,* and Mr. *Bournell,* have their Diſpatche from the Council to your Lordſhip, offeringe them ſelfes with all Humilitie, to doe unto the Queenes Majeſtie, and her Realme, trew and faithfull Service ; which Cowrſe yf they take and followe, I dowbte nothing of your Lordſhips Goodnes towardes them. Yea, and that yow wyl ſhew them Favour, when they ſhall bee ſo well affeeted. Courteyſt Uſage of theſe Men, who have felt ſome Trouble her, will doe moche Good, in my Opinion, for Ad-vancement of the Queenes Service ; and they not feeling any Extremitie, or hard Dealinge, wyll bee the more encouraged to doe good Offices. Thus yow ſee how bowlde I am, to deale with yow frankelie, for the good Wyl I have ever borne your Lordſhip ; and ſo fare you hartelie wel. From the Courte at *Gryne-wyche,* the 23d of *Marche,* 1577.

Your Lordſhips moſt aſſured

to commande,

Tho. Wylſon.

Superſcribed
To the right Honorable my verie good
Lorde, Sir *Henry Sydney,* Knyght,
Lorde Deputie of *Ireland.*

Endorſed,
Received 23 *April,* 1578,
Mr. Secreterey *Wylſon.*

[a] Ex Origin. apud Penſhurſt.

Sir

Sir Henry Sydney *to his Son* Robert Sydney, *afterwards Earl of* Leicester.

R O B I N,

YOUR severall Letters of the 17th of *September,* and 9th of *November,* I have receved ; but that sent by *Carolus Clusyns,* I have not yet hard of. Your Letters are most hartely wellcum to me ; but the unyversall Testymony that is made of you, of the vertuus Course you hold in thys your juvenyle Age, and how mutch you proffyt in the same ; and what excellent Partes God hathe already planted in you, doth so rejoyce me, that the Syght of no earthly Thyng is more, or can be more, to my Comfort, than Heryng in thys Sort from, and of you. Ouer Lord bles you, my sweet Boy. *Perge, perge,* my *Robyn,* in the fylyall Fear of God, and in the meanest Ymaginatyon of your self, and to the lovyng Dyrectyon of your most lovyng Brother.

I lyke very well of your beyng at *Prage,* and of your Intentyon to go to *Vienna.* I wysh you should curyusly looke upon the Fortyfycatyon of that ; and confyderyng the Estate of *Chrystendom,* I can not tell hou to desygne your Travell into *Italy.* I would not have you to go spetyally, for that thear is perpetuall War betwyne the Pope and us. I thynk the Prynces and Potentates of that Regyon, ar confederated wyth hym, and for sum other Respects, I would not have you go thyther. Yet from *Spayne,* we are as it wear under an Inhybytyon ; *France* in endles Troubles ; the *Low Cuntre* in irrecoverable Mysery. So I leave yt to your Brother and your self, whether *Vyenna* beyng sean, you will return into *Ingland,* or spend the next Somer in those Partes ; whych if you do, I thynk best (you beyng satysfyed wyth *Vienna*) you se the pryncypall Cyttees of *Moravia* and *Siletia,* and so to *Cracoua* ; and if you can have any Comodyte, to se the Court of the Kyng of that Realm ; and from thens thoro *Saxon,* to *Holst,* and *Pomerland,* seyng the Prynces Courtes by the Way ; and then into *Denmark,* and *Swedon,* and se those Kyngys Courtes. Aquaynt you sum what wyth the Estate of the fre Steates ; and so at *Hamboro* to imbark, and to wynter wyth me. But what do I blunder at thyes Thyngys, follo the Dyrectyon of your most lovyng Brother, who, in loving you, is comparable with me, or excedyth me. Imitate hys Vertues, Exercyses, Studyes, and Accyons ; he ys a rare Ornament of thys Age, the very Formular, that all well dysposed young Gentylmen of ouer Court, do form allsoe thear Maners and Lyfe by. In Troth I speak yt wythout Flatery of hym, or of my self, he hathe the most rare Vertues that ever I found in any Man. I saw hym not thyes syx Monythes, lyttell to my Comfort. You may here from hym wyth more Ease, then from me. In your Travells, thyes Documentys I wyll gyve you, not as myne but hys Practyses. Seke the Knowlege of the Estate of every Prynce, Court, and Cytte, that you pas thoro. Adres your self to the Company, to learn thys of the elder Sort, and yet neglect not the youngar. By the one you shall gather Learnyng, Wysdom, and Knowlege, by the other Acquayntans, Languages, and Exercyse. Thyes he affectuatly obferved, wyth great Gayn of Understandyng. Ons agayn I say imytate hym. I here you are fallen into Consort and Fellofhyp wyth Sir *Harry Nevellys* Soon and Ayer, and one Mr. *Savell.* I here of syngular Vertues of them bothe. I am glad of your Famylyaryte wyth them.

The 21 of thys present, I received your Letter of the 12th of the same, and wyth yt a Letter from Mr. *Languet,* who semyth as yet to myslyke no Thyng yn you ; for whych I lyke you a great deale the better ; and I hope I shall here furder of your Comendatyon from hym, whych wylbe to my Comfort. I fynd by *Harry Whyte,* that all your Money is gon, whych wyth sum Wunder displeaseth me ; and if you can not frame your Charges, according to that Proportyon I have apoynted you, I must and wyll send for you Home. I have sent Order to Mr. *Languet,* for one hundryth Poundys for you, whych is twenty Pound more than I promysed you ; and thys I looke and order, that it shall

farve

farve you tyll the Laſt of *Marche*, 1580. Affure your felf, I wyll not inlarg one Grote, therfor looke well to your Charges.

I hope by that Tyme you ſhall receve thys Letter, you be at or nere *Strauyſborogh*, from whych, refolve not to depart, tyll the Mydeſt of *Apryll* cum Twelvemonyth ; nor than, I wyll not that you do, on les you fo aply your Study, as by that Tyme you do conceve felyngly, Rethoryk, and Logyk ; and have the Tongues of *Latyne*, *French*, and *Dutch*. Whych I know you may have, if you wyll aply your Wyll, and Wyt, to yt. I am fure you cannot but fynd what Lak in Learnyng you have, by your often Departyng from *Oxford* ; and the lyke, and greater Los ſhall you fynd, yf you refolve not to remayne contynually for the Tyme apoynted, in *Straufborogh*. Wryte to me monythly, and of your Charges partycularly ; and ether in *Latyne* or *French*. I take in good Part, that you have kept Promyfe wyth me ; and on my Bleffyng I charge you to wryte truly to me, from Tyme to Tyme. Whether you kepe yt or no, and if you break it in fum dark Maner, how.

Pray dayly fpeake no Thyng but truly. Do no dyfhoneft Thyng for any Refpect. Love Mr. *Languet*, wyth Reverens, unto whome in moſt harty Manner, comend me ; and to Doctor *Lubetyus*, and Mr. Doctor *Sturmius*. Farewell. If you wyll follo my Councell, you ſhalbe my fweete Boy. From *Baynards Caſtell* in *London*, this 25th of *March*, 1578.

Your Lovyng Father,

Superfcribd,
To hys welbeloved Soon *Robert Sydney*,
    at *Straſborogh ofer Maes*.

H. Sydney.

Sir Philip Sydney *to his* * *Father Sir* Henry Sydney.

Right honorable my ſingular good Lorde and Father,

SO ſtrangely and dyverfely goes the Courfe of the Worlde by the enterchanginge Humors of thofe that governe it, that thoughe it be moſt noble to have allweyes one Mynde and one Conſtancy, yet can it not be allwaies directed to one Pointe ; but muſt needes fometymes alter his Courfe, accordinge to the Force of others Changes dryves it. As now in your Lordſhips, Cafe to whom of late I wrote, wiſhinge your Lordſhip to returne as foone as conveniently yow mighte, encouraged thereunto, by the Affurance, the beſte Sorte had given me, withe what honorable Confiderations yowr Returne ſholde befall : Particularly to yowr Lott, it makes me change my Style, and wryte to your Lordſhip, that keepinge ſtill yowr Minde in one State of vertuoufe Quietnes, yow will yet frame yowr Cource accordinge to them. And as they delay yowr honorable Rewardinge, fo yow by good Meanes to delay yowr Returne, till either That enfue, or fitter Tyme be for This.

Her Majeſties Lettres prefcribed yow a certaine Day I thinke ; the Day was paſte before *Pagnam* came unto yow, and enjoyned to doe fome-things, the Doinge whereof muſte neceſſarily requyre fome longer Tyme. Hereuppon yowr Lordſhip is to wryte back, not as thoughe yow defyred to tarry, but onely ſhewinge that unwillingly yow muſte employ fom Daies thereaboutes ; and if it pleafe yow to add, That the Chaunceilours Prefence ſhall be requifite ; for by him your Lordſhip ſhall either have honorabler Revocation, or Commandement of furdre Stay at leafte till *Michelmas*, which in it felfe ſhall be a fitter Tyme ; confideringe, that then yowr Tearme comes fully out, fo that then yowr Enemies can not glory it is their Procuringe. In the meane Tyme yowr Frendes may labor heere to bringe to a better Paſſe, fuche yowr reafonable and honorable Defyres, which Tyme can better bringe forthe then Speede. Amongs which Frendes, before God there is none proceedes either fo thoroly or fo wyfely, as my Lady my Mother. For myne owne Parte, I have had onely Lighte from her. Now reſtes it in yowr Lordſhip to way the Particularities of

* Ex Orig. apud Penſhurſt.

yowr

yowr owne Eſtate, which no Man can know ſo well as yowr ſelfe ; and accordingely to reſolve. For myne owne Parte (of which Mynde yowr beſte Frendes are heere) this is yowr beſte Way. At leaſte whatſoever yow reſolve, I beſeeche yow with all Speede I may undreſtand, and that if it pleaſe yow with yowr owne Hande ; for truly Sir, I muſte needes impute it ſome greate Diſhoneſtie of ſome abowte yow, that there is little writtne from yow, or to yow, that is not perfittly knowne to yowr profeſſed Enemies. And thus muche I am very willinge they ſhoolde know, that I doe wryte it unto yow : And in that Quarter, yow may, as I thinke, loke precyſely to the Savinge of ſome of thoſe Overpluſſages, or at leaſte not to goe any furdre ; and then the more Tyme paſſes, the better it will be blowen over. Of my beinge ſente to the Queen, being armed with good Accounts and perfitt Reaſons for them, *&c.*   †
25 *Aprill,* 1578.

Sir Henry Sydney *and the Council of* Ireland *to Queen* Elizabeth.

It may pleaſe your moſt excellent Majeſtie,

FOR as moche as it is agreable to oure Dueties, and accordinge to your Majeſties Inſtruccions and Expectacion, to make often and trewe Reporte of the State of this your Realme, vnto your Highnes : We have thought it therefore convenient, not onely to make oure humble Excuſe for oure former Slacknes in that Behalfe ; but alſo nowe by a perfect Informacion particulerlye to ſpeake of the ſeverall Provinces, to Thende your Majeſtie might the more fully conceive, how the Governement ſtandeth of the Whole, which we proteſt fayhtfully to delyver, accordinge as the Tyme preſent geveth Occaſion.

The vniverſall Quiet of *Mounſter, Connaught,* and *Vlſter,* doth geve vs Matter to ſpeake in Commendacion of ſoch of your Majeſties Servauntes, and Subiectes, as either are Directors of youer Services there, or are obedient Executors of the Deſignements ſett downe by thoſe your Majeſties Officers. Wherein to leave the Commendacion dewe to Sir *William Drewrie,* for *Mounſter,* who every Way in oure Opinions hath deſerved his iuſt Praiſe, for the Care he hath had of his Chardge, and his wiſe and diſcrete Governement. We finde that the Earle of *Deſmound* (ſince the Tyme that the Lord Preſident and he were reconcyled by me your Majeſties Deputie) hath carried hym ſelfe in a good and an orderly Courſe, diſperſinge his Men, and ſeakinge Juſtice, from that Governement, and workinge all good Offices to make Shewe of his Obedience and Loyaltie, in ſo moche as he hath diſcovered lately to me, the preſident Practizes nowe in Hand, by *James Fitz Morriſh,* to move Rebellion in *Vlſter,* and *Connaught,* thorough Solicitacion of certeine *Frenche,* and *Iriſh* Men, arrived at *Sligo* in a Shipp of St. *Maloes* ; the Copie of which Advertizements we ſend herewith to your Majeſtie, and the ſame is alſo confirmed by Lettres from Capten *Fiſher* to me, and *Nicolas Malbye* ; ſo as by Conference with me your Deputie, a Plott is laied for the Stay of thoſe *Frenche* Men, and for Apprehencion of ſoch Inſtruments, as come from the Rebell to treate with your Subiects of thoſe Partes. And as this and other good Shewes in the Earle of *Deſmound,* make Demonſtracion that his light and loſe Dealings (whereunto he runneth maney Tymes raſhlye) proceadeth rather of Imperfeccion of Judgement, then of malitious Intendement againſt your Majeſtie. So do we not doubt, but the good Meanes that are vſed to nouriſhe Likinge betwene your Preſident and hym, and to repreſſe Iniuries betwene Partie and Partie, ſhall kepe that whole Province in good Obedience, till your Majeſties Laws ſhall have further Currencie and Allowance there. Which howe moche they have in this ſmall Tyme prevayled, ſhall apeare by a Note ſent herewith, vnder the Teſtimonye of youer Preſident, conteininge a more perticuler Reporte of that

† In Sir *Philip Sydneys* Hand-writing at *Penſhurſt Place,* without his Name, but indorſed by *Robert,* 2d Earl of *Leiceſter* ; as follows: *To my Grandfather from my Vncle.*

Province

Province of *Mounfter*, afwell for the Revenue increafed and revived there to your Majeftie, as for the Difpoficion of the principall Perfons, and the Letts and Hynderauncies why the fame is not alreadye brought to Perfeccion; and for oure owne Opinion generallye we do affirme, that the Countrie is vniverfallye quiet, and that (if forreine Practizes do not dyvert the Myndes of the People) your Majeftie may fhortly have foch a Revenue in that Province, as fhall mainteine a fettled Governement, of as maney or more Men of Warre, and other Officers, as are now mainteined in thofe Partes.

For *Connaught* it fufficeth (becawfe your Majeftie hath received latelye Reporte of that Province) that we confirme that which hath bene formerlye written, namelye, that your Majefties Revenue there is increafed to the yearelye Somme of Mccxxxvij *l.* and that the Collonell hath vniverfall Obedience, Service, and Rent from the perticuler Lords of everye Countrie, and Capteines of everye Surname, whereof *Orwarcke* beinge more fkake then the reft, and noted for Pride amongeft all the *Irifhe*, is at this Inftant, by a private Band of Footemen, fent thether by Sir *Nicholas Malbye*, diftreffed, his Men flayne, his cheife Caftell wonne from hym, the Warde all put to the Swoorde, and he in all Humilitie fubmitteth hym felfe, and appealeth to me your Deputie, for Order betwene hym and the Collonell. Vpon Examinacion of which Matter it appeareth, that this Breache betwene Sir *Nicholas Malbye* and *Orworcke*, grewe vpon Intelligence, that there were certeine Coyners of Money maintened by *Orworcke*, which the Collonell fent for, and were not delyvered by *Orworcke*; for Correctinge of which Infolencye, this late Slaughter was made vpon hym. The reft of the State of *Connaught*, perticular and generall, with the Courfe which he intendeth there to take, and howe your Revenue may yet be farder revived and increafed without Difficultie, your Majeftie fhall vnderftand by a Note vnder the Hande of your faied Collonell, and howe he fortifieth that Plott with probable Reafons to beare the full Chardge of the whole Province: And in the meane Seafon, he feaketh none other Pay for hym felfe, nor for the Horfemen vnder his Leadinge, then of thofe Rentes fo acquyred to your Majeftie. Howe be it, this Impediment he fyndeth, which croffeth all his Defignes, that your Majeftie fo longe fufpendeth your Refolucion touchinge the Proceadinge with the Earle of *Clanrickarde*, for the Hope that is conceived of his Delyverie, and that it is expected he fhould fo fone be fett at Libertie (which fo maney daylye looke for) moveth all his Followers fo moche to be at the Commaundement of his wicked and rebellious Sonnes; which, if the fame were once removed, by a determinate Refolucion from your Highnes, and his Followers thoroughlye affured that the Earle fhould be dealt withall (as he hath deferved) by the ordenarie Courfe of Juftice, they would fcarce geve his Sonnes Breade to put in their Mouthes, which they are nowe not fo moche moved for Love, as for Feare to do, in Refpect of their Fathers Difpleafure; for that once before by Experience they learned, and to their Greives and Oppreffions felt, howe in the like Cafe he dealt with theim for Difobeyinge his Sonnes, affone as he was come amongft theim, and enlarged hence, and reftored to his Libertie.

Of *Vlfter* we may declare, that the fame is vniverfally in Peace both in theim felves (amongft whome no Difcord hath hapned latelye, but a Shewe of a Diftreffe to be taken by *Tirlaugh Lenaugh* againft *Odonnell*, for the Slaughter of one of *Tirlaughs* Sonnes, which was by a Chaunce killed in his Countrey, and that Quarrell nowe compounded) and alfo in good Neighborhode to the Pale, vpon which no Outrage hath bene committed of long Tyme, fo firmely hath *Tirlaugh* obferved his Promife and Covenauntes: And the Baron of *Dungannon* hath alfo bene a good Neighbor, and reftrayneth the Loofenes of foch Borderers as were wonte to difturbe the Quiet of the Countrie. So as vpon the Conformitie of *Tirlaugh*, and the Baron, withe the good Perfwafion alwayes vfed by *Tirlaughes* Wiffe, this Peace doth chiefelye confift; nevertheleffe, amongft your Majefties Servauntes, the beft Inftrument for that Border is the

Marſhall, Sir *Nicholas Bagnall*, who, till of late, that I your Deputye imployed hym in your Service in *Leinſter*, where he hath donne your Majeſtie good and verie acceptable Service, did remayne vpon his own Lands, and was the onelye Countenaunce of that Northeren Border. And this we thinke ſufficient to ſay for *Vlſter*, ſavinge we conceive by that which hath fallen out vpon the Proffes made in *Mounſter* and *Connaught*, that a good Porcion of Revenue, over and above that which the Lords and Freholders have alreadye, by Compoſicion with me your Deputye, conſented to pay, might be eaſilye obteined in *Vlſter*, without violent Meanes, but in Manner by Perſwacion, ſo as the Parties that be Captens and principall Men might receive Eſtates from your Majeſtie, either in Succeſſion or Eleccion, and might knowe the Reſervacions certeine that ſhould be made vpon their Landes, whereof your Majeſtie hath bene heretofore advertized from me your Deputie, and may be more particulerly hereafter informed at your good Pleaſure.

It reſteth, that your Majeſtie be advertized of the State of *Leinſter* and *Meithe*, the wonted Quiet whereof hath bene lately moche diſturbed by twoe Meanes ; the one by the Rebellion of the *Moores* and *Conners* ; the other by a certeine Diſcontentacion in maney of the Lordes and certeine principall Gentlemen of the *Engliſh* Pale, whoſe Cawſe hath depended longe before your Majeſtie and your Privey Counſell in *England*. To the Firſt, touchinge the Rebell *Rorie Oge*, and his Complices, it is ſtraunge that the Proſecucion of hym, havinge bene ſo fervent, his Eſcapes ſo beyonde all Opinion, the Execucion ſo blouddye, by cuttinge of his Company frome 500 to 50, which are nowe his Remayne at the vttermoſt ; thoſe alſo diſtreſſed by Lacke of Victualls, nor daringe to abyde in any Place of the *Iriſhe* Countries, nor the Borders adioyninge, no not ſo long ſcarce, as they may relieve theim ſelves with one Meales Meate, that nevertheleſſe they fynde Favor in the Pale, and other *Engliſhe* Counties, and namelye, *Caterlaugh* and *Kilkennye*, and do ſome Qutragies without Hewgh or Crie, or any Followinge of any other Perſon in Effecte, then of the *Engliſh* Soldiors in your Majeſties Pay, which have and do ſo hunt hym, as there is ſmall Opinion conceived of his Contynuance in any Abilitie to do Hurte. But the other for the Diſcontentacion of the Lords and Gentlemen, is a Matter of more Conſequence, becawſe we ſee theim, as it were, dulled with a Kinde of ſenceles Obſtinacie, as apeareth in the Matter of Submiſſion to your Maieſtie ; wherein howe they ſtand vpon Forme more then vpon any reaſonable Grounde, your Majeſtie hath alreadye vnderſtoode by the Reporte of me your Deputye. And ſince this Diſcontentacion hath not growen vpon any Innovacion or vnwonted Burden layed vpon theim, as hath bene alreadie proved before your Majeſtie, we knowe not whereunto to impute their Behaviours ; but we ſee, that either their owne careles Conſideracion of theim ſelves, or their deiected Myndes, geveth Scope to the Rebell to do the Hurtes which have bene donne in the Pale, and could not have Contynuance, if they did not (for Lacke of Will and Indevor to reſiſt) ſhewe a Kinde of Conſent or an Allowaunce of their owne Harmes.

This Concurrencie with the Iniquitie of the Tyme, we do rather pittie in the Gentlemen then complayne of ; and do hope, that when your Maieſtie ſhall reſolve to diſpatche their Agents with your princelye Direccion, which you will have obeyed, they will then dewtifully conforme theim ſelves, and recover newe Life and Courage bothe to defende, and annoy ſoche as rebell againſt your Majeſtie ; at which Tyme we ſhalbe alſo moſt readye to make Reporte of the better Parte, as we are nowe compelled to diſbourden oure ſelves, and lay the Fault where in dede it is : And touchinge the Rebell, we thinke it mete for your Majeſties Honnor, and for the Safetye of ſoche of the *Engliſhe* Nation, as have bene heretofore planted in thoſe Rebells Landes, that your Majeſtie do contynuallye proſecute theim with youer Forces till they be vtterly extinguiſhed ; the Honnor whereof muſt be the Recompence of the Chardge. This Warre, with the Opinion of *James Fitzmorrice* Landinge, have
bene

bene the Cawfies of extraordenarie Chardge, which neverthelesse have bene so temperatly expended, as nothinge hath bene vnnecessarie or superfluous, so farre as I your Deputye could spare with Honnor and Safetye of this your State and Kingedome.

And, most gratious Sovereigne, when theife, and soche like vnloked for Occasions, do arrise, and drawe some extraordenarie Chardge of Expence, more then your Majesties ordenarie Assignement and Allowaunce; and so fall out somewhat beyonde your Majesties Expectacion in that Pointe, which neverthelesse may neither, in respecte of Honnor, nor Safetie, and Preservacion of your Realme and good Subiects, be well spared, but must of Necessitie be imployed in your Service, as may apear in Parte, by the Declaracion of your last Yeares Accompt : We hope therefore, and even so with all Humilitie, beseache your most excellent Majestie, that it would pleafe the same in like Manner, as you looke into and regarde your Chardge and Expence what it is; so, on the other Side, you would enter into the like Consideracion, howe moch your Revenue is increafed in your perticuler Provinces ; and what Likely-hoods, probable Shewes, and evident Testimonies, there be of the daylie Increafe of more, if this Plott of Governement may be followed and con-fynued : So that, in oure Opinions, savinge your Majesties most grave and princely Reformacion, neither the Purchafe can be well accompted deare, nor the Chardgies estemed great, in respecte of soche a Benifitt, besides the longe hoped and wifhed for Reformacion of this miferable and vnhappie Countrey, in the Tyme of your most blessed and profperous Governement over this your Realme, to the immortall Fame of you and your Posteritie for ever. Wherein we humbly befeach God, that your Majestie may be establifhed with all dewe Obedience from youer Subiectes ; and so we humblye leave your Majestie to the Lord. At your Castell of *Dublin*, the xxth of *April*, 1578.

Your Majesties most humble, obedient, and

faythfull Subiects and Servauntes,

H. Sydney, *&c.*

Sir Henry Sydney *to Queen* Elizabeth, *fent by* Edward Waterhoufe, *Efq;*

May it pleafe your most excellent Majefty,

I Have received your Highnes Lettres, bearinge Date at your Mannor of *Grene-witche*, the xxijth of *Marche* last : And for that the Wynde ferved not foner for Paffage thence hither (notwithstandinge the carefull Dilligence of the Meffen-ger, who lost no Tyme, but tooke the first Wynde that ferved) he arryved not here with your Majesties Lettres before the xxiijth of this prefent *Aprill :* And becawfe your Pleafure and Commaundement to me in theim is, that I fhould put my felfe in a Readines fo to imbarque here with foch Conveniencye, as I fhould prefent my felfe to your Majesties Prefence (if Wynde and Wether were not Im-pediment or further Stay) by the xth of *Maye* next ; I thought it therefore agre-able to my most bounden Dewtye, and your Majesties better Satisfaccion, to ad-vertyze your Highnes, that beinge directed in the former Parte of your Majesties faied Lettres, to deale afwell with the Agentes that were fent over from the Lords and Gentlemen of the Pale, and nowe retorned thence by your Majesties expreffe Order (who arryved not here before the xxvijth of this Prefent) as with the Lords and Gentlemen theim felves. For the Doinge whereof alfo, I am by fpeciall Direccion prefcribed, by an Order from the Lords of your Privey Coun-cell there, what Courfe to hold in that Matter with theim (if I and your Majef-ties Councell here like of their Devife) wherein I am most humblye to thanke your Majestie and theim for that Regarde of me, and the Place I hold here vn-der you ; fo that if it like your Majestie (the Matter hanginge in fome Con-fideracion, and not determined, nor the Lord Chauncellor retorned, who in that

Matter

Matter of Cesse hath bene a great Traveller both there and here, and for that Respecte the more desierous I am to have hym at the Consultacion and Conclusion ; and not to deale therein absolutely my selfe, before his Comminge : And further, for that some Inconvenience might growe of it, if the same should take no Ende before my Goinge) I cannot, theise Cawsies considered, make my Repaier thither so sone as your Majestie hath apointed me, which I thought fitt to make knowen vnto youer Highnes for myne humble Excuse ; and in the meane Tyme as theise Things may growe to their Ripenes (as I hope they will do verye shortlye, your Chauncellor beinge retorned) and I finished that I am directed here to doe by your Majestie in that Parte, I will put my selfe in Order with that Spede that I may possible, to make my Repaier vnto your Presence, except in the meane Tyme I shalbe countermaunded from your Highnes, by your owne Lettres, beinge not vnwillinge, in any Respecte, to serve your Majestie here, or seeke to withdrawe my selfe in a doubtfull or suspected Tyme (as some seame to have geven forth to my Disadvantage) but readdye and desierous, in any Sorte I can, either here or ells where, to serve your Majestie (in what Sort it shall best please you to imploy me) all the Dayes of my Liffe. But farre more willinge, and with a more cherefull Harte I should have performed it (if I may say so moche duetifullye, your Majestie not offended) that I had found that good Acceptacion of my Service, and good Intencion and Meaninge, that in my humble and not vnreasonable Requestes, I had not found your Majestie so harde and difficult with me ; and amongst some other my ill Happs, namelye in this, for the Payment of my Warraunte of MMMJ *l.* which, as the Matter nowe standethe, except your Majestie assigne me more spedye Payment, then I yet fynde by any Apparaunce or Likelyhoode I shall have, it will torne to my Losse, and moche to my Disadvantage, for that my Bills and Speciallties lye for Payment of soch Bills as I received, and my Dayes and Tymes drawe on, that I must see my Creditt dischardged. And, gratious and most dere Lady, for that the Warrauntes are dewe for Service, and Enterteinement past, to faythfull and honest Servitors, that spent their Bloode in your Service, and so consequentlye a dewe Debt to be paied by you : I presume so moche of your gratious Goodnes and Inclynacion towardes me, that you will not have lesse Regarde to pay the same vnto me, the Warrauntes nowe remayninge in my Handes, and restinge vpon my Creditt to satisfie the Owners at their Dayes, then you would have donne at the speciall Sute of theim selves, if they had bene Peticioners in their owne Behalfes, as they would have bene, if I had not dealt with theim ; and I hope my Creditt, for my Rewarde and longe Service, deserve no worse towards your Majestie then theirs. But to come backe to this Matter of Composicion for Cesse, and the Victuallinge of your Garrison here, in Sorte as the Soldiour may lyve of his Wagies, without Encrease of his Pay, and your Majestie no further chardged (wherein by your Highnes I am directed to deale) I fynde the same can growe to no perfecte Conclusion, but by generall Consent, aswell of the Lords of this Countrie Birthe that nowe remayne there, as those that be here ; and so moche the rather I so conceive of it, becawse those Noblemen there have so maney to depende of theim here, who will affirme what they affirme, and denye what they denye (so moche they are at their Devocion) and therefore, without theim, hard it wilbe to make any full Conclusion : Wherefore I humblye pray your Majestie, to order those Lords presentlye to comme over hither, for their Presencies in this Case, and at this Tyme, may do your Majestie good Service ; and then consequentlye there must followe a Parliament, for so it seameth your Majesties Meaninge is, that the Aggrement should be confirmed by Parliament : Wherof I must humblye put your Majestie in Remembraunce, that if it stand not with your Pleasure the same be held in my Tyme, yet you must thinke of it, as of the most speciall Matter that concerneth your Proffitt and Commoditie, and the Contynuaunce of youer Revenue, and cheifelye for your Custome of Impost of Wynes, the Contynuaunce whereof beinge lymitted for Yeares, is nowe almost expired, and therefore either to be lost, to the great Decrease of your Revenue, or els to be con-

tynued

tynued and revyved by Parliament. And for that, at my Repaier thither, glad I would be to be affifted with fomme of this Countrie Birthe, or other grave dif-create Counfellor, to teftifie the Truthe of the State of this Countrie, and of the Proceadings here from Tyme to Tyme, fince the laft Tyme of my Acceptacion of this Governement, and of the Succeffe and Sequell of all Things, I humblye befeache your Majeftie to addreffe your Lettres to fomme foche of your Counfell here, as you fhall thinke moft fitt for their Experience, Knowledge, and Wife-domes, to accompanye me thether, to Thende your Majeftie, by their Teftimo-nies and trewe Reportes may be better certified and confirmed, both of the Trewth of the State of the Countrie ; how I found the fame, and nowe in what Cafe the fame is, when I fhall leave it, as alfo yeld their Opinions for the Plott of the Governement hereafter, if your Majeftie fhall like of it. And even fo prayinge the Almightye, withall Honnor and Happines to contynue your Majefties Reigne longe over vs, your faythfull and humble Subiectes, I humblye take my Leave. From the Caftell of *Dublin,* the Laft of *Aprill,* 1578.

Your Majefties moft humble, obedient, and

faythfull Subiecte and Servaunte,

H. Sydney.

Sir Henry Sydney *to the Lords of the Council in* England.

May it pleafe your good Lordfhips,

YOUR Lettres dated from *Hampton* Courte, the Laft of *Februarye,* and thofe from *Grenewitche,* the xxjth of *Marche,* I received the xxiijth of this *Aprill* ; and becawfe the cheife, and in Effecte, the onelye Pointe of thofe twoe Lettres, conteine an Advife and Direccion from your Lordfhips, howe to procede, afwell with the Agentes of the Pale nowe fent thence (who arryved not here be-fore the xxvijth of this Prefent) as with thofe Noblemen and Gentlemen that re-mayne Prifoners here for that Cawfe ; neither the Lord Chauncellor is come over yet, who, as your Lordfhips writeth, is to refolve me of fondrie other Pointes, which your Lordfhips have referred to his Negotiacion, and efpecially for the Plott laied downe by the Agentes for the Ceffe, wherein the faied Lord Chaun-cellor hath bene, both there and here, a great Traveller : I am therefore the more defierous to have hym at the Confultacion and Conclufion, fo that he be-inge not yet arryved (whofe Retorne I hope wilbe fpedilye) I cannot with any Conveniencye make my Repaier thither, accordinge vnto her Majefties Pleafure and Commaundement, by the xth of the next Moneth, thofe Things being of fo great Importaunce, hanginge yet in Confideracion, and not refolved on, which I befeache your Lordfhips delyver to her Majeftie for myne humble Excufe. And further, for that that Matter (touchinge the Compoficion for Ceffe, and the Vic-tuallinge of her Majefties Garrifon, at foch reafonable Rates, as the Soldior may lyve of his Wagies, and Enterteinement, without further Chardge to the Quene) can not growe to that Perfeccion of Refolucion, without the Confent of thofe Noblemen of this Countrie Birth, nowe attendinge her Majeftie at the Courte, vpon whome depend fo maney Followers ; yea, and fome of the moft princi-pall of theim that are nowe deteined for that Matter here : Your Lordfhips fhall do well (in myne Opinion) for the Furtheraunce of this Service, to move her Majeftie, that thofe Noblemen may be ordered prefentlye to comme over, afwell for the Yeldinge of their Opinions, and for their Affiftaunce and Confents in this Matter, as alfo for that, in this quefye and doubtfull Tyme, their Pre-fence is neceffarie in their Countries and Rules, to anfwere all Events, afwell forreine Attemptes (if any fhould happen) as otherwife, whiche I humblye be-feache your Lordfhips gravelye and advifedlye to thinke of : And where alfo it pleafed your Lordfhips to fignifie vnto me, in your Lettres of the xxjth of *Marche,* of fome Speaches that were blowen Abroade, of the great Waft and

Hurte

Hurte committed vpon the Inhabitaunts of the Towne and Countye of *Kil-kennye*, duringe the Tyme of my late beinge there, afwell by the Diforder of the Soldiors, as for Want of Payment for their Victualls, taken whileft they lay in thofe Partes : I have therefore, accordinge to your Lordfhips Advifes (afwell for your better Satisfaccion, and for the Cleringe of foch Reportes, as to reprove the Reporters of their malitious Vntrothes) addreffed Commiffion to examyne the Matter, and what hath bene founde and delyvered, afwell by the Sheriffe of that Countie (vpon his Examinacion taken vpon his Othe) who was the princi-pall Officer ; as by the Othes and Teftimonies of fome other Noblemen and Gentlemen of the Countrie, beinge nowe prefent with me here this Tearme Tyme, I have fent your Lordfhips, by this Bearer, Mr. *Edward Waterhowfe*, to whome I pray you, afwell in that, as in any other Thinge he hathe by In-ftruccion, in Writinge or otherwife, to imparte to you on my Behalfe, to geve Creditt as to my felfe. And befides, for that I fuppofe your Lordfhips be per-fwaded of his Sufficiencie and Fidellitie, I omitt fome Thinge, which I ment nowe to have committed vnto Writinge, and referre the fame to his Declaraci-on and Reporte, to the which I befeache your Lordfhips to geve Creditt, and even fo I humbly take my Leave. From the Caftell of *Dublin*, the Laft of *Aprill*, 1578.

Your honorable Lordfhips

affured lovinge Freinde,

H. Sydney.

Inftruccions geven by Sir Henry Sydney, *Knight of the Order*, &c. *and Lord Deputie of* Ireland, *to Mr.* Edward Waterhowfe, *beinge fent to her Majeftie and the Lords, for Matters touchinge the Affayres of the State of this Realme. Dated the Firft of* Maij, 1578.

FIRST, You fhall, with that Dilligence you can, make your Repaier to the Courte, and delyver your Lettres to her Majeftie and the Lords of her Privey Counfell, and prefent my humble Service, Duetie, Thankes, and Commendacions to eche, as fhall apperteine.

2. Next you fhall declare to her Majeftie (if you may have Acceffe vnto her Prefence) or to the Lords in generall (if you fhall come before theim) or to foche of her Majefties perticuler Counfellors, as you fhall repaier vnto, the Cawfe of my Stay here longer then her Majeftie hath directed me, which pro-ceadeth, afwell for that I received not her Majefties Lettres in foch Tyme, as I could with any Poffibilitie have bene there, accordinge to her Majefties Direc-cion, by the xth of this prefent *Maye*, as alfo for that I fhould have left the Matter of the Ceffe vndetermined, whereby great Inconvenience would have enfewed, both to the State of the Countrie, and her Majefties Service, and no little Encombrance to hym, that fhould have fucceded me, beinge not acquainted howe the Matter had bene hether to dealt in.

3. You fhall declare vnto her Majeftie, or the Lords, as Occafion fhall fall oute, or when you fhalbe demaunded, that I imparted her Majefties Lettres vnto her Majefties Councell here, and lett theim vnderftand howe willinge and defierous I was to have performed that her Majeftie directed me (as my Duetie was) and prayed their Advifes therein who refolved with me, and even fo have fignified to her Majeftie, that by Reafon of the Shortnes of the Tyme, the Im-portaunce of the Cawfies, and the Neceffitie of the Endinge of theim for the Honnor of her Majeftie, and the Quiet of the Countrie, I could not by any pof-fibilitie retorne fo fone as I was apointed.

4. Touchinge

4. Touchinge the Auditor, you may declare both what daylye Travell he taketh, and howe intricate and crabbed be the Thinges he dealeth withall : So that at the Day appointed, he could not with any Poſſibilitie have bene reddye to have comme with me. Howe be it, he will nowe vpon this Alarum, ſett Thinges as faſt forwarde as he can, and prepare hym ſelfe to come with that Spede and Dilligence, that any Wayes he may diſpatche the Things he hath in Hand.

5. To ſolicite the Payment of the MMM *l.* which is dewe vnto me vpon the Treaſorers Warraunt, and declare howe moche the ſame ſtandeth both vpon my Creditt to ſee my Bills diſchardged, and my Creditors paied at their Dayes, which likewiſe I am bound to doe by my Bills and Specialties to the Parties ; and, therefore, what Hinderance it wilbe vnto me, if I be deferred any longer of my Payment.

6. To declare howe by the firſt Dayes Conference (whereat your ſelfe were preſent) I finde that Diſſentinge in the Matter of Ceſſe, and Contrarietie of Opinions for the Manner of the Compoſicion for the ſame, that the Plott which the Agentes ſett downe, will not be accepted nor allowed of the greater Nomber : For that in Trothe, the Agentes were not ſent from the Boddie, and whole State of the Realme, but from certeine diſcontented Lords and Gentlemen of the Pale : So that ſome other Plott and Deviſe muſt be thought of, for this alreadie ſett downe, will not be generallye concluded and agreed vpon.

7. To report to the Lords, the Courſe of the Proceadinge withe Mr. *White,* for the Office of the Cuſtodie of the *Rolls,* and to ſhewe the Coppie of the Acte and Enterie thereof ſett downe in the Councell Booke.

8. To ſhewe the Certificate and Depoſicions of the Sheriffe, and other Lords and Gentlemen of the Countye of *Kilkennye,* touchinge the Bruites geven out there of the Waſtes and Spoyles donne vpon that Towne and Countye, at the Tyme of my late beinge there ; by the Diſorder of the Soldiors, and Want of Payment for that they tooke, or by other Meane or Occaſion.

9. To ſolicite likewiſe ſome Reſolucion for *Clanrickard,* and yeld the Reaſons whye I thinke it verye-expediente that the Matter be no longer deferred, and what Vncerteintie and Inconvenience growethe therebye to the Service.

10. To obteine Reſolucion of *T. Oneills* Cawſies, if the Lord Chauncellor have not alreadie procured it.

11. To declare the Neceſſitie to have a Parliament for the Contynuaunce and Encreaſe of her Majeſties Revenue, which muſt be thought of with Spede, otherwayes the Impoſt for Wynes, which is a Matter lymitted for Yeares, wilbe expired, and being once diſcontynued, hardly wilbe revived.

12. To ſolicite a Quarterage, if by Occaſion of Letts and Impediments which may arriſe by the Difficultie and Waywardneſs of the Countrie, or otherwayes, Things cannot be reſolved vpon in ſo ſhort a Tyme as is expected for my Retorne.

13. Touchinge the Fines impoſed vpon the Lords and Gentlemen nowe remayninge in the Caſtell here, for Reſiſtinge her Majeſties Prerogatyve for Ceſſe ; that there Fynes may not be remitted by abſolute Order from thence, but left to me and the Councell here.

14. To ſhewe ſoche Lettres as my Lord, and the Lord Preſident received, touchinge the Practize of *James Fitzmorrize,* and the Doubt that is conceived of ſome forreine Attempts.

15. The Accydent of the Lords of *Lowth,* and other Gentlemen of that Countye, the Second of *Maii,* by *Mac Mahon.*

16. To declare the State of the Countrie, and the Quietnes thereof ; and what Increaſe of Revenue there is alreadie in everye perticuler Province, and what Hope there is conceived of Encreaſe of more, if this Plott of Governement may be dewelye followed. In like Manner you may declare the Likelyhood I fynde of the ſpedie Overthrowe of the Rebell nowe in Proſecucion. And of all other Things that ſhalbe demaunded of you, which I have neither by private Speache imparted to you, nor expreſſed in theiſe Memorialls and Notes : I pray

† you

you accordinge to the Tyme and Place to satisfie their Demaundes for the prefent as you can ; and if there be further Matter of Difficultie that you nowe conceive not of, or by theife are not delyvered vnto you, I requyre you advertize me prefentlye thereof, that I may fupply you with further Matter and Inftruccion.

Sir Philip Sydney *to* Edward Mollineux, *Efq; Secretary to his Father as Lord Deputy.*

Mr. *Mollineax,*

FEW Woordes are befte. My Lettres to my Father have come to the Eys of fome. Neither can I condemne any but yow for it. If it be fo, yow have plaide the very Knave with me ; and fo I will make yow know if I have good Proofe of it. But that for fo muche as is paft. For that is to come, I affure yow before God, that if ever I know yow do fo muche as reede any Lettre I wryte to my Father, without his Commaundement, or my Confente, I will thrufte my Dagger into yow. And trufte to it, for I fpeake it in Earneft. In the meane Time farwell. From Courte, this Lafte of *May,* 1578.

Indorfed, Mr. *Philippe Sidney* to me, browght 1578, by my L. Chauncellor ; receiued the 21 of *June.*

By me,

Philippe Sidney.

Edward Mollineux, *Efq; to* Philip Sydney, *in Anfwer to the abovefaid Letter.*

S I R,

I Have receaved a Lettre from you, which, as it is the firft, fo the fame is the fharpeft that I ever receaved from any : And therfore it amafethe me the more to receave fuche a one from you, fince I have (the World can be Iudge) deferved better fomwhere, how fo ever it pleafethe you to condempne me now. But fince it is (I proteft to God) withowt Cawfe, or yet iuft Grownde of Sufpicion you vfe me thus : I bear the Iniurie moore patiently for a Tyme, and mine Innocencie, I hoope in the Ende, fhall trie mine Honeftie ; and then I truft you will confeffe you have done me Wronge. And fince your Pleafure fo is expreffed, that I fhall not henceforthe reade any of your Lettres ; althowghe I muft confeffe, I have heretofore taken bothe greate Delite and Profet in Readinge fomme of them : Yet vpon fo harde a Condicion (as you feeme to offer) I will not hereafter adventure fo greate a Perill, but obey you herein. Howbeit if it had pleafed you, you might have commaunded me in a farre greater Matter, with a farre leffe Penaltie. From the Caftell of *Dwblin,* the Firft of *Julie,* 1578.

Yours, when it fhall pleafe you better to

conceive of me, humblie to commaunde,

E. Mollineux.

Sir Francis Walfyngham *to* Sir Henry Sydney.

My *verie good Lord,*

THE Difpatche of my Lords Lettres touching *Stukeleys* Preparations, and Readineffe to attempt fomewhat agaynft that Realme of *Ireland,* cawfethe mee to fend awaye this Meffinger, *William Grawnfam,* in fome Haft ; and my felfe to bee the fhorter in Writyng. Thus muche only, therefore, I thought good to let your Lordfhip vnderftand, that the Chawncellor departed from

hence

I

hence the Laſt of *Maye*, and will, yf not ſo ſoone, yet ſhortly after the Arrivall of this Bearer, bee with you. And for that your Lordſhip ſhall perceave by ſuche Lettres as the Chawncellor bryngethe, and as before have been ſent from hence vnto you, that the Government of that Realme is, at your Departure, to bee committed chiefly to the Lord Preſident of *Mounſter*, I can not, in Reſpeçt of the Care I have hir Majeſties Service; thoughe I am aſſured your Lordſhip of your ſelfe will have a ſpeciall Care thereof, but wiſhe you leave the Matter of the Ceſſe, and all other Thinges within the *Engliſhe* Pale, in ſo good and peaceable an Order as poſſibly you maye, that the ſayd Preſident maye the better order him ſelfe in that Government: Alſo, that your Lordſhip, before your Commyng awaye, gyve him the beſt Aduiſe and Direçtion that you can, for his better Abilitie, to meete withe the Attempts of the ſayd *Stukeley*, or anie other Forces, either Forayne, or ſuche as may be levyed within that Realme by ill diſpoſed Subieçts. And ſo moſt hartely commendyng your Lordſhip to God, I take my Leave. *Greenwich*, the Second of *June*, 1578.

This Daye the Earl of *Leyceſter*
departed towards *Briſtoul*.

Your Lordſhips aſſured Frend,

Fra. Walſyngham.

Apud Dublin.

Remembrauncies geven by Sir Henrie Sydney, *Knight of the Order,* &c. *and Lord Deputie of* Ireland, *to* Thomas Snagg, *Eſq; her Majeſties Attorney Generall of this Realme, for Thinges to be donne by hym at his Arryvall at the Court. Dated* xj° *Junii,* 1578.

FIRST, To declare, if he be demaunded of her Majeſtie, or any of the Lords, when Oportunitie beſt ſerveth, the State of the Countrey, and the vniverſall Quiet thereof, for the preſent; and then to deſcend (as Occaſion ſhalbe offered) into the State of eche perticuler Province; and howe everye Officer that hath principall Chardge vnder me, carrieth hym ſelfe in his Governement.

2. To requyre the ſpedie Sendinge over of the Lord Chancellour, and namelye, for the Matters of Ceſſe and Ceſſe Cawſies, and the rather to haſten hym, for that he hath bene a principall Dealer both there and here in thoſe Matters.

3. To declare the State of the Courtes and of the Cyvill Magiſtrates; and therein to ſhowe howe Thyngs did proceade at your Comminge, and howe Thinges proceade nowe, and ſpeciallye for the Matter of Revenue.

4. To declare the Neceſſitie of a Parliament, aſwell for the Contynuance of the Subſidie of the Wynes, whiche beinge limitted for a Tyme, is almoſt ſpent; as alſo to revyve the Subſidie of the Ploughland, which is now a Yeare agonne expired.

5. To ſolicite ſome Money to be ſent over for the next Quarterage, if Order be not taken for the ſame alreadye.

Sir Henry Sydney, *and the Council of* Ireland, *to the Lords of the Privy Council in* England.

May it pleaſe your honorable Lordſhips;

YOUR Lettres dated from *Grenewitche*, the Laſt of *May*, were brought me by *William Grawnſame*, the Purſevaunt, the xjth of this preſent *June*, aboute viij of the Clocke in the Morninge: And althoughe the ſame were addreſſed vnto me the Deputie alone; yet I thought it convenient (for ſo the Importaunce of the Cawſe neceſſarilye requyred it) to imparte the Matter preſentlye to ſoche of her Majeſties Counſell as were here niere vnto me, who alſo have ſubſcribed this Lettre with me. And after we had amongeſt oure

felves read the fame fondry Tymes over, and confidered of the Pointes and Subftaunce thereof, touchinge the Advertizements geven oute of *Stewkley*, and of his Intencions and Deffeignes: They concurred fo evenlye in a Manner both with foche, as I, the Deputie, had formerly received, and fome other of vs likewife from fondrie forreine Partes, as we conceived it a Matter fo likelye, and that carrieth in it felfe, foch a Shewe almoft of an vndoubted Certeintie, as we cannot but humblye befeache your Lordfhips to have dewe Confideracion that foch Supply of our Wantes may prefently be had from thence, as we may in due Tyme prevent that which we evidentlye fee at Hand before oure Eies, we have Cawfe fo moch to doubt; which if we fhall want (when Tyme commeth) we may well make Shewe and Demonftracion of oure good Willes (as oure Dueties be) but almoft no Poffibilitie remayneth in vs to do that which is Neade full and our Duties in deede requireth, and your Lordfhips wifheth fhould be donne in foch a Cafe. And, firft, where your Lordfhips have apointed certeine of her Majefties Shipps to repaier to the Seas, vnder fome Perfons of Honnor and Skill, who, duringe this Sommer, may have Regarde to the Landinge of *Stewkley*: We humblye thanke your Lordfhips for it; and in like Manner befeach the fame, that the faide Shippinge may be haftned to bend towardes theife Coafts, fo to prevent the Matter, as by reafon of any further Stay of theim, no fuddein Daungere and Perrill enfue in the meane Tyme: And we, one the other Side (as oure Dueties byndeth us) forecaftinge the worft that may happen to this her Maiefties Realme (whereof vnder her Majeftie we have the Chardge) which God defend. And defieringe as moch as in vs lyeth to avoyd the imminent Perrill (as we take it) are to reveale vnto your Lordfhips the Streingth and Force of the Countrie, which, in Troth, we fynde to be very weake, and not to have fuch a Nomber of Mens Boddies; namely, foch as we may affuredly trufte (for all we may not, fince fo maney, for good Refpectes, are to be doubted) as wilbe a fufficient Strength and Boddie to make Head and refifte foch an Attempt, as it feameth by *Stewkeley* is intended. And therefore we are humbly to pray, that your Lordfhips would geve prefent Order that thofe twoe thowfand Men your Lordfhips write of, which are to be levied out of the Principallitie of *Wales*, and the Counties of *Dorfett, Somerfet, Devon*, and *Corne-wall*, may be ordered prefentlye to comme over, and fpedilye to be imbarqued; and that thofe that are to comme out of Sowth *Wales*, and the Weft Partes of *England*, may be apointed by your Lordfhips Order to land at *Waterforde*, and thofe of North *Wales*, and the Shires adioyninge, may be fent to *Dublin*, without further Expectinge any Lettre from vs; and a greater Nomber forthwith to be put in Order and a Readines to be fent vnto vs, as Neade fhall requier. And we humbly pray your Lordfhips, that fince there are fo maney Penfioners, expert Cap-tens, and other fufficient Leaders here, that your Lordfhips apointe no Captens of Bandes there, but referre the fame to oure Difcreacion and Confideracion here, for fo her Majeftie (in oure Opinions) fhalbe beft ferved, and be fure of experte, able, and fufficient Men to leade her Soldiors, which otherwife may be dowbted, and when it commeth to Tryall, we feare will be found, and then it wilbe too late to remedie it. And likewife that a fufficient Maffe of Victualls for the Victuallinge of iiij M. Men for iiij Monethes, may be provided for and fent ac-cordinge to the Note and Docquett, which herewith we fend to your Lordfhips, of eche feverall Proporcion and Kinde, for that the vniverfall Scarcetie and Dearthe of all Things is foch here, afwell of Corne as all other Provifion, of what Kind foever the fame be, as the Provifion thereof will not by any Poffi-bilitie be made here, where the fame is not in any Sorte to be had: So that we muft expect to be Furnifhed thence of thofe Victualles for the fyndinge of all theim that fhalbe fent hether; and, in the meane Tyme, to prevent oure Wantes; and confideringe the greate Dearthe and Scarcetie here, and that we are to fende prefentlye Forces into *Mounfter*, as we are advifed and directed by your Lordfhips; whiche otherwife we cannct fupplye with Victualls, but of fuch Store as commeth from thence: We have thought it needefull to fend oure Letters, as well to the Maior of *Briftowe*, as to *William Glafier* of *Chefter*, to
fend

fend over foch Proporcion as they have alreadye provided, fo that fome Maffe may remayne here to ferve what Occafion fo ever hapneth vpon the fuddeine. And we will geve foch ftreight Ordere for the Beftowinge, Preferuinge, and well Employinge of the faied Victualls when they fhall come, as may be for her Majefties moft Profitt and Advantage, fo that your Lordfhips fhall have (we hope) no Cawfe thereof to miflyke. In like Manner we humblye defier, that a competent Proporcion of Municion may be fent to lye in Maffe here of all foch Store and Kindes, as is conteined in the Dockett, which herewith your Lordfhips fhall receive, figned with the Mafter of the Ordinaunce Hand; to be accompted and anfwered for by hym, howe the fame fhalbe iffued from Tyme to Tyme, beinge Thinges fo neadefull as when Service fhould be donne, may not in any Sorte be wantinge or fpared : And for that your Lordfhip may not be ignoraunt of the State of the Store of the Municion here, we have cawfed a Note to be fent to your Lordfhips, under the faid Mafter of the Ordinaunce Hand, to the Ende our great Wante may be the foner fupplied thence : And humbly pray your Lordfhips, that a greater Care may be had to fend that which is good and well conditioned then was of the lafte which was fent; the Particulers of which Defectes, as they were prefented vnto vs, we referre to the Reporte of our lovinge Friende *Henry Sheffeild* (whome we have expreffely fent to attend the Bringinge over of the Municion) who bringeth the fame teftified vnder the Mafter of the Ordinaunce Hand; and the rather for the prefent we defier the fame may be perfect and good, for that we are to deale (as we fuppofe) with Men of other Qualitie and Experience then at other Tymes we had, or heretofore have had moche Cawfe to doubte ; and therefore we befeache you fpedilye to difpatche *Sheffield.* And that likewife we may have fent CC choyfe Laborers, for they are the neceffarieft People that are to be defiered for the fuddeine Service ; whereof although we confeffe that this Countrie hath fome Stoare of Apparaunce of foche Men, yet foch they be of fo fmall Skill, Experience, and Dexteritie in thofe Thinges, as one good Laborer brought from thence will do more Service, then any twoe that canne be picked out here will or can do : Wherefore verie requifite it is, that fome fpeciall Care be had, and Order geven, to fend theim. And towchinge the Places your Lordfhips fuppofeth to be fitt to be imployed for Fortificacion, affuredlye your Lordfhips have had that due and grave Confideracion, of the Scite and Defcripcion of the Countrie, howe the fame lyeth, and is extended, as the apteft Places in Dede for that Purpofe (in oure Opinions) are noted in your Lordfhips Lettres ; and fpeciallye for Defence of the Havens, but not fo apt for Fortificacions (as we fuppofe) as the walled Townes be ; if it fo like her Majeftie, to be at the Chardge to fortifie, as the Strengtheninge of *Lymericke,* by the Lord Prefident the laft Yeare, may in fome Parte teftifie, what Neceffitie there is rather to fortifie the Townes, then the Havens ; for the Townes beinge once ftreingthened and fortefied, are able to defend theim felves, and the Bulwarckes be not fo, for if thofe be made, and then we have no garrizoned People and Soldiors, to lye in theim, to kepe and defend theim, the fame perhapps might be a Loffe, both of the Strengthes and Places theimfelves, and likewife of the Artillerie that fhould be placed and left in theim : So that we thinke it not in oure Advifes convenient (favinge your Lordfhips Reformacions) to attempt to make foche Strengthes, before we fhall have Soldiors thence to put in, and man theim ; otherwife the Loofinge of theim, when they be made, would be rather a Streingthe to the Ennimye, then any Healpe or Ayde to vs. And my Lords, foch be the Stoare and Aboundaunce of Havens, Creekes, and apt Places of Landinge and Difcent, a longe that Coaft, beinge not in Diftaunce of Place, above fyve Myles one from the other (moft of theim as we take it) as a hard Matter it wilbe to fortifie in fo maney Places on that Coaft, as fhalbe neadefull of Defence : But cheifelye the fame muft reft in the Strength and Valor of the good Subiecte and Soldior, who are the beft and moft neceffarie Bulwarcks of Strength and Defence, to empeache the Ennimies Landinge, if they fhould attempt it. And for that the Perfectinge afwell of thefe Thinges, as the Supplie

almoft

almoſt of all other Defeƈtes, cannot be donne without Money ; for without that in theiſe Matters of Service, nothinge can be well donne or attempted, and with that both Mens Boddies here may be had of Abilitie ennough to ſerve (thoughe not in ſome Reſpeƈtes comparable with thoſe that come from thence) which wilbe not onely a Meane to kepe theim from the Ennimye, and Harme Doinge, but alſo ſome Strength and Healpe to vs. We humblye beſeache your Lordſhips, that Conſideracion may be had to ſend twentie thowſand Poundes at the leaſt, beſides the ordenarie Quarterage, to remayne in Maſſe in the Threaſorers Handes, to be iſſued as Occaſion of this Service ſhall requier, whome we have apointed to cawſe his Agent to attend for it, and beſeache your Lordſhips ſpedilye to diſpatche hym away. And then we beinge ſupplied with theiſe Thinges, Men, Money, Municion and Viƈtualls, we will not fayle to do oure Dueties, and beſt Indevors to prevent as moch as in vs lieth any Daunger that may be attempted, and hope to yeld ſo good Accompt of oure Doinges as ſhalbe agreable to her Majeſties Expeƈtacion and youers. Humblye prayinge your Lordſhips, that as we have advertized your Honnors, what Wauntes we preſentlye have, and what Proviſion is convenient for vs in Sorte, as your Lordſhips requyred and direƈted vs, we ſhould do : So that it would nowe pleaſe the ſame both to geve Order, that that we write for, may be ſpedilye ſent vnto vs ; and alſo that it would further pleaſe you to ayde and helpe vs, as Occaſion and Matter from Tyme to Tyme ſhall requier. And as Things ſhall fall oute, we will (as becommeth vs) carefullye advertize your Lordſhips, from Tyme to Tyme ; and in the meane Tyme we will geve the beſt Order we can (as partlye we have donne alreadye) generallye to all the Realme, and ſpeciallye to thoſe Partes that are moſt to be doubted and feared in this Caſe ; that they be vpon their Kepinge, and Defence, prepare and fortiſie theim ſelves the beſt they can, and do aſſure theim of oure Healpes, Aydes, Comfortes and Aſſiſtaunce, to the vttermoſt of oure Powers ; beſeachinge your Lordſhips, that for the better Stay of thoſe Partes, you will haſt over as ſpedilye as may be, the Earles of *Kildare*, and *Ormound*, for their Preſences here may ill be ſpared in ſo doubtfull a Tyme, and therefore there Comminge is of no ſmall Conſequence, and we pray your Lordſhips ſo to thinke of it. And even ſo humblye beſeaching your Lordſhips, to have dewe Conſideracion of this Matter, beinge of ſoch Conſequence and Honnor ; and to weigh the ſame, as the Importaunce of ſo great a Cawſe requyrethe, we humblye take oure Leaves. From the Caſtle of *Dublin*, xiiij° *Junij*, 1578.

PS. We have made Choyce of this Bearer, Mr. *Lodovicke Briſkett*, Clarcke of the Counſell here, both to delyver theiſe our Lettres to your Lordſhips, and to ſolicite a ſpedie Anſwere from your Lordſhips ; and have referred to his Creditt and Reporte, aſwell the Declaracion of the State of the Countrie here at this Preſent, as to anſwere to ſoch further Matter (if any be) as may growe of our ſaied Lettres, for that they cannot replye theim ſelves, and for that Purpoſe have delyvered vnto hym certeine Notes and Memorialls. And therefore humbly beſeache your Lordſhips, to geve hym Creditt on oure Behalfes in that he hath to ſay, and with Spede to diſpatche hym thence, and retorne hither to vs agayne.

Your honorable Lordſhips aſſured lovinge Freinds

humblye to commaunde.

H. Sydney, *&c.*

Sir Henry Sydney *to the Mayor of* Briſtol.

AFTER my very hartie Commendacions. I received Lettres of the Date of the Laſt of *Maye*, from the Lords of her Majeſties honnorable Privy Counſell, whereby I was advertized of the great Preparacion that is made by
Stewkeley,

Stewkeley, and other his Complices, and Aydes of forreine Power to do vpon the foddeine fomme Attempt vpon this Realme; whereof, as by their Lordfhips Lettres, I have bene forewarned, and commaunded to be carefull, and with all Policie and Spede, to prevent the fame; fo I am likewife put in Comforte from their Lordfhips, that I fhall have my Wantes from Tyme to Tyme fo fupplied from thence, as I fhall have leffe Cawfe to doubt of any Thinge, the Traytor is able to do againft me; and amongeft other Supplies, I am geven to vnderftand by their Lordfhips, that they have taken Order for the Provifion of a certeine Maffe of Victualls, which fhould be in a Readines there, and that vpon my Lettre and Direecion to you fhould prefently be fent vnto me hether: Wherefore theife fhalbe effectuallye in her Majefties Name, to requier and chardge you, that vpon Receipte hereof, you cawfe the faied Maffe of Victualls, that you have in a Readynes alreadye, or that you can prefently provide for there (beinge apointed for this Purpofe) to be prefentlye imbarckqued to be tranfported thence, and (Wynd and Wether fervinge) to be landed at *Waterford*; and provide the reft with all Spede poffible you can, and delyver over that which you fhall nowe fend over vpon this my Lettre, by dewe Accompte, vnto *John Thickepennye,* whom I have of Purpofe apointed to remayne there, and to receive the fame at your Handes, and to delyver you his Bill, for the Receipte thereof, as apperteineth. And therefore I will, and in her Majefties Name chardge you, as you will anfwere the contrarie at youer Perrill, to fee the Effecte hereof accomplifhed accordinglye. And even fo I bid you Farewell. From the Caftell of *Dublin* the xiiijth of *June,* 1578.

Your lovinge Freinde,

H. Sydney.

The like Lettre to Mr. *William Glafier* of *Chefter,* for Victuals remayning there, to be fent to *Dublin,* and delyvered to *Robart Woodfford.*

Memorialls and Notes for Mr. Lodovicke Brifkett, *touchinge the State of the Realme, beinge fent by the Lord Deputie and Councell to the Courte. Dated from the Caftell of* Dublin *the xiiijth of* June, 1578.

1. **F**IRST, to declare to the Lords, when you fhalbe demaunded, or when you fhall fynde the beft Oportunitie to delyver the fame, in what State the Countrie remayneth at this Prefente.

2. For *Vlfter* you may declare, that the fame of longe Tyme ftoode not in better Termes, for *Tirelaugh Lenaugh* is duetiefull and conformable to any Thinge he fhalbe directed and commaunded, and that *Mac Mahon* although he hath of late bene thouroughly plauged, for the Death of that noble and worthy Gentleman, the Lord of *Lowth* (who for his Loyaltie and Fidellitie, deferveth perpetuall Memorie) yet he is contented nowe to fubmitt hym felfe to reafonable Order; foch as we fhall thinke honorable for the Quene to accept, notwithftandinge the Hurtes and Spoyles he hath received, and that the *Dartrye* the beft and ftrongeft Parte of his Countrie is taken from hym, and geven to an other, who hath put in Pledge and good Affuraunce to anfwere Rente and Service to her Majeftie. For the fame, *Oreiley* likewife, whofe Country was fomewhat fufpected of Harme Doinge, and Receivinge of Stealthes and Spoyles and fome other Diforders, hath put in Pledgies and Securitie, for hym felfe, his Sonnes, and Bretheren, and came hither hym felfe vnto vs, and departed not from vs, before Affuraunce geven for the Anfweringe of foch Hurtes and Performaunce of foch Orders, for the Quiet of the Pale, as we tooke with hym; fo that to conclude, you may affure their Lordfhips, that the State of that Province of *Vlfter,* and of *Oreilies* Countrie adioyninge to the fame, is in verye good Cafe.

3. *Connaught* we learne from Sir *Nicolas Malbye*, the Collonell, who prefently is there, is quiet and in Tune, and fo will contynue, if their be any that hath an Eye vnto theim.

4. *Mounfter* in like Manner is verie well in Order, and not vnlike fo to contynue if the People be not otherwife animated by Forreine Practize, or vnderhand Dealinge by fome that reforte from theim, which nowe is moche to be, confideringe the naturall Difpoficion of the People, howe inclyned they be to Chaunge, and howe apt to receive Newes, and to delyver Bruites, that may ftirre Vnquietnes.

5. *Leinfter*, Thankes be to God, is not in ill Cafe, fave onely the Rebell *Rorie Oge*, who is daylie perfecuted and hath loft maney of his Men, fince the Beginninge of his Profecucion, and of late, fome of his principall Counfellors, and thofe that in Right (of his pretended Title) are next hym felfe, as namely *Neill Mac Lyfagh*, *Omore*, and others, which *Neill Mac Lyfagh* murdered *Ony Mac Hugh*, whereby it is to be hoped, that he cannot longe ftand vp.

6. To folicite with all Care and Dilligence, and according to the Truft repofed in you, the fpedy Sendinge hether of Money, Men, Municion, and Victualls, accordinge as we have written to the Lords ; and declare the State we ftand in, for Waunt of thofe Thinges, and howe vnable we are, by any Poffibilitie, without full Supplye of theim to make Head againft the forreine Ennimie, if he vpon the fuddeine fhould come in, and therefore befeache their Lordfhips, to have that due Care of the Matter, as the Weight and Importaunce of fo great a Cawfe requyreth.

7. To folicite the Sendinge over of xxtie Cariage Horfies with their Furniture, which are fpecially remembred in the Mafter of the Ordinaunce Note.

8. Finallye, we would have you to fhewe, as Occafion offerethe, foch Lettres, Reportes, Examinacions and Notes from Sir *Nicolas Malbye*, and others, as we delyvered vnto you ; and you your felfe fpedilye to retorne againe vnto vs.

Sir Henry Sydney *to the Lords of the Privy Council in* England.

May it pleafe your honorable Lordfhips,

IMmediatelye after my Difpatche made to your Lordfhips by Mr. *Brifkett*, I fent a Gentleman of Creditt, of purpofe, to the Earle of *Defmounde*, with Lettres and Meffage to founde his Difpoficion, and to difcover how he liked of theife Bruites which were fpread, of the Entencions and Defeignes of *Stukeley* and his Kinfman, *James Fitzmorrize*, what Preparacion he made to refift theim (if vpon the Suddeine they fhould attempt any Thinge) and what Affuraunce the State might make of hym in this doubtfull Tyme. And becawfe the Meffenger I fent is a Man fomewhat liked of the Earle, and one of that Skill and Experience, as can well temper with his Humor, I fhall finde at his Retorne (which I looke for fhortlye) I doubt not, fo fpeciall and certeine Reporte, as I fhall knowe what I may truft vnto of hym, and foch as he fhalbe able to leade or governe ; which, al be it I have no Cawfe to doubt of his honnorable and duetiefull Proceedinge, yet for that, in theife waveringe Tymes, Men, that are not fo thoroughlye reclaymed as were in all Pointes to be wifhed, may vnwarrs fall into fome Errours, beinge mifled by ill Counfell : I have cawfed his beft and foundeft Counfellors to remayne aboute hym, and not to departe from hym, till theife Broyles be overblowen, and Things better quieted and fettled : I have likewife written fpeciall Lettres to all the Porte Townes, and to the moft of the Noblemen and Gentlemen of Accompte and Note, that be in the Sowth and Weft Partes, and have prefcribed theim Order what they have to doe, afwell for Matter of Streingth and Fortificacion, as for neceffarie Preparacion and Provifion, whereby they fhalbe better able to refift any fuddeine Attempt, when fo ever the fame fhall hap to be offered. The Lettres that were brought me this Day, by Mr. *Croft*, I have geven Order for the Sendinge theim away. Thofe of her Majefties, addreffed to the Earle of *Defmounde*, and

fome

fome other of the great ones of thofe Partes, I have fent by Mr. *Crofte* hym felfe, and recommended hym to theim by my private Lettres : The reft I have diftributed by other Meffengers, and have directed the Blanks, whiche he brought, to foch as I hope will take the greateft Comforte to receive theim, and be readieft, when Occafion is offered, to do her Majeftie the beft and moft faythfulleft Service. And even fo humbly prayinge your Lordfhips to difpatche away *Brifkett* and *Sheffield*, with your Anfwere and Refolucion for thofe Thinges I write for, whereof I hope your Lordfhips will geve Order I fhalbe prefentlye fupplied, I humbly take my Leave. From the Caftell of *Dublin*, the xxjth of *June*, 1578.

POST SCRIPT.

THE Day after my laft Difpatche to your Lordfhips, I chaunced vpon the Tranfcript of a Paffporte brought from *Spaine*, by a Merchaunte of this Cittie, which the Traytor, *Stewkley*, had geven to certeine *Englifhmen* (it feamed) he had redemed from Captiuitie at *Rome* ; which herewith I fend to your Lordfhips, to acquainte you withe his vayne and pretended Titles, vfurpinge the Names and Stile of other Mens Poffeffions, that I hope wilbe hable to defende their owne well enough from hym, come when he fhall.

The Copie of Stewkeleys *Paffeporte.*

Weixford, and *Caterlaugh Duffercy.* } I *Thomas Stewkeley*, Knight, Baron of *Roffe* and *Idrone*, Vifcounte of *Murrowes* and *Rinfhelagh*, Earle of *Gufort* and *Cathelonfi*, Marques of *Leinfter*, Generall of oure moft Holye Father, *Gregorie the xiijth*, *Pontifico Maximo.*

WE do certifie, in ample and infallible Manner, that from this prefent Porte of *Cadiz*, departeth *Benedict Veglan Gregorie Sylueftre*, and *Dauid Martin*, *Englifhmen*, the which were taken in *Rome* by the Holly Inquifition, of whofe Perfons the Holy Father hath geven vs the Favor and Lycenze to enlardge theim : Declaring hereby the aboue named to be honeft Men, and of good Converfacion, fearing God. And for their Retorne to their Howfies, and Dwelling Placeis, haue praied and befaught me to geve theim this prefent Paffeport, by the which I do commaund to all Manner of Perfons to geve theim free Paffage, and, for Gods Love, to healpe and fauor theim with their Almes, to the Ende they may paffe to the Countrey. And in Confirmacion that we have thus commaunded, we have cawfed theife Prefentes to be paffed by oure Secretaries Hand, and figned withe oure owne Hand, and fealed with oure accuftomed Seale. Geaven at the Porte of *Cadiz*, in the Shipp called the *Saint John Baptift*, the Eight of *Aprill*, 1578.

By Commaundement of his Excellencye.

Sir Henry Sydney *to the Lords of the Council in* England.

My humble Duetie remembred to your honnorable Lordfhips,

THIS Day, in the Morninge, Word was brought me of the Killinge of the Rebell, *Rorie Oge Omoore*, who although fondrie Tymes before he hath bene fo hotlye purfued, and fo hardly fett, as leaving Targett, Skull, Swoorde, Mantle, and all ; he hath efcaped beyonde all Expectacion, either by Swiftenes of his Footemanfhipp, or ells rather (if it be lawfull fo to deme) by Sorcerie or Enchauntement ; for never Wretche, beinge fo longe and earneftlye followed, hath contynued on Foote fo longe ; yet nowe in the Ende he is chaunced by a Devife of his owne he laied to entrapp others (as it is geven forth) into the Handes of theim he fought to betray, which was on this Sorte : On the xxixth of *June*, *Rorie* put forthe a Spiall, which he had framed apt for

that

that Purpofe, to goe to my Lord of *Vpper Offerie*, to tell hym, as it were by Way of great Freindfhipp and Secrecie, that *Rorie* had bene of late in the Countie of *Kilkennye*, and there had taken a great Pray and Spoile of Pottes, Pannes, Pewter, Napperie, Lynnen, and Store of other Howfehold Stuffe and Implements, which eafilye he might come by; and with all Hazarde, *Rorie* and all his Companie (which he pretended were but fewe in Nomber) fo that he would attempt the Matter boldlye with a meane Force: For faieth he, if you come with maney, you wilbe difcovered, and then the Enterprife will quayle. My Lord of *Vpper Offerie*, neither fullye believinge the Reporte of this Companion, nor yet altogether miftruftinge hym, put hym felfe in Areadynes to followe the Occafion that was prefented; and comminge niere the Place where the Baite was laied (as it fhould feame) to have entrapped hym, he fent xxx^tie of his Men into the Woodes to fearche the Rebell, and he hym felfe ftayed with certeine Horfemen and Shott in the Plaines, to attende the Iffue of this Matter, and if Neade were, to refkue his Men he had fett a Woorcke. This Companie were no foner entered ihe Woodes, but the Rebell fhewed hym felfe with a fewe in Nomber, not excedinge xx^tie or xxiiij^tle Perfons, the reft beinge in Ambufhe; beinge of Opinion, that he carried that Fame and Eftimacion a-mongeft the *Irifhrie* for his Valor, as no *Kerne* durft venter vpon hym, if they once fawe his Prefence, wherein he found hym felfe verye moche deceived: For at the firft Viewe, the Lord of *Vpperofferies Kerne*, gave the Chardge upon hym, and at their Reencounter one of theim light vpon hym, and thruft hym prefentlye thorough the Boddie with his Swoorde, which was no foner donne, but twoe or three more likewife hacked vpon hym at once, and gave hym foch mortall Woundes, as downe he fell; and this was the Ende of this rancke Rebell, the laft Day of *June*, in the Morninge, who by the Maintenaunce of his Neighbors, and Supplie of Ayde and Reliefe of fomme of his freindly Borderers, whiche he wanted not in the Tyme of his Neceffities, had fo longe Contynu-aunce, to the Chardge of her Majeftie and the Difquiett of the State. The Re-mayne he hath leaft are not maney, and I hope either, verie fhortlye, to fcaile theim, or ells to make your Lordfhips as good Accompte of theim, as I haue donne of hym. And in the meane Tyme, I humblye befeach your Lordfhips effectuallye to thanke my Lord of *Vpper Offerie*, who of his owne Chardge, and with his owne Forces onelye, without her Majefties Pay, hath adventured hym felfe in this Service, and fo happelye hath atchieved it to his greate Eftimacion and Creditt; which I am the gladder of on his Behalfe, for that all Men have not had that found Opinion of his Fidellitie, which he, afwell in this Service as in maney other Thinges, hathe verye well deferved, in myne Opini-on.

Since the Writinge of my Laft, the Gentleman I fent to my Lord of *Defmound* is retorned, who hath brought fo found Tokens and Teftimonies of the Earles Fidellitie (whereof although for myne owne Parte I had never Cawfe to doubt) as her Majeftie may make as an affured Accompte of his Loyaltie, and of all the Freindes and Forces he is able to make to ferve her Majeftie, as of any one Subiecte fhe hath in this Land; foche hath bene his publique Speaches and Demonftracions, and fo plainelye hath he nowe difcovered hym felfe to the World, as a greater Proffe cannot be made of any Man, then he hath in this Tyme made of hyme felfe. And amongeft other Thinges, I havinge conceived fome Sufpicion of his Brother, Sir *James*, beinge in this queifye Tyme accom-panied with a greater Trayne then I thought it convenient, confideringe the wa-veringe Opinions of fomme Men, howe eafilye they will conceive the Woorft of the leaft Pointe that may be doubtfullye taken (and yet the Suppofall was more then the Matter was in dede, when the Troth was knowen) I requyred of the Earle, by my Meffenger, the better to fatisfie the World, and put me out of Doubt of his Brother, Sir *James*, that he would either vndertake for hym hym felfe, fo that thereby I might be affured of hym, that he fhould lyve due-tifullye, and do no Harme, or ells that he would fend hym vnto me. He an-fwered my Meffenger, that he would doe in the one and the other as I would

direct

direct hym. And there vpon (hopinge by this Meanes the better to affure me) delyvered his Brother by the Hand to my Meffenger, who, together in Companie withe the Bifshopp of *Lymericke* and *Morrice Shean*, the Earles Secretarie, came hither to me to *Dublin*, and offered to juftifie hym felfe in any Thinge he fhould be iuftlye chardged with, and withall proffered, if it pleafed me, in any Thinge to commaund or imploy hym, he would make that good Prouffe of his affured Loyaltie and Fidellitie to her Majeftie, as I fhould have Cawfe to geve hym further Creditt : I was glad to heare it, and hope that when I fhall have Occafion of Triall for her Majefties Service, that I fhall fynd it. Thus moch, my good Lords, I thought convenient to advertize your Lordfhips of the Earles Loyaltie, and of his honorable and found Proceadings, to Thende your Lordfhips may hereafter take fomme Occafion to thanke hym, and even fo I humblye take my Leave. From the Caftell of *Dublin*, the firft Day of *Julye*, 1578.

Your honorable Lordfhips affured lovinge

Freinde humblye to commaunde,

H. Sydney.

Edward Waterhoufe *to Sir* Henry Sydney.

It may pleafe your Lordfhip,

ACcording to your Commaundement, I haue had Conference with Mr. *Brifket* and Mr. *Sheffild*, towching the Lettres which they brought, and haue, as they know, vfed the vttermoft of my Endevour, towching Men, Money, Municion and Victualls : And after long Travall with my Lord Threaferour and Mr. Secretary *Wilfon*, with whome I cheefely delt, I perceiue that a Proportion of Municion fhall be fent by Mr. *Sheffeld*, but not haftely, becaufe he muft ftay till the Raits be made for Cariage of it ; neuertheles, towching Armour, it fhuld feeme her Majeftie had bene enformid of a thowfand Pounds, deliuerid to your Lordfhip in *Wales*, for which the Countrey is not fatisfied. I faid that I knew not how the Matter ftood, but I thought that the Provifion was made by you as farre as euer you had eny Imprefts, and that if the Parcells were not deliuerid, yet I iudged it was left in fome Place of Store, to the Countreis Vfe. The Secreterry told me, that her Majefty wold write vnto you towching that Matter, and that it had bene complainid of here. I cold not inform my felf who were the Complainours, but Sir *John Parrott* hath bene a great Courtier, and reportith that her Majeftie woud faine have him Deputy of *Irland*, and I fufpiCt him the Auctor of the Informacion.

For Victualls, the Queens Shipps are now difchargid, and the Victualls appointid to be fold ; vppon which Direction I made a Motion, that the Bifket and Grayne might be fent to your Lordfhip, but it is otherwife concludid ; for heere is no Sufpicion of Invafion in *Irland*, and becaufe your Lordfhips Intelligence was not frefhe, but your Peticions groundid vppon the Lettres fent from hence by *Graunfbury*, the Purfuvaunt, their is fmall Receuing made of the Matters which we folicyt ; for they fay that in *Fraunce* is no Preparacion, and that the King of *Portugall* hath affurid hir Majefty of all good Dealing : *Stewkeley* is alfo emploied in *Affrique* ; fo, for myne owne Opinion, I think that if the 10000 *l*. lately fent, were heere again, it wold not paffe with a fmall Difficulty. In Conclufion, becaufe your Arrivall heere is expectid, your Lordfhips Frends are cold in Procuering of thes Wants : And therfore I look for no good Succeffe of your laft Lettres, other then for Municion ; and yet I am fuer, both Mr. *Brifkett*, and *Hary Sheffeld*, haue vfid all poffible Dilligence and Erneftenes in the perticuler Points of your Letter ; and what I haue done my felfe, I referre to theim. It fufficeth me that your Lordfhip hath done your Part, and fo preventid the Blame that might be laid to your Lordfhip and the Counfell there for Silence. But *Irifhe* Allarmes are fo farre from waking Courtiers

out

out of their Sleapes, as I am fuer, till they heare that the Enemye is landid, they will neuer think of Aide, that may cary with it extraordinary Charge. Their is now no Speach of the Retorne of the Erles of *Ormond*, and *Kildare*, but all Eies and Eares are convertid to the Doings in the *Lowe Countreyes*, where the States air ftrong, and the Kings Force doth alfo encreafe. The States have made *John Norries* Generall of all the *Englifhe* and *Scottes*, his Regiment 6000, which are vnder iiij Colonells, *Balfour*, *Cauendifhe*, eldeft Son to the Lord of *Shrewefbury*, *Morgan* the Soldier, and *Cromwell*, as I take it; and thus having held your Lordfhip with Matter of fmall Emportaunce, I humbly end. At *London*, the iiijth of *July*, 1578.

Your Lordfhips moft dewtifull

and moft bounden,

Ed. Waterhous.

Sir Henry Sydney *and the Lords of the Council in* Ireland, *to the Lords of the Council in* England.

Oure Dueties to your Honnors humblye remembred,

IT may like the fame to vnderftand, that the Weeke after the Landinge of me, *William Gerrarde*, we called together the Nobilitie, and of everie of the Counties of *Dublin*, *Meith*, *Lowth*, *Kildare*, *Ophaley*, *Leix*, *Caterlaugh*, *Wexford*, *Kilkennye*, and *Typperarie*, certeine of the beft Callinge. We have fpent the Tyme fithence in Conference vpon the Offer made in the Behalfe of the Countrey to victuall the Nomber of one thowfand Soldiours, and to allowe nyne thowfand Pecks of Oates for the Fyndinge of three hundered Horfe, in the Confideracion to have the fame in foche Affuraunce, as her Majefties Service fhould take no Want therebye, and to graunte theim the Contribucion of foch Countries as they requyred, and Lybertie to lay an equall Rate vpon all Landes, afwell foch as clayme to have auntient Fredomes, as vpon other Landes vfuallie chardged; whereunto dyvers diffented, fell out fondrie neceffarie Perticulers, worthie of Debatinge, which held vs longer in Conference then ment; although touchinge the Subftaunce of the Matter, and the Affuraunce, we have drawen the Cawfies to fome Hedds, yet differre we in fome Things requyred of vs in her Majefties Behalfe, and denied by theim, and of other Things requyred by theim, and not confented vnto by vs. Therefore we thought convenient, in a Cafe of fo great Importaunce, before we fhould breake of, or fullie affent, to order to acquaint your Honnors with the Effect of oure Proceadings, all which we have conteined vnder the Titles of the Requefts and Anfwers of vs in her Majefties Behalfe, and of thofe in the Behalfe of the Countrey, and the fame in Notes inclofed fend to your Honnors. And although I, the Deputie, do nowe prepare me with the convenient Spede I may, to take Shippinge, and after my Landinge, to make Repaier vp accordinge to her Majefties Direccion, and then to bringe with me foch further Matters, as are to be imparted to your Honnors, and which neceffarilie concerne this Cawfe of Compoficion, afwell of the Chardge her Majeftie hath fufteined Yerelye by Loffe of Victualls nowe to be faved, if this Compoficion be perfected, and what alfo fhe fhall foregoe, by Loffe of the Subfidie, and otherwife the Compoficion takinge Place: And fo after Confideracion thereof, withe your honnorable Advice to fett downe fome Refolucion; yet becawfe we cannot fatisfie the Requeft which is made on the Behalfe of the Countrie, to have the Impreft of one Quarters Pay to the Soldiour (which we thinke reafonable to graunte) except we firft receive fome Warraunt from her Majeftie to the Treaforer: Therefore have we alfo thought good, in the meane Tyme, to fend this Bearer. The Quarters Impreft is MCxl *l.* The Day appointed to delyver the fame is the xijth of *September* for their Provifion. The fyve thowfand Poundes for the Quarterage is referved to

† be

be defrayed accordinge to her Majefties Direccion ; the other fyve thowfand Poundes is referved, accordinge to her Majefties like Apointement, to be imployed, if Cawfies of forreine Invafion do requyre the fame ; fo as, without her Majefties fpeciall Warraunt, the Impreft requyred cannot be delyvered, with which Warraunt we requyre your Honnors fpedilie to retorne this Bearer, if your Honnors, vpon Confideracion of the faied Notes, conteininge oure Proceadings, fhall fo thinke good. Vpon the Delyverie whereof to the Countrie, there fhalbe Affuraunce taken, that if your Honnors, vpon the Repaier of me the Deputie, fhall miflyke with the Compoficion, and leave vs to the Imponinge of Ceffe, as hath bene accuftomed ; that the fame fhall affuredly be repaied againe to the Treaforer. And thus ceafinge to trouble your Honnors with any further Difcourfies of that Matter, or other Cawfies concerninge the State of the Land, vntill the Repaier of me the Deputie, we humblye take oure Leaves. From the Caftell of *Dublin,* the Firft of *Auguft,* 1578.

Your honnorable Lordfhips affured lovinge

Freindes to commaund,

H. Sydney, *&c.*

Sir Henry Sydney, *and the Lords of the Council in* Ireland, *to the Lords of the Council in* England.

May it pleafe your good Lordfhips,

IN a Poftfcript of youer Lettres, bearinge Date the xxth of *Auguft,* touchinge the Compoficion of the Countrie, we fynde your Lordfhips have conceived fome hard Opinion of Auditor *Jenifon,* for his Protractinge of Tyme, in Finifhinge of his Accompts, imputinge the fame to proceade of the Gayne gotten by his Allowaunce of Entereteineinent, and withall, your Lordfhips do requier he might be difpatched hence with the faied Accomptes.

And for that we have knowen, and fene from Day to Day, the great Dilligence both of the Auditor hym felfe, and of foche Clarcks as he hath apointed and waged for that Purpofe ; that no Day hath overpaffed hym, but that he hath continuallye applied his Office with that Paine and Travell, as hath bene nothinge beneficiall to his Health, befides the great Carefulnes he ever had for the Endinge of the faied Woorke, beinge heped daylie vpon hym, vpon fondrie Occafions as they have fallen oute, and fo intricate, as requyred a more Tyme then was at the firft expected and looked for : We cannot but geve Teftimonie on his Behalfe, that he is altogether to be excufed of Negligence, and hath fo well difchardged hym felfe in the faied Office, as, in oure Opinions, none other whofoever could have donne more, or better for the Tyme then he hath donne. And therefore to with drawe your Lordfhips ill Opinion of hym (if your Lordfhips have conceived any) we have thought good with theife fewe Lynes, in regarde of his honeft, plaine, and fincere Dealinge, to befeache your Lordfhips to accept and allowe of hym, as of a trewe Minifter to her Majeftie, who with all Fidellitie hath imployed hym felfe, as hath becommed a difcrete, carefull, and good Servaunt too doo. And nowe we have difpatched hym away vnto your Lordfhips, beinge in full Readines to have taken his Jorney before the Receipt of your Lordfhips faied Lettres ; and even fo recommendinge hym to your Lordfhips former Favors, do humblye take oure Leaves. From the Caftell of *Dublin,* the xijth of *Auguft,* 1578.

Your Lordfhips affured lovinge Freindes,

humblye to commaund,

H. Sydney, *&c.*

Sir Henry Sydney, *&c. to the Lords of the Council in* England.

It may like your Honnors,

THAT, notwithſtandinge, we heretofore, vpon the Complainte of the Viſcount *Baltinglas*, cawled Sir *Nicholas Bagnoll*, Knight, to anſwere ſoch Hurtes as the ſaied Viſcount ſurmiſed, were committed by hym and his Soldiors, in there one Nights Lodginge at *Baltinglas*, in the Tyme of his Servinge vpon the Rebell *Roorie Oge* : And vpon the Reply of the ſaied Viſcount, to the Anſwere of the ſaied Marſhall, apointed Sir *Lucas Dillon*, her Majeſties Chiefe Baron, and Sir *Thomas Fitzwilliam*, Knights, to examyne ſoch Witneſſes as the ſaied Viſcount would bringe in Proffe of his ſaied Surmiſe : Yet, perceivinge by Lettres latelye received from your Honnors, that the ſaied Viſcounte, before the Retorne of the ſaied Commiſſion and Depoſicions, had written to the Earle of *Ormound* his Lettres, certifienge ſuch Spoiles taken, and of ſuch Value, as a in Note incloſed in the ſame Lettres were conteined ; which beinge preferred by the ſaied Earle to your Honnors, it pleaſed the ſame to retorne to vs, for ſpeadie Order to be taken.

We have, eft ſones, for a more perfect Vnderſtandinge of the Truth of the ſaied Surmiſe, cawled the ſaied Sir *Nicholas Bagnoll* to anſwere, and have procured the Retorne of the ſaied Commiſſion ; and have not onelye reexamined, before oure ſelves, all the former Witneſſes, but alſo, all ſoch other Witneſſes as could be further produced by the ſaied Viſcounte.

Vpon due Conſideracion whereof, and ſyndinge the ſame to differ in Truthe from the Contents of the Surmiſe, and at the Requeſt of the ſaied Sir *Nicholas*, who thinketh hym greatlye touched in Creditt, if the Troth of his Dealinges be not made knowen vnto Honnors : We thought good to ſignifie vnto the ſame in Breife, what falleth out vpon this oure Proceadings, leavinge to your honnorable Judgements, what juſt Cawſe the ſaied Viſcounte had ſo to exclaine againſt the ſaied Sir *Nicholas*, or to fynde hym greived for Want of Juſtice.

The Viſcountes Complainte reſted in Hurtes donne vnto hym ſelfe, whereof (beinge then from Home) he was to take Knowledge of his Servaunts who kept his Howſe.

The cheife Perſonne who kept his Howſe, before vs all, burthened the ſaied Sir *Nicholas*, with no more Hurtes donne vnto the ſaid Viſcount hym ſelfe, then the Takinge of a Barrell of Drincke; a Bacon, and certeine Oetes, all which his Man delyvered for Enterteinemente, beinge of no ſoche Value, as for ſoche a Perſonne, to ſoch a Servitor, in his Tyme of Service to be accompted of.

The Man denied not, but for the ſame there was iiij Kyne paied, in oure Eſtimacion, more in Value, than the Things drouncken or eaten.

The Surmiſe of the reſt of the Goodes ſuppoſed to be taken from hym ſelfe, and conteined in the Note delyvered to your Honnors, *viz.* lv Kyne, xxviij Sheppe, ij Swyne, and Howſehold Stuffe to the Value of vj *l.* before vs all his Man vtterlye denied, that either his Maſter left any ſoche, or that any ſoche were taken.

The Goodes ſurmiſed to be taken from his Tenaunts, beſides the Nombres of Cowes conteined in his ſaied Noates, he valued at CC *l.* for Proofe whereof, he produced of his Tenaunts, a Nombre of poore ſimple Creatures, everie one declaringe what was taken from theim ſelves, not one bringinge the Teſtimonie of any other, to fortifie his Saienge ; amongeſt whome vj of theim, beinge examined before, fell into manifeſt Periurie, vpon there Reexaminacion, which Periurie one of theim beinge puniſhed for, hath confeſſed.

Neverthelesſe, allowinge all their ſingle Allegacions for Truthe, yet the Value of the Goodes taken, exceded not xx *l.* ratinge the ſame after their owne Values.

And

And we be of Opinion, except fome pettie Theftes committed by the Kerne, that there was no Parte of thofe Goodes fo valued at xx *l.* taken, as furmifed.

For by the Declaration of *Henrie Davills,* *Robert Harpooll,* Capten *Mac-woorthe,* and v or vj other Perfonnes of Creditt, who were with Sir *Nicholas,* it apearethe, that after he tooke vp Lodginge, he gave Chardge to everie Capten, to forefee that there fhould be no Spoile committed by the Soldiours, beinge in Nombre Cxl, nor any Thinge to be taken withoute Payment, pro-teftinge Hanginge to any, that fhould take the Value of a Mutton.

And by the like Declaracion vpon their Othes, that there was not one Cowe taken, but foche as was brought with *Mac Shane,* and one *Carragh,* a knowen Rebell, and all put into a Bawne, to the Sight of all Perfons.

They affirmed alfo, that he made Proclamacion at feverall Tymes in the Morninge, thoroughe out all the Towne, before his Departure, that if there was anye, who had Cawfe of Complainte, for Takinge of any Cattell (beinge no Perceil of *Hugh Mac Shanes,* or the *Carraghes* Goodes) the fame fhould be harde and reftored, and that vpon Complainte of.dyvers, there was Clxxiij re-ftored, which the Kerne had dryven with the Pray.

They depofed alfo, that he fent his Servaunts, and the Vifcounts cheife Man, thorough the Towne, with Money to pay for that could be demaunded, and taried hym felfe behinde the Soldiors a Tyme, to fee if any would com-plaine.

By all which Circumftaunces, and the Othes of everie one of thofe, nowe brought to be fworne, who confeffe, that they neither complained then to the Marfhall, nor to the Vifcounte his Servaunt, neither found theim greived of a Quarter of a Yere after, at what Tyme they fay they told the Lord of *Bal-tinglas* thereof. We can hardly be perfwaded to thinke they nowe fpeake trewlye.

Nevertheleffe, vpon that they have depofed, there fhalbe a further Tryall; and vpon due Proffe, wee fhall forefee bothe to do Punifhment, and Reftitu-cion, if any Thinge fall oute to be taken.

And whereas in the faied Lettres, fent to the Earle of *Ormound,* and by your Honnors inclofed, directed to vs; the Vifcounte hath not onelye with great Ve-hemencie affirmed the Truthe of his heynous Spoile, his Vnhabilitie to lyve with out Redreffe. The oft Complayninge with out Countenaunce to have the Cawfe hard, or Hope of Redreffe, no Truft repofed in theim, as may be ga-thered in hym, and the reft of the Nobilitie.

Wee humblye befeach your Honnors, feinge the furmifed Vntruthes fo nierelye touche vs, and oure Service, that it would pleafe your Honnors, fo to write vnto hym, as thereby, he and others may be terrefied, howe by Prac-tize to devife foch Vntruthes to, be preferred to youer Honnors.

And to fortifie the Troth of that we have written, this Bearer hath an Ab-ftracte of the Depoficions to be fene to your Honnors, if it fo pleafe the fame. And fo ceafinge to trouble your Honnors, moft humblye take oure Leaves. From the Caftell of *Dublin,* the xxiiijth of *Auguft,* 1578.

Your good Lordfhips affured lovinge Freinds

humblye to commaund,

H. Sydney, *&c.*

Sir Henry Sydney *and the Council of* Ireland, *to the Lords of the Council in* England.

Oure Dueties humblye remembred to your honnorable Lordſhips,

IN your Lettres of the xiijth of *Julye*, dated from the Courte at *Haveringe*, the Anſwere of ours ſent by Mr. *Briſkett*, touchinge ſoch Supplies as we thought then moſt neceſſarie to be ſent hether (if the Bruite of Thenterpriſe of *Stukeley* had taken Place) amongeſt other Things your Lordſhips noted vnto vs, that for as moche as the Certeintie of the Remayne in the Office of the Ordinaunce was not ſent vnto you together with oure Lettres, you could not ſend ſo full a Proporcion, as we then writt for : Which aſſuredlye, my Lords, was not by the Default of the Maſter of the Ordinaunce, who delyvered a perfeſt Booke of the State of his Office, ſubſcribed with his Hand, to be ſent vnto your Lordſhips ; but the Booke beinge miſlaied, and (yet not by the Negligence of the Clarcke of the Counſell) when the Packett was cloſed vpp, it was omitted to be ſent, as was apointed to have bene ; for vpon the Viewe of that Booke of the Remayne delyvered vnto vs by hym, we ſett downe a Proporcion ſoch as we thought convenient, not onelye to ſupplye the preſent Want, but alſo to have a Store for the better Furniſhinge of the Bandes of Footemen, intended to have bene ſent hether for that Service, which was then moſt neadefull to have bene donne. And where your Lordſhips Pleaſure was to have a ſpeciall Commiſſion addreſſed to the Auditor, and others, to take Viewe of the State of the ſaied Office of the Ordinaunce, and to certifie howe moche remayned in Store before *Michelmas*, *An.* 1576 ; and what hath bene brought in ſince that Tyme, either out of that Realme, or otherwiſe provided, and to certifie what Quantitie of thoſe Remaynes and Proviſions have bene iſſued, and by what Warrants, and what Money is anſwered or anſwerable for the ſame. The Maſter of the Ordinaunce beinge acquainted with your Lordſhips Pleaſures herein, made earneſt Requeſt and Peticion to vs, that a Survey might not be taken for that Tyme onelye, but becawſe his Doinges might be made more apparaunt and knowen vnto your Lordſhips, which he ſuſpeſted were doubtfullye conceived ; that therefore, a Viewe might be made by the Commiſſioners, and a Reckninge and Accompt demaunded and taken of all that had paſſed in his Office from the Tyme of his firſt Accompte, affirminge vnto vs, that in everie Governors Tyme, he hath deſiered and obteined that Commiſſioners might be apointed to take Survey of the Office ; and for Proofe, ſhewed vnto vs, vj ſeverall Surveis, taken by ſeverall Governors Apointements, ſince the Tyme that Auditor *Dix* left this Realme. And where your Lordſhips requyreth further, that ſoch Municion as you nowe ſent, ſhould be more carefullye looked vnto, then that which was laſt ſent ; for that it ſeameth it was reported to your Lordſhips, the Corſeletts were caſt in on Heapes, without any Care of Scowringe or Kepinge theim cleane, whereby the ſaied Corſeletts and Callyvers were ſpoiled with Ruſt, and ſo becomme vnſerviceable : We finde by Reporte of the Commiſſioners, that that laſt Proviſion which was ſent by *Binghame*, was otherwiſe vſed, then your Lordſhips have bene enformed ; for they ſay, that after the Viewe taken of theim, the Maſter of the Ordinaunce cawſed a ſpeciall Place in the Cittie of *Dublin* to be prepared for the Dreſſinge and Oylinge, not onelye of ſoch Corſeletts and Callyvers as were then brought, but alſo of thoſe that remayned afore in the Office, and cawſed Frames of Tymber to be made to hange theim vp, to the Ende they might be preſerved ſerviceable, and kept in Order, as nowe they be. And for that we cannot perceive by any Triall or Examinacion, but that the ſaied Maſter of the Ordinaunce hath carried hym ſelfe in his Office ſince his firſt Enterie verie direſtlye and honeſtlye everie Way. We hope your Lordſhips (if heretofore happelie he have bene vnfreindlye, or hardly reported of to your Lordſhips for that Matter) that it wold pleaſe your Lordſhips to conceive better of hym, and to geve Creditt to vs for his Dealings : For, in

oure

oure Opinions, he hath carried hym felfe verie circumfpectlye and carefullye, and fullye difchardged the Truſt committed vnto hym in the faied Office, as we hope ſhall more plainelye and evidentlye appere vnto your Lordſhips by the Retorne of the Commiſſion, which herewith we ſend your Lordſhips, teſtified vnder the Commiſſioners Handes and Seales. And even ſo befeachinge the Almightie longe and hapelye to preſerve your Lordſhips, we humblye take oure Leaves. From the Caſtell of *Dublin*, the xijth of *September*, 1578.

Your good Lordſhips aſſured lovinge

Freindes humblye to commaund,

H. Sydney, &c.

Lady Mary Sydney *to* Edmund Mollineux, *Eſq;*

Molenox,

I Thoght good to put you in Remembrance to moue my Lord Chamberlein, in my Lords Name, to haue ſome uther Roome then my Chamber, for my Lord to haue his Reſort unto, as he was woont to haue; or ells my Lord wilbe greatly trubled, when he ſhall haue enny Maters of Diſpache: My Lodginge, you ſee, beinge very lytle, and my ſealfe continewaly ſyke, and not able to be mouche out of my Bed. For the Night Tyme, on Roofe, with Gods Grace, ſhall ſerue vs; for the Day Tyme the Quen will louke to haue my Chamber always in a Redines, for her Maieſties Cominge thether; and thoghe my Lord him ſealfe cann be no Impediment thearto by his owen Preſens, yet his Lordſhipe truſtinge to no Playce ells to be provyded for him, wilbe, as I ſayd before, trubled for Want of a conuenient Playce, for the Diſpache of ſouche People as ſhall haue Occaſion to come to him. Therefore I pray you, in my Lords owen Name, moue my Lord of *Suſex* for a Room forthat Porpoſe, and I will haue hit hanged, and Lyned for him, with Stoof from hens. I wiſh you not to be vnmyndfull hear of: And ſo for this Tyme I leue you to the Almyghty. From *Chiſwike* this xi of *October*, 1578.

Your uery aſſured, louing

Miſtris and Frend,

M. Sydney.

Sir Henry Sydney *to his Son* Robert Sydney, *after Earl of* Leiceſter.

Robin,

I Hear well of you, and the Company you keep, which is of great Comforte to me. To be of noble Parentage, uſuallye raiſes an Emulation to follo their great Examples. Thear can be no greater Love than of long Tyme hath byn, and yet ys, betwyne Sir *Harry Nevell* and me; and ſo wyll contynu tyll our Lyves end. Love you thoas we have doon, and do. One Thyng I warn you of; arrogate no Precedency nether of your Cuntremen nor of Strangers; but take your Place promiſcues, with others, accordyng to your Degree and Byrthryght, with Alyens. Follo your dyſcrete and virteius Brothers Rule, who with great Dyſcretyon to hys great Commendatyon, won Love, and could varioſsly ply Ceremony with Ceremony. I here you have the *Dutch* Tourg ſuffycyently, wherof I am glad. You may thearfore ſave Money and diſcharge your *Dutchman*; and do it in deed, and ſend for Mr. *Whyte*; he ys an honeſt young Man, and hys fairely honeſt, and good and ſound to me and my Freyndys. I ſend you now by *Stephen*, 30 *l.* whytch you call Arrerages; tearm yt as you wyll, it ys all I ow you tyll *Eaſter*; and 20 *l.* of that, as *Gryffyn Madox* tellyth me, is *Harry Whytes*. I wyll ſend you at or before *Frankfort* Mart, 60 *l.* ether to bryng you Home, or to fynd you Abrode, as you and your Brother ſhall agre, for half a

Year

Year endyng at *Mychaelmaſs* ; ſo *Harry Whyte* nether hath nor ſhall have Cauſe to thynk, that I am offendyd with hym ; for I cannot look for, nor almoſt wyſh to here better of a Man, than I here of hym ; and how I intend to deale with hym, you may ſe by the Letter I ſend hym. He ſhall have his *l.* 20 yearly, and you your 100 *l.* and ſo be as mery as you may. I thank you, my deer Boy, for the Martern Skynys you wryte of. It ys more than ever your elder Brother ſent me ; and I wyll thank you more if they cum, for yet I here not of them, nor ever ſaw *Caſſymyres* Pyćture. The Meſſenger (of the Pyćture I mean) played the Knave with you, and me ; and after that Sort you may wryte to hym ; but if your Tokens cum, I wyll ſend you ſutch a Sute of Apparell, as ſhall beſeme your Father Sonn to wear, in any Court in *Germany.* Commend me to the Doćtor *Symconys* Father. I love the Boy well. I have no more ; but God bles you, my ſweete Chyld in this World, and forever ; as I in thys World fynd my ſelf happy by my Chyldren. From *Ludlo* Caſtell this 28th of *Oćtober,* 1578.

Your very lovyng Father,

H. Sydney.

Lady Mary Sydney *to* Edmund Mollineux, *Eſq;*

YOU have vſed the Matter very well ; but we muſt do more yet for the good dear Lord then let him thus be dealt with all. *Hampton Courght* I never yet knue ſo full, as ther wer not ſpare Rooms in hit, whan hit hath ben thryſe better fylled then at this Preſenn hit is. But ſome would be ſory, perhaps, my Lord ſhould haue ſo ſuer Footinge in the Courght. Well, all may be as well when the good God will. The whylſt, I pray let us do what we may for our Lords Eas and Quyet. Whear vnto I think, yf you go to my Lord *Howard,* and in my Lords Name alſo moue his Lordſhipe, to ſhew his Brother, my Lord, as they cawle eache other, to ſhew him a Caſt of his Offis, and that hit ſhall not be knone, and aleadge your former Cawſis, I think he will fynd out ſome Place to ſerve that Purpoſe ; and alſo, yf you go to Mr. *Bowyer,* the Gentelman Vſher, and tell him, his Mouther requyreth him, which is my ſealf, to healpe my Lord with ſome on Room, but only for the Diſpache of the Multitude of *Iriſh* and *Welſh* People, that follow him ; and that you will giue your Wourd in my Lords Behalf and myne, hit ſhall not be accounted as a Lodginge, nor knone of. I beleue he will make what Shyft he cann ; you muſt aſſure him hit is but for the Day Tyme for his Beſines, as indead hit is for my Brothers Anſwer of my Stay hear for five or ſix Dayes ; he knowes I have ventured farr allredy, with ſo long Abſens, and am ill thought on for hit, ſo as that may not be. But when the woorſt is knowne, old Lord *Hary* and his old *Moll,* will do as well as the cann in partinge lyck good Frends, the ſmall Porſion alotted our longe Servis in Courght ; which, as lytle as hit is, ſeams ſomethynge to mooche. And this beinge all I cann ſay to the Matter. Farewell, Mr. *Ned.* In Haſt this *Mondaye,* 1578.

Your aſſured lovinge Miſtris and Frend,

M. Sydney.

Yf all this will not ſerve prove Mr. *Huggins,* for I know my Lord would not for no Good be deſtitude in this Time for ſome convenient Playce for his Folowers and Frends to reſort to him, which in this Caſe I am in, is not poſyble to be in my Chamber, tell after Sun ſet ; when the dear good Lord, ſhalbe as beſt becoms him, Lord of his owen.

Sir Thomas Wylkes *to Sir* Henry Sydney *Lord Prefident of* Wales.

My verie good Lorde,

ALthoughe it is not to be doubted, but that your Lordfhip is more particularlie advertifed from hence what is don and occurreth here, than I can of myne owne Knowlege be hable to write vnto yow; yeat to defcharge my Duetie and Promife, made vnto your Lordfhip at your Departure towardes *Wales*, I will not ommitte to write what I my felfe lerne.

Our great Doubte we had of the *Spanifhe* Navie and Preparacion is at this prefent almofte taken waye, by fome flyeng Newes arrived that the faid Navie and Preparacion by the late Deathe of the King of *Portingall*, is divertid into *Portingall*; and nowe is it faid that the fame was in no Sorte fo greate as it was bruited here.

The firft Refolucion taken in Councell for the Withftanding of anie Attempt intended either for this Realme, or the Realme of *Irlande*, waer that the whole Power of *Englande* fhoulde be firft put in areadines, and fpeciall Order taken for the Garding and Defending of the maritaine Shores and Places of Difcente in verie fubftancial Maner; that the whole Navie of her Majeftie fhould be fette furthe, and xii other Shippes of the beft of the Realme, to accompany them. But fince we are become foche (after our old Manner) that there is nothing meant againft her Majeftie and her Dominions, our whole Refolucion is tourned to thre Shippes onlie of the Quenes, to be fett to the Seae and no more. Neuertheles the generall Mufters through the Realme are like to goe forwarde.

Yt is faied here, that prefentlie after the Deathe of this late King of *Portingall*, there is proclaimed Quene of that Realme, a Wief of the Duke of *Bragenza*, a Ladye defcended of Don *Edouardo*, fixt Sonne to *Emanuell*; to defeat *Phulip* of *Spaigne* defcended of *Jfabell*, fecond Daughter to *Emanuel*. Your Lordfhip is not unaqueynted with the naturall Hatred of the *Portingall* againft the *Spaynarde*, and therefore I fuppofe that the King of *Spaigne* will come by that Kingdom with fome Difficultie.

In *Flanders* the whole Fundacion of the Refolucion of the States, for the Continuance of their Warres, is defered to be agreed on and determined this Monethe of *Marche*, at *Antwerpe*, by a full Affemblie of the Provinces vnited: In the meane Whyle the Prince of *Orange* hathe ben in *Freifeland*, ys com to *Vtrecht*, and from thence comythe to *La Haye*, where the States of *Holland* and *Zelande* do mete him. I pray God their Temporifacion be more profitable vnto them then our Coldnes and Securitie here, may chance to be vnto our felfes. In the *Lowe Countries* thay ftande yeat vppon the Calling in of *Monfier*; and in Courte here, as farre as I perceive, the Caufe of his Comyng heither, is either becom tepide, or altogether colde; there be Euafions funde in *France* and Doubts here at Home. And this is as muche brieflie, my good Lorde, as at this Tyme I am hable to write; and fo defiring God to fende yow good Healthe, long Life, and a fpedie Retourne to the Courte, where I wyfhe all you Like. I take my Leave moft humblie. From the Courte at *Whytehall* the vith of *Marche*, 1579.

Your Lordfhip mofte humblie to commaund,

Tho. Wylkes.

Sir Francis Walfyngham *to Sir* Henry Sydney, *Lord Prefident of* Wales.

My verie good Lord,

BY Advertifements lately receaved owt of *Ireland*, as well of the vncertaine Loyaltie and Devotion of the Nobilitie and Gentlemen of *Munfter*, to hir Majeftie, as of certaine Ayd that is expected by the Rebelles there, from the King of *Spaine* (which notwithftanding can not fall owt fo great as ether was intended, or they looked for, by Reafon of the vnlooked for Refiftance of the *Portugals* againft the King of *Spaine*, againft whofe Preparacions, hee fhall bee conftrained to imploy moft of his Forces, if hee entend any Thing that Way) hir Majeftie hath been moved to fend a Supplie of eight hundred Men into *Ireland*, as well to keepe thofe doubtfull Subiects in Obedience, as to make a fpeedier End with the Troubles that the Rebels have caft hir Highnes into, beyng of Opinion that theis with the reft that are there aireadie, and hir Shippes, that lye vppon the Coaftes of that Realme, and are to remaine there, vntill *September*, wilbee a fufficient Power to withftand all fuch foreine Ayd as in any Likelihode is to come vnto them this Yere. And this is the Cawfe of that Levie, which by Direction from hir Majeftie your Lordfhip is to make in thofe Parts. It may pleafe your Lordfhip furthermore to vnderftand, that hir Majeftie willed mee to acquaint your Lordfhip with hir Pleafure, for your continuall Refidence within your Charge, without any Kind of removing from thence, thefe dangerous Tymes, wherin Occafion may bee offred vppon the fodeine of Services to bee done, which in your Abfence can not ether fo well, or fo convenientlie bee perfourmed, as the Neceffitie of hir Highnes Service may require. And this Care fhee hath commanded mee to recommend vnto your Lordfhip the more earneftlie, for that fhee is given to vnderftand, that your Lordfhip doth fometime refort to *Wylton*; which for the Reafons aforefaid fhee fomewhat mifliketh. And fo I take my Leave of your Lordfhip. From the Court at *Nonefuch* the xxiith of *June,* 1580.

Your Lordfhips to commaund

Fra. Walfyngham.

The Prince of *Cardyn* arryved at *Sandwich* in fecret Sorte the xix of this Prefent. The Ende of his Repeyre hether is to acquaynte her Majeftye, with the great Wronges they dayly fuftayne, and to demaunde Supports, whereunto I feare they fhall receyve a cowld Awntfwer.

I thowght good to let your Lordfhip underftande, that my Lords are dyfpofed to commyt the lendynge of 100 Men to *Vaughan Jones*, whome your Lordfhip recommends.

The Sheriff and Juftices of Peace of the County of Glamorgan, *to Sir* Henry Sydney, *Lord Prefident of* Wales.

Pleafeth it your Lordfhip to vnderftande,

THAT whereas, vppon Peticion founded on miftaken Grounde, you addreffed your Lettres, thereby requiring the Sherif and Juftices of Peace of this Cowntie of *Glamorgan*, to bynde all thofe that fhall refufe to contribute ratablye towardes the Finifhinge of *Cardif* Bridge, accordinge to the Statute in that Cafe made, wee have thought requifite (leaft the feared Yll might hinder the wifhed Good) to crave the Revokinge of thofe Lettres by others ; in that the State of the Bridge ftandeth prefentlye vppon thefe Termes. After fome Queftion betwene the Towne and Countrey, whether of them weare to be chardged by Lawe to bwilde the fame : The Towne fuppofinge the Countrey to be chargeable therewith, and the Countrey the Towne, wherevppon Likelyhod of Sute grewe betwene them : And after feuerall Attempts to compownde the Queftion, and as many Breaches enfewinge, the Countrey ftill offeringe, by Waye of Benevolence, to affifte them to bwilde the Bridge : The right honorable the Earle of *Pembroke* beinge made prevy therof, directed his Townefmen of *Cardif* to take a milder Courfe, which notifyed to the Juftices of Peace of this Countie, they (havinge alfo fome other Occation to conferre for her Majefties Service) directed fourth Warrantts to the Highe Coneftables of euerye Hundred within this Countie, requiringe them to geve Admonition to Thinhabitaunts of euerye Parifhe within their Limytts, to appointe ij, iiij, or more, accordinge to the Greatnes of the Parifhe, auĉthorifed for them to aſſente to, or diſagree from Points to be confidered, aſwell for the Bridge as for other Matters, at an Aſſemblye called to *Cowbridge* on the *Eve* of *Palme Sondaye* was Twelve Moneth : At which, after longe Diſcourſe, and ſeuerall Opinyons yealded, hit was at length agreed on all Sides (without Diſſent of any) that a Stone Bridge fhoulde be bwilt at the common Charge, and the Judges to be confulted, whether Towne, Countrey, or both, weare chargeable by Lawe with Bwildinge thereof ; and if the Burden laye on the Contrey, then wee to ac-cept our Quittaunce, for our Money payed as due by Lawe ; if on the Towne, then they to yelde vs Quittaunce, as of a Some graunted of our Be-nevolens. And in the meane Tyme, hit was agreed that Tafke fhoulde be ge-ven, the Some rated with moſt Indifferencye, and the fame imediatly levyed, which hath bene done, beinge proportionably rated accordinge to the ancient Cuſtome through owt the Cowntie, vppon euerye Hundred, Parifhe, and Perſon within the fame, beinge judged by all Men to be the moſte indifferent Waye : Sith which Time, as a great Nomber have paied, fo are there not fewe whoe ſtaye Payment, of whom wee rather judge the greateſt Nomber to be vnprovided of what riſeth vppon them to be preſentlye difburfed, then malici-ouſlye difpofed to hinder fo charitable a Woorke, yet can wee not denye but divers have diuerflye caveled thereat, which not with ſtandinge, wee thincke the moſt obſtinate rather doubted, leaſt the Courfe taken might tende to Exaĉtion, then plainlye denyed to geve as Benevolens : Therefore, as before, thefe are to befech your Lordſhip by thefe Lettres to be graunted, to commaunde, that all thofe be bounde to appeare, that fhall refuſe to paie their Benevolence, by generall Aſſents graunted, and by Thadvice of the Juſtices of Peace (as the myldeſt Waie) ratably proportioned ; vpon the which Lettres received and pub-liſhed, wee truſte wee fhall make an Ende of all your Lordſhips Troubles and ours in that Behalf. Thus wee humbly take our Leave, the viijth of *Julye*, 1580.

Your Lordſhips at Commaundment,

> N. Herbertt, Edwarde Manfell, William Mathew, Mathias Herbert, Ley. Pryce, Edward Stradlynge, Thomas Lewys, Anthony Mawe, Myles Dutton, William Carne.

Sir Francis Walfyngham *to Sir* Henry Sydney.

My verie good Lord,

I Have receaved your Lordſhips Lettre of the vjth of this Prefent, and towch-ing the Placyng of my Lord *Stafford,* a Cownfellor in the Marches, for ſuche Cawfes as you have expreſſed, I think it inconvenient : And therefore mynd, accordinge to your Defyre, to ſtay this Matter, vntill fuch Tyme as all his Cawfes dependyng in that Court bee determined ; and yf Need be, herein alfo to move hir Majeſtie. I am nowe further to defyre your Lordſhip, that where of late you writte to me, towching fome Thinges to bee added to the Commiſſion, you have to deale with Recuſants ; the fame, your Lettre, beyng by fome Mifhappe loft, you would fend me the lyke ; wherevppon I will ac-complifhe as foone as I can that you require. Howbeit for that, in the Mend-yng of the Defeĉt in the fayd Commiſſion, hir Majeſtie hir felfe is to be dealt withall ; which peraduenture will require fome longer Tyme : Myne Opinion is, that it weare good your Lordſhip, with the reft, proceaded agaynſt the Re-cufants, in the meane Tyme as well as maye bee, by Vertue of the Commiſſion in fuche Forme as allreadie you have it ; and fo moſt hartely commendynge

your

your Lordſhip to God, I take my Leave. From the Court at *Nonſuche*, the viijth of *Julye*, 1580.

Your Lordſhips aſſured loving Frend,

Fra. Walſyngham.

The ſeldome Meetyng of my Lords of the Counſell, is the Cauſe why the Delaye of Awntſwer is made.

And as for Thinges that are made to paſſe the Queenes Signature, yf they be not obteyned with that Speed you deſyer ; your Lordſhip and the Counſell ther, muſt beare with us the Secretaryes ; for we cannot doe therin as we woold.

Sir Francis Walſyngham *to Sir* Henry Sydney, *Lord Preſident of* Wales.

My verie good Lord,

MY Lords of late callynge here to Remembrance the Commiſſion that was more than a Yeare agoe given out to your Lordſhip, and certayne others, for the Reformation of the Recuſants and obſtinate Perſons in Religion, within *Wales* and the Marches thereof, marvayled verie muche, that in all this Tyme they have heard of nothing done therein by you and the reſt ; and truly, my Lord, the Neceſſitie of this Tyme requiryng ſo greatly to have thoſe Kynd of Men dilligently and ſharply proceaded agaynſt, there will here a verie hard Conſtruction bee made, I feare mee of you, to reteine with you the ſayd Com- miſſion ſo longe, doyng no Good therein. Of late, nowe I receaved your Lordſhips Lettre towching ſuche Perſons as you think meet to have the Cuſ- todie and Overſight of *Mongomerie* Caſtle, by which it appearethe you have begone, in your preſent Iorneys in *Wales*, to doe ſomewhat in Cawſes of Rel- ligion ; but having a ſpeciall Commiſſion for that Purpoſe, in which are named ſpeciall and verie apt Perſons to ioyne with you in thoſe Matters, it will bee thought ſtrange to my Lords to heare of your Proceading in thoſe Cawſes, withowt their Aſſiſtance : And therfore, to the End their Lordſhips ſhould conceave no otherwiſe than well of your Dealyng withowt them, I have for- borne to acquaynt them withe our late Lettre, wiſhyng your Lordſhip, for the better Handlyng and Succeſſe of thoſe Matters in Relligion, you called vnto you the Buſhoppe of *Worceſter*, Mr. *Phillips*, and certayne others ſpecially named in the Commiſſion. They will, I am ſure, be glad to wayte on you in ſo good a Service, and your Proceading together with them in theiſe Matters will bee the better allowed of here ; and ſo, with my hartie Commendations to your Lordſhip, I take my Leave. *Otelands, the ixth of Auguſt,* 1580.

Your Lordſhips aſſured loving Frend,

Fra. Walſyngham.

Your Lordſhip had neade to walk warely, for your Doings are narrowely obſerved, and her Majeſtie is apt to geve Eare to any that ſhall yll you. Great Howlde is taken by your Ennemyes, for Neglectyng the Executyon of this Com- miſſion.

Sir Henry Sydney's *Account of the State of Lands,* &c. *in* Angleſey, *be- tween* Robert Dudley, *Earl of* Leiceſter, *and Sir* Richard Buckeley, 2d *of* September, 1580. Anno Regine, &c. xxij.

THE ſaid Daye it pleaſed my Lord Preſident to wryte his Lettres to Sir *Richard Buckeley*, ſignefieng to him therby, the Receipte of her Majeſ- ties Lettres, and of his verie good Lord and Brothers, my Lord of *Leiceſter*, his Lettres, touchinge the Forreſt Cauſes in *Angleſey*. And that he ſhold come over

I

óver to his Lordſhip, to ſignefie his Travell and Furtheraunce he had taken in the Service, as it was expected for by my Lord of *Leiceſter* ; which ſaid Lettre was deliuered by *Whyte*, my Lord Preſidents Servaunt, the iijde Day of the ſaid *September*, in the Morninge.

The Fifte of the ſame Moneth, Mr. *Thomas Buckeley*, Vncle vnto Sir *Richard*, deliuered in Meſſage to my Lord Preſedent at *Denbighe*, from Sir *Richard* ; that his Nephewe wold have wayted vpon his Lordſhip accordinge to Dutie, but that he was partly ſicke, and not apte to travell ; with further Speach, tending to that End, in Excuſe of Sir *Richards* Abſence. And at that Inſtant, afore further Speach vſed, came Sir *John Huband*, Mr. *Towneſhend*, and Doctor *Ellice*, whom his Lordſhip did call vnto him.

And then my Lord Preſident, in the Preſence of the ſaid Gentlemen, and the ſaid Mr. *Buckeley*, declared what Meſſage he had receved from Sir *Richard Buckeley* ; and then Mr. *Buckeley* further ſaid, that he had in Commiſſion from his Nephew, to imparte vnto his Lordſhip what Travell and Corſe he had taken for the Service in *Angleſey (viz.)*

That he had called before him, at ſeuerall Times, all his owne Tenaunts, his Frends, and his and there Followers, and had demaunded of them to geve there Conſents, that two thouſand Pounds might be leavied in the ſaid Counȧty, to gratifie my Lord of *Leiceſter*, with ; vſing theſe Reaſons to perſwade them :

Furſt, That my Lord of *Leiceſter* was Aman of great Honor, Power and Strength, and ſuch a one, that for his owne Parte, he found him ſelf to weake to contend with, and that he would aſſiſte and defend them no longer ; and that if there Eſtats were loked to, they wold be found verie weake, with other Speaches, howe others were dealt with, and had yelded, and ſaid that it was anſwered by thoſe his Tenaunts and Frends *(viz.)*

They thought there Eſtats perfect and ſure, the Proclomacion that was ſet furth of late did helpe them, and that they feared not, but they ſhold have Juſtice, and ſawe no Cauſe whye they ſhold contribute to geve any Some of Money ; to which Anſwers the ſaid Sir *Richard Buckely* replyed, ſaing, *viz.*

I wiſhe you to be better adviſed, and yet iterated his former Perſwaſions vnȧto them, wiſhing them to be adviſed vntill a certen ſhort Day, at which Day they gave full Reſolucion, that they were all contented to be Contributaries for the ſaid two thouſand Pounds, ſo as the Buſshops Tenaunts, Sir *William Harberts* Tenaunts, Mr. *Bagnolts* Tenaunts, *Owen Woodds* Tenaunts, and all others of the ſaid County, wold be Contributaries for the ſaid Some alſo ; after which Meting, he reported that his Nephew, Sir *Richard*, dealt with diuerſe Gentlemen, Freholders, and Frends in the ſaid County, and found them to be gret Hinderers, and not willing to the ſaid Payments ; concludinge, that his Nephewe deſiered to knowe his Lordſhips Opinyon and Adviſe what to doe, and that for his owne Parte he was at my Lord of *Leiceſters* Comaundment.

The ſaid Lord Preſident finding the ſaid *Thomas Buckley*, in this his Meſſage and Circumſtances, to be verey diſcret and wiſe, his Lordſhip therfore adviſedly anſwered, and wiſhed him ſo to imparte vnto his Nephewe ; that albeit he reȧceved by him no Letter of the Mynde of his Nephewe, yet for that, he deliuerȧed the ſame ſo fully, and in ſuch good Sort and Termes, he therfore accepted the ſame in good Parte. And for the Matter, his Lordſhip ſaid, that he well knewe, that Sir *Richard Buckley* had no ſuch Comiſſion from my Lord of *Leiȧceſter*, nether to demaund no ſuch Somme of Money, nor yet to take any ſuch Corſe in this Service there ; therby to ſattisfie his Lordſhips Expectacion ; affirmyng further, that the Gentlemen and Freholders had gret Reaſon to deny Sir *Richards* Requeſt, in that they ſhold be required to make Payment, and no Conſideracion on my Lord of *Leiceſters* Parte to ſatisfie them for the ſame ; adȧding further, that this Mans Offering of Service was not honorable to his Lordȧ

ſhip,

fhip; and as my Lord Prefident termed yt, yt was but a Kind of Comerthe; and rather then his Lordfhip fhold geve Place herevnto, or that yt fhold be faid, that the Lord Prefident, travelling hether by her Majefties expreffe Commaundement, fhold confent hervnto, he wold furft fell a C *l.* Land of his owne Inheritance, to his Lordfhips Vfe; concludeinge an vtter Miflike, and that there was no good nor fynfere Meanynge in Sir *Richard,* in this Handling this Caufe.

To this Effect alfo, Sir *John Huband* vfed the like effectuall Speaches, faing that Sir *Richard* before hand did well knowe that this Offer wold not be accepted, nor Procedings liked, and that yf no other Corfe wold be taken by Sir *Richard,* the Service wold proceede accordinge as heretofore hit hath bene well begonne, for that there was no Reafon that the Ynocent fhold be Contributor as well as the Offender; and then the Lord Prefident faid he wold travell thether in Perfon, rather then this Service fhold have no good Paffage and Succeffe.

And Mr. *Townefhend* then adding, that he wifhed that Sir *Richard Buckley* fhold faull from this Corfe, and that he him felf and his Tenaunts fhold furft come and compound with my Lord Prefident, for thofe Lands of his already found by Office in the Counties of *Anglefey,* and *Carnarvon;* and thereby he fhuld bothe fhowe agood Begynninge towards the Fynyfhinge of the Service, and his laft profeffed good Will to his Lordfhip; but by any other Kinde of Travell herin, yt was but Wynnynge of Tyme, and but Showe of Frendfhippe; which Doctor *Ellice* affirmed.

And nowe thefe laft Speaches, my Lord Prefident and Sir *John Huband* thoroghlie confirmed; my Lord Prefident requieringe Mr. *Buckeley* to departe, and to returne with Anfwere furthwith, advifing Sir *Richard,* that he fhold vfe plaine and honeft Dealing towards my Lord of *Leicefter,* and not to forgett his honorable Frendfhipps and Countenaunce he often fhewes towards him, to the Augmentacion of his Credyt and Lyving, thre or fower C Marks Ayere. And thus Mr. *Buckley* being fully fatisfied with Anfwere, departed, with Promes to returne fpedelye.

Sir Richard Buckley *to* Sir Henry Sydney, *Lord Prefident of* Wales.

My very good Lord,

WHERAS vppon the Receipt of your Lettre I forthwith fent over my Men and Horfes, puttinge my felfe in a Redines at the next full Sea to be tranfported over, for more Expedicion of my Repaier towards your Lordfhip, to whom both in Dutie and good Will, I long fythens fownde my felfe verry muche bownden; yet beinge in the meane Tyme taken with an extreme Paine and Stiche in my Syd, was inforfed for that Prefent to omytte my Determynacions; and beinge by the Vehemencye of my Greefe vnable to writt, to avoyd Loffe of Tyme, thought beft to adreffe vnto you, my Vncle, as well to fignifie the Caufe of my Staye, as alfoe to receve from your Lordfhip fuche Direction as pleafed you to deliver for Fortherans and Accomplifhment of my verrye good Lords Procedinges in this Countie, which, above all Things, in Sort as his Lordfhip gave me Order, I wyfhe and will labor to advaunce; at whofe Retorne and Report of your Lordfhips Pleafure in that Behalfe, I am verelye brought to thinke that he hathe muche mifconceaved of your Speaches, for that the Order of Procedinge, which, as he faithe, your Lordfhip wifhethe me to take, dothe varye, and is all together from the Direction delivered vnto me by my Lord, afwell by Worde as by his Lordfhips Lettres, one wherof I receaved within this Fortnight. Somme Eafe I finde of my Stitche, and as fone as I fhal be able to endure Ridinge, I will attend your Lordfhips forther Plefure; and I truft vpon Conferance with your Lordfhip, yf it pleafe you, Matters in this Ile may be brought to fuche End as my Lord wifhethe. Soe ftill, with my humble Comendacion, wifhe the Continuaunce of your Lordfhips well Doinge. *Bewmarryes,* September 7, 1580.

Your Lordfhips to command,
Richard Buckland.

Sir

Sir Henry Sydney's *Anſwer.*

After my verrie hartie Comendacions,

I Receaved your Lettre, dated at *Bewmarries* the viijth of this preſent *Septem-ber,* the viijth of the ſame at Night, delivered vnto me by this Bearer your Servaunt; declaringe your Willingenes and Redines to come vnto me ; but pre-vented by a ſodden Payne and Greiſe in your Syd, the Vehemencie whereof mad you bothe vnable to Write, and cut of youre former Determynacion to com ; yet for the avoydinge the Loſſe of Tyme, you adreſſed youre Vncle vnto me aſwell to ſignifie the Cawſe of your Staye, as to receive Direction for the Furtherance of my Lord of *Leiceſter* Cauſes in that Countie, which you ſeme to be verry deſirous to advaunce. And as I am of Opinion that your Example in doinge that effectually which you may doe, will doe great Good, for that the greater Number within that Countie will nott refuſe to followe that Courſe, which you ſhall lead. Soe if you comm and offer Compoſicion for your ſelfe, and your Frends, Tenaunts and Kinsfolkes, for thoſe Lands you and they have encroched in the Counties of *Angleſey* and *Carnarvon* ; the ſame wilbe an Argu-mente of your good Will in ded ; and ſuche as here tofore you have manie Tymes offered and profeſſed : And therfore in this Point I ame deſirous to receave your private Anſwere what you will doe. And whereas you write, that you are brought to thinke that your Vncle hathe miſconſtered of my Speeches ; yf you had eyther written vnto me what he reported from me, or ſent him backe againe with your Awnſwer vnto me, which I expected, you might therin have bene better reſolved, and I muche more ſatisfied ; and where you ſaye, that the Order of Proceedinge nowe intended doth varrie, and is altogether from the Di-rection delivered you by my Lord of *Leiceſter,* as well by Word as by Lettre ; for that you ſhewe not what Direction you receaved, I am not eaſelie to be in-duced to thinke, that you have been preſcribed to hold any other Courſes but ſuche as hath bene generally reſolved vpon for the Advauncement of the Cauſe, wherin you of all ſhewe your ſelfe moſte conformable, yf you will geve the Ex-ample, to come to compownde for your ſelfe and Tenaunts, for thoſe Lands you and they have encroched. And evenſoe expectinge your Anſwere herein with convenient Speed, I bid you Farewell. From *Denbighe* the ixth of *September,* 1580.

Your lovinge Frend,

H. Sydney.

Sir Henry Sydney *to* Arthur *Lord* Grey, *Lord Deputy of* Ireland ; *how to proceed in his Government of that Kingdom.*

I Doe remember, my verry good Lord, that I wrought unto you ; I would by Auditor *Jeniſon* wright more at Large, whoſe Comminge hether to me, put me in Remembraunce of the ſame. And now, my Lord, in Satisfaction of your Requeſts, and Eaſynge of my deſirous Mynde of your happie Suc-ceſſe, in that vnhapie Countrie ; in the louingeſt Manner that I canne, I ſende vnto your Lordſhip theis Notes followinge, which, if I ſhold laye downe as Principles of Gouernment to your Lordſhippe, I might well be likened to the Puttock, that taught the Faulcon to flie ; or, if I ſhold wright vnto you any Inſtructions for martiall Deſſiines, or Actions, I might well be ſcorned with that Scholler that offred to reade to *Hanibale, De Arte Militare.*

But nowe to beginne, and that with Godde Almightie : As I knowe you are relidgious, ſo I wiſhe your Lordſhippe to frequent Sermons and Praier in pub-lique Places ; it would comforte the fewe Proteſtants you haue there, and abaſhe the Papiſtes, whereof you haue many.

Haue ſpeciall Regarde to the Helthe of your Bodie ; be not withowte a Phiſition of your owne ; and he of this Lands Birthe ; and as you haue ben al-waies

waies delighted in vertuous and noble Exerſiſes ; ſo what Buſines ſoever you haue, vſe wekely ſome Daies, or rather dailie ſome Howers, to continewe the ſame ; otherwiſe ye ſhall bothe dull your Sprights, and mak your Bodie vnhable to ſerue.

Prouide carfull and bowlde Officers for your Howſhold, and put on a Determinacion, to live within the Compas of your Allowaunce ; wherin I wiſhe you to make a Patterne of other Men, rather then of me ; who by ſpending there (and yet in Truthe not prodigalie) am forced to ſpoile my Patrimonye heere ; with what Reward or Thank, I knowe your Lordſhip cannot be ignorant ; and lett one of the princepall Officers of your Howſhold haue a Care for the Collection of your Ceſſe for the ſame : And now *vt vno Verbo dicam*, never agree withowte Ceſſe, for if you take Money, it wilbe made a greate Matter heere, and yet not ſerue your Torne their. Truſt me, my Lord, this one Perticuler was the Thinge that chefely brak my Backe, which I only releaſed, to bringe the People more wiling to advaunce the Reuenewe of the Crowne ; and ſo I did, as herafter your Lordſhip ſhall perceive in this Lettre : This Officer I termed my Clarke Controwler ; and albeit I had bothe Threaſorer and Controwler ; his Precedents in Ranke ; yet had I never a one that I truſted better : If your Lordſhip, or your Officers, have Neede of any Formiler of my Howſhold held there, if you wright vnto me for it, I will ſende it you, ſo ſone as I can gette it ; for here I have none for that Countrie : Be ſuer of a juſte and painfull Man, to be Gentleman of your Horſe, who ſhall have Neede to have a Yoman vnder him ; in theis two Officers reſteth mvch, importinge bothe Honnor and Proffitte. There liveth yet an owld Man, *Powle Greene* by Name, vnto whome, by the Waie, I beſeche your Lordſhip to be good Lord ; he can inſtructe, and I am ſuer will, for ſo have I written to him, who ſoever he be, that your Lordſhip will putte in that Office.

Your beinge in actuall Warres, I neede not to aduiſe your Lordſhip to make none, withowte the Conſente of the Councell ; but for any Charge that may be for the ſame Warres layde vppon the Countrie, doe it not withowte calling them to it, and others of the Nobilitie, as hath ben accuſtomed ; for althoughe you have not all to conſente with you, yet I dowte not but you ſhall have ſo ſtrong a Partie, as alwaies ſhalbe ſufficient for your Diſchardge : One greate Matter you ſhall have to deale in at the Councell Borde, which is the Ceſſe for the Armie, and your Howſhold ; and, my Lord, as this aduiſed, compownde not for any Moneye, they will offer you. I did, and, as I writ beſore, vndid my ſelf by the ſame ; for, vppon their greuous Complaintes, afirminge that ſome one Ploughe Land was chardged with twelue Pounds, and I think might prove theye were chardged with eight, I compounded with them for five Marks *Sterlinge* ; which five Marks *Starlinge*, vppon everie Ploughe Lande, amownted to two thowſand and ſower hundred Pownds *Sterlinge*, for one Yeare, and the ſame received within one hundred Pownds, little more or leſſe, by the aboue named Clarke Controwler ; and the ſame might haue ben fixed to the Crowne Imperiall for ever, yf it had ben well ſtode to here : The Limites and Counties chardged to this, I thinke wil apere in the Councell Booke ; if not, I knowe none ſo able to informe you as the Secritery *Chalinor* ; my Opinion is, your Lordſhip ſhold be reſolute in this, that you ceſſe them accordinge to Theſtate of your Howſhold, and Nomber of your Gariſon ; the Man laſte named I ever fownde painfull, ſkilfulle and faithfull, and praie your Lordſhip to be good Lord to him, and lette him knowe that I forgette him not. My deere Lord, in Conſultacion of this Matter, and of all other Matters that muſt be treated of at Councell Borde, ſuppreſſe Paſſion ; you ſhalbe tempted in *Summo grade* : I had forgotten one late Thinge, and yet materiall, and that is, the Choiſe of Ceſſers for the Gariſon, and Raters for your Howſhold ; for albeit I fownde ſome more honeſter then other, yet amongeſt them all, never a perfect honeſt Man.

For

For the Warres nowe in Action, I wotte not what to wright, for that not long agoe my Lord of *Lecefter* wright vnto me of your Lordfhips fafe Arivall there, of the Deathe of Sir *Jeames* of *Defmond*, and of Thouerthrowe of Sir *John* his Brother, and howe everie Thing wente well ther ; but fince I have harde of a fhrewde Conflicte in *Goulranell*, and divers principall Men flaine in the fame, and that the *Defmonds*,aer of fuch Force as they be able to kepe two Armyes ; and to whether of theis Factions I fhold aduife your Lordfhip to adreffe your felf, confideringe the Nerenefs of the one to *Dublin*, Thopinion and Poffibilitie of the Landinge of forren Force, to Thaide of thother, to-wards which if this Yeare you doe aduaunce, leaue à ftronge Guarde vppon the Pale behinde you ; for a Cottage burnte there wilbe made more here, then a Towne burnte in *Mounfter*. If you will this Yeare goe abowt Thextirpinge of thofe Caniballs of *Goulranell*, and theire Neighbowres, or when you will, if your Lordfhip lette me knowe it, I think I will laye you downe a better Plotte then ever any yet of your Predeceffors for thefe two hvndred Yeares ever followed ; and lette it not troble you, that your People tok fome Blowe there, for I doe not remember that ever any Attempte was made there, nor yet ever harde by my Elders, but that we had more Loffe then Gaine ; thofe Vermin have lived there offenfivelie to *Englifhe* Men, and *Irifhe* Gouernment, aboue iiij C. Yeares : And yet I thinke it verry poffible, and verry feycible, to fubdue or expulfe them ; and dowteles an Acre wonne there is more honorable and prof-fitable for the State, then a Myle in any other remote Place. Once again, my Lord, if you goe into *Mownfter*, leave a ftronger Garde vppon the Pale, and fpare not to burden them of the Countrie to doe it ; it is for them felues ; and what Maffe of Threafure this Crowne exhaufteth, befides that they yerelye doe, they cannot be ignorant of ; I wifhe your Lordfhip fhould in Perfon be in either Action.

If you goe into *Mounfter*, I cannot perceive that there is any Maner of Pro-cedinge yet, but marcially ; this I had forgotten that you leaue all of that Coun-trie Birthe behinde you, that are Men to make any Defence, and trufte to your Soldiers. Some Covnfellors of the Countrie you fhall Neede to haue, with you ; the Potentates of that Province trufte not, till you have tried them, yet hap-pely you mvfte vfe them, but lette them comme imbrued, before you greatelie allowe them.

And fince it is marciallie that you mvfte proceede, and confidering your Ex-perience and Judgmente, I feaffe to treate any more of that, left as I wright in the Begininge of my Lettre, I might power more Follie out of my felf, then put Wifdome into you ; only this, that you fpare for no Cofte to gette Spies ; Knaves wilbe bought for Money, and for helpinge of you to fuche. I knowe none fo apte Men, as *Thomas Mafterfon*, *Robert Pipno*, and *Robert Harpole*, all which I fownde honefte, feruifable, and faithfull ; all which I doe recomend vn-to your good Lordfhips Fauoure.

My thinks it is nowe owte of Seafon to mak any Treatife or Difcorfe of a generall Reformacion, for that were like as if a Man feinge his Howfe on Fire, wold fette downe and drawe a Plotte for a newe, before he wold put his help-inge Hande to quenche the owlde. Neither yet doe I knowe, what Courfe you fhalbe directed, or of your felf are inclined to howld ; for if your Courfe be ei-ther by Direction or Inclinacion to temporife, then mvfte you proceede in dif-ferent Maner, from that Courfe which you mvfte howld ; if you afpire to a per-fecte Reformacion of that acurfed Countrie. Here will come in Queftion whe-ther provinciall Councells and Forces be to be mainteined, or not, and as theis Courfes be different, fo mvfte you vfe Difference of Action, Councellers, and Mynifters ; and herin, when foever you will make me priuey, you fhall have the befte Aduice that I fhalbe able to geve you ; proteftinge that if *Philip Sid-ney* were in your Place, who moft erneftlie and often hath fpoken and writen to doe this louinge Office, he I faie fhold haue no more of me, then I mofte willinglie will wright to you from Tyme to Tyme. But it wilbe befte, that you oppofe me by Queftions, I will anfwer them afwell as I can.

And nowe my good Lord, and beloued Companion, I will feafe to wright of any Matter, and to treate a little of Men ; the mofte fufficient mofte faithfull Kinde that ever I fownde there, were the Barron of *Vperoffery*, Sir *Lucas Dillon*, and Sir *Nicholas Malbie*, thefe for princepall Men both for Councell and Action, and who ever mofte dilligentlie and faithfullie difcharged that which I comitted to them, and trulie they be Men of greate Sufficiencie : Make mvch of this Bringer, for he may and I am fuer will ftand your Lordfhip in Stede, I have alwaies fownde him a jufte fownde Frende : If he be a live there is an honeft Gentleman called *Thomas le Strange*, he was fome Tymes Henchman to Kings, and at the lafte Seruaunte to me, and nowe to the Quene planted there by me ; yf it pleafe you to call him to you at Tymes and geve him good Countenaunce, he will well informe you of that Tracte of the Countrie where he dwelleth : I recomend to your Lordfhip allfo *Launcelot Alforde* the Survaior ; all theis I have fownde fownde and fafte Frends to me : I had almofte forgotten my nereft and dereft Frend and Kinfman, and Knight of myne owne Makinge, Nephew and Godfon, Sir *Henry Harrington :* I befeche your Lordfhip beftowe on him your fauowrable and lovinge Cowntenaunce, you fhall finde in him Nobiletie of Mynde, and that he is not voide of good Councell throughe Experience. It is not for Lack of Loue that I place not aright, your Martiall there, Sir *Nicholas Bagnall*, whom I have ever fownde a faithfull conftant Frend, and fervifable and mofte fafte and affured to that Famelie wherwith I am matched, and with which your Lordfhip is allied ; his Sonne my Godfon and Knight, I recomende vnto your Lordfhip : I defier your Lordfhip to geve your good Covntenaunce to my owld Coffen *Jaques Wingfeld*, I trufte he will deferve it, and nowe lafte thoughe not leaft in Likinge, the Bifhop of *Methe*, whom I ever fownde a good Councellor, for the State, a good Countrieman for the Comon Wealthe, a good Howfekeper, and alwaies my fafte and fownde Frend : Thefe that I have thus writen of, I pray you lette them knowe that I have not forgotten them to your Lordfhip.

I might wright of many other, but I will wright Evell of none, yet Evell have I fownde of fome whome you mvft vfe, for hapelie God ordeined them to be Scourges for my Sinnes, and yet they may be good and fruitefull Inftruments, to further your Seruice (which if you finde) vfe them therafter, and lik them never the leffe for any Thinge don to me ; but if Benefit wold have bownde, I fhold have fownde fafte where I fownde lofe.

As I finde your Lordfhip liketh this, I will fupplie you with more, and nowe defire you to comend me to the Newcomes of *Ireland*, *Videlicet* my Coffen *John Chek*, who withowte Challenge be it fpoken, paffed by *Chefter* and fawe me not albeit he tarried there Daies enoughe ; and to my good Allie *John Zouche* whom I thanke for Comminge to me to this Towne, and to my Gouerner and deere Frend Mr. *Edward Denny*, vnto all which I wifhe from my Harte all Good and Happynes.

My Lord, I had forgotten thre Kinfmen of myne, Sir *Edward More*, *Owen More*, and *Thomas More* ; one of them was my Man and nowe the Quenes, thother my Lord of *Warwicks* and nowe a Knight, the Third my Man ftill : I pray your Lordfhip lette them knowe that I forgette them not ; the befte worthy of Captens that I lefte behinde me was *Humfrie Mackworth*, he was a Boye of myne owne Bredinge, I praie your Lordfhip fauower him the rather for my Sak ; I knowe I fhall have many other that in Refpecte of me will defire Grace at your Hands, and according to the Goodnes of the Cawfe I befeche you to extend the fame vnto them : I wold that they for whome I have written might knowe that I haue not forgotten theim, and that you would kepe this Lettre fecret, leaft others not named might take Occafion to deme them felves of me condemned.

My Lord, I did omitte to wright this Lettre my felf, only for the Shaking of my Hande, which is fuch as with Difficultie I wright myne owne Name, but allfo for that my Lettres written, are to any Reader, yea almofte to my felf illegible, and fo I praye you accept it thoughe fette downe by the Penne of my Man, yet deliuered by the Tonge of my felf : Finalie I comend my felf. my

Sonne

Sonne *Phillip* (who is not here) and the Frendſhip and Seruice of vs bothe, to your good Lordſhip, whom you ſhall finde your faſte and ſownde Frends. From *Denbighe* the xvijth of *September*, 1580.

Your Lordſhips ancient Allie lovinge Companion,

and faithfull Frend,

H. Sydney.

POSTSCRIPT.

My Lord,

THERE is a Debte due vnto me by *Oreilie*, for the Recoveringe wherof I have put *Launcelot Alforde* in Truſte ; but for that Men of his Sorte, who are not commōnlie to be delte withall by ordinarie Auĉthoritie, become ſlowe Paiers of theire Debtts excepte they be verrie earneſtely ſolicited, I praie your Lordſhip therfore (if Neede be) to aſiſte *Alforde* by your Covntenaunce and Commiſſion, the rather to quicken him to procure me Paimente. My good Lord, I had almoſte forgotten by Reaſon of the Diuerſitie of other Matter, to recomende vnto you amongeſt other of my Frends, Sir *Henry Cowley*, a Knight of myne owne makinge, who whilſte he was yonge and the Habilitie and Strengthe of his Bodie ſerued, was valliant fortunate and a good Servante, and havinge by my Appointement the Charge of the Kings Covntie, kepte the Countrie well ordred and in good Obedience : He is as good a Borderer as ever I ſownde any there. I lefte him at my Cominge thence a Councellor, and tried him for his Experience and Judgment, verry ſufficient for the Rome he was called vnto : He was a ſownde and faſte Frend to me, and ſo I dowte not but your Lordſhip ſhall finde when you haue Occaſion to imploye him : And once more, my Lord, I praye you to be good to *Thomas Maſterſon*, he is one of the ancienteſte Followers I had there, and one that hathe ben of longeſt Acquaintaunce with me ; you ſhall finde him valliant, of greate Experience and a verry good Borderer, and fitte to be vſed when you ſhall have any Occaſion to trie his Seruice : Finaly my Lord, tak this for my laſte Precepte, make not many Miniſters for the Layinge owte of your Money, and to deale with your Purſer : What Loſſe I ſuſteined that Waie, no Man can better informe your Lordſhip, then this Bearer, who knewe my Eſtate, and by what Meanes and Degrees I toke the moſte Harme.

Sir *Philip Sydney to his Brother*, Robert Sydney, *who wns the firſt Earle of* Leiceſter *of that Name.*

My deere Brother,

FOR the Mony yow have receaued, aſſure your ſelfe (for it is true) there is nothing I ſpend ſo pleaſeth me, as that which is for yow. If euer I haue Abilitie you will finde it, if not, yet ſhall not any Brother liuing be better beloued then yow of Mee. I cannot write now to *N. White*, doe yow excuſe me. For his Nephew, they are but Paſſions in my Father, which wee muſt beare with Reuerence ; but I am ſory he ſhould returne till he had the Circuite of his Travell, for you ſhall neuer haue ſuch a Servant as he would proue ; vſe your owne Diſcretion therin. For your Countenaunce I would for no Cauſe haue it diminiſhed in *Germany* ; in *Italy* your greateſt Expence muſt be vpon worthy Men, and not vpon Houſholding. Looke to your Diet (ſweete *Robin*) and hould vpp your Hart in Courage and Vertue, truly greate Part of my Comfort is in yow. I know not my ſelfe what I ment by Brauerie in yow, ſo greatly yow may ſee I condemne yow ; be carefull of your ſelfe, and I ſhall neuer haue Cares. I haue written to Mr. *Savell*, I wiſh yow kept ſtill togeather, he is an excellent Man ; and there may if yow liſt paſſe good Exerciſes betwixt yow and Mr. *Nevell*, there is greate Expeĉtation of yow both. For the Method of writing Hiſtorie, *Boden* hath written at large ; yow may reade him, and gather out of many Wordes ſome Matter.

This

This I thinke in Hafte, a Story is either to be confidered as a Storie, or as a Treatife, which, befides that, addeth many Thinges for Profite and Ornament ; as a Story, he is nothing but a Narration of Thinges done, with the Beginings, Cawfes, and Appendences therof ; in that Kinde your Method muft be to haue *Seriem temporum* very exactlie, which the Chronologies of *Melancthon, Tarchagnora, Languet,* and fuch other, will helpe yow to. Then to confider by that as yow not your felfe, *Zenophon* to follow *Thucidides,* fo doth *Thucidides* follow *Herodotus,* and *Diodorus Siculus* follow *Zenophon :* So generally doe the *Roman* Stories follow the *Greeke,* and the perticuler Stories of prefent Monarchies follow the *Roman.* In that Kinde yow haue principally to note the Examples of Vertue or Vice, with their good or evell Succeffes, the Eftablifhments or Ruines of greate Eftates, with the Cawfes, the Tyme, and Circumftances of the Lawes then write of, the Entrings and Endings of Warrs, and therin, the Stratagems againft the Enimy, and the Difcipline vpon the Soldiour ; and thus much as a very Hiftoriographer. Befides this, the Hiftorian makes himfelfe a Difcourfer for Profite, and an Orator, yea a Poet fometimes for Ornament. An Orator, in making excellent Orations, *e re nata,* which are to be marked, but marked with the Note of Rhetoricall Remembrances : A Poet, in painting forth the Effects, the Motions, the Whifperings of the People, which though in Difputation, one might fay were true, yet who will marke them well, fhall finde them tafte of a Poeticall Vaine, and in that Kinde are gallantly to be marked, for though perchance they were not fo, yet it is enough they might be fo. The laft Poynt which tendes to teach Profite, is of a Difcourfer, which Name I giue to who foeuer fpeakes, *Non fimpliciter de facto, fed de qualitatibus et circumftantijs facti* ; and that is it which makes me, and many others, rather note much with our Penn then with our Minde, becaufe wee leaue all thes Difcourfes to the confufed Truft of our Memory, becaufe they being not tyed to the Tenor of a Queftion, as Philofophers vfe fometimes Places ; the Divine, in telling his Opinion and Reafons in Religion ; fometimes the Lawyer, in fhewing the Cawfes and Benefites of Lawes ; fometimes a Naturall Philofopher, in fettinge downe the Cawfes of any ftrange Thing, which the Story bindes him to fpeake of ; but moft commonly a Morall Philofopher, either in the Ethick Part, when he fetts forth Vertues or Vices, and the Natures of Paffions, or in the Politick, when he doth (as often he doth) meddle fententiouflie with Matters of Eftate. Againe, fometimes he giues Precept of Warr, both offenfiue and defenfiue ; and fo laftlie, not profeffing any Art, as his Matter leades him he deales with all Arts, which becaufe it carrieth the Life of a liuely Example, it is wonderfull what Light it giues to the Arts themfelues, fo as the greate Ciuillians helpe themfelues with the Difcourfes of the Hiftorians ; fo doe Soldiours, and even Philofophers, and Aftronomers ; but that I wifh herein, is this, that when yow reade any fuch Thing, yow ftraite bring it to his Heade, not only of what Art, but by your Logicall Subdiuifions, to the next Member and Parcell of the Art. And fo as in a Table, be it wittie Words, of which *Tacitus* is full ; Sentences of which *Liuy,* or Similitudes wherof *Plutarch* ; ftraite to lay it vpp in the right Place of his Storehoufe, as either Militarie, or more fpetiallie defenfiue Militarie, or more perticulerlie, defenfiue by Fortification, and fo lay it vpp. So likewife in Politick Matters, and fuch a little Table yow may eafelie make, wherwith I would haue yow ever ioyne the Hiftoricall Part, which is only the Example of fome Stratageme, or good Cownfaile, or fuch like. This write I to yow in greate Haft, of Method without Method, but with more Leyfure and Studie (if I doe not finde fome Booke that fatisfies) I will venter to write more largely of it vnto yow. Mr. *Sauell* will with Eafe helpe yow to fett downe fuch a Table of Remembrance to your felfe, and for your Sake I perceaue he will doe much, and if ever I be able I will deferue it of him ; one only Thing, as it comes vnto my Minde, lett me remember you of, that yow confider wherin the Hiftorian excelleth, and that to note, as *Dion Nicæus,* in the Searching the Seacreats of Gouerment ; *Tacitus,* in the pithy Opening the Venome of Wickednes, and fo of the reft. My Time exceedingly

fhort

ſhort, will ſuffer me to write no more leiſurely ; *Stephen* can tell yow who ſtands with me while I am writing. Now (deere Brother) take Delight likewiſe in the Mathematicalls, Mr. *Sauell* is excellent in them. I thinke ·yow vnderſtand the Sphere, if yow doe, I care little for any more Aſtronomie in yow. Arithmatick, and Geometry, I would wiſh yow well ſeene in, ſo as both in Matter of Nomber and Meaſure yow might haue a Feeling, and actiue Judgment : I would you did beare the Mechanicall Inſtruments, wherin the *Dutch* excell. I write this to you as one, that for my ſelfe haue given over the Delight in the World, but wiſh to yow as much, if not more, then to my ſelfe. So yow can ſpeake and write *Latine*, not barbarouſly, I never require great Study in *Ciceronianiſme*, the cheiſe Abuſe of *Oxford*, *Qui dum verba ſectantur, res ipſas negligunt*. My toyfull Books I will ſend, with Gods Helpe, by *February*, at which Time yow ſhall haue your Mony : And for 200 *l.* a Yeare, aſſure your ſelfe, if the Eſtates of *England* remaine, yow ſhall not faile of it, vſe it to your beſte Profite. My Lord of *Leiceſter* ſendes yow forty Pownds, as I vnderſtand by *Stephen*, and promiſeth he will continue that Stipend Yearely at the leaſt, then that is aboue Commons ; in any Caſe write largely and dilligently vnto him, for in Troth I haue good Proofe, that he meanes to be every Way good vnto you ; the odd 30 *l.* ſhall come with the Hundred, or els my Father and I will iarle. Now, ſweete Brother, take a Delight to keepe and increaſe your Muſick, yow will not beleiue what a Want I finde of it in my melancholie Times. At Horſemanſhipp when you exerciſe it, reade *Criſon Claudio*, and a Book that is called *La Gloria de l' Cauallo*, withall, that yow may ioyne the through Contemplation of it with the Exerciſe ; and ſo ſhall yow profite more in a Moneth, then others in a Yeare, and marke the Bitting, Sadling, and Curing of Horſes. I would by the Way your Worſhip would learne a better Hand, you write worſe then I, and I write evell enough ; once againe haue a Care of your Dyet, and conſequently of your Complexion ; remember *Gratior eſt veniens in pulchro corpore Virtus*. Now, Sir, for Newes, I referr my ſelfe to this Bearer, he can tell yow how idle wee looke on our Neighbours Fyres, and nothing is happened notable at Home, ſaue only *Drakes* Returne, of which yet I know not the ſeacreat Poyntes ; but about the World he hath bene, and rich he is returned. *Portugall* we ſay is loſt, and. to conclude, my Eies are almoſt cloſed vpp, overwatched with tedeous Buſines. God bleſs yow, ſweete Boy, and accompliſh the ioyfull Hope I conceiue of yow. Once againe commend me to Mr. *Nevell*, Mr. *Sauell*, and honeſt *Harry White*, and bid him be merry. When you play at Weapons, I would haue yow gett thick Cappes and Braſers, and play out your Play luſtilie, for indeed Tickes and Daliances are nothing in earneſt, for the Time of the one and the other greatlie differs, and vſe aſwell the Blow as the Thruſt ; it is good in it ſelfe, and beſides exerciſeth your Breath and Strength, and will make yow a ſtrong Man at the Tournej and Barriers. Firſt in any Caſe practize the ſingle Sword, and then with the Dagger ; lett no Day paſſe without an Hower or two ſuch Exerciſe ; the reſt ſtudie, or conferr diligentlie, and ſo ſhall yow come Home to my Comfort and Creditt. Lord how I haue babled, once againe farewell deereſt Brother.

Your moſt louing and carefull Brother,

At *Leſterhouſe*, this
18th of *October*, 1580.

Philip Sidney.

Robert, *firſt Earl of* Leiceſter, *to his Father,* Sir Henry Sydney.

My Duty moſt humbly remembred to yovr Lordſhip,

THOGH I haue no greate Matter to write to yov of, yet hauing the Opportunite by a Gentleman, the Bearer heerof, I thought it my Part not to let him go into *England* without writing to your Lordſhip. Yeſterday I came hether, where I meane to ſtay a good Part of this Winter, and if I may, will learne to ride. My Brother, in his laſt Letter, put it to my Choiſe, whether I wonld go next Yeare into *France* or into *Italy* ; I haue choſen *Italy*, becauſe it is not fo farr from hence, and afterwards into *France* ; and fo will do, if yovr Lordfhip fhall thinck it good, and will giue me Leaue. My Brother likewife, in his Letter to *Harry White*, wrote that if there were any good Warrs I fhowld go to them, but as yet I haue hard of none. But befides that the Setting out will not ftand me in a little, if I go, any Thing like to them ; what for Horfe and Armor, and my Charges, before I can come where they are. But before any fuch Wars will be, I hope to heare forther from yowr Lordfhip. As towching my Iorney from *Nurenberghe* hether ; firft wee came to *Ingolftadt*, then to *Augf-bourg*, *Munchen*, and *Regeufbourg* ; laftly hether. After *Chriftmas* wee thinck to go towards *Vienna*, and there to remaine till it be yowr Lordfhips, or my Bro-thers Will, I fhowld go forther ; and in the meane Time fee fo much of *Hun-garie*, as I may ; and *Cracow*, if the King of *Poland* come thether. And fo be-ing forced by the Haft of the Meffenger to make an End, I take my Leaue ; moft humbly befeching yowr Lordfhip of yowr dayly Bleffing. From *Prag*, the Firft of *Nouember*, 1580.

Your Lordfhips moft humble and obedient Son,

during Life,

Robert Sidney.

Sir Francis Walfyngham *to Sir* Henry Sydney.

My verie good Lord,

HAving fo convenient a Meffinger as this Bearer, my Nephewe *Amyas*, I thought good in a Word or twoe to aduertife you of our Proceadyngs here in Court. Here is at this Prefent one *Marchemond* come owt of *Fraunce* from Monfieur, whoe verie earneftly follicitethe hir Majefties Refolution in the Matter of the Mariage ; but what the End thereof will bee God only knowethe. Thoughe hir Majeftie hir felfe feeme to hearken verie muche therevnto, yet when it fhall come to a Conclufion, it may peraduenture bee as doubtfull as heretofore. In the Northe Matters goe ill forward ; for the Erle of *Morton* continewethe ftyll Pri-foner in *Dvmbritton*, and Mr. *Randolphe*, thoughe he preffe verie earneftly that he may bee brought to his Triall, yet hitherto hathe prevayled litle or nothing : For fo great Creditt cariethe *D' Awbignie* there, as the Kynge will rather hazard the Love hir Majeftie hathe allwayes borne him, and the Amitie betwen bothe Crownes, than offend him. Hir Majeftie hath readie vppon the Borders, as well for Defence of the fame, as Reliefe of hir Partie in *Scotland* (and Need bee) ij M. Footemen and v C. Horfemen. Vppon the xxth of this Prefent a great Conven-tion of the Nobilitie of that Realme was appoynted in *Edenburghe*, at what Tyme and Place is expected what will bee their Refolution towching their troublefome State, as alfo their Anfweare to Mr. *Randolphe*. As wee fhall receave further Aduertifments, fo I will make your Lordfhip Partaker of the fame. This Bearer having maryed my Neece, and beyng peraduenture fo happie as hereafter to lyve and ferve vnder your Lordfhips Governement there ; yf it fo fall owt I muft neds, and fo doe moft hartely recommend him vnto your Favor, for which as he fhall reft greatly bownd, and I behoulding to your Lordfhip ; fo I doubt not but you fhall fynd him a Gentleman of fo good Difpofition and Parts, as you will well lyke of. And thus commendyng your Lordfhip to God, I take my Leave. From the Court, the xxiiijth of *Februarie*, 1580.

Your Lordfhips affured loving Frend to command,

Fra. Walfyngham.

Sir Philip Sydney *to Queen* Elizabeth, *An.* 1580, *perſwading her not to marry with the Duke of* Anjou.

Moſt feared and beloved, moſt ſweet and gracious Sovereign,

TO ſeek out Excuſes of this my Boldneſs, and to arm the Acknowledging of a Fault with Reaſons for it, might better ſhew I knew I did amis, than any Way diminiſh the Attempt, eſpecially in your Judgment ; who being able to diſcern lively into the Nature of the Thing done, it were Folly to hope, by laying on better Colours, to make it more acceptable. Therefore carrying no other Olive-branch of Interceſſion, then the Laying of my ſelf at your Feet ; nor no other Inſinuation, either for Attention or Pardon, but the true vowed Sacrifice of unfeigned Love ; I will, in ſimple and direct Terms (as hoping they ſhall only come to your mercifull Eyes) ſet down the Overflowing of my Mind in this moſt important Matter, importing, as I think, the Continuance of your Safety ; and, as I know, the Joys of my Life. And becauſe my Words (I confeſs ſhallow, but coming from the deep Well-ſpring of moſt loyal Affection) have delivered to your moſt gracious Ear, what is the general Sum of my travelling Thoughts therein ; I will now but only declare, what be the Reaſons that make me think, that the Marriage with Monſieur will be unprofitable unto you ; then will I anſwer the Objection of thoſe Fears, which might procure ſo violent a Refuge.

The Good or Evils that will come by it, muſt be conſidered, either according to your Eſtate or Perſon. To your Eſtate, what can be added to the being an abſolute born, and accordingly reſpected, Princeſs? But, as they ſay the *Iriſhmen*, are wont to call over them that die, *They are rich, they are fair, what needed they to dye ſo cruelly :* Not unfitly of You, endowed with Felicity above all others, a Man might well ask ; what makes you in ſuch a Calm to change Courſe ; to ſo healthfull a Body, to apply ſo unſavory a Medicine : What can recompence ſo hazardous an Adventure : Indeed, were it but the Altering of a well maintained, and well approved Trade : For, as in Bodies natural, every ſudden Change is full of Peril ; ſo in this Body Politick, whereof you are are the only Head, it is ſo much the more dangerous, as there are more Humours to receive a hurtful Impreſſion. But Hazards are then moſt to be reguarded, when the Nature of the Patient is fitly compoſed to occaſion them.

The Patient I account your Realm ; the Agent Monſieur, and his Deſign ; for neither outward Accidents do much prevail againſt a true inward Strength ; nor doth inward Weakneſs lightly ſubvert it ſelf, without being thruſt at by ſome outward Force.

Your inward Force (for as for your Treaſures indeed, the Sinews of your Crown, your Majeſty doth beſt and only know) conſiſteth in your Subjects, generally unexpert in warlike Defence ; and as they are divided now into mighty Factions (and Factions bound on the never dying Knot of Religion) the one of them, to whom your happy Goverment hath granted the free Exerciſe of the eternal Truth ; with this, by the Continuance of Time, by the Multitude of them ; by the principal Offices, and Strength they hold ; and laſtly, by your Dealings both at Home and Abroad againſt the adverſe Party ; your State is ſo entrapped, as it were impoſſible for you, without exceſſive Trouble, to pull your ſelf out of the Party ſo long maintained: For ſuch a Courſe once taken in Hand, is not much unlike a Ship in a Tempeſt, which how dangerouſly ſoever it may be beaten with Waves, yet is there no Safety or Succour without it : Theſe, therefore, as their Soules live by your happy Goverment, ſo are they your chief, if not your ſole Strength : Theſe, howſoever the Neceſſity of humane Life makes them lack, yet can they not look for better Conditions then preſently they enjoy : Theſe, how their Hearts will be galled,

† if

if not aliened, when they fhall fee you take a Hufband, a *Frenchman* and a Papift, in whom (howfoever fine Wits may find further Dealings or painted Excufes) the very common People well know this, that he is the Son of a *Jezebel* of our Age : That his Brother made Oblation of his own Sifters Marriage, the eafier to make Maffacres of our Brethren in Belief : That he himfelf, contrary to his Promife, and all Gratefulnefs, having his Liberty and principal Eftate by the *Hugonots* Means, did fack *Lacharifts*, and utterly fpoil them with Fire and Sword. This, I fay, even at firft Sight, gives Occafion to all, truly religious, to abhor fuch a Mafter, and confequently to diminifh much of the hopefull Love, they have long held to you.

The other Faction, moft rightly indeed, to be called a Faction, is the Papifts ; Men, whofe Spirits are full of Anguifh, fome being infefted by others, whom they accounted damnable ; fome having their Ambition ftopped, becaufe they are not in the Way of Advancement ; fome in Prifon and Difgrace; fome whofe beft Friends are banifhed Practifers ; many thinking you are an Vfurper ; many thinking alfo you had difanulled your Right, becaufe of the Popes Excommunication ; all burthened with the Weight of their Confcience ; Men of great Numbers, of great Riches (becaufe the Affaires of State have not lain on them) of united-Minds (as all Men that deem themfelves oppreffed naturally are)With thefe, I would willingly join all difcontented Perfons, fuch as Want and Difgrace keep lower than they have fet their Hearts; fuch as have refolved what to look for at your Hands; fuch as *Cæfar* faid, *Quibus opus eft bello civili*, and are of his Mind, *malo in acie, quam in foro cadere*. Thefe be Men fo much the more to be doubted, becaufe, as they do embrace all Eftates ; fo are they commonly of the braveft and wakefulleft Sort ; and that know the Advantage of the World moft. This double Rank of People, how their Minds have ftood, the Northern Rebellion, and infinite other Practifes, have well taught you ; which, if it be faid, it did not prevail, that is true indeed ; for if they had prevailed, it were too late now to deliberate. But, at this prefent, they want nothing fo much as a Head, who, in Effect, needs not but to receive their Inftructions ; fince they may do Mifchief only with his Countenance. Let the *Singiniam* in *Henry the Fourths* Time, *Perkin Warbeck* in your Grandfathers ; but of all the moft lively and proper, is that of *Lewis* the *French* Kings Son, in *Henry the Thirds* Time ; who having at all no Shew of *Title*, yet did he caufe the Nobility, and more, to fwear direct Fealty and Vaffalage; and they delivered the ftrongeft Holds unto him. I fay, let thefe be fufficient to prove, that Occafion gives Mindes and Scope to ftranger Things, than ever would would have been imagined. If then the affectionate Side, have their Affections weakned, and the Difcontented have a Gap to utter their Difcontent ; I think it will feem an ill Preparative for the Patient (I mean your Eftate) to a a great Sicknefs.

Now the Agent Party, which is Monfieur : Whether he be not apt to work on the Difadvantage of your Eftate, he is to be judged by his Will and Power; his Will to be as full of light Ambition, as is poffible ; befides the *French* Difpofition, and his own Education ; his inconftant Temper againft his Brother ; his Thrufting himfelf into the *Low Country* Matters ; his fometimes Seeking the King of *Spains* Daughter ; fometimes your Majefty ; are evident Teftimonyes of his being carried away with every Wind of Hope ; taught to love Greatnefs any Way gotten ; and having for the Motioners and Minifters of the Mind, only fuch young Men, as have fhewed they think evil Contentment a Ground of any Rebellion, who have feen no Commonwealth, but in Faction ; and divers of which have defiled their Hands in odious Murthers : With fuch Fancies and Favourites, what is to be hoped for; or that he will contain himfelf within the Limits of your Conditions ; fince, in Truth, it were ftrange, that he that cannot be contented to be the fecond Perfon in *France*, and Heir apparent, fhould be content to come to be a fecond Perfon, where he fhould

I

pretend

pretend no Way to Sovereignty. His Power, I imagine, is not to be defpifed, fince he is come into a Country, where the Way of evil Doing will be prefented unto him; where there needs nothing but a Head, to draw together all the ill-affected Members: Himfelf a Prince of great Revenues, of the moft popular Nation of the World, full of Souldiery, and fuch as are ufed to ferve without Pay, fo as they may have Shew of Spoil; and, without Queftion, fhall have his Brother ready to help him, as well for old Revenge, as to divert him from troubling *France*; and to deliver his own Country from evil Humours. Neither is King *Philips* Marriage here any Example; fince then it was between two of one Religion, fo that only he in *England*, ftood only upon her Strength, and had Abroad King *Henry* of *France*, ready to impeach any Enterprize he fhould make for his Greatnefs that Way. And, yet, what Events Time would have brought forth of that Marriage, your moft bleffid Reign hath made vain all fuch Confiderations. But Things holding in prefent State, I think I may eafily conclude, that your Country as well by long Peace, and Fruits of Peace, as by the Poifon of Divifion, wherewith the Faithfull fhall by this Meanes be wounded, and the contrary enabled, made fit to receive Hurt; and Monfieur being every Way likely to ufe the Occafions to hurt, there can almoft happen no worldly Thing of more eminent Danger to your Eftate Royal. And as to your Perfon, in the Scale of your Happinefs, what Good there may come by it, to ballance with the Lofs of fo honourable a Conftancy; truly, yet I perceive not. I will not fhew fo much Malice, as to object the univerfal Doubt, the *Races* Unfaithfulnefs; neither will I lay to his Charge the Ague-like Manner of Proceedings, fometimes hot and fometimes cold, in the Time of Purfuit; which always rightly is moft fervent: And I will temper my Speeches from any other unreverend Difgracings of him, in particular; (though they might be never fo true) this only will I fay, that if he do come hither, he muft live here in far lefs Reputation than his Mind will well brook, having no other Royalty to countenance himfelf with; or elfe you muft deliver him the Keys of your Kingdom, and live at his Difcretion; or, laftly, he muft be feperate himfelf, with more Difhonour, and further Difuniting of Heart, than ever before. Often have I heard you, with Proteftation, fay, no private Pleafure, nor Self-affection, could lead you to it; but if it be both unprofitable for your Kingdom, and unpleafant to you, certainly it were a dear Purchafe of Repentance; nothing can it add unto you, but the Blifs of Children, which, I confefs, were a moft unfpeakable Comfort; but yet no more appertaining unto him, than to any other, to whom the Height of all good Haps, were alloted to be your Hufband; and therefore I may affuredly affirm, that what Good foever can follow Marriage, is no more his than any Bodies; but the Evils and Dangers are peculiarly annexed to his Perfon, and Condition. For, as for the Enriching of your Country with Treafure, which either he hath not, or hath otherwife beftowed it; or the Staying of your Servants Minds with new Expectations and Liberality, which is more dangerous than fruitfull; or the Eafing of your Majefty of Cafes, which is as much as to fay, as the Eafing of you to be Queen and Soveraign: I think every one perceives this Way to be full of Hurt, or void of Help. Now refteth to confider, what be the Motives of this fudden Change, as I have heard you in moft fweet Words deliver; Fear of ftanding alone, in Refpect of foreign Dealings; and in them, from whom you fhould have Refpect, doubt of Contempt. Truly, Standing alone, with good Forefight of Goverment, both in Peace and Warlike Defence, is the honourableft Thing that can be, to a well eftablifhed Monarchy; thofe Buildings being ever moft ftrongly durable, which lean to none other, but remain from their own Foundation.

So yet in the Particulars of your Eftate at prefent, I will not altogether deny that a true *Maffiniffa*, were fit to countermine the Enterprife of mighty

Carthage: But how this general Truth, can be applied to Monfieur; in Truth I perceive not. The Wifeft that have given beft Rules, where fureft Leagues are made, have faid, that it muft be between fuch as either vehement Defire of a 3d Thing, or as vehement Fear, doth knit their Minds together. Defire is counted the weaker Bond, but yet that bound fo many Princes to the *Holy Land.* It united that invincible King *Henry* V, and that good Duke of *Burgundy*; the one defiring to win the Crown of *France* from the *Dauphin,* the other defiring to revenge his Fathers Murther upon the *Dauphin*; which both tended to one. That coupled *Lewis* XII, and *Ferdinando* of *Spain* to the Conqueft of *Naples.* Of Fear, there are innumerable Examples: Monfieurs Defires, and yours, how they fhall meet in publick Matters, I think no Oracle can tell; for as the Geomatricians fay, that Parallels, becaufe they maintain divers Lines, can never join: So truly, two, having in the Beginning contrary Principles, to bring forth one Doctrine, muft be fome Miracle. He of the *Romifh* Religion; and if he be a Man, muft needs have that manlike Property, to defire that all Men be of his Mind: You the Erector and Defender of the contrary, and the only Sun that dafleth their Eyes: He *French,* and defiring to make *France* great: Your Majefty *Englifh,* and defiring nothing lefs than that *France* fhould not grow great: He both by own Fancy and his youthfull Governors, embracing all ambitious Hopes; having *Alexanders* Image in his Head, but, perhaps, evil painted: Your Majefty with excellent Virtue, taught what you fhould hope, and by no lefs Wifdom, what you may Hope; with a Council renowned over all *Chriftendom,* for their well-temperd Minds, having fet the utmoft of their Ambition in your Favour, and the Study of their Souls, in your Safety.

Fear hath as little Shew of outward Appearance, as Reafon, to match you together; for in this Eftate he is in, whom fhould he fear, his Brother; alas! his Brother is afraid, fince the King of *Navar* is to ftep into his Place. Neither can his Brother be the fafer by his Fall, but he may be the greater by his Brothers; whereto, whether you will be an Acceffary, you are to determine. The King of *Spain* certainly cannot make Warr upon him, but it muft be upon all the Crown of *France,* which is no Likelyhood he will do: Well may Monfieur, (as he hath done) feek to enlarge the Bounds of *France* upon this State; which likewife, whether it be fafe for you to be a Countenance to, any other Way, may be feen: So that if neither Defire nor Fear be fuch in him, as are to bind any publick Faftnefs, it may be faid, that the only Fortrefs of this your Marriage, is of his private Affection; a Thing too incident to the Perfon, laying it up in fuch Knots.

The other Objection of Contempt in the Subjects: I affure your Majefty, if I had heard it proceed out of your Mouth, which of all other I do moft dearly reverence, it would as foon (confidering the Perfections of Body and Mind, have fet all Mens Eyes by the Height of your Eftate) have come to the Poffibility of my Imagination, if one fhould have told me on the contrary Side, that the greateft Princefs of the World, fhould envy the State of fome poor deformed Pilgrim. What is there, either within you or without you, that can poffibly fall into the Danger of Contempt, to whom Fortunes are tyed by fo long Defcent of your Royal Anceftors? But our Minds rejoyce with the Experience of your inward Virtues, and our Eyes are delighted with the Sight of you. But becaufe your own Eyes cannot fee yourfelf, neither can there be in the World any Example fit to blafe you by, I befeech you vouchfafe to weigh the Grounds thereof. The naturall Caufes are Length of Goverment, and Uncertainty of Succeffion: The Effects, as you term them, appear by cherifhing fome abominable Speeches, which fome hellifh Minds have uttered. The longer a Prince reigneth, it is certain the more he is efteemed; there is no Man ever was weary of well-being. And Good encreafed to Good, maketh the fame Good, both greater and ftronger; for it ufeth Men to know no other Cares, when either Men are born in the Time, and fo never

faw

faw other ; or have fpent much of their flourifhing Time, and fo have no Joy to feek other ; in evil Princes, Abufe growing upon Abufe, according to the Nature of Evil ; with the Encreafe of Time, ruins it felf. But in fo rare a Goverment, where Neighbours Fires give us Light to fee our Quietnefs, where nothing wants that true Adminiftration of Juftice brings forth ; certainly the Length of Time, rather breeds a Mind to think there is no other Life, but in it, than that there is any Tedioufnefs in fo fruitfull a Government. Examples of good Princes do ever confirm this, who the longer they lived, the deeper they funk into their Subjects Hearts. Neither will I trouble you with Examples, being fo many and manifeft. Look into your own Eftate, how willingly they grant, and how dutifully they pay fuch Subfidies, as you demand of them : How they are no lefs troublefome to your Majefty in certain Requefts, than they were in the Beginning of your Reign ; and your Majefty fhall find you have a People more than ever devoted to you.

As for the Uncertainty of Succeffion, although for mine own Part I have caft the utmoft Anchor of my Hope ; yet for *England*'s Sake, I would not fay any Thing againft fuch Determination ; but that uncertain Good fhould bring a Contempt to a certain Good, I think it is beyond all Reach of Reafon ; nay becaufe if there were no other Caufe (as there are infinite) common Reafon and Profit would teach us to hold that Jewel dear, the Lofs of which would bring us to we know not what ; which likewife is to be faid of your Majefties Speech of the Rifing Sun ; a Speech firft ufed by *Sylla* to *Pompey*, in *Rome*, as then a popular Citty, where indeed Men were to rife and fall, according to the Flourifh and Breath of a many headed Confufion. But in fo lineal a Monarchy, where ever the Infants fuck the Love of their rightfull Prince, who would leave the Beams of fo fair a Sun, for the dreadfull Expectation of a divided Company of Stars : Virtue and Juftice are the only Bonds of Peoples Love ; and as for that Point, many Princes have loft their Crowns, whofe own Children were manifeft Succeffors ; and fome that had their own Children vfed as Inftruments of their Ruin ; not that I deny the Blifs of Children, but only to fhew Religion and Equity to be of themfelves fufficient Stays. Neither is the Love born in the Queen your Sifters Days, any Contradiction hereunto ; for fhe was the Oppreffor of that Religion, which lived in many Mens Hearts, and whereof you were known to be the Fauvorer ; by her Lofs was the moft excellent Prince in the World to fucceed ; by your Lofs, all Blindnefs light upon him, that fees not our Mifery. *Laftly*, and moft properly for this Purpofe, fhe had made an odious Marriage with a Stranger (which is now in Queftion whether your Majeftie fhall do or no) fo that if your Subjects do at this Time look for any Afterchance, it is but as the Pilot doth to the Ship-boat, if his Ship fhould perifh ; driven by Extremity to the one, but as long as he can with his Life, tending the other. And this I fay, not only for the lively Parts that be in you ; but even for their own Sakes, for they muft needs fee what Tempefts threaten them.

The laft Proof in this Contempt, fhould be the venemous Matter, certain Men impofthum'd with Wickednefs fhould utter againft you. Certainly not to be evil fpoken of, neither *Chrifts* Holinefs, nor *Cæfar*'s Might, could ever prevent or warrant ; there being for that no other Rule than fo to do, as that they may not juftly fay Evil of you ; which whether your Majefty have not done, I leave it in you, to the Sincerenefs of your own Confcience, and Wifdom of your Judgment in the World, to your moft manifeft Fruits and Fame throughout *Europe*. *Auguftus* was told, that Men fpeake of him much Hurt : *It is no Matter*, faid he, *fo long as they cannot do much Hurt.* And laftly *Charles* V, to one that told him, *Les Hollandois parlent mal ; maiz ilz patient bien*, anfwered he. I might make a fcholar-like Reckoning of many fuch Examples ; it fufficeth that thefe great Princes knew well enough upon what Way they flew, and cared little for the Barking of a few Currs : And truly in the Behalf of your Subjects, I durft with

my

my Blood anſwer it, that there was never Monarch held in more precious Reck-oning of her People ; and before God how can it be otherwiſe ? For mine own Part, when I hear ſome loſt Wretch hath defiled ſuch a Name with his Mouth, I conſider the right Name of Blaſphemy, whoſe unbridled Soul doth delight to deprave that, which is accounted generally moſt high and holy. No, no, moſt excellent Lady, do not raze out the Impreſſion you have made in ſuch a Multi-tude of Hearts ; and let not the Schum of ſuch vile Minds, bear any Witneſs a-gainſt your Subjects Devotions : Which to proceed one Point further, if it were otherwiſe, could little be helped, but rather nouriſhed, and in Effect began by this. The only Meanes of avoiding Contempt, are Love and Fear ; Love, as you have by divers Meanes ſent into the Depth of their Souls ; ſo if any Thing can ſtain ſo true a Form, it muſt be the Trimming your ſelf, not in your own Likeneſs, but in new Colours unto them ; their Fear by him cannot be encreaſed, without the Appearaunce of *Frenche* Forces, the manifeſt Death of your Eſtate ; but well may it againſt him, bear that Face, which (as the tragick *Seneca* ſaith) *Metus in authorem redit*, as becauſe both in Will and Power, he is like enough to do Harm. Since then it is dangerous for your State, as well becauſe by inward Weakneſs (principally cauſed by Diviſion) it is fit to receive Harm ; ſince to your Perſon it can be no Way comfortable, you not deſiring Marriage ; and neither to Perſon nor Eſtate, he is to bring any more Good than any Body ; but more Evil he may, ſince the Cauſes that ſhould drive you to this, are either Fears of that which cannot happen, or by this Meanes cannot be prevented : I do with moſt humble Heart ſay unto your Majeſtie (having aſſayed this dangerous Help) for your Standing alone, you muſt take it for a ſingular Honour God hath done you, to be indeed the only Protector of his Church ; and yet in worldly Re-ſpects your Kingdom very ſufficient ſo to do, if you make that Religion, upon which you ſtand, to carry the only Strength, and have Abroad thoſe that ſtill maintain the ſame Courſe ; who as long as they may be kept from utter Falling, your Majeſty is ſure enough from your mightieſt Enemies. As for this Man, as long as he is but *Monſieur* in Might, and a Papiſt in Profeſſion, he neither can, nor will, greatly ſhield you ; and if he get once to be King, his Defence will be like *Ajax*'s Shield, which rather weighed them down, than defended thoſe that bare it. Againſt Contempt, if there be any, which I will never believe, let your excellent Virtues of Piety, Juſtice, and Liberality, daily, if it be poſſible, more and more ſhine. Let ſuch particular Actions be found out (which be eaſy as I think to be done) by which you may gratify all the Hearts of your People : Let thoſe in whom you find Truſt, and to whom you have comitted Truſt, in your weighty Affairs, be held up in the Eyes of your Subjects : *Laſtly*, doing as you do, you ſhall be as you be, the Example of Princes, the Ornament of this Age, and the moſt excellent Fruit of your Progenitors, and the perfect Mirror of your Poſterity.

Your Majeſties faythfull, humble,

and obedient Subject,

P. Sydney.

Sir

Sir Philip Sidney *to* Edmund Molyneux, *Efq;*

I Pray yow, for my Sake, yow will not make yowr felf an Inftrument to croffe my Cofin *Fowkes [Grevill]* Tytle in any Part, or Conftruction of his Letters Patentes. It will turne to other Boddies Good, and to hurte him willingly weare a foolifh Difcourteify. I pray yow, as yow make Accownt of me, lett me be fure yow will deale heerein according to my Requeft, and fo I leaue yow to God. At *Bainards* Caftell, this 10th of *Aprill,* 1581.

Your louing Frend,

Philipp Sidney.

Sir Francis Walfyngham *to Sir* Henry Sydney.

My verie good Lord,

A BOWT the End of *Februarie* laft, I writt to your Lordfhip on the Behalfe of my Coufen *Foulke Grievell,* for the Proffitts of the Office fallen vnto him there in the Merches, by Mr. *Dudleys* Death. At that Tyme alfo, I writt to Mr. *Fox,* frendly advifing him to fuffer my Coufen quietly to enioy the fayd Office, with all fuch Commodities as Mr. *Dudley* had, which no Doubt was ment vnto him by hir Majeftie ; and, I thincke, to bee caried away by fufficient Words of his Patent. Howebeit, as I vnderftand by your Lordfhips Lettre, and more plainly by Mr. *Fox* him felf, hee intendeth to ftand in Lawe with my Coufen for the Proffitts which Mr. *Dudley* had by the late Increafe of Fees in everie Proceffe paffing the Signett. Yf Mr. *Dudley,* ferving but a Noble Man, could enioy that Encreafe of Fees, much more, I hope, my Coufen fhall, being hir Majefties Servant, and a Gentleman of whome fhee maketh, as your Lordfhip doth knowe, fome good Accompt. I knowe your Lordfhips good Affection towards my Coufen, and therfore doubt not, but you have allreadie, and will further doe what you may with Mr. *Foxe,* to yeald to that is Reafon without Lawe, which if hee will not, but that Lawe muft needes be commenced between them, furely the fame fhall bee profequuted in fuch effectuall Sort, as Mr. *Fox,* in the End, will have fmall Cawfe to reioice of the Iffue therof : Whereas nowe, by yealding to that is required, hee may avoyd Trouble, and purchafe to him felf, not only Affurance of the good Love of my felfe, but alfo of all other my Coufen *Greivells* Frends, which are manie, and of great Callyng, and may ftead Mr. *Fox,* and his, in Matters poffible of greater Importance than this Thing nowe in Queftion is. Much to this Effect I have nowe written to Mr. *Fox,* in whome, if you fhall fynd no prefent Difpofition to yeald to my Requeft, then I wyfhe it would pleafe your Lordfhip to fequefter the Proffits in Controverfie between them (as in former Lettres was required) vntill this Cawfe bee determined by Lawe, or otherwife. And thus, with my hartieft Commendations to your good Lordfhip, I take my Leave. From the Court, the xith of *Aprill,* 1581.

Your Lordfhips affured loving Frend,

Fra. Walfyngham.

Edmund Molyneux, *Efq; to Sir* Philip Sidney.

S I R,

I Have receaved your Lettres, and doe acknowledge the fame as a fpeciall Note of your lovinge Favour, that it wold pleafe you to write vnto me ; and what may lye in me in any Sorte to doe, you fhall not need to requier me : But you have (yf it may foe lyke you) full Power and good Warrant to commaund me. Sir, yt femethe by your faid Lettres, that you have beene enformed, that I either have already, or in fome Sorte pretend hereafter, to be an Adverfarie to Mr. *Grivell* in his Sute heere; and that I make not that good Accounte of the Validitie and Goodnes of his Patent, as in Reafone and cowr-tewfe frindlie Dealinge, I fhould doe, fomwhat, as you gather, to his Difad-vantage, beinge a Matter, as you faye, of noe Bennefite to my felfe; which, yf I fhowld foe forgett my felfe (yf it were only in Refpect that you efteeme Mr. *Gryvell* as your deere and entier Frend) I fhowld juftlie condemne my felfe of vnadvifed and twoe great inconfiderat Dealinges. And therfore I pray you, and foe effectuallye defyre him to hold a better Opinion of me, till you have further Proofe howe I doe deale, and have dealt, in the Cawfe from the Begin-ynge. And as I have neither Will nor Power to hurt in this Cafe if I wolde, havinge onlie to walke in the Pathe I am directed : So yf I had either, beinge otherwife directed by you, I wold not. And therfore befeche you, what foever Cowrfe be held in the Matter, lay noe further Fawlt in me, then I juftlie de-ferve : For affure your felfe, you and yours have, and ever fhall have, that vndowbted Intereft in me, as I will obey your Commaundement, as farre as in Dewtie and Credit I may, which I crave yt maye lyke you to accept. And evenfo I take my Leave. From *Salloppe,* the xxviijth of *Aprill,* 1581.

Yours ever in all to be comaunded

as your obedient Servant,

E. Molyneux.

The King of Portugal *to Sir* Philip Sydney, *tranflated from the Original.*

Illuftrious Nephew Philip Sidney,

I Write this not only to inclofe and forward to you Captain *Allen*'s Letters, but alfo to defire you to write to me often, and preferve me in your Friend-fhip. My Affairs (praifed be God) go on extreemly well. The Fleet is ready to fail fully manned and well equipt, and I do expect to receive a confiderable Quantity of Stores or Ammunitions by the Ships from *Flanders,* in order to equip a fecond Expedition, on Board which I intend to go, with about fix or feven thoufand Men; which Number is getting ready by three or four Friends, who are willing to rifque the fame Fate with me; thefe are Monfieur *De Ba-bues,* Monfieur *de St. Luc,* Monfieur *de Sordiac,* and Monfieur *de Belleville* (that is, if they can get Leave for that Purpofe) there will come alfo Count *Roxafocar,* who is now in *Flanders.* Befides the abovenamed, there are other Gentlemen that will go in the beft Manner they can : This is to be under-ftood, if they continue in the fame Mind, and do not retract : But I am of Opinion they will not, or at leaft the four above named ; and though many more fhould go, if I did not fee you in the Company, I fhall fay, *Numerum non habet illa fuum.*

I have received good News from *Portugal,* both in Regard to the Natives, as well as to *Spaniards*; the former wifhing my Prefence, and the latter defi-ring to return into their own Country. The King of *France* affifts me fufficient-ly, his Mother ftill better, the States of *Flanders* very well ; and only *Dominga* keeps filent, but fhe is not to be blamed, confidering her Hufband's Affairs. I remain in Health, God grant you the fame, according to my Wifhes. *Tunis,* the Third of *May,* 1581.

Your greateft Friend,

The King.

Sir

Sir Francis Walfyngham *to Sir* Henry Sydney.

My verie good Lord,

I Vnderſtand, that vppon the Recommendacion of my Coſin *Greuills* Matter, concerning his Office in the Marches of *Wales,* and grauntid vnto him by her Majeſtie, the whole Cauſe was by your Lordſhip, and the reſt of the Counſell, referred to the Iudgment and Ordering of Sir *Thomas Leighton,* and Mr. *Philip Sydney* ; who, according to the Authoritie geuen them in that Be-half, haue proceedid to the Setting downe of an Awarde betwin the Partyes, which they ſend downe vnto your Lordſhip, and the reſt of the Counſell. There reſteth nowe, that I do put your Lordſhip in Mynd, that yt will pleaſe youe to haue a Care, and to further with your Authoritye, that the Order ſet downe for the Putting of the ſaid Arbitrators Awarde in Execucion, maie dulie be accompliſhed and perfourmid. I neede not to alleadge any more Reaſons vnto your Lordſhip in the Gentlemans Behalf, then I thincke youe do already knowe, that maie moue youe to fauor him in the Right of his Cauſe ; and vppon ſo reaſonable a Requeſt for his quiet Enioyinge the Beneffit of her Maje-ſties Liberalitye and good Meaning towards him, whereof, I doubt not, but that youe haue that Regarde that aperteyneth. I will only tell your Lordſhip, that in Reſpect of th'Accompt I make of the Gentleman, I ſhall accept any Fauor yt ſhall pleaſe youe to extend towards him herein for my Sake, and vp-pon this my Recommendacion as don to me ſelf, whom youe ſhall not fynd vnthanckfull for the ſame, in any Thing wherein I maie requite yt ; beſides that, youe ſhall therebie greatelie bind him vnto youe, to do you any Seruis he may. And ſo I commit your Lordſhip to God. At *Barnellms,* the xxjth of *June,* 1581.

Your Lordſhips aſſured Frend,

Fra. Walſyngham.

Certein ſpeciall Notes to be imparted to Mr. Philippe Sidney, *in the Hand-writting of* Edm. Molineux, *Eſq; and ſigned by Sir* Henry Sydney, *27 April,* 1582.

1. FIRST, that the principall and chiefe Cawſe that moveth him to fancie, or have any Likinge to take the Charge of the Governement of *Irlande* (if the ſame be offered him) is the Reſpect he bearethe to him. So that if he will aſſuredlie promeſſe him to goe with him thither, and withall will put on a determinate Minde to remaine and continew ther after him, and to ſuc-cede him in the Governement (if it may ſo like her Majeſtie to allowe him) he will then yeld his Conſent to goe ; otherwaiſe, he will not leave his quiet and contented Lief at Hoome, conſideringe his Yeares, and the Defectes of Na-ture, that comonly accompaynie Age, to enter into ſo toilſomme a Place, bothe of Bodie and Minde, but only to leave ſomme Memorie and worthie Marke to his Poſteritie.

2. Next, that if her Majeſtie doe not conceive and iudge that he hathe done as good Service (if not better) as any other Man hathe done, either afore his Tyme, or ſince his Tyme, or that any other Man can doe. But that her Majeſtie will ſtande on the Termes with him, that he hathe beene a charge-owſe and waſtfull Servant, the Place (as he ſuppoſethe) is not fitt for him to accept with that Diſgrace.

3. Then if his former Service be allowed, he is of Opinion, that it can not carrie dew Countenance of Credit, withowt ſome Badge of publique Favour be annexed : As Rewarde by Titell of Nobilitation, both ther, and heare ; toge-ther with ſomme Lande or Fee Farme (as may beſt ſtande with her Maje-

sties Pleafure to beftowe vpon him) that it may be knowen, and made apparant to the World, that her Majeftie hathe had graciowfe Confideracion of his Service paft, for his better Encoragement hereafter.

4. That if it fall out, that he be fent into *Irlande*, he wifhe the rather to carrie the Titell of Liewtenant, then Deputie.

H. Sydney.

Sir Henry Sydney *to Mr.* Sackford, *Mafter of the Requefts.*

After my mofte hartye Comeandaciones vnto you (mofte louinge Cozene)

SMALE Favors at others Handes in that Office, as yett haue I founde, yett hope I (my good Cozene) to tafte fumme better Frendfhippe at your Handes ; and therefore, as Confcyence bynedethe me to favor the Innocente, as alfoe to fee the Deferver have Punyfhemente, doe nowe make my felf the boulder with you, to crave your Helpe one the Behaulf of twoe poore Menne, whoe are indyĉted of Manflaughtor, for the fuppofed Kyllinge of a verye commone Dronckarde : And this is the Totall of my Defier, that you will receue the Bill of my Servaunte *Edmunde Mulleneuxe,* and to preferre the fame vnto the Quenes Majeftie for them. In Truethe I examyned the Matter, and canne fynde noe Matter to be layed to their Chardge but Troble : Therefore once againe I praye you forther their Caufe, the rather at my Requefte ; and what you fhall doe heryn, I fhall take the fame, as a Thinge donne to my felf. And foe hauing noe other Matter to wrytte to you of, I bydd you Farewell. From the Cyttye of *Hereforde,* the vjth of *June,* 1582.

Your affured louinge Cozene,

Good Cofyn, freynd me effeĉtually in thys fmall Matter, and I wyll requyte yt.

H. Sydney.

Sir Philip Sydney *to* Edm. Molyneux, *Efq;*

Mollineaux,

I pray thee write to me diligently. I woold yow came down your felf. Solicitt my Lord Treafurer, and Mr. Vice Chamberlain for my beeing of the Cownceill. I woold fain bring in my Cofin *Conningefby* if it wear poffible : Yow fhall do me much Pleafur to labour it. Farewell, even very well, for fo I wifh you. From *Hereford,* this 23d of *Juli,* 1582.

Your louing Frend,

Philip Sidney.

Robert Sidney (*after Earl of* Leicefter) *to* Edm. Molyneux.

Good Mr. Mullinax,

I Pray yow fett doune in Writing the Reafons why her Maieftie fhowlde ereĉt the Office I fue for. Yow muft doe it in good Terms, for it is to be fhewed to her Maieftie. I pray yow lett me hcare quickly from yow, for the Queene will be fpoken to, very fhortly about it. Farewell. Court, this *Sonday,* 1582.

Yours affuredly,

Robert Sidney.

William

William *Lord* Burghley, *Lord High Treasurer of* England, *to Sir* Henry Sydney, *concerning the Queens House at* Otford.

After my very hartie Commendacions to your Lordship,

I Haue of late receved Certificat from Mr. *Bossevyle,* and Mr. *Lambard,* of the Decaies that are at hir Majesties Howse at *Otford,* and the Spoyles that have bene made there, through the Default of such as having Charge thereof, vnder your Lordship, shold have had better Regard therevnto. The Charges whereof for the Howse, are by them estemed to xx *l.* and for the Pale being xij Rods, and the Making of a new Gate, v *l.* amounting in the Whole to xxv *l.* And forasmuch as I vnderstand, the same do require present Repaire ; and that your Lordship hath the Collection of certein hir Majesties Revenues belonging to that Howse, your Lordship maie geve Order for the present Doing thereof. For the which, this my Lettre, together with a Certificat of the Employment, shall be sufficient Warrant to the Auditor, to geve Allowaunce thereof, not exceeding the said Some of xxv *l.* vppon the next Accompt to be made of that Revenue. After which Reparacions so done, it shall be well that some speciall Charge were geven for the Preservacion thereof from the lyke Spoyles hereafter ; for that such voluntary Wastes are to be re-payred by your Lordship, having Custodie of the Howse, as I think my self ought to be, where I haue lyke Charge, if any such Spoyles shold happen to be committed. Whereof I nothing doubt but your Lordship will haue Care accordingly. And so I bidd your good Lordship right hartely Farewell. From my Howse at *Westminster,* this xxvjth of *June,* 1583.

Your Lordships assured loving Frend,

W. Burghley.

Robert Dudley *Earl of* Leicester *to* William *Lord* Burghley *Lord High Treasurer.*

[a] *My good Lord,*

H ER Majestie willed me to delyver a Message to my Lord Chancelor and you, and I thought yt had ben a *Starr Chamber* Day, and coming this Morning to my Lords House I told him of yt and prayd his Lordship to imparte yt to you also : Hit concerned the Staplers.

I wold also my self have gladly spoke with your Lordship, but my Busines was such as I could not stey, and I know your Lordship was to be occupied this Forenone. Hit was to lett you se how true ye late Informacions to her Majestie was, that I procured xxx M Clothes Yerely for ye Merchants, and had I cannot tell how many thousand Pounds for yt. But as I was assured of the contrary, so I partly told your Lordship ye other Day, how untrew yt was. For Confirmation whereof, I doe send your Lordship the Counterparte of all that passed betwene me and the Merchants. And yet I se ther ys sett down a 1000 *l.* more then ever I had. I send yt to your Lordship, that hit may please you that her Majestie may know the Informacion was very false, yf Occasions may serve you. And I partly now know, who informyd hir. Truly as God lyveth, I never made Sute for them, nor ever had Penny nor Farthing of them for yt. And you shall now see that I was forst to condytion with them, that my iiii score M Clothes should be over and beside xxx M that hir Majestie had, and might have Power to grant them.

Lastly, I wold have intreated your Lordship to graunt me, during my Lady *Warwyks* Lunacye, the Keping and Mastershipp of the Game of the Chase of *Malvern,* which I hear ys almost destroyed. Hit lyeth not farr from a Lord-

[a] Letter 38, Not. 161. C. 8. in Bibl. Harley

ſhip, a lytle Howſe I have. I wold be carefull of the Game, and the rather, being once my Fathers, and the auncyent Inherytance of the Erles of *War-wick.* Yf yt pleaſe you to graunt yt me; that your Lordſhip wyll take Order for yt preſently. Ther ys no Boddy now lookes to yt, and Mr. *Vmpton* left yt out of his Porcyon, for thir ys nothing but Pleaſur of the Game to yt. I am buſye about the Forreſt Cauſes, [b] agenſt *Fryday* Morning at *Waltham.* And ſo byd your Lordſhipp Farewell; in ſome Haſt this *Tueſday* Morning.

Your Lordſhips aſſured Frend

July 8, 1584.

R. Leyceſter.

[c] *Sir* Philip Sidney *to Sir* Edward Stafford.

S I R,

THE Caws of my ſending at this Tyme, this Bearer Mr. *Burnam* will tell yow. Onely lett me ſalute yow in the kyndeſt Manner that one nere Frend can do an other.

I woold gladli know how yow and your noble Lady do, and what yow do in this Abſence of the Kinges.

We are heer all *Solito.* Me thinkes yow ſhoold do well to begyn betymes to demand ſomething of her Majeſti as might be found fitt for yow. And lett Folkes chafe as well when yow aſk, as when yow do not. Her Majeſti ſeemes affected to deal in the *Low Contrey* Matters, but I think nothing will com of it. We are haulf perſwaded to enter into the Journey of Sir *Humphry Gilbert* very eagerli; whereunto your Mr. *Hackluit* hath ſerved for a very good Trumpet.

I can wryte no more, but that I pray for your long and happy Life. And ſo I commit yow both to the Giver of it. At Court this 21th of *Juli* 1584.

Yours aſſuredli

Superſcribed

Philip Sidney.

To the right honorable *Edward Stafford* Knight, Embaſſadour for her Majeſtie in the Court of *France.*

Sir William Borlas [d] *to Sir* Robert Sydney *Lord Governor of* Fluſhing.

My very good Lorde,

I Haue written divers Lettres to your Lordſhip to Thende that yow woulde eſtabliſhe your Garriſonne, and that I maie knowe what Companies yow ſhall kepe here continually, and that your Lordſhip woulde ſet downe the Names of thoſe Companies which muſt remayne as cavtionary Companies. For I aſſure your Lordſhep I am daily troubled with Lettres, from the States, and Mr. *Bodeley,* to have owt ſome of theis olde Companies that be here for the preſent Service that they have in Hande, and to receave in their Places ſome of the Companies that be come out of *Portingall,* which I have refuſed to doe, for that I have no Order therefore from your Lordſhip. Mr. *Gilpin* came hether for no other Purpoſe, but onely to deale with me about it.

I have accordinge to my Lords of the Cownſells Letter and your Lordſhips, placed Captene *Smith*; and I aſſuer your Lordſhip if Mr. *Champernons* Companie had bene of any Strength, or armed, I had receaved him into this Garri-

[b] Being Lord Chief Juſtice in *Eyre.* [c] *Gallia* Letters from 1584, to 1589 in his Majeſtys Office for Papers and Records of State, Ex Origin. [d] This Sir *William Borlas,* was Leivtenant Governor of *Fluſhing,* and was a Commander of Note, during the whole War in the *Low Countries,* where he greatly diſtinguiſhed himſelf. From this Sir *William Borlaſe,* deſcended Sir *John Borlaſe* of *Buckmer* in *Buckinghamſhire,* Bart, whoſe 2d Son *William Borlas* of *Great Marlow* in the ſame County, Eſq. left Iſſue *Alicia* one of his Coheirs, Mother to the Right Honourable *John Wallop,* the preſent Earl of *Portſmouth.*

ſonne

fonne, and fent *Smith* prefently owt into the Feilde ; but there is no Time pafte : By this Time I thinke Mr. *Champernons* Companie is in better Order, for there are Men come over to fill it. I can foone have him from *Bergen* hether, if it be your Lordfhips Pleafure ; and fende owt any other Companie that your Lordfhip fhall apointe.

Theis newe Orders are arrived here, and accordinge to your Lordfhips Lettre, they have muftered the Garrifonne, but I affure you, it is impoffible to be kept, there are fo many of Mr. *Digges* his Articles, fuche as were never fene nor hearde of amongft martiall Men. All his Articles are to be concluded in onely three ; but the one of them I fee no Meanes howe it can be kept.

The *Firft* of the three is to mufter ftreightly.

The *Seconde* is to punifhe either Captaine or Soldier, that dothe deceave the Queene, feverely.

The *Thirde* is to paie well, if it may be.

And if theis three be well obferved, wee fhall have no Neede of Mr. *Diggs* his fine Heade amongft Souldiers ; and her Majeftie fhalbe a great Deale better ferved. Befides there muft Choife be made of fuche Men to be Comiffaries, as are both honeft, and have a Care to ferve their Prince truly, and not to fende fuch Men as wilbe corrupted by anie Captaine. For he that muft come to take fuch a Mufter as this is, beinge a generall Mufter of all her Majefties Forces, muft be a Man of fome Countenaunce and one of Creditt.

I fende your Lordfhip the Names of all the Companes in this Garrifonne, becaufe if I fhoulde be commaunded to fende out any Companie, your Lordfhip maie name him, or fuch as yow will have fent owt, and alfo to name whome yow will have come in their Places.

I am very fory to heare of the Death of my very good Freinde Captene *Henry White*, in whome I knowe your Lordfhip hath loft a very good Servaunt : I woulde wifhe your Lordfhip to take fome Care whom yow admit into the Place which yow had appointed for him, for that he had neede be a Man of fome Governement that fhall occupie that Roome.

Thus with my humble Dutie to your Lordfhip, I leave yow to the Tuition of Almightie God. *Vlifhinge* this xvth of *September*, 1584.

Your Lordfhips moft affured to comaunde,

Wylliam Borlas.

Geo. Gilpin, *Efq;* Refident at the Hague, to Sir Robert Sydney.

My very good Lorde,

THopportunitie of this Bearer I would not overflippe, though otherwife vnfurnifhed of Matter worth the troubling you, onely that a few Dayes paft I fent to Sir *William Brown* a Packet, to be conveyed by the firft falfely to your Lordfhip, coming from Monfieur *Aldegonde*, whofe Defyre was fuch, and will, as your Leafure fhall permit, expecte an Aunfwere ; and I alfo no leffe gladde to heare of your Lordfhips Health, with whatfoever els you fhall pleafe to beftowe vppon me. Here we have not any Thinge, all reftinge in Tearmes, as by my laft, exfpectinge to heare of the Deputies Succeffe in *Fraunce*, whofe Lettres from *Angiers*, conteyned no other then of their Audience and gracious Vfuage by the Kinge, whofe Inclination they fownd not fuch to any Peace, but might be diuerted, yf he could obteyne the defyred Helpe, to the better Redreffe of his Eftate, and Eafe of thofe complayne of the Miferies the Warre hath brought with yt. Mr. Secretary they had feene and conferred with, but fownd not his Commiffion or Order, other then to heare and fee how Matters had paffed about the Conference of an Accord, and what would be propownded or offred. This litle lyke them, and breedes a generall Doubt that other Inconveniences will followe, the Peace being more

here

here talked of openly, and fondry Difcourfes made by fuch as wifh, yt might fo fall out, though to the Harme and Alteracion of thofe Perfonnes that hitherto haue mainteyned the Caufe ; and if that fucceede, it is much dowbted all will not continew conftant that are now of Tharmie : Havinge alfo giuen fom Subiect to thofe that are flow, in contributing to feek and vfe Delayes, whatfoeuer their Purpofe may be befides otherwayes, to the Grief of the wel affected, whofe Feare is moft, that the Enimie will get much by thefe Courfes, and that yf one beginne more will followe, fuch being commonly the Humor of all Commonalties or popular Gouernments. After the Retorne of thabfent Deputies, more wilbe knowen ; and for other particular Matters (being felt) I refarre to the Report of this Bearer Captain *Cary.* And fo ceafing to be furder troublefome, befeech Thalmightie for the longe and profperous Eftate of your Lordfhip. From the *Haeghe,* this 25 of *Aprill,* 1590.

Your good Lordfhips moft affured

to do you all Service,

Geo. Gilpin.

Sir Thomas Bodley *to Sir* Robert Sydney.

I Haue perufed thofe Articles, which your Lordfhip fent vnto me, and I haue fhortly fette downe, what I thinke of euery Point. There is very great Reafon in the moft of them ; but becaufe the chiefeft can not well be performed, without fome further Order from her Majeftie, you fhall finde it a great Eafe to delay your Anfwear till my Lord of *Buckhurfts* Comming hither, and then to put them in good Hope of fome fpeedy Redreffe, to their full Contentment. This Courfe is the beft that I can thinke vpon ; which yet your Lordfhip will vfe with better Dexteritie then I can expreffe. Whervppon I commend it, and all your other Actions, to Gods good Direction. From the *Hage, May* 29, 1590.

Your Lordfhips at Commaundement,

Thomas Bodley.

Vppon the Clofing up of this Letter, I receaued your Lordfhips of the 25, and haue dealt with the Councel in your Behalf. Howbeit they will take no Anfwear to hold your Lordfhip altogether excufed, vnles they may haue, at the left, one Company.

1. This Article doth carie a Shew of Equitie, but I fufpend my Iugement until I heare the Allegacions of thofe of the Garrifon.

2. It is fo required by the Treatie, and it hath bin lately promifed by my Lords of the Councel to the States and Councel heer. Howbeit, becaufe the cautionarie Companies are incomplete, the Treatie muft bee fo vnderftood, as it may always ftand with the Safetie of the Yeare.

3. Their Orders of Mvfters were neuer approved by my Lords in *England,* nor the late Orders fett downe by my Lords, allowed heer by the States of thes Provinces, who haue alwaies reiected the 15 dead Paies, and fondrie other Points of the faid Orders. In which Refpect there can bee no Satisfaction giuen vnto them, vntil there bee a mutual Eftablifhement of fuch Orders as are to be obferued, which I hope will be perfourmed at my Lord of *Buckhurfts* Coming hether.

4, 5. Your Lordfhip will confyder whether thes frebuting Souldiers bee neceffarie Euils in that Garrifon ; for otherwife in other Places, it is found by Experience, that the dailie Wrongs and Enormities committed by Frebuters, are full of Danger and Inconuenience.

6. Vnles

6. Vnles it be in extraordinarie Cafes, the Graunt of fuch Kinde of Paffe-ports doth wholie belong to the Councel of State, and this Prohibition ought to bee general. Neuertheles, the Gouuernors of thefe Prouinces vfurp that Authoritie daily.

7, 8. The 7 and 8 Articles feem to be confonant with the Contract. The States of *Holland* have complained of late to my Lords of the Councel againft the Officers of the *Briel*, for your late Impeachment of their Nauigation; and I have bin required by my Lords to take fuch Order as it fhould bee prac-tized no more.

9. No Officer is exempted by the Contract from paieng Impofte and Accife, for which I fee not, for my Part, how any can claime that Priuiledge without their fpecial Permiffion.

10. It is fo required by the Treatie, and, for ought that I can learne, it is fo obferued.

Geo. Gilpin, *Efq; to Sir* Robert Sydney.

Moft honorable Knight,

YOURE Refolve how to deale touchinge your Comminge hither, or Sending efpecially, now his Excellencie is abfent, me thinks, vnder Cor-rection, would farue to fmall Purpofe, for youe fhould fynd no fitt Com-panie: And will better pleafe thefe Men, that your Lordfhip being (as it were) but niewly arryved, ftay yet a Whyle in your Gouuernment, til fuch Order be eftablyfhed as youe fhall haue fownde needfull, and thinke conuenient for the Difcharge of your Place, to the Contentment of all Syds. Mr. *Bodly* hath written youe his Mynde vppon the Articles youe fent him, fo as I neede fay nothinge, onely this, that I have fownd by Experience, that to giue thefe Men good Words, and not to contend with them, in that depends on the Difpofition of others, is moft Wifdom, and workes both more Good and Credit to the Parties in Action, and tends alfo to the better Sarvice of hir Majeftie. Mr. *Wilkes* is now fayd to com ouer, and by that I can perceaue this People do not fhew any great Lykinge, but of the Iffew cannot be iudged, til his Erraunt be knowen. All Things continewe at one Stay; his Excel-lencie remaynes at the Campe; fom fmall Skermifhinge now and then betweene Thennemies and owr Men; the Forte goeth forwarde apace, which being finifhed, there wilbe other Sarvices attempted worthie the being at. In *Groe-ninghen* there is a niew Stirre, by reafon *Verdinge* had a Practyfe to bring in Soldiars by Intelligence within the Towne, meaning to haue taken a Gate in the Morninge of the Watch, and fo to have let his Men in, which fayled, Count *William* wrote for Horfemen, meaninge to have attempted fom Sarvice, whyleft they are (as yt were) denyded in the Towne, but can gett no Helpe hince, til the Sarvices intended by his fayd Excellencie be finifhed. And thus, for Want of other, do take my Leave, committing your Lordfhip to the Protection of the Allmightie. From the *Haghe* this 2 of *June*, 1590. *Stilo Angliæ.*

Your Lordfhips at commaundment,

Geo. Gilpin.

* *Sir* Thomas Heneage *to Sir* Robert Sydney.

S I R,

I Muft defire you, to vnderftand my good Will, rather by my Wurks then my Words; for having prefently both my Hands and my Hedd full of Bufnes, a fhorte Lettre muft not be interpreted as of fhorte good Will; and hauyng told you I love you, you may looke for enowgh from me, yf I be an honeft Man.

Now, by her Majefties Commandment, I wrighte this vnto you, that her Highnes hath Intelligens, that ther is fome Devyfe in Hammeringe for an Enterpryfe againft *Flufhing*, that you have in Chardge; and that it is therefore very needfull, that you be very heedfull and vigilant, to meete with Practyfe, or Attempt, that may be vfed agaynft you, either within or withowt. Ther ys an Opinyon that *Bodnam*, that is at *Dunkyrke*, fetts owt prefently 2 Shipps well manned and furnyfhed, yt is thought to paffe to *Andwerpe* by *Flufhing*, with Gooddes to returne, to which yt wear good to haue an Eye; and fo both to the Maryners and the Armour of the Towne, which your Brother I knowe was euer iealoufe of; and you, I am fure will think of. More I haue not nowe to wryte, but to wyfh you euer as my felf. At the Courte this xiijth of *June*, 1590.

Your affured Frend,

When *Burnham* coomes to you,
you fhall knowe more.   T. Heneage.

Superfcribed, To my honorable good Frend Sir *Robert Sidney*, Knight, Gouerner of *Fluffinge*.

Sir Thomas Wylkes *to Sir* Robert Sydney.

My verie good Lord,

VERDUGO, with 2000 Horfe, and 500 Foote, is entred vpon the Skyrt of *Frize*, ioyning vpon the Lande of *Groeningen*, where he hath taken (fithence my Arrival here,) a Forte from the States, caled *Cemetyl*; and from thence is marched vp towards the Sea Syde, and maketh his Approches to a fecond Fort of very great Importance, which, if he can take, he will thereby greately annoy the whole Province of *Frize*. Yt feemeth that Cont *William* is in verie great Feare, not hauing fufficient Strength to make Head againft the Enemy, and therefore hath written hether for fome fpeedy Succour to be fent vnto him: And bycaufe Cont *Maurice* is in no Cafe able to fpare any Parte of his Forces, and but fewe to be had of thefe Countrie People on the foddeyn, to be employed in this Seruice. The Councell of State haue bene conftrayned to write vnto you for the two Auxiliarie Companies remayning vnder your Gouernment, which it may pleafe you (confidering the Neceffitie) not to refufe; but that, according to fuch Direction as you fhall receyue from the faid Councell, you will vouchfave to fend them furth: And if you fhall fo thinke fyt, geue Notice of the Neceffitie, and Sending of them, to my Lord Threfurer. Your Lordfhip were beft to confider how vnfit yt were to refufe to fend them at this Tyme, both in Refpect of the Seruice, and of my Negotiation, which

---

* Sir *Thomas Heneage* was Captain of the Guards to Queen *Elizabeth*, alfo Treafurer of her Chamber, Vice-Chamberlain of her Houfhold, Chancellor of the Dutchy of *Lancafter*, and one of her Privy Council. He married *Anne*, Daughter of Sir *Nicholas Poyntz*, Knight, by *Joan*, Daughter of *Thomas* Lord *Berkley* of *Berkley* Caftle, two of the moft antient and noble Families in *Gloucefter-fhire*, whofe Anceftors had been eminent by their Quality and great Alliances from the Time of the Conqueft. By which Match, he left an only Daughter and Heir, *Elizabeth*, married to Sir *Moyle Finch*, Knight, who was by King *James the Firft* advanced to the Dignity of Vifcountefs *Maidftone*, in *Kent*; and by King *Charles the Firft* to the Title of Countefs of *Winchelfea*, in *Suffex*, with Limitation of thofe Honours to the Heirs Male of her Body, lawfully begotten. She died on the 13th of *March*, 1633, and from her Ladyfhip the prefent Earl of *Winchelfea* is defcended.

I

hitherto

hitherto is muche applauded by the States, and great Hope and Expectacion had of the Iffue thereof: And fo (with many Thanks to your Lordfhip for myne honorable Enterteynment at *Vlyffing*) I committe you to the Protection of Almighty God. From the *Haghe*, this xvth of *June*, 1590.

Your Lordfhips verie affured to commaunde,

Tho. Wylkes.

Sir Thomas Wylkes *to Sir* Robert Sydney.

My verie good Lord,

THE Counfell of *Oftat* are fent by the States Generall to refide at *Arnham*, there to fecond the Purpofes of the Count *Maurice*, for fome furder Attempt vppon the Forte before *Zutphen*, &c. fo as I cannot aqueynt them with the Lettre to your Lordfhip from my Lord Threfurer: How be it, if there fhalbe Caufe for your better Excufe, I will take the Opportunitie to acqueynt them with it by Writing. We haue here no Newes, but an Incling or Imaginacion of the Cominge of the Duke of *Parma* to *Nuymeghen*, and that *Verdugo* attempteth the Fort of *Nieuzell* in *Frife*. Yf your Lordfhip fhall heare any Newes out of *England*, or any Thing of *France*, I befeach you let vs be Partakers with you here. Yt hath ben an olde Cuftome at Home, that when Men are Abroade in any publike Services, they are written vnto at Leyfure; I feare the Continuaunce of that Cuftome nowe the more, bycaufe there is no Secretarye. I will not forget the Mater of your Lordfhips Poftfcript, as Tyme fhall ferve. I fynde hetherto, the States verie flowe, and am as yeat hardly hable to make Conftruction of their Meanings or Inclinations towards her Majeftie. As I fhall lerne furder, your Lordfhip fhall be aduertifed; and till then, I will recomend you to God, and my felf to the Continuaunce of your good Love and Fauor. From the *Haghe*, the xxiijth of *June*, 1590.

Your Lordfhips affured to comand,

Tho. Wylkes.

Sir Thomas Wylkes *to Sir* Robert Sydney.

My verie good Lord,

YOUR Lettre of the xxvth of the laft Moneth, I received this Morning by a Soldior comyng from the Camp, fignifieng the Refufall of the *Dutche* Commiffioner to joyne with him for her Majeftie, in the Signing of the weeklie Certificate, and Taking of the Mufters. Yt hath ben a Thing vfuall with the States not to joyne with vs in any Mufters offered to be taken by our felfe, in Refpect of the common Fraudes vfed by our Captaines; and therefore, in that Pointe, it is not to be wondred at, if they refufe the like ftill: And, as I remember, ther is Direction geven by Lettres from my Lords, either to your Lordfhip, or your Lieutenant Gouernor, to mufter at all Tymes when the States fhall fo require. For not Signing the weeklie Certificats, I fuppofe they doe it, as not allowing (as yeat) of the Orders eftablifhed for the Maner of the Paye, &c. All thefe Things I fhall in their Courfes fo remedie; and, in the meane Tyme, your Lordfhip may doe verie well, to will the Commiffarie *Englyfhe*, to procede in the Execucion of her Majefties Orders as he hath, by inviting the *Dutche* Commiffary thereunto; which, if he fhall refufe, to take fome Wittneffe of his Refufall, of the Townes People, and him felf to procede as he hathe accuftomed.

I am here entertayned with verie ftrang Delayes, and as hetherto can receive no Anfwer to fuche Propofitions as I haue exhibited, fo that my whole Tyme,

to

to this Inftant, hath ben fpent with out Fruite. They feame glad of my Comyng, and of the Maters I haue deliuered, but do nothing : I fuppofe their Dellayes to growe by Lacke of fufficient Auctoritie, wherewith they dare not aqueynt me, in Refpect of their Lettres lately writen to my Lords of the Counfaill, giving them to vnderftand, that they haue Auctoritie to treat with any fuche as her Majeftie fhold fend, which I fynd not to be fo. As I fhall procede, your Lordfhip fhall heare furder from me : In the meane Tyme, I will committ you to the Tuition of Almightie God. From the *Haghe,* the Firft of *Julie,* 1590.

Your Lordfhips affured to comand,

Tho. Wylkes.

I befeache your Lordfhip, caufe the Lettre fent herewith, to be, by fome truftie Perfon, deliuered to Mr. *Meredethe,* who is furthwith to repare hether, to enter into the Maters of the Accompts. Before this was clofed vp, Mr. *Meredeth* arived here.

Sir Thomas Wylkes *to* Sir Robert Sydney.

My verie good Lord,

I Received your two Lettres, the one of the iiijth, and the other of the viijth of the Prefente, this *Mondaye* the xiijth, in a Packet inclofed to Mr. *Gilpin,* for the which I thank your Lordfhip with all my Harte ; for althoughe I receive Lettres often out of *England,* yeat they com for the mofte Parte from fuche as doe not write me muche Newes (as from the Lord Threforer, and Lords of the Counfaill) or from fuche as cannot write, but of Maters currant in Th'exchange, or in the Horfefaire in *Powles,* where (as you Lordfhip knoweth) many Things are daily, and fowndlie reported, and with Advantage.

I doe wounder who fhould be the Auctor of the Bruicte of her Majefties Treating of Peace with *Spaigne,* or that I fhould be employed hether about any fuche Mater : I doe proteft vnto your Lordfhip, that for my felf, I haue no Commiffion to that or the like Pourpofe, nor doe vnderftand that there was any fuch Thing in Handling at my Comyng out of *England* ; but am of Opinion, that if her Majeftie did affecte a Peace, fhe fhould more hardlie obtayne it nowe, then euer at any Tyme heretofore. I haue had fome Aer of this Conceipt deliuered here vnto me by *Artfens,* the Greffier to the States, who declared vnto me plainlie, that the States feared fome fuche Devife : I anfwered him directly, and with Proteftation, that there was no fuche Mater, and might affure his Mafters thereof, if he would, from me.

But, my good Lord, I hold nothing fo ftrange as the Delaies and Dallyance vfed with me by theife Perfons : I am fo farre beyond my Latin therwith, as I cannot tell what to coniecture rightly of the Caufes thereof : Howbeit, I fynde that fuche as are evell affected to *England,* haue playd their Partes egregiouflie here, bothe before and fithence my Comyng, to drawe this People from all Liking towards her Majeftie, and to affect their Humors to *France* ; a Thing not a litle to be reguarded, and yet not like to be prevented, but with fome Danger. Affure your Lordfhip, the Difcontentements of theis Men have ben let runn fomewhat to long.

Valke hath deliuered vnto me certen Reafons to be imparted to my Lords of the Counfell, towching the Debts of the two Companies mentioned in your Lettres, which remayneth with me not fent, bycaufe I forefee there wilbe nothing don in the Mater, vntill it fhall appeare what Courfe wilbe taken in the greateft and chiefeft nowe in Handling.

I will, according to your Lordfhips Requeft, write Home to the Lords concerning your Powder, and will give all the Furderance thereunto that I maye ; and as that wilbe nedefull for your Defence, fo I think it as neceffary for

† you

you to haue your Eye bent vppon your Charge, having in some Degree sithence my Comyng hether, changed my Opinion of the Integritie and plaine Dealing of theise Countreys towards her Majestie, as I will give your Lordship more to vnderstand hereafter.

Here we are aduertised of the Coming of the Duke of *Parma* to *Bruffelles,* where *Richardot* hath ben, and is with him, who from the King hath, in an Affemblie of the States in that Place, deliuered many Things vnto them: That there is some Practife in Hande to fett *Brabant* and *Flanders* on Work to mediate a Peace with theis Provinces Vnited : That the Duke of *Parma* maketh Leavies of Men within the Counteys to fill the Garrifons of the chefeft Places, and from them to drawe out all the olde Regiments and Companies, and with them to marche fourthwith into *France,* to the Succor of the Ligueurs : Your Lordship may happilie in thefe Partes lerne more of this then I shall here, and more Certaintie. I befeach you, therefore, fynde the Meanes to be informed, and let me be Partaker with you. And fo for this Tyme, with my moft hartie Salutacions, I committ your Lordship to the Protection of Almightie God. From the *Haghe,* the xiijth of *July,* 1590.

Your Lordships euer affured to comand,

and ready to doe you Service,

Tho. Wylkes.

De Conte Maurice *de* Naffau, *a Monfieur Monfieur de* Sidnay, *Governeur de* Flifshinge.

Monfieur,

LE Captaine *Metkerke* vous fera entendre a que i'ay trouue bon que ce faffe au faict que cognoiffes, i'ay efcript a Meffieurs de *Zelande,* qu' il laiffent fumire des hommes pour l' executer et fi vous en ay encores faict donner d' *Hollande,* comme il vous dira plus particulierement, et auffi tout a ceque, fe paffe icy pour le prefent, et ne feruant ceftes a autre fin je prie Dieu.

Monfieur, qu'il vous donne en fante longue vie et heureufe, et l' Heur que voftre entreprinfe puiffe reufier a honne fin ce que vous fouhaitte.

Voftre tres affectionne Amy

Du Camp deuant *Nimeghen,*
15 De *Juillet,* 1590.

de vous faire Servece,

Maurice de Naffau.

Sir Thomas Wylkes *to Sir* Robert Sydney.

My verie good Lord,

TO bothe yours of the xiiijth and xvijth (which I would haue feuerally anfwered, but that by your Promife I hoped to haue fene yow here) I am bold to anfwer yow by this : *Firft,* I thanke yow humblie for your Newes, whereof we are here but too barren, and thereof I am afhamed : Then concerning myne owne Procedings with thes People, I doe affure my felfe they are as hedftrong as fo many Bulles ; no Reguard of her Majefties Merites towards them, nor fo muche as good Maner to thanke her for their Prefervacion ; which I fynde to proceede of two Caufes, the one of Want of Witte and Judgement, and vppon the Advantage they haue, that their Coniunction dothe more import her Majeftie, then the Succours of *England* dothe benefitt them ; and the other, of the comon Gawles we haue given to them, which to this Houre are refted vnplaftred, and *Quia magis injuriæ quam beneficij memores,* whereof we haue ben a litle too negligent towards them. Neuertheles, I haue not as yeat loft all my

6 K Hope,

Hope, but that with a fewe Daies more Travell, I fhall reduce them to a better Temper, albeit hetherto I haue don iuft nothing, and yet haue fpent fome Daies with them in Conference, fcolding and brawling, thoughe to no Porpofe.

I haue offered fome fmale Overture to the States of the Matter I fpake of to your Lordfhip, but I fynd them not to byte at it, to my Liking, but meane not to leave it fo, and will take a fitter Opportunitie for it hereafter.

For the Practife for *France*, there is doubtles fome Canvaffing vnder Hande, but by fome perticular Perfones, who, the better to frame the Humores of the People thereunto, goe about to engorge the People with flanderoufe Reports and Conceipts of her Majefties Actions towards theife Countreys ; it wilbe daungeroufe to let it goe foreward, and therefore I haue geven fome Advife hence howe it may be prevented, and infifted vppon the Execution thereof, if it be liked. I feare no Peace with *Spaigne*, they are fixed fo ftrongly vppon their Libertie, and hate with a moft perfect Hatred, as well the *Spaniard*, as any other Monarchical Comaundement over them.

I haue heard of a fharp Lettre writen latelie vnto yow from the Counfaill of Eftate, about the ij Companies auxiliarie vnder your Charge ; I doubt not but yow will anfwer them as appertaineth ; and I could wifhe for that Refpect, and bycaufe they wilbe erneft with yow here for thofe 2 Companies, that you did forebeare yet a While to com hether, vnles there be fome Caufe of Importance concerning your felf, or any publik Service that · may preffe your Comyng. Thus, my Lord, refting wholy at your Lordfhips Comandement, I ende my Epiftle, with my moft hartie Salutacions to your felf and to my Lady. From the *Haghe*, the xxijth of *July*, 1590.

Your Lordfhips euer affured, and ready to

do yow Service,

Tho. Wylkes.

Conte Maurice *de* Naffau, *a Monfieur Monfieur de* Sidnay, *Gouverneur de* Flifshinge.

Monfieur,

I'AY entendu par le Chevalier *Vere*, que vous feriez d'intention de nous venir trouver, fi toft que vous fcaviez que nous nous viendrions camper aultre part. Surquoi Ie n'ay voulu laiffer de vouis advertir, que Ie fuis refolu de defloger de devant cefte Ville, endedans deulx ou trois jours, & mettre le Camp en quelque aultre endroit, ou l'efpere nous en rapporterons plus de Paffetemps, que devant cefte Ville. Et pourtant Ie vous prie Monfieur fi voftre commoditè peult fouffrir de nous venir trouver, accompaigne avec quelque nombre des voftres, jufques a *Gornicfom*, qu'il Vous plaife, Vous y encheminer, ou que Vous me trouverez, ou finon, de madvertir de la, de Voftre venue illec, affinque Ie Vous y puiffe trouver. Et me remettant avec ce a Vôtre arrivement, lequel j'attens a bonne devotion ; Ie me recommanderay tres affecteufement en Voz bonnes graces, en priant Dieu Vous maintenir.

Monfieur,
En fa fainte Protection du Camp devant *Nimeghen*, le 10 de *Aougft*, 1590.

Voftre tres affectionné Amy

de vous faire Service,

Maurice de Naffau.

Sir

Sir Thomas Wylkes *to Sir* Robert Sydney.

My Lord,

SIthence my laft vnto yow by Mr. *Kiffin,* I tooke Occafion to make a Voiage to fee the Townes of *Nort Holland,* and was abfent from the *Haghe* about x Daies, fynding at my Retourne 2 Lettres from your Lordfhip, one of the 29 of *July,* and another of the 6 of this Prefent ; the firft contayning your Opinion of the Dealings of theife Men nowe towards her Majeftie, wherein yow concurre in Opinion with my felfe, and others, that can difcerne any Thing of their Doings ; and for myne owne Parte I hope of no better at this Tyme, what fo euer may alter hereafter, vppon any dangeroufe Accident growing to their Eftate, either from the Enemy Abroade, or from their civill Diuifions at Home ; the Seconde mentioneth, for the Place, as muche as your Lordfhip promifed in the Firft, wherein I wifhe all happie Succes and Honor to your felf.

The longer I ftaye expecting my Anfwer, the more Delaye appeareth ; for theife Men have refolued vppon Temporifation, to Th'ende they may difcouuer what wilbe the Succes in *France,* that thereby they may ftraighten or enlarge them felfs in graunting or denying our Demaunds. But if your Lordfhip could difcovuer what they doe in *Zelande,* and give me Knowledge thereof before Hande, I fhould thereby gheffe of all the reft : The Man that is nowe imployed thither, is very lewdly affected vnto vs, and yet maketh Shewe of verie great Af-fection to her Majefties Service. It is *Vander Warke,* I befeach your Lordfhip, if yow may haue Meanes, procure him to be obferved.

I truft by the next Difpatche from the Lords, to haue Newes of my Revocaci-on, which will fome what repaire her Majefties Honor in fending hether to fo litle Pourpofe, and leffe Reguard and Accompt made of her Goodnes towards theife Countreys ; albeit this Backwardnes procedeth not from the Generalitie of the Townes and People, but from 2 or 3 Companions here, that affect ambiti-oufly to continnue the Gouernement in their owne Handes, which (if her Ma-jeftie wold be counfailled) might eafyly be avoided, and they fuppreffed in fome Tyme.

I am forie to vnderftand of the Garboil like to growe in *Scotland,* whereof I haue received 2 or 3 Aduertyfements from Home ; it will happen in a verie vn-feafonable Tyme, onles the Liguours be tymely and well beaten, which God graunt for his Mercye.

Your Lordfhip knoweth we haue nothing here of the Doings of the Worlde on that Syde, but it comyth along by yow, and from yow ; and therefore I can-not make yow beholding vnto me for any Newes worth the Writing from hence ; which doth the more increafe my Debt to your Lordfhip, in that it pleafeth yow to afford me fo many of your Lettres, contayning Variety of good Mater, and I can requite yow with nothing, but with the Complaints of my Difcontentments, and the frowarde Procedings of theife Men : I will therefore here make an Ende with many Thankes, and comitt your Lordfhip to the Protection of Almightie God. From the *Haghe,* the xth of *Auguft,* 1590.

Your Lordfhips euer moft affured to comaund,

Tho. Wylkes.

Sir Thomas Wylkes *to Sir* Robert Sydney.

My verie good Lord,

I Am forced to take my Leave of your Lordfhip by Lettre, in Refpect of the Conveniencie of my Paffage from hence, being now revoked and defire-oufe to be at Home. I retourne in all Things *re infecta,* and haue no better Hope of any Succes from the States. I would to God there were in me, any Thing that were agreable to your Lordfhip, and that as it hathe pleafed yow to vfe me with muche Fauour fithence my being here in thies Partes, that it wold

alfo

alfo pleafe yow to vfe and commaund me at Home to doe yow Service, where although I fhalbe leaft hable of a great many, yeat no Man more ready and willing then my felf. And fo with this Brevitie, in Refpect of the haftie Departure of the Berer ; and my felf in fome other Bufynes to be at this Tyme difpatched, bicaufe I looke to imbarke this Afternoone ; I committ your Lordfhip to the Protection of Almighty God, with my mofte hartie Salutacions. From the *Briell*, the xxijth of *Auguft*, 1590.

Your Lordfhips euer affured to commaunde,

Tho. Wylkes.

George Gilpin *Efq*; *Secretary to the Ambaffy to the States General, to Sir* Robert Sidney.

My very good Lorde,

AFTER Mr. *Wilkes* his Departure, fince the Bufines were of that fmall Importaunce, as gaue us rather an Occafion to be occupyed in feinge the Contrye Abroade, then to ftay at Home and doo nothinge ; which made Mr. *Bodley* (whome I accompaigned) make a fhorte Progres, towards *Vytrecht* and thofe Partes, whence wee retornyd not vntil *Friday* laft, when as I determyned to wryte to your Lordfhipe, ftayinge onely Thopportunitie of a Meffenger, which could not light vppon til this Prefent. And may now pleafe youe to vnderftande that I haue receavyd your laft of the Seconde of this Monthe, thereby perceavinge myne to haue come in Saeftie to your Lordfhips Handes with thinclofed Copies. As yet the States haue made no Aunfwere to the Propofitions deliuered them by Mr. *Wilks*, neyther can I learne of any Lykelyhood to haften yt, but do rather iudge they wil deferre the Time exfpectinge the Succeffe in *Fraunce* ; and thereafter to frame their Courfe. The Ambaffadors or Commiffioners of Thempyre and *Liege*, haue not yet their Aunfwere, but is a framinge, and whyle they exfpecte yt, new Matters of Complaynt fall owt, havinge received the Newes that the States Men haue gotten the Towne of *Burick*, and the Ennimies Garrifon forfakinge the fame retyred with their Baggage into the Caftel or Fort there, which being beaten with a Peece or tweyne was furrendred and is poffeffed by owrs, who fince lay Siege with thofe few Forces they haue to a Fort againft *Wefol*, called *Graeve*, and hope to gett yt. Sir *Frauncys Vere* is in thoofe Partes, with Commiffion to attempte the Reskewinge of *Lattekenhome*, a Place in *Munfter* or *Weftphalia*, a Fortyres, furpryfed by owr Men, and befet by Thenemy ; he hath with him nier 600 Horfe and 1000 Footemen wherouer he commaunds. The Wawters growinge hye lately, hath forced the Ennnemy to abandon the Fielde, where he lay in the Frontyers of *Foyfe*, and is retyred with his Troupes into the Countie of *Benthain*, being fo difcontented that they lacke but the beinge in a gud Towne to make a Mutiny: Count *William* hath retorned the 400 Horfe that were fent to his Ayde, and remaynes ftill ; exfpectinge what *Verdugo* will doo, and then eyther to attempte furder or to give ouer and place his Men in Garrifon ; which is thought wilbe Thende of thofe Warres, now their Lymits are freed ; eech caringe for him felfe and no furder. The Count *Maurice* is here, and paffeth the Tyme in Huntinge and Hawkinge, feeing he cannot get the States to fett him a Worke Abroade ; being ftraunge that Men can fuffer fo fit Opportunitie to ouerpaffe and do nothinge.

The Count *Hohenlo* hath bin a Whyle at *Burey*, to accompanie the Ladye of *Orange*; which made fom Speache as yf the Mariage fhould goo forwarde ; the fayd Count is com this Night to this Towne, but do not heare where he lefte the Lady, neyther that any fuch Matter was meant.

There haue bin diuers Entreprifes offred and debated vppon, but none will goo forwarde, eech fearinge the Charges. And fo thefe Warres continewinge onely defenfiue, wil laft this feven Yeres and more. The Counfell have writen to your Lordfhip about fom Difordre or euil Dealinge of your Soldiars, againft

I

the

the Searchers for difcharging their Deutie in fiftinge owte fraudulent Dealings. Alfo touchinge the Trenche or Fort youe meane to make on *Flaunders* Syde o-uer againft *Flufhing.* Yf your Lordfhip com not hither fhortly, I could. wifh I had fomme good Errand into *Zélande* which I labor to efpye or meete with. The meane Whyle yf your Lordfhip continew, in Mynde to com, yt wilbe necef-fary wee knew thereof about your Lodginge, for they are fcaunt here; the Innes being exceffiff deare, and dayntie, to receave any of oure Nation, and to be prouyded by the Harbinger is longe Worke; the beft were to feeke to hyer fom fit Place for a Tyme and there to make your owne Dyet. Which to furdur yf youe pleafe to fend any one afore, I wilbe ready to yelde my Helpe and Aduyce. Receavinge of late a Lettre from *Augufta,* what the Newes were there the in-clofed Copie doth conteyne, which makes me think that the Duke of *Parma* will not fight with the Kinge till all the Forces be together, in hope by Nom-ber to be the better; but the Lord of Hoftes can alter the Matter and difap-poynt his Purpofes. From the *Haeghe* this 7 of *Sept.* 1590.

Your Lordfhips moft ready at Comaundment,

Geo. Gilpin,

Geo. Gilpen, *Efq; to Sir* Robert Sydney.

My very good Lorde,

THIS Night the Generall States beftow and make a greate Bancket to Thymbaffadors of ThEmpyre, whofe Aunfwere is framed and wilbe fent or deliuered within a Day or tweyne: And then I will fynd Meanes to pro-cure and fend your Lordfhip a Copie. Sir *Frauncis Vere,* as him felfe, wrote the Thirde of this prefent comminge, nere the Houfe of *Luttekenhome,* did fynd Thennemy yntrenched very ftrongly, lyke in a Forte, on Thadvenue to the faid Houfe, lying in a Marrifhe, havinge no other Accefs vnto yt : He firft fom-moned them to yelde the Place; they refufed flatly, declaringe plainly, that they meant to holde and mayntaine their Fort to the laft Man. Vppon which Aunfwere, he refoluyd prefently, on all Sydes, to affalte them; and foo the feconde Charge took yt by Force, puttinge aboue 300 Men to the Sworde, and foo refkewed the Affieged; havinge fince furthered the Bringinge of thofe Contryes vnder Contribucion, and was purpofed to haue imployed his Forces about fom other Sarvice in thofe Partes; bvt his Excellencie havinge purpofed to proceede with an Entreprife of fom Moment, Sir *Frauncis Vere* writtes to comme downe with all Diligence with his Forces. *Verdugo* conti-neweth in the Land of *Benthan,* and can do no more then his Men lift and lyke of. Other I faw not at this prefent; and therefore humbly takinge my Leave, do befeech Almightie God for your Lordfhips profperous Eftate, long Lyffe, and Increafe of daily Honors. From the *Haeghe,* this 12th of *September,* 1590.

Your Lordfhips at Commaundment,

Geo. Gilpen.

Occurrences fent with the Letter beforementioned.

LE Roy d'*Efpaigne* fait fort hafter ce qui ce fait perdra, qui eft de fix mille chevaulx, & de 36 compaignies de *Lanfquenetz,* leur rendez vous eft prez de *Bacarach,* au deffus de *Bonne.* Les noms des Colonells de la Caval-lerie font Sr *Bellomont,* qui mefne douze cens chevaulx; le Baron de *Kenbergh* 12^c, *Jan Prendel* 12^c, *Schlegel* 12^c, le frere de l'Evefque de *Treves* 12^c. Les Colonells de Infanterie, font le Conte de *Schwartzembourgh,* *Arkenlergh,* *Bentin* Gouverneur de *Venlo :* les quelles Forces doibuent au plus tard eftre en Campagne, le 16 *Septembre,* ou ce joindront les forces du Ducq de *Lorraygne,* def-quelles forces eftant affemblees le Duc de *Parma,* en doibt eftre le Chief & Conducteur au nom du Roy d'*Efpaigne,* pour entrer en *France,* les Forces du Pape, qu'aultres Potentatz d'*Italye,* ce joindront au Ducq de *Savoye,* qui fera auffij un aultre Chieff, pour entrer en *Provence,* & *Daulphin,* un *Dotain Dorie Geneuois* fera cheff de l'armée de mer, pour l'*Efpaignol,* pour fournir des vivres & chofes neceffaires d'artilleries & munitions de guerre. L'armée du *Savoyat* en fomme ils font eftat aux deux armées de terre, de foixante a 80 mil homes, tant de piet que de cheval, pour attaquer la *France,* a la refolution du Roy d'*Efpaigne,* cheff de la Ligue, eft demployer entierement tous fes moyens & forces, pour ce faire Maître de la *France,* s'il peult par le moyen de la Ligue de *France,* qui ly attire, de la craincte, qu'il a du Roy de *France,* & de la Royne d'*Angleterre,* qu'il tient fes Enemiez mortelz : car quant aux aultres il n'en fait pas eftat, eftimant de les corrompre ayfement par argent, & les affaires du Roy de *France* retardées ou recullées, a faulte d'argent, fans lequel lon ne faict rien pardeca ; non obftant les dilligences poffibles de 3 Ambaffadeurs, que le Roy de *France* a en ces pais. Il ne parle, ou parlera des paix Roy du d'*Efpaigne,* avec eulx ou l'Empereur, & les Princes de l'Empire y doibuent eftre employez. L'on dict que les forces ont fourny l'argent pour la prefente levée qui ce fait en *Allemaigne* pour le Roy d'*Efpaigne.*

Conte Maurice *de* Naffau, *a Monfieur Monfieur de* Sydney.

Monfieur,

IL a eftè refolu, par Meffieurs du confeil d'Eftat, de faire affembler quelque bon nombre de gens de guerre ; & les employer en fervice du pays. Et dau-tant que J'eftime, que vous defirez de vous y trouver. Je vous prieray Monfieur tres affecteufement, fi voftre commoditè le permettera, de me venir trouver a *Willemftadt,* pour le dimanche prochain : Venant avec tout des Soldats, de Voftre Garnifon & Gouvernement, qu'il vous fera aulcunement poffible, & que ce foyent des Compaignies entierres. Et en efperant que nous ferons chofe dont nous rapporterons honneur, Je me recommanderay en voz bonnes graces, en priant Dieu vous maintenir.

Monfieur, En fa faincte de

la Haye, *ce* xix *de* Septembre, 1590.

Voftre tres affectionnè Amy a

vous faire Service,

Maurice de Naffau.

Sir William Borlas *to Sir* Robert Sydney.

My verie good Lord,

THIS prefente *Saterday* I receaved a Packet of Letters from my Lords of the Counfell, directed to Mr. *Bodley,* and to be deliuered here to your Lordfhip, or to me in your Abfence to convey them vnto him. I opened it not, becaufe I knewe not of what Importaunce it might be, but haue fent it vnto him, with Requeft, that if there be any Lettres for your Lordfhip therein, he will convey them vnto you, as fpeedilie as he maie, which, I doubt not, but he will performe. Newes here is none, but as I wrote your Lordfhip in my laft Letter, my Lady and your Children are in good Health, and thofe Women which fhe fent for are come over to her from *Englande.* This Lettre enclofed was intercepted in *Flaunders* by the Freebuiters. I haue thought beft to fende it to your Lordfhip, that you might

haue

haue the Perufinge of it. And fo with my humble Dutie, I leave your Lordfhip to the Almightie. *Flufhinge,* this xxvjth of *September,* 1590.

> *Your Lordfhips moft affured*
>
> *to commaunde,*
>
> Wylliam Borlas.

Geo. Gilpin, *Efq;* to *Sir* Robert Sydney.

My very good Lorde,

ACcordinge to my laft Wrytinge, there is an Aunfwere giuen to the Deputies of Thempire, whofe Propofitions, though fomwhat longe in Words, tended chiefly, that all Places fubiect to Thempyre, and prefently poffeffed by the States, fhould be furrendred vnto them; and that from hence fourth nothinge fhould be any more attempted vppon the lyke; and that the Subiects of all *Germain* Princes, or others, vnder ThEmperiall Iurifdiction, fhould remayne vntroubled, and to be vfed as Neighbours and Newtrals: Herevppon is refoluyd (as I vnderftand) that the Townes and Places aforefayd, fhalbe voyded by owr Garryfons, and delivered to the fayd Deputies, or whome thereto they fhall thinke good to appoynt; and to that Ende there is written to the Commaunders in thofe Places; but the Forte of *Gravenweert* is not comprehended in the Nomber; and though the Deputies infifted hard with Threatenings of Profcription by ThEmpyre (which indeed is not much more cared for then the Pope his Ban or Curfe) yet at laft haue in that Behalfe accepted of the Aunfwere, being fmouth and delatory.

Thofe of *Liege* are not yett aunfwered; but yt is thought the States wil accompte and vfe them as Neyghbors and Frends; Lettres havinge in lyke Sorte fins bin writte to the Governors of *Bargues* and *Breda,* that they fhall releafe all Prifoners, being Liegoys, and not to take any more hereafter, without Commaundment from the Superiors.

The Count *Maurice* is thought to be com ere this Tyme at the Place of Rendezvous, and that the other Troupes being come to *Huy,* he will prefently proceede with Thenterprife, wherein he hopeth to haue good Succez, and then to take others in Hande neerer your Quarters.

Here is a Bruyte that Sir *Frauncis Vere* fhould have affalted the *Graeve,* a Forte afore *Wefel,* and was repulfed, but that he was determined to recharge them the nexte Morninge; whereof this Day wee fhall heare the Certaintie.

Verdugo his Men do ftil fpende on the Boores, which he cannot yett, for Feare of Alteration, the *Spaniards* (as fom of them that haue bin taken Prifonners declare) being at afterhande of their Pay aboue ten Monthes. Al other Things remayne at one Staye.

By Letters owt of *Englande* wee heare, that her Majeftye diflykes much the Vfage of thefe Men towards Mr. *Wilkes,* but will not take any Refolution vntil fhe fie their Aunfwere to his Propofitions, which was promyfed, fhould be delivered to Mr. *Bodley,* but hitherto harde nothinge thereof.

Thus your Lordfhip heareth how the World goeth; and fo moft humbly comit myfelf to your Favours. From the *Haeghe,* this 26 of *Sepiember,* 1590. *Stilo nouo.*

> *Your Lordfhips at Commaundment,*
>
> Geo. Gilpin.

Sir

Sir Thomas Wylkes *to Sir* Robert Sydney.

My good Lorde,

I Haue received bothe your Lettres, the one written at the *Haghe*, and the other at *Flushing*, sent by Capt. *Browne.* To the first, whereas you haue ben informed, that you should stand, in some Sort, in her Majesties Indignacion, in respect of your Privitie to the Mariage of my Lord of *Essex.* I dare assure your Lordship, vppon my poore Credit, there is no suche Mater ; for besides the good and gratiouse Speeches vsed to me by her Majestie of your Lordship, at the Tyme I signified the same vnto you, she hath sithence vppon other Conferences to me expressed the like. And becaufe I would not altogether trust myne own Sense and Conceipt therein, I haue sithence the Receipt of your Lettre (in as discrete Maner as I coulde) inquired among suche as could well informe me, and cannot fynde there hathe ben any suche Mater at all. So as, without all Doubt, the Partyes that haue geven you Notice of this Mater, have misconceived or misvn-derstood the same.

There was some Likelihoode of sending over 4000 Men from hence, the Men being put in a Redynes, and a daily Expectation of their Going ; the Pvr-pose was by some convenient Armie in Feild to haue wrought a Diuision of the Duke of *Parma* from *France*; but sithence vppon some Aduertisement of the Distresses, Want, and Sicknesse of the Duke and of his Armie, who, by this Meanes (as her Majestie is aduertised) is ready to retourne Home ; our Resolu-tion of sending groweth cold, so as, in my Conceipt, there will nothing be don. Yf it go forewarde, I will not faile to remember your Lordship according to your Request.

I can write you nothing of our Home Causes, in respect there is no Alteration in any Thing here ; my Lord Treasurer being still Secretarie, and so like (in my Conceipt) to continue in his Handes as long as he shall live, and be hable to travell. And thus, with my verie duetifull Salutation to yourself and my Ladye, I leave you to Gods Protection. From *Windsor*, the xvjth of *October*, 1590.

Your Lordships assured Frend to command,

Thomas Wylkes.

Roger Seys, *Esq;* † *to Sir* Robert Sydney, *concerning* Robert Dudley *Earl of* Leicesters *Inheritance.*

Right Honorable,

Y T muche rewyfethe your good Lordships Folowers, to heare of the good and happie Deliuerance of my good Ladye ; I praye God yt may move your Honor the sooner to loke to your owne Estate more ; I cane wryt lyttell Comfort to your good Lordship of any greate Hope to come of my Lord of *Leycesters* Inheritance to your Lordship : I would to God I had Cause otherwyese to wryt. Mr. Seriant *Harryes* havinge only entryd into the Cause, drewe yt, and layd yt downe. Your Lordships Counsell, my Lord of *Huntingdon*, and my Lord of *Pembrokes* Counsell, meet at the Beginninge of the Terme, to resolve vpon Mr. Seriant *Harryes* Case, which stode vppon twoe Poynts : The one, whether the Revocacyone made by my Lord of *Leycester* were good, which ys the chefeste Thinge we must yet stycke vnto ; the other was, that by a Fyne levyed by my Lord of *Leycester*, in *Anno* xxiiij. *Elizabethe* after the Deede of xxi. and before the Revocacyone in *Anno* xxvj. the Lands therin contayned was

---

† This *Roger Seys*, Esq; was a Councellor of *Lincoln's Inn*, and was imploied by Sir *Robert Sydney*, to look into his Estate in *Wales*, and the Counties adjoining, and reposed in him an entire Confidence, for his Integrity and Abilityes. From him descended *Richard Seys* of *Boverton* in *Gla-morganshire*, Esq; whose Daughter *Anne* was married to *Peter* Lord *King*, Baron of *Ockham* in *Surry*, and Lord High Chancellor of *England*, who had Issue by her *Peter* the present Lord *King*, &c.

I

forfeated, be that noe Revocacyone myghte after ferve. Thes twoe Poynats be-inge agreed vppon, the one that ys whether the Revocacyone were good or noe, leafte doutfull ; the other agreed to be a Forfeature. Then was there à Courfe dyreatyd to drawe the Office, which I toke in Hand, hopinge of muche Good therof to your Honor ; but after the Entrance into the Caufe and dewe Confide-racyons had of the Lands mencioned in the firfte Deede of xxiv, of the Lands in the twoe Fynes ; the one to confirme the Deed in xxj, the other made in xxiiij ; vpon which Forfeature muche was hopyd of. I found noe Lands to be forfeated, but only twoe Lordfhipes in *Worcefterfhire*, that ys to faye, *Hampton Magna*, and *Hampton Parva*, that any good Licklod myght growe to your Lordfhip, thys beinge impartyd to Mr. Seriant *Harryes*, whoe was the Auator of the great Hope, he could not tell howe to anfwer yt ; this ys trewe, my good Lord; I thought yt better to fynd yt nowe, then to contynewe your Lordfhip in Hopes of Thinges, which would be found by others ; there be maney Queftiones rayfene vppon the Opening of the Cafe by me. It is neceffarye that the Office be founde vppon Hope thatthe Revocatyone wyl be imperfea ; but *Hampton Magna* and *Hampton Parva*, wilbe your Lordfhips without Doubt, I hope : The Affurance made by *Thomas James* his Direattione to Sir *Thomas Sherley*, ferethe euery other Mane to deale with anye the *Suffex* Lands, feeinge there was yealded to him other Lands in Securytie, and he wyll agree for Sales of Lands, and appoynat whate Affurance and Waranties fhalbe made ; and then your Counfell muft pro-cede accordinge to that Agreement, whatfoeuer yt be refonable, or not refonable, his Senfure muft ftand in that, as in all other Thinges. I praye your Lordfhipe looke to his Procedinge for your owne Goode. Is there any honeft Man, that wylbe (yf yt were throwene one him) Surveyor ; the only Agreer for Fynes (and Rents, and none but him felfe to know yt) the Maker of all Leafes, the only Baylyf and Rent-gatherer, the Receuer of all other Profits, Heryots, Fynes, and Amercyaments, and to yeald whate Accompt he wyll ; cane any Mane con-troule yt, or fynd Fault with yt, whoe hathe foe many Offices ? Pardone me, I praye your Lordfhip, to remember you of this ; there be many marvaylethe at yt ; you maye at your good Lordfhipes Pleafure reforme yt. Thus reftinge redye to doe your good Lordfhip any Servyce I maye, I leaue you to Gods Pro-teation. From *Lyncolns Inn*, the lafte Daye of this *Nouember, Anno* 1590.

Your Lordfhips affured to comaunde,

Roger Seys.

Roger Seys, *Efq; to Sir* Robert Sydney.

I Receved, my honorable good Lorde, your moft honorable louinge Lettre, wherby yt pleafethe your Honor to promiefe, that Order fhalbe fhortly takene concerninge your owne Eftate, I praye you haue Care of yt for your owne Good ; I neuer knewe any foe far out of Order, and where is Diforder ther is Confucyon. Your Lordfhipes Lands lyethe extendid, the Profits the Queene will fewerly haue, vntyll Pardones be fewed ; ther is diuers Extents in *Wales*, fome for fome Moneys vnpayed to Mr. *Goringe*, fome for not Entringe the firft Fruits for *Coyte*, fome for Tenthes in Courte Coulmane, fome for fix Shillinges eyght Pence Pencone, which goethe Yearly out of *Coyte* Benefice, fome for Refpit of Homage ; the Chardge is duble, when hit comethe to the Shirifes Hands. *Thomas James* will paye none ; he thinkethe to carye hit in Clouds, but allthoe hit be deferred for a Tyme, hit will faule duble Chardg vppon your Honor ; your poore Tenants, whom you muft difchardge, fhalbe trubled ; therefore, good my Lord, lett fuche as your Honor thinkethe meete ; confider whate muftbe Yearlie payed, and laye that downe vnder their Hands, that your Receuer may difchardg hit ; and lett not one Man haue fo many Offices, that he may not be controuled in hit. To be Surveyor, Leafe Maker, only Bargayne Maker for all your Reuenewe, Rent Gatherer, Taker vp of all Cafualties, and Difpofer of all Thinges, as him pleafethe : Whoe cane controule him, as the moft ys to be made of Thinges ? Which ys one Thinge neceffary by your Officers to be locked vnto, foe thother Thinge as neceffary ; and that is in all Things that your Honor muft be at Chardge with, to haue Care that ther be not more in fuche Sort fpent, then needithe ; and that is leaft locked vnto in the moft of your Honors Caufes. Mr. *Bofwell* hauinge gevene ouer his Office, and Mr. *Hare* in his Place, the Lyvery fued out for my Lords Lands in *Wales* ys cauled for agayne to be enrouled ; Mr. *Gooldinge* faythe yt is not in the Evidence Howfe, your Lordfhip muft take Order that yt be found. Your Lordfhip haue beftowed *Rogyat*, which ys voyd by the Bufhops Deathe ; one *Moore* maketh Clayme to fome Parte of hit, yt muft be locked vnto, for I doubt whether he that hathe the Advoufone will defend hit. Therfore, my good Lord, yt was neuer my Counfell to graunt any Advoufon, but to fuche as fhould protect yt ; for by grauntinge of Advoufons meny hathe byn difherited. I haue wifhed your Lordfhip firft to fee the Hand of fome one that is learned to euery your Graunts, before you figne hit, foe dothe Men of Experience ; and althoe your Lordfhips Pleafure be not I fhould doe yt, yet for your Lordfhips Good lett fome doe yt : Mr. *Jeford* defierethe to deale for *Michillmarfhe,* and prayed me to wrytt foe to your Lordfhipe ; Mr. *Carne* makethe Tytell to certen Wood in *Coyd* Mufter for Eftovers to his Howfe of *Ewenny,* he would haue had me to deale with his Counfell therin. I tould him I had noe Warant foe to doe ; yf he writt to your Lordfhip concerninge that Caufe, I woulde wifhe your Lordfhip not to anfwer hit in Hafte ; yf yt will pleafe you to aquaynt me with his Lettre, I fhall help your Lordfhip to frame ane Anfwer to the fame : Your Lordfhip had a Leafe from my Ladye of *Effex,* in her Wydowod, of Parte of her Dower at a certene Rent ; at the Exchange of *Lee* Perfonage for *Vdyame* ; yt was agred there fhould be a leffe Rent payed, and a newe Leafe made therof ; I would wifhe your Lordfhip to writt therof to my Lord of *Effex* and my Ladye, that your newe Leafe myght be fealed. There ys a *Kentifhe* Mane that hathe Tytle to fome two or three Acres of Lands in *Lee* Perfonage, that fhould haue byn affured to Mr. Secretory, but yt was not ; therfore yt is good that Order be takene, that yt may be affured to your Lordfhip. My Lorde of *Pembrocke* wifhethe to place me in Mr. *Atkins* Rome at the Marches, whoe fuppliethe the Place of her Majefties Attorneye ; I haue agreed with Mr. *Atkynes.* My Lord of *Pembrock* defirethe that the Benche of *Lyncolns Inn* fhould yeald their Opinyon of me, which they have promifed ; my Lord Chef Juftice of *England* beinge the Chef of the Howfe, I praye your Lordfhip, yf yt fhall foe pleafe you, to write your Lettre in my Favor to my Lord Chef Juftice to joyne with the reft of the Benche, and to that End I haue drawen a Lettre, yf hit pleafe you to licke of hit, or eles as your Lordfhip fhall think well ; with twoe other Lettres, the one to my Lord of *Effex,* and the other to Mr. *Robert Cycill,* to praye their Favors in my Behalfe therin. The Copie of which Lettres that I wifhe to haue, or the lyke in Effecte, be herin contayned ; thus humbly takinge my Leave, I comitt your Lordfhip to Gods Protection. From *Lyncolnes Inne,* the xvth of this *January,* Anno 1590.

POST SCRIPT.

Yf I cane fynd any Courfe, without fyndinge of ane Office for the Recouery to your Lordfhip of *Hampton Magna* and *Hampton Parva,* I think it beft to followe that Courfe, for yt wilbe chardgable for your Lordfhip to fynd ane Office of the Whole, and to haue the Benefit but of that twoe Things ; for I cannot fynd, by the generall Opinione, that the Revocacyon wilbe made voyd ; and then haue your Lordfhip noe Tytle but to that whervnto I would wyfh Entry to be fhortly made ; but firft I will confer with the reft of your Councell, and writt therof to your Lordfhip.

Your Lordfhipes affured to comaund,

Roger Seys.

Sir

To my Lord Chef *Juſtice of* England.

A Frynd of myne, one Mr. *Seyes,* of *Lincolnes Inne,* ane vtter Bariſter of eyght Yeares Standinge, by my Lord of *Pembrocks* Favor is promiſed to be placed in the Rome of Mr. *Atkynes,* her Majeſties Attorney in the Marches of *Wales* ; but my Lord of *Pembrocke* wiſhing to haue ſome Comendacione of the Sufficiencye of the Gentleman for ſupplienge of the ſayd Rome, wiſheth him to procuer the Benche, or ſome of them of *Lyncolnes Inn* to comend hym, which they haue willingly promiſed : Becauſe your Lordſhip was of that Howſe, and ys the chefeſt, I praye your Lordſhip to vouchſalfe to joyne with them in Certificat in his Favor, for the which I ſhalbe thankfull vnto your Lordſhip.

To Mr. Robart Cycill.

T H E R ys a Gentleman, a Frynd of myne, one Mr. *Seys,* ane vtter Bariſter of *Lincolnes Inn,* of viijth Yeares Standinge, whoe hathe agreed with one Mr. *Atkynes,* the Queenes Attorney in the Marches of *Wales,* for Yealding to him his Place ; Mr. *Atkynes* ys appoynted ther vnto by certen Inſtrucyones vnder her Majeſties Hande for the Directinge of the Councells Procedings there. I heare the Inſtructiones be ſhortly to be altered, my Deſier ys, yt may pleaſe you for my Sake to move my Lord your Father in his Behalfe, that vppone the next Renewinge of the ſayd Inſtructiones, his Name may be placed in the Rome of Mr. *Atkynes* ; my Lorde of *Pembrocke* hathe a Certiff-cat from *Lincolnes Inn* of the Sufficyencye of the Gentleman.

To my Lord of Eſſex.

T H E R E ys a Gentleman, a Frynd of myne, one Mr. *Seyes,* ane vtter Bariſter of *Lyncolnes Inn,* of viijth Yeares Standinge, whoe hathe agreed with Mr. *Atkynes,* the Queenes Attorney in the Marches of *Wales,* for Yealdinge to him his Place ; Mr. *Atkynes* ys appoyncted thervnto by certen Inſtructiones vnder her Majeſties Hand, for the Dyrectinge of the Counſells Procedings there. I heare the Inſtructiones be ſhortly to be altered, my Deſier ys, hit will pleaſe you for my Sake to moue my Lord Treſuror, or ſuche other, as Mr. *Seys* ſhall pray your Help herin, that vppon the next Renewinge of the ſayd Inſtruccyones, his Name may be placyd in the Rome of Mr. *Atkynes* ; my Lord of *Pembrocke* hath a Certificat from *Lyncolnes Inn* of the Sufficyency of the Gentleman.

Sir Thomas Bodley *to Sir* Robert Sydney.

May it pleaſe your Lordſhip,

T H E more that I haue to impart to your Lordſhip, the leſſe is my Leaſure to impart it as I would, for my often Meeting with the States and Councel, and my neceſſarie Diſpatches into *England,* doe ſo occupie all my Time, as I am forced to be ſhort or ſilent with my Frindes. Sir *John Norreis* hath ſent his Letters and Meſſengers to cauſe the Companies to marche ; and in Caſe they cannot for the Contrey, that then euery Captain ſhall caſhe his owne Company. The States, to withſtand his Proceeding, haue ſent their Letters of Charge to all their Townes and Officers, where the *Engliſhe* are in Garriſon, not to miniſter any Meanes whereby they may paſſe. They haue alſo framed a Forme of Proteſt, which they haue ſent to Sir *John Norreis,* with an auctenical Inſinuation of the ſame to Sir *Francis Vere,* Sir *Thomas Morgan,* Sir *Edward Norreis,* and my ſelf. And to tell yow very truly, I neuer ſee them in any Thing ſo perplexed as in this ; wherof I knowe not what Succeſſe Sir *John Norreis* doth expect. But for my ſelf I am againſt his Caſhing of Companies, it tending to no other but to the Ruine of the Companies, to the Loſſe of thoſe

Townes,

Townes, where the *Englishe* only are in Garrison, and to the general Detriment of the State of these Prouinces.   Becaufe in this Mater I am put in fome Truft, and muft anfwear for my Truft, if I doe not confaile for the beft, I am fully refolued, whatfoeuer other Courfe fhall be taken by others, to direct mine owne Actions to the Indemnitie of the Contrey.   I am not vnmindful of your Lordfhips Requeft, about your Cornet of Horfe, but I take it to be a fitter Opportunie to moue it, when this Mater of Sir *John Norreis* is fomwhat more ouerblowen ; and fo for this Prefent I bidde your Lordfhip moft hartely Farewell.   From the *Hage*, *Feb.* 9, *Anno* 1590.

Your Lordfhips at Commaundement,

Thomas Bodley.

Sir Thomas Bodley *to Sir* Robert Sydney.

IN my laft Lettre vnto your Lordfhip, I forgatte to make Mention of Capt. *Wray*, who is purpofed to be fhortly with yow, and to craue your good Furtherance in the Mater of Enterprife, whiche I imparted heere vnto yow. Becaufe yow knowe it is not meete, to put a Letter in Truft, with Affaires of that Importance, I am to refer your Lordfhip to his Report, and to befeeche yow very earneftly, to affift him in his Purpofe with your beft Aduife and Direction ; to which Effect I haue written into *England*, that I would deale with your Lordfhip.   Of our other Maters heere, I writte vnto yow in a former by Capt. *Spring*, which I truft is deliured, and fo I bidde your Lordfhip moft hartely Farewell.   From the *Hage*, *Feb.* 12, 1590.

Your Lordfhips moft affured

at Commaundement,

Thomas Bodley.

Sir Thomas Wylkes *to Sir* Robert Sydney.

BY your Lordfhips Lettre of the Fowerth of this Prefent, I am advertifed of the gentle Opinion conceyued of me, on that Side, that I fhold haue ben a great Advancer of the prefent Negotiacion of Sir *John Norreys* : In good Truth, I am not any Way Partaker of the Counfaill or Aduife geven in that Behalf, but cold haue wifhed the Contrarie for fome Refpects ; although for myne owne Parte, I cold haue alfo wifhed that the whole Troopes had ben drawen downe to the fower Townes, there to haue remained without any further Imploiement, vntill her Majeftie might haue receyued Anfweares of better Satisfaction to her late Demands.   I receiue from other Hands, that the States are notablie diftempered with her Majefties Purpofe in that Point ; and that they have caufed to be geven out, that when the Commiffioners from the Emperour fhalbe arriued, they will incline to a Peace with *Spayne* ; by which Deuife they thinke to terefie her Majeftie.   Yt feemeth your Lordfhip hath ben aduertifed, that my Lords of the Counfaill fhold like that the former Orders for the Manner of the Paie and Victuell fhold be continued in your Garrifon, and in that of *Oftend* : I am of Opinion yf you defire yt fo, yt wilbe yelded vnto ; howebeit, bicaufe your Burghers haue alwayes mifliked of the Victuelling, it wold be confidered, whether nowe it is reformed, it wold not increafe their Offence.   But if your Companies were paid by the Pole in Money, after Half a Crowne by the Weeke, referving the ij *d*. for their Armes, I thinke yt wold be beft, both for the Soldior, and for the Burgher.   If your Lordfhip fhall defire either of theife, and will write to the Lords, and aduife me to mediate the fame for you, I will doe my vttermoft therein ; as alfo in aduifing that Care be had for the fufficient Defence of the Places vnder your Charge.

†

I cannot

I cannot write to your Lordſhip any Certainety of the Affaires in *France*, but as we are aduertiſed here, the Duke of *Savoye* is entred with his Forces into the Towne of *Aix* in *Province*, and withall, as yt is thought, is admitted into the Towne of *Marſalles*. Yt is expected that the Duke of *Alvas* Sonne ſhall paſs into *France* by the Way of *Nauarre* with 8000 Men ; we are credibly informed that the Preparations in *Spayne* by Sea for *Brytaine* are verie great, and like to be ſpeedely ready : And what Proviſion is made by the Duke of *Parma* to retorne into *France* this next Spring, you may be beſt aduertiſed where you are.

All theſe Preparacions concurring, and we here doubting what will become of the poore King, her Majeſtie hath diſpatched vnto him Mr. *Edmund Yorke*, to be informed of his Caſe and Eſtate, to Thend ſhe may proportion her Succors accordinglie, for his Reliefe. By this Meanes my Lord of *Eſſex* is in ſome Hope (if her Majeſtie doe increaſe her Nombers intended to be ſent into *France*) that he ſhall haue the chiefe Conduction of them as Generall. *Sed hec ſub ſigillo dicet.*

I haue no home Newes to write vnto you, more then of the Queenes Removing to *Greenwich* this Daie, and the Death of my Fellowe Mr. *Daniell Rogers* ; and ſo reſtinge at your Lordſhips Devotion alwayes ready to doe you Seruice, I betake you to God. From *London*, the xiijth of *February*, 1590.

Your Lordſhips aſſured alwaies

to Commaund,

Tho. Wylkes.

Roger Seys, *Eſq*; *to Sir* Robert Sydney.

YT doth, right honorable, appeere, by the Letter herin encloſed, howe your Lordſhips Landes are encumbred, which wilbe noe ſmall Hinderaunce of the Sale entended by your Lordſhip, yf all Things fawle not out according to *Thomas James* Aſſertion : Yf I endevor to aſſiſt hime, with all the Furtheraunce I may, whatſoever ſhall happen to be amiſſe, wilbe obiected againſt me, as heretofore yt hathe byn. He procured your Lordſhips Lettre vnto me, to Thende I ſhold not Allowe of any Leaſes, butt of ſuche as were good (as thoughe I wold doe otherwiſe, had not your Lordſhips Lettre byn) he enforced, that I allowed a poore Mans Leaſe, beinge nought, and of noe Force, knowinge the ſame : Whervnto I am perſwaded your Lordſhip gave ſuche Creditt as yt deſerved : Yet his Obſtinacy wold not otherwiſe be ſatisfyed, vntill the poore Man obtayned Mr. Attorney Generalls Hande vnto his Leaſe, that yt was good : This is his conteenewall Order of Abvſe, bothe of your good Lordſhip, and of ſuche as moſt inwardly wiſhe your Proſperyty. Wherfore I humbly beſeeche your good Lordſhip, vnleſſe ſome one other more, at leaſt, be appointed to deale, that I my ſelfe alone doe not ioyne with hime in thoſe Actions. The Reaſon of thys my Requeſt ys, for that he hathe coſooned your Lordſhip, beſydes other notoryous Abvſes : Of which, yf your Lordſhips Pleaſure be to allowe, then have I not Cawſe to diſlike therwith. The Chardge he puttethe your Lordſhip vnto yerely ys not ſmall, which I have wiſhed to come to your owne Purſe, and may eaſily herafter be brought to paſſe ; and allſoe your yearly Revenewes trewly awnſwered by ſome other your Lordſhips Servaunts. Not, I proteſt, becawſe I meane to crave any his Offices to my ſelfe, or any of myn ; what Profitt ſoe ever he repethe thereby ; but ame ſory to ſee hime ſoe prey vpon your Lordſhip without controwle : *Mychelmarche* mught be well ſowld : And ſome one may be fownd for Money to begge the Reverſion. *Arkyngwalls* Farme is ſought ; yf your Lordſhip were here your ſelfe, I doubt not Money (ſeeing yt muſt ſoe needs be) wold be hade. At your Lordſhips Appointment (notwithſtandinge yt be agaynſt my Stomacke) I will by every Means further any Thinge for your Lordſhips Good. And foe reftinge redy at your Lordfhips Commaundement, with my Duty remembred vnto my good Lady, I commit your Lordfhip to Thalmighty. From *Lincols Inne,* the xxiijth of *February, An.* 1590.

Your Lordfhips affured,

Roger Seys.

Geo. Gilpin, *Efq;* to Sir Robert Sydney.

My Lorde,

THIS Day I receavyd a Letter from the Deputie of the Marchaunts, and therein one from you to Mr. *Bodly,* which I delivered him fourthwith, and will by the furft Retorne aunfwer. Your Sute to his Excellencie about the Companie of your Lordfhips Horfemen, has not bin forgotten : And Yefterday, uppon Mr. *Bodlyes* Motion to him in Counfell, was determyned to wryte to thofe of *Gelderlandt* ; and tolyke Effecte Letters directed to Monfieur *de Locres.* Their Aunfwere is expected, and then fhall your Lordfhip be advertyfed thereof, to Thend yow may fend to Quarter them. I fee his Excellencie favoureth and affecteth yow greatly, but cannot doo as he would. Sir *John Norreys* hath obteyned the Graunt of the ten Companies ; and do thinke that he will com towards yow on *Monday* or *Tuefday* Night. Wee feare that the Duke of *Parma* will not go for *Fraunce,* but fend Men and a Commaunder ; meaninge him felfe to com towards *Nimeghen,* whoe threaten to agree with the States yf they be not holpen, and the laft Yeres Forte made by the States taken within a very fhorte Tyme. What the Succeffe wilbe, wee fhall fee ere longe. His Excellencie purpofeth, fo foone as he fhall heare of any Affembly of the Ennemy, to draw all the Forces he can nere the Field, and oppofe againft his Deffingns. Thus, for Want of other, I humbly take my Leave, and committ your Lordfhip to the Favour of the Allmightie. From the *Hagh,* this 14th of *Marche,* 1590.

Your Lordfhips at Commandemente,

Geo. Gilpin.

* Sir Thomas Bodley *to* Sir Robert Sydney.

YOUR Lordfhips of the 10th, came two Daies paft vnto my Hands, with the inclofed from my Lorde. I attended no Commiffion to perfourme ye Contents : But yet the Negligence was great, of thofe that kept it fo long, before they fent it vnto yow. I have caufed his Excellencie to deale with this Councell, for the remouing of your Cornet ; which they haue refolved to fend to *Waggening,* and to that Effect, they haue written to Monfieur *de Locres,* the Gouernor, to fignifie their Intention. Within thefe 3 Daies, we expect his Anfwear, wherof yow fhall haue Knowledge, and a Patent fent vnto yow. I am forie Capt. *Littleton* hath failed of his Purpofe, which is knowen all Abroade. The Occurrences heere, and howe Sir *John Norreis* hath fpedde with the States, he himfelf will fignifie, being almoft ready to depart affoone as this Meffenger. And fo for this Prefent I bidde your Lordfhip farewell. From the *Hage, Marche* 16, 1590.

Your Lordfhips at Commaundement,

Tho. Bodley.

Captain *Sampfon* is newly come vnto the *Haghe,* who fhall Want no Affiftance that I can giue, albeit his Requeft will, no Doubt, be rejected by the Councel of State.

---

* This was the famous Sir *Thomas Bodley,* who left to the Univerfity of *Oxford,* the public Library, which bears his Name. He ferved his Country in feveral Ambaffies, with great Applaufe ; as may be feen in his Life, printed at *Oxon.* 1647, *Quarto* ; and in *Wood's Athenæ Oxonienfes,* Vol. I.

Sir Thomas Bodley *to* Sir Robert Sydney.

THERE was nothing in my Letter, but your Lordſhip might ſee, nor I neuer have any, but yow may open very freely ; albeit, I am aſſured, it was not what you wiſh. With muche a doe, I haue ouerintreated this Councel, for a couple of Companies to be ſent to *Oſtend*. But they muſt be *Dutche*, and they muſt be returned, when the reſt of their Forces ſhall goe into the Fielde. And this they haue done, to ſatisfie her Majeſtie ; for otherwiſe they knowe, that theſe Alarmes are deuiſed by the Gouernour. His Courſes in all Thinges are wonderfull diſpleaſing to the States and the Councell ; and if his Care be not the greater, to governe to their Liking, he will purchaſe to himſelf a great Deale of Trouble. To that Sir *Airnſina* propoſed to your Lordſhip, I was neuer made privie ; nor I knowe not as yet, by whome he was autoriſed, or what it was that he deliuered. But I thinke he was ſette a Worke by thoſe of *Zeland*. There is nothing with vs, that is ether Newes, or like to Newes ; but Sir *Tho. Baſkeuille*, can diſcourſe it all at large. I would be glad to heare from your Lordſhip of Capt. *Wraies* Imploiement, and of your good Proceeding in that Enterpriſe. And ſo for this Preſent, I commend your Endeavors to Gods good Direction. From the *Hage*, 23 *Marche*, 1590.

Your Lordſhips at Commaundement,

Tho. Bodley.

Sir Thomas Bodley *to* Sir Henry Sydney.

CAPT. *Wray* hath bin heere, and we haue conferred of the Mater of your Lordſhips Letters ; of which I receaued one by him, and another this Morning. Before the Meſſenger can returne, that your Lordſhip ſhall imploy to viſit the Places, the Nightes will be too ſhort to goe in Hand with that Enterpriſe. To diſcloſe the Mater to the States, for mine owne Part I dare not, without Warrant from Home ; which yow knowe the Time will not ſuffer to attend. I am of Opinion, which is alſo the Iudgement of Sir *Fra. Vere*, that it will be beſt to differ it till *October* next, at which Time, if there be no Alteration of Circumſtances, but that it muſt be imparted of Force to the States, it may be then done, as her Highnes ſhall preſcribe. For it would ſteede her Majeſtie exceedingly, if it could be compaſſed by her ſelf, without the States, and that for ſundrie very weightie Reſpects. I am nothing in Doubt of the Diſcoverie of theſe Maters by any of thoſe Perſons, that deliuered them to me ; and your Lordſhip, I hope, can promiſe for the reſt. I beſeech your Lordſhip, becauſe the Partie ſent thither of late, was imploied by your ſelf, and hath made Relation but to you, howe it ſtandeth in the Towne, to aduertiſe her Highnes what yow thinke of the Matter, as I, in my next, will referre my ſelf therein to your Lordſhips Report ; wiſhing yow the While, all Health and Happineſſe. *Hage*, 26 *Mar.* 1591.

Your Lordſhips at Commaundement,

Tho. Bodley.

I have newly receiued a Letter from Sir *Horace Pallauicine* ; by which I am aduertiſed, that the Princes of *Germany* are better affected then he could expect, promiſing ſuche Succors as haue bin required, which he is in Hope ſhall be ready to marche the middle of *May*. After I had written my former Letter, I receaued your Lordſhips of the 24 of this Month. The Companies expected here from your Lordſhip, for ought that I haue vnderſtoode, are but two, which you did alwaies promiſe, and may alwaies be ſuche, as yow ſhall appoint.

point. Other two, to witt, Capt. *Wingfildes*, and Capt. *Hinders* Companies, were chofen by Sir *John Norreis*, by Order from Home. If your Lordfhip defire to haue any Thing changed, his Excellencie will be with you the next Weeke, who I knowe will be willing to affent to any Courfe that you fhall require.

Sir *Thomas* Bodley *to Sir* Robert Sydney.

THIS Bearer came to fignifie of his Going to *Flufhing*, when your Lord-fhips Letter came vnto me, of the Laft of *Marche*. And for the Enterprife whereof yow write, if it can be atchieued without the States, then better fo, then not at all. But happely Tract of Time will minifter fome Ouerture, to Effect it well enough; without their Priuitie. Count *Maurice* hath promifed this Councell, at his Arriual in *Zeland*, to Caufe two Companies of their owne to be fent to *Oftend*. If it come, your Lordfhips well to paffe, as I thinke it will, to fpeake with him of it, a Word or two vnto him, to haften his Pro-mife, will be very requifit. For as farre as I can perceaue by the Gouerment of *Berghen*, he was not willed by her Majefties Letter, to fend any thither, vn-les the States did neglect it. I knowe Sir *Edward Norris* will be very muche trobled, to be then difappointed; but the Councell heere is trobled more, that they can not Commaund in a Towne of their owne. For mine owne Part, I thinke I knowe their Humor fo well, as I fuppofe they will rather doe, as at *Gertrudenburgh*, give the Towne to the Enemie, then be bridled of their Willes. It doth reuiue among fome, a finifter Sufpition, that her Majefties Minifters would be Mafters of their Townes, and bring their Contrey into Thraldome as muche as the *Spaniard*: Whofe Gouernment they abiured for Defenfe of their Liberties. In Effect, the End of this Courfe will but falle to be Troblefome and Preiudiciall, both to her Majeftie, himfelf, and to all our Nation, and her Ma-jefties Seruice aduanced nothing by it. Sir *Fra. Vere* hath written from *Vtrecht* vnto me, that it hath bin his owne good Happe, to finde the Theefe that rob-bed him. His Mony is all come to 15 *l*. but it feemeth his Apparyll will be all recouered. Hauing no other Mater, I End with all good Wifhes to your Lordfhips Endeuors. From the *Hage*, *Aprill*, 4. 1591.

Your Lordfhips at Commaundement,

Tho. Bodley.

Sir *Tho.* Bodley *to Sir* Robert Sydney.

I Affure your Lordfhip there hath wanted no Willingnes in the Councel of State, to take fome Order, about your Company. But thofe of *Waggening* (for other Place they knowe not) haue bin vrged by their Letters, very ear-neftly twice, and will not hearken to any Thing. For they will nether ad-mitte any Companies more, nor no *Englifhe* Men at any Hand. Hereof they haue aduertifed his Excellencie, with whome if your Lordfhip fhall pleafe to Conferre, fome other Meanes may be found; efpecially nowe, that their Forces are ready to be drawen into the Filde. Your Lieutenant was defirous to have the Councels Patent for remouing out of *Berghen*, and of him felf would make a Shift, to be receaued fome where in thofe Vpper Quarters. But the Councel would wonder, if I fhould make fuche a Motion, and they will neuer proceede in that diforderly Sort. Howbeit, I doe not Doubt, but your Lordfhip, with his Excellencie, will take fome other Courfe, that may be more to your owne, and the Contreis Satisfaction. And fo I bidde your Lordfhip moft hartely Farewell. *April* 8, 1591.

Your Lordfhips at Commaundement,

Tho. Bodley.

†

I writte

I writte this Letter, to be fent by Lieutenant *White*; but though I fignified fo muche vnto him, and vfed him Courteoufly, he went his Way without my Letter, and without any Farewell.

Sir Tho. Bodley *to Sir* Robert Sydney.

VPON the receat of your Lordfhips Letter of the 12. of this Prefent, I acquainted the Councel both with the Tenor of her Majefties Letter, and with your Lordfhips defire to be excufed vpon it; which they tooke in good Part in Refpect of your Lordfhip, but difliked Count *Maurice* foe detracting the Time in fending the two Companies of their owne Nation. For had they bin fent, as it was refolued, yow might well haue forboaren the fending of any Company. When that Anfwear is come hither, which is fignified by her Majeftie to be fent vnto them heare, they are fully purpofed to replie againe, with a good Remonftrance. For in Truth it is needfull. And for mine owne Part, becaufe I fee the Inconuenience that is like to enfewe of thefe croffe Proceedinges of Sir *Edw. Norreis*, I will doe that Duty perteneth to my Place, both by aduertifing home, and by telling Sir *Edward* my frindly Opinion; fo as I may anfwear all heereafter, whatfoeuer fhall befalle between her Highnes and this Contrey. I doe onely attend the Courtes coming hither, which I hope will be to Day, or to Morowe at the furtheft, and then I will intreat him to take fome better Courfe, for difpofing of your Cornet, in fome other Garrifon. For Mater of Newes, all that I can fignifie, is an Enterprife that was intended to be perfourmed as Yefterday, by the Count *Ouerftein*, and Sir *Fra. Vere*, vpon *Straeten* in *Guelderland*, a Place of fmalle Importance, but yet held with a Garrifon, and, as it is thought, a very good Booty for the Souldiers. I have no other Mater, but to wifhe your Lordfhips Actions all happy Succeffe. From the *Hage*. *Aprill* 16, 1591.

Your Lordfhips wholy at Comaundement,

Tho. Bodley.

Sir Tho. Bodley *to Sir* Robert Sydney.

SINS my Laft vnto your Lordfhip I receaued that Letter for the Generall States, which her Majeftie doth mention in her Letter vnto yow. They doe greatly diflike this Maner of Proceeding, and have replied very effectually to her Majeftie vpon it. Becaufe I thought yow might defire, to fee the Forme of their Anfwear, I haue fent yow here inclofed the Tranfcript of it, which your Lordfhip will be pleafed to referue vnto your felf. Count *Maurice* is come Home, but fate not yet in Counfell; but by my next, I will aduertife, what may be done about your Company. The Surprize of *Straeten* hath failed, from whens Capt. *Wray*, and Capt. *Clifford*, are returned a litle hurt, and fome Twenty of our Souldiers, and 7 or 8 were flaine. I thinke Sir *Fra. Vere* will be at the *Hage* within 3 or fower Daies, by whome we fhall be informed of euery particularitie of the Enemies Proceedinges, we knowe nothing more, then your Lordfhip may fee by the Letter of the Counfel, for which I End with my wanted; which are alwaies my beft and moft affectionat Wifhes to your Lordfhips Eftate. From the *Hage*, *Ap.* 19. 1591.

Your Lordfhips affured

and at Commaundement

Tho. Bodley.

George Gilpin, *Efq*; to *Sir* Robert Sydney.

My very good Lorde,

NEyther forgetfulnes of Dewtie, nor any other Occafion, haue or could haue caufed my Sylence thus longe, yf there had bin any Niewes or other Subiect, offred worthy the troublinge of your Lordfhip; all havinge bin of late foo quyet and ftill, that I afure yow, I know not what to write ; and therefore befeech your Lordfhip, not to take any Offence there at, neyther to dowbt of my fincere Affection towards yow, with no leffe defyre to doo youe all ready Sarvyce to thuttermoft of my Power, when, and where foeuer yt fhall pleafe youe to commaunde me. At this Prefent we haue not any Niewes, but fuch as com from your Partes ; here is continual Meetinge of the States, but heare not what they do as yett ; his Excellencie is very earneft to furder thintended Campe, whereto all the Prouifions and Neceffaryes, are all moft in a Readynes, and Thofficers for the Fielde fett downe ; refteth onely to draw the Men togither, and determyne vppon the Place of Sarvice, which I think will fall owt towards *Gelderlande.* The wurft is that yt feemeth they of *Frieflande* are not foo redy to fend the Men, were promyfed. All the Horfe Companies of thefe Contryes are renforced and muftred to 120 Horfe ; They of *Vtrecht* make ftill denial to pay the Horfemen of the Count *Ouerfteyn,* and to yelde to any extraordinary Contribution towards the Campe, pleadinge their Pouertie. Owt of *Germanie* no Certaintie harde of the Army, but the Reportes diuers ; the Count *Hohenlo* had fent a Meffenger with Lettres, but are intercepted by thofe of *Nimeghen.* From the *Haeghe,* this 28 of *Aprill,* 1591.

Your Lordfhips, &c.

Geo. Gilpin.

Sir Thomas Bodley *to Sir* Robert Sydney.

I Was at *Enchufen,* when your Lordfhips Letter came hither of the 20 of this prefent ; which was the Caufe of my Stay, from anfwearing fooner, albeit there was no Mater that required a fpeedy Anfwear. Your Lordfhips Coniecture is very right concerning Sir *Edward Norris,* who giveth great Occafion, and euery Day more, of iuft Difcontentment to the Councel of State.

If your Lordfhip haue fuche Stoare, as you can fpare me a Copie of thofe *Browniftes* Bookes, I will giue them the reading; and your Lordfhip harty Thankes. I would your going for *England* at *Michaelmas,* were brought to *Midfummer,* for that it is eafier at firft to hinder ill Impreffions, then to route them out after, being once conceaued. Albeit for your Lordfhip, I can not gheffe at any Mater, that fhould caufe a Diflike, vnles it be not to be liked, that you keepe fo well in Tune, with the States of theife Contreis : which I knowe is the beft for her Majefties Seruice, and fhall be alwais my Endeuour ; and if it be not well conftrued, it will occafion, I hope, that I fhall be revoked ; which hath bin very lately my humble Sute vnto her Majeftie. I haue moued his Excellencie about your Lordfhips Company, in whome there wanteth no Willingnes, as he hath fhewed by his Speeches, in conferring with the Councel. But they can not for the prefent, affigne you any Place, and they think it not needfull, confidering they are ready to goe into the Feelde. Wanting other Mater, I commend your Lordfhips Defigns to Gods good Direction. From the *Hage,* April 29, 1591.

Your Lordfhips euer, and at comaundement,

Tho. Bodley.

Geo.

Geo. Gilpin, *Esq;* to *Sir* Henry Sydney.

My very good Lorde,

HIS Excellencie thinkes long till he be in Field, and omitteth no Meanes to furder the same. Sir *Frauncis Vere* departed this Morninge towards his Quarter, with Chardge to haue Care and Regard, that there be no Prouisions put into *Deventer* or *Sutpfin,* but to attempt the letting thereof. *Verdugo* is retorned to *Groeninghen,* where he entred on *Sonday* last, and was receavyd of the Magistrates, and those that favour him, very ioyfully, with Shewting of Thordinaunce, and such lyke Thinges of Joye, but Men brought he none hither ; and these Fellowes he hath in Felde, are in poor Ordre and Weake. In *Nimeghen* the Burgers beginne to feare, and are lik to fall into Diuision, and would er this haue bin by the Ears together, had not the Garrison setled yt, being thought yf his Excellencie go thither, that they would not holde ovt, but com to an Agreement presently. . I heare that within thes six or eyght Days, his Excellencie will depart towards the Rendezvous. All Things els stand and continew after the old Course and Order : From *Germany* yt is written the Levy for the *French* King goeth forwardes apace, and that the Emperoor studyes to practise a Peace. From the *Hague,* this 8 of *May,* 1591.

Your Lordships at commaundment,

Geo. Gilpin.

Sir Thomas Bodley *to Sir* Robert Sydney.

I Assure your Lordship, I knowe not what to make of that Siege of the Towne of *Ostend* ; for methinkes that Garrison is more trobled with a Siege in report, then some other would be troubled with a Siege in Action. We shall see by this Winde, what Answear will be made to that Letter of the Councel, which was sent vnto her Majestie. To your Lordships Letter, with the Booke of *Barowe,* for which I thanke you very hartely ; I sent a present Answear the next Day after, which I cannot nowe remember to whom I delivered, nor what other Mater it contened. And though I thinke there were nothing that could turne me to Anger, yet, in Truth, I am angrie that any Letter should miscarrie. Our Councel of State is removed to *Vtrecht,* and will reside ether there, or in some other Place, that is near to the Campe : Where I purpose to goe after, but that I looke by this Winde for some Letter from Home, which I would willingly receaue before I go from the *Hage.* Since the taking of *Zutphen* Sconce, I know not what Action is vndertaken at the Campe ; for in the Absence of the Councell our Intelligence heere is exceeding Slender. Howbeit it is given out, that they are busily occupied about the planting of Artillerie before the Towne it self of *Zutphen.* As any Certaintie cometh hither of any Mater of Worthe, I will aduertise your Lordship with the spediest Opportunitie ; which I would not haue omitted for a Weeke or two past, but that I made full Account, that your Lordship was departed, and would before this have bin at the Campe. The *Germany* Levie goeth forward very slowely ; for I am newly nowe aduertised from Sir *Horace Palavicine,* that they will not be ready to come forward till the 12 of *July.* Their Nombers will be suche as were demaunded at the first ; 6000 Horse and 9000 Foote, 1200 Pioners, 6 Canons, and 12 Feeld Peeces ; which Way they shall passe it is not yet resolued. And so I ceafe at this present from troubling your Lordship, till other Mater be offered. From the *Hage, May* 20, 1591.

Your Lordships wholy, and at commaundement,

Tho. Bodley.

Sir

Sir Tho. Bodley *to Sir* Robert Sydney.

SINS the Writing of my former, which I fent your Lordfhip by this Bearer, we haue Intelligence from the Campe, that the Count of *Ouerftein*, attended by certaine Souldiers of the Enemie, that lay in Ambufcado, was fhotte in the Head, wherof he died prefently. Sir *Francis Vere* being with him, efcaped very narrowly, his Horfe being hurt. *May* 21, 1591.

Your Lordfhips at commaundement,

Tho. Bodley.

Sir Tho. Bodley *to Sir* Robert Sydney.

TO fhewe your Lordfhip my Opinion in the Mater of *Dunkerk*, there is no danger in Delay. For the fvreft Seafon is the Moneth of *October*, when the Nightes beginne to lengthen ; for which, me thinkes, at your Leafure, you may talke with Count *Maurice*. To this Effect I haue written into *England* ; and withall I haue fignified, that I will wholy proceede, with your Lordfhips priuitie, not doubting but what her Majeftie doth defire fhall be accomplifhed in good Time. This Bearers haft doth affourd me no Leafure to be longer with your Lordfhip, for which I wifh you, as alwaies, all Maner of good Succeffe. From the *Hague*, *June* 4, 1591.

Your Lordfhips at commaundement,

Tho. Bodley.

Sir Thomas Bodley *to Sir* Robert Sydney.

FOR want of good Leafure to difcourfe, as I would, I fend your Lordfhip herewith the Copie of a Letter, which I writte this Morning vnto my Lord Treafurer. I thinke the Party will embarke at *Flufhing*, and, as I am per-fuaded, will come to your Lordfhip. Sins his going from hens I doe learne, that he is very full of Mony, to a greater Summe then a common Souldier, and a Man of his Shewe is wont to carie. His Anfwer was to one that fawe his Mo-ny, that he had it of your Lordfhip to pay at the Campe : Which maketh me fufpect, that he may have bin hired for fome worfe Intent then he pretendeth, and that he vfeth my Letter, but in fteade of a Paffeport, to gette in to *England*. I pray your Lordfhip, if he chance to come vnto you, or otherwife, if by enquirie you fhall find him in *Flufhing*, to examine him ftrictly, to fuche Pur-pofe as your felf fhall fee Caufe, and if you finde it requifite, to take my Let-ter from him ; and to detene him, till fuche Time as you haue aduertifed my Lord Treafurer of him ; which I referre to your Lordfhips Wifdome. The Man is of a lowe Stature, of the Age of 53, or thereabout, apparelled meane-ley, with a Cloke of the Colour of this Bearer, a greene Paire of nether Stockes, and an old embrodered Sattin Doublet. Our Camp this Morning remoued to-wardes *Groeninghen* ; but their Artillerie was embarked 4 Daies before. If your Lordfhip pleafe to fend your Letters to Mr. *Copert*, I haue giuen fuch Order, as he will fend them very fafely. From the *Hage*, *June* 6, 1591.

Your Lordfhips euer and

at commaundement,

Tho. Bodley.

Sir

Sir Thomas Bodley *to* William *Lord* Burghley.

May it pleafe your good Lordfhip,

THE Bearer hereof, *Ihon Minche*, hauing ferued a long Time in thefe Countreys, was taken Prifonner by the Ennemy about 5 Weekes paft, and brought Prifoner to *Bolduc*, and from thence to *Bruxels*, and lafte of all to *Andwerpe*. In the Time of his Emprifonment, he had Conference in *Bruxels* with one *Ihon Dampor*, a *Chefhire* Gentleman, and a Penfioner to the King of *Spaine*, who feeming to be weary of the Kings Seruice, and defirous to forfake the Companie of the *Englifhe* Fugitiues, difcouered his Minde to this Bearer, and willed him without all Delay, to repaire into *England*, and there notifie fpeedile, that there were certain *Englifhmen* in *Bruxels* which had a mifchievous Practife in Hand vpon her Majefties Shippes. For the effecting wherof they had fent certain Mariners into *England*, and appareled like *Burgers*, which were addreffed to a *Duche* Mans Houfe in St. *Katherins*, near to the *Towre*, who beftoweth them in Seruice in the forefaid Shippes, with Inftruction to watche an Opportunity to fett them on fire. The Truthe hereof I knowe no otherwife but by his owne Report, who as far as I can perceaue, hath no other Proofe nor Coniecture, but by the Speeches of *Ihon Damport*, which alfo I knowe not how truly he avoucheth. Neuertheles, becaufe he offereth of him felf to make this Voyage, requiring nothing of mee but to giue him Meanes by a Letter vnto your Lordfhips, or fome other of my Lords, to haue acceffe, I thought to write thus much by him, and to fignifie heer vnto him, that yf by his Travell and Seruice the Parties be defcried, he wilbee well rewarded, otherwife I could make him no Promife, nor he mighte not build vpon it, for his onely good Will, and this bare Declaration to receaue any Recompenfe. And thus, &c. *Hage, June 6,* 1591.

Your Lordfhips, &c.

Thomas Bodley.

* *Sir* Thomas Wylkes *to Sir* Robert Sydney.

YOUR Lordfhips Lettre of the xxviijth of *April* came to my Hand the xxvth of *May*: I beeing at that Tyme at my Houfe in *Wiltefhire*, where by her Majefties fpeciall Licence I had continued fome xx^{tie} Daies, not having feene it twoe Yeares before. This Occafion of myne Abfence hath fomewhat interrupted my Courfe of Writing vnto you, which I will amend nowe I am againe in Place.

I doe affure your Lordfhip, vpon the Faith and Trewth of an honeft Man, and by the Loue I beare vnto you (which I befeech you beleeue, not to be inferior to the Affection of any Man borne towards you) that I doe not finde in the Counfaill here any other then a verie good and honorable Opinion conceaued of you in the Managing of your Governement on that Side, which they

---

* Sir *Thomas Wylkes* had his Education in *All Souls* Colledge in *Oxford*, and was firft Secretary to Dr. *Valentine Dale*, Ambaffador from Queen *Elizabeth* to the King of *France*. While he continued there, he comforted the King of *Narvar*, and the Duke of *Allenfon* (after of *Anjou*) in the Queen of *England*'s Name, when they were in Cuftody by Order of the Queen Mother, for plotting to remove her from the Goverment. On which the Queen Mother forced him to withdraw into *England*, where fhe alfo followed him with Letters of Complaint ; and to pacify her he was fent back into *France*, and there humbly craved her Pardon. But the King of *Narvar*, when he came to be King of *France*, retained fo grateful a Remembrance of him, that when he faw him in *Normandy* 25 Yeares after, he conferred on him the Degree of Knighthood, and fhewed much Favor to him. In 1577 he was fent Ambaffador into *Spain* ; and the Year after was fent to Don *John* of *Auftria*. In 1593 he was fent into *France*, on the Report of the *French* King's being reconciled to the Church of *Rome*, and to diffuade him from it. Alfo in 1598, he was againe fent into *France* with Sir *Robert Cecill*, but died there foon after he landed.

doe not lett by Speech to fignifie oftentimes, when your Name and Doing doe come in Queftion : And Sir, I doe affure you there is noe leffe good liking had of your good Correfpondencie with the People of that Countrye, confidering yt is mixed with the Care of your Charge and Preferuacion of the Place to her Majeftie. I am of Opinion there wilbe noe Defeftion in them from her Majef-tie, fo long as they fhall finde we feeke not to maifter them, or depriue them of their vfuall Trade and Commoditie by their Traffique and Shipping ; and with-all you will confider howe beneficiall a Thing yt is vnto them to haue a Gar-rifon well governed amongft them, from the which they drawe fo continuall a Profitt and Benefitt, as they doe from our Nation, in that Place vnder your Conduftion. Ther hath ben of late fome Suite attempted by Mr. *Raph Lane* to drawe from her Majeftie the Difpofing of the *Ramekins* vpon him, which hath ben incountred by my Lord Threforer and other your Freinds here, who made yt appeare, that the fame was in your Lettres Patentes, and therefore the Difpofition therof in your felf, which is fome good Effeft of their Care and Re-fpeft had of you. Yf there fhall at any Tyme happen, that there be Caufe to aduife you, concerninge your Charge and Honor in that Place, I befeech you beleue that my poore felf fhalbe one of the firft that will give you Notice, and acquaint you with the Errour, that yow may knowe howe to reforme yt. But I maie fay truelie vnto you without Flaterie, that if the reft of your Governe-ment doe anfwere that which hath ben hitherto, you fhall continue and end with Honour.

I fuppofe you haue hard of her Majefties great Entertainement of late at Tib-balls, of her Knighting of Mr. *Robert Cicill,* and of the Expeftacion of his Ad-uauncement to the Secretarifhipp : But foe yt is (as we faie in Court) that the Knighthoode muft ferue for both. Other Alteracion there is none in Court, but all Things fwaie after the old Manner, faving that we are of late gladded with the good Succeffe of the Counte *Maurice,* and of Sir *John Norreys,* in *Britayne,* wherof I wold write vnto your Lordfhip at large, but that you fhall receaue the whole Difcourfe herewith from Mr. *Richard Wigmore,* my good Freind, and a Man that doth loue and honour you ; to whom if yt fhall pleafe your Lordfhip to write, I will fee your Lettres fafelie conveyed ; and fo reft-ing at your Lordfhips Devotion and Comandement, I comitt you to the Pro-teftion of Almightie God. From the Court at *Greenwiche* the viijth of *June,* 1591.

Your Lordfhips affured euer to Commande,

Tho. Wylkes.

This Daie, Sir *John Perrott* is for the laft Tyme examined at the *Tower,* by my Lords of the Counfaill, and before the Ende of this Terme he is to be in-dited of fondrie Treafons, and fo further proceeded withall at her Majefties Pleafure.

Sir Thomas Wylkes *to Sir* Robert Sydney.

I Haue receiued your Lordfhips of the fecond of this Prefent, in the which you make noe Anfweare to my former, nor any mention therof, fo as I feare yt came not to your Hands : Yt conteyned Matter of Anfweare to another from your felfe, which I greatlie defiered might come to your Know-ledge.

The Knowledge of your owne Vertues haue made me loue you, befides the Inclinacion I haue alwayes had to doe Seruice to your Houfe : I profeffe to loue but a fewe, and every of thofe are affured of a large Portion of my Harte, which when they haue, they haue all : For, befides my Loue I haue nothing in Habilitie or Place to expreffe yt, as you knowe. And therfore my Debt is
† the

the greater vnto you, that you accompt of my Loue, which can yeild you no better Effects.

In the Matter of the *Ramekins*, so earneftlie profecuted by Mr. *Lane*, I finde my Lords of the Counfaill, your good and affured Freinds; for although yt was once refolued by her Majeftie, and her Pleafure to haue ben fignified from the Lords vnto you, and I receiued Inftructions to write vnto you, that notwith-ftanding the Difpofing of that Place were left vnto you by your Lettres Patents, the fame fhold be beftowed on Mr. *Lane*; the Lettres being thervpon drawen and prefented to the Borde, they were vpon fome fmall Motion of myne re-iected. Wherein my Lord Chancellor and my Lord Threforer cheefely did fhewe their Affections towards you, deliuering many good and honorable Speeches of you. You are fo wife as I fhall not neede to aduife you, to enter-taine the good Opinions of thofe two Men, by all the Meanes you may.

You are beholding greatlie to Sir *Thomas Sherley*, who vppon all Occafions that doe concerne you, or your Reputacion, ommitteth noe Office of a true Freinde.

The xxth of this Moneth my Lord of *Effex* intendeth to imbarque with his Troopes of 4000 Men for *Normandy*; in which Expedicion Sir *Thomas Sherley* and my felf were appointed Counfaillors to the Earle, which with much adoe we haue auoyded (as I hope). And I haue not knowen fo gallant a Troope goe out of *England* with fo many young and vntrained Commanders.

Your Opinion of the Humour of that Contrey People (I feare) will happen to be more trewe, then were fitte for her Majeftie to finde; and yt is as im-poffible to alter the Courfes here, which doe and will prouoke them to fo dan-gerous Alteracions, as yt was facile at the firft, to haue remoued all Jealoufyes on both Sides. Good Sir, I muft faie truelie vnto you, I finde no Man that hath Place about her Majeftie take Care of theife future Inconveniences; and for Men of meaner Place to moue any Remembrance of thofe Matters, were but to breede himfelf an Opinion in them, to be more curious and officious then becometh him. Yf you hadd feene the Anfweares of the States to the Propo-fitions deliuered by me at my laft being in thofe *Lowe Contreys*, they wold not a little confirme your prefent Conceipte; and therefore for my Parte, I will praie for the Better and feare the Worft. We doe not a little marvaile of the prefent Actions and Intentions of the Duke of *Parma*; we haue Newes that the Army of *Germany* marcheth: Sir *John Norreys* with the Army in *Britaigne* prof-per and goe forewarde; we take Courage here in Court, and expecte fome good Yffue of this Sommer. What is intended by Sea againft the *Indias* Fleete, you haue ben aduertifed by Lettres from my Lords: And thus much you muft vnderftand, that although *Holland* and *Zealand* affift vs not in that Enterprife, yet doe we prepare fufficient Strength of our owne; and fo with my moft hartie Salutacions I leaue you to Gods Protection. From *London* the xjth of *July*, 1591.

Your Lordfhips affured euer to Commande,

Thomas Wylkes.

Sir Thomas Bodley *to Sir* Robert Sydney.

I Told your Lordfhip, at your being at *Arnham*, howe muche the States are difcontented with the Gouernour of *Oftend*, who continueth his Proceed-inges fo offenfiuely vnto them, as he had neede of a great St. *Chreftopher* to carie him out of the Danger of a hard Refolution to be taken againft him. I pray yowr Lordfhip, when you knowe what is done by Mr. *Lakes*, to lette me vnderftand it. For I can not be perfuaded, that it fhould be to communicat any Mater of fuche Secrecie; for his Treaty about a Peace was imparted by his Letters, and I doubt a greater Mater, or more deferving to be clofely caried,

he

he can hardly haue any. Howſoeuer, in my Opinion, all his Secrets and Deuiſes are but Wordes and Winde, and mere Chimeres, which purchaſe in the Ende the Diſcredit of his Actions. His Excellencie for *Hulſt*, doth expect euery Houre ſome Informacion from Count *Holmes*, and I thinke therupon will attempt it preſently, for the Contrey calleth on him to doe ſomewhat ſomwhere. The Enemie, we are informed, doth marche to *Maſtrich*, which cauſeth thoſe of *Guelders* to calle againe for the Forces, to be imploied againſt *Nimeueghen*. If any Thing of Worthe be determined here, or any good Occurrence come to vs, I will not faile to lett yow knowe it, as I wiſhe continually your Happines in all Thinges. From the *Hage*, *Aug*. 31, 1591.

Your Lordſhips at Commaundement,

Tho. Bodley.

* Thomas, *Lord* Buckehurſt *to Sir* Robert Sydney.

S I R,

THE Bearer, Mr. *Ratlif*, can at large informe you of the good Succes of his Caus. Toching your owne I moved her Majeſtie twiſe for your Leave, but found her at both Times unwilling ; and at the later preſſing her Majeſti very hard, with ſuch Reaſons as cold not in Reaſon be gainſaied. I found that in her Majeſties Breſt there reſteth ſome what of a bye Matter, in which ſhe ſtandeth not ſo well pleaſed towards you. Her Wordes were thes, wherby I think you may eſely conjecture the Matter. Namely, That you were at a Bankett here, *&c.* Thes Thinges I impart unto you, as in my true Love unto you, praieing you to hold the ſame to your ſelf, as never imparted by me ; for that might prejudice me for my good Will to you. Nevertheles I am at this Inſtant returning to the Court, and mene againe and againe to preſſe her for you, and if I can obtain her Licens, you ſhall heere from me ; if I write not, then the Succes is not ſuch as I wiſhe. I ſhall not now ſtay at the Court above 4 or 5 Daies, and if in that Time I can not effect it, I will erneſtly move my Lord Threſorer to doe it for you in mine Abſens ; for untill *Michelmas* I ſhall not be at the Court, which wold be to late for your Purpoſe. For lack of Leaſure, I muſt pray you to commend me very hartely to Mr. *Borlaiſe*, with many Thanckes for his courteous Writing, and to excuſe me for not writing to him againe. I will requite him with a better turne ; namely, to reſt redy on all Occaſions to frend him. The ſame Requeſt I muſt alſo make to your ſelf, from whom receving many courteous Letters, I return few, not for lack of good Will, but of acceptable Matter to write. I reſt al and ever yours. From *Draiton*, 13 *Aug.* 1591.

Your very loving and aſſuird Frend,

Superſcribed, T. Buckhurſt.

To my very loving and aſſuired Frend, Sir *Robert Sidney*, Knight, Governor of *Fluſhinge*.

* His Lordſhip was Lord High Treaſurer of *England*, both in the Reigns of Queen *Elizabeth* and King *James* ; was created Earl of *Dorſet* ; and is celebrated by our Hiſtorians for the Brightneſs of his Parts, Integrity in the Service of his Country, and all thoſe Virtues which adorn every good Man. And it is no leſs remarkable, That every of his Deſcendants, have inherited as well his Abilities, as his Titles ; and have born the higheſt Stations in the Goverment, honoured and eſteemed by Men of all Parties and Perſwations. And his Grace *Lionel*, Duke of *Dorſet*, the 5th. in Deſcent from him, (but 6th Earl of *Dorſet*) was, in Conſideration of his great Merits, created Duke of *Dorſet* by his late Majeſty ; and is now Lord Preſident of his moſt honourable Privy Councll.

Sir

Sir Thomas Wylkes *to Sir* Robert Sydney.

S I R,

THE Occasion of the Repaier of Mr. *Lakes* into thofe Countries, hath geven me this Opportunitie to write vnto you, more to fignifie my Affection and Devotion to doe you Seruice, then to aduertife you of any Noveltie from hence ; for that Mr. *Lake* is well acquainted with the State of all Things here, and can beft informe you of fuch Particularities as are worthie of your Knowledg.

Sir *Robert Cecill* (as you may haue hearde) is fworne of the Counfell, though not Secretarie ; whofe Election (as I conceaue) will be a Barre to the Choice of any Secretary during the Life of his Father.

Out of *France* we receiue, that the King is marching towards the Confines of *Bourgondie,* to receaue the *Germane* Army, which is alreadie paffed through *Loraine* ; by Meanes wherof my Lord of *Effex* continueth ftill about *Diepe* with his Armie.

Out of *Bretaigne,* by Lettres of the Laft of *Julie,* we are aduertifed of the Death of *Monfieur de la Noüe,* of a Wounde receiued in the Heade before *Lamballis :* He departed this Life the xxiiijth of *Julie.*

Monfieur de la Verdin is ioyned with the Prince *de D' Ombes,* and renforced his Troopes with 1200 Foote, and 200 Horfe ; whervpon there is a Refolution taken, to offer Battaile to the Ducke *de Mercure,* which we fuppofe is alreadie given, or the Enemy forced to forfake the Fielde. This briefelie is as much as I can at this Tyme write vnto you, and therefore I will ende with my verie humble and hartie Salutacions. From *London,* the xvijth of *Auguft,* 1591.

Yours, affured ever to Commande,

Tho. Wylkes.

Geo. Gilpin, *Efq; to Sir* Robert Sydney.

May yt pleafe your Lordfhip,

YOUR Lordfhip wrytes, yowe vnderftand nothinge of *Hulft,* and his Excellencie of late fayd, that he expected to heare from thofe Partes, naminge the Count *Solnis* and youe ; thus much I perceive, that he will not lightly Attempt any Place, without certain Lykelyhood to Speede ; here is not any Niewes ftirringe, vnleffe yt be that owr Men, which were fent to fcarre the Levy of Men by *Lingen,* haue effected nothing, onely in their retorne, light vppon Kowes, Swyne, and other Cattle, and brought greate Stoare for Prouifion againft Winter : Yf yt had bin Thenemies al would be wel, but they are Newetrals, and Lettres com from all Places full of Complaynts and Exclamations ; what Reafon they fhall haue wilbe feene : The Gatheringe of the Duke of *Lawnborgh,* is about *Munfter,* and had fom 6 or 700 Men ; yt feemeth his Nomber fhall ftay and be imployed in thefe Contryes. We looke for Sir *Frauncys Vere* euery Day, and yf he bringe vs any Niewes, your Lordfhip fhalbe Pertaker ; in Recompenfe of thefe my humble Defyre is, we may heare of Mr. *Lakes* Negociation with Sir *Edwarde,* whome fom do Dowbt to haue proceeded to farre by Dealinge in Matters beyond his Charge of Gouernorfhip, and can be no other Fruytes expected, then to breede niew Jeloufies and Diffidencies wich make thefe Men loathe, and loth to imploy owr Nation ; whereof at our Meetinge may be difcourfed furder. From the *Haeghe,* this 31th of *Auguft,* 1591.

Your Lordfhips, &c.

Geo. Gilpin.

Conte Maurice *de* Naſſau *a Monſieur Monſieur de* Sydney.

Monſieur,

JE ſuis arrivè en ce lieu de *Cathbech,* avec bon Nombre des gens de guerre, & aultres Proviſions, a Intention de Mettre fin a noſtre Enterpriſe ſur la Ville de *Hulſt,* la quelle J'eſpere moyennant la Grace et Aide de Dieu, remettre ſoubz l'obeiſſance de Meſſieurs Les Eſtats Generaulx. Je vous prie Monſieur ſi voſtre Commodité le peut ſouffrir, de me faire ce plaiſir, que de me Venir trouver, et ſi poſſible eſt avec une bonne Compaignie de Voſtre Gouvernement, laquelle je Vous prie tenir preſte, ſi faire ſe peult, pour quand je paſſeray par devant Uliſſinghe : Car par la fault il que je prenne mon Chemin. Et ſur ce apres mes humble Recommendacions, et voz bonnes Graces, je prieray Dieu vous avoir.

Monſieur,

En ſa ſainéte Proteétion. De mon batteau a *Cathboech,* ce xviii de *Septembre,* 1591.

Voſtre tres affeétionnè amy

a vous faire Service,

Maurice de Naſſau.

Conte Maurice *de* Naſſau *to Monſieur Monſieur de* Sydney.

Monſieur,

JE ſuis reſolu, ſuivant ce que je vous ay eſcript ce Joùrdhuy, de faire Voile ce ſoir, pour me trouver demain à laute de jour a *Hulſterhaven* et *Calverſtert.* Et pourtant, je vous prie une aultre fois, ſi voſtre Diſpoſition et Affaires permettent, de me faire aultant du plaiſir, aultant du plaiſir, que de me venir trover au meſme licu, avec la Compagnie que je voùs ay prie ce Jourdhuy. Et de meſme chemin prendre avec vous, tous les meilleurs Cannoniers que vous avez a *Fliſſinghe,* pour ſervir a ceſt exploiét : Cur ſe ſera comme j'erpere, ſinon que pour bien peu de joues. Et ſur ce apres humbles Recommendations en voz bonnes Graces, je prieray Dieu Vous maintenir.

Monſieur,

En ſa ſainéte Proteétion. De mon batteau a l'oppoſite de *Arnemuyden,* ce xviii de *Septembre,* 1591.

Voſtre tres affeétionnè amy

a vous faire Service,

Maurice de Naſſau.

Sir Thomas Bodley *to Sir* Robert Sydney.

HEERE is nothing ſturring, that is worth the Writing to your Lordſhip. Only as this Day we are informed, that the Caſtel of *Anholt* is in Parley with thoſe of *Gueders.* I thinke your Lordſhip hath heard of the Taking of the Town, which was done by Captain *Lambert,* without Commiſſion from hens, and in that Reſpeét diſliked ; but yet the Contrey is contented to reape the Benefit of his Seruice. We looke euery Houre for Count *Maurice* Returne, till when it will not be reſolved what is next to be attempted. Howbeit, *Nieumeghen* is chiefly thought vpon. I would gladly heare from you, how you propoſe to execut your long intended Surpriſe. Whether you hitte or faile, there is nether Danger nor Diſhonor. But your Lordſhip that knoweth euery Circumſtance, will putte in Praétiſe what is beſt. If your Leaue for *England* be graunted, I beſeeche you lett me knowe ſome litle Time before. For I

would

would write a Worde by your Lordſhip about my Reuocation; and, withall' I would intreat yow, to afforde me of your Fauor, if it come yow well to paſſe. I haue all the Reaſon in the World to alleage for my ſelf, as your Lordſhip, er yow goe, ſhall be thorowly inſtruſted: Beſides, I haue her Maieſties Promiſe for the End of this Sommer. In this, or any Thing els, I will make that Reckning of your Willingnes to pleaſure me, as yow, I hope, will account that I am yours at all Eſſaies. And ſo I bidde yow moſt hartely and happely farewell. From the *Hage, Sept.* 21, 1591.

Your Lordſhips at Commaundement,

Tho. Bodley.

＊ *Sir* Thomas Lake *to Sir* Robert Sydney.

YOUR Lordſhips Letters I receaued at the Court on *Wedneſday*, with Letters to my Lord of *Buckhurſt*, and Mr. *Stanhope*, ſent vnto me by Mr. *Burnham*, which I deliuered. They ſpeake well both, but what they will doe you ſhall beſt iudge as you fynde. Our Matters of *Oſtend* are very much encumbred. The States reſiſt very bitterly. Mr. *Bodley* doubtfully, and Sir *Edward Norris* hath fallen into the high Indignation of my Lord Threſurer, which chanced during the Tyme that I was there. For Matters ſtartid to tedious to expreſſe in a Letter, but in Effeſt for nouryſhing a Dependency vppon others, beſides his Lordſhip, which will hardly be put vp. And therefore, if your Lordſhip have any Thing to doe here, move as few Frends as you can beſides; for it is ill taken. I thought good to put you in Mynde of it, becauſe I fynde him in a good Opinion of you, and enquired of me manie Particularites of your Gouerment. It is good to hold in; olde *Saturnus* is a melancholy and Weyward Planet, but yet predominant here, and if you haue Turne thus do doe, it muſt be don that Way; and whatſoever Hope you haue of anie other, belieue it not.

Our *French* Matters goe very Waywardly, the Queen is fallen out with the King, for miſbehaving of him ſelfe towards her People, as ſhe conceaveth it. And both the Lord and his Troupes are peremptorily ſent for, yet his Frendes here doubt he will not come.

Mr. *Burnham* I thinke will writt to your Lordſhip ſuch Newes as are Currant, here and the Reports that are come here, of our Fleets at Sea, which are very diſcomfortable. Sir *Richard Grenfeld* is ſayd to be taken with the *Revenge*.

＊ Sir *Thomas Lake* was born at *Southampton*, and having a learned Education, and good natural Parts, was imployed by the memorable Sir *Francis Walſingham*, Secretary of State, as his Amanuenſis; and by him recommended to Queen *Elizabeth*, to read to her *French* and *Latin*, who made him Clerk of her Signet. On the Demiſe of the Queen, he was by the Regency, ſent to attend King *James the Firſt* from *Berwick*, who after Knighted him, and made uſe of his Service in *French* Affairs. Alſo by Patent dated 2 *January*, in the 7th Year of his Reign, conſtitutes him (being then one of the Clerks of the Signet) his Secretary for the *Latin* Tongue, during Life. His Sufficiency further appearing, he was ſworn of the Privy Council, 29th of *March*, 1614; and on the 3d of *June*, 1616, was ſworn one of the principal Secretaries of State: But in *February* following, having married his eldeſt Daughter to *William Cecill*, Lord *Roos*, only Son and Heir of *William*, Earl of *Exeter*, by his 1ſt Wife; he was involved into the Quarrel of his Wife and Daughter, with the Counteſs Dowager of *Exeter*, which was the chief and only Cauſe of his Ruin; for thereupon he was diſmiſſed from his Office of Secretary of State, and ſent to the *Tower* 15th of *February*, 1619; having continued till then in the honourable Eſteem of all Men, and of the King himſelf, who adviſed Sir *Thomas*, to leave his Wife and Daughter to the Law. Whereunto he humbly thanked his Majeſty, but ſaid, *He could not refuſe to be a Father, and a Huſband.* On the Hearing in the *Star-Chamber*, he and his Lady were fined 10000 *l.* to the King, 5000 *l.* to the Counteſs, and 50 *l.* to one Mr. *Hutton*. The King is ſaid to compare their Crimes to the firſt Plot, of the firſt *Sin in Paradiſe*: The Lady *Lake* to the Serpent, her Daughter unto *Eve*, and Sir *Thomas* to poor *Adam*, whom he thought in his *Conſcience*, that his *Love* to his *Wife*, had beguiled him. And he was truly pittied by all the Court. His Wife was *Mary*, eldeſt Daughter of Sir *William Ryther*, Lord Mayor of *London*, by whom he had Sons and Daughters. *Aulicus Coquinariæ*, P. 98, & Seq. *Wood's Faſti Oxoniencis*, Vol. I. *Camden's Annals*, &c.

The

The Lord *Harry Vettingale* is come out of *France*, and bringeth Word that *Gournt* is taken, and that the Army is marching towards *Candebec*, to attempt that, and the Caftle of *Bleynvill*, while the Horfe is coming forward with the Reyfties, which I thinke wilbe long firft, for we heare he is marched towards *Franch* Coumte to make Head againft the Popes Forces.

There are in the Army of *Normandy*, Mar. *Byron* with 7000 of Horfe and Foote, *Hallot Montmorency*, and Lieutenant to the Duke *Montpenfer* 4000 Foot, and 500 Horfe. The *English* 4000 Foot, 200 Horfe, 10 Cannons out of *England*; 8 of the *Low Countryes*, 8 from *Calais*; but that Marefchall *Byron* hath but little Prouifion of Munition anfwerable thereto.

I writt not much becaufe I loue not to writt but the Truth of that I meddle with. And fo leaue your Lordfhip to the Protection of the Almighty God. From *London* the Firft of *October*, 1591.

Your Lordfhips to command,

Tho, Lake.

Thomas *Lord* Buckhurft *to* Sir Robert Sydney.

S I R,

I Moved her Majeftie upon *Saturday* laft, for her gracious Licens for your Returne. I found her Majeftie much more inclinable than heretofore ; and yet fhe touched a little upon the old Greife, wherein I prefumed to juftefy you, and as to me femeth, it wrought fome good Effect with her. And fhe faid, that as touching your Returne, fhe would firft be affured of the Duke of *Parma*'s Intentions, either for his Journey into *Wormes*, or for his Defignes in the *Low-Countries*. I told her Majeftie, that by *Albantide*, that would aparantly be fene ; and though fhe mifliked not of that Time for your Returne, as I gathered, yet fhe wold not have me to certify you, but willed me to ftay a While longer. And talking with my Lord Threfurer, he feemed to underftand her Majeftie, that it were not fit you returned til the End of the Terme. So as though the Time of your Return be not yet certain. Yet her Majefties gracious Agrement for your Returne within a very fhort Time, is certain. You fhalbe fure, that I will not forget to follicite it to her Majeftie, till I bring it to a final End. And fo al, and ever yours, I end. Her Majeftie is now plefed to continue my Lord of *Effex*, and the Forces in *France*, for one Month longer. In Haft this 6 of *October*, 1591.

Your very loving and affurid Frend,

T. Buckehurft.

My very good Lorde,

SIR *Thomas Bafkefielde*, deliuered me yours of the 21 of the Laft, beinge fory the Entrepryfe had no better Succes, which in fom Sorte I feared afore becaufe the chief Mover and Informer of the fame, is fomwhat Infortunate, as appearees by other attempted Sarvices ; and yet is thought by fom not to be fo ftraunge, becaufe if a certain Humour doth in fom Sorte poffeffe him, whereof I omit to wryte furder, in Hope, ere longe, to meet with your Lordfhip. I was at my Being in *Middleboroughe* to vifit Mr. *Villers*, where I fownde my Interteynement coalder then heretofore ; what the Caufe is I cannot imagine, but fure I am, that I defarvyd better, and will Content my felfe, though yt had bin Leffe ; the Copies your Lordfhip defyres, I will haue written frefhe, and fhalbe fent by my next, if they be difpatched, with certain Copies of intercepted Lettres written by the Kinge of *Spayne*, to his Ambaffador in *Germaine manie* beinge of Importaunce : His Excellencie is here, and as wee heare meanes to be Abroade agayne ere longe, but diuers thinke he will firft vnto *Vytrecht* to take Poffeffion of the Gouerment and eftablifh fom better Order. They of *Gelderland* infifte to haue him accepte of their Offer, and that the Counfell of State would difpenfe with the Mediation which the Treatie appoynteth, but that is not yet refolved of. Yet I perceive they will affent to the Choyce made of him ; here were certain Speaches that Sir *John Norrys* was fent for owt of *Ireland*, to com hither, with certain Troupes, but I perceave his Welcom fhould be coalde ; Count *Hohenlo* is ftil Abroade in *Kemperland*, but nothinge faid what he effecteth. They of *Zelande*, haue bin earneft in complayninge a-gainft the ftaying of Shypes bownd for *Spayne*, and haue at laft obtayned an Aunfwere, that Deputes fhalbe fent ouer to hir Majeftye ; whoe they fhalbe not known as yet. From the *Haege* this 1 *November*, 1591.

Your Lordfhips, &c.

Geo. Gilpin.

Sir Thomas Bodley *to Sir* Robert Sydney.

I Doe not doubt but your Lordfhip is informed of her Majefties Defire to haue fome Companies from hens for the Seruice of *Rouen.* There was ne-ver worfe Time to propofe fuche a Mater, for that the Deputies of the States are all in their Prouinces, and no Affemblie held at all ; and as for this Court, it is impoffible to drawe them to determine vpon it, for that it paffeth their Commiffion, to fend any Forces out of the Territories of the Contrey. How-beit, with muche adoe, and with long Debate, I haue brought them to this, that albeit they can giue no Licenfe, yet they will be contented, by Way of Conniuation and fecret Permiffion, to fuffer them to paffe, and to caft it vpon vs, that are heere for her Majeftie ; which I thought expedient to certifie with all poffible Speede, to the End that fuche Prouifion, as your Lordfhip is to make, may be prefently prepared. For the Commiffary *Sparhawke* is already difpatched with Patents to thofe Places, where the Companies are in Garrifon. All is fo filent and quiet heere with vs, that I have nothing els of Worth to be written vnto your Lordfhip ; for whiche I bid you for this Prefent moft hartely Farewel. From the *Hage,* Nov. 21, 1591.

Your Lordfhips moft affured,

and at Comaundement,

Tho. Bodley.

George Gilpin, *Efq; to Sir* Robert Sidney.

My good Lord,

I Was very gladde to vnderftande, by yours of the 28th received Yefterday, your Lordfhips good Paffage and faife Arryvall, as I allfoe fhalbe when I fhall heare your Leave to be com, though I would be fory your Abfence fhould be a Hinderaunce any Wayes to thintended Service, whereof, in my Feelinge, the Succeffe is very likely to be certain and good. Here is not any Thinge paffed fince your Lordfhips Departure ; the Princeffe exfpects and wifsheth with greate Deuotion, that the Winde would come to the *Eaft,* and the yong Lady beginnes to think the Time longer ; Meffieurs *Les* Deputies, that fhould go into *Fraunce* will fcarce be ready thefe 10 Daies, and the others for *Eng-land* meane to departe at the fame Time, preparinge harde on all Sides ; and Monfieur *Buzenwall* Vrgeth as harde forwarde, findinge Fault with their Long-nes. I have by Order from fome, made thefe Men acquainted with the Proceedinge of Monsieur *de Maisse*, and her Majesties Anfwere concerninge the Treatie betweene the Kings Ministers and the Cardinals, about an Agreement, wherevnto it feemes hir Majestie inclines fo farre, that fhee wilbe content to fee what Aucthoritie the Cardinal hath to deale, and afterwards confider furder of all : What thefe Men will fay to yt I fhall heare fhortly, but me thinkes they could rather haue wifhed hir Majesties Aunfwer other, though it be affured that withowt theim no Accord wilbe entred vnto, neither that they neede to dowbt of any Separacion ; it will haften theer Deputation to hir Majeftie the more, and what fhalbe refoluid I fhall vnderftand ere longe : And thus watinge other I humbly take my Leaue, committinge yowr Honour to to God his Proteċtion.

Haugh, the 30th
of *Dec.* 1591.

Your good Lordfhips moft ready

to doe you Service,

George Gilpin.

Sir Thomas Bodley *to Sir* Robert Sydney.

ALthough I come very weery from a tedious Difpatche, that I haue made by this Bearer, yet I may not lette him paffe without a Letter to your Lordfhip, which I would ftuffe as full of Thankes, as I can any Way deuife, for the Kindnes of your Letter that yow fent by Capt. *Browne*. But becaufe I am perfuaded yow are no Louer of Ceremonies, I hold it fufficient to giue yow harty Thankes: I would your Lordfhip being in *England*, could haften my Returne, which I haue earneftly of late, and oftentimes folicited. But I am willed by her Majeftie to haue Patience till the Spring, which yet I feare very muche will paffe the Equinoction: It doth come me greatly ill to paffe in my privat Eftat. If the Opportunitie fhould ferue you, a Worde of your Mouth might further that Suite, I pray yow affourd it. For any Thing els I haue nothing to requeft yow, but to keepe your Loue vnto me, and to defend me where yow come ; and where yow fee there is Occafion, which if any fpecial Service, or Token of kinde Affeċtion, towardes yow or any of yow, may requite in any Sort, I proteft vnto yow vnfainedly it fhall not be omittede. I haue no Direċtion out of *England*, for any Company to be fent vnto yow, nor any Kind of Newes to aduertife yow from hens, which is not knowen to this Bearer. Ther is a Paffeport graunted by the Counfel of State, to the Baron of *Reide*, one of the Emperors Ambaffadors at *Bruffels*, who earneftly folicited, to be fuffered to come hither. And becaufe he is taken for an honeft Fauourer of their Caufe, and well affeċted in Religion, they are willing he fhould come, hoping by his Prefence to returne him with an Anfwear, that fhall fhake of all the reft. Hauing no more Mater nor Leafure, I take my Leaue of your Lordfhip. *Haghe, Jan.* 10, 1591.

Your Lordfhips moft affeċtionat,

and at Comaundement,

Tho. Bodley.

Sir Thomas Bodley *to Sir* Robert Sydney.

I Doe affure your Lordfhip, if I goe not Home the fooner, I fhall be ficke with Melancholie ; for I haue fpent all my Patience a great While agoe. Many Thinges doe moue me to feeke it very earneftly, but nothing fo much as my priuat Eftate. If Importunitie would ferue, I haue written about it fower or fiue Times. For an Anfwear at firft, I was bidde to attend till Sommer were paft ; and next, till an other were found to fucceede me : After that I was
willed

willed to tarie till the Spring, and nowe at laft I am told, that as long as this Peace is in Daunger of a Parle, I can not be fpared. Once the Spring is at Hand, and I thinke this Peace will come to nothing, or will proue litle better then a paltrey Practife of the *Spaniards*, to gette Aduantage in dealing with a credulous People ; we fhall fee er be long whereto it will come ; and I thinke for Certaine, there will be no fuche Caufe as to ftay me heere about it. But whether I come or tarie, be it fooner or later, I am your Lordfhips to be vfed both heere and at Home in all your Occafions. To tell yow freely my O-pinion of your Going into *England*, I thinke they finde it inconvenient, that the Cautionery Townes fhould be both at one Time without the Prefence of their Gouernors. I knowe nothing at all of thofe Reportes that are caried A-broade about your Lords *Burgh* ; I am right well affured that the Bur-ghers loue him well, and thinke it longe till he returne. But yet of late they haue bin forced for many Weekes together, to pay the Souldiers there in Garri-fon their Weekely Impreftes : Wherupon they haue complained, and fought to be rembourfed by the States of *Holland*, who haue addreffed them tō me. The Summe that they demaunde doth amount at the left to 1200 *l. Sterling*. I doe not doubt but her Majeftie doth pay that Garrifon as duly, as any of the reft, that I feare there is a Fault, though I knowe not yet in whome, which will hardly be anfweared.

It doth ftand very odly between Sir *Edward Norreis*, and the Councel of State, as yow may fee by that Letter, which they fent of late vnto her Majef-tie, wherof I fend yow the Copie, to be read in your Study. There is no An-fwear yet vnto it, and I can not coniecture what Anfwear can be made ; for he hath vfed ftrange Deuifes to engage her Majeftie and my Lords, with the Ex-cufe of his Actions. And yet the Abufes are fo great, as they will fee them in the Ende, and muft yelde of Neceffitie, and in common Equitie, to caufe him to fatisfie and anfwear the Contrey. The Count, and Sir *Francis Vere* are about fome Enterprife, which is contriued by themfelues, and vnknowen as yet to the Counfel of State, I would otherwife willingly impart it to your Lordfhip. Although the Winde hath ferued, to bring vs Newes out of *France* or *England*, any Time this 4 Daies, we haue yet no Letters, nor Aduertifements from any ; howbeit we hope we fhall haue toMorowe. In the meane While I recommend my felf and my Seruice to your Lordfhips Difpofition, and I wifhe yow Happi-nes in all Thinges, to your greateft Contentacion. From the *Hage*, Marche 1, 1591.

Your Lordfhips at Commaundement,

Tho. Bodley.

Sir Thomas Bodley *to Sir* Robert Sydney.

I Doe not Wonder a Whitte at that Maner of Proceeding of my Mafters of *Zeland* ; for I affure your Lordfhip, I did neuer yet perceaue any harty good Will, in any one of this People, ether towardes her Majeftie, or any one of our Nation. Our good Offices, and good Cariadge, bothe towardes this State in general, and towardes fome in particular, may haue forced fome one, or fome fewe, to make a Shewe at fome Time of Frindfhip and good Will, but vndoubtedly in a Caufe of any Moment, you fhall fee them fo falter in the Duties of Affection, as a Man would hardly credit, that their Plaines were accompanied with fuch notable Cunning. It is a great While agoe, fins by Means of my Imploiments, I haue noted in their Actions their badde Difpofiti-on. And therefor for my felf, without any Jote of Refpect to their Faults or Diffaults, what is fitte to be perfourmed for her Majefties Service, I doe it roundly and vprightly. And, for ought I can perceaue, in Regard of their good Wifhes, I may account as much vpon it, as any other that is heere of her Majefties Minifters.

Their

Their Dealing with your Lordſhip was too, too rude and iniurous : But what will yow haue ? It is not poſſible to drawe Wine out of Veſſels full of Vineger. In my Opinion, it was greatly requiſit, that yow ſhould write, as you did, to the States of that Place, to the End they might not thinke, that they walke inuiſible. But I knowe they will anſwear yow with Courteoſie and Wordes, and litle to the Purpoſe, for your Satisfaction. This I can aſſure yow, that there was neuer no Ouerture of that Exploit to this Councel, vntill they heard it had failed. To impart to your Lordſhip, as you Deſire by your Letter, my ſimple Aduiſe ; methinkes, that for the better Manifeſtation of the Wronge done vnto yow, and to her Majeſtie in your Perſon, and for your owne Diſcharge heereafter, it will be needefull yow ſhould ſignifie that Abuſe to this Councel, as being appointed by the Contract to manage all Affaires appertening to theſe Warres, and to giue yow Audience to any Motion, that ſhall tende to the Seruice of her Majeſtie, or Preſeruation of the Place that is committed to your Charge. Your Lordſhips Writing to them, to ſuche Effect, as yow pleaſe, if yow ſend your Letter vnto me, I will accompany the Deliuerie with ſome verbal Remonſtrance. At this very Preſent, Count *Maurice* is Abroade about ſome Mater of Surpriſe, as we are perſuaded, vpon the Towne of *Maſtricht* ; which is alſo attempted without the Priuitie of this Councel ; wherat they doe diſdaine, and purpoſe, as they ſay, to tell him plainely of it. Sir *Francis Vere* is alſo with him, and hath imparted nothing to me ; whereat I meruell very muche : But of this I would ſay more, if I were in any Place, to conferre with yow by Worde : For truly, to ſpeake plainely, I am flatly of Opinion, that continuall Soothing, and Courting, and Flattering of ſome Perſons that we knowe, or may knowe, to be alienat in Hart from her Majeſtie, and the Nation, doth but giue them more Occaſion, to watche a fitte Opportunitie, when their Turne may beſt be ſerued, to abuſe the good Meaning of her Majeſties owne Seruants, to her notable Preiudice. But that it is a Mater not fitte for Inke and Paper, I would hold you longer with this Talke, which nowe I leaue to your Diſcretion, and wiſhe your ſelf and your Eſtate that Happe, that your Hart doth chiefeſt Deſire. From the *Hage*, 10 *Marche*, 1591.

Your Lordſhips moſt affectionat,

and at Commaundement,

Tho. Bodley.

Conte Maurice *de* Naſſau, *a* Monſieur Monſieur *de* Sidney.

Monſieur,

AIANT par les lettres que puis naguerres vous mavez eſcript, veu vôtre bon deſir, afin que pour les raiſons touchées, Je vouldrois pour quelque temps, vous preſter ma Maiſon a *Fliſſinghen*. Et deſirant non ſeullement en ceſte occaſion, mais auſſy en choſe plus grande, dependant de mon pouvoir et autoritè, vous faire pue bono effects, parroître l'eſtat que Je faiz de vôtre amitiè, et l'entiere et ſincere affection, que Je vous porte. J'ay pour vous accommoder d'une bonne partie de ma dite maiſon bien voulu vous dire, que Je ſuis content que vous entriez quand il vous plairra, en la dite maiſon ; prenant pour vôtre commoditè, et de vôtre famille, tout le quartier d'enhault, avec une des Sales d'embas, et quelques caves, mes mes auſſy telle part au Jardyn, qu'il vous plaiſra : Suivant que J'en eſcrips preſentement auſſy a mon Recepueur et Couchierge Illecy, Lequel Je deſire, que pour la garde de la dite maiſon, demeurer au qaartier qu'il tient : Laiſſant auſſy les aultres Chambres Joignants ſondict quartier (excepte l'une des Salles ſuſdites) a la garde du dit Conchierge, pour la commoditè de Madame la Princeſſe ma belle mere, et la avenue a fin de vous pouvoir ſervir, lois que Madame ou moy pourrons vous

trouver

trouver a *Fliſſinghen.* Et n'eſtant ceſte a aultre effeéte. Je la finiray par mes. Tres affeétueuſes recommendacions, en voz bonnes graces. Priant Dieu vous donner.

Monſieur,

En parfaite ſainétè heureuſe et longue Vie. *A la Haye,* le 3me d'*Aupril,* 1592.

Voſtre tres affeétionne Amy,

a vous faire Service,

Maurice de Naſſau,

Sir Thomas Bodley *to Sir* Robert Sydney.

I Am glad that my Lettres was opened by your Lordſhip, for it gaue yow ſome Occaſion to write that Lettre vnto me, which happely otherwiſe I had miſſed for that Time. I pray yow aſke me no Pardon for Opening of Lettres, for I doe giue yow a Warrant dormant to doe it of Purpoſe, as well as vnawares. To what Termes Sir *Ed. Norreis* hath reduced his Affaires, I know Mr. *Gilpin* will informe yow at large. I doe not Doubt, but though he write to ſome Frindes to ſolicit his Returne, yet he writeth to the chiefeſt to ſolicit the Contrary ; for I knowe not who at Home will prouide him ſo well. My Lord Treaſurer doth intreat me ſomwhat earneſtly, to finde him what I can ; and I purpoſe for my Lord to doe my vttermoſt Endeuor, though Sir *Edward,* and his Frindes, deſerue but litle at my Handes. And though I ſee not as yet, howe Maters can be caried, but with a ſpecial Staine vnto his Credit : Yet, I thinke, in the End, if he will folowe good Aduiſe, he ſhall eſcape better cheape, then his Dealing doth deſerue. Heere is nothing ſturring, that is worth the telling to your Lordſhip. This I haue written, to giue this Bearer ſome Cariage. If your Lordſhip ſee Mr. *Gent,* I pray yow, for my Sake, as wel as his owne, to bidde him Welcome to *Fluſhing.* From the *Hag, Ap.* 9. 1592.

Your Lordſhips all at Commaundement,

Tho. Bodley.

Conte Maurice *de* Naſſau, *a Monſieur Monſieur de* Sidnay.

Monſieur,

VOUS entenduez ſans doubte par les lettres, que Meſſieurs du Conſeil d'eſtat vous eſcrivent, la reſolution qu'ilz ont prinſe, de mettre quelque bon nombre des gens en Campaigne. Et ores que Je m'aſſeure, que vous lour aſſiſterez tres volontiers en la demande qu'ilz vous font, touchant ce fait. Si eſt ce, que Je ne puis laiſſer d'accompaigner leur Lettres avec ce menure, qu'eſt pour vous prier Monſieur bien affeéteunſement, et ſi avant que le garde de la Villa de *Fliſſinghe* le peult aulcunement permettre, qu'il vous plaiſe les ſeconder, avec deulx bonnes compaignies de voſtre gouvernement. Et de les tenir preſts pourle temps, que Je les pourray mander, que comme J'eſpere ſera bien toſt. Et furce apres mes tres affeétuenſes recommendacions, en voz bonnes graces, Je prieray Dieu vous avoir.

Monſieur,

En ſa ſainéte proteétion. De la *Haye,* ce 10 de *Aupril,* 1592.

Voſtre tres affeétionne Amy,

a vous faire Service,

Maurice de Naſſau.

Sir

Sir Thomas Bodley *to Sir* Robert Sydney.

THOUGH I knowe not a Iote of any Newes, that is worth the Writing to your Lordſhip, yet the Opportunitie of this Bearer, and the Receipt of your Lettre of the 20 of this Preſent, which was brought me this Morning, will not ſuffer me to be ſilent. We doe nothing but hearken what Occurrence this Winde will bring vs out of *France*, which we hope will redound to all our good Likinges. And if it come ſo well to paſſe, we muſt caſt a watchefull Eye to the Doinges of this People : For vndoubtedly there are ſome, that will aduiſe vpon the ſoddaine, to play a iadiſhe Tricke. I feare Mr. *Bulenual* doth no very good Offices ; for that I ſee that the chiefeſt are exceedingly *frenchefied*, as in deede they were alwaies ; but lately more then euer. I am wholy of your Opinion for Sir *Edward Norreis* Proceeding. It may amend for a Month, or perhaps a litle more : But, in the Ende, there is no Remedie ; they muſt be contented to lette him liue as *Regulus*. Which doth make me to Prognoſticat, that his Dealing, in Time, will cauſe a great Deale of Trouble, between her Highnes and this Contrey. But of this at your Coming ; till when, and alwaies, I wiſhe very hartely your greateſt Proſperitie. From the *Hage, Ap.* 26, 1592.

> *Your Lordſhips moſt affeĉtionate*
>
> *and at Commaundement,*
>
> Tho. Bodley.

Conte Maurice *de* Naſſau *a Monſieur Monſieur de* Sidney.

Monſieur,

JE ſuis reſolu de me mettre en campaigne avec les trouppes, que Je pourray aſſembler, pour le 20 de ce Mois. Et pource, Je ne voullu failler, ſuivant ce qu'il vous plaiſoit me declarer eſtant chez vous, de Vous prier bien affectueuſement de me faire ceſt Semain que de me Venir trouver icy, pour le meſme temps. J'eſpere en la bonté de Dieu, que le paſſetemps que nous aurons, redondera au Service de Sa Majeſtè et du Pays. Et furce, apres me tres affectueuſes recommendacions en voz bonnes graces, Je prie Dieu vous maintenir.
Monſieur,
En ſa ſaincte Proteĉtion. De la *Haye*, le 8 de *May*, 1592.

> *Voſtre tres affeĉtionne Amy,*
>
> *a vous Servir,*
>
> Maurice de Naſſau.

Je vous prie Monſieur, d'aultant que Je partiray d'icy le 20 de ce Mois au plus tard, de me venir trouver pour le meſme temps, ou ſi vous le pouvez faire pluſtoſt.

Sir Thomas Bodley *to Sir* Robert Sydney.

YOUR Lordſhip may perceaue by the Copie of that Letter, which I ſent my Lord Treaſurer, to what Effeĉt I haue dealt with my Maſters, the States. I haue praied Sir *Francis* [*Vere*] to impart it vnto yow; but I knowe not in what Sort, nor with whome I might requeſt yow to further the Mater ; for both the Court, and the Councel, and this Aſſemblie of the States, is as deafe as is poſſible. Methinks, in the End, it will but proue a Sommer Storme. As any Thing commeth of it, either heere in Conference, for that I haue not

yet

yet their Anfwear, or from Home by other Lettres, I will acquaint your Lord-fhip with it, and leaue yow for this Prefent. At the *Hage, June* 2, 1592.

Your Lordfhips at Commaundement,

Thô. Bodley.

Sir Thomas Bodley *to Sir* Robert Sydney.

I Doe rather falute your Lordfhip, for that this Bearer doth come fo fittely, then for any Kinde of Mater that is worthy of a Letter. For here, at the *Hage*, there is nothing fturring ; and we have litle from the Campe, but your Lordfhip hath it quickly. They are buified at this Prefent in Drieng vp the Ditche, which is eafely done, if there come no Raine ; and fo, it is thought, they fhall be Mafters of the Place ; there is other wife litle Hope, as the Oc-currences goeth heere. The Leuie of *Juliers* doth daily repaire to the Towne of *Sherembergh*, fo as many Men giue out, that there are at this Prefent 700 at the left : Befides, their Forces out of *France*, are expected to returne with the very firft Winde, which will make in all a good Supplie, for the with-drawing of the *Englifhe*, which I fee her Highnes is refolued to fend for by the next : But of that, I thinke your Lordfhip knoweth more then my felf. For which I will not nowe trouble with Intelligence of no Moment, but com-mend yow moft earneftly to Gods good Protection. From the *Hage, Aug.* 11. 1592.

Your Lordfhips at Commaundement,

Thô. Bodley.

Sir Thomas Bodley *to Sir* Robert Sydney.

I Doe affure your Lordfhip, this Mater of withdrawing the Companies from hens, doth moue this People not a litle. But to fay the very Truth, they have no fuch Occafion, as they do pretend ; for the Troupes of Count *Philip*, which are lately returned, and the Leuie of *Juliers*, which are come a great Part to *Sheremberg* already, will amount to a greater Nomber, then all the *Eng-lifhe* that are fent for. For mine owne Part, what with deliuering her Majef-ties Meffages, reporting againe their Anfwers, and replieng continually, with o-ther Thinges Appertinent, both my Head and my Handes haue euery Day their fill. When the Companies are departed, I haue had fo many Promifes to be reuoked from hens, the Time of my Imploiment hath ben fo long in this Ser-uice, and I haue notified fo plainely the Neceffitie of my State, as then me thinkes, I fhould not Doubt of fome prefent Perfourmance. But if it fhould not fo happen, I muft addreffe my felf Perforce with fome greater Importunitie to her Majeftie and the Lords. If my Houfe in *London* had bin voide, it had bin for your Lordfhip, and for no Man fo foone. But truly my State is fo mightily difordered, as I can lette it goe no longer, but that ether I, or my Wife muft be alwaies at Home, and that will Caufe her to remaine, till I doe returne ; and then I Purpofe, God willing, to paffe by your Gouernment, not to be requited for any Cheere that I haue made yow (for yow knowe, I nether did it, and I am not in Place) but to fee your Lordfhip and my Lady, and the Place of your Charge, and to knowe in what Sort I may further your Defires, in my Speeches with her Majefties, which I pray you be perfuaded, that I will frame to doe yow Honour, and to giue yow good Content in all that I am able. It is fiue Daies agoe, fins I heard from the Campe, that I can write yow very litle, to be accounted worth the Writing. As then the Count was in Hope, to difpatche his Maters quickly : Howbeit, if the Enemie be approched with fuche Forces, as is faid, to witte 20 Enfeignes of *Spaniardes*, 16 of *Dutche*, and

6 of

6 of *Wallons*, it may happen to coſt vs broaken Headdes. I thinke with the *Engliſhe*, there are at the Campe, and neere vnto the Campe, to giue Aſſiſtance at a Pinche, at the leſt 8000 Foote, beſides the Horſmen. Hauing no other Mater, that is vnknowen vnto yow, I bidde your Lordſhip for this Preſent, moſt hartely Farewell. At the *Hage, Aug.* 23. 1592.

Your Lordſhips moſt Affectionat at Commaundment,

Tho. Bodley.

Sir Thomas Bodley *to* Sir Robert Sydney.

YOUR Lordſhips Letter of your Hand, was my firſt certaine Tidinges of your good Recouerie ; for which it was welcome a thouſand Times more. I hope that Capt. *Browne* hath receaued my Letter, and is ſatisfied fully of my Affection to his Suite, if it lay in my Power. There are 4 of the Companies of your Garriſon required by Name to be ſhipped for *France*, of which his is one, and Capt. *Purleis*, for whome Sir *Mat. Morgan* ſhould be ſent out of *France*. And for the other two, to witte Capt. *Randolphe*, and Capt. *Ratcliffe*, Sir *Comiers Clifford*, and Capt. *Foukes*. If the Troupe of Sir *Mat. Morgan*, be not ſent, there is nothing written to me, what Order ſhould be taken. But I knowe your Lordſhip vnderſtanding her Majeſties earneſtnes, to haue theſe Companies for *France*, and knowing what is requiſit for the Aſſurance of your Garriſon, will take a fitte Courſe to giue her Highneſs Contentment. But if yow ſhould not ſend them both, me thinkes in Regard of Sir *Fra. Veres* Company, there may one of them be ſpared conueniently ; your Lordſhip, I am ſure, will diſpoſe of all Thinges for the beſt; for which I trouble yow no further, but with my hartieſt Commendations. From the *Hage, Sept.* 16. 1592.

Your Lordſhips at commaundement.

Tho. Bodley.

Sir Tho. Bodley *to* Sir Robert Sydney.

I Would I were departing together with your Lordſhip, being wonderfully weery of this *Hage*, and this Soile, and this paltrie Kinde of People. I haue written about it, by this Bearer, and vſed ſome Termes of ſo earneſt Requeſt, as nowe I thinke or neuer, I ſhall Speede of my Purpoſe. If I doe not, I am here to doe your Lordſhip any Seruice, and ſo I am whereſoeuer, with my vttermoſt endeuour. If your Lordſhip goe ſo ſhortly, I beſeeche yow beſtowe, when yow come to the Court, a Letter vpon me, and ſignifie your Opinion of my Likelihood to Returne. Which I knowe yow can deuiſe to learne by many Meanes. If I ſee, I ſhall be kept in this *Tantalus* Paine, with Promiſes and Hopes and no Perfourmance in the End, I will take ſome other Courſe, to procure ſome greater Grace. Wherein I will be ruled by any Note of Aduiſe, that yow ſhall pleaſe to ſend vnto me, as in the meane Seaſon, I am alwaies as I haue bin, and yow ſhall finde me in all Occaſions, moſt affectionatly bent to doe yow any Seruice. From the *Hage, Oct.* 24. 1592.

Your Lordſhips at Commaundement,

Tho. Bodley.

Sir Thomas Bodley *to* Sir Robert Sydney.

I Doe not write with any Hope, that this my Letter will find your Lordſhip in *Fluſhing*. But yet this Poſt comming to me, and hauing newly nowe receaued by my Lord *Burgkes* Servaunt, a Letter from your Lordſhip, of the

Laſt

Laſt of *October*. I could not but ſignifie of the ſlacke Deliuerie, and alſo thanke yow moſt hartely for the Mater of your Letter. It hath eaſed me greatly of a great Deale of Melancholie. For I Doubt not a Whitte, but that yow may haue good Meanes, to knowe what is intended, as touching my Returne ; and what yow knowe, I make Account, yow will ſignifie vnto me, aſſoone as yow may, which in Truth I ſhall Eſteeme as a ſingulare Benefit, among a great many former, for which I hold my ſelf deepely indebted, to your Lordſhip. I am ſorie for that yow write of the Weakenes of your Body, that it ſhould ſo continue. But yet I truſt the Aire of *England,* and the Sight of your Frindes, will reſtoare yow very quickly. I pray yow hartely if yow heare, what is ſaid to be the Errand of Sir *Thomas Wilkes,* vnto the States, lette me haue a Letter from yow, though I thinke yow will be gone, before this come vnto yow. And ſo I bidde yow for this Preſent, moſt hartely Farewel. From the *Hage,* *Nov.* 16, 1592.

Your Lordſhips aſſured and at Commaundement,

Tho. Bodley.

Sir Thomas Bodley *to Sir* Robert Sydney.

BY your Lordſhips Letter by this Bearer, and by an other before, which was ſent me from *Fluſhing,* I ſee yow haue no Care, how farre you putte me in your Debt, before yow knowe in what Sort I am able to diſcharge it. But I finde methinkes againe, that my Affection ys as muche, as yow deſire for Repaiment, till your turne may be ſerued with ſome better requital. And if that be your Meaning, yow ſhall ſee I will able to croſſe out your Booke. It doth trouble me greatly, and is exceeding preiudicial to my priuate Eſtate, that not onely I cannot gette from this Place, but that I cannot come to Knowledge wherto I may truſt ; for which no Order can be taken, in muche of my Buiſneſs. I doe ſee in the End, I muſt addreſſe my Petition to her Majeſties Handes, and put it in Aduenture how other Men will like it. As in the meane Seaſon I am to thanke your Lordſhip infinitly, for your loving remembrance in inquiring about me. The Affairs of this Contrey doe ſtand I knowe not howe : For they are half in a maner, lie what to doe this Sommer, ſome inclining to doe litle, and ſome to make a Levie, as I writte yow in my laſt ; but I thinke in Concluſion, they will fall to do litle. For it will be this Moneth, before the Prouinces will meete to ſhewe what Summe they will contribute, to the making of a Leuie. Count *Solmes* is heere to gette ſome Souldiers out of *Holland,* for an Incurſion into *Flanders,* whereto, as I thinke, they will willingly aſſent. It is alſo propoſed, and like to take Place, that there may be a Succour of ten thouſand Pound *Sterling* yelded to the *Frenche* King, for the Levie of 2000 Men for certaine Monethes. Other Mater heere is none that is worthy the Writing, and I will not take all from this Bearers Relation ; but ſtill I recommend my laſt Suite to your Lordſhip, as I pray you vnto me recommend what you pleaſe, where my Seruice may advaunce any Buiſnes of yours. From the *Hage,* 22 *Jan.* 1592.

Your Lordſhips moſt ready

at Commaundement,

Tho. Bodley.

The Lord Threafurers Lettre, written to the feveral Partes of the Realme, in Behalf of the Town of Flufhing, *and directed to Sir* Robert Sydney.

After my hartie Commendacions,

WHEREAS her Majeftie, by her Warrant vnder her Signature, dated the xxviith Daye of *Maye* laft, hath bene pleafed, in favor of the Magiftrats and Inhabitants of the Towne of *Flufhinge* in *Zeland*, to yelde to them her Priviledge, that all Manner of Grains that fhalbe tranfported by Licence out of any Part of this Realme, for the *Lowe Countries*, fhould be carried to the fayde Towne of *Flufhing*, there to be vfed, as in lyke Cafes other foraine Commodities are fpeciallie directed, by Way of Stapling the fame in other Townes in *Holland*, and *Zealand*, commanding me by the fame her Warrant, to give Order to all the Ports of her Realme, where anie fuch Corne vppon Lycence fhalbe laden, that the tranfporters thereof be bound with fufficient Suerties to performe her Majefties fayd Order. Thefe are therefore ftreigtly to Will and Command you, that according to her Majefties faid Placaert and Priviledge graunted to the fayd Towne of *Flufhing*, as above is recited, you doe take good Bond, with fufficient Suerties of all Manner of Perfons whatfoever, that fhall lade att that Port anie Manner of Graine, to be tranfported to anie Part of the *Lowe Countries*, by Vertue and Force of any Licence, to difcharge the fame Corne and Graine att the faid Towne of *Flufhing*; and thereof to bring good and fufficient Certificat from the Magiftrates of the fayde Town of *Flufhing*.

Geo. Gilpin, *Efq; to Sir* Robert Sydney.

My very good Lorde,

DO not, I humbly befeech youe, thinke much that thefe many Monthes I haue omitted to wryte vnto youe, for Excufes, I might alledge fondry; but, amongft the reft, and that not the leaft, that your comminge ouer hath bin looked for and defyred this good Whyle. Theffects remayne yet uncertain, and my felf cannot forbare longher, efpecially havinge dealt in a Matter that concerned your Lordfhips Gouuernment; procured as I am fure by the Care had of the Place, for her Majefties Service, and the Good of thefe Contryes. The 5th of the Laft, brought me her Majefties Lettres; and within 4 or 5 Dayes after, the furder Inftructions, refarringe me for the reft to their Pencionary of *Flufhinge*, who in due Sorte fhewed me the Copies of their Priuiledges; and fo being requefted by them to diferre a few Dayes from delivering of the Letters and my Charge, for Reafons which I Leave til our Meetinge, I prepared my Propofitions; and this Daye, with hir Majefties Lettre, prefented the fame to the States General, as by other Copies I fend your Lordfhip herewith will appeare; meaninge to do all Indeavours in the procuringe of this Refolution and Aunfwere; and then of all to aduertife your Lordfhip, with humble Defire yf there be any Thinge wherein my Service may ftande youe in furder fteede, yt may be your Pleafure to command him that have profeffed, and fo remayne, deuoted to your Lordfhips Service. Mr. *Bodly* remaynes ftil here, attending fome Kynde of Anfwere from the States to his Propofitions, which, for the firft, wilbe very coulde, and confifting of the Difficulties they fynd in the mouuing of yt to the Prouinces, which (yf I fhould fpeake truly, in my Opinion) tends onely to Delayes, and requyres a more particular Reafoning, then can be handled by Lettres: When this perfect Aunfwere will com I know not, being dyfferred vntil the Affembly of all the States; and then to your Reply, yt may be as much or more Tyme wilbe fought to be wonne, vnleffe they be dealt rowndly with, and the Matter infifted on; whereto I think yt wil com vnto at laft. I would I might make a Steppe ouer, but know not how to beginne to compas Leave in that Sorte I wyfh; to Mr. *Bodly* I haue tolde my Intention, but many Exceptions are mouuyd; yt may be, I wil feele my honourable Friends what they will fay vnto yt, and the whyleft prepare and refolue my felfe for all. The States prepare for Warres ; *Huy* is furpryfed, and wilbe kept ; the Ambaffadors of *Liegeborg* aunfwered, that *Bernk* being reftored, the other fhalbe yælded. The Troupes that are in *Fraunce* wil ftay there no longer ; fo il is their Interteyne-ment lyked ; and yet haue from hence Mony fent to them Monthly. His Ex-cellencie increafeth in Acthoritie daily ; the Prouinces auledge their Contributions, and the Companies fhalbe reformed, being purpofed that by the 21 of *April,* New Style, the Camp fhould to Fielde, but weather, unknown as yet. All Things els after the olde Sort. From the *Haeghe* the 14 of *Marche,* 1594.

Your Lordfhips moft affured, and ready at Command,

Geo. Gilpin.

George Gilpin, *Efq; to Sir* Robert Sydney.

My very good Lorde,

MR. *Bodly* lyveth here with me : Yefterday he had Audience in full Colledge ; hir Majefties Lettre, and his Propofitions, little contented them ; having requyred anfwere in Wrytinge to confider and refolve what to be donne, that may ftand both with their Eftate, and fatisfie her Majeftie in any good Sorte : I could not yet devyne what fhoul followe ; but fure I am, yt much trou-bleth them every Way ; whereof hereafter wee fhall fpeake furder. From the Camp which lyeth by *Wefel,* not much cometh ; the Ennemie fent 600 Horfe to view his Excellencies Camp, but ere it was refolued to Chardge them they re-tyred, and is thought yf the States would lyken thereof, theie would be fought ere *Mondragan* repaffe the *Rhyn.* Yf any Thinge come to my Knowledge be-fore your Lordfhips comminge, and that I fynde fit Conueyaunce, I will not fayle to make you Partaker. *Haegh,* 15th *Auguft,* 1595.

Your good Lordfhips moft humble to vfe,

Geo. Gilpin.

Sir Thomas Lake *to Sir* Robert Sydney.

S I R,

THE laft Weeke I had difchafged my felfe of my Debt, but that Mr. *Burnham,* who fhould haue been my Conveyance, was fent by my Lord of *Effex* out of the Way ; and I am wary in fending of Lettres, for we are now fo iealous here, as the Poftes Lettres are often vifited. To fatisfie your Requefts, or anie Thing els, wherein my Seruice may fteed you, I fhall be very ready, as one that holdeth your Vertues in Price, and will not fayle to haue an Ey to the Coorfe in-termitted, both by Conference with my Lord *H.* and by myne own attentivenes, to all Accidents that may further it. And I was of late in hope, that the Appre-henfions we had taken of Danger from forraine Parts, wold haue caufed vs to thinke of ftrengthning Councell, and Speech was of it, but quitted againe either by flacking of our Feares, or by Cunning ; which, in Truth, was the Ground for to lett you vnderftand plainely how Thinges are heare. We dwell in a moft certain expectation of being attempted the next Yeare, ether directly here at Home, or by the Way of *Scotland,* where there is very great Practice enter-taigned, not altogither by the Kings Confent, but yet not without Connivence to worke fome Turnes with vs. We ground not this our Apprehenfion onely, vppon the certain Knowledge we have of the Preparations in *Spaine,* to be farre greater then in the Year 88 ; but vppon Aduertifements of the Purpofe for which they were made ; from both private Perfons and Princes, fuch as I may not name. The expectation of this Danger bred here great Diverfity of Opi-nions, of the Proceeding of our Sea Voyage. They that wold have it ftayd,

alleaging

alleaging the impoſſibility of their returne in a ſmall Tyme, fitt to ſerue our Turne, if need required ; the hazard of the Loſſe of ſo manye Mariners going into hott Cuntryes ; the Abſence of the Shippes and Ordonance. The other Partie alleaging the Loſſe of the Queene, and the Adventurers if it brake of. The Diſhonnor, becauſe it wold be imputed to feare, and a probability that the return might be tymely enoughe, with hope of Treaſure, which is our greateſt deſire and want. Some Propoſition was made by the actiue Sort (you may gheſſe whom) to convert this Fleet, aſſimbled with ſome Enforcement, to an offenſiue Courſe, vppon the Ports of *Spaine* ; but checked from aboue, or croſſed vnder Hand, not without a great Diſtemper of Humures on both Sides, for a few Dayes ; yet, in moſt Mens Iudgements, the likelyeſt Way to divert our preſent Feares. But now in the End, they are directed to proceed, and in them reſteth much of our Hopes ; for it beginneth now to be ſpoken, that theſe great Rumors of Preparations are partely for feare of vs, and partely to have ſtayd this Voyage ; *exitus acta probat.* But I am of Opinion, that ſeing we reſt here in theſe Doubts, you may doe ſome Service to cauſe ſuch of thoſe Countrey Men as trade to *Spayne,* to make ſome ſpeciall Obſervation, and thereof to aduertiſe vs by you : We are no léſſe grieued with the Affairs of *Ireland,* where we do yet little good, but conſume very muche Money vppon ſmale Hopes. I think Sir *John Norris* will ſhortely return from thence. Here is come within theſe three Dayes a Maſter of Requeſts, called *Chevalier,* ſent from the Prince of *Conty,* D. *Neners,* D. *Bouillon,* and the Towne of *Paris,* with a very lamentable Declaration of the Loſſe at *Dourlans* adjoyning ; that there are ſlain 550 Gentlemen, of Name and Armes, beſides the Vulgar : That *Cambray* is heald for loſt, they having no Meanes to ſuccor it, and the Town willing enough to leave the *French* Gouuernment ; whereuppon they haue made Requeſt to haue an Ayd of 4000 Foote, at the Charge of the Towne of *Paris,* who ſhall giue Caution to pay them. Of this we falle to Conſultation ; and if we were ſure to haue ſome of our old Footinge in *Pycardy,* for a Place of Retraiet, or in Pawne, it wold be. I think it wilbe moued, and ſome hope that Need will make it be done, if the Gouvernor hynder not, with whome ſome Traficke will be had ; but this is to you onely.

I hope you will now hold me acquitted of any Debte by this tedious ſcribling, which I haue made the longer and more particular, becauſe you conceauing here-by the Humors that now we reſt in, and being not ignorant, as you cannot be, of ſuch Things as ſhall happen in the World, that may ether confirme or alter them. You ſhall not looke to haue many Lettres from me, who am a very ſpare Writer ; but when I ſhall ſee Cauſe to aduertiſe you of any Thing that may giue you ground to frame any Conceipt vppon for your own ſelfe : Other Things that ordinarily falls out. I know you haue here Frends enough to lett you know them. I forgotte to lett you vnderſtand before, that to aſſure vs of the Intention againſt vs, there is a Plotte ledde by the King of *Spaine* for a Peace with the *Turks,* not without ſome good round Charge to him. And ſo I leaue you to a Subiect of many Diſcourſes. From *Nonſuch,* where this Night we are arriued, this xxijth of *Auguſt,* 1595.

Yours to command,

Tho. Lake.

Robert Beale, *Eſq;* *Clerk of the Council,* to *Sir* Robert Sydney.

My very good Lorde,

I Haue of late receaved your Lordſhips of the xijth of the Laſt Monethe, and thincke my ſelf greatlie beholdinge vnto you, that it pleaſethe you to make ſome Accompte of my poor Frindſhippe, and to haue begon to wryte vnto me. Trulie, Sir, I haue allwayes vnfainedlie loued and honoured you, for diuers good and commendable Partes that are in you, and haue wiſhed tó haue ſome good Meanes, whereby I might declare the Affection which I haue borne and doe

beare,

beare, to doe you anie Seruice that I fhalbe hable : You haue feen, that I haue lytle Credit here, and trulie in this thankles Worlde, I haue not fougte nor feek to entermedle in any Matters, more then fuche whereto I am by others forced. And therfore it maye be, that I fhall not be hable to fatisfie your expectation in fuche Thinges, as you maye looke for at my Handes. But I truft you will accepte my good Will in frendlie Parte. I lyked not Mr. *Bodlyes* eger and peremptorie Commiffion ; for eger and bitter Meffages neuer did good with fuch Democraticall Eftates. Monarches maye well vfe them at Home, but they were neuer commendable Abroade, efpeciallye where they be vfed in an vnfeafonable Time, as I take this to be ; for the common Enemye, by raifing of the Siege of *Groll,* and the late Overthrowe of the *Frenche* Forces in *Picardie,* waxethe infolent. We are here putt in feare of greate Preparations by Sea in *Spaine* ; and it cannot be, but that the greater Tempeft is meant to fall vppon thefe Partes. It hathe ben accompted a good and neceffary Pointe of Policie, when Prince or Eftate hath to do with a puiffant Enemye, to make fayre Weather with the reft of his Neighbours, that if he cannot procure them to be ioyned with him, yet he maye at the leaft keepe them from Ayding him, that intendethe to doe Mifchiefe. But how is this cared for now ? The *Eafterlings,* and *Hannfes* [Towns] are (I feare me) at our Enemyes Deuotion, and will affift him. *Fraunce* lytle efteemeth our pettye Succours, and fmall regarde that he thinckethe hath ben and is had of him. If *Baligny* be fo foone entred into Communication with the Count of *Fuentes,* I feare that the next Newes wilbe worfe. It is wrytten out of *Italye,* that there fhould fhould be a Truce made for xxx^tie Monethes, betwine the *Frenche* Kinge and the Duke of *Sauoye,* which is lyke inoughe to drawe on an-other with *Spaine* ; for I haue allwayes feared, that confideringe the fmall Ac-compte which they efteeme to be made of him here, thofe Counfellors that broughte him to forfake his Religion, will alfo finde plaufible Reafons for him to forfake our Amitye, notwithftandinge that Proteftation which you brought from thence: And the Kinges longe lingringe in thofe Partes, maye be fufpected to be for fuche a Purpofe. From your Eftates he can exporte lytle ; and here the Troubles of *Irelande,* and preparacions to refifte the Inuafion of *Spaine,* will fo occupie vs, that we fhall not be hable to yielde Favours to anye other. Wher-for this Meffage of Mr. *Bodlye,* cannot but breede both a Diflyke in the Eftates, and the *Frenche* Kinge alfo. And if afterwardes we be left alone ; confideringe our manifolde inwarde Weakneffes, what will become of vs in the Ende ? Sir *Henrye Killegrewe,* Mr. *Atye,* and my felf, haue of late ben appointed to looke into the Accomptes between her Majeftie and the Eftates ; and, in Trothe, finde the Matter fo, that they haue ben to cunninge for vs, accordinge to the olde Imperfection, which *Philip de Comines* reportethe to be in our Nation, to be ouertaken by others with whom we are to treate. But yet it is no Time now to breake with them, neyther doe I thincke that it is meant. And therefore I could wifhe, that they would be contented to condefcende to fend fome Commiffiones out, to referre the Poyntes that in the Treatie are amiffe, rather than to kindle more Stryfe and Contencion, which can but reioyce the common Enemye, and turne to bothe our Preiudices. They haue receaued greate Benefitts at her Ma-iefties Handes, and it becomethe them to feeke to haue Thinges frendlie com-pounded, rather then to be fought vnto. If the Vnkindneffes doe continewe and increafe, it behouethe you to looke vnto your Charge ; and that was (as I fuppofe) the principall Caufe of the fending out of the Lord *Boroughe,* and your felfe, at this prefent. God forbid that anie Breache fhoulde fall out ; but yet in former Tymes, popular and headye Gouernmentes, have grown to Poyntes ey-ther of Defputacion, or of Hoftilitie : *Quicquid delirant Reges, plectuntur Achiui* ; and wherefoever the Favlt fhalbe, yet Princes will not feeme to committ anye Errors, but the Blame is caft vppon inferior Officers, that are leaft culpable. You knowe how to deale with your Burgers there, and haue the late Prince of *Orange* for a good Example to imitate, who by his popular familiaritye kept them more in, than with anie Force ; hauinge a vigilant Eye vnto their Doinges. By fuche Meanes, you maye (with Gods good Affiftance) preuent the Mifchiefe,

if

if anie, fhould be intended, and continuwe them in good Deuotion to her Majeftie and our Nation ftill. And fo befeechinge Allmightie God to take bothe vs here, and you there, into his holie Protection; I humblie take my Leaue. From my poor Houfe in *London*, the Second of *September*, 1595.

Yours affuredly at commandment,

Robert Beale.

This Day I hear other Newes of the Overthrowe of Count *Morrices* Troopes, whereat the common Enemy will greatly reioyce; and therefore it is not good, that Frinds fhold fall out, but feeke all Means of a frendly Reconciliation and Attonment, which I pray God may enfue betwene her Majeftie and the Eftates.

Geo. Gilpin, *Efq; to Sir* Robert Sydney.

My very good Lorde,

HAvinge fince your Departure hence taken Occafion to conferre with fom of thefe Men, I perceave they find it altogether expedient to vfe Matters fo, that her Majefties Favor towards them may be continued, and a Refolution will followe, to fend ouer Deputies ere longe, though happely it may chaunce that they will feeke to winne Time, to fee what wil becom of *Cambray*, which being not fo much diftreffed as was imagined, can holde owt til the King his Succors be ready: And to force it afore, it is thought *Fuentes* would, if he were ftronge enough to do that, and fend Ayde to the Conftable of *Caftille*, whoe is fo leffend in *Burgomguie*, that if the King can leave fufficient Strength there to make his Partie good, he wil conquere him by intercepted Lettres: At our Camp they haue the Niewes that *Mondragan* is written for, and is removuid higher ouer the *Rhoer* already, but what to doe not yet known; if he departe, his Excellencie will not giue ouer fo fowne, though thefe Men will haue certain Troupes haftened towards *Fraunce*; he had an Enterprife vppon *Meurs*, and were paffed twoe Palifados, but the Day approaching, durft not aduenture furder, thofe that fhould haue feconded them, comming to flowly forwarde; but the Fault being in the Chieff (as is muttered) fuch Peccadillos are ouerpaffed. The States Deputies are not yet retorned from Camp, but looked for daily; fhortly after we fhall fee how my Lord Ambaffador is like to fpeede, for he then meanes to preffe them forwarde, and if that fhall paffe, when Occafion fauourith, your Lordfhip fhallbe made Partaker. *Haeghe*, this 11th of *September*, 1595.

Your Lordfhips, &c.

Geo. Gilpin.

Geo. Gilpin, *Efq; to Sir* Robert Sydney.

My very good Lorde,

THE Deputies of the Generall States that were at the Camp, being retourned, we fhall ere longe heare what Aunfwere they bringe vppon Mr. *Bodlyes* Propofition, from his Excellencie and the Counfell of State: Touchinge the Aide that fhould be fent into *Fraunce*, the States Refolution fhalbe performed, and 20 Companies appointed fourthwith to be fent toowards *Callays*, whereof tene are *Scots*, and the other of thefe Contriemen. Owr Nation was fpoken of, and I thinke were as likely to haue bin fent as any other, and Sir *Francis Vere* to haue had the Commaunde; but the Dowbt thefe Men conceave, that it may chaunce her Majeftie will call them away fowdainly, hindreth all: Yt feemeth his Excellencie as yet purpofeth to kepe in the Fielde, though

though like enough to remoue to fom other Quarter, all Fourage being fpent vp where they lie now. *Mondragan* continueth where he was, neere *Keyfers-Wert*, and fortifieth his Camp with Trenchefs and other Defences, which makes us thinke he meaneth to fend Parte of his Troupes (as was vnderftood by thintercepted Lettres) to the Count *Fuentes*, whoe is refoluid to ftay and abide the King of *Fraunce* his Coming. Of late there was fent vnto me from the Camp certain Difcours about a Peace, written by fom one of Thenemies Side vnto Themperors Court, and lighted into owr Mens Hands. I find it wel donne, and worthie the Readinge, whiche is the Caufe that I fend a Copie to your Lordfhip ; my Lord Ambaffador fent the like into *England*. *Haege*, this 15th of *Septembre*, 1595.

Your Lordfhips, &c.

Geo. Gilpin.

Your Lordfhip muft make *French* of Thinclofed, being written in Hafte, and by me neuer pervfed.

CAllinge to Remembraunce, that your Lordfhip meant to vfe for your Exercife, to diftil and make Extraxtions, I haue thought good to fertifie, that while wee were in *Amfterdam*, there was one Doctor *Carwer*, whoe I heare is very fkilfull therein, and otherwife wel learned and practifed ; if your Lordfhip could like of his Labor and Service, he would be very glad to imploye him felfe, and am of Opinion, your Lordfhip would like wel of him ; vppon your leaft Aunfwere (which I humbly craue) he wilbe willinge and readie to make his Repaire vnto yow, and vppon Conference difpofe of his Bufines and him felfe accordingly.

Rowland Whyte, *Efq*; to Sir Robert Sydney.

My Lord,

THIS Morning there came to vs from *Ireland* aduertifment, that *Tiron* had drawen our Force to fight of Neceffity ; that Sir *John Norreis* was fhot in the Belly ; that Sir *Thomas Norreis* was fhott in the Thigh ; that Capt. *Richard Wingfeld* was fhott in the Elbow with a Mufkett, and likelie to loofe Life or Arme, thother are not in daunger of Liffe. The Hope we had here of a Peace is now turned to an affured War, for twere to much Difhonor to dally longer.

I fownd, at my Return from *Tibbols*, Capt. *Browns* Man with a Packett for me, and another for my Lord Treafurer ; I fent him with them away this Night, and I goe to Morrow with your Lettres to the Court, whom thefe Occafions will draw my Lord Treafurer fooner then he thought to doe ; there I will procure an Anfwer of your Lettre of Importance. As for Sir *John Fortefcue*, you gaue me no Direction to fpeak vnto him, nor Lettre for him, but willed me to let it alone, left it might hinder your Return ; only this I know, that he neuer moued your Sute fince your Departure, as *Pendant* affures me.

My Lord *Rich* is not in Town, and theirfore I know not what to fay of him ; Sir *John Wingfeld* tels me, that he delivered all your Lettres. I haue written to Mr. *Hary Sidney*, but yet cold not heare from him. Touching your Lordfhips Lettre to Mr. *Golding*, I find my Ladie greatly pleafed with your Lordfhips honorable Love and Care of her.

Fookes and I doe goe vp and down to feeke a convenient Houfe for your Lordfhip and my Lady, and doe vfe all my Frends Help in it ; as yet we can not fpeede. I wilbe carefull to know how it ftands for your Lodging promifed in *Epfom* Houfe. In my Lettres by *Waghorn*, I fignified that *Afkaing* had fent your Bookes to his Factor in *Flufhing*, to be deliuered vnto you. I cannot as yet hear of *Cuff*, your Booke he faies it is with Doctor *Gifford* in *Lewfam*. I

fpake

ſpake twice to Sir *George Carew* for your 2 Pikes, he differs it till their be a Deliuerer in that Office, which is voyd.

Forgett not, my Lord, to wright often to my Lady of *Huutingdon*, whoe of late begins againe to mourn the Death of your Brother. Sarjeant *Flemming* tels me, that it is moſt neceſſary to record the Deed of Intaile, which my Lady will haue donne at your Return, and not before.

I will goe to all your Frends, and will harken after ſuch News as happen. I am going with your Lettres to my Lord *Eſſex*, and the reſt at Court, and will now humbly take my Leaue, and euer remain

Your Lordſhips moſt obedient,

and moſt bownden Saruant,

R. Whyte.

London, this *Friday* the
19th of *September*, 1595.

Rowland Whyte, *Eſq;* to *Sir* Robert Sydney.

My Duty very humbly remembred,

YOUR Lettres ſent by Capt. *Brownes* Man were pleaſing to my Lord Treaſorer, for he allowed him v *l.* for his Pains, but comanded him to attend the Anſwers, and to carry them vnto you. Sir *Robert Cecill* diliuered me the Diſpatche, but with this Charge, that I ſhould cary it to his Father, encloſed within his Lettre, which I did this Morning, and ſownd my Lord Treaſurer at *Lambeth*, ready to goe to Court; he took all the Lettres with him, and bid me to Morrow attend his further Pleaſure. My Lord of *Eſſex*, when he had read a Lettre I gave him, he demaunded another, which I told him I had not, but the next Day, Sir *Robert Cecill* brought him it from *Tibbols*, as it ſhuld ſeem incloſed within my Lord Treaſurers Packett.

Mr. *Rays* Man left a Packett at my Lodging for me, which now I receued. I haue already ſent my Lord of *Pembroke* and my Ladies vnto them, and will goe, when I haue donne this Lettre, with my Lady *Huntingdons* vnto her, and the reſt to Morrow I will deliuer at Court. In your Lordſhips Lettre to me, you will me to goe to Sarieant *Wilbys* about the Fine, which I will doe, and haue bene carefull of, but he is not yet returned; your Coſen *Montague*, the Lawyer, hath your Lettres ſent him, and aſſone as euer he comes he will deliver it, and will him not to proceed further in it. You marvaile why you heare nothing of *Beecher*, I haue by Sarieant *Main* written at lardge of that Matter, and wold haue donne ſooner, but that *Beecher* was at the Marriage of *Stephen le Sieur* in *Hampſhire*, whoe is married to Mr. *Warders* Daughter by *Yorke* Howſe, when his other Wiffe died. My Lord *Rich* is not in Town, and his Lady is in *Staffordſhire* with her Mother: My Lords Lettres was encloſed with Lettres in a Packett, and directed vnto her, which may be the Cauſe he had it not ſoone as you did deſire.

Touching Sir *Edward Vvedals* Return, his Man Cooke by *Mainard* hath diſcouered the Likelihood of your Return. And he demanded of me, if I ſtayed about ſuch Buſines, which I denied, and that it was about the Buſines of the Town; if he doe come ouer, it will very muuch hinder yours, and your Lordſhip ſhall doe well to give few Captains Leaue to come ouer. I did follow my Lord Treaſorer dilligently about Municion; he euer anſwered, that at his Return to Court he wold mention it, and now I will not doubt, but that one Way or another I ſhall haue a Reſolution.

I was told that Sir *William Cornwalles*, doth often trouble her Majeſties Eares with Tales of my Lord of *Eſſex*, who is thought to be an Obſeruer of all his Doings, and to examine *Mudriff*, which brings Vnquietnes in the Quene, and occaſions the like in my Lord.

My Lord of *Southhampton*, doth with to much Familiarity court the faire Mrs. *Varnon*, while his Frends obſerving the Quenes Humors towards my Lord

of

of *Eſſex,* doe what they can to bring her to fauor him, but it is yet in vaine.

The Quene is nothiug moued at the Newes which I writt vnto you by the Poſt in my laſt Lettres of *Ireland,* though it is ſaid that our braueſt Comanders are hurt, and in Danger, but Sir *John Norres* and his Brother are like to doe well.

Tis aduertiſed, that in *Duncarcke* their are many great Chains of Yron made, to blocke vp Hauens.

That a *Spaniard* that wold haue kild the King, and *Antonio de Perez,* is taken and impriſoned.

Your Honours, &c.

London, 23 of Septemb.
1595.

R. Whyte.

Robert Beale, *Eſq; Clerk of the Council,* to Sir Robert Sydney.

My verye good Lorde,

BEinge vppon the Beginninge of a Iourneye, which (God willinge) I minde to make into *Warwykeſhire,* for ſome three Weekes or a Monethe, I receaued your Lordſhips Lettre of the xijth of this Preſent, ſignyfying the Receipte of my former, which I would not ſuffer vnaunſwered, allthoughe my Leyſure be at this Preſent verye ſmall. It cannot be, but that the Stayinge of the Eſtates Shippes in *Spaine,* and the late Loſſe beſides *Weſell,* will make Mr. *Bodleyes* Meſſage vnpleaſant vnto them that gouerne ; and beſides cauſe the inconſtant People to enter into ſondrie Conceiptes, if the Matter be ſo ſeuerelie vrged. And yet her Majeſties Goodnes hathe ben ſuche towardes them, as that it hathe deſerued to be more accepted of by ſuche, as will pretende to be wiſe Rulers, and haue no better Staye, then vppon the vncertaine and wandringe Impreſſions of a Populace, then hitherto they haue don. But the Common Cauſe is more to be regarded, then their Ingratitude ; and it cannot be, but if they be abandonned or alienated from vs, we ſhall neither obteyne that which we require at their Handes, nor be warranted from the Annoyance of the Common Enemye. Wherfore I thinke (all Circumſtances conſidered) that that Meſſage will not be ſo ſtrictlie followed, eſpeciallie if they will goe about to yielde vnto her Majeſtie anie reaſonable Satisfaction : Her Charge, how meane ſoeuer it be eſteemed, hath ben greate in thoſe Partes, and ſuche as no other Prince would haue yielded vnto them. Therfore it behouethe them, bothe thankfullye to acknowledge it, and ſeeke by all good Meanes to continewe it. I am of the ſame Opinion that your Lordſhip is of, that the Makinge of a newe Treatie would carrye ſome Difficultie and Inconuenience with it, as the Time now is : But yet if ſome of them, that were Commiſſioners in the Making of the former Treatye, be nowe ſent ouer, to explane ſuch Pointes, as maye ſeeme doubtfull, and geue Occacion of Correction hereafter. I ſuppoſe, that the Colledge of Eſtates hathe ſufficient Power to deale in ſuche a Cauſe, without anie further newe Authoritie from the particular Prouinces : And ſo her Majeſtie might, by receauinge from them ſome better Satisfaction and Aſſurance, be moued to forbeare the Proſecution of Mr. *Bodleyes* Demaundes, and lykewiſe continewe towards them her accuſtomed Succour. And if they refuſe to doe ſo ſmall a Matter, they will ſhewe them ſelues to waywarde, and not to care either for their owne Preſeruacion, or for their Frendes. The Enterpriſes and Preparacions, which the Kinge of *Spayne* makethe in thoſe Prouinces, *France, Spayne,* and *Britayne,* ſhewe his Reſolucions to goe throughe with the Matter, that he hathe taken in Hande, and is lyk to atchieue, if ſuche againſt whome his Miſchiefe is intended, ſhall not ſeeke by all Meanes to reſiſt and annoye him, as he purpoſethe to hurte others. Suerlye our Irreſolutenes and Careleſſenes at Home, and the lytle Eſtimacion that is made of vs Abroade, makethe me feare, that beinge abandoned of

other,

other, and left to our felues, we fhall receaue fome Blowe, if the Lorde doe not prouide for vs otherwife then we haue deferued : Howbeit he will not be allwayes tempted, but at lengthe punifhe the Ingratitude of fuche, as hitherto haue receaued fo greate Benefittes at his Handes, and are fo lytle thankfull for the fame. I feare the Matter of *Irelande*, fett on and mainteyned by the Subornacion of *Spayne*, will proue greater then it was at the firft thought of. You fhall heare from others of a late Bickeringe there, wherin Sir *John Norryes* is faid to be hurte ; and allthough it was geuen out not longe fythe, that the Erle of *Tiron* was come in, and all Thinges compounded ; yet by Lettres out of *Irelande* it femethe, that no fuche Thinge was meant, nor lykely, but rather Apparaunce of further Hoftilitie and Charge ; which will fo occupye vs here, as that our Neighbors cannot looke for any greate Supplie or Ayde from hence. And if heruppon *France* yields to a Peace, and anye Alteracion happen in the *Lowe Countreyes*, we fhall hardlie be able to beare the Burthen of the greate Tempeft, that is lyke to fall vppon thefe Partes. It behouethe vs therfore to praye vnto the Lorde, and to amende our Liues, if happelie he will heare vs, and ouerthrow *Sennacharib*, that threateneth fo greate a Mifchiefe to his Churches and People euerye where.

I heare that of late a verye vile Booke hathe ben printed in *Englifhe*, in *Antwerp*, touchinge the Succeffion of this Crowne, diffaminge her Majeftie, and difhablinge all the Tytles of fuche, that herafter maye pretende anye Intereft therunto, and deriuinge a ftrange Pretence from *John of Gaunt*, Duke of *Lancafter*, vppon the Kinge of *Spaine*, which he mindethe fhortlye to challenge : I truft the Lorde will neuer fuffer him to preuayle in fo wicked and vniuft a Caufe. If you could procure me anye one of the faid Bookes, I fhould thinke my felfe much beholdinge vnto yow, for I would gladlie fee, vppon what Grounde he eftablifhethe fo vnlaufull a Surmife : I heare alfo, that it is dedicated to the Erle of *Effex*, of an Intent furlie to bringe him in Ialoufye and Difgrace here. And fo hauinge nothing els to trouble yow with at this Prefent, I committ you to the Lorde, whome I humblie befeeche to receaue bothe vs here, and yow there, with all fuche as feare him, into his mercifull and almightie Protection. From my Houfe at *Barnes*, in Haft, the xxvth of *September*, 1595.

Your Lordfhips affuredly at Commaundement,

Robt. Beale.

Sir Thomas Wylkes *to Sir* Robert Sydney.

My Lord Govuernor,

I Haue of late receiued from yow two Lettres, the one written here before your Departure, and thother at *Flufhing* : By the firft yow defire to be made acquainted with fuch Orders as might paffe here concerning your Garrifon ; fithence which Tyme there hath ben fomething don, to reforme a notable Diforder difcouered by *Birchenfhawe*, and fome others, faid to be practifed chiefly by the Captaines of your Garrifon. I doubte not out yow haue ben made acquainted with that Order by Mr. *Thomkins* the Commiffarie, which happely yow will miflike, bicaufe it is ordayned, that no Man may paffe from hence for the Supplie of your Companies, but with my Priuetie and Certificate, which maye be an Impediment to fuch as fhall take vp Men in *Effex*, *Kent*, and other Places remote from *London*. Which Difficultie was had in Confideracion, and verbally ordered, that in that Cafe, Teftimonial from two Juftices of the Peace, fignifying the Perfons taken vp, their Names, and other Accidents, and for what Companies, fhould warrante me for my Certificate, to be given for their Admiffion. I was gladd to obtaine this Qualification, for reforming the Diforder, otherwife I doe affure yow, vpon my Creditt, the former Order fo bene-

ficially

ficially fett downe, for the Captaines, had ben abfolutely revoked ; and fithence the Paffinge hereof I haue receaved expreffe Commandement from her Majeftie, by the Mouth of Sir *John Fortefcue,* that no Supplyes be fuffred to paffe ouer, nor I giue Certificate for their Admiffion, without her Priuety and Allowance. So as yow will hereafter find it a Thing very difficulte to haue any Supplyes at all, which growing out of the Diforders of your Captaines, doth make them Aucthors of their owne Harmes.

Your fecond Lettre concerning Mr. *Thomkins,* I haue well confidered, and wilbe ready to doe any Thing to procure him his whole Entertainement, althoughe I cannot deuife howe old *Higham* will liue, if that Portion be taken from him.

We haue ben lately aduertifed out of *Ireland,* of a Conflicte between Sir *John Norreys,* going to victuell the Forte by *Blackewater,* and the Troupes of the Earle of *Tyrone* : Yt happened, after the Place victualled, on the Retourne of Sir *John Norreys,* towards the *Newrye,* wherein he was affayled by 500 Horfe and 2000 Foote of the Ennemy, Sir *John* having only one thoufand Foote and 120 Horfe. In this Rencounter Sir *John Norreys* was hurte with two Mufkett Shotte, the one throughe the left Arme, and th'other athwarte the Belly, but neither of them daungerous : Sir *Thomas Norreys* receaued a Mufket Shott through one of his Thighes, and diuers Captaines and Officers were hurte in that Fighte, which fheweth the fame to haue ben warmely attempted : Fewe of ours were flaine, but iiij C of Thenemy left dead in the Field.

This notwithftanding, we haue here an Expectacion of the Earl of *Tirones* Coming in vpon Pardon for himfelf, *Odonell,* and *Macguire* ; and to that End Aucthoritie is giuen to the Lord Deputie.

This is all worthie of your Knowledge, that I can write at this Tyme : Yow knowe I am yours, and wilbe ever ready to doe yow Service, and with this Conclufion I will here end, and commytt yow to the Protection of Almightie God. From *London,* the xxvijth of *September,* 1595.

Yours affured to be commanded,

Tho. Wylkes.

George Gilpin, *Efq; to* Sir Robert Sidney.

May it pleafe your good Lordfhip,

THE Commoditie of this prefent Bearer, was Occafion of the wrytinge of thefe few Lynes, onely to fend thenclofed Copie of an intercepted Lettre, which we got this Sommer, and is Thopinion of *Yuerra* vnto *Fuentes,* vppon the Negotiation of *Leifvelt* in *Zeland,* with his Excellencie, about the Motion of Peace ; wherein appears the vnlykelyhood of any good to be donne with the *Spaniards* : Ere longe, I will fend your Lordfhip a Copie of the laft State of Warre, conteyninge the Number of Men in Service, the Charge they amount vnto, with certain Particularities that may be, and is, very appearaunt ; that this Winter another wilbe made, being many Things chaunged fince the laft. My Lord Ambaffador continueth at one Stay. The Counfell of State is thought wilbe here this Weeke, and then will a Refolution be taken, which, methinks, the Loffe of *Cambray* will forwarde, fearing that the Kings Abolition with the Pope looketh furder ; and that yt will behoeue her Majeftie and them here, to ftick harde together. The Camp ftil continueth ; a Bridge there is ouer the *Rhyn,* where our Horfemen goo a Fouraginge. *Mondragan* never ftirreth ; but fom of his Men fayled of late to furpryfe *Duffeldorp,* and yf he can, he wil poffeffe one Place or other in *Cleueland,* to farve for his bet-

i   ter

ter Warrant, if euer he fhould chaunce to com agayne another Tyme in thofe Quarters. From the *Haughe*, this 1 *Oct.* 1595.

Your good Lordfhips, &c.

Geo. Gilpin.

Sir Thomas Lake *to Sir* Robert Sydney.

S I R,

I Will not ufe manie Wordes of Reciprocation to your kinde Offer in your Lettres. My Compoficion is not of Wordes. I hope you fhall fynde e-hough by other Proofe, what Value I make of your Favour and Love. If I fhould write much to you of the Condition of our Affairs here, I fhould but repeat what already I have lett you know ; for anie Thing that hath happened fince then, either here or beyond Sea, doth but confirme that which I fignified to you by my laft. I doubt not, but the Particularityes of fuch Things as haue happened of late in *Ireland*, have been written to you by fo manie Frendes as you have here. By that you may perceave, that our Enemies there are of another Proofe then we expected. Judge you whether either Syde have Caufe to boaft of Wynning, when twice they have fought with our Armye, and departed without Hurt. At this laft Encounter, our Generall, and all the Commanders in the Field hurt ; and howfoever Things be fomewhat favourably reported to the Advantage of our Generall, I can affure you, he was never better put to the Tryal of his Courage and Skill. Two Armyes of ours, within three Months Space, broken up and difperfed into Garrifon, without eyer Entring into his Country, or Slaughter of 100 of his Men. There is a Report come, that *Tirlagh Dermagh* being dead, the K. hath taken upon him the Title of *Oneale*, whereby you may gheffe how farre he is from O-bedience.

From *Florence*, we know now for certain, by Lettres Yefterday brought, that *Du Mane* is reconciled. The King to be abfolved at *Rome* on his Demand thereof. In which Purpofe, fome honorable Perfons are to go thither prefent-ly. And as its advertifed alfo, that imediately upon his Abfolution, the Pope is mynded to fend Legats unto both thofe great Princes for a Peace. Of whom here is fome Doubte juftely to be conceaved, that the Plotte is privately agreed on already. Among other Conjectures, one is, what the *French* King paed *Alonfo d'Idiarges*, amountes to 50000 Crownes, who prefently went into *Spaine*, fpeaking firft with the Dukes of *Lorraine*, and *Mane*. *St. Luc*, and the States of *Bretagne*, have fent hither to demand Aid, for preventing the Mifcheafe of the *Spaniards* Troops there, writing a very lamentable Lettre. In which, among other Thinges, they mention, that befides the Forts of *Beaval* and *Frouldaly*, Don *John d'Aquilar*, is now planted with all his Force upon the River of *Radon*, and buildeth on each Syde the Mouth of it a ftrong Fort. Befides that, one *Fontenelles*, a Gentleman of the Cuntrey, hath paffed to their Ufe an Ifle in *Bafe Bretagne*, which he doth fortefy in Sort, as if he may continew but two Monthes, to joyne Art, to that which already is by Nature ; it will be, as they fay, one of the moft inpregnable Places of *Fraunce :* So that, in Effect, they are Mafters of the Coafte.

For the Matter of *Scotland.* It is very true, that fuch a Worke hath been in Hand there, to get the young Prince out of the Cuftody of *Marre* ; of which the Heads were the Queen, and the Chauncellor. The King hath very refolutely expreffed himfelf againft it hitherto, knowing that his own Lyfe wold thereby reft at Difcreation. And it is thought he hath broken the Plott. But heare, for certain, that moft of thofe that were Supporters of the Devife, were of the Devotion of *Spain*, and the Chauncellor himfelfe. The Kings Dif-pleafure hath fhewed it felfe fo great againft him, as he hath abfented himfelfe from Court, and of late hath been fick, and fome Speech that he is dead ; which,

†

which, if it be true, that Pofte is at an End. The fame Parties that fhould have been the Doers in that Attempt, are all our Borderers; as *Hume*, and *Cesford*, &c. who have committed and doe dayly great Spoyles upon our People, without Redreffe.

Concerning your felfe, I can fay nothing; and Things reft here as they did, without Likelyhood yet of Change. My Lord of *Rutland* hath Leave to Travayle, and departed within ten Days; his firft Vifit fhalbe to you. My Lord of *Suffex* is returned, but we cannot hear by what Occafion. I leave further to Trouble you. From *Nonfuch*, the firft of *October*, 1595.

Your Lordfhips to command,

Tho. Lake.

Rowland Whyte, *Efq;* to Sir Robert Sydney.

Right honorable,

I Receued at this Inftant a great Pacquet from you, dated 29 *September*, by the *Dutch* Poft; I haue already deliuered my Lord Treaforer his, and fent my Lord of *Effex* his Lettre, the reft I will deliuer at more Leifure. You are to receue from me yet, a Pacquett from Sir *Robert Cecill*, and my Lord *Effex*.

The Skins for the young Prince wilbe ready within 7 Dayes, and I will befpeake the filke Stokings. At my Lord Treafurers next going to the Court, I will follow hym, both for Municion, and to fee what he will fay for your Leaue; if he will giue that Liffe, I will then acquaint my Lord of *Effex*, my Lord Admirall, and the reft of your Honors Frends; but I doubt yt is yet fomewhat to foone. I am exceedingly troubled that your Lordfhips Buifnes concerning her Majefties Service, hath, by my Solliciting, no fpeedier End. How I fhall fpeed for your Leaue, God knows; but that drawen to a Refolution, I will very humbly requeft to be recalled; and neuer will I, with my Will, come hither again, to fpend your Lordfhips Allowance to fo fmall Purpofe; but this Comfort I haue, that your Lordfhip knowes the Court.

My Lord Treaforer is come to Town; becaufe the Terme begins to Morrow, he tooke Phifick this Day, which doth not worke, and difquiets hym.

Serieant *Williams* is come, and doth affure me, that he will never deale further in the Matter of the Fyne, to *Buck*, till he haue Warrant from you, vnder your Hand and Seale. Thus much hath he promifed in the Prefence of your Cofen *Montague* the Lawier.

Great a doe there is about the Deed of Intaile you haue. My Lord of *Pembroke* thinks that yt will come to his Children: But I am of another Belieffe, and trufte in God your Name fhall live many hundred Years, to enioy the Benefitt that may come of yt. His Lordfhips Lettre vnto you, is only concerning the Deed, and Ufes. I heare no mention at all of your Office in *Wales*, which he hath difpofed of. *Maffinger* continues not with hym long. *Sanford* is come vp to follow his Cawfes, and my Lord hymfelf, with my Lord *Harbart*, come vp to fee the Queen, and (as I heare) to deale in the Matter of a Marriage with Sir *George Careys* Daughter.

Maffinger is threatened, although he did not but what he was commanded, to let you haue yt, when by you twas defired. Now my Lord fayes, that *Maffinger* fhould haue gon with the Deed at all Tymes your Lordfhip had Occafion to ufe yt. Yt concerns your Lordfhip to be very well aduifed, er you part with yt. Yt inftantly appertaining more to you and yours, then to all the World befides.

I did wryte in fome of my Lettres, how carefull I was for a Houfe in *London* for your Lordfhip, and that at laft, Alderman *Catcher* was contented to let you haue his for a Rent. I expect hourely to heare my Ladys Refolution of hauing yt, or not hauing yt. Tis 50 *l.* for half a Yeare Rent; but tis furnifht of all Things neceffary, faue Bedding.

My Lord *Rich* is not yet come to Town: I haue left a Lettre for hym at *Effex* Houfe.

Yf yt wold pleafe your Lordfhip to haue a View taken of all her Majefties Municion, and to certify in what State you fynd yt, feruiceable or vnferuiceable, yt wold further your Buifnes here.

When my Lord Treaforer mentioned, why the Companies in *Flufhing* were not fupplied of Powder by the States, as well as in *Brill*, I anfwered, that yt was an Error *ab initio*, for no Gouernor had yt ; and now I thought yt wold be hardly granted or obtained.

There is no Speach of the Queens Remoue. I haue bene once more at *Heigat* ; but can neither come to my Ladys Speach [Countefs of *Huntingdon*] nor haue any Anfwer of your Lordfhips Lettres. They fay her Ladyfhip is ftill Sorrowing your Brothers vntimely Death.

I humbly take my Leave ; and will pray to God to blefs all your Vertuos Actions. From *London*, this *Wednefday* Night, 8 of *October*, 1595.

Your Lordfhipsmoft bounden and obedient Seruant,

R. Whyte.

Sir Thomas Lake *to Sir* Robert Sydney.

S I R,

ALthough within thefe few Dayes I writte to you, which were more then my Covenant, yet I thought to lett you have this more of Supereroga-tion, becaufe it conteyneth Matter that concerneth you. Sir *Roger Williams* is of late returned, and with him one *Lomeney*, a Secretary of the Kings Chamber ; who both by the Kings Lettres, and by his own Speech, have dealt fo plainely and roundely with the Queen and our Councell, as hath moved here great Offence. The Subftance is, to let the Queen underftand, that he hath his Abfolution, that there are deputed to him four Cardinals, to give him the Solemnity thereof; but their chief Errant to draw him to a Peace with *Spaine*, and unite againft all that are divided from the Church. That he is affured to receive for himfelfe honourable Conditions ; but knowing that he fhalbe fought to be divided from the Queen and the *Low Countreys*, defireth by her to be enabled by a common Concurrency of both their Forces, that he be not compelled to fuch a Peace, as willingly he wold not make, but fuch as may comprehend them all in fuch Termes, as holding always together, they might be a Ballance againft the *Spanifh* Greatnefs. That yf fhe refufe him in it, he muft provide for himfelfe as he may. Thes Lettres delivired with very ftout Speeches, hath greatly offended the Queen, who loveth not to be terrefyed. The Gentleman is difpatched without anie Hope of obtaining Relief from hence. So as you may ghefse what will follow. He hath withall advertifed her Majefty by his Lettres to this Effect, That if fhe be not well informed of the Preparations and Intentions againft her, fhe is then abufed or betrayed. Which being by fome taken as meant to themfelves, hath moved the more Coller. He defired a Conference to be had between the Duke of *Nevers*, and *Bovillon*, whom he would fend to *Calais*, or *Bolyon*, and fome of the Queens Councell ; which is denyed. But that which I wold let you know, is, That he hath written very roundly, to require the Queen to forbear the Calling for her Money from the States, as a Thinge farr out of Seafon. And hath fpoken plainely to Sir *Roger Williams*, that thefe Cuntryes love not the Queen. And that he doth affure himfelfe, that whenfoever he fhall enter into Treaty with *Spaine*, he can difpofe of them, as he fhall thinke good, and that they will turne his Corfe. And that of late they have required him not to forget them. Whether this may be well grounded, or fpoken onely of Boaft, you may ghefse. And, I thinke, will not be amifse for you to have an Eye unto. For if all be true that hath been here alleaged by the *French* Gent, uppon his Returne, the King is like to frame his Drift another Way. The King hath alfo advertifed, and fhewed Sir *Roger Williams* fome Lettres to make it good, that the whole Navy of *England* is returned from all Places where they were Abroad (the *Indian* Fleet

Fleet being fafe come Home, and affembled at *Lisbone*, to the Number of viii Score Sayle). And that it will not be long, eyre they be in *Bretagne*, and from thence difpatch fome Part into *Ireland* ; wherewith fome other Advertifement of ours doe concurre. I have nothing els to trouble you with, but to kifs your Handes. From *Stepney*, this ixth of *October*, 1595.

Yours to command,

Tho. Lake.

Rowland Whyte, *Efq; to Sir* Robert Sydney.

Right Honorable,

MY Lady *Borrow* hauing, as I wryt vnto your Lordfhip, an abfolut Denial for his Return, hath fent his Man *Mynne* to giue Notice vnto my Lord of *Effex*, that his Sicknes is growen to a Confumtion, and he is fallen fo weake, that he cannot recouer, but with the Change of Aire, which he hopes the Queen wilbe fo carefull of, as to fend for hym, he not daring to defire a Thing that is not pleafing to her Majeftie.

Burchinfhaw had 100 Crownes giuen hym by the Queens Comandment, and, as I heare, is cowntenanced by Mr. *Brooke.* My Lady of *Effex*, and Lady *Walfingham*, are come to the Town, and doe hope to fee you here, although my Lord of *Effex* told them he faw litle Hope of yt. my Lady *Walfingham* hath deliuered vnto me old *Languets* Picture, which fhe promifed you. I will fend yt to *Penfhurft.*

My Lord of *Pembrookes* Comming is put of, vpon a Speach of my Lord Treaforers at Cownfell Bord. That confidering the dangerous Tyme, it were good her Majeftie fent my Lord of *Pembroke* to ly about *Milford Hauen*, for half a Yeare, to ftrengthen thofe Parts with his Prefence. At his Comming, I heare the Queen meanes to deale with his Lordfhip in yt. Here is a Speach that *Tiron*, vpon the Sight of her Majefties Pardon, fent for hym, and all that entered into Thaction with hym, is come in ; but this is much doubted by Men of Judgment.

Mr. Vice Chamberlain is ficke, fo is my Lord Chamberlain, both of the Goute.

My Lord of *Effex* promifes to write fomewhat, that he wold haue fent carefully and fafely. I doe attend it. Court 18 of *October*, 1595.

Yours, &c.

R. Whyte.

My Lord Treaforer is at *London*, and not looked for at Court till the Queen come to *Richmond.* I will then ofte fhew my felf vnto hym, and let hym know, I doe only attend the Tyme his Honor fhall thinke fitt to moue her Majeftie for your Return. Thefe *Spanifh* Preparations, I affure your Lordfhip, doth breed incredible Feares in the Mynds of moft Men.

Geo. Gilpin, *Efq; to Sir* Robert Sydney.

My very good Lorde,

AT Length, and with much adoe, the States haue taken a kinde of Refolution ; not to fend (as was purpofed, and had bin the beft for boath Sydes) but to wryte to her Majeftie, excufing their Delay in makinge an Anfwere ; and withall, by other Lettres at large, to fett downe to my Lords of the Counfell, their Impoffibilitie to yelde to that defyred, and what Inconveniences they fynd and feare, in mouing the Matter to the Prouinces ; the Difpatch is made, the Poft departed ; and my Lord Ambaffador hath written his Opinion ; and my felfe, to fome pryuate Friends, haue deliuered my Feelinge. What wee fhall now receaue from Home, I longe to fee, a fayre Opportunitie beinge ouer flipped : Wee do now reft owr felues a Whyle, and yf there were Poft Horfes

† betweene

betweene this and *Flushinge*, your Lordship should, ere this, haue seene me ; and now, I hope, ere longe, to see youe here with my Lord of *Rutland :* His Excellency wee expecte this Weeke ; and of the Gettinge of the House of *Weerdt*, and other lyke, I leave to Captain *Morgans* Report. From the *Haughe*, this 22th *October*, 1595.

Your good Lordships, &c.

Geo. Gilpin.

Rowland White, *Esq*; *to Sir* Robert Sydney.

MY Lord of *Hertford* was sent for by a Messinger, is come vp, and co- mytted to his own Howse. The Cawse sayd to be a Record secretly put into the Court of Th'arches, to prove his first Marriage lawfull, and his Chil- dren Legitimate. Yt was discouered by a Case found amongest Doctor *Aw- bries* Papers, by hym studied, with Thopinion of Strangers. Tis sayd he is one of the wealthiest Subiects of *England*.

My Lord *Shrosbery* is like to fall into new Trouble about the old Matters, for *Wood* is called in Question to the *Star Chamber*, vpon better Proofes of his former Doinges.

Probi is comanded to wayt at Court ; hath spoken with her Majestie, and is sayd he shall haue the Disbursing of the Treasory of the Chamber, till her Majestie be pleased to bestow yt. Sir *H. Umpton*, and Mr. *John Stanhope*, stands for yt.

Here haue bene 6 Borderers of *Cumberland*, in the Name of the Prouinces frontring on *Scotland* ; they complaine of great Incursions and Spoiles donne vnto them at plaine Noone Dayes by the *Scots*. They haue Order for 100 Horse or Foote to recouer their own, becaufe the King doth not punish Th- offenders, nor reforme their Proceedings, although desired by her Majestie vnto yt.

My Lord of *Pembroke* is a great Further and Persuader to fortifie *Milford Hauen* ; the Charges are thought intollerable : There is Care giuen vnto yt, and in the meane Tyme, Sir *Tho. Morgan* is dispatcht to lie in *Pembroke* Cas- tell, and 500*l.* wilbe allowed to fortifie and Repair yt ; he shall haue a Gar- rison for that Place. Their are 3 and 4 Deputie Liftenants apointed in all Shires, and we now credibly belieue the *Spaniards* prepare against us.

Beare of *Grauesend* was with me here. I shewed vnto hym, and the Search- ers of that Town, your Lordships Letters Patents. They say, that if your Lordship will haue any Thing transported from *Grauesend*, they will shew their lawfull Fauor, if yt please you to autorise *Beare*, vnder your Hand and Seale, to send you over what you want. Your Lordship, in my Opinion, shall doe well not to allow *Beare* a general Warrant, but when you wold haue any Thing transported, to signe and seale those Parcels you require, and soe euery Tyme that you want to do yt, for there is left Abuse in yt. From *Catchers* House, this 29 of *October*, at 10 a Clock in the Night.

Yours, &c.

R. White.

Rowland Whyte, *Esq*; *to Sir* Robert Sydney.

My Lord,

I Haue had much adoe about the transporting of 5 Ton of Beere to your Lordship ; the Searchers made Stay of it vntill a Warrant might be pro- cured from my Lord Treasurer, which I obtained at last, upon this Condicion mentioned in the Letter, that I should enter into Bond to return your Lordships Certificat to the Custom-house, that you have receued yt for your own Vse. I brought your Lordships Lettres Patents to the Officers in the Custornes ;

they

they promise your Lordship all Fauor they can, if they can fynd any Words to keepe them from Blame. My Lord Treasurer hath sent a generall Reftraint that no Beer or Corn shalbe transported.

I haue received your Lordships Letter sent by Mr. *Finch*, and yours of the 26 of *October*. All your Lettres to my Lord *Harry*, to Mr. *Standen*, to Mr. *Locke*, are deliuered ; and my Lord of *Essex* burnt your Lettre I gaue him, and promises to wryte.

For your Letter sent by *William* to my Lord Treasurer, I made mention in my Laft of the 29 *October*, that yt was argued before the Queen by the Lords of the Council, and since that Tyme my Lord of *Essex* tells me, that the Queen was pleafed your Wants fhuld be furnifht ; fo saith my Lord Treaforer to, but he wills me to beare with him for 2 or 3 Days ; but I perceiue by Mr. *Mainards* Speeches, yt will not be in as lardge a Manner as the Queen com-manded yt.

Touching your Leave ; tis advifed by your Frends at Court to put yt of till the Queens comming to *London* 12 Dayes hence, and then yt shalbe moued to better Purpole than now. The Queen herfelf, and the Lords of her Cown-fell, being exceedingly bufyed in giving Directions for all Things fitt to hynder an Invafion. The Matters of *Ireland* are troublefome ; and the Rebells ftands vpon more high Termes than with Honor can be granted ; but the Daunger of the Tyme may yeld vnto much.

My Lord *Boroughs* Leave is ftill denied ; but I vnderftand his Lady fhuld say, that he is refolued to come ouer without Leaue for to recouer his Health.

For my Lady *Huntingdon*, your Lordship now fhall heare fhortly from her, and Mr. *Bromley* tels me, fhe takes very kindly your Letters, and often fending to know howhe doth. I heare that Sir *Pofthumus Hoby* hath had Accefs to your Sifter *Sydney*, and likes her fo well, that he means to return out of Hand. I heare fhe fhold say, that fhe is in Subftance much worfe than when fhe knew your Brother.

My Lord of *Pembroke* is here ftill, talking of the Deed of Intaile.

London, 3 *November,* 1595.

> Your Lordships, &c.
>
> R. Whyte.

I fend your Lordship the 4 Bookes of the Civil War imprinted ; and a *French* Difcours.

Rowland Whyte, *Efq; to* Sir Robert Sydney.

My Lord,

VPON *Monday* laft, 1500 [Queen *Eliz.*] fhewed 1000 [Earl of *Essex*] a printed Book of *t—t*, Title to *a—a* : In yt their is, as I here, daun-gerous Praifes of 1000 of his Valour and Worthines, which doth hym harme here. At his comming from Court he was obferued to looke wan and pale, being exceedinglie troubled at this great Piece of Villanie donne vnto hym ; he is Sick, and continewes very ill. 1500 vifited hym Yefterday in Thafternoone. He is mightelie croffed in all Things ; for *Bacon* is gone without the Place of Sollicitor ; and as yet *Flemings* Bill figned ys at a Stay, but fhall un-doubtedly paffe ; 24, ys gonne to the Country ; but his Frends are many and great, and, as I heare, haue foe preuailed, that he fhalbe fent for again. The Chauncelorfhip of the Dutchie ys committed to eight Commiffioners. Iudg *Owen*, *Clinch*, *Beaumont*, *Bragrave*, Thatturney, Sir *Philip Butler*, *Wrener*, and the 2 Auditors ; and the Queen herfelf keepes the Seale, and my Lord Treaforer, as Occafion ferues, doth Seale and Difpatch all the Bufines : *Peter Proby* hath a Chamber in her Court, with Thallowaunce of 3 Difhes of Meat, and paies the

Money

Money till a Treaforer of the Chamber be chofen, which will not be in. haft. Many late Occafions is like to breed a deadly Vnkindens betwen 1000 [*Effex*] and 900. 6000 is in the Cuftodie of 700. The World iudging his heaping of Wealth, and Amors, to be to no good End; his Trouble may be pleafing to fome of our Neighbours. Their is a Refolution taken for all Things, if any Invafion be attempted, as well for our Forces by Land as the Fleet. Out of *Yreland* tis aduertifed, that Sir *Richard Bingham* went to fuccor a Caftell diftreffed, of which fome Rebels in *Conaught* hauing Intelligence, met him in his Iorney, and fought with hym; the Ennemy loft 80, and he but 20; yet the Place ys not deliuered. My Lord Treaforer, as I wrytt to your Lordfhip fome 4 Days paft, defired me to forbear him for 4 or 5 Dayes; but now he ys come to *London*, and lies in Bed fo ill of the Gowte in his Hands, Armes, Knees and Toes, that his Paines make hym pitifully grone. Your Lord-fhips fees, by this Accident, that the Difpatch of my Buifines, though by her Majeftie determined, is like to haue no End till his Recovery. I haue bene here long about thofe 2 Points, of your Wants and Leaue; and, I proteft before God, haue bene very carefull and diligent in them, and therefore yt greves me to fee thefe Delaies not to be remedied but with Patience. I humbly befeech your Lordfhip, in your own Wifdom, to confider the Tyme and the Perfon I attend here, and the Nature of his Place. For your Wants, he promifed a Difpatch before he fell fick; but now their ys no Body that muft trouble hym for any Thing. For your Leaue, I was aduifed by fome of your Frends not to haue yt moued till the Queen commes.

I haue bene foe often with my Lady of *Huntingdon*, that now I am affured fhe takes yt very kindly you care fo much to heare of her Health; for I am comanded to attend a Letter fhe will wryte vnto you.

My Lady of *Bedford* is in Town, and fayd to be with Child. My Lady of *Effex* is not.

At Court, this 5th of *November*, 1595, late.

Your Lordfhips, &c.

R. Whyte

Vpon *Monday* Night the Court Gates were fhutt, my Lord Chamberlain had the Keyes, and *Brown* the Controller carried a Torch; I doe not yet know what the Story might be.

The Book I fpake of is dedicated to my Lord *Effex*, and printed beyond Sea, and tis thought to be Treafon to haue it. To wryte of thefe Things are dangerous in fo perillous a Tyme; but I hope yt wilbe no Offence to impart vnto you Thactions of this Place.

† Sir Edm. Vvedale *to* Sir Robert Sydney.

My good Lord,

I Haue not bene at the Corte this fortene Dayes and more, and ther for I refer the Reporte of the Accountes of that Place to Mr. *White*; he is there often folloinge harde to haue you furnifhed of thofe Wantes of Powder, &c. you defier, and hath good Hope to obtayn it; but my Lord Treafurer being now ficke of the Gowte, is fome ftaye therof.

The Lord of *Harforde* was Yefterdaye carried to the *Tower*, and two of the *Stanopes*, and dyvars other commetted about that Matter.

Sir *Harrebotle* is commetted to the Fleate for fome Matter that hath paft be-twene my Lord of *Pembroocke* and him, and fined 1500 *l.*

I haue not refeaued any Letter from your Lordfhip fines my commeng over, when I do, whatfoeuer hit fhal pleafe you therin to commaund, I

---

† This Sir *Edm. Vevedale* was Lieutenant Governor of *Flufhing*, and very much diftinguifht him-felf in the Wars of the *Low Countries*.

wilbe carfull to performe; and, in the mean Time, I leaue you to the Protec-
fion of the Aulmighti. *Fleetftreet*, the 7th of *November*, 1595.

Your Lordfhips in all Servis,

Edm. Vvedall.

This Booke, which I fend you herwith inclofed, is latli fet forth, and is
peruyfed and difprayfed by mane.

Rowland Whyte, *Efq*; *to Sir* Robert Sydney.

My Lord,

YOU are to receue from me Lettres, from Mr. *Grivel* and Sir *John Wingfeld*,
of the 5 of *Nouember*. This I fend by Mr. *Mufby*, who is difpatched
to Mr. *Bodeley*. My Lord of *Effex*, as I wryt vnto you in my laft, was infinitly troubled with a printed Booke the Queen fhewed hym; but fince he is
prepared to endure the Malice of his Ennemies; yet doth he keepe his Chamber. My Lord of *Hartford* is comytted to the *Tower*, and, as I heare, 2 *Stan-
hops* with hym, but not the Courtiers; Sir *Hen. Barkley* is comytted to the *Fleet*,
and fined in 100 *l.* for the Riott againft my Lord of *Pembroke*; fo are nine of
his Men, and fined in 100 *l.* a piece. The Matter was hard at *Starr Chamber*
vpon *Wednefday*.

My Lord Treaforer is fick a Bed, and my Buifnes lies dead till his Recouery. I hope within 4 or 5 Dayes we fhall have accefs vnto hym, for now
few come neare hym. Capten *Sauvage* promifes me to haue his Father in Law
moue Sir *John Fortefcue* about your Cheques, as theafier to be compaffed at this
Tyme; when by her Majefties Lettre you had Leave to come ouer to recouer
your Health, and after were fent to *France*, a Iorney full of Charge, and
never receved Recompence. My Lady of *Northumberland* is now knowen to
be with Child.

My Lady of *Huntingdon* is gon to take the Ayre of *Heigate*, but very pri-
uatly, leauing the beft Part of her Family at *Sauoy*, and within 4 Daies to return.
My Lady *Lefter*, and Lady *Rich*, are Yefternight come to *London*, and my Lord
Riche will wryte vnto you about his Hangings; I fynd by hym, that if thofe
Hangings that are made doe not anfwer the Note he fent vnto *Bloq*, they will
not ferue their Turn. But by his own Letter you fhall heare more. Here is a
Rumor that their are *Spanifh* Forces landed in *Brittagnie*, and that Part of
his Nauy is come to *Groine*. That the King of *Fraunce* calles a Parlement at
Amiens. And here is a Speach of a Parlement about *Candlemas*. Sir *Antony Sherley*
goes forward on his Voiadge very well furnifht, lead by the ftraung Fortune
of his Marriage, to vndertake any Cowrfe that may occupy his Mynd, from
thincking on her vaineft Words. I humbly take my Leaue. At *London*, this
Friday Night, 7 of *Nouember*, 1595.

Your Lordfhips, &c.

R. Whyte.

Rowland Whyte, *Efq*; *to Sir* Robert Sydney.

My Duty very humbly remembred,

YEfterday in Thafter Noone I was at my Lord Treaforers, who ftill lies a
Bed. Mr. *Mainard* did me the fauor to let his Lordfhip know I was
theire; who returnod me this Anfwer: That he wold fend for *Windibanck*, and
giue hym Directions what the Queens Pleafure is touching the Wants of *Flufhing*. I will carefvlly attend *Windibanck*, becaufe I will know what Quantities are
fett down; that I may aduertize you accordingly. For your Leaue, my Lady

is

is fo carefull in yt, that I am daily fent to my Lord Admirall, and my Lady *War-wicke* about yt. They Promife at the Queens comming hither, which wilbe this Weeke, to haue yt moued, when my Lord Treafurer is with her, who ftill continewes willing to procure yt for 2 or 3 Moneths, yt fo much and foe nearly concerning your Lordfhip. This Day yt appeares, that Mrs. *Mary* hath the Mefels, but, God be thancked, fhe is nothing Sicke withall; the feare we haue here is of my Lady herfelf, who is apt in this State fhe now is, to take them: Yet will fhe not by any Perfuafion be moued to keape from her, and with much ado brought to lie from her. The Child her felf humbly be-feaching my Lady to haue a Care of her own Health, as fhe loued her. Mr. *William* is very well, and forbears not to come to his Sifter; for, he faies, his Turn wilbe next. I wryt vnto you, that my Lord of *Hartford* was comytted to the *Tower*; fince then yt is giuen out, that by Comandment his Sonne fhall no more be called Lord *Beawchamp*, but *Seimor*, and that he is fent for. And yt is credibly fayd, that my Lady *Hartford* is become ftarck Madde. The Doctor *Stanhop*, and *Stanhope* the Lawier, of *Graies Inn*, that were comytted about that Matter, as being acquainted with Thappeale, with divers others, are put at Liberty, and, for a Day or two, Mr. *Michael Stanhope* came not to the Court. Yt is mut-tred here, that 200 had fome inckling in thefe Cawfes, which doe trouble 900. My Lord of *Effex* hath put off the Melancholy he fell vnto, by a printed Booke deliuered to the Queen; wherin the Harme was meant hym, by her Ma-jefties gracious Fauor and Wifdom, is turned to his good, and ftrengthens her Loue vnto hym; for I heare, that within thefe 4 Days, many Letters fent to her felf, from forren Countries, were deliuered only to my Lord of *Effex*, and he to anfwer them.

The Matter of Vittaile lies dead, vntill your Letters to the Queen revive yt again. Mr. *Beecher* hath wrytt vnto you his Opinion of yt, and expects your Anfwer. So hath he donne about your Account and Reckoning; for vnlefs your Lordfhip be willing to yeld fome Satisfaction vnto him, and *Hix*, I fynd hym not fo willing to deale in it, though you pay well for yt; he ftill alledging your Lordfhip can make no great Commodity of yt, in 4 Years or more.

My Lord of *Pembroke* is here, and, as I am told, is very inquifitive for the Deede of Intaile; I haue bene earneftly delt withall by divers to know what is become of yt: For the Conference defired by my Lady *Warwickes* Officers, I befeeche your Lordfhip, wryte to Mr. *Montague* and *Golding*, to be here at yt, and to give Order which of your Counfell you will haue at yt, and to appoint their Fees. In a Matter of fuch Confequence as this is, I defire to haue the Affift-ance both of your Cofen *Montague*, and your own Officers.

The Queens Sollicitor *Flemming*, and Serieant *Harris*, doe now accord, that yt wilbe nothing hurtfull to your Lordfhip, but rather more good, becaufe yt will giue them more Light, if they produce any new Matter, I meane their Counfell. *London*, this *Tuefday* Morning the 12 of *Nouember*, 1595.

Your Lordfhips, &c.

R. Whyte.

Sir *Ed. Harbarts* Sonne and Heyr, was examined by my Lord of *Canterbury*, and doth goe to Church; and now fhalbe a Deputy Liffenant in *Mongomery* Shire.

Rowland Whyte, *Efq*; to Sir Robert Sydney.

My Lord,

I Send your Lordfhip, by *Will* of the Scullery, the Piece of Hanging. My Lord *Rich* faies that the Border is too deep, and that it is not fo deep as he defires by the Note *Bloq* hath of his; my Lady *Lefter* fayd, that if it be aboue 10 *s.* the Sticke, it is to deere. I anfwered, that it feemed Hangings were good Cheap, when fhe bought any. Sure I was that your Lordfhip wold

buy

buy them as good Cheape for my Lady *Ritch* as for your felfe, and fo was my Lady *Ritch* affured, who liked the Hangings very well. I fhewed the Piece to Mr. *Mainard*, he fent for an Arras Man, who truly did efteeme the Goodnes of it as it is, and thinkes it well worth 16 or 18 *s.* the Sticke. My Lady *Warwick* tels me this Euening, that my Lord of *Effex* has bene very earneft for my Lord *Boroughs* Leaue, and brought her Majeftie to pitty his Weakenes, and confuming away ; fo that now a Hope is had, that the Queen wilbe pleafed to licenfe his Return. My Lady *Warwick* being by, faies, that fhe told her Majeftie the Defire your Lordfhip had to come ouer for 2 Monethes, about a very earneft Occafion in Law, that concernd the Good of your Children ; but the Queen fayd, that the Time was to daungerous, and that fhe cold not beleue you your felfe defired it. And fhe bid me goe to my Lord of *Effex*, who promifed her to fecond it. Your Lordfhip may iudge of this as you pleafe. My Ladies Determinacion is, to haue it moued by my Lord Treafurer, Lord Admirall, and Sir *Robert Cecill*, who I hope will be able to effecte it.

The Letters to the States Generall are not yet figned, I talked with one that faies, the firft Part of the Letter doth comprehend an Account taken by her Majefty of her Officers, that haue the Charge of her Artillery and Municion, who inform, that their was fent to *Flufhing*, of late Yeares, a great Quantity of Powder, which the Queen now was aduifed to vfe for the Furnifhing of her own Ships at Sea, againft the Common Ennemy ; and hauing written to your Lordfhip of it, you return the Anfwer I fett down at lardg in my Letter yefterday Morning by the Poft. I cannot come by any Meanes to fpeake with my Lord Treaforer, and theirfore I went to Sir *Robert Cecill*, humbly to defire him to put my Lord, his Father, in mind of the great Wants of *Flufhing*, and to pitty my long Stay here, that attended thefe 3 Moneths, the Queens Pleafure. He then told me that I fhuld haue Lettres to the States ; and when I replied, that it were to dangerous to expect their Refolutions, and befought him your Lordfhip might enioy the Benefitt of her Majefties Comandment, who was pleafed (as my Lord Treafurer told me himfelf) to giue Money to prouide our Wants. *Whyte*, faid he, I know your Wants are great in *Flufhing*, but the Queen faies, the States fhall fpeedely fupply them. This is all I can gett from them ; if your Lordfhip were not exceeding wife, and very well acquainted with thofe vncertain Proceedings of Things, you might much blame me, that aduertife one Day what the next Day is altred ; but God is my Judge, I write nothing but what I haue delivered vnto me by them felues, or fome of their Miniftry from them, I know to be honeft, and of Creditt ; lett the Event fall out as it will.

I wold I had bene fent any other where, when I came hither, for it greiues me, that the Paines and Care I take to doe you Seruice, brings no better Succeffe. Sir *Pofthumus Hoby* is rid down again towards your Sifter *Sydney*, and hath carried with him good Store of faire Jewels and Pearls, and my Lord Treafurers Lettres to my Lord of *Huntingdon*, to make that Marriage.

My noble and worthie Cofen, Mr. *Dean Wood,* the Queens Chaplen, is married to *Ritch* Ballets Widow of *Cheapfide* ; he hath by her 300 *l.* a Yeare Iointer, and fhe is befides worth 4000 *l.* Here is great Preparacion for thefe Triumphes, and fuch Deuifes promifed as our Age hath not feen the like. Mrs. *Touchet* hath catcht Mr. *Thinnes* Son and Heire, and married her felfe vnto him, to his Fathers Miflike, for with hur fhall he haue nothing, but thofe vertuous Qualities fhe brought from Court.

Their are Lettres fent Abroad, to difcharg the Watch of Beacons till *March* next, and that in all our trained Bands, all our Billes be converted to Pikes. My Lord of *Pembroke* neuer fent but once to fee my Lady. My Lord *Herbart* came once to vifit her.

My Lord of *Effex*, and my Lord Treafurer haue their Bore Pies, and this Day the reft are prefented, my Lady referuing none for her felf, beftowing her two vpon Sir *Robert Cecill*, in Hope he wilbe careful for your Leave. God keep you in Health, and fo I take my Leaue. *London*, this *Sonday* Morning, xvjth of *Nouember*, 1595.

　　　　　　　　　　　　　　　　　　　　Your Lordfhips, &c.

　　　　　　　　　　　　　　　　　　　　　　R. Whyte.

Rowland Whyte, *Efq*; to *Sir* Robert Sydney.

My Duty very humbly remembred,

THE Bore Pies are all deliuered, and fpecialliy much comended for their well Seafoning. Sir *Rob. Cecil*, as I was twice credibly informed, refufed the Prefent Sir *Edward Vvedale* fent him, and hath denied to medle in the Bufines for his Accownts, which maketh him much to maruell.

Capt. *Sauage* begins to come Abroade, and promifes to deale for your Checks ; he is of Opinion, it is not good to mingle thold Accownt with it.

I told Sir *Robert Cecill*, that the Wants of Flufhing, were extreme and daungerous in fuch a Town, if any foddain Vprore vnlooked for might happen ; he anfwred that he knew it, but cold not remedy it, for this was the Queens Pleafure.

My Lord of *Effexs* Deuife is much comended in thefe late Triumphes, fome pretty While before he came in him felf to the Tilt, he fent his Page with fome Speach to the Queen, who returned with her Majefties Gloue. And when he came himfelf, he was mett with an old Hermitt, a Secretary of State, a braue Soldier, and an Efquier. The firft prefented him with a Booke of Meditations ; the fecond with pollitical Difcourfes ; the third with Oracions of braue fought Battles ; the fourth was but his own Follower, to whom thother three imparted much of their Purpofe, before his Coming in. Another devifed with him, perfuading him to this and that Courfe of Liffe, according to their Inclinations. Comes into the Tilt Yard vnthought vpon, thordinary Poft Boy of *London*, a ragged Villain all bemired, vpon a poore leane Jade, gallaping and blowing for Liff, and deliuered the Secretary a Packet of Lettres, which he prefently offred my Lord of *Effex* ; and with this dumb Shew our Eyes were fed for that Time. In thafter Supper, before the Queen, they firft deliuered a well pend Speach to moue this worthy Knight, to leaue his vaine following of Loue, and to betake him to hevenly Meditacion ; the Secretaries all tending to haue him follow Matters of State, the Soldiers perfuading him to the Warr ; but the Efquier anfwered them all ; and concluded with an excellent, but to plaine *Englifh*, that this Knight wold neuer forfake his Miftreffes Love, whofe Vertue made all his Thoughts Deuine, whofe Wifdom tought him all true Pollicy, whofe Beauty and Worth, were at all Times able to make him fitt to comand Armies. He fhewed all the Defects and Imperfections of all ther Times, and theirfore thought his Courfe of Liffe to be beft in feruing his Miftres. Thold Man was he, that in *Cambridg* plaied *Giraldy*, *Morley* plaied the Secretary, and he that plaied Pedantiq, was the Soldior, and *Toby Matthew* acted the Squires Part. The World makes many vntrue Conftructions of thefe Speaches, comparing the Hermitt and the Secretary, to two of the Lords, and the Soldier to Sir *Roger Williams* ; but the Queen faid, that if fhe had thought their had bene fo moch faid of her, fhe wold not haue bene their that Night, and foe went to Bed.

Their are Lettres come out of *Ireland*, with good Newes of *Tirons* Submiffion, which brought my Lord Treafurer to the Court, from his ficke Bed. The Lords haue bene thefe 3 Daies in Cownfell, about this *Irifh* Peace ; a formale Pardon according to our Lawe is now a drawing. Sir *Henry Bagnell* is landed, and looked for hire daily. *Tiron* blames him much for Wrongs done vnto him.

As for D——d I hard that all his Gouernment is wholy mifliked, if he doe any Thing without firft acquainting 140 here ; he is to rafh, if he direct by
the

the Aduife of 140 their ; then is he thought to take to much vpon him ; and thus is he like to endure Difgrace, while *E———e* is only imploied, and graced, his Opinion beft allowed of and followed. I hard it is like to grow to a Faction between them.

Vpon *Thurfday*, Sir *Thomas Heneges* Funerals were folemnifed, his Offices all vnbeftowed. Here is a Speach that Mr. *Arthur Gorge* fhalbe fent into *France*.

The Speach of Marriage betwen 9000 and *q q* is quite broke of, by his not liking ; and I feare me, their is like to grow great Vnkindnefs between 1000 [*Effex*] and 2000 ; when I know the true Caufe, I will aduertife your Lordfhip. My Lady *Pembroke* hath bene dangeroufly ill of a Swelling in the Throat ; *Goodirich* went down, and is faid to lawnch it.

My Lord Treafurer, my Lord Admirall, and Sir *Robert Cecill*, promife to moue your Leaue, when they haue difpatcht for *Irelande* ; and that the Sheriffs are prickt. I will lofe no Time in attending their Pleafure.

Sir *Edward Harberts* eldeft Daughter is married to Sir *William Stanleis* eldeft Sonne, which makes my Lord of *Pembroke* very melancholy.

My Lady of *Hertford* is nowe better then fhe was, and yet *Rowland* tels me, fhe is very ill.

My Lady and all your fweet Children are well, my Lady praying for your Leaue, and that God will pleafe to fend her a good Howre, for fhe is very bigg and neare her Time. *London*, this *Saturday* Morning, 22th of *Nouember*, 1595.

Your Lordfhips, &c.

R. Whyte.

Rowland Whyte, *Efq; to Sir* Robert Sydney.

Right Honorable,

I Haue receued your great Packet of Lettres, fent by Capt. *Brownes* Soldior vpon *Tuefday* laft, and according to their Directions haue deliuered them all. Sir *Robert Cecill* hath thofe you fent to his Father, for he told me this Afternoone, I cold haue no Anfwer of them thefe 5 or 6 Daies. My Lord of *Effex* told me, he cold do no good in the leaft for your Return ; but my Confidence is in my Lord Treaforer, and my Lord Admirall, and Sir *Robert Cecill*, who promife to take a fitt Time to moue her Majeftie about it. And vpon *Monday*, my Lady dines at Court, and then will vifit all her Frends about it. I ftaied at Court till 6 a Clocke, and faw the States Lettres figned and fealed ; and fearing left my Lord Treafurer might forgett to fend you a Copie, I haue procured them Word for Word, examined, and hereinclofed fend them. The Lettres them felues, Sir *Robert Cecill* carried to his Father, who promifes to write this Night, if he haue Leifure : I haue left my Man to ftay their for them till my Lord Treaforers going to Bed, defiring Mr. *Mainard* to deliuer them vnto him, if his Lord will fend any Difpatch. I heare *Tiron* is accepted, and Sir *George Carew* of the Ordonance fhalbe prefently fent ouer to take his Othe, and to be Comiffioner in that Buifnes with my Lord Deputy, to whom fmale Cowntenance or Truft is comitted, in this or in any Thing els ; and the Credit of all Thinges giuen to Sir *John Norres*. This is the Bufines my Lord Treaforer hath now in Hand, which peraduenture will ftay the Difpatch I expect, for one or two Daies longer. My Lord *Staffords* Sonne is bafely married to his Mothers Chambermaid.

The Poft is come, and deliuered vnto me a very great Packett of Letters from your Lordfhip. To morrow Morning I will goe to the Court, and deliuer them all with my own Hands, and will not faile to lett Mr. *Stanhop*, *Griuell*, and *Manners*, know what you comand me. About the Conference I will defire Mr. *Mountagues* Prefence and Aduife, and doe looke for Mr. *Golding* here vpon *Monday* ; then will Mr. *Olfworth* apoint a Time of Meeting, and will haue

their

their Refolution vnder their Hands. My Lady is exceedingly pleafed that your Lordfhip is fo carefull of her, in fending of cordiall Things for her. Here was the honeft Doctor *Brown*, who bid her in no Cafe to medle with the *Laudamum*, becaufe it was very daungerous.

I faw the fame Mr. *Cox* you fpeake of, at my Lord of *Effexs* Chamber this Day, who told me, that he had often put my Lord in mind to anfwer the Lettres he brought vnto him from you. Affone as my Lady is brought to Bed, what you wryte of Gofhips fhalbe.obferued.

My Man is returned from my Lord Treafurer, and Mr. *Mainard* fends me Word I muft come to my Lord to Morrow Morning for the Lettres, about 9 a Clocke, and I will not faile to afke him what the Town fhall doe for Powder, while the States are refoluing. At *London*, this *Saturday* Night, 22 of *Nouember*, 1595.

Your Lordfhips, &c.

Row. Whyte.

Rowland Whyte, *Efq*; *to Sir* Robert Sydney.

My good Lord,

THIS Day my Lord Treaforer is very priuat, that I cold not come to his Sight, but Mr. *Mainard* deliuered vnto me the Packet for the States, and affures me, that if they do not fpedely furnifh your Wants, he hard his Lordfhip fay the Queen wold do it, for fhe is very carefull of the Town. I am aduifed by him not to deliuer this laft Lettre I had from you, about your Leaue, till his Lordfhip hath ended fome Bufines, he now hath in Hand, about *Ireland*. In the meane Time I will deliuer to Mr. *Manners*, Mr. *Stanhop*, Mr. *Grivell*, their Lettres, which I cold not doe this *Sonday*, becaufe it was a great Court ; but I found my Lady *Warwicke* at Leifure, fhe read your Lettre, and tels me, that fhe is much beholding vnto you, for, according to this Conference, it fhall much content her, to heare what her Cownfell will fay vnto it. I protefted vnto her, that your Lordfhip, before you euer ftirrd in it, tooke fo good Aduife as poffibly you cold get, and being by them affured of your Title, you were willing to giue it Liffe ; and as far as I cold perceaue by you, you were not minded to proceed in it, till her Honor, by her own Cownfell, might haue Time to know and confider of your Right ; fhe refolued, that if it were yours, fhe was farr from hindring any Good vnto you, but moft ready in her felf, to make the World know how much you were efteemed of her for your own Worth, and nearnes of Kin to her late Lord ; and when this Matter between her and the Queen were ended, your Lordfhip fhuld fee her Care of you. To which I anfwered, that her Ladyfhip cold not beftow her Favors vpon any liuing Creature, that wold with more Humblenes doe her Seruice ; and told her, that Mr. *Golding* and I wold attend the Time Mr. *Olfworth* wold fett down for the Meeting.

My Lord of *Effex* being at Dinner, and many Lords with him, cald me vnto him, and faid, by God I cannot perfuade the Queen to giue your Mafter Leaue to returne, though I told her that he was troubled with an Ague, which might proue dangerous, and that it concernd him, for to fettle his own Fortune, to be here. She anfwered, that fhe hard *Flufhing* was worfs in the Somer then the Winter, and to giue him Leaue now to come ouer, were to feeke to liue ftill from his Charg. That he replied, you did not defire to be here but for one Month or 6 Weeks. To which fhe faid, that the Cardinal was daily expected, and fhe wold not haue you away at his firft Comming, vntill it were feen what he purpofed : This he wills me to aduertife, an promifes to write himfelf, though I find he hath no Hope of it. All this my Lady *Warwicke* confirmes, who was by, when my Lord of *Effex* tooke as good a Time as might be be to moue it. I will carfully follow Mr. *Stankops* and *Griuels* Aduise, as you comand me. I rest,

Your Lordships, &c.

Sonday Night, 23 No-
vemb. 1595.

R. Whyte.

Rowland Whyte, *Esq; to* Sir Robert Sydney.

Right Honorable,

IN my late Lettre vnto you, I aduertised that my Lord Treforer told me, the Queen was pleased to supply the Wants of Powder in *Flushing*, by deliuering of Money, becaufe that Municion was very fcarfe here. He at that Inftant cawfed an Allowance to be fett down, which was caft vp by Mr. *Mainard,* and then viewed by him felf, and I promifed to haue it difpatcht ; my Lord of *Essex*, as I writ vnto you, told me, that the Queen gaue Comandment their fhuld be 500 *l.* deliuered for to prouide Powder. Notwithftanding all this, my Lord Treaforer now doth feeke to fupply all your Wants, by fending her Majeftys earneft Letters to the States Generall, and likewife to them of *Zealand*; and in fuch Manner, as your Lordfhip peraduenture will much marvaile at it, when you fee them.

Their was deliuered vpon *Thurfday*, in thafter Noone, to Sir *Robert Cecill,* by his Father, the Minutes or Draughts of the faid Lettres, to be put into *French*, and, as I am informed, they cheifly contain thefe Points : That her Majefty, in this Time of Daunger, arminge and preparing all Things neceffary for the Defence of her own Cowntry, cawfed Lettres to be fent vnto you, to aduertife her of the particular State of your Gouernment, which fhe had a fpeciall Care of, and how you were prouided of Things fitt for the Safety of it.

That your Lordfhip in Anfwer of thefe, doth by your Lettres at lardge make knowen, their is no Powder lefte in the Town ; that the States being by you defired, haue delayd the Supplying of your Wants, and theirfore you were forced to fpend the Store of Powder (which from hence was from Time to Time fent ouer to ly their for the Defence of the Town) vpon the Soldiors and Artillery, wherin you are much blamed by her Majeftie ; that the Fortificacions are in many Places weake, the Ramparts and Diches decayed, and vnrepaired ; that the Ordounances vpon the Walles ly vnmounted. Her Majeftie doth therfore much maruaile at it, and according to the Contract, doth pray and require them fpeedely to furnifh your prefent Want with a good Supply of Powder, and alfo to reftore back all the full Quantity of Powder by her fent ouer (which contrary to her Meaning was fpent) becaufe fhe wold haue it here againe to ferue her own Turne ; that they mount all your Artillery, repaire your Fortifications, Ramparts, and Diches ; and to all this fhe expects their fpeedy Anfwer and Refolution.

I thought good to aduertife your Lordfhip of this with all poffible Speed, and to let you knowe, that I thincke thefe Cowrfes are confulted vpon by the Father and the Son only, the Lords not priuy vnto them all.. And I dare not acquaint others with thefe Proceedings, becaufe I wold not offend your Lordfhip in erring from your Directions, to follicit my Lord Treaforer only. Yet this I conceue, that the Queen and his Lordfhip wold haue the Town prouided for, and if the States refufe to furnifh your Wants, that then their is no Remedy, the Supply muft come from hence. When the Letters are figned and read, I purpofe to fend my Man *George* with them.

The Queen came to *Whyt Hall* Yefternight, my Lady to Morrow goes to the Court, to haue your Leaue moued, and to make her beft Frends know, how much it imports you to be here for 2 or 3 Moneths. God fend her better Succefs then my Lady *Borough* had, whofe Defire was abfolutely denied, and the

Queen toke it very ill, that in fuch a Time he wold defire to be from his Gouernment.

I am now going to the Court, and what I can hear I will this Night by the
Poft fend vnto you. *London*, this *Saturday* Morning, 25 of *Nouember*, 1595.

Your Lordfhips, &c.

R. Whyte.

Rowland Whyte, *Efq*; *to Sir* Robert Sydney.

My Lord,

YEfterday my Lady was at Court, where my Lord Admirall, and all that
Tribe, were exceeding glad to fee her. She alledged the Want of your
Health, the Greatnes of your Bufines, for the Good of your Children only, fince
the Death of your Brother ; and defired my Lord Admirall to promife your
Return back fhuld be within 2 or 3 Moneths. After that he had much pitied
her Iorney, being fo big and fo neare her Time, he went vp to the Queen,
and, as bufy as they were there about the Pricking of Sheriffs, he fpoke to my
Lord Treaforer, my Lord of *Effex*, and my Lord Chomberlain, to ioine with
him in this Motion to the Queen, for your Leaue for fo fhort a Time. And
they all are willing vnto it, and they fay they will doe it before the Queen remoue back again to *Richmond*, which wilbe vpon *Thurfday*. My Lord of *Effex*
being bufy aboue, fent Mr. *Carew Reinals* twice vnto her, to excufe his not
Comming himfelf, and now that he was fo well backt, he hoped to bring her
the firft News of your Leaue himfelf, to her Houfe in *Brodftreet*. My Lady of
Kildare was fent purpofely to keep my Lady Company, who had my Lady *Ho-
bies* Chamber alone to her felf to dine at.

I muft not forget to acquaint your Lordfhip, with Mr. *Cholmleys* exceeding
Care of my Lady, who vpon his own Coft prepared fuch a Dinner for my Lady,
of good Meat and well dreffed, that for 12 Difhes I neuer faw better in my Liffe.
She vifited my Lady *Warwick*, my Lady *Skudmore*, and my Lady of *Hartford*,
who is now more comforted then fhe was.

As my Lady paffed thorough the Garden, fhe mett by Chaunce with the two
Sifters, my Lady *Elizabeth*, and *Katharine Somerfett*, and they were very glad to
falute her and fee her.

My Lady tooke with her Mrs. *Mary*, Mr. *William*, and Mrs. *Katharine*; my
Lord Admiral fware, if it had not bene fo bufy a Time, his beft Cofen and her
Children fhuld haue feen the Queen, but he wold tell her of their being at
Court. I haue, according to your Directions, deliuered Mr. *Stanhop* and Mr.
Griuell your Lettres, who promife much ; and this Day I goe to my Lord Trea-
forer and Mr. *Mannors*. As I can difpatch your Bufines, I will advertize your
Lordfhip.

This Lettre, I now fend you from my Lord of *Effex*, I thinck doth confirme
what I writ vnto you of his Motion to the Queen for your Leaue, and her Denial ; but my Lady being at Court, hath giuen it new Liffe : She was at *Baynards*
Caftell with my Lord of *Pembroke*.

My Lord Admiral did very much ioy in your Children, and told Mrs. *Mary*
fhe was already a fitt Maid for the Queen. God blefs them, and make you
long liue to be carefull of them ; for goodlier Children this World hath not.
London, 25 of *Nouemb*. 1595.

Your Lordfhips, &c.

R. Whyte.

Sir

Sir Thomas Bodley *to Sir* Robert Sydney.

S I R,

THE Letter heerwith was fent me to convey, with which I haue no Matter to fend yow befides, but that the Queen hath written hither, That for her D=mande fhe will vrge it no longer for the Prefent, if fo be they will affift her with 30 of their beft Shippes againft the *Spanifhe* Preparations, and defray the Expenfes of her Auxiliarie Forces, which is but Half of the Offer which was made by my Ouverture; and yet it will not be accorded. For we will afke it as a Debt, by Vertue of the Contract, which they contend we ought to keepe as a Matter of Right, and a iuft Stipulation, and dare not fignifie to the People, that the Queene will diffolue it; and therfore, in the Ende, if any Thing be gotten, it muft come by the Meanes of an other newe Treatie: But for the Shippinge required, they doe promife altogether, to come well prouided. The Sending of Deputies, to enforme her Majeftie at full of the State of their Affaires, is once againe a Foote, and I thinke they intende it out of Hande, and haue fignified fo muche by a Lettre to her Majeftie. Heere is no other Matter fo much worth as a Sheate of Paper; for which I leaue yow, and comend yow to Gods good Tuition. *Hage,* 25 *Nouemb.* 1595.

Your Lordfhips at commandement,

Tho. Bodley.

Rowland Whyte, *Efq; to Sir* Robert Sydney.

My Lord,

YOUR laft Lettre to my Lord Treaforer, that came in your Packet vnto me by the Poft of the 19 of *Nouember,* I thought had concerned your Leave only, and therefore I chofe out a fitt Tyme to fend yt in to hym by Mr. *Mainard,* hauing attended two Dayes to fynd hym at Leifure. Yt was fo ill wrytten, that my Lord hymfelf cold not reade yt; fo Mr. *Mainard* was faine to helpe hym in yt. Your Lordfhip giues my Lord Treaforer Thanckes, for hauing moued the Queen to yeld vnto the Supply of the Wants of Powder in *Flufhing,* as I had certified, his Lordfhip had informed me, which I proteft before the living God, was true, though he now denies yt. As Mr. *Mainard* can well witnefs, when I put hym in Mynd how that he and I caft vp a leffer Proportion of Powder, according to a reformed Allowance: To this he fhruged vp his Sholder, and fayes, that my Lord forgets yt. My Lord tels me I mifvnderftood hym; that yt was true, he moued the Queen, but that fhe was not willing to giue the Supply of Powder, till the States Intent were firft known, who, by their Contract, were to do it, as in *Brill* and *Oftend:* Let me neuer be belieued, if at that Tyme he vfed any fuch Speach vnto me. My Lord of *Effex* is honorable, and I know will not forgett he told me the very fame Day, that yt was argued and difputed before the Queen, and that fhe was pleafed, that 500 *l.* fhould be deliuered for that Supply. I did not thincke yt Wifdom to contend with fuch a mighty Lord, but to beare this Wrong patiently; that he affured the Queen when fhe blamed you, yt was not a Fault of yours, but an Error of theirs that went before you. I humbly thancked his Lordfhip, for hauing fayd fo much in your Behalf; that fure I was your Lordfhip, was moft vnwilling to draw the Queen to any of thefe Charges, if you cold haue fownd any other Way to have remedied yt: That now hauing her Majefties Lettres to warrant you, you wold deale very carefully, to bring the States to performe this Article of the contract. But my Lord fayd I, their is no Powder in the Town, and what fhall we doe for Powder, while the States be refoluing. To this he made Anfwer, that he wold acquaint her Majeftie once more with yt; and that he had earneftly delt with her, to deliuer Powder, to

be

be anfwered vpon the Soldiors generall Pay, but fhe wold not confent vnto yt; but was content, yf yt might be defalked out of their weekly Lendings; that is a Thing impoffible, quoth I, for they doe moft hardly liue vpon yt, and doe murmur, that their full pay is kept from them.

Well fayd he, for the Wants of the Queens Ordonnance, I will wryt a Warrant to Sir *George Carew*, for Carriages, and to certifie what your Demandes comes vnto, which Lettre I haue fent hyme.

And underftanding his Lordfhip was to goe to the Queen, I humbly befought hym to remember to fpeake vnto her Majeftie, for your Leaue, but for 6 Weks or 2 Moneths, to which he anfwered that he wold doe his beft; though your Lordfhip, in no Letter you wryt vnto hym of late, made any Mention of yt. But it is one Parte of my Bufines here, to follicyt yt, and in all your Lettres vnto me, I am comanded to defire his honorable Fauor and Furtherance in yt; foe I departed from hym, and he went vp to the Queen, but did no good in this; but only delt for Thanfwer of your laft Pacquett of Importance vnto hym, fent by Capt. *Browns* Soldier, and this enclofed is Thanfwer, as Mr. *Mainard* tels me. Now to anfwer all other Points of your Lettres vnto me, by the Poft, which came to my Hands, the 22 of *November*.

I will begin with Mr. *Roger Manners*, when I deliuered him your Lordfhips Lettre, he brake yt vp, and went to his Window, and from one Corner to the other, for more Light; at laft he cald me vnto hym, and fayd that he wold not take 100 *l.* to read this Lettre. I was faine to read yt for hym, and he was exceeding glad to heare fuch Praife, of my Lord of *Rutland*, becaufe yt came from your felf, that he knowes can rightly iudge of the Hopes he expectes in his Nephue; and for hym felf (when I had deliuered vnto hym, the Meffage you comand me) he protefted, that he was now the fame, he was then, and in all other Occafions, he wilbe right glad, and willing to fhew his Love and Affection vnto you.

I acquainted Mr. *Griuell*, with the Reafons that moued you to defire to return, but for 6 Weekes, and befought hym to direct me the Courfe I fhuld obferue in yt; he hauing underftood how farre yt was proceeded in by my Lord of *Effex*, and how my Lord Treafurer, and Lord Admirall, wold againe moue yt. He affured me, that he liked the Cours, but he was affrayd that my Lord *Borough*, and your Lordfhip, both iumping at one Tyme for Leaue, might hynder each other, yet willed he me, to follow them, and bring yt to fome Refolution; and that he would not faile to doe all kynd Offices to further yt.

Mr. *Stanhope* affured me, that he efteemed yt as a Fauor, your Lordfhip did repofe fuch Confidence in hym, that he wold not faile, both to take a fitt Tyme with the Queen, and to put my Lord Treafurer in Mynd of yt.

I have followed my Lord of *Effex*, and my Lady *Warwicke*, very diligently, and they both affure me, that yt muft be my Lord Treafurer that muft doe yt, if yt wilbe donne at all. For my Lord Admirall fpeaking of yt, with my Lord of *Effex*, for his Affiftance, he anfwered that he wold back hym, telling hym how far he had already delt with the Queen, and what abfolut deniall was giuen hym.

With Mr. *Mainard* I brake the Matter, as from my felf; his Opinion is, that we fhall haue no Parlement, till the laft Subfedy be payd, that the Speach of a Parlement was vpon the Preparacion of *Spaine*, which being waxen cold, he thought the Speach wold dy to, of a Parlement. As for the Creation of Noblemen, he of hym felf remembred, that your Lordfhip was once named, and made no Doubt, but you wold be named againe; and deepely protefted, that if their were any fuch Thing intended, or when yt fhall be, he will moft carefully give me Notice of yt, and would grace my Saruice here, in any Thing I had Occafion to vfe hym: That he knew his Lord loued you, that he hard hym fay, you had many good Parts in you, able to doe your Cowntrey Seruice, and wifhed your Lordfhip to beare with his Age and Buifnes; if you had not affone as you expected Refolutions, in thofe Things that concern your
Gouernment;

Gouernment; that vpon the Anfwer of the States, you fhall fpeedely receue Contentment, aduifing me, to wryte vnto you as from my felf, to deale fo effectually with theim, as her Majeftie may vnderftand you are willing this Charg fhuld light vpon them.

I mett Mr. *Lake* at Court, and told hym I was comanded by your Lordfhip to attend hym, and to be directed by hym, if their were Occafion, to which he anfwered. That in the Buifnes I fpake of, their was no fturring; for that the Report of a Parlement was ended, and that he had wrytten vnto you of yt already, and lefte his Lettre at Mr. *Burnhams*, to be fent vnto you.

Mr. *Golding* was here, and we went to Mr. Sollicitor, who hauing better thought vpon this Conference, deliuered his Opinion plainly vnto us. That her Cownfeill [Lady *Warwicks*] and yours, would neuer agree, but wold ftand vpon fuch Doubts and Cauels, as cold neuer be ended but by Triall and Judgment; and therefore, his Opinion was, that to fatisfie my Lady *Warwicke*, Mr. *Finch* fhould acquaint fome of her younger Cownfaill with the Cafe, but not giue yt them in Writing; and in the meane Tyme, your Lordfhip might furceafe your Sute in Law.

I went to Mr. *Oldfworth* and told hym, that Mr. *Finch* was ready to meet with fome of my Ladyes younger Cownfell, to talke of this Cafe, which he liked of very well; they mett Yefterday, and as Mr. *Finch* tels me, he will handle the Matter foe, that he will draw from theim, more then they fhall from hym; and if my Lady *Warwicke* will needs haue a Meeting of both Cownfels, yt may be the next Terme, which *Oldfworth* rather defires then, then now; becaufe all my Ladys Cownfell may haue Tyme to be better inftructed, and prepared for a Conference.

Mr. *Finch* told me, that he hard your Lordfhip would ftand to be Knight of the Shire in *Kent*, that the Cowntrey wold be glad of yt, and that he wold fhew many Offices of his Seruice, if Occafion required; to this I cold fay nothing, as hauing neuer hard any Word of your Lordfhips Inclination that way. I iudged yt to be fome Motion of your Frends, that peradventure thincke to doe you a Pleafure in yt.

Mr. *Beecher* hath broken the Matter of your Accownts to *Hix*, who already hath made Sir *Robert Cecill*, priuy vnto yt; and as I heare, his Anfwer was, that your Lordfhip was denied yt in the fame Kind that *Becher* Demands yt out of the *Checquer*, but Mr. *Hix* anfwered, that your Lordfhip in Confideracion of great reckonings between you and *Beecher*, was content to turn ouer vnto hym, that Debt of the Queens, which now was no more your Lordfhips, but the Intereft in *Beecher*, and vpon that Grownd followes the Sute. Mr. *Hix* hath yt a Foote, and will loofe no Tyme to bring yt to fome End. Yt was told me, that the Queen of late gaue fpeciall Comandment to my Lord Treafurer, and Sir *John Fortefcue*, that out of the generall Cheques, no Paiment fhuld be made without her own Warrant.

I haue fought amongeft many Papers, your Brothers Aduife of Trauell vnto you, but yet cannot fynd yt, and I am not fure I haue yt.

Mr. *Hen. Sidney* is fo bufy and carefull, about this Affurance, for the Purchafe he makes, that Night and Day he liues with his Lawiers. *Whiting* tels me, that he fynds by his Mafter, that he continews his former Purpofe towards you, and yours; but as yet hath not fetled his Eftate, or figned any Will or Conueighance; when he doth, your Lordfhip fhalbe affured of his Seruice, and Furtherance. That if his Miftris knew, how he was inclined towards you, he might receue blame, and theirfore refers all Conference to his comming to *London*, which wilbe euery Term, and defires to haue no Lettres fent vnto hym. Mr. *Sidney* tooke your Lettre very kindly, and will anfwer yt er he goe away.

The Queen went Yefterday to *Richmond*, my Lady *Hartford* was at *Whitehall*, with my Lord *Effex*, my Lord Treaforer, Sir *Robert Cecill*, and others, very meanly attired. I hard, the Queen fhould fay, that her Hufbands Liffe nor Liuing, fhuld be called in Queftion.

The Mafter of the Rowles, was fent to examine my Lady *Shrosbery*, who an-fwers very difcretly and prudently to thofe Articles obiected by the Phifician againft her.

This Matter is to hotly purfued by Mr. *Talbot.*

My Lord *Shrofbery*, and my Lady liue here, hard by us.

London, this *Saturday*   *Your Lordfhips,* &c.
Noone, 29 *Nouem.*
1595.
                                                                                R. Whyte.

My Lord *Pembroke* is gon out of Town this Day, and the Matters between hym, and my Lord of *Effex* not ended, about *Norwod* Parcke. My Lord *Pembroke* faies, that my Lord *Effex* doth not perform Covenants. My Lord of *Effex* faies, that he wold haue that for 6000 *l.* which he may haue 12000 *l.* for. But their is fome Fault attributed to *Sanford,* who was by my Lord *Pembroke* imploied, to my Lord of *Effex*'s Officers, about this Buifnes, and thought to haue bene to peremptory in his Speach, which he faies, were the Meffages of his Lord.   The feeking to ouerthrow Sir *Hen. Berklees* Leafe, vpon fo nice a Point, as the Paiment, of his Rent, to a Bailiffe, that entred not into Bond, according to the Statute, and theirfore was vnlawfull; is very much fpoken of euery where. Sir *Harry,* hath deliuered his Petition to the Queen, who is angry at foch Corfes. Yet is yt, *Summum Jus.* My Lord of *Effex* is weary of yt, and wold haue my Lord of *Pembroke* comence the Sute in his own Name. What will grow of this between them, I know not.

Rowland Whyte, *Efq; to* Sir Robert Sydney.

My Lord,

ALL this Day my Lady hath kept her Bed, and now it appeares to be the very Meafels; fhe is not ficke with them, but as the Children were when they had them. Doctor *Brown* was here, and faies, that feeing my Lady is foe neare her Time, Godwilling, it will not proue daungereous. The Midwiffe is in the Houfe, and Mrs. *Bacon.* I know not now what to fay for Gofhips, for fure I am, thefe great ones you name wilbe vnwilling to come, and theirfore will attend your Lordfhips further Directions. I was going to the Court to morrow Morning, to bring your Leaue to a Refolution, but I am comanded by my Lady to attend here, till I fee what will grow of this, which I truft in God wilbe paft within two Daies, as the Children were. My Lord Treaforer is in Town, and vntill his being at Court, I doe not know to what great Purpofe I fhold be their, only to follow my Lord Admirall, who I am vnwilling fhuld moue it without my Lord Treaforers Prefence. For the Inftruction you giue me to deale with my Lord of *Effex,* I wilbe aduifed by Mr. *Lake.* My Lady receues great Comfort by her Children, who are continually with her; fo is Mr. *William,* that hithervnto hath efcaped them. *London,* this *Saturday* Night, 29 of *Nouemb.* 1595.

                                                        Your Honors, &c.

                                                                                R. Whyte.

Rowland Whyte, *Efq; to* Sir Robert Sydney.

MY Lady was fafely brought to Bed Yefternight, at 9 a Clocke, of a goodly Sonne, being *Monday,* the 1ft of *December,* 1595; and now I will tell yow the Circumftances: Thefe 3 Daies paft my Lady was full of the Meafals, had withall a great Cough, and a gentele Feuor, it made vs all very fearfull; and my Lady herfelf all Day Yefterday tooke your Lordfhips Abfence as a great Part of her Affliction, and burft out into thefe Words: *That now fhe had moft Cawfe for your Prefence and Comforte, it was not Gods Will for her to haue it.* About 4 a Clocke in thafter Noone, *Rifley* came in with Lettres vnto

                                    †   her

her from your Lordſhip, which indeed brought great Comfort vnto her, ſeeing your Lordſhip cold not be here, you were moſt carefull of her ; and to heare of her weldoing, in ſending him of Purpoſe ouer to that Intent ; and when ſhe had oft and oft aſked him how you did of your Ague, ſhe gaue him Leaue to goe to my Lord Treaſorer. I went with him, and let *Mainard* know he was ſent of Purpoſe with thoſe Lettres, and ſpeedely to return. He went in with the Lettres, came out againe, and told *Riſley* he neaded not ſtay ; by 7 a Clocke we were come backe againe to my Ladys Houſe ; half an Houre after ſhe began to haue Paines ; her Midwiffe, by her own Leaue, was at the Labor of one in the *Spitle* ; we ſent for her ſpeedely, and hauing a convenient Nomber of Women about her, I ſent for *Jacob*, Doĉtor *Brown*, and *Naſh*, who all 3 preſently came ; her Ladyſhip receaued great Comfort by their being in the Houſe ; but, I thank God, ſhe had no Occaſion to vſe *Jacob* or the other, for from 8 to 9 her Paines were ſharpe and naturall, and God, according to his wonted Goodnes towards her, deliuered her of the Paine, by ſending into this World a goodly fatt Boy, but as full of the Meaſels in the Face as can be. They gaue it ſome of the Nurſes Milke and Safron, which he ſuckt out of a Spoone, and they keape him very warme ; he ſuckes as well as any Child doth, and cries as ſtrongly *. Soe that we hope in God he ſhall liue long, to both your Comforts.

Doĉtor *Brown* lay here all Night, and is the moſt carefull Man in the World of his Profeſſion. All your Children are in very good Health. As for the fooleſh Brutes giuen out of her Majeſtie, beleue me my Lord they proceed from ſome ill diſpoſed Humors, for I know their was no Cauſe to lead them to it, her Highnes daily ſhewing her ſelf to her faithfull Subieĉts, and they moſt ioying in her Sight, as well appeared at the Triumphes of her Coronation, and at her Remoue from hence vpon *Thurſday* laſt. I doe duly obſerue her Weldoing, which God grant may be long among vs. *Riſley* is gone to the Court with my Lord of *Eſſexs* Lettres, becauſe the Capt. of the Ship is gon to *Stretam* to *Charon*, and will not away till to morrow Morning. I thought good to ſend this Lettre, becauſe I know your Lordſhip is deſirus to heare of my Lady. She is in good State, as Doĉtor *Brown* and the Wives tels mé, and God will ſtrengthen her. Your Leaue being denied to my Lord of *Eſſex*, I am aduiſed not to haue it moued again, but by my Lord Treaſorer, who goes to Court this Weeke, and I will attend him. In Haſt, this *Tueſday* Morning, 2d of *Decemb.* 1595.

Your Lordſhips, &c.

R. Whyte.

Rowland Whyte, *Eſq*; *to Sir* Robert Sydney.

My Lord,

IN my laſt, of the 2d of *December*, I ſignified my Ladys ſafe Deliuerance of a goodly Sonne, which was born vpon *Monday* Night, at 9 a Clocke, the 1ſt of *December* ; and in it I ſpecified how my Lady and the Child had the Meaſels ; that my Lady fownd as great Care had of her, as was poſſible to be had of any in the ſame Caſe, which ſhe knew proceded from ſome former Direĉtions of your Lordſhips vnto me, in your deereſt Loue to her. Your Letter to my Lady *Rich*, ſent by *Riſley*, as ſhe ſayes, was to deſire her to be a Godmother, which ſhe doth moſt willingly agree to, and ſo deſired me to let you know, which ſhe wold her ſelf haue donne, but that ſhe was going to *Epſom*. I then told her, That long before I knew both your Lordſhip and my Lady had an Intent to deſire that Honor at her Hand, but as Thinges fell out, I was aſſured that neither of you wold, for any Thing in the World, requeſt her vnto it. And ſhe being moſt deſirous to know why, I anſwered her, that my Lady and the

---

* This was *Robert Sydney* the ſecond Earl of *Leiceſter,* who highly diſtinguiſht himſelf by his eminent Abilities and Services ; and when he died, was eighty-one Years and eleven Months old, *viz.* the 2d of *November,* 1677.

Child

Child born had the Meafels : To which fhe fodainly replied, that after 8 Dayes their was no Daunger to be feared, and theirfore it fhalbe no Occafion to keape me from doing Sir *Robert Sydney* and my Lady a greater Kindnes. When I faw her fo defperat, I humbly befought her Ladyfhip to take a longer Time to thincke vpon the Daunger, which fhe did till that after Noone ; and then comming to her to *Effex* Houfe, fhe told me fhe was refolued, and theirfore defired me to let your Lordfhip and my Lady know it. She afked me who was thought vpon to be the Godfathers ; I faid my Lord *Monjoy* for one, but I cold not well tell who the other fhuld be. Thence I went to *Holborn*, and found my Lord *Monjoy* at his Houfe ; I faid my Lady fent me vnto him, to defire him, both in your Name and hers, to chriften your Sonne that was newly born, which he very honorably promifed to doe ; and when I told him my Lady *Rich* was Godmother, he was much pleafed at it ; and affuring me, whenfoeuer the Day was apointed, he wold not faile to be theire.

My Lady cannot yet bethincke her felf of an other Godfather, but defires your Lordfhip to name one, and to giue her Leaue that his Name be *Robert*. Her Ladyfhip meanes (if your Leaue cannot be obtained) to haue Sir *Edmund Vuedall*, and Capt. *Savage* here, to bid your Gofhips welcom. And Mr. *Cholmley*, with my felf, will vndertake to prouide the Banquet, of what Goodnes, your Lordfhip fhall pleafe to fet down.

My Lady *Rich* defires the Chriftning may be fome 3 or 4 Daies before *Chriftmas*, becaufe till then fhe wilbe in the Countrey ; my Lady by me fent her Word, that it fhuld be then, or when els fhe wold pleafe to appoint it.

Rifley and I haue bene euery Day at my Lord Treaforers for an Anfwer to thofe Lettres he brought, and yet can haue none ; only this I learn, that he fent them to Sir *Robert Cecill* to the Court.

My Lord of *Effex*, euer fince *Monday*, was at *Petworth*, and came this after Noone to the Court ; *Rifley* deliuered him your Lettres with his own Hands, but is returned without Anfwer.

Sir *Michael Blunt* is put out of his Place, and this I heare faid to be the Caufe : He grew very familiar with Mr. *Neuell*, alias *Latimer*, and Capt. *Wainman* ; and in Difcours with them, they began to talke of the Dangers of the Time ; from that to argue of the Towne, how it might be made defenfible, what Provifion, what Men wold ferue the Turn, what a braue Comand it was in a Change ; then they grew madder, as to talke of Titles, and tis reported the Lifetenant deliuered his Mind how he was affected ; that he and his Frends wold keape that Place till he faw great Reafon to yeld it. But when they had waded fo far, Mafters, faid he, thefe Matters we fpeake of are perrilus, and theirfore I will haue nothing to doe with it. But *Latimer* and *Wainman*, fownd Meanes to difcouer it firft to the Queen, wherevpon the Lieftenant was examined by the Lords, and is now comitted in the *Towre*. Upon *Tuefday* laft, Sir *Drue Drury* was fworne in his Place.

Sir *Henry Bagnoll* is come to *London*, and finds fo few Frends here, that he lies ficke at his Lodging, and fends his Lettres to the Lords.

Sir *George Carey* takes it very vnkindly, that my Lord of *Pembroke* broke of the Match intended between my Lord *Herbart* and his Daughter, and told the Queen it was becawfe he wold not affure him 1000 *l.* a Yeare, which comes to his Daughter, as next a Kinne to Queen *Ann Bullen*. He hath now concluded a Marriage between his Daughter and my Lord *Barkleys* Sonne and Heire.

The Queen vfed my Lord of *Pembroke* very well at his Departure, and fent my Lady your Sifter a Jewell, but hath not graunted my Lord *Harbart* his Sute for *Clarindon*. Truly I hard, that if my Lord of *Pembroke* fhuld die, who is very purfife and maladife, the Tribe of *Hunfdon* doe laye Waite for the Wardfhip of the braue yong Lord.

I mett this Day with a Cofen of mine, the Cuftomer of *Lynne*, who in Secret told me, that he had, within thefe few Daies, Conference with Mr. *Hen. Sydney*, and that he findes him fo well bent towards you, and your Name, that he will leaue you all his Lands..

I

My Lady *Darbys* great with Child, ſtaies ſtill at Court, and many wonder that ſhe doth not return.

As for your Buſines, touching Creation, I wilbe, as I write vnto you, aduiſed by Mr. *Lake* in what Sort I ſhall deale with my Lord of *Eſſex*, vpon the Inſtruction you gaue me, and will watch Opportunities to find him alone.

My Lady not being well, hath kept me from the Cort theſe 7 Daies, but I had Buſines enough in Town, about ſome Supplies now granted from the *Towre*, for the Queens Ordonnance in *Fluſhing*; as by another Letter, I will preſently write purpoſely of that Seruice vnto yow, becauſe I will make an End of this.

London, Friday the 5th of
December, 1595.

Your Lordſhips, &c.

Row. Whyte,

Rowland Whyte, *Eſq;* to *Sir* Robert Sydney.

My Lord,

I Deliuered Sir *George Carew* my Lord Treaſorers Letter, which containd a Collection of certain Parcels, neceſſarey for the Queens Demi Canons, taken out of the Note of the generall Wants of *Fluſhing*, deliuered by the Maſter Gunner at his being here; which ſeuerall Parcels were by my Lord Treaſurers Direction prized by the Officers of the *Towre*. And now their is a Warrant and a Priuy Seale fairly ingroſſed, for the Queen to ſign, which hath bene my three Dayes Labor: Aſſone as it is diſpatched at Court, the Officers of the *Towre* promiſe to tranſport them ſpeedely vnto you, which I will alſoe haue a Care of. The Store that ſhalbe ſent at this Time comes to 192 *l.* 15 *s.* 8 *d.* As for Pikes, Powder, Muſket, Calliuer, Match, Lead, which are the principall and neceſſary Wants of *Fluſhing*, I can haue no Anſwer of, only that the States muſt firſt Anſwer her Majeſties Letters for Powder, er any Order wilbe taken; but I will ſollicit an Anſwer to this Lettre you ſent by *Riſley*, to know what you ſhall doe while the States be reſoluing for Powder.

As for Shott for *Culuering, Saker, Minion,* &c. the States are to doe it. As for Vittailes, your Lordſhip muſt nouriſh Liſſe in it by your Lettres, els will it dye.

London, 5 *Decemb.*
1595.

Your Lordſhips, &c.

R. Whyte.

Rowland Whyte, *Eſq;* to *Sir* Robert Sydney.

My Lord,

MY Lord of *Eſſex* tels me, that when he acquainted the Queen with the Contents of your Lettres, ſent by the Page, ſhe demanded where the Boy was, and wold haue let him come to her Preſence, but being comanded by my Lady not to ſtay at Court, he miſſed of that Hapines; it may perchaunce neuer come ſo again as long as he liue.

Sir *Hen. Vmpton* was in a good Forwardnes of going into *Fraunce*, but within theiſe 2 Daies their is ſome Backwardnes in it, and the Cawſe muttred, to be *Villeroyes* preſent Imploiment from that King to the King of *Spaine*; which Aduertiſement I doe not heare comes from Mr. *Edmonds*, and theirfore held doubtful, but if it be true, their is great Negligence imputed vnto him.

I heare that Mr. *Killigrew* ſhall receue and pay the Treaſure of the Chamber, till the Queen find one fitt for it; but if this continew true, Mr. *Killigrew* will haue it in the End himſelf. Sir *Henry Bagnall* is at Court, and doth anſwer diſcreetly and ſtoutly to what is ſaid vnto him; he is ſomwhat blamed for being to ſevere in his Gouernment.

Wood, Yeſterday in *Cheapſyd,* vpon a Pillory, had one Eare cut of, and three Lettres burnt in his Forehead. He made an Oracion to the People, that the

Fact

Fact was his own, procured vnto it by others ; that his own Confeſſion was vo-luntary, leade vnto it by the horrible Sting of his Conſcience, to accuſe him of his owne Villanies, which els cold neuer haue bene diſcouered ; that he had ra-ther goe to Heauen with one Eare, then to Hell with both Eares, and deſired the People to pray with him, that God wold receaue his Contrition.

In his Examinacion, he doth charge my Lady *Shruſbury* very deepely with the Matter, but her Honor denies it ; and thother brings no Proofe but himſelf to confirme it, which in Reaſon, beinge a perjured Fellow, ought not to be be-leued.

I can haue no Anſwer what the Queen will have you doe for Powder, while the States be reſoluing, nor what her Pleaſure is for Pikes, Muſkett, Calliuer, Match, and Lead, with a Proportion of Vittailes. My Lord Treaſorer will not be here till *Tueſday* or *Wedneſday*, then will I ſollicit the Reſolucion for your Leaue to return, the Time is fitt for it, becauſe Men ſpeake litle of the *Spaniſh* Preparacion, only the Cardinalls comming down is the Thing that is thought to bring many Matters with it. I heare by diuers, that the Queen was very angry when my Lord of *Eſſex* moued her for you, but all your Frends here doe wiſh me to ſee the End of my Lord Treaſorers, and Admirals Promiſes, which, God willing, I will doe.

Here is all Speach of Parlement quite dead, and for the Matter, you will me to breake with my Lord of *Eſſex*, I muſt attend my Time to doe it. I will call vpon *Lake*, *Stanhop*, *Grivell*, and *Ferdinando*, to write vnto you. I will attend your Lordſhips Pleaſure for the Banquet, and what Honor you will haue donne to my Lady *Rich*.

I was deſired by my Lady *Warwicke* to comend her very kindly vnto you. My Lady *Huntingdon* promiſes to write ; I cold neuer haue Acceſs vnto her, ſhe hath gotten my Lords Leaue to come vp.

My Lady *Elizabeth Clinton*, and my Lady, mett at my Lady *Comberlands* be-fore her lying down, and ſhe ſent twice to ſee how my Lady did ſince her Deliuery. Your Coſen, Mr. *Henry Sydney*, is gon into the Cowntry, and deſires you to excuſe his not anſwering of your Lettre, for Want of Time ; he promiſes much, and that he loues you ; God ſend him to perform it in Deedes. I know *Whiting* will continew all good Offices.

Your Lordſhips, &c.

At Court, this *Sonday*
7 of *December,* 1595.

R. Whyte.

Rowland Whyte, *Eſq;* to *Sir* Robert Sidney.

My Lord,

I Signified the Cauſe of Vnkindnes betwen 1000 [Earl of *Eſſex*] and 2000 [*Pem-broke*] which yet continewes, but the Queen takes the Matter in Hand, and migh-tely fauors the Weſtern Knight, is angry with 1000 for taking ſo violent a Courſe, and tels 2000 he ſhall goe without the Thing in Queſtion, who ſware vnto her Majeſtie, that he wold neuer deliver vp the Couenants and Aſſurances he had, and that to be denied the Cours of Law, was an Injury donne to the meaneſt Subiect. But away is he gonne, being at his Departure graciouſly vſed, and a Iewell ſent to C————c ; but ſince here are like many Stormes to fall vpon him, by Com-plaints growing vpon ſome of his Proceedings within his Gouernment, and here hath he now no Frend to leane vnto ; 500 truly touched with a Scorn, as he thinkes donne vnto him, by refuſall of the intended Marriage, and indeed bent to fauor all that are his Aduerſaries. My Lady, your Siſter, is very well : *Beecher* hath, as he tels me, written to you what his Opinion is touching the Vittaile, which is not to medle in it without an Impreſt, and withall to haue your Lord-ſhips Fauor to ſell it from Time to Time, but ſtill to haue a Care to the Safety of the Town and your Honor. I haue had Speach with Mr. *Lake* about Thin-ſtruction you ſent me, who wills me to forbeare doing your Comandment for a While, becauſe the Speach of a Parlement is dead againe. Yet doth honeſt **11**

tell

tell me, that though it receue many Checks, it will forward, becaufe it brings neceffary Profitt with it, and that vpon *Sonday* he hard it fhold be ; but I will haue an Eare opened and an Eye vnto your Lordfhip, and wilbe aduifed by Mr. *Lake*, whom I fynd very carefull to doe you Seruice. I writt vnto you I had bene with my Lord *Monjoy*, and my Lady *Rich*, and now here are refolued of the 3. I will goe in your Name and my Lady, to my Lord *Compton*.

As for the Wants I writ vnto you of the Artillery, they fhalbe fupplied, for the Warrants I deliuered to Sir *Robert Cecill* for the Queen to figne, are recomended by my Lord Treaforer with his own Hand. As to your Leave, I was comanded by my Lord Admiral, my Lady *Warwick*, and Mr. *Stanhope*, to fignifie this much vnto you : That the Queen talking of *Low Cowntrey* Matters with my Lord Admiral, told him what Reports were giuen out of her, and that your Lordfhip had fent very carefully a Page ouer of Purpofe, to bring you affured Word how fhe did.

This Opportunity he tooke to moue her about your Return, and kneeling down befought her Majeftie to heare him. He faid, that the Death of your Brother occafionned a great Alteracion in your priuat Eftate ; that one of his Cownfell, whoe was alfo one of yours, affured him, that it did much concern you to be here for one Terme, to fettle your Fortune ; that this Care in you was fpecially for the Good of your Children, his very neare Kinred, that wold be much preiudiced, if any Thing otherwife then well hapned vnto you before you returned, and theirfore humbly defired her Majeftie to licenfe your Return but for fix Weekes ; that he wold giue his Word you fhuld ftay no longer. Thofe 6 Weekes you fpeake of wold be 6 Moneths, faid the Queen, and I will not haue him away when the Cardinall comes there. My Lady *Warwick* affured her, that if there were any Occafion of her Seruice to call you away, you wold prefer it before all your priuat Bufines, and return, leauinge it vndonne. And Mr. *Stanhope* kneeled, and told her, that fhe needed not feare your Return to your Gouernment, if her Seruice required it ; for if fhe wold, at your being here, but lay her Comandments vpon you to begone, he euer knew you foe refpectiuely Obedient of them, that you wold depart in 6 Howres. But for all this fhe wold nether grant it, nor denie it. And in deed no Refolution wilbe had till my Lord Treaforers being at Court, who is at *Strand*, and by the Queens own Comandment (left he fhuld take cold) to ftay thire till milder Weather. The Lords came of Purpofe from the Court vnto hym, and fatt in Cownfell this after Noone, about *French* Bufines, which indeed troubles them very much, for as I hear, the King anfwers, that as a Prince carefull of his Subiects ; he muft by fome Meanes or other looke vnto their Safety, and keape his Cowntry from vtter Ruin, that is like to perifh, if fome Remedy be not found out to comfort it, which is laid open vnto him by many of his faithfull Subiects, but that he is moft vnwilling to harken vnto it, being vnplefing vnto him, as long as he can poffibly ftand without it ; but to what Cours foeuer he be driuen vnto, he will neuer forgett her exceeding Fauors donne vnto him. And I heare that the Duke *d'Efpernon*, having of late loft by Reuolt 3 Townes in *Prouence*, is now content to accept of Thoffers the King heretofore made vnto him. That the Cardinals Stay is not wholy for the Chriftning in *Sauoy*, but to nourifh thofe Factions and Broiles at *Marfeiles*, and *Prouence* ; to give Orders for the Levying of new Troops, and the Furnifhing of all Things neceffary for the War, if the States refufe the Peace he brings with him.

At our Court the Queen is well (euer may it be foe) and the faire Ladies doe daily trip the Meafures in the *Counfell Chamber*. Sir *H. Vmpton* is vpon his Difpatch, but is moft vnwilling to goe this Iorney ; fome of his Frends tell him, that the Queen meanes to beftow fome Honor vpon him before he goe, but it is much doubted of by others. Sir *Roger Williams* hath bene dangeroufly fick of a hot burning Ague, that came by a Surfett, but is a very little better.

At *London*, this *Monday* Night,   *Your Lordfhips*, &c.
8 of *December*, 1595.

Row. Whyte.

Conte

Conte Maurice *de* Naſſau, *a Monſieur Monſieur de* Sidney.

Monſieur,

J'AY eſtè adverti par Meſſieurs les Eſtatz de *Zelande,* que l'ennemi ſeroit dintention, daſſieger la Ville de *Ooſtende* ; Laquelle comme Ilz me mandent, ſeroit mal proveue tant de gens guerre comme auſſi de Commandeur. Et d'autant, que vous ſcavez combien que la conſervation de la dite place Importe, pour le Service de ſa Majeſtè et de ces pays. Je n'ay peu laiſſer de vous prier Monſieur, que vous plaiſe envoier cent et cinquante hommes de *Fliſſingne,* Illec pour peu de Jours ſeulement, et Juſques a ce que nous puiſſions voire ce que l'ennemi vouldra entreprendre J'envoie auſſy quatre Companies de ces Garniſons, nonobſtant ce temps de geïee : Il ne ſe peult faire ſans meltre les places en danger. De ce que vous m'aviez mandè des fortifications de *Fliſſingne,* j'ay le faict a Meſſieurs les Eſtats ſerieuſement, et tiendray la main qu'il y ſoit proveu. Et ſur ceſte fin apres mes humbles Recommendations en vos bonnes graces, je prie Dieu vous maintenir.

Monſieur & la ſaincte Protection. A la *Hay* le 11 de *December,* 1595.

Voſtre tres Affectionnè a vous

faire Service,

Maurice *de* Naſſau.

Rowland Whyte, *Eſq; to Sir* Robert Sydney.

My Lord,

HER Majeſtie is in very good Health, and comes much Abroad: Vpon *Thurſday* ſhe dined at *Kow,* my Lord Keapers Howſe (who lately obtained of her Majeſtie his Sute for 100 *l.* a Yeare Land in Fee Farm.) Her Intertainment for that Meale was great and exceeding coſtly. At her firſt Lighting, ſhe had a fine Fanne, with a Handle garniſht with Diamonds. When ſhe was in the midle Way, between the Garden Gate and the Howſe, there came Running towards her, one with a Noſegay in his Hand, deliuered yt vnto her, with a ſhort well pened Speach ; it had in yt a very rich Iewell, with many Pendants of vnfirld Diamonds, valewed at 400 *l.* at leaſt. After Dinner, in her Privy Chamber, he gaue her a faire Paire of Virginals. In her Bed Chamber, preſented her with a fine Gown and a Juppin, which Things were pleaſing to her Highnes ; and, to grace his Lordſhip the more, ſhe, of her ſelf, tooke from him a Salt, a Spoone, and a Forcke, of faire Agatte.

Your Lordſhips Leave ſtands as yt did, not moued ſince my Lord Treaſorers Comming to the Court ; but all promiſing to doe yt within 3 or 4 Dayes. If your honourable Frends doe me Right, they can witneſs, with what Care and Diligence I ſollicyt and attend them, humbly deſiring the Queens Reſolution for your Returne ; and daily alledging vnto them Thoccaſions, and the Shortneſs of the Tyme, deſired to ſtay here. They all anſwer me, that now they are buſy about Sir *Hen. Vmptons* Diſpatch into *Fraunce,* that ended, they hope to fynd the Queen at better Leiſure to be ſpoken vnto.

Here was Yeſterday, *Mynn,* my Lord *Boroughes* Man, who is departed with an abſolute Denial for his Leave ; yet did he aſſure me, that his Lordſhip wold be here before *Candlemas,* let hap what liſt. He likewiſe told me, that in *Suſſex* and *Kent,* whence he was newly come, yt was bruited Abrode, that your Lordſhip was ſent for to be made a Counſailor, and aſked me if yt were ſo or no. I did wonder how yt ſhould riſe.

The Lords ſatt this Forenoon about Sir *H. Vmptons* Inſtructions ; ſome doe further his Going, ſome are more cold. Their is a Complaint come to the Lords againſt Mr. *Foulk Griuell,* for ſome Abuſes in *Kanck Wood,* and an Information of 14000 *l.* Spoile, by good Certificat of Gentlemen dwelling their abouts.

abouts. Yt will grow hardly with hym : The Matter is referd to my Lord Treaforer, and Sir *John Fortefcue*.

Sir *Roger Williams* died of a Surfett in *B. Caftle*, Yefterday, at 3 a Clocke after Midnight. He gaue all he had to my Lord of *Effex*, who, indeed, faued his Sowle, for none but he cold make hym take a Feeling of his End ; but he died well, and very repentant. His Iewels are valewed at 1000*l*. Tis fayd he had 1200*l*. out at Intereft. In ready Gold he had 200*l*. and 60*l*. in Silver. His Plate is worth 60*l*. his Garments 30*l*. his Horfes 60*l*. and this is his End. He defires to be buried in *Powles*, and I heare my Lord of *Effex* meanes to haue it donne in very good martiall Sort.

My Lady *Hartford* is here, fues to haue her Hufband at Liberty, or at left-wife to be comytted to my Lord *Canterbury*, or my Lord Keepers. The Queen fees her not, though fhe be in the Privy Lodgings, but fends her gracious Mef-fages, that neither his Life or Fortune fhalbe touched ; fends her Brothes in a Morning, and at Meales, Meat from her Trencher.

My Lady *Dacres* is here, an earneft Suter for her 2 Sonnes Pardon, and takes a Courfe to make her Way eafy ; fhe is promifed to come to the Queens Pre-fence. And I heare yt feared, my Lady *Shrofbery* wil be called in publique Queftion for *Woods* Perjuries ; yet hath fhe here many great Frends of both kinds.

Their is great Meanes made for Sir *Wal. Rawleighs* Comming to the Court, he lives about *London* very gallant ; his Voiage goes forward, and my Lord Treafo-rer venters with hym 500*l*. in Money : Sir *Robt. Cecill* venters a new Ship brave-ly furnifht, the very Hull ftands in 800*l*.

My Lord *Monjoy* was here, and fpake with the Queen in privat, having his Gown girt about hym, becaufe of an Ague : Some fay he would faine be a Cownfailor. And I hard that 200 fhould in priuat fay to another, whome he trufted much, that the *Long Slang*, meaning 1000 [Earl of *Effex*] fince *d d* going away, was never from 1500 ; and that.... now wold doe nothing but what he and my Lord knew.

To Morrow Morning, Sir *Edward Vvedall* deliuers to the Lords his Peticion for his old Accounts, and makes no Doubt but to obtain yt in 12 Days, becaufe all the Lords doe promes to further yt, and none will crofs yt. But I beleeue the Queen her felf will not grant yt. At Court, this *Saterday*, 13 of *December*, 1595.

I am your Lordfhips, &c.

R. White.

Geo. Gilpin, *Efq*; *to* Sir Robert Sydney.

My very good Lorde,

BY Captain *Lamberts* Hands, I receavyd yours of the 4th ; and for the firft Point, touching *Oftende*, the Matters being ended, and Sir *Edwarde* retorned thether, there needeth no Aunfwer, leavinge the Particulars, vntil I fee your Lordfhip. And as for my owne Caufe, I would be loath to be troublefome vnto any, and befeech youe to pardon the Boldnes yf I vfed any, leavinge that, and any other, to your honorable Difcretion and Pleafure. Want of Matter hath made me fylent this few Days ; and had it not bin to fertifie youe of the Recepte of your aforefayd Lettre, I would, as yet, not have troubled your Lordfhip. This thawe fell owt very fitly, for the Enimie, as by intercepted Letters was dif-covered, prepared to have paffed the Rivers into *Hollande*, which to oppofe a-gainft, though his Excellencies Will was good, I infure youe, his Forces would haue bin flender, the Companies being weake, and the Places many, where he might haue entred. Of the mutynied *Italians* comminge agayne to *Turnbow*, I am fure youe haue vnderftood they have ryfled the Villages in thofe Quarters, de-maunding 3 Months Contribution owt of Hand, threateninge all with Fire and Flame, yf they performe yt not. Thefe Men do nothinge lyke of this Courfe, but how to amend yt, that is the Difficultie, havinge fauoured them thus longe. Moft of the States Deputies that affembled here, are gonne to their Provinces to furder the Graunt of Contributions for the nexte Yere; fo as here is no great Meetinge, and leffe Refoluinge. As yet, wee know not whome they will fend ouer, ftayinge for Aunfwere to their laft Lettres, weather hir Majefty lyke of thofe ment to fend. Monfieur *Buzenval* hath lately affured the States, in the Behalfe of his Mafter, that he will make noe Peace nor Agreement with the King of *Spayne*, without their Knowledge and Lykinge; but what Holde may be taken on fuch Affuraunce that confifts in bare Words, I leaue to others Iudgement. *Haeghe*, this 13 of *December*, 1595.

Your Lordfhips, &c.

Geo. Gilpin.

Sir Thomas Lake *to Sir* Robert Sydney.

S I R,

ALthough I haue no Newes to writte, yet meeting here with Mr. *White*, who from Tyme to Tyme hath acquainted me with his Proceedings in your Bufines, afwell for your Leaue, as for the Supplyes, I thought it not amiffe, doubting, leaft the Succeffe of Things, being not altogether as you perhaps expected, may caufe you to impute it, to Want of Diligence in him, to anfwer, or that he hath exceeded all Rules of Dilligence, fo farre, that he hath rather been troublefome with Importunity; and without it, had neuer brought Things fo far as they are; your Leaue is yet in Hope. My Lord *Borroughes* abfolutely denyed, and his Man fent away; your Supplyes are yet vncertain, fome Thing perhapps from hence, but not vntill we finde it defperate, to be don by the States. We are now difpatching Sir *Henry Vmpton*, to the *French* King, hoping to diuert him from a Courfe with *Spayne*, which by his own Aunfweares, and Mr. *Edmonds*, and by other Coniectures, it feemeth he is lyke to enter into, the Pope working earneftly to bring it fo to paffe. And almoft all his Councell difcouering no good Conceipt of our Amity. I know not yet what wilbe the Succeffe of his Iorney, nor what we fhall offer him, fufficient to diuert him from anie other Way, whereby he come to the Quiet Poffeffion of his Kingdome. The cunning of Princes are great, and cannot be difcernyd by euery Countenance; but if he be in deed in Hope of a Peace, vppon any reafonable Conditions, I doe not fee what we are able to offer and performe, that may incourage him to continew the Warre.

We heare ftill of the Preparations of *Spaine*, which me thinketh you fhould haue better Meanes to gett Knowledge of, then we. And becaufe I would be glad that you might doe euery Thing, that may make you gratefull here, I thought good to lett you know, that we begynne to haue fo feeling an Apprehenfion of the Deffeigns of *Spayne*, as we wold be glad to be at fome Cofte, to difcouuer the Certainty of the Preparations. And therefore if you could bethink of anie fitt Perfon there, that might make a Iorney into *Spayn* for that Purpofe; I thinke fuch an Offer being probable, wold be welcome.

I leaue to you, if it fhall be your Chance to light on any fuch Conceipt, you muft be thinke your Witts, by whom here you will prefent it; for you are not ignorant of the Iealoufyes; peraduentur it were beft to make it to the Queen. I leaue further to trouble you. From *Richmond* this xiijth *Decemb.* 1595,

Yours to command,

Tho. Lake.

Rowland Whyte, *Efq; to Sir* Robert Sydney.

My Lord,

WOrd came hither Yefterday, that my Lord of *Huntington*, was lefte in *Yorcke*, fo ficke, as that yt is now feared he is dead. The Queen fent my Lord of *Effex* in Poft vnto hym, and as I heare, to fee Things well ordered

in

in thofe Quarters, vntill the Queen can fynd a trufty Prefident, to fend in his Place, if God fhuld call hym away. My Lady of *Huntington*, knows nothing of this, and by the Queens Comand kept from her.

Here were fent for certain of Thaldermen of *London*, who are comanded to furnifh fpeedely, 15 of their beft Ships. And Letters are fent to all the Ports of *England*, to prepare fuch Ships, as by the Statute they are injoined, and to be ready out of Hand. My Lord Admirall is gonne to *Chatam*, to fee the Nauie prepared, and that fome be prefently put to Sea, for here is a Sufpicion conceued, that *Fuentes*, will with his Army now a Foote, attempt fomething againft *Cales*.

My Lord Admiral fpake very earneftly to my Lord Treafurer to move the Queen for your return for one Moneth, and that he wold giue his Honor, you fhuld ftay here no longer, which he hath promifed to doe, and byd me attend yt. My Lady *Warwick*, and Mr. *Stanhope* tells me as much, fo doth Mr. *Ferdinando*. I will not ftur hence, till I know what my Lord Treafurer hath fayd to the Queen, and what her Pleafure is.

Yt was told me, that my Lord *Boroughes* Frends defpairing of his Leaue, gaue yt quite over ; but now fynding that your Return is like to be, they ftand againe for yt ; and why fhuld not he return as well as you. So fearing left yt might hynder yours, I went to my Lady *Warwick*, and Mr. *Stanhop*, and befought them to fatisfie my Lord *Boroughes* Frends fo far, as to affure them, your Lordfhip wold not ftay here longer then *Candlemas*, at which Tyme he might come and ftay here as long as he pleafed ; and that this Cours might Occafion no Hyndrance to either of you, which they promes to doe.

Moreouer I did affure them, that Sir *Edmond Vveaall*, wold leaue all Buifnefs, and carry ouer the Leaue hymfelf, which will further yt much, and foe doth Sir *Edmond* hymfelf offer, as he promifed you, and truly acknowledges the Fauors you doe hym. His Buifnes is like to haue but cold Succefs, for all his great Hopes and Promifes. The Queen is very well.

The two Warrants are figned for the Wants of the Queens great Ordinance in *Flufhing*, and I will fend my Man to the Town to haften yt away. As for the Powder, Pikes, Vittailes, here is little Good, to be looked for ; and the States Letters are expected, what they will fay to powder.

Court 16 *December*,
1595

Your Lordfhips, &c.

Rowland White.

Sir Tho. Bodley *to* Sir Robert Sydney.

S I R,

FOR as much as yow had written to haue her Majefties Letters addreffed vnto me, and it hath bin, notwithftanding configned to yourfelf, without any Thing to me, of any fuche Mater ; and becaufe, in very Truth, I am vtterly vnacquainted with any Part of thofe Affaires, ether touching the Prouifion of Powder fent vnto yow, or the State of thofe Places, that yow require to be fortified, or other particularities contained in the Lettre. In my Conceat it was intended, that as Maters appertaining to your owne Charge, and wherein yow could beft pleade for her Majefties Right, and anfwer all Obiections, they fhould be folowed by your felf, as methinkes the Lettre it felf, doth expreffe it very plainely, by referring them vnto yow. For in me, yow knowe it were no Grace, to prefent a Lettre publickly, which is not fent vnto me, and wherein I am not named (as I am alwaies in all, that I am willed to exhibit) and of the Subiect whereof I am nothing fo informed, as that I am able, to anfwear, and replie, and debate it with them, as is fitte. In which Refpect, left the Lettre fhould mifcarie, with wandring too and fro, I will retaine it with me heere, that if your Leafure and Comoditie will ferue therunto, it may be prefented by yourfelf in Perfon ; if not, I fhould wifhe yow to write to the General States,

and

and fignifie fome Reafon of your not comming hither, and fuche Mater withall, as yow fhall thinke expedient, for the Furtherance of your Buifneffe; wherupon I will take Order, that her Majefties Lettres, together with yours, fhall be deliuered to the Prefident of their College, and that they fhall be folicited for an Anfwer out of Hande; which is the very beft Courfe, that I thinke vpon yet, to be taken in your Behalf. The Copie of the Lettre I returne heere inclofed. As yet I haue no Anfwer to my laft Difpatche into *England*, nor a Scrappe of any Newes, that is worth your Paines to reade it, for which I leaue yow faluted and refaluted very hartely.

Your moft affectionat Frende

From the *Hage*,
Dec. 17. 1595.

to doe yow Seruice,

Tho. Bodley.

Rowland White, *Efq; to Sir* Robert Sydney.

My Lord,

IN my laft, of the 16 of *December*, from the Court, I fignified my Lord of *Huntingdons* being ill at *Yorke*; in this, that he is affuredly dead: The Certainty of yt was brought to the Queen, upon *Wednefday* Morning, by one Mr. *Nevell*, a Kinfman and a Seruant of his own, who was with hym all the While he was Sick, which was 9 Dayes, and at the Howre of his Deathe, whiche was vpon *Sunday* laft. He reports, that the Bifhop of *York* being with hym, defired two Things of his Hands; to prepare hymfelf to dye, which he did; not vfing many Words but fuch as did giue good Affurance he died a good Chriftian; and to difpofe of his Eftate, which by no Meanes he wold harken vnto; and fayd litle to yt, only that it was a wild World, which he wold not thincke vpon. This is kept from my Lady *Huntingdon*; but the Queen of Purpofe is come to *Whytehall* on fuch a foddayn that yt makes the World much wonder at yt, and iudge Thinges that neuer were, what yt is, but to comfort her, and to breake yt vnto her herfelf. My Lord Keaper was fent to her to tell her from the Queen, that my Lord was ficke, and therefore if he had not fetled his Eftat to her content, fhe wold fee and fend about that yt fhuld be donne. In the After noon he came againe vnto her, to let her know, that the Queen was aduertifed he was in fome Danger, and theirfore befought her to confider what fhe wold haue donne about his Eftate. And thus, you fee, her Majefties gracious Care of her; and now that the Way is prepared, the Queen this Day will let her know the Truth. Affone as I could find Oportunity I went to my Lady *Warwicke* and Mr. *Stanhope*, and told them, that I was carefull to impart vnto them, what, in my Opinion, did much concern you, which was, that my Lord of *Huntingdon* was dead: I knew yt would infinitly grieve you, both for his Loffe, and that you cold not be here both to comfort your difconfolate Aunt, and to do her Service in this Tyme; fhe, without Queftion, fhuld haue Occafion to vfe one that truly loved her, and honoured her; and that none was fitter for yt then your felf, being now fole left, as yt were, of her Blood. They allowed very well of my Reafons; and my Lady *Warwick* broke yt to the Queen; my Lady *Hoby*, and Mr. *Stanhope* being by. Who then fayd, *She had rather than* 100 l. *you were here, for none fo fit as your felf to looke vnto her.* Whereupon fhe gave Order to my Lord Treafurer, to fignifie this hur Pleafure vnto you, by his Lettre, which moft willingly he did, and fent for me, gaue me this enclofed vnto you, which he wryt with his own Hand; and, as he faies, for you to prepare your felf againft the Queens own Lettre came, which fhalbe donne at the firft Signing Day. He byd me tell you, that he fends you no Word of my Lord *Huntingdons* Death, becaufe he wold not fend you any Thing to trouble you. I had a whole Howres talke with him of our Wants of *Flufhing*, of your Living and my Ladys, of your Children, Sonnes and Daughters, which being a Difcourfe apart, and of great Length, I haue at this Tyme no Leifure to deliuer yt vnto you, becaufe of my haft to fend this away. But I will fay thus much,

that

that your Lordſhip is as much beholding vnto hym for his good Speaches of you, as I know any Gentleman of *England*, that is of no Kin vnto him, and ſoe ſay his neereſt Seruants. Mr. *Lake* ſent vnto me from Sir *Robert Cecill*, to know who your Lordſhip wold Leave in your Place, now that Sir *Edm. Vuedale* was here. I ſent him this Word, that the Charge of the Town you wold be moſt carefull of : That you had in the Town at this Howre Capt. *Brown*, a Gentleman your Lordſhip knew to be diſcrete, valiant, well affected in Religion, well languaged, and one that was ſpecially well acquainted with the Humors of the Burgers and Mariners, and euery Way ſuch a one as your Lordſhip wold be anſwerable for. But if Sir *Edm. Vuedall* being here were any Hindrance to your Leaue, he was right willing to return with your Licenſe. Mr. *Lake* imparted yt to Sir *Robert Cecill*, who ſayd, that their was litle Reaſon to poſt Sir *Edm. Vuedall* ouer again in ſuch haſt, having a Sute in Hand that his Preſence might help to obtain, and that his vndoing did depend vpon yt. And theirfore he was glad your Lordſhip had ſo ſufficient a Man to leaue behynd you : Then went Mr. *Lake* to draw your Lettre, which contains, that her Majeſtie being ofte earneſtly delt withall for your Return about ſome vrgent Buiſnes, of your own, ſhe was won to graunt yt ; although yt was but lately you had been here : That you might ſo determine as to be returned to your Charge againe by *Candilmas*, and to leaue in your Place the eldeſt Captain. For this Purpoſe, if yt be not altered is this Lettre, the Shortneſs of the Tyme is put in to ſatisfie my Lord *Boroughes* Frends, who ſtorme at this, and think them ſelues injuried ; but when you are here, your Lordſhip ſhall find Occaſions to ſtay longer. I will attend and ſollicit the Queens Letter ; have a Care to the Fine was left with my Lord of *Hunting-don* for Capt. *Bucke* ; and harken after my Lady of *Riches* Pleaſure for the Chriſtning, who ſendith Word, ſhe will not be here till *Chriſtmas* Eve. My Lord *Monjoy*, and my Lord *Compton*, do willingly accept of this Kindneſs you deſire them vnto. My Lady is well, and exceedingly glad of your Leue, and your laſt Lettre did more content her than euer any you wryt vnto her. All the Children are well, ſaue Mrs. *Betty*, who is troubled with a great Cold, and burnes much. Your Lordſhip is beholding to my Lord Admirall, as my Lord Treaſurer told me, for his good Speeches of you to the Queen, and his earnyſtneſs to procure Leaue. Soe are you to my Lady *Warwick*, Mr. *Stanhope*, and Sir *Robert Cecill*. They looke for Thanckes, and it is due vnto them. The two Warrants. are diſpatched, and ſent to the *Towre* ; and they tell me, they will ſend ouer thoſe Wants with as much Speed as they can. All Things are ready ſaue the 4 Carriages, which are in Hand. My Ladys *Elizabeth*, and *Katharine Somerſet*, take my Lord *Huntingdons* Death moſt grievouſly.

Mr. *Arthur Gorge* makes Sute for the great Park of *Winſor* ; and they are in Paine whare to fynd one fit to ſucceed hym in his Goverment of the North, Some name my Lord of *Worceſter*. I beſeech your Lordſhip except my ſcrolled Lettre : My haſt is great becauſe of the Tyde. From *White-Hall*, this *Friday* Morning 19 of *December*, 1595.

Your Lordſhips, &c.

Roland Whyte.

Rowland Whyte, *Eſq*; to *Sir* Robert Sydney.

Right honorable,

BY *Chriſtopher Brown*, I ſent my Lord Treaſorers Letter, ſignifieng the Queens Letters for your Return. To-morrow I ſhall have the Queens Letters ſigned, which I will ſend you. This encloſed is from my Lord of *Eſſex* ; and Sir *Robert Cecil* tels me, he hath wrytten vnto you, and ſent yt by the Poſt, with a Packett to Mr. *Bodeley*. The Queen goes backe againe to *Richmond* vpon *Monday*. Here is a Speach that the Queen will make both Cownſailers and Officers of Houſhold ; I hear named Lord *Monioy*, Lord *North*, Maſter of the *Rowles*, the Chieff Juftice Sir *Henry Leigh*. Vpon this Report I went to 12, and tooke an Occafion to fpeake of yt. He made ftraunge of yt, and thought their wold be none made in haft ; but, fayd he, yt will encreafe the Queens New Yeares Giftes. Sir *Hen. Vmpton* is difpatched, fave one Lettre to be figned, to the Duke of *Monmorency*, which not being redy to Day, was the Caufe that yours was not prefented to the Queen till To-morrow, to haue them both figned together, as Mr. *Lake* affures me. The Queen hath promifed hym the Thre-furefhip of the Chamber, and ftands conftant in yt, and at his Return to haue yt. But yf 900 and 200, that wold 40 had yt, can hynder yt, thother fhall goe without yt. The Vnkindnes doth continew between 1000 [Earl of *Effex*] and 2000 [Earl of *Pembroke*] and for the Cawfe I wryt vnto you ; 2000 by no Meanes will releafe thofe Bonds and Covenants thother entred vnto, who now faies, he was drawen to doe he knew not what hym felf. But 1500 (Queen) is much of-fended with all, and faies 2000 fhall doe yt.

My Lord Chamberlain, and my Lord Admirall, were in the *Towre* to view the Remain of all Things ; and a fpeciall Care is taken for all Kind of Armes and Municion fit for the Defence of the Land.

The City muft furnifh 16 Ships and 4 Pinnafes, and arme 10000 Men, which they thincke to be to much. I hard yt faid, that within thefe 20 Dayes theire are 30 Marchants, that were efteemed wealthy, become Banckrowpts.

I was defired by an honeft Gentleman that is in Ward with 1000 [Earl *Effex*] to tell you, that he hoped your Return wold be for your good, if his Fauor and Creditt, I mean 1000, cold effeft yt ; for to all he can name, Exceptions are taken, vnles yt be your felf, of whom 900 and the reft, doe hold no ill Opinion of.

Your Lordfhip, by my former Lettres, have hard of my Lord of *Huntingdons* Death ; and now I will wryte of my Lady your Aunts vnhard of Sorrowes. Vpon *Thurfday* Night (having before hard by my Lord Keeper of her Huf-bands being but ill, fufpecting more, fhe cawfed all the Men and Women in the Howfe to come before her, and by their very Countenances, who could not choofe but lament, fhe apprehended the Greiffe that fo much afflicts her ; and yet all that Night none durft not breake the Matter vnto her. Vpon *Friday* Morning, my Lady *Puckering* came to fee her, and finding her fo difquieted, fhe told her by Circumftaunces that his Daunger was great, and fmale Hope of Recouery ; but being defired by my Lady to tell her the very Truth of it, fhe then told her, that indeed affured Word was come he was dead. I am not able to deliuer vnto you the Paffions fhe fell into, and which yet fhe continues in. Sure I am, I was greued to here a Gentlewoman of hers with weeping and crying, made me know it ; who faid, that none but your felf were fitt to Comfort her, and there-fore fhe hoped you were fent for ; which I did affure her was true ; and befought her to lett my Lady know of yt, as fhe found Occafion to doe yt. The Queen her felf, in a Litter, went to vifit her about 4 o'Clocke this Euening ; I will goe To-morrow Morning, and know what Comfort fhe receiued by yt, and daily aduertife your Lordfhip of her Eftat.

I hard that a Gentleman, whofe Name I cold not yet learn, having had 300 *l.* a Yeare Land conveied vnto hym, of Truft by my Lord of *Huntingdon*, to the Vfe of my Lady, in lieu of fo much Land of her Iointer fold, makes refufall to do yt vnto her, but to the new Earle, whofe Sonne *Frauncis* died Lord *Haft-ings*, vpon *Monday* laft, as yt is here by Letters advertifed. I thincke his Wiffe was Sir *John Harringtons* Sifter, whoe by her is now Lady *Haftings*, her Husband not enioying that Honor a whole Day.

The Queen, much offended hereat, comanded my Lord Keeper, my Lord of *Buckhurft*, Sir *John Fortefcue*, and the Mafter of the *Rolles*, to examine the Caufe ; and, as I heare more of yt, I will impart yt vnto you.

I vnderftand he died a very poore Lord, extremely in Debt, wold make no Will, and therby my Lady hath nothing but her bare Iointer left her. God fend your Lordfhip foon ouer to Comfort her, and to looke to fuch Things as her Sor-rows will not giue her leave to doe.

Her

Her Officers are looked for daily : I will enquire after the Fine your Lordſhip lefte with hym for Capt. *Bucks* Matter.

Sir *Roger Williams* is buried vpon *Tueſday* in *Powles.* Sir *Tho. Morgan* continewes ſtill very ill, and ſmal Hope conceaved of his Recouery.

My Lady *Darby,* was brought to Bed Yeſterday of a Boy, to the great Comfort of her Grandfather. My Lady *Rich* will not be here till *Chriſtmas* Eue, and then ſhall ſhe apoint the Day for the Chriſtning. The two Lords do attend her Pleaſure.

Sir *Edmond Vuedall,* wold haue bene as good as his Promes vnto you, to return with your Leaue, if his being here had giuen yt any Hyndrance ; but me thinckes he begins to marvell he hath receued but one Lettre from you, in anſwer of many he ſent, and to fear leaſt your Lordſhips Loue be growen more cold towards hym, then yt was wont to be. For any Thing that euer I cold heare, he hath carried hymſelf here towards you, as one acknowledging to haue receued Creditt and Benefitt by your Fauor.

My Lord Treaſorer, is ordring of a Proportion for your ſpending Powder in *Fluſhing* for thauxilary Companyes, and for a Store for the Safety of the Town. I dare not importune hym much till this Leaue be ſigned, and ſent away ; then will I deliver vnto hym a Petition for Gunpowder, the Town being at this Inſtant without any, and ſo ſend yt with the Wants of Thartillery. He ſtill ſayes, that the States muſt fynd the cawtionary Companies Powder.

15 tells me, that my Lady *Borough* gives yt ovt, that her Lords Return wilbe his undoing ; and wiſhes his Abode where he is ; and for any Thing I heare, he is like to ſtay till your coming and going back again.

The Tyme limited for your Lordſhips ſtay is but till *Candlemas,* you nead theirfore make haſt. My Lord Admiral told me Thanſwer was in *Fluſhing,* which you might keape, if you pleaſed, to bring you ouer. My Lord *Sheffield* is come vp, and hopes for that he ſhall neuer haue.

My Lord of *Eſſex* mournes for my Lord of *Huntingdon,* and takes his Death very grievous.

London, this *Saturday* Night,   *Your Lordſhips,* &c.
xxth of *December,* 1595.

                       Roland Whyte.

Roland Whyte, *Eſq; to Sir* Robert Sydney.

My Lord,

THE Queen ſigned your Leaue this Day at Twelue a Clocke : Sir *Robert Cecill* deliuered yt unto me, and I went to Mr. *Lake,* who ſealed yt, and directed yt vnto you. A true Copie whereof I here encloſed ſend you, and deliuered the Queens Letter yt ſelf to my Ladys own Hands. I fearing leaſt my Man *George* might come to ſome Miſhap at Sea, take this Courſe of ſending the Copie vnto you. I was with my Lord Treaſorer, who only wiſhes you a ſafe Paſſage. I made my Lord of *Eſſex* acquainted with it, who ſalutes you. So doth Sir *Robert Cecill,* and my Lady *Warwicke,* who tooke exceeding Care in this ; and the honorable Mr. *John Stanhope,* whoe indeed tooke Paines to induce ſome of the Lords to Diſpatch yt. Now, my Lord, you ſee yt is donne, let me tell you what Cheques were giuen vnto yt theſe 2 Dayes. My Lord *Boroughes* Frends hearing that the Queen had graunted your Lordſhips Leaue to Return, gaue yt out that he was ſo ſicke, that their was no Hope of Recouery, but by the Chaunge of Ayre ; and that if her Majeſtie were reſolued to keape hym theire, ſhe ſhould ſhortly heare of his Death. My Lady *Shandos,* my Lady *Thomas Howard,* Mrs. *Bridges,* and my Lady *Borough,* were in my Lady *Cecills* Chamber, which, indeed, made me ſo jealous, that I went to my Lady of *Huntingdons,* and beſought Mrs. *Malby* to let my Lady know what Hindrance I fownd were giuen to your Return ; and therefore I humbly deſired

I

fired her to fend one to the Queen about my Difpatch : She brought me this Word, that the Queen her felf told my Lady, your Lordfhip was fent for, and theirfore fhe knew none durft be againft yt. I then affured her yt was not foe, and humbly befeeched her to fend a Gentleman to the Court with me about yt, which was donne, and my Ladys *Warwick*, and *Scroope*, told the Queen of yt, and by that Means your Lordfhip hath your Leaue obtained.

The Queen was with my Lady *Huntingdon* very priuat vpon *Saturday*, as I wryt vnto you, which much comforted her. Her Gentlewomen and Gentlemen tell me, fhe exceedingly defires your fpeedy Return ; and affure me, fhe is very ill, and continewes full of Sorrow. Here is no Body to looke to her Buifnes ; if your Lordfhip were here, yt is very like fhe wold comytt the Truft of all to your Hands. I fhall need to fay no more, but to referre your fpeedy Coming to your own Wifdom, which can beft direct you ; but if fhe be foe ill as they tell me, I wold wifh your Lordfhip to make great Haft. I will daily goe to fee how fhe doth, and now muft attend my Ladys Chriftning ; and the Sending of the Prouifions from the Towne. My Lady *Rich* is not yet come, yt wilbe *Chriftmas Eve* ; fhe muft appoint the Day and Tyme for yt.

Her Majeftie thought to haue gone to *Richmond* to Day ; but, by Reafon of the fowle Weather, deffers yt till to Morrow. Sir *Henry Vmpton* is pofted away. Newes are here, that the King hath wonne *la Fere*. That from the States, there fhall come Comiffioners to the Queen. That from *Genoa*, are gonne to *Spaine* 12 new built Ships well appointed, and called the 12 *Apoftles*. That our Fleet is a making ready, and a Stay made of all Sortes of Ships of Warre in all our Portes.

To Morrow Sir *Roger Williams* is buried, and I feare Sir *Tho. Morgan* will dy this Night, for all that come from hym are of that Opinion.

I forgat to wryte vnto you, that the rich Gentleman was knighted by the Queen at *Kew* Sir *Hugh Portman*. *d d d*, follows his Buifnes at Court with wonderfull Care ; and I was affured by *c c*, that 200 was neuer knowen to be foe earneft in any Thinge as in yt ; and that he fhuld fay, their was no Reafon why he fhuld be fent away before 1500 [Queen] had giuen hym Satisfaction. 100 prefents the Peticion, 900 comends yt, and 200 drawes as many to doe it as he can ; but 300 faid at 130, that their were many Sutes of the fame Nature, and how fhuld yt be knowen if the Soldiers hired or were paid, what he now demanded for them.

I acquainted Sir *Edmund* [*Vvedale*] with your Leaue, and fhewed yt hym, who proteftes, that when your Lordfhips comes, if you will haue hym goe to *Flufhing*, he will leaue all, and obey your Comandments. But feeing his being here doth not hynder yours, he hopes your Lordfhip will not be offended withall, feeing all his Fortune depends vpon this Sute he now hath in Hand.

Affoon as ever I heare of your Landing, which I hope wilbe affone as may be, left Th'occafions of this Tyme might countermand your Return. I will attend your Pleafure where you will comand me. And referre many Thinges to that Tyme. God fend your Lordfhip a good Wynd ; and I befeach you be carefull to haue a good Shippe to carry you. *London*, this *Monday* Night 10 a Clocke, 22 *December*, 1595.

Your Lordfhips, &c.

Rowland Whyte.

I haue made knowen the Wants of Powder, but I fee no Haft made to Supply you. My Lord Treaforer talkes of yt with Sir *Tho. Brooks*, who giues yt Furtherance.

Rowland

Rowland Whyte, *Esq;* to *Sir* Robert Sydney.

My Lord,

MY Lord *Boroughes* frends do mightely ftorme that he hath no Leave, and doe begin to fynd Fault with 1000 [Earl of *Effex*], who is thought to be the Occafioner of yours ; but beleue me, though 900 put me euer in good Hope, I of late began to difpaire of your Leaue, and am perfuaded, that if my Lady *Huntingdons* Defire to fee you, had not moued the Queen to grant yt, you had not come ouer in Haft. And foe doth 1000 affure them, as 14 tells me. My Lady *Rich* is come to the Town, yet the Chriftning is put of till *Wednefday* New Yeares Eue. She fayes that my Lord *Compton* defired her to differ yt till then, becaufe of fome vrgent Buifnes he hath in the Countrey, that will keepe hym away till *Tuefday* Night ; but I doe rather thincke yt to be a Tetter, that fodainly broke out in her faire whyte Forheade, which will not be well in 5 or 6 Days, that keapes your Son from being chriftned. But my Lady *Riches* Defires are obeyed as Comandment by my Lady, who, in deed, is forry of this Delay, becaufe fhe wold haue it paft before your Returne. My Lord *Borough* is expected with the next Wynd, though he haue no Leaue, for he is wrytten vnto by 200, and others, that the Queen hath graunted yours. My Lady *Effex* was with my Lady vpon *Chriftmas Eve*, and ftayed here 3 Howres. My Lady, and all the Children are well, and doe pray to God to fend you well and fpeedely ouer.

I am going to the Court, but to harken how the World goes their ; and as long as the Wynd continewes wefterly to wryte vnto you. I am foe affrayd of Countermands, as that I cold wifh you here already : But if they come to my Hands, you fhall not receue them in Haft. *London*, this St. *Stephens* Day.

Your Lordfhips, &c.

Rowland Whyte

Sir *Roger Williams* is buried, and Sir *Thomas Morgan* dead. Here are 2 *Yrifh* Greihownds fent you from *Yreland*, by Capt. *Gorings* Procurement ; I cannot learne from whom.

Rowland Whyte, *Efq;* to *Sir* Robert Sydney.

My Lord,

YF my Seruant *George* be come vnto you, whom I difpatcht hence the 22 of *December* at Night, your Lordfhip hath receued affured Newes that you haue leave to come ouer ; for by hym I fent a true Copie of the Queens own Lettre vnto you, exaimined by Mr. *Lake*. My Lady hath the Warrant yt felf, left yt fhuld perrifh at Sea. And leaft my Man might haue fome Misfortune, I fend now againe a Copie of yt vnto you, befeaching your Lordfhip to haften ouer, for my Lady *Huntingdon* is ill, and continewes ill, vnwilling to receue Comfort. I nead not tell you how much yt may concern you, but refer yt to your own Wifdom. Her Eftate is broken ; and, as I heare, much of her Iointer, by her Confentment made away. At your own Coming, you fhalbe acquainted with the Truth of all Things, which I only can receue by vncertain Reports. I was at Court this Morning, where nothing is fo much thought vpon as Dauncing and Playing. Some were there, hoping for Preferment, as my Lord *North*, and Sir *Henry Leigh*. They play at Cards with the Queen, and it is like to be all the Honor that will fall vnto them this Yeare.

My Lord Treaforer is ill of a Cold in the Neck, and lies at his Houfe in the *Strand*. Sir *Edm. Vvedall* is at Court ; hath exceeding good Words giuen vnto hym, but he doth no good at all in his Buifnes ; 200 [Sir *Robert Cecil*] doth moft for hym, and that brings no Fruit at all. The Bifhop of *Yorke* is made Lord

Prefident of the *North.* My Lady *Darbyes* Son is turned to be a Daughter ; fhe was but brought to Bed vpon *Chriftmas Eve,* though the Newes at Court was that yt was a Boy, 12 Dayes paft.

My Lord *Borough* hath no Leaue, nor like to haue any, though his Frends doe mightely trauaile in yt, efpecially 1000 [Earl of *Effex*], and all in vaine.

The Queen chid my Lord of *Lincolne,* that he doth not give his Daughter better Maintenance.

The Chriftning (as I wryt vnto you in my Lettre Yefterday, which I fent with 2 Greihownds to *Grauefend*) is put of by my Lady *Riches* owne Comandment, till *Wednefday* next. My Lady is well, and all thefe your fweet Children, that howrely pray for your fafe Returne.

The Queen went this Day to the Chappell very Princelike, and in very good Health. *London,* this St. *Johns* Day at Night, 1595.

Your Lordfhips, &c.

R. Whyte.

Roland Whyte, *Efq;* to *Sir* Robert Sydney.

My Lord,

ALthough I hope your Lordfhip become away with the faire Wynd, which appeared here to be good vpon *New Years* Day, I venter the fending of this, which purchance you may meet on the Way.

My Lady of *Huntington* continewes foe ill, as that many Doubt fhe cannot liue ; fhe is fo much by Sorrow weakned as that no Officer of hers, ·dare goe to her fight, to know her Pleafure, either in her own priuat Fortune, or to know what fhall be donne with the dead Body ; you are much wifhed here to comfort her, which I affure them wilbe affone as any Boat be able to put to Sea, the Wynd and Weather being as yt is contrary and tempeftuous.

Your Sonne was chriftnyd vpon *New Years* Eue, by my Lord *Monjoy,* Lord *Compton,* and Lady *Rich.* They named hym *Robert,* by my Lady *Riches* Defire. They gaue 3 very fair ftanding Bowles all of one Fafhion, that may be worth 20 *l.* a Piece. Here was my Lady *Cumberland,* her Daughter ; my Lady of *Effex,* her Daughter and Sonn ; my Lady *Dacres,* her Daughters, and many other Gentlewomen, and Gentlemen. All Thinges were fo prouided, as they had no Cawfe to feare the Meafels.

My Lord *Borough* hath a Grant to come ouer, the Queen being continually importuned vnto yt by his Frends, fince your Leave was figned ; yet is not his Warrant come to the Signet.

My Lord Treafurer is gonne this Day to the Court, I meane Godwilling, to Morrow, to goe and hearken a loofe if their be any Speach of you thefe Holidays, and how the Speach continews of making of Officers, and Counfellors.

A Brute is here, that the King of *Scots* of late hath declared hym felf to be the Succeffor here ; but long may our gracious Soueraigne rayne ouer us. And yt is reported, that the Duke of *Sauoys* Embaffadors are very kindly receued by the King of *France.*

My Lady is Churched, is very well, and all the Children. We all pray for your fafe and fpeedy Return : This enclofed is from my Lady *Rich,* and a Note of the Hangings to be made.

The Carriages for the great Ordinance are not yet ready, I doe follicit the difpatching of them ; the Officers of the *Towre,* put the Fault in the Carpenter.

Yf my Lady *Huntington,* be in that extremyty as many tell me ; I cold wifh your Lordfhip to put to Sea with a contrary Wynd, left you come to late to fee hur in this World ; but I hope they make of yt more then yt is, but my Duty is to aduertife what I foe credibly here to be foe. And no Body hath yet

looked

looked into the Point of her Eſtate, which is thought very poore ; yet ſomthing is ſayd to be lefte vnto her, and her Heires for euer.

London 3 *January,* 1595,   *Your Lordſhips,* &c.
    at Night by Poſt.

R. Whyte.

Geo. Gilpin, Eſq; to Sir Robert Sydney.

My eſpeciall good Lorde,

NO Subject is offred for the Preſent, worth the troublinge of yowe, all re-mayninge in State, as at your Lordſhips being here ; ſomwhat his Ex-cellencie is about, and ready to be put in Execution, but what, none ſhall know, til yt ſpeede or fayle ; Sir *Fra. Vere,* beinge alſo not ydle, but would make ſure Worke, or neuer beginne yt ; my Lord Ambaſſador attends for the retorne of thoſe of *Holland* from *Zurick* Sea, and then will there very ſhortly after, be a Meet-ing here of thoſe, of this Province ; when as, within a Whyle after, I ſhall here what is paſt, and thereby haue a Geſſe of the Succeſs in the preſent Nogocia-tion of his Lordſhip ; whereof your Lordſhip ſhall haue Aduertiſement, as Oc-caſion ſhall ſarve ; ſo I may but know wether and how to directe my Letters vn-to yowe in *London.* At your Lordſhips comming to the Court, I humbly be-ſeech you, I may be remembred for ſom Increaſe of my Interteynement, and yf afore, I could be fauoured by your Lordſhips Meanes withowt that I be made known, yt might much Pleaſure me, eſpecially at this Preſent, for Cauſes which I am loath to manyfeſt. Yf I could get the Priuiledge about the Furnaces, I would thinke to make yt benaficiall to me, and to your Lordſhip worthe the Fauouringe : Forget not *Aertſens,* for he put me in remembraunce of Thoffices by him donne about *John Waringes.*

Here are new Alarmes from *Oſtende,* which I thinke your Lordſhip ſhall there haue harde of : I dowbt the Gouuernour at length wil worke his owne Harme ; Capt. *Olyuer* wil as I ſuppoſe inlarge hereof, what he heareth. *Haugh* this 12th *January,* 1595.

Your Lordſhips, &c.

Geo. Gilpin.

Some Letters being by Miſtake omitted in their proper Places, I have referred to the Pages, where they ſhould have been incerted, *viz.*

Page 8.   *Copy of the Orders, for putting an End to the Differences between the Erls of* Ormond *and* Deſmound. *Sent by Secretary* Cecil, *to Sir* Henry Sydney, *Lord Deputy of* Ireland.

1. *Article*   FIRST, That all their Matters in Controverſy, be hard in the *Chauncerie* in *Irland,* without eny dilatorie Plees.

2. *Secondly,* That after Iſſue joinid, the Queens Majeſty be advertiſed, that Comiſſion be ſent out of *England,* for the Triall of the Iſſue ; then the Com-miſſioners Certificat to be returnid. Firſt to the Lord Deputy, then by hym to the Queene, with his Opinion. And then the Queen to take Order.

3. The Priſe Wines of *Yonghall,* and *Kinſale,* to be ſequeſtrid by the Lord Deputy and Counſaill, till the Queen ſhall determine the Effects and Bonds, to be taken for due aunſwering of the ſame, by the Sequeſtrators.

4. All

4. All Lands. *&c.* whereof the Erle of *Ormound* was poſſeſſed, before the Fraie committid, *viz.* i *Februarii,* 1564, to remaine in the Poſſeſſion of the Erle of *Ormound.*

5. All Lands, in the Erle of *Deſmounds* Poſſeſſion, before the ſaid Fraie, to remaine in Poſſeſſion of the Erle of *Deſmound,* till they be recouerid by Lawe.

6. All Things in the doubtfull Poſſeſſion, to be in the Hands of indifferent Perſons, by the Lord Deputies Sequeſtracion. Whervnto the Erles to be obedient, and the Bonds to be taken of thoſe indifferent Perſons for the Rent, *&c.*

7. That bothe Erles obſerue the Pece, againſt the other, by themſelfs, their Seruaunts and Followers, till her Majeſty ſhall take Order.

8. Both the Erles fined at . . . . the Peece, for the Breach of the Peace in their Conflict.

9. That the Erles be callid to Accompt for the Detts to their Queene.

10. That the Erle of *Ormounde,* within xxty Daies after his Arrival, deliver to the Lord Deputy in Writing, the Names of all Offenders, mainteyned by the Erle of *Deſmound,* or his Frends, by his Conſent or Comaundement; which Offenders, *Deſmound* ſhall bring to Juſtification.

11. That the Erle of *Deſmound* ſhall in like Maner, *Mutatis mutandis.*

12. The Lord Deputy and Counſaill, hath Power to determine Contraverſies, concerning Goods and Cattaills detained; or of eny Perſon or Perſons impriſonned, in ſuch Sort and Maner, as they ſhall think meeteſt, for the Service of the Queenes Majeſty.

13. The Erle of *Ormounde,* within xxty Daies after his Arrival, to put in Pleadges, and thes to be deteined, impriſonned, alterid, or ſett at Liberty, at the Lord Deputies Diſcretion. And that thes Pledges ſhalbe, and remaine, for Perfourmaunce of the Recogniſaunce, knowlegid by the ſaid Erle, 22° *Nouembris,* 1565.

14. The like for the Erle of *Deſmound, Mutatis mutandis.*

Page 59. *Sir* Frances Walſyngham *to Sir* Henry Sydney.

My very good Lord,

I Was gladd to vnderſtande by the Earl of *Eſſex*'s Letter, that your Lordſhip and he is growen to ſo good a Concluſyon towching his Demaundes, wherby his Lordſhip ſeamethe to be greatlye ſatisfyed with your frendely Dealyng towardes him. Soche here as doe wyſhe generally unto that State, and partycularly to your ſelves, doe deſyre nothing more, then the contynewance of good Lyking and ſownde Frendeſhip betwene you. And therfor, good my Lord, lett your Eares be cloſed ageynſt Tale-bearers, who make ther Proffyt of Dyſſentyon. That Natyon, I learne, is cunnyng in the Profeſſyon, and therefore yt behouethe your Lordſhips bothe, to be verry circumſpect in that behalf. I pray God, that peſtylent Humour receive no Neuryſhement from hence. When I ſawle into Conſyderation of the Sowndenes of bothe your Judgements, then doe I ſhake of all feare : But when I caule to my mynd the curſed Deſtyny of that Ilande, I can not put of all Dredd. I hope your owne Wyſdome, and the caulyng en of your Frends here, and the good Myniſters aboute you, they will pevent the Mallyce of ſoeche as ſhall ſeak any Waye to ſlander you. Towching the ſendyng over of your Aſſyſtaunts, I am not unmyndefull thereof. Him whom you chiefly deſyre, I meane Sir *W. Dreury,* wyll not fayle at the Tyme by you appointed, yf God let yt not, or her Majeſty. Mr. *Rookebye,* without ſome impreſt owt of your Lordſhips Hande, and to forniſhe him of ſoeche Neceſſaries as the Place he is appoynted for requyre (having not the Meanes otherwyſe to furniſhe him ſelfe) ſhall be forced to refuſe the ſame, thorowhout Dyſabylytye. When I conſyder the Woorthynes of the Man, howe hardely ſooche an other of his Integryte is to be fownde, and how great Neade that Place hath of ſooche a oane ; I can not but wyſhe your Lordſhip to ſtreyne your ſelf as myche as you may,

✝

to fupplye his Wants. And fo leavyng forther to troble your Lordfhip, I moft hombly take my Leave. At my Houfe at *Odiam*, the 20th of *Octobre*, 1571.

Your Lordfhips affured Frend,

Fra. Walfyngham.

Page 81. *Sir* Francis Walfyngham, *to Sir* Henry Sydney.

After my very hartie Commendacions vnto your good Lordfhip,

WE have here had Newes, to the great Grief of many, of the Deathe of good Sir *Peeter Carew*; a Gentleman, in the Opinion of all Men, of fuch rare Vertue, and fingular good Parts, as is feldom to be found in thefe our Dayes; our Loffe is therbie the greater; but he is in better State then we can wifhe him. Vppon theife Newes, very earneft Suite hath ben made here, for theftablifhinge and maintaininge of his Cofin *Peeter* (whome he hath made his Heire to his Landes in that Realme) in the Barony of *Hidron*, and for fo much as it is geven t'vnderftand, that the fame fhall hardly be kept, vnleffe he have alfo her Majefties Caftell of *Lanhelin* in Keeping, as Sir *Peeter* had. The faid Suite tendeth to make Meanes to your Lordfhip (in whome the Difpoficion of the fame is) that he may have the Graunt therof, and be placed there accordingly. Your Lordfhips Favour to that good Name hath alwayes ben noted, and Sir *Peeter*, in that Suite, did finde the Fruites therof, to his great Beneffitt and Compfort; and fo is the fame acknowledged by his neereft Friendes; and, thervppon, the greater Hope is conceaved, that your Lordfhip will maintaine in his Succeffion, the fame Favour and Goodnes: And, for fo much as I have learned, that the Vphouldinge of a truftie and trew *Englifhman* in thofe Parts; fhall ftand much to Thadvancement of her Majefties Service, afwell in the Repreffinge of the *Irifhrie*, as for other good Purpofes, better knowen to you then to me. I am moved emonge the reft of the Frindes to that Name (that in fo many Ages are witneffed to have ben good Servaunts to this Crowne) to be an Interceffor vnto your Lordfhip, that yt may like you to fhew him fo much Favour as you may, afwell by Placinge of him as aforefaid, as by Aidinge and Affiftinge him with fuch Perfons of Advice and Counfell, in the Practifes of that Realme, as are moft meeteft to hould him in his Strength, for the Keeping of him in his Inheritaunce, and therewithall to hould that Countrey in goode Obedience, to the Furtheraunce of her Majefties Service. And as your Lordfhip hereby fhall fhowe good Allowance of the Title adiudged by you and her Majefties Counfell of that Realme, fo fhall you deferve for ever the Love and good Will of all that Kinred. And whatfoever you fhall doe for my Sake, and for the Interceffion of other of his Frindes, you fhall finde vs ready to requite you with any Pleafure we can fhewe you. And fo I bid your Lordfhip right hartely farewell. From *Windfore*, the ixth of *December*, 1575.

Your Lordfhips affured Frinde;

Fra. Walfyngham.

Page 248. *Sir* Philip Sidney *to* Edward Waterhowfe, *Efq; Secretary of* Ireland.

My good Ned,

NEUER fince yow wente, that euer yow wrote to me, and yet, I haue not failed to do fome frendely Offices for yow heere. How know I that, fay you. I can not tell. But I know that no Lettres I haue receaued frome yow. Thus dothe Vnkyndeneſs make me fall to a Pointe of Kyndenes. Good *Nedd*, either come or wryte. Let me either fee the, heere the, or reede the. Yowr other Frendes that know more, will wryte more fully. I, of my felfe, thus muche. Allwaies one, and in one Cace. *Me folo Exultans totus teres atque Rotundas.* Commende me to my Lord Prefident ; to the noble Sir *Nicholas,* whom I beare fpeciall good Will to ; to my Cofin *Harry Harrington,* whom I longe to fee in Helthe ; Sir *Nicholas Bagnoll* ; Mr. *Agardes* Daughter ; my Cofin *Spikman* for yowr Sake ; and whofoeuer is Maire of *Deulin* [*Dublin*] for my Sake. And euen at his Howfe when yow thinke good. I bidd yow fare well. From *Courte,* this 28th *Aprill,* 1578.

Your uery louing Frende,

Philippe Sidney.

Page 130. *Sir* Henry Sydney *to* Thomas *Earl of* Ormond.

My verie good Lord,

I Am fory you were fo ill delte withall by *Occarell,* that you were forced with that Extremytie to paffe your Cariage over the *Shannyne* ; more neighbourly Dealing mighte haue ben lookid for at his Handes, efpecially towardes your Lordfhip. I expected longe er this, that your Compaynie had ben remayninge in the Plaines of *Connaught,* there to haue refiftid the Force of the *Scotts,* as I writt to my Lord Treaforer thei fhoulde doe ; and be reddie at his Appointment, as Occafion required, to joyne their Force with his, in any Exploite that fhoulde be made : Or els, according to my former Direction, they fhoulde haue taryed for me, at the *Corlew-foote.* Their longe Staie, cheiflie, that I hard not from them, hath ben occafioned of my tarryeng heere, longer then otherwife I had eyther determynid, or woulde haue donne ; to fome Hinderaunce of the Service in Loofinge fo muche Tyme ; and I rather directed them to theife Places, becawfe I woulde haue had them to haue had fome Dealing with the *Scootts,* thereby to haue wonne your Lordfhip fome Honnor ; fince the *Scotts* will not abide the Places nere where I come, I woulde haue driven them in to their Lappes, or to haue been mett withall by fome other Bandes or Companies, that I haue difperced Abroade in like Sorte. Towching the Complaintes you make of your bad Neighboures, and fpecially againft my Lord of *Vpper Offory,* and Sir *William Occarell,* I haue written to them boathe, as by the enclofed your Lordfhip fhall perceive, either to be fente or deliuered vnto them by your Lordfhip ; but fince they be bothe Men ameandable to Juftice, and the Harmes done in myne Abfence ; your Lordfhip, for fpedier Remedie, might have complaynid to my Lord Chauncellor, whoe, in my abfence, would haue done you Juftice. And, for the Execucion of any Orders that I haue taken againft *Occarrel* on your Lordfhips Behalfe, I will fee he fhall performe yt, and doe that toe your Lordfhip that appertaynith to him to doe ; othercors he fhall not haue me to Frende. And where you make Requeft that the Compaynie fent from you, mighte be fente backe to defende the Counties where they dwell : My Lord, fince they be comme, I thinke yt expedient to vfe their Service ; being a Thing moore neceffarye, confidering the Action in Hande, to vfe their Service heere, then to fpare them hence to any other Place, which is not, in Apparance, of fuch Daunger as is dalie looked for here, till the Rebells be fuppreffed. And even fo I bid your good Lordfhip hartelye farewell. From *Gallwaye,* the xxiith of *September,* 1576.

Your Lordfhips, &c.

H. Sydney.

By the Lord Deputie.

Truſtie and right welbeloved, we grete your Lordſhip hartelye well,

IT is complayned vnto vs, by oure verye good Lord, the Earle of *Or-mound,* that ſince the Tyme of oure Departure thence, ſoche perticuler Iniuries and Wronges have bene offered and attempted by you and yours, againſt him and his, in Preyinge and Steelinge from hym and his Tenaunts and Followers nightlye. As we have bene more troubled with thoſe perticular Complaints, and Cawſies of Quarrell and Striffe betwixt you twoe, then with all other accidents of thoſe Parts, wherewith we are not a little offended towardes you. The rather, when we enter into the Conſideracions of the Matter of what Wiſedome and Diſcreacion you are to governe thoſe vnder you, if your Mind and good Will were framed there unto ; afwell to reſtrayne thoſe your badd People, and looſe Followers, for doing any Harme, as to puniſhe and correcte theim if they ſhould offende ; and ſo conſeqentlye, by this Kinde of Dealinge, ioyne in Freindſhippe and good Neighbourhoode with his Lordſhip, to whome you are ſo niere allyed ; which Thinge we expected at your Handes in oure Abſence, rather then to have harde of ſoch Complaints of your Dealings. Theiſe, therefore, ſhalbe, to will and commaunde your Lordſhip, not onelye to amende and repair that which is paſt, and to make preſent Reſtitucion of that, that hath bene taken from the Earle, or any of his Tenaunts and Followers, in this oure Abſence, by you, or any of thoſe vnder you ; but alſo, from hencefoorth, to defift in any Sort, to offer any newe Occaſion of privat Quarrells betwixt you : And ſo, by your Doings, to drawe vs from this publike Action, wherein we are nowe occupied, to converte oure Force, to ſuppreſſe thoſe Contentions and Quarrells : Which we will do, rather then we will endure theiſe contynuall Clamors, and Oppreſſions, which are daylie complayned of by hym ; and on your Parte not amended, for any Thinge that heretofore we have donne. And ſo we bid your Lordſhip hartelye Farewell. From *Galway,* the xxiith of *September,* 1576.

The Forme of this Leter was adreſſed to the Lord *Barron,* of *Vpper Oſſery,* and to Sir *William Occarall,* Knight, and in a Poſt Scripte of my Lords owne Hande, was written to my Lord of *Vpper Oſſery,* theis Wordes : *Trewly I am not a little offended, that yow ſo little regarde Juſtice ; your owne Promiſe, and myne Honor.* In the Letter to Sir *William Occarall,* was wrytten of my Lords owne Hande, theis Wordes : *Be you aſſured yf I finde this trewe, I will make your owne Boddie aunſwer for yt, in the Caſtell of* Dublin.

Page 130. *Sir* Francis Walſyngham *to Sir* Henry Sydney.

My verie good Lord,

YOUR Lordſhip maye eaſely Coniecture howe vnpleaſant the Newes of my Lord of *Eſſex,* dangerouſe Sickneſe, withowt all Hope of his Recoverie, hath been to vs here in Court, knowinge what a Subiect hir Majeſtie ſhall looſe of him, and of howe good an Aſſiſtant your Lordſhip ſhalbe deprived. Towching your Deſyre, to knowe what hathe been done for the Archbuſhoppe of *Dublin,* your Lordſhip may vnderſtand, that bothe my ſelfe, and other his Frends here, have been, and are alwayes myndefull to doe him what Good we maye, ether in Healpinge to tranſlate him into this Realme or otherwiſe ; but as yet the Placynge and Alteration of Buſhops, is not called into Deliberation : Concernynge the Buſhopricke of *Oſſorie,* when Oportunitie ſhall ſerve, I will doe my beſt Endevor to further your Lordſhips Requeſt to hir Majeſtie, for the Preferment of Mr. *Clere.* For the preſent State of *Fraunce, Flanders,* and ſome other foraine Parts, I referre you to theſe ſeverall Occurrents here incloſed.

And

And fo verie defyroufe to heare fome good Newes of your Lordfhips Tra-
vayles, for the appeafynge of *Connaghe*, I humbly take my Leave.   From the
Court at *Readynge*, the xxixth of *September*, 1576.

Your Lordfhips affured Frend,

Fra. Walfyngham.

Page 268. *Sir* Henry Sydney, *to his Son Sir* Philip Sydney.

Philippe,

BY the Lettres you fent me by *Sackeforde*, you have difcovered unto me,
your Intencion to goe over into the *Lowe Countries*, to accompagnie Duke
Caffimiere, who hathe with fo noble Offers, and by fo honorable Meanes con-
vited you: Which Difpofition of your vertuowfe Mind, as I muft needes muche
commende in you: So when I enter into the Confideracion of mine owne
Eftate, and call to Minde, what Practifes, Informacions, and maliciowfe Accufacions, are devifed againft me; and what an Affiftance in the Defenfe of
thofe Cawfies, your Prefence wold be unto me, repofinge my felf fo much,
bothe upon your Helpe and Judgment, I ftrive betwixt Honor and Neceffitie,
what Allowance I may beft geve of that Mocion for your Goinge: How be it,
if you thinke not my Matters of that Weight, and Difficultie (as I hope thei be
not) but that they may be well enowghe by my felf, without yowr Affiftance,
or any other, be browght to an honorable End, I will not be againft your Determinacion.   Yet wolde wifhe yow, before your Departure, that yow come
to me, to the Water Side, * abowt the latter Ende of this Moneth, to take yowr
Leave of me: And fo from thence to departe towardes yowr intended Journey.
Yow muft nowe beare with me, that I write not this unto yow with mine owne
Hande, which I wold have done, if the Indifpocion of my Body, had not beene
fuche, as I cowld not.   God profper yow, in that yow fhall goe abowt, and
fende yow to winne muche Credit and Honor.   And I fend you my daily
Bleffing.

The Firft of *Auguft*, 1578.   *Your very lovyng Father*,

H. Sydney.

Page 296. *Sir* Philip Sydney *to* Robert Dudley, *Earl of* Leicefter.

[a] *Right honorable my very good Lorde*,

I Am bolde to trouble your Lordfhip withe thefe few Wordes.   Humbly to
craue yowr Lordfhips Favour fo furr unto me, as that it will pleafe you to
lett me undreftand, whether I may withe your Lordfhips Leave, and that I
may not offende in Wante of my Service, remaine abfente from the Cowrte this
Chriftemas Tyme.

Some Ocafions bothe of Helthe and otherwife, do make me much defyre it,
but knowing how muche my Dutie goes beyonde any fuche Cawfes, makes me
bolde to befeeche humbly your Lordfhip to know your Direction, which I will
willingly follow, not onely in thefe Duties I am tyed to, but in any Thinge,
wherein I may be hable to doe your Lordfhip Service.

I will no furdre troble your Lordfhip, but withe the Remembrance of my
Dutie to your Lordfhip, and my Lady and Awnte.   And fo I humbly Leave
you both to the Eternall, who allwaies profper you.   Frome *Wilton*, this 16th
of *December*, 1582.

Your Lordfhips humbly at Comandemente.

Philippe Sidney.

* His Houfe was at *Bainards* Caftle by the Water-fide, near St. *Pauls.*   [a] Letter 42, Not. 161.
C. 7. in Bibl. Harley.

I was

I was bolde of late to move your Lordſhip in the Caſe of the poore ſtranger Muſician. He hathe allreddy, ſo furr taſted of yowr Lordſhips Goodnes, as I am rather in his Behalfe, humbly to thanke your Lordſhip. Yet his Caſe is ſuche, as I am conſtrained to continew ſtill a Suiter to your Lordſhip for him.   Superſcribed,
                                        To the Earle of *Leyceſter.*

Sir Philip Sydney *to* William *Lord* Burleigh.

[b] *Right honorable, my ſingular good Lord,*

I Have from my Childhod ben much bownd to your Lordſhip, which as the Meanes of my Fortune keeps me from Hability to requite, ſo gives it me daily Caws to make the Bond greater, by ſeeking and uſing your Favor towardes me.

The Queen, at my Lord of *Warwicks* Requeſt, hath bene moved to joine me in his Office of Ordinance, and, as I learne, her Majeſty yeeldes gratious heering unto it. My Suit is, yowr Lordſhip will favour and furdre it; which I truly affirme unto your Lordſhip, I much more deſyre, for the being buſied in a Thing of ſome ſerviſeable Experience, then for any other Commodity; which I think is but ſmall, that can ariſe of it.

I conclude your Lordſhips troble with this, that I have no Reaſon to be thus bold with your Lordſhip, but the preſuming of yowr honorable Goodwill towardes me, which I can not deſerve, but I can and will greatly Eſteem. I humbly take my Leave, and pray for your long and proſperows Lyfe. At Court, this 27th of *January,* 1582.

Your Lordſhips moſt humble at Commandment,

Superſcribed,   Philip Sidney.

To the Right honourable, and ſingular good Lord, the Lord Threaſorer of *England,* &c.

Page 298. Thomas *Lord* Buckehurſt *to* Robert Dudley, *Earl of* Leiceſter, *on the Death of Sir* Philip Sydney.

My very good Lord,

WITH great Grief do I write theſe Lines unto you, being thereby forced to renew to your Remembrance, the Deceaſe of that noble Gentleman your Nephew, by whoſe Death not only your Lordſhip, and all other his Frends and Kinsfolks, but even her Majeſtie, and the whole Realm beſides, do ſuffer no ſmall Loſs and Detriment. Neverthelefs it may not bring the leaſt Comfort unto you; that as he hath both lived and died, in Fame of Honour and Reputation to his Name, in the worthy Service of his Prince and Country; and with as great Love in his Life, and with as many Tears for his Death, as ever any had; ſo hath he alſo by his good and godly End, ſo greatly teſtified the Aſſurance of Gods infinite Mercy towards him, as ther is no Doubt but that he now liveth with Immortality, free from the Cares and Calamities of mortal Miſery; and in Place thereof, remaineth filled with all heavenly Joys and Felicities, ſuch as cannot be expreſſed: So as I doubt not, but that your Lordſhip in Wiſdom, after you have yielded ſome While to the Imperfection of Mans Nature, will yet in Time remember how happy in Truth he is, and how miſerable and blind we are, that lament his bleſſid Change. Her Majeſtie ſeemeth reſolute to call home your Lordſhip, and intendeth preſently to think of ſome fit Perſonage, that may take your Place and Charge. And in my Opinion, her Majeſtie had never more Cauſe to wiſh you here than now; I pray

[b] Letter 19, Not. 161 C. 8. in Bibl. Harley.

God fend it fpeedily. I fhall not need to enlarge my Letter with any other Matters, for that this Meffenger, your Lordfhips wholly devoted, can fufficientli inform you of all. And fo wifhing all Comfort and Contentacion unto your Lordfhip. I reft your Lordfhips wholly for ever, to ufe and command as your own. From the Court this 3d of *November*, 1586.

Your Lordfhips moft affured to command,

T. Buckehurft.

Page 299. *Sir* William Borlas *to Sir* Robert Sydney.

My verie good Lord,

I Haue thought good, accordinge to Theffect of my laft Lettres, to move your Lordfhip to deale with Mr. Secretarie, and Mr. Threafurer, of the great Want of Shooes, which (at this greateft Time of Neede) the poore Souldier fuftaineth, through the Fault of thofe which are appointed to ferve the Garrifons with Apparell, who are fo vtterlie vnprovided, as that there are not any to be gotten. It is pitifull to fee howe the poore Souldier is pinched this colde Weather, and greivous to heare their dailie Complaints. Befides, the Bread which is given out, fince the Execucion of the newe Orders, is fo exceedinge muftie, that Men are fcarce able to eate it, and the Souldiers crie out exceedinglie againft it. I befeech your Lordfhip to deale for Remedie of both theis Abufes. I haue looked more narrowlie into the Counfells Lettres, and finde the Order not to be for the viij *d.* in Bread only, but in Victualls ; whereby the Captaines make a Doubt to receive it, as they haue done in Bread, but rather to make Suite to receive it in Victualls, as they faie it is the Counfells Will it fhoulde be. I affure your Lordfhip I am greatly troubled with theis Matters, and fo fhall you be, vnles you provide thoroughly for it before your Cominge over, which I hope will nowe fhortlie be ; for the Howfe is nowe ready for you, and the Hangings and all Things vp. There wanteth nothing but your Lordfhips Perfon, which I affure you euery Man here woulde be glad to fee ; and thus with my humble Dutie I leave your Lordfhip to Almightie God. *Flufhinge*, this xxijth of *November*, 1589.

Your Lordfhips moft affured to comaunde,

William Borlas.

The Princeffe here is in great Heavines, by Reafon of the Sicknes of her younge Sonne, whome it hath pleafed God, at this Inftante, verie greatlie to vifite.

Page 299. *Sir* William Borlas *to Sir* Robert Sydney.

My verie good Lorde,

THIS prefent Morninge I receaved Advertifements both from the Lorde Governor and the Captaines of *Oftende*, of fome Enterprife which they fuppofe the Enimie hath in Hande againft that Place, by Reafon of the Repaire of the Prince with his Forces about *Bruges*, and other Places thereabouts. They have therefore requefted me to fende thither twoo Companies out of this Towne, which I haue differred to doe, vntill fuch Time as I fhall receive fome Direction from your Lordfhip in that Behalfe, whereof I befeech your Lordfhip to advertife me your Minde with as convenient Speede as maie be.

The Souldiers here continuallie complaine of their bad Bread, neither can they endure longe to eate, vnles it be amended.

That

This prefent Day there are executed, by the Comandement of the States, about fortie or fiftie Mariners, which were taken about five Daies agone in the *Admirall* of *Dunckerke*, which was brought in hether by the Men of Warre of this Towne, amongft which were diuers Souldiers of *Gravelinge*, whofe Execucion I haue furthered as much as I coulde, for the Maffacre which they made of our Men at Sir *Phillip Sidneyes* beinge at *Gravelinge*; and thus, with my humble Dutie, I leave your Lordfhip to the Almightie. *Flufhinge*, this thirde of *February*, 1589.

Your Lordfhips affured to comaunde,

William Borlas.

Page 299.   George Gilpin, *Efq; to Sir* Robert Sydney.

Moft honorable Knight,

BEinge retorned this Weeke from *Zelande* and *Bargenopzoom*, I fownde your Lettre of the 30 of *January* laft, which was longe by the Way, and yet moft welcom, becaufe wee were put in affurid Hope to haue iniòied your Prefence, whereof I would haue bin moft glad; at my late beinge in *Flufhinge*, where I fownde them all longinge for the fame, as alfoe in *Middelborgh*, and here: His Excellencie, the Count of *Solms, Hohenlo*, and the Admiral *Naffawe*, inquire often of your Comminge. I am now againe voide of any Hope of feeing you for a longe Time, by Reafon of the right honorable Earle of *Warwicke* his Difeafe; and yet truft, that fhall neither be Caufe of your Stay, neither yet alter your Minde and Defire to poffeffe your Govuernment of fo noble a Garrifon, and by Saruice in Warres, to make greate that worthy Name of *Sidneys*; wherein, though your late honorable Brother loft his Liffe, yet did he leave foch a Teftimony of his Zeale to Religion, that the Renown thereof wil laft til the Worlds Ende, and his Soule receave everlafting Ioy, to the Comfort of all his Pofteritie, and an Incouragement to all vertuous Mindes, to afpire and tend to like Honnors. Whenfoeuer you fhalbe arrived in *Flufhinge*, I will looke for your Lettres, and whereinfoeuer I may ftand yow in Steede, my Sarvice is and fhalbe at your Commaundment, which to fhew effectuallie, I could wifh my felfe there at your Comminge; me-thinkes it were good yow could bringe ouer a hundret or twoe of Men, to fil vp the Companies of your Garrifon, which would make them faire and ftrong, and be an Occafion to make thefe Men thinke you beganne with a Defire and Care to keepe the Companies compleete. Other Matters I leave for this Time, wifhinge your Buifnes there to be wel ended, and your felfe with my Lady and Familie wel fettled in *Flufhinge*. Owr Newes are few, not dowbtinge but yow fhall haue vnderftood, ere this, the Particularities of the Takinge of *Breda*; fince the which, Count *Maurice* is com hither, leavinge there the Count of *Hohenlo*, with Capten *Harrogieres*, who commaundeth ouer the Garrifon, which confifteth of 1200 Foote, and 4 Cornets of Horfemen. The Loffe of that Place doth much amafe Thennemy, and will diverte and change al his Intents, havinge drawen a Nomber of Men together. Between *Vendlo* and *Ruremonde* are paffed ouer the *Maefe* about 60 Enfignes of Foote, and 10 Cornets of Horfe, being com as farre as *Helmont*; fo as it is thought he will haue a Layinge to *Breda*, where he fhalbe receaved with Bullet and Pike, and wil find more Play then he looketh for, with Likeliehood, after a longe Siege, to departe with Difhonor. Others write, the Meaninge is onely to victuail the Townes nere to *Breda*, which he cannot doe but ouer Lande, and with a greate Force, for *Bargues* and *Breda* beinge ftrongly garrifoned, will cutt of all Convoies, vnleffe they be very ftronge. Wee vnderftande that *Hanno Veccho*, by Commaundment from the Duke, had the Kees of *Geertrudenbergh* taken from him, and received him Prifoner, beinge in greate Difpleafure. Yt is faid there is not in that Towne for 3 Weekes Victuals, and thofe of *Bolduck* haue refufed flatly to difprouide them felues, and fend thither any; *Stoenberghen, Rofendael*, and *Wouwe*, are likewife flenderlie prouided. The

I   Count

Count *Maurice* infifteth harde to haue the States make a niew Levy of 3 or 4000 Men, whereto they harken, but agree flowly. *Verdugo*, this laft Froft, made a Roade againe into *Freefland*, but did no more Harme, then to fire a Village or twoe, and fo retired. Thence are good Stoare of Men put into *Steenwick* and *Demeter*, where it is prefumed he hath fom Enterprife in Hande ; wee are alfo here practifinge of another Matter or twoe of good Service, God fend the Succes agreable to the laft. Al other Matters continew after the olde Way ; Sir *Frauncys Vere* is readie to departe to his Garrifon in *Defborghe* ; and thus, for Want of other, I humbly take my Leave. From the *Haeghe*, this 7th of *Marche*, 1589. *Sti Angliæ.*

Your Lordfhips at commaundment,

Geo. Gilpin.

Page 383. Robert Beale, *Efq;* (*Clerk of the Council*) to *Sir* Robert Sydney.

My verie good Lorde,

I Moft humblie thancke yow for your Letter of the xiiijth of this Prefent. Concerning the Booke which I wrote for, I was defirous to haue it, not for anie particular Refpect or Intereft of mine owne, but onelye by feinge what flaunderous and wicked Allegacions the Enemies haue againft this Eftate, to be better hable to aunfwar them when Time and Occafion fhould require. I haue hearde that diuers of the faid Bookes haue ben brought into this Realme and difcouered : But fuch a Ialoufie is conceaued, that anie fhould haue the Sight of them, that I can be contented to forbeare to defire it, becaufe I will not incurre the Difpleafure or Sufpicion of anie whatfoeuer.

I thincke the *Spanifhe* Preparacions be the principall Caufe, why the Demaunde of the Moneye is not vrged ; but yet the Eftates ought to make better Accompt of the Benefits that they haue receaued from hence. For whether it hathe proceaded of a Feare, and Provifion for our felues, to keepe the Enemye farre of, or of Loue to them, a greate Maffe of Treafure hathe ben iffued out of this Realme, which they will never paye or requite towardes vs, if the Burthen of the Warre be turned from them vppon vs, as, by thefe great Preparacions in *Spaine*, it is to be feared. The Deathe of your noble Vncle, the Erle of *Huntingdon*, Doctor *Whittakers* in *Cambridge*, and Sir *Roger Williams* here ; all three worthie Men in their Callinge, and hardlie to be feconded againe, portende fome Skourge vppon vs, for the Multitude of our Sinnes and Tranfgreffions. The Lorde geue vs Grace to amende our Liues, fo maye we be affured of his Mercie and Deliverance. To him I commende yow, and fo take my Leaue. From my Houfe in *London*, the xxjft of *December*, 1595.

Your Lordfhips affuredly at Commaundement,

Robert Beale.

Sir *Henry Vmpton* is difpatched into *Fraunce*, I pray God that he cum not to late to do good : Houbeit it is reported, that the Duke of *Mayne* is cume into the King, and that there is good Hope of the Duke of *Mercure* ; but for Lack of Countenance, the Caufe of Religion goeth to wrack. The Lord amend all.

†

T H E

F I N I S.